PRINCIPLES

OF

CRIMINAL LAW

A P SIMESTER

WARREN J BROOKBANKS

with a chapter on Culpable Homicide

by

GERALD ORCHARD

Brooker's

LEGAL INFORMATION

NOTICE OF DISCLAIMER: This publication is intended to provide accurate and adequate information pertaining to the subject matters contained herein within the limitation of the size of this publication. Nevertheless it has been written, edited, and published and is made available to all persons and entities strictly on the basis that its authors, editors, and publishers fully exclude any liability by any or all of them in any way to any person or entity for damages in respect of or arising out of any reliance in part or full, by such person or entity, upon any of the contents of this publication for any purpose.

Published by:
Brooker's Ltd
Level 1 Telecom Networks House
68-86 Jervois Quay
PO Box 43
Wellington

© Brooker's Ltd 1998

ISBN 0-86476-281-8

Publishing editor: Lisa Clephane LLB
Cover design: Anderson Advertising & Design
Typeset in Book Antiqua (9.5 pt) by Brooker's Ltd, Wellington, New Zealand
Printed by Hutcheson, Bowman & Stewart

For
Winnie and Glen

PREFACE

For generations, New Zealand students — including the authors of this book — have learned their criminal law without recourse to a textbook on the subject. They were not, of course, without secondary sources. Both Garrow and Turkington's and Sir Francis Adams' great works have provided valuable guidance over the years, while insight is also to be gleaned from the steady stream of academic papers that continues to flow into our law journals. Yet none of these admirable writings is a textbook, whose first ambition is to address a student audience. The distinction from *Adams* and *Garrow* will be immediately obvious, in that we have departed from a format of annotating the code laid down in the Crimes Act 1961. The differences, however, are rather more than presentational.

In the present work, we have sought to explain the general doctrines of criminal responsibility and the specific law of the core substantive offences. We set out to do so in a manner that both states the law and identifies the issues of principle and policy which gird and shape that law. These underlying issues are not always acknowledged in the reasoning of the courts. Neither are they commonly to be found in the pleadings of counsel. But criminal law is not, and cannot be, a value-free institution. Appellate decisions are rarely mechanical applications of statute or case law rules; they require interpretation and application of the values, philosophies, and standards embedded in such rules. It is sometimes thought that black letter law and legal theory are disjunctive; that the former belongs in the courtroom, the latter in the university. Not so. Both are a part of the law : the difference is merely of emphasis.

Thus we make no apology for the unpragmatic quality of some of this book. As well as reflecting upon the definitions of criminal offences, we evaluate the rationales for those definitions. If this is not done in a university, then where? Nonetheless, conscious of the needs of students, we have sought not to forsake the detail. Good law is made when rules and principles coincide, and the seductiveness of theory must always be tempered by case and statute. Whether we have achieved a successful balance is not for us to judge. That, at least, has been our aim.

The genesis of this work traces back to 1994, when the first-named author was teaching criminal law as a visiting lecturer at Waikato University. Realising that there was no textbook to recommend, he conceived the idea of producing one, and broached the possibility to Warren Brookbanks in Auckland. An agreement to collaborate was reached in principle, although other commitments prevented us from commencing the project until late 1996. When work finally began, we were to some extent unprepared for the scale of the undertaking, and remain very fortunate that Gerald Orchard was available and willing both to read chapters and to produce one himself. Owing to the twin yokes of time and distance, the writing of the book has not been quite the joint endeavour originally envisaged, and the chapters have been produced to some extent independently, with the first-named author and Lisa Clephane, at Brooker's, taking responsibility for the overall presentation. In respect of Parts I and II and the chapters on property offences, which fell to Andrew Simester, we would like to thank Professor Andrew Ashworth, Mr P R Glazebrook, Mr Stephen Shute, and especially Professors A T H Smith and G R Sullivan, for making time to read and greatly improve the writing; also Miss Kelyn Bacon, whose research assistance was both invaluable and superb. A number of the chapters on inchoate offences, defences, and non-fatal and sexual offences, which were written by Warren Brookbanks, were considerably enhanced by the comments of A G V Rogers, Barrister.

We have certain more general debts. Lisa Clephane and her team at Brooker's have produced this book with flair, imagination, and, above all, flexibility. Gerald Orchard, indubitably New Zealand's leading criminal lawyer, has supported our enterprise both with humour and with the material assistance that we are grateful to acknowledge. At Auckland, Bernard Brown has been an inspirational teacher and colleague, and a leading contributor to the development, over the last 35 years, of the law that we have attempted to state.

Finally, a debt that transcends our professional lives. Life, like law, is not a mechanical thing. And it would mean nothing without Winnie and Glen, to whom this book is dedicated.

APS
WJB

CONTENTS

AUTHORS

Andrew Simester
BCom LLB (Auck) DPhil (Oxon)
Senior Lecturer in Law, University of Birmingham

Warren J Brookbanks
LLM BD (Melb)
Barrister and Solicitor of the High Court of New Zealand
Associate Professor of Law, University of Auckland

Gerald Orchard
LLM (Cant) PhD (Nott)
Barrister and Solicitor of the High Court of New Zealand
Professor of Law, University of Canterbury

TABLE OF CASES

A

D

E

F

L

M

N

O

P

Q

R

S

T

X

Y

TABLE OF STATUTES

Crimes Act 1961 — *continued*

1

SELECTED BIBLIOGRAPHY

Books listed in this bibliography are referred to in the text as set out below in the first column. Bibliographical details are given in the second column.

Adams	Robertson (ed), *Adams on Criminal Law* (3rd ed), Wellington, Brooker's, 1992.
Adams (2nd ed)	Adams, *Criminal Law and Practice in New Zealand* (2nd ed), Wellington, Sweet & Maxwell (NZ) Ltd, 1971.
Ashworth, *Principles*	Ashworth, *Principles of Criminal Law* (2nd ed), Oxford, Clarendon Press, 1995.
Garrow and Turkington	Turkington, *Garrow and Turkington's Criminal Law in New Zealand*, Wellington, Butterworths, 1992.
Hart and Honoré	Hart and Honoré, *Causation in the Law* (2nd ed), Oxford, Clarendon Press, 1985.
Smith and Hogan	Smith and Hogan, *Criminal Law* (8th ed), London, Butterworths, 1996.
Williams, *CLGP*	Williams, *Criminal Law: The General Part* (2nd ed), London, Butterworths, 1961.
Williams, *TBCL*	Williams, *Textbook of Criminal Law* (2nd ed), London, Stevens, 1983.

1

Criminal Law: Definition, Application, and the Rule of Law

Our aim in this chapter is to introduce some of the theory that surrounds the criminal law: to explain why the criminal law matters and to highlight the issues it raises. It is a theoretical chapter, and those who are not interested in theory may press on without stopping here. But for those curious to understand the nature and role of the criminal law in more general terms, we provide the chapter as an (admittedly incomplete) introduction to many of the issues that have troubled criminal jurists.

There are three aspects to the discussion. We begin by considering the defining features of the criminal law, which distinguish it from other parts of New Zealand's system of laws. Secondly, we investigate its application — what sorts of actions attract criminalisation, and when is it apt to declare someone a criminal? Finally, we outline some of the constitutional and Rule of Law constraints on the operation of criminal law.

1.1 A SEARCH FOR DEFINITION

Like other types of law, the criminal law is a means by which the state participates in the ordering of its citizens' lives. Yet throughout the world, every society with a formal legal system distinguishes between criminal and civil law.[1] This raises a question about the scope of criminal law: what marks a law out as criminal rather than civil?

One way of approaching that question is to look for a definition of the criminal law. Broadly speaking, a crime is an event that is prohibited by law, one which can be followed by prosecution in a criminal proceeding and, thereafter, by punishment. Criminal law, in turn, is the variety of law that prohibits such crimes.

But to define criminal law only in these procedural terms fails to shed any light on a more fundamental problem: why does the distinction between criminal and other law matter? It is true that criminal prosecutions follow a different legal procedure from their civil counterparts. But if that is the sole difference, and there is no underlying reason for separating the two, drawing the distinction would be pointless.[2]

1.1.1 The harmful nature of the prohibited event

One suggestion might be that the harm proscribed by criminal law is greater in degree than in the civil law, or is somehow public rather than private in nature. However, while it is true that prevention of harm is central to the criminal law, there are difficulties with this type of answer. For one thing, most harms are both public and private. The major oil spillage in Sydney harbour that gave rise to the *Wagon Mound* tort cases affected more than one person,[3] while by contrast an ordinary assault typically involves a single victim. In our view, the events prohibited by criminal law are not inherently different from those regulated by other sorts of law. Indeed, the same act can sometimes lead to both criminal and civil liability. For example, if D takes V's car without V's consent, he may be prosecuted for theft. He can also be sued in tort for conversion.

That having been said, there is intuitive appeal in the idea that criminal wrongs are typically more serious than their civil counterparts; sufficiently serious that, whether or not they also give rise to civil causes of action, the State

---

1   Robinson, "The Criminal-Civil Distinction and the Utility of Desert" (1996) 76 Boston ULR 201 at 201, 202.

2   Moreover there would be a problem explaining why the distinction is maintained in those countries which do not observe the procedural safeguards normally found in criminal law. See Robinson, ibid at 203.

3   *Overseas Tankship (UK) Ltd v Morts Dock and Engineering Co Ltd (The Wagon Mound)* [1961] AC 388, [1961] 1 All ER 404 (PC); *Overseas Tankship (UK) Ltd v Miller Steamship Co Pty* [1967] 1 AC 617, [1966] 2 All ER 709 (PC). Cf public nuisance cases: *Halsey v Esso Petroleum Co Ltd* [1961] 2 All ER 145, [1961] 1 WLR 683.

feels constrained to step in and regulate them directly. This can be seen in the rule that a victim who forgives his attacker may discontinue his civil suit for damages, but cannot stop the prosecution of that attacker. Criminal offences are not merely a private matter; the public as a whole has an interest in their prevention and prosecution. Thus, according to Allen, behaviour is criminalised "because it consists in wrongdoing which directly and in serious degree threatens the security or well-being of society, and because it is not safe to leave it redressable only by compensation of the party injured".[4] Allen's remark is a useful pointer to why assaults are crimes whereas breaches of contract are not. Assault involves an interference with fundamental rights of the victim, rights which the State is perceived to have a duty to protect. By contrast, individuals are normally able to protect themselves against breach of contract, and can satisfactorily undo any damage suffered with the aid of the civil law.

Another possible basis for differentiating civil from criminal law is that criminal acts are intrinsically morally wrong. (Such acts are sometimes called mala in se.) To some extent this is true of the more serious, stigmatic offences – assault, murder, and so forth.[5] But much of the modern criminal law involves prohibitions which are only wrong because they are illegal (mala prohibita). There is no intrinsic moral difference, for instance, between driving at 100 km/h on the highway and driving at 105; but the latter is an offence. And conversely, lying may be immoral, but it is not per se a criminal act.

So there are limits to the extent to which we can safely elaborate on our initial definition by reference to the things that criminal law prohibits. In part, this reflects the fact that criminal law presents political problems as well as legal and academic ones. In § 1.2, we shall discuss some of the reasons why the State criminalises certain harms rather than others. But it should always be borne in mind that, in practice, criminal laws are characteristically deployed to control behaviour and events because there is a public – and political – interest in doing so.

1.1.2 Punishment

So far there has been limited progress. There is, however, another element of the preliminary definition given in § 1.1: punishment. Perhaps the main distinction between criminal and civil law is that the criminal law licenses punishment as opposed to compensation? The latter, it might be said, is the province of the civil law.[6]

---

4   *Legal Duties* (1931) 233, 234. Compare Coffee: "Characteristically, tort law prices, while criminal law prohibits." On this view, the criminal law should be invoked when the "price" of an action, that the defendant would have to pay in tortious damages, is insufficiently prohibitive. Coffee, "Does 'Unlawful' Mean 'Criminal'?: Reflections on the Disappearing Tort/Crime Distinction in American Law" (1991) 71 Boston ULR 193 at 194.

5   Cf Gross, *A Theory of Criminal Justice*, New York, Oxford University Press, 1979, 13.

6   Moore, *Law and Psychiatry: Rethinking the Relationship*, Cambridge, Cambridge University Press, 1984, 81.

Punishment is an important facet of the criminal process. Indeed, it is an indispensable feature of criminal offences. Parliament does not say: "Do not assault other people, *please*." That would not be a law at all. Rather, the law declares: "Do not assault other people, *or else . . .*". Of course, civil laws also specify sanctions. However, as Posner points out, the nature of the civil sanction differs from that found in criminal law. A defendant who is convicted of a crime will normally be imprisoned or fined. By contrast, someone who loses a civil action may face an injunction, an order for specific performance, or a requirement to pay damages.

Posner argues that this difference reflects a crucial distinction between the functions of criminal and civil laws. In his opinion, the criminal law exists to impose punishments such as imprisonment in situations where tortious remedies are an insufficient deterrent.[7] But Posner's explanation is doubtful. Both criminal and tortious remedies can operate as deterrents. Each is likely to be regarded as unwelcome by a defendant, and indeed civil damages awards often far exceed criminal fines in magnitude.

On the other hand, it is instructive to consider the reasons *apart from deterrence* which underlie the imposition of sanctions in these cases. In particular, whether or not they have deterrent effects, civil remedies are not normally regarded as punitive. Punishment involves more than simply imposing something unwelcome upon a defendant. A *punitive* sanction imposes hardship *because the recipient deserves it*. Damages in a contract dispute, for instance, are a sanction; but they are imposed without censure. It is not necessary to show that a defendant is at fault when he breaches his contractual obligations.

Punishment, by contrast, is imposed with censure as an integral aspect. It responds to the fact that the defendant has done something wrong.[8] Indeed, the level of sentence is one way in which a court signals the wrongfulness of the defendant's actions.[9] Of course, there are also fault-based actions in the law of tort. Nonetheless, damages for tort losses are normally compensatory, not punitive, and are understood as such. That is why one may usually insure against contractual or tortious damages, but not against criminal fines.[10]

Punishment, then, is one function of the criminal law. But punishment is not what is unique about crime. Indeed, punishment is not even a specifically legal phenomenon, let alone specifically the province of criminal law. We do not require a criminal conviction before punishing children or for a footballing foul, and it is sometimes possible to obtain exemplary damages in civil cases. One may even be fined or imprisoned for a civil contempt of court. Conversely, neither is a conviction always accompanied by sanctions. Sometimes offenders are discharged without receiving any sentence for their wrongdoing. This

---

7   Posner, "An Economic Theory of the Criminal Law" (1985) 85 Col LR 1193.

8   For discussion, see von Hirsch, *Censure and Sanctions*, Oxford, Claredon Press, 1993.

9   Cf *R v Martineau* (1990) 79 CR (3d) 129 at 138, [1990] 2 SCR 633 at 645 (SCC) (Lamer CJ): it is a "fundamental principle of a morally based system of law that those causing harm intentionally be punished more severely than those causing harm unintentionally".

10   *Askey v Golden Wine Co Ltd* [1948] 2 All ER 35, (1948) 64 TLR 379.

4

suggests that while punishment is *a* characteristic of the criminal law, it is not the defining marque.

1.1.3 Convictions

In addition to prohibition and punishment, a third aspect of the criminal process is the conviction itself — the type of judgment that the court makes. Convictions are the most distinctive aspect of criminal law. In particular, while it also licenses the imposition of sanctions, a criminal conviction (at least for stigmatic offences) is regarded as a penalty *in its own right*, both by legal officials, such as judges, and by the public.[11] This is because it has the effect of labelling the accused as a criminal.[12] A conviction makes a public, condemnatory statement about the defendant: that she is blameworthy for doing the prohibited action. It is, literally, a pronouncement that she is "guilty". By contrast, civil judgments seem merely to pin the salient breach on a defendant, without necessarily saying anything about her moral culpability. Thus, as we have noted, a plaintiff can sue for breach of contract without having to show fault by the defendant.

This facet is not mentioned in the definition of criminal law that we proposed earlier. Rather, it is something that accompanies the procedural differences. Thus the essential distinction between criminal and civil law lies not so much in the operation as in the social significance of the criminal law — in the way criminal laws and convictions are understood. The criminal law has a communicative function which the civil law does not, and its judgments against the accused have a symbolic significance that civil judgments lack. They are a form of condemnation: a declaration that the accused did wrong. Public recognition of this fact can be seen in the relevance of the criminal law to applications for a visa, or for admission to practise as a lawyer, in which applicants are required to disclose any previous convictions. Or consider the difference between publicly denouncing someone as a "convicted criminal" and calling them a "tortfeasor".[13] The law exists in society, not in the abstract. Correspondingly, the law's labelling of a defendant as "criminal" imports all the resonance and social meaning of that term.

1.2 APPLICATION

Three salient functions of criminal law emerge from the discussion so far. The first might be called *criminalisation*: the law sets out for citizens those things

---

11 Otherwise, there would be no reason to distinguish a "conviction and discharge" from a "discharge without conviction", as is done in ss 19 and 20 Criminal Justice Act 1985.

12 "Non-conviction of the blameless should be an informing principle of the substantive criminal law. A conviction for a stigmatic offence is a sanction in its own right and parsimony in the distribution of sanctions should be fostered." Sullivan, "Making Excuses" in Simester and Smith (eds), *Harm and Culpability* Oxford, Clarendon Press, 1996, 131, 152.

13 The former is certainly defamatory. Cf *Carver v Pierce*, an action for slander based on the words, "Thou art a thief, for thou hast stollen my dung". (1648) Sty 66, 82 ER 534.

which must not be done.[14] The second thing the law does is *convict* persons who are proved to have transgressed its prohibitions. Finally, it may *punish* those whom it convicts; and more generally, the criminal law poses the threat of punishment to reinforce its function of criminalisation.

The criminal law, then, is a powerful and condemnatory response by the State. It is also a bluntly coercive system, directed at controlling the behaviour of citizens. To criminalise an action is to declare that it should not be done and, typically, to deploy sanctions as supplementary reasons not to do it. In a sense, criminal law is the means by which the State bullies citizens into complying with its programme for society.

When should the criminal law be invoked? No one, including the State, should coerce others without good reason. The manipulation of people's conduct calls for justification, especially when it is accompanied by censorious and punitive treatment of those who do not comply. Unless there are compelling reasons the criminal law should not be deployed by Parliament.

Nonetheless, sometimes the use of the criminal law *is* justified. Imagine the following scenario:

> One fine September morning, Jim is discovered dead in his home. His skull has been crushed by a blow inflicted with a heavy object. The police are called. Upon further investigation, they establish that he was murdered by his daughter, Alice, who killed him in order to receive her inheritance under his will.

Intuitively, most of us would regard this as a classic example of criminal wrongdoing. It is a paradigm case where the application of the criminal law is warranted. The justification for this is twofold. First, what Alice has done is precisely the sort of activity that the State should prohibit. Murder is both harmful and wrong, and people ought to be protected against it. Secondly, Alice is clearly blameworthy, and deserves of censure for her actions. Thus she is precisely the sort of person who should receive the condemnation of a criminal conviction, as well as the punishment that a conviction exposes her to.

Alice's example is a central case for the application of criminal law. It involves deliberate, culpable infliction of the sort of serious harm that the criminal law is meant to prevent. However, not every case is as clear as this. Suppose the following alternatives:

> Case 1: Jim is discovered dead in his home. This time, the police establish that he died instantly after being struck by a vase. The vase was accidentally dislodged from the bookshelf by Barbara.

> Case 2: During an argument, Clare insults Jim. Jim is deeply hurt by Clare's words.

It is much less obvious that the criminal law should intervene in these situations. In case 1, Barbara has caused Jim's death, but there is no suggestion that she is at fault. Given this, it is inappropriate — and indeed wrong — to apply to her the sanctions of public condemnation and punishment. In case 2, Clare has wronged Jim, and deserves censure. But not by the criminal law. Unlike murder, this is not the sort of behaviour that ordinarily should be prohibited by the draconian technique of criminalisation.

---

14   Or allowed to subsist: see § 2.1.2.

In questioning when application of criminal law is legitimate, guidance may be had from the functions identified earlier. There are two dimensions to the operation of criminal law: ex ante and ex post. Ex ante, the law marks out actions that are prohibited, and warns citizens not to do those actions lest they be punished. Ex post, it censures (convicts) and punishes (sentences) persons who transgress its prohibitions. In the following paragraphs, we investigate these two roles separately, and discuss some of the issues affecting when they should be invoked.

1.2.1 Criminalisation ex ante

Why should some behaviour be criminalised, while other behaviour is permitted? The answer to that question is complex and somewhat fragmented. Prima facie, a Legislature has the power to proscribe almost any sort of conduct,[15] and in New Zealand there has been little attention directed toward the question of whether it is right or wrong to criminalise a particular event or action. Earlier, we pointed out that there is no obvious distinction between actions which are criminal, and those which generate civil liability (§ 1.1.1). When the Legislature marks some action as criminal, however, it condemns it and rules it out as an acceptable option for citizens. A responsible Legislature ought to take such drastic measures only if there are compelling reasons to do so.

The most graphic examples of prohibited behaviour are those where one individual seriously injures another without any justification or excuse. It is impossible to imagine an organised society in which such behaviour were permitted. Similarly, it is difficult to conceive of a society which recognises individual property rights without buttressing that recognition with laws prohibiting theft — indeed, theft is one of the earliest crimes known to the common law.[16] In these examples, prohibition through the criminal law is obviously appropriate. People ought to be stopped from inflicting such harm on others. The prevention of harm is a legitimate purpose of criminal law, and the seriousness of the harms involved in these cases justifies their criminalisation.

Other examples may be less straightforward, yet still explicable in terms of harm. One example is legislation controlling the possession of guns. The harm motivating such law lies not in the possession of a gun, but rather in the prospect of its misuse. Criminalisation of unlawful possession is a convenient if indirect means of regulating that harm.

---

15 Except perhaps in extreme cases: "Some common law rights presumably lie so deep that even Parliament could not override them." *Taylor v New Zealand Poultry Board* [1984] 1 NZLR 394 at 398 (Cooke J). See also Mann, "Britain's Bill of Rights" (1978) 94 LQR 512; Rishworth, "Affirming the Fundamental Values of the Nation" in Huscroft and Rishworth (eds), *Rights and Freedoms: the New Zealand Bill of Rights Act 1990 and the Human Rights Act 1993*, Wellington, Brooker's Ltd, 1995, chapter 3; *Snyder v Massachusetts* 291 US 97 at 105 (1934). The question of substantive limits on the powers of Parliament is not specific to criminal law, and will not be pursued here.

16 Stephen, *History of the Criminal Law of England*, vol III, London, Macmillan, 1883, chapter 28.

More generally, harm is the standard reason for criminalisation. A conscientious Parliament ought normally to decide whether to prohibit particular behaviour by considering the probability and magnitude of the harmful consequences of that behaviour, and by balancing these factors against the social value of the behaviour itself.[17] If the risk and gravity of the harm sufficiently outweighs the positive aspects of the conduct at issue, there is prima facie reason to criminalise that conduct. Often this balancing act can involve difficult judgments. It is generally agreed that the risk of road deaths is good reason for setting a maximum speed limit. But at what level should that limit be set? Although the risks might be minimised by setting a maximum of 10 km/h, this must be weighed against the effect that doing so would have on mobility and transportation in society. It would be an impractical step, and the speed limit is therefore higher despite the increased risks of injury and fatalities that it brings.

The victim of the harm need not always be an individual. The State often criminalises harms to collective interests. Even a minimalist State is likely to use the criminal law to enforce the obligations of citizens with respect to defence and national security, eg through laws criminalising treason. Beyond these measures, there may be laws to implement certain collective goals. If a society resolves to establish, say, a public health system, this will give rise to co-operative obligations on the part of individuals, for example to pay tax, which may require enforcement, as a last resort, by means of the criminal law. Similarly, modern anti-pollution laws reflect the community's view that protection of the environment is an important objective, even though transgressions may not harm the legal rights of any particular individual.

1.2.1.1 *Should there be criminalisation without harm?*

The harm principle cuts two ways. While harmful consequences may be a reason in favour of criminalising behaviour, conversely behaviour should normally *not* be criminalised *unless* it causes harm. So, according to this argument, the creation of thought-crimes by the State is illegitimate. The pedigree of this limiting principle is considerable. According to John Stuart Mill, "the only purpose for which power can be rightfully exercised over any other member of a civilised community, against his will, is to prevent harm to others".[18] Sometimes, however, the criminal law appears not to observe the harm principle, and to criminalise actions in the absence of harm. One example is the English case of *Shaw v DPP*,[19] in which the defendant was charged with an offence of conspiring to corrupt public morals.[20] On appeal, his indictment was upheld by the House of Lords. According to Lord Simonds, "there remains in the courts of law a residual power to enforce the supreme and fundamental

---

17   Cf Feinberg, *Harm to Others*, New York, Oxford University Press, 1984, chapter 5.
18   *On Liberty*, chapter 1, § 9.
19   [1962] AC 220, [1961] 2 All ER 446 (HL).
20   Until then unknown: see § 1.4.2.

purpose of the law, to conserve not only the safety and order but also the moral welfare of the State".[21]

The rationale for criminalisation in *Shaw* was not consequential harm, but instead the immorality or sinfulness of the defendant's behaviour. As such, the decision is objectionable. Criminalisation merely on the basis of immorality leaves a great deal to the whims and fashions of the times (and, indeed, of the prevailing location or culture: adultery, not proscribed at all in many countries, is a capital offence in others). Thus a private, consenting homosexual act might be a serious crime at one point in time, and no crime whatsoever at another[22] — yet the essential nature of the conduct has not changed in the interim. Perhaps surprisingly, this variability is actually celebrated as a virtue by Lord Devlin: "*Shaw*'s case settles for the purposes of the law that morality in England means what twelve men and women think it means — in other words it is to be ascertained as a question of fact."[23] Yet many areas of morality are open to honest and reasoned disagreement. Abortion and homosexuality, for example, are obvious cases where different juries may reach opposite conclusions over what is moral and what is immoral. This suggests that it will not do to criminalise conduct merely on the basis of its "objective" immorality.

Were New Zealand a uniform society comprised of citizens with identical values, Lord Devlin's approach might present few problems. But that is not the case. New Zealand is a multicultural environment, incorporating diverse ethnic, religious, moral, and philosophical perspectives. The law regulates in order to assist in the smooth functioning of our society, but a multicultural society also needs tolerance. The guidance provided by the harm principle is an important aid in ensuring that tolerance, by ruling out criminal censure for mere immorality.[24]

Joel Feinberg has argued persuasively for middle ground in this debate, by proposing that, in addition to more obvious forms of harm, Mill's principle could legitimately be extended to include *offence* to others as an additional ground for criminalisation. This suggestion would not support the prohibition of an activity merely because other people disapprove of it. Rather, Feinberg has in mind public displays which are profoundly offensive to others and which cannot easily be avoided by those offended. In these cases, criminalisation would be founded on the offensiveness rather than the immorality of the display, and would not turn on whether the conduct would be immoral when performed in private. An example might be the prohibition of sexual intercourse by two passengers on a bus, which is sufficiently offensive even if the participants happen to be married.[25]

---

21 [1962] AC 220 at 267, [1961] 2 All ER 446 at 452 (HL). For an example of more recent legal moralism see the majority judgment by Lord Templeman in *R v Brown* [1994] 1 AC 212, [1993] 2 All ER 75 (HL); discussed in Kell, "Social Disutility and the Law of Consent" (1994) 14 OJLS 121.

22 Cf substitution of s 142 Crimes Act 1961 by s 5 Homosexual Law Reform Act 1986.

23 "Law, Democracy and Morality" (1962) 110 Pa L Rev 635 at 648.

24 See generally Feinberg, *Harmless Wrongdoing*, New York, Oxford University Press, 1988.

25 Cf Feinberg, *Offense to Others*, New York, Oxford University Press, 1985, 12.

The harm principle allows for the prohibition of conduct causing harm to others. What about harm caused by the defendant to herself? Many criminal theorists who oppose using the criminal law to enforce morality nonetheless admit the legitimacy of *paternalism*, the principle that the State may use coercion against D to further D's own interests. The principle is attractive when the imposition on D is minimal and the gains in D's welfare (and, indirectly, in the welfare of society) are substantial. Indeed, it is by reference to paternalism that seat-belt legislation is best justified. However, the justifying force of paternalism is limited. Arguments for criminalisation based on paternalism should always be analysed with care, since they very often conceal a moral rationale. An example is legislation prohibiting marijuana, which is frequently defended on the basis of paternalism. Yet on that ground, the benefits of enforcement for both individuals and society have been doubted.[26] It is likely that a potent underlying reason for its criminalisation is simply disapproval of drug-taking.[27] Moreover, if paternalism is admitted as a basis for State coercion, it has no obvious limits. Suicide is no longer a crime in this country;[28] nor should it be, despite the harm to D's well-being that it involves. Yet its criminalisation is prima facie warranted by paternalism. So, too, was the era of National Prohibition.

1.2.1.2 *Why criminalisation should be parsimonious*
The decision whether a particular action or state of affairs is sufficiently harmful to warrant criminalisation always involves difficult judgments for the Legislature, and will be affected by the political values and social structure of a society. In New Zealand, there is no sphere of industrial, commercial, or administrative activity untouched by the criminal law. As criminal lawyers, however, we may still inquire whether conduct is ever made criminal which does not merit that designation. It is submitted that, within the limits of harm and offence, individuals should be left free by the State to pursue their own goals and priorities. There are a number of reasons to oppose the overuse of criminal law. While the present discussion cannot hope to outline them in full, it is useful to highlight some of the main factors.

The most important consideration is *autonomy*. The need for tolerance within a society, which we mentioned in the preceding section, is grounded in autonomy. Prohibiting whatever is "sinful" is likely to intrude much too far on the liberties of citizens. This is not only to say that, in a liberal society, freedom of choice is to be fostered. It is also to claim that if the law is to respect the right of citizens to control their own lives, it should not deprive them of that control without good reason.

---

26 Husak, "Recreational Drugs and Paternalism" (1989) 8 Law and Phil 353; Feinberg, *Harm to Self*, Oxford University Press, 1986, chapter 17.

27 As Alldridge points out, "if what is going on really is an exercise in paternalism then one might expect the sentences on the user to be of the same order as those for seat belt and crash-helmet offences". "Dealing with Drug Dealing" in Simester and Smith (eds), *Harm and Culpability*, Oxford, Clarendon Press, 1996, 239, 245.

28 Contrast the old common law rule that suicide was a form of murder: *R v Dyson* (1823) Russ & Ry 523, 168 ER 930.

10

The criminal law stands in the way of free choice. It coerces people by threatening them with criminal liability unless they submit to its commands. Consequently, it circumscribes the individual's capacity to live her own life, in a manner that she herself dictates. By restricting the ways in which a person may shape her life, the law has the potential to prevent her from pursuing the goals and aspirations which matter to her. Indirectly, the criminal law imposes the Legislature's view of how society should behave on its citizens.

Intrusion by the State into people's lives should not be done gratuitously. Individual freedom is valuable. Even though it is right, and indeed necessary, to have criminal prohibitions, the fact that they restrict autonomy means we should be careful of overextending the reach of the criminal law, and of damaging the right of self-determination. As Nagel remarks, that right is fundamental:

> Why not interfere with someone else's shaping of his own life? . . . I conjecture that the answer is connected with that elusive and difficult notion: the meaning of life. A person's shaping his life in accordance with some overall plan is his way of giving meaning to his life; only a being with the capacity to so shape his life can have or strive for a meaningful life.[29]

When a person's choices are not voluntary, but instead decided by laws, the life she lives is not entirely her own.[30] Of course, if one considers each crime separately, a criminal prohibition is unlikely to interfere with someone's freedom in any substantial, pervasive, or long-term sense. Outlawing arson still leaves us with a wide range of alternative activities, most of which are law-abiding. But the point about autonomy is more general than that. The effect of criminalisation must be assessed cumulatively, not in isolation. There are already thousands of things the State forbids. Autonomy requires us to have good reason before extending the reach of the criminal law.

None of this is to say that people ought to be allowed to disregard the interests of others, or that there is anything wrong with most of the criminal prohibitions we presently have. But it is a ground for the criminal law to beware of interfering more than the minimum necessary — a prima facie reason against the use of criminal sanctions.

Another consideration to be borne in mind when contemplating criminalisation is practical. It may be ineffective, unnecessary, or uneconomic to use the criminal law,[31] especially if civil legislation would be adequate to deal with the problem.[32] Criminal censures are always intrusive, and may

---

29   Nozick, *Anarchy, State and Utopia*, Oxford, Blackwell, 1974, 50. See Feinberg, *Harm to Self*, New York, Oxford University Press, 1986, 54, and chapters 17-19 more generally.

30   Raz, *The Morality of Freedom*, Oxford, Clarendon, 1986, 382.

31   Or the side-effects of doing so may be too drastic. See, for example, Alldridge's argument in "Dealing with Drug Dealing" in Simester and Smith (eds), *Harm and Culpability*, Oxford, Clarendon Press, 1996, 239, 243, 244, 255, 256.

32   Bentham, *Introduction to the Principles of Morals and Legislation* (1789), chapter 13; cf Feinberg, *Harm to Others*, New York, Oxford University Press, 1984, 26: there is a good reason to criminalise only provided that "there is probably no other means that is equally effective at no greater cost to other values." Per Jareborg, criminalisation "should be used only as a last resort or for the most reprehensible types of wrongdoing." "What

11

frequently be disastrous for the person falling foul of them. Therefore, they should not be deployed merely as a tool of convenience, and where possible other forms of control ought to be used in their stead.

1.2.2 Ex post: censure and sanction
Our search for definition fastened on the pronouncement of guilt through conviction as the distinguishing mark of criminal law. This pronouncement connotes fault on the part of the criminal. When the court finds an accused guilty of committing a crime, and purports to punish her through sentencing, there is a public implication that she is blameworthy. Of course, there are offences of a minor character (eg related to parking infringements) where this element of reproof may be relatively trivial — such offences are often characterised as not being "truly" criminal in nature. Paradigmatically, though, censure is inherent in criminal convictions.

1.2.2.1 *The need for mens rea*
An institution which condemns and punishes people must take care to do so accurately. Being just matters. In particular, if a person is not to blame when something goes wrong, the censure of the criminal law is not appropriate — and if it is inflicted on her, the public will tend to think that is because she *is* to blame. When the law labels a defendant as "criminal", it simply cannot avoid this implication. Consequently, it should not convict those for whom that implication is unjustified.

The grounds for wanting to avoid mislabelling defendants are twofold. First, it is unfair and unjust to stigmatise someone as a criminal when they do not deserve condemnation. Secondly, if the criminal law is seen regularly to make mistakes, it will lose its moral credibility. This, Robinson points out, will diminish its effectiveness as a tool of social control:

> The criminal law can also be more directly effective in increasing compliance with its commands. If it earns a reputation as a reliable statement of what the community perceives as condemnable and not condemnable, people are more likely to defer to its commands as morally authoritative ... A distribution of liability that the community perceives as doing justice enhances the criminal law's moral credibility; a distribution of liability that deviates from community perceptions of justice undermines it.[33]

For these reasons, the criminal law ought not to convict people unless they are culpable for doing a prohibited action.[34] Therefore, in so far as possible, criminal offences should be structured so that there can be no conviction

---

Kind of Criminal Law do We Want?" in Snare (ed), *Scandinavian Studies in Criminology* Vol 14 (1995) 17, 22.

33 "The Criminal-Civil Distinction and the Utility of Desert" (1996) 76 Boston ULR 201 at 212, 213. Robinson's point is made about criminalisation, but applies in this context also.

34 For an interesting debate which touches on this proposition, see Reiman and van den Haag, "On the Common Saying that it is Better that Ten Guilty Persons Escape than that One Innocent Suffer: *Pro* and *Con*" in Paul, Miller and Paul (eds), *Crime, Culpability, and Remedy*, 1990, 226.

without fault. This is achieved by including within every criminal offence some element that reflects culpability.

Suppose the following example:

> Pam has killed Alex. Pam is a doctor, and Alex was one of her patients. Pam gave him a painkiller, to which he had an allergic reaction and died. Causing another's death is generally regarded as a very undesirable thing, and the police investigate. Pam's actions satisfy the definition of "homicide" within s 158 Crimes Act: the killing of a human being by another, directly or indirectly, by any means whatsoever. Pam, the police conclude, has committed homicide.

On these facts alone, is Pam therefore bad, or blameworthy? Should we convict her of murder? The answer is no. Alex may have been the one patient in a million who was unknowably allergic to the painkiller and died as a consequence. It is important not to kill people, but it does not follow from the fact that killing is undesirable, and normally prohibited, that someone should automatically be convicted or punished for causing another's death. In the criminal law, this principle is expressed by the maxim, actus non facit reum nisi mens sit rea: an act does not make a man guilty unless his mind is (also) guilty. There must be mens rea — a guilty mind. The action must be done intentionally or recklessly, or wilfully or knowingly, or negligently, or with some other mental state as a result of which we can say that the defendant is culpable. In Kenny's words, "no external conduct, however serious or even fatal its consequences may have been, is ever punished unless it is produced by some form of *mens rea*".[35]

1.2.2.2 *Theories of culpability*

The argument for having a mens rea element in criminal offences assumes that proof of mens rea establishes culpability. However, to what extent this is true is debated by criminal theorists.[36] Academics commonly argue over two accounts of when we may legitimately blame someone for her actions, which can only be sketched here. The first, which is reflected in the law regarding serious crimes,

---

35 *Outlines of Criminal Law* (2nd ed), 1904, 39. This proposition is subject to qualification in respect of strict liability. See § 1.2.2.3, and chapter 4. Note that the present claim is only that mens rea is *necessary* for culpability. As is illustrated in *R v Kingston* [1995] 2 AC 355 at 364-366, [1994] 3 All ER 353 at 359-361 (HL); *Yip Chiu-Cheung v R* [1995] 1 AC 111, [1994] 2 All ER 924 (PC); and *Gordon v Schubert* [1956] NZLR 431, proof of mens rea may not be sufficient to establish moral fault. Where this is so, absence of fault is usually (but unfortunately not always) recognised by the availability of defences. See § 1.2.2.4; Fletcher, *Rethinking Criminal Law*, Boston, Little Brown & Co, 1978, 511f, 799f.

36 See, for example, Hampton, "Mens Rea" in Paul, Miller & Paul (eds), *Crime, Culpability, and Remedy*, 1990, 1 (also in (1990) 7 Social Philosophy and Policy 1); Moore, "Choice, Character, and Excuse" in Paul, Miller and Paul (eds), *Crime, Culpability and Remedy*, 1990, 29; Bayles, "Character, Purpose and Criminal Responsibility" (1982) 1 Law & Phil 5; Arenella, "Character, Choice, and Moral Agency" in Paul, Miller and Paul (eds), *Crime, Culpability and Remedy*, 1990, 59; Duff, "Choice, Character and Criminal Liability" (1993) 12 Law & Phil 345; Hart, "Negligence, Mens Rea, and Criminal Responsibility" in *Punishment and Responsibility: Essays in the Philosophy of Law*, Oxford, Clarendon Press, 1968, 136; Sullivan, "Making Excuses" in Simester and Smith (eds), *Harm and Culpability*, Oxford, Clarendon Press, 1996.

is sometimes called a "subjective" analysis: that culpability depends on morally defective *choices*. We blame someone for choosing to do a wrong action — for instance, for choosing to set fire to the house. Conversely, fault is not made out unless someone *deliberately* does something bad.

The upshot of this approach is that the actus non facit reum nisi mens sit rea maxim transforms into a requirement that we should not convict without advertence. As will be seen in chapter 3 on mens rea, in New Zealand this would include such mental states as intention and recklessness. If Pam gave Alex the painkiller in order to kill him, we can blame her for causing his death because she intended to do so. Conversely, on the subjective account, it is perfectly reasonable for Pam to dose Alex if she is unaware that the medicine will kill him. Failing to take account of the risk of death is not something for which she can be blamed.

The alternative account is "objective". It grounds fault in *conduct* rather than choices, arguing that an action attracts blame if it inflicts harm when a reasonable person would not have acted that way. Under the objective analysis, awareness of wrongdoing is not essential. If homicide is undesirable, then Pam has a reason not to do it whether or not she foresees the risk. Homicide does not become acceptable just because it is done inadvertently. Since it involves harm, not only does Pam have a moral (and, in this case, legal) duty not to do it, but she also has a duty to *take care* so that she does not do it inadvertently either. On this account, Pam may legitimately be convicted of a crime if she is unreasonably careless.

The objective view works best when explaining why someone may be blamed for negligence, and in giving substance to the idea of the "reasonable man". The "reasonable man" is archetypally a person of decent character. Thus if the defendant has failed to behave like a reasonable person, we may infer culpability, since her conduct has fallen short of reflecting that decent character.

These subjective and objective approaches are extreme alternatives, and middle ground is available. In New Zealand, inadvertent negligence *is* thought to be a standard of fault, but foresight of wrongdoing is regarded as involving *greater* culpability. As we shall see in chapter 3, New Zealand has adopted a more subjectivist stance than England, particularly over the interpretation of "recklessness", which is the minimum fault requirement for many stigmatic criminal offences. Suppose that David causes a fire in his house and is charged with reckless arson. In many jurisdictions, including New Zealand, recklessness requires some degree of actual foresight. So for David to be guilty he must have actually foreseen the risk of setting fire to the house when he did the act that caused it. Were he merely negligent (or even grossly so), he would have to be acquitted. In these jurisdictions, the subjectivist holds sway. On the other hand, the law in England regarding this offence is objective:[37] David can be convicted of reckless arson even though he did not notice the risk, at least if the risk was an obvious one.

---

37 *Commr of Police of the Metropolis v Caldwell* [1982] AC 341, [1981] 1 All ER 961 (HL).

If fault is a prerequisite of criminal liability then it is easy to see why recklessness or other foresight-based mental states are so often required before a defendant can be convicted for his actions. Much more difficult are statutes that define an action to be an offence when it is done negligently. Indeed, subjectivists often argue that people should never be convicted for negligence.[38] We disagree, and it seems to us that one may fairly be blamed for an unreasonable failure to take care; though no doubt the criminalisation of such cases ought to be sparing. But whether one adopts a subjective or objective stance, and whatever one's views regarding the culpability of negligence, one thing is clear. Without at least some form of fault, a defendant should not be convicted of a crime. This proposition is reflected in New Zealand's criminal law, where in the absence of advertence to the harm (or, in some cases, of negligence), a defendant must be acquitted of any serious criminal offence.

1.2.2.3 *Regulatory offences*
What, then, of strict liability? There are many crimes for which the prosecution need not prove any element of fault before the defendant may be convicted. In these offences, the defendant's liability is said to be "strict", and the actus non fit reum maxim is said not to apply. For example, under the Water and Soil Conservation Act 1967 a defendant may be convicted for discharging waste into natural water if the prosecution shows merely that waste was discharged.[39] There is no need to prove that the defendant's involvement was a culpable one.

We deal with strict liability offences more fully in chapter 4. For now, two observations may be made. The first is that, as we shall see, the courts have moved to make "strict" liability in effect a standard of fault — where culpability on the part of the defendant is presumed, but may be rebutted. If D can prove that the harm was not at all his fault, then he will be acquitted. Thus the essential difference between offences of strict liability and those of negligence is the burden of proof. It is at least arguable that in some minor offences, it may be appropriate for that burden to rest on the defendant rather than the prosecution.

The fact that such offences are minor raises a second point. Strict liability offences tend not to involve the same level of public censure as serious crimes. A parking offence, for example, comprises an altogether different order of wrongdoing from murder. This is not to deny that traffic offences and their like are part of the criminal law, although perhaps they should not be.[40] But most people in ordinary life distinguish minor, regulatory-type offences from "true" crimes, and the element of public condemnation is and should be conveyed

---

38 See § 3.5.5.

39 Section 34(1)(b). See *Hastings CC v Simons* [1984] 2 NZLR 502 (CA).

40 According to Robinson, "Serious deterrent sanctions can and ought to be imposed [for regulatory violations] but they can as easily and effectively be imposed under an administrative system distinct from criminal law that carries a noncriminal label, such as 'violation'." "The Criminal-Civil Distinction and the Utility of Desert" (1996) 76 Boston ULR 201 at 214. Cf Mann's proposal for a separate system of justice to deal with such minor crimes, in "Punitive Civil Sanctions: The Middle Ground Between Criminal and Civil Law" (1992) 101 Yale LJ 1795.

only by a conviction of the latter type. The difference in social significance is illustrated by the question we mentioned earlier, commonly found in visa and employment applications, about an applicant's criminal record. It is not a request that is intended to elicit disclosure of minor infractions such as parking infringements.

1.2.2.4 *Allowing defences*

The medical homicide example (§ 1.2.2.1), in which Pam kills Alex, illustrates one way in which the defendant may be absolved of fault when a prohibited consequence occurs. Her answer is that, although she killed Alex, it was an accident. She neither intended his death, nor was she negligent in bringing it about: she lacked mens rea. Sometimes, however, a person may not be culpable even though she harms another person deliberately. For example:

> Anne is a police officer in the Armed Offenders Squad. She is standing outside a bank when a robbery occurs. John, who is one of the robbers, comes out of the bank and runs toward her, pointing a gun. In order to protect herself, Anne shoots and injures John.

Prima facie, this is an assault. Anne cannot claim that she shot John by accident. Nevertheless, Anne is not to blame. Her action, we would say, is *justified*, and she does not deserve to be convicted of any crime.

In order to deal with this sort of case, the law recognises a number of general defences, under which the defendant may acknowledge that he did an otherwise prohibited act and yet escape conviction. Examples of these justificatory defences are self-defence, prevention of crime, and defence of property. In effect such defences allege that, although D's conduct was harmful and normally unlawful, his conduct was nevertheless appropriate in the circumstances.[41] They claim that the defendant's conduct was the right (or an acceptable) thing to do, and so was not deserving of censure. As such, justifications are generalised: they involve judgments about the situation which apply to all the participants; so, for example, John is not entitled to resist Anne's justified use of force.

There are other predicaments where inflicting harm can be defensible on a more restricted basis. In these cases a person may choose to do something wrong, ie unjustified, but we may nevertheless think her insufficiently blameworthy to warrant the censure of the criminal law. For example:

> Susan is arrested after taking part in the bombing of a Government building. She had driven the car in which the bombers, a gang of terrorists, had made their escape. After her arrest, it is discovered that she did so only because the terrorists had threatened to kill her otherwise.

---

41   Indeed one may say of such cases that no prohibited harm occurred. Thus Smith remarks, "Where the defendant's conduct can fairly be described as coming within the terms of the proscribed activity, an offence has, prima facie, been committed: liability will ensue unless he advances some explanation of his conduct which shows that it was justified, in which case there is no *actus reus*". "On Actus Reus and Mens Rea" in Glazebrook (ed), *Reshaping the Criminal Law: Essays in Honour of Glanville Williams*, London, Stevens & Sons, 1978, 95, 97.

16

In this type of case, Susan's conduct may not be justified, and other people would be entitled to try to stop her. Nevertheless her culpability is lessened by the fact that she was coerced. Thus she has an *excuse*. The rationale for allowing excusatory defences is that advanced by Hart: "unless a man has the capacity and a fair opportunity or chance to alter his behaviour to the law its penalties ought not to be applied to him".[42] Susan's wrongdoing was deliberate, but understandable. By admitting compulsion as a defence,[43] the criminal law acknowledges that Susan did not have a genuine and fair opportunity to choose not to break the law. We may have no reason to praise her. But she does not warrant the penalties of the criminal law, because she is below the threshold of blameworthiness that is appropriate to criminal liability.

1.2.2.5 *Accountability*

So far in § 1.2, we have argued that the criminal law should only convict people who are culpable when a prohibited event occurs, and that events should only be prohibited when they are sufficiently harmful to override considerations such as the need to protect the autonomy of citizens. There is, however, a further requirement to be met before the criminal law will convict someone of a crime: accountability. Recall the example with which we began this discussion:

> Jim is discovered dead in his home. His skull has been crushed by a blow inflicted with a heavy object. The police are called. Upon investigation, they establish that he was murdered by his daughter, Alice, who killed him in order to receive her inheritance under his will.

This, as we said earlier, is a plain case. But it is not just the fact that Alice is culpable which licenses her conviction. Culpability, by itself, is insufficient. Suppose that Jim's brother, David, had suspected Alice might try to murder Jim, and had done nothing to warn him? David may be blameworthy, but ought we to prosecute him? Certainly not for homicide, at any rate. The difference between David and Alice is that only Alice is legally accountable, or *responsible*, for Jim's death. Only Alice has performed an action that caused Jim's death.

Because he is not legally responsible, there is simply no point in prosecuting David, however much we may disapprove of his conduct.[44] Sometimes, however, the question of accountability raises difficult issues. Suppose another variation:

> Case 3: Jim is discovered dead in his home. The police establish that he died after being struck by a vase which fell accidentally from the bookshelf. However, his daughter, Edith, had observed the scene and deliberately failed to summon an ambulance in time to save him.

---

42 "Punishment and the Elimination of Responsibility" in *Punishment and Responsibility: Essays in the Philosophy of Law*, Oxford, Clarendon Press, 1968, 158, 181.

43 Cf s 24; see also chapter 10.

44 Or, as Lord Esher MR put it, "A man is entitled to be as negligent as he pleases towards the whole world if he owes no duty to them." *Le Lievre v Gould* [1893] 1 QB 491 at 497 (CA).

This is very similar to Alice's case, except for one aspect: our complaint here is not about what Edith did, but about what she *failed* or *omitted* to do. Another way of expressing the difference might be to say that, unlike Alice, Edith did not *cause* Jim's death.[45] Either way, however, because of that distinction, criminal liability does not necessarily follow.

The issues of omission and causation will be discussed in more detail in chapter 2, but it is important to note that these, too, are crucial matters affecting the range and intrusiveness of the criminal law. Prohibiting an omission is not like prohibiting an action. When the law prevents Ian from (say) punching Bob, it leaves him with plenty of options and rules out only one. Ian is free to choose what to do or not do instead. By contrast, when the law proscribes an omission, it tells him exactly what to do. If Jim is dying, Edith *must* rescue him — she is not free to choose what to do or not do instead. One option is *required*, and all the other options are ruled out. Thus liability for omissions is much more likely to impinge on individual autonomy and freedom of action.

In a liberal community, the right to autonomy is fundamental.[46] If the law is to acknowledge and respect individuals as independent members of society, then it must judge them according to their own actions, and not those of others. The process of shaping and controlling a person's life should be left to that person, and would be undermined were citizens constantly forced to assume responsibility for events they do not bring about.[47] For this reason, it is a guiding principle of the law that defendants are liable according to what *they* do, not what others do and they might prevent; correspondingly, they should be left free to live their own lives and pursue their own goals without having legal duties to act or intervene constantly thrust on them, unanticipated, unpredictable, and unwanted, because of the actions of others. This is why there is no general duty to prevent crime.[48] It is also why principles of accountability are so important.[49]

Implicit in this reasoning, however, is that omissions are special not because they deny culpability, but because of the implications of their proscription for individual freedom. Thus they are not ruled out tout court. In practice, a criminal law duty to intervene is imposed, if at all, only when the defendant has a special connection to the harm — for example, when the defendant is the victim's parent.[50] But even that need not be true. Sometimes an altruistic reason

---

45 Cf Moore, *Act and Crime: the Theory of Action and its Implications for Criminal Law*, Oxford, Clarendon Press, 1993, 267-278. But the law may disagree: see § 2.2.4.1.

46 See § 1.2.1.2.

47 Thus Hart and Honoré "respect for ourselves and others as distinct persons would be much weakened, if not dissolved, if we could not think of ourselves as the separate authors of the changes we make in the world." For further discussion, see § 2.1.1.

48 Cf *R v Coney* (1882) 8 QBD 534 at 557, 558; *R v Clarkson* [1971] 3 All ER 344 at 347.

49 There is a pragmatic side to accountability. If a swimmer drowns, the law cannot afford to prosecute every person on the beach. More generally, the State could not possibly contemplate prosecuting everyone who might have prevented it each time a prohibited harm occurs. So the general principle against liability for omissions has a realistic air about it as well as a philosophical justification.

50 See § 2.1.1.2.

for a stranger to get involved may justify the extension of responsibility. Suppose that Ian, a passer-by, sees a child drowning in a paddling pool. He can rescue the child at no risk to himself. In this situation, for Ian not to intervene would be monstrous. Although New Zealand criminal law does not at the moment criminalise such cases, it might justifiably do so, depending on such factors as the seriousness of the impending harm and the degrees of risk and inconvenience involved in averting it. In many other jurisdictions, it is a crime not to rescue someone in peril when doing so involves no personal danger.[51]

Similarly, the criminal law need not always require D's behaviour to *cause* a specified consequence. For example, the law of secondary liability recognises the responsibility of those who do not themselves perpetrate a crime, but are nevertheless parties to its commission.[52] Suppose, for example, that David plans to kill Tony. Knowing this, Rebecca lends David her gun. Rebecca is a participant in Tony's murder, and his death may be attributed to her as a secondary party. The point here is that Rebecca does not cause Tony's death.[53] (David would have killed him anyway, using someone else's gun.) But she is not like a mere bystander, who can claim that David's action has nothing to do with her; that it is none of her business. Instead, she has involved herself in the murder, and *made* it her business. Thus, although it is David who kills Tony, Rebecca shares in the responsibility for his death.

Like liability for omissions, derivative liability involves an extension of the criminal law beyond the core cases of wrongdoing. As such, it involves a greater intrusion on people's freedom of action: not only may D not strike V, he may not do anything to help someone else strike V either, a much greater limitation upon what he is left free to do. This raises difficult questions of policy: if Rebecca is a shopkeeper, should she refuse to sell a gun to David if she suspects or believes he has an illicit purpose? Derivative liability has the potential to force individuals to police the actions of others, and squarely raises issues of autonomy once more.[54] It is a hard question how far such extensions of responsibility should go, since like vicarious liability[55] they can have the

---

51   See Ashworth, "The Scope of Criminal Liability for Omissions" (1989) 105 LQR 424.

52   See chapter 5.

53   See, for example, *Hart and Honoré* 51ff, 363ff; Smith, "Aid, Abet, Counsel, or Procure" in Glazebrook (ed), *Reshaping the Criminal Law: Essays in Honour of Glanville Williams*, London, Stevens & Sons, 1978, 120, 131-134.

54   Particularly in cases of complicit liability for omissions, which may arise when the secondary party has some form of control over the wrongdoer. See, for example, *Du Cros v Lambourne* [1907] 1 KB 40, in which the passenger in a car was convicted of being a party to dangerous driving, on the basis that he owned the car and failed to exercise his right of control over the driver's actions.

55   The doctrine of vicarious liability provides a second route with which a causal requirement may be bypassed. However, vicarious liability is normally to be avoided in criminal law, since it arises out of a more general relationship between the defendant and the actual perpetrator of a wrong, and so is not specific to the wrongful action; consequently the defendant risks being convicted of a crime for which he is not morally responsible. As a rule, "*Qui peccat per alium peccat per se* is not a maxim of criminal law". *Tesco Supermarkets Ltd v Nattrass* [1972] AC 153 at 199, [1971] 2 All ER 127 at 155 (HL) (Lord Diplock). See further § 5.2.

effect of imposing liability largely on the basis of the defendant's status rather than his behaviour. Yet, once again, accountability is not ruled out tout court.

1.3 THE STRUCTURE OF A CRIMINAL OFFENCE

The discussion in this chapter has practical implications for criminal offences. We have characterised the criminal law as a system of prohibition and censure. Correspondingly, the main elements of crimes are twofold, harm and fault. The first of these is primarily an external element:[56] an event or conduct which causes the harm that the law is designed to prevent. For example, the external element in murder is the killing of one human being by another.[57] This external element is known as the *actus reus* of the offence. It sets out the physical thing that must happen before the criminal law can be invoked, and will be discussed in detail in chapter 2.

Generally, the actus reus is not enough by itself to constitute an offence. In § 1.2.2.1 we discussed the example of Pam, a doctor, who killed Alex by injecting him with a painkiller to which he was allergic. Pam has done the actus reus of a murder. But if Alex's allergy was unknowable, then Pam is not to blame, and should not be convicted. Alex's death is simply a tragic accident. The need for fault in an offence gives us the second element, which is known as *mens rea*. This is what might be termed the "mental" element — the guilty mind, such as the intention, knowledge, or recklessness, of the defendant with respect to the actus reus. Mens rea is the subject of chapter 3.

Like the actus reus, the mens rea varies for each offence. In some crimes, intention or recklessness will be required before D can be convicted, while in others negligence or some other fault element may suffice. An example will help to illustrate. Suppose that Tom has been charged with an offence against s 205(1)(b) Crimes Act 1961. He recently married Jill, who he believed was a widower. Jill's first husband, Sam, had been lost at sea some years ago. However, it later turns out that Sam had not drowned, as everyone thought, and was still alive at the time of Tom's wedding. Hence Jill was already married, and her marriage to Tom was bigamous. The relevant section provides as follows:

205(1) Bigamy is ...

.   .   .   .   .

(b) The act of a person who goes through a form of marriage in New Zealand with any other person whom he or she knows to be married ...

In this crime, the actus reus is going through a form of marriage in New Zealand with a married person. The mens rea of the crime is knowledge, ie believing (correctly) that the other party to the ceremony is already married.

---

56 Although it may not be entirely external. Sometimes actions acquire a harmful or criminal character only when done with a particular mental state. For illustrative discussion of this point, see Horder, "Crimes of Ulterior Intent" in Simester and Smith (eds), *Harm and Culpability*, Oxford, Clarendon Press, 1996, 153; also § 3.3.

57 Section 160.

On the facts given, Tom will not be guilty of bigamy as he lacks the mens rea required for an offence against s 205(1)(b).

Sometimes the mens rea can be present without the actus reus. Imagine this time that Tom believes Jill is married, but that (unknown to either of them) Jill's previous husband had suddenly died on the day before the wedding. In this case Jill is no longer married to Sam, and Tom does not commit bigamy because the actus reus is missing.[58]

1.3.1 Defences: a separate element

The examples above illustrate that both specified parts of the offence, the actus reus and the mens rea, must be proved before there is any question of D's being guilty of a crime. Even if both parts are proved, however, there might still be a defence available, and so we have a third basic element of every crime: the absence of a valid defence.

Suppose, for example, that Tom had indeed known Jill was married, but had been forced to go through the ceremony because Jill's father had "asked" him to do so, while wielding a shotgun suggestively. Tom has performed the actus reus of s 205(1)(b), with the required mens rea. So we can say that he has committed a *prima facie offence*. Despite this, he will not be convicted since he has a further defence of duress or compulsion.

The word "defence" can sometimes be misleading, because it tends to be used by lawyers to describe any reason why the defendant should be acquitted. Thus if the defendant has an alibi, he will rely on this for his defence. More precisely, however, an alibi is not a defence but rather a denial that there was a prima facie offence at all. If the alibi is accepted, it means that the defendant did not do the actus reus. Similarly, automatism is not so much a defence as a denial of responsibility for the actus reus. Duress and self-defence, by contrast, deny neither actus reus nor mens rea, but rather seek to defend the commission of a prima facie offence by reference to events not contemplated in the actus reus.[59]

Normally, defences are dealt with in a separate section of the Crimes Act, and are not expressly set out as part of each offence. Similarly, they are treated in separate chapters of this text. This is because they are of general application to all crimes, unless expressly or impliedly excluded by the statute which creates a particular crime. Indeed many defences are not referred to at all in the Crimes Act, and are merely incorporated by s 20, which preserves the common law defences without their needing to be restated. The fact that defences make up a third element was accepted by Lord Wilberforce in *DPP for Northern Ireland v Lynch*. Duress, he stated:

> is something which is superimposed upon the other ingredients which by themselves would make up an offence, ie upon act and intention. "Coactus volui" sums up the combination: the victim completes the act and knows that he is doing

---

58   Cf *R v Deller* (1952) 36 Cr App R 184 (CCA).

59   Cf Smith, "On Actus Reus and Mens Rea" in Glazebrook (ed), *Reshaping the Criminal Law: Essays in Honour of Glanville Williams*, London, Stevens & Sons, 1978, 95, 97ff; Simester, "Mistakes in Defence" (1992) 12 OJLS 295 at 295, 296.

so; but the addition of the element of duress prevents the law from treating what he has done as a crime.[60]

In case it is helpful, we represent this relationship by the following diagram:

The offence of bigamy

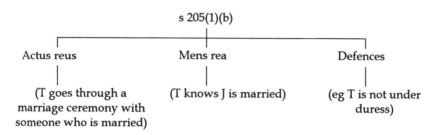

s 205(1)(b)

Actus reus	Mens rea	Defences
(T goes through a marriage ceremony with someone who is married)	(T knows J is married)	(eg T is not under duress)

1.4 LIMITATIONS: THE RULE OF LAW

It is temptingly easy for a government to misuse the criminal legal system as a convenient means of social ordering. The criminal law, in seeking to secure benefits to society at large, can be a major threat of *in*security for any individual charged with the commission of a crime. Indeed, in some respects the criminal justice system constitutes New Zealand's most potent peace-time threat to the civil rights of those citizens suspected of and prosecuted for crimes. Accordingly society, while endeavouring to control and reduce criminal conduct, must be sensitive to the rights and legitimate expectations of those charged with crime.

Central to the protection of those rights and expectations is the Rule of Law, which demands that those under the State's control should be dealt with by fixed and knowable law, and not according to the discretion of State (including judicial) officials. As such, the Rule of Law embodies a cluster of legal values, including certainty, clarity, and prospectivity; which have at their heart not merely the constitutional premise that Government should operate under the law, but also the ideal that citizens themselves should be able successfully to live within the law, by deriving guidance from the law itself.[61]

This, in turn, requires that the criminal law must be an organised, ascertainable system of legal rules — and not ad hoc responses to the conduct of individuals. It is not possible, in the present text, to explore this implication fully. Nonetheless, in the remainder of this chapter we shall consider some of the main principles associated with the Rule of Law, in the context of their significance for the criminal law.

---

60   [1975] AC 653 at 679, 680, [1975] 2 WLR 641 at 655 (HL).

61   See Raz, *The Authority of Law: Essays on Law and Morality*, Oxford, Clarendon Press, 1979, chapter 11; Colvin, "Criminal Law and the Rule of Law" in Fitzgerald (ed), *Crime, Justice and Codification: Essays in Commemoration of Jacques Fortin*, Toronto, Carswells, 1986, 125.

1.4.1 No conviction without criminalisation

The first limiting principle is inherent in the definition of criminal law offered at the beginning of this chapter: that a crime involves, among other things, an event prohibited by law.[62] This implies that nobody should be convicted of a criminal offence unless what was done is, in law, a crime.[63] Nullum crimen sine lege, the maxim goes: no crime without law.[64] Suppose, for example, that Jane is a visitor from another country where adultery is a criminal offence. While in New Zealand she has an affair with a married man. Even though she believes she is committing a crime, she cannot be convicted of any offence, since adultery is not illegal under New Zealand's criminal law. A case which illustrates this principle is *R v Deller*.[65] The defendant sold a car, stating as he did so that it was free of encumbrances. In fact, he thought the car was encumbered, because he had earlier mortgaged it to a finance company. Deller was charged with obtaining the proceeds of the car sale under false pretences. As it happened however, the earlier mortgage was apparently invalid, and hence the car *was* unencumbered. By chance, his pretence was not false. He could not be convicted since he had broken no law.[66]

1.4.2 Retrospective crimes

A corollary of the nullum crimen principle is that there should be no retrospective criminalisation, whereby citizens might be convicted on the basis of conduct which was not, *when they did it*, an offence. In such cases, it is not enough that relevant law is to hand at the time of the trial. It would still be true that at the time of D's conduct he committed no applicable crime. Remedying the legal deficiency by passing a retrospective law, which deemed the offence into existence at the time of its commission, would be to contradict rather than uphold the Rule of Law. Particularly given the dramatic implications of criminal penalties for the lives of individuals, criminal liability is not the sort of nasty surprise that should be sprung on citizens ex post facto.

In England, the evolutionary nature of the common law has resulted in a less than scrupulous observance of this constraint. In *R v R*, for example, the House of Lords recently abolished an exemption in the common law crime of rape, which had meant that a husband could not be convicted of raping his wife.[67] While that change is to be welcomed as a matter of social and legal

---

62 See § 1.1.

63 In New Zealand this requirement is codified by s 9 Crimes Act 1961, the effect of which is to exclude criminal liability unless an offence has been committed against a New Zealand statute. The section is subject to exceptions for contempt and courts martial.

64 Sometimes called the principle of *legality*, especially in the United States. See Hall, *General Principles of Criminal Law* (2nd ed), Indianapolis, Bobbs-Merrill, 1960, 27f.

65 (1952) 36 Cr App R 184 (CCA).

66 At least, at that time. Under modern law, it appears that Deller could now be convicted of an attempt. See chapter 6.

67 [1992] 1 AC 599, [1991] 4 All ER 481 (HL). Technically, the House of Lords did not abolish the exception but rather purported to recognise that, by the time of the defendant's actions, the historical immunity for spouses was no longer part of the law. (Cf the decision by the European Court of Human Rights in *SW v UK* Case

policy, the retrospective rather than de futuro manner in which it was achieved is more controversial, since it led to R's being convicted for conduct that was apparently not a criminal rape when done. The decision is defensible, perhaps, on the footing that R's conduct did constitute a crime when done by anyone else, and that the reasons for criminalisation apply just as forcefully to a husband as to anyone else. A more extreme case is that of *Shaw v DPP*.[68] Shaw was charged with conspiring to corrupt public morals — an offence that had not existed until he was indicted for it. His indictment was upheld by the House of Lords. *Whether or not* the defendant's actions were covered by an existing law, the courts were said to have residual power to criminalise his conduct.[69]

In our view, it is simply wrong to expect people to abide by a criminal law unless that law is stated in advance. Moreover, it undermines the entire operation of the law, as a system of rules designed to guide society's behaviour, when the rules are unknown. Retroactive crimes are inconsistent with both s 10A Crimes Act 1961 and s 26(1) New Zealand Bill of Rights Act 1990, which provide that no criminal enactment shall have a retrospective effect. Although ss 10A and 26(1) may be overridden by an express legislative enactment, they provide a signal protection against that possibility. Their existence should at least ensure that courts will, in the absence of the clearest language, be very loath to infer that a newly created crime, or a statutory increase in penalty, is to be given retrospective effect.[70] Moreover, conflict with ss 10A and 26(1) will make it obvious that a part of the criminal law transgresses the Rule of Law, and contravenes the defendant's basic human rights.

1.4.3 Fair warning

Apart from its constitutional implications, the most important reason for requiring criminal offences to be created prospectively is that failure to do so undermines predictability in the law. In *Shaw v DPP* (above), the enterprising Mr Shaw had been assured by his lawyer that his proposed publication, *The Ladies' Directory*, passed muster in legal terms. Yet the House of Lords found

---

No 47/1994/494/576.) Given acknowledgement of the exemption in quite recent cases such as *Steele* (1976) 65 Cr App R 22, and *Sharples* [1990] Crim LR 198, this otherwise vital distinction smacks of sophistry. From D's (and most lawyers') point of view, the immunity *was* effectively abolished by their Lordships.

68 *Shaw v DPP* [1962] AC 220, [1961] 2 All ER 446 (HL).

69 *Shaw* is objectionable on two counts: it is also discussed earlier in this chapter, with respect to criminalising *immoral* activity. See § 1.2.1.1. The House of Lords has since disavowed further extensions of the common law to enforce morality: *Knuller (Publishing, Printing and Promotions) Ltd v DPP* [1973] AC 435, [1972] 3 WLR 143 (HL). See Goodhart, "The *Shaw* Case: The Law and Public Morals" (1961) 77 LQR 560; Note (1962) 75 Harv LR 1652; Smith, "Judicial Law Making in the Criminal Law" (1984) 100 LQR 46.

70 Cf *R v King* [1995] 3 NZLR 409; *Hedges v Waitakere CC* 21/5/92, Barker J, HC Auckland AP114/92; *Dept of Labour v Latailakepa* [1982] 1 NZLR 632. Note that s 10A applies "notwithstanding any other enactment", so is subject to implied repeal only by *later* statutes.

that he, with others, had conspired to corrupt public morality. If even competent legal advice cannot predict the unlawfulness of a defendant's conduct, his attempt to live within the law is a farce.

However, it is important to notice that, in *Shaw*, predictability was threatened not merely because the offence was created retrospectively. Suppose, as some have argued, that the House of Lords resurrected rather than invented this species of conspiracy, and that the principle against retroactivity was not breached. Either way, the nebulous terms of the offence leave to speculation what kinds of thing one must not conspire to do.

This shows that non-retroactive legislation is not the only standard set by the Rule of Law, and that the need for predictability has more general implications. The criminal law is not there solely to tell police and judges what to do after someone offends, but also to tell *citizens* what not to do in advance. As such, it is not enough for there to be a law in place before people can commit a crime. They should also be told about it. This is the reason why non-publication or unavailability of a statutory instrument may be a defence, if a person commits a crime under that instrument while unaware of its existence.[71] There must be an opportunity for defendants to know the law before they are convicted of breaking it:

> Respect for law, which is the most cogent force in prompting orderly conduct in a civilised community, is weakened, if men are punished for acts which according to the general consensus of opinion they were justified in believing to be morally right *and in accordance with law*.[72]

The Rule of Law mandates that people should be governed "by rules which are fixed, knowable, and certain".[73] This requires both that the rule be stated in advance, and also that it be stated clearly. Clarity is essential if citizens are to have *fair warning*, that by their prospective actions they are in danger of incurring a criminal sanction.[74] If individuals understand the law, they will be

---

71 *Grant v Borg* [1982] 2 All ER 357, [1982] 1 WLR 638 (HL); *Burns v Nowell* (1880) 5 QBD 444 (CA); *Lim Chin Aik v R* [1963] AC 160, [1963] 1 All ER 223 (PC); *Golden-Brown v Hunt* (1972) 19 Fed LR 438; *R v Catholique* (1979) 104 DLR (3d) 161.

72 *State v O'Neil* (1910) 126 NW 454 at 456 (emphasis added). See Brett, "Mistake of Law as a Criminal Defence" (1966) 5 MULR 179 at 204.

73 Ashworth, *Principles*, 67, and see § 3.4 generally; also Raz, *The Authority of Law: Essays on Law and Morality*, Oxford, Clarendon Press, 1979, 214, 215.

74 Cf *Papachristou v City of Jacksonville* 405 US 156 at 162, 31 L Ed 2d 110 at 115 (1972) (vagrancy ordinance void for vagueness). Fair warning is also relevant to inadvertence-based liability, for example, for negligence. It is one reason why criminal liability for serious crimes should normally be confined to reckless or intentional wrongdoing. This is because if there were widespread exposure to state interference for inadvertent wrongdoing, then it would be much harder for citizens to plan and get on with their lives, without fearing the unforeseen disruption that facing criminal charges entails. See, for example, Hart, "Punishment and the Elimination of Responsibility" in *Punishment and Responsibility: Essays in the Philosophy of Law*, Oxford, Clarendon Press, 1968, 158, 181, 182. However, this argument is not insuperable. To the extent that the Rule of Law interdicts unpredictable interference by the State, liability for negligence is reasonably predictable. Moreover, unless negligence liability were no deterrent, the argument prima

able properly to decide what to do in light of the guidance that the law is meant to provide. Only then can the law act as the deterrent it is intended to be. And only then do citizens have a fair opportunity to steer themselves clear of criminal liability.

1.4.3.1 *Use of evaluative concepts*

A legal system, then, should seek to provide as much guidance and predictability as it can. However, realism is required when deciding what degree of certainty is attainable in particular laws. Explicitness is necessarily compromised in offences which involve vague and open-ended concepts such as "unreasonable", "excessive",[75] and "fraudulent". Similarly, if we drive a car we know, or should know, that we must drive with "due care and attention". The phrase sets a standard for a myriad of driving contexts and inevitably must leave an ultimate assessment to the court, which will find the phrase of no more than open-ended guidance. What degree of error or inattention will turn us into criminals cannot be stated with exactitude. If the criminal law is to involve itself with standards of safety, which surely it must, it cannot give a rigid specification of the circumstances under which criminal liability will follow.

Nonetheless, both Legislature and Judiciary should be cautious about the deployment and interpretation of such expressions. Consider, for example, the imposition of negligence-based criminal liability, through offences which are typically couched in terms of the "unreasonableness" of the defendant's behaviour. The touchstone, be it "unreasonable" or "negligent", is not susceptible of accurate or formal definition. What is "reasonable"? Nowhere does the law say, and to some extent the individual must judge the law's standard for herself, and risk the Court's disagreeing with her. Such gambles ought to be minimised,[76] and where possible these discretionary terms should be replaced by more concrete definitions of what counts as illegal, and what as legitimate.

This reservation should not be overstated, and it cannot be claimed that such terms deprive individuals of advance warning altogether. The defendant's judgment is not purely a guess: words such as "reasonable" are not meaningless.[77] We understand them, and know how to apply the implicit judgments they import. The use of broad evaluative terms such as "negligent" and "fraudulent" may well provide an acceptable level of guidance where

---

facie deprives victims of protection from similarly unlooked-for intrusions by other citizens.

75 Cf s 62 Crimes Act 1961.

76 "A statute which either forbids or requires the doing of an act in terms so vague that men of common intelligence must necessarily guess at its meaning and differ as to its application, violates the first essential of due process of law." *Conally v General Construction Company* 269 US 385 at 391 (1926). Cf Rawls, *A Theory of Justice*, Massachusetts, Belknap Press of Harvard University Press, 1971, 239: "if the precept of no crime without a law is violated, say by statutes being vague and imprecise, what we are at liberty to do is likewise vague and imprecise."

77 Lucas, "The Philosophy of the Reasonable Man" (1963) 13 Phil Qtrly 97.

there is a high degree of social consensus about appropriate behaviour in the area of activity under regulation. One may assume that degree of necessary consensus, for instance, in matters of road safety; accordingly a requirement to drive with due care and attention may tell us all we really need to know.[78]

Moreover, evaluative standards are useful. Terms like "reasonable", and "dangerous", give the law flexibility to deal with cases that a legislator might not foresee. It is too much to expect a statute to list every single mode of negligent homicide, and meaningful terms like "unreasonable" save us from being straightjacketed by a rigid specification of the circumstances under which criminal liability will or will not follow. Indeed, without such flexibility, the law would be unfair and incomplete. There will always be matters which require regulation, but where a degree of imprecision is inevitable.[79] Despite this, such terms *are* imprecise, and for that reason, at least in serious crimes, should normally be used only sparingly and for clear cases of wrongdoing.[80]

1.4.4 Statutory interpretation

In the previous section, we noted that the Rule of Law should not be cast as a demand for unattainable measures of predictability and certainty. A degree of imprecision is inherent in the enterprise of legal ordering. Statutes are necessarily expressed general terms, and must be interpreted and applied to particular cases. The agent of this process is the court.[81]

In practice, the Judicial task is more substantial than it need be. While legislators cannot be expected to foresee every variant case that might arise when they create an offence, the standard of drafting in this country is such that offences frequently omit to specify quite obvious matters, such as what (if any) mental element an offence requires, on whom a burden of persuasion may lay, and whether omissions as well as acts are within the conduct proscribed. Moreover, some fundamental aspects of the criminal law, such as causation, are

---

78 On the other hand, it is doubtful whether there is a sufficient degree of consensus about the acceptable contents of literature, plays and film to render the standards, "indecent" and "obscene", employed in indecency laws, a sufficient guide to producers and publishers of artefacts in those fields. (Cf s 124 Crimes Act 1961, and the Indecent Publications Act 1963.) If a government wishes to maintain a regulatory presence there, it is better that it regulates by description, expressly identifying those things which are not to be written, photographed or filmed: hence the use of a classification system under the Films, Videos, and Publications Classification Act 1993.

79 For example, for many years the courts sought a legal definition of when an act was sufficiently close to the commission of a crime to constitute an attempt to commit the crime. Various tests were tried; all were unsatisfactory. Nowadays it is simply asked whether an act was "more than merely preparatory". See chapter 6.

80 Cf the common law's requirement that negligence be "gross" before one may be guilty of manslaughter. See chapter 14.

81 For general discussion, see Ashworth, "Interpreting Criminal Statutes: a Crisis of Legality?" (1991) 107 LQR 419; Hall, "Strict or Liberal Construction of Penal Statutes" (1935) 48 Harv LR 748; MacCormick and Summers (eds), *Interpreting Statutes: a Comparative Study*, 1991; Jeffries, "Legality, Vagueness, and the Construction of Penal Statutes" (1985) 71 Va LR 189; Kremnitzer, "Interpretation in Criminal Law" (1986) 21 Israel LR 358.

largely untouched by statute. Consequently, the role of judges is pivotal and powerful.

One way of observing the rights and expectations of citizens under the Rule of Law is for judges to show a proper restraint when interpreting the rules of the criminal law. In the civil law — say, a case involving the law of restitution — a judgment may earn praise for the way it reconceptualises the grounds of restitution, thereby vindicating new restitutionary claims. Similar creativity in the criminal law is generally to be avoided, since the scope for condemnation and punishment is thereby enlarged. In *Kokkinakas v Greece*, the European Court of Human Rights spoke of the principle that:

> [T]he criminal law must not be extensively construed to the accused's detriment, for instance by analogy; it follows from this that an offence must be clearly defined in law. This condition is satisfied where the individual can know from the wording of the relevant provision and, if need be, with the assistance of the courts' interpretation of it, what acts and omissions will make him liable.[82]

This need for restraint means that the approach to interpretation of a criminal statute differs slightly from the proper approach to statutory interpretation in the civil law. It is not possible in a text of this nature to provide more than a brief overview of the relevant principles, and what follows is necessarily incomplete. When questions about the meaning of an offence arise, there are three steps for a court to take.

In the first instance, the interpretation of a criminal statute will not differ in technique from the interpretation of a civil statute. Modern statutory interpretation, both civil and criminal, should first take the form of ascertaining the *ordinary meaning in context*.[83] The reference to context is particularly important. It is a feature of language that meaning is not merely lexical, but also depends on the surrounding words and the purpose of the writer. For example, s 246 creates an offence, among other things, of procuring, by false pretence, another person to endorse a valuable security. On one lexical meaning, to "endorse" something is to express approval of it. But it is quite clear, both from the lexical context (a valuable security) and the purpose of the offence (to criminalise obtaining by false pretences), that the intended meaning is to assign by writing.

Even the best-drafted statute can require interpretive decisions by the court. If context as well as lexical meaning is addressed, one meaning will usually emerge as clearly the best suited to effect the purposes of the statute or the relevant part thereof. The technique outlined here is endorsed by s 5(j) Acts Interpretation Act 1924, which applies to both civil and criminal statutes, and

---

82 Case No 3/1992/348/421. The passage is apropos of art 7 European Convention on Human Rights, which proscribes convictions except for an offence in existence at the time of the relevant conduct.

83 Cf Bell and Engle, *Cross on Statutory Interpretation* (3rd ed), 1995, 31-33, 48f; Evans, *Statutory Interpretation: Problems of Communication*, Auckland, Oxford University Press, 1988, 19-22, 59f.

requires courts to construe a statutory provision in keeping with the purpose of the statute which enacts it.[84]

Sometimes the meaning cannot be determined within the four corners of the statute itself. In such cases, the courts have the power to investigate the legislative background of an Act in order to ascertain the intention of Parliament.[85] Unfortunately, whether or not the legislative history is consulted depends upon the inclination of judges. In the notorious case of *Commr of Police of the Metropolis v Caldwell*,[86] to which we return in chapter 3, Lord Diplock conceded that there was an issue of interpretation in respect of the meaning to be given to the culpability term "reckless". He resolved the issue by recourse to "ordinary" English, which informed him that the term comprehended not only defendants who perceived the likely consequences of their conduct, but also defendants who failed to give thought to the obvious consequences of that conduct. He signally failed to make resort to a Law Commission report which stated, unequivocally, that only defendants who actually perceived the consequences of their conduct were to be found reckless in cases of criminal damage.

Finally, if, after examining the statuary context, there is still some uncertainty about which interpretation is preferable, then the court should give the benefit of that uncertainty to the accused. This is a presumption of strict construction. It is justified by the requirement to give fair warning, which implies that ambiguity in offences should not be understood to create unpredictable offences; statutes should not require citizens to guess at their meaning, and so should be construed against imposing liability on a defendant who reasonably thought she was within the terms of the law. The principle of strict interpretation, confined to criminal and taxation statutes, may be expressed as follows:

> if a penal provision is reasonably capable of two interpretations that interpretation which is most favourable to the accused must be adopted.[87]

This is not to say that *any* measure of doubt over the meaning of a statute should be construed in the defendant's favour. The strict construction principle is a default rule, one to rely on if the meaning of the statute cannot be ascertained by other standard techniques. In the past, the principle of strict construction has been read as entailing that the benefit of *any* favourable

---

84   Per s 5(j), every Act shall be deemed remedial and receive a "fair, large, and liberal construction and interpretation" so as best to achieve its object according to its true intent, meaning, and spirit.

85   *Pepper (Inspector of taxes) v Hart* [1993] AC 593, [1993] 1 All ER 42 (HL). In terms of the Rule of Law, consultation of such sources as Hansard is unobjectionable provided the source is adequately made available to the public, so that potential defendants have fair warning of its import. See Evans, *Statutory Interpretation: Problems of Communication*, Auckland, Oxford University Press, 1988, 289.

86   [1982] AC 341, [1981] 1 All ER 961 (HL).

87   Per Lord Reid in *Sweet v Parsley* [1970] AC 132 at 149, [1969] 1 All ER 347 at 350 (HL). Cited by the Court of Appeal in *Millar v MOT* [1986] 1 NZLR 660 at 668, (1986) 2 CRNZ 216 at 224 (CA).

interpretation which passes a minimal threshold of plausibility must always be given to the defendant.[88] Yet, as Lord Reid recognised in *DPP v Ottewell*,[89] this extreme reading is untenable. Particularly in light of s 5(j) Acts Interpretation Act 1924, a lexically-possible meaning should not be adopted if the statutory context makes clear that an alternative interpretation is best suited to the purposes of the statute. Nonetheless, as a subsidiary principle, strict construction should be retained in modern criminal law.

The correct approach, it is submitted, is first to seek the ordinary meaning in context. Where, like the example of "endorse" in s 246, the meaning of a phrase emerges clearly from the context and purpose of the statute, there can be no objection, even for a criminal statute, to an interpretation which goes against the defendant. Otherwise, if the meaning is not apparent from the Act or the relevant part of the Act, a thorough review of the legislative history should be undertaken. If, after that exercise, the interpretation of the provision remains a matter of reasonable dispute, the benefit of the doubt should be given to the defendant. In practice, of course, the approach argued for here will always be vulnerable to judges minded to suppress interpretive uncertainty in the interests of crime control. That, however, would be to subvert the Rule of Law.

1.4.5 Fair labelling

We have seen that the ex ante guidance the law is meant to provide requires it to be clearly stated. There is, however, another reason for expecting clarity in criminal offences. When a crime occurs, justice must not only be done, it must be *seen* to be done. The law needs precision in order to identify exactly what offence the wrongdoer has committed. If he is publicly convicted of "murder", D should *be* a murderer and not a parking offender. At the same time, neither would it be satisfactory for the law simply to label all convicted offenders unspecifically as "criminals", for that would equate the convictions of rapists with pickpockets. The criminal law speaks to society as well as wrongdoers when it convicts them, and it should communicate its judgment with precision, by accurately naming the crime of which they are convicted. This requirement is known as the principle of fair labelling.[90]

The need for fair labelling is one reason why we should not combine the separate offences of murder and manslaughter into a single crime of culpable homicide, as was proposed in the Crimes Bill 1989. In the eyes of society, these are two different types of wrongdoing, and the communicative function of the law would be impaired were the law to blur that difference. Sir Robin Cooke (as he then was) recognised this when he criticised the Crimes Bill proposal:

---

88 For example, *R v Harris* (1836) 7 C & P 446, 173 ER 198.

89 [1970] AC 642 at 649, [1968] 3 All ER 153 at 157 (HL); cf *Tuck & Sons v Priester* (1887) 19 QBD 629 at 638 (CA).

90 Cf Ashworth, "The Elasticity of *Mens Rea*" in Tapper (ed), *Crime, Proof and Punishment: Essays in Memory of Sir Rupert Cross*, London, Butterworths, 1981, 45, 53-56; Williams, "Convictions and Fair Labelling" [1983] 42 CLJ 85.

[t]he issue is social as much as legal ... it should remain open to a jury, having heard the evidence, to condemn a crime as so heinous as to cry out for the name of murder ...[91]

Underlying this objection is the point that different offences criminalise actions which have differing social significance. So, for example, it would be a mistake to assimilate vandalism with negligent damage to property. Even though the harm to property is the same, vandalism expresses a certain sort of contempt for society, and the victim, that negligent damage does not. If the criminal law were not to distinguish between the two, a conviction would be potentially misleading.

The law must make clear what sort of criminal each offender is — what the conviction is *for*. It should communicate this to the defendant, so that he may know exactly what he has done wrong and why he is being punished; in order that his punishment appears meaningful to him, not just an arbitrary harsh treatment. In addition, the law should communicate the crime to the public, in order that they too may understand the nature of his transgression. The public record matters. While an employer may have few qualms about hiring a convicted fraudster as an orderly in a children's hospital, it would be an entirely different matter to contemplate employing someone who has been in jail for pædophilia.

---

91   "The Crimes Bill 1989: A Judge's Response" [1989] NZLJ 235 at 239.

2

The Actus Reus

In the last chapter we discussed some of the reasons why a person cannot and should not be guilty of a crime unless both (i) he has caused or is otherwise responsible for the external event prohibited by law — the actus reus; and (ii) he had a specified mental state (falling within the requirements of the particular crime) with respect to that external event — the mens rea. If D kills P, she may have brought about the actus reus of murder, but it does not follow that she has committed any offence. When the doctor gives a painkiller to her patient, who turns out to be unknowably allergic to it, she may kill that patient: but it is an accident, and no criminal liability will follow. The mens rea is missing. Conversely, if she administers the drug intending it to kill him, and he dies of an unrelated heart attack, then she does not murder him.[1] The actus reus is missing. In the next two chapters, we investigate the orthodox general principles of criminal law regarding these two elements. It is convenient to begin here with the actus reus.

---

1   *R v White* [1910] 2 KB 124, [1908-10] All ER Rep 340.

The actus reus of a crime is that part of the definition which does not refer to the defendant's mental state. It can usefully be divided into three types of ingredient: behaviour, consequences, and circumstances. Often the circumstances or consequences surrounding something the defendant does are relevant to her wrongdoing, and so the offence does not just turn on D's behaviour. It is an essential part of our concept of murder, for instance, that someone dies. Thus the victim's death — a consequence — is a constitutive part of the actus reus of murder in the Crimes Act 1961. Such offences are sometimes called "result crimes"[2] because they cannot be committed unless the defendant's actions cause the specified result or consequence actually to occur.

An example of a crime requiring *circumstances* is bigamy, which involves D's going through a marriage ceremony (the behaviour) while being married to someone else (the circumstance). It is important to realise that since specification of the actus reus of each offence differs, and is a matter for the Legislature to decide,[3] there is no requirement that all three types of ingredient be present in the actus reus of each offence. Hence the actus reus of murder — ie the killing of one person by another — requires that there be (i) some (unspecified) behaviour on the part of the defendant with (ii) the consequence that another person dies. By contrast, the actus reus of rape is made out if there is (i) behaviour (sexual intercourse) by the defendant with the victim, in (ii) circumstances where the victim does not consent to it. No consequence is necessary.

2.1 THE BEHAVIOUR ELEMENT

Normally, the actus reus doctrine requires an action of some sort; something *done* by the defendant. This is not always obvious. It might sometimes appear as though result crimes such as murder could be specified solely by reference to the consequence, and without the actus reus containing any behavioural element. Thus it is the outcome which is emphasised in Kenny's definition of actus reus: "such result of human conduct as the law seeks to prevent."[4] And consider, for instance, the crime of murder. Surely it is the result, death, which is central to that crime? People's lives are valuable, their deaths to be avoided if possible: were this not so, there would be no crime of murder. V's death is the harmful result that, as Kenny puts it, the law seeks to prevent. Without that death, murder is not and cannot be committed. The relevant harm has not occurred.

But the view that it is only the consequence or result that matters is not quite right. The law is not concerned with deaths *per se*, but rather with deaths that other people bring about. "A dead man with a knife in his back is not the *actus reus* of a murder. It is putting the knife in the back thereby causing the

---

2   The term is Gordon, *Criminal Law of Scotland* (2nd ed), Edinburgh, Green [for] the Scottish Universities Law Institute, 1978, 61. ·

3   Bearing in mind the sorts of constraints mentioned in the previous chapter, for example, of ordinary language (§ 1.4.4), and political morality (§ 1.2.1.1).

4   Turner, *Kenny's Outlines of Criminal Law* (19th ed), Cambridge, Cambridge University Press, 1966, 17.

death which is the *actus reus*."[5] Correspondingly, s 158 Crimes Act 1961 defines homicide not as "the death of a human being", but as "the killing of a human being by another". We agree that the result *is* important: it helps to mark out what type of wrongdoing the law is concerned with. Indeed, it is the nature of the result, rather than of the behaviour which causes it, that gives homicide its moral and social significance. Murder is murder whether done by knife or poison, and this is why the behaviour element of the actus reus is unspecific. But it exists all the same.

On the other hand, it is possible for an actus reus to consist *only* of behaviour. This is especially true of inchoate crimes, such as incitement and attempt, where there is no requirement that the incitement be effective or that the attempt be successful.[6] Crimes of this type are sometimes termed "conduct crimes", since the actus reus requires proof only of specified conduct by the defendant, without the need for any accompanying circumstances or consequences.

2.1.1 Behaviour and omissions

Where behaviour is an element of the actus reus, standard legal doctrine stipulates that the behaviour requirement is a requirement that there be a positive action by the defendant. Except occasionally, an omission will not do. Thus it is a crime for D to deliberately drown P, but no crime for D gleefully to stand on the beach and watch while his enemy, P, is caught in the tide and drowns nearby.[7]

This standard doctrine in fact comprises two rules. First, behaviour specified in an actus reus can prima facie only be satisfied by a positive act on the part of the defendant, and not by the defendant's omission. Secondly, there are certain exceptions to the first, prima facie rule. These exceptions usually arise when the defendant has a *duty* to intervene and prevent the rest of the actus reus from occuring; whereupon his failure to do so counts as an omission satisfying the behavioural element of that actus reus. The first rule is general in nature: the exceptions, and the duties upon which they are based, are specific and confined.

In the above approach the criminal law resembles the civil law, which is generally averse to imposing liability for omissions,[8] and is willing to do so

---

5   *Smith and Hogan*, 31.

6   Chapter 6.

7   Cf Stephen, *Digest of the Criminal Law* (4th ed), 1887, art 212. Other writing includes Glazebrook, "Criminal Omissions: The Duty Requirement in Offences Against the Person" (1960) 76 LQR 386; Hughes, "Criminal Omissions" (1958) 67 Yale LJ 590; Ashworth, "The Scope of Criminal Liability for Omissions" (1989) 105 LQR 424.

8   Cf *Zoernsch v Waldock* [1964] 2 All ER 256 at 262, [1964] 1 WLR 675 at 685; *Curran v Northern Ireland Co-ownership Housing Association Ltd* [1987] AC 718, [1987] 2 All ER 13; *Gautret v Egerton* (1867) LR 2 CP 371 at 375; *Quinn v Hill* [1957] VR 439 at 446, [1957] ALR 1127 at 1133; *Hill v Chief Constable of West Yorkshire* [1987] 1 All ER 1173, [1987] 2 WLR 1126; *East Suffolk Rivers Catchment Board v Kent* [1941] AC 74, [1940] 4 All ER 527. Per Salmond & Heuston, *The Law of Torts* (20th ed), London, Sweet & Maxwell, 1992, 224, "in

only in special cases where the reasons in favour are strong enough to override that aversion. The distinction between misfeasance and non-feasance is, as Fleming has said, "deeply rooted in the common law".[9] Duties to intervene are dependent upon, for example, the defendant's having created the risk[10] or in some other way having assumed responsibility for it.[11] Similarly, an omission to reject a contractual offer cannot constitute its acceptance.[12] Silence is no representation in the tort of deceit;[13] nor is it per se a misrepresentation when negotiating a contract.[14]

2.1.1.1 *Why omissions are special*

One might, of course, accept that the law often does distinguish between acts and omissions, but still ask why that distinction *should* make any practical difference to criminal liability. There are various reasons. One is based on considerations of autonomy. We value living in a society where citizens are respected as individuals — where they are free to live their own lives and pursue their own priorities without having their choices determined by legal duties to act or intervene. The prohibition of omissions is far more intrusive upon individuals' autonomy and freedom than is the prohibition of acts, which is why the systematic imposition of (criminal or civil) liability for failures to act is to be resisted.[15]

This is not to suggest that there should never be liability for omissions. Rather, it is an argument that liability for omissions should be exceptional, and not as widespread as liability for actions. At any moment in time, the number of positive actions we are doing is very small. But the number of things we are failing to do is enormous. This is because there are very few ways in which one can do an action, whereas the number of ways in which one can fail to do something is much greater. For example, while D is not saving the drowning swimmer she may be walking, reading a book, swimming herself, playing cricket, etc. But she cannot do any of these things while she *is* saving the

---

the absence of some existing duty the general principle is that there is no liability for a mere omission to act".

9   Fleming, *The Law of Torts* (8th ed), Sydney, Law Book Co, 1992, 146.

10 *Johnson v Rea Ltd* [1962] 1 QB 373, [1961] 1 WLR 1400; *Racine v CNR* [1923] 1 DLR 572.

11 For example *Horsley v MacLaren* [1972] SCR 441, 22 DLR (3d) 545.

12 *Felthouse v Bindley* (1862) 11 CB (NS) 869, 142 ER 1037.

13 *Peek v Gurney* (1873) LR 6 HL 377 at 392, 403, [1861-73] All ER Rep 116 at 124, 128; *Arkwright v Newbold* (1881) 17 Ch D 301, 318; *Lietzke (Installations) Pty Ltd v EMJ Morgan Pty Ltd* (1973) 5 SASR 88.

14 *Fox v Mackreth* (1788) 2 Cox Eq Cas 320 at 321; *Keates v The Earl of Cadogan* (1851) 10 CB 591, 138 ER 234; *Bell v Lever Bros Ltd* [1932] AC 161 at 227 [1931] All ER Rep 1 at 32.

15 See, very generally, Simester, "Why Omissions are Special" (1995) 1 Legal Theory 311; also the earlier discussion in §§ 1.2.1.2, 1.2.2.5. We do not claim (for it is controversial to do so — see Simester, ibid) that the act-omission distinction, of and by itself, is morally significant. However, it is worth mentioning that usually acts manifest a greater level of hostility than do omissions, and we tend to feel very differently about killers than about non-savers. Omissions are often incidental to the defendant's practical deliberations — they disclose a different and lesser fault, of limited imagination or empathy, rather than malice.

swimmer. The burden the law imposes when it prohibits a person from doing something is therefore lighter and less intrusive than when it orders that person to act. Enforced forbearance involves the sacrifice of fewer options, and is more likely to leave the defendant with a chance of conforming to law without significant derangement. "Compare being banished to Liechtenstein with being banished from Liechtenstein."[16] Or, in a more apposite example, compare being prohibited from drowning the other swimmers when sunbathing at a beach to being required to save (or, indeed, drown) them. Wholesale liability for omissions would force us constantly to interrupt our own actions and plans in order to prevent outcomes that are brought about by others: to become, in effect, our brothers' keepers. It would be incompatible with New Zealand's political nature as a liberal State.

A second consideration is that if prohibited omissions involve the sacrifice of more options, then they are also likely to require a greater sacrifice of our own interests. If D buys a piece of furniture for his home, why is he not held responsible for the lives that money would save in, say, Ethiopia? One factor is our acceptance that people are to some extent entitled to prefer their own interests, and the interests of those near to them, above the interests of others. A mother who gives her own child pocket money warrants no reproof when she does not do the same for the child next door. Of course, such a view may be no more than a moral mistake. But if so, it is an inescapable feature (flaw?) of our society, and the law must bow to its almost universal acceptance. Moreover, given that individuals exist in different and specific situations, they are typically better placed to assess and contribute to their own lives, and to the lives of those they know, than to the lives of strangers. It is better that parents look after their children themselves, rather than rely upon an agency to do so. These points help to explain examples where someone does not save starving children in foreign countries: they limit the extent to which the needs of strangers take precedence over and mandate the sacrifice of our own plans and interests. We cannot do everything, and it would be absurd to expect us to try. When we decide what to do we are entitled to acknowledge that our own lives, and the lives of people we are close to, are important to us. So, even apart from questions of autonomy, the law's adoption of the act-omission doctrine can be justified as a simple and workable means by which the law can recognise the priority individuals are entitled to accord the content of their own lives.

2.1.1.2 *The exceptions*

2.1.1.2(a) *Specific statutes*
Many statutes now contain offences which expressly impose liability for an omission. Often these are offences which can *only* be committed by omission, such as failing to provide a breath specimen, or failing to file a return to the Inland Revenue Department or the Companies Office. Such offences involve

---

16 Bennett, "Morality and Consequences" in McMurrin (ed), *The Tanner Lectures on Human Values*, Salt Lake City, University of Utah Press, 1981, 47, 78; cf Bennett, *The Act Itself* (1995) 92. A similar principle applies in the context of false imprisonment: *Bird v Jones* (1845) 7 QB 742, 115 ER 668.

specific reference to a behavioural element on the part of the defendant. A second variety of statutory crime which can be done, indirectly, by omission is that where the actus reus names no behavioural element at all, and requires only proof of certain events or circumstances.[17] (We discuss this type of offence below, in § 2.1.2.) Characteristically, offences of this sort are an indirect imposition of liability for D's omission to prevent the specified event or outcome occurring. Of course, in these cases liability will also lie for bringing the outcome about by a positive act. But no such act is *required*.

In the context of homicide, the Crimes Act 1961 has enacted certain specific categories of liability for omission. Because they are similar to the duties existing at common law, these will be noted where relevant in the discussion below.[18]

2.1.1.2(b) *Duties imposed on persons in a special relationship to the victim*

Sometimes, even without statutory intervention, the law holds that considerations such as autonomy and self-interest are outweighed. This occurs when the defendant is found to be under a legal duty, such as the duty parents have to their children. A stranger can stand by and watch a child starve or drown, but that child's parent cannot.

The law does not normally require us to be guardians of the interests of others. But parents already *are* the guardians of their children, and are responsible for their welfare. The law does no more than reflect that by imposing a legal duty upon parents to intervene on behalf of their children. In the context of homicide, these particular duties are expressly reflected in the Crimes Act 1961. Section 152, for example, sets out the duty of parents to provide the necessaries of life to their children.[19] It must be remarked, however, that the duties of parents are more wide-ranging than this. A parent's failure easily to rescue her child would count as the actus reus of murder even though it is scarcely a failure to supply "necessaries". And more generally, a parent who willingly permits another to assault his child (when he can prevent this happening) is himself guilty of an assault.[20]

So a parent has a duty to rescue his child from harm. But is this so if the child is 30? Where the child is no longer dependent upon her parents, a special relationship still exists between them, but it no longer involves the same commitment to responsibility for the child's welfare.[21] It is the latter, we think, that is the more important feature. Thus, in our view, parents do not ordinarily

---

17   For example, the offence in *Finau v Dept of Labour* [1984] 2 NZLR 396 (CA).

18   To the extent that these statutory provisions define the scope of particular common law duties, they appear to exclude homicide liability based upon any wider existing common law duty. See *Adams* § CA160.14; chapter 14. The provisions appear to be capable of applying to other offences. See, for example, § 15.4.

19   Cf ss 151 and 154; also, at common law, *R v Gibbins and Proctor* (1918) 13 Cr App R 134.

20   Cf *R v Emery* (1993) 14 Cr App R (S) 394; *R v Russell* [1933] VLR 59, [1993] ALR 76.

21   Compare s 152, the application of which terminates when the child reaches the age of 16 years.

owe legal duties to rescue their adult children.[22] Nor do children owe such duties to their parents.[23] This is not to deny that people have moral obligations to their relatives. But it is quite a different matter to hold them criminally liable for failing to discharge those obligations.

The view that, rather than the closeness of their emotional or other relationship, it is D's responsibility for V's welfare that is the decisive feature is reflected in s 151. This section places a duty to provide the necessaries of life on the shoulders of those with "charge" of anyone "unable to provide himself with the necessaries of life". The same view ties in also with the case law regarding legal duties owed toward someone who is in the defendant's care. In *R v Stone and Dobinson*,[24] S and his mistress D (both somewhat backward) were held to have assumed responsibility for the care of S's sister, who died from a combination of anorexia nervosa and their incompetent neglect. *Both* were convicted of manslaughter, irrespective of the fact that only S was related to V.[25]

It would seem that a marriage or similar relationship contains, by its nature, a mutual obligation to protect one's spouse or partner. In *R v Russell*, R's wife had drowned herself and their sons while R was present. R was convicted of the manslaughter of not only the sons but also the wife.[26] Presumably that responsibility would not extend to a mere sexual relationship.[27]

2.1.1.2(c) *Duties imposed on persons assuming a particular responsibility*

The cases discussed so far have been concerned with duties arising from a wide-ranging and unspecific responsibility for another's welfare. Such duties tend to be general in nature, with the result that the criminal law treats omissions like actions for most purposes. A more complex relationship is that between the doctor and her patient.[28] This duty is a confined one — a doctor on

---

22   *R v Smith* (1826) 2 C & P 449, 172 ER 203; *R v Shepherd* (1862) 9 Cox CC 123; contra *R v Chattaway* (1922) 17 Cr App R 7.

23   Contra *Smith and Hogan*, 51; but see 53, 54.

24   [1977] QB 354. Arguably, the Court's finding of an assumed responsibility was doubtful on the facts; see the short discussion of the case by Ashworth, "The Scope of Criminal Liability for Omissions" (1989) 105 LQR 424 at 443.

25   Cf *R v West London Coroner's Court, ex p Gray* [1988] QB 467, [1987] 2 All ER 129; *R v Gibbins and Proctor* (1918) 13 Cr App R 134; *R v Conde* (1867) 10 Cox CC 547; *R v MacDonald* [1904] St R Qd 151; *R v Foster* (1906) 26 NZLR 1254; *R v Instan* [1893] 1 QB 450; *R v Marriott* (1838) 8 Car & P 425, 173 ER 559; *R v Nicholls* (1874) 13 Cox CC 75. See Williams, "Criminal Omissions — The Conventional View" (1991) 107 LQR 86, 90. A valuable and wide-ranging discussion may be found in *R v Taktak* (1988) 14 NSWLR 226, 34 A Crim R 334.

26   [1933] VLR 59, [1933] ALR 76 (McArthur J dissenting).

27   Cf *People v Beardsley* 113 NW 1128 (1907). Or, nowadays, to an estranged spouse: contra *R v Plummer* (1844) 1 C & K 600, 174 ER 954. In *R v Smith* [1979] Crim LR 251 the Court of Appeal assumed that the institution of marriage did not of itself generate a duty of care between spouses. See France, "The Law of Omissions — Proposals for Reform" (1992) 7 Otago LR 625.

28   Cf s 155. For other examples of a role-based responsibility, see *R v Dythams* [1979] QB 772, [1979] 3 All ER 641 (duty of a police officer to protect others) and *R v Curtis* (1885)

her way home may drive past the scene of an accident without attracting criminal liability for doing so. The duty applies only to the patients in her care. In such cases, injury resulting from the doctor's failure to provide proper care is regarded by the criminal law just as if it were brought about by an act of improper treatment.

Even to her patients, however, the doctor's duty is not all-encompassing. She may not kill by positive act, but it appears that she may withdraw care, with judicial approval, from a patient in a persistent vegetative state.[29] The duty is not to keep the patient alive, but to make reasonable efforts to do so, consonant with proper medical practice,[30] and only insofar as doing so is in the patient's best interests.[31]

Another source of specific criminal law duties is civil law obligations. The classic case is *R v Pittwood*.[32] D had been employed by a railway company to keep the gate at a level crossing. He went to lunch forgetting to close the gate. A haycart subsequently entered the crossing and was struck by a train. D was convicted of manslaughter. It is not clear whether D's duty depends on his having been hired to discharge a duty to the public that was owed by his employers,[33] or is grounded on the fact that he was hired to protect other people and that they were likely to be injured by his dereliction. The latter seems to have been the rationale adopted by Wright J.[34] Either way, however, cases such as *Pittwood* will now usually fall within the scope of s 157, which establishes a legal duty whenever D "undertakes" to do an act the omission of which may be dangerous to life.

2.1.1.2(d) *The continuing act doctrine*

Sometimes a defendant brings about an actus reus without mens rea but then, while the harmful consequences continue, intentionally omits to remedy or discontinue them. In such cases the "continuing act" doctrine may be applied, and liability imposed without the need to find a legal duty owed by the

---

15 Cox CC 746 (duty of a local authority officer to provide medical assistance to a destitute person).

29 *Auckland Area Health Board v AG* [1993] 1 NZLR 235; *Airedale NHS Trust v Bland* [1993] AC 789, [1993] 1 All ER 821. See also the case note by Finnis, "*Bland*: Crossing the Rubicon?" (1993) 109 LQR 329.

30 Cf *TBCL*, 236.

31 *Airedale NHS Trust v Bland* [1993] AC 789 at 868, 869, [1993] 1 All ER 821 at 869, 870 (Lord Goff). See also the difficult cases involving the degree of care owed by doctors to handicapped neonates: *Arthur* (1981) 12 B Med LR 1; *Re B* (1981) [1990] 3 All ER 927; *Re F* [1990] 2 AC 1, [1989] 2 WLR 1025.

32 (1902) 19 TLR 37. See also *R v Hughes* (1857) Dears & Bell 248, 169 ER 996; approved in *R v Roberts* [1942] 1 All ER 187 at 192; *Kelly v R* [1923] VLR 704 at 708 (reversed on a different ground in 32 CLR 509).

33 Compare *R v Smith* (1869) 11 Cox CC 210, where a watchman who deserted his post was held not liable for manslaughter because his employer has no duty to provide a watchman. The decision is criticised by Turner in Kenny's *Outlines of Criminal Law* (17th ed), 1958, 169.

34 "The man was paid to keep the gate shut and protect the public . . . A man might incur criminal liability from a duty arising out of contract." (1902) 19 TLR 37 at 38.

defendant. In *Fagan v Metropolitan Police Commr*,[35] F accidentally drove onto a policeman's foot. When apprised of his action, he refused to move the car. He was convicted of assault on the basis that his refusal to remove the vehicle amounted to a continuation of the original (positive) act of battery,[36] and was not a mere omission. Hence it could satisfy the actus reus requirement.

2.1.1.2(e) *Duties imposed on persons with a special relationship to the harm*

In *R v Miller*,[37] a vagrant set fire to his mattress with a cigarette while sleeping. He awoke to find the mattress smouldering. Without taking any steps to extinguish the fire, he simply moved to the next room and went to sleep. The house itself caught fire, and he was charged with arson. Although the English Court of Appeal upheld his conviction on the basis of a continuing act, the House of Lords took an alternative approach. It acknowledged that the arson had been committed by M's knowing omission to deal with the fire, and held that this omission could satisfy the actus reus requirement because M's unintentional starting of the fire *created* a legal duty. The duty is "to take measures that lie within one's power to counteract a danger that one has oneself created."[38] The relevant sorts of "danger" are those which threaten an interest protected by the criminal law — thus the duty arises where, unless D intervenes, his earlier (positive) act will bring about the actus reus. (*Miller*, therefore, can be distinguished where necessary[39] from *Fagan* (above), where the actus reus had already occurred.)

Note that a defendant's subsequent failure to prevent the risk will not by itself constitute an offence — it must be accompanied by such other elements of the offence as are required, eg mens rea.

2.1.1.3 *Restrictions by statutory language*

Some offences exclude liability for omissions by specifying the particular type of behaviour that is required. For example, s 199 creates an offence of, among other things, "throwing" acid. It would seem that this manner of behaving can only be done by a positive act. Similarly, the actus reus of rape and other forms of sexual violation requires an active sexual connection with the victim; an omission cannot suffice.[40]

In these offences, liability for omissions is restricted because the behavioural element of the actus reus has been specified quite precisely by statute. Conversely, omission-based liability should normally be possible where an offence has an unspecific behaviour element, and its actus reus is defined mainly by reference to consequences or circumstances. An example of this is

---

35   [1969] 1 QB 439, [1968] 3 All ER 442.

36   Which had not itself been an assault because F lacked mens rea at that time.

37   [1983] 2 AC 161, [1983] 3 All ER 978. Cf Smith [1982] Crim LR 527; Williams [1982] Crim LR 773. For an extension of this type of case see *R v Speck* [1977] 2 All ER 859, (1977) 65 Cr App R 161, in which D was convicted of gross indecency because he passively allowed an 8-year-old girl to touch him indecently.

38   [1983] 2 AC 161 at 176, [1983] 1 All ER 978 at 981.

39   For example, § 2.1.1.3.

40   Section 128.

"homicide", in s 158, which is defined as "the killing of a human being by another, directly or indirectly, by any means whatsoever" — in essence, as the causing of death by D.

Homicide is a clear case. It is settled law that culpable homicide can be committed by omission.[41] But what about other offences? Assault, for example, is defined inter alia as the act of intentionally applying force to the person of another. Can this be done by omission? *Adams* is doubtful,[42] a view France shares:[43]

> Assault is defined as *the act* of intentionally applying force to the person of another. Such a definition leaves little scope for assault by omission although factually it is very easy to conceive of such an event. One who intentionally leaves a leg out to see V fall over it knowing V has not seen the danger surely assaults V as much as by putting the leg out to trip V. The section, however, by employing the term "act" would not embrace this conduct.

But no authority is cited. With respect to these authors, it seems implausible to say that a parent who intentionally trips his child in the way France describes cannot be convicted of assault. He certainly ought to be. It is submitted that where an offence is unspecific as to the manner of behaviour required, it should be possible to commit that offence by omission. The fact that an offence is defined in terms of "action", as such, should not be determinative. This is especially since positive action is the default requirement of offences with a behavioural element anyway — the entire sphere of omissions liability is predicated on an exception from that requirement.

Sometimes, as we have seen, the action requirement *is* excluded by linguistic considerations. It would be unfair to convict a defendant for conduct the statutory language clearly excludes.[44] But such instances are and should be rare. There is no judicial compunction about saying that a parent can kill a child by failing to feed it, however odd that might sound,[45] and it is submitted that mere linguistic variations, which do not reflect valid moral principles or distinctions, should normally be secondary in importance to the general legal doctrine which applies to omissions.

---

41   Cf s 160(2)(b); *R v Gibbins and Proctor* (1918) 13 Cr App R 134.

42   "The requirement of an 'act' suggests that assault can never be committed by a mere omission": § CA196.10.

43   France "The Law of Omissions — Proposals for Reform" (1992) 7 Otago LR 625 at 628.

44   See the fair warning discussion in § 1.4.3. (An example might be arson in s 294, which requires that the defendant "sets fire to" the item in question.) For this reason Williams argues in a letter to the editor of the Criminal Law Review that "the courts should not create liability for omissions without statutory authority. Verbs used in defining offences and prima facie implying active conduct should not be stretched by interpretation to include omissions": [1982] Crim LR 773. See also his "Criminal Omissions — The Conventional View" (1991) 107 LQR 86 at 87-89; "What should the Code do about Omissions" (1987) 7 LS 92 at 94, 95.

45   And for other examples, see *R v Shama* [1990] 2 All ER 602, [1990] 1 WLR 661; *R v Firth* (1990) 91 Cr App R 217, [1990] Crim LR 326.

If such harms as "killing", "wounding",[46] and "injuring"[47] can be done by omission, and if the difference between various offences as to whether one can be convicted for an omission is not to be arbitrary and piecemeal, then a coherent general approach should be taken. Unless the Legislature has demonstrated a contrary intention by specifying the particular manner of behaviour in which the offence must be committed, a criminal offence should be capable of being committed by omission. This is the only approach capable of producing predictable and consistent rather than random law. Any concern over the width of that approach should be tempered by the realisation that the defendant would have to be under a legal duty to act, and that mens rea would still have to be proved.

One important point to emphasise is that, even where omission-based liability is excluded by the terms of the offence, a conviction may still be obtained under the continuing act doctrine (§ 2.1.1.2(d)). Suppose that D and V are having consensual sexual intercourse, and that sexual connection has already occurred. During intercourse, V withdraws her consent. D, however, knowingly remains in a state of sexual connection with V. His passive failure to desist is a continuation of the original act of having sexual connection with V. Since it is no longer consented to, he commits the actus reus of rape.[48]

2.1.1.4 *Omissions and consequences: causation*
One problem that arises for omissions is whether or not they can be said to "cause" things. Characteristically, what is significant about omissions is that they fail to prevent *other* factors from bringing about the harm. If D watches from the beach while V drowns, a post-mortem will conclude that V's death was caused by excessive time underwater. D merely failed to intervene: can she truly be said to have caused V's death? We shall consider this question more fully in § 2.2.4, when we discuss causation. But it is clear that in the law, omissions can be causes — or perhaps one should say, causal factors. If D could have saved V, then her failure to do so was *a* reason why V died. And if D had a legal duty to save her, then that failure will be a cause of death in law.

2.1.1.5 *Distinguishing acts from omissions*
Given that, as we have seen, there is normally no liability for omissions, it is important to be able to distinguish acts from omissions in order to decide whether a defendant's behaviour counts as one or the other. Unfortunately, the line between them is not easily drawn:[49]

> If a doctor is keeping a patient alive by cranking the handle of a machine and he stops, this looks like a clear case of omission. So too if the machine is electrically operated but switches itself off every 24 hours and the doctor deliberately does not

---

46 Cf s 188 (wounding with intent), which is expressed in causal terms *simpliciter*, without any restriction regarding the manner of D's behaviour.

47 Section 2(1) Crimes Act 1961, merely "to cause actual bodily harm".

48 *Kaitamaki v R* [1984] 1 NZLR 385, [1985] AC 147 (PC).

49 *Smith and Hogan*, 52. See, in respect of the examples, Williams, *TBCL*, 236, 237; Kennedy, "Switching Off Life Support Machines: The Legal Implications" [1977] Crim LR 443; Benyon, "Doctors as Murderers" [1982] Crim LR 17.

re-start it. Switching off a functioning machine looks like an act; but is it any different in substance from the first two cases? On the other hand, is it any different from cutting the high-wire on which a tight-rope walker is balancing? — which is an act, if ever there was one. Is the ending of a programme of dialysis an omission, while switching off a ventilator is an act? Is the discontinuance of a drip feed, which is keeping a patient alive, by withdrawing the tube from his body an act? and failure to replace an emptied bag an omission? It seems offensive if liability for homicide depends on distinctions of this kind; but it appears to be so.

Why is switching off a ventilator an act, and failing to (re)start it an omission? The difference seems to be that the former *requires* certain bodily movements, whereas the latter does not. Switching the ventilator off can be done in only one way,[50] but failing to switch the ventilator on (or off) can be done while doing any number of things — one might be talking to the nurse, reading a journal, taking a walk, booking dinner at a restaurant, etc. Similarly, cranking the handle of a machine and cutting the high-wire are actions because they require very specific behaviour by D: not cranking the handle, and not replacing the emptied bag, are not specific about D's behaviour at all.

As we saw earlier, this difference is an important facet of the rationale for separating omissions from acts when it comes to criminalisation. Prohibiting omissions rules out many more options than does prohibiting acts. If D is enjoined by law not to strike V, that leaves him with plenty of freedom for legal movement of his arm, not to mention the rest of his body. But if D is *required* to strike V (ie prohibited from omitting to do so) then his freedom of movement is severely curtailed. His options are down to one.

The difference is legally irrelevant, however, where the defendant is held responsible for the actus reus through the existence of a legal duty. With this in mind, we should reconsider Sir John Smith's remark that "it seems offensive if liability for homicide depends on distinctions of this kind; but it appears to be so". The obvious response is that liability does not *just* depend on the act/omission distinction, but also on the issue in each case whether D is under a duty to intervene. What his examples do suggest, though, is that one might be doubtful of the judicial reasoning in life-and-death medical cases. In *Airedale NHS Trust v Bland*,[51] B had been in a persistent vegetative state for 3½ years without medical hope of improvement. Having obtained parental consent, the hospital applied for a declaration that it would be lawful to discontinue artificial ventilation, feeding, and hydration, with the intention that B should be allowed to die. The House of Lords upheld the declaration. Their Lordships affirmed that for the doctors to bring about B's death by lethal injection or suchlike would be murder, but reasoned that (i) what was proposed was an omission rather than an act, and (ii) the legal duty of the doctors did not extend to prolonging treatment of a patient when it was no longer in his best interests to do so.[52]

---

50   Or, at most, in only a few ways.
51   [1993] AC 789, [1993] 1 All ER 821.
52   Ibid at 868, 869, at 869, 870 (Lord Goff).

The difficulty with this reasoning is that ceasing of treatment involved switching off the ventilator. That is an act, not an omission. An intruder who does such a thing commits murder, even though she has no legal duty to save the patient's life. The true explanation of these cases must surely be that there is a very limited justification available to doctors, in certain circumstances, to take some quite specific measures toward ending life. Those measures can include particular acts as well as omissions.

2.1.2 Crimes with no behaviour element

Some academic writers have suggested that there can be no criminal liability without a "voluntary act" on the part of the defendant; meaning by this that there must be (i) a behavioural element specified in every actus reus, which (ii) must be done "voluntarily" by the defendant.[53] We agree with the second aspect of this suggestion, which is discussed in more detail later (§ 2.3). The first claim, however, is less plausible.

It is certainly true that crimes such as murder, rape, and assault — with which ordinary citizens are most familiar, and which have the greatest moral resonance — are crimes which require wrong*doing*, and necessarily involve some behaviour (whether act or omission) by the defendant. But many less well-known crimes need involve no behavioural element on the part of the defendant. These are offences which penalise a defendant on the basis of the situation in which she finds herself. It is the circumstances themselves which make up the harm that the criminal law is designed to address, and so it is possible to specify the actus reus of these crimes solely by reference to those circumstances.

For convenience, we can divide offences of this sort into two main types: crimes where the actus reus specifies only the occurrence of some state of affairs; and crimes of possession.

2.1.2.1 *Crimes involving states of affairs*

Sometimes known as crimes of "situational liability",[54] these are crimes where the actus reus is simply an event or circumstance that is in some way connected to the defendant. An example is provided by s 56(4) Dog Control and Hydatids Act 1982:

---

53 For example, Stephen, *A History of the Criminal Law of England* vol II, London, Macmillan and Co, 1883, 97; Cross and Jones, *An Introduction to Criminal Law* (3rd ed), 1953, 32; Turner, Kenny's *Outlines of Criminal Law* (17th ed), 1958, 26, 27; O'Connor and Fairall, *Criminal Defences* (2nd ed), 1988, 2, 6, 7; Moore, *Act and Crime: the theory of action and its implications for criminal law*, Oxford, Clarendon Press, 1993, chapter 2. The claim made is normally, in fact, even stronger: that there must be a positive (and voluntary) act by the defendant specified in every actus reus. Our phrasing is designed to allow for omissions.

54 Glazebrook, "Situational Liability" in Glazebrook (ed), *Reshaping the Criminal Law: Essays in Honour of Glanville Williams*, London, Stevens, 1978, 108; Cohen, "The 'Actus Reus' and Offences of 'Situation'" (1972) 7 Israel LR 186. Crimes of this sort are sometimes ruled unconstitutional in the US: *Robinson v California* (1962) 370 US 660, 8 L Ed 2d 758 (being addicted to narcotics); *Papachristou v City of Jacksonville* (1972) 405 US 156, 31 L Ed 2d 110 (being a vagrant).

> The owner of any dog that makes any such attack [on any person, stock, or poultry] commits an offence and is liable on summary conviction to a fine not exceeding $500

Here the actus reus of the offence is apparently complete without the need to prove any act or omission on the part of the defendant.

Of course, it is not enough for a defendant to be criminally liable for an offence just because something bad happens — for example, because a dog attacks another person. The defendant must in some way be connected to, and responsible for, the actus reus. Normally this connection is through his having a particular status, or relationship, with respect to that actus reus. If a dog attacks someone, it is only the dog's *owner* who is picked out for attention by the criminal law, and not, for instance, every person living on that street. Situational offences are in this respect similar to offences of omission, in that they raise the problem of attribution to defendants, discussed earlier (§ 1.2.2.5). The potential for over-broad criminalisation means that there is a need on the part of the legislator to contain liability by specifying only defendants who are responsible for, and in a position to control, the prohibited situation.

The requirement for a particular status or relationship is typically found in another type of situational liability, being the vicarious criminal liability sometimes imposed on employers for the acts of their employees. Vicarious liability is dealt with further in chapter 5.[55] A third form of connection may be seen in the notorious English case *R v Larsonneur*.[56] In that case, L was convicted of being found in the UK when permission for her to enter the country had previously been refused. It was, however, undisputed that the only reason for her being back on UK soil was that she had been brought there against her will by the police. In convicting her of a situational liability offence, the law has picked out Larsonneur because it was she to whom the actus reus happened, and not because of anything she did.[57]

Larsonneur has been widely criticised, and rightly so.[58] But the proper reason for criticising it is less clear. One problem with the case is that the language used in many situational offences does not appear to require any mens rea or fault element on the part of the defendant. This is an important criticism, and we shall return to it in chapter 4. But that has not been the only ground of opposition. Ashworth, for instance, disapproves of "defining an offence in a way that seems to require no act by the defendant as a basis for liability".[59] His objection is that, quite apart from there being no mens rea element, there is no behavioural requirement in the actus reus. However, in our view Ashworth's

---

55 See also § 1.2.2.5.

56 (1933) 149 LT 542. See too *Winzar v Chief Constable of Kent*, The Times, 28 March 1983; contrast that case with *Palmer-Brown v Police* [1985] 1 NZLR 365, also reported as *Palmer-Brown v Hohaia* (1984) 1 CRNZ 306 (CA); also *O'Sullivan v Fisher* [1954] SASR 33.

57 Though see Lanham, "Larsonneur Revisited" [1976] Crim LR 276, who suggests the possibility of prior fault.

58 For example, Hall, *GPCL*, 329, n 14; Williams, *CLGP* 11; Howard, *Strict Responsibility*, London, Sweet & Maxwell, 1963, 47.

59 *Principles*, 105.

point is not a valid objection. There is nothing inherently defective or unjust about an offence which contains no behaviour element.

To see this, *Larsonneur* may be contrasted with the New Zealand case *Finau v Dept of Labour*,[60] where F was prosecuted under the Immigration Act 1964 for remaining in New Zealand after the expiry of her visitor's permit. The Court of Appeal upheld F's appeal against conviction on the basis that it had been impossible for her to leave the country, owing to her pregnancy and the consequent refusal of any airline to carry her.

At the level of principle, *Finau* and *Larsonneur* are inconsistent decisions. It is, of course, the former which is authoritative in New Zealand. Yet even at the more abstract level of principle, *Finau* is to be preferred. The result in that case demonstrates that there need be no injustice, and there is nothing intrinsically wrong, in criminalising states of affairs, so long as the class of potential defendants is clearly identified. What *Finau* does is to make clear a further proviso: that the defendant could have done something about it. The actus reus, although it specifies no act or omission, must still have been *voluntary*. More on this in § 2.3. But it is the failure to observe *this* requirement which seems to us the main problem with *Larsonneur*, and (even apart from its inconsistency with *Finau*) the reason why that case should not be followed.

It is submitted that, unless there is a requirement of voluntariness, situational offences are at odds with the deepest presuppositions of the criminal law. The very notion of a trial, of a plea, assumes putative answerability for something. One is not answerable for a state of affairs (eg having red hair), and it should not be the actus reus of an offence, unless one is able to avoid that state of affairs (eg by shaving one's head or dyeing the hair another colour).

Where, by contrast with the facts of *Finau* and *Larsonneur*, the defendant *could* have prevented the actus reus from occurring, then situational liability is, in effect, very much like liability for voluntary omissions. Indirectly, it involves the defendant being prosecuted for her failure or omission to prevent the actus reus from happening. A case of this sort is *Tifaga v Dept of Labour*.[61] There D *was* convicted of overstaying, following the termination of his temporary entry permit, because his inability to leave the country was due to his own failure to retain sufficient funds to do so.

2.1.2.2 *Crimes of possession*

Possessory offences are a creation of statute. They are not found in the common law.[62] There are a number of such offences on the books, especially relating to drugs, and to weapons or tools of crime.[63] According to s 7 Misuse of Drugs Act

---

60 [1984] 2 NZLR 396; also with *Martin v State of Alabama* (1944) 17 So 2d 427. Contrast the approach of the House of Lords in *Porter v Honey* [1988] 3 All ER 1045, [1988] 1 WLR 1420.

61 [1980] 2 NZLR 235.

62 Compare, for example, *R v Heath* (1810) Russ & Ry 184, 168 ER 750; *Dugdale v R* (1853) 1 E & B 435, 118 ER 499.

63 For example, s 244 Crimes Act 1961 (instruments of burglary); s 50 Arms Act 1983 (pistol or restricted weapon).

1975, for example, it is a crime to a person to "have in his possession . . . any controlled drug". The offence makes no reference to the defendant's conduct.

Characteristically, possession is criminalised as a convenient substitute for the harm that is really objected to, being the *use* of the thing possessed. Criminalisation at the earlier stage both simplifies evidential issues and makes an offence out of behaviour which might otherwise not even count as an *attempt* to do the ultimate crime contemplated. Thus, if offences of this sort did not exist, the police would not be able to intervene at an early stage to prevent many crimes without the prospective offender's escaping the clutches of the criminal law. It is undesirable as well as wasteful of resources that they should have to wait until the offence has commenced before making an arrest.[64]

In crimes of possession, there is no formal requirement for an act or omission by the defendant.[65] No doubt D put the crowbar in his car before heading out to commit a burglary, but the offence requires only that he *has* it.[66] It does not matter how that situation came about.[67] Nonetheless, like offences of situational liability, possessory offences can be thought of as having an implicit behavioural element, albeit one that the prosecution need not prove. In effect, criminalisation of D's possession of the crowbar may be treated as imposing an indirect liability, *either* for the act of obtaining the crowbar (ie acquiring possession), or for the omission by D to dispose of it.[68]

So possession and situational offences do not contain the normal requirement for proof of a behavioural element on the part of the defendant. Despite this, criminal convictions in these cases do not really violate the so-called "voluntary act" requirement, since they can each be explained in terms which incorporate an underlying behavioural component. Although the prosecution need not establish any particular conduct by the defendant, recognition of this underlying component helps to explain some of the more difficult cases where D did not obtain the prohibited item by means of his own efforts. Suppose that D is stopped while in his car, and is found to have with him a package containing cannabis. He claims, however, that he had nothing to

---

64 For criticism of this rationale, see Fletcher, *Rethinking Criminal Law* Boston, Little, Brown & Co, 1978, 197-205.

65 It is otherwise in the US; § 2.01(4) Model Penal Code states that possession is established "if the possessor knowingly procured or received the thing possessed or was aware of his control thereof for a sufficient period to have been able to terminate his possession".

66 The nature of this requirement of physical custody will vary for different offences. It may be enough that the crowbar is held by a third party who will give it immediately to D if asked: *R v McRae* (1993) 10 CRNZ 61 at 66, 67 (CA). In the case of drugs, the physical element of possession will be established if the substance is present at a place which is subject to D's dominion or control: *Police v Emirali* [1976] 2 NZLR 476; *Rose v Loo Kee* [1927] GLR 403.

67 The possibility of inadvertent possession, however, is usually excluded by the mens rea requirement for knowledge that the courts have held is implicit in the word "possess". Cf *R v Cox* [1990] 2 NZLR 275, (1990) 5 CRNZ 653 (CA); *R v Cugullere* [1961] 1 WLR 858.

68 Cf Williams, *CLGP*, 8; Husak, *Philosophy of the Criminal Law* Totowa, NJ, Rowan to Littlefield, 1987, 12; Moore, *Act and Crime: the Theory of Action and its Implications for Criminal Law*, Oxford, Clarendon Press, 1993, 21.

do with the presence of the package in his car, and that it had been placed there by a friend. While that claim would suggest that D is not responsible — and therefore should not be criminally liable[69] — for the fact that the cannabis is in his possession, the law may still be justified in imposing criminal liability because of his voluntary failure to dispose of the item.[70] The more difficult problem for this analysis is posed by the second half of the "voluntary act" requirement: that D's possession (whether by acquisition or non-disposal) must be *voluntary*. We shall return to this issue in § 2.3.2.

2.2 CONSEQUENCES: THE NEED FOR CAUSATION

Not all consequences involve persons. For example, the unexpected arrival of a very large meteor is thought to have caused the extinction of dinosaurs; and the collapse of many of Napier's buildings in 1931 is ascribed to an earthquake rather than human hand. But for the purposes of the criminal law, consequences are those circumstances, events, or states of affairs which are the result of (ie *caused* by) the defendant's behaviour. Thus, whenever a consequence, such as death, is specified as part of the actus reus of an offence, the prosecution must prove both that the consequence occurred, and that the defendant's behaviour caused that consequence.

From this it may be seen that the requirement of causation is fundamental to our understanding of the actus reus in criminal law. Suppose, for example, that V dies. The result (death) is an element of the actus reus of murder. But it would normally be wrong to hold someone guilty of murder who does not cause V's death. Imagine B is a bystander who happens to be standing beside V when, suddenly, D rushes up to V and stabs him fatally. Then it is not B who kills V, but D, because it is D who causes V's death. Here our criminal law takes a very individualistic approach, emphasising the distinctive responsibility of citizens for their own actions. Thus the law does not prosecute D's parents, who brought D up in such a way that he was not adequately instilled with the values that would have stopped him from killing V. Nor would it hold B guilty of murder even if B had, in fact, been planning to kill V himself, and had delightedly stood aside upon perceiving D's murderous intentions.[71] In short, there is no doctrine of collective responsibility in our criminal law. This reflects the nature of our society. Even in team games, such as a rugby match, the newspaper statistics record the names of those who

---

69 Cf § 1.2.2ff; also § 2.3.

70 Pace, *R v Thomas* (1981) 6 A Crim R 66, in which the disposing of cannabis by D was held to be the assertion of a right of control "amounting to" possession. The decision can be explained on different grounds: that D had knowingly refrained from disposing of the drugs until the police arrived, and that the disposition was not an irrecoverable one; it was, rather, a "secreting".

71 B may, however, become guilty of murder if he manifests his delight in a manner which is intended to encourage D. Not all liability for outcomes is predicated on *the defendant's* having caused the outcome; he may be held responsible for the consequence of someone else's actions as a secondary party. See chapter 5.

scored tries. Of course, other approaches are possible.[72] At one time, it was the practice in Greece to hold the entire city punishable for the crimes of its leaders. Similarly, the Chinese doctrine of *lian-tsua* would result in a whole family or village being punished for the wrongdoing of one of its members. But these are not the ways of modern New Zealand society. Moreover, to impose criminal liability upon someone for the actions of others would not only be out of step with public perceptions, but would also substantially restrict individual liberty.[73] It is inappropriate in a liberal culture to force us to be the guardian of others on pain of criminal conviction.

2.2.1 The rule of thumb

The starting, and frequently finishing, point of any causation problem is the "but for" or sine qua non test: would the consequence specified in the actus reus have occurred *but for* the defendant's behaviour? If it would not have occurred except for the defendant's acting as he did, then prima facie his behaviour caused that consequence. Conversely, if it would have occurred anyway, that is a reason to deny the existence of causation (and consequently, to refrain from holding the defendant criminally liable for the occurrence of the actus reus).

Suppose, for example, that a doctor injects his patient with a painkiller, and the patient subsequently dies. Whether or not the doctor is guilty of manslaughter or murder depends upon a number of factors, but he definitely commits neither unless injecting the painkiller caused that patient's death. If the patient would have died when she did whether or not the doctor had injected her (eg of an unrelated heart attack), then the *but for* test is not satisfied and we have grounds for saying that the doctor's actions did not cause her death.[74] Conversely, if it can be proved that she would not have died when she did without the doctor's intervention, then prima facie he killed her.

Most of the time, the sine qua non test will be an entirely adequate yardstick of causation, and in the absence of any unusual circumstances the prima facie answer it gives will be a conclusive one. But it is important to realise that *but for* causation is no more than indicative of true legal causation. Suppose, for instance, that D invites V to meet her for lunch. Unfortunately, while driving to their rendezvous, V's car is hit by a truck, the brakes of which have failed. But for D's inviting V to lunch, the accident would not have occurred. Yet D did not cause the accident. Another useful illustration is *R v Hensler*.[75] D sent V a begging letter in which he misrepresented his plight. V was not deceived, but nevertheless sent D some money. On these facts, although V would not have sent the money but for D's letter, D could not be

---

72   See, for example, Fauconnet, *La Responsabilité: Étude de Sociologie*, 1920.

73   Cf the argument against liability for omissions at § 2.1.1.1; also the discussion in chapter 1.

74   Cf *R v Dalloway* (1847) 2 Cox CC 273; *R v White* [1910] 2 KB 124.

75   (1870) 11 Cox CC 570.

convicted of obtaining by false pretences, because the false pretence had not caused D to send the money.[76]

So the presence of *but for* causation does not mean that there is true legal causation. Conversely, the absence of *but for* causation does not imply an absence of true legal causation either. Suppose this time that D sets fire to V's house, razing it. It turns out, however, that there was a faulty electrical circuit in the house that was about to overheat and cause a similar fire. We cannot say that, but for D's conduct, V's house would not have burned down. Yet despite this, it *is* D who causes the damage.

The difficulty arises because so-called *but for* "causation" *is actually not a species of causation at all*. Rather, it is a formula which merely expresses a certain sort of relationship between two things: that, in the circumstances, it was impossible for the second event (the "consequence") to happen without the first action (the "cause") having occurred. As such, the sine qua non relationship is simply a logical relationship, and not a causal one. What really matters in the law is not whether there is a *but for* relationship between the defendant's behaviour and the prohibited consequence, but whether there is a true causal relationship *at law*.

2.2.2 Causation in law

Some causal relationships are very mechanical, and present no problems for the law. This sort of causation occurs when the action leads to the relevant consequence through the ordinary workings of physics, biology, and the like. Thus the connection between D's knocking over the tumbler and its watery contents pouring out is a simple mechanical one; the consequence follows straightforwardly given the existence of gravity and the fluidity of the liquid inside, without the intervention of subsequent events. The connection between D's shooting V, and V's consequential death, is normally just as straightforward, something that a pathologist might be able to discuss in technical rather than, say, legal or moral terms.

The real difficulties arise when there are other actions, or events of nature, which *also* play a role in bringing about the relevant consequence. Consider, for example, the facts in R v Pittwood,[77] where D failed to close the gate at a railway crossing, with the result that a cart entered the crossing and was hit by a train. One can say, of this case, that the arrival of the train was itself a causal factor in the accident. Yet we can still agree that D's negligence caused the crash. Why?

It is not possible to give a definitive analysis of the principles of causation here.[78] But over the next few pages we will suggest a number of guiding

---

76   D was, however, convicted of an attempt to obtain by false pretences. Compare *R v Mills* (1857) 7 Cox CC 263, 1 Dears & Bell 205, 169 ER 978.
77   (1902) 19 TLR 37.
78   The classic work is *Hart and Honoré*. See also Kadish, *Blame and Punishment*, 1987, chapter 8; Williams, *TBCL*, chapter 14. For more philosophical discussion, see Honoré, "Necessary and Sufficient Conditions in Tort Law" in Owen (ed), *Philosophical Foundations of Tort Law*, 1995, 363; Mackie, "Causes and Conditions" in Sosa (ed), *Causation and Conditionals*, London, Oxford University Press, 1975, 15.

principles. (In the context of homicide, some of these common law principles of causation have been modified by statute: see chapter 14.)

Perhaps the most important point to remember during the discussion which follows is that, while causation frequently depends upon physical, mechanical relationships between actions and outcomes (such as the relationship that D's firing a gun may bear to V's death a moment later), causation is also and very often a function of moral evaluations. When we state that Pittwood's dereliction "caused" an accident, we are articulating a view that his behaviour was responsible for that accident. In other words, the ascription of causation in *Pittwood* is not so much a *prerequisite* of his being held responsible as it is an expression of the moral *conclusion* that, through his behaviour, he is responsible, and legally answerable, for the accident that resulted.

2.2.2.1 *Significant cause*

Whatever other causes play a role in bringing the actus reus about, the first requirement is that D's behaviour must contribute in some significant way to its occurrence. In *R v White*,[79] W gave his mother poison. Before it could take effect, however, she died of an unrelated heart attack. W was guilty of an attempted murder. But he did not commit murder because the poison played no role in his mother's death.

The contribution that D makes must be more than insignificant, or de minimis.[80] If a doctor takes a blood sample from a patient who is dying from gunshot wounds, the additional loss of blood for the sample may further weaken the patient and hasten death by a few moments. But the doctor's role in the patient's death is, in this context, causally insignificant, and the law will impute the death solely to the gunshot wounds.[81]

However, the defendant's contribution need not be a substantial one. In *R v Hennigan*,[82] for example, it was ruled wrong to direct a jury that D was not liable if less than one-fifth to blame for the actus reus. Certainly, D's behaviour need not be the main cause of death. It is enough that her conduct played a part which was not "insubstantial", or "insignificant".[83]

2.2.2.2 *Causal salience*

As well as making a "not insignificant" contribution, D's causal role must also be *salient*. Suppose that D is driving to work at a speed in excess of the speed limit. He slows to the correct speed in advance of an intersection, but is involved in an accident on the intersection with another car. If he had not been speeding he would not have arrived at the intersection when he did, and the accident would not have occurred. But his speeding is not a cause of the accident. Its only role was to ensure that D was present in a particular place at a particular time, and this in no way affected the likelihood of an accident

---

79   [1910] 2 KB 124.

80   See *R v Cato* (1976) 62 Cr App R 41 at 45.

81   Cf Palmer "Dr Adam's Trial for Murder" [1957] Crim LR 365.

82   [1971] 3 All ER 133.

83   *R v Myatt* [1991] 1 NZLR 674 at 682, 683, (1990) 7 CRNZ 304 at 312, 313; *R v Cato* (1976) 62 Cr App R 41 at 46; *R v Cheshire* [1991] 3 All ER 670 at 677, [1991] 1 WLR 844 at 852.

occurring. The risk would have been just as great had he arrived later;[84] indeed, neither would the accident have happened if his speed had been even *more* excessive. A slightly different example is put by Hart and Honoré:[85]

> If it is negligent of the defendant to hand a child a loaded gun, and the child drops the gun on his foot and injures it, the injury to the foot is not within the risk (shooting) that made it negligent to hand the child the loaded gun. It is also true that the aspect of the defendant's conduct which made it negligent, the fact that the gun was loaded, was not causally relevant to the injury, since that fact did not significantly increase the gun's weight.

Here D, by giving the gun to the child at all (whether loaded or not), played a causal role in V's subsequent injury. But the reasons why D is at fault are in no way salient to the injury that V sustains.

2.2.2.3 *Multiple causes*

A further principle is that there may be multiple causes. In *Pittwood*,[86] both the arrival of the train and the defendant's failure to close the gate were causes of the accident. This may be true even when more than one person is at fault.[87] Suppose that D shoots V, who is taken to hospital. While in hospital, V is attended to by E, an inexperienced doctor who negligently fails to recognise the true extent of her injuries. V dies because those injuries are improperly left untreated. In this case, the actions of both D and E cause V's death, and (depending on mens rea considerations) both D and E may be guilty of homicide-related offences. Similarly, if both A and B simultaneously shoot C fatally through the heart, and C dies instantly, then both A and B kill him; even though we cannot say "but for" each shot, C would not have died. It is enough that the actus reus or consequence can be attributed to the defendant's conduct as *a*, not *the*, cause. The general test when there are multiple causes is whether the defendant's contribution was, by the time the consequence came about, still a "significant and operating cause".[88] If so, then it is irrelevant whether that same consequence can also be attributed to other defendants.[89]

Neither does it matter whether the consequence can also be attributed to other events or actions of the defendant. In *R v McKinnon*,[90] D struck V on the head, rendering him unconscious. He subsequently manhandled V, eventually leaving him lying on the ground. At some stage V suffered a minor injury to his nose which resulted in bleeding. This injury may have been in itself accidental.

---

84 Cf *Berry v Sugar Notch Borough* (1899) 43 Atl 240 (Pa); *Hart and Honoré*, 168-170; Williams, *TBCL*, § 16.7.

85 *Hart and Honoré*, lxiii. Cf *Gorris v Scott* (1874) LR 9 Ex 125; Fleming, *The Law of Torts* (7th ed), Sydney, Law Book Co, 1987, 174.

86 § 2.2.2.

87 Cf *R v Benge* (1865) 4 F & F 504, 176 ER 665.

88 Usually "substantial and operating" — cf *Adams* § CA158.07; *R v Smith* [1959] 2 QB 35 at 42, 43, [1959] 2 All ER 193 at 198; but see § 2.2.2.1.

89 *R v McKinnon* [1980] 2 NZLR 31; *R v Storey* [1931] NZLR 417 (even to the defendant's own negligence); *A-G's Reference (No 4 of 1980)* [1981] 2 All ER 617, (1981) 73 Cr App R 40. Cf *R v Blaue* [1975] 3 All ER 446, [1975] 1 WLR 1411.

90 [1980] 2 NZLR 31 (CA).

Unfortunately, while V was lying on the ground unconscious, the bleeding went into his lung and he suffocated. Had he not been unconscious, the bleeding would have been no serious matter. The Court of Appeal held that, while the injury to V's nose was a cause of death, it was so *concurrently* with the blow to V's head that rendered him unconscious and so unable to deal with the effects of the bleeding. Thus V's death could properly also be attributed to the assault by D.

When multiple causes are concurrently at work, a defendant's conduct may still be held to cause death even though it was not enough to do so on its own. An example of this is the case of *R v Lewis*,[91] where (on one view of the evidence), two attackers separately injured V, the injuries being fatal only because they were cumulative. In such case *each* attacker has caused V's death. Once again, the general test is the same: whether the particular defendant's own conduct was a significant contributor in bringing about the actus reus.

2.2.3 Intervening causes

In such cases as *Pittwood, McKinnon,* and *Lewis,* the other causal factors operated in tandem with D's conduct to bring about the prohibited harm. Sometimes, however, D's contribution is followed by an action by someone else, or a coincidental event, that is the more immediate (or "proximate") cause of death and which displaces D's causal responsibility for the actus reus. A good example of this is the case of *White*, mentioned earlier. Suppose that in the normal course of events the poison D gave his mother would have caused her death.[92] Nonetheless, it was a subsequent, unrelated heart attack that killed her. The occurrence of the heart attack overtook the effects of D's conduct and usurped his causal responsibility for her death.

Where the later event displaces D's responsibility in this way, it is often called a novus actus interveniens. A novus actus is an action or event which "intervenes" to "break the causal chain" leading from D to the eventual harm. Where the prohibited consequence is attributable to a novus actus, D is not criminally liable for bringing that consequence about. His behaviour is no longer a significant and operating cause.

We look now at the main types of intervening causes in more detail.

2.2.3.1 *Natural events*

Where the other causal factors involve natural events rather than persons, the basic rule is that causation is attributed to the defendant *unless* the intervening natural event was not reasonably foreseeable. In *R v Hart*,[93] D assaulted V, leaving her lying unconscious on a beach below the high-water mark. V was subsequently drowned by the incoming tide. The Court of Appeal held that D had caused the death of the victim. It is thought that D would not have killed

---

91 [1975] 1 NZLR 222 at 226, 227.

92 In fact, although D probably thought otherwise, it appears that the quantity given was insufficient to cause death, save perhaps as part of a cumulative dose.

93 [1986] 2 NZLR 408. See also *R v Hallett* [1969] SASR 141; *R v Phillips* [1971] ALR 740, (1971) 45 ALJR 467; *Hill* [1953] NZLR 688 at 694, 695.

her had V been left lying above the high-water mark and had only drowned because of a freak tidal wave.[94]

The idea here is that the further cause is not merely a coincidence. Rather, it is the sort of risk that is created or increased by D's initial actions; and the prospect of the prohibited consequence coming about by that further means is one of the reasons we might sensibly give when stating why D should not act as he does.[95] Thus in *R v Forrest*,[96] where D inflicted an injury upon V, thereby making V susceptible to an infection which V later contracted and from which he died, it was held that D's conduct, in rendering V especially vulnerable to the further, immediate cause of death, was a sufficient cause for the death to be attributable to D. A contrasting case with a different result is *Bush v Commonwealth*.[97] In that case D shot V, who subsequently died of scarlet fever, transmitted to him in hospital by the surgeon who operated on the bullet wound. D was acquitted of unlawful homicide. His attack on V did not substantially increase the risk of V's contracting scarlet fever; neither was that risk a significant reason why we would think D's initial actions wrong.

The outcome in *Bush v Commonwealth* would be different if the fever had only caused death *in conjunction with* the fact that V was weakened by the wound D had inflicted. This would be a case of multiple concurrent causes, rather than of novus actus, since the original injury would still be making an ongoing (operating) contribution to V's death.

There is another important exception to the rule that unforeseeable events are capable of breaking the causal chain linking defendant to eventual outcome. A coincidental or fortuitous route involving natural events will not normally be a novus actus when the ultimate result was *intended* by the defendant.[98] For example:

D shoots at V on a mountainside, meaning to kill him. She misses, but the noise of her shot triggers an avalanche in which V is swept away and killed. In our view, D is guilty of murder. She has brought about the intended result, and cannot escape responsibility by pointing to the unexpected causal detour of the means that she herself initiated.

This exception is sometimes described as a rule that "intended consequences are never too remote". We prefer not to characterise it in that way, and indeed to do so would be inaccurate. For example, D's intended contribution to an outcome may be superseded by the novus actus of a third party.[99] It is to that possibility that we now turn.

---

94 Perkins, "The Law of Homicide" (1946) 36 J Crim L 391 at 393, 394.

95 Cf the requirement for salience at § 2.2.2.2.

96 (1886) 20 SALR 78.

97 (1880) 78 Ky 268.

98 *R v Demirian* [1989] VR 97 at 113, 114, (1988) 33 A Crim R 441 at 457, 458; *R v Michael* (1840) 9 C & P 356, 173 ER 867.

99 The rule would also be subject to a salience requirement regarding unexpected interventions: § 2.2.2.2.

2.2.3.2 *Other persons*

In some respects, there are similarities between the causal status of natural events and the intervening actions of third parties. If D stabs V, and V later dies, D is nevertheless not causally responsible if it turns out that V dies because the ambulance within which he was being carried to hospital was crushed by a runaway lorry. Nor does D kill V if, after being fatally wounded and left for dead, V is chanced upon by his old enemy T, who shoots V, killing him instantly.[100] In these situations, the unforeseeable intervention of another breaks the causal chain between D's contribution and the eventual outcome. However, there are also significant differences between the attribution of causation where there are intervening natural events and that where there are intervening actions by other persons. In the former case, the main test is one of reasonable foreseeability. In the latter, this is only one aspect of a more complex inquiry.

At a very generalised level, there are two main principles guiding causation when a third person intervenes. First is the proposition that T's intervention which causes the actus reus will normally be a novus actus, and absolve D of responsibility, when that intervention is "free, deliberate and informed".[101] This occurs when T *knowingly* intervenes to bring about the prohibited outcome, without her choice to do so being induced, fettered, or constrained by the situation D has created. In that situation T assumes full responsibility for the outcome, displacing or pre-empting its attribution to D. The rationale for this is ably expressed by Glanville Williams:[102]

> Underlying this rule there is, undoubtedly, a philosophical attitude. Moralists and lawyers regard the individual's will as the autonomous prime cause of his behaviour. What a person does (if he has reached adult years, is of sound mind and is not acting under mistake, intimidation or similar pressure) is his own responsibility, and is not regarded as having been caused by other people. An intervening act of this kind, therefore, breaks the causal connection that would otherwise have been perceived between previous acts and the forbidden consequence.

Very often T's knowing intercession will not meet those criteria. The doctor's intervention in treating V is not free or unconstrained, but rather is a justified response to the need for treatment that D has engendered. This point can be stated more generally: T's participation in begetting the actus reus is insufficiently free, and *cannot* be a novus actus, when it is justified or excused by the demands of the situation that D's conduct has placed her in. While T's

---

100 *R v Evans & Gardiner (No 2)* [1976] VR 523 at 527, 528. The decision of the Court of Appeal in *R v Lewis* [1975] 1 NZLR 222 at 226, 227 is prima facie contrary to this proposition, in that the language used in the judgment would result in both D and T being guilty of murder. But that case perhaps turns on its facts, which were less than entirely clear. The context appears to have been one in which the injuries inflicted by the second assailant would have compounded rather than superceded those inflicted by D. Moreover, nothing in the judgment of the Court suggests an intention to abandon the common law position stated in the text here. See § 2.2.3.2.(b).

101 *R v Pagett* (1983) 76 Cr App R 279 at 288, 289.

102 *TBCL*, 391.

conduct may itself be a cause of the harm, it is not an independent cause; rather, in law, it has the status of being itself a consequence of D's wrongdoing. Thus, instead of T's becoming fully (and exclusively) responsible for the eventual outcome, D remains at least partly responsible for that intervention by T, and for its effects.

Neither will T's input be "free, deliberate and informed" when T is ignorant of the relevant facts. In this sort of case, T's contribution to the harm is an inadvertent one. Her role may be innocent or accidental, but need not be, and may instead be negligent. Either way, there is no deliberate choice by T to bring the harm about, and so she cannot be said to assume full responsibility for that harm to the exclusion of D.

The second main principle applies where, because of her ignorance or mistake, T's intervention does not meet the "free, deliberate and informed" criteria. In that case the third party intervention is, in effect, no different from a natural event. Thus it is subject to the further tests that govern intervention by a natural event. In particular, it can only count as a novus actus if its occurrence was independent of D's wrongdoing and was not reasonably foreseeable. One new factor in examining this issue will be T's culpability for her conduct: if the eventual harm was due to T's gross negligence, it is less likely to be reasonably foreseeable and the sort of risk which provides a reason why D should not have acted as he did in the first place.[103]

As with any intervening cause, whether natural or human, a third principle also applies: that even if the intervention was independent of D and unforeseeable, it will be no more than a concurrent cause if D's contribution is still playing a direct, contributory role at the time the harm eventually occurs. This is a straightforward application of the proposition that there can be multiple causes of an outcome.[104]

In the following subsections, we will consider these rather abstract principles in the more practical context of the leading cases, and in light of judicial dicta.

2.2.3.2(a) *Foreseeable and innocent interventions*

Cases where another's intervention does not break the causal chain occur in a variety of ways. In some of the most dramatic examples, D will still be ascribed with causal responsibility if the contribution of the other party is both predictable (ie reasonably foreseeable) and itself innocent.

A famous case of this variety is *R v Michael*.[105] D wished to murder her illegitimate child, who was in the care of a foster mother. She gave a bottle

---

103 § 2.2.3.1. Less likely, but not impossible: cf *R v Fleeting (No 1)* [1977] 1 NZLR 343 at 348, where Barker J opined that T's intervention would not necessarily be a novus actus even if negligent or unlawful. Compare *R v Benge* (1865) 4 F & F 504, 176 ER 665; *Smyth v Police* [1973] 1 NZLR 56 at 58. See further § 2.2.3.2.3.

104 See § 2.2.2.3. This appears to be the best explanation of *R v Jemielita* (1995) 81 A Crim R 409.

105 (1840) 9 C & P 356, 173 ER 867; see also *Tessymond's case* (1828) 1 Lew CC 169, 168 ER 1000.

of poison to the foster mother, telling her it was medicine and instructing her to administer it to the baby. The foster mother decided not to give the medicine and put it on the mantelpiece. Some days later the foster mother's own five-year-old child removed the bottle and administered a fatal dose to the child. D was convicted of murder.[106]

The events in *Michael* involved the input of a young child, undoubtedly an innocent for the purposes of legal responsibility. But they would be treated no differently by the law if T were an adult whose foreseeable intervention was inadvertent and blameless. An example of the latter is supplied by *R v Fleeting*,[107] where in an altercation D pushed V, who stumbled onto the street and was run over and killed by a passing car. Being a busy street in Auckland, the intervention of the car (unintended by its driver) could not be regarded as a novus actus, and D could properly be treated as having caused V's death.

By contrast, the innocent intervention will be regarded as a novus actus where it is unforeseeable.[108] *Fleeting* may instructively be contrasted with *R v Knutsen*,[109] where D had left V unconscious in a quiet and well-lit street, and could not be held responsible for her death when she was subsequently run over by a drunk driver who had ample opportunity to avoid her.

Where T's actions are not inadvertent but instead justified or excused because of the situation D has created, T will effectively be counted as an innocent intervener. The most important case of this type is *R v Pagett*,[110] in which the defendant holed up in a building, then emerged firing at police and using his hostage as a human shield. The police returned fire in the dark, killing the hostage. The consequence, that the police would — quite reasonably — return fire, and so kill the girl, was an entirely foreseeable upshot of what the defendant did, and so could not break the chain of causation which led from his behaviour to the hostage's death.

It was said in *Pagett* that the policeman's reaction in returning fire was instinctive and "involuntary". But it need not be involuntary. It was enough that the reaction was a reasonable response, justifiable either in terms of self-defence or the execution of a legal duty.[111] Either way, it is not sufficiently "free" to usurp the defendant's causal responsibility for the eventual consequences.

An extension of the decision in *Pagett* may be seen in *R v Tomars*,[112] where D gave chase to a motorcyclist, driving in such a manner that the motorcyclist (V)

---

106 It is thought that T's intervention was reasonably foreseeable. (See *TBCL*, 394.) However, even if it were not foreseeable, D's conviction can be justified on the basis that, T's intervention being innocent, it should be treated like a natural event and the rule about intended consequences applied. See § 2.2.3.1.

107 [1977] 1 NZLR 343.

108 This must be the explanation of *R v Martin* (1827) 3 C & P 211, 172 ER 390.

109 [1963] Qd R 157. See also *Smyth v Police* [1973] 1 NZLR 56 at 58.

110 (1983) 76 Cr App R 279.

111 Contrast this with a response to provocation, no more than a mitigating excuse: *R v Dubois* (1959) 32 CR 187.

112 [1978] 2 NZLR 505.

was caused to swerve in front of another car. V died in the ensuing accident. It was held that D's actions were capable of being a cause of V's death, since V's conduct was reasonably foreseeable. The case is slightly different from *Pagett*, in that V's reaction was a mistake, and as such excusable rather than justifiable.[113] But it was reasonably foreseeable, and moreover one for which V could not be blamed — an error induced by the circumstances that D himself had generated. Thus V's reaction is allowed to be a mistake, provided it is a reasonable or understandable one made in the heat or emergency of the moment. Although *Tomars* involves an intervention by the victim rather than a third party, and as such may be governed by rules which are even less favourable to the defendant,[114] it is thought that the principle in that case also extends to interventions by strangers.

2.2.3.2(b) *Foreseeable and intentional interventions*
The cases above illustrate the general rule that, where the intervention is both innocent and foreseeable, it will not normally suffice to break the causal chain linking the defendant to the actus reus. But what if the third party's free intervention is foreseeable, yet not innocent or blameless? Here things get a little more complicated. The reason for this is the importance of individual autonomy and responsibility in the law. A person's actions are not usually regarded as caused by others, and the law stipulates that a defendant is responsible for her own actions but is normally not responsible for the wrongdoing of a third party even if it was foreseeable, and would not have occurred but for the defendant's contribution. So if D inflicts serious injuries upon V during a mugging, and another assailant later chances upon and shoots V (killing him instantly) then D does not cause death even if it was foreseeable[115] that another person might subsequently kill V. Similarly, the result in *Michael*[116] would have been different if T had been a mature adult who knew the details of D's plans when she administered the poison to D's baby.[117]

Where the third party's wrongful intervention is itself intentional, something other than causation is required before the outcome can *also* be ascribed to the original actor-defendant. Characteristically, the extra ingredient is supplied when the third party's intervention is in some way induced or underwritten by the defendant. In these cases, D's liability is predicated on a

---

113 Cf *R v Williams* [1992] 2 All ER 183, [1992] 1 WLR 380; *R v Martin* (1881) 8 QBD 54.

114 See § 2.2.3.3.

115 Or even made "likely" by D's actions: *R v Dalby* [1982] 1 All ER 916, [1982] 1 WLR 425 (CA). As Glanville Williams states, "The fact that [D's] own conduct, rightful or wrongful, provided the background for a subsequent voluntary and wrong act by another does not make him responsible for it. What he does may be a but-for cause of the injurious act, but he did not do it. "*Finis* for *Novus Actus*?" (1989) 48 CLJ 391.

116 § 2.2.3.2.(a).

117 *Grant* [1966] NZLR 968 at 973, 974 (CA); *People v Elder* (1894) 100 Mich 515, 59 NW 237; compare *Hilton's case* (1838) 2 Lew CC 214, 168 ER 1132 with *R v Lowe* (1850) 3 Car & Kir 123, 175 ER 489; also *R v Dubois* (1959) 32 CR 187, where T's intervention was provoked by D. Cf the "free, deliberate and informed" criterion in § 3.2.3.2.

derivative, or secondary party basis, rather than upon causation.[118] Thus when D deliberately incites or assists T to commit a crime, D too will be criminally liable alongside T for its commission. Secondary liability is dealt with separately in chapter 5.

Sometimes an intervention to bring about the actus reus may be intentional without necessarily being culpable. As we saw in the preceding section, where this occurs because of a justification or excuse arising from D's conduct, T is treated as if his were an innocent intervention. However where T's intervention is intentional, free, and unconstrained by justificatory or excusatory circumstances, it will usually break the causal link between defendant and outcome. In *R v Latif*,[119] D was charged, inter alia, with importing a controlled drug. The drug was in fact brought into the country by a customs officer with full knowledge of the contents of the packages he carried. The House of Lords held that the officer's voluntary and knowing intervention relieved D of causal responsibility for importation of the drugs, and that the most he could be convicted of was an attempt to commit the offence.[120]

2.2.3.2(c) *Foreseeable and culpable interventions*

Normally, when there is no *intentional* wrongdoing by the intervener, it is less likely, but not impossible, that the culpable intervention will break the causal link between D and the eventual outcome. This is because, as was stated in § 2.2.3.2, T cannot be said to have assumed a full responsibility for the effects of her intervention. Nonetheless, it is still possible for T's conduct to disrupt the causal path joining D with the actus reus. For example, where V is injured by D, but killed in an accident en route to hospital, the fact that the accident was unintended by T is no bar to an application of the novus actus doctrine and denial of D's responsibility. The most instructive legal examples of this variety arise in a medical context, where D inflicts injuries upon V the extent of which are at least exacerbated by the medical treatment V subsequently receives.

A case where "palpably" bad medical treatment was held to cause death to the exclusion of D's original actions is *R v Jordan*.[121] In that case the defendant had stabbed V, who was admitted to hospital and died 8 days later. On appeal, evidence was admitted to show that when he died, the original injury had substantially healed. V's death was in fact caused by his allergic reaction to the antibiotic he was given in hospital and by the intravenous administration of too much liquid. Moreover, the antibiotic was introduced to prevent infection only after he had shown he was intolerant of it. The Court of Criminal Appeal, in quashing Jordan's conviction, held that the grossly negligent[122] medical treatment broke the causal link between the stabbing and V's death.

---

118 Cf Fletcher, *Rethinking Criminal Law*, Boston, Little, Brown & Co, 1978, 582.

119 [1996] 1 All ER 353, [1996] 1 WLR 104 (HL).

120 It is possible that the officer's intervention could be regarded as culpable since the House of Lords treated him as having committed an offence himself. But this was not required in *R v Horsey* (1862) 3 F & F 287, 176 ER 129.

121 (1956) 40 Cr App Rep 152.

122 See Williams, "Causation in Homicide" [1957] Crim LR 429.

While we submit that *Jordan* was rightly decided, it must be regarded as a very unusual case, distinguished by its rather extreme facts. Acknowledging this, the Court was "disposed to accept it as law that death resulting from any normal treatment employed to deal with a felonious injury may be regarded as caused by the felonious injury".[123] Thus where death results from normal treatment applied to the injury, then both the treatment and the injury are causes of death and the treatment does not break the chain of causation from the original injury to death.

Even if the intervening treatment is abnormal, however, it will not necessarily count as a novus actus. In *R v Smith*,[124] V was stabbed by P with a bayonet. His lung was pierced, but this injury went unrecognised by those who attended to him. He was dropped twice on the way to the medical reception station. There the medical officer failed to diagnose the seriousness of the situation and gave the wrong treatment, which very likely increased the risk of death.[125] On appeal, it was held that where the original injury is still an operating and significant[126] cause of death, then, regardless of other contributing causes, the death can still be attributed to the defendant. It is only if the original wound is merely a *historical setting* for the second injury (here, the treatment), which is then the major operating cause of death, that there can be a break in the causal chain. By contrast with the facts in *Jordan*, in *Smith* the stab wound and consequent haemorrhage were still immediate medical factors explaining V's death.

There appear, therefore, to be two conditions which must be satisfied before the intervening behaviour can supercede the defendant's causal role. First, the original harm inflicted by D must no longer be contributing to the occurrence of the eventual result. This condition applies even if T's wrongdoing is intentional. For example, if D inflicts a non-fatal stab wound upon V, then D (as well as T) causes V's death if T later also stabs V and the loss of blood from both wounds is a contributing factor bringing about V's death.[127] Contrast this example with the example mentioned earlier, where D stabs V and T later chances upon V and shoots her, killing her instantly. In that case T and not D causes V's death.

The second condition is that the relevant intervention by T must, as well as being culpable, itself *not* be a consequence of the original wrongdoing by V. This condition was pivotal in *R v Kirikiri*.[128] In that case, V was the victim of a serious assault by D, which caused structural damage to her face. At the hospital where she was first treated, a temporary tracheostomy was performed

---

123 (1956) 40 Cr App R 152 at 157.

124 [1959] 2 QB 35, [1959] 2 All ER 193.

125 Indeed, it was said in evidence at the trial that V's chances of recovery were 75 percent given proper treatment.

126 "Substantial" in the speech of Lord Parker CJ [1959] 2 QB 35 at 42, 43, [1959] 2 All ER 193 at 198. But see § 2.2.2.1.

127 This may be the best explanation of *R v Dear* [1996] Crim LR 595.

128 [1982] 2 NZLR 648; also of *R v Cheshire* [1991] 3 All ER 670, [1991] 1 WLR 844, where the doctors' conduct was admittedly negligent.

in order to assist her breathing. She was then transferred for reconstructive surgery, which was to take place 4 days later and was not essential to save her life. Before surgery, however, the inserted tracheal tube slipped. Attempts to replace it failed and V died. The High Court held, on a pre-trial motion, that there was "ample evidence" on these facts for a jury to hold that D caused V's death. This seems right. The immediate cause of death was the failure of the tracheostomy and of the surgeons' attempts to repair it. But the tracheostomy itself was a medically-appropriate response, made necessary by the injuries D had inflicted upon V. D might therefore be regarded as causally responsible for the (necessitous, appropriate) intervention that, in turn, led to V's death.[129]

It may be helpful to illustrate the different legal character of the causal sequences in these cases with diagrams. In *Jordan*, the conduct of the doctor amounted to a novus actus independent of D's actions:

Jordan: $C_D \longrightarrow$ stabs V $\longrightarrow\!\!\mid$ C_T $\mid\!\!\longrightarrow$ injects antibiotics $\longrightarrow$ V dies

By contrast, in *Kirikiri* the doctor's intervention was a direct response to the injuries D had inflicted, and thus could be treated as a consequence of D's actions:

Kirikiri: $C_D \longrightarrow$ shoots V $\longrightarrow$ T performs tracheostomy $\longrightarrow$ V dies

In *Smith*, the doctor's conduct made an independent contribution to V's death. But the stab wound inflicted by D remained a concurrent, operating cause of death:

Smith: $C_D \longrightarrow$ stabs V $\longrightarrow\!\!\!\Big]$

$\qquad\qquad\qquad\qquad\qquad\qquad\qquad \longrightarrow$ V dies

$\qquad C_T \longrightarrow$ exacerbates wounds $\longrightarrow\!\!\!\Big]$

2.2.3.2(d) *Distinction from the innocent agent doctrine*

Sometimes persons bring about outcomes deliberately through the agency of another person. If D gives P's daughter a lethal draught of poison, telling her it is for P's cold, and the daughter administers the poison to P, D is guilty of murder as if he had administered the poison himself.[130] Similarly, D may be convicted of importing prohibited drugs even though the means of conveyance was an airline.[131] The doctrine of innocent agency renders the intervening participant the mere instrument of D, enabling courts to find that D has committed the offence as a principal offender.[132]

---

129 Note that s 166, which applies to cases of homicide, was treated for the purpose of argument in *Kirikiri* as declaratory of the common law: [1982] 2 NZLR 648 at 651. For further discussion of this case, see chapter 14.

130 *Anon* (1634) Kel 53, 84 ER 1079.

131 *White v Ridley* (1978) 140 CLR 342, 52 ALJR 724.

132 *R v Paterson* [1976] 2 NZLR 394 at 396 (CA).

Discussion of this doctrine belongs in chapter 5 on secondary parties. It is mentioned here in order to distinguish it from the causation question that arises upon an innocent third party's intervention. Innocent agency requires that D knowingly uses T as his agent to bring about the prohibited result. Thus *Michael*, where a child later and independently administered the poison that D had instructed V's nurse to give to V, is not a suitable case for application of the doctrine.

Innocent agency and causal principles nonetheless share some common ground. Like causation, innocent agency requires that T should be ignorant of the true nature of her actions. Where this is not so, and T is aware that her conduct constitutes an actus reus, responsibility for her actions and their result cannot then be imputed back to D.

2.3.3.3 *The victim*

If the intervention is by V himself, rather than by a third party, the general rule is that the consequences of V's intervention are attributable to D provided that:

(i) V's conduct is in reaction to D's wrongdoing; and

(ii) V's reaction was a reasonably foreseeable possibility.

In *R v Roberts*[133] the defendant made sexual advances to V while driving a car. V leapt out of the moving vehicle and suffered resulting injuries. D's conviction for assault occasioning actual bodily harm was upheld by the Court of Appeal, which asked whether the injury was "the natural result of what the alleged assailant said and did, in the sense that it was something that could reasonably have been foreseen as the consequence of what he was saying or doing?"[134] The same principle is capable of explaining the American case of *People v Lewis*,[135] in which V, who was dying painfully from a gunshot wound, committed suicide by cutting his throat. D was held to have caused V's death.[136] It would be otherwise, however, if V had killed himself not in reaction to the suffering that D had inflicted, but rather in order to shield D.

The second requirement, of reasonable foreseeability, may not be met where the victim's reaction is disproportionate. Although it is sometimes said that "the victim must be taken as he is found",[137] in *People v Lewis* D would not have been guilty of murder if the wound had merely been painful rather than

---

133 (1971) 56 Cr App R 95, [1972] Crim LR 27. Other cases include *R v Tomars* [1978] 2 NZLR 505 (CA); *DPP v Daley* [1980] AC 237, [1979] 2 WLR 239; *R v Williams* [1992] 2 All ER 183, [1992] 1 WLR 380; *R v Pitts* (1842) Car & M 284, 174 ER 509; *R v Halliday* (1889) 61 LT 701; *R v Lewis* [1970] Crim LR 647. The Crimes Act also sometimes provides for attribution to the defendant where there is indirect causation: eg s 160(2)(e), (inducing self-destruction by threats, fear or deception).

134 (1971) 56 Cr App R 95 at 102, [1972] Crim LR 27 at 27, 28.

135 (1899) 124 Cal 551, 57 P 470.

136 Although the *ratio* of the decision was multiple causes (that V died from loss of blood from the combined wounds), the court would have been prepared to decide the case on this ground if the facts had been clear regarding D's motive for cutting his own throat. See also *State v Angelina* (1913) 73 WVa 146, 80 SE 141; *Jones v State* (1942) 220 Ind 384, 43 NE 2d 1017; *Stephenson v State* (1932) 205 Ind 141, 179 NE 633 (torture).

137 For example *R v Blaue* [1975] 3 All ER 446 at 450, [1975] 1 WLR 1411 at 1415; § 2.2.4.2.

dangerous, and, knowing this, V had taken his life only in order to escape pain. In general, V's reaction will not be a novus actus where it is "in the foreseeable range",[138] and is not "daft".[139] This remains so even if that reaction is negligent or unlawful.[140]

As is the case with third party interventions, the possibility of a victim's contribution being a novus actus interveniens remains subject to the proviso that the original harm inflicted by D must no longer be contributing to the occurrence of the eventual result. In *Wall*,[141] the defendant (a colonial governor) sentenced V to an illegal flogging of some 800 lashes. V died from the punishment. It appeared that V had drunk alcohol after the flogging, which may well have accelerated his death. If so, however, it did so in combination with the effects of the flogging, and so would have been no more than an accompanying rather than overriding causal factor. The defendant therefore remained causally responsible for V's death.

2.2.4 Omissions

2.2.4.1 *As causes*

It is sometimes suggested that omissions cannot be causes.[142] This idea is founded on the notion that non-events, like failures to intercede and rescue a drowning victim, cannot bring things about: they are merely failures to prevent. To some extent this is true. If D watches without intervening while in a position to save V, her causal contribution to D's death is not of the same order as that when D herself holds V's head under water. One thing that is distinctive about omissions is that they do not initiate causal processes. Instead, they permit other causal processes to bring about the harm.

Nonetheless, neither ordinary language nor the law has much compunction about attributing causal responsibility to omissions. Both within and outside the courtroom it is acceptable to say that the railway gatekeeper's failure in *R v Pittwood*[143] to close the gate before the train came through caused the resulting accident. By contrast, it would be misleading just to state that the train's arrival

---

138 *R v Corbett* [1996] Crim LR 594 (CA); *R v Dear* [1996] Crim LR 595 (CA). It is submitted that the former case is to be preferred on this point, being consistent with existing case law.

139 *R v Roberts* (1971) 56 Cr App R 95 at 102, [1972] Crim LR 27 at 28.

140 Cf *R v Fleeting (No 1)* [1977] 1 NZLR 343 at 347, 348.

141 (1802) 28 St Tr 51 at 145. See also *R v Flynn* (1867) 16 WR 319 (Ir); *R v Mubila* [1956] 1 SA 31.

142 For example Moore, *Act and Crime: the Theory of Action and its Implications for Criminal Law*, Oxford, Clarendon Press, 1993, 267-278. For discussion, see Hughes, "Criminal Omissions" (1958) 67 Yale LJ 590 at 627-631; Husak, *Philosophy of Criminal Law* Totawa, NJ, Rowan to Littlefield, 1987, chapter 6; Leavens, "A Causative Approach to Criminal Omissions" (1988) 76 Cal LR 547; Benyon, "Causation, Omissions and Complicity" [1987] Crim LR 539. Fletcher, "On the Moral Irrelevance of Bodily Movements" (1994) 142 U Pa L Rev 1443; Hart and Honoré, 38; Fletcher, *Rethinking Criminal Law* Boston, Little Brown & Co 1978, 589ff.

143 (1902) 19 TLR 37. Cf the discussion in *Hart and Honoré*, 32ff; also Feinberg, *Harm to Others* (1984) 172ff.

caused the accident, although that was also a causal factor. We tend to reserve the language of causation for those factors which are most relevant to our explanations.

All this reflects the point made earlier in § 2.2.2, that causation in law is rarely a simple mechanical issue. Rather, it is intimately connected with the process of ascribing *responsibility* for the actus reus. Active intervention, while an obvious means of "causing" harm in the mechanical sense, is not the only way of being involved in bringing that harm about. In law, responsibility for the consequences of omissions involves a twofold test. D is normally held legally responsible for the consequences of an omission when (i) he has a duty to prevent those consequences from occurring (considered earlier in § 2.1.1.2), and when (ii) *his omission to intervene made a difference*. Part (ii) is the causal test.[144] For omissions, it is usually satisfied by proof of "but for" causation. In other words, D's omission causes an outcome if, but for that omission by D, the outcome would not have occurred.[145] If it would have resulted anyway, then D's omission made no difference and D cannot be held causally responsible for that outcome. As an example:

> Suppose that D, a doctor, does not notice that V has stopped breathing and fails to give him artificial respiration. She cannot be held causally responsible for his death unless it can be shown that V would have survived if D had discharged her duty to intervene and artificially respirate him.

A similar example is *Dalloway*,[146] in which D was driving a cart without retaining a proper grip on the reins. A young child ran out in front of the cart and was struck and killed. It was ruled that D might be convicted of manslaughter only if it were proved that, had D been using the reins correctly, the child would have been saved.

Ex abundante cautela, it is worth emphasising that even where it can be shown that D's omission is a "but for" cause of the harm, the omission will not be a legal cause if a novus actus intervenes. It is also subject to the requirement of salience.[147] Suppose, for example, that A makes a luncheon appointment with J. Later A discovers that she will not be free on the day they have arranged. Unfortunately, she discourteously fails to telephone J and cancel the appointment. While *en route* to the restaurant, J is killed in an automobile accident. If A had remembered to cancel, J would have eaten lunch at his office. Thus, but for A's omission, J would not have died. In this situation, however, A's omission is not a cause of death.

---

144 Quaere whether this requirement was overlooked in *Stone and Dobinson* [1977] QB 354, [1977] 2 All ER 341.

145 *R v Myatt* [1991] 1 NZLR 674 at 682, 683; (1990) 7 CRNZ 304 at 312, 313 (CA); *R v Morby* (1882) 8 QBD 571; *Barnett v Chelsea & Kensington Hospital Mgmt Cttee* [1969] 1 QB 428, [1968] 1 All ER 1068.

146 (1847) 2 Cox CC 273.

147 § 2.2.2.2.

2.2.4.2 As interventions

The general rule is that, while an omission by a third party can be a causal factor, it cannot be a novus actus interveniens. Where D omits to prevent harm, his omission may be a legal cause of that harm, but it is always a *concurrent* cause, ie alongside those causal processes that the omission has failed to prevent. To illustrate:

> Suppose that D stabs V, who is admitted to hospital with substantial loss of blood and in urgent need of a blood transfusion to save her life. Apart from the loss of blood, V's injuries are not life-threatening. T, the doctor who attends V, recognises that she needs a blood transfusion and prepares to give her one. While waiting for the blood to arrive, he goes to check on another patient. Unfortunately, he is distracted by a conversation with the patient and forgets to return and administer the transfusion to V. V dies from the loss of blood. Had the transfusion been performed, she would have survived.

In this case, *both* D and T cause V's death. Diagrammatically, their actions are multiple concurrent causes:

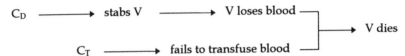

T's omission is not a novus actus which intervenes to break the causal chain from D's conduct to V's death. The whole reason why T's omission is causally significant is that it *fails to break* the causal sequence from D's action's to V's death. Indeed, we fault T and hold him (as well as D) liable for V's death precisely because he should have intervened and broken that chain before it reached its fatal culmination.

The proposition that an omission cannot break a pre-existing causal chain is the proper explanation of *R v Blaue*.[148] In that case V was stabbed, and was admitted to hospital having lost a large quantity of blood. She was a Jehovah's Witness, and refused the blood transfusion that was necessary to save her life. Thus the following day she died. D was convicted of her manslaughter. He appealed, contending that V's refusal to have a blood transfusion had broken the causal chain between the stabbing and V's death.

While it was accepted by the Crown that V's refusal to have a transfusion was *a* cause of her death, the Court of Appeal quite rightly ruled, using an analogy with *Smith*,[149] that the original wound inflicted by D was still an operating cause of death. However, faced with the submission by D's counsel that V's decision was an unreasonable one, the Court responded that:[150]

> It has long been the policy of the law that those who use violence on other people must take their victims as they find them. This in our judgment means the whole man, not just the physical man. It does not lie in the mouth of the assailant to say

---

148 [1975] 3 All ER 446, [1975] 1 WLR 1411. Since this is a case involving homicide, in New Zealand it would now be covered by s 165. See chapter 14.

149 See § 2.2.3.2(c).

150 [1975] 3 All ER 446 at 450, [1975] 1 WLR 1411 at 1415.

that his victim's religious beliefs which inhibited him from accepting certain kinds of treatment were unreasonable.

As a general proposition, this is not valid law. Cases such as *Roberts*, discussed in § 2.2.3.3, establish that an intervening reaction by V *does* break the chain of causation where it is not a reasonably foreseeable possibility — or, as was said in that case, where the reaction is "so daft" that it is really V's own voluntary act.[151] This means that D does not have to take his victim however he finds her, but only in so far as her reaction is a reasonably foreseeable or understandable one.

Suppose, then, that V's refusal of a transfusion *was* "daft", and not a sensible or foreseeable possibility (this was not decided by the Court). Prima facie, on the authority of *Roberts* and similar cases, this would then be a novus actus for which D was not responsible. In *Blaue*, however, the difference from those other cases was that V's intervening conduct involved not an act but an omission.[152] Thus, while it played a causal role in bringing about her death, and was a factor (unlike *Roberts*) for which D was not responsible, it did not break the causal chain from the stabbing to V's death. D's appeal, in effect, was that by her refusing to break the causal sequence D had set in motion, V broke the chain of causation. But an omission cannot do that.[153]

The difference between the two cases can be illustrated, once again, with causal diagrams:

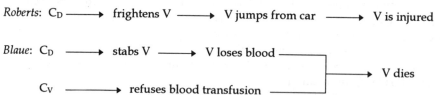

Roberts: C_D ⟶ frightens V ⟶ V jumps from car ⟶ V is injured

Blaue: C_D ⟶ stabs V ⟶ V loses blood —
⎤
⎥⟶ V dies
⎦
C_V ⟶ refuses blood transfusion —

2.3 THE REQUIREMENT OF VOLUNTARINESS

It is a fundamental requirement of the criminal law that D cannot be held liable for the occurrence of an actus reus unless he was *responsible* for it, ie unless its occurrence can in some way be attributed to D.

We noted in chapter 1 that when an actus reus occurs (for example, Jim is murdered), the criminal law begins with every member of society as a potential defendant.[154] The legal criteria that define responsibility for an actus reus also help to tell us which members of society are suitable defendants. Suppose that while investigating Jim's death, the police learn that his daughter Alice had secretly wished him dead because she stood to gain from his will. Despite her desires, the need for responsibility means that Alice is not guilty of murder unless she actually played some role in bringing about his death.

---

151 (1971) 56 Cr App R 95 at 102.

152 More precisely, an action (refusal) whose causal role depends upon an omission (non-transfusion).

153 Contra *Hart and Honoré*, 361.

154 See § 1.2.2.5

In respect of consequences, responsibility is established by showing causation. The police may conclude that although Alice wanted Jim's death, she did not cause it. Then she did not murder Jim. More generally, causation is necessary to establish a link between D's behaviour and the prohibited consequences. If an actus reus includes specification of such consequences (eg a person's death), the prosecution must prove causation in order to show that D's behaviour was responsible for that consequence, as part of showing that the actus reus as a whole can be attributed to D.

However, before she can be criminally liable the defendant must also be responsible for the *behaviour* element of the actus reus. This requirement is met when her behaviour is voluntary. Suppose that Alice did in fact cause Jim's death, but that she did so while suffering an epileptic seizure, during which her movements caused a heavy object to fall and crush Jim. Alice's behaviour, which causes Jim's death, is not voluntary. She is not responsible for his death, and cannot be convicted of murder.

Very often, acquittal in these circumstances need not be based upon involuntariness. Crimes such as murder require proof of some mental element on the part of the defendant, ie proof of some form of mens rea.[155] In most cases, murder itself cannot be committed unless D intends or is reckless about the victim's death.[156] Thus, even though Alice's behaviour may have caused death, she lacks the mental element required to be guilty of murder. She lacks mens rea.

But it is important to emphasise that involuntariness is *not* merely a denial of intention, or of other forms of mens rea, or even a denial of fault in general.[157] Alice does not claim that she killed Jim by *accident*. Her denial is much more profound. It is a claim that the movements of her body which caused Jim's death do not belong to Alice as a reasoning person.

This deserves elaboration. As part of our conception of what it is to be a human being, we draw a distinction between a deliberative person and her body. Not all movements of one's body can be identified with the person whose body it is that moves. When the doctor tests Simon's reflexes by tapping him on the knee, the swinging of his leg cannot be attributed to Simon. It is merely an event in the history of his body, rather like the lurching of passengers standing in a crowded bus. These are not actions that a person is answerable for doing. They are things that happen to him, over which he has no control,[158] and for which he is not responsible. So it is with Alice. Her behaviour is part of her body's history, but is not traceable to her as a reasoning person. It is not produced by any exercise of the capacities which mark Alice out as a moral agent. In the words of Hart:[159]

---

155 Chapter 3.

156 Chapter 14.

157 For useful discussion of this point, see Patient, "Some Remarks about the Element of Voluntariness in Offences of Absolute Liability" [1968] Crim LR 23.

158 Cf *R v Milloy* (1991) 54 A Crim R 340, [1993] 1 Qd R 298.

159 Hart, "Acts of Will and Responsibility" in *Punishment and Responsibility: Essays in the Philosophy of Law*, Oxford, Clarendon Press, 1968, 90, 107.

What is missing in these cases appears to most people as a vital link between mind and body; and both the ordinary man and the lawyer might well insist on this by saying that in these cases there is not "really" a human action at all and certainly nothing for which anyone should be made criminally responsible however "strict" legal responsibility might be.

2.3.1 Involuntary behaviour

In general, D's deliberative control over her behaviour can be lost or impaired in two ways. First, D's normal capacity to reason about her behaviour may be suppressed because of an impaired consciousness. Alternatively, even if D is able to reason normally about her actions, she may have lost physical control over the movements of her body. In either case, her actions are not responsive to reason. They are "movements of the body which occurred though the agent had no reason for moving his body in that way".[160]

2.3.1.1 Loss of physical control

Imagine the following assault:

> Deborah is standing between Vicky and Tanya. Suddenly, Tanya grasps Deborah's arm and forces it into Vicky's midriff. Tanya is more powerful than Deborah, and Deborah has no chance to resist her. Vicky is winded.

In this situation, Deborah does not commit an assault on Vicky, because her behaviour is involuntary.[161] The movement of Deborah's arm does not occur under her control, and she cannot prevent its occurrence. Thus she is not responsible for the actus reus which eventuates. (Indeed, it is Tanya who assaults Vicky, using Deborah's arm.) Comparable instances would be where D's arm strikes V as the result of a reflex movement or a muscular convulsion or spasm.[162]

2.3.1.2 Impaired consciousness

It has also been held that if D, while driving, is stunned by a blow and rendered incapable of controlling his car, his consequent failure to give way to a pedestrian at a pedestrian crossing would be involuntary and not subject to criminal liability.[163] An analogous situation is sleepwalking. In *Hughes*, a woman had got out of bed during the night and had gone to the kitchen "to

---

160 The definition of involuntariness proposed by Hart, *Punishment and Responsibility: Essays in the Philosophy of Law*, Oxford, Clarendon Press, 1968, 255, 256.

161 *R v Farduto* (1912) 10 DLR 669 at 673, 21 CCC 144 at 149; compare *O'Sullivan v Fisher* [1954] SASR 33 at 39, 40; *Purdie v Maxwell* [1960] NZLR 599 at 606.

162 *Bratty v A-G for Northern Ireland* [1963] AC 386 at 409, [1961] 3 All ER 523 at 532 (HL).

163 *Hill v Baxter* [1958] 1 QB 277 at 282-283, 286, [1958] 1 All ER 193 at 195, 197; *Burns v Bidder* [1967] 2 QB 227 at 240, [1966] 3 All ER 29 at 36; *Kay v Butterworth* (1945) 61 TLR 452 at 453; *R v Spurge* [1961] 2 QB 205, [1961] 2 All ER 688; *McCone v Police* [1971] NZLR 105 at 109; *Sione v Labour Dept* [1972] NZLR 278; *R v Bell* [1984] 3 All ER 842 at 846, [1984] Crim CR 685 at 686.

peel potatoes", whence she had taken a knife and returned to the bedroom to stab her husband. She was acquitted of wounding with intent.[164]

Sleepwalking is an instructive case, because D's behaviour in this state may well be purposive,[165] and exhibit many outward signs of intentionality. Glanville makes this point vividly:

> The sleep-walker does not always proceed as the cartoonists imagine him, with eyes tightly closed and arms outstretched. His eyes may be open and he may appear to be in perfect control. He will open a door and turn a corner, walk downstairs, open a drawer, take out a carving-knife, and return to the bedroom where his wife is asleep. But after waking up he will not remember his deed (except sometimes as a dream). Although his acts have a certain purpose (indeed, he may have an understandable reason for killing his wife), it is the purpose of a dream-state. He is not acting with his normal conscious mind.[166]

When Lady MacBeth is observed "washing" her hands at night,[167] her movements are hardly random or uncontrolled. They exude purpose. Her actions are, in some sense, a subintentional product of her unconscious or subconscious mind. Certainly they are not mere reflex movements. But the control that Lady MacBeth has over them is in no way a conscious control — indeed, she is incapable of acting intentionally at all. Her "acts" are, in law, involuntary.

In the criminal law, these forms of involuntary behaviour are known as automatism. Like Lady MacBeth, the defendant may be unconscious or semi-conscious when she does the actus reus. Where this is so, and her actions are the product of that impaired consciousness, those actions are described as automatic. Automatism will be considered in more detail in chapter 8. However, as the assault example involving Deborah, Tanya, and Vicky shows, automatism predicated upon unconsciousness or impaired consciousness is not *required* for the defendant to be absolved of responsibility for her behaviour. Whether she was conscious or unconscious, what is essential to the denial of responsibility for a defendant's involuntary behaviour is that *she was unable deliberatively to control that behaviour and to prevent it from occurring.*[168]

In most cases, there will be a connection between consciousness and control: the greater the degree of consciousness a defendant has, the greater the degree of conscious or deliberative control she will have over her actions. This raises the further question: where D's claim of involuntariness is based upon automatism and an impaired consciousness, must D have lost *all* conscious control over her limbs?

It would appear not. Certainly there is no requirement that D be altogether unconscious. In *R v Charlson* D was not denied the defence even though he

---

164 Reported in *The Times* 3 May 1978, p 5. Cf *Bratty v A-G for Northern Ireland* [1963] AC 386 at 403, 409, [1961] 3 All ER 523 at 528, 532; *R v Carpenter* (1976) The Times, October 14; *R v Carter* [1959] VR 105, [1959] ALR 335; *Fain v Commonwealth* (1879) 39 Am Rep 213.

165 Cf also *R v Charlson* [1955] 1 All ER 859, [1955] 1 WLR 317.

166 *TBCL*, 665.

167 *MacBeth*, Act V, scene i.

168 *R v Milloy* (1991) 54 A Crim R 340, [1993] 1 Qd R 298.

could recall hitting V on the head.[169] Similarly, in *R v Quick*, D was allowed to claim automatism consequent upon hypoglaecemia, notwithstanding that his condition was one of semi-consciousness.[170] North P considered the question in *Burr*, where he concluded that the claim of automatism:[171]

> does not mean that the accused person must be absolutely unconscious because you cannot move a muscle without a direction given by the mind . . . All the *deliberative* functions of the mind must be absent so that the accused person acts automatically.

This, with respect, seems correct.[172] What counts is the inability *deliberatively* to control one's conduct — that one's movements are not responsive to a capacity to reason and deliberate about one's conduct. Obviously, where the defendant is altogether unconscious her reasoning capacities will be inactive. But a defendant need *not* be unconscious before those capacities may be suppressed or inoperative. A hypnotised patient who carries out the instructions of the hypnotist must be able to comprehend and implement those instructions at some level of consciousness. Yet he has no capacity to deliberate about what actions to take or his reasons for taking them. He is an automaton, and is not responsible for his behaviour.[173]

Apart from sleepwalking and hypnotism, standard cases of semi-conscious conduct which are capable of qualifying as automatic and involuntary behaviour include acts done while in a state of concussion,[174] dissociation,[175]

---

169 [1955] 1 All ER 859 at 862I, 863F, [1955] 1 WLR 317 at 322, 323.

170 [1973] QB 910 at 916B, [1973] 3 All ER 347 at 350. The possibility of semi-conscious automatism appears to have been accepted also in *R v Carter* [1959] VR 105 at 108, 109, [1959] ALR 335 at 338, 339; *R v Stripp* (1978) 69 Cr App R 318 at 320, 321.

171 [1969] NZLR 736 at 744, 745 (emphasis added). For a somewhat extreme illustration, see *R v T* [1990] Crim LR 256, discussed in Horder, "Pleading Involuntary Lack of Capacity" [1993] 52 CLJ 298 at 313-315.

172 Notwithstanding the suggestion in *Watmore v Jenkins* [1962] 2 QB 572 at 586, [1962] 2 All ER 868 at 874 that automatic conduct must be "wholly uncontrolled and uninitiated by any function of conscious will"; cf *A-G's Reference (No 2 of 1992)* [1994] QB 91, [1993] 4 All ER 683; *Broome v Perkins* (1987) 85 Cr App R 321, [1987] Crim LR 271. These decisions must be regarded as inconsistent with the case-law and as contrary to principle (cf *TBCL*, 679). In *Broome v Perkins*, the prosecution's submission (at 325) that "automatism meant an act which was done by the muscles without any control by the mind such as a spasm, a reflex action or a convulsion" reveals a fundamental confusion between automatism and loss of physical control over one's limbs (§ 2.3.1.1). This went unnoticed by the Divisional Court, which repeated (at 330, 331) the characterisation of automatism found in *Watmore v Jenkins* [1962] 2 QB 572 at 586, [1962] 2 All ER 868 at 874, as connoting no "wider or looser concept than involuntary movement of the body or limbs". Note that *R v Isitt* (1977) 67 Cr App R 44, [1978] Crim LR 159 is sometimes cited as similar authority, but on the facts appears to have involved action for a purpose, merely without moral inhibition (see at 48, 49).

173 For interesting discussion, see Williams, "The Actus Reus of Dr Caligari" (1994) 142 U Pa L Rev 1661 at 1667f.

174 Cf *Bratty v A-G for Northern Ireland* [1963] AC 386 at 403, [1961] 3 All ER 523 at 528 (HL); *R v Quick* [1973] QB 910 at 918, 920-922, [1973] 3 All ER 347 at 352, 354-56.

175 Cf *R v Toner* (1991) 93 Cr App R 382, [1991] Crim LR 627; *R v T* [1990] Crim LR 256; *R v Rabey* (1980) 15 CR (3d) 225, [1980] 2 SCR 513.

and advanced stages of hypoglycaemia.[176] (These will be discussed further in chapter 8.) In each of these instances, a loss of the capacity deliberatively to control D's behaviour will mean that he cannot be held criminally responsible for his actions and their consequences.

The view taken here may be contrasted with that found in *Police v Bannin,* where Fisher J suggests that automatism turns on whether D had the capacity to form the mental elements required for the crime:[177]

> the defence of automatism can be reduced to the question whether at the material time the accused had the mental capacity to form the particular mental ingredients of the crime with which he is charged . . . The mental ingredients of the crime will vary from one case to another but in every case the accused must have (i) some appreciation of each of the key facts relevant to the crime; (ii) some capacity to make a decision to act with respect to those facts; and (iii) some capacity to form each of the residual elements of the particular mens rea involved.

With respect to his Honour, to claim that D's conduct was involuntary is to make a claim about D's responsibility for the actus reus, not about her capacity to satisfy the mens rea requirements. The test for involuntariness does not, and should not, vary according to the mens rea requirement of each particular offence. Indeed, where an offence includes mental ingredients, it is not necessary to show automatism: D will be absolved of criminal liability so long as one of those mental ingredients was absent, whether or not she had the capacity to form it at the time.[178] Furthermore, it is not at all clear how his Honour's analysis could be applied to offences which do not require proof of mens rea.[179]

In practice, although our approach is based on rather different principles than those embraced by Fisher J, the practical effect will probably be little, at least in respect of offences where proof of a mental element is necessary. Where D is incapable of forming, for example, an intention, she will surely also be incapable of exercising deliberative control over her behaviour, and will thus be automatic. Nonetheless, the test of deliberative control may be more generous to the defendant than that espoused in *Police v Bannin.* It is conceivable that a defendant with impaired consciousness may be *capable* of forming a limited intention, even though her ability to deliberate about her behaviour is effectively suppressed.[180] (Indeed, this may well be true of hypoglycaemic actors.) In such cases, it is submitted that the approach taken here, which acknowledges the fundamental importance of responsibility and voluntariness, is to be preferred.

It must be emphasised, however, that where D *does* in fact form an intention to commit a crime, then "however clouded, confused, and distant" D's

---

176 *R v Quick* [1973] QB 910, [1973] 3 All ER 347.

177 [1991] 2 NZLR 237 at 254, also reported as *R v Police* (1990) 7 CRNZ 55.

178 *R v G* (1984) 1 CRNZ 275; *R v Tucker* [1984] 36 SASR 135 at 139, (1984) 13 A Crim R 447 at 451; *R v Martin* [1983] 32 SASR 419, (1983) 9 A Crim R 376.

179 See § 2.3.3.

180 Cf *Burnskey v Police* (1992) 8 CRNZ 582, in which evidence of impaired consciousness was treated as raising the possibility of automatism.

awareness may have been, automatism is excluded.[181] It is no defence that D acted upon an "irresistible impulse", for example, if he knew what he was doing and acted intentionally. An impulsive action is conscious and intentional — it is action for a reason, not action uncontrolled by reason.[182]

Nor is responsibility for behaviour denied merely because D's deliberative faculties are not "fully functioning",[183] or "not working in top gear".[184] "Not thinking clearly" implies that D is still thinking about his actions, even if not very well. He is still exercising deliberative control over his conduct, and cannot claim that his conduct was involuntary — it is a far cry from this state to one in which D is not reasoning at all. Rather than automatism, the appropriate defence (if applicable) is one of absence of mens rea. An instructive case is *R v Kingston*, the facts of which were as follows:[185]

D was invited to a flat for ostensibly innocent purposes. While there, he was given coffee laced with disinhibiting drugs. He was then taken into a bedroom where a 15-year-old boy lay, also drugged, on a bed. D performed sexual acts with the boy, and was subsequently charged with an indecent assault. His conviction was upheld by the House of Lords.

It is quite likely that D would not have acted as he did had he not (unknown to him) ingested the drugs, which may well have affected his judgment by freeing him of his usual self-restraint. But a disinhibited intent is still an intent, and the explanation cannot amount to a denial of responsibility for D. He acts for reasons — albeit perhaps not reasons that would normally motivate him — and thus is not automatic.[186]

2.3.1.2(a) *Insane automatism*

Whenever a defendant's involuntariness is found to be due to automatism, the court must then determine whether it is to be classified as *sane* or *insane* automatism. This classification depends upon the cause of the automatism. Where the defendant loses consciousness as a result of a blow on the head, for example, his behaviour will be regarded as occurring in a state of sane automatism. By contrast, behaviour occuring during an epileptic fit will be exculpated on the footing of insane automatism.

The test for differentiating these types of automatism will be discussed in chapter 8. The importance of the distinction is that sane automatism operates as

---

181 *Police v Bannin* [1991] 2 NZLR 237 at 253, also reported as *R v Police* (1990) 7 CRNZ 55.

182 Cf *R v Burr* [1969] NZLR 736 (CA).

183 *R v Burr* [1969] NZLR 736 at 745 (CA).

184 *R v Isitt* (1977) 67 Cr App R 44 at 48, [1978] Crim LR 159.

185 [1995] 2 AC 355, [1994] 3 All ER 353; considered in detail at § 9.2.8.

186 Cf *HM Advocate v Kidd* [1960] SLT 82; *Burr* [1969] NZLR 736; *R v Isitt* (1977) 67 Cr App R 44 at 49, [1978] Crim LR 159; *A-G for South Australia v Brown* [1960] AC 432, [1960] 1 All ER 734; *Bratty v A-G for Northern Ireland* [1963] AC 386 at 409, [1961] 3 All ER 523 at 532 (HL). A similar analysis would apply to provocation; D's provoked intention is still an intention. Thus the defence functions as an excuse rather than as a denial of voluntariness. See below, chapter 14. For an interesting argument that Kingston might deserve an excusatory defence, see Sullivan, "Making Excuses" in Simester and Smith (eds), *Harm and Culpability*, Oxford, Clarendon Press, 1995, 131.

a straightforward denial of voluntariness and thus leads to an outright acquittal. By contrast, insane automatism is treated in law as a species of insanity for which there is a special vedict and a different burden of proof upon the defendant. Insanity is considered below, in chapter 8.

2.3.2 Omissions, states of affairs, and possession

So far we have considered involuntariness in the context of positive actions by a defendant. However, we saw earlier in this chapter (§ 2.1) that not every actus reus requires a positive action. For example, offences can sometimes be committed by omission. When D stands by while her child drowns in the bath, her failure to save him is prima facie the actus reus of culpable homicide.[187]

Obviously, the involuntariness of omissions cannot be explained in the same way as actions. It would be odd indeed to talk of a reflex or convulsive omission. Nonetheless, even for omissions the criminal law requires that D must be responsible for her behaviour before she commits the actus reus of a crime. D's omission is involuntary, and her responsibility for the actus reus is negated, when she fails to discharge a duty to intervene because it was *impossible* for her to do so.[188] For instance:

After an earthquake, D observes that his daughter is suffocating under a pile of rubble. D fails to rescue her because he is pinned beneath some collapsed masonry from which he cannot escape. D is not responsible for failing to rescue his daughter, and cannot be attributed with the actus reus of a homicide.

This is true even if, for some reason, D had wanted his daughter dead, and would not have rescued her had it been possible to do so.[189]

In such cases, where a defendant would not have complied with the law even if possible, it is sometimes important to distinguish between involuntary *behaviour* and unavoidable *consequences*. In the earthquake example, D has no control over his behaviour. But imagine the following case:

E is sunbathing on the beach when he observes his young daughter entering the sea and starting to swim in shallow water. Unfortunately, she encounters difficulties and is caught in an outgoing tide. E does not lift a finger to help, despite her cries to him, and watches as she is swept out to sea and drowned.

E may be able to deny responsibility for his daughter's death on the basis of *causation*. In a prosecution for murder or manslaughter, the prosecution must prove that E's omission to intervene caused his daughter's death. If in fact there was a riptide, and E would have been unable to save her anyway, then he is not responsible for the fatal consequence and cannot be convicted of a homicide offence.

The difference between this case and the earthquake example is that E denies responsibility for a *consequence* of his omission on the basis of causation,

---

187 § 2.1.1.2.(b).

188 *R v Bamber* (1843) 5 QB 279, 114 ER 1254; *Stockdale v Coulson* [1974] 3 All ER 154, [1974] 1 WLR 1192; *R v Mary Hogan* (1851) 2 Den 277, 169 ER 504. A valuable discussion is Smart, "Criminal Responsibility for Failing to Do the Impossible" (1987) 103 LQR 532. See also Williams, *CLGP*, 746-748.

189 *Starri v SA Police* (1995) 80 A Crim R 197.

while D denies responsibility for his *behaviour* on the basis of involuntariness. Either way, a vital element of the actus reus of homicide is missing. But unlike D, E may still be criminally liable for an *attempt*.[190] Because E's behaviour was not involuntary, it is capable of constituting the actus reus of an attempted murder. (Whether or not he would be convicted then depends upon questions of mens rea and proximity.) By contrast, it is impossible for D even to attempt a rescue. Therefore he cannot be held responsible for failing to do so.

The test of responsibility is very similar for crimes which specify no behavioural element, and which criminalise states of affairs[191] or possession.[192] This would seem to follow from the point made earlier (in § 2.1.2.1, 2) that such offences, while formally needing no proof of particular behaviour by the defendant, can be seen as indirectly imposing liability for a defendant's omission to prevent the actus reus from occurring. In *Kilbride v Lake*,[193] D was charged with permitting his car to be on the road without displaying a warrant of fitness. After he had parked and left the car, the warrant somehow became detached. It was conceded that D had no opportunity to rectify this state of affairs, and thus that his omission to do so, and consequently the existence of the actus reus, was involuntary. On this footing Woodhouse J ruled that D should be acquitted. It is a cardinal principle, his Honour said, that:[194]

> a person cannot be made criminally responsible for an act or omission unless it was done or omitted in circumstances where there was some other course open to him. If this condition is absent, any act or omission must be involuntary . . . In the present case there was no opportunity at all to take a different course, and any inactivity on the part of the appellant after the warrant was removed was involuntary and unrelated to the offence.

Without an opportunity to avoid the actus reus, D is not responsible for its occurrence. Similarly, in *Finau v Dept of Labour*[195] the defendant was acquitted of the situational-liability offence of remaining in New Zealand after the expiry of her temporary entry permit. Owing to her pregnancy, she had been refused carriage by an airline. Therefore, even though the actus reus had occurred, Finau was not criminally responsible for that actus, since it was impossible for her to prevent it.[196]

---

190 Or for any other relevant offence where consequences are not part of the actus reus: compare *R v Brown* (1841) Car & M 314 at 318, 174 ER 522 at 524.

191 § 2.1.2.1.

192 § 2.1.2.2.

193 [1962] NZLR 590. See Clark, "Accident — Or What Became of Kilbride v Lake?" in Clark (ed), *Essays on Criminal Law in New Zealand*, Wellington, Sweet & Maxwell, 1971, 47; Budd and Lynch, "Voluntariness, Causation and Strict Liability" [1978] Crim LR 74.

194 [1962] NZLR 590 at 593. Contra, in England, *Strowger v John* [1974] RTR 124, [1974] Crim LR 123; *Pilgram v Dean* [1974] 2 All ER 751, [1974] 1 WLR 601.

195 [1984] 2 NZLR 396 (CA).

196 See also *Tifaga v Dept of Labour* [1980] 2 NZLR 235 at 237-239, 241, 242 (CA); *O'Sullivan v Fisher* [1954] SASR 33; *Burns v Nowell* (1880) 5 QBD 444 at 454. English law is rather more draconian than New Zealand law on this point: see the discussion and citations above, § 2.1.2.1.

Like situational offences, criminal possession (for example, of an instrument of burglary[197] or of a controlled drug[198]) can be established without proving any behaviour by D. The physical element of "being in possession" is a state of affairs in which D has control, with or without custody,[199] of the prohibited item. It is usually sufficient for the actus reus to show that the item is at a location where it is subject to D's power of control.[200]

Suppose that D acquires possession of controlled drugs but not by means of his own voluntary actions; for example, if a visitor to his house leaves the drugs behind when she departs. D may not be responsible for acquiring possession, but normally he is still responsible for *being* in possession because he fails to divest himself of the drugs. Suppose further, however, that D knows that he has been left the drugs yet happens to be bed-ridden through illness and is thus unable to dispose of them. It is submitted that, by analogy with offences involving states of affairs, D is not responsible for the actus reus and possession should not be attributed to him for the purposes of criminal liability.[201]

2.3.2.1 *Distinction between impossibility and ignorance of duty*

Impossibility amounting to involuntariness should be distinguished from situations where D is reasonably unaware of the existence of facts that trigger a duty to act in a certain manner. For example, one does not, apparently, commit an offence of remaining in Singapore when one's presence there becomes unlawful pursuant to an unpublished law.[202] Exculpation in such cases does not depend upon any claim of involuntariness, but rather upon an absence of mens rea and the reasonableness and cause of D's ignorance of law or fact. It is thus a matter for particular defences.

2.3.3 Involuntariness: responsibility by antecedent fault

Sometimes, even though the actus reus occurs involuntarily, D may still be held criminally responsible. One way in which this may occur is through vicarious liability, which is discussed below in chapter 5. Leaving that possibility aside, however, D may also be liable for an offence if his involuntariness, and in turn the actus reus, was the consequence of earlier conduct by D at a time when he also had the mens rea required for that offence.

---

197 Section 244 Crimes Act 1961.

198 Section 7 Misuse of Drugs Act 1975.

199 Cf *R v McRae* (1993) 10 CRNZ 61 (CA); *R v Delon* (1992) 29 NSWLR 29; s 2(2) Misuse of Drugs Act 1975.

200 *Police v Emirali* [1976] 2 NZLR 476 (CA); *Rose v Loo Kee* [1927] GLR 403. In some offences control without the availability of imminent custody may not suffice: *R v Rollo* [1956] NZLR 522 (CA); *R v Lester* (1955) 39 Cr App R 157.

201 As it happens, most offences of possession in New Zealand also require proof of mens rea going beyond mere knowledge of possession: cf *Dong Wai v Audley* [1937] NZLR 290; *R v Cox* [1990] 2 NZLR 275 (CA); *Police v Emirali* [1976] 1 NZLR 286 (CA).

202 *Lim Chin Aik v R* [1963] AC 160, [1963] 1 All ER 223. Cf *Harding v Price* [1948] 1 KB 695, [1948] 1 All ER 283 (failing to report an accident when D did not know it had occurred). See chapter 12.

An example might be the phenomenon sometimes called "Dutch Courage": where D, planning to perpetrate an assault, drinks himself into a virtual stupor in order to commit it.[203] Even if the Court accepts his claim that the assault occurred while D was an automaton, it will not negate his criminal responsibility for the actus reus. Rather than focussing upon D's actions while automatic, his responsibility will be based upon his earlier conduct, which caused the eventual actus reus, and which was itself accompanied by the fault element required for the crime of assault.

This approach was accepted by the Court of Appeal as a possible analysis in *R v Wickliffe*.[204] In that case, D attempted to rob a jeweller's shop. He threatened those in the shop by pointing a loaded and cocked gun at them with his finger on the trigger. It appears that V then sprang at him. D was jolted back against the door, causing his finger to depress the trigger involuntarily. V was killed when the gun went off. Under s 167(d), D is guilty of murder if, for an unlawful object, he "does an act that he knows to be likely to cause death, and *thereby kills any person*". In the Court's view,[205] although the immediate cause of death was an involuntary act by D, that was not a novus actus interveniens; his actions leading up to that point, in threatening V and other people in the shop by pointing a gun at them with his finger on the trigger, were still a cause of death.[206] Thus D's earlier conduct, rather than the firing of the gun itself, could be the act for the purposes of s 167(d) which "thereby kills any person".

There is no general doctrine that allows for responsibility to be ascribed to an involuntary or automatic person merely because she was previously at fault for becoming automatic.[207] Consider the facts of *R v Lipman*:[208]

> L and his female friend, V, took a quantity of LSD while in V's flat. During the hallucination which followed, L suffocated V by cramming bed sheet into her mouth. He believed when he did so that he was fighting snakes while descending to the centre of the earth.

L's behaviour while hallucinating is analogous to sleepwalking. It does not occur under his conscious or deliberative control. However, the automatism is

---

203 *A-G for Northern Ireland v Gallagher* [1963] AC 349 at 382, [1961] 3 All ER 299 at 314 (HL) (Lord Denning).

204 [1987] 1 NZLR 55 at 60, (1986) 2 CRNZ 310 at 314 (CA). Cf *Ryan v R* (1967) 121 CLR 205 at 218, 219, 231, 233, 239, [1967] ALR 577 at 586, 594, 596, 600; Elliott, "Responsibility for Involuntary Acts: Ryan v The Queen" (1968) 41 ALJ 497; *R v Howe* [1987] AC 417 at 458, also reported as *R v Burke* [1987] Crim LR 480 at 484.

205 At least, on the view of the facts most favourable to the accused.

206 See also the discussion of causation earlier in this chapter, § 2.2.3ff.

207 Cf *R v Bailey* [1983] 2 All ER 503, [1983] 1 WLR 760, overruling the earlier decision in *R v Quick* [1973] QB 910 at 922, [1973] 3 All ER 347 at 356, where it was said that automatism would not be available where its onset "could have been reasonably foreseen as a result of either doing, or omitting to do something, as, for example, taking alcohol against medical advice after using certain prescribed drugs, or failing to have regular meals while taking insulin." See generally Ashworth, "Reason, Logic and Criminal Liability" (1975) 91 LQR 102, 106-109; Robinson, "Causing the Conditions of One's Own Defence: A Study in the Limits of Theory in Criminal Law Doctrine" (1985) 71 Va LR 1.

208 [1970] 1 QB 152, [1969] 3 All ER 410.

self-induced, and moreover induced by D's own fault in becoming intoxicated. In England, his claim to be exculpated on the basis of automatism was refused, and L was convicted of manslaughter.[209]

In New Zealand, automatism would be available and L would not be convicted.[210] Even though L is responsible for his automatism, becoming automatic is not a criminal offence. It does *not* follow that he is responsible for the further consequences of his automatism. Before that can be the case, L must have the required mens rea not merely in respect of becoming automatic, but also in respect of those further consequences which make up the actus reus. For example, if an offence requires proof that the defendant foresaw the actus reus, the claim of automatism or involuntariness denies responsibility unless she actually foresaw the possibility of her incapacity *and* the resulting offence.[211]

The analysis is perhaps more difficult for offences that do not require proof of mens rea. Such offences, involving what is known as strict or absolute liability, are considered in chapter 4. It is submitted that because voluntariness is fundamental to D's responsibility for the actus reus, and not merely relevant to mens rea, in principle its absence will still result in there being no criminal liability for D's conduct.[212]

Nonetheless, responsibility may again be established antecedently. It will be open to the prosecution to show that earlier, voluntary, behaviour by D is responsible for the later (involuntary) events which brought about the actus reus. As will be seen in chapter 4, in strict liability offences the defendant may exculpate himself by proving that his actions were without fault. It follows that, where D's involuntariness, and in turn the actus reus, *is* a consequence of his earlier, voluntary conduct, then in order to exculpate himself D will be required to show that the later situation in which he found himself was not a foreseeable consequence of earlier behaviour for which he was at fault.

---

209 Approved in *DPP v Majewski* [1977] AC 443, [1977] Crim LR 532. See MacKay, "Intoxication as a Factor in Automatism" [1982] Crim LR 146; Horder, "Pleading Involuntary Lack of Capacity" [1993] 52 CLJ 298 at 304ff. The refusal of a defence in England seems to be predicated on the fact that its self-induced cause specifically involves intoxication, rather than some other faultworthy origin. Intoxication does not have the same inculpating status in New Zealand: *R v Kamipeli* [1975] 2 NZLR 610; *R v Hart* [1986] 2 NZLR 408, (1986) 3 CRNZ 474; *Steinberg v Police* (1983) 1 CRNZ 129; chapter 9.

210 *R v Cottle* [1958] NZLR 999 at 1002, 1007 (CA) (Gresson P); *R v O'Connor* (1980) 146 CLR 64, (1980) 29 ALR 449; *R v Martin* (1984) 51 ALR 540, 16 A Crim R 376; Orchard, "Surviving without Majewski — A View from Down Under" [1993] Crim LR 426.

211 *R v O'Connor* (1980) 146 CLR 64 at 73, 29 ALR 449 at 456, 477 (Barwick CJ), 103 (Stephen J); cf *R v Egan* (1897) 23 VLR 159, [1897] ALR 37; *Sione v Labour Dept* [1972] NZLR 278; *Ryan v R* (1967) 121 CLR 205, [1967] ALR 577. Thus Lipman might be convicted of manslaughter if the risk of killing someone while under the influence of LSD were such as to make his taking the drug "grossly negligent". (For discussion of the mens rea element in manslaughter see chapter 14.)

212 *R v O'Connor* (1980) 146 CLR 64, 29 ALR 449; *Hill v Baxter* [1958] 1 QB 277, [1958] 1 All ER 193; Williams, "Absolute Liability in Traffic Offences" [1967] Crim LR 142 and 194, 199ff. But see *Keech v Pratt* [1994] 1 NZLR 65 at 72, also reported as *Police v Pratt* (1993) 10 CRNZ 659 at 666, 667.

In practice, therefore, the requirement of absence of fault is the more important excusing condition for strict liability offences. But it does not subsume the requirement for voluntariness.[213] If the proscecution cannot show that the actus reus was a foreseeable consequence of earlier conduct by D, D will be entitled to an acquittal without having to prove an absence of fault.

2.3.4 Evidential issues

A claim of involuntariness or automatism is often described by lawyers as a "defence". In terms of substantive legal doctrine, it is not. It is a denial of the actus reus, rather than a plea that the defendant's actions were justified or excused. As such, it is for the prosecution to prove voluntariness on the part of the defendant alongside the rest of the actus reus. So far as the burden of proof is concerned, however, automatism *is* like a defence. In practice, there is a presumption of deliberative capacity to control one's actions, and voluntariness will become an issue only if there is evidence which genuinely raises the issue.[214] Thus, if the defendant wishes to deny responsibility on this basis, she must point to credible evidence which supports her claim. It is said that "blackout is one of the first refuges of a guilty conscience."[215] In general, since it is so easily feigned the defendant's testimony of automatism will not be accepted unless it is buttressed by relevant evidence of surrounding circumstances or medical conditions.[216]

---

213 Contra *MOT v Strong* [1987] 2 NZLR 295. See the criticism of that decision in *Adams* § CA20.49(2). Note too that if an offence imposes strict liability only as to part of the actus reus, and requires mens rea for some other part, then involuntariness will of course preclude liability in the normal way.

214 *Bratty v A-G for Northern Ireland* [1963] AC 386 at 406, 407, 413, 416, 417, [1961] 3 All ER 523 at 530, 531, 535, 536, 537 (HL); *R v Cottle* [1958] NZLR 999 at 1025 (CA). Similarly for impossibility: cf *R v Bailey* [1983] 2 All ER 503 at 507, 508, [1983] 1 WLR 760 at 765, 766. For further discussion of the burden of proof, see § 4.1.

215 *Cooper v McKenna, ex parte Cooper* [1960] Qd R 406 at 419 (Stable J); *Bratty v A-G for Northern Ireland* [1963] AC 386 at 413, 414, [1961] 3 All ER 523 at 535, 536 (Lord Denning).

216 *Cook v Atchison* [1968] Crim LR 266; cf *Hill v Baxter* [1958] 1 QB 277, [1958] 1 All ER 193; *R v Stripp* (1978) 69 Cr App R 318; contrast *R v Budd* [1962] Crim LR 49. A more detailed treatment of this point is to be found in *Adams* §§ CA23.44-46; also chapter 8.

3

Mens Rea

The mens rea of a crime is, generally speaking, that part of the offence which refers to the defendant's mental state. Returning to a familiar example from chapter 1, bigamy, recall s 205(1) Crimes Act 1961:

Bigamy defined—(1) Bigamy is:

. . . . .

(b) The act of a person who goes through a form of marriage in New Zealand with any other person whom he or she knows to be married . . .

When Tom is charged with committing an offence against s 205(1)(b), the offence may only be established if Tom *knew that his "bride" was already married*. The italicised part of the last sentence is the mens rea requirement.

In the case of s 205(1)(b), only one mental element is specified. But it is also possible for an offence to contain a variety of actus reus elements for which the corresponding mens rea requirements differ. Consider, for example, the offence of wilful damage contrary to s 298(1) Crimes Act:

(1) Every one is liable to imprisonment for a term not exceeding 14 years who wilfully destroys or damages—
(a) Any property, whether he has an interest in it or not, if he knows or ought to know that danger to life is likely to ensue . . .

Section 298(1)(a) requires proof of more than one actus reus ingredient. Correspondingly, there are two parts to the mens rea for this offence. A defendant must (a) have *wilfully* damaged property, and (b) have *known or ought to have known* that doing so was likely to create a danger to life.

Although "mens rea" is often regarded as the requirement that the defendant have a "guilty mind", and is taken to contain the fault elements of each offence, it is in practice a rather technical area of law. For a prosecutor, mens rea requires her to establish only that the defendant had the specified mental state toward the actus reus which is required for that crime. In particular, proof that the defendant had the requisite mens rea of an offence does not mean that she must know her conduct is illegal,[1] or wrong. Similarly, a law-abiding motive which prompts the defendant to commit an offence is no defence. In *R v Smith*,[2] for instance, the defendant offered a bribe to the town mayor. He did so in order to expose the mayor as corrupt. Despite his good motive, he was convicted of offering a bribe to a public servant since he had intentionally (the mens rea) offered the bribe (the actus reus). At that stage the offence was complete, and his motive could not help him.[3]

---

1   Cf s 25 (Ignorance of law).

2   [1960] 2 QB 423, [1960] 1 All ER 256.

3   The decision does not sit well with *R v Clarke* (1984) 80 Cr App R 344, [1985] Crim LR 209, which holds that a citizen has a defence if acting honestly and solely to reveal crime and recover its proceeds. However, the view that mens rea means no more than the mental element for the offence is endorsed in *R v Hicklin* (1868) 3 QB 360 at 370-372; *Gordon v Schubert* [1956] NZLR 431; *Yip Chiu-cheung v R* [1995] 1 AC 111, [1994] 2 All ER 924; also *R v Kingston* [1995] 2 AC 355, [1994] 3 All ER 353. This approach, which disconnects a finding of mens rea from the presence of fault, is appropriate only if a suitable range of defences is available. See § 1.2.2; also Brett, *Inquiry into Criminal Guilt*,

There are three steps to be taken in establishing whether a defendant has mens rea. The first step is to determine what mens rea standard is required in respect of each separate element of the actus reus. The second is to interpret the criteria of those mens rea element(s). Third is the factual question: did the defendant in fact act with the mens rea element(s) required?

We will come back to the first step, deciding which mens rea standard, in chapter 4, once we have looked more closely at the main types of mens rea which the law might require. There are in fact a great variety of possible mens rea states; the Crimes Act mentions, among others, intention, recklessness, wilfulness, knowledge, belief, the lack of a belief on reasonable grounds, fraudulence, dishonesty, failure to use reasonable care, purpose, calculation and corruption. However, in this chapter we will confine our discussion to the most common, and most important, types of fault element.

3.1 INTENTION[4]

As was mentioned in chapter 1, New Zealand's criminal law has travelled a relatively subjective road when it comes to serious offences, with criminal fault being predicated upon the accused's knowing or deliberate choice to do or risk doing the actus reus. This means that, at least for serious offences, the law's emphasis and a textbook's concentration is upon intention and recklessness, together with their cognitive counterparts, knowledge and belief. It is the defendant's recognition that he is doing the act that constitutes an offence, and his choice to do so, which condemns him.

The central, and usually the most grave, case of wrongdoing occurs when the defendant's crime is intentional. For the majority of offences, it is not necessary to prove that the actus reus was intended, since recklessness will normally suffice for a conviction. (Intention will therefore, often be most relevant at the sentencing stage.) But this is not always so — the offence of attempting to commit a crime, for example, can only be done intentionally[5]. Similarly, an assault can only be committed by applying force intentionally; recklessness will not suffice.[6] There are other important reasons for distinguishing intention from recklessness, and we shall return to these later.

1960. Compare too *R v Gordon* (1993) 10 CRNZ 430 at 438, 439, 441 (CA): "sympathy for the appellant cannot prevail over the current statutory provisions".

4   See, for example, Smith, "Intention in Criminal Law" (1974) 27 CLP 93; White, "Intention, Purpose, Foresight and Desire" (1976) 92 LQR 569; Buzzard, " 'Intent' " [1978] Crim LR 5; Smith, " 'Intent': A Reply" [1978] Crim LR 14; Orchard, "Criminal Intention" [1986] NZLJ 208; Duff, "The Obscure Intentions of the House of Lords" [1986] Crim LR 771; Williams, "Oblique Intention" (1987) 46 CLJ 417; Buxton, "Some Simple Thoughts on Intention" [1988] Crim LR 484; Duff, "Intentions Legal and Philosophical" (1989) 9 OJLS 76; Smith, "A Note on 'Intention' " [1990] Crim LR 85; Simester and Chan, "Intention Thus Far" [1997] Crim LR 704.

5   See s 72 Crimes Act 1961.

6   Section 2; cf *R v Young* 9/7/92, CA86/92.

3.1.1 Ways of speaking about intention

There is normally no need for an elaborate definition of intention in order to decide whether an actus reus was intended. A few peculiar cases may present difficulty, but usually the analysis will be intuitively obvious:

> The general legal opinion is that "intention" cannot be satisfactorily defined and does not need a definition, since everybody knows what it means.[7]

Nonetheless, the fact that some cases are difficult means that we do need guidelines about what intention means.

As a starting point, it may be helpful to look at how "intention" has been paraphrased by Judges and academic writers. In *Cunliffe v Goodman*, Lord Asquith stated that intention "connotes a state of affairs which the party 'intending'. . . does more than merely contemplate: it connotes a state of affairs which, on the contrary, he decides, so far as in him lies, to bring about".[8] In other words, D generally intends an outcome if it is something that he decides, or seeks, to bring about.

It is also clear that D intends a result if he acts with the *purpose*,[9] or object, of bringing it about. In Smith and Hogan's useful example:[10]

> If D has resolved to kill P and he fires a loaded gun at him with the object of doing so, he intends to kill. It is immaterial that he is aware that he is a poor shot, that P is nearly out of range, and that his chances of success are small. It is sufficient that killing is his object or purpose, . . . that he acts in order to kill.

At the heart of this approach is a recognition that D intends to kill P if he means to bring about P's death by his actions — if he acts with the aim, objective, or purpose of killing P.[11]

Antony Duff has built on this idea. Suppose that D fires a gun knowing that P is nearby, and we are trying to decide whether he intended to kill P. Duff argues that if D aims to cause P's death by his actions, then we can say that D *attempts* to kill P.[12] Furthermore, an attempt can either be a success or a failure. Therefore, Duff shows, one feature of intention is that a defendant who intends (aims, tries, attempts) to kill P would regard himself as having "failed" in some

---

7   Williams, *TBCL*, 74. Per Lord Bridge, in *R v Moloney* [1985] AC 905 at 926, [1985] 1 All ER 1025 at 1036, 1037 (HL). "The golden rule should be that . . . the judge should avoid any elaboration or paraphrase of what is meant by intent, and leave it to the jury's good sense to decide whether the accused acted with the necessary intent . . .". Cf *R v Belfon* [1976] 3 All ER 46, [1976] 1 WLR 741 (CA); *R v Nedrick* [1986] 3 All ER 1, [1986] 1 WLR 1025 at 1027 (CA).

8   [1950] 2 KB 237 at 253.

9   *R v Burke* [1991] 1 AC 135 at 147, [1990] 2 WLR 1313 at 1318 (HL).

10 *Smith and Hogan*, 57.

11 Cf *Gollins v Gollins* [1964] AC 644 at 663, [1963] 2 All ER 966 at 971 (HL) (Lord Reid); *DPP v Smith* [1961] AC 290 at 327, also reported as *R v Smith* [1960] 2 All ER 450 (HL) (Viscount Kilmour LC); *Hyam v DPP* [1975] AC 55 at 79, [1974] 2 All ER 41 (HL) (Lord Hailsham).

12 This point was made by the Court of Appeal in *R v Moloney* The Times (London), 22 December 1983 (May LJ); see *R v Moloney* [1985] AC 905 at 919, [1985] 1 All ER 1025 (HL) (Lord Bridge). Compare also *Walker* (1989) 90 Cr App R 226 at 230, [1990] Crim LR 44.

sense if P does not die.[13] By contrast, if he does not intend P's death, then he would not think he has failed if P survives. So this is another way of testing whether D intended P's death.

An illustration of Duff's argument is provided by the case of *Hyam*.[14] D had poured petrol through the letterbox of V's house and set fire to the petrol, intending only to frighten V but realising her actions risked causing death. Duff remarks:[15]

> Mrs Hyam intended to set fire to Mrs Booth's house; her action would have failed had the house not caught fire . . . She intended thereby to frighten Mrs Booth: had the fire not frightened Mrs Booth, her action (though successful as one of "setting fire to the house") would have failed as one of "frightening Mrs Booth". But she did not intend to cause death or injury: though she foresaw death or injury as a likely effect of her action, her action would not have been a failure had no one been killed or injured; death or injury were foreseen side-effects, not intended effects, of her action.

By frightening Mrs Booth, the defendant would have succeeded in her purpose; her actions would not have been a failure if no one had died, since it was no part of her purpose to kill. Nor, we would say, was she trying to kill anyone. Thus the deaths were not intended.

3.1.2 A formal definition

The differences noted above between intended and unintended actions can also be set out in terms of means, ends, and side-effects. Things done as means or ends are intended; side-effects are not.[16] In *Hyam*, D set fire to the house as a means of frightening Mrs Booth. Hence, both setting fire to the house and frightening Mrs Booth were intended. But the ensuing fatalities were neither a means nor an end. They were side-effects of her actions, and as such unintended.

Ideas of means, ends, and purpose point to a more formal way of thinking about intention. The purposes or ends for which one acts are the reasons *why* one acts. They motivate and explain one's action. Intention embraces both these and the intermediate steps (the means) that one undertakes in order to achieve those ends. Formally, we can capture the central cases of intention as follows. D intends to do an action (or to bring about some consequence) if:

(i)   He *wants* to do that action (or to bring about that consequence), or

(ii) He *believes* it is possible for him to achieve something he wants by doing that action (or by bringing about that consequence),

and

---

13   Duff, *Intention, Agency and Criminal Liability: philosophy of action and the criminal law*, Oxford, Blackwell, 1990, 61-63.

14   [1975] AC 55, [1974] 2 All ER 41 (HL).

15   Duff, *Intention, Agency and Criminal Liability: philosophy of action and the criminal law*, Oxford, Blackwell, 1990, 61.

16   Williams, "Oblique Intention" (1987) 46 CLJ 417 at 421.

(iii) He behaves as he does *because*[17] of his desire in (i) or his belief in (ii).

The combination of (i) with (iii) covers actions which are done as ends:

(i)   He *wants* to do that action (or to bring about that consequence); and

(iii) He behaves as he does *because* of that desire.

Mrs Hyam wanted to frighten Mrs Booth, and she set fire to the house because she wanted to frighten her. Therefore she intended to frighten Mrs Booth. Her desire to frighten, which is the desire contemplated in (i) above, is often termed the defendant's *motive*. But it is important to recognise that a mere desire, or motive, is not enough by itself to establish intention:[18]

> It is a dangerous doctrine to lay down that the mere proof of a motive, even in the absence of any apparent motive in any other persons who could have committed the act, is held to be conclusive proof of guilt.

Often people want things which they never set out to achieve. The mere wish that another person were deceased is not an intention to kill. Distinguishing between desire and intention here is (iii), the requirement that the defendant act because of that motive. A motive is irrelevant to intention unless it is also *why* D did the actus reus.

On the other hand, desire is not an essential component of intention.[19] Often, we bring things about not because we want them, but because they are a *means* to something else (that we do want).[20] The lecturer who fails her student may do so regretfully, believing it to be her only option and wishing very much that there were something else she could do; yet she intends to fail the student all the same.[21] What she wants is to mark the exam fairly, and she fails the student in order to be fair. But she does not desire his failure, at least not for its own sake. This sort of case, where the actus reus is done as a means to an end, is captured by the combination of (ii) with (iii):

(ii)   He *believes* it is possible for him to achieve something he wants by doing that action (or by bringing about that consequence); and

(iii) He behaves as he does *because* of that belief.

In *Smith*,[22] D believed that by bribing the mayor he would be able to expose him. This was why he acted as he did. Therefore he intended to bribe the official, even though his ultimate aim was to expose him. Similarly, Mrs Hyam

---

17   Or, at least *in part because*. We consider the possibility of multiple intentions below, in § 3.1.6.

18   *Woods v Brown* (1907) 26 NZLR 1312 at 1315, 10 GLR 70 at 71. Cf Lord Bridge in *R v Moloney* [1985] AC 905 at 926, [1985] 1 All ER 1025 at 1037 (HL): "intention is something quite different from motive or desire."

19   Cf *Mohan* [1976] QB 1 at 11, [1975] 2 All ER 193 at 200 (CA) (James LJ): intention is "a decision to bring about, in so far as it lies within the accused's power, the commission of the offence . . . no matter whether the accused desired that consequence of his act or not".

20   See *Hyam v DPP* [1975] AC 55 at 74, [1974] 2 All ER 41 at 62 (Lord Hailsham): intention includes "the means as well as the end". See also Williams, *CLGP*, § 16.

21   Compare *Lang v Lang* [1955] AC 402 at 428, 429, [1954] 3 All ER 571 at 579, 580.

22   [1960] 2 QB 423, [1960] 1 All ER 256. See § 3.

believed that by setting fire to the house she would be able to frighten Mrs Booth. That was why she acted as she did. Therefore she intended to set fire to the house.

In practice, of course, looking at the defendant's desires and beliefs is an indispensable aid in helping us to ascertain her intentions. Even in (ii), the case of doing something as a means to an end, there must be a motive in the background. And although it does not matter in principle what that background motive is, often it will be important for evidential purposes. "To prove the intention, you may show the motive, and this is a link in the chain of evidence."[23]

3.1.3 Foresight of consequences is not enough

The key ingredient of any account of intention is (iii), that the defendant acts because of her desire or belief. Without it, there cannot be intention. If D foresees an outcome, and indeed welcomes it, but that outcome nevertheless plays no part in her decision to act, then she does *not* intend it. Mrs Hyam foresaw the possibility of killing Mrs Booth, but she did not set fire to the house *because* of her belief that doing so might bring about Mrs Booth's death. Hence, although she was reckless,[24] she did not intend to kill. Similarly, a Judge who awards compensatory damages against a defendant may realise that, in so doing, he might cause the bankruptcy of the defendant, but that has nothing to do with why he awards the damages. The bankruptcy is no more than a foreseen but unintended side-effect.

The law has not always been clear on this point. In *Hardy v Motor Insurers' Bureau*, for instance, it was said of the accused that "he must have foreseen, when he did the act, that it would in all probability injure the other person. Therefore he had the intent to injure the other person."[25] And in *R v Jakac*, the Supreme Court of Victoria was of similar mind: if the defendant "knew what the consequences were likely to be, and with that knowledge he deliberately did the act and if the consequences in fact did follow, he must be taken to intend them."[26] Notoriously, the House of Lords in *DPP v Smith* simply presumed (inter alia) that Jim Smith intended whatever he foresaw.[27] The House of Lords later divided on this question in *Hyam*. Although Lord Hailsham declared it "clear that 'intention' is clearly to be distinguished alike

---

23 *R v Heeson* (1878) 14 Cox 40 at 44 (Lush J).

24 See § 3.2.

25 [1964] 2 QB 745 at 764, [1964] 2 All ER 742 at 748 (Pearson LJ); see also at 758 (Lord Denning MR). See also Lord Devlin's definition of "purpose" in *Chandler v DPP* [1964] AC 763 at 805 to "designate those objects which he knows will probably be achieved by the act, whether he wants them or not."

26 [1961] VR 367 at 371. Cf Saunders, *Mozley & Whitley's Law Dictionary* (9th ed) 1977, 175: "a person who contemplates any result, as not unlikely to follow from a deliberate act of his own, may be said to intend that result, whether he desire it or not".

27 [1961] AC 290. Cf Viscount Kilmuir LC, at 326: "the test of what a reasonable man would contemplate as the probable result of his acts and therefore, would intend". See also *R v Ward* [1956] 1 QB 351, [1956] 1 All ER 565; Kenny, "Intention and Purpose in Law" in Summers (ed), *Essays in Legal Philosophy* Oxford, Blackwell, 1968, 146.

from 'desire' and from foresight of the probable consequences",[28] his Lordship's view does not reflect a consensus. Viscount Dilhorne, for instance, remarked that if someone does an act "knowing when he does it that it is highly probable that grievous bodily harm will result, I think that most people would say and be justified in saying that whatever other intentions he may have had as well, he at least intended grievous bodily harm".[29] Indeed, Lord Diplock felt able, following *Hyam*, to hold that the law was now "well-settled":

> [W]here intention to produce a particular result was a necessary element of an offence, no distinction was to be drawn in law between the state of mind of one who did an act because he desired it to produce that particular result and the state of mind of one who, when he did the act, was aware that it was likely to produce that result but was prepared to take the risk that it might do so . . .[30]

The distinction between intention and mere foresight seems, however, to have been accepted more recently in *R v Moloney*, where Lord Bridge expressed himself to be "firmly of opinion that foresight of consequences, as an element bearing on the issue of intention in murder, or indeed any other crime of specific intent, belongs, not to the substantive law, but to the law of evidence".[31] The same view was subsequently taken in *R v Hancock and Shankland*,[32] and it may safely be regarded as prevailing in New Zealand. *DPP v Smith* itself was effectively overruled by the Privy Council in *Frankland and Moore v R*.[33]

3.1.4 Morally certain consequences

Mere foresight of a consequence, then, does not establish an intention. But one question is still unresolved: what if the consequence is foreseen not merely as possible, but as *certain* to occur − does "intention" include such a case? In *R v*

---

28   [1975] AC 55 at 74, [1974] 2 All ER 41 at 52 (HL). See also *R v Belfon* [1976] 3 All ER 46, (1976) 63 Cr App R 59 (CA).

29   [1975] AC 55 at 82, [1974] 2 All ER 41 at 59 (HL).

30   *R v Lemon; R v Gay News Ltd* [1979] AC 617 at 638, [1979] 1 All ER 898 at 905. See also a similar dictum in *Hyam* [1975] AC 55 at 86, [1974] 2 All ER 41 (HL).

31   [1985] AC 905 at 928, [1985] 1 All ER 1025 at 1038 (HL). Contrast this with the trial judge's direction (ibid at 917), based as it was upon *Hyam*: "a man intends the consequence of his voluntary act (a) when he desires it to happen, whether or not he foresees that it probably will happen, and (b) when he foresees that it will happen, whether he desires it or not".

32   [1986] 1 AC 455 at 474, [1986] 1 All ER 641 at 651 (HL) (Lord Scarman): "the greater the probability of a consequence the more likely it is that the consequence was foreseen and . . . if that consequence was foreseen the greater the probability is that that consequence was also intended . . . [T]he probability, however high, of a consequence is only a factor". See also *R v Nedrick* [1986] 3 All ER 1, [1986] 1 WLR 1025 (CA).

33   [1987] AC 576, [1987] 2 WLR 1251 (PC). In the *Law Quarterly Review*, Lord Goff concludes that "after the journey through *Smith, Hyam, Moloney* and *Hancock*, the law is really back where it was . . . Foresight of consequences is not the same as intent, but is material from which the jury may, having regard to all the circumstances of the case, infer that the defendant actually had the relevant intent." Goff "The Mental Element in the Crime of Murder" [1988] 104 LQR 30 at 41.

Richards [aiding and abetting],[34] Fisher J suggested that the answer might be yes, when he held that intention includes not only those consequences which are sought, but also those which are foreseen with sufficient certainty. In this context, it is worth noting the definition of intention proposed in the *Report of the Crimes Consultative Committee*.[35] A person intends the result of an act when he does the act:[36]

> (a) Meaning to bring about that result; or
>
> (b) Being aware or believing that that result *will* happen.

It is the second limb that reflects the suggestion in *Richards*. The use of the emphatic "will" reflects the need for something more than just foresight that the result is likely. The latter would be a case of recklessness, something defined in the same Report as requiring that the person do an act "being aware that there is a risk that the result will happen."[37]

The English Courts, which have considered the point more fully than their New Zealand counterparts, remain equivocal. Although Lord Hailsham did not think that "foresight as such of a high degree of probability is at all the same thing as intention",[38] he nevertheless stated explicitly that intention includes not only those things done as ends or means but also "the inseparable consequences of the end as well as the means". The extension is supported by reference to an example developed by Glanville Williams:[39]

> suppose that a villain of the deepest dye blows up an aircraft in flight with a time-bomb, merely for the purpose of collecting on insurance. It is not his aim to cause the people on board to perish, but he knows that success in his scheme will inevitably involve their deaths as a side-effect.

According to Lord Hailsham, "if any passengers are killed he is guilty of murder, as their death will be a moral certainty if he carries out his intention."[40] In *Moloney*, Lord Bridge, too, accepted that there may be cases where things which are seemingly not sought as ends or means should be analysed as cases of intention:

> A man who, at London Airport, boards a plane which he knows to be bound for Manchester, clearly intends to travel to Manchester, even though Manchester is the last place he wants to be and his motive for boarding the plane is simply to escape pursuit ... By boarding the Manchester plane, the man conclusively demonstrates his intention to go there, because it is a moral certainty that that is where he will arrive.[41]

---

34 (1992) 9 CRNZ 355 at 361.

35 *Crimes Bill 1989*, Crimes Consultative Committee, Department of Justice, 1991.

36 Sections 21, 92 (emphasis added).

37 Ibid ss 22, 93.

38 *Hyam v DPP* [1975] AC 55 at 77, [1974] 2 All ER 41 at 54 (HL).

39 "Oblique Intention" (1987) 46 CLJ 417 at 423; cf his earlier *The Mental Element in Crime*, 1965, 34, 35.

40 *Hyam v DPP* [1975] AC 55 at 74, [1974] 2 All ER 41 at 52 (HL).

41 *R v Moloney* [1985] AC 905 at 926, [1985] 1 All ER 1025 at 1039 (HL).

In such a case the law would say that the "morally certain" consequence is intended. But the basis on which it does so is unclear.[42] There are two alternatives: either morally certain consequences are *by definition* intended, or the link is only evidential. In the latter case, foresight of a moral certainty is no more than a ground for inferring that the consequence was intended, and the inference may be rebutted by other evidence.

There is much to be said for thinking the link is merely evidential. The certainty of a consequence is surely not enough by itself to make that consequence intended. If D drinks a bottle of scotch one evening, he may be sure that he will get a hangover in the morning, but he does not drink the scotch with the intention of having a hangover.[43] Support for this position is found in decisions subsequent to *Moloney*, where the Courts have tended to read Lord Bridge's remarks as pertaining to evidential matters. In *R v Nedrick*, Lord Lane CJ held that:

> if the jury are satisfied that at the material time the defendant recognised that death or serious harm would be virtually certain (barring some unforeseen intervention) to result from his voluntary act, then that is a fact from which they may find it easy to infer that he intended to kill or do serious bodily harm . . .[44]

Writing extra-judicially in 1987, Lord Goff condemned the extension of intention to embrace moral certainty as "illegitimate".[45] If that is right, then the explanation of cases like the flight to Manchester has nothing to do with moral certainty. Rather, it is that the fugitive intentionally travels to Manchester as a *means* of leaving London.

But this answer does not help to deal with the insurance-bombing case proposed by Glanville Williams, where the deaths of the airline passengers are clearly not a means to anything. Despite this, it does seem that the deaths are so intimately bound up with the villain's intended actions as to be inseparable, and it would be wrong to call them mere side-effects. We suggest that the rule once proposed by Hart applies to such cases: a foreseen outcome is to be regarded as intended when it:

> is so immediately and invariably connected with the action done that the suggestion that the action might not have that outcome would by ordinary standards be regarded as absurd, or such as a mentally abnormal person would seriously entertain.[46]

---

42 Compare Duff, *Intention, Agency and Criminal Liability*, 1990, 21, 22; also Duff, "The Obscure Intentions of the House of Lords" [1986] Crim LR 771.

43 Duff, *Intention, Agency and Criminal Liability*, Oxford, Blackwell, 1990, 89-90.

44 [1986] 3 All ER 1 at 3, 4, [1986] 1 WLR 1025 at 1028. See also the judgment by Lord Scarman in *Hancock*, above at n 32.

45 "The Mental Element in the Crime of Murder" [1988] 104 LQR 30 at 59.

46 "Intention and Punishment" in *Punishment and Responsibility*, 1968, 113, 120. Hart continues, "the connexion between action and outcome seems therefore to be not merely contingent but rather to be conceptual." See further Simester, "Moral Certainty, and the Boundaries of Intention" (1996) 16 OJLS 445. This is a tighter connection (as with respect it ought to be) than that required by the Canadian Supreme Court in *R v Chartrand* (1994) 116 DLR (4th) 207 at 225-230.

These outcomes are intended by definition, and not just as a matter of evidence. They represent an extension to the core definition of intention stated in § 3.1.2.

3.1.5 Intention and circumstances

The account of intention we have given so far needs qualification when applied to any circumstances which form a part of the actus reus. This is best seen by means of an example. Rape can only be committed by D's having sexual intercourse with V without her consent. The circumstance, that V does not consent, is part of the actus reus of the offence. There are two different ways in which D's mental state regarding V's non-consent can satisfy the demands of intention. The plain case occurs where D rapes V by intentionally having sexual intercourse with her, *hoping* that she does not consent. In this case D intends "sexual intercourse without consent" in its full sense, because it is part of his purpose not merely to have sexual intercourse with V, but to have it without her consent. Duff's test of failure shows this clearly:[47] D would regard himself as having "failed" if V did in fact consent to having sexual intercourse with him.

Although the clearest sort of case, this is the less common variety of intention where circumstances are at issue, and probably applies only to a pathological or sadistic offender. More often, rape is committed intentionally when D neither intends nor hopes that V is not consenting. (He means to have sexual intercourse, and does not care whether or not his victim consents.) In this situation he nevertheless intends to have "sexual intercourse without consent", because he intends to have sexual intercourse *believing* that V does not consent.

So there are two ways of showing that an actus reus is intended when it involves circumstances. The first is by showing that the behaviour and consequences are intended, and that D hopes the circumstances are present. The second is by showing that the behaviour and consequences are intended, and that D believes the circumstances are present. What does "believing" mean in this context? In our view "believing" has the same meaning as "knowing", with one exception. We consider the meaning of knowledge below,[48] but in essence what is required is that the defendant hold a positive belief, amounting to an acceptance, that the circumstance exists.

The one difference between knowledge and belief is that a belief need not be correct. The defendant may believe something wrongly, but she cannot "know" something that is false. Usually the difference will not matter very much. For example, if D wrongly believes that V does not consent to sexual intercourse, then regardless of his mens rea he cannot commit rape, because the actus reus is missing. But sometimes it will still be important to establish whether D has mens rea, since even without the actus reus he might

---

47 See § 3.1.1.

48 See § 3.4. We do not endorse Orchard's remark in "Criminal Intention" [1986] NZLJ 208 at 212, that "it may be that it should suffice [for intention] if D adverted to the *possibility* of the existence of the circumstances"; or the discussion in *Adams* § CA20.21.

nevertheless be guilty of an attempt. In this example, his false belief that V does not consent will be sufficient to help constitute the intention required for attempted rape.[49]

3.1.6 Multiple intentions

Very often, a person has more than one reason for acting as he does. By cooking dinner, John might intend not only to assuage his hunger, but also to use up the contents of the fridge, as well as surprise and please his flatmates. All three results are intended. The mere fact that a defendant can point to some other result that he was also trying to achieve does not mean that he cannot have intended the actus reus. It is no answer for a newspaper that deliberately publishes sub judice material to say that it was really trying to increase its circulation. Ignoring extraneous intentions, the criminal law focuses only on the actus reus and asks, whatever else he intended, did D intend that *actus*?

3.1.7 "With intent" or "ulterior intent" crimes

Sometimes the intentional doing of an actus reus is not itself an offence, and dons criminal garb only when it is done for some further purpose. For example, if D carries a crowbar in his bag he does nothing wrong, but if he carries the crowbar with intent to use it in a burglary, then he is guilty of an offence.[50] Crimes of this sort require what is often called an "ulterior intent". The main feature of such crimes is that they specify, as part of the mens rea, the intent to do something that is not part of the actus reus. In the example above, the actus reus is simple possession of the crowbar — it does not matter whether the crowbar is actually used in a burglary.[51] This is why such crimes are said to involve "ulterior" intent: because the eventual intention is ulterior to the actus reus.

In other respects, however, these crimes are no different from crimes of ordinary intent. In particular, the ulterior intent must exist at the time when the actus reus is performed. This point is illustrated in *Police v Bannin*,[52] where the defendant appealed against convictions inter alia for three offences of entering a house with intent to commit a crime therein, contrary to s 242. Although he was found to have intended to enter the house, the convictions were quashed on the ground that the prosecution had failed to prove that he had already formed an intent to commit an offence by the time at which he entered the house.

Where a crime specifies an ulterior intent as part of the mens rea, it seems clear that mere foresight of the further consequence will not do. The crime can only be committed if the defendant intends that consequence. This seems to be

---

49   The claim here is merely that knowledge or belief satisfies the demands of intention. It is a further question (taken up in chapter 6) whether, with respect to circumstances, intention is *required* to establish the mens rea of attempt offences.

50   Section 244(1)(b).

51   Cf *R v Rodley* (1913) 9 Cr App R 69 at 76.

52   [1991] 2 NZLR 237, also reported as *B v Police* (1990) 7 CRNZ 55.

the explanation of the controversial case of *R v Steane*.[53] Steane had been compelled, through concern for the safety of his family, to make broadcasts on behalf of the Germans during the Second World War. He was prosecuted under English wartime regulations for doing an act likely to assist the enemy (the actus reus), "with intent" to assist the enemy. The Court of Criminal Appeal quashed his conviction for lack of mens rea, holding that although what he did was likely to assist the enemy, the prosecution had failed to prove that this was also his intent (ie a part of his purposes in acting). Steane intended to make the broadcasts, but his ulterior intent in so doing had been to protect his family. It would be otherwise, of course, if the foreseen further consequence were "morally certain" to accompany his intended actions — in which case they too would be intended.[54]

3.1.8 Conditional intent

Sometimes a person is willing to commit a crime but her actions will not necessarily result in one. For example, if a thief makes off with a handbag, meaning to keep the contents, she steals those contents only if there are any. In this situation, her intention to take the contents is conditional upon there being anything to steal. Such cases are not uncommon in the criminal law, especially in the context of offences involving an ulterior intent. The general rule is that an intention to do or bring about something only if particular conditions hold remains, in law, an intention. Thus a burglar who enters a flat with intent to steal a television set only if there is one still, in law, enters with intent to steal.[55] Similarly, in *Wicks v Police*[56] it was held that D intended permanently to deprive V of his property even though D meant to keep the item only if V refused to meet his demands.

3.2 FORESIGHT AND RECKLESSNESS

Often people cause injury without intending to — that is, without acting in order to do so. The doctor who injects her patient with a painkiller may unintentionally kill him if the patient is allergic to the drug she injects him with. But the fact that an injury is unintended does not mean that the person who causes it is blameless; the doctor may have been aware of the risk of injury, a risk that she nevertheless chose to run. In such cases we would say she *foresaw*, but did not intend, the harm.

Not every case of foresight amounts to recklessness. In order for a defendant to be reckless, the risk that she chooses to run must also be an

---

53 [1947] KB 997, [1947] 1 All ER 813 (CA). See, for example, Williams, "Oblique Intention" (1987) 46 CLJ 417 at 428.

54 See § 3.1.4; also *Chartrand* (1994) 116 DLR (4th) 207 at 225-230.

55 *A-G's References (Nos 1 and 2 of 1979)* [1980] QB 180, [1979] 3 All ER 143, distinguishing and confining *Husseyn* (1977) 67 Cr App R 131n, [1978] Crim LR 219 (CA); cf *Police v Wylie* [1976] 2 NZLR 167 at 169.

56 (1984) 1 CRNZ 328. (D came into possession of a barrister's file and refused to return it until the barrister settled an unrelated claim of D's.) See also *R v Hare* (1910) 29 NZLR 641 (CA).

unreasonable one. Although in practice this issue does not often arise, the qualification is important. It means that anaesthetists, who knowingly undertake a slight risk that the patient will have a fatal allergic reaction when anaesthetised before an operation, are not automatically guilty of reckless homicide when the patient dies. The question of what is reasonable is an objective question, and it is not an issue of whether the defendant thought the risk was reasonable; rather, it is a question of whether an ordinary and prudent person would have been prepared to take that risk. To this extent defendants cannot be permitted to displace the law and judge what is right for themselves.[57]

There are a number of factors for the law to consider when deciding whether a particular risk was reasonable or not. These include the probability of the risk occurring, and the nature and gravity of the harm being risked. Driving at 50 km/h on a busy road may be reasonable but driving at 80 km/h may not be, because of the increased risk of accidents and the more serious injuries that are likely to ensue should there be an accident. Against these considerations should be balanced the value and likelihood of achieving what the defendant was trying to do while running that risk. A high-risk surgical operation may be justifiable when it is done as a last resort or in an emergency to save the patient's life. But the risks involved may not be acceptable if less dangerous alternatives are available, or if the purpose of the operation is trivial.[58]

One point that should be made here is that the incorporation of a standard of reasonableness means that there is no need for a separate "threshold" criterion of probability or likelihood.[59] Obviously, if a risk is thought to be minimal or only an "outside chance", running that risk is likely to be unobjectionable.[60] But even a very slight risk will be enough for recklessness if the harm being risked is serious enough and the act concerned has no social

---

57 Thus we do not entirely concur with the view expressed by Tipping J in *Taylor v Police* (1990) 6 CRNZ 470 at 471, that recklessness "is a purely subjective concept". Cf Eichelbaum J in *Dept of Health v Multichem Laboratories* [1987] 1 NZLR 334 at 339 (a strict liability case): "The defendant's own perception of reasonableness cannot govern the situation."

58 Or if reasonable steps were not taken to reduce those risks: cf *Summers v SPCA* [1991] 2 NZLR 469 at 474, 475, (1990) 6 CRNZ 201 at 207, 208.

59 The view expressed here contrasts with that in *Garrow and Turkington* § V.6, and with the words used by the Court of Appeal in *R v Tihi* [1989] 2 NZLR 29 at 32; (1989) 4 CRNZ 289 at 292 (CA), where it was said that "it must be shown that the accused either meant to cause the specified harm, or foresaw that his actions were likely to expose others to the risk of suffering it. This would preserve the subjective test of liability, giving 'likely' the meaning favoured by this Court in *R v Gush* [1980] 2 NZLR 92." In *Gush*, the favoured meaning was "such as could well happen"; but the question there arose in the context of a statutory wording rather than a general test of recklessness. There seems no reason in principle why such a threshold should apply to recklessness, and *Adams* accepts that "in some cases it may suffice if there was a realisation that there was some possibility of it eventuating, at least if this was not dismissed as 'altogether negligible'." (§ CA20.32.)

60 Cf *Hilder v Police* (1989) 4 CRNZ 232 at 236.

value. A game of "Russian roulette" would be reckless even if the chances of being killed were thought to be only 1 in 200. In such cases, it may be necessary to abandon an activity altogether if the defendant cannot eliminate the risk entirely. One example of this is provided by *Chief Constable of Avon and Somerset Constabulary v Shimmen*.[61] D, a martial arts expert, was demonstrating his skill to friends by kicking close to a window without breaking it. He smashed the window. Even though he thought he had "eliminated as much risk as possible", he was nevertheless guilty of reckless criminal damage since he had chosen to run the slight and unjustifiable risk which remained. Conversely, there may be a very substantial risk of injury or death in certain "last resort" surgical operations, but those operations are not necessarily unreasonable when undertaken.

Formally, D does an action recklessly if, in doing it:

(i)   He believes it is possible for him to do that action by behaving as he does; and

(ii) It is unreasonable for D to run the risk that he foresees.

The main difference between intention and recklessness is that while in both cases the defendant must foresee the possibility of doing the actus reus, in recklessness he need not seek or be motivated to bring it about. In recent times, however, there has been a suggestion that element (i), actual foresight of the risk, should not always be required. We consider this possibility in the next section.

3.2.1 The need for foresight

The leading modern case to require that there be actual foresight before a defendant can be reckless is *R v Cunningham*.[62] In that case, D interfered with the coin-operated gas meter in an unoccupied house in order to steal money from it. The gas escaped, seeped into an adjoining house, and endangered the life of a person living there. Upon his appeal against conviction for maliciously administering a noxious thing so as to endanger life,[63] the Court of Criminal Appeal held that "malice" required either intention or recklessness, and that the latter meant that "the accused has foreseen that the particular kind of harm might be done, and yet has gone on to take the risk of it".[64]

On this view, stupidity in failing to think about a risk is not a ground of criminal culpability. An illustration of this principle is found in *R v Stephenson*,[65] where D lit a fire in order to warm himself while sheltering in a haystack, and was charged with reckless arson after the haystack itself caught

---

61   (1987) 84 Cr App R 7, [1986] Crim LR 800.

62   [1957] 2 QB 396, [1957] 2 All ER 412 (CA). Cf *R v Briggs* [1977] 1 All ER 475 at 477; *R v Stephenson* [1979] QB 695; *R v Mullins* [1980] Crim LR 37; *Flack v Hunt* (1979) 70 Cr App R 51, [1980] Crim LR 44.

63   Contrary to s 23 Offences Against the Person Act 1861 (UK).

64   [1957] 2 QB 396 at 399, [1957] 2 All ER 412 at 414 (CA). Quoting with approval from Turner, *Kenny's Outlines of Criminal Law* (16th ed), Cambridge, Cambridge University Press, 1952, 186.

65   [1979] QB 695.

fire and was destroyed. Stephenson's conviction was quashed on appeal because, as he suffered from schizophrenia, he might not have been aware of the risk to the haystack.

On the other hand, the law as stated in *Cunningham* does not entitle a defendant to deliberately close her mind to an obvious risk when she is aware of the risk but does not think about it because she does not care. In *R v Parker*[66] D slammed down a public telephone receiver with such force that he broke it. The Court rejected his defence that he had been too enraged to think about the risk. The inherent association of his violent action with its consequence meant that he could be taken to have appreciated the risk without the awareness of that risk being at the forefront of his mind, and without the need for sober or careful deliberation in advance.

The inference made in *Parker* is not always appropriate.[67] In *Smith v Police*,[68] D had been served with a High Court summons by V. He attempted to push the documents back through the partly-opened window of V's car. As a consequence of D's actions, and perhaps of the movement of V's car, the car window shattered. On appeal, Barker J ruled that D was not reckless, as he had not necessarily given thought to the risks involved.

Unlike *Parker*, the risk created by the defendant in *Smith* was not so inherent in his actions that it was inevitable that D had appreciated it. *Smith* reinforces the point that there must be awareness of the risk at some level of the defendant's consciousness before he can be found reckless.

That was the traditional position after *Cunningham*. In 1981 it was undone by the House of Lords in *Metropolitan Police Commr v Caldwell*[69] and the companion case of *R v Lawrence*.[70] In *Caldwell*, the defendant set fire to a hotel while intoxicated. He was charged, inter alia, with an offence against s 1(1) Criminal Damage Act 1971 (UK), which makes it an offence to damage another's property "being reckless as to whether any such property would be destroyed or damaged". The House of Lords held that a defendant is reckless in law if:

(1) he does an act which in fact creates an obvious risk that property would be destroyed or damaged[71] and (2) when he does the act he either has not given any

---

66   [1977] 2 All ER 37.

67   Indeed, it is arguable that the inference was inappropriate in *Parker* itself. As such the decision by the Court of Appeal may be a precursor of *Caldwell*, discussed below in this section. If so, however, the approach in *Parker* is more narrow than that taken by the House of Lords in *Caldwell*; it would justify inferring recklessness only where D "deliberately closes his mind" to obvious consequences because he is "in a self-induced state of temper", or for a similarly discreditable reason. See [1977] 2 All ER 37 at 40.

68   (1988) 3 CRNZ 262. Cf *Police v L (a young person)* [1990] DCR 172.

69   [1982] AC 341, also reported as *R v Caldwell* [1981] 1 All ER 961 (HL).

70   [1982] AC 510, [1981] 1 All ER 974 (HL). Cf also *Miller* [1983] 1 All ER 978 (HL).

71   Or, in *R v Lawrence* [1982] AC 510 at 527, [1981] 1 All ER 974 at 982 (HL), an "obvious and serious" risk. The requirement of obviousness does not apply where the risk is in fact foreseen: *R v Reid* [1992] 3 All ER 673 at 691, [1992] 1 WLR 793 at 814.

thought to the possibility of there being any such risk or has recognised that there was some risk involved and has nonetheless gone on to do it.[72]

The essence of the decision was to create a second category of recklessness in criminal law. In addition to the cases of actual foresight covered by *Cunningham*, the defendant would also be treated as reckless if he failed to think of a risk when that risk was a glaring one. In effect, recklessness embraces both advertent wrongdoing and gross negligence.[73]

The extension of recklessness proposed in *Caldwell* has been controversial. Its justification, according to Lord Diplock, is that inadvertence to an obvious risk is frequently just as blameworthy as choosing to run a risk which is foreseen, and so should be treated the same way. There is some force in this: it is an unattractive option to acquit a defendant who did not consider the risks because he was too drunk, too temperamental, or too uncaring a person to bother thinking about them.[74] A question might be asked, however, whether that moral equation will always (or almost always) hold — which ought to be the case before a Court makes such a comprehensive extension. In particular, it seems harsh to treat as reckless those whose inadvertence was due to preoccupation or distraction,[75] and who might be utterly horrified when they recognise the consequences of their actions. It is even more harsh to equate with advertent recklessness the actions of those who were *incapable* of perceiving the risk. This is what the English courts apparently did in *Elliott v C (a minor)*.[76] C, a 14-year-old girl of low intelligence, had wandered away from home and spent the night outdoors without sleep before ending up in a garden shed. There she found some white spirit, which she poured on to the floor and ignited by dropping lighted matches on it. The shed was destroyed in the ensuing conflagration. Even though it was found that "in the circumstances this risk [that the shed would be destroyed] would not have been obvious to her or appreciated by her if she had given thought to the matter",[77] she was nevertheless convicted of criminal damage. The Divisional Court held, on the authority of *Caldwell*, that the test whether the risk was obvious is objective: would it be obvious to a reasonable person, rather than, should it have been obvious to the particular defendant.[78]

Although the decision in *Caldwell* exercised a considerable influence over English criminal law during the 1980s, it has never really taken hold in New Zealand.[79] This is despite the fact that at first, in *R v Howe*,[80] the *Caldwell*

---

72 [1982] AC 341 at 354, also reported as *R v Caldwell* [1981] 1 All ER 961 at 967 (HL).

73 See § 3.5.4.

74 Cf Lord Goff in *R v Reid* [1992] 3 All ER 673 at 687ff, [1992] 1 WLR 793 at 809ff.

75 Cf Griew, "Reckless Damage and Reckless Driving: Living with *Caldwell* and *Lawrence*" [1981] Crim LR 743 at 747; in tort, *West Ky Tel Co v Pharis* (1904) 25 Ky LR 1838.

76 [1983] 2 All ER 1005, [1983] 1 WLR 939.

77 [1983] 2 All ER 1005 at 1008, [1983] 1 WLR 939 at 945.

78 See too *R, Stephen* (1984) 79 Cr App R 334.

79 Nor elsewhere: *R v Smith* (1982) 7 A Crim R 437; *Sansregret v R* (1985) 17 DLR (4th) 577, [1985] 1 SCR 570.

80 [1982] 1 NZLR 618 (CA).

definition of recklessness was endorsed by the Court of Appeal in the context of the offence of riotous damage, contrary to s 90. Section 90 (as it then read) provided that it was an offence for a member of a riot to damage any of certain specified types of property. D, a rioter, deliberately damaged a vehicle which was, in fact, a police car. The Court held that D would be guilty of an offence against s 90 if he knew or was reckless — in the *Caldwell* sense — that the vehicle was a police car or one of the other types of property specified in the section. The need for recklessness was not explicitly stated in the statute, and the Court noted that one might well expect an extension into *Caldwell*-style inadvertence to be especially appropriate to such an offence, given that people do not normally stop to ponder the particular nature of the property they are damaging in the midst of a riot.

The subsequent decision by the Court of Appeal in *R v Harney* makes it quite clear that the view taken in *Howe* is not of general application:

> Subject to the requirements of particular contexts, however, we incline to the view that "recklessly" has usually been understood in New Zealand to have the meaning given in pre-*Caldwell* textbooks . . . That is to say, foresight of dangerous consequences that could well happen, together with an intention to continue the course of conduct regardless of the risk.[81]

In our view, the definition of recklessness adopted in *Caldwell* has no place in New Zealand law. Even the "particular context" where it first intruded exists no longer: s 90 was amended in 1987 to include damage to "any property", rendering *Howe* "obsolete".[82] Although possible, it must be regarded as unlikely that the *Caldwell* definition will be extended to other offences.[83] An instructive illustration of the present New Zealand approach is to be found in *R v Tihi*, a case similar to *Howe* in that the statute omitted to specify a mens rea element with respect to the causing of injury when done with intent to commit a crime, contrary to s 191(2):[84]

> Strict liability would run counter to the well-established presumption in favour of mens rea in all criminal offences . . . Accordingly, before he can be guilty, it must be shown that the accused either meant to cause the specified harm, or foresaw that his actions were likely to expose others to the risk of suffering it. This would preserve the subjective test of liability . . .

The tenor of this passage is clear: unless the statute expressly precludes it, the fault element for all criminal offences is a subjective one.

It may be worth reinforcing this view with the point that in England the importance of *Caldwell* is now diminishing. Even the decision of the House of Lords in *Lawrence*,[85] that the offence of reckless driving could be committed without the defendant's having adverted to the risk his driving posed, is no longer relevant, since that offence was abolished in 1991. Nor does *Caldwell*

---

81   [1987] 2 NZLR 576 at 579 (CA).

82   *R v Harney* [1987] 2 NZLR 576 at 579 (CA).

83   For a survey of cases where the courts have refrained from doing so, see *Adams* § CA20.29.

84   [1989] 2 NZLR 29 at 32, (1990) 4 CRNZ 289 at 292 (CA).

85   [1982] AC 510.

apply any longer to the English law of manslaughter,[86] assault,[87] or rape.[88] In effect, its application has been restricted to the offence in the case itself (criminal damage), and to a few other statutory offences.[89] Advertent recklessness is, once more, the dominant test.

3.2.2 Recklessness as an actus reus term

The plausibility of decisions such as *Lawrence* rests upon a distinction that we drew in chapter 2.[90] In *Lawrence*, the actus reus of the offence is concerned only with D's *behaviour* (ie with his reckless driving). By contrast, in many other offences D's behaviour alone is not sufficient to establish the actus reus. There must be an additional element, for example that the victim is not consenting, or that she dies, or that the damaged vehicle is a police car. Where an offence involves circumstances and consequences, it is natural for a lawyer to think of recklessness as a mens rea term, requiring advertence to the specific circumstance or consequence named in that offence. For example, to commit a reckless homicide one has to foresee the possibility of death ensuing. But matters are different when the actus reus is concerned with the behaviour of the defendant. In an offence of reckless driving the Court does not ask, "was the defendant aware of the possibility that she might be driving a car?" Rather, what counts is whether the *manner* of her behaviour is sufficiently dangerous, not what she thought about that behaviour. "Reckless", in this context, qualifies the nature of the behaviour that is needed for the offence. Hence, it is an actus reus term. One might, for example, drive in a reckless manner (the *actus*) deliberately (the *mens*).[91]

3.2.3 Recklessness and circumstances

Just as with consequences, recklessness as to circumstances requires that the defendant acts believing that there is a possibility, or risk, that the circumstance might exist. This is sometimes called "reckless knowledge", but the term is a misleading one, since "knowledge" as such is not needed, and it will be enough if the defendant merely recognises that the circumstance *may* exist.

The definition just stated is derived from general principles. Recklessness requires that the defendant be aware of the possibility that the actus reus, as a whole, may occur. Hence it requires the defendant to be aware that each element of that actus reus may be present, including circumstances. A useful illustration of this can be found in s 135, which creates the offence of indecent assault. One element of that offence is the victim's lack of consent. The mens

---

86 *R v Adomako* [1995] 1 AC 171, [1994] 3 All ER 79, reversing *R v Seymour* [1983] 2 AC 493, [1983] 2 All ER 1058 (HL).

87 *R v Spratt* [1991] 2 All ER 210, (1990) 91 Cr App R 362.

88 *R v Satnam; R v Kewal* (1984) 78 Cr App R 149, [1985] Crim LR 236 (CA).

89 For example, *Large v Mainprize* [1989] Crim LR 213. According to Ashworth, "The *Caldwell* definition is now of little practical significance": *Principles*, 183.

90 See §§ 2, 2.1.

91 Winslade, "Brady on Recklessness" (1972) 33 Analysis 31.

rea for this element appears to be recklessness.[92] Thus the defendant cannot be guilty if he believes that his victim consents, and may only be convicted if he goes ahead recognising that she may not be consenting.

The difference between recklessness and intention can be shown by the following example. If D has sexual intercourse with V recognising (but not caring) that she may not be consenting, then if V does not consent D commits a reckless rape. On the other hand, if D has sexual intercourse *believing* positively that V does not consent, he rapes her intentionally. (In either case D will be guilty of an offence against s 128.[93])

The above states the law in principle. Sometimes, however, this definition leads to difficulties where the defendant acts without giving thought to attendant circumstances. This might occur, for example, where D indecently touches another person but claims it did not occur to him that she might not consent. What if D did not think about the possibility because he did not care, and would have gone ahead anyway? Should he be acquitted? In order to deal with such situations, recent cases have suggested two alternative ways of finding recklessness by the defendant.

The first possible extension is that a defendant may be held reckless about a circumstance, such as non-consent, if he was indifferent to, or could not care less about, whether the victim was consenting. The genesis of this formulation seems to be the "indifference to an obvious risk" test that has informed the English law since *Caldwell*. It is endorsed in a number of English decisions,[94] and has received the imprimatur of the New Zealand Court of Appeal at least twice.[95] Nevertheless it must be doubted whether this extension is valid.[96] *Caldwell*, as we have noted, is not good law in New Zealand. And in the two cases where indifference was contemplated by the Court of Appeal, the remarks made were clearly *obiter* and not demanded by the facts of those cases. Mens rea is not normally concerned with the *attitudes* of defendants; it is

---

92　*R v Nazif* [1987] 2 NZLR 122 at 128 (CA); *Police v Bannin* [1991] 2 NZLR 237 at 245, also reported as *B v Police* (1991) 7 CRNZ 55 at 62. Contrast the application of force itself in an assault, which must be intentional: s 2; *R v Young* 9/7/92, CA86/92. The view taken in *Nazif* may be questionable, since, by contrast with English authorities cited in the case, assault in New Zealand requires intention rather than recklessness on the part of the defendant. The justification for the Court of Appeal's interpretation seems to be that consent is a common law defence, rather than part of the actus reus of assault (cf *Police v Bannin* [1991] 2 NZLR 237 at 245, also reported as *B v Police* (1991) 7 CRNZ 55 at 62). This is inconsistent with the decision by the House of Lords in *DPP v Morgan* [1976] AC 182, [1975] 2 WLR 913. See Simester, "Mistakes in Defence" [1992] 12 OJLS 295.

93　Whether D's recklessness would be sufficient for him to be convicted of an attempt (if V in fact does consent) is discussed in chapter 6.

94　For example *R v Kimber* [1983] 3 All ER 316 at 320, [1983] 1 WLR 1118 at 1123: D's "attitude to [V] was one of indifference to her feelings and wishes. This state of mind is aptly described in the colloquial expression, 'couldn't care less'. In law this is recklessness." Cf *R v Pigg* [1982] 2 All ER 591, (1982) 74 Cr App R 352 (CA); *Millard and Vernon* [1987] Crim LR 393 (CA); *R v Khan* [1990] 2 All ER 783, [1990] 1 WLR 813 (CA).

95　*Waaka v Police* [1987] 1 NZLR 754 at 759, (1987) 2 CRNZ 370 at 375 (CA); *Millar v MOT* [1986] 1 NZLR 660 at 678, (1986) 2 CRNZ 216 at 236 (CA) (Casey J).

96　Cf *Adams* § CA20.38.

concerned with what they intended, knew, and did not know. This is why a worthy attitude, or a good motive, is no defence under the criminal law.[97] It is also why defendants are not to be convicted on the basis of an unworthy attitude or bad motive, eg for indifference.

A second objection to this formulation is that it may well add nothing to the requirement of advertence, or foresight of risk. As Smith and Hogan put it, "it is difficult to understand how a man can be indifferent to something the possibility of which he has not envisaged".[98] If D foresaw the possibility, then he can be convicted anyway; if he did not, then he should not be convicted on the basis of a hypothetical inquiry regarding what his attitude would have been if he had seen the risk.

The second alternative to traditional recklessness is perhaps more plausible. In *R v Nazif* D was charged with indecent assault. He claimed, inter alia, that he believed V consented to his actions. The Court of Appeal accepted that such a belief would be a defence:

> it would be contrary to principle that a person who believes the victim of an assault consented to it should be found guilty of that assault. Where there is evidence of such belief it will be for the Crown to negative it. The reasonableness or otherwise of the grounds of such belief will be material to *the question of whether the accused in fact held it.*[99]

[Emphasis added]

Clearly the Court regarded that question, whether D actually believed that V consented, as legally crucial. The implication of this passage is that a positive belief is required to found D's defence. Thus, for example, where recklessness about non-consent is required to establish mens rea, it suffices *either* if D recognised V might not be consenting, *or* if D did *not* believe that she was consenting. Such a test was accepted in the English case of *R v Satnam and Kewal Singh.*[100] Its effect is that the prosecution need prove only that D lacked a genuine belief that V consented, without having to prove, in addition, that he believed there was a risk that she did not consent. This formulation would not convict defendants who wrongly assume that D consents, but would catch those who proceed to harm V without being mistaken about V's agreement.

Before moving on, note should be taken of *Waaka v Police.*[101] The case is important but, it is submitted, should be approached with caution. D was charged under s 10 Summary Offences Act 1981 with assault of a constable

---

97 Cf *R v Smith* [1960] 2 QB 423, [1960] 1 All ER 256 (CA); see §§ 3, 3.1.2. For the rule that a positive attitude, of hoping the actus reus would not happen, supplies no defence, see *R v Crabbe* (1985) 156 CLR 464 at 470, (1985) 16 A Crim R 19 at 33.

98 *Smith and Hogan*, 472. Cf *Taylor* (1984) 80 Cr App R 327 (CA); *R v Haughian* (1985) 80 Cr App R 334 (CA). See, however, *R v Reid* [1992] 3 All ER 673 at 687, 688, [1992] 1 WLR 793 at 809-811 (Lord Goff).

99 [1987] 2 NZLR 122 at 128 (CA).

100 (1984) 78 Cr App R 149, [1985] Crim LR 236. Contra *R v Bonora* (1994) 35 NSWLR 74, where the Court of Criminal Appeal ruled that D must be aware that V may not be consenting.

101 [1987] 1 NZLR 754, (1987) 2 CRNZ 370 (CA).

acting in execution of his duty. While the mens rea for assault is intention,[102] a question arose whether mens rea was required regarding the rest of the actus reus. In this respect the Court of Appeal's remarks were *obiter*, but they deserve repetition here:[103]

> In *Millar v Ministry of Transport* [1986] 1 NZLR 660 this Court reviewed generally the position in New Zealand as to mens rea in statutory offences. We laid weight on the general principle that mens rea is an ingredient of criminal liability — guilty intent including in this context indifference or wilful blindness . . . the main alternatives for consideration will be a defence of total absence of fault or, more drastic, absolute liability.

> As to s 10 of the Summary Offences Act, there is insufficient reason for not applying the approach in *Millar*. Accordingly we think that mens rea must go to all the ingredients of the offence. The prosecution must prove that the defendant knew that the person assaulted was a police officer and knew that he was acting in the execution of his duty; or that the defendant wilfully shut his eyes to these possibilities or was indifferent to whether or not they were the truth.

> We would leave open for future consideration if need be the position under s 10 of a defendant who knows that the person assaulted is a police constable but gives no thought at all to whether or not he is acting in the execution of his duty.

In accordance with *Millar*, by finding that mens rea was required for the rest of the offence, the Court in effect decides that D must be reckless whether V was a constable acting in execution of his duty, since in the absence of express statutory language, recklessness is the basic standard of mens rea.[104] That much is unexceptionable. However, the Court then states that, regarding the victim being a constable, D must "know" that this is so at the time of the assault. This finding must be regarded as doubtful in principle, since full knowledge is not required: recklessness is satisfied if D merely realises that V might be a constable. Yet the Court then watered down the strenuousness of the test by stating that it would be sufficient if the defendant had "wilfully shut his eyes to those possibilities or was indifferent to whether or not they were the truth".[105]

With respect to the Court, the use of the term "know" is unhelpful here. "Knowledge" has its own meaning,[106] and demands a higher standard of belief than mere recklessness. As we shall see, in those offences where knowledge is expressly required by the statute it is certainly not enough to show that D was merely indifferent. We are left, then, with recklessness. It would have been enough for a conviction if D had recognised that V might be a constable acting in execution of his duty. The Court then suggests two additional ways of finding mens rea. The first, wilful blindness, is sufficient to establish

---

102 Section 2; *R v Young* 9/7/92, CA86/92.

103 [1987] 1 NZLR 754 at 759, (1987) 2 CRNZ 370 at 375 (CA).

104 See § 4.3.1.

105 [1987] 1 NZLR 754 at 759, (1987) 2 CRNZ 370 at 375 (CA). Followed in *Frost v Police* (1988) 4 CRNZ 539.

106 See § 3.4.

recklessness; we shall consider this doctrine below.[107] But whether indifference is enough may be less certain, for the reasons given earlier.

3.3 WHY DISTINGUISH INTENTION FROM RECKLESSNESS?

The fact that recklessness normally satisfies any mens rea requirement in a crime raises an obvious question: why bother discussing a separate category of intention at all? There are three reasons for doing so. First, some actions can only be done intentionally. For example, a person only attempts to harm another if he intends to do so. It would be a misuse of language to describe a knowing risk-taker as "attempting" to inflict harm.

Often this linguistic difference reflects a moral distinction,[108] because the presence of intention can alter the very nature of what is done. As Glanville Williams once pointed out, "The act constituting a crime may in some circumstances be objectively innocent, and take its criminal colouring entirely from the intent with which it is done."[109] It was the defendant's intention which changed the action from innocent to actus reus in *Court*,[110] a case where D spanked a young girl on the seat of her shorts. He was convicted of indecent assault because he had not done so in order to administer discipline, but rather for sexual gratification — his intention made the behaviour "indecent".[111] Similarly, the difference between negligent damage to property and vandalism lies not merely in the degree of culpability but also in the nature of the action itself (even though the physical harm may be the same). Vandalism is not fully specified by its consequence because it expresses a certain sort of contempt for society, and for the victim, which the mere causing of damage does not.

The second rationale for distinguishing intention from recklessness is that, as we have seen, recklessness is only established if the defendant risked doing the actus reus *unreasonably*. By contrast, there is no condition of unreasonableness attaching to intention. Nor is there a general defence known to the criminal law of reasonable action.[112]

The third ground also involves defences, which is a topic we have not yet discussed. As the law presently stands, in order to claim a defence such as self-defence, the defendant must *intend* to defend himself when he does the actus reus. This point is illustrated by the well-known case of *R v Dadson*,[113] in which

---

107 See § 3.4.1.

108 See, for example, Duff, "Attempted Homicide" (1995) 1 Legal Theory 149; Horder, "Crimes of Ulterior Intent" in Simester and Smith (eds) , *Harm and Culpability*, 1996, 153.

109 *CLGP*, 22. See also Lynch, "The Mental Element in the Actus Reus" (1982) 98 LQR 109.

110 [1989] AC 28, [1988] 2 All ER 221 (HL).

111 Per Lord Ackner (at 43; at 230): "To decide whether or not right-minded persons might think that the assault was indecent, the following factors were clearly relevant: the relationship of the defendant to this victim . . ., how had the defendant come to embark on this conduct and *why* was he behaving in this way?"

112 For a discussion of this point in the context of medical necessity, see Ashworth, "Criminal Liability in a Medical Context: the Treatment of Good Intentions" in Simester and Smith (eds), *Harm and Culpability*, 1996, 173.

113 (1850) 3 Car & Kir 148, 4 Cox CC 358.

a policeman shot and wounded a thief who was stealing wood. It was then, as now, an offence intentionally to shoot another, and both the actus reus and mens rea were made out in Dadson's case. However, the thief was in fact a felon, and a defence existed at that time to the effect that the policeman would be justified in shooting to prevent the escape of a felon. The difficulty was that the policeman had not realised that the person he was shooting was a felon. He did not intend to prevent the escape of a felon, and he was convicted.[114]

3.4 KNOWLEDGE

Where an offence is formulated so as to require that the defendant act "knowing" that some circumstance exists, this requires a positive (and correct) belief on the part of the defendant that the relevant circumstance does indeed exist. If Tom marries Jill suspecting that she is already married, he commits no offence of bigamy because he does not "know" she is married — he merely suspects it. Belief that a circumstance *may* obtain, which would be sufficient for recklessness, is not knowledge. Hence it is inadequate to satisfy the mens rea of any offence that specifies knowledge or intention.[115] In this respect "knowledge" of circumstances is the cognitive cousin of intention, rather than recklessness.

What is not necessary, however, is that the defendant should think that the relevant circumstance exists with provable certainty. The crucial feature is *acceptance*. The defendant must accept, or "assume",[116] or have no serious doubt, at the time he acts, that the circumstance is present. Hence if Tom refrains from investigating further whether Jill is indeed already married, and goes ahead with the ceremony believing that she may well be, he is not guilty of bigamy. It is not enough for him to believe there is a real possibility or likelihood that Jill is married.[117] But if, despite the fact that he has not actually seen a marriage certificate, he accepts Jill's disclosure to him that she is already married, then he commits bigamy when he goes ahead with the ceremony.

In sum, "knowing" means "knowing, or correctly believing".[118] The qualification, that the belief be a correct one, is implicit in the meaning of knowledge. Suppose that when Tom marries Jill he is sure that she is already married, but in fact she is not. Tom cannot be guilty of an offence against s 205(1)(b), of marrying someone he knows is already married. This is not only because there is no actus reus, but also because he does not "know" Jill is married, since his belief is wrong.

---

114 See also *R v Thain* [1985] NI 457; Sullivan, "Bad Thoughts and Bad Acts" [1990] Crim LR 559; Hogan "The *Dadson* Principle" [1989] Crim LR 679.

115 *R v Crooks* [1981] 2 NZLR 53 (CA); *Hall* (1985) 81 Cr App R 260; [1985] Crim LR 377 (CA).

116 *R v Simpson* [1978] 2 NZLR 221 (CA).

117 Compare *Griffiths* (1974) 60 Cr App R 14 (CA); *R v Woods* [1969] 1 QB 447, [1968] 3 All ER 709 (CA).

118 Cf *R v Baird* (1985) 3 NSWLR 331 at 334; 32 A Crim R 67 at 70. See also the discussion in § 13.4.2.1.

3.4.1 Wilful blindness

The situation where Tom realises there is a chance that Jill is already married, yet deliberately refrains from checking his suspicion, raises the issue of "wilful blindness". Cases of wilful blindness often appear to fall between the mens rea alternatives (i) recklessness as to the circumstance ("reckless knowledge"), and (ii) (actual) knowledge, which satisfies intention. One alternative is straightforward. *Every* case where a defendant realises or suspects the circumstance might exist and refrains from investigating further is a case of reckless knowledge (i). Even without further investigation, the defendant knows already that there is a risk that the circumstance is present. So if the mens rea of an offence requires only recklessness, then the defendant may be convicted.[119]

Finding actual knowledge is more difficult. In some cases of deliberate non-inquiry by a defendant, the Court will invoke what is known as the "doctrine" of wilful blindness. This doctrine applies where the defendant intentionally chooses not to inquire whether something is true because he has no real doubt what the answer is going to be. Its effect is to attribute knowledge of the circumstance to the defendant. In other words, where the wilful blindness doctrine applies, the law will treat the defendant as having actual knowledge (ii), and not merely the reckless knowledge that he would otherwise have.

The conditions under which the doctrine applies are not capable of being stated precisely. Broadly speaking, if there is an obvious way of finding something out and the defendant deliberately shuts his eyes to a risk by failing to find out, then he will not be permitted to exculpate himself by claiming that he did not know the truth. However, wilful blindness cannot be invoked just because he *should* have inquired into the facts, or even if he suspected the truth.[120] He is wilfully blind only if he shuts his eyes and fails to inquire "because he knew what the answer was going to be."[121] This approach squares with the test once proposed by the English Law Commission:

> The standard test of knowledge is — Did the person whose conduct is in issue either know of the relevant circumstances or have no substantial doubt of their existence?[122]

It will be obvious from this that in the bigamy example above, Tom would not be imputed with actual knowledge under the wilful blindness doctrine.

---

119 See § 3.2.3.

120 *R v Crooks* [1981] 2 NZLR 53; see also *Millar v MOT* [1986] 1 NZLR 660 at 674, (1986) 2 CRNZ 216 at 231 (CA).

121 *R v Crooks* [1981] 2 NZLR 53 at 58. See § 13.6.2.1(a).

122 *Draft Criminal Liability (Mental Element) Bill* No 89, London, HMSO, 1978, cl 3(1). This is a more demanding test than that finally endorsed by the Law Commission: *A Criminal Code for England and Wales* No 177, London, HMSO, 1989, cl 18(a). It is also more stringent than the standard set by the House of Lords in *Westminster CC v Croyalgrange Ltd* [1986] 2 All ER 353 at 359, [1986] 1 WLR 674 at 684. For an interesting discussion of earlier Australian and English cases, see Lanham, "Wilful Blindness and the Criminal Law" (1985) 9 Crim LJ 261.

3.5 NEGLIGENCE

Unlike such mens rea varieties as recklessness, intention, and knowledge, negligence does not presuppose any particular state of mind on the part of the defendant. It is, however, a standard that reflects fault on the part of the defendant, and so it is appropriately discussed alongside the other mens rea categories. The main feature distinguishing negligence from the categories we have mentioned so far is that, in negligence, there is no requirement that the defendant foresee the risk that the actus reus might occur. Sometimes we blame people precisely because they have *failed* to think about something — because they were careless, or thoughtless. It is this sort of case that is captured by negligence.

3.5.1 The test for negligence

Even though negligence permits the finding of fault for inadvertent wrongdoing, it does not actually matter whether the defendant attends to or contemplates the risks. As Glanville Williams asserts, "the essential question, at any rate for legal purposes, is whether it was reasonable for you to go ahead with your conduct in the circumstances."[123] Of course, normally one who foresees and runs an unreasonable risk will be reckless as well as negligent. Negligence does not, however, *require* inadvertence. This is for two reasons. The first is that in the criminal law, the lesser fault standard incorporates the greater. A defendant should not be able to exculpate herself by pleading that her actions were reckless or intentional rather than negligent. It follows that where negligence is enough for criminal liability, then, a fortiori, there is liability for intention or recklessness.

The second reason is that, as we mentioned earlier, a defendant can foresee the actus reus without being reckless, yet may still be negligent. For example, an anaesthetist who recognises there is a slight risk of killing his patient is not normally reckless. But if he has unknowingly miscalculated the dose, then he is negligent even though not reckless. Recklessness involves an objective assessment of the subjectively-perceived risk. Negligence involves an objective assessment of an objectively-recognisable risk.[124]

So the emphasis is on the unreasonableness of the defendant's behaviour. Formally, the defendant is negligent if a reasonable person in the same circumstances (i) would have been aware of the risks of doing the actus reus, and (ii) would not have run those risks. It does not matter that the defendant herself was unaware of the risks. What counts is that her behaviour falls short of the standard of conduct that we would expect of a reasonable person — that she failed to take reasonable precautions against the harm specified in the actus reus.

A recent example of the negligence standard in operation is provided by *Yogasakaran*.[125] D, an anaesthetist, was attending an operation when the patient

---

123 Fitzpatrick and Williams, "Carelessness, Indifference and Recklessness: Two Replies" (1962) 25 MLR 49 at 57.

124 Although this proposition will be qualified below, in § 3.5.2.

125 [1990] 1 NZLR 399, (1989) 5 CRNZ 69 (CA).

developed breathing problems. D decided to inject her with a drug known as Dopram. He took a drug container from the drawer marked "Dopram" and, without checking the label on the container, injected its contents into the patient. Unfortunately, the drug he injected was Dopamine. It was correctly labelled but had been placed in the wrong drawer. The patient died in consequence of being injected with the wrong drug. D was convicted of manslaughter, on the footing that a reasonable anaesthetist would be expected to check the label on the drug he was about to inject.

3.5.1.1 *Emergency*

One of the features of *Yogasakaran* was that the situation was urgent. The test of negligence has sometimes been criticised for being insensitive to circumstances, and for assessing emergency judgments in the cold light of the courtroom. Jeremy Horder has argued that in such situations we should not demand clinical accuracy, and that legitimate emotions such as fear and compassion, which sometimes lead us to make mistakes, are not properly allowed for by the orthodox test of negligence.[126] But this underestimates the legal test. We usually excuse a prima facie "negligent" mistake because it was not unreasonable *in the circumstances*. Although the evaluation of a defendant's conduct is done in a courtroom, in each case it must be done in the light of the defendant's particular circumstances and of normal social and personal values — including those of compassion and self-preservation. This is why it is sometimes reasonable to react precipitously.[127] The law does make allowance for emergencies: in *Yogasakaran*, the Court of Appeal pointed out that "instant decisions may have to be taken in an emergency; that must be a major factor to be kept prominently in mind in determining whether there has been a failure to live up to the appropriate professional standard."[128] Or, as Holmes J has noted, "detached reflection cannot be demanded in the presence of an uplifted knife".[129] Horder claims that negligence in such cases "is not culpable". But if it is not culpable, this will be because it is not negligence at all.

3.5.2 Abnormal defendants — does the reasonable man share any of their characteristics?

The test of negligence that we have identified seems at first blush to be an objective one. We complain of the defendant's *conduct*, and decide that she was negligent simply by determining that her conduct does not match a standard of behaviour that would have been acceptable in the circumstances. However, if negligence is truly a measure of culpability, there would seem to be a problem with this approach. In other categories of mens rea, the defendant is

---

126 Horder, "Cognition, Emotion and Criminal Culpability" (1990) 106 LQR 469 at 482. Compare Williams, "Offences and Defences" (1982) 2 Legal Studies 233 at 242.

127 As Bernard Williams notes: *Ethics and the Limits of Philosophy*, Cambridge, Mass, Harvard University Press, 1985, 185. See Horder, "Cognition, Emotion and Criminal Culpability" (1990) 106 LQR 469 at 481.

128 [1990] 1 NZLR 399 at 405, (1989) 5 CRNZ 69 at 74 (CA).

129 *Brown v US* 256 US 335 at 343 (1921). More prosaically, see *Wood v Richards* (1977) 65 Cr App Rep 300, [1977] Crim LR 295; also Williams, *TBCL*, 90.

blameworthy because she *knowingly* does the wrong thing — not merely because her behaviour is wrong. But that ground of fault cannot apply here. In negligence, the law says that the defendant *should* have done whatever the reasonable man would have done: but why? Why should the defendant be regarded as blameworthy, and attract the odium of criminal culpability, just because her behaviour causes some harm that she did not foresee?

The law's response is to assume that the reasonable man test incorporates the requirements of blame. If the defendant's conduct is objectively unreasonable, then it manifests a failing on the part of the defendant for which she may properly be blamed. Putting things the other way around, had she not been deserving of blame, her behaviour would not have failed the reasonable man test.

Most of the time this is a satisfactory answer. For example, if D had been a properly attentive and caring parent, she would not have left her child unattended by the swimming pool — we may hold her negligent, and blame her for doing so where a reasonable parent would not. And the fact that D was not a naturally caring parent is no excuse. But not every case is so straightforward. What if D is in some way abnormal? Suppose, for example, that D fails to observe a child climbing into the pool. A normal person would have seen the child. Is D negligent? Perhaps not, if it turns out that D is blind. The example suggests that, although the reasonable man test is mostly independent of the particular defendant, it is not entirely so. We do not expect D to behave as if she were sighted, but rather as a reasonable blind person would.

Generally speaking, the law states that behaviour is negligent if it involves a failure to exercise "care and caution which a reasonable and prudent person ordinarily would exercise under like conditions or circumstances."[130] But what exactly is meant by the "reasonable and prudent person"? The illustration above suggests that we do not replace the defendant altogether with objective characteristics, otherwise the youngest child would receive no allowance for immaturity[131] and the blind would be expected to see.[132] *Adams*, however, characterises the reasonable man standard rather more robustly:[133]

> The test is "objective" in that it depends on what the hypothetical reasonable person would have foreseen and done: it does not matter that the individual did not actually advert to the risk, and may have had personal attributes which were such

---

130 *Cordas v Peerless Transportation Co* 27 NYS 2D 198 at 200 (1941).

131 Gray, "The Standard of Care for Children Revisited" (1980) 45 Mo LR 597; Shulman, "The Standard of Care Required of Children" (1928) 37 Yale LJ 618. See, for example, *Charbonneau v MacRury* 153 A 457 (1931); *McHale v Watson* (1966) 115 CLR 199, [1966] ALR 513; *Yorkton Agricultural & Industrial Exhibition Assoc v Morley* (1967) 66 DLR (2d) 37. Compare *DPP v Camplin* [1978] AC 705 at 718, [1978] 2 All ER 168 (HL) (provocation).

132 Cf, in tort law, *Bernard v Russell* 164 A 2d 577 (1960); *Keith v Worcester St RR* 82 NE 680 (1907); *Balcom v City of Independence* 160 NW 305 (1916). See Weisiger, "Negligence of the Physically Infirm" (1946) 24 NCLR 187; Lowry, "The Blind and the Law of Tort" (1972) 20 Chittys LJ 253.

133 § CA20.39.

that he or she would not normally be expected to achieve a higher standard of care than was in fact achieved.

It will be clear that we disagree. The test is mostly objective, but it is also, in part, subjective. In particular, the reasonable man should be endowed with any peculiar physical characteristic of the defendant — including sight, hearing,[134] and age.[135] If his colleague's electrocution could have been avoided by simply throwing the mains switch, D is not negligent if he fails to do so because he is a paraplegic.

Sometimes this can work against the defendant. If she has additional knowledge, over and above that which a reasonable man would possess, then she will be held to the standard of that extra knowledge.[136] Thus a driver with abnormally good vision would be expected to avoid the cyclist she espies ahead of her even if ordinary drivers would not see that cyclist in time. And a professional, acting in a professional capacity,[137] will be judged by the standard of "a reasonably skilful and competent practitioner";[138] not by the standard of a layman.

In what other ways is the reasonable man test to be influenced by facts about the particular defendant? In order to answer that question, consider why we would expect the apparently "objective" standard in negligence to be affected by a defendant's physical limitations. The reason is that to convict a blind person for failing to see would be wrong and unfair. The blind do not deserve blame for failing to see. This, it is submitted, is the right way to approach the question of objectivity in negligence. The reasonable man test should be subjective to the extent that the defendant's shortcomings do not disclose fault. In particular, apart from physical limitations there is one other failing for which an abnormal defendant should not be blamed: intelligence. Recall the facts of *Elliott v C*.[139] C was a 14-year-old in a remedial class at school who had been awake all night before playing with matches and white spirit. Although someone of normal intelligence would no doubt have appreciated the risk of burning down the shed, it was found as a fact that the risk would not have been obvious to one of her limited capacities. It is submitted that to regard her as having destroyed the shed negligently would be wrong.

That having been said, however, it is not at all clear whether the criminal law currently makes any allowance for low intelligence when assessing negligence. The above passage from *Adams* suggests not. And in England,

---

134 Cf *SA Ambulance Transport Inc v Wahlheim* (1948) 77 CLR 215, [1949] ALR 1.

135 N 131 above. Cf *R v Cox* 7/11/96, CA213/96.

136 Cf *R v Lamb* [1967] 2 QB 981, [1967] 2 All ER 1282 (CA); *R v Gossell* (1993) 105 DLR (4th) 681 at 694-696.

137 This qualification may not apply in tort: *McComiskey v McDermott* [1974] IR 75.

138 *R v Yogasakaran* [1990] 1 NZLR 399 at 405, (1989) 5 CRNZ 69 at 75 (CA).

139 § 3.2.1.

according to Smith and Hogan, "if D has less knowledge or capacity for foresight than the reasonable man this, it seems, will not generally help him."[140]

Academic argument favours taking account of personal incapacities. Hart has proposed a general precondition for criminal liability of the form, "*could the accused, given his mental and physical capacities have taken [the required] precautions?*"[141] Outside Canada,[142] however, there is little relevant legal authority. In England, the suggestion of a test like Hart's may be found in *R v Hudson*,[143] but is impliedly excluded by *Elliott v C*.[144] In New Zealand things are a little more promising: *Elliott v C* seems to have been regarded as "harsh" in *Harney*,[145] and — in a different context — Fisher J suggests in *Police v Bannin*[146] that to be convicted a defendant should possess the capacity to form the mental elements required for the crime charged.

3.5.3 Negligence as an actus reus standard

Like recklessness, negligence sometimes operates as an actus reus term. It does so when it qualifies the behavioural element in the actus reus. So, for example, in an offence of dangerous driving the dangerousness — ie negligence — of the driving is not a mens rea term meaning that a reasonable person would (and the defendant should) have realised that he was driving. Rather, it is an actus reus term meaning that the defendant was driving in a *manner* that fell short of the standard a reasonable person would set. Thus dangerous driving is a different type of negligence offence from negligent rape, where the law's concern is not so much with the manner of the defendant's action as with the fact that it was done at all.

Most of the time the difference will not be important since even as a mens rea term negligence is assessed by reference to the defendant's conduct. However, it seems that the subjective elements of the reasonable man test may

---

140 *Criminal Law* (7th ed), 1992, 93; also Williams, *TBCL,* 94. Note that an objective approach to the absence of fault *is* taken in New Zealand in the context of strict liability offences. See § 4.2.1.2.

141 Hart "Negligence, Mens Rea and Criminal Responsibility" in *Punishment and Responsibility* Oxford, Clarendon Press, 1968, 136, 154. See also Ashworth, *Principles,* 190, 191; Orchard, "Culpable Homicide — Part II" [1977] NZLJ 447 at 451-453.

142 A similar test was endorsed by the Supreme Court in *R v Creighton* (1993) 105 DLR (4th) 632.

143 [1966] 1 QB 448, [1965] 1 All ER 721. See also *R v Hardie* [1984] 3 All ER 848, [1985] 1 WLR 64 (CA).

144 [1983] 1 WLR 939; also *R v Stephen* (1984) 79 Cr App R 334; *R v Ward* [1956] 1 QB 351, [1956] 1 All ER 565. See now, however, *R v Adomako* [1995] 1 AC 171, [1994] 3 All ER 79, which suggests that fault should be assessed by reference to the capacities of the particular defendant; also *R v Reid* [1992] 3 All ER 673 at 675, 696 (CA).

145 [1987] 2 NZLR 576 at 579. But see *R v P* (1993) 10 CRNZ 250 at 252, 253, 255, where D's intellectual impairment was said to be irrelevant to the question whether grounds for a belief held by D were reasonable. (Compare also *R v Clarke* [1992] 1 NZLR 147, [1992] 1 WLR 793 at 796, 819.) The unfortunate ruling in *R v P* is perhaps dependent upon the particular wording of s 128(2)(b).

146 [1991] 2 NZLR 237 at 254, also reported as *B v Police* (1991) 7 CRNZ 55 at 73.

not apply when negligence is operating as an actus reus standard. Hence in *McCrone v Riding* it was said that the standard of care in driving:

> is an objective standard, impersonal and universal, fixed in relation to the safety of other users of the highway. It is in no way related to the degree of proficiency or degree of experience attained by the individual driver.[147]

The justification for this is the need for a co-operative standard that other drivers can rely upon, together with the fact that driving is a voluntary activity, and those who engage in it may be thought to hold themselves out as being reasonably competent to do so.

3.5.4 Gross negligence

The criminal law knows two types of negligence: ordinary negligence and gross negligence. So far we have only considered ordinary negligence. Sometimes, however, the mens rea of an offence cannot be satisfied by anything less than gross negligence. While the difference between the two is a matter of degree and judgment in each case, broadly speaking, negligence will be gross if the defendant's conduct not merely fails to meet the standard set by the reasonable man test, but falls short of that standard by a considerable margin — ie if the defendant's conduct is not merely unreasonable, but *very* unreasonable.[148] It may be negligent to drive around a particular bend at 50 km/h; if so, it is grossly negligent to do so at 80 km/h. It will also be gross negligence if the risk created by the defendant is very obvious — C's inadvertent burning down of the shed in *Elliott v C* would have been grossly negligent had she been a normal adult. Hart puts the test another way: "Negligence is gross if the precautions to be taken against harm are very simple, such as persons who are but poorly endowed with physical and mental capacities can easily take."[149]

3.5.5 The place of negligence

A number of writers have argued that people should never be subject to criminal liability on the basis of negligence,[150] and that its place lies properly in

---

147 [1938] 1 All ER 157 at 158. See too *R v Gosney* [1971] 2 QB 674 at 680, [1971] 2 All ER 220.

148 Cf *R v Bateman* [1925] All ER Rep 45 at 48, (1925) 19 Cr App R 8 at 11 (CA): "in order to establish criminal liability the facts must be such that, in the opinion of the jury, the negligence of the accused went beyond a mere matter of compensation between subjects and showed such disregard for the life and safety of others as to amount to a crime against the State and conduct deserving punishment."

149 "Negligence, Mens Rea, and Criminal Responsibility" in *Punishment and Responsibility*, 1968, 136, 149.

150 Hall, "Negligent Behaviour Should be Excluded from Penal Liability" (1963) 63 Columbia LR 632; Turner, "The Mental Element in Crimes at Common Law" in Radzinowicz and Turner (eds), *The Modern Approach to Criminal Law* (1948) 195, 207-211; Hall, *General Principles of Criminal Law* (2nd ed), Indianapolis, Bobbs-Merrill, 1960, 138. Hart's refutation of Turner's argument is convincing: "Negligence, Mens Rea, and Criminal Responsibility" in *Punishment and Responsibility*, 1968, 136. See also Moore, "Choice, Character, and Excuse" in Paul, Miller and Paul (eds), *Crime, Culpability and Remedy*, 1990, 29, 58; Keedy, "Ignorance and Mistake in the Criminal Law" (1908) 22 Harv LR 75 at 83-85.

the arena of torts and compensation rather than of crimes and punishment. There is force in this argument, since it would normally be harsh to equate those who do wrong inadvertently with others who break the law intentionally or recklessly. The person who inadvertently does harm might well have refrained from doing so, had she only realised the risk. But the fact that negligence is often not as bad as recklessness or intention does not mean that it is never serious enough to warrant criminalisation. Baker's example is instructive:

> Carelessly handling loaded firearms in a crowded area, or speeding through a school zone at lunch hour oblivious to the dangers to others because one is absorbed in an interesting conversation, is more culpable . . . than deliberately taking a $0.50 store item without payment or than many other knowing offences against property.[151]

Sometimes, one who knowingly takes the risk of a minor crime is not so deserving of a criminal sanction as another who carelessly risks serious harm. It would be wrong for the criminal law only ever to convict in the former case.

However, such instances are exceptional, and normally the law is reluctant to inflict serious criminal (rather than civil) sanctions upon people who have merely been negligent. The general rule for serious criminal offences is that, in the few crimes where negligence is a sufficient to meet the mens rea requirements (such as manslaughter), then the negligence must be "gross" before the defendant can be convicted.[152] However, where the statute specifies the standard of care required in its own terms, eg as "reasonable care", then ordinary negligence will suffice.[153]

Although rare among serious crimes, it would be a mistake to discount the significance of negligence. As we shall see in chapter 4, it is extremely important in the context of strict liability, where the main ground of exculpation is essentially an absence of negligence.

3.6 OTHER MENS REA STATES

We have mentioned that there are a variety of other mens rea terms used in the criminal law. Some of these, such as "dishonestly", occur primarily in the context of property crimes such as theft, and will be explored in some detail when we come to look at the specific offences.[154] Another fairly common term is "wilfully", which appears in a number of offences contained in the Crimes Act.[155] In essence, it appears that wilfulness is an alternative term for

---

151 "Mens Rea, Negligence and Criminal Law Reform" (1987) 6 Law & Philosophy 53 at 81. In *Principles*, 191, Ashworth posits the following example: "D, a shot-gun champion, fires at a target, knowing that there is a slight risk that the bullet will ricochet and injure a spectator, which it does; E, who rarely handles guns, is invited to participate in a shooting party and fires wildly into bushes, failing to consider the possibility of others being there, and one is injured. Is D manifestly more culpable than E?"

152 *R v Burney* [1958] NZLR 745; *Bateman* [1925] All ER Rep 45, (1925) 19 Cr App R 8 (CA).

153 *R v Storey* [1931] NZLR 417; *R v Yogasakaran* [1990] 1 NZLR 399, (1989) 5 CRNZ 69 (CA).

154 Chapter 17.

155 See *Adams* (2nd ed) § 2263.

(subjective[156]) recklessness, and is satisfied if the defendant either intends or foresees the prohibited outcome. Inadvertence will not do.[157]

Recklessness requires that the actus reus is an unreasonable risk. It is possible that "wilfully" imports no such requirement. If so, then a surgeon who carries out a risky yet medically-justified operation might injure her patient wilfully, even though she is not reckless. However, while this may be true of ordinary language, we submit that in the context of the criminal law "wilfully" should bear the more restricted meaning of (intent or) subjective recklessness. In our view, the defendant who, without intending the actus reus, advertently takes a reasonable risk of bringing that actus about should not be regarded as having brought it about wilfully.

3.7 TRANSFERRED MENS REA

It is a general rule that, if the defendant does an actus reus with the required mens rea (and without being able to plead any relevant defence), she is guilty of an offence even though the occurrence of the actus reus may be unexpected in a way which is immaterial to the definition.[158] To illustrate:

Suppose that Duncan takes aim at Tom with intent to kill him, and pulls the trigger. Just as Duncan shoots, however, Tom bends down to pick a flower. Duncan's shot misses Tom and hits Bill, who was standing behind Tom. Bill is killed instantly. In this situation Duncan is guilty of murdering Bill, notwithstanding that he did not foresee that possible outcome. The actus reus of murder is to kill a *person*.[159] Thus, although Duncan intended to kill Tom rather than Bill, he had the mens rea for murder since he intended to kill a *person*; the identity of that person is immaterial to the definition of the offence.

The "transferred malice" doctrine (as it is popularly known) is not confined to murder.[160] If Ian steals a cheap painting because he thinks it is a valuable Constable, he has the mens rea (and commits the actus reus) of theft since the specific identity of the property stolen forms no necessary part of the offence

---

156 *R v Sheppard* [1981] AC 394, [1980] 3 All ER 899, which suggests that *Caldwell* recklessness is sufficient. In general, English case law should not be relied upon for the interpretation of wilfulness, since its meaning appears to vary across the English offences. For discussion, see Andrews, "Wilfulness: a Lesson in Ambiguity" (1981) 1 LS 303 at 315ff.

157 *Durey v Police* (1984) 1 CRNZ 392; *Donnelly v CIR* [1960] NZLR 469. See also *Summers v SPCA* (1990) 6 CRNZ 201 at 207, and the cases there discussed. For consideration of the effect upon "wilfulness" of a mistake of law, see *Police v Cunard* [1975] 1 NZLR 511; *Police v Shadbolt* [1976] 2 NZLR 409; also *Donnelly v CIR* [1960] NZLR 469 at 472, 473.

158 For critical discussion, see Ashworth, "Transferred Malice and Punishment for Unforeseen Consequences: essays in honour of Glanville Williams" in Glazebrook (ed), *Reshaping the Criminal Law*, London, Stevens & Son, 1978, 77; Ashworth, "The Elasticity of Mens Rea" in Tapper (ed), *Crime, Proof and Punishment*, 1981, 45; Williams, "Convictions and Fair Labelling" (1983) 42 CLJ 85.

159 *Agnes Gore's Case* (1611) 9 Co Rep 81, 77 ER 853; *A-G's Reference (No 3 of 1994), Re* [1996] QB 581, [1996] 2 All ER 10; *R v Hopwood* (1913) 8 Cr App R 143. Note that, in s 167(c), explicit statutory provision is made for transferred malice in homicide.

160 For example, *Gross* (1913) 77 JP 352; *Latimer* (1886) 17 QBD 359, [1886-90] All ER Rep 386; *McCullum* (1973) 57 Cr App R 645, [1973] Crim LR 582 (CA).

definition. It is enough that he takes "anything capable of being stolen", whether or not the thing stolen is of great value.[161]

Neither is it a doctrine merely of transferred *intention*. Suppose, this time, that Jane bears a grudge against Daniel. She throws a stone at No 6 King Street, thinking that it is Daniel's house. She recognises that the stone might break a window, although she does not intend it to do so. In fact Daniel lives at No 8, and the stone breaks Pat's window. Jane's recklessness is sufficient mens rea for the crime of wilful damage,[162] and is transferable to the (otherwise unanticipated) result: damage to *Pat's* property.

However, transferred malice does not operate when the divergence between actus reus and mens rea *is* relevant to the definition of the offence. In particular, it is not possible to convict someone on the basis of an actus reus for one offence accompanied by the mens rea for a different offence. If Jane were to throw a stone at Daniel and miss but inadvertently break his window, she is not guilty of wilful damage.[163] Her intent to injure Daniel does not satisfy the mens rea requirement for damage to property.

When malice is transferred, so also are defences. Imagine one last variant: Duncan attempts to shoot Tom only because Tom is attacking him and Duncan is in immediate peril of his life. He misses and unexpectedly kills Bill. Duncan's intention may be transferred, but so too is his claim of self-defence. He is not guilty of murder.[164]

3.8 CONCURRENCE

As a general rule, the actus reus and mens rea of a crime must coincide in time. That is, the behavioural and circumstantial elements of the actus reus must occur at the same time as the mens rea requirements are satisfied. Unless there is a scintilla temporis at which these elements are all present, the crime is not committed.[165] Consider the following illustration:

> D is an assassin who has been hired to kill V. One evening she drives over to V's house in order to shoot him when he comes home. On the way, however, she is involved in an accident when she collides with a cyclist who has suddenly cut in front of her car. Upon getting out of the car, D recognises that the cyclist is V. Thinking V is unconscious but alive, she shoots him through the heart. V, however, was already dead as a result of the accident.

---

161 Section 220; cf *R v Wrigley* [1957] Crim LR 57. See chapter 17.

162 See ss 298, 293.

163 Compare *R v Pembliton* (1874) LR 2 CCR 119; *R v Taaffe* [1984] AC 539, [1984] 1 All ER 747 (HL). However, compare *R v Ellis and Street* (1986) 84 Cr App R 235, [1987] Crim LR 44 (CA), which pays lip service to the principle that the actus reus and mens rea must correspond, but at the same time subverts that fundamental requirement for the sake of enforcement convenience.

164 Cf *Gross* (1913) 77 JP 352 (provocation). Note that the transfer of a defence will not necessarily preclude liability for an independent offence. It may, for example, have been grossly negligent to shoot at Tom because of the risk of hitting Bill.

165 Cf *R v Terry* 9/9/96, CA50/96; *R v Scott* [1967] VR 276.

D has not murdered V. Although she may have caused his death (the actus reus) by driving into him, when she did so she did not have a present intention to kill. Later, when she shot V, she had the mens rea for murder but her behaviour did not cause his death, so could not constitute the actus reus. Thus there is no moment in time at which both the actus reus and mens rea of murder are present.

Neither can an antecedent mens rea be added to a subsequent actus reus in order to support a conviction. For example:

> D takes a new umbrella to the law library one morning. When she departs, she realises that she cannot remember exactly what her umbrella looked like. However, seeing an attractive umbrella in the stand, she decides to take and keep that one instead — not realising that it is in fact her own umbrella. Later, she begins to feel guilty. She returns to the law library, and replaces the attractive umbrella. In its place, she takes with her a different umbrella which she mistakenly thinks is the one she originally came with.

When D first leaves the library, she attempts to steal an umbrella but fails to do so because the one she takes is her own. She has the mens rea for theft but does not commit the actus reus.[166] Later, when she departs for a second time, she commits the actus reus of theft by taking another person's umbrella, but does so innocently — without an "intent to deprive the owner". There is no scintilla temporis at which all elements of the definition of theft are co-existent.

Where the actus reus includes consequences, the requirement for concurrence applies to the behavioural element rather than its consequence. If D deliberately poisons V, and V takes some hours to die, the fact that D repents in the meantime will not absolve her of murder.[167] Conversely, if D is driving and accidentally hits a cyclist, the fact that she realises the cyclist is V, her enemy, and rejoices while he is dying of his injuries will not make her guilty of a homicide offence. For the purposes of concurrence, the actus reus has already occurred.

Although concurrence is a standard requirement for offences involving mens rea, there are some situations where the need for concurrence does not operate or can be circumnavigated.[168] We consider these below.

3.8.1 Circumventing the concurrence requirement

3.8.1.1 *Fresh acts, continuing acts, and subsequent omissions*

Where an actus reus by D precedes his having mens rea, one technique available to the prosecutor is to show another, later, occurrence of the actus reus which coincides with D's mens rea — ie to look for a different scintilla temporis at which the offence can be proved to have occurred.

A standard, if unusual, case of this would be where D does a second, positive act which also brings about the actus reus.[169] Suppose, in the days

---

166 The taking is not a trespass: see § 17.2.2.1(a).

167 Cf *Jakeman* (1983) 76 Cr App R 223, [1983] Crim LR 104 (CA).

168 Marston, "Contemporaneity of Act and Intention in Crimes" [1970] 86 LQR 208.

169 Cf, on one view of the facts, *R v Chignell* [1991] 2 NZLR 257, also reported as *R v Chignell and Walker* (1990) 6 CRNZ 103 (CA).

when tort actions died with the plaintiff,[170] that while driving D accidentally runs over V, fatally injuring him. D is uninsured and, panicking, she backs up hoping thereby to avoid tortious liability. If the further injuries D inflicts by reversing over V play any causal role in V's death, then D becomes guilty of murder, on the basis of the second and not the first incident.

Absent a fresh causative act by the defendant, the prosecution may try instead to show a *continuing* act: that the actus reus, although initiated by D without mens rea, is still occurring or being perpetrated by D at later moment when D now has the required mens rea. This type of case is discussed in § 2.1.1.2.4. It is exemplified by *Fagan v Metropolitan Police Commissioner*,[171] in which D accidentally stopped his car on a policeman's foot. That itself was no assault, since D did not yet have mens rea. However, when he deliberately refrained from moving his car, an assault was established. There was an ongoing application of force to the policeman by D (the actus reus), which was now accompanied by mens rea.[172]

Alternatively, the prosecution can try to bring its case within the ambit of *R v Miller*.[173] In this situation, a subsequent omission to prevent harm may constitute the actus reus if it amounts to a failure to prevent a danger that D has himself created by his earlier actions. *Miller* is discussed further in § 2.1.1.2.5.

3.8.1.2 *The complex single transaction*

The law is different when the actus reus of an offence occurs *after* D has mens rea. Here it will sometimes be possible to convict D on the basis that the particular act that caused harm was part of a larger, complex series of actions which should be viewed as a whole, where D has mens rea at some earlier point during that "transaction".

The classic case is *Thabo Meli v R*[174] in which four defendants conspired to kill V and dispose of his body. In accordance with their plan, they struck V on the head (with intent thereby to kill him). Thinking him dead, they rolled him over a cliff. In fact, V was not killed by the blow and died from exposure suffered after falling down the cliff. Prima facie, the act of disposal, which caused V's death, was unaccompanied by the mens rea for murder since the defendants believed he was already dead. Nonetheless, the Privy Council upheld their convictions for murder. Rather than slicing up the events of the killing into component moments of time and then looking for a scintilla temporis at which actus reus and mens rea coincide:

> It appears to their Lordships impossible to divide up what was really one series of acts in this way. There is no doubt that the accused set out to do all these acts in order to achieve their plan, and as parts of their plan; and it is much too refined a

---

170 Winfield, "Death as Affecting Liability in Tort" (1929) 29 Col L Rev 239.

171 [1969] 1 QB 439, [1968] 3 All ER 442.

172 See also *Kaitamaki v R* [1984] 1 NZLR 385, [1985] AC 147 (PC); *R v Cooper* [1994] Crim LR 531.

173 [1983] 2 AC 161, [1983] 1 All ER 978 (HL).

174 [1954] 1 All ER 373; [1954] 1 WLR 228 (PC).

ground of judgment to say that, because they were under a misapprehension at one stage and thought that their guilty purpose was achieved before, in fact, it was achieved, therefore they are to escape the penalties of the law. [175]

It is hard to disagree with this decision, which represents a genuine exception to the concurrence requirement. The defendants did exactly what they planned to do, and the result they intended to achieve did occur. The fact that the manner in which their success occurred was unexpected seems no ground for exculpation. However, it is salient that their actions were pursuant to a preconceived plan. This feature is crucial to the application of *Thabo Meli* in New Zealand. In *R v Ramsay*,[176] D had assaulted and gagged V, whose death was caused by one or other of those acts. However, it appeared that D may not have had the mens rea of murder when gagging V. The Court of Appeal ruled that the assault and the gagging could not be treated as a continuous single course of conduct: there was not a preconceived plan by D to behave as he did, and his conduct could not be regarded as a series of actions governed throughout by a "dominating intention" to produce the actus reus. Hence D's mens rea when he assaulted D could not be combined with the actus reus when he gagged her to satisfy the requirements of murder. Although the rationale underlying *Thabo Meli* might have suggested a different conclusion,[177] the Court of Appeal has taken a firm stance against further exceptions to the concurrence principle.

It follows from the decision in *Ramsay* that the *Thabo Meli* doctrine will not apply to crimes of recklessness or negligence. The New Zealand law on this point differs from applicable law elsewhere,[178] but is perhaps defensible on the basis that it fosters certainty, by confining exceptions to the concurrence requirement to those cases where there is a preconceived plan.

3.8.1.3 A causation approach

Where the defendant's mens rea precedes the action that most obviously constitutes the actus reus, another way of circumventing concurrence difficulties is to show that some earlier action by the defendant, done at the time when he had mens rea, was *also* a cause of the prohibited harm. An

---

175 Ibid at 374.

176 [1967] NZLR 1005 (CA); cf *R v Chignell* [1991] 2 NZLR 257 at 265, also reported as *R v Chignell and Walker* (1990) 6 CRNZ 103 at 111 (CA); *R v Dixon* [1979] 1 NZLR 641 at 646, 647 (CA).

177 Cf Adams, "Homicide and the Supposed Corpse" (1968) 1 Otago LR 278 at 290. However, as Adams acknowledges, it is arguable that the approach in *Thabo Meli* — that at common law, a homicide committed in such a manner is murder — is less easily adopted where murder has a statutory definition specifying the particular intent(s) required.

178 *Shoukatallie v R* [1962] AC 81, [1961] 3 All ER 966; *R v Church* [1966] 1 QB 59, [1965] 2 All ER 72 (CA); *R v Moore and Dorn* [1975] Crim LR 229 (CA); *R v Le Brun* [1992] 1 QB 61, [1991] 4 All ER 673 (CA); *A-G's Reference (No 4 of 1980)* [1981] 2 All ER 617, [1981] 1 WLR 705 (CA). For discussion, see Sullivan, "Cause and the Contemporaneity of Actus Reus and Mens Rea" (1993) 52 CLJ 487 at 495-499.

example of this approach is *R v McKinnon*.[179] In that case D assaulted V and knocked him unconscious. D then manhandled V, apparently causing an accidental nose-bleed, before leaving V lying on the ground and running off. While V was lying unconscious, the blood from his nose entered his lungs and he suffocated. The Court of Appeal upheld D's conviction for murder. Although D may not have had the required mens rea when he caused the injury to V's nose, he did have mens rea when he struck V and knocked him unconscious. Moreover, the Court ruled, D's striking V was a contributory cause of his death, in combination with the nose-bleed, since it rendered V unable to deal with the bleeding. Thus there was no need to invoke a series-of-acts analysis, of the sort found in *Thabo Meli*, since there was already a scintilla temporis at which both an actus reus and the mens rea of murder were present.[180]

3.8.1.4 *Involuntariness and antecedent fault*

If D perpetrates an actus reus while in an automatic state, normally the concurrence requirement will not be satisfied. Exceptionally, however, it may be possible to convict D on the basis that his automatism is a consequence of his own earlier actions which occurred at a time when he had the mens rea for the offence. This type of case is discussed more fully in § 2.3.3. Suppose, for example, that David is a diabetic. One day he deliberately takes insulin without eating any food. He does this in the hope of reducing himself into a semi-conscious state where he knows that he is likely to become violent and assault his flatmate whom he does not like. Should his plan be successful, David will be guilty of an intentional assault, notwithstanding his automatism at the time the assault occurs.

Sometimes the offence may be proved without reference to the defendant's subsequent, involuntary conduct. In *Kay v Butterworth*,[181] D fell asleep while driving and collided with soldiers marching on the road. He was convicted of careless driving, but not because he drove into the soldiers. (At that time he was asleep and his behaviour was involuntary.) Rather, the offence was complete when he continued to drive while drowsy — that, in itself, was careless driving. Indeed, D would have committed the offence even if he had not run into the soldiers.[182] Glanville Williams illustrates this point in a lucid example:

---

179 [1980] 2 NZLR 31 (CA). For discussion of multiple causes see § 2.2.2.3. Cf *S v Masilela* 1968 (2) SA 558.

180 Indeed, it is arguable that *Thabo Meli* could itself have been decided on a causation basis: Adams, "Homicide and the Supposed Corpse" (1968) 1 Otago LR 278 at 287; *R v McKinnon* [1980] 2 NZLR 31 at 36, 37 (CA). On this approach, the *Thabo Meli* doctrine would still be necessary in some cases, but only where the second event was overwhelmingly the cause of death, and amounted to a *novus actus interveniens*. (For example, where V is killed instantly by the impact after he is thrown over a cliff: compare *R v Le Brun* [1992] 1 QB 61, [1991] 4 All ER 673.)

181 (1945) 173 LT 191. Cf *Moses v Winder* [1980] Crim LR 232. For a rather more dramatic example, see *People v Decina* 2 NY 2d 133 (1956).

182 *R v Spurge* [1961] 2 QB 205 at 210, [1961] 2 All ER 688 at 690.

When, for example, a driver proceeds along Church Lane in a sleepy condition, and falls asleep at the wheel just before entering High Street, where he is involved in an accident, he cannot be convicted of careless driving in High Street, because in contemplation of law he did not "drive" in High Street, and it makes no difference that his involuntary accident in High Street was the result of his own previous fault. He can, indeed, be convicted of careless driving, but this must be laid as having taken place in Church Lane, when the driver was undoubtedly "driving". [183]

The scintilla temporis of the offence occurs in Church Lane.

---

183 *TBCL,* 682. Obviously, this analysis works only if the time-frame for commission of the actus reus is sufficiently elastic, and not tied to a particular incident. Contrast *Burns v Bidder* [1967] 2 QB 227, [1966] 3 All ER 29 (failing to accord precedence at a pedestrian crossing). A nice illustration is *MOT v Beregi* [1992] DCR 261, in which D had a petit mal epileptic attack while driving. He was convicted on a dangerous driving charge, because it was held reasonably foreseeable that D could endanger others on the road by having an epileptic fit. Nonetheless, he was discharged on the second count of failing to stop after an accident.

4

Strict Liability and the
Burden of Proof

4.1 THE BURDEN OF PROVING ACTUS REUS AND MENS REA

In chapter 1, we argued that convicting an innocent person would be seriously to defame him. Punishing him, of course, compounds the wrong. Because criminal liability is so serious, every citizen has the right not to have the State inflict such liability on him unless he is, in fact, guilty. That right is fundamental: it is profoundly wrong for the State to mistreat an innocent person, and to do so breaches one of the keystones of an individual's relationship with the State.

So when the State brands someone a criminal, it needs to be sure that it is right — or at least, in the absence of omniscience, as sure as it can be.[1] For that reason, there is a basic presumption in New Zealand (and in many other jurisdictions) that the defendant in a trial is innocent until proved guilty. The presumption is codified by s 25(c) New Zealand Bill of Rights Act 1990. But it predates that Act, and has been a part of the common law at least since the English case of *Woolmington v DPP*.[2] In *Woolmington*, on a charge of murder,

---

1   Cf the judgment of Brennan J in *Re Winship* 397 US 358, 25 L Ed 2d 368 (1970) (USSC).
2   [1935] AC 462, [1935] All ER Rep 1 (HL).

the trial Judge had relied on earlier authorities to direct the jury that, once the prosecution has proved the actus reus, mens rea can be presumed and it was up to the defendant to "satisfy" the jury either that mens rea was absent and the killing had been accidental, or that it had been justified. On this view, the prosecution had to prove only the actus reus, and the burden then lay on the defendant to prove either the lack of mens rea or any defence. Not so, said the House of Lords:[3]

> Throughout the web of the English Criminal Law one golden thread is always to be seen, that it is the duty of the prosecution to prove the prisoner's guilt . . . If, at the end of and on the whole of the case, there is a reasonable doubt, created by the evidence given by either the prosecution or the prisoner, as to whether the prisoner killed the deceased with a malicious intention, the prosecution has not made out the case and the prisoner is entitled to an acquittal. No matter what the charge or where the trial, the principle that the prosecution must prove the guilt of the prisoner is part of the common law of England and no attempt to whittle it down can be entertained.

The effect of *Woolmington* may be summarised in the following steps:

(i)   The prosecution has the burden to bring evidence which prima facie proves all actus reus and mens rea elements of the offence *beyond reasonable doubt*.

(ii)   Once the prosecution has done so, then it is open to the defendant either to refute the evidence the prosecution has brought, or to point to some further evidence which raises a doubt whether the prosecution's evidence is in fact sufficient to prove both actus reus[4] and mens rea beyond reasonable doubt.

(iii) Alternatively, if the prosecution proves both actus reus and mens rea, the defendant has an *evidentiary burden* to raise any evidence which suggests the possible availability of a defence (for example, that the actus reus was done in self-defence).[5] If he does so, or if the evidence introduced by the prosecution does so,[6] then the prosecution assumes the burden of proving beyond reasonable doubt that the relevant

---

3   [1935] AC 462 at 481, 482, [1935] All ER Rep 1 at 8 (HL) (Viscount Sankey LC).

4   This includes claims of involuntariness or automatism: *R v Burr* [1969] NZLR 736 at 748 (CA); *Police v Bannin* [1991] 2 NZLR 237 at 241, 242, also reported as *B v Police* (1990) 7 CRNZ 55 at 58, 59; *Millar v MOT* [1986] 1 NZLR 660 at 667, 668, (1986) 2 CRNZ 216 at 224, 225 (CA); *Bratty v A-G for Northern Ireland* [1963] AC 386 at 406, 407, 413, 414, [1961] 3 All ER 523 at 530, 531, 534-536 (HL). See § 2.3.4.

5   *R v Matoka* [1987] 1 NZLR 340 at 344 (CA); *R v Nepia* [1983] NZLR 754. The evidentiary burden to introduce defences differs from the option to refute evidence of actus reus or mens rea in step (ii). The latter is sometimes called a *tactical burden* on the defendant. The difference is that, where there is an evidential burden on D to suggest (for example) a defence, its absence will be *presumed* by the Court unless D discharges that burden. By contrast, a tactical burden involves no presumption. Thus, D may choose not to respond to the prosecution's evidence of actus reus and mens rea, and simply hope that the jury is not convinced by it.

6   Thus the defence must be considered even if the defendant has not raised it himself — or, indeed, disclaims it. See *R v Tavete* [1988] 1 NZLR 428; (1987) 2 CRNZ 579 (CA).

defence is not available in this case.[7] This rule applies to statutory as well as common law defences unless the statute provides otherwise.[8]

The defendant does *not* have to prove that he is innocent. The jury may think that he is a scoundrel, and be unconvinced by his story. But if it thinks there is a reasonable possibility that he is not guilty of the crime charged, then he must be acquitted.

The crux is the standard: "beyond reasonable doubt". It means that the jury must acquit if there is a realistic or genuine doubt about the defendant's guilt, although not if the doubt is only vague or fanciful.[9] Such a high standard is needed for the State to be sufficiently sure that it is imposing criminal liability accurately. It is not enough that the defendant "very likely", or even "probably", did the crime; otherwise there would be too many cases of error and consequent miscarriages of justice. The possibility of error is all the greater when it is also remembered that the State typically has far greater resources with which to conduct a prosecution than the defendant has with which to defend himself. In addition, the high standard of proof acts as a constraint upon the decision to prosecute. Without the presumption of innocence, those who make that decision would have an immense and potentially oppressive power to disrupt the lives of citizens.[10]

4.1.1 Exceptions

4.1.1.1 *Parliament*
It is not uncommon for a statute to modify the normal burden of proof, especially in respect of a statutory defence. An example of this is s 134(3) Crimes Act 1961, which provides a defence to the crime of sexual intercourse or indecency with a girl aged between 12 and 16 "if the person charged proves that the girl consented and that he is younger than the girl". In this case, once the prosecution has proved the elements of an offence against s 134(1) or s 134(2), the defendant has a legal (and not merely evidential) burden to prove that the conditions of the defence exist. In all such cases, the defendant must prove to the civil standard, of balance of probabilities.[11]

This is not a textbook on evidence. However, it is submitted that for the reasons given in the last section, and especially in light of s 25(c) New Zealand

---

7   *R v Kahu* [1947] NZLR 368 (CA); *R v Kerr* [1976] 1 NZLR 335 at 340.

8   *R v Rangi* [1992] 1 NZLR 385 (CA); *Bay of Plenty Regional Council v Bay Milk Products* [1996] 3 NZLR 120; cf s 25(c) New Zealand Bill of Rights Act 1990; *R v Phillips* [1991] 3 NZLR 175 (CA). (The position in England appears to be different: *R v Hunt* [1987] AC 352, [1987] 1 All ER 1.) An important statutory exception to this rule is s 67(8) Summary Proceedings Act 1957, which places on the accused in summary proceedings the burden of proving any statutory defence, to the balance of probabilities. For discussion, see *Adams* § Ch2.1.05, 06.

9   *R v Harbour* [1995] 1 NZLR 440 at 448, (1995) 12 CRNZ 317 at 324 (CA); *R v S* 20/12/91, CA273/91.

10   As Ashworth points out: *Principles*, 81.

11   See the discussion in *Robertson v Police* [1957] NZLR 1193; also Orchard, "The Golden Thread — Somewhat Frayed" (1988) 6 Otago LR 615.

Bill of Rights Act 1990, statutory exceptions of this sort are generally to be deplored.[12] Effectively, they reverse the presumption of innocence, and replace it with a presumption of criminality, whereby the defendant is to be convicted of a crime unless she exculpates herself. As such, they expose the defendant to conviction for a crime without the prosecution being required, at any stage, to lead evidence which proves her guilt beyond reasonable doubt. There *are* occasions when it may be apt to require the defendant, who may have more information about salient events than the prosecutor, to suggest reasons why she should not be convicted.[13] But even then the desired result can usually be achieved by imposing an *evidential* burden to introduce defences upon the defendant, without requiring her to discharge the full legal burden of persuading the Court that she is innocent.

4.1.1.2 *Insanity*

A second exception is the defence of insanity. In line with the common law,[14] the Crimes Act 1961 makes a statutory presumption of sanity in s 23(1). Once again, the defendant must prove this defence on the balance of probabilities[15] — an incongruous anomaly given that the defendant bears only an evidential burden in respect of other general defences; and that the consequence of proving insanity may be incarceration.[16] The need to do so, however, arises only if the prosecution can prove both actus reus and mens rea beyond reasonable doubt in the normal way.[17] Insanity is discussed in detail in chapter 8.

4.1.1.3 *Strict liability*

A most important exception is the one to which we shall come in § 4.2. In offences of strict liability, the defendant carries the burden of proving a defence of absence of fault, once again to the balance of probabilities.

4.1.1.4 *Where the statute is silent as to mens rea*

There is one situation where mens rea is required, but the prosecution does not bear the initial burden of proving it beyond reasonable doubt. As we shall see in the discussion of strict liability (below), frequently the statute creating an offence specifies only the actus reus elements of that offence, and neglects to mention the need for mens rea. In such instances the Courts must determine

---

12 See, for example, Roberts, "Taking the Burden of Proof Seriously" [1995] Crim LR 783; Jeffreys and Stephan, "Defences, Presumptions and Burden of Proof in Criminal Law" (1979) 88 Yale LJ 1325.

13 See the discussion of (and reservations about) strict liability, at §§ 4.2.1.3(b), 4.3.2.2(a)–(b).

14 Cf the *M'Naghten* rules, [1843] 10 Cl & F 200 at 210, 8 ER 718 at 722; *Woolmington v DPP* [1935] AC 462 at 475, [1935] All ER Rep 1 at 5 (HL).

15 *R v Roulston* [1976] 2 NZLR 644, *R v Cottle* [1958] NZLR 999 at 1014, 1022 (CA). The same is true regarding unfitness to plead.

16 For excellent discussion, see Jones, "Insanity, Automatism, and the Burden of Proof on the Accused" (1995) 111 LQR 475.

17 Or at least if, following proof of the actus reus, mens rea can be inferred upon presumption of the defendant's sanity.

whether the offence is one of strict liability or, alternatively, one in which mens rea is unexpressed but in fact required (sometimes called an "implied mens rea offence"). In the latter case, the burden of proof can best be summarised as follows:

(i)   Where the statute states expressly that something is an element of the offence, then the prosecution must prove that and every other specified element beyond reasonable doubt, in accordance with step (i) above (§ 4.1). In particular, the prosecution must actively prove any specifed mental elements, and those mental elements may not be presumed.[18]

(ii)   However, if mens rea is not specified in the statute but is instead an implied requirement, then step (i) above applies only to the actus reus. The mens rea will be presumed, once the prosecution has proved the actus reus, unless there is evidence suggesting that mens rea was lacking. In the absence of such evidence, the defendant has an *evidential* onus to point to evidence that suggests why there might be a reasonable doubt whether the mens rea element was present. The onus on the defendant is no more than evidential; once it is discharged, the prosecution must prove mens rea beyond reasonable doubt.

That the latter rule applies for crimes of implied mens rea was recognised by the Court of Appeal in *R v Strawbridge*.[19] We shall return to its discussion once we have considered strict and absolute liability offences.

4.1.2 No presumption of intention
Proving mens rea is often difficult. It is impossible to look directly into the minds of defendants in order to know whether they had mens rea at the time of the offence. Usually, if the defendant does not himself confess to having it, the prosecution will be put to proving the relevant state of mind through supporting evidence, eg of the defendant's actions before, during, and after the actus reus occurred. Suppose that D is found to have shot V. If there is evidence that D planned the shooting in advance, this may be admissible to support the allegation that D's actions were intentional. The same is true if it is shown that D took careful aim at V's heart before pulling the trigger. In this case, proof by the prosecution that the prohibited harm (ie V's death) was a natural consequence of D's actions will support the inference that D intended it. Similarly, proof that the defendant foresaw the outcome (for example, because D knew the gun was loaded) may also help to support such a conclusion. Inferences of this variety depend upon a recognition that there is no reasonable interpretation of the evidence other than that the defendant had mens rea.

But such inferences are a matter of evidence only. They are neither irrebuttable, nor are they substantive rules of criminal law. In New Zealand, intention is a purely subjective concept, and any inference made from the evidence is *not* a presumption. It may, for instance, be undermined by the fact that when D pointed the gun at V, she was too intoxicated to recognise the

---

18   *R v Strawbridge* [1970] NZLR 909 at 915 (CA).

19   [1970] NZLR 909 at 915 (CA). See § 4.3.2.2.

obvious consequence.[20] Where the prosecution is obliged to prove mens rea, it must do so beyond reasonable doubt. Supporting evidence, for example, of foresight, is simply a part of what the prosecution may show in order to convince the court that, in light of all the evidence, it may safely conclude, beyond reasonable doubt, that D had the required mens rea.[21]

4.2 STRICT AND ABSOLUTE LIABILITY

Not every offence against the criminal law involves the sort of public condemnation that is implicit in a conviction for homicide. We argued in chapter 1 that serious criminal offences, where considerable public stigma attaches to a conviction, should always stipulate some form of mens rea element that must be proved before the defendant may be convicted, in order to avoid inflicting "the disgrace of criminality"[22] upon defendants who are not at fault when harm occurs. By contrast a parking offence, for instance, involves little or no stigma, so the need for a mens rea element is not as pressing.

There are many offences of a regulatory nature (sometimes called Public Welfare Regulatory Offences) which do not have a true mens rea ingredient. These fall into two categories, strict and absolute liability. For convenience, we will summarise the two categories before discussing them below:

(i)   *Strict liability*: The prosecution is required to prove the actus reus, but in relation to one or more elements of the actus reus,[23] there is no mens rea element to prove. However, the defendant can prove absence of fault on his part in order to exculpate himself.

(ii) *Absolute liability*: The offence is complete upon proof of the actus reus. There is no requirement to prove mens rea, nor can the defendant claim an absence of fault in his own defence.[24]

---

20   *R v Kamipeli* [1975] 2 NZLR 610 at 617 (CA). Contrast the English case *DPP v Smith* [1961] AC 290, also reported as *R v Smith* [1960] 3 All ER 161 (HL), which held that (i) if the reasonable person would have foreseen that outcome, then the defendant must be taken to have done so; and (ii) if the defendant foresaw it, then he intended it. *Smith* was later reversed in the UK by legislation, and was treated as wrongly decided by the Privy Council in *Frankland and Moore v R* [1987] AC 576, [1987] 2 WLR 1251 (PC).

21   Cf *R v Noel* [1960] NZLR 212 at 215, 216.

22   *Warner v Metropolitan Police Commr* [1969] 2 AC 256 at 272, [1968] 2 All ER 356 at 360 (HL) (Lord Reid).

23   An offence may properly be regarded as being of strict liability even though mens rea is required regarding other elements of the actus reus: *R v Lemon; R v Gay News Ltd* [1979] AC 617 at 656, [1979] 1 All ER 898 at 920 (HL) (Lord Edmund-Davies). This classification will sometimes be misleading, for example where strict liability goes only to a foreseeable consequence of the other actus reus elements, which themselves require mens rea. Careless driving causing death, contrary to s 56 Transport Act 1962, is an offence of this form: the fact that no additional fault is required about the death itself hardly makes it in substance an offence of strict liability. Indeed, fatalities are precisely the sort of reason why careless driving is culpable.

24   In both strict liability and absolute liability offences the prosecution must still prove the actus reus beyond reasonable doubt.

(One word of caution. In England, the terms "strict liability" and "absolute liability" are used almost interchangeably, a phenomenon that is likely to mislead the unwary from another jurisdiction. The same is true of cases decided in New Zealand before 1983. A distinction between the two types of regulatory offence was first drawn explicitly in New Zealand by the Court of Appeal in *Civil Aviation Dept v MacKenzie*.[25])

Strict and (in particular) absolute liability offences appear to have emerged in England during the nineteenth century, in the wake of the industrial revolution, as a convenient means with which to deal with rapidly changing social and industrial practices.[26] They are a creation of statute rather than the common law.[27] Most often they owe their existence to a perception that the need to protect the public might on occasion justify convicting people of offences even where they were not necessarily at fault; especially though not invariably where the harm involved resulted from a specialised activity, one which might naturally lend itself to control by regulatory rather than "truly criminal" prohibitions. Even the enforcement of such offences tends to be distinctive. They are frequently patrolled not by the police, but by specialist agencies created to monitor and control the effects of particular types of activity such as pollution and industrial safety. Habits of prosecution differ also. In practice, it appears that while prosecution is a typical response of the police to breaches of the law, regulatory agencies by contrast tend to prosecute only for recurring or very serious breaches of the law.[28]

4.2.1 Strict liability

The leading modern case on strict liability is Canadian. Traditionally, English law has consigned regulatory offences to the category of absolute liability unless the offence involved is "truly criminal"[29] in nature (in which case mens rea will be required), or the statute expressly directs otherwise. This approach leaves the courts with only a rather simplistic choice between the extremes of requiring full mens rea and making an offence absolute.[30] In *R v City of Sault Ste Marie*,[31] the Supreme Court of Canada decided that although mens rea need not be an essential ingredient of an offence, an alternative to absolute liability was nonetheless possible: there might be a defence available of "total absence of

---

25 [1983] NZLR 78, also reported as *MacKenzie v Civil Aviation Dept* (1983) 1 CRNZ 38 (CA).

26 See, for example, Carson, "Symbolic and Instrumental Dimensions of Early Factory Legislation" in Hood (ed), *Crime, Criminology and Public Policy*, London, Heinemann Educational, 1974; Carson, "The Conventionalisation of Early Factory Crime" (1979) 7 Int J Soc Law 37.

27 With the isolated exceptions, at common law, of public nuisance and criminal libel.

28 See, for example, Hawkins, *Environment and Enforcement*, Oxford, Clarendon Press, 1984; Hutter, *The Reasonable Arm of the Law*, 1988.

29 Cf *Gammon v A-G of Hong Kong* [1985] AC 1 at 14, [1984] 2 All ER 503 at 508 (Lord Scarman).

30 *Sweet v Parsley* [1970] AC 132, [1969] 1 All ER 347.

31 (1978) 85 DLR (3d) 161 (water pollution). See, for analysis, Hutchinson, "*Sault Ste Marie*, Mens Rea and the Halfway House: Public Welfare Offences Get a Home of Their Own" (1979) 17 Osgoode Hall LJ 415.

fault", the onus of proof for which would lie on the defendant. This third category, which the Court named strict liability, was characterised as follows:[32]

the doing of the prohibited act *prima facie* imports the offence, leaving it open to the accused to avoid liability by proving that he took all reasonable care. This involves consideration of what a reasonable man would have done in the circumstances. The defence will be available if the accused reasonably believed in a mistaken set of facts which, if true, would render the act or omission innocent,[33] or if he took all reasonable steps to avoid the particular event.

The Supreme Court thus claimed a middle ground that the House of Lords has denied itself. Indeed, it went further and held that public welfare regulatory offences, if they were not found to require proof of full mens rea, should presumptively involve strict rather than absolute liability.[34] In New Zealand, the view of the Canadian Supreme Court was endorsed by the Court of Appeal in *Civil Aviation Dept v MacKenzie*[35] and the other leading case, *Millar v MOT*.[36] A large number of offences have now been held to be of strict liability.[37]

The effect of these decisions is that proof of strict liability offences is prima facie complete as soon as the prosecution proves, beyond reasonable doubt, that the actus reus has occurred. However, it is possible for the defendant to show that the occurrence of the actus reus was not something for which he was at fault. By contrast with the actus reus, and with normal rules about proof of mens rea, the burden of proving absence of fault rests with the defendant, on the balance of probabilities.

4.2.1.1 *The nature of the defence*

Usually described as "absence of fault", in essence the defence can be made out by showing that the occurrence of the actus reus was not something the defendant could reasonably have prevented, or — if he in fact caused the actus reus — that he did so without being at fault (ie without being negligent). If the actus reus occurred because of factual ignorance or mistake on the defendant's part, then he will be required to prove that his ignorance or mistake was a reasonable one. An example where the facts would support such a defence is provided by *Finau v Dept of Labour*,[38] in which D was prosecuted for remaining in New Zealand beyond the expiry date of her temporary entry permit. D's defence succeeded: owing to pregnancy she had been refused carriage upon an

---

32 (1978) 85 DLR (3d) 161 at 181, 182, [1978] 2 SCR 1299 at1326.

33 The *R v Tolson* defence: (1889) 23 QBD 168, [1886-90] All ER Rep 26. Compare, in Australia, *Proudman v Dayman* (1941) 67 CLR 536 at 540, [1944] ALR 64 at 65 (Dixon J); Howard, "Strict Responsibility in the High Court of Australia" (1960) 76 LQR 547. See also Brett, "Strict Responsibility: Possible Solutions" (1974) 37 MLR 417.

34 (1978) 85 DLR (3d) 161 at 182, [1978] 2 SCR 1299 at 1326. See § 4.3.3.2(d). The policy reasons for preferring strict liability are stated at 171, at 1310.

35 [1983] NZLR 78, also reported as *MacKenzie v Civil Aviation Dept* (1983) 1 CRNZ 38 (CA) (dangerous flying).

36 [1986] 1 NZLR 660, (1986) 2 CRNZ 216 (CA) (driving while disqualified).

37 A collection can be found in *Adams* § CA20.47.

38 [1984] 2 NZLR 396 (CA).

airline, and it was therefore impossible for her to avoid committing the actus reus.

Impossibility is not itself required to sustain the defence; what counts is an absence of fault. In *Dept of Health v Multichem Laboratories Ltd*,[39] D was charged with supplying a medicine to the Auckland Hospital Board Pharmacy before consent to its distribution had been obtained from the Department of Health. Even though it was possible for D to choose not to supply the medicine, and also possible for D to have checked that consent had been obtained, the High Court accepted D's defence that the omission to do so was reasonable.

Although impossibility or involuntariness will generally also deny criminal responsibility for the actus reus,[40] sometimes that impossibility may be a consequence of earlier conduct by D.[41] In such cases the absence of fault defence will still be needed.[42] To illustrate, the facts of *Finau* may be contrasted with those in the earlier case *Tifaga v Dept of Labour*.[43] In *Tifaga*, D's entry permit had similarly expired. He claimed that it had proved impossible for him to leave the country because he had not enough money to purchase an air ticket. Rejecting his claim, the Court of Appeal opined that D's failure to retain enough funds was his own fault, and therefore a defence did not arise.

4.2.1.2 *The standard of care required*
It may be that a scenario akin to *Tifaga* is what is contemplated when the defence is termed one of *total* absence of fault.[44] Although in considering the phrase Barker J has held that "total" adds nothing to "absence of fault",[45] it does help to emphasise that the defence is not established merely by proving the defendant was not at fault during the very moments that the actus reus occurred. The defendant must show also that he was blameless antecedently,[46] ie that he took "*all* reasonable care", and not merely some reasonable steps. This point was once made by Chapman J in the context of a similarly-worded statutory defence:

> an acquittal on this ground is not secured by showing that in the ordinary sense reasonable care has been taken; the very words of the section must be pursued, and

---

39   [1987] 1 NZLR 334. Note that the defence in this case was statutory.

40   §§ 3.3, 3.3.2.

41   See § 3.3.3.

42   Compare *Keech v Pratt* [1994] 1 NZLR 65, also reported as *Police v Pratt* (1993) 10 CRNZ 659. Thus it seems that automatism will not excuse a defendant whose automatism is due to antecedent fault, such as self-induced intoxication. *O'Neill v MOT* [1985] 2 NZLR 513 suggests that involuntariness due to intoxication will only be a defence to strict liability offences where the defendant did not know that she was consuming alcohol (or drugs). There is no defence where the defendant ought to have known she could be affected by alcohol; nor where she voluntarily consumes alcohol without knowing that it was too much.

43   [1980] 2 NZLR 235 (CA). Note that this case was decided before *MacKenzie*; thus see also § 4.2.2 (absolute liability).

44   Cf *Millar v MOT* [1986] 1 NZLR 660 at 668, (1986) 2 CRNZ 216 at 225 (CA).

45   *Police v Starkey* [1989] 2 NZLR 373 at 379, (1989) 4 CRNZ 400 at 405, 406.

46   Cf *Police v Creedon* [1976] 1 NZLR 571 at 582, lines 35-39 (Richmond J).

the defendant must prove that all reasonable steps have been taken to avoid an offence.[47]

If that represents a difference at all from ordinary negligence, it is surely a minor one.[48] More significantly, it also appears that the defence is a purely objective one and seemingly independent of any of the defendant's personal inadequacies. This suggests that the standard of care demanded is that of negligence when operating as an actus reus, rather than mens rea, term.[49] Thus the defence will not be available if the defendant's mistake was one which a person of average intellect should not have made, notwithstanding that the defendant himself was of low intelligence. According to Richardson J, in *MacKenzie*:

> a high standard of care is properly expected of a defendant in such a case and he must prove that he did what a reasonable man would have done. It would not in our view be appropriate to have a variable standard of negligence depending on subjective considerations affecting the individual concerned, as was suggested in argument at one point.[50]

This statement clearly excludes consideration of the defendant's capacities. It will be no answer for her to claim that because of individual peculiarities he was incapable of attaining the standard of reasonableness that the no-fault defence requires.[51] His Honour cited in support of this proposition the earlier case of *Police v Creedon*,[52] in which Cooke J had approved the assertion by Megaw LJ in *R v Gosney* that fault does not "necessarily involve moral blame":

> Thus there is fault if an inexperienced or a naturally poor driver, while straining every nerve to do the right thing, falls below the standard of a competent and careful driver. Fault involves a failure, a falling below the care or skill of a competent and experienced driver, in relation to the manner of the driving and to the relevant circumstances of the case.[53]

The "failure", then, need not be one for which the individual is culpable.

4.2.1.3 *The justification of strict liability*

4.2.1.3(a) *The no-fault defence*

The argument for having a strict liability fault standard in certain offences is made in two stages. The first step involves arguing that to require something less than full mens rea (intention or recklessness etc) is appropriate in such

---

47 *Canterbury Central Co-op Dairy Co Ltd v McKenzie* [1923] NZLR 426 at 428.

48 Cf *Buchanans Foundry Ltd v Dept of Labour* [1996] 3 NZLR 112 at 119.

49 See § 3.5.3.

50 [1983] NZLR 78 at 85, also reported as *MacKenzie v Civil Aviation Dept* (1983) 1 CRNZ 38 at 45 (CA).

51 Cf France, "Absolute liability since *MacKenzie*" [1987] NZLJ 50 at 51; Orchard, "The Judicial Categorisation of Offences" (1983) 2 Canterbury LR 81 at 93, 94; Orchard, "The Defence of Absence of Fault in Australasia and Canada" in Smith (ed), *Criminal Law: Essays in Honour of J C Smith*, London, Butterworths, 1987, 114, 118.

52 [1976] 1 NZLR 571 at 586, 587. See also at 575, line 40 (McCarthy P), 582, line 35 (Richmond J), and 586, lines 38, 39 (Cooke J).

53 [1971] 2 QB 674 at 680, [1971] 3 All ER 220.

offences. The second stage is the claim that the other major alternative, absolute liability, is *not* appropriate. This second limb is dealt with below, in the discussion of absolute liability (§ 4.2.2).

The reason most often given for abandoning a full mens rea requirement is that protection of the public sometimes requires a high standard of care on the part of those who undertake risk-creating activities.[54] Proper care needs to be taken by such persons, and without liability for negligence the careless will be able to transfer the considerable costs of their negligence to the rest of society, without having any serious incentive to reduce or eliminate those risks. The threat of criminal liability supplies a motive for persons in risk-generating activities to adopt precautions, which might not otherwise be taken, in order to ensure mishaps and errors are eliminated.[55]

In practice, this point seems to be reflected in the law. Regulatory offences are often found where there is a need to protect the public from risks created by industrial and other specialist activities. Yet this surely cannot be a decisive justification. The public needs also to be protected from assaults, damage to property, and the like, yet these are not strict liability offences; they require proof of mens rea in the ordinary way.

Fortunately for strict liability, the force of this initial point is reinforced by other factors. One is that, in New Zealand, strict liability is a partial substitute for tortious liability for personal injury, which has been displaced by accident compensation legislation. Thus the usual economic incentive to avoid negligent accidents — the prospect of civil liability — is much less effective here than it may be overseas. Additionally, strict liability is particularly appropriate where the offence is directed toward controlling the activity of corporations. There are three reasons for this. First, corporate convictions do not normally involve the same level of stigma as do those attaching to individuals, nor the same practical implications. Secondly, corporate activity is characteristically on a larger scale than that by individuals, and correspondingly creates greater levels of social threat. Finally, and most importantly, the proof of mens rea presents special difficulty in the context of corporate bodies, since there is no one person who can be identified as the agent when a corporation acts. The negligence standard contained in strict liability, by contrast, is particularly appropriate to companies and the like, since it is measured by reference to conduct rather than mental state.

All this having been said, it is arguable that there is a case for reform. The above considerations do not establish why criminal rather than civil sanctions should be used to regulate the activities involved. Even if private individuals cannot pursue a claim for damages, it may be open to the State (by legislative reform) to pursue miscreants through an administrative system of regulations that applies a standard of strict liability without the accompanying

---

54   This may help to explain why an objective, rather than subjective, non-fault standard is demanded of the defendant (§ 4.2.1.2). For an elaboration of the assumption of risk argument, see Honoré, "Responsibility and Luck — the Moral Basis of Strict Liability" (1988) 104 LQR 530.

55   *R v City of Sault Ste Marie* (1978) 85 DLR (3d) 161 at 171, [1978] 2 SCR 1299 at 1310, 1311.

connotations of a criminal conviction. The moral authority of the criminal law is undermined by the extension of liability to what are, in essence, mere regulatory violations.[56]

On the other hand, however, against this argument it may be said that the description, "mere regulatory violations", somewhat underplays the vital public protection role that construction standards, work-safety standards, pollution standards, etc discharge. Setting up a new system to try these matters as civil infractions rather than crimes would be a major task, and might be seen as downgrading the importance of effective regulation. There is little evidence that the proliferation of regulatory crimes has blunted the distinction between doing wrong and getting something wrong.

4.2.1.3(b) *The burden of proof*

While absolute liability is controversial since it involves convicting the blameless, strict liability is primarily a fault-based standard,[57] and the main issue it raises for justification is a different one: is it right to reverse the onus of proof in these offences?

Most plausibly, the motive for abandoning ordinary proof requirements is convenience. Administration of justice would be more expensive and greatly slowed if the prosecution were put to proving mens rea in respect of every minor offence before the courts. This is perhaps the simplest reason why one might be prepared to require the defendant to exculpate himself, as strict liability does. However, it is buttressed by the fact that frequently in areas regulated by public welfare offences, the defendant is better-placed to explain the nature of his own specialist activity, and the precautions he has taken, than is the prosecutor. This is all the more true of activities (and transgressions) by large and complex corporations, where it may be very difficult for an external prosecutor to prove the conduct of particular individuals within such organisations. Given these factors, it is arguable that, as well as being more efficient, the shift in evidential burdens may also result in better justice. In many cases it may be problematic for the prosecution to disprove a false claim of no-fault — even one that would not be established on the balance of probabilities.

Regulatory enforcement needs to be done efficiently — a Government cannot afford to spend large amounts of money on prosecutions, especially where the offences involved are common and involve no serious harm. (Where serious harm does ensue, the prosecution should in any event be for a more serious crime involving mens rea.) The costs of controlling economic activity are, in truth, part of the costs of carrying on that activity, and it therefore makes some sense that the burden of establishing an absence of fault should be borne as a form of production expense by those who voluntarily initiate risk-creating activities.

---

56   Compare Robinson, "The Criminal-Civil Distinction and the Utility of Desert" (1996) 76 Boston ULR 201 at 212-214.

57   Though, for exceptions, see § 4.2.1.2.

Yet it is important to note that, as with a no-fault defence (above), the argument here trades upon the fact that conviction for a strict liability offence does not carry the same moral opprobrium and social stigma as does conviction for an offence that is "truly" criminal in nature. Indeed, that was the basis on which both the New Zealand Court of Appeal and the Supreme Court of Canada distinguished *Woolmington*.[58] Therefore, a cautionary note is appropriate. In *Woolmington*, Viscount Sankey LC had stated that, apart from insanity and statutory exceptions, the prosecution must prove guilt "no matter what the charge or where the trial".[59] Danger lies in the fact that, if a defendant's interests are to be subordinated to those of the general public in "regulatory" offences, the line denied in *Woolmington* between such offences and "true" crimes is not always easy to draw. *MacKenzie* itself involved an offence punishable by imprisonment; surely placing it in the category of serious rather than minor transgressions? It is worth noting that the US Model Penal Code eschews such a possibility, asserting that the possibility of imprisonment should be a conclusive reason against imposing strict liability.[60] We return to the difficulty of categorising offences below (§ 4.3.3). But if a clear distinction between "regulatory" and "truly criminal" offences cannot be drawn, or if that distinction fails to capture the public imagination, then the arguments[61] for retaining the presumption of innocence — and against reversing the onus of proof in strict liability — are much harder to surmount.

Placing the onus upon the defendant in strict liability cases may now be inconsistent with s 25(c) New Zealand Bill of Rights Act 1990, which secures to everyone charged with an offence "the right to be presumed innocent until proved guilty according to law". However, if it does contravene s 25(c), strict liability in its present form had been held by the courts to be saved by s 5 of that same Act, which permits limitations to the rights contained in the Act so long as they "can be demonstrably justified in a free and democratic society".[62]

4.2.2 Absolute liability

In offences of absolute liability, proof beyond reasonable doubt of the actus reus is sufficient to convict the defendant, and even absence of fault is no defence:[63]

---

58 *R v City of Sault Ste Marie* (1978) 85 DLR (3d) 161 at 174, 175, [1978] 2 SCR 1299 at 1316; *Civil Aviation Dept v MacKenzie* [1983] NZLR 78 at 84, 85, also reported as *MacKenzie v Civil Aviation Dept* (1983) 1 CRNZ 38 at 44, 45 (CA).

59 [1935] AC 462 at 481, [1935] All ER Rep 1 at 8 (HL); compare *Mancini v DPP* [1942] AC 1 at 11, [1941] 3 All ER 272 at 279 (Viscount Simon LC); Orchard, "The Judicial Categorisation of Offences" (1983) 2 Canterbury LR 81 at 94.

60 § 6.02(4). Though a contrary statute would not be unconstitutional: *US v Freed* 401 US 601, 28 L Ed 2d 356 (1971).

61 See §§ 4.1, 4.1.1.1.

62 *Joe v Police* 21/12/95, Goddard J, HC Wellington AP230/95; following *R v Wholesale Travel Group Inc* (1991) 84 DLR (4th) 161, [1991] 3 SCR 154, a decision by the Supreme Court on corresponding provisions in the Canadian Charter of Rights and Freedoms.

63 *R v City of Sault Ste Marie* (1978) 85 DLR (3d) 161 at 170, [1978] 2 SCR 1299 at 1310.

"absolute liability" entails conviction on proof merely that the defendant committed the prohibited act constituting the *actus reus* of the offence. There is no relevant mental element. It is no defence that the accused was entirely without fault. He may be morally innocent in every sense, yet be branded as a malefactor and punished as such.

An example of such an offence may be found in s 17(1) Machinery Act 1950, which requires owners of machinery to ensure that dangerous parts thereof are securely fenced. In *AHI Operations Ltd v Dept of Labour*,[64] the defendant was convicted under the section notwithstanding that its machine did originally have a guard mechanism, which had been removed (contrary to instructions) by an employee. Heron J held that the offence was complete upon proof merely that the guard was absent.

However, it does appear that a combination of involuntariness (or, as the case may be, impossibility) *and* absence of fault on the part of a defendant will be sufficient to exculpate. The roots of this defence are to be found in *Kilbride v Lake*.[65] In that case, D was convicted at first instance of permitting his car to be on the road without displaying a current warrant of fitness.[66] The car had been parked by D on a street. At the time of parking, a warrant of fitness was on display. However, while the car was unattended, the warrant of fitness became detached; hence D's prosecution. His appeal was argued before the Supreme Court on the issue whether the offence was one of absolute liability or mens rea. Woodhouse J, however, decided the case on a different footing. The actus reus of the offence, his Honour said, was "the presence of the car combined with the absence of the warrant".[67] Given the facts, D's liability could only be predicated, if at all, upon his failure immediately to replace the warrant when it became detached. But (it was conceded) that failure was involuntary since D had had no opportunity to rectify the situation. On this basis, D should not be convicted even if the offence was absolute:

a person cannot be made criminally responsible for an act or omission unless it was done or omitted in circumstances where there was some other course open to him. If this condition is absent, any act or omission must be involuntary.[68]

The qualification, that the involuntariness must be accompanied by an absence of fault, was articulated by the Court of Appeal in *Tifaga v Dept of Labour*.[69] In that case, the impossible situation in which D found himself was self-induced: his inability to leave the country before his immigration permit expired was attributable to his own failure to retain enough money to buy an air ticket. It would have been different, and he would have escaped conviction,

---

64 [1986] 1 NZLR 645. Criticised by France, "Absolute Liability Since *MacKenzie*" [1987] NZLJ 50 at 52. The defendant was found in any event not to have been without fault, so would have been convicted even had the offence been one of strict liability. For a survey of other cases imposing absolute liability, see *Adams* § CA20.51.

65 [1962] NZLR 590. Also discussed at § 3.3.2.

66 Contrary to reg 52 Traffic Regulations 1956.

67 [1962] NZLR 590 at 592.

68 Ibid at 593.

69 [1980] 2 NZLR 235 (CA).

if the impossibility had arisen for reasons beyond his control: if, for instance, D had been robbed of the money while en route to buy his ticket, or had been injured and hospitalised when going to the airport;[70] or if, as in *Finau v Dept of Labour*, she had been refused passage on grounds of pregnancy.[71]

The discussion in *Tifaga* suggests that, in addition to involuntariness or impossibility, necessity may also be available as a defence provided the circumstances of the necessity do not arise through any fault of the defendant.[72] The necessity, however, would have to be such as to leave the defendant with no practical alternative but to permit or bring about the actus reus.[73]

One question arises regarding the burden of proof. There appears to be no decision on this point, but since absolute liability is not subsumed by *Civil Aviation Dept v MacKenzie* it is prima facie governed by *Woolmington v DPP*, and the prosecution has the burden of disproving any defence suggested by the evidence. Nonetheless it may be arguable, by analogy with the onus upon defendants in strict liability cases, that in offences of absolute liability the defendant should bear the burden of proving his defence to the balance of probabilities.

4.2.2.1 *The place of absolute liability*

By contrast with England, where regulatory offences are characteristically absolute rather than strict, in New Zealand the conclusion that an offence is of absolute liability should only be made where the statute imposes it "in clear terms or by necessary implication".[74] It is submitted that this approach is the correct one: there is no other justification for a court to hold an offence absolute rather than strict.

It is not sensible for the law to demand that defendants do more than what is reasonable. The effect of doing so would be to force a defendant either to desist from the risk-creating activity altogether, or to persist and accept that he must run all risks, however esoteric and unlikely, of the prohibited harm occurring; and incur the ensuing conviction. The first option cannot be taken

---

70 Examples cited by Richardson J in *Tifaga* [1980] 2 NZLR 235 at 245, 246 (CA). See also *Sione v Labour Dept* [1972] NZLR 278; *Burns v Bidder* [1967] 2 QB 227, [1966] 3 All ER 29; *McCone v Police* [1971] NZLR 105 at 109 (CA); *R v Bamber* (1843) 5 QB 279, 114 ER 1254; *Stockdale v Coulson* [1974] 3 All ER 154, [1974] 1 WLR 1192 (distinguishing *Park v Lawton* [1911] 1 KB 588 on the basis that the impossibility in the earlier case arose through the defendant's own default); Patient, "Some Remarks about the Element of Voluntariness in Offences of Absolute Liability" [1968] Crim LR 23.

71 [1984] 2 NZLR 396 (CA). Section 14(5), under which Finau was prosecuted, was held in *Murray v Ongoongo* [1985] BCL 1843 to impose absolute liability — the right decision for the wrong reasons, according to Orchard: "Quasi-absolute Liability under the Immigration Act 1964" [1986] NZLJ 66.

72 [1980] 2 NZLR 235 at 243, 244 (CA). Compare, in England, *Smith and Hogan*, 116, 117; in Canada, *R v Cancoil Thermal Corp and Parkinson* (1986) 27 CCC (3d) 295 at 301, 302, 52 CR (3d) 188 at 197; *R v Walker* (1979) 48 CCC (2d) 126 at 134, 135; *R v Kennedy* (1972) 7 CCC (2d) 42; *R v Breau* (1959) 125 CCC 84, 32 CR 13.

73 Cf *Burns v Nowell* (1880) 5 QBD 444. There is a brief discussion of these questions in Sayre, "Public Welfare Offences" (1933) 33 Col LR 55 at 75-78.

74 *Millar v MOT* [1986] 1 NZLR 660, (1986) 2 CRNZ 216 (CA).

seriously. It is surely not the intention of the law to discourage people from entering into productive activity altogether. The nation's economy would not last very long if that were the outcome. Rather, the aim of regulatory laws must be to discourage people from entering into an activity (or from executing it in a manner) which creates *unreasonable* risks of the unwanted harm occurring. But *that* aim can be achieved by strict liability. Absolute liability forces the blameless defendant to become a gratuitous risk-taker, subject to a criminal legal lottery over which she has no reasonable control. If she is unlucky, she will be convicted. A lottery is no basis on which to conduct the nation's criminal law. Such a draconian system, moreover, is likely to promote cynicism and disrespect for the law among innocent people who are labelled criminal "offenders" by their conviction.

It is doubtful whether there are any significant advantages whatsoever to be gained from the device of absolute liability. While it simplifies the prosecution's task, that may also be achieved through the use of strict liability, and since the defendant's lack of fault will be relevant both to a defence of impossibility and (otherwise) to sentencing, the evidence may as well be heard straightforwardly before conviction. Neither is it clear that absolute liability is a more effective deterrent than mens rea offences or strict liability.[75]

Most importantly of all, it is just wrong to convict the innocent. To do so is, quite simply, a misuse of the criminal law, which is the most condemnatory institution available to society. If someone does not deserve to be convicted then they should not be. To convict innocent people violates the most basic tenet of criminal liability. It is unjust.[76] It also breaches the requirement for fair warning, since citizens have no way of knowing or predicting when they might be about to incur criminal liability.[77] No doubt the public need to be protected from the harms that regulatory offences are designed to prevent. But the public need to be protected, too, from random liability.

To the claim that absolute liability tends to be imposed only for offences which involve little or no public stigma, it may be responded that transgressors still suffer the rigours of the criminal process, with associated costs and loss of time, not to mention the fact of a conviction. And if the conviction is a trivial consideration, why make the wrongdoing a criminal rather than civil or administrative matter? Thor's hammer was not meant for driving nails. We undermine and belittle the criminal law when we use it for trivial tasks.

4.3 THE MENS REA CATEGORISATION OF PARTICULAR OFFENCES

So far in this and the previous chapter we have concentrated on explaining the leading varieties of mens rea that may be required in an offence. But a further question arises every time we consider a particular offence. *Which* mens rea state is required to satisfy *that* offence? The answer varies from offence to

---

75 See Jackson, "*Storkwain*: A Case Study in Strict liability and Self-Regulation" [1991] Crim LR 892; Richardson, "Strict Liability for Regulatory Crime: The Empirical Research" [1987] Crim LR 295; Baldwin, "Why Rules Don't Work" (1990) 53 MLR 321.

76 See § 1.2.2.1.

77 Cf § 1.4.3.

offence: for rape, negligence will suffice; for assault, intention is required; operating an overloaded vehicle, by contrast, is an offence of strict liability. Often the answer will be found straightforwardly in the explicit words of the statute that creates the offence. For example, s 197 Crimes Act 1961 makes it an offence "wilfully" to disable another person: the offence cannot be committed inadvertently. But frequently, a statute will specify only the actus reus elements, and be silent regarding whether a form of mens rea is required. In such instances the courts must decide.

4.3.1 The options available before *Millar v MOT*

It now appears that there are four alternative determinations that a Court can make regarding a statute that does not itself state what mens rea if any is required. Before the Court of Appeal's decision in *Millar v MOT*, there had been at least seven. The seven categories, which were set out by Cooke P and Richardson J in *Millar*, are differentiated by whether or not mens rea is required, and by various combinations of the burden of proof and the availability of an exculpatory defence:[78]

(1) *Simple mens rea*: This is the standard category for truly criminal offences. Mens rea here means intention or recklessness (or knowledge or belief, as appropriate). Actual foresight is required, and negligence will not do.[79] The prosecution has a full probative burden to prove mens rea beyond reasonable doubt. (It should be emphasised that in all seven categories the prosecution has to prove the actus reus beyond reasonable doubt.)

(2) *Assumed mens rea rebutted by an honest belief*: In this type of case the prosecution must prove the actus reus as usual, but mens rea will then be presumed in the absence of any evidence to the contrary. Mens rea once again means intention or recklessness. Thus there is an evidential burden on the defendant to point to evidence suggesting that he did not foresee the possibility of the actus reus (ie that he was not reckless). Upon such evidence being raised, the prosecution then assumes the full burden of proving mens rea beyond reasonable doubt.[80]

(3) *Assumed mens rea rebutted by a defence of honest and reasonable belief*: Here mens rea is once again presumed, and the defendant has an evidential onus to argue that she had an honest and reasonable belief in facts that, if true, would have made her actions innocent. If such evidence is raised, the burden reverts to the prosecution to prove, beyond reasonable doubt, that she did not have an honest and reasonable belief. This category had earlier been recognised by the Court of Appeal in *R v*

---

78 [1986] 1 NZLR 660 at 664-666, (1986) 2 CRNZ 216 at 221-223 (CA).

79 *R v Walker* [1958] NZLR 810 at 815, 816 (CA); also *R v Howe* [1982] 1 NZLR 618 at 623 (CA), as modified by *R v Harney* [1987] 2 NZLR 576 (CA).

80 See *R v Wood* [1982] 2 NZLR 233 at 237 (CA); *R v Metuariki* [1986] 1 NZLR 488, (1986) 2 CRNZ 116 (CA).

Strawbridge,[81] in the context of an offence of cultivating prohibited drugs.

(4) *No mens rea required, but a defence is available of honest and reasonable mistake*: In this category the probative burden rests upon the defendant to prove on the balance of probabilities that he had an honest and reasonable belief in facts that, if true, would have made his actions innocent.[82]

(5) *Strict liability*: As in § 4.2.1: no mens rea is required, but the defence of absence of fault is available. The burden of proving that defence rests upon the defendant (to the balance of probabilities). This category was regarded by the Court as broader in scope than (4), as it does not confine the available defence to one involving a mistake.

(6) *Assumed mens rea rebutted by a defence of honest belief*: The prosecution need not prove mens rea, and the defendant has the burden of proving, on the balance of probabilities, that she did not advert to the actus reus (in effect, that she lacked mens rea). This category is similar to that in (2), except that the defendant bears a higher onus of proof. It had been applied to the offence of selling an indecent publication[83] by the Court of Appeal in *R v Ewart*,[84] but was disapproved by the Privy Council in *Lim Chin Aik v R*,[85] and was effectively abolished by the Court of Appeal in *Strawbridge*.[86]

(7) *Absolute liability*.

4.3.2 The options available today

The Court of Appeal in *Millar* then proceeded to abolish three of these categories, by assimilating category (2) with simple mens rea (1), and by absorbing categories (4) and (6) within strict liability (5). Including the case where the statute itself specifies a mens rea requirement, this leaves a total of five options available, as follows.

---

81 [1970] NZLR 909 (CA). Cf the Australian cases of *He Kaw Teh v R* (1985) 157 CLR 523, 59 ALJR 620; *Kidd v Reeves* [1972] VR 563 and *Mayer v Marchant* (1973) 5 SASR 567; Adams, "Onus of Proof in Criminal Cases" in Clark (ed), *Essays on Criminal Law in New Zealand*, Wellington, Sweet & Maxwell, 1971, 67, 80-82.

82 *R v Tolson* (1889) 23 QBD 168, [1886-90] All ER Rep 26. See Howard, "Strict Responsibility in the High Court of Australia" (1960) 76 LQR 547; Campbell, "Crime by Omission" in Clark (ed), *Essays on Criminal Law in New Zealand*, Wellington, Sweet & Maxwell, 1971, 1, 16; Orchard, "The Defence of Absence of Fault in Australasia and Canada" in Smith (ed), *Criminal Law: Essays in Honour of J C Smith*, London, Butterworths, 1987, 114.

83 Contrary to the (then) Offensive Publications Act 1892.

84 (1906) 25 NZLR 709. Early English authority for this category includes *R v Prince* (1875) LR 2 CCR 154 at 161, 162, [1874-80] All ER Rep 881 at 890, 891 (Brett J); *Sherras v De Rutzen* [1895] 1 QB 918 at 921, [1895-99] All ER Rep 1167 at 1169 (Day J); also *Harding v Price* [1948] 1 KB 695 at 700, [1948] 1 All ER 283 at 284 (Goddard LCJ).

85 [1963] AC 160 at 173, [1963] 1 All ER 223 at 227, 228 (on appeal from Singapore). Compare *Warner v Metropolitan Police Commr* [1969] 2 AC 256 at 303, [1968] 2 All ER 356 at 386 (HL) (Lord Pierce).

86 [1970] NZLR 909 at 915, lines 24-26.

4.3.2.1 *Statutory mens rea elements*

Where the statute explicitly states a mens rea requirement, the situation is like category (1) above. The prosecution must prove that requirement beyond reasonable doubt.[87] This rule was left undisturbed in *Millar*, since the analysis by Cooke P and Richardson J was concerned only with cases where the statute does not state what, if any, mens rea element is required.[88]

4.3.2.2 *Implied mens rea*

It was said in *Millar* that "if there is any distinction between classes (1) and (2) in the foregoing list, it seems so narrow as not to be worth preserving".[89] Unfortunately, the Court of Appeal did not clearly resolve the further question: if there *is* a difference between the two categories, which one was abolished?

Beginning with the first part of that question, there is indeed a distinction between categories (1) and (2).[90] The difference is that in category (1) the prosecution has both a persuasive and an evidential burden to prove mens rea. In category (2) the evidential burden is on the defendant. This means that, upon proof by the prosecution of the actus reus, mens rea will be *presumed* in the absence of evidence to the contrary. It then falls to the defendant herself to adduce evidence, or point to evidence adduced by the prosecution,[91] which raises a reasonable doubt whether she in fact had mens rea. Once this evidential burden is discharged, the prosecution has the persuasive burden to prove mens rea beyond reasonable doubt.

By contrast, in category (1), the defendant only has a case to answer once the prosecution, besides proving the actus reus, has adduced sufficient evidence from which mens rea can be inferred. Often, this will impose upon the prosecution no greater burden than exists in category (2), since proof of the actus reus will usually supply evidence from which mens rea too can be inferred. If D loads his pistol, points it at V, and pulls the trigger, it is a natural inference that D intended to shoot V. Here a presumption adds nothing to the inference. Sometimes, however, the distinction will make a difference. Suppose that D is charged with possession of a prohibited drug, being a "magic mushroom".[92] Evidence is given that D picked the mushroom, which had been growing wild on a beach, just before he was arrested. Such evidence, which establishes the actus reus, might not support the inference that D knew the nature of the mushroom. If the offence falls within category (1), the prosecution will fail unless further evidence is introduced from which mens rea may be inferred as a fact. By contrast, if it belongs in category (2), mens rea will prima

---

87   Ibid at 915. Compare R v *Kamipeli* [1975] 2 NZLR 610 at 617, *Cvil Aviation Dept v MacKenzie* [1983] NZLR 78 at 85, also reported as *MacKenzie v Civil Aviation Dept* (1983) 1 CRNZ 38 at 45, 46 (CA) (negligence).

88   [1986] 1 NZLR 660 at 664, line 52, (1986) 2 CRNZ 216 at 221 (CA).

89   Ibid at 667, at 224.

90   For excellent discussion, see Orchard, "The Judicial Categorisation of Offences" (1983) 2 Canterbury LR 81 at 87-90.

91   *MacKenzie v Hawkins* [1975] 1 NZLR 165; *Police v Creedon* [1976] 1 NZLR 571 at 584 (Richmond J).

92   Cf R v *Metuariki* [1986] 1 NZLR 488, (1986) 2 CRNZ 116 (CA).

facie be presumed, where the presumption is rebuttable by evidence raising a reasonable doubt about the matter.

It might be thought that the upshot of the merger effected by *Millar* was to abolish category (2). In fact, although there is rarely any practical difference, it appears that the Court did away with category (1):

> absence of guilty knowledge is like the defences of provocation, automatism, self-defence and compulsion. There must be some evidence or material, either from the prosecution case or called by the defence, to raise the issue. In the absence of a foundation for a contrary view the offence will be inferred to have been committed unprovoked, knowingly, not in self-defence, free from compulsion.[93]

It is settled law that the defendant has an evidential onus to raise matters such as provocation, automatism, self-defence etc, and that their absence is presumed unless there is evidence to the contrary.[94] By likening mens rea to these elements, Cooke P and Richardson J seem to have held that where mens rea is an implied and not expressly-stated element of the offence, the defendant has an evidential onus to raise a reasonable doubt about the presence of mens rea. If it appears that the defendant may not have foreseen or intended the actus reus (ie that she did not have mens rea), that onus reverts to the prosecution, who must then prove mens rea beyond reasonable doubt.[95]

Our analysis may be controversial. In particular, note should be taken of Casey J's judgment, in which, he said, "I accept the conclusion that there is no practical difference between classes (1) and (2), involving offences in which mens rea is an ingredient . . . In such cases both the evidentiary and persuasive onus remain on the Crown."[96] This suggests that it is category (2), rather than (1), which has been displaced. However, the preservation of category (2) is consistent with the earlier decision by the Court of Appeal in *Strawbridge*, where North P had asserted that:

> . . . in New Zealand we have never interpreted *Woolmington*'s case as going any further than determining that the burden of proof at the end of, and on the whole of, the case lay on the Crown . . . we have however distinguished between cases where the offence consists in "knowingly" doing an act and cases where the word "knowingly" has been omitted. In the former class of case the Crown must prove knowledge on the part of the accused before it can be said that a *prima facie* case has been made out. In the latter class of case, on the other hand, knowledge of the wrongful nature of the act will be presumed in the absence of any evidence to the contrary . . . it is still true to say that it lies on the accused to point to some evidence which creates a reasonable doubt that he did not have a guilty mind.[97]

The language of *Strawbridge* is unequivocally that of presumption rather than inference. Neither the judgment by Casey J, nor any of the other

---

93   [1986] 1 NZLR 660 at 667, (1986) 2 CRNZ 216 at 224 (CA).

94   § 4.1, nn 4, 5.

95   Per § 4.1.1.4.

96   [1986] 1 NZLR 660 at 678, (1986) 2 CRNZ 216 at 236 (CA).

97   [1970] NZLR 909 at 915 (CA); concurring with Lord Diplock's dissent in *Sweet v Parsley* [1970] AC 132 at 164, [1969] 1 All ER 347 at 362, 363. See too *Sherras v De Rutzen* [1895] 1 QB 918, [1895-1899] All ER Rep 1167.

judgments in *Millar*, purports to overrule *Strawbridge* on this point. Rather, they appear to endorse it.[98] The reality that there is little practical difference between the two approaches can be seen, however, in the judgment of Somers J, who freely intermingles the language of presumption with that of inference.[99] Subsequent cases have been mixed in their analysis of this point. In *Police v Starkey*, Barker J cited Cooke P in *Millar*, and stated:

> Where the necessary mens rea is expressly set out as part of the definition of the offence . . . clearly that mental state must be affirmatively proved by the prosecution beyond reasonable doubt, with no evidential onus on the accused. But where, as in the present case, the requisite intention is merely implicit in the section, the necessary mens rea will be assumed in the absence of evidence to the contrary . . . It will then be open to the accused to lay a foundation for the defence of lack of mens rea, and the onus will be on the prosecution to prove mens rea beyond reasonable doubt.[100]

By contrast, in *Police v Bannin*, Fisher J uses the language of inference.[101] However, his Honour was not required to consider the point as carefully as did Barker J, and it is the latter who appears to have stated the law.[102]

For all that, should the issue ever come before the Court of Appeal for authoritative resolution, it is submitted that, to the extent that there *is* a difference between the two approaches, the one taken by Casey J is to be preferred. Suppose a case where proof of the actus reus does not, by itself, unambiguously support the inference that the defendant acted with mens rea.[103] Given that, as was said in *Strawbridge*, the prosecution has the burden of proving mens rea on the whole of, and at the end of, the case, there would seem no reason why the defendant should bear an evidential onus — and mens rea be presumed — where the prima facie evidence does not necessarily support that presumption. The language of inference is, in our view, to be preferred.

4.3.2.3 *Category (3): Strawbridge*

Category (3) occurs in *R v Strawbridge*. D was prosecuted for cultivation of cannabis. She sought to deny knowledge of the nature of the plant. The Court of Appeal held that, while the prosecution did not need to prove knowledge in order to make out a prima facie case, and knowledge should be presumed in the absence of evidence to the contrary, it was open to the defendant to point to

---

98   See [1986] 1 NZLR 660 at 667 (Cooke P and Richardson J), 675 (McMullin J), 676, 677 (Somers J), 678 (Casey J), (1986) 2 CRNZ 216 at 224, 232, 233, 234, 236 (CA).

99   Ibid at 676, 677, at 233, 234; compare at 678, at 236 (Casey J).

100 [1989] 2 NZLR 373 at 378, (1989) 4 CRNZ 400 at 404, 405.

101 [1991] 2 NZLR 237 at 246, also reported as *R v Police* (1990) 7 CRNZ 55 at 63: "The fact that the accused physically entered the house would, in the absence of mental abnormality, imply that he intended to do so." Note that the ulterior intention also needed for the offence in that case was an express statutory requirement.

102 Cf *R v Metuariki* [1986] 1 NZLR 488, (1986) 2 CRNZ 116 (CA); *R v Wood* [1982] 2 NZLR 233 at 237 (CA); *Summers v SPCA* [1991] 2 NZLR 469 at 473-475, (1990) 6 CRNZ 201 at 205-208. See generally *Adams* §§ CA20.42-20.44.

103 Cf *R v Keane* [1921] NZLR 581 at 584.

evidence that she honestly believed on reasonable grounds that her act was innocent.

This class of offence was described in *Millar* as "a troublesome anomaly, probably best done away with or severely confined".[104] Even by the time of *Millar*, most cases falling within its scope had already migrated to category (2), which "may be called *Strawbridge* without reasonable grounds".[105] The requirement that D's belief be reasonable was abandoned by the Court of Appeal following the English case of *DPP v Morgan*;[106] and it is now said that the reasonableness of D's claimed belief is relevant only to the evidential question whether that belief was in fact honestly held by D.

It seems, therefore, unlikely that an offence will now be held to fall within the *Strawbridge* category. Yet we cannot say for sure that this class of offence has been abolished. *Millar* does not expressly take that step. Moreover, the offence in *Strawbridge* is unlike those found in categories (4) through (6), which are now absorbed by strict liability. The case involves a serious criminal offence, punishable by a maximum of 14 years' imprisonment. Thus, it should now either become a full mens rea offence, or remain sui generis.

Strawbridge may be contrasted with *Police v Creedon*,[107] a case in which D was prosecuted for failing to yield the right of way at an intersection, in circumstances where (it was conceded) he was not at fault. Although the case was said in *Millar* to belong properly in category (5), the original decision fell within category (3), since the Court of Appeal in fact held that D bore only an evidential onus to suggest a lack of fault.[108] It is clear that *Creedon*, a mere traffic offence, does not survive *MacKenzie* and *Millar*.

4.3.2.4 *Strict liability*

See § 4.2.1 above. In *Millar*, strict liability was endorsed by the Court of Appeal as being best-placed to achieve "the object of justice aimed at by the other three classes" of offence, viz (3), (4), and (6).

4.3.2.5 *Absolute liability*

See § 4.2.2 above. This category of offence has survived unmolested. However, as was made clear in *Millar*, "there is a good deal less room for class 7, absolute liability, once it is accepted that class 5 is an available alternative under which the onus is on the defendant of proving total absence of fault".[109]

---

104 [1986] 1 NZLR 660 at 668, (1986) 2 CRNZ 216 at 224, 225 (CA) (Cooke P).

105 Ibid at 667, at 224.

106 [1976] AC 182, [1975] 2 WLR 913. See *R v Wood* [1982] 2 NZLR 233 at 237 (CA); *R v Metuariki* [1986] 1 NZLR 488 at 490, 493, 497, (1986) 2 CRNZ 116 at 118, 120, 125 (CA).

107 [1976] 1 NZLR 571.

108 Ibid at 575, 576, 584, 586. See *Civil Aviation Dept v MacKenzie* [1983] NZLR 78 at 83, also reported as *MacKenzie v Civil Aviation Dept* (1983) 1 CRNZ 38 at 43 (CA).

109 [1986] 1 NZLR 660 at 668, (1986) 2 CRNZ 216 at 224 (CA).

4.3.3 Deciding which fault standard applies

4.3.3.1. *Clear cases*

The starting place is the statute that creates the offence. If the statute specifies a particular mens rea standard, that is decisive. Even where it does not do so explicitly, the scheme of the statute may give a clear indication of the Legislature's intent. France cites, by way of example, s 56(4) Dog Control and Hydatids Act 1982 (now repealed), which provides that:

> The owner of any dog that makes any such attack [specified in s 56(1)] commits an offence and is liable on summary conviction to a fine not exceeding $500 . . .; and where the dog has not been destroyed, the Court may, on convicting the owner, make an order for the destruction of the dog.

According to France, this creates an absolute liability offence by necessary implication:

> The drafting of this provision makes the Court's ability to order destruction of the dog dependent upon conviction of the owner. If an owner were allowed a no-fault defence, the Court would become unable to deal with the animal. Yet, if the dog has attacked even though the owner has done all that could reasonably be expected, that would seem exactly the situation when a Court may wish to order destruction. This could only be achieved by holding the offence to be absolute.[110]

We agree, though we deplore this manner of drafting.

Absent clear legislative guidance, there may be an "overriding judicial history".[111] That is to say, the mens rea standard for the offence may have been settled by judicial precedent. For example, the offence of operating an overloaded vehicle has been held to impose strict liability in *SM Savill Ltd v MOT*[112] and *MOT v Coastal Carriers Ltd*.[113] In light of this, and unless the offence is altered by legislation, there would seem to be no reason for another court to reconsider the question in future.

It is worth remembering that different parts of the actus reus may correspond to different standards of mens rea. In the previous chapter we discussed an example where the statute was explicit.[114] But the situation may arise even where the statute is silent. An illustrative case is *Police v Starkey*,[115] which involved an offence against s 55 Local Elections and Polls Act 1976. Section 55 prohibits (a) publication of a document containing (b) an untrue, (c) and defamatory, statement (d) which was calculated to influence the vote of any elector. Barker J held that the mens rea requirements are, as to (a) intention; (b) strict liability; (c) none, since it was a question of law; and (d) knowledge of likelihood to influence.

---

110 France, "Absolute Liability since *MacKenzie*" [1987] NZLJ 50 at 53.

111 *Millar v MOT* [1986] 1 NZLR 660 at 668, (1986) 2 CRNZ 216 at 225 (CA).

112 [1986] 1 NZLR 653.

113 [1990] DCR 529.

114 Section 205(1)(b).

115 [1989] 2 NZLR 373, (1989) 4 CRNZ 400.

4.3.3.2 *Guiding principles*

If the mens rea standard for the offence is not settled by its being a clear case (above), the following may be taken as guiding principles.

4.3.3.2(a) *The initial presumption*

The basic presumption from which one starts is that mens rea is required for every offence.[116] Traditional authority for this presumption is *Sherras v De Rutzen*: "There is a presumption that mens rea . . . is an essential ingredient in every offence; but that presumption is liable to be displaced either by the words of the statute creating the offence or by the subject matter with which it deals, and both must be considered." [117] The justification for this starting-point rests in the issues discussed earlier in this chapter, and in chapter 1. According to Lord Diplock:

> the mere fact that Parliament has made the conduct a criminal offence gives rise to *some* implication about the mental element of the conduct proscribed . . . This implication stems from the principle that it is contrary to a rational and civilised criminal code . . . to penalise one who has performed his duty as a citizen to ascertain what acts are prohibited by law (*ignorantia juris non excusat*) and has taken all proper care to inform himself of any facts which would make his conduct lawful.[118]

Parliament normally does not, and indeed should not, intend to make criminals of those who are not blameworthy and do not warrant that label.

In most cases, the presumption in *Sherras v De Rutzen* will represent merely a formal point of departure, a prelude to assessment of the considerations noted below, in the next section. But its substantive force is that mens rea is the default position for an offence unless its implication is *clearly* outweighed by other factors. This implication is buttressed by the passage from Lord Reid's judgment in *Sweet v Parsley* which finds recitation in both *Civil Aviation Dept v MacKenzie* and in *Millar v MOT*: "it is a universal principle that if a penal provision is reasonably capable of two interpretations, that interpretation which is most favourable to the accused must be adopted". [119]

Thus the presumption for mens rea is abrogated, in favour of strict or absolute liability, only when it would be positively unreasonable (in light of the factors stated below) to interpret the offence as requiring mens rea. We should remark, however, that this constraint is in practice not as forceful as it sounds. Usually, according to the courts, it turns out that the only reasonable

---

116 Endorsed as the "ordinary rule" by Cooke P and Richardson J (at 668, 224), and as the "starting point" by Somers J (at 676, 234), in *Millar v MOT* [1986] 1 NZLR 660, (1986) 2 CRNZ 216 (CA).

117 [1895] 1 QB 918 at 921, [1895-99] All ER Rep 1167 at 1169.

118 *Sweet v Parsley* [1970] AC 132 at 162, 163, [1969] 1 All ER 347 at 361, 362. See also at 148, 349 (Lord Reid), 153, 353 (Lord Morris).

119 Ibid at 149. See *Civil Aviation Dept v MacKenzie* [1983] NZLR 78 at 81, also reported as *MacKenzie v Civil Aviation Dept* (1983) 1 CRNZ 38 at 41 (CA); *Millar v MOT* [1986] 1 NZLR 660 at 668, (1986) 2 CRNZ 216 at 224 (CA).

construction of public welfare regulatory offences is that they are intended to be of strict liability.[120]

We emphasise that, as was said earlier, the presumption of mens rea generally means intention or recklessness (or, as appropriate, knowledge or belief). Negligence is thought to be not blameworthy enough to warrant criminal sanctions for "truly criminal" offences. In *R v Walker*, the Court of Appeal adverted to this point expressly: "negligence or inadvertence is in general insufficient to constitute the guilty mind, which is necessary where mens rea is not ruled out by the words of the section creating the offence".[121]

4.3.3.2(b) *Whether or not to override the presumption*

In deciding this question, regard should be had to a number of considerations.

Put most broadly, the main concern is whether the offence is "serious" or "truly criminal", as opposed to a "public welfare or regulatory" offence. At the heart of this issue is the nature of the mischief the offence is designed to suppress. Very obviously, an offence will be of the former variety, and require mens rea, when it prohibits an activity that is, in itself, overtly wrongful.[122] In these cases the activity might occasion moral condemnation even without being criminalised, and a conviction is therefore likely to attract a substantial level of moral stigma.

More difficult are cases where the defendant's activity is not necessarily wrongful, but becomes the actus reus of an offence when done in a particular manner. Driving a vehicle may be a legitimate activity, but driving a vehicle while overloaded is a strict liability offence.[123] Factors relevant to the assessment of such offences include whether the offence is directed at regulating trades, activities, and the like, especially those which involve specialist skills and those for which one must be licensed. Where this is the case, it is more likely to be treated as a public welfare offence: "the essentially regulatory nature of the legislation justifies the interpretation that proof or an inference of mens rea is not required as part of the prosecution's case".[124] An example of this reasoning can be seen in *Re Wairarapa Election Petition*.[125] In that

---

120 Cf *R v City of Sault Ste Marie* (1978) 85 DLR (3d) 161 at 182, [1978] 2 SCR 1299 at 1326: public welfare offences would "prima facie" involve strict liability. In *Millar v MOT* [1986] 1 NZLR 660 at 668, (1986) 2 CRNZ 216 at 224 (CA), it was stated that "the qualification *reasonably* is also important and prevents an overweighting in favour of the accused".

121 [1958] NZLR 810 at 816; *MacKenzie v Hawkins* [1975] 1 NZLR 165, at 167, 168; *Civil Aviation Dept v MacKenzie* [1983] NZLR 78 at 84, also reported as *MacKenzie v Civil Aviation Dept* (1983) 1 CRNZ 38 at 44 (CA); *R v City of Sault Ste Marie* (1978) 85 DLR (3d) 161 at 170, [1978] 2 SCR 1299 at 1309, 1310; § 4.3.1.

122 For example, assault on a constable in the execution of his duty: *Waaka v Police* [1987] 1 NZLR 754 at 758, 759, (1987) 2 CRNZ 370 at 373-375 (CA); also possession of a controlled drug: *R v Cox* [1990] 2 NZLR 275, (1990) 5 CRNZ 653 (CA).

123 *SM Savill Ltd v MOT* [1986] 1 NZLR 653.

124 *Millar v MOT* [1986] 1 NZLR 660 at 669, (1986) 2 CRNZ 216 at 226 (CA).

125 [1988] 2 NZLR 74 at 117, 118.

case, speaking about the prohibition of expenditure in excess of $5,000 on a candidate's electoral campaign, the High Court said:

> This is not an offence such as the other corrupt practices of bribery or treating which import moral turpitude and which have all the attributes of true criminal offending . . . Rather this is a means of controlling the conduct of an election to prevent excesses and to avoid unfair competition and unfair advantage simply because of the more ready availability of money in one case than in another.[126]

Unlike other corrupt practices, the offence was held to impose strict liability because it regulates and controls excesses in an otherwise acceptable practice.

The fact that the activity is a specialist one increases the probability that its regulation will involve strict liability. One reason for this is that the use of strict liability simplifies prosecutions, a factor that is especially salient when the defendant may be expected to know far better than the prosecutor what went wrong and how to prevent it. According to the Court of Appeal:

> there are a significant group of statutory provisions, aimed at regulating the carrying on of various trades or activities, where . . . it may be unreasonable to read in the ordinary implication of mens rea. For instance, . . . it may be unreasonable to suppose that the prosecutor will be able to acquire any accurate knowledge of the workings of the defendant's business organisation. The object of this type of provision is best served by imposing liability prima facie if the defendant or his or its servants or agents are shown to have committed the unlawful act, while allowing exculpation if the defendant can prove total absence of fault.[127]

The Court's reasoning is reinforced by the fact that regulation of a specialist activity does not lead to the conviction of citizens for doing ordinary things without being on notice that their conduct was in danger of breaching the criminal law. Concerns about fair warning[128] are thus less pressing where the defendant may be said to some extent to have assumed the risks of liability by voluntarily bringing herself within the particular sphere of operation of a regulatory law. A similar point was made in *Sweet v Parsley* by Lord Diplock:

> Where penal provisions are of general application to the conduct of ordinary citizens in the course of their everyday life, the presumption is that the standard of care required of them in informing themselves of facts which would make their conduct unlawful, is that of the familiar common law duty of care. But where the subject-matter of a statute is the regulation of a particular activity involving potential danger to public health, safety or morals, in which citizens have a choice whether they participate or not, the court may feel driven to infer an intention of Parliament

---

126 Ibid at 117, 118. The remarks are made apropos of distinguishing the offence from one of absolute liability, but are relevant also to the distinction from mens rea offences — compare also at 118 lines 33-39, 119 lines 12-15.

127 *Millar v MOT* [1986] 1 NZLR 660 at 668, (1986) 2 CRNZ 216 at 225 (CA). Per *Civil Aviation Dept v MacKenzie* [1983] NZLR 78 at 85, also reported as *MacKenzie v Civil Aviation Dept* (1983) 1 CRNZ 38 at 45 (CA), "the defendant will ordinarily know far better than the prosecution how the breach occurred and what he had done to avoid it." Cf *Helleman v Collector of Customs* [1966] NZLR 705.

128 See § 1.4.3.

to impose, by penal sanctions, a higher duty of care on those who choose to participate.[129]

As Lord Diplock contemplates, the likelihood of a law's being declared strict is also increased if the activities it regulates have a tendency to endanger sections of the public[130] (or, in recent times, the environment[131]). An obvious place for such laws would be Health and Safety regulations, governing the quality of food products or safety in a workplace.[132]

Another consideration is the range and severity of punishments prescribed upon conviction. In *Strawbridge*, for example, it was said by the Court of Appeal to be "unthinkable that Parliament ever intended to expose citizens to a liability of up to fourteen years' imprisonment where the accused person did not know that the plant he or she was cultivating was a prohibited plant".[133] In general, where the offence is punishable by imprisonment, the presumption that mens rea is an implied element is very unlikely to be overridden.[134]

Finally, if one element of the actus reus involves the arbitrary drawing of a line over such matters as age, time, quantity, or size, mens rea may be less likely to be required in respect of that particular aspect.[135] At the other end of the spectrum, if an element of the actus reus involves the legal assessment of certain facts, then the defendant need only possess whatever mens rea is required regarding the facts themselves, and their legal assessment will be a matter of absolute liability.[136] In *Police v Starkey*, D was prosecuted for publishing matter defamatory of a candidate in an election.[137] Barker J held,

---

129 [1970] AC 132 at 163, [1969] All ER 347 at 362. One interesting philosophical discussion which makes a point of this type is Honoré, "Responsibility and Luck: the Moral Basis of Strict Liability" (1988) 104 LQR 530.

130 *Millar v MOT* [1986] 1 NZLR 660 at 669, (1986) 2 CRNZ 216 at 226 (CA).

131 Cf *Hastings CC v Simons* [1984] 2 NZLR 502. This notwithstanding that environmental offences now appear to involve significant social stigma.

132 Cf *Civil Aviation Dept v MacKenzie* [1983] NZLR 78 at 85 line 15ff, also reported as *MacKenzie v Civil Aviation Dept* (1983) 1 CRNZ 38 at 45 (CA).

133 [1970] NZLR 909 at 916. Cf *R v Tihi* [1989] 2 NZLR 29 at 32, (1989) 4 CRNZ 289 at 292 (CA).

134 The position appears to be otherwise in English law. Compare *Gammon (Hong Kong) Ltd v A-G of Hong Kong* [1985] AC 1 at 17, [1984] 2 All ER 502 at 511: "The severity of the maximum penalties [a $250,000 fine and imprisonment for 3 years] is a more formidable point. But ... there is nothing inconsistent with the purpose of the Ordinance in imposing severe penalties for offences of strict liability." Need there be such an inconsistency before strict liability is foreclosed?

135 See the references collected in *Adams* § CA20.15. An example where this point might have been relevant (but was not considered) is *Re Wairarapa Election Petition* [1988] 2 NZLR 74.

136 But compare the dissent on this point by Barwick CJ in *Iannella v French* (1968) 119 CLR 84 at 97, [1986] ALR 385 at 393. The presence of a legal assessment within the actus reus raises conflicting concerns; between the need to prevent individuals from "second guessing" the law's values, and the need to give them fair warning of the criminal implications of their conduct. See further the discussion of ignorance of law, at § 12.2.

137 [1989] 2 NZLR 373, (1989) 4 CRNZ 400. Other cases are noted in *Adams* § CA20.15.

inter alia, that while D must have intended to publish the material, whether the material was defamatory was a question of law, regarding which no fault element was required.

4.3.3.2(c) *Implying mens rea*

Sometimes, rather than presumed or explicit, or established by the judicial history, a mens rea requirement can be *implied* directly from the words of the statute. For example, s 306 creates an offence of threatening to kill another person. Although the section contains no express mention of mens rea, it has been held that the word "threaten" itself involves an intention to influence the mind of another — simply as a matter of ordinary language. Absent that intention, the defendant's conduct could not be described as a "threat".[138] Similarly, it has been held that the action of "publishing" defamatory matter, contrary to s 55 Local Elections and Polls Act 1976, can only be done intentionally. It is not possible to "publish" a document inadvertently.[139]

4.3.3.2(d) *When mens rea is not implied, and the presumption is overridden*

If the presumption of mens rea is overridden, the court must then decide whether the offence is of strict or absolute liability.[140] Factors in that determination are as follows. First, and most importantly, absolute liability ought to be very rare. The courts should find that an offence is one of absolute liability only when it is imposed in express terms or by necessary implication.[141] An example of the former, where the language of the statute evinces a clear intention by Parliament to impose absolute liability, was said in *Millar* to reside in ss 17 and 27 Machinery Act 1950: amendment of that Act to require "due" and not merely "faithful" compliance with the obligations therein has been held to indicate that no defence should be available.[142] Perhaps more important is the alternative possibility, that absolute liability may be a necessary implication, particularly in light of the scheme and purpose of the Act. In *IRD v Thomas*,[143] Barker J held that failing to file a tax return elicited absolute liability, since otherwise the purpose of the offence would be frustrated by the ability of a taxpayer to shelter behind the failings of his accountant.[144]

---

138 *R v Meek* [1981] 1 NZLR 499.

139 *Police v Starkey* [1989] 2 NZLR 373, (1989) 4 CRNZ 400.

140 Cf *Millar v MOT* [1986] 1 NZLR 660 at 668 lines 35-37 (Cooke P and Richardson J), 676 line 36ff (Somers J), (1986) 2 CRNZ 216 at 225, 233, 234 (CA).

141 *Millar v MOT* [1986] 1 NZLR 660 at 668, (1986) 2 CRNZ 216 at 225.

142 *AHI Operations Ltd v Dept of Labour* [1986] 1 NZLR 645. See the criticism by France, "Absolute Liability Since *MacKenzie*" [1987] NZLJ 50 at 52, 53.

143 (1989) 13 TRNZ 697.

144 Cf § 4.3.3.1. It is arguable that this case could instead have been decided on the basis that the offence imported strict liability but that D may be vicariously liable for the fault of his agent.

The reluctance to find that an offence imports absolute liability is surely right, both on principles of strict construction[145] and because strict liability will normally achieve the desired object of an offence anyway. In addition, there are at least three specific features that will further incline a Court away from imposing absolute liability. The first is the presence of an evaluative term in the actus reus, such as "fair" or "reasonable". Because this type of element cannot be determined by the defendant, in advance, with total certainty, but must always await the subsequent assessment of a judge, it raises a problem of fair warning.[146] Absolute liability, if it is imposed at all, should be threatened only in the clearest terms, so that it is at least possible for a defendant to know in advance what the boundaries of the offence are. This argument was recognised by the High Court in *Re Wairarapa Election Petition*:

> the provisions of subs (4) of s 139 provide that a fair proportion of expenses when carried on earlier than the three months period may be attributed to that period as election expenses. It would be wrong that, no matter how conscientiously a candidate had assessed that fair proportion, he should be absolutely liable for the excess of payment if in the end the Electoral Court concluded that his fair proportion was erroneous. When there is absolute liability there ought to be absolute certainty as to the ingredients of the offence so that the offender cannot say that he was unable beforehand to conduct himself so as to avoid the offence.[147]

For similar reasons, the Courts are very reluctant to ascribe absolute liability in cases where the defendant's activity is affected by what others are doing. In *Police v Creedon*, a prosecution for failing to yield the right of way at an intersection, McCarthy P emphasised the importance of the fact that "the regulation requires a driver of a motor vehicle to take a specific course of action if, and only if, something else is being done by someone else".[148] By contrast, say, with failing to stop at an intersection governed by a stop sign, the offence in *Creedon* does "not impose an omnipresent and unvarying obligation".[149] Its uncertain boundaries thus militate against absolute liability. An additional and buttressing rationale is that the regulation, in effect, gives another person the power to place the defendant under a criminal legal duty (in this case, by approaching the intersection from another direction). The vesting of such powers in third parties should never be accompanied by absolute liability on the part of the defendant.[150]

Another factor is the severity of the penalty prescribed for a breach. In *Re Wairarapa Election Petition*, where the mandatory penalty was described as "truly draconian", this was taken to be a reason against imposing absolute

---

145 Cf the principle asserted by Lord Reid in *Sweet v Parsley* [1970] AC 132 at 149, [1969] 1 All ER 347 at 350; § 4.3.3.2(a). See also § 1.4.4.

146 § 1.4.3.

147 [1988] 2 NZLR 74 at 117.

148 [1976] 1 NZLR 571 at 573.

149 Ibid at 574.

150 Cf *Re Wairarapa Election Petition* [1988] 2 NZLR 74 at 117, lines 36-38. For related discussion of this point, see § 2.1.1.1.

liability: "it is contrary to sense and justice that a person should be subject to the ultimate penalty, no matter how careful or innocent he may be".[151]

On the other hand, one consideration in favour of implying absolute liability arises if the statute itself designates a more specific defence, such as the taking of detailed steps by the defendant. *McLaren Transport Ltd v MOT* provides one such example: offences against s 23(2)(a) Road User Charges Act 1977 were held to be of absolute liability, subject to particular statutory defences contained in the Act. According to Hardie Boys J, "the statute itself prescribes 'avenues of escape' which are of limited availability and which would be entirely subverted were absence of fault in a more general sense to be available as a defence".[152] Where the function of the more specific defences is not "entirely subverted", of course, this argument would seem not to apply.

---

151 Ibid at 117.

152 [1986] 2 NZLR 81 at 83. Compare *McKnight v NZ Biogas Industries Ltd* [1994] 2 NZLR 664 at 667-669 (CA).

5

Derivative Liability

In chapter 1, we considered the following example:[1]

> One fine September morning, Jim is discovered dead in his home. His skull has been crushed by a blow inflicted with a heavy object. The police are called. Upon investigation, they establish that he was murdered by his daughter, Alice, who killed him in order to receive her inheritance under his will.

This, as we said earlier, is a paradigm case of criminal wrongdoing by Alice, involving deliberate, culpable infliction of the sort of serious harm that the criminal law is meant to prevent. Alice is precisely the sort of person who deserves the condemnation of a criminal conviction. But she may not be the

---

1   § 1.2 and, especially, § 1.2.2.5.

only person culpable in respect of Jim's death. Imagine the following additional details:

> During the course of their investigation, the police unearth a number of related facts. Frank, Jim's cousin, had learned by accident of Alice's plan to murder Jim, but had done nothing because he, too, stood to inherit under the will. Alice had planned the murder with the help of Gertrude, whom she had consulted about possible methods of carrying out the killing. The baseball bat that Alice eventually used belongs to Harry, who lent it to Alice for the purpose.

When an offence is committed it is not only the immediate perpetrator of the actus reus who may incur criminal liability. Others may also be held accountable by the criminal law. Usually, this will occur when those others have participated in the commission of the crime, albeit without themselves carrying out the actus reus. Such persons, when they are held to be criminally accountable, are said to be *parties* to the offence.

The difficult question, for both theory and doctrine in criminal law, is *when* persons other than the perpetrator of a crime should be held liable. When Jim dies the criminal law begins with every person within the jurisdiction as potential defendants, yet it is inappropriate to regard every member of society as involved in the crime that Alice commits. But how do we narrow the field in a principled way? In short, when a crime occurs, who are the suitable defendants?

In chapter 2 we considered the criminal law's doctrines of omission and causation, which play a vital role in identifying those persons who may be attributed with legal responsibility for committing a crime. Because of the law regarding omissions, for example, Frank will not be held responsible for Jim's death. On the other hand, these are not the only doctrines of responsibility in criminal law. Gertrude and Harry did not cause Jim's death: Alice's action was a free and unconstrained one and, as such, a novus actus.[2] Yet they, as well as Alice, will be held guilty of Jim's murder.

In this chapter, we consider the doctrines by which a defendant may be held responsible for a crime she does not herself commit. There are two main ways in which this may occur. The first gives rise to *secondary liability*. Although they did not perpetrate the crime, Gertrude and Harry have participated in Jim's murder by rendering aid and encouragement to Alice. Hence, they are known as secondary parties to the murder and are guilty of the offence alongside Alice. The second doctrine of responsibility occurs when a person is held responsible, at large, for the various acts of another person. This is known as *vicarious liability* and is much more common in civil than in criminal law. For example, a parent may sometimes be sued in tort for the damage her child causes to a neighbour's property, but she cannot herself be prosecuted for vandalism.

Both forms of liability are *derivative*. The defendant is indirectly held responsible for a crime committed by another and, as such, her liability is

---

2   See § 2.2ff. Their assistance need not even be a sine qua non of the crime — Alice, we may suppose, would have received the same advice and aid from others had Gertrude and Harry been unavailable or unwilling.

dependent upon the criminal actions of that other person. If no crime is committed, there is nothing of a criminal character with which the defendant can be secondarily or vicariously attributed.[3] As was noted in § 1.2.2.5, and will be seen below, the fact that liability is derived from the crime of another raises difficult questions of policy. The level of involvement required to make D guilty when P commits a crime must balance the consideration that D is often just as culpable as P (and indeed sometimes more culpable), even though it was not D who ultimately pulled the trigger, against the difficulty that derivative liability casts the net of criminalisation well beyond the direct infliction of criminal harms, to catch ostensibly innocent conduct such as lending (or selling[4]) Alice a baseball bat or even sitting as a passenger in a car.[5] It is for this reason that the mens rea requirements of secondary liability, in particular, are generally more stringent than those for the underlying offence.

For similar reasons, vicarious liability is normally to be avoided altogether in criminal law, since it arises simply out of a pre-existing relationship between the defendant and the actual perpetrator of a crime, and so is not specific to the crime or to any conduct by D relevant to that crime. It follows that D risks being convicted of a crime to which he has not contributed and for which he is in no way at fault. As we saw in chapter 1, that would be an undesirable outcome, especially in the context of stigmatic crimes. Consequently, vicarious liability is normally restricted to regulatory offences,[6] and is imposed only when it is found that Parliament must have intended it.

In the final part of this chapter, we will turn our attention to the liability of corporations. Although corporations are sometimes credited with a legal capacity to act, or omit, and to commit crimes directly, as will be seen, corporate liability is often to be explained as a specialised variety of vicarious liability.

5.1 MODES OF PARTICIPATION

The law governing forms of participation in a crime is stated in s 66 Crimes Act 1961.[7] The section reads as follows:

l **Parties to offences** — (1) Every one is a party to and guilty of an offence who —

    (a)   Actually commits the offence; or

    (b)   Does or omits an act for the purpose of aiding any person to commit the offence; or

    (c)   Abets any person in the commission of the offence; or

---

3   Kadish, *Blame and Punishment*, 1987, 146ff.

4   Cf *National Coal Board v Gamble* [1959] 11 QB 11, [1958] 3 All ER 203. See, for example, Duff, " 'Can I help you?': Accessorial Liability and the Intention to Assist" (1990) 10 LS 165; Williams, "Complicity, Purpose and the Draft Code" [1990] Crim LR 4.

5   For example *Ashton v Police* [1964] NZLR 429; *Du Cros v Lambourne* [1907] 1 KB 40; § 5.1.2.3.

6   Cf *SM Savill Ltd v MOT* [1986] 1 NZLR 653. See also § 5.2.

7   Except in the case of a crime committed outside New Zealand, for which the liability of parties is pursuant to ss 68, 69.

(d)   Incites, counsels, or procures any person to commit the offence.

(2) Where 2 or more persons form a common intention to prosecute any unlawful purpose, and to assist each other therein, each of them is a party to every offence committed by any one of them in the prosecution of the common purpose if the commission of that offence was known to be a probable consequence of the prosecution of the common purpose.

Conventionally, we distinguish between the *principal* — the person or persons who actually perpetrate the crime — and the *secondary party*. Secondary parties are those persons whose assistance, abetment, etc is sufficient to make them, under s 66, also participants in and guilty of the crime committed by the principal, notwithstanding that the secondary party does not herself commit that crime.[8]

A secondary party should be distinguished from an *accessory after the fact*. The latter is a person who assists someone else (who may be either a principal or secondary party) who has committed an offence *after* the crime has been completed. Thus the accessory after the fact does not participate in the crime itself, and his liability is not for the original crime committed, but instead arises independently as an offence under ss 71 and 312. By contrast, participation by a party to the offence must occur before that offence is completed.[9]

As s 66 makes clear, the distinction between principals and secondary offenders is now of little practical significance in criminal law since each is deemed to be guilty of the full offence. Thus it will not affect his resulting conviction for, say, murder, whether D himself killed another person or was simply a secondary party. Indeed, it can be very difficult on the facts of some cases to differentiate between principals and secondary parties,[10] and the form of charge need not reveal the nature of D's participation, but may simply allege guilt.[11] Nonetheless, the terminology is still to be found in the case law. One reason for this is that the distinction is still crucial to the operation of s 66 itself. If D was not a principal, the inquiry whether D was a secondary party will depend in part upon the existence of a principal who did perpetrate the offence, and will take a different form (with a different actus reus and different

---

8   At common law, secondary parties were further categorised as "principals in the second degree" or as "accessories before the fact", depending whether their participating conduct occurred during or before the commission of the relevant crime. The finer point is now of mere terminological interest.

9   *R v Beuth* [1937] NZLR 282 (CA); *R v Gosney* [1977] 2 NZLR 130 (CA); *Larkins v Police* [1987] 2 NZLR 282, (1987) 3 CRNZ 49; *S v Thomo* [1969] (1) SA 385 (AD). In the case of a continuing offence, such as rape (cf *R v Kaitamaki* [1984] 1 NZLR 385, also cited as *Kaitamaki v R* (1984) 1 CRNZ 211 (PC) the participation may occur after commencement of the offence but must happen before its completion (ie prior to withdrawal by the rapist): *Mayberry* [1973] Qd R 211. For discussion, see *Adams* § CA66.19.

10   Consider, for example, the facts of *R v Samuels* [1985] 1 NZLR 350 (CA); *Abbott v R* [1977] AC 755, [1976] 3 All ER 140 (PC); *R v Lewis* [1975] 1 NZLR 222 (CA).

11   Section 343 Crimes Act 1961; s 76 Summary Proceedings Act 1957. However, it is desirable wherever possible for the prosecution to specify the form of participation when laying the charge: *Adams* § CA66.12; *DPP for Northern Ireland v Maxwell* [1978] 3 All ER 1140, [1978] 1 WLR 1350 (HL).

mens rea) from the inquiry into the principal's liability. The elements of the principal's liability will be as set out in s 167 (and surrounding sections) and s 66(1)(a); the elements of the secondary party's liability are set out in s 66(1)(b)-(d) and (2).

The difference between principals and secondary parties matters for at least two other reasons. First, some offences are defined so that certain participants are excluded from liability, either because only a named class of persons may commit the offence as a principal or (more rarely) because the possibility of secondary participation is excluded.[12] Secondly, there is no vicarious liability for the acts of secondary parties.[13]

5.1.1 The principal: s 66(1)(a)

Before considering the varieties of secondary participation falling within s 66, it is necessary to make some observations regarding the participation of principal offenders. First, there may be more than one principal offender. If P and Q assault V by jointly raining blows on him, they are each principals. If V dies from the combination of blows, they will each be guilty of manslaughter or murder.[14] There are two ways in which multiple defendants may be held to be principals. First, each may separately satisfy all the required ingredients of the relevant offence. In the above example, P and Q are each independently guilty of an assault. This form of liability requires no reference to s 66, although it falls within the scope of s 66(1). Alternatively, under s 66(1)(a) each may separately satisfy *some* part of the actus reus for the offence where their actions, in combination, fulfil the complete actus reus requirement and each has the requisite mens rea. The latter is a true case of joint principals, in that it is sufficient for liability that each party does a part of the actus reus.[15]

Note, however, that there must be *some* contribution to the occurrence of the actus reus before one can be held to have committed the offence as a principal.[16] This requirement was disregarded — it is submitted, wrongly — by the Court of Appeal in *R v Harawira*,[17] in which D had been present during an attack on V by a number of assailants, and had assaulted but not injured V. Nonetheless, her conviction for injuring with intent as a principal under s 66(1)(a) was upheld, the Court of Appeal stating that it was sufficient that she had "participated in concert" with the persons who actually injured the victim. With respect, although her conviction for injuring with intent was obviously warranted, the proper basis for the conviction is clearly one of secondary participation, of aiding and abetting, rather than the actual commission of the offence.

---

12 See § 5.1.4.2.

13 *Ferguson v Weaving* [1951] 1 KB 814, [1951] 1 All ER 412.

14 Cf *R v Lewis* [1975] 1 NZLR 222 (CA); *R v Bingley* (1821) Russ & Ry 446, 168 ER 890.

15 *R v Wyles* [1977] Qd R 169; Williams, *TBCL*, 330; Lanham, "Complicity, Concert and Conspiracy" (1980) 4 Crim LJ 276.

16 *R v Demirian* [1989] VR 97, (1988) 33 A Crim R 441.

17 [1989] 2 NZLR 714, (1989) 4 CRNZ 348 (CA).

5.1.1.1 *Innocent agents*

Sometimes the actus reus is not perpetrated personally by the defendant, but is instead brought about by another who is unaware of the significance of his actions. Where the defendant deliberately[18] *uses* an "innocent agent" to bring about the actus reus, the intervening actor is not regarded as a participant in the crime, and the law treats the defendant as the principal.[19] An example would be when the host at a party gives a waiter a glass of wine to take out to the victim, when only the host knows that the wine contains poison. Although the waiter gives the victim poison, he is merely an innocent agent and it is the host who is the perpetrator of the crime.[20] This rule was applied by the Court of Appeal in *R v Paterson*,[21] in which D, who procured T to uplift a television for him from V's flat by pretending the flat was his, was held "actually" to have committed the offence of burglary within the terms of s 66(1)(a).

The doctrine of innocent agency may only be invoked, and the intervening actor can only be categorised as an *innocent* agent, if she either does not know that she was doing the *actus reus*, or if she lacks criminal capacity, in particular through being insane or an infant.[22] There are also some crimes for which the doctrine is excluded altogether because, by the very nature of those crimes, it cannot be said that D has personally committed the actus reus. This will depend upon the construction of the legislation creating each offence,[23] but is more likely to occur where the essence of the crime is specified *behaviour* by the criminal, rather than the bringing about of some *consequence*.[24] In bigamy, for example, it seems impossible to say that D has gone through a ceremony of marriage with V when he has procured T to do so. The same is true for rape,[25]

---

18 Exceptionally, an actus reus brought about by an innocent agent may also be attributed to D if it resulted from D's negligence, when negligence is sufficient to establish mens rea: *Tessymond's Case* (1828) 1 Lewin 169, 168 ER 1000.

19 For discussion, see Alldridge, "The Doctrine of Innocent Agency" (1990) 2 Crim L Forum 45; Williams, "Innocent Agency and Causation" (1992) 3 Crim L Forum 289; Alldridge, "Common Sense, Innocent Agency, and Causation" (1992) 3 Crim L Forum 299; Orchard, "Criminal Responsibility for the Acts of Innocent Agents" [1977] NZLJ 4. By contrast, secondary liability is thought to depend upon the existence of a principal offender: see, for example, *R v Bowern* (1915) 34 NZLR 696 (CA). This requirement is considered at § 5.1.4.1.

20 Cf *Anon* (1634) Kel 53; *R v Michael* (1840) 9 C & P 356, 173 ER 867; *R v Butt* (1884) 15 Cox CC 564; *White v Ridley* (1978) 140 CLR 342 (HCA).

21 [1976] 2 NZLR 394 (CA).

22 Cf *R v Tyler* (1838) 8 C & P 616, 173 ER 643; *R v Manley* (1844) 1 Cox CC 104; *R v Mazeau* (1840) 9 C & P 676, 173 ER 1006.

23 Contrast the definition of "rape" in s 128(2) ("his penis" would appear to exclude innocent agents) with that of "sexual connection" in s 128(5)(a) ("any other person").

24 See the distinction made between behavioural, circumstantial, and consequential elements of the actus reus, § 2.

25 Notwithstanding *R v Cogan* [1976] QB 217, [1975] 2 All ER 1059 (CA). But see *R v Cooper* 29/6/88, Williamson J, HC Christchurch T16/88.

and for crimes such as careless driving[26] and driving with excess alcohol.[27] The doctrine of innocent agency conceives D to "stand in the shoes" of the agent, whose own contribution disappears. That is straightforwardly done where the actus reus does not specify particular behaviour by the defendant. For example, in murder, which simply requires the causing of another's death, it is apt to view D as having killed V herself, even though she in fact procures the waiter to deliver the poison. It is rather less easy to treat D as having done the actus reus personally when the gist of the wrong is T's actual conduct, rather than its consequence.[28]

Innocent agency is also excluded if D is not a member of the class of persons eligible to commit the offence as a principal. *Adams* illustrates this point with the example of an offence that can be committed only by certain "licensees":

> If A, who is not a licensee, procures B, an innocent licensee, to commit such an offence, it seems inappropriate to say that A "actually commits" the offence. To do so implies that A is a licensee when that is not so. But A may properly be regarded as having actually committed the offence in the reverse situation where, being a licensee, A procures B, an innocent non-licensee, to perform the physical acts constituting the offence.[29]

5.1.2 Secondary parties who assist or encourage crime: s 66(1)(b)-(d)

Persons who involve themselves in a crime by giving assistance or encouragement to its commission are deemed to be parties if they fall within the terms of s 66(1)(b), (c), or (d). These subsections mention five varieties of conduct counting as secondary participation: aiding, abetting, inciting, counselling, and procuring. Apart from incitement (which in any event overlaps with abetment, counselling, and procurement), these are also the categories of participation recognised at common law, and the common law applicable to these concepts necessarily informs their interpretation in s 66. Because, as we shall see, the categories overlap, it appears that they effectively include the actus reus of any form of assistance, encouragement, contribution to, or causing of a crime by the principal.

5.1.2.1 *The conduct element*

Although s 66(1) identifies five disparate types of conduct constituting participation, it is arguably a mistake to treat them as independent, alternative,

---

26 *Thornton v Mitchell* [1940] 1 All ER 339; see also § 5.1.4.1. Cf *R v Harrison* [1941] NZLR 354 (CA); *Sweetman v Industries and Commerce Department* [1970] NZLR 139 at 146, 147.

27 Cf *A-G's Reference (No 1 of 1975)* [1975] QB 773, [1975] 2 All ER 684 (CA), in which D secretly laced P's drink. (Note that the offence in that case was held to be one of absolute liability, and that P was therefore guilty of committing the offence as a principal, notwithstanding his "innocence". D, in turn, was a secondary party.)

28 This difficulty may be thought a reason to doubt the application of the innocent agency doctrine to assault, as occurred in *R v S* [1994] DCR 76. See Dawkins, "Criminal Law" [1995] NZ Recent LR 34 at 51. On the other hand, innocent agency was applicable to burglary in *R v Paterson* [1976] 2 NZLR 394 (CA), arguably as much a "behaviour" crime as rape. See Orchard, "Criminal Responsibility for the Acts of Innocent Agents" [1977] NZLJ 4.

29 § CA66.17(1).

actus reus elements,[30] and it is not necessary in the charge to specify which type of conduct is relied on. The section is clearly designed to capture all forms of non-trivial assistance or encouragement for crimes committed by others, when rendered with the requisite mens rea,[31] and it may be artificial to analyse the terms separately. Nonetheless, the manner in which the statute is drafted, by dividing the alternatives into different subsections, makes this unavoidable.

5.1.2.1(a) *Aiding*

S aids P by assisting, helping, or giving support to P in the commission of a crime. There must be actual assistance: merely trying to help is not enough.[32] If S, knowing that P is going to rob a bank, plans to lend P her gun, she does not aid the offence if her car breaks down on the way over to P's house and P leaves to commit the robbery before S arrives. On the other hand, the assistance need not be substantial. Merely being available as a back-up person in the event of need would be sufficient.[33] By implication, it is not necessary that the assistance should take place at the actual scene of the offence. A helpful illustration of these principles may be found in the facts of *R v Turanga*.[34] Two secondary parties aided the perpetrators of an aggravated robbery by supplying a second getaway car, for use in completing the escape after the robbers had abandoned their first getaway car (utilised to flee the scene of the robbery itself). In the event, the second car was never used, because the principal robbers were arrested first. Despite the fact that their agreed role was never performed, and despite their distance from the scene of the crime, the defendants' applications to discharge counts of aiding the robbery were refused. The accused had helped the principals by providing their *means* of escape.

Neither is it always necessary that the principal should be aware of the assistance, provided she is in fact assisted.[35] Suppose that P plans a robbery, intending to use her gun. The day before the robbery takes place, S notices that P's gun is missing from its drawer. Without telling P, he places his own gun, a similar model, in the drawer for P to use instead. P carries out the robbery using S's gun. In this case S has aided P and is a party to the robbery even though P is ignorant of S's contribution.[36]

Sometimes, however, the question whether assistance is actually provided may be more difficult because the principal is unaware of the assistance. Consider

---

30 Cf *Adams* (2nd ed) § 648.

31 Outlined at § 5.1.2.4.

32 *Larkins v Police* [1987] 2 NZLR 282, (1987) 3 CRNZ 49.

33 *R v George* 16/5/96, CA550/95. But see the discussion of *Larkins v Police* [1987] 2 NZLR 282, (1987) 3 CRNZ 49, below.

34 [1993] 1 NZLR 685.

35 *Larkins v Police* [1987] 2 NZLR 282, (1987) 3 CRNZ 49.

36 See *State v Talley* 102 Ala 25 (1894): S prevented a third party from warning V of the danger, thereby making it easier for P to kill V. S was guilty of aiding murder, notwithstanding that P was unaware of the assistance.

the following facts, which arose in *Larkins v Police*.[37] Some associates of S had decided to burgle a bottle store. After they had broken into the rear of the store, S, who was on the street fronting the store, decided to act as a lookout in case the police arrived. The persons inside the store were unaware of S's decision to keep watch. As it happened, however, he made no contribution to events, since someone else saw the police arrive and called out the warning. S was charged with (being a party to) the offence of breaking and entering. Although his conviction was quashed on another ground,[38] Eichelbaum J considered that "the appellant's action in providing the principal offenders with, as counsel put it, an extra pair of eyes was at least evidence of actual assistance regardless whether those offenders were aware of its availability".[39]

Adams doubts this view, describing the case as one "of completely ineffectual aid which might have had some effect only if events had turned out differently . . . His act amounted to no more than a completely ineffective attempt to aid, and attempting to aid is not an offence".[40] But, in our opinion, the analysis of Eichelbaum J is plausible. Where the participation of a lookout is known by the principal offenders, *Adams* seems to suggest the principals are aided because they rely on the presence of the lookout, whether or not the lookout has cause actually to give any warning. Yet it is arguable that reliance does not constitute assistance. Consider the case where S tricks P by promising to act as lookout but not in fact doing so. Although P relies on S to keep watch, it would be odd to say that S "aids" P. If so, the gist of the assistance in *Larkins* is not the reliance, which by itself would seem more relevant to abetment or counselling, but rather the fact that S supplies P with an extra pair of eyes. And this occurs in *Larkins v Police* even though P is unaware that S does so. This case is not like the example given earlier, in which S attempts but fails to lend P her gun.

5.1.2.1(b) *Abetting*

In terms of its dictionary definition, "to abet" means to incite by aid, to instigate, or to encourage. In practice, because of its overlap with the other forms of participation in s 66(1), abetment is typically associated with encouragement.[41] Indeed, as was suggested in § 5.1.2(a), in cases where S is alleged to "assist" P by providing support on which P relies, the reliance itself may be sufficient for P to be abetted, whether or not any assistance is in fact provided. The encouragement may be by words or conduct — nodding one's head in endorsement of a plan may be just as effective as a verbal indication of

---

37 *Larkins v Police* [1987] 2 NZLR 282, (1987) 3 CRNZ 49.

38 Namely, that S's assistance occurred after the break-in was complete. Thus the offence had already been committed and S could only be charged with being an accessory after the fact. See § 5.1.

39 *Larkins v Police* [1987] 2 NZLR 282 at 290, (1987) 3 CRNZ 49 at 57.

40 § CA66.18(1). See Dawkins, "The Unknown Look-out and Liability for 'Aiding' an Offence" [1989] NZLJ 30. For the rule that attempting to be a party to an offence is not itself an offence, see § 5.1.4.3.

41 Cf *R v Galey* [1985] 1 NZLR 230 (CA).

agreement. Indeed, provided S has the requisite mens rea, mere presence may constitute abetment where that amounts to an incentive to the principal to go ahead. For example, in *R v Coney*[42] it was said that attendance at an illegal prize fight might be evidence of abetting battery by the fighters, since as Mathew J observed:

> the chief incentive to the wretched combatants to fight on until (as happens too often) dreadful injuries have been inflicted and life endangered or sacrificed, is the presence of spectators watching with keen interest every incident of the fight.[43]

Simply by watching, S may encourage the fighters (although, as we shall see below, the mens rea requirement means that S must also *intend* this result). However, it is necessary to show that S did *in fact* encourage P in the commission of a crime. Mere presence by itself, which does not encourage, is insufficient.[44]

In practice, the inference of encouragement will usually require something further, such as proof of some additional action by S or of a particular circumstance that implies support, for example that P and S are members of the same gang.[45] Alternatively, it appears to be sufficient that S is part of a group offering encouragement, and that P is aware of the group's behaviour, albeit unaware of S's individual conduct.[46]

5.1.2.1(c) *Inciting*

The meaning of incitement, which is also an inchoate offence, is considered below (§ 6.3). In essence, incitement requires persuasion, inducement, coercion, or at least a greater pressure than mere encouragement, which would normally constitute abetting.[47]

5.1.2.1(d) *Counselling*

"Counselling" has two varieties of meaning which both overlap with the other terms used in s 66(1). First, it includes the provision of advice or information, though such conduct may also amount to aiding or abetting.[48] Alternatively, counselling may contemplate "urging" someone to commit an offence[49] — in which context the overlap is with incitement of the offence.

5.1.2.1(e) *Procuring*

By contrast with the other varieties of secondary participation, procurement of an offence requires that the secondary party deliberately *causes* the principal to

---

42 (1882) 8 QBD 534.

43 Ibid at 544 (dissenting).

44 *R v Atkinson* (1869) 11 Cox CC 330; *R v Clarkson* [1971] 3 All ER 344, [1971] 1 WLR 1402; *R v Allan* [1965] 1 QB 130, [1963] 2 All ER 897 (CCA). This point is considered further at § 5.1.2.2.

45 See also *Wilcox v Jeffrey* [1951] 1 All ER 464, where S attended an unlawful concert performance in his capacity as a jazz critic and, further, paid a fee to attend.

46 *R v Schriek* [1997] 2 NZLR 139, (1996) 14 CRNZ 449, 3 HRNZ 583 (CA).

47 Cf *R v Hendrickson* [1977] Crim LR 356 (CA); *Burnard v Police* [1996] 1 NZLR 566.

48 Cf *R v Baker* (1909) 28 NZLR 536 (CA); *Martyn v Police* [1967] NZLR 396.

49 *Stuart v R* (1974) 134 CLR 426, 4 ALR 545 (HCA).

commit the offence. Therefore the requisite connection between S and the commission of the offence must be rather stronger than for aiding, abetting, counselling, or incitement. By contrast with those other terms, which require only that S play some part in the crime:

> To procure means to produce by endeavour. You procure a thing by setting out to see that it happens and taking the appropriate steps to produce that happening.[50]

Thus the perpetration of the principal crime must in some sense be a consequence of the procurement by S.[51] However, S's contribution need not be a decisive, or sine qua non ingredient of the decision by P to commit the offence: it is enough that the procurement was influential. Even though P may well have chosen to commit the offence anyway, if S in fact influenced P's reasoning for his decision then S will be guilty of procurement.[52]

Normally, procurement by S will take the form of persuasion, inducement, or threats. Sometimes, however, the causation element of a procurement may operate without influencing P's reasons; indeed, P may be entirely ignorant of S's role. In cases where an offence can be committed without mens rea, and the innocent agent doctrine does not apply,[53] S may be a secondary party to an offence by causing P to commit it. In *A-G's Reference (No 1 of 1975)*[54] S secretly laced the drinks of P, who was subsequently convicted of driving with excess alcohol (in that jurisdiction, an absolute liability offence). S was guilty of procuring the offence.

5.1.2.2 *The need for a connection*

Secondary liability is derived from S's *involvement* in the principal offence, and not merely her attempt to become involved. It follows that S's conduct must somehow be connected to the commission of the offence by P. As we have seen, in the case of aiding this requirement is manifested by the need to demonstrate that assistance of some sort *was in fact* provided to P; similarly, in the case of procuring, it is reflected in the need to show a causal link between S's conduct and perpetration of the offence. The same is true for abetting, inciting, and counselling. Although causation need not be shown, it must be established by the prosecution that the principal received encouragement, incitement, or advice, before S's conduct may count as participation falling within s 66.[55]

---

50 *A-G's Reference (No 1 of 1975)* [1975] QB 773, [1975] 2 All ER 684 (CA). See also *Cardin Laurant Ltd v CC* [1990] 3 NZLR 563, (1989) 3 TCLR 470; *MOT v Barnett* (1986) 3 DCR 382.

51 See the summary by Smith, "Aid, Abet, Counsel, or Procure" in Glazebrook (ed), *Reshaping the Criminal Law: Essays in Honour of Glanville Williams*, London, Stevens and Sons, 1978, 120, 134.

52 *Blakey v DPP* [1991] Crim LR 763, [1991] RTR 405.

53 § 5.1.1.1.

54 [1975] QB 773, [1975] 2 All ER 684 (CA). The decision has considerable untapped potential for the liability of hosts and publicans: see, for example, Williams, *TBCL*, 339, 341.

55 *R v Clarkson* [1971] 3 All ER 344, [1971] 1 WLR 1402 (abetting); *R v Calhaem* [1985] QB 808, [1985] 2 All ER 226 (CA) (counselling). Cf Smith, "Aid, Abet, Counsel, or Procure" in Glazebrook (ed), *Reshaping the Criminal Law: Essays in Honour of Glanville Williams*, London, Stevens and Sons, 1978, 120 at 131-134.

This point is sometimes misunderstood, and was left open by the Court of Appeal in *R v Padlie*.[56] Nonetheless, it is fundamental to the nature of secondary participation. Derivative liability is *not* a form of inchoate liability. Liability is not based on S's act of incitement (for example), as it is in the corresponding inchoate offence punishable under s 311(2). Rather, it is derived from S's *participation in* the offence perpetrated by P. If P is not aware of the encouragement, incitement, or advice, S necessarily fails to participate in the commission of the offence. In such a case, S cannot be a party to its commission.

The result is the same if the encouragement was so long ago that P has forgotten about it by the time she resolves to commit the offence; in which case S will not be a party to the offence.[57] This type of "forgotten advice" case is covered by a further *connection-based* requirement, suggested in the extraordinary case of *R v Calhaem*:[58] P must be aware not only of S's encouragement (for example), but also that he is acting in accordance with, or within the scope of, the endorsement provided by S's encouragement. The Court of Appeal provided the following illustration:

> For example, if the principal offender happened to be involved in a football riot in the course of which he laid about him with a weapon of some sort and killed someone who, unknown to him, was the person whom he had been counselled to kill, he would not, in our view, have been acting within the scope of his authority; he would have been acting outside it, albeit what he had done was what he had been counselled to do.[59]

This is not to require that the encouragement, counselling, etc actually "made a difference" in influencing P to commit the offence. As Woolf J stated in *A-G v Able*, "it does not make any difference that the person [counselled] would have tried to commit suicide anyway".[60] P must have received and been aware of, say, encouragement by S, but the encouragement need not have played a significant role.

5.1.2.3 *Omissions*

S may aid or abet an offence by omission.[61] Most obviously, this may occur where S's failure to discharge a legal duty assists P to commit an offence: for example, when the security guard at a warehouse deliberately fails to lock a door, intending that P may readily gain entry into the building and steal some of the goods stored inside.

Rather more problematic are cases where a person is held liable as a party for omitting to interfere and prevent an offence when she has a duty to do so

---

56   28/11/95, CA209/95; CA232/95; CA237/95: the Court chose not to decide the question whether abetting requires proof that the principal was aware of the encouragement.

57   Cf *A-G v Able* [1984] QB 795, [1984] 1 All ER 277.

58   [1985] QB 808, [1985] 2 All ER 266 (CA).

59   Ibid at 813, 269.

60   *A-G v Able* [1984] QB 795 at 812, [1984] 1 All ER 277 at 288.

61   See, for example, *Ashton v Police* [1964] NZLR 429; *Theeman v Police* [1966] NZLR 605; *Cooper v MOT* [1991] 2 NZLR 693. For general discussion, see Finn, "Culpable Non-Intervention: Reconsidering the Basis for Party Liability by Omission" (1994) 18 Crim LJ 90.

and (or alternatively, or) a power of control over the principal or the victim. Standard examples of this variety of abetment are said to occur if a parent permits another to commit an offence against her child, or if the owner of a car, while sitting in the passenger seat, permits the driver to break the law. However, these are not the same type of case.

Consider, first, the case where S, a parent, permits another to inflict fatal injuries upon his child when he is in a position to prevent the assault from taking place. In *R v Witika*,[62] the Court of Appeal stated that such a person would be party to a culpable homicide if, by not intervening, S encouraged (and — the mens rea element — intended to encourage) the principal offender. As far as secondary liability is concerned, this seems to understate the position. It is submitted that where S has a legal duty and the present ability to prevent some event, his failure to do so is, *in itself*, constitutive of *aiding*, and not merely evidence of encouragement. The case is analogous to that of the warehouse security guard (above); in both examples, the conduct would be aiding whether or not P knew of the decision by S to refrain from performing his duty. This view is now supported by a more recent decision of the Court of Appeal in *R v Brough*, where it is said:

> An intention to encourage is normally an essential ingredient: *R v Witika* (1991) 7 CRNZ 621 Cooke P at 622. However, this element is not always necessary. Liability for an omission will arise where A, who has a legal duty to act and a right or power of control over B, fails to observe or discharge the duty by exercising that control to prevent B committing an offence . . .[63]

Indeed, arguably S is not merely a secondary party; he may be independently guilty of homicide without reference to s 66. Provided that his intervention would have been causally efficacious in preventing the actus reus from occurring, it seems open to conclude that death results from his culpable failure to discharge his duty as a parent to intervene,[64] in which case this is a plain case of direct liability for murder or manslaughter resulting from his omission to perform a legal duty.[65]

At the other end of the scale is the case where S, a stranger, chances upon the commission of a crime and remains to watch. As we have noted already (§ 5.1.2.1(b)), such facts by themselves are insufficient to make S a party to the crime. In *R v Clarkson*,[66] two soldiers entered a room where a rape was taking place. They stayed to observe the events, purportedly without either encouraging or discouraging commission of the offence. Their convictions for

---

62   (1991) 7 CRNZ 621 (CA); [1993] 2 NZLR 424, (1992) 9 CRNZ 272 (CA).

63   27/2/97, CA507/96 at 10.

64   This would require analysis of the case as involving concurrent causes (ie P's action and S's omission), rather than a novus actus by P. Yet such an approach seems plausible, provided that S is able to prevent P's conduct. This is not to criticise the decision in *Witika* itself. Arguably, on the particular facts of the case, one of the defendants was not in a position to prevent the violence. As such, her liability would have to be predicated on secondary participation.

65   The existence of such a duty is discussed at § 2.1.1.2(b).

66   [1971] 3 All ER 344, [1971] 1 WLR 1402 (CA).

aiding and abetting were quashed by the English Court of Appeal. In the absence of actual and intended encouragement, their failure to intervene attracted no criminal liability, since they were under no duty to intervene.

The difficult case arises when S is not under a duty but has a legal power to control P's activity. Consider the facts of *Du Cros v Lambourne*, an English case.[67] S was the owner of a car that had been driven dangerously, but it was not clear who of S and his companion, P, was driving at the time and who was in the passenger seat. Nonetheless, S was convicted of being a party to dangerous driving, it being irrelevant whether he was principal or abettor. If P was driving, S had the legal power to direct the manner in which P drove; his acquiescence in the manner of P's driving was therefore held to constitute abetment of the offence of dangerous driving.

In England, then, failure by S to exercise a legal *power* (not duty[68]) of control over P's activity may be, without more, constitutive of secondary participation in crime. However, is that the law in New Zealand? In 1964, *Du Cros v Lambourne* was applied without qualification by the Supreme Court.[69] However, the conclusion to be drawn from the Court of Appeal's decision in *R v Witika*[70] (above) is a resounding "No".[71] Not only must there be a failure to intervene, but the non-intervention must in fact encourage (and be intended to encourage) P in her commission of the offence.

In light of *Witika* and *Brough*[72], we conclude that the current New Zealand law regarding omissions is as follows:

(i)   If S has a *legal duty* to prevent an offence (for example, in the case of a parent to protect his child), then a failure by S to take reasonable steps to intervene *in itself* constitutes the actus reus of aiding.

(ii) If S has no such duty, then he must intend by his non-intervention to encourage P, and, in fact, his inaction must also encourage P.

If *Witika* is right, the owner-passenger is in exactly the same legal position as the onlookers to the rape in *Clarkson*, or the casual spectators at a prizefight in *R v Coney*.[73] Arguably, however, the English position is to be preferred. In the difficult case, S is not a mere stranger, a passer-by who stumbles upon a crime that she is under no duty to prevent. Although there is no general obligation to prevent crime,[74] it seems reasonable to conclude that those with

---

67   [1907] 1 KB 40; followed in New Zealand in *Ashton v Police* [1964] NZLR 429. Cf *Tuck v Robson* [1970] 1 All ER 1171, [1970] 1 WLR 741.

68   Contrast the case of *Rubie v Faulkner* [1940] 1 KB 571, [1940] 1 All ER 285, in which a driving instructor was under a *duty* to intervene and prevent a dangerous manoeuvre by the learner-driver. See Wasik, "A Learner's Careless Driving" [1982] Crim LR 411; Lanham, "Drivers, Control, and Accomplices" [1982] Crim LR 419. The distinction between right and duty is unnoticed in *Smith and Hogan*, 136.

69   *Ashton v Police* [1964] NZLR 429.

70   (1991) 7 CRNZ 621 (CA), [1993] 2 NZLR 424, (1992) 9 CRNZ 272 (CA).

71   Cf *Adams* § CA66.18(1)(b).

72   27/2/97, CA507/96.

73   (1882) 8 QBD 534; see § 5.1.2.1(b).

74   Cf *Allan* [1965] 1 QB 130, [1963] 2 All ER 897 (CCA).

the legal power to prevent a crime *do* contribute to — hence, participate in — the wrongdoing by refraining from exercising their authority and, thus, deliberately permitting that crime to occur.

On the other hand, a countervailing consideration is that to impose liability in such cases is, effectively, to extend criminal liability for omissions. As we saw in chapter 2, the law is reluctant to impose liability for omissions, and for good reason. Forcing persons to intervene and regulate the actions of others (for example requiring property owners to police the actions of users) substantially widens the umbrella of criminal responsibility for wrongdoing and in turn risks intruding severely upon the autonomy of citizens.[75] Thus the New Zealand position, as asserted in *R v Witika*, is not without justification.

5.1.2.4 *Mens rea for participation under s 66(1)(b)-(d)*

The mens rea for secondary participation is intention: S must intend to participate in the crime committed by P. Stated in this way, the fault element appears straightforward. However, it is in fact quite complex, because the mens rea element must relate to two different matters: S's own conduct, in assisting or encouraging P's actions and the fact that P's actions are criminal in nature. We may summarise the mens rea requirement as follows.

(i)   S must intend:

    (a)   His conduct (ie the conduct that in fact assists or encourages P); and

    (b)   That his conduct will help or encourage P's actions; and

(ii) S must know the nature of P's actions. That is, S must know the "essential matters" relating to P's actions which make those actions an offence.

5.1.2.4(a) *Intention to aid, abet, etc*

The essence of aiding and abetting is intentional help or encouragement.[76] This means that not only must S intend her actions, but she must also act with the intent thereby to aid, abet, incite, counsel, or procure P's conduct. It is therefore insufficient that S is reckless whether P is assisted or encouraged: mere knowledge that her actions are likely to aid or abet P's conduct does not establish the intent required under s 66(1).[77]

The criteria of intention are considered at § 3.1. In the context of s 66(1), it is worth emphasising that there is no requirement for S to desire that P commit the offence she aids (abets, etc). It is the *assistance*, not the ultimate crime, that must be intended by S. Consider, for example, the following facts, which are based on *R v Richards*:[78]

> S is a pharmacist. He sells large quantities of Panadeine tablets to P, which he knows
> P will use to manufacture heroin. S does not sell the Panadeine because he wants P

---

75   For elaboration of this argument, see §§ 2.1.1.1; 1.2.1.2; 1.2.2.5.

76   *R v Samuels* [1985] 1 NZLR 350 (CA).

77   *R v Pene* 1/7/80, CA63/80 at 5. For the distinction between intention and foresight, see § 3.1.3.

78   (1992) 9 CRNZ 355.

to manufacture heroin, but rather because he wants the money that P is prepared to pay for the tablets.

The claim that S does not want or intend P to manufacture heroin is irrelevant. It may be characterised as a claim about S's motive, or ultimate purpose, which is of course to make money. But what matters is whether he intended to assist P. The answer to that question is yes. S intended to provide P with the essential ingredient for manufacturing heroin, *knowing* that this would, *necessarily*, assist P. Thus the case is one of moral certainty,[79] in which the assistance is constituted by the very outcome (P's receiving the Panadeine) that S intends.

Cases of moral certainty are, of course, rare. In the example above, supplying the tablets amounts *of itself* to assisting P. By contrast, it would not be enough that S merely knows it is likely that P will be assisted. Thus if S were to supply P with unlabelled tablets, being unsure whether the tablets were Panadeine or a placebo, he would lack the mens rea for secondary participation.

This variety of case should be contrasted with that where S intends that her conduct should assist P, but is uncertain whether the contemplated offence will eventually occur. The latter is clearly a case of intentional assistance. If S lacks mens rea at all, it will be on the basis of the second limb, knowledge of essential matters. Under the first limb, it is the help, not the ultimate offence, that must be intended.[80]

It might be thought that s 66(1)(b) creates an exception to the requirement for intention, at least in respect of participation by aiding. The subsection specifies that every person is a party to an offence if she "does or omits an act *for the purpose* of aiding any person to commit the offence". In *Richards*, counsel for the defendant sought to argue that use of the term "purpose" implies a stricter requirement: that S's assistance should be motivated by a desire that the offence itself be committed.

Fisher J rejected counsel's submission,[81] and rightly so. The crucial test under s 66(1)(b) is whether S's action is taken for the purpose of aiding; whether or not that aid is itself rendered for the *further*, or *ultimate*, purpose of bringing about the offence is simply a different question, and irrelevant to secondary liability. In this context, "purpose" adds nothing to "intention", and, like intention, S may have more than one purpose when she acts. There is no requirement under s 66(1) that S's purpose of aiding be the sole, primary, or motivating reason for her behaviour — indeed, the limitation proposed by counsel in *Richards* would deprive s 66 of much of its role, excluding from liability even secondary parties whose participation is integral to the eventual

---

79 § 3.1.4.

80 Cf *National Coal Board v Gamble* [1959] 1 QB 11, [1958] 3 All ER 203; *DPP for Northern Ireland v Lynch* [1975] AC 653, [1975] 1 All ER 913 (HL); *A-G v Able* [1984] QB 795, [1984] 1 All ER 277.

81 [1992] 9 CRNZ 352 at 362, 363.

commission of a crime, whenever they have some further reason (for example payment or fear[82]) explaining why they assisted.

5.1.2.4(b) *Knowledge of essential matters*

The classic statement of this requirement is to be found in *Johnson v Youdan*, where it was said that the secondary party to an offence must "know the essential matters which constitute that offence".[83] Two issues arise: (i) what mens rea standard is set by "knowledge", and (ii) what "essential matters" of an offence must S know about?

The meaning of "knowledge" is considered at § 3.4: S must accept, or assume, or have no substantial doubt that the relevant facts are true.[84] A suspicion that they may well be true is insufficient, even if accompanied by a deliberate failure to inquire into the facts;[85] although in the extreme case of wilful blindness, S will be treated as having knowledge.[86] This analysis is consistent with the statement, in the previous section, that the essence of aiding and abetting is intentional help. Mere belief in the possible existence of a set of facts amounts to recklessness, not intention.[87]

The exception to this requirement for knowledge is in respect of unknowable facts, such as future circumstances or P's future conduct. In these instances, knowledge of the probable existence of such facts will suffice.[88]

Although the foregoing states the relevant law, the merits of requiring knowledge rather than recklessness have been doubted. *Adams* questions:

> whether, as a general requirement, such a degree of knowledge should be necessary for there to be an intention to help or encourage the principal party ... While a secondary party must know of any relevant circumstance where knowledge is required of the principal party, it is difficult to see why recklessness should not be sufficient for a secondary party when it suffices for the principal party. A fortiori, belief in the probable existence of a circumstance [ie an "essential matter"] should satisfy the mental element for a secondary party where neither knowledge nor recklessness in respect of that circumstance is required of the principal party.[89]

With respect, however, the basis of secondary liability is different from that of a principal. There is no suggestion that the secondary party actually committed the offence himself or that he satisfies the actus reus requirements of the relevant crime. The actus reus element of secondary participation is entirely independent of the actus reus of the principal offence. This being so, there seems no reason why the mens rea requirement for participation should be

---

82　Cf *R v Joyce* [1968] NZLR 1070 (CA); *R v Pollock* [1973] 2 NZLR 491 (CA). However, such fear may be sufficient to underpin a defence of compulsion within s 24: see chapter 10.

83　[1950] 1 KB 544 at 546, [1950] 1 All ER 300 at 302. For general discussion of this requirement in New Zealand, see *Cooper v MOT* [1991] 2 NZLR 693.

84　*Giorgianni v R* (1985) 156 CLR 473, (1985) 58 ALR 641 (HCA).

85　*R v Crooks* [1981] 2 NZLR 53 (CA); *Millar v MOT* [1986] 1 NZLR 660 at 674 (CA).

86　The doctrine of wilful blindness is examined at § 3.4.1.

87　See §§ 3.2.3, 3.4.

88　See *Cooper v MOT* [1991] 2 NZLR 693; *R v Rees* [1990] 1 NZLR 555 at 558, (1990) 5 CRNZ 487 at 489 (CA).

89　§ CA66.20(1)(b).

determined by that principal offence. Moreover, derivative liability of any variety involves widening the net of the criminal law beyond those who actually perpetrate offences: not only may S not strike V, she may not do anything to help anyone else strike V either.[90] Because of this widening, the grounds of derivative liability ought correspondingly to be constricted, in order to prevent excessive criminalisation of conduct that does not itself cause a criminal harm. Otherwise, over-criminalisation would lead, in turn, to an excessive intrusion upon the freedoms of citizens who do not themselves commit crimes, forcing them constantly to modify their own actions because of the potential conduct of others.

The second question, relating to the range of "essential matters" which must be known by a secondary party, is perhaps more difficult. However, certain propositions may be asserted.

First, S must know that P intends or contemplates doing actions which constitute the actus reus of an offence, although S need not recognise that those actions in fact constitute an offence.[91] Secondly, S need not know all the details of the proposed offence, such as the time or place of its commission.[92] However, he must at least know either:

(i)   The *type* of offence intended (and eventually committed) by P;[93] or

(ii) That P was likely to commit any one of a number of offences, the "list" of which includes the offence eventually committed. [94]

The leading decision which states these criteria is that of the Court of Appeal in *R v Kimura*.[95] In that case, S was charged with aiding and abetting aggravated burglary, as defined in s 240A(b). The principal offence consisted, essentially, of burglary accompanied by possession or use of a weapon by P, and the Court of Appeal ruled that it was a misdirection for the trial Judge to state that S need not know P had a weapon with him. Instead, the Court held that possession or use of a weapon was an "essential element" of the offence of aggravated burglary, and that aggravated burglary could therefore not be regarded as being of the same *type* as simple burglary. S could only be convicted as a party to aggravated burglary if, as well as knowing that P contemplated a burglary, he also knew that P would have a weapon with him at the time.

---

90   § 1.2.2.5.

91   *Cardin Laurant Ltd v CC* [1990] 3 NZLR 563, (1989) 3 TCLR 470.

92   *R v Baker* (1909) 28 NZLR 536 (CA); *R v Witika* [1993] 2 NZLR 424, (1992) 9 CRNZ 272 (CA). Cf s 70(1), which confirms that a secondary party remains liable even though the principal commits the offence "in a way different from that which was incited, counselled, or suggested"; also s 70(2). For further discussion, see *Adams* § CA66.11.

93   *R v Baker* (1909) 28 NZLR 536 (CA); *R v Bainbridge* [1960] 1 QB 129, [1959] 3 All ER 200 (CCA).

94   *DPP for Northern Ireland v Maxwell* [1978] 3 All ER 1140; [1978] 1 WLR 1350 (HL).

95   (1992) 9 CRNZ 115 (CA). Thus mere knowledge that "something illegal" is intended by P is not enough: *R v Bainbridge* [1960] 1 QB 129, [1959] 3 All ER 200 (CCA); *R v Scott* (1978) 68 Cr App R 164 (CA).

Thirdly, S must know that P will do the actus reus with the level of mens rea required for it to amount to an offence. Thus, for example, S cannot abet murder if S recognises that P is about to kill V negligently; since negligence is insufficient mens rea for P to be guilty of murder.[96] Similarly, on a charge of abetting possession of a controlled drug for sale or supply,[97] S must know not only about P's possession, but also about her purpose of sale or supply.[98]

Finally, in the case of consequences which are specified in the actus reus but to which the fault requirement does not extend, such consequences are not essential matters of the offence. For example, S need not foresee the consequence (death) in order to abet the offence of "dangerous driving causing death". For the purposes of secondary participation, only the dangerous driving counts as an essential element.[99]

5.1.3 Secondary parties pursuant to a common intention: s 66(2)

Under s 66(1), liability is established on the basis that the offender assists or encourages the principal in the commission of an offence, by aiding, abetting, inciting, counselling, or procuring the commission of that offence. As an accessory, the offender knows the facts which constitute the offence charged and intends to assist the principal in committing the offence.

Section 66(2) contemplates liability in a different situation. The secondary party may not know the facts that constitute the offence with which he is ultimately charged. He becomes a party if he knew that the offence committed was a "probable consequence" of committing the original planned offence, even though he may not have intended or even have been directly involved in the commission of the new, or "collateral", offence that ultimately was perpetrated. In simple terms, we may say that the parties set out to commit one crime and become liable for a different one. The difference between the two sections, in so far as the mental element is concerned, is that s 66(1) requires knowledge plus intention to assist or encourage, while within s 66(2) knowledge of probability suffices.[100]

Under s 66(2), where S and P form a common intention to prosecute an unlawful purpose, which generally means committing a crime, S is liable for every offence committed by P in carrying out that purpose which S knew to be a "probable consequence" of carrying out the common purpose. Although the rule is commonly applied in cases where homicide is the consequence of the planned offence, it is a rule of general application and is not limited to homicide cases. It could apply where, for example, P plans to commit the crime of burglary and with S's assistance, breaks into V's home. In the course of the

---

96   *R v Chignell* [1991] 2 NZLR 257, (1990) 6 CRNZ 103 (CA); *R v Hamilton* [1985] 2 NZLR 245 (CA).

97   Contrary to the Misuse of Drugs Act 1975.

98   *R v Samuels* [1985] 1 NZLR 350 (CA).

99   *Giorgianni v R* (1985) 156 CLR 473, 58 ALR 641 (HCA). See also *R v Renata* [1992] 2 NZLR 346, (1991) 7 CRNZ 616 (CA), in respect of manslaughter by unlawful act.

100 See Orchard, "Parties to an offence: The function of s 66(2) of the Crimes Act" [1988] NZLJ 151.

burglary, P is challenged by V whom he attacks and violently assaults. Suppose that S does not participate in the actual assault, but knows P to be of a violent disposition: the jury, on a charge of assault causing actual bodily harm, would be invited to infer that he knew that the assault of the householder was a probable consequence of executing their common purpose. It does not matter that S did not intend the offence of assault to be committed, nor that he did not intend to help or encourage its commission. Liability arises simply because S has participated in a criminal enterprise with P, pursuant to which P has committed a different "collateral" offence which S knew could well occur.

Although, typically, the collateral offence is one different in character from the offence the parties planned to commit, this is not necessarily so. The subsection is not phrased in terms limited to offences strictly collateral to the main purpose.[101] In *R v Currie*,[102] the Court of Appeal noted that the words "to every offence committed by any one of them" in s 66(2) do not exclude the offence which was the immediate object of the common purpose. So if the immediate object of the common purpose was to administer a severe beating to the victim and included an intention to cause bodily injury known to the accessories to be likely to cause death, together with a reckless disregard whether death ensued or not, evidence that one of the accessories struck a blow with the necessary knowledge of its consequences would be sufficient to bring the case within the terms of s 66(2).[103]

On the other hand, where the parties achieve what they set out to do, s 66(2) should not normally be invoked. This is because s 66(1) is concerned with *intentional* acts of aiding, abetting etc, whereas s 66(2) contemplates the situation where certain consequences are merely foreseen. In *R v Curtis*,[104] the Court of Appeal said that s 66(2):

is concerned, not with an act which is the very unlawful act to which an offender lends his aid or his encouragement, but with any act done by the principal party which, while not the result aimed at, was a probable consequence of the prosecution of the unlawful common purpose ... Liability turns on the contemplated, albeit unwanted, consequences of the criminal enterprise.[105]

Contemplating consequences that are unwanted will normally be incompatible with an intention to do the very thing which is the object of the criminal enterprise, so that in putting its case the prosecution will need to

101 *R v Nathan* [1981] 2 NZLR 473 at 475 (Prichard J).

102 [1969] NZLR 193 (CA).

103 *R v Nathan* [1981] 2 NZLR 473 at 475. But see *R v Simpson* (1988) 46 DLR (4th) 466, [1988] 1 SCR 3 (SCC), where the Supreme Court of Canada held that "unlawful purpose" must be different from the "offence" charged. See also *R v MacDonald* (1990) 75 CR (3d) 238, 54 CCC (3d) 97.

104 [1988] 1 NZLR 734 at 739, 740 (CA).

105 See *R v Hamilton* [1985] 2 NZLR 245 at 250 (CA) (Cooke J); also *R v Gush* [1980] 2 NZLR 92 (CA); *Chan Wing-Siu v R* [1985] AC 168, [1984] 3 All ER 877 (PC); *R v Powell* [1997] 4 All ER 545, [1997] 3 WLR 959 (HL).

choose between s 66(1) or s 66(2). Both bases of accessory liability cannot be alleged together in respect of the same facts.[106]

5.1.3.1 *The "all or nothing" question*

An important question which has periodically troubled the courts is whether, in a prosecution for murder alleging liability under s 66(2), an accessory must necessarily be convicted of the same offence as the principal or acquitted altogether if the evidence against the accessory is insufficient to sustain a conviction for murder. In other words, is a manslaughter verdict open in such cases, or is it murder or nothing?

The issue first arose in New Zealand in *R v Malcolm*.[107] In that case, two men attacked another in his home for the purpose of robbing him of opium. While the offender delivered with an axe the blows which caused death, the accessory withdrew to the back yard, later claiming that he had disassociated himself from further participation in the common purpose. The Court of Appeal held that because the evidence proved murder or nothing, the presiding Judge was entitled to tell the jury that it could not find a verdict of manslaughter — that is, where the evidence clearly supported a verdict of murder and there was nothing in the evidence to justify the verdict's being reduced to manslaughter. The reasoning behind this rule was that where the principal offender has struck the blows which caused death, and the evidence against him points exclusively to murder, the accessory is equally guilty of murder by virtue of s 66(2), on the basis of common intention.[108]

One problem with this rule is that it denies a constitutional right which, arguably, the jury has, on a charge of murder to return a verdict of manslaughter, even though the jury is satisfied that every element necessary to constitute the crime of murder has been established.[109]

In *R v Morrison*[110] the Court of Appeal appeared to doubt whether the view expressed in *Malcolm* any longer represented the law in the light of later authorities. However, it refused to consider the question because the Judge had clearly given a direction that even where the evidence, if accepted, proves murder or nothing, the jury has the power to return a verdict of manslaughter. In that case, the two accused had formed a common intention to escape from custody in police cells. The appellant, M, struck the constable in attendance with a wooden broom handle and his associate, W, further disabled him with blows struck with a wooden handled scrubber. The constable died the next day as a result of the blows with the scrubber. It was held that since M had intended to inflict grievous bodily harm, he could not rely on a defence that his associate had acted with an "independent murderous intent", such that M could not be guilty of murder. It was held that once the jury concluded that there was a common intention to escape by the use of force, then there was

---

106 *R v Curtis* [1988] 1 NZLR 734 at 740 (CA).

107 [1951] NZLR 470 (CA).

108 Ibid at 483 (Gresson J).

109 See *R v Ryan* [1966] VR 553. For discussion of this point, see *Adams* § CA171.21.

110 [1968] NZLR 156 at 161 (CA).

overwhelming evidence that the force contemplated was such as would render the constable unconscious or otherwise incapacitated. That was sufficient to fix M with knowledge that the constable's murder was a "probable consequence" in terms of s 66(2).

5.1.3.2 *Different verdicts for culpable homicide*

It is now settled that where murder is charged for a killing committed in the prosecution of an unlawful common purpose, different verdicts may be available against the different persons charged as parties under s 66(2). The general rule is that on an indictment for murder it is open to a jury to find a verdict of either murder or manslaughter. However, the onus is always on the prosecution to prove that the offence amounts to murder if that is the verdict sought. If, on the whole of the evidence, there is nothing which could entitle a jury to return a verdict of manslaughter the judge is not bound to leave it to them to find murder or manslaughter, although there is nothing to prevent a jury returning a manslaughter verdict should it choose to do so. But where there is evidence sufficient to justify a verdict of manslaughter then, whether the defence have relied on it or not, the judge must bring it to the attention of the jury, because if the jury accepts or is left in reasonable doubt about the possibility of manslaughter, the prosecution have not affirmatively proved a case of murder.[111] In *R v Hartley*,[112] the Court of Appeal expressed its unwillingness to accept that under s 66(2) a secondary offender may never be convicted of a lesser form of homicide than the principal offender. The Court has, in a line of cases, indicated the range of possible verdicts that will now be appropriate in cases involving an alleged common purpose.

In order to understand how these rules have developed we need briefly to consider the facts of the two principal cases. In *R v Hamilton*,[113] H was a passenger in a car driven by W. The car drew up beside a stationary car, the occupants of which H and W had been seeking. The car was driven by L, a rival gang leader. H then fired a single shot from a cut-down rifle which struck L below the neck, killing him instantly. There was little dispute about H's liability for murder. However, W appealed against his conviction for murder on the ground that the trial Judge had failed to put manslaughter as a possible verdict, even though it had not been raised by the defence at the trial. It was held that there was a sufficient foundation in the evidence for there to have been a possibility of a verdict of murder against H and a verdict of manslaughter against W and, because that possibility had not been put before the jury in plain terms, a new trial was ordered for W.

R v Tomkins[114] concerned a prosecution for murder arising out of the robbery and abduction of a taxi driver. T admitted that he and his two associates planned to rob a taxi driver and to this end armed themselves with

111 *Kwaku Mensah v R* [1946] AC 83 at 92 (PC). See also *R v Hamilton* [1985] 2 NZLR 245 at 251 (CA).

112 [1978] 2 NZLR 199 (CA).

113 [1985] 2 NZLR 245 (CA).

114 [1985] 2 NZLR 253, (1985) 1 CRNZ 627 (CA); noted in (1986) 10 Crim LJ 191.

knives and a barbecue fork. After robbing the driver in his taxi, they made him drive to an isolated spot and get out of his taxi. T and one associate pushed the victim into some bushes and he fell to the ground. T snatched the victim's glasses from his face and stood by, knife in hand but not raised, while the associate stabbed the victim twice, killing him. The Court of Appeal noted that while the admissions were evidence upon which T could properly have been found guilty of murder by aiding and abetting the principal, T had maintained that the weapons were taken to scare and that the three conspirators did not intend to kill the driver.

The Court approved the general proposition that if a defendant joins in a criminal enterprise intending that knives will be used, even if only to threaten, he is or may be guilty of manslaughter if another party to the enterprise uses a knife to kill with murderous intent.[115] The Court said:

> The availability of manslaughter as a verdict in such cases gives effect to the community's sense that a man who joins in a criminal enterprise with the knowledge that knives (or other weapons such as loaded guns) are being carried should bear a share of criminal responsibility for an ensuing death; but that, if he did not think that the weapons would be intentionally used to kill, it may be unduly harsh to convict him of murder.[116]

In both cases the Court of Appeal concluded its judgment by making some general observations about the circumstances in which verdicts of either murder or manslaughter may be available in any case involving a common purpose. We shall consider these alternate verdicts under the separate heads of murder and manslaughter.

5.1.3.2(a) *Murder*

The relevant principles are as follows. First, in any case in which the accessory meant to encourage the murder he may be charged as a party to murder under s 167(a) and s 66(1).[117]

Secondly, if the jury is satisfied that the accessory knew there was a real risk that his confederate would kill with murderous intent in circumstances similar to those that arose, he will be guilty of murder.[118] Here the charge will be framed in terms of s 167(a) or (b) and s 66(2). In such a case, the prosecution will need to prove that the secondary party realised (subjectively) that there was a real risk that the principal meant to kill or intended to cause bodily injury known to the principal to be likely to cause death. Relevant knowledge in such a case may be inferred from the secondary party's conduct and any other evidence tending to prove his comprehension of the risk at the time.[119]

---

115 Ibid at 629, at 254.

116 Ibid at 629, at 255. See also *R v Reid* (1975) 62 Cr App R 109, [1976] Crim LR 570 (CA).

117 *R v Tomkins* [1985] 2 NZLR 253 at 256, (1985) 1 CRNZ 627 at 630 (CA).

118 Ibid. The accessory must foresee the risk as "substantial" or as something that "could well happen". In other jurisdictions, evidence that the accessory foresaw the act contemplated as a *possible* incident of the original venture would also seem to suffice. See *Chan Wing-Siu v R* [1985] AC 168 at 176, [1984] 3 All ER 877 at 881 (PC); *Johns v R* (1980) 143 CLR 108, (1980) 28 ALR 155 (HCA).

119 *Chan Wing-Siu v R* [1985] AC 168, [1984] 3 All ER 877 (PC).

Thirdly, a murder verdict will also be available where, in a prosecution under s 168, the accessory did not foresee the risk of death. In *R v Hardiman*,[120] this was said to be so because murder, as defined in s 168, does not require knowledge by the principal party that death is likely to ensue. Therefore, it will be enough that the accessory knew that the infliction of grievous bodily harm was a probable consequence of carrying out the common purpose. Although *Hardiman* currently states the law on this point, the interpretation adopted in that case may be criticised on the ground that, because death is an essential element of any form of murder, a secondary party surely must always know that death is a probable consequence.[121]

5.1.3.2(b) *Manslaughter*

R v Tomkins and *R v Hamilton* have identified a number of cases where a verdict of manslaughter will be appropriate against an accessory charged with murder on the basis of s 66(2). The common feature of these "rather less grave cases"[122] is that the subjective foresight necessary to make the accused guilty of the murder is lacking. Nevertheless, the cases generally show that the accused knew that a killing in some way could occur. The courts have identified the following instances where a verdict of manslaughter alone will be available.

(i)   Where the accessory knew only that at some stage in the course of the carrying out of the criminal plan there was a real risk of a killing short of murder.[123]

An example might be where it was known that the principal offender(s) intended to beat the victim violently in order to "teach him a lesson" or, as in *Hamilton*, where there was a common intention to frighten the victim or take an item of adornment (a gang patch) by force less than shooting.

(ii) If the accessory foresaw a real risk of murder, but the homicide was in fact committed at a time or in circumstances very different from anything he ever contemplated.[124]

The evidence may raise a possibility, for example, that while P may not have departed from the "tacit agreement" so as to justify S's complete acquittal (§ 5.1.3.2(c)), nonetheless it was *totally unforeseen* by S that P would be so audacious as to shoot the intended victim in broad daylight with an innocent eyewitness present.[125] Even though in such a case the killing occurred in circumstances very different from anything ever contemplated, manslaughter is still an available verdict provided the jury is satisfied that S must have known that, with lethal weapons being carried, there was an ever-present risk

---

120   [1995] 2 NZLR 650, (1995) 13 CRNZ 68 (CA); see *R v Morrison* [1968] NZLR 156 (CA); *R v Trinneer* (1970) 10 DLR (3d) 568, [1970] SCR 638 (SCC).

121   See Orchard, "Strict liability and Parties to Murder and Manslaughter" [1997] NZ Recent LR 93; *R v Greening* (1990) 6 CRNZ 191; *Adams* § CA66.26.

122   *R v Tomkins* [1985] 2 NZLR 253 at 256, (1985) 1 CRNZ 627 at 630 (CA).

123   Ibid.

124   Ibid.

125   *R v Hamilton* [1985] 2 NZLR 245 at 252 (CA).

of a killing in some way.[126] This new form of manslaughter has rightly been criticised, on the basis that it is doubtful whether such a concession ought to be made simply because the circumstances of the killing were "very different" to those foreseen by S, particularly where the only apparent significance of the difference is that there is a high probability of apprehension.[127]

(iii) Where the common intention was only to frighten the victim or to use a degree of force less than potentially lethal violence, but the principal party went beyond the plan and committed murder.[128]

In this case, the secondary party need not have foreseen death as a probable consequence of prosecuting the common purpose. It has been noted that this alternative verdict also entails a departure from the requirement in s 66(2) that the offence be committed "in the prosecution of the common purpose".[129]

(iv) Where the accessory has foreseen some risk of murder but the possibility of murder was so remote that it was never a real risk in the accused's mind.[130]

This finding is also consistent with the common law, where it has been recognised that D should not be convicted of murder if he had genuinely dismissed the risk of such a crime as "altogether negligible".[131] This issue arose on the facts in *Chan Wing-Siu* where, on a charge of wounding with intent, there was evidence that one of the co-accused had suddenly "out of the blue" gratuitously suggested that someone should "stab down" a woman who was kneeling on the floor and offering no resistance.

5.1.3.2(c) *Complete acquittal*
There is some authority for the proposition that in some circumstances an accessory in a "common purpose" case may be entitled to a complete acquittal. In *R v Anderson*,[132] the English Court of Criminal Appeal held that where P, in pursuance of a joint enterprise, goes beyond what has been "tacitly agreed" as part of the joint enterprise, S is not liable for the consequences of P's unauthorised act. At common law, this means that if the perpetrator, P, intentionally kills in pursuance of a joint enterprise where he and S had agreed only to inflict some minor injury on the victim, the fact that P's act was beyond the common design and uncontemplated by S would absolve S from liability even for manslaughter, notwithstanding that S might otherwise (ie but for P's departure from the common design) have had sufficient culpability for manslaughter.[133] However, in *R v Hamilton*[134] the Court of Appeal stated that in

---

126 *R v Tomkins* (1985) 1 CRNZ 627 at 630 (CA).

127 Orchard, "Joint and Several Murder and Manslaughter" [1986] NZLJ 45 at 48.

128 *R v Hamilton* [1985] 2 NZLR 245 at 252 (CA). See the discussion in *Adams* § CA66.26.

129 See Orchard, "Joint and Several Murder and Manslaughter" [1986] NZLJ 45.

130 *R v Tomkins* [1985] 2 NZLR 253 at 256, (1985) 1 CRNZ 627 at 630 (CA). See also Orchard, "Joint and Several Murder and Manslaughter" [1986] NZLJ 45 at 47.

131 See *Chan Wing- Siu v R* [1985] AC 168 at 179, [1984] 3 All ER 877 at 883 (PC).

132 [1966] 2 QB 110, [1966] 2 All ER 644 (CCA).

133 *R v Powell* [1997] 4 All ER 545, [1997] 3 WLR 959 (HL); *R v Lovesey* [1970] 1 QB 352, [1969] 2 All ER 1077 (CA); *R v Dunbar* [1988] Crim LR 693 (CA).

the circumstances where there was a common intention to frighten and to use less than lethal force, a finding of manslaughter could be justified if the principal "went beyond the plan and committed murder". This approach is difficult to reconcile with the common law authorities and departs from the strict reading of the requirement in s 66(2) that the offence be committed "in the prosecution of the common purpose".[135] Orchard suggests that in view of the common law authorities S will "presumably" be entitled to complete acquittal if killing or serious injury was not a "likely" consequence of the common purpose, so that P's actions went "completely beyond" its scope (although in such a case whether S knew P had or might use a weapon is likely to be of vital importance on that issue).[136] This approach has been endorsed in a recent decision of the New Zealand Court of Appeal, where it was held that if a group of persons embarks on a fight involving only punching and kicking, but one of them kills the victim with a weapon, the other parties to the common purpose will not be criminally responsible for the death under s 66(2) if they were unaware that the weapon was being carried by a member of the group.[137]

5.1.4 General principles applying to commission of offences

Secondary liability under either s 66(1)(b)-(d) or s 66(2) is subject to certain general doctrines governing the nature of the link required between the participant's actions and the commission of the offence to which she is party. We consider these doctrines in the following subsections.

5.1.4.1 *Liability is dependent on commission of the offence*

As we have observed already, and unlike inchoate crimes such as attempt, secondary participation is derivative and not itself an offence. Rather, it involves S in being attributed, alongside P, with legal responsibility for the offence that P commits. It follows that S may only be attributed with that offence *if it is actually committed*.[138] For example:

> S urges P to shoot V, a common enemy. P purchases a gun, but before he has the opportunity to purchase any ammunition the gun dealer becomes suspicious and alerts the police, who cancel P's gun licence and confiscate the weapon.

S is guilty of the inchoate offence of incitement to commit a crime, but since P does not actually commit the crime, S cannot be a party to murder.

That is a straightforward example. However, there are some situations where the requirement that P commit the relevant offence may not apply. The first occurs when P commits the actus reus of the offence, but is not criminally responsible for doing so and therefore cannot be convicted of that offence. The main exceptions of this variety are contained in ss 21(2), 22(2), and 23(4), and

---

134 [1985] 2 NZLR 245 at 252.

135 Orchard, "Joint and Several Murder and Manslaughter" [1986] NZLJ 45 at 47.

136 Ibid.

137 See *R v Hirawani, Wilson, and Henry* 30/11/90, CA134; 165; 172/90.

138 *R v Bowern* (1915) 34 NZLR 696 (CA); *R v Harrison* [1941] NZLR 354 (CA); *R v Paterson* [1976] 2 NZLR 394 (CA); *R v Nathan* [1981] 2 NZLR 473.

apply when P is exculpated by infancy (ss 21 and 22)[139] or insanity (s 23). To illustrate, consider the following example:

> P, a 9-year-old child, tells her father (S) that she hates her mother, who will not let her eat dessert until she has finished her vegetables. S, who shares P's view, tells P that there is poison in the cupboard and that if P wants to kill her mother she should take her a glass of water with some of the poison in it. This P does.

Prima facie, P has committed murder, since the actus reus and mens rea elements of that offence are present. However (as we shall see in chapter 7), she cannot be convicted because of her infancy. Therefore, no offence has been committed by P. Despite this, S may be convicted of being a secondary party to murder, by virtue of s 21(2).

It is undecided to what extent, in New Zealand, further exceptions exist. In particular:

(i) Are there any other defences that P may claim which will not negate S's liability as a party?

(ii) Can S be guilty as a party if P does the actus reus of an offence but lacks mens rea?

In answer to the first question, there is at least one such general defence:[140] that of compulsion, when S is the source of compulsion. In *R v Bourne*,[141] S forced his wife to have sexual connection with an animal. S was convicted of abetting her to commit buggery notwithstanding that it was assumed his wife, had she been charged with the same offence, would have been acquitted owing to the availability of a defence of coercion. It appears that this defence operates only as a personal excuse, and similar reasoning would not, therefore, carry over to situations where (for example) P acted in justifying self-defence.[142]

Authority for the second proposition, that S may be liable as a secondary party when she assists P to commit the actus reus of an offence for which P lacks mens rea, is the decision of the Court of Appeal in the English case of *R v Cogan*.[143] In that case, P had sexual intercourse with S's wife, apparently believing (on the basis of what S told him) that the wife was consenting. On appeal, P's conviction for rape was quashed, but S's conviction was upheld. The main ground for upholding his conviction was said to be that P was an innocent agent through whom S had acted as a principal in committing the offence. However, as Smith and Hogan point out, "[t]he agency theory is misconceived. If it were right, a woman could be convicted of rape as the principal and it is plain that she cannot commit that offence".[144] Rape is one of a variety of offence that cannot be committed through an innocent agent.[145]

---

139 Cf *DPP v K and B* [1997] 1 Cr App R 36.

140 And see also § 5.1.4.1(a).

141 (1952) 36 Cr App R 125 (CCA).

142 Cf *R v Howe* [1987] AC 417 at 458, [1987] 1 All ER 771 at 799 (HL), where Lord Mackay highlighted the fact that duress involved a "reason special to [P] himself".

143 [1976] QB 217, [1975] 2 All ER 1059 (CA).

144 *Smith and Hogan*, 156.

145 § 5.1.1.1.

Alternatively, the Court of Appeal reasoned that S was guilty of procuring rape, since even though P could not be convicted, S's wife had "clearly" been raped: "Cogan had had sexual intercourse with her without her consent. The fact that Cogan was innocent of rape because he believed that she was consenting does not affect the position that she was raped."[146]

This, with respect, is poor reasoning. Rape is not an absolute liability crime, constituted simply by its actus reus. The fact that P was innocent of rape because of his belief means that, for the purposes of the criminal law, no rape occurred. Nonetheless, S's conviction seems a just result. If so, the proper basis appears to be that, where S *procures* P to commit the actus reus of an offence without mens rea, S may be convicted of procuring that offence.[147] It remains to be seen whether this analysis will be accepted in New Zealand,[148] but in any event such cases will be rare, since whenever the actus reus involves consequences, S may normally be convicted as a principal offender (either on the basis of having caused the actus reus personally or by means of the innocent agent doctrine).

There can, at least, be no secondary liability without proof of an actus reus. Consider the facts of *Thornton v Mitchell*.[149] S, a bus conductor, negligently directed the bus driver to reverse. Two pedestrians were in consequence hit by the bus. However, the driver was acquitted of careless driving, since he had quite properly relied upon the instructions of the conductor. In these circumstances, S was acquitted of aiding and abetting the offence of careless driving. There was no actus reus by the bus driver — he had not been driving carelessly[150] — and thus nothing at all of a criminal character from which S's liability might derive.

5.1.4.1(a) *Conviction for different offences with the same actus reus*
A variant situation arises when there are two offences constituted by the same actus reus, and differentiated only by degree of culpability. The leading example of this is murder and manslaughter. It appears that, in such instances, S and P need not be convicted of the same offence, and that where P is guilty of murder, S may be guilty only of manslaughter.[151] The case of s 66(2) has already been considered in § 5.1.3.1-2.[152] In the case of s 66(1), the basis of such a finding would be that S's participation was with the intention of assisting or encouraging P, whose proposed conduct was such that were V to die, P would

---

146 *R v Cogan* [1976] QB 217 at 223, [1975] 2 All ER 1059 at 1062 (CA).

147 *R v Millward* [1994] Crim LR 527 (CA); *R v Wheelhouse* [1994] Crim LR 756 (CA).

148 The issue was undecided by the Court of Appeal in *R v Lewis* [1975] 1 NZLR 222 (CA).

149 [1940] 1 All ER 339. See Taylor, "Complicity and Excuses" [1983] Crim LR 656.

150 For explanation, see § 3.5.3.

151 *R v Tomkins* [1985] 2 NZLR 253, (1985) 1 CRNZ 627 (CA); *R v Hamilton* [1985] 2 NZLR 245 (CA).

152 See also Orchard, "Joint and Several Murder and Manslaughter" [1986] NZLJ 45 at 47, 48.

be guilty of manslaughter; in circumstances where, ultimately, P acted with sufficient mens rea for murder.[153]

The fact that these offences share the same actus reus means that any incursion upon the principle, that S's liability is derivative upon P's, is minimal. Indeed, manslaughter may be regarded as a lesser included offence within murder. However, the reverse is not true, and it seems right, as was said in *R v Hartley*,[154] that S may not be convicted of murder if the principal party is guilty only of manslaughter.[155]

The exception to this is, consistent with the case of compulsion in the preceding section, in respect of personal excusatory defences available to P. Culpable homicide acknowledges palliative defences; in particular, for provocation, suicide pacts, and infanticide. Where such a defence is available to the principal, the secondary party's liability for murder will not be correspondingly reduced.[156]

Hartley appears to exclude the second exception discussed in the preceding section, whereby S may still be guilty of murder when P is guilty of manslaughter because of lack of mens rea. At common law, however, the English Court of Appeal[157] has since expressed an obiter view contrary to that found in *Hartley* and the possibility may remain open.

5.1.4.2 *Limitations on the application of s 66*
Sometimes party liability is excluded by statute. An example is provided by s 132(4), in the context of sexual intercourse with a girl under the age of 12 years. Prima facie, consensual intercourse with an 11-year-old would involve the girl's being a party under s 66 to the offence committed by her adult partner. The express legislative exception reflects the fact that the relevant offence exists for the *protection* of such persons, even "against themselves", and that they are regarded by the statute as victims rather than co-offenders.

Arguably, express statutory exceptions, while welcome, are not required to achieve this result. The same principle excepting victims from participation in crimes against themselves exists at common law. In *R v Tyrell*, it was held that D, a girl under the age of 16 years, could not be convicted of abetting unlawful sexual intercourse with herself, because the Act that created the offence was passed "[w]ith the purpose of protecting women and girls against themselves".[158] However, the common law principle espoused in *Tyrell* is of

---

153 Cf *R v Murtagh* [1955] Crim LR 315; *R v Malcolm* [1951] NZLR 470 at 485 (CA).

154 [1978] 2 NZLR 199 (CA). See *R v Lewis* [1975] 1 NZLR 222 (CA); *Remillard v R* (1921) 59 DLR 340, 62 SCR 21 (SCC).

155 For contrary thinking in Australia, see *Warren v R* [1987] WAR 314, (1985) 15 A Crim R 317.

156 Cf s 169(7) (provocation); s 178(8) (infanticide); s 180(5) (suicide pact). In the case of infanticide, S's liability may be for either murder or manslaughter.)

157 *R v Howe* [1986] QB 626 at 641, 642, [1986] 1 All ER 833 at 839, 840 (CA), affirmed sub nom *R v Howe* [1987] AC 417, [1987] 1 All ER 771 (HL); disapproving the reasoning in *R v Richards* [1974] QB 776, [1973] 3 All ER 1088 (CA).

158 [1894] 1 QB 710 at 712 (Lord Coleridge CJ). See also *Scott v Killian* (1985) 40 SASR 37, 19 A Crim R 187; *R v Whitehouse* [1977] QB 868.

somewhat uncertain scope[159] and its application may be doubtful in areas other than offences against young persons and persons suffering from a disability.

It should also be mentioned that, on occasion, the relevant primary offence may be defined by statute in such a way that it specifies the class of participants who may commit that offence. In such instances, participation under s 66 is excluded except in so far as such participants qualify within the class stipulated by the primary offence. However, these cases are rare.[160] More commonly, the statute may define a class of persons who may commit the offence *as a principal*, without restricting the range of persons who may be guilty of the offence as a secondary party.[161] A good example is the offence of rape within s 128(1)(a), which can only be committed by a "male" against a "female". The definition makes clear that a female cannot commit rape as a principal party (though she may commit sexual violation under s 128). But she may nonetheless aid and abet a rape committed by someone else.[162]

5.1.4.3 *Secondary liability and inchoate offences*

Section 66 does not create offences. Therefore, S cannot commit an inchoate offence of attempting, inciting, or conspiring to aid and abet.[163] Conceptually, this seems right. If S has failed to participate in a crime, she has no connection to it and should not be convicted. Her conduct is, one might say, too remote from manifest criminality to warrant the attention of the criminal law; attention that would be tantamount to punishing for little more than wrongful thoughts.[164] Conversely, however, the inchoate offences *are* offences independent of the further crime that is attempted, incited, or conspired toward. Therefore, S may be a party to (aid, abet, etc) an attempt,[165] incitement, or conspiracy[166] by P to commit an offence. The exception to the latter rule is that S may not be a party under s 66(2) to a conspiracy. In view of the overlap

---

159 Williams, "Victims and other Exempt Parties in Crime" (1990) 10 LS 245.

160 See, for example, *R v Mickle* [1978] 1 NZLR 720. For a fuller discussion of cases where the language of the primary offence appears to exclude secondary liability, see *Adams* § CA66.05.

161 For example *Sweetman v Industries and Commerce Dept* [1970] NZLR 139. See also *R v Sockett* (1908) 72 JP 428.

162 See *R v Ram* (1893) 17 Cox CC 609.

163 Smith, "Secondary Participation and Inchoate Offences" in Tapper (ed), *Crime, Proof and Punishment*, London, Butterworths, 1981, 21; *Adams* § CA66.14(1); § 5.1.2.1(a). Contrast an *offence*, such as aiding suicide under s 179(b), which is defined in terms of aiding and abetting. S may be guilty of attempting to commit such an offence: *R v Stack* [1986] 1 NZLR 257, (1986) 2 CRNZ 238 (CA); *R v McShane* (1977) 66 Cr App R 97, [1977] Crim LR 737 (CA).

164 Per Fletcher, *Rethinking Criminal Law*, 1978, 680, 681: "there is no social wrong in acting to aid the crime of another, unless the aid actually furthers the criminal objective . . ." See also Dawkins, "The Unknown Look-out and Liability for 'Aiding' an Offence" [1989] NZLJ 30 at 34, 35.

165 *R v Baker* (1909) 28 NZLR 536 (CA); *R v Mackie* [1957] NZLR 669 (CA); *Drewery v Police* (1988) 3 CRNZ 499; cf *R v Hapgood* (1870) LR 1 CCR 221, 11 Cox CC 471.

166 *R v Anderson* (1984) 80 Cr App R 64, [1984] Crim LR 550 (CA); *R v McNamara (No 1)* (1981) 56 CCC (2d) 193. Cf *R v Gemmell* [1985] 2 NZLR 740, (1985) 1 CRNZ 496 (CA).

between that subsection and the requirements of conspiracy, S will be liable in such cases only if she is an fact a member of the conspiracy itself.[167]

5.1.4.4 *Withdrawal*

In the case of inchoate (and substantive) offences, an offender cannot undo his crime. Once the elements of the offence are concurrently satisfied the offence is committed and cannot be "uncommitted". By contrast, participation *can* be undone. S may withdraw her participation, although she must do so before the crime is committed or attempted. Withdrawal, however, is not easy. Repentance is insufficient.[168] The participation must not merely be discontinued. It must be countermanded.

5.1.4.4(a) *Withdrawal from participation by common intention under s 66(2)*

Where S has participated simply by joining in a common intention to commit a crime, the common intention may be abandoned by S's communicating his withdrawal in an unequivocal and timely way. The leading statement of the requirement is found in *R v Whitehouse*:

> where practical and reasonable there must be timely communication of the intention to abandon the common purpose from those who wish to dissociate themselves from the contemplated crime to those who decide to continue in it.[169]

The notice of withdrawal, whether made by words or actions, must be unequivocal; a perfunctory disclaimer is likely to be insufficient,[170] as is merely leaving the scene.[171] It must also be timely, occurring before the crime is committed.[172] Where, however, the situation is such that communication of withdrawal to the other parties is impossible or impractical, withdrawal may alternatively be effected by taking steps to prevent the commission of the offence, for example by warning the victim or the police.[173]

5.1.4.4(b) *Withdrawal from assistance or encouragement under s 66(1)(b)-(d)*

When S has actually provided assistance or encouragement toward the commission of a crime, countermanding that participation is more onerous. Mere cessation of further participatory activity will be insufficient.[174] Withdrawal may only be effected by taking all reasonable steps to undo the effect of his previous actions.[175] What is "reasonable" will, it seems, depend upon the circumstances and upon the extent of S's prior participation: the

---

167 *R v Gemmell* [1985] 2 NZLR 740, (1985) 1 CRNZ 496 (CA); Orchard, "The Mental Element of Conspiracy" (1985) 2 Canterbury LR 353.

168 *R v Croft* [1944] 1 KB 295, [1944] 2 All ER 483 (CCA); 1 Hale PC 618.

169 [1941] 1 DLR 683 at 685, (1940) 75 CCC 65. See also *Henderson v R* [1949] 2 DLR 121; *R v Becerra* (1975) 62 Cr App R 212 (CA); *R v Wilcox* [1982] 1 NZLR 191 (CA).

170 *R v Malcolm* [1951] NZLR 470 (CA).

171 *R v Whitehouse* [1941] 1 DLR 683, (1940) 75 CCC 65.

172 *R v Witika* [1993] 2 NZLR 424, (1992) 9 CRNZ 272 (CA).

173 *R v Becerra* (1975) 62 Cr App R 212 (CA); *R v Jensen* [1980] VR 194.

174 *R v Johnson* (1841) Car & M 218, 174 ER 479.

175 *R v Menniti* [1985] 1 Qd R 520, (1984) 13 A Crim R 417, noted at (1986) 10 Crim LJ 236; *R v Wilton* (1993) 64 A Crim R 359.

greater the involvement, the more S must do to withdraw.[176] Incitement can normally be undone by an express statement to the opposite effect.[177] However, if material assistance has been rendered, there may have to be some form of physical intervention to impede the crime. For example, S may have to try to recover the weapon loaned to P or attempt to protect the victim.[178] Advice or counsel, on the other hand, cannot as such be undone, but may be countermanded by attempts to dissuade P from proceeding with the crime.[179]

5.2 VICARIOUS LIABILITY

Unlike secondary liability, which involves *participation* by the defendant in the crime of another, vicarious liability involves the *attribution* to one individual or corporation of criminal liability for the acts of another. The defendant bears liability *on behalf of* another. In general, the possibility of vicarious liability is rejected at common law, the basic rule being that a master or principal is not criminally liable for an offence committed by his servant or agent: "they must each answer for their own acts, and stand or fall by their own behaviour".[180] The courts have resiled from the idea that D might be held criminally responsible for an event brought about by another which it was impossible for him to prevent, in circumstances where he could not personally take the precautions enjoined upon by the relevant statute.[181] In effect, vicarious liability imposes criminal responsibility on the basis of status; yet, unlike ordinary "state-of-affairs" offences that may be committed by a principal,[182] there is no implicit behavioural element of the offence and no defence of involuntariness. Such liability is, therefore, repugnant to the fundamental principles of criminal law.

Nonetheless, vicarious liability may sometimes be imposed by the express terms or necessary implication of a statute, and occasionally on the basis of a master-and-servant or principal-and-agent relationship.[183] At common law, there were two notable exceptions to the principle that a master could never be liable for the criminal acts of his servant. They concerned public nuisance and criminal libel, where a master could be held liable for his servant's acts even though he was completely innocent. However, these exceptions were overtaken in the late nineteenth century, when it became increasingly common to use vicarious liability to regulate the activities of persons and corporations who held licences to perform specific activities, in circumstances where it was common practice to delegate the statutory functions and responsibilities of the

---

176 For discussion of variant cases, see *Adams* § CA66.15.

177 *R v Saunders* (1573) 2 Plowd 473; 75 ER 706. Cf *R v Croft* [1944] KB 295, [1944] 2 All ER 483; *R v Rook* [1993] 2 All ER 955, [1993] 1 WLR 1005 (CA).

178 *R v Becerra* (1975) 62 Cr App R 212 (CA); *R v Baker* [1994] Crim LR 444 (CA).

179 *R v Grundy* [1977] Crim LR 534 (CA).

180 *R v Huggins* (1730) 2 State Tr 883 at 885, 93 ER 915 at 917 (Raymond CJ). See *Woodgate v Knatchbull* 2 TR 148; *Smith and Hogan*, 174ff.

181 *Hardcastle v Bielby* [1892] 1 QB 709 at 713 (Collins J).

182 Discussed at § 2.1.2.1.

183 See *Crawford v Haughton Ltd* [1972] 1 All ER 535.

licensee to an employee or agent. In limited circumstances of this type, it was considered not unreasonable to make the principal liable for those acts of her employee committed within the scope of employment.[184]

To determine whether a statute impliedly imposes vicarious liability, it is necessary to consider the object of the statute, the words used, the nature of the duty laid down, the person upon whom it is imposed, the person by whom it would in ordinary circumstances be performed, and the person upon whom the penalty is imposed.[185] Where the duty is one which would ordinarily be performed by a servant of the owner or other person having responsibility, the courts have often been willing to find an intention by the Legislature to impose vicarious liability. The rationale for this willingness is that, where a penalty is imposed for a breach of duty, it may be reasonable to infer that the penalty was imposed for a default of the person by whom the duty would ordinarily be performed, namely the employee, regardless of the state of mind of the employer. This point is buttressed by the fact that it is normally the employer who is best placed to ensure her employee complies with the law.[186]

Once an offence is held to import the doctrine, there are two principal bases upon which vicarious liability may be established: the "delegation" principle, and the "scope of employment" principle. According to the delegation principle, which applies in the case of mens rea offences, a person may be held liable for the acts of another where he has delegated the performance of statutory duties to that other person. According to the scope of employment principle, which applies to strict and absolute liability offences, a master may be held liable because the servant has been given authority to do the very kind of act involved in the offence.

5.2.1 "Delegation" theory
The delegation principle only applies in those cases where, by the terms of the relevant statutory provision, "knowledge" or some similar mens rea element is required as a condition of liability. In such a case, liability may be imposed where the principal knows the relevant facts, or where she has delegated her powers and duties. In *Vane v Yiannopoullos*[187] the licensee of a restaurant had been granted a licence subject to the condition that liquor was only to be sold to persons ordering meals. A waitress, despite being instructed only to serve drinks to customers ordering meals, had served drinks to two youths who had not ordered meals while the licensee was in another part of the restaurant and knew nothing of the sale. Upon an appeal against the dismissal of an information alleging that the licensee had "knowingly" sold intoxicating liquor contrary to the conditions of the licence, it was held that since there had been no delegation and the licensee had no knowledge of the offence, he was rightly

---

184 *Mousell Brothers v London and North-Western Railway Co* [1917] 2 KB 836, [1916] All ER Rep 110.

185 Ibid at 845 (Atkin J).

186 For the moral objection to an analogous argument, see the discussion of absolute liability at § 4.2.2.

187 [1965] AC 486, [1964] 3 All ER 820 (HL).

acquitted. However, a delegation was found to have occurred in *Allen v Whitehead*[188] where the occupier of a cafe had been charged and convicted of "knowingly permitting" prostitutes to remain in a place where refreshments were sold and consumed. He had left his manager in charge of the business with instructions that no prostitutes were to be allowed to congregate on the premises. However, on a number of occasions this instruction was ignored and a number of prostitutes had been allowed to remain on the premises contrary to the statutory requirements. On appeal, it was held that D's ignorance of the facts was no defence. The manager's acts and his mens rea were to be imputed to the occupier because it was found that the management of the cafe had been delegated to him.[189]

The distinction between these two cases suggests that for vicarious liability to arise there must be a real and effective delegation of powers and the corresponding duties, such that the activity delegated is under the exclusive control of the delegate, free from the principal's supervision.[190]

The delegation principle has been described as "anomalous"[191] and as "hard to justify".[192] It allows a person to be liable for an offence requiring mens rea on the basis that the defendant had put in her own place a substitute who did the proscribed acts and had the relevant mental element at the time. The defendant is thus made answerable for the acts and mental element of another.[193] Perhaps, however, it can be said that the defendant voluntarily assumes that risk by her act of delegation? As such, vicarious liability by delegation may be justifiable on the basis that, in certain areas of regulatory activity, legislative compliance would be difficult to achieve if the person upon whom certain statutory duties have been cast were able to avoid responsibility for ensuring compliance by choosing not to exercise the requisite control, and simply passing to a delegate the control of the premises.[194] It is arguable that in those areas in which it has traditionally been applied, vicarious liability is a useful vehicle for ensuring that a master is answerable for her servant's actions and, particularly in the area of liquor licensing, that it serves the interests of public policy. However, it remains a controversial form of criminal liability, which probably should not be

---

188   [1930] 1 KB 211, [1929] All ER Rep 13.

189   See also *Linnet v Commr of Metropolitan Police* [1946] KB 290, [1946] 1 All ER 380, in which a co-licensee was held liable for acts of the other licensee for "knowingly permitting disorderly conduct", on the basis of delegation in keeping the premises.

190   See *Somerset v Hart* (1884) 12 QBD 360. Regarding the extent of delegation necessary for the principle to apply, see *Adams* § Ch4.1.02(6).

191   *Adams* § Ch4.1.02(5).

192   Cf the comments of Lord Reid in *Vane v Yiannopoullos* [1965] AC 486, [1964] 3 All ER 820 (HL); *Smith and Hogan*, 177.

193   For trenchant criticism of *Allen v Whitehead*, see Williams, *TBCL*, § 43.3.

194   See the discussion in *Adams* § Ch4.1.02(5). In particular, it is not clear that the tactic mentioned in the text could be outflanked by the use of strict liability offences.

extended beyond the area it has traditionally occupied, namely liquor licensing.[195]

5.2.2 "Scope of employment"

Where a vicarious liability offence imposes strict[196] or absolute[197] liability and is not one to which the delegation principle applies, the defendant may alternatively be liable for the conduct of any person who has been authorised to do the very type of act involved in the offence. In these circumstances, the principal is held liable because the acts done physically by the servant may, in law, be considered the master's acts. The basis of liability under the "scope of employment" rule is that authority has been vested in a substitute, regardless of the nature of the relationship existing between the parties.

The scope of employment rule reflects the practical reality that, in most cases, the business of selling, for example, liquor by a licensee holding a licence to do so is carried on by other persons on behalf of the licensee. Consequently, it is thought that unless the licensee is held responsible for the behaviour of his servants when acting within the scope of their employment, the object of the legislation would be defeated. Thus, in *Gifford v Police*,[198] the appellant was held liable for the act of a friend, whom he had temporarily authorised to supervise a hotel bar, after the friend supplied beer to a person under the age of 21.

However, where the substitute acts outside the scope of his employment or of the authority conferred, the defendant will not be liable. For example, if a cleaner, lacking any authority to do so, opens a hotel bar outside the legal hours and sells liquor to customers, the licensee will not be liable.[199] The cleaner's acts are clearly outside the scope of his employment and cannot bind the licensee who employs him. Similarly, in *Adams v Camfoni*[200] it was held that a master was not liable when a servant boy, who had no authority to do so, supplied his master's liquor to a customer out of hours. On the other hand, a servant will not necessarily go outside the scope of his authority simply because he acts in a way contrary to instructions given. Accordingly, an assistant's selling hams as "scotch ham", despite the employer's express instructions that they were only to be sold as "breakfast hams", was held in *Coppen v Moore (No 2)*[201] to constitute a prima facie case of an offence vicariously committed by the employer.

Whenever an employee acts within the scope of her employment, the act of the employee is deemed to be the act of the master. The standard cases of this

---

195 See *Bradshaw v Ewart-James* [1983] QB 671, [1983] 1 All ER 12. For New Zealand cases in which the delegation principle has been applied, see *Gifford v Police* [1965] NZLR 484 (CA); *Murphy v Weir* [1986] NZLR 657.

196 Cf *S M Savill Ltd v MOT* [1986] 1 NZLR 653.

197 *Barker v Levinson* [1951] 1 KB 342 at 345, [1950] 2 All ER 825 at 827; *Bradshaw v Ewart-James* [1983] QB 671 at 676, [1983] 1 All ER 12 at 14.

198 [1965] NZLR 484 (CA). See also *Sivyer v Taylor* [1916] NZLR 586.

199 See *Jull v Treanor* (1896) 14 NZLR 513.

200 [1929] 1 KB 95.

201 [1898] 2 QB 306.

variety arise where the legislation prohibits the performance of a particular type of activity like "selling" or "possessing". These offences typically involve strict or absolute liability, where it is not necessary for the prosecution to prove that the offender knew the relevant facts. Liability attaches to the master or employer because, using a broad construction of the words which constitute the actus reus of the offence, the employer is treated as performing the relevant acts through the employee's actions. Smith and Hogan observe:

> Now a "sale" consists in the transfer of property in goods from A to B and the seller, in law, is necessarily the person in whom the property is vested at the commencement of the transaction. It is not a great step, therefore, for the court to say that the employer has committed the *actus reus* of "selling" even though he was nowhere near when the incident took place.[202]

Analogously, on the basis of the scope of employment principle, a company as the "master" was held liable for the acts of an employee who "used" a motor vehicle with defective brakes contrary to regulations.[203] Similarly, in *Sopp v Long*[204] the defendant, a licensee of a number of railway refreshment rooms, was held liable for the acts of a waitress, whom he had never met, for "causing" to be delivered to a customer whiskey short of the measure purported to be sold. The Court held that, being absent from the premises the licensee sold through his servant, the waitress, and that by every sale he conducted through her, he "caused" to be delivered that which was sold.[205]

5.2.2.1 *A due diligence defence?*

Where the relevant offence is one of strict liability, the Canadian Supreme Court has suggested that an employer would have the usual strict liability defence of due diligence, if charged as vicariously responsible for that offence committed by an employee, provided the defendant had set up and monitored a system intended to prevent the offence.[206] Although inconsistent with the principles of vicarious liability, this is a development to be welcomed. However, the substance of any such defence may well depend on the degree to which the preventive system is actually monitored. It would seem that merely drafting and circulating instructions to managers aimed at ensuring strict compliance with the law will not suffice.[207] The issue has yet to be decided in New Zealand.

---

202 Smith and Hogan, *Criminal Law* (7th ed), London, Butterworths, 1992, 175.

203 *James & Son Ltd v Smee* [1955] 1 QB 78, [1954] 3 All ER 273.

204 [1970] 1 QB 518, [1969] 1 All ER 855 (CA).

205 Ibid at 526, at 860 (Edmund Davies LJ). See also *Strutt v Clift* [1911] 1 KB 1 ("keeps").

206 *R v City of Sault Ste Marie* (1978) 85 DLR (3d) 161, [1978] 2 SCR 1299 (SCC).

207 See *Sopp v Long* [1970] 1 QB 518, [1969] 1 All ER 855 (CA); *Coppen v Moore (No 2)* [1898] 2 QB 306; *Director General of Fair Trading v Pioneer Concrete UK* [1995] 1 AC 456, [1994] 3 WLR 1249 (HL).

5.3 THE LIABILITY OF CORPORATIONS

For a long time the common law considered that corporations were beyond the reach of the criminal law.[208] There were many reasons why this was thought to be the case. A principal difficulty concerned the meaning given to the word "person". Where "persons" could be punished for offences committed by them, the phrase seemed inapt to include an incorporated association.[209] This merely linguistic difficulty was eventually overcome by legislation, which stipulated that the word "person" may be construed to include a legal, as well as a natural, person.[210] A further problem was that because personal appearance was necessary at assizes and quartersessions, a company, which lacked a physical existence, could not appear. However, this perceived difficulty was eventually overcome by the practice of having a representative appear and enter a plea on behalf of the company, for which provision is now made in legislation.[211]

In addition, at one time a major obstacle to the prosecution of corporations for crimes (felonies) was that all felonies were punishable by death, and since a corporation could not be put to death it was, in that sense, incapable of committing a crime. This objection has been overcome by legislation enabling a court to sentence the offender to pay a fine in lieu of imprisonment.[212] Furthermore, the objection that a corporate body has no mind or soul and, as such, is incapable of possessing the mental element necessary for most serious offences, can be met by saying that a corporation can have knowledge and form an intention *through its human agents,* so that the knowledge and intention of its agents may be *imputed* to the body corporate.[213]

The general position at common law today is that a corporation is in the same position in relation to criminal liability as a natural person, and may be convicted of common law and statutory crimes including those requiring mens rea.[214] In a now celebrated passage in *Lennard's Carrying Company Ltd v Asiatic Petroleum Company Ltd*, Lord Haldane said:

> A corporation is an abstraction. It has no mind of its own any more than it has a body of its own; its active and directing will must consequently be sought in the person of somebody who for some purposes may be called an agent, but who is really the directing mind and will of the corporation, the very ego and centre of the personality of the corporation . . . The fault or privity [of the company] is the fault or privity of somebody who is not merely a servant or agent for whom the company is

---

208 For discussion, see *Garrow and Turkington,* § VI.2.

209 See, for example, *Pharmaceutical Society v London Provincial Supply Association* 5 App Cas 857 at 869, where it was held that "person" in the Act under consideration did not include an incorporated company.

210 See s 2 Interpretation Act 1889 (UK): "person" defined to include "a body of persons corporate or unincorporate". A similar stipulation is now made in s 2 Crimes Act 1961.

211 See s 361 Crimes Act 1961 ("Plea on behalf of corporation").

212 Section 26 Criminal Justice Act 1985.

213 *DPP v Kent and Sussex Contractors Ltd* [1944] 1 KB 146 at 155, [1944] 1 All ER 119 at 123 (Lord Caldecote CJ).

214 *Halsbury's Laws of England,* vol 11(1), (4th ed Reissue), § 35.

liable upon the footing of respondeat superior, but somebody for whom the company is liable because his action is the *very action* of the company itself.[215]

In New Zealand there are now only a few crimes for which a company may not be convicted.[216] For example, a corporation cannot, by its nature, commit the offence of perjury (an offence which cannot be committed vicariously) or bigamy, which can only be committed by a natural person.[217] Homicide, including both murder and manslaughter, cannot be committed by a company as a principal because of its definition, in s 160 Crimes Act 1961, as the "killing of one human being by another".[218] For this reason, it was held in *R v Murray Wright*[219] that the defendant company, which conducted a chemist business, could not be liable as a principal offender on a charge of negligent manslaughter when the incorrect preparation of a prescribed medicine was the cause of death. However, this is not to deny that a company may be liable as a party to homicide. Liability as a principal is merely limited by s 160 in respect of the act causing death, which must be committed by a "human being". Section 66, governing secondary participation, contains no such limitation. Hence a company may still be held liable as a party to offences committed by an individual. In *R v Robert Millar (Contractors) Ltd*,[220] the company was convicted of counselling and procuring the death by dangerous driving of six occupants of a car, which had been struck by a truck owned and operated by the company. The accident was caused by a tyre blowing out on the truck. The company was jointly charged with one of its directors, who had instructed an employee to drive the truck knowing that it had a dangerously defective tyre and that there was a serious risk of harm resulting to other road users. Rejecting the company's appeal, the Court approved the view that where a corporate employer, with imputed knowledge of the defective mechanical state of the vehicle, permits an employee to take that vehicle out on the road, it is counselling and procuring the employee to drive the vehicle in that state.

Although it is sometimes argued that a punitive approach to corporate responsibility does little to ensure compliance with the law,[221] it seems plausible to assume that corporate liability coupled with the doctrine of strict liability in public welfare regulatory offences, with its defence of lack of fault, means that the management of a corporation has a real incentive to make diligent efforts to ensure compliance with the law.[222] It may be that a variety of approaches, including both punitive and preventive, are needed to restrain the

---

215 [1915] AC 705 at 713, [1914-15] All ER Rep 280 at 283 (emphasis added).

216 *Purser Asphalts & Contractors Ltd v Police* [1990] 1 NZLR 693 at 695, (1988) 3 CRNZ 540 at 543 (Eichelbaum J).

217 *R v ICR Haulage Ltd* [1944] 1 KB 551 at 554, [1944] 1 All ER 691 at 693 (CCA).

218 *R v Murray Wright Ltd* [1970] NZLR 476 (CA).

219 Ibid.

220 [1970] 2 QB 54, [1970] 1 All ER 577 (CA).

221 See, for example, Fisse, "Responsibility, Prevention and Corporate Crime" (1973) 5 NZULR 250 at 253.

222 *Adams* § Ch4.1.01.

immense power of corporations in modern society and to protect citizens from the effects of misuse, or careless use, of that power.

5.3.1 The presumed criminal liability of corporations

As was noted above, corporate criminal liability has been provided for by extending the meaning of the word "person" to include bodies corporate,[223] implying that all criminal statutes are presumed to apply to artificial as well as natural legal persons. This presumption can be overridden, especially if the particular statute indicates a contrary intention. For example, a company cannot be nominated as a "pharmacist" for the purposes of certain proceedings under the Misuse of Drugs Act 1975.[224] The definition of "pharmacist" in the Act is clearly limited to a "*person* for the time being registered as a pharmacist", which necessarily excludes a corporation.[225] We have already noted another statutory exception, that a company cannot, by definition, be guilty of homicide as a principal. The presumption of corporate liability may also be rebutted in respect of most sexual offences, at least in respect of liability as a principal.

Sometimes legislation requires that a mandatory penalty be imposed in respect of certain offences which, by its nature, is inapplicable to a corporation. In the rare cases where this occurs, it may not be possible to prosecute a corporation, and the presumption in favour of corporate liability may be rebutted. This might occur where, for example, legislation prescribes a mandatory minimum sentence of imprisonment or community service for a particular offence. However, as was noted earlier, exclusive minimum sentences are rare and in almost every case the courts may alternatively impose a fine in lieu of imprisonment.[226]

Even in cases where the legislation imposes a mandatory form of penalty that is not amenable to a company (for example, a mandatory period of disqualification), the presumption will not necessarily be rebutted if other penalties may be imposed such that the mandatory penalty may be regarded in the context as "mere surplusage" to the other penalties available. An illustrative case is *Police v Purser Asphalts & Contractors Ltd*,[227] where a company was charged under s 56 Transport Act 1962 with causing death by the careless use of a motor vehicle. The mandatory period of disqualification from driving, which can apply only to a natural person convicted of the offence, was held simply to be inapplicable to the company, which would nonetheless be subject to other penalties under the statute. The Court was influenced to reach this result by the fact that any other outcome would be inconsistent not only with the legislative presumption in favour of including companies, but also with the very purpose of s 56. As Eichelbaum J observed:

---

223   See s 6(1) Acts Interpretation Act 1924, and s 2 Crimes Act 1961.
224   See *R v Richards* (1992) 9 CRNZ 355.
225   Section 2 Misuse of Drugs Act 1975 (emphasis added).
226   Section 26(1) Criminal Justice Act 1985.
227   [1990] 1 NZLR 693, also reported as *Purser Asphalt & Contractors Ltd v Police* (1988) 3 CRNZ 540.

It is notorious that numerous vehicles on the roads are in commercial use and owned by companies. There would be a significant gap in the scope of s 56(1) if incorporated owners were exempt from prosecution. The general direction of the Transport Act toward promotion of road safety is therefore in favour of the applicability of the section to bodies corporate.[228]

We may therefore state, as a general principle, that where legislation expressly mandates a particular penalty which is apposite only to natural persons, a company may still be prosecuted, provided at least one other penalty (applicable to companies) is available. This requirement is usually met by the possibility of imposing a fine, which for most offences is available by way of alternative to imprisonment.

5.3.2 Distinguishing between direct and vicarious liability of companies

Because a company is a legal person without a physical existence, it is incapable of acting or forming an intention to act other than through its human agents. There are two ways in which a corporation may be liable for an offence. First, it may be liable for the conduct of employees or agents through the doctrine of *vicarious* liability (§ 5.2), at least whenever a statute admits of vicarious liability. Alternatively, the corporation may be liable because acts done by its agents, servants, or directors are treated as acts done by the corporation itself, in circumstances where the human agents are deemed to be the "directing mind and will" of the company. In a sense, this is a false distinction, since under either approach the liabilities of the company are vicarious, being based upon an identification of the defendant company with the conduct of its agents, rather than upon any acts by the defendant itself. Nonetheless, although there is potential for confusing the two doctrines, their distinction reflects some important differences in the manner in which the acts of the human agents of a corporation may become, in law, the acts of the company itself. Whereas corporate liability depends upon an *identification* being made between the acts of a human agent and the company itself, vicarious liability involves the *attribution* of criminal liability to one individual or corporation for the acts of another.

5.3.3 Vicarious liability of corporations

Normally, vicarious liability, which makes the defendant answerable for the acts of its deputy, will not be imposed unless there are in the statute creating the offence very clear words imposing responsibility upon a defendant for the acts of its servant or agent. It should be remembered that vicarious liability was virtually unknown in the criminal law until quite recently, even though civil law has long held that an employer may be responsible for the torts of its employees acting in the course of their employment. In the criminal law, a defendant will normally only be liable for the actions of its servants on the

---

228 Ibid at 543, at 696.

basis of being a party to those actions. For the most part offenders are answerable only for their own acts.[229]

However, vicarious liability may be found where to fail to hold a master liable for the acts of its servant would be to "render nugatory" the statute and thus defeat the will of Parliament.[230] Especially in the context of regulatory offences, a particular statute may be open to the interpretation that it was the Legislature's intention to regulate certain types of activity by making the defendant liable for the acts of a servant, on the presumed basis that imposing liability on employers for contraventions by employees will more effectively achieve compliance with the legislation. The issue in each case will be whether the relevant statutory provision, which imposes a penalty on (say) an owner, is capable of making the defendant liable for an act of its employee when that act is done within the scope of employment but without the knowledge or instructions of the defendant. Because, in such cases, liability may be established without mens rea on the part of the defendant, it follows that this form of liability is likely to be relatively rare. However, as we saw in § 5.2 there are some limited areas of commercial activity where, historically, the Legislature has sought to regulate the activity by imposing vicarious liability. There does not appear to be any legislative tendency to expand the scope of vicarious liability.

A company may become vicariously liable for the actions of its servant (provided she is acting within the scope of her employment[231] or pursuant to a delegation[232]) in any circumstances in which vicarious liability may be imposed on an individual defendant. Typically, vicarious liability is found in legislation which regulates the sale or distribution of foodstuffs and other related activities, and in the area of liquor licensing. In such activities, it is not uncommon for the Legislature to attach criminal responsibility to an employer, whether or not a company, for the acts done by an employee in the course of his employment, or (in the case of mens rea offences) pursuant to a delegation of the employer's powers and duties, even though the particular acts were not authorised by the master, and may even have been expressly prohibited.[233] The details of this doctrine are considered in § 5.2.

5.3.4 Rules for attributing direct (non-vicarious) liability to a company

Any proposition about a company necessarily involves reference to a set of rules. A company exists because there is a statutory rule which says that a fictional person is deemed to exist and which has the powers, rights, and duties

---

229 *R v Huggins* (1730) 2 Str 883 at 885, 93 ER 915 at 917.

230 Allen, *Textbook on Criminal Law* (3rd ed), 1991, 200.

231 § 5.2.2.

232 § 5.2.1.

233 See, for example, *Coppen v Moore (no 2)* [1898] 2 QB 306, where vicarious liability was found to exist in relation to the offence of selling goods to which a forged trademark or false trade description is applied.

of a natural person.[234] However, the creation of such a fictional person is only meaningful if rules exist that are able to tell us which acts count as acts of the company. Such rules are called "the rules of attribution". Their particular form depends upon the constitutional rules of the company, rules ordinarily implied in company law, and other rules which have been formulated by the courts in order to distinguish between employees and other company officials whose acts may be attributed to the company itself. The application of these rules determines the circumstances in which a company may be liable for the acts and mental state of an individual.

The basic rule of attribution is that, for an individual's conduct and state of mind to be identified with the company, *she must be in control of the company or a sphere of its activities.* However, this rule, as we shall see, is no more than a generalisation.

It is tempting to argue that the rules of attribution are general and invariant in nature, so that the liability of corporations for the acts of wayward employees or agents could be conveniently limited to acts done within the permissive powers of the company: for example, where the act is specifically authorised by a resolution of the board or a unanimous agreement of shareholders. Unfortunately, issues of liability are seldom as simple as this. First, where nominal and effective authority within a company differ, the courts will attribute on the basis of the particular company's actual as well as legal management structures. For example, in *Meridian Global Funds Management Asia Ltd v Securities Commission*[235] the company was held liable for the activities of employees who were left in de facto control of an area of the company's activities, though nominally authority was in the hands of a superior. It was held that the fact that an investment manager had undertaken a deal to purchase shares for a corrupt purpose, and did not give notice as required by the New Zealand Securities Amendment Act 1988 because he did not want his employers to find out, did not prevent that knowledge and the duty to give notice from being attributed to the company. Provided the person speaks and acts as the company, and is in actual control of company operations, liability may attach to the company.[236]

Secondly, and perhaps even more importantly, a simple insistence upon generalised rules of attribution would sometimes defeat the legislative intention that a particular law was intended to apply to companies. In such cases the court must fashion a special rule of attribution "tailored . . . to the terms and policies" of the particular substantive rule.[237] We may see the

---

234 See s 6(1)(a) Acts Interpretation Act 1924; *Meridian Global Funds Management Asia Ltd v Securities Commission* [1995] 3 NZLR 7, [1995] 2 AC 500 (PC).

235 Ibid. See also *Morris v Wellington City Corp* [1969] NZLR 1038. Cf *John Henshell (Quarries) Ltd v Harvey* [1965] 2 QB 233, [1965] 1 All ER 725: knowledge of an employee (a weighbridge operator) who has no real control over the company's activities is not enough.

236 See *Nordik Industries v Regional Controller of Inland Revenue* [1976] 1 NZLR 194.

237 *Meridian Global Funds Management Asia Ltd v Securities Commission* [1995] 3 NZLR 7 at 16, 17, [1995] 2 AC 500 at 512 (PC) (Lord Hoffmann).

tailoring of generalised attribution principles in a number of recent decisions, considered in the following paragraphs.

In early cases, the courts often utilised a distinction between individuals who were the "brains" or "minds " of the company and those who were merely its "hands", implying that inferior employment status may never bind a company in respect of unauthorised acts done within the scope of an individual's employment.[238] The analogy of "brains" and "hands" was applied in *Tesco Supermarkets Ltd v Nattrass*.[239] Tesco had been prosecuted under the Trade Descriptions Act 1968 for displaying a notice that goods were being offered at a price less than that at which they were in fact being offered. The prosecution had arisen because the shop manager of one of the 200-odd supermarket branches had negligently failed to notice that he had run out of specially marked low-price packets of washing powder, one of which was sold to a customer at a price higher than that stated on the display notice. The Act provided a defence for a shop owner who could prove that the commission of the offence was caused by "another person" and that he took "all reasonable precautions . . . to avoid the commission of such an offence by himself or anyone under his control". The House of Lords held that the branch manager could not be considered a controlling mind of the company, such that his negligence could be attributable to the company (he was, in law, "another person"), and that the precautions taken by the board of directors were sufficient to count as precautions taken by the company. However, the case was not resolved simply at the level of general principle, by distinguishing between "brains" and "hands", but also by examining the substantive rule in the particular statute which, the Court concluded, was intended to give effect to a policy of consumer protection, the rationale for which did not require the conclusion that the acts and defaults of the manager were to be attributed to the company. It is this particularised element that makes the modern cases on corporate attribution distinguishable from each other.

In contrast with *Tesco* is the decision in *Director General of Fair Trading v Pioneer Concrete (UK)*.[240] There a restrictive arrangement, in breach of an undertaking by a company to the Restrictive Practices Court, was made by executives of the company acting within the scope of their employment. The board of directors knew nothing of the arrangement and had given instructions to company employees that they were not to make such arrangements. However, the House of Lords held that for the purposes of deciding whether the company was in contempt, the act and the state of mind of an employee who entered into an arrangement in the course of his employment should be attributed to the company. Again, the particular attribution rule was derived from a construction of the undertaking against the background of the Restrictive Trade Practices Act 1976. The Court concluded that such undertakings would be worth little if the company could avoid liability for

---

238 See *HL Bolton (Engineering) Co Ltd v TJ Graham & Sons Ltd* [1957] 1 QB 159 at 172, [1956] 3 All ER 624 at 630 (CA).

239 [1972] AC 153, [1971] 2 All ER 127 (HL).

240 [1995] 1 AC 456, [1994] 3 WLR 1249 (HL).

what its employees had actually done on the ground that the board did not know about it. An uncritical application of the *Nattrass* rule, the Court found, would effectively mean that the "higher management" of a company could benefit from restrictive arrangements, outlawed by Parliament, by hiding behind the actions of an employee who had individually accepted, implemented, and arranged prohibited activities which benefited the company, while claiming that he was not authorised to do so.[241]

The conclusion which emerges from these cases is that it will be a question of construction in each case whether enforcement of the particular statute or regulation requires that knowledge of an act, or the state of mind with which it is done, should be attributed to the company. In particular, it should not be assumed that whenever a servant of a company has authority to do an act on the company's behalf, knowledge of that act will for all purposes be attributed to the company.[242] For example, the fact that a company authorises an employee to drive a heavy vehicle does not automatically imply that, if he kills someone by reckless driving, his actions and state of mind must be attributed to the company for the purposes of establishing its criminal liability. In each case, the rule of attribution must be tailored to the terms and policies of the substantive rule.[243]

5.3.4.1 *"Alter ego" v "embodiment" or "identification"?*

In older case law it is sometimes suggested that identification between the company and its human agents was based on the theory that when speaking and acting for the company, the agent was acting as the "alter ego" of the company. In *Tesco Supermarkets Ltd v Nattrass* Lord Pearson indicated that he saw a place for the phrase "alter ego":

> A company may have an alter ego, if those persons who are or have its ego delegate to some other person the control and management, with full discretionary powers, of some section of the company's business.[244]

However, in the same case Lord Reid deprecated the use of the phrase "alter ego" in this context:

> I think it is misleading. When dealing with a company the word alter is I think misleading. The person who speaks and acts as the company is not alter. *He is identified with the company.* And when dealing with an individual no other individual can be his alter ego. The other individual can be a servant, agent, delegate or representative but I know of neither principle nor authority which warrants the confusion . . . of two separate individuals.[245]

The essence of corporate personality, as Lord Reid notes in an earlier passage in the judgement,[246] is that when a person acts or speaks for a company he is

---

241 See the comments of Lord Templeman, ibid at 465, 1254, 1255.

242 *Meridian Global Funds Management Asia Ltd v Securities Commission* [1995] 3 NZLR 7 at 16, 17, [1995] 2 AC 500 at 512 (PC)

243 Ibid.

244 [1972] AC 153 at 193, [1971] 2 All ER 127 at 150.

245 Ibid at 171,172, at 132, 133 (emphasis added).

246 Ibid at 170, at 131.

acting *as* the company and his mind which directs his acts is the mind of the company:

> There is no question of the company being vicariously liable. He is not acting as a servant, representative, agent or delegate. He is an embodiment of the company or, one could say, he hears and speaks through the persona of the company, within his appropriate sphere, and his mind is the mind of the company.[247]

In *Meridian Global Funds Management Asia Ltd v Securities Commission*,[248] the New Zealand Court of Appeal based attribution upon the notion that the investment manager was the "directing mind and will" of the company.[249] The concept of a "directing mind and will" is closer to Lord Reid's idea that the person acting for the company is "an embodiment of the company" and is, with respect, to be preferred to the "alter ego" theory. However, as has been noted, whether a particular individual can be described as the "directing mind and will" whose knowledge that an act has been done may be attributed to a company, remains a matter for construction in each case. In *Meridian*, the Privy Council said:

> In such a case, the court must fashion a special rule of attribution for the particular substantive rule. This is always a matter of interpretation: given that it was intended to apply to a company, how was it intended to apply? Whose act (or knowledge, or state of mind) was *for this purpose* intended to count as the act etc of the company? One finds the answer to this question by applying the usual canons of interpretation, taking into account the language of the rule (if it is a statute) and its content and policy.[250]

The notion of the "directing mind" is the basis of the "identification" doctrine in Canada. In *R v Church of Scientology*[251] the Ontario Court of Appeal applied the identification doctrine to a non-profit religious corporation on the basis that since corporations (including non-profit corporations) occupy such a central role in society, it would be "intolerable" to leave them outside the purview of the criminal law.[252] Of the identification doctrine itself, the Court said:

> The identification doctrine is a pragmatic, but rational, way of making a corporation liable for the criminal acts committed on its behalf or at least partly for its benefit. It imposes liability only for the acts of the corporate governing body and those to whom that body has delegated executive authority. Moreover, even if the employee is deemed to be a directing mind of the corporation, the corporation will not be liable for that employee's acts if they are in total fraud of the corporation.

The reason for the latter limitation would seem to be that an employee who acts in fraud of a company cannot be said to be carrying out his assigned function in the corporation and, as such, is acting outside the scope of his

---

247 Ibid.

248 [1994] 2 NZLR 291 (CA).

249 The phrase "directing mind and will" comes from a celebrated speech of Viscount Haldane, in *Lennard's Carrying Co Ltd v Asiatic Petroeum Co Ltd* [1915] AC 705, [1914-15] All ER Rep 280 (HL).

250 [1995] 3 NZLR 7 at 12, 13, [1995] 2 AC 500 at 507.

251 (1997) 33 OR (3d) 65.

252 Ibid at 131.

authority. In *R v Safety-Kleen Canada*[253] it was held that where the identification theory applies in the absence of a statutory basis for corporate liability, the inquiry is a "fact-driven" one which looks beyond titles and job descriptions to the reality of any given situation.

5.3.4.2 *Liability for negligence in failing to supervise a company's activities*

Alternatively, depending upon the particular statute, a company may be directly liable for offences of negligence in failing to prevent the actus reus from occurring. Because negligence liability does not require proof either of particular acts or of a particular state of mind, the company is more easily affixed with responsibility for its omission to prevent harm. In these cases, the company will normally escape criminal liability if it has acted reasonably to select suitable persons to oversee the corporation's activities and to carry out a reasonable policy to ensure compliance with the law. Conversely, in the absence of a reasonable standard of conduct and management, liability may be imputed to a company. In *The Lady Gwendolen*[254] the defendant company was the owner of a ship which had been involved in a collision with another vessel. The collision occurred because the master, as was his practice, had taken his fully-laden vessel up the Mersey Channel at full speed in dense fog without more than an odd glance at his radar. Owning ships was a subsidiary part of the company's activities. It had a traffic department which managed the ships under the overall supervision of a member of the board who was a brewer and took little interest in the safety of their navigation. The marine superintendent who was below the traffic manger in the company's hierarchy failed to observe that the ship's master was given to dangerous navigation. In attributing liability to the company, the Court said:

> In their capacity as shipowners they must be judged by the standard of conduct of the ordinary reasonable shipowner in the management and control of a vessel . . .[255]

The Court found that a reasonable shipowner would have realised what was happening and would have given the master proper instruction in the use of radar.

While a corporation will not normally be liable for the negligent conduct of junior employees, the breach, by a superior officer of a company, of a duty to check the conduct of a junior may result in liability being attributed to the company itself. However, such a duty would not normally arise where the junior employee is experienced at the work in question, unless there were special facts to suggest a need for closer oversight.[256] Such a person could properly be described as the "hands" of the company, whose actions would not

---

253 (1997) 145 DLR (4th) 276, 114 CCC (3d) 214.

254 [1965] P 294, [1965] 2 All ER 283 (CA).

255 Ibid at 333, at 288 (Sellers LJ).

256 *Adams* § Ch4.1.01; and see *Lewin v Bland* [1985] RTR 171.

normally be attributable to the company because they do not represent the mind and will of the company.[257]

5.3.4.3 *Mens rea offences*

Where the offence committed requires proof of a specific intent, a corporate defendant cannot be found guilty unless the requisite intent was a state of mind of one or more of the natural persons who constituted the company's directing mind and will.[258] By contrast, where the offence is one of strict or absolute liability, the company may be held liable for the acts of any of its servants or agents once those acts are proved to be, in law, the company's acts.[259] Where (a third alternative) it is a defence for an employer to prove that the offence was due to the act or default of another, and that the employer took all reasonable precautions, this defence is available to a corporation. In such circumstances, "another person" is any person other than the directors or other superior officers who control the corporation's affairs.[260]

If a defence requires evidence of a belief or other state of mind, this must normally be the belief or state of mind of the controlling officer[261] since she is acting as the company and it is her mind which directs the company.[262] However, such a belief may be negated if another superior officer knows that the belief is ill-founded.[263] This is because the supervening belief held by the superior officer becomes the knowledge or belief of the corporation itself, provided that officer at the point at which he acquires the knowledge is acting within the scope of his employment.

Relevant knowledge or beliefs may also be attributed to the company, even where the impugned individual cannot be described as a or the "directing mind and will" of a company, provided it is established that the individual concerned had been delegated the "governing executive authority" of the company within the scope of her authority: that is to say, where she has been left with the decision-making power in a relevant sphere of corporate activity.[264]

5.3.5 Personal liability of company employees

As a general rule, a director or controlling member of a company is not criminally liable for the acts of the company simply because of his position. Liability is not automatically vicarious. Furthermore, it does not follow that because a company may be criminally liable for the acts of its officers acting

---

257 See *Re H Bolton (Engineering) Co Ltd v TJ Graham and Sons Ltd* [1957] 1 QB 159 at 172, [1956] 3 All ER 624 at 630 (CA) (Denning LJ).

258 *Wings Ltd v Ellis* [1984] 1 All ER 1046 at 1053; and see *Tesco Supermarkets Ltd v Nattrass* [1972] AC 153, [1971] 2 All ER 127 (HL).

259 Smith and Hogan, *Criminal Law* (7th ed), London, Butterworths, 1992, 182.

260 *Tesco Supermarkets v Nattrass* [1972] AC 153, [1971] 2 All ER 127 (HL).

261 *GF Coles & Co Ltd v Goldsworthy* [1958] WAR 183.

262 *Nordik Industries v Regional Controller of Inland Revenue* [1976] 1 NZLR 194 at 203.

263 *Brambles Holdings Ltd v Carey* (1976) 15 SASR 270.

264 *Rhone (The) v Peter AB Widener (The)* (1993) 101 DLR (4th) 188 at 209, 210, [1993] 1 SCR 497 at 520, 521 (SCC) (Iacobucci J).

within the scope of their employment, an individual officer must be criminally liable because the company has been found to be criminally liable. The company's acts are defined by the actions of those who are identified as the "directing mind and will" of the company. But an individual officer of the company may avoid liability if he did not know of the facts which were constitutive of the offence or offences committed by other senior officials of the company and by which the company was itself impugned. In *Cardin Laurant Ltd v Commerce Commission*,[265] which involved a prosecution under the Fair Trading Act 1986 for offering to supply a garment which failed to comply with product safety standards, the High Court held that the principal in a company could not be held a party to any offence committed by the company unless he had knowledge of the essential matters which constitute the offence.[266] However, where the principal of a company is knowingly concerned in the commission of offences committed by the company, there can be no objection to prosecuting the principal personally for the identical acts and decisions that were relied on as the acts of the company.[267] There is nothing conceptually wrong with such a course because a person may function in two capacities.[268] The relevant principle has been expressed in these terms:

> the company, being a legal entity apart from its members, is also a legal person apart from the legal personality of the individual controller of the company, and that he in his personal capacity can aid and abet what the company speaking through his mouth or acting through his hand may have done.[269]

But the same principle does not apply when a conspiracy is alleged. The basis of conspiracy is the acting in concert of two or more persons. Although a company is a separate legal entity, where the sole responsible person in a company is the defendant herself, there cannot be two or more persons or minds and so there can be no conspiracy between the defendant and the company.[270] On the other hand, this rationale does not exclude the possibility of a conspiracy involving the company where two or more directors have agreed together to do an unlawful act, since the guilty mind of only one human agent, acting within the scope of his employment, is necessary to impugn the company.

---

265 [1990] 3 NZLR 563, (1989) 3 TCLR 470.

266 Ibid at 569, at 477 (Fisher J). Of course, the person need not actually know that an offence has been committed, because he may not know that the facts constitute an offence and ignorance of the law is not a defence: *Johnson v Youden* [1950] 1 KB 544 at 546, [1950] 1 All ER 300 at 302.

267 See *Hamilton v Whitehead* (1988) 166 CLR 121 at 125, 82 ALR 626 at 628 (HCA).

268 Ibid at 128, at 630.

269 *R v Goodall* (1975) 11 SASR 94 at 101 (Bray CJ).

270 *R v McDonnell* [1966] 1 QB 233, [1966] 1 All ER 193 (CCA).

Individual liability may also attach to the directors of a company in respect of an offence committed by a corporation where the statute creating the offence specifically provides, for example, that the directors or persons involved in the management of the corporation are liable unless they can prove that they did not know that the offence was being committed or that they took reasonable steps to prevent its commission.[271]

---

271 See, for example, s 340 Resource Management Act 1991; *Machinery Movers Ltd v Auckland Regional Council* [1994] 1 NZLR 492, (1993) 2 NZRMA 661.

6

The Inchoate Offences

Attempt, conspiracy, and incitement are inchoate crimes. Their designation as "inchoate" reflects the fact that they criminalise conduct by D which is incomplete or imperfect, in the sense that it has not resulted in the commission of some particular, substantive offence. Thus they criminalise the conduct of a person who has the purpose of committing a substantive offence, where her conduct has the *potential* to culminate in that offence, without the need for the offence actually to occur.[1]

In general, the rationale for having inchoate crimes is derivative from the rationale for criminalising a substantive offence. If particular conduct — say, causing another's death — is sufficiently harmful to warrant criminalisation, it is thought that so, too, is the attempt (conspiracy, incitement) to bring that harm about. It may not be so bad to try unsuccessfully to kill V as it is to succeed, but it is both culpable and wrongful to do so all the same. It would be odd if V were to react as if nothing untoward had happened. Society endorses this view, by recognising that the proximity of her attempt to the substantive crime gives D's behaviour and intentions a criminal character in their own right.

Moreover, there are deterrence and law-enforcement reasons for criminalising inchoate activity. In order to deter persons from killing others, it seems desirable also to deter them from attempting (plotting, inciting others) to do so.[2] Having inchoate offences also enables the police to intervene and prevent crime before it occurs, without foregoing the chance of a conviction. It would be bizarre indeed if the police were, in order to save V's life, forced to arrest D and in so doing enable her to escape criminal liability.

6.1 ATTEMPTS

Section 72 Crimes Act 1961 provides:

> (1) Every one who, having an intent to commit an offence, does or omits an act for the purpose of accomplishing his object, is guilty of an attempt to commit the offence intended, whether in the circumstances it was possible to commit the offence or not.
>
> (2) The question whether an act done or omitted with intent to commit an offence is or is not only preparation for the commission of that offence, and too remote to constitute an attempt to commit it, is a question of law.
>
> (3) An act done or omitted with intent to commit an offence may constitute an attempt if it is immediately or proximately connected with the intended offence, whether or not there was any act unequivocally showing the intent to commit that offence.

The law of attempts has a long history, dating back at least to the ancient Greek and Roman civilisations. However, it is noticeably absent from early common law, where it was generally said that "a miss was as good as a mile". Only in 1801 was the general principle established that an attempt to commit a crime is, itself, a crime.[3]

Section 72 does not create offences, but rather defines the circumstances in which an attempt may be committed. Punishment for attempts is found under a number of other provisions in the Crimes Act 1961, most of which criminalise

---

1   Gillies *Criminal Law*, 1985, 512.
2   See *DPP v Nock* [1978] AC 979 at 997, [1978] 2 All ER 654 at 661 (Lord Scarman).
3   See *R v Higgins* (1801) 2 East 5, 102 ER 269.

attempts to commit specific offences.[4] The general provision punishing attempts is contained in s 311, which covers every situation falling within s 72 where no punishment is otherwise provided for. The effect of s 311 is to criminalise any attempt to commit a criminal offence (including all summary offences). In general, a person guilty of an attempted crime under s 311 is liable to one half of the maximum penalty to which a person guilty of the completed offence is liable.[5]

The law of attempts focuses on four principal types of element: mens rea, actus reus, proximity, and impossibility. Each of these aspects will be discussed below. The first three relate to the minimum requirements for a criminal attempt; the fourth, impossibility, represents an important limitation on liability for an attempt.

6.1.1 Mens rea

Mens rea is the most important element of criminal attempts, because the actus reus does not, as a matter of definition, require proof of a completed crime. Indeed, although some conduct by the accused is required before there can be an attempt, that conduct need not be obviously criminal in nature; and the criminal element of the offence may lie solely in the intent.[6] In many attempts, the actus reus may be a quite harmless act which, of itself, would not attract any adverse comment were it not for the intention of the offender to commit a crime.

Therefore, it is essential to determine the precise state of mind of the accused at the time of the act which allegedly constituted the attempt. The phrase in s 72(1) "having an intent to commit an offence" prima facie suggests that only an intention to commit the offence will suffice. In most jurisdictions, the meaning of intent in relation to attempts is construed quite narrowly. In England, for example, whereas recklessness is sufficient mens rea for most non-fatal offences against the person, and for offences of criminal damage, it is not a sufficient mens rea on a charge of attempting to commit any of those offences.[7] This is almost certainly the position in New Zealand, although the point has not been formally decided upon by the courts.

However, while it appears that the mens rea element of the crime of attempt is unaffected by the mens rea required to be convicted of the relevant full offence, and is specific to s 72, it cannot be said for certain that *only* intent suffices for the mens rea requirements of s 72. There is some debate on this point.

There is authority in England to the effect that while intent is required regarding the behaviour and consequence elements of the full offence,

---

4   See s 95 (Attempts to commit piracy); s 129 (Attempt to commit sexual violation); s 173 (Attempt to murder); s 295 (Attempted arson); s 302 (Attempting to wreck).

5   Regarding the summary trial of offences under s 311, see s 6(2) Summary Proceedings Act 1957, as amended by s 3(1) Summary Proceedings Amendment Act 1961 and s 4(2) Summary Proceedings Amendment Act 1973.

6   *R v Ancio* (1984) 10 CCC (3d) 385 at 402, [1984] 1 SCR 225 at 248 (SCC).

7   Smith and Hogan, *Criminal Law* (5th ed), London, Butterworths, 1983, 256.

recklessness will be sufficient regarding any *circumstances* specified in the actus reus.[8] Similarly, it has been argued by Smith and Hogan that merely because the notion of attempt requires an intended result, it does not necessarily require intention with respect to material circumstances.[9] The authors contend that the mens rea of a completed crime should be modified only in so far as it is necessary in order to accommodate the concept of attempt; and that if recklessness as to circumstances is a sufficient mens rea for the complete crime, so also should it be for an attempt.[10] On the other hand, Professor Griew has argued that the phrase "with intent to commit an offence" requires, as a matter of construction, that the intention must apply to the whole situation necessary to constitute the offence.[11] According to this analysis a man attempting to have sexual intercourse with a woman who does not in fact consent will not be guilty of attempted rape if he is merely reckless whether she is consenting or not. His aim must be not merely sexual intercourse, but non-consensual intercourse.

The latter, seemingly narrow, approach to the mens rea requirements of attempt has been criticised on the ground that it creates an absurdity when applied to crimes such as rape, in which the circumstantial element of non-consent is central to the offence. Ashworth[12] gives the example of two men who set out to have sexual intercourse with two women, not caring whether they consent or not. He notes that it would be absurd if the one who achieved penetration was convicted of rape, while the other, who failed to achieve penetration despite trying, was not even liable for attempted rape. In both cases the degree of moral culpability is identical, yet the attempter would avoid conviction because, being reckless, he failed to achieve his objective.

In other jurisdictions, the approach to the mens rea requirement for attempts varies. The Court of Criminal Appeal of South Australia has taken an approach similar to the English Court of Appeal, holding that the mens rea of attempted rape is an intention to have sexual intercourse being recklessly indifferent whether there is absence of consent.[13] However, in *R v Colburne*[14] the Quebec Court of Appeal has held that an attempt requires a specific intent to carry out the crime, even if the completed offence requires a lesser intent. This has led one commentator to suggest that, arguably, an attempted sexual assault in Quebec must be based on D's subjective intent to engage in non-consensual sexual activity, even though a person could now be convicted of the completed

---

8 For example *R v Khan* [1990] 2 All ER 783, (1990) 91 Cr App R 29. See also White, "Three Points on *Pigg*" [1989] Crim LR 539.

9 Smith and Hogan, *Criminal Law* (5th ed), London, Butterworths, 1983, 257.

10 Ibid.

11 Griew, *Current Law Statutes*; cited in Smith and Hogan, *Criminal Law* (5th ed), London, Butterworths, 1983, 257. The wording is that of s 1 Criminal Attempts Act 1981 (UK), and parallels the requirements of s 72 Crimes Act 1961: "having an intent to commit an offence."

12 *Principles*, 146.

13 *R v Evans* (1987) 30 A Crim R 262. Cf *R v Zorad* [1979] 2 NSWLR 764 at 773.

14 (1991) 66 CCC (3d) 235 at 240, 248, 249 (Que CA).

offence of sexual assault on the basis of recklessness, wilful blindness, or a failure to "take reasonable steps, in the circumstances known to the accused at the time, to ascertain that the complainant was consenting".[15] That would be to adopt the "narrow" approach advocated by Griew.

The theoretical basis for the narrow approach is, in essence, that where attempt is in issue, "the intent is the essence of the crime";[16] hence the conviction that the mental element in an attempt should be expressed as an intent to bring about each of the constituent elements of the offence attempted.[17] Anything less would be to create a very different inchoate offence from attempt, in which the marque of criminality was not supplied by D's *seeking through his actions* to commit a crime, but by the fact that his conduct merely ran the risk of being wrongful.

However, while there would seem to be little merit in any proposal to amend the New Zealand law of attempts to establish a more general doctrine of "reckless attempts", and indeed the problems presented by criminal attempts in New Zealand are not so grave as to justify such an extension to the reach of the criminal law, Ashworth's example makes a powerful case for accepting recklessness as sufficient mens rea for the circumstantial elements of the offence attempted.[18] It makes little sense if an offender could be convicted of rape for failure to take "reasonable steps" to ascertain a victim's consent,[19] while his counterpart, unsuccessfully attempting the same offence and despite even recognising that the victim may not be consenting, could avoid conviction because the prosecution had been unable to prove "subjective intent" (ie knowledge or belief that consent was absent).[20] The issue, however, has not yet been considered by a New Zealand court.[21]

Ultimately, the law's willingness to extend attempts liability to include reckless attempts is likely to be determined as a matter of public policy. The issues that need to be considered are as follows. First, should liability for an

---

15 Section 273.2 Criminal Code 1954 (Canada). See Roach, *Criminal Law*, 1996, 72.

16 *R v Whybrow* (1951) 35 Cr App R 141 at 146, 147 (Lord Goddard CJ).

17 English Law Commission, "Criminal Law: Attempt, and Impossibility in Relation to Attempt, Conspiracy and Incitement", London, HMSO, Report No 102, 1980, 10, 11.

18 For further discussion of "reckless attempts", see Moloney, "Attempts" (1991) 15 Crim LJ 175 at 179; Duff, "The Circumstances of an Attempt" [1991] 50 CLJ 100, and now his *Criminal Attempts*, Oxford, Clarendon Press, 1996.

19 Sufficient mens rea for the completed crime: see s 128(2)(b) Crimes Act 1961.

20 § 3.1.5, 3.4.

21 Neither have the New Zealand courts yet ruled on the question whether foresight of consequences as a "moral" or "virtual" certainty will be sufficient mens rea for an attempt. In principle, this issue should be approached on the basis discussed above, in § 3.1.4. In practice, the question may be regarded as unlikely to arise, since foresight of certainty will be a fact from which a jury may find it easy to infer intent. Where, for example, A, charged with attempting to injure B with intent, is apprehended before he is able to deliver a blow to the unsuspecting B's head with a heavy piece of timber, his protestations that he was not "100 percent sure" that the blow, had it been delivered, would have injured B, should hardly be a ground for avoiding conviction on the attempt charge. Every normal instinct would inform us that A had intended to injure B.

attempt depend principally on the meaning of particular words, like "intent"? Should the fact that attempt normally connotes trying and, by extension, purposeful behaviour, necessarily imply that all other elements of mens rea in an attempt must also conform to the same linguistic limitation? Secondly, is the fact that the law has historically given "intent" a narrow meaning in relation to attempts a sufficient reason for rejecting the concept of reckless attempts? Finally, would a more broadly-based mens rea for attempts be better able to protect the public against those who *would* cause harm apart from the fortuities of insufficiency of means, incompetence, or factual impossibility?

6.1.2 Actus reus

From the discussion above, it will be apparent that the mens rea of an attempt is of paramount importance. This is not to say that the actus reus is a trivial matter, but rather that it is D's mens rea that will determine whether a particular act relied on by the prosecution amounts to an attempt. For example, to enter a bank with a motor-cycle helmet in one's hand may or may not constitute an attempt to rob the bank, depending on whether there is an intent to rob the bank or merely to make a withdrawal. It is the intent which determines the character of the act. The actus reus of an attempt, on the other hand, determines when acts done by the accused in pursuit of that intention are sufficiently proximate to the envisaged crime to warrant criminal liability.[22] In a pragmatic sense, the task of the courts here is to determine when an act is sufficiently close to the intended offence to constitute a real danger to the public and justify intervention by enforcement agencies.

Under s 72(1), the actus reus of an attempt is an act or omission done "for the purpose of accomplishing his object". However, not every act or omission done for the purpose of accomplishing the criminal object will necessarily be sufficient to lead to a conviction. It has been observed that the quoted words are so general by themselves that they would include acts of mere preparation.[23] It is necessary, therefore, in applying the section, to read subsection (1) subject to the statutory limitation placed on those words by the rest of s 72. It must be shown that the criminal intent has been accompanied by an act or omission which is "immediately or proximately connected with the intended offence";[24] it is not sufficient to prove activity which is "only preparation for the commission of that offence, and too remote".[25]

Conduct which constitutes mere preparation, as opposed to an actual attempt, is on display in the facts of R v Wilcox.[26] In that case, the appellant had been charged with attempted aggravated robbery of a suburban post office. He admitted that he had planned to rob the post office, and that two air rifles and two balaclavas had been purchased for that purpose. He also admitted that he had arranged with a friend for transportation and had embarked on the

---

22   Cross & Jones, *Criminal Law* (10th ed), 1984, 419, § 17.32
23   *R v Wilcox* [1982] 1 NZLR 191 at 193 (CA),
24   Section 72(3).
25   Section 72(2).
26   [1982] 1 NZLR 191 (CA).

journey. His plan was, however, frustrated: the police had received a warning of the planned robbery from an associate of the appellant, and stopped the car carrying the offenders when it was about 1 km from the post office.

In directing the jury, the trial Judge had ruled that the evidence of purchasing the weapons and balaclavas, giving false names, persuading someone to act as a driver, loading the weapons, and travelling to within a kilometre of the objective were not simply matters of preparation and were not too remote to constitute an attempt. The Judge also implied that the individual acts could be regarded *cumulatively* as acts done for the purpose of accomplishing the object of robbery and as such sufficient to amount to an attempt.

The Court of Appeal rejected this approach. It held that independent acts of mere preparation cannot take on the quality of attempt merely by being added together. Although the Court's decision appears to leave open the question whether a judge may direct a jury to consider the whole pattern of conduct and not any individual parts of it as constituting an attempt, the Court was nevertheless satisfied on the facts of this case that the purchase of weapons and balaclavas were only acts of preparation and were incapable of giving "increased significance" as a matter of law to the car journey. It concluded, in allowing the appeal, that the appellant, at the point that he was apprehended — still some distance away from the post office — was doing no more than *getting himself into a position* from which he could embark on an actual attempt at robbery.

In reaching its decision, the Court was influenced by the reasoning of Taschereau J in a dissenting opinion in *Henderson v R*, where his Honour said:

> I do not believe that it can be held that the mere fact of going to the place where the contemplated crime is to be committed, constitutes an attempt. There must be a closer relation between the victim and the author of the crime; there must be an act done which displays not only a preparation for an attempt, but *a commencement of execution, a step in the commission of the actual crime itself.*[27]

Thus, at least for the purposes of New Zealand law, it is possible to discern two preliminary threshold tests for determining the point at which an act of mere preparation *may* become an attempt. Each may be postulated as a question:

(i) Has the offender done anything more than *getting himself into a position* from which he could embark on an actual attempt? Or,

(ii) Has the offender actually *commenced execution*; that is to say, has he *taken a step in the actual crime itself*?

If the answer to either question is "yes", then we may safely say that there has been an attempt as a matter of law. Otherwise, the conduct remains in the realm of preparation and is not a crime.

In most cases, applying either of these tests should straightforwardly resolve whether relevant conduct amounts to an attempt without the necessity of being drawn into a discussion of the complex and often inconclusive

---

27   (1948) 91 CCC 97 at 105 (emphasis added).

threshold tests developed at common law. Nonetheless, because some cases do present difficulty, it will be necessary to consider the other threshold tests which have been developed at common law and which continue to be applied by the courts. However, before doing so, we first consider the circumstances in which, under New Zealand law, either an act or an omission may provide the basis of a prosecution for attempt.

6.1.2.1 Modes in which attempts may be made

6.1.2.1(a) Words

As was noted above, the actus reus of an attempt may be either an act or omission. Where the attempt is by a positive act, it may include words used as a means of accomplishing the offence and indicating the criminal attempt. However, as with other forms of conduct, the courts distinguish between words which are *mere propositions* and at worst preparation for an attempt, and words which are *constitutive* of an attempt. In the celebrated case of *R v Barker*, Salmond J observed that in certain kinds of crime, words used by the accused which are expressive of his criminal purpose may be themselves the means or part of the means by which he endeavours to fulfil his purpose.[28] For example, D's words themselves may be the overt acts which constitute her attempt. However, before words alone will be constitutive of an attempt there must be a clear proximity between the words uttered and the offence contemplated, such that it can be said that the words constitute an attempt or part of an attempt to commit the offence. Accordingly, there will be a significant difference between the words "meet me at the park at 6 o'clock, and we will have some fun" in the context of a charge of attempted sexual indecency, and the words "come with me and we will commit a burglary". In the former example, liability for an attempt may be established, because the nearness to consummation of the crime and the accused's ability to control the course of events should the invitation be accepted suggest that there is a substantial likelihood of success. In the other example, however, the lack of specificity of time and place and the number of acts required to transform the proposition into a consummated act would strongly suggest the existence of mere words too remote to constitute even preparation, let alone an attempt. In *R v Barker*, a letter delivered to a 16-year-old boy inviting him to meet at a park with a view to "some good fun" was held to be a sufficiently overt act to constitute attempted sodomy. Similarly, in *R v Yelds*,[29] the accused's words to a girl, "you are getting a big girl now. Have you got hair growing there?" while pointing to his private parts was held, together with evidence that he had accosted the child and endeavoured to entice her to accompany him to a park, to be evidence of an attempt.

In these examples, D's spoken or written words amounted to an attempt partially because they made a link, explicit or implicit, with the substantive offence being attempted. By contrast, this link was missing in *R v Rowley*.[30] In

---

28   [1924] NZLR 865 at 876 (CA).
29   [1928] NZLR 18 (CA).
30   [1991] 4 All ER 649, [1991] 1 WLR 1020.

that case, D was convicted of attempted incitement to commit gross indecency. He had left a number of notes in different public places designed to lure young boys for immoral purposes. In allowing D's appeal, the English Court of Appeal held the notes could not be regarded as more than a preparatory act because they went no further than to seek to meet with the boy or boys in question. To constitute an attempt at incitement to commit gross indecency would have required a proposition to be made *for that specific purpose*.[31] The Court differentiated between letter-writing that sought merely to engineer a preliminary meeting, and letter-writing in which a specific invitation to commit gross indecency is made. Only the latter would amount to an attempt, since only then would D have done all he could towards inciting the commission of an offence.[32]

6.1.2.1(b) *Possession*
There has been some judicial debate on the question whether the status of possession, or other criminal status created by unlawful involvement in defined factual circumstances, could be the subject of an attempt charge. The status of possession is, strictly speaking, neither an act nor an omission. Accordingly, since s 72 requires proof of "do[ing] or omit[ting] an *act* for the purpose" of committing an offence, the acquisition of a particular status as the basis of an attempt may seem to be inconsistent with the express wording of the statute.

This issue arose in *R v Grant*,[33] which involved a prosecution for attempted possession of marijuana. The accused had picked up a bag which he thought contained marijuana. However, the police had removed the drug and replaced it with newspaper and had the bag under surveillance when the accused uplifted it. Mahon J, noting that the offence of having in possession does not entail an act by the defendant but a status created by involvement with specified factual circumstances, held that possession is itself an inchoate offence and cannot be attempted. His Honour's reason for so holding was that since the offence of possession is itself an "inchoate attempt", it would seem contrary to policy to further create an offence of attempting to be in possession.[34]

Arguably, Mahon J's reasoning reflects an unnecessarily doctrinaire approach to the requirement for an "act". In particular, he cites approvingly the statement of Glanville Williams that the actus reus of an attempt is the commission of an act and is almost always an overt act, concluding that because s 72 requires as a criterion of liability an act coupled by an intention on the part of the offender to commit an offence, it can only refer to the commission of an *act* as opposed to the acquisition (by design or otherwise) of some criminal status, created by unlawful involvement in defined factual circumstances; ie possession. Yet in *Grant*, the accused had sought to acquire

---

31 Ibid at 654, at 1025.
32 See *R v Ransford* (1874) 31 LT 488.
33 [1975] 2 NZLR 165.
34 [1975] 2 NZLR 165 at 169, 170.

(the criminal status of) possession *by an act*; ie by picking up the bag. The act requirement in s 72 was clearly satisfied.

The decision in *Grant* should be contrasted with that in *R v Willoughby*,[35] a prosecution for attempting to have possession for supply. There the Court took a broader view of the meaning of "act", at least for the purposes of attempts liability. Speight J reasoned that the notion of possession can be both "active" and "passive", and since it may include both the positive conduct of holding or transporting the thing in possession, and the passive recognition that an article is within one's power and control while permitting it to remain there, it is possible to say that an act or omission demonstrating control must always be proved in a case of possession.[36] In addition, the Court noted that the wording of the Misuse of Drugs Act 1975 referred, in the relevant section, to the conduct of possessing heroin for supply as an "offence". His Honour concluded that if, in terms of s 72, D has an intention to commit that offence (ie intends to have heroin in his possession), and does an act such as purchasing or attempting to purchase to that end, then he comes within the plain wording of s 72.

In our view, this reasoning is to be preferred to the approach of Mahon J in *Grant*. It is consistent with the theory of criminal attempts, and avoids ascribing too narrow a scope to the concept of an attempt. It is conceded that while statutory language is sometimes infelicitous in its insistence on using language which fails to reflect important developments in criminal jurisprudence, it is the task of the courts to apply the law in a manner which respects and gives expression to the policy behind the provision in question.[37]

6.1.2.1(c) *Omissions*

We have noted that s 72 allows a prosecution for attempt based on an omission by D as opposed to a positive act. It follows that where D deliberately omits to perform a legal duty but fails to bring about the (intended) consequence specified in the principal offence, the failure may constitute an attempt. However, because omissions liability is by its nature rare, an omission will seldom be the basis of an attempt prosecution.

By way of example, attempt liability may occur where D, an anaesthetist, owing V a duty to avoid omissions dangerous to life, deliberately fails to supply oxygen when V begins to turn blue in the course of an operation; but D's plan to cause the death of V is foiled before V can succumb to oxygen starvation.

This analysis applies in those rare cases where a *result* crime may be committed by an omission. However, it will not apply where the offence charged alleges a simple omission that does not require any consequences for its commission. For example, it would not normally be possible to be convicted of the offence of attempting to fail to stop after an accident, or of attempting to

---

35 [1980] 1 NZLR 66.

36 Ibid at 68. See § 2.1.2.2.

37 For a more detailed discussion see Dawkins, "Attempting to have in possession" (1981) 5 Otago LR 172. See § 1.4.4.

fail to furnish an income tax return.[38] In such cases, D's omission constitutes not merely an attempt but a successful commission of the full offence. There is no middle ground.

6.1.2.2 *"For the purpose of accomplishing his object"*

Before moving on to discussion of the boundary between attempt and preparation, it is necessary briefly to consider the phrase "for the purpose of accomplishing his object" which appears in s 72(1). The phrase limits the types of acts or omissions which may properly be considered as the basis of a charge of attempt.

The fact that D intends to commit an offence does not mean that every act she subsequently does is directed toward commission of that offence. In order to establish the actus reus of an attempted crime, there must be an act (or omission) by D which is done *for the purpose* of committing that offence. Unrelated actions, even actions coincidentally proximate to execution of the intended offence,[39] do not count.

For example, imagine a variation of the facts of *Wilcox* (§ 6.1.2). Suppose that D intended to rob Bank V. He proceeded to the scene of the robbery, alighted from his car, and was apprehended by police as he proceeded up the steps of the neighbouring Bank X with a loaded air rifle under his jacket. Assuming that walking up the steps would normally be an act going beyond mere preparation,[40] D should still avoid liability for attempted robbery on the basis that he approached the bank not (yet) in order to rob, but rather to meet his girlfriend beforehand. Whatever offences the accused may be guilty of in such circumstances, attempted robbery is not one of them.

6.1.3 From preparation to attempt

6.1.3.1 *Common law tests for proximity*

At the heart of any discussion of criminal attempts is the question where to set the threshold between an attempt and an act of "mere" preparation. To set the threshold too high means that many people who may have come dangerously close to achieving their criminal objective will avoid criminal liability, thus compromising public safety. To set it too low presents the danger of penalising those whose criminal "conduct" may have proceeded not much further than unexecuted thoughts. Unfortunately, judicial debate on this question has not always been enlightening, and many of the judicial attempts to define the threshold do little more than state the obvious in terms that are often trite and tautological. Glanville Williams notes that:

> Almost all the judgments content themselves with elaborate tautologies, reiterating in an infinite variety of language the basic rule that the attempt must be 'proximate' and not "mere preparation", but furnishing no helpful definition of the meaning of

---

38   See s 65 Transport Act 1962; s 91(a) Income Tax Act 1976.

39   See § 6.1.3.

40   *R v Campbell* (1991) 93 Cr App R 350, [1991] Crim LR 268, a decision of dubious application. Cf *R v Kelly* [1992] Crim LR 181.

these terms. Where a test is indicated by the judges it turns out on examination to be useless.[41]

In addition, statutory tests are often unhelpful in providing guidance on the issue of proximity. For example, the test contained in the English Criminal Attempts Act 1981, which has been described as "a triumph of trumpery over triviality",[42] asks simply whether "a person does an act which is more than merely preparatory to the commission of the offence",[43] and gives no guidance about when that line between preparation and attempt might have been crossed. Arguably, the test in the New Zealand Crimes Act 1961,[44] which defines an attempt in terms of an act or omission that is "immediately or proximately connected with the intended offence", is equally trite and inconclusive. Such vague standards make the application of the law very difficult, and indeed risk leaving D without fair warning that his next step may be illegal.[45] To aggravate the difficulty, judicial dicta are often contradictory and confusing. For example, it is difficult to reconcile the statement:

all acts done for the purpose of committing a crime are not attempts, for they may be merely acts of *preparation.*[46]

With the proposition that:

preparation is not an attempt. But *some* preparations may amount to an attempt.[47]

While both statements are true, they may, taken together, seem to suggest that the accumulation of independent acts of mere preparation may be sufficient to constitute an attempt, a proposition clearly rejected by the New Zealand Court of Appeal.[48]

The truth is that the mere language of proximity, as reflected in phrases like "proximately connected", "immediately connected", "more than preparation", "too remote to constitute an attempt" etc conveys much less legal meaning than might be expected of a code, and raises a serious question about the utility of attempting to define liability for attempts at all. If, as has been suggested, endeavours to define the difference between a proximate attempt and preparation are efforts to define the indefinable and are doomed to failure,[49] efforts to do so may be discounted as being at best unenlightening and at worst irrelevant. As the Court of Appeal observed in *R v Wilcox*,[50] the "broad" answer by D that his alleged conduct amounted to nothing more than preparation depends simply on an assessment of that conduct; and since the question

---

41 "Police Control of Intending Criminals" [1955] Crim LR 66 at 68.

42 Meehan, *The Law of Criminal Attempt: A Treatise*, Alberta, Carswell, 1984, 92.

43 Section 1(1) Criminal Attempts Act 1981 (England).

44 See s 72(3).

45 · Cf § 1.4.3.

46 *R v Linneker* [1906] 2 KB 99 at 104 (Walton J) (emphasis added).

47 *Commonwealth v Peaslee* 177 Mass 267 at 272, 59 NE 55 at 56 (1900) (Holmes CJ) (emphasis added).

48 *R v Wilcox* [1982] 1 NZLR 191 at 194 (CA) (Woodhouse J).

49 *Adams* (2nd ed) § 700.

50 [1982] 1 NZLR 191 at 193 (CA).

whether preparation or attempt is one of law, it ought to be possible for judges to direct themselves on that issue having regard to the quality of the accused's acts, and the time and circumstances of their occurrence, without the need to resort to an abstract test.

Nevertheless, the courts continue to assess liability for attempts with reference to various tests for proximity, despite the fact that liability invariably turns on the facts and circumstances of each case. It is necessary, therefore, to examine more closely the different tests that have been developed by the judges.

6.1.3.1(a) *The tests in Eagleton*

It is sometimes suggested that at common law over the last 100 years, two different tests as to the actus reus of attempt have predominated.[51] The first was exemplified by the decision in *R v Eagleton*.[52] In that case, the defendant was alleged to have attempted to obtain money from the guardians of a parish by falsely pretending to the relieving officer that he had delivered loaves of bread of the proper weight to the poor, when in fact the loaves were deficient in weight. In giving the judgment of the Court, Parke B said:

> Acts *remotely leading* towards the commission of the offence are not to be considered as attempts to commit it, but acts *immediately connected* with it are; and if, in this case, after the credit with the relieving officer for the fraudulent overcharge, any further step on the part of the defendant had been necessary to obtain payment, as the making out a further account or producing the vouchers to the Board, we should have thought that the obtaining credit in account with the relieving officer would not have been sufficiently proximate to obtaining the money. But, on the statement in this case, no other act on the part of the defendant would have been required. It was the *last act*, depending on himself towards the payment of the money, and therefore it ought to be considered as an attempt.[53]

Eagleton has had an important influence on the law of criminal attempts in common law jurisdictions, and the dictum quoted above is probably more often cited than any other authority in this area of the criminal law. For over 100 years, the passage has been quoted as representing a correct statement of the law, and has been adopted by law-makers in crafting statutory tests for attempts liability. Yet its use of such broad concepts as "acts remotely leading towards" and "acts immediately connected with", which purport to state a legal rule, begs the question of how to distinguish mere preparation from attempt.[54] The truth is that despite its obvious appeal to generations of judges, the dictum has served to inhibit the development of the law of attempts by limiting the conceptual framework within which the doctrine has developed.

In practice, apart from these broad conceptual phrases, the most influential aspect of the *Eagleton* approach has been its endorsement of the so-called "last

---

51 See *R v Gullefer* [1990] 3 All ER 882 at 884, [1990] 1 WLR 1063 at 1065; *R v Jones* [1990] 3 ALL ER 886 at 888, [1990] 1 WLR 1057 at 1060.

52 (1855) Dears CC 515, [1843-60] All ER Rep 363.

53 Ibid at 538, at 367 (emphasis added).

54 Meehan, *The Law of Criminal Attempt: A Treatise*, Alberta, Carswell, 1984, 90.

act" test. As we will demonstrate later in this discussion, this test, together with other "final stage theories",[55] presupposes that attempt liability can only exist where the accused has completed the last necessary act needed for the offence to occur, or has set in motion events which would normally result in an offence, without further action on his part.

6.1.3.1(b) *The "series of acts" test*

The second major approach as to the actus reus in attempt focuses not on the requirement for a discrete act that is sufficiently proximate to amount to an attempt, but rather on the question whether a "series" of acts, if uninterrupted, would amount to the crime sought. This approach is attributed to Stephen, in whose view:

> An attempt to commit a crime is an act done with intent to commit that crime, and forming part of a series of acts which would constitute its actual commission if it were not interrupted.[56]

According to Stephen, the point at which such a series of acts begins cannot be defined, but depends on the circumstances of each case. On the face of it, this suggests a very loose test of liability and allows for the threshold for liability to be constantly shifted according to the fact situation in each case. Indeed, in one passage of an earlier edition of the *Digest*, Stephen appears to imply that there may be some situations where even an act of preparation could make a person criminally liable.[57] Such an approach to attempts liability may be characterised as a radical "first stage" theory, because it offers a basis for liability much earlier than other conventional theories would allow. And for that reason we think it must be rejected. As one commentator has observed, if *any* act were a sufficient actus reus for attempt, when combined with the presence of mens rea, the non-criminal preparation/criminal attempt dichotomy would disappear, because all acts of "preparation" would suffice for an attempt.[58] This would effectively amount to punishing for mens rea alone.

Despite its approval in a number of English cases since 1906,[59] Stephen's test must be criticised for lacking practical usefulness, and for its ambiguity, since it fails to define the exact point at which a series of acts can be said to begin.

6.1.3.1(c) *The "Rubicon" test*

Other tests have sometimes gained judicial currency. The first of these derives from the judgment of Lord Diplock in *DPP v Stonehouse*.[60] There the

---

55 The phrase is due to Meehan, who formulated it to describe those theories of attempt liability which focus on conduct occurring at a late stage of a transaction or series of events and which indicate the existence of an attempt. See Meehan at 103ff.

56 *Stephen's Digest of the Criminal Law* (5th ed), 1894, art 50.

57 "I should hesitate to say no act leading up to a crime could be criminal unless it amounted to an attempt": *Stephen's Digest of the Criminal Law* (1877) Note IV, 337.

58 Meehan, *The Law of Criminal Attempt: A Treatise*, Alberta, Carswells, 1984, 99.

59 See *R v Linneker* [1906] 2 KB 99; *Hope v Brown* [1954] 1 All ER 330 at 332, [1954] 1 WLR 250 at 253; *Davey v Lee* [1967] 2 All ER 423 at 425, [1967] 3 WLR 105 at 108 (Lord Parker CJ).

60 [1978] AC 55, [1977] 2 All ER 909.

accused, an English member of Parliament and Privy Councillor, staged his own drowning in order to effect a false insurance claim. Lord Diplock held that before an act of preparation may be held to be sufficiently proximate to amount to an attempt, it must indicate a "fixed irrevocable intention to go on to commit the complete offence unless involuntarily prevented from doing so".[61] Quoting the classic words of Parke B in *R v Eagleton* ("acts remotely leading towards the commission of the offence are not to be considered as attempts to commit it, but acts immediately connected with it are"[62]), Lord Diplock then summarised the test in the now-celebrated phrase: "In other words, the offender must have crossed the Rubicon and burnt his boats."[63] The Rubicon is the ancient name of a small stream which formed part of the boundary between Italy and Cisalpine Gaul; the crossing of the stream by Caesar marked the beginning of the war with Pompey. The phrase "to cross the Rubicon" thus signifies the making of a decisive or final step. In *Stonehouse*, the House of Lords held that D's staging of his own drowning was sufficiently proximate to the commission of a complete offence of obtaining property by deception to amount to an attempt to commit that offence. His acts were held not to be mere preparatory steps towards the commission of the complete offence, since he had done all the physical acts *in his power* necessary for completion of the full offence.

6.1.3.1(d) The "commencement of execution" test

This test, various formulations of which have proved popular in both common law and civil law jurisdictions,[64] falls somewhere between *Eagleton's* "last act" test and Stephen's "uninterrupted series of acts" test. Typical statutory formulations of this test make it a crime where a person, intending to commit a crime, *begins to put his intention into execution.*[65] Arguably, a form of the "commencement of execution" test is also implicit in *Eagleton* in the assertion that "acts immediately connected with it" are to be considered attempts to commit the offence. What the commencement of execution test requires is an act (or omission) which indicates that the accused has started to do the very thing which he had planned. However, the test attracts the same criticism as does Stephen's test, in that it tends to beg the question whether the conduct is preparation or attempt, and, as the cases demonstrate, is not easy to apply to a particular set of facts. Consider the following example:

> D decides to commit an aggravated robbery, having a particular victim in mind. To this end he acquires a large hunting knife, locates a map indicating the victim's address and likely walking route, purchases a carry-bag to carry the anticipated "spoils", and having disguised himself with a balaclava purchased for the purpose, lies in wait for his victim. The victim is seen walking towards D, but when she is 100 metres from where the offender is hiding, she, for no apparent reason, turns around

---

61   Ibid at 68, at 917.

62   (1855) Dears CC 515 at 538, [1843-60] All ER Rep 363 at 367.

63   *DPP v Stonehouse* [1978] AC 55 at 68, [1977] 2 All ER 909 at 917.

64   See Meehan, *The Law of Criminal Attempt: A Treatise*, Alberta, Carswells, 1984, 101.

65   See, for example, Queensland Criminal Code 1899, as amended, s 4 (1964); Western Australia Criminal Code, Stat no 28 of 1913, as amended, s 4 (1978).

and begins to retrace her steps. Because he considers it too risky to attack the victim in the changed circumstances, D abandons his plan.

Is he guilty of an attempt? We could not say that, because he has made elaborate preparations for the crime and has got himself physically into a position from which the crime may be launched, he has done an act forming part of a series of acts which would constitute the commission of the crime of aggravated robbery if not interrupted. He would not satisfy the test in Stephen's *Digest*. By the same token, can we really say he has commenced "execution" of the crime intended? The specific elements of the crime of aggravated robbery require theft accompanied by violence or the use of a weapon. Has D come so close that he can be said to have commenced the execution of that crime? The notion of "execution" implies a degree of propinquity that goes beyond acts that are merely suggestive of criminal intent. But how far beyond? In the dissenting dictum of Taschereau J in *Henderson v R*,[66] his Honour required a "closer relation between the victim and the author of the crime" than D's merely going to the place where the contemplated crime was to be committed; but his Honour gave no guidance about the point at which the required "closer relation" was established.

In all probability, on the facts given, D would be judged not to have attempted an aggravated robbery. This conclusion is certainly consistent with the commencement of execution test in principle. But at a pragmatic level, the test appears to offer little guidance for triers of fact, and leaves the threshold question substantially unresolved. It has, nonetheless, been approved in principle by the New Zealand Court of Appeal, and may be regarded as an applicable test for determining the threshold question in New Zealand.[67] Further support for the test has also been given by the High Court in *Drewery v Police*, where Williamson J approved the dictum of Lord Reid in *Haughton v Smith*[68] that for an act to be proximate for the purposes of attempt, "the accused must have *begun to perpetrate* the crime".[69]

6.1.3.1(e) *The "last act" test*
As we have noted, the "last act" test has its origins in the dictum of Lord Parke in *R v Eagleton*.[70] The true significance of the test is that it nominates the "last act depending on [the defendant]" as the threshold at which an act of preparation becomes an attempt. According to this test an accused commits an attempt when she does the last act necessary to be done, or has set in motion physical or human factors which in the normal course of events would result in an offence, without her doing anything further.[71] The test was approved and applied by the English Court of Appeal in *R v Ilyas*,[72] where the accused had

---

66 (1948) 91 CCC 97.

67 See *R v Wilcox* [1982] 1 NZLR 191 at 195 (CA).

68 [1975] AC 476 at 499, [1973] 3 All ER 1109 at 1120, 1121 (HL).

69 (1988) 3 CRNZ 499 at 502 (emphasis added).

70 (1855) Dears CC 515 at 538, [1843-60] All ER 363 at 367.

71 Meehan, *The Law of Criminal Attempt: A Treatise*, Alberta, Carswells, 1984, 103, 104.

72 (1984) 78 Cr App R 17.

falsely reported his car stolen and had obtained, but not completed, an insurance claim form. In allowing the appeal, the Court held that the appellant had not done every act which it was necessary for him to do in order to achieve the result he intended, and as such his conduct, in so far as it had gone, was merely preparatory and too remote from the contemplated offence.

The "last act" test was also applied in the controversial decision in *R v Robinson*,[73] a case involving facts reminiscent of *Ilyas*. R was a jeweller who, having insured himself against theft, simulated a robbery against himself with a view to falsely claiming the insurance money. He concealed some of his stock, tied himself up with string, and called for help. He told a policeman who broke in to "rescue" him that he had been knocked down and his safe robbed. However, the policeman was not satisfied with the story, and while searching the premises discovered the concealed property. In allowing his appeal against conviction, the Court of Appeal held, applying the approach in *Eagleton*, that because R had taken no steps towards communicating the claim to the insurers his act of faking the robbery was an act only remotely connected with the commission of the full offence, and was not immediately connected with it. Furthermore, it was not the last act that depended on R himself to achieve the intended result.

It could be argued that the "last act" test is overly generous to those accused of crimes, and that it has the potential to allow too many criminals to escape liability. The test does, after all, allow potential criminals to proceed dangerously close to achieving their criminal purpose before enforcement authorities may intervene. This is certainly true where the sequence of events between the consummated crime and the acts of preparation is foreshortened, as may be likely to occur in crimes such as attempted rape or attempted murder. In these instances, the last act depending on the accused is likely to be the very act constituting the crime itself — ie pulling the trigger in attempted murder, and achieving penetration in the case of rape or sexual violation. In such cases, application of the last act standard appears to be inappropriate because of its tendency to leave the public unprotected against clearly dangerous conduct. This can be illustrated with reference to the case of *R v Linneker*.[74] L had drawn a loaded revolver from his pocket during an argument, but his arm was seized before he could take aim. His conviction for attempting to discharge a revolver with intent to cause grievous bodily harm was upheld on the basis that L's act in drawing the revolver from his pocket was sufficiently proximate to constitute the actus reus of an attempt. However, had the last act test been applied, at least two further stages would have had to be passed; namely, taking aim and pulling the trigger. On this basis, L would have been acquitted. It is submitted that his conviction was correct.

The better view, it is submitted, is that the "last act" is a *sufficient* but not a *necessary* basis for attempts liability. The mere fact that the accused gets so close to achieving her object but fails to complete the last act dependent on her does not necessarily imply that every act before the last act is an act of mere

---

73   [1915] 2 KB 342, [1914-15] All ER Rep Ext 1299.

74   [1906] 2 KB 99.

preparation. This analysis is supported by *O'Connor v Killian*,[75] a decision of the Supreme Court of South Australia. The appellant had received cheques sent to the previous occupant of the house in which she lived. She went to a building society and tried unsuccessfully to cash the cheques, and then opened an account in the name of the previous occupant and deposited the cheques. The appellant did not make any request to withdraw the money because she realised that she was unable to produce appropriate identification. Her defence, when charged with attempting to obtain money by false pretences, was that the conduct alleged was not sufficiently proximate to the completed offence. In particular, the defence argued, applying *Eagleton*, that because identification and a further demand for money was required, the last act depending on the appellant herself had not occurred, and therefore the offence was not made out.

In response, the Court refused to rely on the last act theory, which it held was not a condition precedent to conviction. Observing that the fact D had more to do did not prevent her attempt to commit the offence from being commenced,[76] the Court preferred the view of Salmond J in *R v Barker* that:

> to constitute a criminal attempt the first step along the way of criminal intent is not necessarily sufficient and the final step is not necessarily required.[77]

The Supreme Court concluded that the appellant's conduct was purposive, and that the prosecution had proved a sufficiently proximate act to warrant conviction. It dismissed D's appeal. The decision is surely correct. To have conceded D's argument would have meant the appellant would virtually have to have committed the intended offence before she could be guilty of an attempt. In such circumstances there is, as one writer has observed, a consequential risk for the victim; since completion of the last act before success will often be followed by complete success.[78] The consequences of setting the threshold of attempt liability at a very late stage in a series of acts could be disastrous for the victims of attempted crimes, and may be one reason why the courts have appeared unwilling to fully embrace the "last act" test. This appears from the facts in *R v Jones*.[79] D, a married man, had formed a relationship with another woman who, despite a strong attachment to D, had decided to break off the relationship in favour of another man. Subsequently, D climbed into the back seat of a car driven by his former mistress's new lover, whom he had never met, and pointed a loaded sawn-off shotgun at him, saying "You are not going to like this". The victim managed to grab the gun and push it away, and in the course of a struggle threw the gun out of the car window. The victim then escaped and rang the police.

---

75   (1985) 15 A Crim R 353. See also commentary on *O'Connor v Killian* at (1985) 9 Crim LJ 367.

76   Cf *R v Page* [1933] VLR 351, [1933] ALR 374.

77   [1924] NZLR 865 at 874 (CA).

78   Meehan, *The Law of Criminal Attempt: A Treatise*, Alberta, Carswells, 1984, 106.

79   [1990] 3 All ER 886, [1990] 1 WLR 1057.

At his trial for attempted murder, there was evidence that the safety catch of the gun was on at the time of the attack, and the victim was unable to say that the appellant's finger had ever been on the trigger. It was argued that since D would have had to perform at least three more acts before the full offence could have been completed (ie remove the safety catch, put his finger on the trigger, and pull it), the evidence was insufficient to support the charge. However, the trial Judge ruled against the submission and, after D had given evidence, the jury convicted him of attempted murder.

In construing the meaning of the corresponding attempts provision in the English Criminal Attempts Act 1981,[80] the Court of Appeal rejected D's contention that the *Eagleton* "last act" test should have been adopted by the trial Judge. Neither did it consider itself bound by the test derived from *Stephen's Digest of the Criminal Law*. Rather, the Court appeared to deny the relevance of both tests, preferring the approach taken in *R v Gullefer* that the Criminal Attempts Act steers a "midway course" between the two: an attempt "begins when the merely preparatory acts come to an end and the defendant embarks on the crime proper", ie on the actual commission of the offence.[81]

There can be little doubt that Jones ought to have been convicted. However, the approach taken by the Court to justify that conclusion is hardly satisfactory. In reality, the distinction articulated by the Court is a non-distinction. It tells us nothing further about where the line is to be drawn and reduces analysis to mere casuistry. It certainly does not tell us *why* Jones's acts were an attempt to kill, as opposed to preparation to do so.

6.1.3.1(f). *The "equivocality" test*

One theory of proximity, which dominated attempts theory in New Zealand for many years, was the so-called "equivocality" rule. The rule derives from a threshold theory developed by Salmond J in *R v Barker*.[82] Salmond J held that in order to be sufficiently proximate, the acts relied on as constituting an attempt must be "sufficient in themselves to declare and proclaim the guilty purpose with which they are done". That is to say, the case must be one of res ipsa loquitur. The "equivocality" rule was accepted by *R v Yelds*[83] as stating the law in New Zealand in 1928. It remained as the principal threshold test for attempts in New Zealand until being criticised by Adams J in *Campbell v Ward*,[84] on the grounds that it tended to exclude overt acts that were proximate and which were proved by other evidence to have been done with the necessary intent.[85]

---

80 Section 1(1) of the UK Act provides: "If with intent to commit an offence to which this section applies, a person does an act which is *more than merely preparatory to the commission of the* offence, he is guilty of attempting to commit the offence." (emphasis added).

81 *R v Gullefer* [1990] 3 All ER 882 at 885, [1990] 1 WLR 1063 at 1066.

82 [1924] NZLR 865 (CA).

83 [1928] NZLR 18 (CA).

84 [1955] NZLR 471. See also *R v Mackie* [1957] NZLR 669 (CA); also Sim, "The Actus Reus in Criminal Attempt" (1955) 8 MLR 620.

85 [1955] NZLR 471 at 476.

The rule was explicitly abrogated by s 72(3) Crimes Act 1961,[86] which provides that an intentional act immediately or proximately connected with the intended offence may be an attempt, regardless whether there was any act "unequivocally showing the intent to commit that offence". However, it seems the unequivocality rule may not be completely dead. A partial revival of the theory would seem to be implicit in comments of Williamson J in *Drewery v Police*.[87] In that case, his Honour suggested in construing s 72(3), that in any case where the act is one which *does* unequivocally show intent to commit an offence, the question whether the act is only preparation or is too remote cannot be answered by inquiring only whether that act was *immediately* or *proximately connected* with the intended offence:

> It would seem to be a matter of degree so that if the evidence of intent is strong and clear the proximity or immediacy may not have to be as great as in cases where evidence of intent is reliant upon inferences to be drawn from the nature of the act itself.[88]

That is to say, where D's actions unequivocally disclose a criminal purpose, that factor may be taken into account when deciding whether D's actions were sufficiently proximate to commission of the full offence to count as an attempt. In our view, this proposition cannot be accepted without reservation.[89] First, the suggested qualification to subs (3) would seem to introduce new, extra-statutory criteria for determining proximity, when the Legislature had been concerned to limit the effect of such criteria by deliberate abrogation of the equivocality rule. Secondly, it is arguable that s 72(3) is not only or primarily concerned with situations where the nature of the act fails unequivocally to show an intent to commit a crime, and that it stipulates a general test of proximity whether or not there was any act unequivocally showing the intent to commit the offence.[90] Williamson J's interpretation of s 72(3) has itself been questioned. In *R v Drummond*,[91] a prosecution for attempting to manufacture amphetamine, Holland J queried the approach of Williamson J in the passage quoted. Noting that subsection (3) does not apply unless the act has been proved to have been done or omitted with the necessary intent, his Honour expressed difficulty in seeing how the strength of the evidence of the intent can affect the interpretation of the subsection if the court must be satisfied about D's intent even before the subsection applies.[92] We agree. It seems unnecessarily confusing to reintroduce, in any form, the language of unequivocal acts when the Legislature has clearly been at pains to avoid the complications implicit in such an approach.[93]

---

86 *Adams* § CA72.10.
87 (1988) 3 CRNZ 499 at 503.
88 Ibid at 503.
89 *Adams* § CA72.10.
90 Ibid.
91 (1993) 9 CRNZ 228.
92 Ibid at 233.
93 Regarding the impact of the equivocality rule outside New Zealand, see the brief discussion in *Adams* § CA72.10A.

6.1.3.2 *Inadequacy of proximity theory*

Proximity has always been "of the essence" in determining liability for an attempt. In the Crimes Act 1961, the notion of "proximity" stands opposed to that of "remoteness", suggesting the conceptual threshold between an act of preparation and an attempt. However, it is a circular and an ultimately unhelpful distinction because an attempt is intentional conduct which is sufficiently proximate to the intended crime and not so remote as to be regarded as mere preparation; preparation is intentional conduct which is insufficiently proximate to an intended crime and too remote to be regarded as an attempt. Neither proposition gets us very far. Neither tells us what it is about the *character* of an act that allows us to say "that act is only preparation" or "that act is an attempt".

One of the factors that has bedevilled the law's attempts to articulate a simple, universal test to determine the threshold question in attempts is its insistence on identifying discrete "acts" or "omissions" as the harbingers of criminal conduct, rather than considering the character of the conduct taken as a whole. Yet, this is done freely in other areas of the criminal law. For example, we do not insist on a minute analysis of each separate act or omission preceding the prohibited event to determine whether an accused was acting voluntarily. Rather, we examine the whole context of events to determine whether the accused's "behaviour" was consistent with the claim that he was acting involuntarily.[94] Similarly, when determining liability in respect of result crimes such as murder, we do not analyse the multiplicity of individual acts and omissions that comprise the actus reus. We usually simply ask the jury, "did D 'kill' V?" We know, as a matter of common understanding, that the act of killing has composite elements which must necessarily occur before the crime of murder can be said to be complete. And while each element is susceptible to proof or disproof, liability ultimately turns on the existence of broad patterns of conduct which establish the accused's responsibility for the crime. It seldom turns on the existence or non-existence of a particular bodily movement.

Nonetheless, it seems that this is just what attempts "theory" seeks to do. As long as we continue to insist on a fine line being drawn between attempt and mere preparation, we necessarily consign ourselves to the sorts of analyses discussed above that are ultimately incapable of clear or definite resolution. In fact we are no closer to determining the point at which preparation ends and an attempt begins than when that inquiry first began in earnest over 100 years ago. This truth, it is submitted, reveals something about the theoretical tools being used.

6.1.3.3 *A way forward?*

The difficulty involved in devising an adequate abstract test to determine whether, in a particular case, the accused has gone beyond mere preparation, has led some judges to conclude that the issue must be determined by

---

94 See, for example, *Ryan v R* (1967) 121 CLR 205, [1967] ALR 577.

"common sense".[95] This was the preferred approach of the Court of Appeal in *Police v Wylie*.[96] On a charge of attempting to procure cocaine, D had got as far as inspecting the drugs but had not agreed on the price or made an actual offer to purchase. For these reasons the Supreme Court on appeal quashed D's conviction, holding that there had been nothing more than an invitation to trade. The Court of Appeal, on the contrary, held there was an attempt, applying its "common sense" to decide that D's conduct amounted to a "real and practical step" towards the actual commission of the crime rather than mere preparation.[97] Yet "common sense" is itself a very elusive concept. What may appear to one judge as a solution based on practical wisdom, may appear to another as unreasonable. Each will bring her own values and preconceptions to the determination of "common sense". It is a highly subjective criterion.

It seems that something more than "common sense" or epithets like "real and practical step", "commencement of execution", "last proximate act", "a step in the actual crime itself" etc may be necessary if we are to make any headway in accounting for the proximity of attempts. The problem, as one writer has observed,[98] is finding the mean that is compatible with the requirement for clear legislative definition of punishable conduct, and yet consistent with the practical value of early police intervention. Many legal systems have now moved away from the view that to be guilty of an attempt one must do everything in one's power to effectuate the offence, on the basis that it is incompatible with the policy of early intervention and the prevention of harm.[99] If, as may be thought, early intervention and prevention of harm are cardinal criminal justice values that the law on criminal attempts seeks to uphold, a threshold test which best supports those values might seem to be worth considering. In our view, a test of "dangerous proximity" is well suited to uphold those values, while providing a fair threshold for marking out punishable conduct.

6.1.3.4 *"Dangerous" proximity*

A theory of "dangerous" proximity focuses on the *character* of the conduct we judge to be proximate, in order to determine whether it is the sort of preparatory conduct that ought to be visited with criminal sanctions. There are two ways in which relevant "dangerousness" may be judged: (i) by considering the *degree* of closeness to completion of the intended crime; or (ii) by considering the *nature* of the preparatory conduct undertaken, in terms of the actual risk presented to public health or safety. Either or both criteria may be considered in evaluating the proximity of the alleged conduct to the intended offence. If, for example, on an altered version of the facts in *R v Wilcox*,[100] the

---

95   See *Haughton v Smith* [1975] AC 476 at 499, [1973] 3 All ER 1109 at 1121 (Lord Reid). See also *Drewery v Police* (1988) 3 CRNZ 499 at 502; *R v Peneha* (1993) 11 CRNZ 183 at 184.

96   [1976] 2 NZLR 167 (CA).

97   Ibid at 170.

98   Fletcher, *Rethinking Criminal Law*, Boston, Little, Brown, 1978, 136.

99   Ibid.

100 [1982] 1 NZLR 191 (CA).

offenders had been stopped by the police as their car pulled up outside the bank, it could be argued that, on both counts, they were *dangerously* close to achieving their object. Regardless of how many discrete acts may have been required to have effected the actual robbery, the degree of closeness inherent in driving to within metres of the planned crime would suggest that a major issue of prevention of harm had arisen, justifying immediate (early) intervention. Assuming the robbers were armed and intent on completing their object, their presence could be said to have posed an immediate and serious threat to any innocent person within the immediate vicinity of the bank, a threat which the police may justifiably act to eliminate.

A similar analysis could be applied to the facts of *R v Wylie*.[101] At the point at which the prospective purchaser of cocaine was holding the cash in his hands and was proceeding to examine the cocaine with a view to its purchase, it could be said that he was "dangerously close" to achieving his object. (Bear in mind that he must *intend* to commit the crime.) At any moment he could simply have extended his hand with the cash in it and said: "I'll have it". At that point, the crime of procuring would have been complete. Had he done so, it would not have been necessary to ask whether the appellant's conduct would also have presented an actual risk to public health or safety, since the threshold for an attempt had already been established. Arguably, even without doing so, a person who so determinedly pursues the object of purchasing dangerous narcotic drugs represents a similar social threat.

The test of "dangerous proximity" may be more difficult to apply in factual situations where the accused has done everything in his power to assist another in the commission of a crime, but more steps remained to be undertaken by others before the substantive offence is complete. The problem is demonstrated in *Drewery v Police*,[102] where D was charged with arson and attempted false pretences after he had destroyed the vehicle owned by the principal offender as part of a fraudulent insurance claim. There D carried out the only and final act he was to perform in the offence, namely destroying the principal's car, while more steps remained to be taken by the principal to effect the false claim. It is arguable in such a case that it is not straining language to say that D came "dangerously close" to achieving his object because there was nothing more he could have done or was required to do as part of the agreement. However, although it does not affect the theory of proximity being advocated here, it has been suggested that *Drewery* may have been wrongly decided. D did not intend to commit the offence himself, and he could only be guilty of an attempt on the basis that he was a secondary party to a sufficiently proximate act by the owner of the car who was the intended principal.[103] Since the owner did not appear to have gone beyond arranging for D to destroy the car (a mere preparation), it may be doubted whether D himself could be said to have proceeded beyond mere preparation.

---

101 [1976] 2 NZLR 167 at 170 (CA).

102 (1988) 3 CRNZ 499.

103 *Adams* § CA72.09G.

In spite of the difficulties presented in cases such as *Drewery*, where the liability of a secondary party for attempt may depend on whether the principal has committed an act sufficiently proximate to amount to an attempt,[104] the test of dangerous proximity would seem to work well in other situations of attempt. For example, it is appropriate to the facts of a case like *R v Jones*,[105] where the accused, apparently intent on murdering his putative victim, had entered the victim's car and pointed a loaded shotgun at him at a range of 10 to 12 inches, while saying "You are not going to like this". It would seem an inescapable conclusion that the accused was "dangerously close" to achieving his object of killing the victim, regardless of whether there were one, two, three, etc discrete acts required to be performed by him before the full offence could be completed.[106] Indeed, it may be argued that the application of threshold tests like the "last act" test to such a case make a mockery of prevention of harm policies, and establish an impossibly narrow "window of opportunity" for police intervention.

The theory of "dangerous proximity" aims to make clearer when the threshold between proximity and attempt has been reached, by focussing on the point at which it may be said the accused's conduct has become "dangerous". It seeks to capture the point of difference between acts of preparation which, while notionally close to the complete offence, are in themselves innocuous and unthreatening, and acts which, by their nature, demonstrate that the accused is significantly close to success and may even be endangering the lives/interests of other people already. In our view, it is this element of propinquity and threat, coupled with an intention to commit a crime, that justifies the attribution of attempt and calls for the intervention of the police.

6.1.4 Withdrawal

Once the threshold from preparation to attempt is crossed, the attempt is committed and cannot be undone. The accused is then unable to withdraw, or to seek to distance himself from the enterprise by a change of heart or repentance, and the intervention of others into the enterprise before completion of the crime cannot affect its character as an attempt.

Therefore, the crucial question is up until what time does an accused have a locus poenitentiae[107] during which he may withdraw from the enterprise without attracting criminal liability? Applying the "dangerous proximity"

---

104 But see *R v Peneha* (1993) 11 CRNZ 183, where Williamson J was "unrepentant" in his view that if a person intends to be a party to an offence and then carries out the physical act which is his part in the offence then the tests in s 72(1) are met, regardless of whether the principal has carried out the physical act necessary to complete the offence. However, with respect, the essential issue in the statute (s 72(2)) is whether the act done or omitted "with intent" was sufficiently proximate to the "commission of [the] offence" intended, not whether the party, whether secondary or principal, had done all that she could to complete the offence.

105 [1990] 3 All ER 886, [1990] 1 WLR 1057.

106 Ibid at 887, at 1059.

107 Literally, a place of repentance.

analysis, we may say that a locus poenitentiae should remain so long as the accused's acts of preparation are merely innocuous and unthreatening, and do not represent a threat to the safety or interests of other persons. So, in *R v Page*,[108] the Australian Court rightly found an attempt proved where the accused had inserted a tyre lever to break open a window, but changed his mind before applying any force. Similarly, when the defendant in *R v Taylor*[109] approached a stack of corn with a lighted match in his hand for the purpose of setting the stack on fire, but abandoned the plan once aware that he was being watched, he was properly convicted of an attempt. In principle, withdrawal should make no difference to liability for an attempt where the accused, by her conduct up until the time of withdrawal, has demonstrated a contumelious disregard for the safety or interests of others and has demonstrated a fixed determination to achieve her object. Withdrawal, signalling a change of heart, may be a factor relevant to sentencing but does not affect liability for an attempt where the accused has already shown her hand, and demonstrated a dangerous willingness to harm the interests of others. New Zealand law does not recognise any defence of free and voluntary desistance; nor, in our view, should it. Repentance and desistance is always available while conduct remains in the realm of preparation. Once an accused moves into the uncharted waters of the threshold between preparation and attempt she takes the risk that she may already have gone too far, and cannot be heard to plead, after the event, "I'm sorry. I wish I had abandoned the plan earlier".

The argument against allowing a defence of free and voluntary desistance may be illustrated by a simple example. D, intent on raping P, has pinned her to the ground by the weight of his own body. She is terrified and alone. But before he has touched her in any indecent manner or attempted to remove her clothes, he suddenly has a change of heart and decides to abandon the assault. Should he be able to avoid liability on a charge of attempted rape simply because he has voluntarily desisted? The answer must surely be "no". D has callously inflicted P's plight. Even though he has not physically harmed her, the emotional scars of his conduct — which is recognised by P as an attempted rape, and which will affect her as such — will remain with P for a long time.

6.1.5 Impossibility

The issue of impossible attempts has been a subject of fascination for generations of criminal law students.[110] Although it provides an excellent framework in which to tease out fascinating theoretical issues of criminal responsibility, and indeed to set examination questions, the issue of impossibility does, periodically, give rise to important practical questions that are reflected in the case law. In cases of attempts to do the impossible, the defendant was labouring under some kind of mistake, since no sane person

---

108 [1933] VLR 351, [1993] ALR 374.

109 (1859) 1 F & F 511, 175 ER 831.

110 See Smith, "Attempts, Impossibility and the Test of Rational Motivation" in *Auckland Law School Centenary Lectures*, Auckland, Legal Research Foundation, 1983.

will intend to do what he knows to be impossible.[111] In so far as impossible attempts always involve a mistake of some kind, the legal status of relevant mistakes depends on whether the mistake gives rise to a situation of "factual" impossibility, or to one of "legal" impossibility.

Section 72(1) includes the phrase "whether in the circumstances it was possible to commit the offence or not". The phrase, which has appeared in New Zealand criminal legislation since 1893, was intended to express the common law as stated in *R v Ring*.[112] In that case, the accused was convicted of attempted theft after he placed his hand in an empty pocket with a view to stealing the purse he hoped was there. The impossibility of success was no impediment to his conviction. At the same time, the subsection abrogates the effect of *R v Collins*[113] where, on facts similar to those in *Ring*, it was held that a person who put his hand into the pocket of another was not guilty of an attempt to steal because, as it happened, no theft was possible since the pocket was empty. In favouring *Ring* over *Collins*, Parliament has foreshadowed that mere "factual" impossibility will not be a bar to conviction.

This approach is generally consistent with the position in other jurisdictions, where the common law defence of impossibility has been largely foreclosed by legislation. For example, English legislation (which has abolished the offence of attempt at common law and substituted a statutory offence) contains an expression similar to s 72(1), according to which a person may be guilty of attempting to commit an offence "even though the facts are such that the commission of the offence is impossible".[114] The effect of this provision is that a person may be convicted of an attempt where she has accomplished that which she set out to do, but because of some mistake on her part her conduct does not after all amount to an offence. This is demonstrated in the House of Lords decision in *R v Shivpuri*.[115] In that case, D was charged with attempting to be knowingly concerned in dealing with a prohibited drug. While on a visit to India, D had been approached by a man who offered him a sum of money if, on return to England, he would receive a suitcase containing packages of "drugs" and then distribute them. Having duly received the suitcase, D arranged to meet a third person with a view to delivering a package of drugs. While they were meeting, the police arrested them. D frankly admitted his involvement in receiving and distributing the drug, which he believed was either cannabis or heroin. However, on a scientific analysis the packages were found to contain only a harmless vegetable substance.

In upholding D's conviction, the House of Lords overruled its earlier decision in *Anderton v Ryan*,[116] in which it had held that a person could not be liable for conviction of an attempt where his actions were "objectively innocent" even though he erroneously believed in facts which, if true, would

---

111 Ibid at 27.
112 (1892) 17 Cox CC 491.
113 (1864) 9 Cox CC 497.
114 See s 1(2) Criminal Attempts Act 1981 (UK).
115 [1987] AC 1, [1986] 2 All ER 334 (HL).
116 [1985] AC 567, [1985] 2 All ER 355

make those actions criminal. In *Shivpuri*, Lord Bridge declared that the concept of "objective innocence" is "incapable of sensible application in relation to the law of criminal attempts".[117]

6.1.5.1 *"Legal" impossibility as a defence*

It is sometimes said that a distinction should be drawn between attempts which are impossible owing to some "physical" or "factual" impediment (eg D's crowbar is in fact not strong enough to lever open V's safe), and those which are impossible owing to some required legal status or element (eg because V — though D does not know it — is already dead, he is no longer a human being within the meaning of s 158, and therefore cannot be murdered).

One significant implication of *Shivpuri*, which interprets statutory language similar to that found in s 72, is that UK law no longer recognises any distinction between situations of "legal" and "physical" impossibility. A person will be guilty of an attempt provided simply that she has an intent to commit an offence, and has done an act which is more than merely preparatory to the commission of that offence.[118]

However, it appears that New Zealand law still recognises a distinction between "legal" and "factual" impossibility. Its recognition derives from the seminal case of *R v Donnelly*.[119] D had been charged with attempted receiving after he had presented a ticket at the left luggage office of the Auckland Railway Station with a view to collecting some gramophone records which he believed had been stolen. In fact, the records had been uplifted earlier by the police, after being identified by their owner as property stolen from her home. It was held that, in those circumstances, it was impossible *in law* for D to commit the offence of receiving, because of the operation of s 261 Crimes Act 1961, which states that it is not an offence to receive property once it has been restored to its owner.

The Court of Appeal agreed that the fact that the goods had been *physically* removed from the place where D believed them to be did not affect his liability for attempt, because such a case of *factual* impossibility was clearly covered by s 72(1). However, the majority held that this was a case of *legal* impossibility, which precluded the appellant's liability for an attempt. Since he could not have been convicted of the completed offence of receiving, it was held that he could not be convicted of attempt. The Court identified six situations in which a person who sets out to commit a crime might fail.[120] They are:

(i)   Change of mind before committing an act sufficiently "overt" to amount to an attempt.

(ii) Change of mind but too late to deny an attempt.

(iii) Prevention by some outside agency from doing an act necessary to complete the crime.

(iv) Ineptitude, inefficiency, or insufficiency of means.

---

117 [1987] AC 1 at 21, [1986] 2 All ER 334 at 344 (HL).
118 See s 1(1) Criminal Attempts Act 1981 (UK).
119 [1970] NZLR 980 (CA).
120 Ibid at 990, 991 (Turner J).

(v)   Physical impossibility.

(vi) Legal impossibility.

Only in respect of the first and sixth categories can there be no liability for attempt under the present New Zealand law. It was into the sixth category that the case was held to fall.

The approach taken in *Donnelly* has been criticised on the grounds that it admits a technical and unmeritorious defence, based on fortuitous circumstances unrelated to D's social dangerousness and moral blameworthiness.[121] Furthermore, the decision implicitly endorses the theory of "objective innocence", now rejected in the English courts, by emphasising that the appellant's actions, considered alone, "would leave him guiltless in the eyes of the law".[122] Yet, as Haslam J rightly points out in his dissenting judgment, the concluding phrase in s 72(1) — "whether in the circumstances it was possible to commit the offence or not" — makes "objective impossibility" an irrelevant consideration.[123]

In our view, the Court's conceptualisation of D's intention is flawed, leading it falsely to attribute him with intention to do something which was not an offence. The Court said:

> What the appellant intended to do, therefore, was *to do something which was not an offence*. If he is to be convicted of a criminal attempt, it must be simply because of his erroneous belief that what he was attempting to do was an offence in law, when actually it was not one.[124]

This would be true if the appellant's intention had been "to receive [previously] stolen goods *that had been restored to their owner*". But that was *not* his intention. His intention was "to receive stolen goods" simpliciter. That is an intention to do something which is an offence.

The complexity of these cases arises in part because the legal status of the goods (ie as no longer stolen) depends itself on the presence of relevant facts (ie that the goods have been recovered on behalf of their owner). It may be a failure to recognise this connection that explains why the majority judgment seems to contain a confusion between "imaginary crimes", which we shall discuss below and which can never be attempted, and the situation in which the defendant's objective, if it could be attained, would be a crime but where, because he is making a mistake *of fact*, he believes it to be possible when it is not. In relation to the latter, impossibility should not be a bar to conviction. It is

---

121 See Dawkins, "Parties, conspiracies and attempts" in Cameron and France (eds), *Essays on Criminal Law in New Zealand: Towards Reform?*, Wellington, Victoria University of Wellington Law Review, 1990, 141. For further criticism of the "illusory and analytically suspect" distinction between factual and legal impossibility, see Meehan, *The Law of Criminal Attempt: A Treatise*, Alberta, Carswells, 1984, 151-153.

122 *R v Donnelly* [1970] NZLR 980 at 992 (Turner J).

123 Ibid at 994.

124 Ibid at 992 (Turner J).

a case of failure where, if the accused had succeeded and the facts been as he thought they were, he would have committed a crime.[125]

6.1.5.2 *Factual impossibility*

By contrast, as we stated at the beginning of § 6.1.5, factual impossibility has never been a bar to conviction in New Zealand. In *Police v Jay*,[126] a conviction for attempting to receive cannabis was upheld when the accused received hedge-clippings by deception. This was held to fall within the fifth category in *Donnelly*. In *Jay*, the Court followed *R v Austin*,[127] where a person was found guilty of attempting to unlawfully supply a pregnant woman a "noxious thing" knowing that it was intended to be used to procure a miscarriage. The thing was not noxious at all. In *Higgins v Police*,[128] factual impossibility was held to be no defence to a charge of attempting to cultivate cannabis, in circumstances where positive identification of the seedlings was not possible because of their immaturity.

In such cases, liability follows because the accused, intending to commit an offence, does *something* (going beyond preparation) for the purpose of accomplishing the offence. Although the means chosen was not sufficient for the object sought, or a supervening event made completion impossible, the accused nevertheless did a relevant act for the purpose of accomplishing her object, fulfilling the essential requirements for an attempt.

While the distinction between factual and legal impossibility remains in New Zealand, it is difficult to justify in the light of the reasoning in *Shivpuri*. In particular, the decision in *Donnelly* has been the subject of strong criticism, and although the decision has thus far survived challenge in the Court of Appeal, its continuing usefulness as an authority on impossibility must be doubted.[129] Above all, the distinction drawn between legal and factual impossibility lacks a clear or coherent basis, and is contrary to the plain meaning of the words in s 72(1).

6.1.5.3 *The "imaginary crime" exception*

A noteworthy feature of developments in the UK is that they signal a clear movement away from a focus on the objective quality of the act, toward an emphasis on the subjective intention of the accused coupled with proof of a relevant post-preparatory act. However, although *Shivpuri* appears to have foreclosed virtually all situations that might previously have qualified (at common law) as exculpatory "impossible" attempts,[130] there is one remaining situation where it would seem an attempt cannot be committed.

---

125 Smith, "Attempts, Impossibility and the Test of Rational Motivation" in *Auckland Law School Centenary Lectures*, Auckland, Legal Research Foundation, 1983, 30.

126 [1974] 2 NZLR 204.

127 (1905) 24 NZLR 983 (CA).

128 (1984) 1 CRNZ 187; and see *Collector of Customs v Kozanic* (1983) 1 CRNZ 135.

129 See Orchard, "Impossibility and inchoate crimes — Another hook in a red herring" [1993] NZLJ 426.

130 For example, the man who attempts to steal from an empty pocket, or attempts to steal his own umbrella, or who attempts to receive an item he believes to be stolen which is

The exception occurs when the accused makes no mistake about any material fact, but wrongly believes that what he is attempting to do is a crime. His object need not be impossible to attain yet, when it is attained, no crime will have been committed. In such a case, even if his "attempt" is successful, it is not a proximate step toward the commission of a crime.[131] Consider the following examples:

(i) D has sexual intercourse with a 17-year-old girl. He believes that the criminal law prohibits sexual intercourse with girls under the age of 18. However, contrary to his belief, the relevant age is 16. He has not committed a crime or an attempted crime.

(ii) D believes that it is unlawful to shoot opossums without a licence. She shoots six opossums which are eating turnips in a farm paddock. There is nothing unlawful in her actions.

These do not amount to attempts to commit crimes in law. There is no actus reus, because the act done is lawful; there is no crime that D's conduct can be an attempt to commit. Neither is there mens rea, because the mens rea of an attempt requires an intention to cause a result forbidden by law. A mere belief by D that her act is a criminal offence is insufficient.[132]

In these cases, the language of impossible attempts is inapt, because impossibility in this context implies the existence of an offence the completion of which is impossible in the circumstances. Similarly, applying the test of "dangerous proximity" postulated earlier, the conduct described in the examples above could not amount to an attempt because the conduct is neither *inherently* dangerous nor can it be said to be *dangerously* close to achieving the object sought, since the object is already accomplished and is not per se criminal. Most jurisdictions recognise that the "imaginary crime" is a legitimate exception in cases of liability for impossible attempts.[133]

6.2 CONSPIRACY

A person does not become guilty of a crime by merely thinking about it. There must always be some external manifestation of conduct to transform a criminal thought into culpable conduct. Even more than attempts and incitement, however, conspiracy, by its nature, is a crime that comes very close to punishing a person for his thoughts alone. Yet even here mere evidence of a criminal intention, in the absence of an actual *agreement* between two or more persons to commit a crime, will be insufficient to constitute an offence. On the face of it the reason seems clear enough. If two people have actually agreed on

---

not: see *R v Collins* (1864) 9 Cox CC 497; *Anderton v Ryan* [1985] AC 560, [1985] 2 All ER 355.

131 Smith, "Attempts, Impossibility and the Test of Rational Motivation" in *Auckland Law School Centenary Lectures*, Auckland, Legal Research Foundation, 1983, 27.

132 Ibid at 28.

133 See, for example, *Britten v Alpogut* [1987] VR 929, (1986) 23 A Crim R 254. See also *R v Sew Hoy* [1994] NZLR 257 at 267, (1993) 10 CRNZ 581 at 591: "But certainly it cannot be a crime to agree to commit an 'imaginary crime'." (Hardie Boys J). The concept of "imaginary crime" is also discussed by Glanville Williams in "The Lords and Impossible Attempts, or *Quis Custodiet Ipsos Custodes*" (1986) 45 CLJ 33 at 55ff.

a course of conduct it is much more likely that it will be carried out than if one person, scheming alone in the solitude of his mind, merely imagines the completion of a criminal enterprise.

The question whether conduct amounts to a conspiracy is not, like criminal attempts, merely a difficult threshold problem of determining when there is sufficient proximity to the intended crime. Instead, the focus of the wrongdoing is quite sharply defined: what must be proved is an actual agreement to commit an offence. However, while defining the elements of a conspiracy has all the appearance of simplicity, the jurisprudence of conspiracy is quite complex and requires careful analysis. Conspiracy has been described as one of the most difficult and controversial branches of the criminal law.[134] To say that the essence of conspiracy is agreement is very much to oversimplify the relevant law.

6.2.1 The scope of conspiracy

Although successive New Zealand criminal codes have established liability for conspiracy, neither the elements nor the scope of the offence has ever been defined by statute.[135] The principal substantive provision, s 310 Crimes Act 1961, is primarily a penalty provision. However, it does clarify the rule that conspiracy is only a crime in New Zealand if the conspiracy is to commit a statutory offence or "to do or omit, in any part of the world, anything of which the doing or omission in New Zealand, would be an offence . . ."[136] By contrast, where the Crimes Act 1961 defines particular conspiracies, for example conspiracy to defraud in s 257, it is clear that the conspiracy need not be aimed at the commission of an offence.[137] Similarly, the offence of conspiring to defeat justice[138] is not limited to conspiracies to commit offences per se, and includes conspiracies to do acts that if done by individuals might not be offences.[139] Nonetheless, in the vast majority of cases, the conduct impugned as conspiracy will comprise an agreement to commit an offence; and, if impugned under s 310, it *must* do so.

The reasons for this are historical. When the Criminal Code Bill Commissioners presented their report containing the Draft Code,[140] they recommended that crimes should no longer be indictable at common law.[141] One effect of this recommendation was to prevent indictments at common law

---

134 *Kamara v DPP* [1974] AC 104 at 116, [1973] 2 All ER 1242 at 1248 (Lord Hailsham).

135 Dawkins, "Parties, conspiracies and attempts" in N Cameron & S France (eds) *Essays on Criminal Law in New Zealand — Towards Reform?* VUW Law Review Monograph 3, Wellington, Victoria University Press, 1990, 130.

136 Section 310(1). See *R v Gemmell* [1985] 2 NZLR 740 at 743, (1985) 1 CRNZ 496 at 499 (CA).

137 See § 19.3; also *Adams* (2nd ed) § 2084.

138 Section 116.

139 See *Adams* (2nd ed) § 880; also *R v Newland* [1954] 1 QB 158, [1953] 2 All ER 1067.

140 See *Report of the Royal Commission Appointed to Consider The Law Relating to Indictable Offences*, London, Eyre & Spottiswode for HMSO, 1879, C.- 2345

141 See Draft Code s 5 — Offenders to be Tried under this Act and see Crimes Act 1961; also s 9 Crimes Act 1961 — Offences not to be punishable except under New Zealand Acts.

for conspiracy. Having identified the individual conspiracies that could be prosecuted under the Draft Code,[142] the Commissioners expressed doubt whether there was any "distinct authority" that other common law conspiracies exist. They did concede, however, that a "degree of obscurity exists on the subject".[143] Consequently, the decision to abolish common law conspiracies reflects a perception that it is unsatisfactory to have any indictable offence where the elements are left in uncertainty and doubt.[144]

This is in contrast to the position in the UK, where the courts have held that the common law definition of conspiracy does not limit liability to agreements to commit crimes but may also include agreements to commit some torts, to defraud, to corrupt public morals, and to outrage public decency.[145] While in England the categories of conspiracy to effect a public mischief may not be closed, the House of Lords has cautioned that any extension should be closely and jealously watched by the courts because of the difficulty of "riding the horse of public policy".[146]

In New Zealand, then, all conspiracies are necessarily statutory. Under s 310 Crimes Act 1961, where the conspiracy is to commit a summary offence, the conspiracy itself is a crime and may be tried indictably. Suppose, for example, that A and B conspire to light a fire in a rubbish skip belonging to their neighbour X, with whom they have had a long-running feud. Even though the summary offence[147] they plan to commit is punishable only by a fine of $200 and carries no right of election, the conspiracy becomes an electable offence; albeit that the penalty for conspiracy is limited to the maximum for the substantive offence, ie $200.[148]

6.2.2 When is a conspiracy complete?

Before examining the elements of conspiracy, it may be useful to reflect on the question: "when is a conspiracy complete?" Because the actus reus in a conspiracy is an agreement to execute an offence, it is now settled law that a conspiracy is complete when the agreement is made.[149] "Complete", in this sense, means that all that is necessary for the offence has occurred. The offence has been committed and all the conspirators can be prosecuted, even though no performance may have taken place. But it does not mean that the conspiratorial

---

142 Including treasonable conspiracies, seditious conspiracies, conspiracies to bring false accusations, to pervert justice, to defile women, to murder, to defraud, to commit indictable offences, and to prevent by force the collection of rates and taxes. See Draft Code ss 79, 102, 126, 127, 149, 180, 284, 419, 420, 421.

143 Draft Code Report, 16.

144 Ibid. Cf discussion of the Rule of Law § 1.4.

145 Allen, *Textbook on Criminal Law* (2nd ed), 1991, 202. See §§ 1.2.1.1, 1.4.3.

146 *Kamara v DPP* [1974] AC 104 at 123, [1973] 2 All ER 1242 at 1254 (Lord Hailsham). See, in particular, *DPP v Withers* [1975] AC 842, [1974] 3 All ER 984.

147 See s 36 Summary Offences Act 1981 (lighting fires).

148 Per s 310(1).

149 See *Kamara v DPP* [1974] AC 104 at 119, [1973] 2 All ER 1242 at 1251; *R v Gemmell* [1985] 2 NZLR 740 at 744, (1985) 1 CRNZ 496 at 500 (CA). See also the *Poulterer's Case* (1610) 9 Co Rep 55b, 77 ER 813.

agreement is finished with.[150] As long as the conspirators continue to perform their agreement the conspiracy remains alive and operating and it continues to operate until it is discharged by being performed in full or until it is abandoned or frustrated.[151] So if A and B agree together to commit a robbery, but before the robbery actually commences B is shot and killed by a security guard, then while A may still be guilty of conspiracy to rob, the conspiracy itself would be deemed to have terminated because it is incapable of further agreement. Any further acts of A in pursuance of the common design would necessarily be the acts of A alone and not pursuant to a continuing agreement.

It follows that, where the conspiracy has been conceived and commenced in one jurisdiction but acts necessary to its execution are committed in New Zealand, it is open to a court to find that the conspiracy continues and is not discharged until all that is necessary for the offence has occurred. This is illustrated in *R v Johnston*.[152] In that case D, while on holiday in England, had arranged to send some Class A drugs to New Zealand. His appeal was based on the fact that he never received the drugs, which were intercepted by customs officers, and did not plan the operation in New Zealand. He argued that the New Zealand courts had no jurisdiction. In rejecting these arguments and dismissing the appeal against conviction, the Court of Appeal held that the use of the New Zealand Customs and Postal Services was part of the conspiracy, which brought the offence within the jurisdiction of the New Zealand courts. The Court was influenced by the fact that s 7 Crimes Act 1961 confers jurisdiction and deems an offence to be committed in New Zealand:

where [i] any act or omission forming part of any offence, or [ii] any event necessary to the completion of any offence, occurs in New Zealand, the offence shall be deemed to be committed in New Zealand, whether the person charged with the offence was in New Zealand or not at the time of the act, omission, or event. [Item numbering added.]

In the Court's words:

It is well settled that though the offence of conspiracy is complete when the agreement to do the unlawful act is made a conspiracy does not end with the making of the agreement. The conspiratorial agreement continues in operation and therefore in existence until it is ended by completion of its performance or abandonment or in any other manner by which agreements are discharged.[153]

Richardson J, delivering the judgment of the Court, noted that the expressions "complete" and "completion" may be used in the different sense of having come into existence and having been at an end.[154] The Court ruled that in the context of the phrase "any event necessary to the completion of any offence" under limb (ii) of s 7, "completion" must be read as meaning "coming into existence" — ie *formation* of the conspiracy. The use of the post office

---

150 *R v Johnston* (1986) 2 CRNZ 289 at 291 (CA); *DPP v Doot* [1973] AC 807 at 827, [1973] 1 All ER 940 at 951.

151 *DPP v Doot* [1973] AC 807 at 827, [1973] 1 All ER 940 at 951 (Lord Pearson).

152 (1986) 2 CRNZ 289 (CA).

153 Ibid at 290.

154 See, for example, *R v Kaitamaki* [1984] 1 NZLR 385 (PC).

therefore fell outside the second limb, since the conspiracy had already been formed. However, D's conviction stood, because the handling of the letter by the post office fell within limb (i). It constituted an action "forming part of the offence [of conspiracy]" — ie an action within the envisaged conduct of the conspiracy, which occurred before the conspiracy was terminated.

6.2.3 The elements of conspiracy

In *R v Gemmell*,[155] the Court of Appeal approved the following statement from *Mulcahy v R*,[156] as being the "locus classicus" of the definition of conspiracy:

> A conspiracy consists not merely in the intention of two or more, but in the agreement of two or more to do an unlawful act, or to do a lawful act by unlawful means. So long as such a design rests in intention only, it is not indictable. *When two agree to carry it into effect, the very plot is an act in itself, and the act of each of the parties, promise against promise, actus contra actum, capable of being enforced, if lawful, punishable if for a criminal object or for the use of criminal means.*[157]

This statement, while useful, is not exhaustive. For example, it fails to identify the fact, implicit in s 310, that a conspiracy may have as its object an omission. Thus, a couple conspire to commit an offence by omission if they agree not to feed their young child, or not to provide it with medical attention when ill, thereby intending to cause the child's death.[158] Of course, it would still be necessary in such a case to establish the existence of a plot — an actual agreement to effect the child's death by a wilful omission. Mere negligence in failing to provide the necessaries of life[159] accompanied by the intention of one party to injure the child by such neglect would not, without more, amount to a conspiracy.

Nonetheless, as the quotation makes clear, at the heart of a criminal conspiracy is "the very plot", the element of agreement or consensus, ie the joint resolution of two or more persons. Such an agreement is entered into by the operation of both physical and mental faculties and consists, as with all true crimes, in an actus reus and mens rea. Other important elements within the nature of conspiracy concern parties' liability and the circumstances which pertain following the acquittal of other alleged conspirators. We will look at each element in turn.

6.2.4 The actus reus of conspiracy

It is common ground that the actus reus of a conspiracy is the agreement to execute the illegal conduct, and not the execution of it. The crime is complete when the agreement is made. The actual conduct comprising the actus reus consists in the physical acts, words, or gestures whereby the conspirators

---

155 [1985] 2 NZLR 740, (1985) 1 CRNZ 496 (CA).

156 (1868) LR 3 HL 306.

157 [1985] 2 NZLR 740 at 743, (1985) 1 CRNZ 496 at 499 (CA).

158 The example is due to Dawkins, "Parties, conspiracies and attempts" in Cameron & France (eds) *Essays on Criminal Law in New Zealand — Towards Reform?*, VUW Law Review Monograph 3, Wellington, Victoria University Press, 1990, 130, 131.

159 Section 151 Crimes Act 1961.

indicate their agreement. The agreement may be express or implied, or in part express and in part implied.[160] However, for a conspiracy to exist, it is not necessary for the prosecution to establish that the individuals are in direct communication with each other, or that they directly consulted together. It is enough that they entered an agreement with a common design.[161]

A conspiracy will not necessarily be present simply because two or more persons pursued the same unlawful objects at the same time or in the same place; it is necessary to show a meeting of minds, a consensus to effect an unlawful purpose. In *R v Walker*,[162] it was held that mere negotiation of an agreement was insufficient for a conspiracy. In that case, D's conviction was quashed because, although D had discussed with the others the idea of stealing a payroll, it was not proved that the alleged conspirators had got beyond the stage of negotiation when D withdrew.

For a conspiracy to exist it is not necessary that each conspirator should have been in communication with every other. In *R v Parnell*, Grose J said:

> It may be that the alleged conspirators have never seen each other, and have never corresponded, one may have never heard the name of the other, and yet by the law they may be parties to the same common criminal agreement. Thus, in some of the Fenian cases tried in this country, it frequently happened that one of the conspirators was in America, the other in this country; that they had never seen each other, but that there were acts on both sides which led the jury to the inference, and they drew it, that they were engaged in accomplishing the same common object, and when they had arrived at this conclusion, the acts of the one became evidence against the other.[163]

From this statement it is clear that persons may conspire together, even though there is no direct communication between each and all of them. What must be established is that they entered into an agreement with a common design.[164] In describing the different ways in which such agreements may be made the courts have resorted to the use of various metaphors, including those of a "wheel" and of a "chain". We shall consider these particular varieties below (§ 6.2.4.4-5).

6.2.4.1 *Acts subsequent to the formation but during the continuation of the conspiracy*

It has been held that any subsequent acts performed in the commission or attempted commission of the unlawful object are not part of the actus reus of

---

160 *Halsbury's Laws*, vol 11(1), (4th ed), § 64.

161 *R v Gemmell* [1985] 2 NZLR 740 at 744, (1985) 1 CRNZ 496 at 500 (CA). Because direct evidence of the making of the agreement and its nature and terms is rarely available, proof will almost always depend on evidence of subsequent acts or declarations by persons alleged to be parties to the conspiracy, and on the inferences to be drawn from them (eg that the acts are pursuant to a concluded agreement). However, it is important to note that those acts do not themselves constitute the conspiracy. They are only the evidence from which the agreement may be inferred.

162 [1962] Crim LR 458. See also *R v Mills* [1963] 1 QB 522, (1962) 47 Cr App Rep 49 (CCA).

163 (1881) 14 Cox CC 508 at 515.

164 *R v Meyrick* (1929) 21 Cr App R 94 at 102.

conspiracy, although they may be evidence from which an inference can be drawn regarding the existence of an illegal agreement.[165] While this is clearly true in the case of a simple conspiracy which is complete on the agreement's being made, it is also apparent from cases like *R v Johnston*[166] and *R v Sanders*,[167] involving extraterritorial conspiracies, that subsequent acts may be regarded as part of the actus reus of a *continuing* conspiracy. Indeed, unless such acts were treated as part of the continuing actus reus, it would be impossible to obtain convictions of co-conspirators who reside outside the jurisdiction in which the conspiracy is initially formed.

However, if the alleged agreement is identical to and coterminous with the very crime which is the object of the conspiracy (the "object crime") there cannot be a conspiracy because the agreement must precede, or be anterior to, the object crime contemplated in the agreement; it cannot be synonymous with the object crime itself.[168] For this reason, particular problems may arise in determining the appropriate charge where the statute, in addition to nominating conspiracy as a possible offence, specifies other general offences like "supplying", which is capable of being interpreted to include "*agreeing* to supply".[169] Where the Crown, in such a case, relies on a form of "supply" consisting of the act of entering into an agreement to sell drugs, there can be no charge of conspiracy because there would be no agreement anterior in time to the object crime (the agreement to supply).[170]

6.2.4.2 *Proof of the agreement*

As was noted above, the essence of conspiracy is an *agreement* or *consensus* between two or more persons in certain terms. The actus reus consists in the physical acts, words, or gestures by which the conspirators indicate their agreement.

Often, however, it may be unenlightening to talk of the actus reus of conspiracy, in so far as actus reus typically speaks of the acts or omissions of an accused that are proscribed by law. Realistically, to establish conspiracy such acts or omissions need not necessarily be proved. Indeed, in many criminal conspiracies the actual agreement will not be capable of identification or proof. The precise manner in which agreement was reached may even be irrelevant, provided the fact of an agreement in the terms alleged can be established.[171] The formation of the agreement can be proved *either* (i) by evidence that the parties actually met together and concluded an agreement, or (ii) indirectly, by proof of the overt acts done in the transaction of the agreement — provided

---

165 See *R v Janis* 28/5/92, Heron J, HC Wellington T91-95/91.

166 (1986) 2 CRNZ 289 (CA).

167 [1984] 1 NZLR 636 (CA).

168 *R v Richards [conspiracy]* (1992) 9 CRNZ 403 at 407. See also *R v Chow* (1987) 11 NSWLR 561, 30 A Crim R 103 (CA).

169 *R v Richards [conspiracy]* (1992) 9 CRNZ 403 at 407. See s 6(1)(c) and s 6(2A) Misuse of Drugs Act 1975.

170 Ibid.

171 Ibid.

these acts are sufficient, when taken with any relevant surrounding circumstances, to compel the inference that their commission was the product of concert between the alleged parties.[172] One consequence of this possibility is that the prosecution need not prove the exact moment at which the conspiracy began.

6.2.4.3 Conspiring with "persons unknown"

There must be at least two parties to a conspiracy. But it is not essential to prove the actual number and identity of the co-conspirators. An accused may be convicted of conspiring "with a person or persons unknown" to commit an unlawful act.[173] On the other hand, the number and identity of the co-conspirators may be relevant or even essential to the identification of the subject matter of the alleged conspiracy and to the proof of its actual existence. For example, the question whether the intended perpetrator of an unlawful act is actually a party to a conspiracy is likely to be of critical importance to the question whether the relevant conspiracy is a conspiracy to commit the act as distinct from a conspiracy to procure its commission by another.[174] In *Gerakiteys*,[175] the identity of the alleged co-conspirators was of importance in determining whether the conspiracy charged was a conspiracy to make fraudulent claims, or a conspiracy to procure or enable the making of those claims by persons who were not conspirators.

Where an indictment alleges conspiracy with "a person or persons unknown", there must be some evidence from which a conspiracy could be inferred.[176] In *White*, where W appealed against a conviction for conspiring with L and other persons unknown to utter forged petrol coupons, Myers CJ stated:

> The charges however in the present case are not confined to a conspiracy ... with the other and with other persons unknown. It follows, therefore ... that even if there were no evidence against *White* of having conspired with L and there were no evidence ... of his having conspired with other persons unknown and if in consequence of there being no evidence against him he is entitled to be acquitted, L might still be convicted if the evidence showed that *he* had conspired with other persons unknown, that is to say, persons other than White whose identity the evidence did not disclose.[177]

Often, inferences of conspiracy may legitimately be drawn from the criminal acts of the parties accused, done in pursuance of an apparent common purpose. But mere conjecture is insufficient. A court must be careful to ensure

---

172 *R v Janis* 28/5/92, Heron J, HC Wellington T91-95/91, at 3. See also Gillies, *The Law of Criminal Conspiracy* (1st ed), Sydney, Law Book Co, 1981, 13.

173 See *R v Howes* (1971) 2 SASR 293; *R v Anthony* [1965] 2 QB 189. Sometimes a statute may depart from this rule, and specify that a person can be charged as having conspired with various people, provided that at least one of them is named. See, for example, s 393 Crimes Act 1900 (NSW).

174 *Gerakiteys v R* (1984) 153 CLR 317 at 334, 51 ALR 417 at 431, per Deane J.

175 Ibid.

176 *R v White* [1945] GLR 108 at 112.

177 Ibid at 111, 112.

that a person is not convicted of a crime simply on suspicion, speculation, or guesswork.[178] Thus, in *White*,[179] it was held that evidence that one accused was seen to pass his wallet into the pocket of another alleged conspirator, and that the wallet contained what looked like folded cards of coupons, was not evidence that they were forged coupons sufficient to infer a conspiracy to utter forged coupons. A mere series of assumptions, each in the nature of a guess unsupported by other evidence, is insufficient to prove a conspiracy charge.[180]

6.2.4.4 *The "wheel" conspiracy*

The essence of this kind of conspiracy is the notion that there is one global agreement made by all the conspirators, through the intermediary of a central person or group of persons. The persons at the centre (hub) form links (spokes) to the other individual members of the conspiracy, each of whom has no contact with any other conspirator apart from the central persons. However, there are some important limitations to this analysis. First, a person should not be joined in a charge alleging a *general* conspiracy unless there is real evidence from which a jury can infer that their minds went beyond a conspiracy to do a particular act or acts. This objection may be illustrated by the following example:

> A employs an accountant, C, to prepare his tax return. He and his clerk B are present when A is about to sign the return. A notices and queries an item in his expenses of $100 and indicates that he doesn't remember incurring the expense. B concedes that A did not put the item in but that it had been added by B on his own initiative on the basis that A "would not object to a few dollars being saved". The accountant agrees with the arrangement and after some hesitation A also agrees to let it stand.[181]

On those bare facts A and B could be charged with conspiring with C to defraud the Inland Revenue Department. However, the same evidence could not justify a charge against A of conspiring with 20 other people to defraud the Inland Revenue Department of $10,000 simply because the accountant and B had persuaded 100 other clients to make false returns. A would not be guilty of the general conspiracy because he has not knowingly attached himself to a general agreement to defraud.

In *R v Griffiths*,[182] the Court of Criminal Appeal allowed appeals against conviction on the grounds that there was no evidence that the appellants, a group of farmers who had allegedly conspired to defraud the Government by inducing a Department of State to pay excessive contributions under an Agriculture Lime Scheme, had any link with each other or knew what contracts other than their own had been entered into by the principal alleged conspirator to supply lime.

---

178 Ibid.
179 Ibid at 112.
180 *R v Sadler* (1911) 14 GLR 117 at 123, per Denniston J.
181 *R v Griffiths* [1966] 1 QB 589 at 598, 599, [1965] 2 All ER 448 at 454.
182 Ibid.

A second objection is that, with both "wheel" and "chain" conspiracies (below), the concept of "agreement" is replaced by "common design".[183] Yet for the common design to become a common agreement, there must have been some manifestation of assent to the agreement.[184] Where wheel or chain conspiracies are in issue, it appears that the courts sometimes derive the necessary manifestation of assent by treating some conspirators as making the agreement on behalf of themselves and others.[185] This approach is problematic. It is probably going too far to suggest that the concept of a "wheel conspiracy" is not known to the criminal law, as was suggested in the headnote to one English case.[186] However, it is equally clear that a person should not be convicted of complicity in a "wheel" conspiracy unless the trier of fact is convinced that each alleged conspirator was a party to a single, common conspiracy.[187] This implies that individual conspirators must at least have *knowingly* attached themselves to a conspiracy, whether or not their minds have gone beyond a conspiracy to do a particular act or acts. A person cannot enter a conspiracy inadvertently.

6.2.4.5 *The "chain" conspiracy*

In a "chain" conspiracy, the overall agreement is made by a series of groups of conspirators. Each group includes only some of the people who are members of the other groups. Thus, A communicates with B, B with C, C with D, and so on until the end of the list of conspirators. What has to be ascertained is whether the acts of the accused were done in pursuance of a criminal purpose held in common between the individual conspirators.[188] The courts treat each conspirator as being a party to the common design, and therefore as being a party to the agreement or conspiracy. On this basis, direct communication between all the co-conspirators is unnecessary. Neither is it required that any one co-conspirator knows of the existence of all the others.[189] What must be established is that the individual conspirators did have the common purpose to achieve some unlawful end. But if two conspirators agree to effect several unlawful objects and a third person agrees with them to effect only some of those objects, there are two conspiracies, not one. The original conspirators are parties to both conspiracies, the third person is party only to the conspiracy with the more limited objects.[190]

---

183 *Adams* § CA310.06.

184 Ibid.

185 Ibid.

186 See *R v Griffiths* (1965) 49 Cr App Rep 279 and see discussion in *R v Ardalan* [1972] 2 All ER 257 at 262, [1972] 1 WLR 463 at 470.

187 Ibid at 262, 470.

188 *R v Meyrick* (1929) 21 Cr App Rep 94 at 102.

189 *Adams* § CA310.06.

190 *Gerakiteys v R* (1984) 153 CLR 317 at 327, 51 ALR 417 at 425.

Note that where a single conspiracy has been charged, it is not open to the jury to find the accused guilty of a consequential but different conspiracy which flowed from that which is the subject of the actual charge.[191]

6.2.5 The mens rea of conspiracy

In general, the mens rea for conspiracy is present where there is an intention that the requisite course of conduct shall be pursued.[192] Accordingly, it is no defence for the accused to plead that the intended course of conduct was in fact impossible to pursue; because the essence of conspiracy is what the accused *agreed to do*, not what was *achieved*. In *R v Sew Hoy*,[193] the Court of Appeal held that it is the making of the agreement that is inimical to the public good, regardless of whether it proceeds further.[194]

In *R v Gemmell*[195] it was held that, to have the necessary knowledge for conspiracy, a person must know what he is supposed to have agreed to do. That is, D must intend to be a party to an agreement to commit the specific offence to which the conspiracy is directed.[196] However, it is not necessary that the accused should know the intended conduct will amount to an offence.[197] Thus if A and B agree together to take a 15-year-old girl out of the possession of her parents the fact that B believed the girl to be 17 would be no defence to a charge of conspiracy to abduct.[198] However, if on the same facts the evidence was that B believed the girl was a family friend of A's, and that the parents had consented to A and B having the temporary custody of the child, he would not be guilty of conspiracy because it could not be said that on the facts known to B what they agreed to do amounted to an unlawful act.[199] In *Churchill v Walton*, Viscount Dilhorne held:[200]

> If what they agreed to do was, on the facts known to them, an unlawful act, they are guilty of conspiracy and cannot excuse themselves by saying that, owing to their ignorance of the law, they did not realise that such an act was a crime. If, on the facts known to them, what they agreed to do was lawful, they are not rendered artificially

---

191 Ibid at 334, at 431, per Deane J.

192 *Halsbury's Laws of England*, vol 11(1), (4th ed), § 65.

193 [1994] 1 NZLR 257, (1993) 10 CRNZ 581 (CA).

194 This is in contrast to the position at common law, where if the conspiracy could not possibly have been successful, the parties were not guilty of conspiracy though they believed otherwise. See *DPP v Nock* [1978] AC 979, (1978) 67 Cr App R 116 (HL); *R v Bennett* (1978) 68 Cr App Rep 168 (CA). However, in the UK, the common law position has now been reversed by statute, to the effect that a person may be guilty of conspiracy even though the facts were such that the commission of the offence was impossible. See s 1(1) Criminal Law Act 1977 (UK), as amended by the Criminal Attempts Act 1981 (UK).

195 [1985] 2 NZLR 740 at 744, (1985) 1 CRNZ 496 at 500 (CA).

196 Ibid. See also *Churchill v Walton* [1967] 2 AC 224 at 237, [1967] 1 All ER 497 at 503.

197 Ibid.

198 Section 210. This is because, for an offence to be committed under s 210, it is not necessary that D should know the age of the girl (per s 210(2)).

199 Cf s 210(3).

200 *Churchill v Walton* [1967] AC 224 at 237, [1967] 1 All ER 497 at 503.

guilty by the existence of other facts, not known to them, giving a different and criminal quality to the act agreed upon.

It follows, therefore, that while a mistake of law will not afford a defence, an honest belief in a state of facts which, if true, would render the conduct lawful, will be an answer to any charge of conspiracy.[201] It would also follow, for example, that if T, charged with conspiracy to trespass, asserted a belief in a state of facts which would give rise to an enforceable right-of-way, that too would deny mens rea. Similarly, on a charge of conspiracy to publish defamatory matter during an election campaign,[202] it would normally be a defence that the accused genuinely believed in facts which would establish a privilege.[203] In these examples the burden of proof would rest on the prosecution to exclude the defences.[204]

6.2.5.1 *Agreements and acquiescence*

While an accused need not know that what she has agreed to do is unlawful, an apparent agreement which stops short of an intention to carry the offence through to completion is generally regarded as being insufficient for a conspiracy.[205] For example, if B and C, while having a quiet drink at the local pub, begin to discuss the possibility of committing a burglary, but before they can agree on the location and timing of the crime there is a disturbance in the hotel and they have to vacate the bar, there will be no conspiracy because there has been no intention manifested to carry the offence through to completion.

In this example, the charge of conspiracy would seem to be doomed because of the apparent absence of any agreement. One might think that merely discussing, in a speculative and abstract way, the possibility of committing an offence at an undefined future date defies the notion of agreeing to carry a criminal design into effect. Is it not the fact of consensus to participation in a common design that transforms mere discussion into a conspiracy? At first blush, it would seem reasonable to suggest that an accused person should not be guilty of conspiracy if she has not agreed and intended to do something of a positive nature herself to further the criminal design.

However, the authorities are not easily reconcilable on this point. In *R v Mulcahy*, in the dictum quoted earlier,[206] Willes J noted that the agreement to carry a criminal design into effect is a "plot" which constitutes the actus reus of conspiracy. A plot, by its nature, is a plan to carry something out or to accomplish something. Nevertheless, it appears that a requirement that the accused, to be a conspirator, must have intended *to play some part* in the agreed course of conduct,[207] may overstate the legal requirements. If it were to be

---

201 *Kamara v DPP* [1974] AC 104 at 119, [1973] 2 All ER 1242 at 1252.

202 See s 55 Local Elections and Polls Act 1976, and *Police v Starkey* [1989] 2 NZLR 373, (1989) 4 CRNZ 400.

203 *Kamara v DPP* [1974] AC 104 at 120, [1973] 2 All ER 1242 at 1252.

204 Ibid.

205 *R v Gemmell* [1985] 2 NZLR 740 at 744, (1985) 1 CRNZ 496 at 500 (CA).

206 § 6.2.3.

207 See *R v Anderson* [1986] AC 27 at 39, [1985] 2 All ER 961 at 965 (Bridge J).

insisted on, it would effectively confer impunity on the organiser of a crime who recruited others to carry it out. Such a person would, on this view, not herself be guilty of conspiracy unless it could be proved that she also intended to play an active part thereafter.[208]

On the other hand, acquiescence in a course of conduct over which a person would in any event have no influence does not qualify as an agreement for the purposes of conspiracy. The agreement should at least require that an accused assent to something in circumstances where, had he withheld assent, the withholding would have been of practical consequence.[209]

Accordingly, there is no conspiracy where a prospective offender has merely discussed with another person his own intention to commit an offence, to which course of conduct the other person acquiesces. The absence of a causal nexus between the discussion and any offence that follows would seem to defeat the possibility of a conspiracy charge.[210] However, where the second person, as a consequence of the conversation, offers to provide equipment or tools for the commission of the "object" crime, or otherwise intentionally encourages the intending offender to proceed with the crime, the act of expressing agreement in such practical terms might well amount to the real nexus required for a conspiracy charge.[211]

6.2.5.2 *Partial conspiracy?*

As we have seen, New Zealand courts have held that there must be an intention that the agreement be carried out, and that the agreement must be common to the minds of the conspirators. This requirement presents difficult problems in cases where D "agrees" with two or more others, who themselves intend to pursue a course of conduct which will necessarily involve the commission of an offence, but where D in fact has a secret intention to participate in only part of that course of conduct. Is D also guilty of conspiracy to commit an offence?

Commonwealth courts have diverged from the English courts on this question. In *Gemmell*, the Court of Appeal approved the decision of the Supreme Court of Canada in *R v O'Brien*,[212] where the majority agreed that because one of the co-conspirators did not have any intention to carry though the common design he could not be a party to the conspiracy. In *O'Brien*, this mental element was expressed as the *intention to put the common design into effect*. So if A and B purport to enter into an agreement to manufacture a Class A prohibited drug but B, acting as an informer for the police, has determined that he will have no part in the manufacture of drugs and will pull out of the agreement as soon as certain information has been disclosed, there is no conspiracy because, in reality, there is no common intention to put the design

---

208 See *R v Siracusa* (1990) 90 Cr App R 340 at 349, where the English Court of Appeal "explained " Lord Bridge's dictum.

209 *R v Richards* (1992) 9 CRNZ 403 at 411 (Fisher J).

210 Ibid.

211 This causal link must be both present and intended: ibid at 412.

212 [1955] 2 DLR 311, [1954] SCR 666 (SCC).

into effect. It has also been held that where a criminal enterprise is well advanced in the course of preparation, and it comes to the notice of the police or some other honest citizen in such circumstances that the only prospect of exposing and frustrating the criminals is that some innocent person should play the role of an intending collaborator in the proposed criminal conduct, the innocent person will be regarded as being innocent of conspiracy even though that person may be obliged to agree to a course of conduct involving the commission of a crime.[213] Public policy reasons dictate that an intention to frustrate the objects of a conspiracy ought to be allowed as a special defence.[214]

In *Anderson*,[215] the House of Lords took a different approach. The defendant was convicted of conspiring with a number of other men to effect the escape of one of them from jail. For a fee of £20,000 he had agreed to supply diamond wire to cut through metal cell bars, but claimed that he never intended the plan to be put into effect and did not believe that the plan could succeed. In rejecting this defence, it was held that it was sufficient that the accused agreed to perform certain of the acts contemplated for the achievement of an illegal end, even though he did not intend to go further with the scheme or believe that the offence could be committed.

Lord Bridge pointed out that to find in favour of the defendant would lead to an absurdity, because it would mean that a person could assist in aiding and abetting the commission of a crime by supplying the means to effect it and be fully aware of the agreed course of conduct yet be able to avoid a conviction for conspiracy on the basis that he was completely indifferent whether the offence was committed or not and therefore could not be said to have intended that the offence be committed. In Lord Bridge's view, a person who is fully aware of the circumstances of the commission of an offence and has provided assistance instrumental for its successful completion is "plainly" a party to the conspiracy to commit the offence.

The suggested justification for this approach is the fact that, in these days of highly organised crime, the most serious statutory conspiracies will frequently involve an elaborate and complex agreed course of conduct in which many will consent to play necessary but subordinate roles, which do not involve any direct participation in the commission of the offence at the heart of the conspiracy:[216]

"Parliament cannot have intended that such parties should escape conviction of conspiracy on the basis that it cannot be proved against them that they intended that the relevant offence or offences should be committed."

However, while the policy argument appears sound it may also be criticised as producing an absurdity. It has been observed that if no intention need be proved on the part of one alleged principal offender in conspiracy, it need not be proved on the part of another. Yet a conspiracy which no one intended to

---

213 *R v Anderson* [1986] AC 27, [1985] 2 All ER 961 (HL).

214 See Smith & Hogan, *Criminal Law* (7th ed), London, Butterworths, 1992, 274.

215 [1986] AC 27, [1985] 2 All ER 961 (HL).

216 [1986] AC 27 at 38, [1985] 2 All ER 961 at 965 (HL) (Lord Bridge).

carry out is an absurdity, if not an impossibility.[217] For these reasons it is suggested that *Anderson* should not be followed on this point.[218]

However, a conspiracy may be committed if a person acts with an intention to carry out the object of the conspiracy even though the ulterior motive is to gather evidence as part of a surveillance operation and where the party would not have been prosecuted if he carried out the plan agreed to. In *Yip Chiu-Cheung v R*,[219] A met N in Thailand and arranged to act as a courier to carry heroin from Hong Kong to Australia, for which he was to be paid US$16,000. N was, in fact, a US undercover drug enforcement officer whom the Australian and Hong Kong authorities had permitted to carry drugs from Hong Kong to Australia in the hope of breaking the drug ring to which the appellant belonged. Although the plan was not carried through and N did not fly to Hong Kong, the appellant A was arrested in Hong Kong and charged with conspiring with N to import heroin.

The Privy Council upheld the appellant's conviction for conspiracy. Their Lordships held that the fact that N would not have been prosecuted if he had carried out the plan to import the drugs into Australia as intended did not mean that he did not intend to commit the criminal offence, even though this was part of a wider scheme to combat drug dealing. Since N intended to commit the drug importation offence, it followed that there had been a conspiracy and A was properly convicted. The existence of a good motive did not negate the mens rea for the conspiracy. Suppose that N's undeclared intention had been to abscond to South America with the heroin upon successfully importing it to Australia and that he had, unknown to his superiors, arranged for an innocent "mule" to undertake the actual importation. Would these facts have negated the existence of a conspiracy to traffic in heroin? On the grounds of general principle N would have been regarded as the principal and the act of importing by the innocent agent would have been deemed to be his act.[220] The existence of the conspiracy would have been unaffected by the fact that N had acted with an impure motive.

6.2.6 Attempted conspiracy?

The language of the Crimes Act 1961 appears not to exclude the possibility that one may be convicted of attempting to form a conspiracy to commit an offence, and it was possible at common law to attempt to conspire.[221] However, it is arguably undesirable to extend the ambit of the criminal law by heaping preliminary crime upon preliminary crime, and it remains possible for the courts to refrain from acknowledging the possible "offence". In practice,

---

217 Smith and Hogan, *Criminal Law* (7th ed), London, Butterworths, 1992, 273.

218 Ibid.

219 [1995] 1 AC 111, [1994] 2 All ER 924 (PC).

220 *R v Paterson* [1976] 2 NZLR 394 (CA). See also *R v Jakeman* (1983) 76 Cr App R 223, [1983] Crim LR 104.

221 Smith and Hogan, *Criminal Law* (7th ed), London, Butterworths,1992, 267. However, the offences of incitement and attempt to conspire were abolished in England by s 5(7) Criminal Law Act 1977 (UK).

moreover, because liability for the attempt to commit a crime requires an intention to carry out that crime, where the absence of intention to carry the offence through to completion is a bar to the substantive crime of conspiracy, it would seem also to debar a successful prosecution for attempt.[222]

6.2.7 Conspiracy and party liability

The essence of a conspiracy is two or more persons participating in a common agreement to commit a crime. In that sense conspirators may properly be described as "parties" to a conspiracy. They are co-participants in a joint enterprise. Strictly speaking, this is where any assumed similarity between party liability and conspiracy should rest.

However, because New Zealand's statutory provision governing party liability refers, in one subsection, to persons "forming a common intention to prosecute an unlawful purpose",[223] it has sometimes been assumed that liability as a secondary party to an offence will necessarily make an offender liable as a party to conspiracy. In *R v Gemmell*,[224] the Court of Appeal rejected this approach, emphasising that a conspiracy is not the same thing as aiding and abetting, since the two offences have different ingredients. The Court approved the view that a person who knows other persons have agreed to commit a crime, but who is not a party to the agreement, and who does certain acts designed to assist in carrying out the crime, is not an accomplice to the offence of conspiracy. The person may, of course, be an accomplice to the substantive offence (the "object offence") if it is committed.[225]

The reason why the accomplice should not be guilty of conspiracy in such a case is that, although she may do or have done things which assist the principal to commit the object offence, the agreement is complete before those things are done and it cannot be said that there is a causal nexus between the agreement and the acts of the accomplice done in pursuance of the substantive offence.[226]

Regarding the specific relationship between conspiracy and the notion of common intention in s 66(2), the Court said:

> Viewed simply in conceptual terms we incline to the view that s 66(2) has no application to a conspiracy charge for the reason that the concept of probable consequences of a common purpose used in that provision is inconsistent with the concept of conspiracy. It is of the essence of a conspiracy that there must be a common design, a meeting of minds directed to the crime which is to be committed. That points to a state of knowledge on the part of the accused at the time the agreement is made between the conspirators. Reference to an offence which is a

---

222 There is some debate as to whether the offence of attempting to conspire exists at common law. On one view it is objectionable in principle to extend the ambit of the criminal law by heaping preliminary crime on preliminary crime. See GF Orchard, *Impossibility and the Inchoate Crimes* [1978] NZLJ 403 at 412.

223 Section 66(2) Crimes Act 1961.

224 [1985] 2 NZLR 740 at 746, (1985) 1 CRNZ 496 at 502 (CA).

225 *R v Gemmell* [1985] 2 NZLR 740 at 747, (1985) 1 CRNZ 496 at 502 (CA). See also *R v Clark* [1951] OR 791, (1951) 101 CCC 166; also *R v Koury* (1964) 43 DLR (2d) 637 at 650, [1964] SCR 212 at 217 (Spence J).

226 *R v Richards* (1992) 9 CRNZ 403 at 411.

probable consequence of the crime which the conspirators have actually agreed to commit is at odds with an agreed common design to commit an agreed particular crime.[227]

6.2.8 Extraterritorial conspiracies

It was noted in § 6.2.2 that a conspiracy may be conceived and commenced in one jurisdiction while acts necessary to its completion are committed in another. These are called "extra-territorial" conspiracies. It is clear from s 310(3) that the New Zealand courts have jurisdiction in respect of an agreement made in New Zealand to commit an offence overseas. However, difficulties may arise where the alleged conspiracy is an agreement to commit an offence in New Zealand but the agreement is made outside the country. A fundamental requirement of criminal liability in New Zealand is that a person may not be tried in respect of any "act done or omitted" outside New Zealand, unless the act or omission is an offence by virtue of the Crimes Act itself or some other enactment.[228] But where an act or omission forming *part of* an offence, or an event necessary to complete any offence, occurs in New Zealand, the offence is *deemed* to be committed in New Zealand, regardless whether the person charged was in New Zealand at the time of the act or omission.[229] The effect of these provisions taken together is to give the New Zealand courts jurisdiction over all offences completely performed in this country and also over offences where any act or omission forming part of the offence occurs here. Relying on these provisions, the Court of Appeal in *R v Sanders*[230] found that New Zealand courts had the jurisdiction to try conspirators who formed an agreement in Australia to import drugs into New Zealand because the conspirators had gone on to perform acts in New Zealand in furtherance of the execution of the conspiracy. D and E had agreed in Australia to import heroin into New Zealand. D then came to New Zealand and, after speaking with E by telephone, went to the airport to meet E. E arrived with the drug but was apprehended at the airport. In affirming D's conviction for conspiracy to import heroin, the Court held that conspiracy is a continuing offence, which is committed when the agreement is made but which continues as long as the agreement is in existence. Considering the effect of s 7, the Court said:

> the agreement in the present case had its origins in Australia but remained effective as a continuing agreement in New Zealand. In the words of s 310, the offenders were continuing to conspire at the moment the applicant was apprehended at Auckland airport.[231]

---

227 *R v Gemmell* [1985] 2 NZLR 740 at 748, (1985) 1 CRNZ 476 at 504 (CA).

228 Section 6.

229 Section 7.

230 [1984] 1 NZLR 636 (CA).

231 Ibid at 640 (McMullin J). The objection that a conspiracy to import is completely performed the moment the drug is brought within the territory, may be answered by noting that although this constitutes importing, that process also continues for a time, at least until the goods are released by the carrier, Customs, or the Post Office. See *Purdy v Collector of Customs* [1979] NZ Recent Law 43.

The reasoning in *Sanders* was extended in *R v Johnston*,[232] where the Court of Appeal affirmed the view of the trial Judge that a conspiracy to import a controlled drug was within the jurisdiction of the New Zealand courts. In that case, although the agreement had been formed abroad, one of the conspirators had come to New Zealand and a drug had been sent pursuant to the conspiracy. In such a case jurisdiction might be established on the basis that a conspiracy can be held to be committed wherever *anything* occurs pursuant to it in New Zealand during its continuance.[233] In *Johnston*, the only acts done in New Zealand (including the handling of a letter containing hashish sent by a co-conspirator in England) were done by innocent agents, namely members of the customs and post office. Nevertheless, these were held to be acts "within the contemplation of the conspirators in the performance of the continuing conspiracy" and were part of the continuing offence.

With respect to the Court of Appeal, it is arguable whether acts of innocent agents that are done in furtherance of the common object are to be regarded as constituting the offence, since they are not essential ingredients of the offence of conspiracy — which, of course, consists in a formed and continuing *agreement* between two or more people. The better approach may be to regard them as acts and events which provide *evidence* of the continued existence and performance of the agreement, rather than as constituent elements of the offence itself.[234]

6.2.9 Acquittal of other conspirators

If A is charged with conspiring with B and B is acquitted, can A be convicted? At common law there was some doubt whether a jury trying several conspirators could convict one and acquit the others. To convict A and acquit B would contravene the requirement that the verdicts on co-conspirators be formally consistent.[235] However, there are good reasons why it may be appropriate to convict one conspirator and acquit the other(s). For example, A may have made a confession which is admissible against him but not against B, which indicates that A conspired with B. Similarly, if A and B are tried separately the evidence presented at each trial may be different in some material respect, or the cases may be conducted differently, producing inconsistent verdicts.[236] It may also be that the convicted co-conspirator had conspired with a person other than the one acquitted.[237]

It is doubtful whether the strict rule requiring consistency of verdicts for co-conspirators now applies in New Zealand following its rejection at common law. In the UK, the question has been put beyond doubt by the Criminal Law

---

232 (1986) 2 CRNZ 289 (CA). See discussion at § 6.2.2.

233 See Orchard, "Jurisdiction over extraterritorial conspiracy" [1986] NZLJ 185.

234 Ibid at 186. And see further discussion Orchard, "Jurisdiction over extraterritorial conspiracy — an addendum" [1986] NZLJ 335.

235 See *Kannangara Aratchige Dharmasena v R* [1951] AC 1.

236 Allen, *Textbook on Criminal Law*, 1991, 205. See *DPP v Shannon* [1975] AC 717, [1974] 3 WLR 546.

237 *R v Ahearne* (1852) 6 Cox CC 6.

Act 1977 (UK), which provides that the mere fact that the others, supposedly party to an agreement on which the conviction of one conspirator is based, are acquitted, is not a ground for quashing the one conviction unless the conviction is inconsistent with the acquittal of the others.[238]

The effect of this rule is that where the evidence against C and D is of equal weight the judge should direct the jury that they must either acquit both or convict both, and if they are in any doubt, to acquit both.[239] There is no comparable rule under New Zealand statute law. It is suggested that the law in New Zealand is likely to follow the approach taken by the High Court of Australia, to the effect that there need be no impermissible inconsistency where there is a *significant difference* in the evidence admissible against the co-accused.[240] If there is a significant difference in the evidence admissible against the co-conspirators, or if the findings are by different tribunals, different verdicts are not necessarily inconsistent.[241]

6.2.10 Impossibility and conspiracy

Impossibility in the inchoate crimes of conspiracy, incitement, and attempts is conceptually distinct from the defence of impossibility of compliance and the related defence of necessity. Obviously, where a crime is impossible to commit, no one can be convicted of it. However, the law has long recognised that a person may, in some circumstances, still be convicted of conspiring to commit an offence even though the commission of that offence was impossible. Impossibility may be relevant to conspiracy in two situations:

(i) Where the agreement made was to perform conduct which was wrongly believed to amount to an offence; or

(ii) Where the agreement was to perform only certain types of conduct which could not, in fact, produce the desired end result.

6.2.10.1 *Conduct wrongly believed to be an offence*

This case is reasonably straightforward: no offence is committed. Thus if A comes to New Zealand believing that opossums are a protected species which it is illegal to kill, because it is a crime in some Australian states, he may freely agree to kill opossums for commercial gain. In fact the offence which he contemplates does not exist, its "commission" is legally impossible, and he has committed no offence.[242]

---

238 Criminal Law Act 1977 (UK), s 5(8) and (9).

239 *R v Longman* (1980) 72 Cr App R 121, [1982] Crim LR 54.

240 *Adams* § CA310.10.

241 Ibid.

242 See *R v Taaffe* [1984] AC 539, [1984] 1 All ER 747 (HL). D imported packages into the UK thinking they contained foreign currency which he believed (wrongly) it was a crime to import. Since there was no such crime, he could not be convicted of an offence even though the packages in fact contained cannabis. Although he committed the actus reus of importing cannabis he had no mens rea to do so.

6.2.10.2 *Desired end impossible to produce*

At common law, impossibility was generally an answer to a charge of conspiracy. In *DPP v Nock*,[243] the accused persons had agreed to attempt to produce cocaine from a certain substance in their possession by subjecting it to a particular chemical process. In reality the substance did not contain cocaine. They were held not guilty of conspiracy to produce a controlled drug since the performance of the agreement could never have resulted in the commission of an offence.

By contrast, *Nock* was not applied by the New Zealand Court of Appeal in *R v Sew Hoy*.[244] In that case, the company owned by the respondent had imported a shipment of clothing, described on accompanying documents as women's clothing. A customs inspection revealed it was men's clothing, and it was so classified by the Customs Department. The duty payable was higher for men's clothing and the company held insufficient import licences for the clothing. When asked to produce further documentation the accused again produced documents showing the clothing to be woman's clothing. However, the false documents would not have affected the classification because the classification decision had already been made.

The trial Judge applied *Nock* and held that because at all material times the documents could not have deceived the Customs Department in the way intended, the agreement was incapable of commission from the outset. However, the Court of Appeal distinguished *Nock*. It distinguished between an agreement which, if carried out, *could not* result in the commission of the alleged offence because of legal or physical impossibility, and an agreement which would result in the commission of the crime alleged if carried out in accordance with the intention of the parties but which cannot be carried out because some person not a party to the agreement is unwilling or unable to do something necessary for its performance.[245]

The Court held that in this case the respondents intended to defraud and did all they intended to do to realise that intention. They failed because the means they adopted were inappropriate to realise their intention. Whereas in *Nock* the substances employed were incapable under any circumstances of achieving the narrow purpose of the conspiracy, in *Sew Hoy* the means employed *were* capable of deceiving. The respondents were frustrated in achieving their purpose simply because the Customs Department instituted its own assessment procedures to prevent this kind of fraud. The case was held to fall within the fourth category of attempts identified by Turner J in *R v Donnelly*,[246] namely inefficiency or insufficiency of means, and therefore the respondents were guilty of both an attempt and conspiracy.

The decision indicates the Court's approval of an approach to conspiracy which emphasises the inherent *culpability* of the criminal agreement, rather

---

243 [1978] AC 979, [1978] 2 All ER 654.

244 [1994] 1 NZLR 257, (1993) 10 CRNZ 581 (CA).

245 *R v Bennett* (1978) 68 Cr App R 168 at 178, [1979] Crim LR 454 at 455. See also *R v Harris* (1979) 69 Cr App R 122.

246 [1970] NZLR 980 at 990 (CA).

than an approach which focuses on *results* that may or may not happen.[247] In *Sew Hoy* Hardie Boys J said:

> The essence of conspiracy is an intention to agree coupled with a common design to commit an offence, that is, to put the design into effect. The mens rea is the intention to achieve the common design, the actus reus is the fact of the agreement . . . The offence is therefore complete when the agreement is made. *It is the making of the agreement itself that is seen as inimical to the public good* whether it proceeds further or not. It should therefore be irrelevant that it may not be possible in fact to carry out the agreement. This does not mean that the parties are punished on the basis of guilty intention alone. They will have gone further, and have acted upon their intention by making their agreement.[248]

6.2.11 Charging conspiracy together with the substantive offence

Generally it is inappropriate to include a charge of conspiracy in an indictment alleging the substantive offence. The reasons commonly given for this are that evidence admissible only on the conspiracy count could have a prejudicial effect in relation to other counts. In particular, by bringing a conspiracy count the prosecution can combine into an indictment a variety of offences. If two or more persons are arraigned on an indictment which includes a conspiracy count, everything said or done by either accused which is relevant to that count is admissible in evidence against both accused at their joint trial. However, without the conspiracy count, even though an application for separate trials may not succeed, the trial judge must be careful in directing the jury about which evidence is admissible against each individual accused. In addition to these considerations, adding a count of conspiracy may unnecessarily complicate and prolong a trial.[249]

Including conspiracy and a substantive count in one indictment will normally be justifiable only where there is real evidence from which a jury may infer that the alleged conspirators were acting in pursuance of a criminal purpose held in common between them.[250] However, a charge of conspiracy might properly be included in an indictment where the substantive offences charged do not represent the total criminality.[251] Where there is a joinder of substantive offences and conspiracy the correct approach is to deal with the substantive charges first, before deciding whether the conspiracy charge should be considered.[252]

---

247 See *Maxwell v HM Advocate* [1980] SLT 241.

248 *R v Sew Hoy* [1994] 1 NZLR 257 at 267, (1993) 10 CRNZ 581 at 591 (CA) (emphasis added).

249 *R v Humphries* [1982] 1 NZLR 353 at 355 (CA). See also *Verrier v DPP* [1967] 2 AC 195, [1966] 3 All ER 568.

250 *R v Griffiths* [1966] 1 QB 589, [1965] 2 All ER 379.

251 *R v Jones* (1974) 59 Cr App R 120, [1974] Crim LR 663.

252 *R v Dawson and Wenlock* [1960] 1 All ER 558, [1960] 1 WLR 163.

6.3 INCITEMENT

Incitement is not defined in the Crimes Act 1961, but a general provision governing the penalty for the offence is provided in s 311(2).[253] If D incites *any* person to commit *any* offence *which is not in fact committed*, she is liable to the same punishment as if she had attempted to commit that offence, except where a punishment for that offence is expressly provided by statute.[254] "Offence" may be taken to include all penal offences and not merely crimes defined in the Crimes Act.[255] The reason why the offence created by s 311(2) applies only where the incited offence is not committed, is that, if the offence is committed, a person who incites, counsels, or procures the commission of an offence will be liable as a secondary party under s 66(1)(d). The provision thus supplements the rules on parties by providing for the situation where, because no principal offence has actually been committed, secondary liability cannot be imposed under s 66.

In addition to the general offence of incitement, punishable under s 311(2), certain grave incitement offences are punished independently by specific provisions. For example, s 68(2) provides for a prison term not exceeding 10 years for every person who incites the commission of an act outside New Zealand which would be murder if done or omitted in New Zealand, where no such act is done or omitted.[256] Separate provision is also made for the crime of inciting the murder of any other person in New Zealand, when murder is not in fact committed.[257]

There is one special case. In all these varieties of incitement, incitement may be charged only where the substantive offence is *not* committed. By contrast, the crime of inciting suicide is committed only if the person *actually commits* or attempts to commit suicide in consequence of the incitement.[258] This is because if the suicide is committed, the inciter cannot be charged as a party to the commission of an offence, since suicide itself is no longer a crime. Accordingly incitement becomes, in effect, the substantive offence. This means that advising V to commit suicide does not amount to incitement unless and until V does commit or attempt suicide.[259] In turn, since incitement is the principal offence, it has been accepted that an offence exists of attempting to incite suicide; thus D's "unsuccessful" advice or encouragement, which does not result in a suicide attempt by V, may be punishable as an attempt by D.[260]

---

253 The offence is electable: s 6(2) Summary Proceedings Act 1957, as amended by s 3 Summary Proceedings Amendment Act 1961.

254 Section 311(2) Crimes Act 1961.

255 See s 2; also *Clyne v Bowman* (1987) 33 A Crim R 280 at 285, 286.

256 See also s 69 (party to any other crime outside New Zealand).

257 Section 174.

258 Section 179(a).

259 Smith and Hogan, *Criminal Law* (7th ed), London, Butterworths, 1992, 380.

260 Ibid. See *R v McShane* (1977) 66 Crim App R 97, [1977] Crim LR 737 (CA).

6.3.1 The actus reus

As has been remarked, incitement is not defined in the Crimes Act. Its meaning is derived from the common law. A person who incites:

> is one who reaches and seeks to influence the mind of another to the commission of a crime. The machinations of criminal ingenuity being legion, the approach to the other's mind may take various forms, such as suggestion, proposal, request, exhortation, gesture, argument, persuasion, inducement, goading or arousal of cupidity.[261]

In *Young v Cassels*,[262] "incite" was held to mean "to rouse", "to stimulate", "to urge or spur on", "to stir up", "to animate". In that case, the appellant had been charged with inciting persons to resist constables in the execution of their duty when, in a speech to striking waterside workers, he had used the words, "if a police constable uses his baton to you, give him one back, and if one won't do, make it a double header". Stout CJ held that there is no requirement that the incited actors must be ready to commit the crime, or that anyone must have acted on the incitement before D could be convicted of inciting; rather, what was required, generally speaking, was simply that the time of the incitement was antecedent to the time when the crime was to be committed or attempted. On the facts of *Young v Cassels*, this meant that it was not necessary for an arrest to be about to take place before the offence of inciting to resist arrest could be committed.[263]

As the quotation above makes clear, the modes and forms of incitement are many and varied. For example, incitement may be committed where D threatens or puts pressure on another to commit an offence. The incitement does not have to take the form of persuasion.[264] Additionally, the target of the incitement may be a particular individual or people generally.[265] In *R v Most*,[266] the defendant published an article urging readers throughout the world to follow the example of Russian revolutionaries and murder their heads of State. This was held to be an incitement to murder.

Further, incitement need not be express but may be implied. This includes a disguised or encoded invitation in a letter to commit an offence that can only be understood by the recipient.[267] So advertising a police radar detection device in a magazine, emphasising its value in detecting police radar traps, was held in *Invicta Plastics v Clare*[268] to amount to inciting the offence of using unlicensed apparatus for wireless telegraphy contrary to the Wireless Telegraphy Act 1949.

---

261 *S v Nkosiyana* [1966] (4) SA 655 at 658 (Holmes JA); cited in Smith and Hogan, *Criminal Law* (7th ed), London, Butterworths, 1992, 265.

262 (1914) 16 GLR 391 at 392.

263 Ibid at 393.

264 *Race Relations Board v Applin* [1973] 1 QB 815 at 825, [1973] 2 All ER 1190 at 1194 (Lord Denning MR).

265 *Walsh v Sainsbury* (1925) 36 CLR 464 at 476, [1925] ALR 343.

266 (1881) 7 QBD 244. (Prosecution under s 4 Offences Against the Person Act 1861 (UK)).

267 *R v Cope* (1921) 16 Cr App R 77.

268 [1976] Crim LR 131, [1976] RTR 251. The point here is not that D was inciting speeding, but that D was inciting *use* of the radar detector, which itself constituted an offence.

However, it is not incitement *per se* to manufacture and sell a device which has no function other than one involving the commission of an offence.[269] There must be a promotion of the offence; unless D actually seeks to persuade or encourage another, there can be no incitement.[270] On this basis an advertisement for a product which was known to be capable of assisting people to break the law, but in which no words of endorsement, inducement, or encouragement appear, would not amount to incitement to commit an offence.[271]

Another limitation is that since the terms of s 311(2) are confined to persuasion and attempted procuring, the offence does not include assistance to commit an offence.[272] Thus, if P, intent on committing a crime, asks D to supply him with services or materials to be used in the commission of the offence, the supply of those materials or services would not make D liable under s 311(2) when B does not in fact commit the offence.

6.3.1.1 *Communication of incitement*

For an incitement to be complete there must be some form of actual communication with a person whom it is intended to incite. Where a communication is sent with a view to incite, but does not reach the intended recipient, the sender can be guilty only of an attempt to incite.[273] Accordingly, in *R v Banks*,[274] where the accused send a letter to her niece advising her how to kill her infant using poison, it was held that even though the letter was intercepted D could be convicted of an attempt to incite her niece to murder the child.

Banks illustrates the requirement that a criminal incitement must be communicated to the other party. However, it need not in fact influence the recipient.[275] In *R v Dimozantos*,[276] which involved an appeal against conviction for incitement to murder, the Court of Criminal Appeal of Victoria had to construe a provision in the Crimes Act 1958 (Vic) which provided that a person will be guilty of incitement "if the inciting *is acted on* in accordance with the inciter's intention".[277] The Court agreed with the interpretation of the trial Judge who held that it was not necessary to prove that the person incited *in fact* acted upon the incitement, but rather that it was essential to prove that the course of conduct urged would, *if* it had been acted upon as the inciter intended, amount to the commission of the offence. In the view of the Victorian

---

269 *R v James* (1985) 82 Cr App R 226 at 232, [1986] Crim LR 118 at 119.

270 *Halsbury's Laws of England* , vol 11(1), (4th ed, reissue), § 58.

271 See *R v Dionne* (1987) 38 CCC (3d) 171.

272 *Adams* § CA311.08.

273 See *R v Cope* (1921) 16 Cr App R 77; *R v Ransford* (1874) 13 Cox CC 9.

274 (1873) 12 Cox CC 393.

275 *R v Krause* (1902) 66 JP 121.

276 (1991) 56 A Crim R 345.

277 Section 321G Crimes Act 1958 (Vic). (Emphasis added.)

Court, the offence of incitement is constituted "solely by what the inciter says or does and intends".[278]

This interpretation is consistent with the common law, which has held that incitement is complete even though the mind of the person incited is unaffected.[279] The law has never required any consequent step towards the completion of the substantive offence before incitement may be established. Thus incitement would be complete even if the person incited (for example) intended to inform on the inciter.

6.3.1.2 *Renunciation of incitement*

Similarly, in *R v Gonzague*[280] D was charged with procuring C to commit murder after he had allegedly arranged for C to have a business competitor "wiped off the mat". The Ontario Court of Appeal held that the offence of procuring (the equivalent of inciting) is complete when the solicitation or incitement occurs, even though it is immediately rejected by the person solicited, or even though the person solicited merely pretends assent and has no intention of committing the offence. The Court rejected the appellant's contention that a renunciation by the appellant of a previous act of incitement constituted a defence, stating that there is no authority supporting the view that renunciation of the criminal purpose constitutes a defence to a charge of inciting.[281] The rationale for this rule would appear to be that the essence of the crime of incitement lies in D's seeking to influence the mind of another, and that this action is complete once the solicitous words have been uttered or otherwise articulated, regardless of their eventual impact on the mind of the audience. Subsequent renunciation of the criminal purpose cannot retrieve those words already uttered, whether or not they actually incite the commission of an offence.

6.3.1.3 *Attempted incitement*

An attempt to incite the commission of an offence requires proof of an act which is more than merely preparatory to the commission of the full offence. In *R v Rowley*,[282] the accused was charged, among other things, with attempting by written notes to incite a child under the age of 14 to commit an act of gross indecency. However, the fact that the notes relied on went no further than seeking to meet with the boys in question, and contained nothing "lewd, obscene or of a disgusting nature", led the Court to find that the acts were no more than preparatory even on the assumption that the ultimate intention of the appellant was gross indecency. It was held that incitement to commit gross indecency would require a proposition to be made for that specific purpose.[283]

---

278 *R v Dimozantos* (1991) 56 A Crim R 345 at 349.
279 See *R v Diamond* (1920) 84 JP 211.
280 (1983) 4 CCC (3d) 505 at 508.
281 Ibid at 508, 509. See also Wasik, "Abandoning Criminal Intent" [1980] Crim LR 785.
282 [1991] 4 All ER 649, [1991] 1 WLR 1020.
283 Ibid at 654, at 1025.

6.3.2 Mens rea

To prove incitement, it is necessary to show that the accused sought to persuade or encourage another to commit an act that would constitute a crime if done by that other.[284] Thus the offence requires two mental elements, which correspond to those necessary to establish secondary liability under s 66(1):

(a) Knowledge of the circumstances which would make the act of the person incited an offence; and

(b) An intention that the person incited should commit the act constituting the offence.

In relation to (a), the meaning of knowledge has been considered earlier in this book, and would include cases of wilful blindness where the accused deliberately closed his eyes to the circumstances of the act incited which are elements of the crime in question.[285] The relevant circumstances include the mens rea of the incitee. For example, if D incites V to commit theft by representing to her that the item to be stolen actually belongs to D, and V believes D, D could not be guilty of incitement to steal (assuming the item is not actually stolen), because V, the innocent agent, will have acted without any mens rea for theft. Of course, D would be liable as the principal if the offence is committed, or otherwise for attempted theft if the venture has proceeded beyond mere preparation.

In relation to (b), D must intend the consequences specified in the actus reus of the offence incited. Suppose that D, walking with his girlfriend, comes across two men arguing in the street. D yells out to them both, "give him one from me!", being indifferent whether a fight ensues but intending to show off to his girlfriend. On these facts, D is not guilty of inciting to assault. He is reckless whether an assault results but does not intend that it should do so. It is an *intention* to bring about the criminal result, when coupled with an act of persuasion, that is the essence of incitement.[286]

6.3.3 Incitement to murder

This offence is defined separately in s 174 Crimes Act 1961. The elements of the offence are:

(i) Inciting any person,

(ii) To murder any other person in New Zealand,

(iii) The murder is not in fact committed.

Where the murder is committed, there is no offence under s 174, although if there has been counselling or inciting s 66(1) will apply, and the offender may be liable for the substantive offence of murder. Where the murder incited is attempted but not committed, the inciter may be charged with attempted murder under s 173 in addition to inciting murder under s 174. So, if D publishes an article in a "hard-core" nationalist magazine extolling the virtues of those who kill "white" politicians, which inspires P to attempt to kill such a

---

284 *R v Curr* [1968] 2 QB 944, [1967] 1 All ER 478.

285 § 3.4.

286 Smith and Hogan, *Criminal Law* (7th ed), London, Butterworths, 1992, 268.

person, D may be guilty of both attempted murder and incitement.[287] In such circumstances it is not necessary that the proposed victims be named, provided they form a sufficiently well-defined class.[288]

As with incitement generally, it must be proved that communication of the incitement to murder reached a person whom D intended to incite, although it is not necessary to show that the recipient's mind was affected thereby.[289]

It remains unclear from the cases whether it is necessary that the person being incited should actually understand the communication ie that they are being solicited to commit a particular offence. However, it is arguable that since the essence of incitement is what the inciter says or does (and intends),[290] it does not matter whether the person being incited actually understands the communication, provided it is proved to have reached her.

6.3.3.1 Inciting "any person"

It is submitted that the words "any person" in s 174 may be given their natural meaning, and may therefore include an "innocent agent" or a person who is incapable of understanding the solicitation. However, if D knew that P (the person incited) was mentally disordered and lacked the capacity to understand that what he was being incited to do was an offence, it could not be said that D had knowledge of the circumstances which would make P's act an offence.[291] On the other hand, if the intended offence is committed D may still be guilty as the principal.

6.3.3.2 To murder "any other person"

In R v Shephard,[292] the Court of Criminal Appeal held that the phrase "any other person"[293] applied when D solicited a pregnant woman (P) to kill her child when it was born. At the time of D's writing the solicitous letter, P was only six weeks pregnant. The proposed victim did not have to exist as a human being at the date of the incitement, but the Court left open the question whether the offence could be committed if the child had not been born alive, and thus could never have been a potential victim of murder. However, since incitement is a relational crime and is not dependent on any "permissive" facts being in existence before the crime may be committed (the person inciting need only believe that the crime incited is capable of being committed at some future time), there would seem to be no reason why incitement could not be committed even if the child were stillborn. The requirement that the child be born alive is a necessary condition for murder. It is not an element of incitement to do the same. In New Zealand, this analysis is reinforced by the fact that s 174 expressly excludes the commission of the substantive offence as

---

287 R v Diamond (1920) 84 JP 211.

288 Smith and Hogan, Criminal Law (7th ed), London, Butterworths, 1992, 376. See R v Most (1881) 7 QBD 244; R v Antonelli and Barberi (1905) 70 JP 4.

289 R v Fox (1870) 19 WR 109 (CCR); R v Krause (1902) 66 JP 121.

290 R v Dimozantos (1991) 56 A Crim R 345 at 349.

291 See Adams § CA311.09.

292 [1919] 2 KB 125.

293 Also contained in s 4 Offences Against the Person Act 1861 (UK).

an element of incitement. Given this, it would seem to be of no consequence whether the intended victim is ultimately capable of being killed.

6.3.4 Impossibility

Although s 311 makes no direct reference to impossibility, it is clear that situations may and do arise where one person incites, counsels, or attempts to procure another to commit an offence which it is impossible in law or in fact to commit. In *R v Fitzmaurice*,[294] the appellant's father conceived a plan to defraud a security firm of reward money by informing the police of a plan to rob a security van and then simulating a street robbery to make it appear that the advice was instrumental in preventing a major robbery from occurring. The appellant, believing the plan to commit the street robbery was genuine, had secured the services of two men to rob a woman carrying wages between a factory and a bank. However, before the "robbery" could take place the two men were arrested and charged with conspiracy to rob. The appellant was charged with and convicted of unlawfully inciting the two men to rob the woman. In dismissing the appeal, the Court of Appeal held that in approaching an inchoate crime at common law it was necessary to decide in each case what was the course of conduct incited, agreed, or attempted. In particular, the evidence might establish incitement in general terms, while the subsequent agreement might be directed at a specific crime in greater detail. In such a case, although a successful committal of the specific crime (in the manner agreed) may be impossible, it might nonetheless be possible for the inciter to be convicted. This occurred in *Fitzmaurice* itself. Because D had taken steps to recruit the men at a time when he *believed* that there was to be a robbery, he was encouraging the men to participate in a robbery, and accordingly there was incitement to commit an offence which was not, in itself, an impossible offence to carry out.

This analysis is consistent with the general principle concerning incitement, that it is what the accused does or says with intent that constitutes the wrongdoing — not whether her incitement has any effect on the mind of the incitee, nor whether it is capable of fulfillment. For this reason, in *R v McDonough*,[295] on a charge of incitement to receive stolen goods, it was held to be unnecessary that any stolen goods should be in existence as envisaged at the time of the incitement.

---

294 [1983] 1 QB 1083, [1983] 1 All ER 189.
295 (1962) 47 Cr App R 37 (CCA).

7

Infancy

7.1 RATIONAL CAPACITY

A hallmark of criminal responsibility is that at the time of the alleged offence the offender possessed the rational capacity to be charged with and convicted of a crime. Rational capacity generally requires that the person be capable of understanding what she is doing, in the sense of being able to understand the nature, circumstances, and consequences of her actions and of having the ability to control those actions. It follows that criminal culpability should not attach to a person who at the time of an alleged offence was incapable of understanding either what she was doing, or the legal and social significance of her conduct, and/or who was unable control her actions.[1] The principle of rational capacity is thus a *precondition* of one's eligibility for punishment.[2] Defences based on the absence of rational capacity include infancy, insanity, and automatism. They operate on a different theoretical basis to those "defences", including intoxication and certain mistakes of fact,[3] which gainsay criminal liability by denying some (usually, mens rea) element of the offence charged. For example, intoxication is not a defence of incapacity under New Zealand law because the essential question is not whether the accused was *incapable* of forming the necessary intent, owing to the effect of alcohol or drugs, but instead whether the requisite intent or recklessness by D *was in fact* present.[4] Intoxication is merely evidence from which a tribunal of fact may

---

1   See Barlow, "Drug Intoxication and the Principle of *Capacitas Rationalis*" (1984) 100 LQR 639.
2   See Allen, *Textbook on Criminal Law* (2nd ed), 1991, 98; also the requirement for "deliberative control" over one's conduct, at § 2.3.
3   See chapter 12.
4   *R v Kamipeli* [1975] 2 NZLR 610 at 616 (CA).

infer that the mens rea for an offence was lacking. It is therefore inapt to describe it as a fundamental incapacity.

Similarly, defences like self-defence, compulsion, duress of circumstances, and necessity are not based on a claim of rational incapacity. Rather, they operate as justification or excuse. They depend upon a recognition that although the accused was capable of understanding relevant actions, circumstances, and consequences, his free choice was circumscribed by threats or exigent circumstances so that he had no reasonable choice but to break the law.

Lack of rational capacity is not the only form of incapacity known to the law. As we saw in § 2.3, in cases of impossibility or physical involuntariness, responsibility for the actus reus is avoided because of the operation of imperious forces over which the accused had no control. The defence is one of involuntariness based not on *rational incapacity* but rather on *causative impotence*. The accused is simply *physically* incapable of conduct that would result in compliance with the law, or of avoiding the circumstances which constitute a criminal offence.

7.2 YOUNG CHILDREN: AN IRREBUTTABLE PRESUMPTION

At common law the rule was that children under the age of 7 years were doli incapax. This meant that they were considered to be incapable of crime regardless of evidence of actus reus or mens rea. Under s 21 Crimes Act 1961, which is otherwise declaratory of the common law,[5] the triggering age is now 10 years. Section 21 lays down an irrebuttable presumption that a person under the age of 10 years is incapable of committing an offence:

Children under 10 – (1) No person shall be convicted of an offence by reason of any act done or omitted by him when under the age of 10 years.

Consequently, where an offender is under 10 years of age, the State is absolutely prohibited from acting against that child in respect of any "offence" committed by him, regardless of the degree of understanding in fact possessed by the child regarding the nature and consequences of his offending. The formula in s 21, "no person shall be convicted", does not alter the common law by suggesting that a criminal offence *is* committed by the infant but that he is merely exempted from being convicted. A child of relevant age is by stipulation incapable of *committing* a crime.

Because at common law the child cannot commit a crime, it would normally follow that someone who instigates the commission of an offence by that child cannot be a party to that offence. This exclusion appears to be overridden by s 21(2), which provides that s 21 "shall not affect the question whether any other person who is alleged to be a party to that offence is guilty of that offence". However, reliance on s 21(2) is generally not necessary, since even at common law, any person acting through the child to commit a crime would be liable as the principal offender under the doctrine of innocent agency.[6] This

---

5   *R v Brooks* [1945] NZLR 584 at 595 (CA) (Myers CJ).

6   See § 5.1.1.1.

might occur where, for example, D, an adult, instructs C, a child aged 7, to steal an item from a shop. In those circumstances D would be deemed to be the principal offender because C is presumptively incapable of committing an offence. In law, C's body is merely the "agency" through which D has acted to commit the offence. In such a case C is not criminally responsible, not because she lacked mens rea, but because (as with the defence of insanity) she lacked the legal capacity to commit a crime.

However, this does not mean that the State is powerless to intervene in any way in respect of a young child who is suspected of having deliberately committed an offence. Where there is evidence that the child under the age of 10 is behaving in a way which is harmful to the child's well-being, or where the child's parent, guardian, or other person having the care of the child is unwilling or unable to care for the child, proceedings for "care and protection" may be commenced under Part II Children, Young Persons, and Their Families Act 1989.[7] The purpose of this jurisdiction is not to punish but rather to protect such children from harm and to promote their welfare.[8]

7.3 CHILDREN OVER THE AGE OF 10

Where a child is over the age of 10 years a different set of rules applies. A child in the "twilight zone"[9] between the ages of 10 and 14 cannot be convicted unless it is proved not only that the child did the act in circumstances which would involve an adult in criminal liability but also that he knew that he was doing wrong. That is to say, for children aged between 10 and 14 years there is a rebuttable presumption that they are doli incapax.

Another way of expressing this rule is to say that, in the case of wrongdoing by such a child, knowledge that her act or omission was wrong becomes a necessary ingredient of the charge against her, and the existence of this necessary ingredient must be proved by the Crown before the child can be convicted.[10] Criminal responsibility would result upon proof of actus reus and mens rea together with what was known at common law as "mischievous discretion".[11] The relevant principles are defined in s 22 Crimes Act 1961:

> **Children between 10 and 14**—(1) No person shall be convicted of an offence by reason of any act done or omitted by him when of the age of 10 but under the age of 14 years, unless he knew either that the act or omission was wrong or that it was contrary to law.

In effect, a child between the ages of 10 and 14 will be presumed to be incapable of committing an offence, but this presumption may be rebutted by

---

7   See s 14(1)(d) and (f) Children, Young Persons, and Their Families Act 1989.

8   Section 13 Children, Young Persons, and Their Families Act 1989. For a comprehensive discussion of the principles underlying the protective jurisdiction for children and young persons, see *Trapski's Family Law* vol 1, Wellington, Brooker's, 1991, § CP.1.

9   Stuart, *Canadian Criminal Law* (3rd ed), 1995, 336. See also Williams, "The Criminal Responsibility of Children" [1954] Crim LR 493.

10 *R v Brooks* [1945] NZLR 584 at 595 (CA).

11 Stuart, *Canadian Criminal Law* (3rd ed), 1995, 336. See also Hale 1 PC, 630.

proof that the child "knew" her act or omission was "wrong" or that it was "contrary to law".[12] The onus of such proof lies on the prosecution.[13]

However, although s 22(1) implies that a child may be prosecuted where such knowledge is present and the doli incapax presumption is rebutted, in practice such prosecutions are very unlikely because of the operation of s 272(1) Children, Young Persons, and Their Families Act 1989. Section 272(1) of that Act stipulates that a child over the age of 10 shall not be subject to proceedings brought under the Summary Proceedings Act 1957, except where the charges involve murder or manslaughter. In the event of a prosecution for murder or manslaughter, the preliminary hearing must take place before a Youth Court under the terms of the Children, Young Persons, and Their Families Act 1989.

7.3.1 Care and protection proceedings

While prosecution of children between 10 and 14 is very rare, such child offenders may, like those under 10, be subject to care and protection proceedings where the offending by the child is such as to give "serious concern for the well-being of the child".[14] Since the child cannot normally be charged with the relevant offence (except where the offence is murder or manslaughter), the commission of the offences by the child will seldom be established by criminal conviction.[15] This means that any applicant for a declaration that the child is in need of care or protection will have to prove the commission of the offences during the civil proceedings, either by proving that the child admitted the offences or by calling evidence.[16] In any case where application has been made for a declaration that the child is in need of care and protection, where the application is based on the fact of offending by the child, a declaration cannot be made unless the following conditions are met:

(i) It must be established that the court would have found the child guilty of an offence if the proceedings had been pursuant to an information laid under the Summary Proceedings Act 1957, charging the child with an offence; and

(ii) The court must be satisfied the child knew either that the act or omission constituting the offence was wrong or that it was contrary to law.[17]

The criminal standard of proof and rules of evidence apply in such proceedings.[18]

7.3.2 Burden of proof in rebutting the doli incapax presumption

At common law, the presumption that a child between the ages of 10 and 14 was doli incapax at the time of the alleged offending can be rebutted only by

---

12 Section 22(1) Crimes Act 1961.

13 *R v Brooks* [1945] NZLR 584 (CA)

14 Section 14(1)(e) Children, Young Persons, and Their Families Act 1989.

15 *Trapski's Family Law* vol 1, Wellington, Brooker's, 1991, § CP.1.

16 Ibid.

17 Section 198 Children, Young Persons, and Their Families Act 1989.

18 Section 198(2) Children, Young Persons, and Their Families Act 1989.

clear positive evidence that the child knew that her act was *seriously* wrong, and evidence of acts amounting to the offence itself will not be enough to rebut the presumption.[19] In *C (A Minor) v DPP*, evidence that the 12-year-old offender had done substantial damage to a motorcycle that he was intending to steal and the fact that he ran from the police leaving behind a crowbar was held by the House of Lords not to be sufficient of itself to rebut the presumption.

Although "conceptually obscure", the meaning of the common law test, which requires that the child should know that her act is "seriously wrong" in a moral sense,[20] is reasonably clear when the phrase is contrasted with "merely naughty or mischievous".[21] Mere knowledge of illegality will not necessarily suffice.

While it appears to be generally accepted that, in modern times, the presumption of incapacity is not always appropriate, especially in the case of older children within the range to which it applies, it provides a "benevolent safeguard" against children being treated as if they ought to know the wrongfulness of their acts when, in reality, they may not. The safeguard may, however, be overcome by the prosecution's positively proving that the child was of normal mental capacity and as such was able to distinguish right from wrong and to form a criminal intent.[22] But it is *not* for the child to disprove the presumption that she is a normal child of her age; the courts will not countenance, as a means of rebutting the presumption, the "sensible" argument that any child of the defendant's age would know she was doing what was wrong.[23]

Knowledge of right and wrong may be proved by evidence of previous convictions. However, the convictions must be relevant. For example, at common law on a charge of blackmail, evidence of a conviction for assault or for riding a bicycle on a footpath would normally be excluded as irrelevant, whereas a conviction for theft may be relevant.[24] Other relevant evidence may include anything the child said or did before or after the conduct in question, the results of an interview or psychiatric examination, and evidence from someone who knows the child well.[25] Evidence of normal development is admissible, but may not be "really cogent". Evidence that the child ran away following detection may be equivocal, because it shows that the child appreciated the conduct was "naughty" and does not necessarily establish knowledge that the conduct was "seriously wrong". What is required is proof of guilty knowledge that is clear "and beyond all possibility of doubt", or

---

19 *C (A Minor) v DPP* [1996] AC 1, [1995] 2 WLR 383 (HL).

20 See *JBH and JH (Minors) v O'Connell* [1981] Crim LR 632, where Donaldson J described the relevant test as being that the prosecutor had to prove the appellants knew that what they were doing was wrong morally, whether or not they knew it was an offence.

21 *C (A Minor) v DPP* [1996] AC 1 at 33, [1995] 2 WLR 383 at 397 (HL).

22 Ibid.

23 See *IPH v Chief Constable of South Wales* [1987] Crim LR 42.

24 *C (A Minor) v DPP* [1996] 1 AC 1 at 35, [1995] 2 WLR 383 at 398 (HL) (Lord Lowry).

25 *Adams* § CA22.06

evidence that is "very clear and complete",[26] so that there is no danger of merely naughty children being convicted of crimes.

Despite the existence of quite sophisticated law on the matter, for the purposes of criminal law, because of the operation of the Children, Young Persons, and Their Families Act 1989, the defence of infancy based upon a child's lack of knowledge that the act or omission was wrong is seldom likely to be advanced. It will only ever be relevant in a case where the offence charged is murder or manslaughter. For practical purposes, the presumption of incapacity by infants has such a narrow scope of operation in New Zealand that its utility as a general defence must be doubted. The increasingly common criticisms that the rule "reflects an outworn mode of thought", "is stepped in absurdity", is "unreal" and "contrary to common sense" may foreshadow its future demise.[27]

---

26 *R v Gorrie* (1918) 83 JP 136.

27 See, for example, Law Commission No 143 (UK), *Criminal Law, Codification of the Criminal Law: a Report to the Law Commission*, London, HMSO, 1985, § 11.22, 11.23.

8

Insanity

8.1 INTRODUCTION

The defence of insanity is concerned with an individual's mental capacity for crime. Although it is commonly conceptualised as a "defence", in earlier textbooks on criminal law it was common to treat insanity as an instance of legal abnormality, a status shared at common law by the Sovereign, children, corporations, and clerks in holy orders.[1] On this basis, criminal responsibility was denied because the offender was said to lack the legal *capacity* to be held responsible for a crime, rather than because the prosecution had failed to prove an essential element in the definition of the offence. For practical purposes, the distinction may have little significance, because it will often be the case that an "insane" offender, on account of the relevant mental disorder, did not possess whatever mens rea is required to establish the charge. We will, therefore, adopt the common convention of referring to insanity as a defence. Nonetheless, it is important to acknowledge that in some instances of insanity the *mens* may not be *rea* not because the accused did not know or intend what he was doing, but rather because the mental illness has removed part of the very foundation for criminal responsibility, ie rationality, which distinguishes between an *actus* and a mere event or happening.

Although in the courtroom we continue to use the word "insanity", it is important to realise that it is not a medically recognised concept, and does not fit within any diagnostic standard. It is a legal term of art, and is used exclusively to describe the state of mind which, in a criminal prosecution, will produce a verdict of not guilty by reason of mental disorder.

8.1.1 Under disability

Mental disorder or disability other than at the time of committing the offence may also be relevant during the trial process. Before briefly considering these situations, some comment about language is appropriate. In New Zealand, the term "insanity" refers exclusively to the insanity defence. In the past, "insanity" also included the mental state of a person who had been found by a court to be unfit to plead or unfit to be tried, which in New Zealand is referred to as being "under disability".[2] To be under disability, a person must necessarily be "mentally disordered" as defined in the Mental Health (Compulsory Assessment and Treatment) Act 1992. However, it by no means follows that because an offender is found to be under disability that he must also be legally insane. Indeed, it is possible and may often be the case that an offender is mentally disordered and under disability at the time of trial but legally sane at the time of the commission of the crime. Conversely, a person may be proven to have been insane when the offence was committed yet not be under disability at the time of the trial. It is, therefore, essential to separate

---

1   See, for example Turner (ed), *Kenny's Outlines of Criminal Law* (19th ed), Cambridge, Cambridge University Press, 1966, 74ff.

2   See ss 108-111 Criminal Justice Act 1985. For a full discussion of the origins and current status of the law governing "under disability" in New Zealand see Brookbanks, "A Contemporary Analysis of the Doctrine of Fitness to Plead" [1982] NZ Recent Law 84; Brookbanks, "Judicial Determination of Fitness to Plead — The Fitness Hearing" [1992] 7 Otago LR 520; Brookbanks, "Fitness to Plead and the Intellectually Disabled Offender" [1994] Psychiatry, Psychology and Law 171. See also commentary on "Special Patients" in *Trapski's Family Law* Vol III, Wellington, Brooker's, 1995. See also, Legal Research Foundation, *Fitness to Plead: Under Disability in the 90's*, Legal Research Foundation, Auckland, 1995.

carefully the particular context and purpose for which mental state is being assessed, appreciating that mental abnormality is not a unitary concept in criminal law and that it is capable of broad and diverse applications.[3]

Under s 108 Criminal Justice Act 1985, a person may be found "under disability" where, because of the extent to which she is mentally disordered, that person is unable to plead, to understand the nature or purpose of the proceedings, or to communicate adequately with counsel for the purposes of conducting a defence. The evidence of two medical practitioners is required.[4] If satisfied that the person is under disability, the court is required to make an order that she be detained either as a special patient or as a patient under the provisions of the Mental Health (Compulsory Assessment and Treatment) Act 1992 as a patient where it is in the interests of the public to do so.[5] Where the interests of public safety are satisfied, the court has a discretion to order a person's "immediate release".[6]

In New Zealand the question whether D is under disability is always determined by a judge alone (by contrast with the UK, where the issue of an accused's fitness to plead is always determined by a jury[7]). However, there is still some debate whether in New Zealand a jury may be empanelled to determine the preliminary issue of muteness, where a person "wilfully refuses to plead". The better view seems to be that in order to achieve conformity of practice between the High Court and the District Court the jurisdiction to determine muteness should lie, as it does in determining fitness to plead, with a judge alone and that the procedure should be identical to that prescribed for determining whether an offender is under disability.[8]

8.1.2 Mental disorder at sentencing

The question of the mental state of an accused person may also be relevant at the sentencing stage, following conviction. Sometimes the issue of mental illness or disorder, not evident during the trial or in the remand period, may flare up after the offender has been convicted, perhaps as a traumatic reaction to the fear of imprisonment or to the experience of custodial detention while awaiting sentence. There are two main ways in which the legal process may be affected by the intervention of mental illness or disorder at this stage. First, where an accused has pleaded guilty to an imprisonable offence but appears to be under disability either at the time the sentence is imposed or when the sentence is about to commence, the sentence should be deferred and the

---

3 The phrase "mental abnormality" does not appear in New Zealand law but may be used to describe the broad range of aberrant mental states encompassed by the legal concepts of insanity, disability, and mental disorder.
4 See s 111 Criminal Justice Act 1985.
5 Section 115(1)(a) and (2)(a) Criminal Justice Act 1985.
6 Section 115(2)(b) Criminal Justice Act 1985.
7 Section 4(5) Criminal Procedure (Insanity) Act 1964 (UK).
8 See discussion in *Adams* §§ CA356.08, 09.

accused's ability to be sentenced determined in the normal way.[9] Although the question whether the accused is under disability normally arises before or during the course of the trial or hearing,[10] the common law continues to apply to the effect that the question of fitness to plead may be raised at any stage of the proceedings, including verdict and sentencing. In *R v Skokolic*[11] the Supreme Court noted that the practice of deferring sentence where, after conviction, a criminal becomes "insane" was designed to protect a prisoner who had become incapable of advancing "some plea which if sane he could urge in stay of execution".

The second way in which the sentencing process may be affected by the intervention of mental disorder is where, having convicted the accused, the court is concerned that the offender's mental state is such that treatment for mental disorder is *required*, in the person's own interest or for the purpose of protecting the public. In these circumstances s 118 Criminal Justice Act 1985 empowers a judge, as a "benevolent alternative to a custodial sentence in a penal institution",[12] to make an order that the offender be detained in a hospital as a patient.[13] An order under s 118 is only one of the alternatives for consideration by the judge in determining what if any sentence to impose on an offender, and "Its function in the statutory scheme is to provide a more suitable individualised sentence operating in the interests of the offender and in the wider public interest than would otherwise be available".[14]

In *R v Elliot* the Court of Appeal held that s 118 should not be used to detain a minor offender as a committed patient,[15] and should not be invoked without regard to the gravity of the offending because of the need to maintain a reasonable proportionality between the offending and the "severe curtailment of liberty inherent in an order for detention as a committed patient".[16] We will consider the appropriateness of detaining mentally disturbed offenders in hospitals later in the chapter, when we examine the issue of disposition.

---

9   That is, by a judicial hearing to determine whether she is under disability in terms of Part VII Criminal Justice Act 1985.

10   Section 109 Criminal Justice Act 1985 specifies, inter alia, that a court may make a finding of disability "after the defendant has been committed for trial, whether or not the defendant has pleaded to the indictment".

11   [1929] NZLR 521 at 523 (Blair J). See also *R v Berry* (1876) 1 QBD 447 at 449, where the Court held that the accused could not be *convicted* because he was incapable of understanding the proceedings.

12   *R v Elliot* [1981] 1 NZLR 295 at 302 (CA).

13   Section 118 Criminal Justice Act 1985.

14   *R v Elliot* [1981] 1 NZLR 295 at 302 (CA). For a more thorough discussion of the law and practice in relation to hospital orders in New Zealand see Brookbanks, "The Sentencing and Disposition of Mentally Disordered Offenders" in Brookbanks (ed), *Psychiatry and the Law: Clinical and Legal Issues*, Wellington, Brooker's, 1996, 308ff. See also the useful discussion of s 118 in Hall, *Sentencing Guide*, Wellington, Butterworths, 1994, D/1076-D/1081.

15   *R v Elliot* [1981] 1 NZLR 295 at 302.

16   Ibid.

8.1.3 Mental disorder during incarceration

Frequently, sentenced offenders, or those in custody on remand pending either trial or the hearing of charges, become mentally unwell while in a penal institution. Mental illness or disorder in such circumstances may be the product of stress caused by the isolation and harshness of the prison environment or anxiety at the outcome of legal proceedings. Where the superintendent of a prison has reasonable grounds to believe that an inmate may be mentally disordered she may apply for the person to be assessed under the provisions of the Mental Health (Compulsory Assessment and Treatment) Act 1992.[17] In the event that the assessment confirms the superintendent's belief that the inmate is mentally disordered, she may be formally transferred to a hospital to be detained for as long as is necessary to treat the illness. If the patient responds to treatment and recovers her mental health she may be returned to the institution in which she was previously detained to undergo the remainder of the sentence.[18] Offenders dealt with in this manner are designated "special patients"[19] because, unlike offenders committed under s 118 Criminal Justice Act 1985, their mental health status does not represent a final disposition of the matter and will change upon return to the penal institution or upon reclassification if the sentence expires while the patient is still detained in hospital.[20]

8.2 THE ORIGINS OF THE INSANITY DEFENCE

The foundations of the insanity defence can be traced back at least to the thirteenth century. Prior to this, in the period of pre-Norman English law, there was no insanity defence as such because contemporary practice required the family of an insane person who committed a serious offence to pay compensation to the family of the victim, without presenting the offender for trial.[21] Early formulations of a test for legal insanity, such as Bracton's idea that an insane person was "one who does not know what he is doing, who is lacking in mind and reason, and who is not far removed *from the brutes*",[22] tended to draw descriptive analogies with the mental capacities of children and

---

17 Section 45(3) Mental Health (Compulsory Assessment and Treatment) Act 1992.
18 Section 47(1) Mental Health (Compulsory Assessment and Treatment) Act 1992.
19 "Special patient" is defined in s 2 Mental Health (Compulsory Assessment and Treatment) Act 1992. Essentially, the classification encompasses offenders found under disability, those acquitted on account of insanity, those remanded for psychiatric assessment, and those detained in a hospital under ss 45 and 46 of that Act. For a comprehensive account of special patient status see *Trapski's Family Law* Vol III, Wellington, Brooker's, 1995, para MH2.25.01-2.25.33.
20 Section 48(3) Mental Health (Compulsory Assessment and Treatment) Act 1992.
21 Walker, *Crime and Insanity in England*, Edinburgh, Edinburgh University Press, 1968, 26; discussed in McAuley, *Insanity, Psychiatry and Criminal Responsibility*, Dublin, Roundhall Press, 1993, 18 fn 1.
22 Henri de Bracton, *On the Laws and Customs of England*.

animals.[23] While these descriptions were intended as metaphors for a radical want of reason and not as prosaic descriptions of a subhuman species,[24] their effect was to limit the availability of exculpatory insanity to evidence of unrestrained irrationality, so that as late as 1723, in *R v Arnold*, the jury was properly directed that to be found insane, "it must be a man that is *totally deprived* of his understanding and memory and doth not know what he is doing, no more than an infant, than a brute, or a wild beast".[25] It is safe to assume that only very serious mental disorder would have been recognised as giving exemption from serious crime, particularly homicide.[26]

8.2.1 The insanity defence during the eighteenth and nineteenth centuries

A succession of cases during the eighteenth and early nineteenth centuries appeared to harden the notion that only those who were completely bereft of reason were entitled to the defence of insanity.[27] However, towards the end of the eighteenth century there was a growing acceptance amongst commentators that if the purpose of punishment is the prevention of offences, the punishment of a person mentally ill at the time of the crime simply fails to achieve its object. Accordingly, by 1800, when James Hadfield was tried for the attempted murder of George III, there had been a softening of the rigid test applied in *Arnold*, such that the jury was now able to acquit upon being satisfied that the defendant suffered from a delusion which prompted his act.[28] On this basis, Hadfield was acquitted after firing a pistol at George III as he entered his box in the Drury Lane Theatre.[29]

However, the acquittal of Hadfield immediately highlighted an important lacuna in the legislation, in that there existed no statutory means of securing Hadfield's safe keeping following the finding of insanity. Accordingly, in 1800 the English Legislature passed the Criminal Lunatics Act, described in its Long Title as "an Act for the Safe Keeping of Insane Persons Charged with Offences". The statute was passed in great haste and made retrospective. It provided that if any person charged with treason, murder, or felony was found to be insane at the time of committing the offence and acquitted, "the Court shall . . . order

---

23 See also Hale, who suggested that the insane are not criminally responsible "for they have not the use of understanding, and act not as reasonable creatures, but their actions are in *effect in the condition of brutes*": 1 Hale PC 31 (emphasis added).

24 McAuley, *Insanity, Psychiatry and Criminal Responsibility*, Dublin, Roundhall Press, 1993, 19.

25 (1724) 16 St Tr 695 at 765 (emphasis added).

26 Prins, *Offenders, Deviants or Patients?* (2nd ed), London, 1995, 13.

27 See *R v Ferrers* (1760) 19 St Tr 885; *R v Hadfield* (1800) 27 St Tr 1281; *R v Bellingham* Coll Lun 636; *R v Oxford* (1840) 4 St Tr (NS) 498.

28 McAuley, *Insanity, Psychiatry and Criminal Responsibility*, Dublin, Roundhall Press, 1993, 21.

29 It has been suggested that an important factor in securing Hadfield's acquittal may have been public sympathy engendered by the long-standing intermittent mental illness of King George III. See Prins, *Offenders, Deviants or Patients?* (2nd ed), London, 1995, 13.

such Persons to be kept in strict custody, in such place and in such Manner as to the Court shall seem fit, until His Majesty's Pleasure shall be known".

Hadfield's case is noteworthy in that it provided for the first time for a special verdict "Not guilty, he being under the influence of Insanity at the time the act was committed" and created a new category of offenders, to be known as "criminal lunatics".[30]

8.2.2 M'Naghten Rules

The most significant development in the insanity defence came in 1843 with the decision of the House of Lords in M'Naghten's Case.[31] M'Naghten, a former woodcarver who suffered from paranoid delusions, was charged with murder when he shot and killed Edward Drummond, having mistaken him for the then Prime Minister of England, Sir Robert Peel. M'Naghten believed, amongst other things, that the Tories were conspiring to kill him. Although he was acquitted at his trial on the grounds of insanity, the furore created by his acquittal led the House of Lords to demand of the fifteen common law judges a statement of the law governing such cases. The judges, summoned under considerable pressure, were required to answer, in the abstract, five questions on the subject of insanity as a defence to criminal charges. In answering on behalf of the other judges, Lord Chief Justice Tyndal laid out two rules which have become the basis of the legal test for insanity in many western jurisdictions. The Rules are as follows:

(1) The jurors ought to be told in all cases that . . . to establish a defence on the ground of insanity, it must be clearly proved that, at the time of committing the act, the party accused was labouring under such a defect of reason, from disease of the mind, as not to know the nature and quality of the act he was doing, or if he did know, that he did not know he was doing what was wrong.

(2) Where one labours under partial delusions only and is not in other respects insane, and commits an offence due to that fact, he must be considered in the same situation as to responsibility as if the facts with respect to which the delusion exists were real.[32]

This statement of the law has been followed in most common law jurisdictions and has remained substantially unchallenged as the test for legal insanity for over 150 years. The M'Naghten Rules emphasise the importance of the patient's notions of right and wrong, the causal relationship between the content of delusions and the crime, and the status of the offence if the content of the delusions is true. Interestingly, it has been observed that the "rules" were more stringent in their formulation than the guides given in the earlier cases, such that if the "right from wrong" test had been applied at the time of M'Naghten's trial, he could *not* have been found not guilty on the grounds of

---

30 See Forshaw and Rollin, "The History of Forensic Psychiatry in England" in Bluglass and Bowden (eds), *Principles and Practice of Forensic Psychiatry*, Edinburgh, Churchill Livingstone, 1990, 84.

31 (1843) 10 Cl & Finn 200, 8 ER 718, [1843–60] All ER Rep 229 (HL).

32 Ibid.

insanity.[33] Yet *M'Naghten* demonstrates, and subsequent cases have also shown, that a person may know precisely what she is doing and even be aware that she is committing a criminal act, yet be excused because her firmly-held delusions have compelled her to act as she did. The strength of delusions may be such as to force the conclusion that the offender did not know the *moral quality* of the act she is charged with committing. Delusions which appear to be limited to an isolated topic, (as with M'Naghten) may in reality be symptoms of a more general condition and indicate a diseased condition of the brain which is said to affect the *volition* of the person exhibiting them.[34]

Another point to note is that the Rules do not address the issues of lack of control, irresistible drives, or impulses.[35] The mere claim that the impulse to kill or seriously injure someone was *irresistible* or *uncontrollable* will not excuse in the absence of evidence that the accused was suffering from a mental disease at the time of the crime.[36] We will examine the claims of irresistible impulse in more detail later in the chapter.

8.3 THE ELEMENTS OF INSANITY IN NEW ZEALAND

The essential elements of the M'Naghten Rules were first incorporated into New Zealand's criminal law in the Criminal Code Act 1893. The Criminal Code Act was itself based upon the Draft Code of the English Criminal Code Bill Commission, published in 1879, and indeed s 23 of the 1893 Act enacted in almost identical terms the text of s 22 of the Draft Code, although the arrangement of the text differed in some respects. Because of the close linguistic relationship which exists between the two provisions, it may be instructive to consider the comments made in relation to s 22 by the drafters of the Draft Code,[37] bearing in mind also that New Zealand's insanity defence has been relatively unaffected by subsequent revisions of our criminal legislation.

Acknowledging that s 22 expresses the existing law, the Commissioners conceded, perhaps somewhat despairingly, that:

> The obscurity which hangs over the subject cannot be altogether dispelled until our existing ignorance as to the nature of the will and the mind, the nature of the organs by which they operate, the manner and degree in which those operations are interfered with by disease, and the nature of the diseases which interfere with them, are greatly diminished. The framing of the definition has caused us much labour and anxiety; and although we cannot deem the definition to be altogether

---

33   Forshaw and Rollin, "The History of Forensic Psychiatry in England" in Bluglass and Bowden (eds), *Principles and Practice of Forensic Psychiatry*, Edinburgh, Churchill Livingstone, 1990, 84.

34   See, for example, *R v Monkhouse* [1923] GLR 13 (Chapman J).

35   Forshaw and Rollin, "The History of Forensic Psychiatry in England" in Bluglass and Bowden (eds), *Principles and Practice of Forensic Psychiatry*, Edinburgh, Churchill Livingstone, 1990, 84 at 88.

36   *R v Deighton* (1900) 18 NZLR 891.

37   See Criminal Code Bill Commission, *Report of the Royal Commission Appointed to Consider The Law Relating to Indictable Offences: With an Appendix Containing a Draft Code Embodying the Suggestions of the Commissioners*, London, Eyre & Spottiswode for HMSO, 1879, C-345.

satisfactory, we consider it as satisfactory as the nature of the subject admits of. Much latitude must in any case be left to the tribunal which has to apply the law to the facts in each particular case.[38]

Three points in particular deserve comment. First, the alleged "obscurity" which hangs over the subject of exculpatory insanity still remains. One reason for this is that, despite the developments in medical science over the last 150 years our knowledge of the nature and causes of mental illness is still limited and subject to ongoing change. But perhaps even more importantly, there seems to be little interest in handing over the judicial task of determining the legal status of mental illness or disease exclusively to medical experts.[39] While judges continue to be invested with the responsibility of determining the legal content of insanity, the "obscurity" will continue, simply because a judge's function is not to declare the *clinical parameters* of a particular disease process but rather to state whether a mental disease fits within the legal criteria for insanity laid down by Parliament. Ultimately, medical evidence on such matters provides useful guidance for a judge but is never determinative of the issues to be decided by the court.

Secondly, it is probably impossible to formulate a perfect legal test of insanity. There have been many attempts over the years to recast the law's insanity criteria to reflect modern psychiatric developments and understanding. Few of the formulations that have departed radically from the M'Naghten Rules have survived, and most modern western versions of the insanity defence are modelled on the Rules in one form or another. They are for the most part thoroughly cognitive in emphasis and, arguably, fail to give adequate consideration to disorders of the will or the emotions. Indeed, the main focus of modern debate tends to be not on whether the M'Naghten Rules should be replaced, but rather whether they ought to be supplemented by statutory rules which are better able to reflect differing levels of criminal culpability of those affected by mental illness falling short of legal insanity.

Thirdly, because the M'Naghten Rules are very narrowly formulated, it is not uncommon for judges to interpret them liberally in order to accommodate difficult but deserving cases. This being the case, it might be argued that any attempt to redefine insanity according to a detailed prescriptive formula may inhibit the ability of trial judges to apply the law generously in order to ensure that severely mentally disordered offenders are not unfairly treated by the courts.

To the extent that these observations are accurate it could be said that the comments of the Commissioners reflect even present realities, and remind us of the thoroughly elusive nature of legal insanity. The following discussion will demonstrate that insanity is a remarkably fluid concept.

New Zealand's current version of the Rules is set out in s 23 Crimes Act 1961. In Australia the common law states of New South Wales, Victoria, and South Australia still follow the M'Naghten Rules, although statutory

---

38 Ibid at 17.

39 For a directly opposing view see Nygaard, "On Responsibility: or the Insanity of Mental Defences and Punishment" (1996) 41 Villanova LR 951 at 952.

provisions in these jurisdictions also deal with ancillary matters. Under the Criminal Codes of Queensland, Western Australia, the Northern Territory, and Tasmania provision is also made for a volitional criterion, based on the capacity of the accused to control his actions; which is, as noted above, not part of the common law criteria for insanity. Section 23 states:

Insanity—(1) Every one shall be presumed to be sane at the time of doing or omitting any act until the contrary is proved.

(2) No person shall be convicted of an offence by reason of an act done or omitted by him when labouring under natural imbecility or disease of the mind to such an extent as to render him incapable—

(a) Of understanding the nature and quality of the act or omission; or

(b) Of knowing that the act or omission was morally wrong, having regard to the commonly accepted standards of right and wrong.

(3) Insanity before or after the time when he did or omitted the act, and insane delusions, though only partial, may be evidence that the offender was, at the time when he did or omitted the act, in such a condition of mind as to render him irresponsible for the act or omission.

(4) The fact that by virtue of this section any person has not been or is not liable to be convicted of an offence shall not affect the question whether any other person who is alleged to be a party to that offence is guilty of that offence.

The principal difference between the M'Naghten Rules and s 23 is that the New Zealand Parliament has defined insanity in terms of the accused's *capacity* to understand the nature and quality of an act or omission, or to know that it was morally wrong; whereas the M'Naghten Rules were concerned with the accused's actual knowledge of those matters. In addition, the Criminal Code Act 1893 added "natural imbecility" as one of the factors which might bring an accused within the scope of the insanity defence.

The M'Naghten Rules and earlier New Zealand legislation contained a provision that persons suffering "specific delusions", but otherwise sane, were not to be acquitted on the ground of insanity unless the delusions would, if true, have justified or excused the act.[40] However, as was recognised in *R v Monkhouse*,[41] where the accused was charged with the attempted murder of a farm manager after he had been heard to mutter "Him and I for it. If I don't kill him he'll kill me", that delusions which appear to be limited to an isolated topic may really be symptoms of a more general condition and possibly indicative of deep-seated insanity. In that case, the evidence of delusions was accepted as being evidence of insanity and the accused was acquitted on the ground of insanity. The provision concerning delusions was not re-enacted in the present New Zealand provision, in part because s 23(2) probably covers such cases, and also because its insistence on legal justification or excuse might conflict with the introduction of "moral" wrongness in s 23(2)(b).[42]

---

40   See s 22 Draft Code 1879; s 23(3) Criminal Code Act 1893; s 43(2) Crimes Act 1908.

41   [1923] GLR 13.

42   Adams (2nd ed) § 414. We consider delusions further at § 8.3.6.

8.3.1 The presumption of sanity and burden of proof

Section 23 commences with a presumption that "every one" is sane at the time of doing or admitting any act "until the contrary is proved".[43] This is where any inquiry concerning insanity must begin.[44] Every person is deemed to be sane until he is proved to be insane. This requires that the *accused* must show (has the burden of proving) that he was insane when he committed the relevant act. Apart from statutory exceptions and case law developments in relation to public welfare regulatory offences, insanity is the only qualification to the general rule that it is the duty of the prosecution to prove an accused's guilt.[45] What this means in practice is that it not enough, as would be the case with other "defences", for the accused simply to point to evidence that raises the issue of insanity for consideration by the court. Rather, the accused has the legal burden (the burden of persuasion) to persuade the court of the fact in issue, namely, that he was insane at the time of committing the crime. It is insufficient for the accused to discharge an ordinary evidentiary burden. He must persuade the court of his insanity, on the balance of probabilities, which will normally mean adducing medical testimony regarding his state of mind at the time. A mere assertion that he was insane, without more, will not be sufficient to discharge the duty. However, the onus on the accused to prove insanity is not as heavy as that which remains on the prosecution to establish other elements of the offence charged. The accused is not required to prove insanity beyond reasonable doubt, but only need prove it to the satisfaction of the jury on the balance of probabilities, the standard of proof required of a plaintiff in a civil action.[46] Thus the accused must be acquitted if the jury think it more likely than not that he was insane at the relevant time.

It has been held in South Africa that even where sufficient evidence has been led to show that there was a *reasonable chance* that the accused may have suffered from a mental disease which prevented him from knowing what he was doing, the accused must nevertheless prove the alleged mental disease on the balance of probabilities. There can no obligation, in such a case, for the prosecution to prove that the mental disease did not have the effect claimed.[47] New Zealand courts have also held, in relation to proof of disease of the mind, that it is not enough for the accused to provide evidence that merely indicated such a disease. It is necessary to prove the *probable presence* of a disease of the mind.[48] In *Proctor v Police*[49] evidence that the accused had probably inhaled quantities of paint vapour prior to consuming liquor was insufficient to show

---

43   Section 23(1) Crimes Act 1961.

44   See *R v Deighton* (1900) 18 NZLR 891 at 892.

45   *Woolmington v DPP* [1935] AC 462, [1935] All ER Rep 1 (HL). See § 4.1

46   *R v Cottle* [1958] NZLR 999 at 1014, 1022 (CA) (Gresson P); *Sodeman v R* (1936) 55 CLR 192.

47   *S v Kennedy* (1951) 4 SA 431 (A).

48   *R v Roulston* [1976] 2 NZLR 644 (CA); *Proctor v Police* 5/4/84, Vautier J, HC Auckland M1333/83, (1981-87) 1 Consol Case Annotations, 1st Series, C-233.

49   5/4/84, Vaultier J, HC Auckland M1333/83, (1981-87) 1 Consol Case Annotations, 1st Series, C-233.

the probable presence of disease of the mind even though the evidence was led by witnesses who included both members of the police and psychiatrists.

Similarly, in New Zealand the courts have rejected the proposition that the accused need only lay some foundation for the defence of insanity and when that is done the general burden of proving the charge would require the Crown to prove it beyond reasonable doubt. In *R v Roulston*,[50] the Court of Appeal approved the view that while the *ultimate* burden rests on the Crown to prove every element essential in the crime, in order to prove that the act was voluntary, the Crown may rely on the presumption of sanity and if the defence wishes to displace the presumption they must give some evidence from which the contrary may reasonably be inferred.

Sometimes the fact that the burden of proving insanity is on the accused may create difficulties, particularly where joint defences of insanity and involuntariness are raised. This will include situations where there is an evidential foundation for both insanity and sane automatism to be considered. Involuntariness (sane automatism) places only an evidentiary burden on the accused, and the defence must be negatived by the prosecution beyond a reasonable doubt, whereas insanity must be affirmatively proved by the accused. One approach to this difficulty suggested by the High Court of Australia is that the accused should receive an unqualified acquittal if the evidence leaves the jury in a reasonable doubt on the issue of sane automatism. The issue of whether insanity has been proved should be considered only if the prosecution excludes such reasonable doubt.[51]

The requirement that a defendant must affirmatively prove insanity derives, as has been observed, from the common law presumption that an accused is legally sane until the contrary is proved. In Canada a similar statutory presumption in s 16(4) Criminal Code has been criticised as being a historical anomaly, unfair to the accused, unnecessary as a matter of policy, and an irrational exception to the ordinary onus of proof. Nonetheless, in that jurisdiction the Supreme Court has recently held, in a majority decision, that although the reverse onus in insanity violates the presumption of innocence in s 11(d) Charter of Rights and Freedoms, it is nevertheless a "reasonable limitation" under s 1 of the Charter.[52]

The argument that the burden on the accused to prove insanity is both anomalous and without justification has some powerful supporters, and indeed the English Criminal Law Revision Committee in its Eleventh Report (1972) and Fourteenth Report (1980) has recommended that the burden of proof be changed so that the accused need only raise a reasonable doubt to support the insanity verdict. However, despite these objections to the reverse onus, the predominant direction of legal reform seems to be towards retention of the traditional burden of proof rules for insanity. In the US, as a result of reforms

---

50 [1976] 2 NZLR 644 at 648 (CA). See also *Bratty v A-G for Northern Ireland* [1963] AC 386, [1961] 3 All ER 523 (HL); *R v Cottle* [1958] NZLR 999 at 1029 (CA); *R v Burr* [1969] NZLR 736 at 743 (CA).

51 See *R v Falconer* (1990) 171 CLR 30 at 63, 65 ALJR 20 at 34 (HCA).

52 *Chaulk v R* (1991) 62 CCC (3d) 193, [1990] 3 SCR 1303 (SCC).

made since the Hinckley trial, approximately two-thirds of the States which accept the insanity plea place the burden of proof on the defendant, usually by a preponderance of the evidence.[53]

Although the common law burden of proof requirements for insanity have been criticised for having the effect of making exculpation more difficult for the insane than the sane defendant, ultimately where the burden of proof lies will depend on policy considerations prevailing in particular jurisdictions, and public perceptions of how readily defendants are able to avoid conviction through "unconvincing" insanity defence pleas. In New Zealand, there has been no pressure upon the Legislature to abolish the presumption of sanity, presumably because the insanity defence is numerically insignificant in this country and has not given rise to the perceived social and legal injustices which have accompanied recent American show trials involving the insanity defence.

8.3.2 Natural imbecility

Proof of either natural imbecility or disease of the mind is the necessary foundation of any insanity defence in New Zealand. The expression "natural imbecility" (which may be translated as "subnormality" or "mental retardation") clearly includes a congenital defect, as well as a disorder which develops later in life. In Australia the expression has been equated with "Arrested or retarded development of mind".[54] In practice, the defence of insanity is seldom based on the presence of natural imbecility, because most potential offenders who would be identified as intellectually disabled would normally be within some form of protective custody and would have limited opportunities to become involved in serious crime. Like the phrase "disease of the mind", "natural imbecility" is a legal concept and it is therefore a question of law for the trial judge whether particular mental conditions are included within the term.[55] The concept is wider than disease or "injury" in that it does not necessitate permanence, though it does connote durability.[56] The condition of autism, for example, which is a chronic, lifelong disorder characterised by impaired social interactions and impaired ability to communicate, could fall within the definition of "natural imbecility" for the purposes of the insanity defence, even though it is not uniformly associated with mental retardation.[57]

In Canada, recent legislative changes have meant that the term "insane" has been replaced with the term "not criminally responsible". In addition, the phrase "state of natural imbecility or has disease of the mind" has been replaced with the term "mental disorder", which in turn is defined as meaning

---

53 See Mackay, "Post-Hinckley Insanity in the USA" [1988] Crim LR 88 at 93.

54 *R v Rolph* [1962] Qd R 262 at 271.

55 See *Bratty v A-G for Northern Ireland* [1963] AC 387 at 412, [1961] 3 All ER 523 at 534 (HL) (Lord Denning).

56 Campbell, *Mental Disorder and Criminal Law in Australia and New Zealand*, Wellington, Butterworths, 1988, 126.

57 Andreasen and Black, *Introductory Textbook of Psychiatry*, Washington, 1991, 439: up to 70 percent of autistic patients show some evidence of mental retardation, although others have normal intelligence and may demonstrate very specific talents or abilities.

"disease of the mind".[58] Prior to these modifications, "natural imbecility" had been held to involve an "imperfect condition of mental power from congenital defect or natural decay as distinguished from a mind once normal which has become diseased".[59] This unfortunate circularity left the status of "natural imbecility" somewhat uncertain in that jurisdiction, although it is thought that with the re-adoption of the phrase "disease of the mind" in the definition of "mental disorder", much of the case law decided under the predecessor legislation is applicable to the new provision[60]. While it is not clear that the Canadian case law on "natural imbecility" will necessarily carry over to the new provision, it would seem to follow that a mentally retarded person should be granted protection within the defence of "mental disorder" if her mind is affected to such a degree that she cannot appreciate the nature and quality of her act or know the act is wrong. As most psychiatrists distinguish subnormality from other forms of mental disorder, any legal standard ought also to reflect that distinction.

8.3.3 Disease of the mind

Under existing law, medical witnesses are permitted to give an opinion whether a disorder may be regarded as a "disease of the mind". They may also testify to the causes and symptoms of the condition diagnosed. Since "disease of the mind" (or natural imbecility) is an irreducible, though not a sufficient, requirement for legal insanity, such testimony will always be crucial in an insanity trial. However, as has been noted already, disease of the mind is a legal not a medical concept and it is therefore a question of law what mental abnormalities are included within the term. While it is for the jury, not medical experts, to decide whether the particular mental disease the accused suffered from rendered her incapable of knowing the nature and quality of her actions or of knowing that they were morally wrong, the jury's verdict must be founded on evidence. Medical evidence supported by other relevant evidence cannot arbitrarily be put aside.[61]

In New Zealand, disease of the mind is said to be "a term which defies precise definition and which can comprehend mental derangement in the widest sense".[62] Our courts have never attempted to define it precisely or comprehensively. When considering the meaning of "disease of the mind" it is important to understand that the criminal law is not concerned with the *origin* of the disease so much as with its *effects*.[63] This means that it is unimportant whether the relevant incapacity is due to degeneration of the brain, or to some other form of mental derangement, or to a physical disorder, such as arteriosclerosis or brain tumour, provided it has the effect of impairing the

---

58   See Criminal Code (Canada) R.S.C 1985, Chap C-46, s 2.

59   *R v Cooper* (1978) 40 CCC (2d) 145 at 159.

60   Greenspan (ed), *Martin's Annual Criminal Code 1997*, Aurora, Ontario, Canada Law Book Co, 1996, cc/48.

61   *R v Rotana* (1995) 12 CRNZ 650 (CA). See further below, § 8.3.9.

62   *R v Cottle* [1958] NZLR 999 at 1011 (CA) (Gresson P).

63   *Halsbury's Laws of England*, vol 11(1) , (4th ed reissue), § 31.

reasoning process. It follows that the law will normally only accommodate those disorders which affect the mind, that is to say the faculties of reasoning, memory, and understanding; it is unconcerned with disorders which simply produce disturbed *behaviour*.

However, from the perspective of medical professionals who may be called upon to give evidence in an "insanity" trial, this approach may be problematic. Psychiatrists distinguish between *psychoneurosis* and *psychosis*, conditions which cause subjective distress in patients, and are professionally committed to treating both. However, neurotic disorders, including such conditions as anxiety states, obsessional states, hysteria, and various mood (affective) disorders are normally excluded from the category "disease of the mind". Most psychoses, on the other hand, satisfy the criteria for legal insanity.[64] Because a psychiatrist operates from a professional desire to assist in the alleviation of subjective mental distress, she may have difficulty in accepting the law's insistence that only mental states which affect the accused's rationality are fit candidates for inclusion within this archaic legal category. She may legitimately reason that any aberrant mental state that produces distress and affects individual behaviour should be considered in evaluating an offender's criminal responsibility, and may seek to introduce evidence to this effect. However, to do so would be to misconceive the purpose of the insanity defence, which is designed not for the therapeutic benefit of the offender, but as a measure and symbol of criminal responsibility and as a means of protecting the public against the recurrence of dangerous conduct.[65] The role of the psychiatrist in giving evidence of insanity has been well expressed in the following passage from Gunn and Taylor:

> The psychiatrist should resist, within the bounds of propriety, the temptation to give a medical view on the question of the level of responsibility. Instead, he should set out the medical evidence, give an account of the relationship of the killing (if admitted) to those medical facts (especially the mental state) and indicate how far, in his opinion, the medical features and/or diagnosis influenced the aggressive and other relevant behaviour. The reply to direct questioning about the diminution of responsibility should reiterate the nature of any mental disorder discovered and then the point should be made that only a layman's view about the ultimate question can be given.[66]

The danger is that if the psychiatrist attempts to translate medical terms into legal terms, he may subvert the role of the jury by answering questions that are for their sole consideration.[67]

However, we are still left with the question of what constitutes a "disease of the mind". We may accept that the term embraces any illness, disorder, or abnormal condition which actually impairs the human mind and its functioning, although this must be taken to exclude self-induced intoxication caused by alcohol or drugs, as well as transitory states such as hysteria or

---

64 Allen, *Textbook on Criminal Law*, London, 1991, 106.

65 See *R v Sullivan* [1984] AC 156 at 172, [1983] 2 All ER 673 at 677, 678 (HL) (Lord Diplock).

66 Gunn and Taylor, *Forensic Psychiatry: Clinical, Legal and Ethical Issues*, Oxford, 1993, 54.

67 Allen, *Textbook on Criminal Law*, London, 1991, 106.

concussion.[68] Concussion might, however, qualify as a disease of the mind if it was associated with an enduring brain injury which caused the offender to act irrationally at the relevant time. Similarly, in *R v Kemp*,[69] where the accused, in an entirely motiveless attack, struck his wife with a hammer severely injuring her, it was held that arteriosclerosis, from which he suffered and which caused a restriction of the flow of blood to his brain producing a temporary loss of consciousness, was a disease of the mind for the purpose of the insanity defence. In that case Lord Devlin made the following important observation:

> The law is not concerned with the brain but with the mind, in the sense that "mind" is ordinarily used, the mental faculties of reason, memory and understanding. If one read for "disease of the mind" "disease of the brain", it would follow that in many cases pleas of insanity would not be established because it could not be proved that the brain had been affected in any way, either by degeneration of the cells or in any other way.[70]

This recognises the fact that while psychiatry may, for classification and therapeutic purposes, distinguish between *functional* and *organic* mental "diseases",[71] these distinctions are of no consequence for legal purposes, because the law's concern is not with the origin of the disease or the cause of it but simply with the mental condition that has brought about the act.[72]

The decision in *Kemp* may be compared with the case of *R v Charlson*.[73] In the latter case a father, without any provocation or motive, struck his 10-year-old son with a mallet and threw him out of a window. The defence was non-insane automatism. Insanity was not raised as a defence, although medical evidence revealed a possibility that the accused had a brain tumour which, if it existed, could have caused an outburst of impulsive violence over which he would have no control. The jury followed the Judge's direction that unless they were satisfied, when he struck his son, that the accused was acting consciously knowing what he was doing, they should return a verdict of "Not guilty", and acquitted him. The case turned on the fact that it had not been "given in evidence"[74] that the accused was insane; indeed, the evidence of the only medical witness was that he was sane. Clearly, the case turned on its own facts

---

68 Greenspan (ed), *Martin's Annual Criminal Code 1997*, Aurora, Ontario, Canada Law Book Co, 1996, cc/48.

69 [1957] 1 QB 399, [1956] 3 All ER 249.

70 Ibid at 407, at 253.

71 In fact, modern psychiatry knows nothing of the concept of mental "disease" as such, but does distinguish between functional and organic psychoses — psychological or behavioural abnormalities associated with serious mental dysfunction. See *Bratty v A-G for Northern Ireland* [1963] AC 387 at 412, [1961] 3 All ER 523 (HL), where Lord Denning noted that the *major* mental diseases (psychoses), such as schizophrenia, are "clearly" diseases of the mind.

72 Ibid.

73 [1955] 1 All ER 859, (1955) 39 Cr App R 37.

74 As required by s 2 Trial of Lunatics Act 1883 (UK), as amended by s 1 Criminal Procedure (Insanity) Act 1964 (UK). The phrase "appears in evidence" also occurs in s 113(3) Criminal Justice Act 1985, as a condition of the provision allowing a judge to direct a jury to consider the question of insanity.

and should not be taken as any authority that a cerebral tumour can never be a disease of the mind. Had there been probative evidence going beyond mere speculation that the accused did suffer from a brain tumour, it would have been open to Barry J to conclude that he was suffering from a disease of the mind such that at the time of the assault he did not know what he was doing.

In *R v Sullivan*,[75] which also involved an unprovoked and apparently motiveless attack on an innocent victim, the issue was whether psychomotor epilepsy constituted a disease of the mind for the purpose of determining whether the accused could rely on a defence of "non-insane" automatism. The accused, apparently in the post-ictal phase of a petit mal seizure, had struck the elderly victim and knocked him to the ground and then proceeded to kick him about the head and body, causing him severe injuries. Lord Diplock, with whom the other Law Lords agreed, concluded that psychomotor epilepsy was a disease of the mind constituting insanity because it impaired the mental faculties of reason, memory, and understanding to the extent that the sufferer did not know what he was doing.[76] Provided such a disease subsists at the time of the commission of the act, it does not matter whether the origin of the impairment is organic, as in epilepsy, or functional; or whether the impairment itself is permanent, or transient, or intermittent.[77]

One suggested means of identifying a disease of the mind is to ask: is it a mental disease which has "manifested itself in violence" and is it "prone to recur"? This test was first formulated by Lord Denning in *Bratty v A-G for Northern Ireland*.[78] has, however, been criticised as being "ill considered"[79] and possibly too sweeping.[80] The difficulty with this test is that it appears to exclude mental diseases which manifest in ways that do not include violence, such as pyromania or kleptomania, and fails to recognise that some conditions which manifest themselves in violence may not legally be diseases of the mind.[81] However, Lord Diplock's statement in *R v Sullivan* that the purpose of the legislation relating to the defence of insanity "has been to protect society against the recurrence of dangerous conduct"[82] has been judicially interpreted as endorsing the consideration of recurrence as a relevant if non-determinative factor in the insanity inquiry.[83] The danger of recurrence has also been

---

75 [1984] AC 156, [1983] 2 All ER 673 (HL).

76 Lord Diplock stated that the expression "He did not know what he was doing" was a more apt way to explain to a jury the expression in the M'Naghten Rules "as not to know the nature and quality of the act he was doing", which may also be taken to include the case of a person who does an act while unconscious: ibid at 173. See also the discussion on this point in *R v Cottle* [1958] NZLR 999 at 1009 (CA).

77 *R v Sullivan* [1984] AC 156 at 173, [1983] 2 All ER 673 at 678 (HL).

78 [1963] AC 386, [1961] 3 All ER 523 (HL).

79 See Allen, *Textbook on Criminal Law*, London, 1991, 107.

80 *Adams* § CA23.09.

81 Allen, *Textbook on Criminal Law*, London, 1991, 107.

82 *R v Sullivan* [1984] AC 156 at 172, [1983] 2 All ER 673 at 678 (HL).

83 *R v Parks* (1992) 15 CR (4th) 289 at 303, (1992) 95 DLR (4th) 27 at 50; [1992] 2 SCR 871 at 906 (SCC) (La Forest J).

approved recently by the English Court of Appeal as an "added reason" for categorising sleepwalking as a disease of the mind.[84] Perhaps the proper conclusion to draw from this discussion is that while recurrence is one of a number of policy factors to be considered in the disease of the mind inquiry, the absence of a danger of recurrence will not automatically exclude the possibility of a finding of insanity.[85]

8.3.3.1 *The "internal v external cause" test*

At the same time, some conditions which do manifest themselves in violence may not fall within the definition of disease of the mind. This is because of a distinction recognised at law between "external" and "internal" causes when determining the existence of legal insanity. A temporary mental aberration may be caused by some factor "external" to the accused. This could include a blow on the head, consumption of alcohol or drugs, absorption of an anaesthetic, hypnotism, hypoglycaemia, or delirium produced by the toxins of infection.[86] In such cases, the aberrant mental state is properly regarded as externally *imposed* upon the offender's otherwise normal and rational mental state. Accordingly, any act committed while in that state would be treated as involuntary for the purposes of criminal responsibility and would lead to an unqualified acquittal. An offender would be said to have been acting as a "sane" automaton. Such mental states are distinguishable from those contemplated by the phrase "disease of the mind", which uniformly embraces mental or bodily disorders endemic to the physical or psychological makeup of the offender herself which affect the balance of her mind and/or produce a state of automatism. Because these states of mental aberration arise from within the individual herself and are unrelated to any external causality, they are referred to as "internal" causes. In this regard the concepts of insanity and automatism merge, and a person so afflicted would be detained subject to the special verdict of "not guilty by reason of insanity". This is so even if her actions were done in an automatic state (a case of "insane automatism").

The gravamen of "internal" causes is that the malfunction or abnormality of the mind arises from some cause *within the individual herself*, and has its source in the person's psychological or emotional make-up, or in some organic pathology. Included within the concept of an "internal cause" are purely functional disorders which, so far as is presently known, have no physical cause. Generally speaking, any malfunctioning of the mind which has its source primarily in some subjective condition or weakness that is internal to the accused (whether or not it is fully understood) may be a disease of the mind.

Because it cannot be limited to a clinical model of mental illness, the concept of "disease of the mind" is capable of extension by the courts. The types of mental disorder it embraces have never been closed. It certainly includes

---

84 See *R v Burgess* [1991] 2 QB 92 at 99, [1991] 2 All ER 769 at 774 (CA).

85 *R v Parks* (1992) 95 DLR (4th) 27 at 50, 15 CR (4th) 289 at 303, [1992] 2 SCR 871 at 906 (SCC) (La Forest J).

86 *R v Rabey* (1977) 79 DLR (3d) 414, 37 CCC (2d) 461.

medically recognised mental disorder or mental illness, but may also embrace subjective states of mind that would not normally be associated with mental disorder or illness. This may be because the notion of legal insanity serves public policy goals other than therapy. The case of *Rabey v R*[87] illustrates the point. The accused had struck a fellow student with a rock after he became aware that she thought little of him. Psychiatric evidence was given that the act was involuntary and was done while the accused was in a state of dissociation caused by a "psychological blow" following discovery of the young woman's rejection of him. A majority of the Supreme Court of Canada, while rejecting the accused's claim of *sane* automatism, acknowledged that transient disorders caused by "specific external factors" are not within the concept of disease of the mind:

> Any malfunctioning of the mind or mental disorder having its source primarily in some subjective condition or weakness internal to the accused (whether fully understood or not) may be "a disease of the mind" if it prevents the accused from knowing what he is doing, but transient disturbances of consciousness due to specific external factors do not fall within the concept of disease of the mind.[88]

The Court held that the notion of an "external factor" did not apply to a case like the present one where dissociation resulted from "the ordinary stresses and disappointments of life which are the common lot of mankind". Such a condition, including the claimed dissociation, was to be considered as having its source principally in the accused's psychological or emotional make-up and was to be regarded as a disease of the mind. However, Dickson J, in his dissenting judgment, suggests that proof of a disease of the mind would normally require evidence of an "underlying pathological condition *which points to a disease requiring detention and treatment*".[89] For the reasons discussed above, we suggest that this represents an incorrect view of the role played by the disease of the mind concept, and confuses the requirement of therapy, which may be an *outcome* of an insanity plea, with legal responsibility and public protection, arguably the principal rationales for the rule.

A point of some interest is whether or not "disease of the mind" includes personality disorders. There does not appear to be a clear view on this. On one view, personality or behavioural disorders classified as "psychopathy" or "neuroses" will not suffice.[90] Other writers suggest that severe personality disorders may be included because they are regarded as functional psychoses.[91] The real issue is simply whether there is medical evidence that the condition should be regarded as a mental illness, regardless whether the defence is able to satisfy the additional tests in s 23(2).[92] Because the notion of insanity serves social and legal purposes quite distinct from other legal standards of mental

---

87   [1980] 2 SCR 513, (1980) 15 CR (3d) 225 (SCC).

88   Ibid at 319, at 233.

89   Ibid at 552, at 260 (emphasis added).

90   See Williams, *CLGP*, §§ 146, 170, 171.

91   See Greenspan (ed), *Martin's Annual Criminal Code 1997*, Aurora, Ontario, Canada Law Book Co, 1996, cc/48; also Allen, *Textbook on Criminal Law*, London, 1991, 106.

92   *Adams* § CA23.08.

disorder and capacity, the attitudes of clinicians to personality disorder in other mental health contexts should not determine its acceptability in this context. It is ultimately for the courts to determine whether it qualifies as mental disease, and for the tribunal of fact to decide whether it affected the accused's mental capacity in a relevant way.

8.3.3.2 *Automatism*

The distinction between "internal" and "external" causes has become critical for courts in relation to claims that the accused was acting as an automaton at the relevant time. Automatism, which, like "disease of the mind", is a legal rather than a medical concept, signifies "action without conscious volition" or an act "which is done by the muscles without any control by the mind".[93] Where the defence of automatism is raised by a defendant, two questions must be decided by the judge before the defence can be left to the jury. The first is whether a proper evidential foundation for the defence of automatism has been laid. The second is whether the evidence shows the case to be one of insane automatism, ie whether it is a case which falls within the M'Naghten Rules, or one of non-insane automatism. As we have noted, cases do periodically arise where the issue of insanity is closely linked to a claim that the offender had acted without conscious awareness, and the main medico-legal question concerns what *caused* the state of altered consciousness. Automatism caused by disease of the mind is subsumed under the insanity defence and will ultimately lead to the special verdict of not guilty on account of insanity.[94] It is often described as "insane" automatism. On the other hand, where automatism is produced by concussion or the consumption of drugs, it may be characterised as "non-insane" or "sane" automatism and constitutes a complete defence to a charge.

The principal cases of non-insane automatism which have been considered by the courts include concussion, and situations where a person has experienced involuntary intoxication due to drugs administered medically.[95] However, there are two additional areas where major difficulties have arisen. They concern, first, the problem of diabetes leading to either *hypoglycaemia* (low blood sugar caused by excessive insulin) or *hyperglycaemia* (elevated blood sugar caused by a failure to take insulin) and, secondly, the case of sleepwalking.

8.3.3.2(a) *Diabetic automatism*

R v Quick[96] concerned a diabetic man who, while employed as a charge nurse, committed an assault upon a disabled patient. At the time of the assault he was suffering from hypoglycaemia caused by his failure to eat and subsequent deficiency of blood sugar. The trial Judge ruled that the defence of automatism amounted to a plea of insanity, whereupon Q, not wanting to put forward a

---

93 *Bratty v A-G For Northern Ireland* [1963] AC 386, [1961] 3 All ER 523 (HL). See § 2.3.
94 Section 113(1) Criminal Justice Act 1985.
95 See, for example, *R v King* (1962) 35 DLR (2d) 386, [1962] SCR 746 (SCC).
96 [1973] QB 910, [1973] 3 All ER 347 (CA).

defence of insanity, changed his plea to one of guilty. In quashing his conviction, the Court of Appeal ruled that because the appellant's mental condition was not caused by his diabetes "but by his use of the insulin prescribed by his doctor" such malfunctioning of the mind as there was was caused by an *external* factor and not by a bodily disorder in the nature of a disease which disturbed the working of his mind.[97] The Court concluded that he was entitled to have his defence of non-insane automatism left to the jury.

In contrast to this case is the decision in *R v Hennesey*.[98] H, also a diabetic, was charged with taking a conveyance without authority and driving whilst disqualified. At his trial, he attempted to raise a defence of non-insane automatism. However, the trial Judge ruled that any impairment of the appellant's mind could not have been caused by anything but diabetes, a disease. H then changed his plea to guilty and was sentenced to imprisonment for 9 months. Dismissing the appeal against conviction, the Court of Appeal agreed with the trial Judge. It held that hyperglycaemia caused by an inherent defect (diabetes), and not corrected by insulin, is a disease; and if it does cause a malfunction of the mind, the case falls within the M'Naghten Rules. This means, in effect, that automatism in a case involving hyperglycaemia is attributable to an "internal" cause and for legal purposes is treated as insanity.

The use of the "internal/external cause" test to distinguish insanity from automatism has been described as "fatuous"[99] and, it is suggested, may cause ordinary people to regard with incredulity those decisions which endorse the distinction — contrary to the warning of Lawton LJ in *Quick* that "the law should not give the words 'defect of reason from disease of the mind' a meaning that would be regarded with incredulity outside a court".[100] Allen asks:

> Is the distinction between a diabetic in hyperglycaemic coma and one in hypoglycaemic coma so marked in its dangers, consequences and risk of recurrence that the former should be found insane while the latter goes free?[101]

The answer is clearly "no", yet the distinction is upheld by the courts. We cannot escape the fact that both hypoglycaemia and hyperglycaemia are conditions derivative of the same medical disease, namely diabetes. The only basis of the differing policy approach to the cases is the occurrence, at different stages of the disease's progression, of low blood sugar as opposed to low insulin. It seems problematic, to say the least, that important legal consequences should turn upon such serendipitous medical episodes. It is enough to observe that the hypoglycaemic (non-insane) automaton one day could become a hyperglycaemic (insane) automaton the next, depending simply upon his failure to take or, alternatively, over-absorption of insulin.[102]

---

97 Ibid at 923, at 356.

98 [1989] 2 All ER 9, [1989] 1 WLR 287 (CA).

99 See Allen, *Textbook on Criminal Law*, London, 1991, 107.

100 Ibid. See *R v Quick* [1973] 1 QB 910 at 919, [1973] 3 All ER 347 at 353 (CA) (Lawton LJ).

101 Allen, *Textbook on Criminal Law*, London, 1991, 109.

102 For a more comprehensive discussion of the problems with the insane/non-insane automatism distinction see Padfield, "Exploring a Quagmire: Insanity and Automatism"

On the other hand, while it seems that a more medically and legally appropriate means of dealing with the problem of hyperglycaemic automatism is called for, it is not at all clear what the solution to the problem should be. A possible answer would be legislatively to declare all diabetically-related automatisms to be the result of (say) "external" causes, thus eliminating, for legal purposes, the distinction between *hyper*glycaemia and *hypo*glycaemia. However, an objection to this solution might be that it unfairly discriminates against other automatistic actors who also suffer from organic disorders but which have been characterised as "internal" causes. Another possible solution is to do nothing, on the basis that cases of diabetic automatism are rare and that any unfairness resulting from the attribution of a diabetic condition as an "internal" cause can be dealt with by dispositional solutions that restrict the offender's freedom to the least extent possible.

8.3.3.2(b) *Sleepwalking and automatism*

Another area of current difficulty concerns the correct characterisation of sleepwalking (somnambulism) as a defence to crime. Traditionally, people who committed offences while asleep were entitled to an unqualified acquittal provided there was no evidence of a condition which could be regarded as a disease.[103] In *Bratty v A-G for Northern Ireland* Lord Denning considered that sleepwalking should be treated in the same way as concussion:

> No act is punishable if it is done involuntarily: and an involuntary act in this context — some people nowadays prefer to speak of it as automatism — means an act which is done by the muscles without any control by the mind such as a spasm, a reflex action or a convulsion, or an act done by a person who is not conscious of what he is doing such as an act done whilst suffering from concussion *or whilst sleepwalking.*[104]

Such dicta in this and other decisions clearly characterise violence in sleepwalking as illustrations of non-insane automatism. However, in *R v Burgess,* [105] the English Court of Appeal held that the case of violence occurring during a sleepwalking episode amounted to insanity under the M'Naghten Rules and was not sane automatism. The Court held that the accused, who had struck the victim on the head with a video recorder while unconscious and sleepwalking, was to be treated as though insane because medical evidence suggested that the sleepwalking was an abnormality resulting from an internal factor which, although transitory, might recur. The appellant had stated that he and the victim had fallen asleep on the evening of the alleged assault and that

---

[1989] 48 CLJ 354 at 354, 355. See also McDonald, "Acquittal for the Intoxicated Automaton?" [1993] NZLJ 44 at 46.

103 See *R v Tolson* (1889) 23 QBD 168 at 187, [1886-90] All ER Rep 26 at 37, where Stephen J said: "can anyone doubt that a man who, though he might be perfectly sane, committed what would otherwise be a crime in a state of somnambulism, would be entitled to be acquitted? And why is this? Simply because he would not know what he was doing."

104 [1963] AC 386 at 409, [1961] 3 All ER 523 at 532 (HL) (emphasis added). See also Viscount Kilmuir LC, who opined (at 403, at 528) "[where] a defence of insanity is raised unsuccessfully [there may be] room for an alternative defence based on automatism. For example [if] . . . the accused . . . was a sleepwalker."

105 [1991] 2 All ER 769, [1991] 2 QB 92 (CA).

when he awoke he felt confused, realising at the same time that he was holding the victim down on the floor. He claimed he did not recall hitting the victim and argued that, because he was sleepwalking when he attacked her, he was suffering from non-insane automatism and accordingly, lacked the mens rea for the offence. In dismissing the appeal, the Court agreed that sleep was a normal condition. However, it was satisfied, on the basis of the medical evidence presented, that in this case the appellant was suffering from a sleep *disorder* which was an abnormality of the brain function and could properly be regarded as a pathological condition. As such it was an internal factor, and because the disorder had manifested itself in violence, and even though the recurrence of serious violence was unlikely, the trial Judge had been right to direct the jury that the defence was one of insanity. Even if, as the prosecution medical witness had opined, this was not a case of sleepwalking but a case of *hysterical dissociation* (where for psychological reasons, such as being overwhelmed with his emotions, a person's brain works in a different way), the disorder would still have been treated as an internal cause with the consequential features of an insanity verdict.

However, the decision in *Burgess* is open to criticism. It has been argued that the Judges' reasoning on the issue whether B suffered from a disease of the mind was flawed,[106] because in claiming to have adopted the definition of "disease of the mind" put forward by Lord Denning in *Bratty*, there was no evidence upon which it could be properly concluded that B suffered from a mental disorder or illness of any kind.[107] In reality, all that was established was that B had suffered from some sort of transitory abnormality of the brain function; and because the evidence fell far short of a disorder that was "prone to recur", it is argued that their Lordships were wrong to conclude that B suffered from a disease of the mind, and the issue of insanity should have ended there.[108] To the extent that the Court was concerned to pursue a social defence policy, it was unnecessary to do so, because this was not the sort of case where the accused should be detained in hospital in order to protect the public.[109]

Burgess contrasts with the decision in *R v Parks*.[110] The appellant in *Parks*, whilst asleep, had driven 23 km and then killed his mother-in-law by stabbing and beating her, and seriously injured his father-in-law. The defence of automatism was left to the jury, on the basis of a direction that if the jury decided that the appellant was in a state of somnambulism at the time of the killing, he was entitled to be acquitted on the basis of non-insane automatism. The Ontario Court of Appeal found the case very troubling but dismissed the Crown's appeal against P's acquittal.

In the Supreme Court of Canada, on a further appeal by the Crown against the acquittals, it was held that sleepwalking was a common disorder in

---

106 Mackay, "The Sleepwalker is not Insane" [1992] 55 MLR 714.

107 Ibid at 717.

108 Ibid at 718.

109 Ibid.

110 (1990) 56 CCC (3d) 449.

children, occasionally found in adults, which involved no neurological, psychiatric, or other illness and which was not treatable. It did not arise from a disease of the mind and, therefore, entitled the accused to a complete acquittal. While the uncontradicted evidence was that the respondent's faculties of reason, memory, and understanding were impaired at the relevant time, there was no evidence that this was because he was suffering from any illness. P's awareness of his actions was impaired (ie he was unconscious) because he was asleep, not because his sleep was disordered. It could not be said, therefore, that there was a causal connection between the impairment of P's faculties and the sleep disorder, and thus his inability to know what he was doing could not be due to a "disease of the mind". The Court found that sleep impairs the human mind and its functioning, but cannot be called an illness, disorder, or abnormal condition because it is a perfectly normal condition.

However, it has been observed that *Parks* is "more striking for its unusual facts than for its advancement of the law".[111] It is not easy to discern the clear basis of the Court's reasoning. For example, Lamer CJC concluded that, because sleep was the cause of the accused's mental state and is a normal condition, P did not suffer from a disease of the mind. His Lordship then stated that for there to be a finding to the contrary, the record would need to disclose evidence that sleepwalking was the cause of the respondent's state of mind which, he concluded, was not the case with P. Yet he intimated that sleepwalking might be a disease of the mind "in another case on different evidence",[112] although the Court did not give any indication what evidence might lead to the classification of sleepwalking as a disease of the mind.

Furthermore, La Forest J appears to reject the internal/external cause criterion as a universal approach to the disease of the mind inquiry, and relegates it the status of an analytical tool rather than an all-encompassing methodology.[113] Again, however, no clear alternative analysis is offered in the judgment.

The effect of these decisions is to leave the law on somnambulistic automatism in a state of confusion. It is difficult to reconcile the divergent legal reasoning represented in both decisions. Indeed, they illustrate how mental abnormality "defences" may be used to serve a variety of diverse and sometimes apparently contradictory social purposes, and to reflect significant differences in criminal justice values. Resolution of the difficulties in future cases may require a more accurate understanding of the underlying mental infirmity.

8.3.4 "Nature and quality" of the act or omission

If the disease of the mind or natural imbecility suffered by the accused is to be effective in establishing a defence of insanity, it must affect her responsibility by producing a relevant incapacity in one of the two ways specified in the Crimes Act 1961. Accordingly, the accused must prove that she was either

---

111 Grant and Spitz, "Case Comment: *R v Parks*" (1993) 72 Can Bar Rev 224.
112 (1992) 95 DLR (4th) 27 at 40, [1992] 2 SCR 871 at 891 (SCC).
113 Ibid at 47, at 902.

"incapable of understanding the nature and quality of the act or omission *or* of knowing that the act or omission was morally wrong having regard to the commonly accepted standards of right and wrong".[114] We first examine the former element of this test.

In most jurisdictions the "nature and quality" of an act refers exclusively to the physical character of the act concerned.[115] It includes cases where the accused is not conscious of acting and situations where the accused is mistaken, through some delusional process, as to the character of the act he is doing. The phrase does not involve any consideration of the accused's moral perception, his knowledge of the moral quality of his act. To succeed under this limb it is necessary for the accused to prove that he did not know what he was doing, or did not appreciate the consequences of his act, or did not appreciate the circumstances in which he was acting.[116] Traditional, if unlikely, examples include someone's strangling the victim while believing he is squeezing a lemon, or cutting a person's throat believing he is slicing a loaf of bread. However because, outside of an encapsulated delusional system,[117] an offender's logic and train of ideas are generally unimpaired, it is highly improbable that an offender could be so deluded as to fail to appreciate the essential character of conduct in the manner suggested by these traditional examples. The older texts are littered with bizarre examples of incapacity to understand the nature and quality of the act, such as the person who cuts off a sleeper's head because "it would be great fun to see him looking for it when he woke up"[118] or the woman who put her child on the fire thinking she was putting on a log of wood. Perhaps these examples reflect the earlier perception that true insanity can only be found where the person was totally devoid of rational capacity. However, as we shall see, the demands of the present law are much less rigorous than this view would suggest.

Virtually all cases falling under the "nature and quality" limb involve (insane) automatism, where D's behaviour is not under his conscious control at all, rather than cases where D's behaviour is voluntary but misunderstood by him. Because this limb of the insanity test is concerned with the incapacity of the accused to appreciate the *physical* consequences of his act, an accused would be unable to rely on this limb of the insanity defence where, for example, he was aware that he was killing the victim and knew that killing was a crime, but believed that the victim was "Satan" and that in killing the deceased he was acting under divine orders.[119] (Such a case would fall under s 23(2)(b), covering "knowledge of . . . wrong".) In reality, a determination of insanity very seldom turns on whether the defendant understood the "nature

---

114 Section 23(2)(a) and (b) Crimes Act 1961.

115 *R v Codere* (1916) 12 Cr App R 21.

116 Allen, *Textbook on Criminal Law*, London, 1991, 110.

117 A technical term, indicating that apart from the delusion or its ramifications, the patient generally behaves in a normal manner.

118 Stephen, *History of the Criminal Law of England* Vol II, London, MacMillan, 1883, 166.

119 Greenspan (ed), *Martin's Annual Criminal Code 1997*, Aurora, Ontario, Canada Law Book Co, 1996, cc/49.

and quality of his act". Apart from instances of automatism, in almost all litigated insanity cases, it is the second limb that is in dispute (ie whether the defendant knew the wrongfulness of the criminal act).

8.3.5 Knowledge of wrongfulness of act

Under the second "limb" of the insanity test a defendant must establish that she did not know that the act was wrong. Historically, there has been much debate over whether, in formulating the test in these terms, the judges intended to inquire into the defendant's knowledge of *legal* or *moral* wrong. Before the 1961 Act there was particular doubt about this because of earlier English authority which had held that "wrong" means contrary to law.[120] In *Windle*, W had been charged with murder when he killed his wife after having been coaxed by his workmate to "give her a dozen aspirin". He gave her 100. His wife was always talking of committing suicide and was certifiably insane. When he gave himself up to the police W said " I suppose they will hang me for this". At his trial evidence was led that W suffered from a form of communicated madness called *folie a deux* whereby if a person was in constant attendance of another person who was mentally ill in some way, insanity can be communicated to the attending person. Experts on both sides agreed that he knew that he was doing an act prohibited by the law, as a result of which the judge withdrew the issue of insanity from the jury and he was convicted.

On appeal to the Court of Appeal, Lord Goddard CJ held that it was not the function of a jury to determine whether a particular act was morally right or wrong and that the test of "wrong" in the M'Naghten Rules means *contrary to law*. Since the appellant knew what he was doing was contrary to law it was appropriate for the defence of insanity to be withdrawn from the jury. The appeal was dismissed.

Some years earlier in the case of *R v Porter*,[121] an Australian Judge had directed a jury, in what has come to be regarded as a classic direction in this country, in the following terms:

> We are not dealing with right or wrong in the abstract. The question is whether he was able to appreciate the wrongness of the particular act he was doing at the particular time. Could this man be said to know in this sense whether his act was wrong if through a disease or defect or disorder of the mind *he could not think rationally of the reasons which to ordinary people make that act right or wrong?* If through the disordered condition of the mind he could not reason about the matter with a moderate degree of sense and composure, it may be said that he could not know that he was doing what was wrong. What is meant by wrong? *What is meant by wrong is wrong having regard to the everyday standards of reasonable people . . .*[122]

This approach to the meaning of "wrong" was later endorsed by the High Court of Australia in *Stapleton v R*.[123] Rejecting *Windle*, the Court held that in

---

120   See *R v Windle* [1952] 2 QB 826, [1952] 2 All ER 1 (CCA).

121   (1933) 55 CLR 182 at 189, 190, [1936] ALR 438 at 441 (HCA) (Dixon J).

122   Ibid.

123   (1952) 86 CLR 358 (HCA). This quote is from the headnote of the CLR. The case is also reported at [1952] ALR 929 (HCA).

applying the second branch of the legal test of insanity in *M'Naghten's case*, the question is "whether the accused knew that his act was wrong according to the ordinary principles of reasonable men, not whether he knew it was wrong as being contrary to law".[124]

This has always been the approach taken by New Zealand courts,[125] and in *R v Macmillan*[126] the Court of Appeal affirmed that what was intended by s 23(2)(b) was to adopt the *Stapleton* direction as appropriate in future trials in New Zealand.[127] The question of the meaning of "wrong" has been put beyond debate in New Zealand by the express language of the statute, which requires proof of knowledge that the act or omission was "*morally* wrong, having regard to the commonly accepted standards of right and wrong".[128] The meaning of the phrase was discussed at length in *Macmillan*. M, who suffered from paranoid schizophrenia, pleaded insanity to a charge of attempting to break out of Mt Eden jail. The essence of his defence was that he did not regard the act as wrong for him to do, although he would have known that people generally would regard it as wrong. At the trial, counsel for the prosecution argued that the inclusion in the statute of the words "having regard to the commonly accepted standards of right and wrong" signified the Legislature's intention to substitute an objective for a subjective standard by which to judge whether an act was morally wrong; a conclusion which, if pressed, would have meant that a large group of persons suffering from paranoia would have been excluded from the defence of insanity.[129]

In rejecting this approach, the Court held that in enacting the present section the Legislature did not intend to change the law as it was understood at the date of its enactment, but rather clearly to indicate its preference for the decision in *Stapleton v R* over *R v Windle*. The introduction of the word "morally" simply reflects this preference.[130] In other words, it seems that insanity will be established in New Zealand even where the accused perceived that the act was "morally wrong in the eyes of other people", if he thought the act was right himself, or thought that his own acts were "above judgment on moral standards".[131] The practical effect of this decision has been to affirm that the statutory test for insanity in New Zealand is based on a *subjective* moral standard. This implies that an accused will not be criminally responsible for his acts if, as a result of mental disease, he believes he is morally justified in his behaviour even though he may have known that his acts were illegal and/or contrary to public standards of morality (ie that he would be condemned in the eyes of "right-thinking people").

---

124 Ibid.
125 See *Murdoch v British Israel World Federation (NZ) Inc* [1942] NZLR 600 at 630 (CA).
126 [1966] NZLR 616 at 622 (CA).
127 Ibid.
128 Section 23(2)(b) Crimes Act 1961 (emphasis added).
129 [1966] NZLR 616 at 620 (CA).
130 Ibid at 621.
131 Ibid at 622.

Although the New Zealand approach has been criticised as being "directly contrary to the words of the Act",[132] it is clear that the Court in *Macmillan* was concerned to avoid an interpretation which would have excluded the defence from a significant class of persons who are clearly insane. The reason why this approach may now be accepted is that it conforms both with the way in which exculpatory insanity has been understood historically, and that it reflects sound common sense. No person should be convicted of a crime whose mind is so disordered that he is unable to make the moral judgments which, in "sane" people, enable them to live socially integrated lives and to choose conduct which conforms with both moral and legal norms. It is that capacity which is so radically lacking in an "insane" person. Indeed, it is difficult to imagine a class of persons less mentally equipped to perform such tasks than those diagnosed as paranoid schizophrenics — whether or not they comprehend the applicable law.

What constitutes a relevant lack of mental "composure" for the purposes of legal insanity is a matter to be considered in the light of the facts of a particular case. There is no formula that can be applied. However, since the test approved in *Stapleton* requires only an ability to reason about a matter with a "moderate" degree of sense and composure, it would seem that not every degree of mental perturbation or upset is necessarily an indication of a relevantly disordered mind. In *R v Macmillan*[133] the Court indicated that the fact that an accused may have methodically and logically planned a crime, such that there was "method in his madness", was not necessarily inconsistent with insanity "but might in fact support it".[134] However, a lack of "appropriate feelings", as in the case of a psychopath who kills a person but lacks a normal person's emotional and affective appreciation of the wrongness of the act, will not secure an insanity acquittal where the psychopath has an intellectual awareness that his act is wrong.[135] What is normally required is that the accused acted "in a state of frenzy, uncontrolled emotion, or suspended reason".[136] The defence will fail if the evidence merely establishes an "absence of moral inhibition, restraint, or conscience" falling short of a state of suspended reason.[137] Therefore if, because of a disease of the mind, D is unable to restrain himself from killing V because he is subject to an emotional impulse which he cannot control (a so-called "irresistible impulse") but, nevertheless, understands the nature of his act and that it is morally wrong, he would not be able to take advantage of the insanity defence.[138] Provided a person's cognitive processes are functioning at a level sufficient to enable the accused to grasp the nature and wrongfulness of his act,

---

132 *Adams* (2nd ed) § 418.

133 [1966] NZLR 616 at 625 (CA).

134 Ibid.

135 See *Willgoss v R* (1960) 105 CLR 295 (HCA).

136 Ibid at 301.

137 *R v Brown* [1968] SASR 467 at 475.

138 See Gillies, *Criminal Law*, Sydney, 1985, 177.

the fact that his emotional and volitional capacities are abnormal will not detract from the judgment that he was legally sane.[139]

This is a further indication of the fact that the insanity defence is grounded in an exclusively cognitive model of rational capacity to know right and wrong and is largely unconcerned with disorders which have their impact principally upon the will or the emotions. Whether this is fair may well be debated, although there is insufficient space to do so here. Yet it is apt at this point to highlight a need for further discussion on how best to accommodate, within the criminal justice system, those offenders who are not insane in this narrow sense yet who suffer from mental abnormalities which impair their ability to conform to the law's requirements.

8.3.6 Delusions

A delusion is an abnormality in the content of thought. Delusions, particularly persecutory and religious delusions, are commonly associated with the insanity defence and have been a feature of legal insanity throughout its history: for example, Daniel M'Naghten suffered from the delusion that he was being persecuted by Tories, while Edward Oxford, who in 1840 fired two pistols at Queen Victoria while she was travelling in her coach, suffered from the grandiose delusion that he was to be the instrument of a plot of an imaginary secret society.[140] In a more recent case the accused shot and killed, without apparent motive, a young female friend because of a delusion that members of a local union had conspired to "destroy" him and that they had given a commission to the victim to kill him.[141]

One of the questions posed to the Judges in *M'Naghten's Case* concerned the liability of a person who, under an insane delusion about existing facts, commits an offence as a consequence of the delusion. The Judges replied:

> the answer must, of course, depend on the nature of the delusion: but making the same assumption as we did before, namely, that he labours under such partial delusion only, and is not in other respects insane, we think he must be considered in the same situation as to responsibility as if the facts with respect to which the delusion exists were real. For example, if under the influence of his delusion he supposes another man to be in the act of attempting to take away his life, and he kills that man, as he supposes in self-defence, he would be exempt from punishment. If his delusion was that the deceased had inflicted a serious injury to his character and fortune, and he killed him in revenge for such supposed injury, he would be liable to punishment.[142]

In some jurisdictions which follow the M'Naghten Rules, this supplementary rule regarding insane delusions has been retained. The effect is that a person will be responsible for an act committed under an insane delusion on the basis that the facts with respect to which the delusion exists were real.

---

139 Ibid. See also *Sodeman v R* (1936) 55 CLR 192, [1936] ALR 156 (HCA).
140 Forshaw and Rollin, "The History of Forensic Psychiatry in England" in Bluglass and Bowden (eds), *Principles and Practice of Forensic Psychiatry*, Edinburgh, 1990, 85.
141 *R v Oommen* (1993) 21 CR (4th) 117.
142 10 Cl & F 200 at 211, 8 ER 718 at 723, [1843-60] All ER Rep 229 at 234.

Although this rule still applies in the UK, it may be that it adds nothing to the Rules because the situation is already covered by the test relating to the nature and quality of the act.[143] In effect, the rule simply emphasises the fact that delusions which do not prevent D from having mens rea will not afford a defence.[144]

Various forms of this rule appear in the criminal legislation of Queensland, Western Australia, Northern Territory, and Tasmania. A similar version appeared in s 16(3) Canadian Criminal Code but was repealed in 1991 on the ground that it was superfluous.[145] The formulation as to insane delusions has been criticised as being far too mechanical to be capable of sensible application, and in any event does not appear to have been applied in any of the reported cases subsequent to M'Naghten[146]. Another criticism is that the rule concerning insane delusions is obsolete and outmoded in that it assumes that a person may be sane in every respect except for a specific delusion. It is suggested that this is faculty psychology at its worst.[147]

The rule has never been part of the law in New Zealand. The matter falls to be decided on ordinary principles. Thus the fact an accused knew that he was killing a person and that killing was wrong, while labouring under a delusion caused by mental disease, will not necessarily exclude him from the protection of the insanity defence. Indeed, under s 23(3) "insane delusions", whatever their character, may be evidence that the offender was mentally irresponsible for his act or omission. The question, as always, is whether he is able to think *rationally* of the reasons which to ordinary people make his act right or wrong. However, in *R v Green*,[148] the New Zealand Court of Appeal expressed doubt whether delusions as to factual matters which, if true, would make an act morally justifiable, can by themselves be sufficient to show that a person is incapable of knowing that an act or omission is morally wrong. While acknowledging that there was some authority for a contrary view,[149] the Court concluded that ultimately the issue was one for the jury to decide. It is, nevertheless, of interest that in *Chaulk v R*[150] the Supreme Court of Canada was satisfied that such a person does not know and is incapable of knowing that the conduct is wrong in the circumstances.

8.3.7 Diminished responsibility

Diminished responsibility is a statutory defence in a number of Commonwealth jurisdictions including Barbados, Bahama, England, New

---

143 See Allen, *Textbook on Criminal Law*, London, Butterworths, 1991, 110; also Smith and Hogan, *Criminal Law* (7th ed), London, 1992, 203.

144 Smith and Hogan, ibid, 204.

145 *R v Chaulk* (1990) 62 CCC (3d) 193, 2 CR (4th) 1 (SCC).

146 Gillies, *Criminal Law*, Sydney, 1985, 185.

147 O'Connor and Fairall, *Criminal Defences* (2nd ed), Sydney, 1988, 249.

148 [1993] 2 NZLR 513 at 525, (1993) 9 CRNZ 523 at 535, 536 (CA).

149 See *Murdoch v British Israel World Federation (NZ) Inc* [1942] NZLR 600 (CA).

150 (1990) 62 CCC (3d) 193 at 235, 236, [1990] 3 SCR 1303 at 1361, 1362 (SCC). See also *R v Oommen* (1994) 91 CCC (3d) 8, [1994] 2 SCR 507 (SCC).

South Wales, Queensland, and the Northern Territory. The defence in each jurisdiction is substantially the same and is based on the English defence defined in s 2 Homicide Act 1957 (UK). Diminished responsibility is only a defence to murder and may reduce what would otherwise be murder to manslaughter. The defence has never been part of New Zealand law, the view having been taken at the time the Crimes Act 1961 was passed that since there was no longer a death penalty in New Zealand there was no need for a separate diminished responsibility defence.[151] Its non-availability as a defence has been recently reaffirmed in a case where psychological evidence was admitted in support of the defence claim that the accused had arranged for her husband's murder while suffering from post-traumatic stress disorder, battered wife syndrome, and depression.[152] In R v Gordon the Court of Appeal held that sympathy for the appellant could not prevail over the current statutory provisions,[153] and that it was unable to accept expert testimony that the accused "had diminished responsibility because of her mental state at the time [of the offence]".[154] The Court did find, however, that where an accused person is suffering from an illness that might affect her responses or judgment, its consequences may be beyond the experience and knowledge of a jury, and so expert evidence may be adduced to show that those consequences may be such as to weaken or negate the inference of intent that could properly be drawn in the case of a normal person.[155] In such a case a jury might acquit, not on the grounds of diminished responsibility, but simply because it is not satisfied beyond a reasonable doubt that the accused possessed mens rea at the relevant time.

It may be argued that in New Zealand there is a "de facto" defence of diminished responsibility, which has been acknowledged by the courts but not yet endorsed by the Legislature. This possibility was first alluded to by the Court of Appeal in R v Aston.[156] In that case, the respondent had been convicted of arson and manslaughter following an incident in which he had shot and killed the proprietor of a service station then set fire to the service station, a museum, and a private home. Under the legal guise of a provocation defence, psychiatric evidence was led at the trial that the respondent was suffering from paranoia at the time and had been provoked into losing his self-control by suggestions from the deceased that he was homosexual. It was accepted by the trial Judge that the respondent's mental illness played a significant part in the crimes.

In surveying sentencing issues, the Court alluded to three Australian cases of manslaughter on the ground of diminished responsibility, observing that

---

151 Brookbanks, "Diminished Responsibility: Balm or Bane" in Legal Research Foundation, *Movements and Markers in Criminal Policy*, Legal Research Foundation, Auckland, 1984, 30.

152 *R v Gordon* (1993) 10 CRNZ 430 (CA).

153 Ibid at 430.

154 Ibid at 439.

155 Ibid at 437.

156 [1989] 2 NZLR 166, (1989) 4 CRNZ 241 (CA).

this was "in substance" the present case.[157] But, apart from additional comparisons drawn from other jurisdictions regarding the sentencing of persons who commit grave crimes while suffering from mental disorder, there is no further reference to a substantive diminished responsibility defence in the judgment. However, in *R v McCarthy*[158] the Court of Appeal suggested that the availability of diminished responsibility, while it has never been expressly accepted by a New Zealand Parliament, may nevertheless, within the limited field of the provocation defence, be seen as the *"inevitable and deliberate effect* of the statutory changes embodied in s 169 of the Crimes Act 1961". [159] The full implications of this concession are not yet entirely clear. Nonetheless, one may safely say that the judicial expansion of the scope of relevant "characteristics"[160] to include such matters as mental deficiency, or a tendency to excessive emotionalism as a result of brain injury,[161] as factors relevant to the determination whether murder should be reduced to manslaughter, clearly foreshadows the emergence of a type of diminished responsibility defence, albeit still under the banner of provocation.[162]

In those jurisdictions in which a diminished responsibility defence is currently available, the "abnormality of mind" which is essential to establish the defence need not be a generally recognised type of "insanity"[163], provided it is a state of mind so different from that of ordinary human beings that the reasonable man would term it abnormal.[164]

8.3.8 Irresistible impulse

Because diminished responsibility also extends to an accused's inability to exercise willpower to control physical acts in accordance with a rational judgment, it may be established where there is evidence that the accused acted under an irresistible impulse. Again, however, apart from the statutory provisions relating to infanticide in s 178 Crimes Act 1961 which arguably allow a limited form of diminished responsibility defence,[165] in New Zealand irresistible impulse is not a defence even if caused by disease of the mind. In *R v Deighton*[166] the accused was charged with the murder of his 3-month-old

---

157 Ibid at 245.

158 [1992] 2 NZLR 550, (1992) 8 CRNZ 58 (CA).

159 Ibid at 558, at 66 (emphasis added).

160 See s 169(2)(a) Crimes Act 1961. Within the statutory scheme a relevant "characteristic" may be added to the profile of an ordinary person in deciding whether some idiosyncratic personal trait may have made the offender more susceptible to a loss of self control caused by provocation than if that characteristic had not been present. For detailed discussion see § 14.4.1.5(c).

161 *R v McCarthy* [1992] 2 NZLR 550 at 557, (1992) 8 CRNZ 58 at 65, 66 (CA).

162 See also Brown, "Provocation: Characteristics, Diminished Responsibility and Reform" in *Movements and Markers in Criminal Policy*, Legal Research Foundation, 1984, 40.

163 *R v Rose* [1961] AC 496.

164 *R v Byrne* [1960] 2 QB 396, [1960] 3 All ER 1 (CCA).

165 See § 14.5.

166 (1900) 18 NZLR 891.

son. Although evidently fond of the child, the accused had become depressed at the state of his home and his wife's continual drunkenness. However, there was no evidence that he was suffering from any mental disease at the time. The only evidence was that, on the day in question, he may have become "excited" and formed a fixed idea to kill the child while claiming to suffer from an impulse which he could not control. In rejecting the defence of irresistible impulse, Stout CJ held that if the accused knew he was killing the child, and knew that it was wrong, he could not be acquitted on the ground of insanity. The other matters, including his fixed idea to kill his child, his wife, and himself, and the claimed impulse which he could not control, could not assist him.

It would seem, therefore, that the only circumstances in which an irresistible impulse may assist a defendant in New Zealand is where there is evidence that an irresistible impulse is a symptom of a mental disease sufficient to exclude knowledge of the physical or moral quality of the act, amounting to legal insanity.[167]

8.3.9 Role of expert evidence

Once a court has ruled on the question whether the particular disorder from which the accused suffered was a disease of the mind, it is for the jury to determine whether he was legally insane at the time of the commission of the offence. The courts have stated on numerous occasions that this function cannot be usurped by medical experts. In *R v Rotana*[168] the appellant had been convicted of the murder of his wife after he had struck her about the head with an axe. At the trial, evidence was given by two psychiatrists to the effect that he was suffering from a disease of the mind at the time of the killing, and although he knew the nature and quality of his actions, he was incapable of knowing they were morally wrong. The Crown did not call rebutting evidence, but extensively cross-examined the defence witnesses in order to provide another explanation for the killing. On appeal it was held that it was for the jury, not medical witnesses, to make a decision in such cases. The fact that the verdict is inconsistent with medical evidence given at the trial will not necessarily provide grounds for holding that a verdict is unreasonable. Nevertheless, the verdict must be based on evidence, and medical evidence which is supported by other relevant evidence cannot arbitrarily be put aside. While a jury may disagree with expert opinions, there has to be some rational basis for doing so, otherwise their decision amounts to an arbitrary substitution of their own view for what appears to be uncontradicted evidence from well qualified professionals.[169]

If, in an appeal against conviction, it "appears" to the Court of Appeal that the appellant was insane at the time of the commission of the offence and should have been acquitted on account of his insanity, the Court may quash the

---

167 *A-G for the State of South Australia v Brown* [1960] AC 432 at 449, 450, [1960] 1 All ER 734 at 742, 743 (PC).

168 (1995) 12 CRNZ 650 (CA).

169 Ibid at 654, 655.

conviction and substitute a special verdict of not guilty on account of insanity.[170] However, this procedure will only be adopted where the Court of Appeal is of the opinion that the jury's verdict was unreasonable and unable to be supported having regard to the evidence[171] — ie where the only available evidence points conclusively to the fact that the accused was insane, particularly where the nature of the offence suggests an "insane driving force at work".[172] Such a case was *R v Clark*.[173] The accused had killed and mutilated the body of a middle-aged man in a motel lavatory. The victim's eyes had been torn out and he was cut or torn in the area of the testicles, although death was caused by strangulation. The unchallenged medical evidence from two psychiatrists suggested that the accused was suffering from schizophrenia and was legally insane at the time of the attack. In allowing the appeal against conviction for murder and substituting an insanity verdict, the Court of Appeal noted that while a verdict inconsistent with medical evidence was not necessarily unreasonable, the verdict must still be founded on evidence. Where the evidence of doctors on insanity is not only unchallenged but actually receives support from the surrounding facts it cannot be rejected. In such circumstances an insanity verdict is unavoidable.[174]

However, the mere fact that an accused is believed by the jury to be suffering from mental abnormality, and deviating in material respects from a condition of complete sanity at the time of the crime, will not necessitate an insanity verdict if the jury is not satisfied that the abnormality amounted to legal insanity.[175] Suppose, for example, that D, while in a state of mild depression, kills V, his anorexic daughter, to "put her out of her misery and save the family further heartache". The depression represents a material deviation from complete sanity. However, it is doubtful whether it could it be said that these circumstances led inevitably to the conclusion that the accused was driven by a deranged mind into a course of conduct about which he was incapable of forming a rational moral judgment.[176] D may have been deeply distressed at V's self-destructive conduct, but that would not of itself be sufficient to constitute a disease of the mind for the purposes of legal insanity. However, it might, as in *R v Gordon*,[177] be sufficiently serious to justify the conclusion that, were a defence of diminished responsibility available in New Zealand, such a defence might well have availed D.

---

170 Section 386(4).

171 Section 385(1)(a).

172 *R v Rotana* (1995) 12 CRNZ 650 at 655 (CA).

173 (1983) 1 CRNZ 132 (CA)

174 Ibid at 133.

175 See *R v Bransgrove* [1954] NZLR 1076 at 1080 (CA).

176 See *R v Smith* (1995) 12 CRNZ 616 at 623 (CA) (Casey J).

177 (1993) 10 CRNZ 430 at 441 (CA).

8.4 THE DISPOSITION OF THE CRIMINALLY INSANE

The power of a court to record an insanity verdict is now contained in s 113 Criminal Justice Act 1985. Such a finding can only be made at a hearing or trial for an offence punishable by death or imprisonment, but must be made where the defendant has pleaded insanity and the jury (or judge) has found that the defendant is not guilty on account of her insanity.[178] In the event that the jury finds the defendant not guilty in a trial where insanity has been pleaded, the judge must request the jury to indicate whether or not the acquittal is on account of the defendant's insanity.[179] In addition, the section empowers a judge to leave the issue of the defendant's insanity to the jury, even where insanity has not been expressly pleaded, "where it appears in evidence" that the accused may have been insane when the offence was committed[180]. The requirement that the possibility of insanity "appears in evidence" eliminates the prospect of a judge or jury making a finding of insanity in the absence of probative evidence to that effect (mere hearsay or anecdotal accounts of the defendant's "odd" behaviour will not suffice) but allows a jury to bring in a special verdict where there is such evidence, even if contrary to the defendant's wishes or express instructions to her counsel.[181]

Prior to 1969, an accused person acquitted on account of insanity was required to be kept in strict custody "until the pleasure of the Minister of Justice is known".[182] This invariably meant indefinite detention in a mental hospital, there being no other form of disposition available to the courts. However, an amendment to the Criminal Justice Act 1954 in 1969[183] inserted a new s 39G into the principal Act, which gave the courts an additional range of dispositional options. These equivalent provisions are now contained in s 115 Criminal Justice Act 1985. Section 115 allows for four options once a person has been either found to be "under disability" or "acquitted on account of his or her insanity". They are:

(i)   An order that the person be detained as a "special patient": s 115(1);

(ii) An order that the person be detained in a hospital as a committed patient: s 115(2)(a);

(iii) An order for the person's immediate release: s 115(2)(b);

(iv) To make no order at all, where the person is already liable to full-time custodial detention: s 115(2)(c).

---

178 Section 113(1) Criminal Justice Act 1985.

179 Ibid at s 113(2).

180 Ibid at s 113(3).

181 The provision is a statutory clarification of *R v Cottle* [1958] NZLR 999 (CA) where, although sane automatism only had been pleaded, the jury acquitted on the ground of insanity.

182 Section 31 Mental Health Act 1911.

183 See s 2 Criminal Justice Amendment Act 1969.

8.4.1 Detention as a "special patient"

In the normal course of events a person acquitted on account of insanity will be detained in a hospital as a "special patient" under the Mental Health (Compulsory Assessment and Treatment) Act 1992.[184] Special patient status is an intermediate designation that describes a range of offenders who have been made subject to therapeutic intervention at various stages of the prosecution process. As applied to an insanity acquittee, it may signify that the person represents a serious danger to the public and must be kept in secure detention and be subject to non-clinical control. Under s 117 Criminal Justice Act 1985, a special patient order continues in force until the defendant is "reclassified" as a committed patient or is discharged. In either event, the direction can only be made by the Minister of Health, who must be satisfied, on the recommendation of two medical practitioners, that neither the person's own interests nor the safety of the public requires that she should continue to be subject to the special patient order. However, it should be noted that disposition under s 117(2) is distinct from disposition under s 115(2). The former presupposes that the defendant has already been made a special patient and is subject to non-clinical oversight. However, where a defendant is made subject to an order under s 115(2), the court is given the *immediate* power either to make the offender a committed patient or to discharge directly. The matter is not subject to the Minister's discretion.

Generally, judges are reluctant to impose special patient status because of its indeterminate character and the difficulties that may be faced by an offender in ultimately achieving reclassification. However, in cases involving homicide it has been held to be an "invariable" practice for judges to make a special patient order and that it is inappropriate to take any other course.[185] In such cases a " wider element of public interest, quite apart from its safety, and quite apart from what might be in the best interests of the individual", may justify detaining an offender as a special patient, even though he may no longer be a public danger.[186]

In some jurisdictions existing law still allows trial judges no discretion but to order that an insanity acquittee be kept in "strict custody" until the pleasure of either a senior minister of the Crown or the Queen's Representative is known.[187] Such dispositions are genuinely indeterminate and are usually intended to ensure that criminally insane offenders are kept out of "circulation" for very lengthy periods, often without formal review. The justification for this approach is said to be societal concern about the possibility that the same mental process which deprived the actor of rationality, and led to the offence charged, will repeat itself to the public detriment. Thus the notion of dangerousness is fundamental to the determination of what is an appropriate disposition in such a case, despite the fact that the link between mental illness of any sort and dangerousness is controversial and unclear.

---

184 Section 115(1)(b) Criminal Justice Act 1985.

185 See *R v GH* [1977] 1 NZLR 50.

186 Ibid at 52.

187 See, for example, ss 292, 293 South Australian Criminal Law Consolidation Act 1935.

However, modern rights-based jurisprudence is having an impact upon this area of the law, and many jurisdictions are moving away from the rigid indeterminacy inherent in the mandatory confinement of persons acquitted by reason of insanity, toward procedures that favour regular review of status, and reassessment on a regular basis of D's present dangerousness. For example, in Canada recent amendments to the Criminal Code have given review boards the role of primary decision-maker in respect of insanity acquittees, a role formerly vested in the Lieutenant-Governor of each province. Under the new provisions, review boards may hold disposition hearings, outlining what actions may be taken in the care of the person, dictating the time limits on incarceration, and stipulating possible treatment to be undertaken. Significantly, the new legislation outlines administrative procedures and the procedural rights of individuals appearing before review boards, including rights to counsel, notice of hearings, and the right to cross-examination. When making a disposition, the court or review board is required, in taking into account all extraneous factors, to make the order "that is the least onerous and least restrictive to the accused".[188] There is at present no similar legal requirement in New Zealand. However, the Mental Health (Compulsory Assessment and Treatment) Act 1992, while not actually eliminating indeterminate dispositions for insanity acquittees, now specifies the right of persons detained as special patients to regular clinical reviews at intervals of not longer than 6 months, following an initial compulsory review 3 months after the original disposition order, and to a Tribunal review whenever a clinical review has taken place.[189]

The effect of these legislative changes is to ensure that no person may now be detained indefinitely as a special patient in New Zealand for reasons other than public safety or the patient's own interest. These are the only specified statutory grounds upon which a Review Tribunal may determine that a person should continue to be subject to an order for detention as a special patient.[190]

8.4.2 Detention as a "patient" under the Mental Health (Compulsory Assessment and Treatment) Act 1992

Detention as a special patient is the appropriate form of disposition where a person has been acquitted on account of insanity whose conduct represents a threat to public safety. However, where the court is satisfied that there is no such threat and that it would be "safe" to do so, it may, as an alternative to special patient status, order the person's detention as a patient in a hospital.[191]

An order that a person be detained in hospital as a patient opens up the possibility of two distinct disposition options. A person may be detained as an *inpatient* or as an *outpatient* subject to a community treatment order.[192] Where

---

188 Section 672.54 Criminal Code.

189 Sections 77(1) and 80(5) Mental Health (Compulsory Assessment and Treatment) Act 1992.

190 Ibid at s 80(5)(a).

191 Section 115(2)(a) Criminal Justice Act 1985.

192 See s 28 Mental Health (Compulsory Assessment and Treatment) Act 1992.

an order is made under s 115(2)(a) Criminal Justice Act 1985 it is deemed to be a compulsory treatment order.[193] The fact that the section specifies that the offender be "detained in a hospital" does not necessarily mean that the person must be received and held in a hospital. In *Police v M (No 2)*,[194] it was held that there is nothing in the statute to suggest that such an order must be treated as an inpatient order. In fact, s 28(2) Mental Health (Compulsory Assessment and Treatment) Act 1992 specifies that in making a compulsory treatment order the court *shall* make a community treatment order unless it considers the patient cannot be treated adequately as an outpatient. What will be determinative of the type of "patient" order that is appropriate will be whether the court is satisfied that services for care and treatment on an outpatient basis *appropriate to the needs of the patient* are available and that the *social circumstances* of the patient are adequate for his care in the community.[195]

8.4.3 Immediate discharge

If the form of disability suffered by the "patient" is not of a type that would justify detention and treatment in a mental hospital and the person does not represent a danger to the public, then it may be appropriate to order the person's immediate release.[196] However, because most persons acquitted on account of insanity will have committed serious crimes and are likely to pose a danger to the public, this option will seldom be appropriate. It may, nevertheless, be appropriate where the offender has been acquitted of an offence that did not involve injury or violence or was otherwise of a relatively minor nature.[197]

---

193 Section 115(4A) Criminal Justice Act 1985 as amended by the Fourth Schedule to the Mental Health (Compulsory Assessment and Treatment) Act 1992.

194 [1994] DCR 388.

195 Section 28(2) Mental Health (Compulsory Assessment and Treatment) Act 1992.

196 *R v S (No 2)* (1991) 7 CRNZ 576.

197 See, for example, *Police v XYZ* [1994] DCR 401.

9

Intoxication

9.1 BACKGROUND

In New Zealand, the defence of incapacity or lack of mens rea owing to intoxication is based on the English common law defence preserved by s 20 Crimes Act 1961. However, the New Zealand defence has developed along different lines to its English forebear, and is less restrictive than the common law defence. While intoxication is currently capable of underwriting a complete defence to most crimes that may be committed intentionally, that was not always the case and for many centuries intoxication was regarded simply as an aggravating factor in assessing criminal liability. A brief overview of the history of intoxication may assist our understanding of some recent developments in the theory of the defence.

The earliest reference to drunkenness occurs in the *Penitential of Theodore*, Archbishop of Canterbury, 668-690 AD. According to Theodore:

> whosoever shall have killed a man while drunk shall be guilty of homicide; he commits one fault by self-indulgence and another by killing a Christian.[1]

---

1   Cited in Singh, "History of the Defence of Drunkenness in English Criminal Law" (1933) 49 LQR 528.

The theme of intoxication amounting to fault *of itself* is picked up in later expositions on the subject, and tends to explain the fact that before the nineteenth century intoxication was no defence to a criminal charge. Writing in 1643, Dalton remarked that "if a man that is drunk killeth another, that is felony of death, for it is a *voluntary ignorance* in him, insomuch as ignorance cometh to him by his own act and folly".[2]

Many early commentators regarded drunkenness as an *aggravation* of an offence, as the following extract from *Beverley's Case* in 1603 illustrates:[3]

> although he who is drunk is for the time *non compos mentis*, yet his drunkenness does not extenuate his act or offence ... but it is a great offence ... and therefore aggravates his offence, and doth not derogate from the act which he did during that time.

The law's unbending condemnation of drunkenness during this period is reflected in an early seventeenth century statute described in its short title as "an Act for repressing the odious and loathsome Sin of Drunkenness",[4] which identified drunkenness as the single cause of a range of additional "enormous sins" including "bloodshed, stabbing, murder, swearing, fornication, adultery". It was also blamed for the "overthrow" of various arts and manual trades, and for the general disablement and impoverishment of the workforce. In such a climate of condemnation, it is not difficult to imagine why it was regarded as an aggravation rather than a mitigation of crime.

For all this, it is unclear what practical effect was actually given to the notion of drunkenness as an aggravation of crime, and whether, in truth, penalties were harsher for those who committed offences while drunk. Even in the seventeenth century, some qualifications to the strict rule that intoxication was an aggravation of an offence had begun to emerge, presaging the future direction of the defence at common law. In a chapter of Sir Matthew Hale's *Historia Placitorum Coronae* entitled "Concerning the defect of ideocy, madness and lunacy",[5] a separate section was devoted to a discussion of "*Dementia affectata, namely Drunkenness*". The gist of this passage was that at English law, voluntary drunkenness was not a "privilege", and that, legally, it left D in the same position as if he were in his right senses. However, certain mitigations were recognised, in particular the acknowledgement that if a person by the "contrivance" of his enemies had eaten or drunk something which caused a temporary or permanent "phrenzy", this put him into the same condition as any other phrenzy and equally excused him. Thus the law began to recognise an important distinction between *voluntary* and *involuntary* intoxication. Furthermore, in a later passage discussing "*Dementia accidentalis*", which might be taken to include cases of involuntary intoxication, Hale appears to lay the

---

2   Ibid at 531.

3   (1603) Co Rep 123b at 125a, 76 ER 1118 at 1123. See also Sir Edward Coke, *Coke on Littleton* 247a, who noted that a drunkard was "voluntarius daemon", who gained no "privilege" from that status, and if any "hurt or ills" were occasioned thereby, "his drunkenness doth aggravate it".

4   4 Jac 1, c5.

5   (1694) 29ff.

groundwork for the future exculpatory defence of intoxication when he contemplates a state of involuntary intoxication so profound as to amount to temporary insanity, such that if the accused was rendered incapable of forming the necessary intent the crime was not made out.[6]

Other early authority on intoxication, which tended to suggest that evidence of intoxication may be relevant to the question whether the accused had the requisite intent for certain grave crimes like homicide, has tended to be discounted by some commentators who argue that the relevant dicta were uttered at a time when the law concerning the mental element of crime, and in particular the place of intoxication within it, was at an early stage of development.[7] However, during the nineteenth century the original common law rule suggesting that intoxication was, if anything, an aggravation of crime, came significantly to be relaxed. In a line of cases, judges accepted that drunkenness could be relied upon to support a defence that the defendant had not formed the intent required to commit the crime charged.[8] During this period a clear distinction began to emerge between criminal liability and moral delinquency, to the extent that intoxication was increasingly allowed as an indirect defence which negatived the existence of a specific intent required for certain serious crimes. This approach is illustrated in *R v Grindley*,[9] where Holroyd J held that, although voluntary drunkenness could never excuse the commission of a crime, on a murder charge, where the material question was whether the act was premeditated or done in the heat of the moment, the fact of intoxication was a relevant consideration to take into account. The case, despite its subsequent overruling,[10] represents a watershed in the development of the intoxication defence and shows the emergence of a change in attitude towards drunkenness and the beginning of judicial resistance to Establishment disapproval of drunkenness.

---

6   See *R v Kingston* [1995] AC 355 at 368, [1994] 3 WLR 519 at 529 (HL) (Lord Mustill). However, Lord Mustill cautions that while the extract from Hale is consistent with the existing law, legal concepts of criminal responsibility in the seventeenth century were so different from those of today that there may be danger in placing too much reliance on them as a starting point for the development of the modern doctrine of intoxication.

7   See, for example, *Pearson's Case* (1835) 2 Lew 144, 168 ER 1108, where Park J suggests that drunkenness may be taken into consideration to explain the probability of a party's intention in the case of violence committed on sudden provocation. See also Singh, "History of the Defence of Drunkenness in English Common Law" (1933) 49 LQR 528; also the discussion in *R v Kingston* [1995] 2 AC 355 at 367, [1994] 3 WLR 519 at 528 (HL) (Lord Mustill).

8   A suggested explanation for this was that in the nineteenth century, judges began to relax the strict common law rule in cases of murder and serious violent crime where the penalties were perceived to be particularly harsh or where there was likely to be much sympathy for the accused. See *R v Majewski* [1977] AC 443 at 456 (Lawton LJ).

9   (1819); cited in *Russell on Crimes and Misdemeanours* (2nd ed) 8.

10   *Grindley* was, however, overruled in *R v Carroll* (1835) 7 C & P 145, 173 ER 64, where the Court held that the language in *Grindley* was capable of such wide application that "there would be no safety for human life if it were to be considered as law".

By the time Stephen J delivered his celebrated dictum in *R v Doherty*,[11] there had been a significant turning of the tide of opinion towards drunkenness, and the broad parameters of a future exculpatory defence could now be seen:

> Although you cannot take drunkenness as any excuse for crime, yet when the crime is such that the intention of the party committing it is one of its constituent elements, you may look at the fact that a man was in drink in considering whether he formed the intention necessary to constitute the crime.[12]

Stephen J's apparent purpose in making this concession was to ensure that in prosecutions for very serious crimes, ie those that required proof of an additional mens rea element (usually intention) going to consequences and beyond the mere intention to behave as D did, evidence of intoxication could be admitted by the trial judge for the purpose of negating the "ulterior" mens rea element, thus reducing the level of culpability of the offender. As one commentator has observed, Stephen J's formulation established the emerging rationale for the "long-desired mitigation of punishment" of grossly inebriated homicides.[13]

9.1.1 Intoxication in English law

In English common law, intoxication is normally irrelevant in determining criminal liability. It is suggested that this is because there are varying degrees of intoxication, and the issue can only be relevant in those relatively rare cases where the intoxication is so serious that it prevents the formation of a mental element.[14] In itself, intoxication has never been a defence to a criminal charge. Crucially, English law has always held that criminal intent and a state of intoxication can be compatible, a view captured in the phrase "a drunken intent is nevertheless an intent".[15] That is to say, provided she had the necessary mens rea for the offence, D cannot avoid criminal liability by saying that intoxication impaired her ability to distinguish between right and wrong, or weakened her inhibitions so that she behaved impulsively or in a way she would not have done if she had been sober.[16] Similarly, the fact that D intentionally committed an offence while intoxicated will be no defence even though he cannot remember what he did.[17] Amnesia is not per se a defence to crime, and does not become one simply because it is associated with intoxication.

Nevertheless, in crimes where proof of a subjective mental element is required, evidence of intoxication may, in very limited circumstances, be relevant to the question whether the required state of mind was present.

---

11   (1887) 16 Cox CC 306.

12   Ibid at 308.

13   Hall, *General Principles of Criminal Law* (2nd ed), Indianapolis, Bobbs-Merrill, 1960, 532 at 533.

14   Virgo, "Reconciling Principle and Policy" [1993] Crim LR 415.

15   *R v Doherty* (1887) 16 Cox CC 306 at 308; *R v Sheehan* [1975] 2 All ER 960 at 964.

16   Criminal Law Reform Committee (NZ), *Report on Intoxication as a Defence to a Criminal Charge*, Wellington, Government Printer, 1984, 44.

17   Ibid.

Intoxication may have the effect of impairing awareness, perception, or foresight; and thus result in the absence of the requisite state of mens rea.[18] Equally, however, for certain crimes, including strict liability offences and other offences requiring proof of negligence or objective recklessness, even extreme intoxication is irrelevant. The rationale for this is, as the case may be, either that there is no mental element to be proven, or that the defendant must comply with the standard of the reasonable person, who would not have been intoxicated and so would not be prevented thereby from foreseeing the risk of harm.[19]

9.1.1.1 *The "basic" v "specific" intent distinction*
In England, the concept of a "specific intent" has been used by the courts to limit the availability of the defence of lack of intent based on intoxication. For those crimes requiring proof of a subjective mens rea, extreme intoxication (such that D lacked mens rea) *may* be relevant, depending on whether the offence is characterised as one of "basic" intent or one of "specific" intent.

It is not entirely clear how the distinction originated. It seems that it may have had its origins in the judicial decisions of the late nineteenth century, where certain judges were concerned to devise a means of partial exculpation for offenders charged with capital offences who, because of the effects of intoxication, were incapable of forming the particular intent required for grave crimes like murder. Where evidence of intoxication was sufficiently powerful to negate the specific mens rea for murder, the offender was eligible for the lesser verdict of manslaughter, and thus able to avoid the mandatory penalty of capital punishment for murder. Initially, intoxication seemed to be relevant only to the question whether an act was premeditated or done only with "sudden heat or impulse" for the purposes of the provocation defence.[20] However, in due course it became common in homicide cases for evidence of intoxication to be admitted, and for judges to direct juries to the effect that although drunkenness is no excuse for crime, it may be of great importance in cases where it is "a question of intention".[21] In such cases, a person may be so drunk as to be utterly unable to form any intention at all, yet be guilty of very great violence.[22] The connection between intoxication and its ability to negate the *specific* mens rea for certain grave crimes is made explicit by the judgments of Patterson J and Coleridge J in *R v Monkhouse*:

> if the defendant is proved to have been intoxicated, the question becomes a more subtle one; but it is of the same kind, namely, was he rendered by intoxication entirely incapable of forming the intent charged ... Drunkenness is ordinarily neither a defence nor excuse for crime, and where it is available *as a partial answer* to

---

18 Ibid.

19 Virgo, "Reconciling Principle and Policy" [1993] Crim LR 415 at 416.

20 See, for example, *R v Grindley*, cited in *Russell on Crimes and Misdemeanours* (2nd ed) 8; also in Singh, "History of the Defence of Drunkenness in English Common Law" (1933) 49 LQR 528 at 537.

21 *R v Cruse* (1838) 8 C & P 541, 173 ER 610.

22 Singh, "History of the Defence of Drunkenness in English Common Law" (1933) 49 LQR 528 at 539.

a charge, it rests on the prisoner to prove it, and it is not enough that he was excited or rendered more irritable, unless the intoxication was such as to prevent his restraining himself from committing the act in question, or to take away from him the power of forming any *specific intention*.[23]

Two things emerge from this extract. First, on the question of exculpation, intoxication was perceived only to be a *palliative* defence, capable of reducing the crime charged to one of lesser seriousness. It was never perceived as a complete defence. Secondly, as to responsibility, its effect, in those rare cases where intoxication was legally relevant, must be to negate the *capacity* to form the intention required for certain crimes. This implies that intoxication was only ever relevant in cases where an offender had reached an advanced state of drunkenness and in that state had committed an act of great violence. It seems that intoxication was only ever intended to provide a narrow release from criminal culpability for offenders charged with grave crimes like murder and attempted murder who, while in a state of profound intoxication, had committed some violent act while lacking the mental capacity to premeditate or otherwise intend that act. It was, arguably, never meant by early jurists to have any wider application, and certainly not to provide a complete exculpation from criminal responsibility.

Thus voluntary (self-induced) intoxication was generally regarded as being presumptively incapable of conferring either justification or excuse for *any* crime. At best, in those relatively rare cases where it was pleaded in extenuation of an offence, it was regarded as being available only as a "partial answer" to a charge.[24] What is contemplated by the notion of a "partial answer" is not absolutely clear, but the best view may be that the negation of mens rea in certain crimes did not lead to avoidance of criminal responsibility altogether but rather only to avoidance of the harsh consequences of conviction for a mandatory capital offence. The importance of the passage from *Monkhouse*, we submit, lies not only in the fact that it is the first direction to point out that evidence of drunkenness is admissible to negative *specific intent*,[25] but also in the apparent analogy it creates between provocation and intoxication as *palliative* defences. The passage as a whole indicates that whether as extenuation of homicide in provocation or as a limited negation of mens rea, intoxication can never excuse and can only ever have the effect of lowering an accused's culpability from the capital offence charged to one involving a lesser degree of culpability.

Until 1920, when the decision of the House of Lords in *DPP v Beard*[26] was handed down, there was no clear authority contradicting the view that intoxication was never intended to allow for more than extenuation of certain grave crimes, and that its application was probably limited to murder, attempted murder, and manslaughter. In respect of lesser crimes the general

---

23   (1849) 4 Cox CC 55 at 56 (Coleridge J). (Emphasis added.)

24   See *R v Monkhouse* (1849) 4 Cox CC 55 at 56 (Coleridge J).

25   See Singh, "History of the Defence of Drunkenness in English Common Law" (1933) 49 LQR 528 at 540.

26   [1920] AC 479, [1920] All ER Rep 21 (HL).

rule was consistently applied; namely, that drunkenness is ordinarily neither a defence nor excuse for crime.

However, the decision in *Beard* irrevocably altered the common law on intoxication. Although the case was an appeal against conviction on a prosecution for murder, certain dicta in the case suggested the basis for a much more broad-based defence of intoxication. Lord Birkenhead asserted the general proposition that evidence of drunkenness which renders the accused incapable of forming a specific intent essential to constitute the crime should be taken into consideration with other facts proved in order to determine whether the accused had that required intent. He proceeded to articulate a significantly wider rule for intoxication; indeed, one which has been criticised on the ground that it extends the defence of drunkenness far beyond the limits assigned to it by the common law and which is opposed to the weight of authority on the point.[27] According to Lord Birkenhead:

> I do not think that the proposition of law deduced from these earlier cases is an exceptional rule applicable only to cases in which it is necessary to prove a specific intent in order to constitute the graver crime — eg wounding with intent to do grievous bodily harm or with intent to kill. It is true that in such cases the specific intent must be proved to constitute the particular crime, but this is, on ultimate analysis, only in accordance with the ordinary law applicable to crime, for, speaking generally (and apart from certain special offences), a person cannot be convicted of a crime unless the *mens* was *rea*.[28]

The implication that intoxication may affect ordinary mens rea has become the conceptual foundation of the intoxication defence as it has developed in New Zealand law. We will consider these developments shortly. However, before doing so it is necessary to make some further brief observations about the development of the common law defence since *Beard*.

Beard appeared to leave open the possibility that a person charged with *any* offence requiring proof of intention could plead intoxication as evidence going to prove that he was *incapable* of forming the intention essential to constitute the crime charged. This implied, in theory at least, that a person charged with a relatively minor crime, say a simple assault, could plead intoxication in order to show that he lacked the capacity to form the intent to assault his victim. Consequently, however, if such a defence were available to a lesser crime like assault, the accused would have to be acquitted altogether — because there would be no lesser crime for which liability could attach once intoxication had been allowed to palliate his liability for assault.

9.1.1.2 DPP v Majewski

This possibility existed in English law until 1977, when the window of opportunity left open by *Beard* was conclusively shut by the decision of the House of Lords in *DPP v Majewski*.[29] In that case, the accused had been

---

27 Singh, "History of the Defence of Drunkenness in English Common Law" (1933) 49 LQR 528 at 544, 545.

28 *DPP v Beard* [1920] AC 479 at 504, [1920] All ER Rep 21 at 30 (HL) (emphasis added).

29 [1977] AC 443, [1976] 2 All ER 142 (HL).

involved in a bar-room brawl as a result of which he was convicted on three counts of assault causing actual bodily harm and on three counts of assault on a police constable in the execution of his duty. There was evidence that at the time of the alleged assaults Majewski was acting under the influence of a combination of voluntarily-consumed alcohol and drugs, and it was suggested that he may not have known what he was doing. The trial Judge directed the jury that the effect of the drink and drugs could provide no defence and should be ignored. On appeal, this ruling was unanimously approved by both the English Court of Appeal and the House of Lords. It was held to be established law in England that the effects of self-induced intoxication could provide a defence only if the offence charged required a "specific" intent; and that intoxication, however extreme it might be, could never support a defence when the mental element was no more than a "basic" intent. In the words of Lord Elwyn-Jones LC:

> In the case of these offences it is no excuse in law that, because of drink or drugs which the accused himself had taken knowingly and willingly, he had deprived himself of the ability to exercise self-control, to realise the possible consequences of what he was doing, or even to be conscious that he was doing it.[30]

Because the offences charged in *Majewski* required proof only of a "basic intent" on the part of the accused, it was held that the jury had been properly directed to ignore intoxication as the possible basis for a defence.

There are three things to be noted here. The first is that a formal distinction between offences of "basic" and "specific" intent did not exist before *Majewski*. It does not represent a logical development of the common law. Secondly, the distinction would be unnecessary if the common law defence had been confined to cases involving really serious physical violence. Thirdly, the distinction does not detract from the widely accepted view that intoxication, of itself, is not a defence to crime but merely evidence from which a lack of intent to commit a serious crime may be inferred. Liability may still attach for any offence for which proof of that intent is not required.

The rule in *Majewski* has its most important impact in cases involving personal violence or damage to property.[31] In such cases, the intoxicated actor may take advantage of a defence of lack of intent in relation to the most serious offences, where intent is of primary importance. However, the rule ensures that voluntary intoxication cannot support a defence of lack of intent to a range of lesser charges which will generally be available.[32] This means that under English law, D may be acquitted of murder by pleading intoxication, but will then be convicted of manslaughter, a "basic" intent crime.

One explanation of the distinction is that specific intent offences are those offences always requiring proof of intention, while offences of basic intent are those offences which can be committed recklessly. In practice, however, the distinction is quite arbitrary, and does not imply, as might be expected, that

---

30 Ibid at 476, at 151.
31 Criminal Law Reform Committee (NZ), *Report on Intoxication as a Defence to a Criminal Charge*, Wellington, Government Printer, 1984, 10.
32 Ibid.

crimes of specific intent are necessarily more serious than crimes of basic intent. For example, while theft is characterised as a crime of specific intent, regardless of the seriousness of the particular charge, rape is characterised as a crime of basic intent,[33] in respect of which intoxication cannot be relied upon to negate mens rea. Furthermore, if the defendant is charged with a basic intent crime then, even if when the harm was caused he could not have foreseen that harm because he was intoxicated, recklessness is deemed to exist from the time the intoxicating substance was taken.[34] In *Majewski*, Lord Elwyn-Jones said that the defendant's course of conduct in reducing himself by drugs and drink to a state of intoxication itself supplies evidence of mens rea sufficient for crimes of basic intent.[35] At common law the very taking of an intoxicating substance is deemed to be reckless, and to be sufficiently culpable to justify conviction for a basic intent charge. However, where intoxication has been caused by a drug whose effects are not well known, recklessness cannot be presumed and the prosecution must prove that the defendant foresaw the risk of unpredictable and uncontrollable conduct as a result of intoxication.[36]

One attempt has been made to mitigate the harshness of the basic intent rule, at least in the case of rape, by holding that the jury should discount the fact that the defendant was intoxicated and ask whether, if the defendant had been sober, he would have foreseen the risk that the victim was not consenting.[37] However, this approach merely demonstrates the absurdity of the basic/specific intent distinction because, as Virgo notes,[38] it means that the defendant may still be acquitted if the jury accepts that he would have lacked the necessary mental element for the offence *had he been sober*! One is bound to ask, if it is necessary to contrive a means of exculpating the drunken defendant on a basic intent crime by postulating a *sober* defendant, what is the point of continuing the distinction at all?

The English Law Commission recently proposed the abolition of the basic/specific intent distinction, and its replacement with a new offence.[39] The effect of this change would have been that there would be a return to fundamental principles of criminal liability; namely, that the accused should be acquitted if she lacked the relevant mental element for an offence. However, in order to reflect public policy concerns that voluntarily intoxicated people who commit the actus reus of a crime should not escape punishment, an offender acquitted of the principal substantive offence on grounds of intoxication would

---

33 See *R v Fotheringham* (1989) 88 Cr App R 206, [1988] Crim CR 846 (CA).

34 Virgo, "Reconciling Principle and Policy" [1993] Crim LR 415 at 416.

35 [1977] AC 443 at 474, 475, [1976] 2 All ER 142 at 150 (HL). As Ashworth points out, this is "plainly a fiction": *Principles*, 211.

36 *R v Bailey* [1983] 2 All ER 503, [1983] 1 WLR 760 (CA); *R v Hardie* [1984] 3 All ER 848, [1985] 1 WLR 64 (CA).

37 *R v Woods* (1981) 74 Cr App R 312, [1982] Crim LR 42 (CA) discussed in Virgo, "Reconciling Principle and Policy" [1993] Crim LR 415 at 417.

38 Ibid.

39 Law Commission Consultation Paper No 127, *Intoxication and Criminal Liability*, London, HMSO, 1993, § 6.30.

still be liable for the offence of causing harm while intoxicated. The mens rea of the new offence would be "deliberate" intoxication, meaning that the accused took the intoxicant of her own will, being aware that, in the quantity she knowingly took, it would or might cause her to become intoxicated. Intoxication would not, however, be deliberate if the intoxicant was taken for medicinal, sedative, or soporific purposes, or if it was taken involuntarily.[40]

Although the Law Commission subsequently resiled from these proposals,[41] they reflect a growing disillusionment with the *Majewski* approach in England.[42] In particular, they evince a concern with its illogicality, and its incompatibility with accepted theory. What, then, is the "accepted theory" concerning the modern defence of intoxication? We illustrate this with reference to New Zealand law.

9.2 THE INTOXICATION DEFENCE IN NEW ZEALAND

There is at present no statutory provision which governs the extent to which intoxication may support a defence to a criminal charge. As will be seen, the approach taken to intoxication in New Zealand is significantly different to that taken in other jurisdictions, including the US, Canada, and the UK.

Judicial development of the defence in New Zealand effectively begins with *DPP v Beard*.[43] New Zealand judges have never sought to limit the availability of the defence to grave crimes, nor to limit its scope by reference to the basic/specific intent distinction. *Beard* was considered in *R v Kamipeli*,[44] the leading authority on intoxication in New Zealand, and from that analysis certain principles emerged which continue to govern the defence. In the following section we examine the decision in *Kamipeli*, and outline the guiding principles identified in that case.

9.2.1 *R v Kamipeli*

The accused was charged with murder, following an incident in which he attacked another man in the street and, after knocking him to the ground, continued to punch him and allegedly kicked him in the head. The prosecution argued that he intended to cause the death of the victim, or that he intended to cause the victim bodily injury known to the offender to be likely to cause death and was reckless whether death ensued.[45] There was no suggestion that the accused had struck the victim unintentionally. Indeed, the appellant claimed in evidence that he thought the deceased was about to assault one of his friends, implying that he struck the deceased in order to defend another. It was argued

---

40 For a detailed discussion of these proposals and comments on them, see Virgo, "Reconciling Principle and Policy" [1993] Crim LR 415 at 421ff.

41 Law Commission No 229, *Legislating the Criminal Code: Intoxication and Criminal Liability*, London, HMSO, 1995. See Paton, "Reforming the Intoxication Rules: The Law Commission's Report" [1995] Crim LR 382.

42 An exception is Gardner, "The Importance of *Majewski*" (1994) 14 OJLS 279.

43 [1920] AC 479, [1920] All ER Rep 21 (HL).

44 [1975] 2 NZLR 610 (CA).

45 See s 167(a) and (b).

that he should be convicted only of manslaughter because he had not acted with the intent required for murder.

Evidence that the accused was heavily intoxicated was relied on in support of his defence of lack of intent. However, the trial Judge directed the jury that the accused must have been so drunk that his mind had "ceased to function, that he was acting as a sort of automaton" [46] without his mind functioning. On appeal, the Court of Appeal held that this was a misdirection because it would have left the jury with the impression that anything less than being so drunk that the accused's mind had ceased to function could not, as a matter of law, leave them with a proper doubt whether intent had been established on all the evidence. The Court made the following observation about the true effect of evidence of intoxication:

> Drunkenness is not a defence of itself. Its true relevance by way of defence . . . is that when a jury is deciding whether an accused has the intention or recklessness required by the charge, they must regard all the evidence, including evidence as to the accused's drunken state, drawing such inferences from the evidence as appears proper in the circumstances. *It is the fact of intent rather than the capacity for intent which must be the subject matter of the inquiry.* [47]

Thus, in a case like *Kamipeli*, a drunken offender might have known what he was doing when he attacked the victim, and he might have intended such an attack, but his intoxication remains relevant to the further question whether he meant to kill or foresaw the risk of causing death. (Indeed, Kamipeli was subsequently retried and acquitted of murder but convicted of manslaughter.)

9.2.1.1 A model direction

In *R v Tihi*,[48] the Court of Appeal approved the following direction on the relevance of intoxication to intention in the context of a murder prosecution:

> It has to be shown that in the state of mind that the offender was in, he recognised the real possibility that what he was doing could lead to death . . . [W]e do not judge it by an objective standard. If we are considering each man's position. . . with the age that he is, what sort of man we judge him to be and his state of mind . . . including how drunk he might have been, must he, in the state that he then was, have realised that there was this risk of death as a real possibility?[49]

The task of the jury in such a prosecution is to have regard to all the evidence, including that relating to drink, in order to determine whether, at the material time, the accused had the requisite intent. The judge is not entitled to give an opinion on the evidence about the degree of the accused's intoxication. That is exclusively a jury question, and no more than one matter to be taken into account in considering all the circumstances when reaching a verdict.[50]

---

46 *R v Kamipeli* [1975] 2 NZLR 610 at 612.

47 Ibid at 616 (emphasis added).

48 [1990] 1 NZLR 540, (1990) 5 CRNZ 472 (CA).

49 Ibid at 545, at 476.

50 Ibid at 546, at 477.

9.2.1.2 *Evidential considerations*

Of course, the claim that D was too drunk to understand the consequences of his actions may usually be regarded with some scepticism. In any case where the defence of intoxication is raised by the accused but there is no evidence of intoxication which could reasonably be thought to have affected the accused's awareness or formation of an intent, a trial judge should so rule and thereby exclude drunkenness from the jury's consideration.[51] Equally, however, general principal would seem to require that wherever evidence of intoxication does arise in the course of a trial which may have a bearing on the question of the accused's intent or foresight, the defence must be put to the jury even where the accused has not pleaded it or even expressly disavowed it.[52] It is always a question of law to be determined by the judge whether there is sufficient evidence of intoxication for the matter to go before the jury

However, the question of the sufficiency of evidence of intoxication to raise the defence as a live issue should not be confused with the question of sufficiency of evidence of intoxication to justify an acquittal. Because intoxication is always a threshold question, it is quite possible that there will be enough evidence to persuade the jury that the accused was indeed intoxicated at the time she committed the offence but insufficient to persuade it that at the time the offence was committed the accused had not formed the intent necessary to constitute the particular crime. It has been observed on many occasions that the mere fact that a defendant was affected by drink so that she acted in a way that she would not have done had she been sober, will not assist her provided the necessary mens rea is present. As has already been remarked, "a drunken intent is nevertheless an intent".[53]

It is for the jury, using its common sense and experience of life, to discern (for example) whether a person using violence in a drunken state possessed an intention to kill.[54] In the absence of proof of such an intent manslaughter would be a proper verdict. However, intoxication is seldom the only relevant consideration and other circumstances, including the duration and degree of violence required to inflict extensive injuries or to cause death, may well weigh with a jury in finding a murderous (albeit drunken) intent proved.[55] So, in a situation where D, in a drunken state, attacks V with an iron bar, without any provocation on V's part, D's liability for the murder of V may well depend in practice as much on the nature of the assault as upon the fact of intoxication. If the assault is prolonged and deliberate, the jury may well conclude that its severity negates the claim that the killing was unintentional, despite D's

---

51   *R v Kamipeli* [1975] 2 NZLR 610 at 617 (CA).

52   See *R v Tavete* [1988] 1 NZLR 428, (1987) 2 CRNZ 579 (CA).

53   *R v Sheehan* [1975] 2 All ER 960 at 964, [1975] 1 WLR 739 at 744; and see *R v Doherty* (1887) 16 Cox CC 306 at 308: "A drunken man may form an intention to kill another, or to do grievous bodily harm to him, or he may not; but if he did form that intention, although a drunken intention, he is just as much guilty of murder as if he had been sober." (Stephen J)

54   *R v Tihi* [1990] 1 NZLR 540 at 546, (1990) 5 CRNZ 472 at 477 (CA).

55   Ibid.

intoxicated state. A single blow, on the other hand, may suggest an impulsive act in which an intention to kill is properly negated by evidence of heavy intoxication.

9.2.2 Capacity and intent

Some earlier judgments on intoxication appear to suggest that intoxication will justify an acquittal only if the accused is "incapable" of forming a required intent. In *DPP v Beard*, Lord Birkenhead said:

> evidence of drunkenness which renders the accused *incapable* of forming the specific intent essential to constitute the crime should be taken into consideration with the other facts proved in order to determine whether or not he had this intent.[56]

In *A-G for Northern Ireland v Gallagher*, Lord Denning made a similar observation, when he asserted:

> If a man is charged with an offence in which a specific intention is essential (as in murder, though not in manslaughter), then evidence of drunkenness, which renders him *incapable* of forming that intention, is an answer.[57]

However, in *Broadhurst v R*,[58] where the Privy Council was required to interpret an express provision in the Malta Criminal Code governing the defence of intoxication, Lord Devlin observed that the passage from *Beard* cited above "is not altogether easy to grasp". He went on to state:

> If an accused is rendered incapable of forming an intent, whatever the other facts in the case may be, he cannot have formed it; and it would not therefore be sensible to take the incapacity into consideration together with the other facts in order to determine whether he had the necessary intent.[59]

If a rigid standard for the defence of incapacity to form intent were insisted upon, it would be open to the criticism that an offender might be *capable* of forming the required intent yet fail *in fact* to form it. As the Court of Appeal observed in *Kamipeli*, if a rigid level of intoxication, such as incapacity, were to be insisted upon, that would result in the jury being deprived of its proper function of deciding on all the evidence, including that of intoxication, whether the Crown has in fact discharged its onus of proving mens rea.[60] For that reason, it is submitted, the Court of Appeal was right to hold that it is the *fact* of intent rather than *capacity* for intent which is the crucial inquiry.

This means that in a case like *Kamipeli*, an intoxicated offender may have known what he was doing when he attacked the victim, and may even have intended the attack. Nevertheless, intoxication will still be relevant to the essential questions, in a charge of murder, whether he either *meant* to kill, or meant to cause bodily injury *foreseeing* the risk of causing death.

---

56   [1920] AC 479 at 501, 502, [1920] All ER Rep at 29 (HL) (emphasis added).

57   [1963] AC 349 at 381, [1961] 3 All ER 299 at 313 (HL) (emphasis added).

58   [1964] AC 441, [1964] 1 All ER 111 (PC).

59   Ibid at 461, at 122.

60   *R v Kamipeli* [1975] 2 NZLR 610 at 614.

9.2.3 Intoxication and recklessness

When a statute fails to define the mental element required for a "true" crime it is generally held that either intention or recklessness will suffice.[61] Sometimes the statute will explicitly specify that recklessness is sufficient mens rea. We saw in ch 3 that New Zealand has traditionally regarded recklessness as a subjective mental state, requiring that the defendant actually foresee that the particular offence might result from her conduct. At the same time, it is clear from *R v Kamipeli* that the Court of Appeal anticipated that intoxication might in some circumstances exclude the mens rea for an offence that could be committed recklessly.[62] The implications of intoxication for recklessness, therefore, are straightforward: if D fails to foresee a risk of bringing about the actus reus because she is too drunk, she is not to be held reckless.

It is worth noting here that the House of Lords decision in *R v Caldwell*[63] would, if followed in this country, produce a different conclusion. In that case, the House of Lords held that when recklessness is sufficient mens rea, a person who damages property will be reckless as to the danger to life if she *actually realised* that there was a risk of danger, *or if she failed to give any thought to* the possibility of such a risk when the risk would have been *obvious* had she given thought to the matter. Consequently, in England it will be no defence that, because of self-induced intoxication, the defendant was unaware of the risk that would have been obvious to him if he had been sober.

Because *Kamipeli* predates *Caldwell*, it is possible that the approach taken by the Court of Appeal would not apply to any New Zealand offences for which the *Caldwell* definition of recklessness is sufficient mens rea.[64] However, as we saw in chapter 3, *Caldwell* appears to have no place in the law of this country. Unless a particular statutory context indicates otherwise, an express or implicit requirement of recklessness requires *actual awareness* of the risk in question.[65] It is very unlikely, therefore, that *Caldwell* will have any impact on the New Zealand law of intoxication.

9.2.4 Intoxication and mistake

In adopting a predominantly subjective approach to mens rea, New Zealand law has accepted as a cardinal principle of criminal responsibility that people are to be judged according to the facts as they believed them to be. As such, if D genuinely believed in a set of facts which, if true, would have made her act innocent, the cause of her mistaken belief ought, strictly speaking, to be irrelevant. Normally, the law does not inquire why D was mistaken, and

---

61 § 4.3.

62 [1975] 2 NZLR 610 at 617.

63 [1982] AC 341, [1981] 1 All ER 961 (HL). Discussed at § 3.2.1.

64 [1982] AC 341, [1981] 1 All ER 961 (HL). See Criminal Law Reform Committee, *Report on Intoxication as a Defence to a Criminal Charge*, Wellington, Government Printer, 1984, 15.

65 See Orchard, "Surviving without Majewski — A View from Down Under" [1993] Crim LR 426 at 427. See also *Hilder v Police* (1989) 4 CRNZ 232; *Taylor v Police* (1990) 6 CRNZ 470.

concerns itself only with the inquiry whether D was *in fact* mistaken; rather less frequently does it ask whether her mistake was *reasonable*.

Intoxication adds a complicating element to this inquiry because, arguably, a person who acts dangerously while voluntarily intoxicated is per se acting unreasonably, and ought not for reasons of public policy to be able to take advantage of a mistake made while in that state. This may be the reason why the English Court of Appeal has held that evidence of voluntary intoxication cannot support a plea of absence of mens rea by reason of mistake unless it negates a specific intent — even when the statute itself provides that the question whether there were reasonable grounds for a mistake is of evidential significance only.[66] Indeed, the general approach in England seems to be that if the defendant made a mistake of fact when intoxicated, such a mistake should be ignored, regardless whether the offence charged is one of specific or basic intent.[67] The approach is illustrated in *O'Grady*, where D's claim of self-defence failed because D had been drunk when he mistakenly believed he needed to defend himself. This seems a harsh outcome, in that it appears to deny the availability of an exculpatory defence on the basis that the accused ought not to have been drunk when he made the mistake.

The approach to intoxicated mistakes in New Zealand is rather different, although the standard of performance expected of a defendant varies according to whether the mistake is one about the *essential circumstances* (ie the actus reus elements), or about *some matter of defence*. The former can be illustrated with reference to the case of *R v Thomas*.[68] The defendant, having been drinking with friends, was driving down a suburban road in the early hours of the morning when she came upon what she mistook to be a police "beating up". In fact the police were attempting to effect a quite lawful arrest. The defendant investigated and intervened in the mistaken belief that the police were using excessive force. Upholding her appeal against conviction, the Court of Appeal held that her honest belief negated the mens rea required for a charge of obstructing a police officer in the execution of his duty. According to the defendant's honestly-held belief, the police were effecting an unlawful arrest, and therefore she did not intend "to obstruct the police while they were acting lawfully".

Concerning the second category, the general rule is that a mistaken belief as to a matter of defence will exclude liability only if it is based on reasonable grounds. So if D, mistakenly believing that his safety is seriously under threat from an imminent hurricane, breaks into V's house in order to take shelter, the

---

66 *R v Woods* (1981) 74 Cr App R 312, [1982] Crim LR 42 (CA). But compare *Jaggard v Dickinson* [1981] QB 527, [1980] 3 All ER 716, where it was held that if a statute expressly provides that some honest but mistaken belief is a defence, such a belief suffices even though it is induced by voluntary intoxication and the offence requires no specific intent.

67 Virgo, "Reconciling Principle and Policy" [1993] Crim LR 415 at 417.

68 [1991] 3 NZLR 141, (1991) 7 CRNZ 123 (CA).

defence of duress of circumstances will be unavailable unless, inter alia, D can point to evidence that his belief was based on reasonable grounds.[69]

Where an excusing mistake is required to be both honest and reasonable, D's voluntary intoxication will be relevant to the determination whether the mistake might actually have been made, but it will be disregarded in assessing the reasonableness of any such mistake.[70] The reasonable person is not drunk. Thus, in the duress example above, if D's mistake arises owing to his intoxication, his intoxication will be relevant to the issue *whether* he mistakenly believed his safety was being threatened. However, if a reasonable sober person would not have made the same mistake, D cannot call his intoxication in aid to explain *why* he made the mistake. Hence, unless there are other grounds for his belief, D will be unable to claim the defence.

There are exceptions to this rule governing defences, which typically arise from the statutory wording of specific defences. For example, where an accused person relies on a mistaken belief in relation to self-defence, the statutory definition of self-defence in s 48 Crimes Act 1961 justifies such defensive force as is reasonable "in the circumstances as the accused believes them to be". (Another example is s 24, governing compulsion.) This statutory formula overrides the general rule, and allows a defendant to rely on a mistaken view of the circumstances even when the mistake is attributable to self-induced intoxication; contrary to the position at common law.[71] Indeed, this was an alternative ground for the decision in *R v Thomas*, since (as the Court of Appeal recognised) D's mistaken belief that the police were using unlawful force also supported the justificatory claim of lawful defence of another under s 48.

9.2.5 Negligence and strict liability offences

Where the mens rea of an offence requires only negligence, rather than intention or recklessness, the approach of the law is similar to that taken to reasonable mistakes (above). Evidence of voluntary intoxication will generally be irrelevant, even in circumstances where the accused claims he was mistaken as to the strength of the alcohol consumed.[72] Once again, the reasonable person is not drunk, and the accused's intoxication is disregarded when determining whether his conduct is reasonable. The same rule applies to the defence of absence of fault in strict liability offences. This principle operates most commonly in the context of offences involving impaired driving, where it reflects the commonsense view that where intoxication is of the essence of the offence it would be contrary to public policy to confer impunity simply

---

69   *Kapi v MOT* [1992] 1 NZLR 227 at 230, (1991) 7 CRNZ 481 at 484 (HC); aff'd (1991) 8 CRNZ 49 (CA).

70   Orchard, "Surviving without *Majewski* − A View from Down Under" [1993] Crim LR 426 at 428. See also *R v McCullough* (1982) 6 A Crim R 274 (Tas CCA); *R v Clarke* [1992] 1 NZLR 147 (CA).

71   Cf *R v O'Grady* [1987] QB 995, [1987] 3 All ER 420 (CA).

72   See *MOT v Crawford* [1988] 1 NZLR 762, (1988) 3 CRNZ 163; *MOT v Strong* [1987] 2 NZLR 295.

because, as a consequence of intoxication, the defendant lacked the relevant awareness or intention to drive while impaired.

9.2.6 Intoxication and automatism

An area of some continuing uncertainty concerns the question whether a person who, through voluntary consumption of alcohol or drugs, becomes an automaton ought to be able to plead automatism as a defence to a charge based on absence of fault.

Automatism at law is action without conscious volition and connotes the state of a person who, though capable of physical movements, is not deliberatively able to control those movements.[73] As such, actions performed in an automatic state are generally said to be "involuntary", and normally attract no criminal liability. The ground for exculpation is twofold: (i) the accused lacks mens rea because she acted without intention or foresight, and (ii) she was not responsible for producing the actus reus because her acts (or omissions) were involuntary.[74]

While automatism, including intoxicated automatism, is a well-established ground of defence in respect of crimes requiring proof of mens rea, its status in the context of public welfare offences, and in offences where intoxication is of the essence of the offence charged, remains unclear. While in principle intoxicated automatism will deny the accused's responsibility for the actus reus, she may nonetheless be liable for her subsequent, involuntary, behaviour, on the basis that it was a foreseeable consequence of her becoming intoxicated beforehand.[75] If so, then although a general defence of "total absence of fault" is available to the accused, it will be difficult to establish given that she became drunk voluntarily.

9.2.7 Manslaughter

Another difficult issue is whether voluntary intoxication should be a defence to a charge of manslaughter. In England, the rule in *Majewski* does not permit evidence of self-induced intoxication to support a defence to manslaughter. This is because manslaughter has been characterised as a crime of *basic* intent.[76] However, this may be thought to be an unsatisfactory situation for two reasons. First, there is the general objection that it is possible to convict a defendant simply for bringing about the actus reus, even though intoxication prevented the formation of mens rea. Second is the more particular objection that manslaughter is itself a very grave crime that requires proof of an unlawful act

---

73   *Bratty v AG for Northern Ireland* [1963] AC 386 at 401, [1961] 3 All ER 523 at 527 (HL). See § 2.3.1.

74   It is accepted by the courts that intoxication may produce a state of automatism sufficient to excuse D from criminal responsibility. See, for example, *R v Cottle* [1958] NZLR 999 at 1007 (CA); *R v Kamipeli* [1975] 2 NZLR 610 at 612. In *Kamipeli*, intoxicated automatism was not discussed directly by the Court of Appeal, but is implicit in the direction of the trial Judge, who is not criticised on that point.

75   See §§ 2.3.3, 4.2.1.1.

76   See *DPP v Beard* [1920] AC 479 at 499, 500, [1920] All ER Rep 21 at 27, 28 (HL); *R v Howell* [1974] 2 All ER 806 at 810; *R v Lipman* [1970] 1 QB 152, [1969] 3 All ER 410 (CA).

(and often, in turn, mens rea) or, at least, that the offender acted voluntarily. Because of its seriousness, it seems odd to allow evidence of intoxication to reduce an offender's culpability for murder but not for manslaughter.

The position in both Australia and New Zealand remains unsettled on this point, although arguments from general principle would seem to favour allowing intoxication to support a defence to manslaughter. The decision in *Kamipeli* establishes the general principle that, on a charge of any criminal offence, evidence of voluntary intoxication may be relied upon to support a defence that the accused lacked a mens rea component required by the definition of the crime, or that she acted unconsciously. Prima facie, this principle would include manslaughter and not merely crimes requiring proof of intent or recklessness.

The general principle has also been endorsed by the majority in the Australian High Court decision in *R v O'Connor*.[77] In that case, D had stabbed a police officer in the arm. There was evidence that a state of voluntary intoxication, produced by alcohol in combination with a hallucinogenic drug, may have meant that D did not intend to act as he did. On appeal, a majority of the High Court refused to apply *Majewski*, and held that in the Australian common law jurisdictions, evidence of self-induced intoxication could support the denial of any requirement that conduct, circumstances, or consequences be intended, known, or foreseen; also of any requirement that the conduct be conscious and voluntary.[78] Further, the High Court endorsed the judgment of the Court of Appeal in *Kamipeli*, which had held that there should be no distinction between offences of "general" intent and offences where a "particular" intent was required, and that evidence of intoxication was relevant even if the mens rea requirement for the crime was only recklessness.[79]

In *O'Connor* itself, because of the existence of earlier common law authorities (pre-dating *Majewski*) to the effect that voluntary intoxication can never support an acquittal of manslaughter,[80] the High Court acknowledged that manslaughter may be an exception, albeit an "entrenched anomaly".[81] But in a more recent decision, the High Court of Australia has held that, because *O'Connor* establishes that evidence of intoxication is relevant in any case where it is necessary to prove the mental element of a crime, intoxication is therefore available to support an acquittal even of manslaughter in a case where the accused's conduct might have been involuntary.[82] It thus appears that in the Australian common law jurisdictions, evidence of intoxication will now support a defence of automatism in a prosecution for manslaughter; although, where the accused was not so drunk as to be an automaton, intoxication may

---

77 (1980) 146 CLR 64 (HCA).

78 See Orchard, "Surviving without *Majewski* — A View from Down Under" [1993] Crim LR 426 at 426.

79 [1975] 2 NZLR 610 at 614.

80 *DPP v Beard* [1920] AC 479 at 499, 500, [1920] All ER Rep 21 at 27, 28 (HL); *R v Howell* [1974] 2 All ER 806 at 810.

81 *R v O'Connor* (1980) 146 CLR 64 at 86.

82 *R v Martin* (1984) 51 ALR 540, Crim R 87 (HCA).

(anomalously) still be inadmissible to support a simple denial of the mens rea for manslaughter.

In New Zealand, the Court of Appeal in *R v Grice*[83] left open the question whether self-induced intoxication can ever support a defence to manslaughter. In *Grice*, D, who was intoxicated, had been fighting with his father. When his father continued shouting at him after D had threatened otherwise to "throw something", D threw a large bottle which struck his father above the left eye. The father later died as a result of the injuries he received. One ground of appeal against a conviction for manslaughter was that the trial Judge had been wrong in declining to put the defence of drunkenness to the jury. D sought to persuade the Court that there was a proper foundation in the evidence for an inference that, although conscious of what he was doing, D may have been so affected by alcohol that he did not appreciate the risk or intend to injure or frighten his father. However, this argument was rejected on the basis that, because D had threatened to throw something at his father unless he left D alone, there was an "inevitable inference" that D intentionally applied force directly to his father, which was sufficient to constitute assault and, in turn, the requisite unlawful act for a manslaughter prosecution.

However, when the decision is examined in the light of *Kamipeli*, decided 4 months later by a differently-constituted Court, it appears that the Court in *Grice* stated the wrong test in finding, as it did, that there was no evidence to go to the jury that D was "incapable of forming any intent" to apply force to his father. It is clear from *Kamipeli* that the proper inquiry is whether the accused actually possessed the relevant intent, not whether he was "capable" of forming the necessary intent. Accordingly, it is arguable that the Court of Appeal in *Grice* may have overstated the legal requirements when it concluded that there was no evidentiary foundation for a defence that drunkenness might have completely precluded D from *having any mens rea whatever*. In truth, D was not contending for such a broad proposition, but simply that he lacked the mens rea to make his act an assault (ie unlawful); for which, it could be argued, there was at least some evidence to enable intoxication to go to the jury.

On the broader policy question whether intoxication can ever be a defence to manslaughter, the Court in *Grice* ventured the very tentative view that "it *may prove to be* the law that, putting aside only rare cases of drunken stupor so complete as to result in automatism, intoxication can never be a defence to manslaughter".[84] However, this view finds support only from the broad proposition from *DPP v Beard*[85] that drunkenness can never do more than reduce the crime from murder to manslaughter. That this fails to adequately represent the current jurisprudence on the intoxication defence hardly need be stated, and certainly does not reflect the trend to expand rather than narrow the scope of exculpatory intoxication. However, the issue still awaits an authoritative ruling from the Court of Appeal.

---

83   [1975] 1 NZLR 760 (CA).

84   Ibid at 767.

85   [1920] AC 479 at 500, [1920] All ER Rep 21 at 28 (HL).

9.2.8 Involuntary intoxication — a new excuse?

In recognising defences, the law allows that, in very limited circumstances, D may be entitled to an acquittal if there is a possibility that although her act was intentional, the intent itself arose out of circumstances for which she bears no blame. Despite its hostility to voluntary intoxication, English law does extend this rationale to situations where D's intoxication was not deliberate. Hale observed that although drunkenness per se was no excuse because it was a "voluntary contracted madness",[86] nonetheless a person might be excused a crime if his intoxication was the result of the "unskilfulness of his physician" or "the contrivance of his enemies".[87] The principle is one which reflects "common justice".[88] Although there is little case law, it appears to be a settled principle that *involuntary* intoxication may be taken into account in determining the existence of a subjective mens rea.[89]

The distinction between voluntary and involuntary intoxication is, of course, irrelevant in New Zealand — where the law simply asks, whatever the reason, *did* D have mens rea? However, it is worth paying some attention to a recent case that suggests the possibility of an excuse-based defence of involuntary intoxication, which would be available even when D does have mens rea. The suggestion is made by the English Court of Appeal in *R v Kingston*.[90]

In *Kingston*, K, a paedophiliac homosexual, was invited by P to P's flat, ostensibly to discuss business matters. While there, he was given coffee laced with soporific drugs. He was then invited into a bedroom where a boy of 15, also drugged, was lying unconscious on the bed. K, at P's instigation, committed indecencies upon the boy. At trial, K's defence was that his actions, although intentional, had been done in a state of involuntary intoxication. The Judge directed the jury that they could convict if they were sure that despite the effect of any drugs he still intended to commit an indecent assault, because a drugged intent is still an intent. The Court of Appeal held that this amounted to a misdirection. Lord Taylor said:

> A man is not responsible for a condition produced "by stratagem, or the fraud of another." If . . . drink or a drug, surreptitiously administered, causes a person to lose his self-control and for that reason to form an intent which he would not otherwise have formed, it is consistent with the principle that the law should exculpate him because the operative fault is not his. The law permits a finding that the intent formed was not a criminal intent or, in other words, that the involuntary intoxication negatives the mens rea . . . [T]here must be evidence capable of giving

---

86 See 1 Hale PC 32. See also *Pearson's Case* (1835) 2 Lew CC 144, 168 ER 1108: "If a party be made drunk by stratagem, or the fraud of another, he is not responsible." (Park J).

87 Ibid.

88 *R v Kingston* [1994] QB 81 at 87, [1993] 4 All ER 373 at 378 (CA) (Lord Taylor).

89 See Smith and Hogan, *Criminal Law* (7th ed), London, Butterworths, 1992, 220, 228; cited with approval in *R v Kingston* [1994] QB 81 at 88, [1993] 4 All ER 373 at 378 (CA); also the UK Law Commission Consultation Paper No 127, *Intoxication and Criminal Liability*, London, HMSO, 1993, § 2.28.

90 [1994] QB 81, [1993] 4 All ER 373 (CA).

rise to the defence of involuntary intoxication before the judge is obliged to leave the issue to the jury. However, once there is an evidential foundation for the defence, the burden is upon the Crown to prove that the relevant intent was formed and that notwithstanding the evidence relied on by the defence it was a criminal intent.[91]

This excuse-based defence of involuntary intoxication, so formulated, is quite different from the defence of intoxication that we been considering in this chapter. As we have seen, the essence of ordinary intoxication as a "defence" is that evidence of intoxication is evidence from which a jury *may* infer that D lacked the mens rea for the crime charged (or, in an extreme case, that D was in a state of automatism). That is, mens rea may be absent because D, being drunk, did not form the required intent. The prosecution is judged to have failed to prove an essential element of the crime charged.

By contrast, where involuntary intoxication is pleaded it may be conceded that an intent is formed to do an act that would otherwise be criminal, but the intent is not attributed to the accused as mens rea because it is not an intent he would have formed had he not been surreptitiously plied with drink. Yet to say that an intent formed as a result of involuntary intoxication is not a criminal intent, or that involuntary intoxication negatives mens rea, is problematic. If an intent is present then a formal element of criminal responsibility has been established. Non-culpability must, therefore, be related to some factor other than the *absence* of mens rea. In *Kingston*, the Court of Appeal hinted that the true basis of exculpation is an analogy to the rationale underlying the defence of duress, although this is not developed in the judgment. If it is desirable as a matter of legal policy to excuse people who commit offences only because of the deliberate actions of other people, the theoretical basis and scope of such a defence needs to be clearly articulated.[92] It should be made clear that, in excusing a person who commits a crime while involuntarily intoxicated, the judgment of non-culpability relates not to the fact that no offence is committed, but rather that punishment in such circumstances is both pointless and unfair. We may excuse because of the commonsense recognition that anyone whose inhibitions may have been involuntarily taken away by the use of unsolicited alcohol or drugs might act with the same degree of disinhibition and commit an offence. It is, strictly speaking, a case of confession and avoidance rather than a claim that an essential element of the offence, namely mens rea, was lacking.

This approach to involuntary intoxication has two important consequences. First, it recognises the error of saying that a person who forms an intent that they would not have formed but for being plied with drink, does not have a criminal intent. If a drunken intent is still an intent,[93] then an involuntarily

---

91   Ibid at 89, at 380.

92   For discussion of one possible theoretical basis for the defence, see Sullivan, "Making Excuses" in Simester and Smith (eds), *Harm and Culpability*, Oxford, Clarendon Press, 1996, 131.

93   In the sense that it is no defence that intoxication removed the defendant's inhibitions and caused him to act in a way he would not have done when sober: *R v Sheehan* [1975] 2 All ER 960, [1975] 1 WLR 739 (CA).

induced drunken intent must also be an intent, albeit perhaps not one which the law regards as criminally culpable.

Secondly, its recognition as an excuse, of confession and avoidance, does not imply that involuntary intoxication should be an unqualified defence. Arguably, there must be limits to the extent to which conduct should be excused on the basis that D deliberately committed the crime only because P had laced his drink. Consider the following variant on the facts in *Kingston*. Imagine that, in addition to the indecencies committed, D also beat the boy with a baseball bat so that he suffered very serious injuries from which he nearly died. Should involuntary intoxication provide a defence? According to the theory of the defence as outlined by the Court of Appeal in *Kingston*, if the drink surreptitiously administered causes D to lose control *and to form an intent he would not have otherwise formed*, he is entitled to an acquittal because the "operative fault" is not his.[94] Yet this seems an outrageous result. While accepting that D intended, albeit drunkenly, to inflict a serious beating on the boy, this view would suggest that he may do so with impunity. In its decision, the Court of Appeal does not suggest that there is any limit to the operation of the doctrine.

The decision of the Court of Appeal in *Kingston* was overturned by the House of Lords,[95] which ruled, first, that the existence of mens rea is a purely formal question, and is not dependent upon whether the accused is blameworthy: an involuntarily-drugged intent is still an intent, and there is no distinction between "intent" and "criminal intent". Secondly, it held that there is no confession-and-avoidance defence of the type the Court of Appeal purported to recognise. Arguably, however, it is open to the New Zealand Court of Appeal to prefer the analysis of the English Court of Appeal to that of the House of Lords were such a case to come before our courts. Yet, without wanting to deny sympathy for one in Kingston's position, objections to recognising an "excuse" of involuntary intoxication are powerful.

First, it seems to strain credulity somewhat to suggest that *only* because a person was involuntarily subject to the effects of drink or drugs, did he deliberately commit a crime he would not otherwise have done. Arguably, the propensity to commit the crime *must already have been present*. The alcohol or drugs merely took away D's inhibitions that would otherwise have suppressed those propensities *on that occasion*.

Secondly, for the reasons outlined above, the defence must be subject to restrictions. There are many situations where a person is placed in a situation (eg temptation, duress) where, if she chooses to commit a crime, she may say that she would not have done so but for her being *involuntarily* placed in that situation. In our view, there is no practical way of drawing a boundary around which crimes may be excused, and under what circumstances. Therefore, in our view, the defence of *exculpatory* involuntary intoxication should be limited to those cases where, because of the effects of intoxication, mens rea is lacking so that the accused is entitled to an unqualified acquittal in any case where

---

94   *R v Kingston* [1994] QB 81 at 89, [1993] 4 All ER 373 at 380 (CA).

95   [1995] 2 AC 355, [1994] 3 All ER 353 (HL).

mens rea is an element of the offence to be proved by the prosecution. Where, however, the involuntary intoxication merely causes disinhibition such that the accused commits a crime he would otherwise not have committed, we submit that intoxication should not be a complete defence, but rather a factor to be considered by the court in mitigation of sentence. We do not believe that involuntary intoxication should be endorsed in New Zealand as an exculpatory defence which in some fictional sense negates mens rea in circumstances where clearly there was an intention to commit an offence, albeit drunkenly.

9.2.8.1 *Breath-alcohol offences*

"Involuntary intoxication" is sometimes also used in another sense in New Zealand. There is a line of cases, involving excess breath-alcohol offences, which suggests that a defence may exist where a person was unaware that she was consuming drink or drugs — the availability of the defence depending on whether the accused had notice of the possible effect of the substance, and whether she had an opportunity of avoiding its effects. However, because the offences concerned have now been formally classified as public welfare regulatory offences,[96] they are now governed by ordinary principles of strict liability. Thus the defence of involuntary intoxication, where it is relevant, will be available only where the defendant is able to prove (on a balance of probabilities) that she was totally without fault. Such a defence will not succeed where a person concerned knew, or ought to have known, that she was affected by alcohol.[97]

---

96   See *O'Neill v MOT* [1985] 2 NZLR 513.

97   Ibid. See also *Flyger v Auckland CC* [1979] 1 NZLR 161; *Rooke v Auckland CC* [1980] 1 NZLR 680.

10

Compulsion

The criminal law concept of compulsion, together with its cognate expression, duress, has been described as an "extremely vague and elusive juristic concept".[1] This may be partly because the defence has developed on an insecure theoretical footing and partly on account of imprecision in the use of definitions. For example, in legal literature the concept of compulsion may be referred to by a bewildering variety of expressions, and it is not always clear from the context in what sense the concept is being employed. The foundational notion of overbearing physical or psychological pressure may be implied in any of the following expressions: physical causation, physical compulsion, causal necessity, absolute causation, coercion, duress per minas,

---

1 *DPP for Northern Ireland v Lynch* [1975] AC 653 at 686, [1975] 1 All ER 913 at 931 (HL) (Lord Simon).

duress of circumstances, teleological necessity, and coactus volui.[2] Some of these expressions will be explained below, as the discussion proceeds. All represent different ways of conceptualising compulsion and show that there is a strong linguistic connection between compulsion and the related notion of necessity, such that the concepts are often confused in legal discussion. Necessity will be considered in chapter 11.

Although the expressions "compulsion" and "duress" are often used interchangeably in the case law, compulsion appears to be the expression first used in the context of overbearing threats which induce criminal action, and is the expression commonly used by common law commentators.[3] It is also the expression preferred by Stephen and, through his influence on the Draft Criminal Code of 1879, is the expression adopted in the Crimes Act 1961 and its antecedents.[4]

10.1 THE HISTORY OF COMPULSION

The law has, from a very early period, endorsed the view that a person is entitled to preserve his life and limb. The right is recognised and preserved in a variety of ways, including the statutory defences of compulsion and self-defence, and the common law defence of necessity. Contrasting somewhat with this rich palette, the statutory defence of compulsion is designed to provide relief from criminal liability only in fairly closely circumscribed situations in which an offender has been "forced" to commit an offence because of the overbearing threats or violence of another person. Moreover, it is clear that not every threat or situation of anxiety generating an apprehension of personal violence will raise the defence. The relevant threats must be immediately to kill or seriously injure the person claiming compulsion, and the person must apprehend a real risk that unless she cooperates the threatener will deliver on the threats.

As the law has developed, it has been established that compulsion is a defence only where the crime is not of a heinous character.[5] In particular, English common law has insisted — an insistence reflected in many modern statutory formulations of the compulsion defence — that the killing of an innocent person can never be justified.[6] This rule dates back at least to the writings of Lord Hale, who said:

> if a man be desperately assaulted, and in peril of death, and cannot otherwise escape, unless to satisfy his assailant's fury he will kill an innocent person then

---

2   Literally, "by his will but coerced".
3   See 1 Hale PC 49; 1 East PC 70.
4   See s 24 Criminal Code Act 1893; s 44 Crimes Act 1908; s 24 Crimes Act 1961.
5   Criminal Code Commission, *Report of the Royal Commission Appointed to Consider the Law Relating to Indictable Offences: With an Appendix Containing a Draft Code Embodying the Suggestions of the Commissioner*, London, Eyre & Spottiswode for HMSO, 1879, 43.
6   Ibid, and see s 24(2)(e) Crimes Act 1961; s 17 Canadian Criminal Code; s 94 Indian Penal Code; s 31 Queensland Criminal Code 1899; s 31 Western Australia Criminal Code 1902.

present, the fear and actual force will not acquit him of the crime and punishment of murder, if he commit the fact; for he *ought rather to die himself, than kill an innocent.*[7]

Many of the early cases involved offenders who sought to defend charges of treason on the grounds that the commands of an invading enemy or rebels backed by threats of force constituted compulsion. In a number of trials for high treason in 1746, the defence of the prisoners was that they were compelled to serve in the rebel army.[8] In these cases the law was fairly generous, and provided that the defence of compulsion applied not only to furnishing provisions to the rebel army, but also to joining and serving in that army.[9] Relief was nonetheless conditional:

> The only force that doth excuse is a *force upon the person and present fear of death* and this force and fear of death *must continue all the time the party remains with the rebels.* It is incumbent on every man who makes force his defence, to show an *actual force,* and that he quitted the service as soon as he could.[10]

New Zealand law does not require actual force as an element of compulsion because the defence, as defined in s 24, is concerned with *moral* force, ie with threats as opposed to direct physical force. However, the other elements in italics generally reflect present requirements of statutory compulsion.

Interestingly, although most of those who raised compulsion as a defence to treason must have fought in battle and killed, or at least assisted in killing, therefore presumably coming within Hale's "stern" rule, it was not suggested in earlier commentary that this made a difference.[11] Evidently the claims of compulsion in the context of treasonable rebellion were viewed differently by the courts to the gratuitous killing of innocent victims under compulsion.

On the other hand, the early cases were quick to recognise a distinction between a fear of destruction of property and a fear of death or injury as a basis for compulsion. In *M'Growther's Case,*[12] it was established that the fear of destruction of property was no excuse for joining with the rebels and that "the only force that excuses is a force upon the person and present fear of death". Why this should be so is not made clear. Nevertheless, it remains a feature of the law. It is not difficult to imagine that for some people the threat to destroy a valuable asset like a car or a building, or to destroy a beloved pet, unless the person complies with the compeller's commands may be, in many cases, as emotionally and psychologically overwhelming as a threat to injure the person herself.[13]

---

7   1 Hale PC 51 (emphasis added).

8   Criminal Code Bill Commission Report, 1879, 43.

9   Ibid.

10   Ibid (emphasis added).

11   Ibid.

12   (1746) Fost 13, 168 ER 8; cited in 1 East PC 71.

13   See *DPP for Northern Ireland v Lynch* [1975] AC 653 at 686, [1975] 1 All ER 913 at 932 (HL) (Lord Simon): "a threat to property may, in certain circumstances, be as potent in overbearing the actor's wish not to perform the prohibited act as a threat of physical harm."

M'Growther's Case also endorses the principle that it is for the accused to show that he quitted the affair as soon as he could. Although this also is not a requirement of the present law, the failure of an accused person to disengage from a criminal enterprise when the opportunity to do so is clearly presented, could be a factor considered by the jury in deciding whether the accused actually was under compulsion by threats of immediate death or grievous bodily harm at the relevant time.

The earliest non-treason case in which compulsion was admitted as a defence is *R v Crutchley*.[14] The charge involved a prosecution for malicious damage arising out of the threshing machine riots. The defendant had been compelled to join a mob and to give a blow at each machine that was broken. He gave evidence that he ran away at the earliest opportunity. Compulsion was admitted as a defence and D was acquitted. Regrettably, the report of the case does not include the direction to the jury, so it is impossible to know the nature of the compulsion.

Up until the early nineteenth century, the law of compulsion had developed exclusively in the case law and through the opinions of the commentators. By 1831, although the defence had been judicially extended to include malicious damage, neither judicial pronouncement nor legislative enactment had purported to make compulsion a defence of general application. It is, therefore, difficult to determine how the limitations subsequently placed on the defence were arrived at, since there was no clear agreement over the circumstances in which the defence should exculpate a defendant, other than an apparently general agreement that it did not apply to charges of murder, high treason, or robbery. The fact that the defence was not commonly encountered by the courts and, accordingly, had seldom been subjected to judicial scrutiny led Stephen to lament that "hardly any branch of the law is more meagre or less satisfactory than the law on this subject".[15]

When the Report of the Law Commissioners was published in 1879, it expressed a view of the scope of compulsion that was much more limited than earlier attempts at codification of the defence would have allowed. This may have been due to the influence of Stephen, who had prepared the Draft Code and considered that compulsion should only ever go to mitigation of penalty and not to excuse. (In this he may have been following the opinion of the Indian Commissioners in the first draft of the Indian Code, who preferred to make compulsion in *no* case a defence, and to have it merely as a ground for appealing to the mercy of the Government.[16]) Nevertheless, the view that a defence of compulsion should be codified prevailed and the Commissioners declared: "we have framed section 23 of the Draft Code to express what we think is the existing law, and what at all events we suggest ought to be the law". The proviso is apt; in adopting compulsion as a general defence and

---

14   (1831) 5 C & P 133, 172 ER 909.

15   Stephen, *History of the Criminal Law of England* vol II, Macmillian, 1883, 107, 108.

16   Criminal Code Commission, *Report of the Royal Commission Appointed to Consider the Law Relating to Indictable Offences: With an Appendix Containing a Draft Code Embodying the Suggestions of the Commissioner*, London, Eyre & Spottiswode for HMSO, 1879, 43.

extending the categories of excluded offences it cannot be said, as the Commissioners claimed, that the draft code accurately represented the then existing law.

It is true that this branch of the criminal law "lacks neatness and consistency",[17] which is largely attributable to the failure of early judges and commentators to articulate a clear theoretical basis for the defence and to draw clear distinctions between the generically related concepts of compulsion, necessity, and self-defence. The following discussion is intended to help clarify these distinctions, and to locate the defence of compulsion within a clearer theoretical framework.

10.2 THE THEORETICAL BASIS OF COMPULSION

The defence of compulsion operates on the basis of "confession and avoidance"; although the accused may have intentionally committed an offence, she is excused because her will or freedom of choice has been "overborne" by threats from another. Typically, a person claiming compulsion is told: "Do this [an act that would amount to a crime in the absence of a defence of compulsion] or you will be killed." In fear for her life, D does what she is commanded to do. At the heart of the defence is the motive of *fear* that certain consequences will occur if the threat is not obeyed. As such, the defence represents an exception to the general rule that motive is never an element of an offence.[18] It is the fact that an offender has acted out of a well-grounded fear in succumbing to illegal threats that provides the true basis of exculpation, since it is argued that anyone of like fortitude would have acted in the same way and, therefore, D should not be punished. Unlike defences which operate to negate *mens rea* (as in the cases of mistake and intoxication) or *actus reus* (as with the defences of involuntariness, automatism, and impossibility) compulsion provides a supervening excuse which negates criminal responsibility for an offence that prima facie *has been committed*. That is to say, in the case of compulsion, the elements of both *actus reus* and *mens rea* are in place, but criminal liability is overridden because D's choice to commit the offence was a constrained one. Exceptionally, therefore, motive may be regarded as an (exculpatory) element of an offence committed under compulsion.

Under English common law, the defence of compulsion is embraced under the name "duress per minas" ("duress by threats"). Traditionally this extended, as the expression suggests, only to threats made by another person. However, in recent years the English courts have recognised another form of duress, duress of *circumstances*; which also depends on the accused committing a crime out of fear, but in circumstances where there was no *person* demanding that she do it. The defence of duress of circumstances is still in its infancy in England, but in that jurisdiction it is developing by analogy to duress by

---

17 *DPP for Northern Ireland v Lynch* [1975] AC 653 at 707, [1975] 1 All ER 913 at 949 (HL).

18 See, for example, Smith and Hogan, *Criminal Law* (7th ed), London, Butterworths, 1992, 79: "If D causes an *actus reus* with *mens rea*, he is guilty of the crime and it is entirely irrelevant to his guilt that he had a good motive."

threats. It is thought that considerations of policy suggest that both defences should be governed by the same principles.[19]

In New Zealand, although the courts have also recognised the new defence,[20] the position is complicated by the fact that compulsion here is codified, while necessity, to which duress of circumstances is analogous, remains as a common law defence of uncertain scope. It may be that duress of circumstances will only be available in New Zealand to the extent that the threat which underlies the claim of duress does not issue from any human agency, on the basis that s 24 Crimes Act 1961 exhaustively defines the extent to which human agent threats are available as a means of exculpation.[21] This issue will be considered in more depth in chapter 11.

10.2.1 Involuntariness as an element of compulsion

It is sometimes said that a person who acts under compulsion acts "involuntarily". However, this is merely a shorthand way of saying that the threat *substantially impaired* the person's free choice, so that he acted purposively but unwillingly. Such a person, though doing an act under duress, may still act voluntarily. In the criminal law, many acts are done under pressure. This does not mean that there was no mens rea or that the act was not voluntary. With compulsion, the element of involuntariness lies in threats which "overbear the ordinary power of human resistance".[22] To say that D's will is "suppressed" or "overborne" in this context is not the same as saying that D acted involuntarily; because the latter would normally imply that D's will had not merely been overpowered but had ceased to be operative at any conscious level.

Furthermore, attributing involuntariness to acts done under compulsion makes it difficult to distinguish conceptually between conduct which is *constrained* (as with compulsion by threats) and conduct which is *driven* by a superior force (as in cases of physical causation). So we may properly say that D acted involuntarily when T, using superior force, shouldered D who in turn struck V, causing V to fall to his death from a narrow walkway. This is qualitatively different to E's claim to have acted "involuntarily" when he succumbed to P's threat to shoot him unless he drove the getaway car for an armed robbery. One person acts involuntarily; the other's choices are merely constrained by threats. Unlike the person "acting" while under physical compulsion (for example the person whose hand is held and directed by superior force to perform some criminal act), the person acting under

---

19 Smith and Hogan, *Criminal Law* (7th ed), London, Butterworths, 1992, 232.

20 See *Kapi v MOT* [1992] 1 NZLR 277, (1991) 8 CRNZ 49 (CA), affirming (1991) 7 CRNZ 481.

21 Ibid at 54, 55. Per Gault J: "When s 24 provides a defence of compulsion (or duress) where the criminal act is done under threat of death or grievous bodily harm from a person who is present when the offence is committed, we do not consider s 20 [Crimes Act] can be said to preserve a common law defence of duress by threat or fear of death or grievous bodily harm from a person not present."

22 *A-G v Whelan* [1934] IR 518 at 526 (CCA) (Murnaghan J).

compulsion is unable to say "I had no choice" (or, indeed, that "my conduct occurred outside my control"). The alternative to not committing the crime may have been extremely unpleasant, but it would be untrue to say there was no choice.

The nature of the choice that is exercised in cases of compulsion can be demonstrated in the following example. D is standing at the window of her room on the third floor of a 20-storey hotel. The hotel is ablaze and fire is threatening to consume her room. D may choose to stay in the hotel and almost certainly burn to death or she may jump, risking serious injury and possibly death. Her decision to jump is the result of a choice in which she weighs the dangers of remaining in the hotel against the risks inherent in jumping and concludes that the odds of surviving the fall are greater than remaining in the burning building. It is truly a choice between evils. Yet it is a choice. This type of invidious decision-making is sometimes referred to as "normative" or "moral" involuntariness, because it is typical of what anyone with normal fortitude could be expected to do under such terrible pressure, even though an ability to choose remains.[23] The heart of the compulsion defence is that no person should be *forced* by threats to have to make such awful choices and be held criminally responsible when they do.

In the case of compulsion it is, therefore, possible that the offender may *intend* to commit the prohibited act yet not *wish*, or desire, that it should happen. Compulsion is consistent with voluntary and deliberate action. What allows exculpation in such cases is not the fact that the accused acted involuntarily but rather the fact that the power of choice — axiomatic to the notion of freedom of the human will and to criminal responsibility — was substantially impaired.[24] However, as Smith and Hogan note,[25] a defence of compulsion should never be available where the prosecution is able to prove that the accused would have done the same act even if the threats had not been made. Where the accused's acts are attributable to other motives in addition to threats, the question that will determine the availability of the defence is whether he would have acted as he did but for the threats.[26]

10.2.2 Relationship between compulsion and necessity

In the development of the criminal law, compulsion has derived from, and is founded on, the same underlying considerations as the broader doctrine of

---

23   The notion of "normative involuntariness" has developed from Canadian criminal jurisprudence. See *R v Perka* (1984) 13 DLR (4th) 1, [1984] 2 SCR 233 (SCC). It is said that an accused whose offence is normatively involuntary cannot be said to be personally at fault because it "is axiomatic that in criminal law there should be no responsibility without personal fault": *R v DeSousa* [1992] 2 SCR 944 at 956, (1992) 76 CCC (3d) 124 at 134 (SCC) (per Sopinka J); discussed in *R v Langlois* (1993) 80 CCC (3d) 28 at 33 (per Fish JA).

24   *DPP for Northern Ireland v Lynch* [1975] AC 653 at 689, [1975] 1 All ER 913 at 933 (HL) (Lord Simon).

25   *Criminal Law* (7th ed), London, Butterworths, 1992, 233.

26   Ibid at 234. See *R v Valderrama-Vega* [1985] Crim LR 220; also *DPP v Bell* [1992] Crim LR 176.

necessity, which is concerned generally with conduct occurring under pressure of external forces or fear of death or serious injury. In *DPP for Northern Ireland v Lynch*[27] Lord Simon explained the close connection between the two concepts as follows:

> The only difference is that in duress the force constraining the choice is a human threat, whereas in "necessity" it can be any circumstance constituting a threat to life (or, perhaps, limb). Duress is, thus considered, merely a particular application of the doctrine of necessity.

In compulsion, the fear originates in threats from another person; in necessity, the fear originates simply from the situation in which the person is found.[28] Jurists distinguish two species of necessity:[29]

(i) "Absolute" necessity, where the conduct is the product of natural cause and effect and lacks voluntariness.

(ii) "Hypothetical" necessity, where the proscribed conduct is not determined by antecedents so much as by the defendant's own choice, yet where the ability to make a choice by free will is severely limited. In these situations it is not uncommon to characterise the choice as being effectively without volition or at least as a choice between evils, in that the defendant would never normally have chosen the course of conduct she did, apart from the overwhelming fear of the circumstances to which she was subjected.

Like the common law defences of duress and necessity, the statutory defence of compulsion falls within the second category, hypothetical necessity, because of its characterisation as choice between evils. A person acting under compulsion, though not lacking in intention and though "acting" with some measure of deliberation, is held not to be criminally responsible because the compulsion is deemed to override his responsibility for the actus reus and mens rea of the crime.

At common law, compulsion developed under the title "duress per minas",[30] as opposed to "coercion", which was a limited defence available to a wife who committed an offence while subject to the influence of her husband. In New Zealand there is no longer any presumption that a woman who commits an offence in her husband's presence was subject to compulsion by him. Some writers prefer to reserve the expression "compulsion" to situations of overpowering physical force, where there is arguably neither mens rea nor actus reus. However, this usage is inappropriate in New Zealand where the

---

27 [1975] AC 653 at 692, [1975] 1 All ER 913 at 936 (HL).

28 For a modern application of the defence of necessity, see *R v Martin* [1989] 1 All ER 652, (1989) 88 Cr App R 343 (CA). "Most commonly this defence arises as duress, that is pressure on the accused's will from the wrongful threats or violence of another. Equally, however, it can arise from other objective dangers threatening the accused or others" (at 653, at 345, 346) (per Simon Brown J).

29 The distinction is attributable to Aristotle, but has been recognised and applied by modern criminal jurists. See Aristotle, *Ethics* (Thompson ed) 77; also Hall, *General Principles of Criminal Law* (2nd ed), Indianapolis, Bobbs-Merrill, 1960, 419-421.

30 See § 10.1.

expression as used in statute is clearly limited to situations where D is constrained by threats to act as he does.

10.3 THE STATUTORY DEFINITION OF COMPULSION IN NEW ZEALAND

The defence of compulsion is defined in s 24 Crimes Act 1961, which states:

> Compulsion — (1) Subject to the provisions of this section, a person who commits an offence under compulsion by threats of immediate death or grievous bodily harm from a person who is present when the offence is committed is protected from criminal responsibility if he believes that the threats will be carried out and if he is not a party to any association or conspiracy whereby he is subject to compulsion.

The remaining subsections itemise the offences which are excluded from the operation of the statutory defence (subs (2)), and repeal the presumption of marital coercion (subs (3)). These will be considered later in this chapter.

As we have noted, the defence may be regarded conceptually as a species of necessity. However, it is distinguishable from other forms of necessity known to New Zealand law (chapter 11) which emphasise the inexorability of external forces. In particular, the statutory defence is concerned primarily with the verbal threats of human agents, although threats implicit in the *conduct* of persons present at the commission of a crime will also qualify, provided they have the consequences defined in the section.[31] However, the defence is not to be viewed as a general catch-all provision to assist offenders of frail personality who crumble at the slightest pressure and are especially susceptible to the threatening behaviour of others. Indeed, the provision has been tightly drawn to prohibit its use in all but the most exigent of circumstances. The Court of Appeal has said:

> The legislation provides a *narrow release from criminal responsibility where its strict requirements are met*. It reflects a policy decision that in those limited circumstances (and where the offence is not in the gravest category excluded from the application of the defence under s 24(2)) a person faced with the threat of immediate death or grievous bodily harm may properly be excused if he chooses the lesser evil of committing the offence.[32]

10.3.1 Battered women who commit offences under compulsion

Generally, mere fear will be insufficient to ground the defence if the strict requirements of the test are not satisfied.[33] The fact that the defendant may have been suborned in her judgment by a stronger, violent man whom she feared, will not provide evidence of compulsion in the absence of threats of the nature and quality contemplated by the Legislature. This has become an issue of some significance in relation to battered women who commit offences while ostensibly under a form of duress. However, the arguments in favour of

---

31 An analogy may be drawn with the cases on self-defence, in which context it has been held that threats to use physical power, as well as the actual use of physical power, are included in the notion of "force" within s 48 Crimes Act 1961. See *R v Terewi* (1985) 1 CRNZ 623 (CA).

32 *R v Teichelman* [1981] 2 NZLR 64 at 66 (CA) (emphasis added).

33 *R v Frickleton* [1984] 2 NZLR 670 (CA).

allowing compulsion in such circumstances are sometimes less than convincing and fail to support the case being contended for. For example, the view has recently been advanced in New Zealand that *every* action a battered woman takes is coerced because of the overwhelming need, in most aspects of daily living, to placate the batterer.[34] It is claimed that crimes (without apparent differentiation) committed by the abused woman are simply an extension of the same duress that leads her to cook the batterer's favourite meal or keep the children quiet.[35] That is to suggest that the whole matrix of a battered woman's life is one of coercion and that every offence committed by her, whatever its nature, is presumptively coerced. Clearly, such a claim is overbroad and unsupportable.[36] The fact is that the vast majority of women who might be classified as battered women do not commit crimes. Furthermore, even if there were evidence to support such a claim, it by no means follows that compulsion is a necessary element of every offence so committed. The acceptance of this argument would lead to the startling view that a person could claim global immunity from criminal liability for every criminal act committed by her (or him) on the basis simply of her status as a battered partner, regardless of the existence or otherwise of a proven causal link between the alleged offence and the fact of abuse. This raises the important question whether the law should be any more inclined to grant immunity to battered women who offend than to other oppressed and marginalised groups within the community who offend under pressure of need or disability, yet who are uniformly prosecuted for their offending (for example persons who shoplift to supplement their low incomes, substance abusers who steal or rob to support their drug addiction, or compulsive gamblers who commit serious fraud to support their gambling addictions). *That* is an important question, requiring careful debate. Yet prima facie, it may be thought that such special immunity as may be justified would be available only to crimes of violence *directed against the batterer*.

Where the facts of a case, involving the prosecution of an offence committed by a battered woman, raise the possibility of compulsion as a live issue, that defence ought to be put to the jury together with any other defence for which there is an evidentiary basis. However, the fact that the defence contains elements that ". . . cannot be easily satisfied by women who are abused"[37] puts battered women at no greater disadvantage than other defendants seeking to plead compulsion. As has already been noted the statutory defence of compulsion has been crafted within clear and precise limits in order to provide a "narrow release from criminal responsibility where its strict requirements are met".[38] If this is perceived to be unfair for battered women who offend, then it

---

34 *New Zealand Law Society Seminar: Women in the Criminal Justice System*, Wellington, New Zealand Law Society, 1997, 66.

35 Ibid.

36 Quite apart from the fact that the tenor of the claim runs contrary to the abolition of the marital coercion presumption by s 24(3).

37 *New Zealand Law Society Seminar: Women in the Criminal Justice System*, Wellington, New Zealand Law Society, 1997, 66.

38 *R v Teichelman* [1981] 2 NZLR 64 at 66 (CA).

is a statutory unfairness that can only be resolved by Parliament as a matter of law reform. Moreover law reform, if effected, ought to be based on an assessment of the specific needs of battered women — an assessment that ought not to be *avoided* by the pretence that the present, unspecific defence of compulsion is appropriate.

10.4 THE ELEMENTS OF COMPULSION

The scope of the statutory provision was examined by the Court of Appeal in *R v Teichelman*,[39] where it was noted that four ingredients were contemplated by the Legislature. First, there must be a threat to kill or cause grievous bodily harm. Secondly, the threat must be to kill or inflict that serious harm immediately following a refusal to commit an offence. Thirdly, the person making the threat must be present during the commission of the offence. Fourthly, the accused must commit the offence in the belief that otherwise the threat will be carried out. We will consider each of these elements in turn.

10.4.1 A threat to kill or cause grievous bodily harm

In *R v Teichelman*[40] the Court of Appeal, interpreting the phrase "immediate death or grievous bodily harm" in s 24, held that it is the "belief in the inevitability of immediate and violent retribution for failure . . . to comply with the threatening demand", that constitutes the gravamen of the defence.[41] In that case the accused, a drug dealer, claimed compulsion on the basis that a drug dealing associate had allegedly made threats to a third person to "blow [his] head off" if he refused to put him in contact with suppliers of drugs; and on the further ground that he "felt frightened" and thought the associate would attack him if he did not supply drugs. On appeal the Court held there was an insufficient evidential foundation for compulsion to be considered by the jury, in particular because there was no evidence, on any of the occasions the appellant had been requested to supply drugs, that threats had been uttered or "threatening gestures" made.[42]

The inclusion of "threatening gestures" in this context may be taken to imply that the requirement in the statute for "threats of immediate death . . ." will be satisfied where there is relevant threatening behaviour that causes the accused to believe that he will be subjected to inevitable and immediate violent retribution if he fails to comply with the threatening demand.[43] This is also consistent with the common law defence of duress per minas, which is taken to include "threats and *menaces*, which induce a fear of death or other bodily harm . . ."[44] In *R v Raroa*[45] the Court of Appeal confirmed that a threat need not

---

39 Ibid.
40 Ibid.
41 Ibid at 67.
42 Ibid.
43 Ibid.
44 Blackstone, *Commentaries on the Laws of England* (19th ed), London, Sweet & Maxwell, 1836, Book IV, chapter II, 30 (emphasis added).
45 [1987] 2 NZLR 486 at 493, (1987) 2 CRNZ 596 at 602 (CA) (Bisson J).

be in words for the purpose of s 24. On the other hand, it must still be a particular kind of threat associated with a particular demand. Therefore mere apprehension, leading an offender to feel "threatened" in some general sense, will be insufficient to satisfy the statutory test in the absence of a clear demand. Yet if D is faced with a large and intimidating aggressor holding a dangerous weapon in a menacing manner, the sense of threat and the felt need to comply with any implicit demand is likely to be as powerful as any imperious verbal command. It is proper that the law should acknowledge this in interpreting "threats". This approach may be further reinforced by the Court of Appeal's insistence, in *Teichelman*, that in the final analysis it is the accused's *belief* in the inevitability of immediate and violent retribution that determines the ground for exculpation, rather than the manner in which the threat is delivered. Despite this, in *Teichelman* itself the Court found that the highest it could reasonably be put on the evidence was that, because of the previous menacing conduct of the associate, the appellant felt that if he did not cooperate he would be in some danger. This, the Court found, fell far short of acting under a continuing threat of immediate grievous bodily harm as contemplated by the section.

The emphasis in *Teichelman* on the "strict requirements" of the statute would seem to require that the threats are actually aimed at forcing the accused to commit an offence. If "mere apprehension" on the part of an accused or an honest belief in non-existent threats is insufficient to provide a defence,[46] it may be difficult to contend that the defence ought to be available to a defendant who is not actually forced to commit an offence. In *R v Raroa*,[47] it was precisely because there was no evidence of any demand, accompanied by threats, having been made on the accused to assist in the disposal of two bodies following an execution-style killing that the Court of Appeal disallowed compulsion and dismissed the appeal. It is arguable that such a requirement is implicit in the insistence by s 24 that the accused act "under compulsion". However, this element was left unresolved in *R v Lamont*.[48] In that case, the appellant sought to defend a charge of causing death by careless use of a motor vehicle on grounds of compulsion (duress of circumstances). The alleged compulsion had been generated by another's car driving up behind him and maintaining a close proximity, in circumstances in which the defendant believed he was being chased and needed to take evasive action to avoid the "threat" of a collision. The Court did not consider it necessary to deal with the issue whether s 24 necessarily requires a "demand" element, because of the appellant's failure to provide any evidence of threats of, and a genuine fear of, immediate death or serious bodily harm. Compulsion (duress by threats) was, however, allowed in *R v Smith*,[49] where the accused, an intoxicated woman charged with driving with excess blood alcohol, had driven to escape her husband's threatened

---

46 Ibid at 494, at 604.

47 Ibid. See also *R v Dawson* [1978] VR 536, where the common law defence was held to be available only when threats were aimed at forcing the accused to commit an offence.

48 27/4/92, CA 442/91. See also chapter 11.

49 [1977] 6 WWR 16.

violence. However, the case is a doubtful authority because of the complete absence of discussion of the legal criteria considered by the Court in allowing the defence. As an oral decision of the Provincial Court it has little persuasive authority, and cannot be relied upon as an accurate expression of the law.

The "strict requirements" approach to interpreting s 24 precludes the acceptance in New Zealand of lesser threats, including threats of serious "hurt" to a person's "comfort", or threats to property,[50] since the statute expressly requires threat of "death or grievous bodily harm". It is now established that these words should be given their ordinary meaning of "really serious bodily harm" or "really serious hurt".[51] However, the words of the statute are sufficiently broad to include threats to inflict a person with a fatal disease and would extend to the situation where, for example, a person is threatened with the infliction of the AIDS virus either through an act of sexual violation or through a contaminated syringe, if he fails to comply with the demand made.[52] Since the expression "grievous bodily harm" now includes serious psychiatric injury,[53] it is arguable that the defence could be made out where there is evidence that an accused genuinely believed that the threatener had the power to inflict psychological devastation upon him unless he complied with the demand.[54] However, such an extension to the law has yet to be tested by the courts.

10.4.1.1 Implied threats and mistake

Under the present law, "mere apprehension" is not enough to give rise to the defence of compulsion.[55] The person must fear the particular type of harm set out in s 24. Often, this will involve proof of a verbal threat communicated to the offender. However, as we have seen there is at present no requirement that the threat must be communicated verbally.[56] At common law it could be express or implied by words or conduct. There is no reason to suppose that s 24 does not include implied threats, although such cases may provide more room

---

50 For a thoughtful discussion of the arguments in favour of allowing lesser threats see Aldridge, "Developing the Defence of Duress" [1986] Crim LR 433 at 435-437.

51 DPP v Smith [1961] AC 290, [1960] 3 All ER 161 (HL); R v Metharam [1961] 3 All ER 200, (1961) 45 Cr App R 304 (CCA); R v Mwai [1995] 3 NZLR 149 at 155, (1995) 13 CRNZ 273 at 280 (CA).

52 For a discussion of the general issues involved in this example see Kirby, "Legal Implications of Aids" in Legal Implications of Aids, Auckland, Legal Research Foundation, 1989, 3.

53 R v Mwai [1995] 3 NZLR 149 at 155, (1995) 13 CRNZ 273 at 280 (CA).

54 Such an extension of the defence would still not assist the defendant in Salaca v R [1967] NZLR 421 (CA), because his fear that "something might happen to me" would be insufficient to establish serious psychiatric injury.

55 R v Frickleton [1984] 2 NZLR 670 at 672 (CA). See R v Tyler (1838) 8 C & P 616 at 620, ER 643 at 645: "[fear of the other] has never been received by the law as an excuse for his crime."

56 See 1 Hale PC 51; M'Growther's Case (1746) Fost 13 at 14, 168 ER 8; Stephen, Digest, Art 10; also DPP for Northern Ireland v Lynch [1975] AC 635, [1975] 1 All ER 913 (HL), in which evidence of duress was allowed to go to the jury although there had been no express threat.

for disputing whether the threat was of the kind required by statute.[57] We have seen from *R v Raroa*[58] that a threat need not be in words for the purposes of s 24, notwithstanding that it must be a particular kind of threat associated with a particular demand. Consequently, it seems that threats implied and "inherent in the situation" in which the defendant found herself would support a compulsion defence, in appropriate circumstances.[59] This might include a situation where, for example, the threateners, who are present in the courtroom, have previously threatened the accused that she will be beaten up unless she gives perjured evidence.[60]

The difficulty arises when D makes a mistake. There are two types of mistake that may be made:

(i) A mistake about what T has done or said, so that D believes he has been threatened;

(ii) A mistaken inference that D is being threatened or is in danger, when the facts as D perceives them to be do not disclose a threat (at least, a threat qualifying under s 24).

The first variety of mistake might occur, for example, when D mishears T, and thinks that T has threatened to shoot him unless he commits a specified crime, when in fact T has merely asked D the time. Although at common law such mistakes must be reasonable to exculpate,[61] under s 24 a subjective belief is sufficient, and D will qualify for the defence of compulsion.[62]

However, in the second case, in the absence of a perceived *actual threat*, an honest (and even reasonable) belief that D is in danger will not be a sufficient basis for a defence of compulsion. The language of s 24 requires "threats of immediate death or grievous bodily harm", which excludes inferences based on non-existent threats.[63] If D mistakenly thinks there is an implied threat by T to shoot him unless D offends, that will be a mistake of the first variety and may exculpate. But if D merely infers a risk of danger to himself without thinking that he has expressly or impliedly actually been threatened in a manner qualifying within s 24, the inference falls within the second category and will not be compulsion.

An example of the latter case occurred in *R v Raroa*.[64] D was charged with being an accessory after the fact with murder, after he had assisted the killers to dispose of two bodies. Although the Court of Appeal acknowledged that "the accused was no doubt very frightened, frightened of what had happened and frightened of what he would see, frightened at the men who could have done

---

57 Orchard, "The Defence of Compulsion" (1980) 9 NZULR 105 at 112.

58 [1987] 2 NZLR 486 at 493, (1987) 2 CRNZ 596 at 602 (CA).

59 Ibid at 493, at 603.

60 See *R v Hudson* [1971] 2 QB 202, [1971] 2 All ER 244 (CA).

61 *R v Graham* [1982] 1 All ER 801, (1982) 74 Cr App R 235 (CA).

62 *R v Raroa* [1987] 2 NZLR 486 at 492, (1987) 2 CRNZ 596 at 602 (CA); *R v Teichelman* [1981] 2 NZLR 64 at 67 (CA).

63 *R v Raroa* [1987] 2 NZLR 486 at 494, (1987) 2 CRNZ 596 at 603, 604 (CA).

64 Ibid.

such a thing",[65] it endorsed the refusal of the trial Judge to allow a defence of compulsion:

> He was fearful of the possibility of harm because of what had happened and because they still had three shells left. He may even have gone [with the killers] because he feared what would happen if he did not but the law is clear that fear is not enough. To be excused under s 24 there must be a particular kind of threat and there is no evidence that there was in this case.[66]

Raroa then states — and tightly circumscribes — the law governing when D may claim the defence.

But it must be said that this is hardly a satisfactory position. If D accompanies T because, even in the absence of an actual threat, she reasonably fears for her life were she not to volunteer, her moral position is just the same as if she acts under a "compulsion" falling within s 24. Given that s 24 applies according to what D believed the facts to be, rather than what the facts are in reality, it would seem that the difference between a belief in implied threats and a belief in danger from non-existent threats is likely in many cases to be marginal. It is certainly doubtful that culpability should turn upon such a tenuous distinction.[67] Nor does it follow that "mere apprehension" (a fear that something may happen) is the same as an honestly held belief, however unfounded in fact, that something is presently happening. It is the *belief* in the imminence of the perceived threat, not its existence in fact, which prompts D's action, and which should determine liability. To allow an honest, albeit mistaken, belief in the existence of a danger to life and limb (even without actual threats) to support a compulsion defence, does not threaten the integrity of the statutory provision.[68] The defendant would still be required to discharge an evidentiary onus that she genuinely believed she was in such danger. Evidence of a belief that was simply the product of the defendant's over-anxious imagination or her unreasonable fears would be relevant to the issue whether or not the belief was in fact held. In the Canadian case of *R v Wilcox*[69] a mistaken belief in threats was accepted as sufficient. It has been suggested that this is the desirable conclusion, because the pressure on the accused is the same whether or not her belief is correct.[70]

10.4.2 Threat to kill or inflict harm immediately following a refusal to commit offence

In *R v Teichelman*[71] the Court of Appeal noted that s 24(1) requires a threat to kill or cause grievous bodily harm "immediately following a refusal to commit

---

65   Ibid at 493, at 602.
66   Ibid at 494, at 603.
67   See also § 10.4.4.
68   See *R v Williams* [1987] 3 All ER 411, (1983) 78 Cr App R 276, where it was held in the context of private defence that D should be judged on the facts as he believed them to be: "it seems inconsistent in principle to apply a different test for duress."
69   (1976) 38 CRNS 40.
70   Orchard, "The Defence of Compulsion", (1980) 9 NZULR 105 at 113.
71   [1981] 2 NZLR 64 at 66, 67 (CA).

the offence", and that the accused must offend "in the belief that otherwise the threat will be carried out immediately". It is not sufficient that the threat was "immediate" in the sense that it was made or continued at the time of the offence. It must also be a threat that the harm will follow immediately on non-compliance with the threatener's demand.[72] In *Salaca v R*,[73] a defence of compulsion was disallowed on a charge of bigamy because there was insufficient evidence that at the time of the ceremony of marriage the appellant was under compulsion of threats of immediate death or grievous bodily harm. S claimed he had bigamously married K because she had, some time before the ceremony, threatened that if he did not marry her she would get the witch doctor "to do something" to him, a threat which he believed. Despite the Court's decision, it may be observed that, while in many cases a threat that "something" will happen will not sufficiently suggest death or serious injury, in the circumstances of *Salaca* such harm might well have been impliedly threatened, at least in the accused's mind.[74] Orchard suggests that the facts of the case provide a good illustration of the desirability of rejecting any legal requirement that a mistake must be reasonable.[75]

At least in the context of the offence of supplying drugs, it is not necessary that the person making the threat be present from the making of the threat onwards while the accused does everything directed towards carrying out the offence up to its completion.[76] A threat antecedent to the commission of the crime will still support a defence of compulsion provided it continues as a threat of immediate violence at the time of the offence.[77] (In this context it is the actual supplying which is the essence of the offence and the critical time for the alleged threat to be operative.) Conversely, the mere presence of the threatener at the time of the offence will not establish compulsion in the absence of relevant threats.

In determining the immediacy of the alleged threats, it is impossible to ignore the accused's beliefs on the matter. Although *Teichelman* requires a belief on the part of the accused that she will be instantly killed or really seriously injured if she does not do what she is told, the question of when and how the threat will be executed is a question of fact and degree. This may mean that, although the accused believes the threat will be executed, it may not be necessary for her to believe that this is inevitable, or that she believes the threatened injury may not follow instantly but after an interval. This is the position at common law, as is illustrated by *Subramaniam v Public Prosecutor*.[78] The appellant had been charged in Malaya with unlawful possession of ammunition. He defended on the basis that he had been captured by terrorists and at all material times was acting under duress. The statute under which he

---

72 Orchard, "The Defence of Compulsion" (1980) 9 NZULR 105 at 113.
73 [1967] NZLR 421 (CA).
74 Orchard, "The Defence of Compulsion" (1980) 9 NZULR 105 at 113.
75 Ibid.
76 *R v Teichelman* [1981] 2 NZLR 65 at 66 (CA).
77 Ibid.
78 [1956] 1 WLR 965 (PC).

was charged required that the threats "reasonably cause the apprehension [of] *instant death*".[79] The Privy Council held that there was evidence of compulsion because the appellant had acted as a result of the terrorists' threats, who, although absent at the time he committed the offence, "may have come back at any moment".

It is possible that the accused may put a wrong interpretation upon the actions of those putting him under compulsion, or even attribute a time framework to events that may be completely misconceived. On this basis, an accused may either underestimate or overestimate the relative immediacy of the execution of the threats. However, it would surely be quite wrong to deprive him of the defence of compulsion because he thought there might be a small time delay in the execution of the threat when, in reality, he had no means of knowing the actual intentions of the threateners. What is important is that he believed the threats were imminent, and that they were compelling.

At common law there is no requirement for a threat of "immediate" harm. Threats of future harm suffice where their effect is to neutralise the accused's freedom of choice at the time of the offence. In *R v Hudson*,[80] the defendants, two young women, were charged with perjury by not identifying W at his trial on a charge of wounding. They admitted their evidence was false, but claimed compulsion on the grounds of having been threatened that they would be "cut up" if they testified against W. The threat was reinforced by the presence of a man in the public gallery who had a reputation for violence and was one of the group who had threatened them. The Court, following *Subramaniam*, held that the Recorder was wrong in ruling that as a matter of law the threats were not sufficiently present and immediate to support the defence of duress, and found that it should have been left to the jury to decide whether the threats had overborne the will of the appellants at the time they gave their evidence. The Court said:

> When ... there is no opportunity for delaying tactics, and the person threatened must make up his mind whether he is to commit the criminal act or not, the existence at that moment of threats sufficient to destroy his will ought to provide him with a defence even though the threatened injury may not follow instantly but after an interval.[81]

Whether this common sense view represents the New Zealand position may be doubted. The problem is the requirement of threats of *immediate* death. On the face of it, this would appear to exclude the defence if the accused knows that a significant time must elapse before the harm is inflicted. Yet if the requirement of strict immediacy is insisted upon in such a case, it would mean that compulsion will never be a defence to oral perjury, even though that is not an offence listed in s 24(2).[82] A possible solution is to ask: "what does the Legislature seek to achieve in its insistence on the immediacy of the threat?" A

---

79   Section 94 Malay Penal Code (emphasis added).

80   [1971] 2 QB 202, [1971] 2 All ER 244 (CA).

81   Ibid at 207, at 247.

82   Orchard, "The Defence of Compulsion" (1980) 9 NZULR 105 at 114.

plausible answer is that what is being aimed at is an assurance that the threat be "present" in the sense that it is effective to neutralise the free will of the accused at the relevant time. If the real issue is the effectiveness of the threat on the accused's mind, and that is certainly the moral crux of the matter, then it cannot matter whether she believes it will be carried out immediately upon non-compliance or after an interval, provided she believes it *will* be carried out and has complied because of that belief.

However, for the meantime the issue would seem to have been put beyond debate by the decision of the Court of Appeal in *R v Joyce*.[83] There the accused, who had been charged with assault with intent to rob under s 237 Crimes Act 1961, gave evidence that at the time the robbery was attempted he had been compelled by threats to keep watch in the street, although he was not physically proximate to the perpetrator of the offence. Citing as authority the Canadian decision of *R v Carker (No 2)*[84] the Court held that the evidence did not disclose threats of "immediate" death or grievous bodily harm from a person present[85] when the appellant did the acts which made him a party to the offence, and held that compulsion had properly been withdrawn from the jury by the trial Judge.

10.4.2.1 *Failure to seek protection*
A related problem for the development of New Zealand law, which emerges from the *Hudson* case, the fact that the Court held that failure to seek the protection of the Court and the police was not a bar to the offence, unless the jury decided that the accused had failed to take an opportunity to render the threat ineffective which was "reasonably open to him".[86] In determining whether there was such opportunity the jury should have regard to the accused's age and circumstances and to any risks to him involved in the course of action relied upon.[87]

It has been suggested that because of the terms of s 24(1), as interpreted in *Teichelman*, such an approach is not possible in New Zealand.[88] However, it is not clear why this should be so. The *Teichelman* decision does not actually address the issue of failure to seek protection, and although the case insists that the statute only provides a basis for excuse where its "strict terms" are met, there is nothing in the common law position on the point that appears directly to contradict the *Teichelman* strictures. It is arguable that failure to seek protection in circumstances where that was possible should be a factor that a jury may consider in determining whether the accused really believed in the efficacy of the threats giving rise to the defence of compulsion (ie that she was

---

83   [1968] NZLR 1070 (CA).

84   [1967] SCR 114, (1968) 2 CRNS 16 (SCC).

85   Although the lack of "presence" of the threatener may be a ground for distinguishing Joyce, as we shall see (when discussing the requirement for presence below, § 10.4.3) the tenor of the decision essentially precludes that possibility.

86   *R v Hudson* [1971] 2 QB 202 at 207, [1971] 2 All ER 244 at 247 (CA).

87   Ibid.

88   Adams § CA24.11.

truly faced by the immediate threat of death), but it should not of itself be a reason for refusing to allow compulsion to go to the jury, if this is what is being suggested. We shall consider this issue in more detail below (§ 10.4.5.1).

10.4.3 Person making threats present during commission of offence

As was noted above, *R v Joyce* is authority for the proposition that threats must come from a person who is actually present at the time of the commission of the offence and in a position to execute the threats. When D said he wanted to withdraw from the planned robbery on becoming aware that P proposed to use a rifle to achieve his object, P threatened to shoot D if he did not continue with the arrangement. In complying with the threat, D had gone with P to the garage. While P went inside and committed the robbery, D remained outside as a lookout. In this capacity as a party to the robbery, D prima facie committed the offence for which he claimed compulsion. Moreover, it was held that because at the time D was offending he was on the street while P was inside, compulsion necessarily failed. It could not be said that D was being threatened with "immediate" harm from a person who was "present". This was decided on the basis that there was no evidence of any threat of immediate death or grievous bodily harm once P left D on the street and entered the building to carry out the robbery. The Court reached this strict interpretation of the meaning of "presence" after reviewing the relevant provisions of the earlier Codes and noting that the word "actually" had been deleted from the original phrase "a person *actually* present" when the provision was re-enacted in 1961. The Court said:

> In our poinion [sic] . . . there is no justification for concluding that the Legislature in making this amendment intended to include as a good defence anything less than threats by a person actually present when the accused committed such acts as were alleged against him, for the very object of the section is to provide a defence to persons who commit offences under "immediate" threats of death or grievous bodily harm from persons who are in a position to execute their threats.[89]

The implicit limitation of the meaning of "present" to physical presence only was affirmed by the decision in *Teichelman*,[90] where the Court of Appeal said:

> there must be evidence of a continuing threat of immediate death or grievous bodily harm made by a person who is present while the offence is being committed and so is in a position to carry out the threat or have it carried out *then and there*.[91]

While the meaning of "present" now seems clear, the strict insistence on physical proximity is likely to produce anomalies in future applications of the rule. For example if, assuming the facts in *Joyce*, D had been present inside the service station so that P was clearly in view and capable of carrying out the threat when P committed the robbery, the presence requirement would have

---

89   [1968] NZLR 1070 at 1077 (CA).
90   [1981] 2 NZLR 64 (CA) (emphasis added).
91   Ibid at 67.

been satisfied and D would have had a defence of compulsion. But what if D was standing on the threshhold of the door to the service station, so that in theory he could have fled and avoided the operation of P's threats. Would he still have a defence of compulsion? Or, to take the scenario a step further, what would be the position if the service station room in which D and P were "present" was divided by a large fixture separating the door and D from the counter where the robbery occurs. In the physical circumstances which pertain, P would be prohibited by the obstruction of the fixture from shooting D if he decided to execute the threat in the event of D's sudden departure. Can we say P is "present" in these circumstances for the purpose of conferring a defence of compulsion on D?

Alternatively, and perhaps more importantly, what if D is a person who is psychologically weak and easily intimidated and more likely to submit to and to be held in thrall by threats of death or injury, even where the law insists that the threatener was not "present" at the relevant time? Since the standard for belief in the carrying out of the threats is subjective and the belief itself need not be reasonable,[92] it must matter that the accused believed that the threatener was effectively "present" and able to carry out the threats even if the requirements of strict physicality of presence cannot be met. In these circumstances, a concept of "constructive" or "psychological" presence may be better able to do justice to defendants who find themselves in situations of compulsion, without seriously damaging the "strict requirements" test. Moreover, such a concept would give some effect to the Legislature's deletion, in 1961, of "actually" from the requirement of presence under s 24.

At common law there is no requirement that the threatener be "actually" present, and a notion of "constructive" presence appears to undergird the relevant case law. In *R v Williamson*[93] the appellant was charged with being an accessory after the fact to murder. The murder had occurred on a Wednesday and W was threatened with death unless he helped to dispose of the body, which he did on the following Sunday. W claimed that throughout the intervening 4-day period the original threat remained operative. He was under constant pressure to comply by the persons who had issued the original threat and, while they had left him alone for most of the period, they had visited him from time to time to reiterate the threat. The New South Wales Court of Appeal held that the issue of duress should have been left to the jury even though the threateners were "not actually present and in a position to execute the threats".

A case in which the parameters of "constructive" presence are more clearly identified is the South Australian case of *Goddard v Osborne*.[94] There a wife, who claimed she was acting under duress from her husband, attempted to obtain a welfare benefit by presenting false documents, while her husband remained outside in the street. The Supreme Court held that the wife was entitled to an acquittal by reason of duress *and* the statutory defence of marital coercion,

---

92   *R v Raroa* [1987] 2 NZLR 486 at 491, (1987) 2 CRNZ 596 at 600 (CA); also §§ 10.4.1, 10.4.1.1.

93   [1972] 2 NSWLR 281.

94   (1978) 18 SASR 481.

which required that the offence be committed "in the presence of" the husband. It was held that the husband was "present" if he was "close enough to influence the wife into doing what he wants done, even if he is not physically present in the room".[95] It has been noted that such constructive presence was probably sufficient to raise the common law presumption of marital coercion, and in view of the deletion of the word "actually", that it should be enough for the purposes of compulsion in s 24.[96]

Despite all this, it seems that the New Zealand courts will continue to insist that "actual presence" is required, and at the present time it is an apparently inescapable feature of New Zealand law that nothing less than the physical presence of the threatener in close proximity to the accused or the ability, in an exceptional case, of instantly executing the threat from a distance, will suffice.[97] This interpretation of the New Zealand position is reinforced by the gloss in *Teichelman*, suggesting the necessary capacity of the threatener to carry out the threat "then and there".

10.4.3.1 *Threats to others apart from the accused*

A remaining area of difficulty regarding the statutory requirement for the person making the threat to be "present" is the change of wording in the 1961 Act from "a person actually present at the commission of the offence" to "a person who is present *when the offence is committed*". While this formula does not specify *where* the person must be present, *Joyce* clearly requires that the threatener be present with the accused when he offends. However, it is not so clear what "present" means when the accused is subject to threats that *others* will be harmed if compliance is not forthcoming. If presence of the threatener with the accused *alone* is insisted upon, that would appear to exclude from the defence those situations where a threat is made to injure a third party, but in circumstances where the threatener is capable of executing the threats even though the putative victim is at a distance from where the offence will be carried out. The issue arose in *R v Hurley*,[98] where the two appellants claimed to have acted under the duress of two escaped prisoners who had threatened to kill the de facto wife of one of them if the appellants did not comply with their demands. At the time the threats were operative the appellants were physically separated from the threateners by a substantial distance, so that the threateners could not be said to be present when the offence of being accessories after the fact to the felony of escape was committed. In a dissenting judgment Smith J outlined the circumstances in which threats to third parties would suffice for the purposes of a defence of duress. His Honour held that a threat made known to the accused to kill or do grievous bodily harm to any human being can be sufficient to found a defence of duress.[99] Thus the doctrine could apply to

---

95 Ibid at 493.
96 Orchard, "The Defence of Compulsion" (1980) 9 NZULR 105 at 116.
97 Orchard suggests that such an exceptional case might be where the threat can be instantly executed; where, for example, a rifle is aimed at the accused from a distance. Ibid at 116.
98 [1967] VR 526 at 543.
99 Ibid (Smith J).

threats against people the accused loves, including, but not limited to, his wife or child, and, equally, to a case where armed men, having taken possession of a house, retain a hostage whom they threaten to kill if their demands are not met.[100]

Applying these dicta, it is arguable that "present" in s 24 may be interpreted to include threats against the accused or someone else, whether or not related to the accused. However, if a strict or "natural" interpretation of s 24(1) is insisted upon, it may seem to require that only threats against an accused will suffice. However, such an approach appears to go against both logic and commonsense and would seriously disadvantage genuine defendants whose only reason for complying with the demands of criminals is to protect innocent parties whose lives are threatened in the event of non-compliance.

In order to deal with this issue, the Crimes Bill 1989 proposed to substitute for the phrase "a person who commits an offence" in s 24(1), the phrase "to that person *or any other person*".[101] The substituted phrase would resolve a question currently left at large in the judicial interpretation of s 24. The proposed solution would bring New Zealand law into conformity with the common law approach, and would endorse the decision in *Hurley* which, it has been suggested,[102] would extend the protection of compulsion to D's family and others to whom he owed a duty and, possibly, even to a complete stranger. Threats that a person held as a hostage would be killed if D did not participate in the crime would, on this view, suffice.

It makes good sense that threats communicated to the accused, regardless of whom they are aimed at, should suffice for the purposes of compulsion. This is consistent with the fact, as one commentator has observed, that the degree of pressure to which the accused is subjected does not necessarily depend upon the identity of the proposed victim, and that when another is threatened the defence has more merit because the element of self-preservation is absent.[103] However, the matter has not yet been directly considered by a New Zealand court and, in the absence of statutory reform, we await an authoritative ruling on the matter.

10.4.4 Belief that the threat will be carried out

The fourth critical feature of statutory compulsion identified in *Teichelman* is that the accused must commit the offence in the belief that otherwise the threat will be carried out. This raises a difficult issue, regarding the nature of the accused's belief.

In *Teichelman*, the Court of Appeal characterised the required belief as "belief in the inevitability of immediate and violent retribution for failure . . . to comply with the threatening demand".[104] In New Zealand there is no requirement that the accused's belief be subject to an objective test of whether a

---

100 Ibid.

101 Clause 31(1) Crimes Bill 1989 (emphasis added).

102 Smith and Hogan, *Criminal Law* (7th ed), London, Butterworths, 1992, 238.

103 Ibid.

104 *R v Teichelman* [1981] 2 NZLR 64 at 67 (CA).

person of reasonable firmness of character could have been expected to resist the threat, as is the position at common law.[105] However, it has been held that although an objective test is not open in New Zealand because the wording of s 24 specifically refers to the belief of the accused, thereby requiring a subjective test, a question of fact still arises as to whether the belief is genuinely held. This must be negated by the prosecution beyond reasonable doubt.[106] Whether such a belief is reasonable or well-grounded will be relevant to the question whether it was genuinely held.[107]

This would seem to suggest that an accused may unreasonably believe that he is facing inevitable and immediate violence if he does not comply with the threatener's demands, even if a sober person of reasonable firmness, sharing the accused's characteristics, would not have acted in the same way. On the face of it this is a rule that an accused is to be judged on the basis of what he actually believed and what he actually feared.[108] Consider the following example:

> T, in D's presence, points a shotgun and shoots and kills V. She then waves the shotgun in the air while performing a dance around V's body. Next, she turns to D and asks him to help dispose of the body. D, who is an associate of T but had no part in or knowledge of the intended shooting, forms the belief that if he doesn't comply T may shoot him also. In the circumstances, should D have a defence of compulsion if he then assists T with disposal of the body?

According to the strict application of a subjective test the answer must be "yes": he is to be judged according to the facts as he believed them to be. If D honestly believed that he was under a threat of death if he failed to comply with T's request, he should be excused. It is not necessary to ask whether a person of reasonable firmness could have been expected to resist. The only question should be, what did D believe? However, it is clear that when we examine the actual approach taken by the courts to the "subjective" test its efficacy seems to evaporate.

Consider the example above. It is instructive to ask, "how does one characterise the 'threat'"? Is it primarily an implied threat that D honestly believed to exist, or is it simply a "non-existent" threat? As we saw above in § 10.4.1.1, if it is a "non-existent" threat then it cannot assist D, however earnestly he believes in its existence, because a non-existent threat cannot give rise to compulsion under s 24.[109] If, on the other hand, the case is characterised as an implied threat which D honestly believed to exist, how is that state of mind different from "mere apprehension" that unless he co-operates he will be shot? "Mere apprehension", unaccompanied by the type of threat set out in s 24, is similarly not enough to raise a defence of compulsion.[110]

---

105 See *R v Howe* [1987] AC 417 at 426, [1987] 1 All ER 771 at 775 (HL) (Lord Hailsham).

106 *R v Raroa* [1987] 2 NZLR 486 at 492, (1987) 2 CRNZ 596 at 602 (CA).

107 Ibid.

108 Smith and Hogan, *Criminal Law* (7th ed), London, Butterworths, 1992, 240.

109 *R v Raroa* [1987] 2 NZLR 486 at 494, (1987) 2 CRNZ 596 at 603 (CA).

110 See *R v Frickleton* [1984] 2 NZLR 670 at 672 (CA); *R v Raroa* [1987] 2 NZLR 486 at 494, (1987) 2 CRNZ 596 at 603 (CA).

Because non-existent threats — even if D honestly believes himself to be "threatened", in the sense of being in danger — are excluded from the operation of compulsion, the utility of the subjective standard in s 24 must be in doubt. It is arguable that in refusing to allow compulsion to operate in purely subjective circumstances the New Zealand courts have determined that the defence be "shackled" by requirements that are relevant to only the most obvious, but less likely, forms of compulsion, requirements which fail to recognize that there are many subtle forces by which people are compelled to betray their own will, including their own subjective fears.[111]

10.4.5 Further restrictions on the defence

10.4.5.1 *Opportunity to escape*

At common law the defence will fail if the accused did not avail herself of an opportunity which was reasonably open to her to render the threat ineffective.[112] However, this requirement is qualified by the further rule that it is essentially a jury question whether the accused had a reasonable opportunity to render the threat ineffective.[113] In determining this question, the jury may have regard to other factors including the offender's age and circumstances, and the ability of the police to provide effective protection. In *Goddard v Osborne*[114] the Supreme Court of South Australia was unimpressed by the fact that the wife could have called the police or sought the help of an official in the Social Services Department by whom she was being interviewed. It accepted that seeking such protection could have terminated the accused's marriage, but concluded that a court should not have to require a wife to terminate her marriage in order to escape bodily injury and compulsion. Thus, the preservation of marriage was seen to be a consideration relevant to the question whether the accused could reasonably have avoided committing the offence.

Section 24 makes no reference to the accused having a "safe avenue of escape" or a means of "seeking effective protection", and the strict terms of the section would seem to militate against importing into the statute a further qualification which Parliament has not seen fit to impose.[115] It is, therefore, arguable that the statutory test is less rigorous in this regard than the common law. However, it appears that this may have little effect in practice, because the necessity for actual threats, and the requirements of immediacy and presence, will operate to exclude the defence where there is a reasonable chance of escape.[116]

---

111 See Coolican, "Compulsion and duress as an excuse for the commission of a criminal offence" (1966) 2 CRNS 21 at 28.

112 *R v Hudson* [1971] 2 QB 202, [1971] 2 All ER 244 (CA).

113 Ibid.

114 (1978) 18 SASR 481.

115 See Orchard, "The Defence of Compulsion (1980) 9 NZULR 105 at 117.

116 Ibid.

Some clarification of these requirements has been achieved in *R v Raroa*.[117] In proposition 3 of the trial Judge's summary of the statutory requirements it was stated that there must be, inter alia, "no chance of escape".[118] The inclusion of this phrase in the required elements, together with the requirement in proposition 2 that "there is no opportunity of seeking help or protection", were challenged by the defence on the grounds that they were unnecessary restrictions upon the application of s 24 and that they were restrictions that did not appear in *Teichelman* when the Court of Appeal outlined the "critical features" of s 24(1). It was submitted that their inclusion, were they to be regarded as "elements" of compulsion, might be taken to mean that if there is an opportunity of seeking help or protection the claim that one was acting under compulsion might be rejected.

In dealing with this issue, Bisson J referred to *DPP for Northern Ireland v Lynch*,[119] in which Lord Morris had cited with approval a statement of the Court of Appeal in *Hudson*:

> it is always open to the Crown to prove that the accused failed to avail himself of some opportunity which was reasonably open to him to render the threat ineffective, and that upon this being established the threat in question can no longer be relied upon by the defence. In deciding whether such an opportunity was reasonably open to the accused the jury should have regard to his age and circumstances, and to any risks to him which may be involved in the course of action relied upon.[120]

His Honour concluded that whether there is a "continuing threat" when there is an opportunity of seeking help or protection or of escaping is a question of fact in each case, the answer to which is relevant to the accused's belief.[121] That is to say, if D recognises the existence of a viable escape route, then his beliefs may not disclose a continuing threat sufficient to qualify as compulsion within s 24. This means that under New Zealand law the stricture suggested in *A-G v Whelan*,[122] that "if there were reasonable opportunity for the will to reassert itself, no justification can be found in antecedent threats", and the suggested limitation of the trial Judge in *Raroa* that "there is no opportunity of seeking help or protection", are not to be taken as absolute requirements of the defence of compulsion, but only as factors to be taken into account by a judge or jury in determining the belief of the accused.[123] However, this qualification will not alter the practical reality that, in the majority of cases, if the accused clearly had a chance of escape or ability to seek protective custody, the efficacy of "immediate" threats and the threatener's "presence" will be called seriously into doubt.

---

117 [1987] 2 NZLR 486, (1987) 2 CRNZ 596 (CA).

118 Ibid at 490, at 600.

119 [1975] AC 653, [1975] 1 All ER 913 (HL).

120 Ibid at 675, at 922.

121 *R v Raroa* [1987] 2 NZLR 486 at 491, (1987) 2 CRNZ 596 at 601 (CA).

122 [1934] IR 518 at 526 (CCA).

123 *R v Raroa* [1987] 2 NZLR 486 at 491, (1987) 2 CRNZ 596 at 601 (CA).

10.4.5.2 *Parties to conspiracies or associations*

A further restriction on the operation of the compulsion defence is the provision in s 24 that the defence will be available only if an accused person "is not a party to any association or conspiracy whereby he is subject to compulsion". The limitation is aimed at preventing the situation where a gang leader threatens an associate with physical violence unless he complies with a criminal demand, thereby effectively conferring immunity on him. However, it does not mean that the defence must fail simply because the compulsion comes from a member of a criminal enterprise which the accused has voluntarily joined. In *R v Joyce*[124] the Court of Appeal held that the limitation only operated where it is proved that:

> the very nature of the association was such that the offender, as a reasonable man, should have been able to foresee that the association was of a kind which at least rendered it possible that at a later stage he might be made subject to compulsion.[125]

On this basis, casual criminal associations in which a group of offenders decide spontaneously to commit an offence like burglary or car theft will seldom qualify for exclusion, because they will fail to meet the "nature of the association" test and will not usually be the type of association for which violence is a foreseeable prospect. However, liability in each case will still turn on the particular features of the group's modus operandi. In *R v Sharp*[126] the appellant was a member of a gang which, to his knowledge, used loaded firearms to carry out robberies of post offices. During one such robbery, in which the appellant was involved, a post office employee was killed. At his trial for murder he pleaded duress, on the basis that he did not want to take part in the robbery when he realised loaded guns were to be used, but did so when the gang leader pointed a gun at him and threatened to "blow his head off" if he did not participate. The Court of Appeal, dismissing the appeal, held that where a person has voluntarily, with knowledge of its nature, joined a criminal organisation or gang which he knew might put him under pressure to commit an offence and was an active member when put under such pressure, he could not rely on duress as a defence to an offence committed as a member of the gang.

Where the organisational and initiatory structure of an organisation is such that violence and threatening behaviour is an endemic characteristic of its identity and social purpose, it will always be more difficult for an offender to avoid the conclusion that in joining the group he must have known that it was one "whereby he [would be] subject to compulsion". This restriction would apply to many ethnic gangs and other organised criminal associations whose existence depends on their ability to threaten and intimidate for the purpose of achieving various social and economic advantages.

However, where the accused has been subject to compulsion from the outset of the association, so that it cannot be said that he has voluntarily joined

---

124 [1968] NZLR 1070 (CA).

125 Ibid at 1076.

126 [1987] QB 853, [1987] 3 All ER 103 (CA).

it, the defence will not fail on that account alone.[127] Further, it has been held that the fact that an accused continues an association with a criminal enterprise in circumstances where there is no immediate fear for his own safety will not necessarily deprive him of the defence if his actions are motivated by a reasonable fear that a third person would be killed if he fails to carry out the threatener's directions.[128]

10.4.5.2(a) *Foreseeability or actual knowledge?*

Notwithstanding the language of foreseeability used in *R v Joyce* (above), there is no case in which the facts have required a determination whether, in voluntarily joining a group, D must have actual knowledge that its members were ready to use violence to further their criminal purposes, or whether he loses the defence if violence was merely reasonably foreseeable. At common law, it has been held that actual knowledge of the "disciplinary code of vengeance" of the criminal gang joined by D may be sufficient to prevent him relying on compulsion.[129] In *R v Fitzpatrick*,[130] the appellant had been convicted of armed robbery and murder after he claimed to have been compelled to take part in the robbery by members of the IRA who had threatened to shoot his parents if he refused. The Court of Appeal for Northern Ireland held that the defence of duress was unavailable to the appellant who, the Court found, had voluntarily joined an organisation which to his knowledge might compel him to commit crimes similar to those with which he was charged. The fact that he had tried to leave the organisation was held to be irrelevant.[131] In rejecting the defence that D had attempted to leave and was prevented from doing so by threats, the Court stated:

> the better organised the conspiracy and the more brutal its internal discipline, the surer would be the defence of duress for its members. It can hardly be supposed that the common law tolerates such an absurdity.[132]

Fitzpatrick is regarded as an authoritative statement of the law on illegal association and has been approved in England.[133] However, it may be that the decision goes somewhat further than s 24 currently allows, by requiring evidence that a person has *knowingly* exposed himself to illegal compulsion by voluntarily joining an organisation *which to his knowledge* might compel him to commit criminal acts. It is submitted that an amendment to s 24, which incorporated these elements, would be useful in eliminating existing ambiguities in the law, and would bring the New Zealand provision into line with common law developments.

---

127 *R v Hurley* [1967] VR 526 at 544.

128 Ibid.

129 See *S v Bradbury* [1967] (1) SA 387; also *R v Lawrence* (1980) 32 ALR 72 at 87.

130 [1977] NI 20 (CCA).

131 Ibid.

132 Ibid at 31.

133 See *R v Sharp* [1987] QB 853 at 860, [1987] 3 All ER 103 at 108 (CA).

10.4.6 Excluded offences

A feature of s 24, which it shares with other codified versions of the compulsion defence but which distinguishes it from the common law, is the inclusion of a list of "grave" offences that compulsion never excuses. The excluded offences are listed in s 24(2), which provides:

> (2) Nothing in subsection (1) of this section shall apply where the offence committed is an offence specified in any of the following provisions of this Act, namely:
>
> (a) Section 73 (treason) or section 78 (communicating secrets):
> (b) Section 79 (sabotage):
> (c) Section 92 (piracy):
> (d) Section 93 (piratical acts):
> (e) Section 167 and 168 (murder):
> (f) Section 173 (attempt to murder):
> (g) Section 188 (wounding with intent):
> (h) Subsection (1) of section 189 (injuring with intent to cause grievous bodily harm):
> (i) Section 208 (abduction):
> (j) Section 209 (kidnapping):
> (k) Section 234 (robbery):
> (ka) Section 235 (aggravated robbery):
> (l) Section 294 (arson).

When the list was first compiled, it was generally agreed that certain "heinous"[134] offences should be excluded from the defence, although in reality the compilation of the list appears to have been somewhat arbitrary. In particular, there is no evidence that all the offences listed in subs (2) ever fell outside the common law defence, which, on the contrary, has allowed it in respect of a number of those offences. For example, it is now recognised that the common law defence of duress per minas is available for some forms of treason,[135] and it has been allowed for arson.[136] Thus the current position at common law would appear to be that duress may now excuse any crime except murder, attempted murder, and possibly some forms of treason. Although in New Zealand the Crimes Bill 1989 proposed to drop the list of excluded offences, this recommendation has not become law and the statutory exclusions remain. These exclusions are anomalous, and as well as being historically unjustified, they produce arbitrary distinctions.[137]

Because s 24(2) precisely identifies each excluded offence by reference to the specific section creating the offence, the courts are prevented "by necessary

---

134 See Criminal Code Commission, *Report of the Royal Commission Appointed to Consider the Law Relating to Indictable Offences: With an Appendix Containing a Draft Code Embodying the Suggestions of the Connissioner*, London, Eyre & Spottiswode for HMSO, 1879, 43.

135 See *M'Growther's Case* (1746) Fost 13, 168 ER 8; *R v Purdy* (1946) 10 J Cr L 182.

136 See Orchard, "The Defence of Compulsion" (1980) 9 NZULR 105 at 108, and cases cited at note 18. But not attempted murder: *R v Gotts* [1992] 2 AC 412, [1992] 1 All ER 832 (HL).

137 Orchard, "The Defence of Compulsion" (1980) 9 NZULR 105 at 108.

implication" from adding other offences to the list.[138]   This produced the absurdity, in *R v Joyce*,[139] that the defence was available to a charge of aggravated robbery (s 235) but not to robbery simpliciter because that is an excluded offence (s 24(2)(k)). It might be thought that this result was so bizarre that it should have prompted a review at least of s 24(2). However, the response of the Legislature was simply to add aggravated robbery to the list[140] while ignoring other important and arguably unjust distinctions. For example, while the defence is apparently available on a charge of assault with intent to rob (s 237), injuring (s 189(2)), and aggravated wounding or injury (s 191), all of which are not listed offences, it is excluded from wounding with intent (s 188) and injuring with intent (s 189(1)).

Prior to February 1986, when an important statutory amendment came into force, another puzzling exclusion was the offence of "aiding or abetting rape". The offence of rape itself was not listed, which meant that compulsion could have been relied upon if the actual commission of rape was alleged, but not if the charge was of aiding or abetting! The reference to aiding or abetting rape has now been deleted by s 7 Crimes Amendment Act (No 3) 1985, with the result that compulsion may now be a defence to a charge of sexual violation,[141] regardless whether the accused actually committed the offence or was a secondary party.

With the possible exceptions of murder and attempted murder (regarding which see § 10.4.6.1), there would seem to be scant justification for maintaining the list of excluded offences, given the anomalies that the list, by its nature, creates. In Canada it has been held that the exclusion, in s 17 Criminal Code, of certain offences from the operation of the compulsion defence is unconstitutional, because it violates the principle of fundamental justice that a person should not be found guilty of a crime if she is morally blameless.[142] In *Langlois*, the accused had been charged with conspiracy, possession of drugs, and trafficking in drugs. Claiming to have been acting under compulsion, he brought drugs into a penitentiary where he worked as a recreation officer. The trial Judge held that s 17 Criminal Code, which would have deprived him of a defence of compulsion by threats, was unconstitutional and permitted the accused to rely on a common law defence of duress. The trial Judge's ruling was upheld on appeal to the Quebec Court of Appeal, which was concerned that because of its narrow scope, s 17 had the potential of allowing a conviction despite the "normatively involuntary" character of the accused's actus reus.

It is arguable that the New Zealand position is even more restrictive than that which existed in Canada given that in New Zealand a defendant is debarred from taking advantage of any residual common law defence of duress

---

138 Ibid.

139 [1968] NZLR 1070 (CA).

140 See s 24(2)(ka), as inserted by s 2 Crimes Amendment Act 1973.

141 The crime of rape was replaced by the generic crime of "sexual violation" in s 2 Crimes Amendment Act (No 3) 1985. "Rape" is retained as an included offence by s 128(1)(a). See chapter 16.

142 *R v Langlois* (1993) 80 CCC (3d) 28 at 33.

by threats even if she is also excluded from the terms of s 24.[143] However, it has been observed[144] that while a similar criticism might be levelled at the statutory exclusions in s 24(2), the current formulation reflects a policy decision that compulsion will only be available as "a narrow release from criminal responsibility where its strict requirements are met".[145] Any existing unfairness is statutory and therefore can only be removed by the Legislature. In any event, a review of the provision would be timely in the light of recent calls for a fresh parliamentary look at the defence of duress in both England and Canada.[146]

10.4.6.1 *Should compulsion be available for murder?*

We have noted that s 24(2) currently excludes the availability of compulsion as a defence to the offences specifically listed and that cl 31 Crimes Bill 1989, by deleting the list of exclusions, would make compulsion available "in all cases".[147] This must be taken to include murder and attempted murder, for which the defence is unavailable even at common law.

In *R v Howe*,[148] the House of Lords in a unanimous decision ruled that the defence of duress is unavailable either to a principal in the first degree to murder (the actual killer) or to the principal in the second degree (the aider and abetter).[149] Essentially, their Lordships were of the opinion that the loss of any right to a defence justifying or excusing the deliberate taking of an innocent life was a proper price to pay in order to emphasise the sanctity of a human life.[150] Lord Hailsham spoke of the availability of administrative as distinct from purely judicial remedies for the hardships that might otherwise occur in the most agonising cases.[151] Lord Griffiths considered it "inconceivable" that in extreme situations involving innocent persons, for example, a woman motorist being hijacked and forced to act as a getaway driver, such persons would be prosecuted.[152]

---

143 *Kapi v MOT* [1992] 1 NZLR 227, (1991) 8 CRNZ 49 at 55 (CA).

144 *Adams* § CA24.18.

145 *R v Teichelman* [1981] 2 NZLR 64 at 66 (CA).

146 See *R v Langlois* (1993) 80 CCC (3d) 28 at 53.

147 See Explanatory Note, vii.

148 [1987] AC 417, [1987] 1 All ER 771 (HL).

149 Expressly overruling its earlier decision in *DPP for Northern Ireland v Lynch* [1975] AC 653, [1975] 1 All ER 913 (HL), while approving and applying the Privy Council decision in *Abbott v R* [1977] AC 755 (PC). The decision in Lynch had precluded the defence only for principals in the first degree.

150 See *R v Howe* [1987] AC 417 at 433, [1987] 1 All ER 771 at 781 (per Lord Hailsham). Lord McKay emphasised that "repugnance" of the law's recognising in any individual "in any circumstances" the right to choose that one innocent person should be killed rather than another (ibid at 456, at 798).

151 Ibid at 433, at 781.

152 Ibid. As a reason for not extending duress to murder, this prognosis is criticised as being "over-optimistic" and a "complete evasion of the responsibilities of the House of Lords to avoid dealing with difficult cases". See Milgate, "Duress and the Criminal Law: Another About Turn by the House of Lords" [1988] CLJ 61 at 70, 71.

Two major grounds of objection have been suggested by critics of the decision in *Howe*. First, it is argued that a "morally innocent person" should not be left to the mercy of administrative discretion on a murder charge, if indeed it is realistic to suppose that Parliament intended to leave it to the discretion of the police not to prosecute in such cases.[153] Secondly, it may be thought that there is an "indefensible anomaly" in allowing a defence of duress if, with the mens rea for murder, the defendant only injures his victim, while taking the defence away if the victim dies within a year and a day.[154]

Dealing with the first of these objections, it seems a rather startling proposition that a person, who with full mens rea kills another innocent person, should be deemed to be innocent, simply because what is done is done out of fear, however well-grounded. Compulsion cannot here be a justification, but, at most, an excuse. Moreover, the fact that it may seem pointless to punish in such cases is not to say that the actor is morally blameless. Such a judgment could be made only if the interests of the victim in a coerced attack represented a value that was not worth preserving. That is clearly not the case. Considered in this light, it is not unreasonable for the law to declare that taking innocent life under compulsion is morally reprehensible, regardless of the options that may be available to reflect the diminished culpability of the offender.

As for the "indefensible anomaly" argument, their Lordships concede that there are anomalies inherent in their decision, but that these are a consequence of the fact that murder is a result-related crime with a mandatory penalty.[155] The anomaly is not one specific to compulsion, but inherent in any legal system where the actual occurrence of results affects one's criminal liability. As Lord Hailsham observes, consistency and logic, though inherently desirable, are not always prime characteristics of a penal code based on custom and common sense.[156] This may be an area where the demands of "consistency" must defer to other moral principles aimed at maximising the protection of innocent persons. In any event, as an ethical principle, it is very doubtful whether automatic priority should be given to saving one's own life, or whether a person ought always to be entitled to protect her own bodily integrity at any cost.

Given that the clear weight of common law authority has been against extending exculpatory defences to those who, in situations of extremity, consider themselves forced to take innocent life, the arguments in favour of extending the defence of duress to persons charged as parties to murder become less persuasive. For New Zealand to maintain the status quo in this regard establishes consistency with other common law jurisdictions, which

---

153 See the commentary on *Howe*, sub nom *R v Burke* [1987] Crim LR 480, by Smith at 481-485.

154 Ibid; cf s 162 Crimes Act 1961.

155 *R v Howe* [1987] AC 417, [1987] 1 All ER 771 (Lord McKay). For a full discussion of the other anomalies created by the decision, see Milgate, "Duress and the Criminal Law: Another About Turn by the House of Lords" [1988] CLJ 61 at 74, 75.

156 *R v Howe* [1987] AC 417 at 457, [1987] 1 All ER 771 at 799 (HL).

generally exclude murder or attempted murder from the ambit of compulsion.[157]

10.4.7 Burden of proof

Where a defendant relies on the defence of compulsion, in practice the burden lies upon him to adduce sufficient evidence to raise compulsion as a "live issue". The possibility of compulsion cannot be considered by the jury unless an evidential foundation for the defence exists.[158] For example, evidence that the accused had been "pressured" or was being "hassled" to supply heroin to a third party, or that he was merely frightened by the actions of another into doing so, will be insufficient to raise the defence of compulsion.[159] However, once compulsion becomes a live issue, the burden is on the prosecution to negative the defence beyond reasonable doubt.[160] In *R v Bone*[161] the English Court of Appeal, in considering the question of burden of proof in cases of duress, said:

> Duress, like self-defence and drunkenness, is something which must in the first instance be raised by the defence, but at the end of the day it is always for the prosecution to prove their case, which involves negativing the defence which has been set up . . . to ensure that the jury are not confused it is not sufficient to give the general direction at the beginning in regard to the burden and standard of proof, but the jury should be told specifically that it is for the prosecution to negative in that case, the self-defence.[162]

In New Zealand there has been some debate whether this rule applies equally to summary trials as to trials on indictment. Adams argued that the rule only applied to trials on indictment, and that in summary proceedings the onus of proof (on the balance of probabilities) rests on the accused.[163] This was based on the assumption that s 67(8) Summary Proceedings Act 1957, which requires the defendant in a summary proceeding to prove any "exception, exemption, proviso, excuse, or qualification, whether it does or does not accompany the description of the offence in the enactment creating the offence", necessarily required the defendant to prove compulsion, which constituted an "excuse" within the meaning of the subsection. However, it may be doubted whether the provision was ever intended to apply to general defences, since the exception, in terms of its common law origins, is limited to "offences arising under enactments which prohibit the doing of an act save in specified circumstances or by persons of specified classes or with specified

---

157 See s 17 Criminal Code of Canada; s 94 Indian Penal Code; s 20 Tasmanian Criminal Code; s 31 Queensland and Western Australian Criminal Codes.

158 *R v Teichelman* [1981] 2 NZLR 64 at 66 (CA).

159 See *R v Frickleton* [1984] 2 NZLR 670.

160 *R v Gill* [1963] 2 All ER 688, [1963] 1 WLR 841 (CCA). See also *Salaca v R* [1967] NZLR 421 at 422 (CA).

161 [1968] 2 All ER 644, [1968] 1 WLR 983 (CA).

162 Ibid at 645, at 985.

163 *Adams* (2nd ed) § 482.

qualifications or with the licence or permission of specified authorities",[164] language which seems inapt to describe a general statutory defence like compulsion. It is arguable that the principle espoused in s 67(8) applies only to statutory provisions that provide limited exceptions to what would otherwise be unlawful conduct *within that same provision*, and not to a provision that negatives criminal responsibility for other offences in general.

---

164 *R v Edwards* [1975] QB 27 at 40, [1974] 3 WLR 285 at 295 (CA) (Lawton LJ).

11

Necessity

11.1 DOES NECESSITY EXIST?

The common law defence of necessity (or "duress of circumstances") has never been codified in New Zealand. In fact, until quite recently its status as a separate defence was seriously in doubt. As late as 1971 the courts in New Zealand had not attempted to lay down any general principle covering necessity. There appeared to be a general perception that because many of the early instances of necessity, including self-defence and compulsion, had acquired recognition as separate defences, there was little need to recognise a general defence of necessity.

At common law, there has also been debate whether a general defence of necessity exists, and, if it does exist, over the scope of the defence. In this context it is worth noting that Sir Samuel Griffith chose to specify a general defence of necessity in his Criminal Code (which provides the basis of the Criminal Codes in the states of Queensland, Western Australia, and Papua New Guinea). Griffith intended to make the statement of common law justification or excuse in his Code comprehensive by including a provision dealing with "sudden or extraordinary emergency" as a residual defence to protect the "morally innocent" where other defences did not apply.[1]

While contemporary academics like Professor Glanville Williams also support the view that there is a general defence of necessity, other distinguished commentators on the criminal law have argued that no such defence exists, or that it is unnecessary.[2] The evidence, however, is broadly in favour of the defence. Over the years, varying measures of recognition have been granted to the concept in a variety of circumstances involving "criminal" behaviour, although acceptance of necessity in particular instances has tended to "wax and wane". For example, in 1803, East, a leading criminal law commentator, suggested that "taking upon necessity" was a defence to larceny,[3] a view which had earlier been condemned by Sir Matthew Hale[4] and one which is not supported by modern authorities.[5] However, if we accept, as Sir William Scott suggests, that even the law must sometimes yield to necessity, where to force compliance would compel someone to "impossibilities",[6] then it is impossible to say that necessity may *never* be a defence to theft. Each case would depend on the *nature* of the physical forces exercising pressure, whether the alleged "harm" (ie theft) has made possible the preservation of some greater interest or value (eg D's life), and whether committing theft was the only means of conserving that value (ie of preserving D's life).[7]

11.1.1 Recognition in the case law

Periodically, celebrated cases have given rise to important debates concerning the scope of the defence of necessity. In the late 1800's the case of *R v Dudley and Stephens*[8] raised the intriguing question whether necessity could ever be a defence to murder, arising out of circumstances which would, undoubtedly, have tested the fortitude of even the most "staunch" of sea-faring adventurers. The merits of the case have been analysed at length by numerous

---

1   O'Regan, *New Essays on the Australian Criminal Codes* Sydney, Law Book Co, 1988, 50, 51.

2   See O'Connor & Fairall, *Criminal Defences* (2nd ed), 1988, 105.

3   11 East PC 656; cited in O'Connor & Fairall, *Criminal Defences* (2nd ed), 1988, 105. East is supported in this view by Bacon, who asserted that "If a man steale viands to satisfie his present hunger, this is no felony nor larceny". (Cited in *DPP for Northern Ireland v Lynch* [1975] AC 653 at 691, [1975] 1 All ER 913 at 935 (HL) per Lord Simon.)

4   1 Hale PC 54.

5   See *DPP for Northern Ireland v Lynch* [1975] AC 653 at 691, [1975] 1 All ER 913 at 935 (HL).

6   Sir William Scott in *The Generous* (1818) 2 Dods 322, 165 ER 1501; discussed in *Brooms Legal Maxims* (10th ed), 1939, 162, and cited in *Tifaga v Department of Labour* [1980] 2 NZLR 235 at 243 (CA).

7   See Hall, *General Principles of Criminal Law* (2nd ed), Indianapolis, Bobbs-Merrill, 1960. See also *R v Lalonde* (1995) 37 CR (4th) 97 at 108 (defence of necessity allowed to charges of fraud on the basis that in the mind of the accused, a battered woman, there was no reasonable alternative and the need to put food on the table for her children, in her financial circumstances, was pressing.)

8   (1884) 14 QBD 273, [1881-85] All ER Rep 61

commentators.[9] The accused were the survivors of a shipwreck. After having drifted in an open boat for 8 days, without food and with no immediate prospect of rescue, they killed and ate the cabin boy in order to save their own lives. They were rescued 4 days later and were later tried for murder.

Lord Coleridge, speaking on behalf of a distinguished bench, completely repudiated the defence of necessity, at least in relation to murder. He considered that to apply the doctrine in a case like this, where no wrongful act had been committed by the deceased, who was "the weakest, the youngest, the most unresisting", would be preposterous.[10] He considered the doctrine of necessity "at once dangerous, immoral, and opposed to all legal principle and analogy"[11] and, repudiating the alleged "duty" of self-preservation, said that the "plainest and highest duty" may sometimes be to sacrifice one's own life.[12]

The effect of the decision in *Dudley and Stephens* was to leave the English law on necessity in a very unsatisfactory state. In 1883, Sir James Fitzjames Stephen expressed the view that the law on necessity was so vague that the judges were virtually free to lay down any rule they thought expedient. In his view, the expediency of breaking the law might occasionally be so great that a defence should be allowed, but such cases could not be defined in advance.[13]

Notwithstanding *Dudley and Stephens*, the common law has recognised necessity in a variety of circumstances. Examples of conduct justified on grounds of necessity include pulling down a house to prevent a fire from spreading, a prisoner's "escaping" from a burning jail, the crew of a ship jettisoning cargo in order to save the lives of passengers, and prison officials force-feeding prisoners to preserve their health and their lives.[14] In *R v Vantandillo*[15] it was held to be lawful to carry an infected child through the streets to seek medical aid, even though such conduct would normally have amounted to the common law misdemeanour of public nuisance. A constable, it would seem, also has the right to direct a driver to disobey traffic regulations where it is necessary to protect life and property.[16] Hitherto, however, while necessity has sometimes been permitted to exculpate otherwise illegal conduct in situations of extremity,[17] these cases have usually been regarded at common

---

9   See, for example, Hall, *General Principles of Criminal Law* Indianapolis, Bobbs-Merrill, 430-436. For a full account of the tragic last voyage of *The Mignonette* and of the ensuing legal issues, see Simpson, *Cannibalism and the Common Law*, Penguin, 1986.

10   Hall, *General Principles of Criminal Law* Indianapolis, Bobbs-Merrill, 1960, 431.

11   Ibid.

12   Ibid at 432.

13   *A History of the Criminal Law of England* vol 2, 108.

14   *Johnson v Phillips* [1975] 3 All ER 682, [1976] 1 WLR 65. See Smith and Hogan, *Criminal Law* (7th ed), London, Butterworths, 1992, 245 and other examples given there.

15   (1815) 4 M & S 73, 105 ER 762.

16   *Johnson v Phillips* [1975] 3 All ER 682, [1976] 1 WLR 65, [1975] Crim LR 580.

17   See, for example, *Southwark London Borough Council v Williams* [1971] Ch 734, [1971] 2 All ER 175 (CA) where Lord Denning held that the law may permit an encroachment on private property in order to preserve life in a case of "great and imminent danger".

law as isolated exceptions, and not as applications of a recognised, more general defence of necessity.

This limitation on necessity has now, it seems, been removed as a result of the decision in *R v Pommell*.[18] The appellant in *Pommell* had been charged with the possession of a loaded sub-machine gun which, he told police, he had persuaded another person to give him, in order to prevent that person from shooting some others. He told the police he intended to wait until morning to give the gun to his brother to hand in to the police. The trial Judge ruled that the failure of the appellant to go to the police immediately deprived him of the defence of necessity. On appeal, it was held that the defence of necessity was open to the appellant in respect of his acquisition of the gun, although a person in possession in such circumstances must desist from committing the crime as soon as he reasonably can.

There are two important points to note about this case. First, the offence under the Firearms Act 1968 (UK) was one of absolute liability.[19] As such, it would have been no defence for the defendant to maintain that he did not know or could not reasonably have been expected to know that the gun was a sub-machine gun as defined in s 5(1) of the Act.[20] Secondly, among the recent English cases on duress of circumstances this was the first case not involving a road traffic offence. In delivering its judgment, the Court made the following observations concerning the scope of the common law defence:

(i) The limited defence of duress of circumstances has been developed in English law in relation to road traffic offences to deal with the situation where someone commendably infringes a regulation in order to prevent a greater evil. In such circumstances it is not satisfactory to leave it to the prosecuting authority not to prosecute, or to individual courts to grant an absolute discharge.

(ii) It is still not clear whether there is a general defence of necessity or, if there is, what are the circumstances in which it is available.

(iii) Necessity can be a defence to a charge of reckless driving where the facts establish duress of circumstances, that is to say when the defendant is constrained to act as he did to avoid death or serious bodily harm to himself or some other person.

(iv) The defence of duress of circumstances may also be available to a person charged with excess breath alcohol who, fearing serious injury, drives his car, provided he drives only for the distance necessary to avoid the threat.[21]

(v) While all the cases involving duress of circumstances have so far concerned road traffic offences, there are no grounds for supposing that the defence is limited to that kind of case. On the contrary, the defence, being closely related to the defence of duress by threats, appears to be

---

18 [1995] 2 Cr App R 607 (CA).

19 See *R v Bradish* [1990] 1 QB 981, (1990) 90 Cr App R 271 (CA); *R v Waller* [1991] Crim LR 381 (CA); also comments in *R v Pommell* [1995] 2 Cr App R 607 at 613 (CA).

20 *R v Bradish* [1990] 1 QB 981 at 992, (1990) 90 Cr App R 271 at 280 (CA) (Auld J).

21 See *DPP v Bell* [1992] RTR 335, [1992] Crim LR 176; *DPP v Jones* (1990) RTR 33.

general, applying to all crimes except murder, attempted murder, and some forms of treason.[22]

From this summary, despite the uncertainty expressed in observation (ii) above, we may tentatively conclude that at common law necessity, whether or not it is characterised as duress of circumstances, is a general defence that is available in respect of any offence, including offences of strict or absolute liability; with the exceptions of murder, attempted murder, and some forms of treason. What is not clear, however, is the *circumstances* in which the defence will in future be available. Presumably, in order to qualify for the defence the evidence will need to establish, as a minimum, that the situation was one of great and imminent danger and that the accused acted as she did in order to avoid death or serious bodily injury to herself or some other person.[23] Beyond this, what else is required will, no doubt, be determined in time with reference to the established case law on duress of circumstances.

11.2 PROBLEMS WITH NECESSITY DOCTRINE

Early attempts in New Zealand to conceptualise a necessity defence by reference to specific examples were viewed as the product of a "fertile imagination",[24] based on situations in which it was impossible to believe that the person concerned would ever be prosecuted, or if prosecuted, that a jury would ever convict him. Adams gives the example of A, who sees a crane about to drop a heavy load on B. He pushes B aside just in time to save B from being killed. Adams observes that it is difficult to visualise A's ever being convicted of assault or of assault causing grievous bodily harm in the event of B being seriously injured, even though A may technically be guilty of either offence. The unlikelihood of prosecution in such cases is supported with reference to ancient authorities like *Reniger v Fogassa*,[25] where the Court said:

> [I]n every law there are some things which when they happen a man may break the words of the law, and yet not break the law itself; and such things are exempted out of the penalty of the law, and the law priviledges [sic] them although they are done against the letter of it, for breaking the words of the law is not breaking the law, so as the intent of the law is not broken. And therefore the words of the law of nature, of the law of this realm, and of other realms, and of the law of God also will yield and give way to some acts and things done against the words of the same laws, and that is, where the words of them are broken to avoid greater inconveniences, or through necessity, or by compulsion . . .[26]

While it is true that jurists and legal commentators have long maintained that in some situations the force of circumstances makes it unrealistic and unjust to attach criminal liability to actions which, prima facie, violate the

---

22 See the comments of Sir John Smith at [1992] Crim LR 176.
23 See *Southwark London Borough Council v Williams* [1971] Ch 734 at 743, [1971] 2 All ER 175 at 179 (CA) (Lord Denning).
24 *Adams* (2nd ed) § 491.
25 (1550) 1 Plowd 2, 75 ER 1.
26 Ibid at 18, at 29 (Pollard, Sergeant at Law).

law,[27] such broad statements of principle often fail to appreciate the complexity of the situations and forms in which a claim of necessity may arise. Neither do they give guidance on how the "defence" ought informally to be applied. In such cases, non-prosecution can never be guaranteed. In particular, to the extent that "extraordinary circumstances" of necessity in the examples commonly given often involve *real* situations of extreme pressure (eg the lost alpinist forced to break into a mountain chalet to escape the perils of a storm) which invoke immediate sympathy for the imperilled defendant, they fail to take account of the fact that many modern claims of necessity are based upon a *mistaken* belief in the emergent peril. Such mistakes, whether reasonable or not, may invoke considerably less sympathy than do the classic examples. It would be unrealistic to hope that prosecutors will always act with absolute fairness, and be able to accommodate the complex jurisprudential issues inherent in a claim of mistaken necessity, when deciding whether or not to prosecute in such a case. The proper place to address such issues is in the courtroom.

It is regrettable that much of the early debate in New Zealand concerning the merits of the necessity defence was highly rhetorical and tended to falter upon the perception that early examples of necessity (for example the moral duties of two persons in the water struggling for the possession of a plank capable of supporting only one) simply existed for the whimsical amusement of "casuists" who have "for centuries" amused themselves with such moral teasers.[28] A similar view is expressed by Adams, who suggests that the courts cannot be drawn into "a morass of moralising" which is the product of the "endless argument" that the (often unrealistic) classic cases of necessity give rise to.[29] However, it should be noted that the claims of casuistry and moralising have largely been associated with a discussion of the merits of necessity as a defence to murder. They bear little relationship to the modern defence, which typically concerns such practical questions as whether necessity should be available to a mother who runs a red light while rushing a sick child to hospital or to an offender who causes death by careless driving when he speeds to avoid the threatening behaviour of the occupants of another car. These questions, we suggest, involve issues of principle that have *real* importance, and should not be dismissed as mere casuistry.

The thrust of this chapter will be to argue that the complexity of modern society demands a more considered and rational response to the claims of exculpatory necessity than that suggested by the early commentators. Traditional accounts of the doctrine have allowed necessity to excuse conduct that would otherwise be criminal in exceptional cases based on the maxim *in casu extremae necessitatis omnia sunt communia* (in cases of extreme necessity all

---

27 See, for example, the comments of Dickson J in *R v Perka* (1984) 14 CCC (3d) 385 at 392, [1984] 2 SCR 233 at 241 (SCC).

28 See Criminal Code Bill Commission, *Report of the Royal Commission Appointed to Consider the Law Relating to Indictable Offences: With an Appendix Containing a Draft Code Embodying the Suggestions of the Commissioners*, London, Eyre & Spottiswoode for HMSO, 1879, Note A to Page 10, 44.

29 *Adams* (2nd ed) § 492.

things are common).[30] However, such broadly expressed principles do not reflect the complexity of a modern doctrine of necessity and fail to give any guidance about how it should be applied in circumstances where the merits of a claim are not intuitively clear. In our view, the doctrine should be clearly expressed in statutory form and should be available as a general defence to all crimes short of murder and attempted murder.

11.2.1 Justification or excuse

The one term, "necessity", in fact comprises two distinct excusing conditions. The difference between these two types of necessity is important and must be borne in mind in evaluating any claim of necessity. The first variety of necessity is concerned with the *avoidance of the greater harm* or the *pursuit of some greater good*. The second type concerns the *difficulty of compliance with the law in emergencies*.

Because the first type often involves situations in which citizens are compelled to break a specific law in order to preserve a greater good (for example a police officer shooting a hostage taker, a mother who breaks the speed restriction to rush her sick child to hospital, the husband who uses fatal force to protect his wife from an attacker), these situations are sometimes said to be "justified". Indeed, in all but one of the examples given the law expressly confers a justification.[31] In such situations we consider D's actions rightful and worthy of praise, not worthy of punishment.

By contrast, the second form of necessity is not one of justification. It recognises that while the accused's actions are "wrong", it would be pointless or even inhumane to punish in such circumstances. Examples might include a backpacker who breaks into a Department of Conservation hut and smashes the lock of a cupboard in order to find food; the man who takes possession of a prohibited weapon to give to someone who will hand it to the police; and a prisoner who escapes from jail because he fears, on good grounds, a severe attack by other inmates. We excuse because, although the conduct is not permissible or to be endorsed, we are not prepared to say that it should be punishable.

However, as these examples demonstrate, it is not easy to say whether, in a particular case, conduct ought to be excused rather than justified. The approach taken in this book is that the "residual" defence of necessity, covering both of the above models, is better conceptualised as an excuse and that the language of justification is best left to apply to those statutory expressions of necessity which the Legislature has determined to be matters of justification. If ever the defence of necessity is codified as a general defence, the Legislature would have to determine whether the relevant conduct was justified or whether the accused was simply to be "protected from criminal responsibility".[32]

---

30 See Hale 1 PC 54 at 55.

31 See Crimes Act 1961, s 39 (force used in executing process or in arrest), s 48 (self-defence and defence of another).

32 For the meaning of the terms "justified" and "protected from criminal responsibility" see s 2 Crimes Act 1961.

In *R v Perka*,[33] Dickson J held that while the defence of necessity may be conceptualised as either a justification or an excuse, it should be recognised in law as an excuse. As such, it:

> [R]ests on a realistic assessment of human weakness, recognising that a liberal and humane criminal law cannot hold people to the strict obedience of laws in emergency situations where normal human instincts, whether of self-preservation or of altruism, overwhelmingly impel disobedience. The objectivity of the criminal law is preserved; such acts are still wrongful, but in the circumstances they are excusable.[34]

Necessity, like its cognate defence compulsion, refers to cases where D is not completely deprived of control over her behaviour but is faced with a choice between evils. She may simply do nothing and allow a harm to occur, or she may "choose" to commit an offence in order to avoid the harm. As was noted in chapter 10 on compulsion, these situations may appropriately be characterised as involving "normative" involuntariness because in practical terms the accused had no true choice. Dickson J explains the concept of "normative" involuntariness in these terms:

> Literally, this voluntariness requirement simply refers to the need that the prohibited physical acts must have been under the conscious control of the actor. Without such control, there is, for purposes of the criminal law, no act. *The excuse of necessity does not go to voluntariness in this sense.* The lost Alpinist who, on the point of freezing to death, breaks open an isolated mountain cabin is not literally behaving in an involuntary fashion. He has control over his actions to the extent of being physically capable of abstaining from the act. Realistically, however, his act is not a "voluntary" one. His "choice" to break the law is no true choice at all; it is remorselessly compelled by normal human instincts. This sort of involuntariness is often described as "moral or normative involuntariness".[35]

This view of necessity has been described as "compulsion of circumstance"[36] and has been equated with the English defence of "duress of circumstances".[37] As Fletcher notes, the "normative" conception of involuntariness must be sharply distinguished from physical involuntariness (causal necessity) even though both expressions may be involved in any talk of "circumstances overpowering the will" or the actor's having "no choice".[38] Stressing the element of involuntariness in a claim of necessity is simply a way of emphasising the moral claim that the offender should not be blamed for (inevitably) making the same choice that other people would make under similar circumstances.[39]

---

33 (1984) 14 CCC (3d) 385, [1984] 2 SCR 233 (SCC).

34 Ibid at 398, at 248.

35 Ibid at 398, at 249 (emphasis added).

36 See Fletcher, *Rethinking Criminal Law*, Boston, 1987.

37 *R v Langlois* (1993) 80 CCC (3D) 28 at 45 (per Fish JA).

38 Fletcher, *Rethinking Criminal Law*, Boston, 1987, 803.

39 Ibid at 856.

This is very different from a claim of physical involuntariness: where the notion of involuntariness strictu sensu[40] is employed, there is not merely a claim that the offender's will was overpowered; it is also implicit that the offender has not acted at all, at least not in any sense that would be of interest to the criminal law, because he is entirely unable consciously to control the course of events.[41] Hale described this species of exculpation by the maxim "quicquid necessitas cogit, defendit" (that may be lawfully done which cannot be forborne).[42]

By contrast, we cannot say the same of a person acting "involuntarily" in the normative sense. Such a person has clearly acted and deliberately so. However, the principle that punishment should be reserved for those who voluntarily break the law, and our intuition that those who lack an adequate choice should be excused their offences out of respect for individual autonomy, dictate that punishment would be pointless in such a case.

Sometimes necessity in this sense is described as "teleological" necessity, because the relevant harm is inflicted *under pressure* of physical forces, as opposed to being caused solely by the *operation* of physical forces.[43] This teleological (ends-directed) necessity does not exclude the operation of physical forces. Rather it implies conduct *in the face of* the serious danger threatened by the impact of physical forces. We may illustrate the difference between the two types of necessity by the following model:

Physical involuntariness ("causal necessity")

Force $\longrightarrow$ D *causally compelled* $\longrightarrow$ consequential harm

Teleological necessity

Force $\longrightarrow$ D *threatened (notionally compelled)* $\longrightarrow$ consequential harm

The modern defence of necessity involves "teleological" necessity rather than involuntariness, because harm is not caused directly by natural forces but indirectly by the *threat* of harm to the offender.[44]

From the foregoing discussion we conclude with the following propositions concerning necessity:

(i)   It is better characterised legally as an excuse rather than as justification.

(ii) Issues of necessity involve important matters of principle that should not be dismissed as mere casuistry.

(iii) The true characterisation of the defence is as a choice between evils rather than as involuntary conduct.

---

40   Hart, *Punishment and Responsiblity: Essays in the Philosophy of Law*, Oxford, Clarendon Press, 1968, 22-24. See § 2.3.

41   For a useful discussion of the various ways in which the notion of involuntariness may be conceptualised with reference to necessity and related concepts see *Tifaga v Dept of Labour* [1980] 2 NZLR 235 at 241 (CA) (Richardson J).

42   1 Hale PC 54.

43   Hall, *General Principles of Criminal Law* (2nd ed), Indianapolis, Bobbs-Merrill, 1960, 425.

44   Sometimes these situations are characterised as "mixed action" because the conduct may be viewed as partly involuntary and partly voluntary: ibid.

(iv) Conduct is excused on the hypothesis that the accused had no reasonable alternative.

(v) Actions performed under "teleological" necessity are excused because of the operation of the threat of physical forces, which overwhelms the free will of the actor.

11.3 NECESSITY IN NEW ZEALAND LAW

The first explicit reference to a defence of necessity in New Zealand occurs in *R v Woolnough*,[45] where the Court of Appeal alluded to the "extreme vagueness of necessity" as a general defence in English criminal law and observed that the defence, if it existed at all, would be available by virtue of s 20 Crimes Act 1961. In *R v Tifaga*,[46] an immigration case in which the accused pleaded "impossibility of compliance" to a charge of overstaying, the Court of Appeal again, somewhat tentatively, conceded the existence of necessity, endorsing its preservation under s 20. Noting that necessity and impossibility are distinct but related concepts, Richardson J approved the dictum of Lord Simon in *DPP for Northern Ireland v Lynch*[47] that, although an action constrained of "true" necessity is one made without any choice of action at all, necessity has come to denote the situation where circumstances present a person not with no choice at all, but with a choice between two evils such that he cannot be blamed if he chooses the lesser. By contrast, impossibility involves the inability to comply with the law at all.

11.3.1 Specific statutory defences of necessity

At present the Crimes Act 1961 does not provide a general defence of necessity, although as has been noted, other defences analogous to necessity have been codified, including compulsion (s 24), self-defence (s 48), and defence of property (ss 52-56). There is also provision in s 61 and s 61A for those who perform surgical operations to be protected from criminal responsibility where the operation is performed with "reasonable care and skill". In addition, legislation occasionally provides that a particular emergency or danger may excuse a specified offence. An example is s 183, which, in combination with s 187A, prohibits procuring the miscarriage of any woman or girl by certain "unlawful" means. Pursuant to s 187A(3), the procurement will not be done "unlawfully" if the person doing it believes the miscarriage is "*necessary* to save the life of the woman or girl". It has been suggested that the word "necessary" as used in this context may require proof that the danger to the woman could not reasonably be averted by any means other than an abortion.[48] However, the use of the word "necessary" alone does not of itself imply that the section must be interpreted in light of established principles governing the operation of the defence at common law. Rather, the meaning of necessity must be judged by

---

45   [1977] 2 NZLR 508 at 516 (CA).
46   [1980] 2 NZLR 235 at 242 (CA).
47   [1975] AC 653 at 690, 691, [1975] 1 All ER 913 at 934, 953 (HL).
48   *Adams* § CA187A.10.

the context in which it occurs, which may in turn be affected by particular case law developments. For example, the interpretation of s 187A, in particular of the term "unlawfully", has been largely influenced by the decision in *R v Woolnough*,[49] where the Court of Appeal held that an abortion would not be performed "unlawfully" for the purposes of s 183(1) if the accused believed in good faith that there was a real risk of danger to the mother's life or of serious harm to her mental and physical health if she continued with the pregnancy.

11.3.1.1 *Trespass offences*

The question of the relationship of the word "necessary" appearing in a statutory definition with the common law defence of necessity has been considered in New Zealand in relation to the offence of trespass as defined by s 3 Trespass Act 1980. That section states:

> (1) Every person commits an offence against this Act who trespasses on any place and, after being warned to leave that place by an occupier of that place, neglects or refuses to do so.
>
> (2) It shall be a defence to a charge under subsection (1) of this section if the defendant proves that it was necessary for him to remain in or on the place concerned for his own protection or the protection of some other person, or because of some emergency involving his property or the property of some other person.

In *Wilcox v Police*,[50] the appellant and nine other persons had gone to a Christchurch hospital with the purpose of preventing the entry of women who were intending to have abortions that day. They were warned to leave, but refused to do so and were then charged under s 3(1) with trespass. They argued that since unlawful abortions were going to be performed at the hospital that morning, they were justified in refusing to leave because it was *necessary* for them to remain for the protection of the unborn children and the mothers concerned.

One issue for the Court to determine was whether the provision of a statutory defence of necessity in subs (2) "overwhelmed" the common law defence of necessity as it applied to trespass or whether the common law defence operated in tandem with the statutory defence. The Court held that under s 3 the question of necessity should be considered only under the defence available in subs (2) and not, additionally, when determining whether there had been a breach of subs (1). If necessity were to arise twice, first within the concept of trespass under subs (1) and then again under the statutory defence in subs (2), it was likely, the Court held, that the statutory defence would become a dead letter in most cases.

In ruling that the defence of necessity was limited to its statutory form, Tipping J considered and distinguished the Court of Appeal decision in *Kapi v MOT*.[51] It was argued by counsel for the appellants that the decision in *Kapi* (in which the possibility of a defence of necessity had been acknowledged, but

---

49   [1977] 2 NZLR 508.
50   [1994] 1 NZLR 243, (1993) 10 CRNZ 704 (Tipping J).
51   (1991) 8 CRNZ 49 (CA). See § 11.3.2.2.

ruled out where the statutory defence of compulsion governed), read together with s 20 Crimes Act 1961, supported the proposition that necessity arises twice, ie under each subsection. His Honour made the following observations:

> The fact that necessity, properly understood, is a justification for trespass at common law is not in doubt. When acting by force of necessity the person concerned does not commit a trespass at all . . . [H]owever, . . . this principle of the common law does not continue to apply if altered by, or inconsistent with, any other enactment. In my judgment the common law principle of justification by necessity is inconsistent with s 3(2) of the Trespass Act 1980 and has in substance been altered thereby. Section 3(2) is in large measure a statutory enactment of the common law doctrine of necessity. While it may not be exactly the same, Parliament has clearly codified in statutory form the essential aspects of the doctrine of necessity.
>
> Necessity has been made a statutory defence to a charge of trespass under s 3(1). It is a defence in respect of which the defendant has the onus of proof on the balance of probabilities. That in my judgment is quite inconsistent with the proposition that the informant must, for the purposes of s 3(1), negative any question of necessity beyond reasonable doubt in order to establish that there has been a trespass. Accordingly, while s 20 . . . prima facie preserves the concept of necessity for the purpose of the law of trespass, s 3 of the Trespass Act has expressly altered the position and is inconsistent with the prima facie preservation. There is nothing in the decision . . . in *Kapi's* case which . . . assists the appellants on this point.[52]

The result is that facts raising necessity which do not fall within the terms of s 3(2) Trespass Act fail to exculpate, arguably as a result of a deliberate legislative intent to restrict the scope of the defence of necessity in that regard.[53] Unfortunately, the decision does not attempt to define the *elements* of necessity within the offence of trespass. Is one to suppose, for example, that the Legislature intends, in defining necessity within the terms of s 3(2), to provide a *narrow* release from criminal responsibility where the strict terms of the statutory requirements are met, as in the case of statutory compulsion?[54] If so, what is implied in the expression "necessary . . . to remain"? Does that require proof of an "extraordinary emergency", as seems to be a general requirement for the common law defence?[55] Does the defence require an honest and reasonable belief that there was an emergency justifying the accused's actions or must a *factual* emergency be proved regardless of the accused's belief? By analogy with the statutory defence of compulsion, it could be argued that mere apprehension of an emergency in the absence of a (factually) critical situation will be insufficient to establish a necessity to remain.[56]

---

52 [1994] 1 NZLR 243 at 247, (1993) 10 CRNZ 704 at 707, 708.

53 *Kapi v MOT* (1991) 8 CRNZ 49 at 54 (CA) (Gault J).

54 See *R v Teichelman* [1981] 2 NZLR 64 at 66 (CA) (Richardson J).

55 *Kapi v MOT* [1992] 1 NZLR 227 at 230, (1991) 7 CRNZ 481 at 484. Jeffries J identified three elements for the defence of necessity: (1) a really extraordinary emergency; (2) an honest belief; (3) reasonable grounds.

56 See *R v Frickleton* [1984] 2 NZLR 670 at 672 (CA) (McMullin J): "once it is shown that an accused person intended to do the act which is forbidden by law mere apprehension is not enough to provide a defence."

Some of these questions were addressed by the Court of Appeal in *Bayer v Police*,[57] which also concerned the actions of anti-abortionists who entered the premises of the Auckland Medical Aid Trust and effectively blocked access. The question of the proper interpretation of s 3(2) Trespass Act 1980 was again in issue. The Court noted that, although the requirement to prove necessity was expressed in absolute terms, the implication of an objective standard of reasonableness qualifying the word "necessary" was called for in order to give realistic scope to the beneficial operation of the subsection. Therefore, the standard was whether a reasonable person aware of all the circumstances would have thought it necessary to remain for the protection of some other person.[58]

Given this objective standard, is there any scope within the statutory defence under s 3(2) for a *mistaken* belief in the existence of an emergency justifying the accused's remaining in or on the place, whether or not that belief is based on reasonable grounds? It would seem not. In *Bayer* the Court held that the language of the section "does not admit of any allowance" for the defendant's honest belief in circumstances justifying necessity.[59] The apparent rationale for this approach is that a statutory defence such as that provided for in s 3(2) confers a "benefit" on an accused and there is no warrant for reading into its terms those common law considerations which are appropriate to "penal" provisions. In particular, the specific references to the accused's belief, made in those sections of the Crimes Act 1961 dealing with matters of justification or defence,[60] by implication excludes consideration of the matter in a "statutory" defence that makes no such mention. This approach has more recently been affirmed in *Wilcox v Police*.[61] Yet the rationale is surely a dubious one. The actual distinction, if any, between a "statutory" defence and a "penal" provision is not made clear, and it is far from self-evident that ordinary principles of criminal responsibility regarding exculpatory mistakes should have no application in the former case. Criminal defences, whether statutory or not, are part of penal provisions. It could also be argued that all defences, statutory and common law based, confer a "benefit" on an accused and in that regard are, or ought to be, indistinguishable. In any event, it does not follow that the sort of benefit conferred by a "statutory" defence is such as to justify the exclusion of other possible exculpatory provisions, particularly where the offence, in respect of which the statutory defence is claimed, is itself truly "penal" and carries the possibility of loss of liberty.[62]

---

57   [1994] 2 NZLR 48 (CA).

58   Ibid at 50. See also *R v Gough* [1993] AC 646, [1993] 2 All ER 724 (HL).

59   See also *O'Neill v Police* 22/11/93, CA392/93, on appeal from *Police v O'Neill* [1993] 3 NZLR 712. The same principle was held to apply.

60   See, for example, ss 41 (prevention of suicide or injury), 44-46 (suppression of riot), and 48 (self-defence).

61   [1995] 2 NZLR 160 at 165, (1995) 12 CRNZ 468 at 474 (CA).

62   The offence defined in s 3(1) Trespass Act 1980 is punishable by a fine not exceeding $1000 or imprisonment for a term not exceeding 3 months.

11.3.1.2 *Emergency operations*

It has been noted that the standard of "reasonable care and skill" mentioned in ss 61 and 61A should be read in the light of the duty imposed by s 155.[63] This section provides that, *except in the case of necessity*, every one who undertakes to administer surgical or medical treatment is under a legal duty to have and to use reasonable knowledge, care, and skill in administering the treatment. In *R v Yogasakaran*,[64] the Court of Appeal rejected a submission that the qualification "except in the case of necessity" had any bearing on the situation where an anaesthetist had to act in haste when an emergency arose during an operation. Of the expression, the Court said:

> That exception is plainly intended to cover the case of persons unqualified or insufficiently qualified who in emergencies undertake surgical or medical treatment or the like. It is not intended to emancipate a professional medical practitioner from the exercise of reasonable professional care and skill in an emergency. Instant decisions may have to be taken in an emergency; that must be a major factor to be kept prominently in mind in determining whether there has been a failure to live up to the appropriate professional standard.

There may be many situations in which an emergency dictates the need for immediate medical intervention and treatment. Almost invariably, it will not be possible to obtain the consent of the patient concerned and obtaining the consent of someone able to give consent on the patient's behalf may be impracticable. If actual patient consent were required for every medical procedure without exception, the administration of emergency medicine would be seriously impaired and doctors would face a choice between operating without such consent (with a possible prosecution for criminal assault to follow) and refusing to operate at all.[65]

At common law, the doctrine of necessity has been extended to allow action to be taken to preserve the life, health, or wellbeing of another who is unable to consent to that action. Whether or not these situations are characterised as arising from an "emergency", there are two basic requirements that must be satisfied before action without consent can be justified on grounds of necessity:

(i) First, there must be a necessity to act when it is not practicable to communicate with the other person;

(ii) Secondly, the action taken must be such as a reasonable person would, in all the circumstances, take action in the best interests of the person being assisted.[66]

The principle of necessity, so formulated, will not justify mere officious intervention.[67] Neither will it justify a medical intervention without consent

---

63 See *Adams* § CA61.05.

64 [1990] 1 NZLR 399 at 405, (1989) 5 CRNZ 69 at 74 (CA).

65 Collins notes that if consent were mandatory in every case of medical intervention it would jeopardise the ethical obligation of doctors to "render all assistance possible to any patient where an urgent need for medical care exists". See Collins, *Medical Law in New Zealand*, Wellington, Brooker & Friend, 1992, § 3.4.1.

66 *Re F (Mental Patient: Sterilisation)* [1990] 2 AC 1 at 75, [1989] 2 WLR 1029 at 1084, 1085 (HL) (Lord Goff of Chieveley).

when another more appropriate person is available and willing to act or when it is contrary to the known wishes of the person in need of assistance (to the extent that the person is rationally capable of forming such a wish).[68] However, provided the above criteria are fulfilled, interference with the person or property of the person being assisted will not be unlawful. So, in the event of a railway accident or plane crash where injured passengers lie trapped in the wreckage, the principle of necessity will render lawful the actions of other persons who offer aid and comfort to victims, even where reasonable assistance given in good faith actually accelerates the death of the person being assisted. This might occur where, for example, a victim is trapped in a fiercely burning carriage and amputation of a limb is necessary to remove him from the immediate threat to his life; notwithstanding that the victim may later die as a result of complications caused by blood-loss from the amputation before intensive life-saving treatment could be administered.

11.3.1.2(a) *Treatment without emergency*

Necessity would also cover the treatment by a doctor or nurse of an elderly person who suffers a stroke which renders him incapable of speech or movement. Any touching or movement of his person aimed at assisting or caring for him will be lawful. Clearly, this situation, although embraced by necessity, is not strictly an emergency and is characterised as a "permanent or semi-permanent state of affairs".[69] In *Re F*,[70] Lord Goff suggested that the principle of necessity should also be applicable to a case of a mentally disordered person who is disabled from giving consent. In such a case, as with a stroke victim, the permanent state of affairs may call for a wider range of care than may be needed in an emergency which arises from accidental injury.

> When the state of affairs is permanent, or semi-permanent, action properly taken to preserve the life, health or well-being of the assisted person may well transcend such measures as surgical operation or substantial medical treatment and may extend to include such humdrum matters as routine medical or dental treatment, even simple care such as dressing and undressing and putting to bed.[71]

A situation or state of affairs characterised as permanent or semi-permanent, as with a mentally impaired person or a patient in a "permanent" coma, may justify a doctor's moving with dispatch to do the thing which secures the patient's best interests, without the need to obtain the patient's consent. However, this stands in contrast to the situation where a doctor performs an operation without consent on a patient temporarily rendered unconscious as a result of an accident. In these circumstances the doctor should do no more than is reasonably essential, in the best interests of the patient, before he recovers consciousness.[72] The latter restriction derives from the

---

67 Ibid at 76, at 1086.
68 Ibid.
69 Ibid.
70 Ibid.
71 Ibid.
72 Ibid at 77, at 1087.

expectation that the patient will, before long, regain consciousness, and may then be consulted about longer term measures. Therefore, the doctrine of necessity may not cover medical interventions where the attending physician does more than is reasonably required to secure the patient's immediate needs. Suppose, for example, that V is severely injured in a motor accident. While V is comatose, D, a surgeon, performs surgery to repair a compound fracture to V's upper left leg. Although the primary operation without V's consent may well be justified on grounds of necessity, D is not at liberty to perform additional surgery of a cosmetic nature to eliminate "ugly scarring" without V's consent, particularly where this involves the surgical removal of skin tissue from some other part of V's body.[73] The suggested standard, that any treatment which is "clearly to the medical benefit of the patient" may be given where there is no reasonable likelihood of the patient regaining competency,[74] clearly needs elaboration in cases where the patient is in fact expected to recover competency.

11.3.2 The general common law defence

As was noted earlier, English courts have in recent years recognised a common law defence of necessity, which has come to be referred to as "duress of circumstances". The modern defence of necessity was first recognised in *R v Willer*.[75] The appellant had been charged with reckless driving after he had driven very slowly on a pavement while attempting to escape from a gang of youths who were intent on subjecting him and his passengers to violence. The trial Judge ruled that the defence of necessity was not open to him. The Court of Appeal quashed the conviction and said that the issue of necessity did not, in any event, arise. Rather, it considered that the appropriate defence to raise was duress, which was not pursued. The foundation of the defence would have been: "I could do no other in the face of this hostility than to take the right turn as I did, to mount the pavement and to drive through the gap out of further harm's way, harm to person and harm to my property."[76] However, as the authors of Smith and Hogan properly observe,[77] this was not an instance of the previously recognised defence of duress by threats. Rather, the Court was allowing the defence of necessity which it had purported to dismiss as unnecessary to the decision. "It should surely make no difference whether D drove on the pavement to escape from the youths, or a herd of charging bulls, a runaway lorry, or a flood, if he did so in order to escape death or serious bodily harm."[78] Conceived of in these terms, the case for a defence of necessity or duress of circumstances might seem so strong as to be unarguable when the

---

73 For further discussion of the issues arising see *Marshall v Curry* [1933] 3 DLR 260, (1933) 60 CCC 136; *Murray v McMurchy* [1949] 2 DLR 442; also the discussion in Collins, *Medical Law in New Zealand* Wellington, Brooker & Friend, 1992, §§ 3.4.4, 3.4.5.

74 Gostin, *Mental Health Services – Law and Practice*, 1986, § 20-16.

75 (1986) 83 Cr App R 225 (CA).

76 Ibid at 227.

77 *Criminal Law* (7th ed), London, Butterworths, 1992, 242.

78 Ibid.

emergent peril involves the threat of death or serious bodily harm. However, as we shall see, the approach taken by the English and New Zealand courts differs significantly, to the extent that it may be doubted whether there is in New Zealand a *separate* defence of necessity based upon threatening *human* behaviour.

11.3.2.1 *Development of the English doctrine*

In *R v Conway*[79] the English Court of Appeal first coined the expression "duress of circumstances". The appellant, D, had been convicted of reckless driving. His evidence was that a passenger, T, had a few weeks earlier narrowly escaped being shot with a shotgun. When on this occasion two young men in civilian clothes had come running towards his car, T screamed "drive off!" and D did so, fearing that the men were potential assassins intent on attacking T. They were in fact police officers, who wanted to talk to T for whom a bench warrant was outstanding. In allowing D's appeal, the Court concluded that only where the facts establish "duress of circumstances" could necessity be a defence to a charge of reckless driving. The defence would be established where, as in *R v Willer*, the defendant was constrained by circumstances to drive as he did, in order to avoid death or serious bodily harm to himself or some other person. On the facts alleged, the trial Judge was bound to leave the defence to the jury and because he failed to do so the conviction was quashed.

The Court in *Conway* accepted that the admission of a defence of "duress of circumstances" is a logical consequence of the existence of the defence of duress, in its commonly understood sense of a threat requiring D to "do this or else".[80] The only difference between the two defences is that whereas duress arises from wrongful threats of violence by *another human being*, necessity or duress of circumstances arises from other *objective dangers* which threaten the accused.[81] In the view of Lord Hailsham the distinction is one without a relevant difference, because duress may be viewed as simply a species of the genus of necessity which is caused by wrongful threats. In either case, the type of pressure on a person's free will is precisely the same.[82]

In *Conway*, the Court of Appeal concluded that necessity could only be a defence to a charge of reckless driving where the facts establish "duress of circumstances", ie where the defendant is constrained to drive as he did to avoid *death or serious bodily harm* to himself or to some other person. It appears from the discussion that there is, in law, no difference between necessity and "duress of circumstances", in that the defence of necessity approved by the Court is subject "to the same limitations as the 'do this or else' species of duress".[83]

In any event, the Court was unwilling to recognise any wider defence to a charge of reckless driving, which would imply that where "duress of

---

79   [1988] 3 All ER 1025, [1988] 3 WLR 1238 (CA).

80   Ibid at 1029, at 1244.

81   *R v Howe* [1987] AC 417 at 429, [1987] 1 All ER 771 at 777 (HL) (per Lord Hailsham LC).

82   Ibid.

83   *R v Conway* [1988] 3 All ER 1025 at 1029, [1988] 3 WLR 1238 at 1244 (CA).

circumstances" is invoked it must always be possible to point to an "objective danger" if not actual threats. What constitutes a relevant "objective danger" is not at all clear. However, by analogy with the common law governing duress of threats,[84] it appears that the feared danger must be either real or, if not, at least reasonably perceived. Mere anxiety that the accused *might* be attacked, or a claim that she was forced to drive recklessly because she wanted to escape the effects of a tidal wave that she feared *might* eventuate, when none in fact existed and there was no reasonable basis for her concern, would seem not to meet the "objective" requirement.

The scope of "duress of circumstances" was also considered in *R v Martin*,[85] where the disqualified defendant drove his son to work because he feared that his wife, who was mentally disturbed, would commit suicide if he refused. The son had overslept and his wife was obsessively fearful that he would lose his job. On an appeal against conviction because of the failure of the trial Judge to leave the defence of "necessity" to the jury, the Court of Appeal held that the defence should have been so put. The Court summarised the relevant principles:

(i) English law recognises a defence of necessity in *extreme circumstances*. The defence most commonly arises as duress, ie pressure on the accused's will from the wrongful threats or violence of others. However, it may arise from other objective dangers threatening the accused or others. In this form it is referred to as "duress of circumstances".

(ii) The defence is only available if, from an *objective* standpoint, the accused can be said to be acting *reasonably* and *proportionately* to avoid the threat of death or serious injury.

(iii) Where the defence is available on the facts, the jury must determine two questions:

   (a) Was the accused impelled to act as he did because, given what he *reasonably believed to be the situation*, he had good cause to fear that death or serious physical injury may otherwise result?

   (b) If so, would a sober person of reasonable firmness, *with the accused's characteristics*, have responded to the situation by acting as the accused did?

(iv) Where the answer to both questions is "yes", the jury should acquit.

In considering the availability of the defence to a charge of driving while disqualified, the Court stated:

We see no material distinction between offences of reckless driving and driving whilst disqualified so far as the . . . scope of this defence is concerned. Equally we can see no distinction in principle between various threats of death; it matters not whether the risk is death by murder or by suicide or indeed by accident. One can illustrate the latter by considering a disqualified driver being driven by his wife, she

---

84   *R v Graham* [1982] 1 All ER 801, [1982] 1 WLR 294 (CA).

85   [1989] 1 All ER 652, (1989) 88 Cr App R 343 (CA).

suffering a heart attack in remote countryside and he needing instantly to get her to hospital.[86]

While the principles seem clear enough, it is strange that the case should have been characterised as one of *duress of circumstances* since it appears to have been a case of duress by threats ("do this or else").[87] However, its characterisation as duress of circumstances may be of little consequence for English law because, as we have seen, the principles governing each defence are identical. The characterisation would be critical under New Zealand law because, as we shall see, any claim of duress of circumstances alleging any type of threat by "human agency" would not fall within the scope of the common law defence, but would, instead, have to comply with the strict terms of s 24 Crimes Act 1961.

11.3.2.1(a) *Relevant characteristics*
An issue which has proved to be of some importance in the development of the English defence of duress and, by extension, duress of circumstances, concerns the extent to which particular characteristics possessed by the accused, eg low intelligence or voluntary consumption of drink or drugs, are relevant in assessing the second objective component, of "reasonable firmness" in responding to the threatening situation. The question, what are the relevant characteristics of the accused to which the jury should have regard in considering the second objective test, was considered by the English Court of Appeal in *R v Bowen*.[88] In that case, the appellant had been convicted of obtaining services by deception after he had purchased various items by paying a proportion of the cost by way of deposit, but had never completed payment on any item purchased. He claimed that throughout the period in question (a period of over 2 years) he had acted under duress imposed by two men, who had accosted him in a public house and had threatened him that he and his family would be petrol-bombed if he did not obtain goods for them. Defence evidence was presented at the trial that the appellant was a man of low intelligence (with an IQ of 68 and reading age of a child of 6 years, 8 months) and that he was abnormally suggestible. The Court of Appeal held that in most cases the only relevant "characteristics", for the purposes of the second objective element, were the offender's age and sex.[89] The Court also took the view that low IQ, short of mental impairment or mental defectiveness, could not be a characteristic that makes those who have it less courageous and less able to withstand threats and pressure. It held that since the objective test predicates a "sober person of reasonable firmness", there could be no scope for

---

86   Ibid at 654, at 356.

87   Smith and Hogan, *Criminal Law* (7th ed), London, Butterworths, 1992, 242.

88   [1996] 4 All ER 837, [1996] 2 Cr App R 157 (CA).

89   In making this determination, the Court was influenced by authorities on provocation — which it considered were similar to duress — where it had been consistently held that age, sex, physical health, and disability may be relevant characteristics. See *R v Howe* [1987] AC 417 at 459, [1987] 1 All ER 771 at 800 (HL); *R v Morhall* [1996] AC 90 at 97, 98, [1995] 3 All ER 659 at 665, 666 (HL).

attributing to that sober and reasonable person the offender's low intelligence, since it was difficult to see how the person of reasonable firmness could be invested with the characteristic of a personality which lacks reasonable firmness.[90] The Court of Appeal identified seven general principles, derived from the relevant authorities:

(i) The fact that the accused is more pliable, vulnerable, timid, or susceptible to threats than a normal person is not a characteristic that may legitimately be invested in the reasonable person for the purpose of considering the objective test.

(ii) The defendant may be in a category of persons whom the jury think is less able to resist pressure than people not within that category. Relevant factors for this purpose include *age* (a young person is not so robust as a mature one); *sex* (though many women would probably consider they had as much moral courage to resist pressure as men); *pregnancy*; *serious physical disability* (which inhibits self-protection); and *recognised mental illness or psychiatric condition* (eg post-traumatic stress disorder).

(iii) Characteristics relevant in considering provocation,[91] relating to the nature of provocation itself, will not necessarily be relevant in cases of duress. This would include homosexuality, since there is no reason to think that homosexuals are less robust in resisting threats of the kind that are relevant in duress cases.

(iv) Self-induced characteristics such as those owing to abuse of alcohol, drugs, and glue are not relevant.

(v) Psychiatric evidence may be admissible to show that the accused suffered from a *mental illness*, *mental impairment*, or *recognised psychiatric condition*, provided, generally, persons suffering from such a condition may be more susceptible to pressure and threats, and to assist the jury in deciding whether a reasonable person suffering from such a condition might have been impelled to act as the defendant did.

(vi) Where counsel wishes to submit that the accused has a relevant characteristic, this must be made plain to the judge who must then rule on the admissibility of supporting medical evidence.

(vii) In most cases it is probable that the age and sex of the accused will be the only characteristics capable of being relevant.

In New Zealand it must be regarded as an open question whether, in an appropriate case, a court would consider itself limited, in determining the second objective limb, to the sorts of characteristics listed in (ii) and (vi) above. Because, as has been noted, provocation and duress are analogous for the purposes of determining the scope of the objective element, a court in ruling on the availability of a defence of duress of circumstances in New Zealand would have to be mindful of the local developments regarding "characteristics" in the defence of provocation. In particular, the New Zealand Court of Appeal has

---

90 [1996] 4 All ER 837 at 842, 843. See also *R v Hegarty* [1994] Crim LR 353; *R v Horne* [1994] Crim LR 584; *R v Hurst* [1995] 1 Cr App R 82.

91 See chapter 14.

expressed the view that the ambit of provocation in New Zealand may have been "unduly restricted" by observations in earlier case law,[92] such that they "go somewhat too far and add needless complexity to the application of [s 169 Crimes Act 1961]".[93] It has been held, for the purposes of New Zealand law, that an accused's racial characteristic, her age and sex, any mental deficiency, or her tendency to excessive emotionalism as a result of brain injury, are all examples of characteristics of the offender to be attributed to the hypothetical person for the purposes of s 169.[94]

However, it is doubtful whether, if a case involving facts similar to *Bowen* had to be determined in New Zealand, the accused's low intelligence would amount to a characteristic under the title of "mental deficiency". The English courts have ruled that "mental impairment" or "mental defectiveness", which may be regarded as analogous to the New Zealand expression "mental deficiency", are to be distinguished from low intelligence which, in itself, is not a characteristic that makes those who have it less courageous and less able to withstand threats and pressure.[95] Nevertheless, it is clearly a question of degree. In each case it will be necessary to ask whether the deficit in intelligence amounted to an intellectual disability so that it can be said that the defendant was "mentally deficient". It will then be up to the jury or trier of fact to determine whether the measure of coercion brought to bear on the mind of the defendant was such as would influence the reaction of a sober person of reasonable firmness, having the characteristic of the defendant as a person of low intelligence; mindful of course that mere pliancy or vulnerability to pressure are not relevant characteristics.[96]

11.3.2.2 *Development of duress of circumstances in New Zealand*

In New Zealand the statutory defence of compulsion (duress of threats) and the common law defence of necessity have developed along conceptually distinct lines, so that it cannot be said that the criteria for determining the availability of compulsion are identical to those for necessity. However, the New Zealand courts have now acknowledged the existence of a defence of necessity, analogous to duress of circumstances and in respect of which the English cases on duress of circumstances have been considered and approved. The critical issue in New Zealand concerns the content and scope of the new defence, an issue which has yet to be determined by the courts. The content and scope of necessity will depend on the courts' perception of the common law, although, as we will see, existing statutory definitions of particular defences that are

---

92 See *R v McCarthy* [1992] 2 NZLR 550 at 558, (1992) 8 CRNZ 58 at 66 (CA), commenting on the limitations suggested in *R v McGregor* [1962] NZLR 1069 at 1080-1083 (CA).

93 *R v McCarthy* [1992] 2 NZLR 550 at 558, (1992) 8 CRNZ 58 at 67 (CA).

94 Ibid.

95 *R v Bowen* [1996] 4 All ER 837 at 845, [1996] 2 Cr App R 157 at 167 (CA).

96 *R v Horne* [1994] Crim LR 584 at 585, 586 (CA); *R v Bowen* [1996] 4 All ER 837 at 843, [1996] 2 Cr App R 157 at 165 (CA). However, where the offender is intellectually disabled, but not sufficiently so to be found unfit to plead, susceptibility to pressure and suggestibility will normally be a feature of his emotional makeup that may make him more readily amenable to threats and compulsion.

related to necessity (compulsion, self-defence, impossibility) are such that it may be difficult for the courts to determine a coherent independent model.[97]

The status of necessity in New Zealand was considered in *Kapi v MOT*.[98] The defendant was charged in the District Court with failing to stop after an accident and failing to ascertain injury. He had been driving home along a suburban street following a rugby practice when he collided with the rear of a parked vehicle which he said he failed to see because of oncoming headlights. He argued that he should not be convicted because he held an honest belief that he might be beaten up if he stopped to ascertain whether any person had been injured, which made it reasonable for him not to do so. His defence was thus one of necessity or, as it was characterised by the Court, duress of circumstances.

The District Court Judge accepted that although there was no authority in New Zealand regarding traffic offences, a common law defence of necessity may be available under s 20 Crimes Act 1961. His Honour concluded, however, that the defence required evidence of an immediate threat of death or serious bodily injury; because there was no reason why the defendant was prevented from at least stopping and backing up, without getting out of the car, to ascertain whether anyone had been injured, it was held there was no reasonable basis for him to be apprehensive for his safety. The defence of necessity failed.

In the High Court, the appeal was argued on the assumption that the defendant had an honest belief that he was in danger of an assault by persons unknown if he stopped following the collision. The defendant contended that for the defence to succeed his belief did not need to be based on reasonable grounds. Jeffries J accepted that a defence of necessity does exist in New Zealand and that the "prospective legislative provision" of a general defence in cl 30 Crimes Bill 1989 "means to put the existence of the defence beyond question for New Zealand".[99]

Concerning the requirement for "reasonable grounds", the Court acknowledged that the defence of self-defence, to which counsel sought to draw an analogy, required only an honest belief that the person was being attacked, regardless whether that belief was reasonable, and that the defence would only be lost on objective grounds if the *reaction* in self-defence was unreasonable. Counsel then argued that in the case of necessity, the honest belief being the subjective element, the objective element is supplied by measuring the response against what a person of ordinary common sense and prudence would do in the circumstances. The Court disagreed. After reviewing the authorities, Jeffries J held that:

> On close analysis most, if not all the cases, reveal three elements. First, a really extraordinary emergency; secondly an honest belief, and thirdly reasonable grounds. There is no authority for an honest belief and an ordinary commonsense and prudence test to the circumstances. The general rule in the decided cases in all

---

97 *Adams* § CA24.28.

98 (1991) 8 CRNZ 49 (CA), affirming [1992] 1 NZLR 227, (1991) 7 CRNZ 481.

99 [1992] 1 NZLR 227 at 230, (1991) 7 CRNZ 481 at 483.

countries is that honest belief is firmly limited to reasonable grounds before the honest belief itself can be accepted.[100]

The Court of Appeal agreed with this analysis, and adverted to the fact that in *Conway* the argument that the defence of necessity should be based upon subjective belief was expressly rejected.[101] Concerning the scope of the defence, the Court of Appeal held that it must be seen as "probable" that in New Zealand the scope of the defence was considered by the Legislature and that s 24 Crimes Act 1961 reflects the extent to which the defence of necessity was adopted in this country. After quoting the text of s 24(1), the Court said:

> In this respect, in *R v Willer* (1986) 83 Cr App R 225 there was evidence of direct threats to kill. In *Conway* there was evidence of people running at the accused (in fact they were plain clothes policemen) and claimed fear of a fatal attack and in *Martin* there was evidence of a threat of suicide. So far as such fact situations would not fall within s 24 this might be said to result from deliberate legislative intent to restrict the scope of the defence of duress or compulsion.[102]

The Court reasoned that because s 24 provides a defence of compulsion (duress of threats) where the criminal act is done under threat of death or grievous bodily harm from a person who is present when the offence is committed, s 20 cannot be said to preserve a common law defence of duress by threat or fear of death or grievous bodily harm from a person not present.[103] The appeal was determined against the appellant on this basis, the clear implication being that in the absence of persons actually (objectively) present making threats, there was no emergency that could give rise to a defence of duress of circumstances, since it was not claimed that the threat came from an "objective danger".

11.3.2.3 Necessity as a general defence

In *Kapi v MOT*, the Court of Appeal appears to concede that there may be a "broader" defence of necessity,[104] although it is by no means clear from the ensuing discussion what are the parameters of that general defence. One thing that appears certain, however, is that for such a defence to be available in New Zealand, the defendant must possess a belief formed on reasonable grounds of *imminent peril of death or serious injury*, notwithstanding that this may appear unreasonably to limit the availability of the defence in respect of relatively trivial offences:

> We consider on the authorities cited to us that a defence of necessity, if available in New Zealand, requires at least a belief formed on reasonable grounds of imminent peril of death or serious injury. Breach of the law then is excused only where there

---

100 Ibid at 230, at 484.

101 *Kapi v MOT* (1991) 8 CRNZ 49 at 54 (CA). "It follows that a defence of 'duress of circumstances' is available only if *from an objective standpoint* the defendant can be said to be acting in order to avoid a threat of death or serious injury." *R v Conway* [1988] 3 All ER 1025 at 1030, [1988] 3 WLR 1238 at 1244 (CA) (Woolf LJ).

102 *Kapi v MOT* (1991) 8 CRNZ 49 at 54 (CA).

103 Ibid at 54, 55.

104 Ibid at 55.

was no realistic choice but to act in that way. Even then the response can be excused only where it is proportionate to the peril.[105]

A breach of the law is excused where there is no realistic choice but to act in that way and where the response is proportionate to the peril.[106] While there is no requirement to prove there was in fact a "really extraordinary emergency", the absence of actual peril will of course be relevant to an assessment of the reasonableness and honesty of the belief.

A useful illustrative case is *R v Lamont*,[107] in which the appellant appealed against conviction on two counts of causing death by careless use of a motor vehicle. The principal ground of appeal was the trial Judge's failure to allow a defence of duress of circumstances to go to the jury. The appellant had driven at an excessive speed and ultimately lost control of and crashed his vehicle after another vehicle had allegedly "tailgated" him, causing him to panic. The Judge refused to allow the defence of duress of circumstances to go to the jury, principally on the basis that there was no evidence that he feared death or serious injury, simply that he feared there would be a collision. The Court of Appeal agreed and dismissed the appeal:

> The type of emergency situations for which these defences may be available are those in which fear for life and limb is such as to compel breach of the law. If a breach of the law is by way of response to such threats and fear it is to be expected that the attribution would be immediate. Yet in this case . . . despite it being put to him more than once the appellant gave no evidence that he feared death or serious injury . . . A concern at having his car hit or even shunted in the rear does not amount to fear of death or serious injury.[108]

It appears, then, that by synthesising the New Zealand case law on necessity with such English case law as is consistent, the following observations, at least, may be made about the operation of the defence of necessity in New Zealand:

(i) The perceived threat must be one of imminent death or serious injury;

(ii) D's perception of the threat must be either correct or reasonably based;

(iii) D's action must be in response to that perceived threat;

(iv) D's response to the threat must be proportionate, in the sense that a sober person of reasonable firmness, sharing certain characteristics of D, would have responded in like manner (where the qualifying characteristics are as yet not authoritatively decided in New Zealand);

(v) The defence is not available to murder or attempted murder;

(vi) The defence is not available whenever the source of the threat is another person (all such cases are covered only by s 24).

We illustrate these observations with a deliberately awkward scenario:

> D is driving his car down a steep hill at night. Suddenly, the large truck which has been travelling at a safe distance behind him appears to speed up and "threatens" to

---

105 Ibid at 57.
106 Ibid.
107 27/4/92, CA442/91.
108 Ibid at 8-10.

ram him from behind. D recognises that being hit by a truck may cause a serious accident. Unbeknown to D, the driver of the truck has had a heart attack and the truck is, in reality, driverless. As D speeds up to escape from the danger he passes a traffic officer hidden in a layby and is ultimately charged with driving at an excessive speed. Should D have a defence of duress of circumstances?

The answer appears to be "yes". Clearly the runaway truck in fact constitutes a danger. Although D thinks the threat is posed by another person, in fact it is not; thus it falls within the scope of necessity rather than statutory compulsion.[109] Assuming the court was willing to accept that there was an objective threat demanding some remedial action, the issues for the jury would be whether the accused had a reasonable belief that death or serious injury would result to him if he did not take action to avoid the danger, that the action taken was reasonably proportionate to the threat, and that a sober person of reasonable firmness would have responded to the danger in the same way.

11.3.2.4 *Strict liability offences*

Where the offence is characterised as a public welfare regulatory offence, the defence of necessity is subsumed by the general defence of absence of fault. The test to be applied in such cases is whether in all the circumstances the accused did what a reasonable person would have done.[110] The defence of absence of fault is one of due diligence or absence of negligence, and extends to situations where the accused reasonably, but mistakenly, believed in facts which, if true, would have made the conduct innocent.[111] Given that necessity is subsumed under absence of fault in relation to public welfare offences, it would appear that an honest but reasonably mistaken belief that the offender is threatened with death or serious injury, necessitating action in breach of the law, will be a good defence to a public welfare offence; even though not to a true crime. This would suggest that the defence has a different, perhaps more liberal, character when applied to public welfare offences. However, in the regulatory context, the accused is required to prove absence of fault, which would include necessity, on the balance of probabilities. In addition, before a trial judge is required to leave the defence to the jury there must be a credible or plausible narrative which might lead the jury to entertain the reasonable possibility of the defence.[112] These requirements would tend to eliminate any notorious or unmeritorious claims.

---

109 See also *R v Morris* (1994) 32 CR (4th) 191 (SC). A new trial was ordered when the Justice of the Peace refused to allow evidence of necessity on the ground that the offence (speeding) was one of absolute liability.

110 See *Civil Aviation Dept v MacKenzie* [1983] NZLR 78 at 81, also reported as *MacKenzie v Civil Aviation Dept* (1983) 1 CRNZ 38 (CA) (Richardson J); also *Tifaga v Dept of Labour* [1980] 2 NZLR 235 at 242, 243 (CA) (Richardson J); *R v Slovack* [1980] 1 WWR 368; *R v Gonder* (1981) 62 CCC (2d) 326.

111 See § 4.2.1.1; *Adams* § CA20.48.

112 *R v Joyce* [1968] NZLR 1070 at 1077 (CA); *R v Grice* [1975] 1 NZLR 760 at 765 (CA).

11.4 CODIFICATION OF NECESSITY

Since the early 1970's, the tide of both law reform and judicial developments has been moving in favour of the recognition of necessity as a defence. In New Zealand, the draft Crimes Bill 1989 contains a proposal for the codification of necessity (cl 30), which has now been redrafted by the Crimes Consultative Committee in order to incorporate some "useful features" of the English Draft Code provision.[113] Clause 30, as originally drafted, provided:

> Necessity — A person is not criminally responsible for any act done or omitted to be done under such circumstances of sudden and extraordinary emergency that a person of ordinary commonsense and prudence could not reasonably be expected to act otherwise.

The clause aimed to protect a person from criminal responsibility for anything done in an emergency, if a person of ordinary common sense and prudence could not reasonably be expected to have acted otherwise. It was based broadly on cl 46 of the proposed Criminal Code (UK) and on § 3.02 Model Penal Code (US).[114] The draft reflects the common law position that where duress of circumstances is advanced as a defence to crime it must be established by reference to objective facts or beliefs. This would imply that a mistaken belief, wholly unfounded in fact, in circumstances of necessity, will be insufficient to give rise to the defence.[115]

The position of mistaken but reasonable beliefs is unclear. The wording of the original cl 30 does not even mention the accused's state of mind, and appears to require only an objective situation of emergent peril, regardless whether it is perceived as such. However, this interpretation, which excludes consideration of the defendant's subjective belief concerning the emergency, is both inconsistent with principle and contrary to the approach taken in respect of other defences recognised under New Zealand criminal law, and must be regarded as unlikely. This anomaly was rectified when the Crimes Consultative Committee recommended a significant redraft of cl 30.[116] The redrafted clause now reads:

> Necessity — (1) A person is not criminally responsible for any act done or omitted to be done under circumstances of emergency in which —
>
> (a) The person *believes* that it is immediately necessary to avoid death or serious bodily harm to that person or any other person; and
>
> (b) A person of ordinary common sense and prudence could not be expected to act otherwise.

---

113 See Crimes Bill Consultative Committee, *Crimes Bill 1989: Report of the Crimes Consultative Committee presented to the Minister of Justice April 1991*, Wellington, Dept of Justice, 1991 at 20.

114 Crimes Bill 1989, Explanatory Note.

115 See *R v Conway* [1988] 3 All ER 1025 at 1029, [1988] 3 WLR 1238 at 1244 (CA): "necessity can only be a defence . . . *where the facts establish* 'duress of circumstances' " (emphasis added).

116 See Crimes Bill Consultative Committee, *Crimes Bill 1989: Report of the Crimes Consultative Committee presented to the Minister of Justice April 1991*, Wellington, Dept of Jusitce, 1991, 95, 96.

(2) Subclause (1) does not apply where the person who does or omits the act has knowingly and without reasonable cause placed himself or herself in or remained in, a situation where there was a risk of such an emergency.

(3) Subclause (1) does not apply to offences of murder or attempted murder. [Emphasis added]

The revised version now clearly includes a subjective element, which, should it ever become law, would bring the statutory defence broadly into line with the other defences already contained in the Crimes Act.

11.5 IMPOSSIBILITY OF COMPLIANCE

A defence which is closely related to necessity is that of impossibility. To distinguish it from impossibility in attempts, which has an entirely different conceptual basis, the defence is sometimes called impossibility of compliance. Impossibility in this sense may arise where, at the time of the prohibited conduct or event, it was not possible to comply with the law. However, there are two important qualifications to the doctrine:

(i) The impossibility must not be attributable to the accused's own fault.

(ii) The claimed impossibility must not create an inconsistency with the enactment creating the particular offence or any other statutory provision.

We examine each of these qualifications below.

11.5.1 Absolute impossibility

Impossibility operates by negativing the actus reus of an offence, in the same way as does physical involuntariness (causal necessity).[117] The essence of the analysis in such cases is that the performance of a legal duty was impossible because of circumstances which absolutely physically prevented the accused from doing the thing required by law. It is a case of actus reus for which the accused is not responsible. Unlike the defence of duress of circumstances (teleological necessity), which may be based upon a mistaken but reasonable belief that a particular course of action is required in order to avoid an emergent peril, impossibility presupposes that the actus reus occurred in circumstances which the accused was entirely unable to avoid. It is not simply a case of choice between evils. In *Tifaga v Dept of Labour*, Richardson J stated, "[i]n contemporary usage *inability to comply at all* is the subject of ... impossibility."[118] There would seem, therefore, to be no room for a mistaken belief in impossibility as a defence to a charge that the accused had failed to perform a duty prescribed by law. Either the duty was impossible to fulfil or it was not, in which case the defence must fail.

Similarly, the notion of impossibility, being a species of involuntariness, does not allow for a qualification based on reasonableness. It does not make sense to say that a proscribed omission was "reasonably impossible" any more than it makes sense to say that the accused's acts were "reasonably

---

117 See § 2.3.

118 [1980] 2 NZLR 235 at 243 (CA).

involuntary". Conduct was either impossible or it was not. It does not assist analysis to ask whether a reasonable person would have considered the duty impossible to fulfil. The essence of the claim is that the defendant was prohibited from fulfilling her legal responsibilities by exigent events.

This may assist us in understanding why some claims of impossibility must fail. The availability of an alternative course of action militates against the notion of impossibility, because it suggests that the course of conduct required by the law was merely *difficult* to fulfil and not impossible. An opportunity to abide by the law is an essential basis for testing responsibility for acts and omissions,[119] and its absence denies D's responsibility for the actus reus of a crime. Any qualification to the exculpatory defence based on *difficulty* of compliance, as opposed to *impossibility*, would negate the purpose of the doctrine and would decrease the effectiveness of criminal sanctions. Many people find difficulty in complying with the law's demands, but that has never seriously been advanced as a reason for reducing the high standard of compliance expected of all responsible citizens.

The *absolute* character of impossibility may be demonstrated by reference to cases. In the old English case of *R v Bamber*,[120] the defendant was indicted for failure to repair a road adjoining the sea. It was held that the accused was not guilty because, as the result of an "act of God", the road, and all the materials with which a road could be made, had been washed away in a storm. Sometimes a defence akin to impossibility is claimed but not expressed as such. For example, in *Stockdale v Coulson*,[121] where the defendant company director had been charged with failing to annex copies of the company's balance sheet to annual returns as required by the Companies Act 1948 (UK), it was held that since there were no balance sheets in existence which had been laid before the company in a general meeting the defendant was not guilty of the offence charged. The Court said that "you cannot be punished for failing to annex something which does not exist".[122]

By contrast, as was noted above, mere difficulty of compliance is no defence. This is demonstrated in *Tifaga v Dept of Labour*,[123] where impossibility had been claimed as a defence to a charge of overstaying under s 14 Immigration Act 1964. The defendant had come to New Zealand on a temporary entry permit. During the period in which the permit was still current, the defendant was convicted of an offence and sentenced to imprisonment for 6 months. While in prison he was advised that his permit was to be revoked. At about the time of his release from prison he received a formal notice which required him to leave New Zealand within 21 days of that date. He failed to do so and was charged with overstaying his permit. His defence was that at the time of his release from prison he had neither savings nor recourse to funds to meet the cost of departing from New Zealand and in

---

119 Ibid at 238 (Woodhouse J).
120 (1843) 5 QB 279, 114 ER 1254.
121 [1974] 3 All ER 154, [1974] 1 WLR 1192.
122 Ibid at 158, at 1196 (per Melford Stevenson J).
123 [1980] 2 NZLR 235 (CA). Discussed at § 4.2.2.

the time available to him had been unable to earn a sufficient amount. He argued that he had no choice about leaving or remaining in New Zealand so that his conduct in that regard was involuntary. Rejecting that argument, the Court of Appeal held that it was the appellant's responsibility to provide the practical means to enable him to leave the country. He had chosen not to have sufficient funds available to meet the fare from New Zealand. Since there was no evidence that it had been impossible to maintain a reserve fund for that purpose, it could not be said that his conduct was involuntary. The appeal was dismissed. Woodhouse J pointed out that it could not be said that some "extraneous cause" produced the situation whereby he was unable to leave, and that having the practical means to leave the country was the continuing responsibility of the defendant throughout his visit. The conviction and subsequent imprisonment of the appellant made compliance with the law more difficult and may have generated some sympathy for the defendant, but did not justify a finding that he was not criminally responsible.[124]

11.5.1.1 *Impossibility given ignorance of duty*
Impossibility of the variety being considered here should be distinguished from a different type of case which arises where D is unaware of his legal duty to act. In *Harding v Price*,[125] it was held that a driver is not liable for failure to report an accident if he does not know the accident has happened. Similarly, in an early case in which the defendant was charged with failing to give notice to a police constable that some animals of his were infected with a contagious disease, it was held that since the defendant did not know the animals were infected he could not be convicted.[126] As Keating J said:

> I cannot understand how . . . it can be said that a man can neglect to give notice with all practicable speed without knowledge of the fact of which he is to give notice.

In these cases exculpation is predicated not on physical impossibility of compliance but upon the meaninglessness of demanding compliance with a duty when D does not know that facts exist which give rise to the duty. As such, however, the determination of D's liability will, like physical impossibility, depend upon the absence of fault or mens rea in respect of those underlying facts.

11.5.2 Freedom from fault
In *Tifaga*, Richardson J noted that a requirement that the accused be free from fault in order to avoid criminal responsibility is implicit in the line of authorities on impossibility. In particular, the law looks first at the defendant's conduct leading up to, and his responsibility for the existence of, the impossibility; and, secondly, at the defendant's efforts and ability to overcome the situation he found himself in, ie whether he used "all practical endeavours"

---

124 See *Oakley-Moore v Robinson* [1982] RTR 74 in which it was held that where "parking" was caused by running out of petrol, no excuse was available to the regulatory offence of parking in the approach limits to a pedestrian crossing.

125 [1948] 1 KB 695, [1948] 1 All ER 283. See § 2.3.2.1.

126 *Nichols v Hall* (1873) LR 8 CP 322.

to overcome the difficulties of his situation but which, in the event, he found insurmountable.[127] A person cannot rely on impossibility of compliance which she has knowingly brought about by her own actions. It is only where the impossibility has arisen in circumstances which are outside the person's "reasonable or possible control" and in which she is not at fault, that liability is negated.[128]

Note that the limitation concerning "reasonable control" should be viewed as attaching only to the first limb of the test, namely, whether the defendant's conduct leading up to and perhaps generating the necessity was reasonable;[129] not to the second limb, concerning her ability to overcome the situation she found herself in (ie the situation of impossibility itself). For the reasons mentioned earlier, impossibility is an absolute concept. A thing cannot be impossible in degrees: it is either impossible or it is not. An objective evaluation is arguably meaningless on this second question.

11.5.3 Public policy

The doctrine of impossibility proceeds from the premise that the legislature is not to be assumed to have intended to punish for failure to perform the impossible. Of course, there will always be a point in a chain of events after which it may be said that the proscribed result is "inevitable".[130] However, the defence of impossibility is unavailable if the prohibited event is *not* caused by circumstances beyond the accused's ability to control:

> A defendant who by due diligence could have avoided the position from which there is no escape does not have a claim in justice for exemption from criminal responsibility for his conduct.[131]

Accordingly, mere inability due to financial stringency to comply with a statutory requirement will not amount to impossibility[132] where the shortage of funds has not been produced by circumstances beyond the defendant's control. For example, D should not park in a metered space unless he has money to feed the meter; and E, on a charge of failing to stop at a controlled intersection, should not drive a car which he knows has brakes that may fail at any time.

The essential principle may be described thus: impossibility is present where there is a complete inability on the part of the defendant to control

---

127 See *The Generous* (1818) 2 Dods 322, 165 ER 1501 (per Sir William Scott); quoted in *Tifaga v Dept of Labour* [1980] 2 NZLR 235 at 243, 244 (CA).

128 *Burns v Bidder* [1967] 2 QB 227 at 240, [1966] 3 All ER 29 at 36 (per James J).

129 This may explain the much criticised decision in *R v Larsonneur* (1933) 24 Cr App R 74, 149 LTR 542 (CCA), despite its being described by one commentator as "the acme of strict injustice!" Hall, *General Principles of Criminal Law*, Indianapolis, Bobbs-Merrill, 1960, 329 n 14. Compare Lanham, "Larsonneur Revisited" [1976] Crim LR 276; § 2.1.2.1.

130 *Tifaga v Dept of Labour* [1980] 2 NZLR 235 at 245 (CA).

131 Ibid (Richardson J).

132 See *MV Yorke Motors v Edwards* [1982] 1 All ER 1024, [1982] 1 WLR 444 (HL): a defendant cannot complain because a financial condition is difficult for him to fulfill; he can only complain when a financial condition is imposed which it is impossible for him to fulfill.

events at the point at which, without fault on her part, she has acquired a duty to perform an act or avoid an omission prescribed by law. It does not matter that the situation of impossibility may, at some earlier point, not have existed, provided the impossibility pertaining has not been generated by a lack of due diligence on the part of the defendant. Thus, in *Finau v Dept of Labour*,[133] it was held that the defendant had a defence of impossibility to a charge of overstaying when, at the time she was due to leave New Zealand, medical advice concerning her pregnancy triggered a refusal by the only available airline carrier to fly her to her destination. It might have been different, however, if there had been evidence that the pregnancy or other matters, for example leaving a booking to such a late stage that it was impossible to obtain a seat, had simply been manoeuvres by the appellant to circumvent the legislation.[134] Such evidence would tend to negate the defendant's claim that the situation was one she was powerless to avoid.

11.5.4 Inconsistency with a statute

The common law defence of impossibility is available in New Zealand by virtue of s 20 Crimes Act 1961, which preserves all common law defences to the extent that they are not "altered by or are inconsistent with" the express terms of legislation. In addition however, the defence reflects deeper principles of legal policy embodied in the maxims impotentia excusat legem (the law does not punish a person for not doing what he lacked the power to do or for being in a situation he was powerless to avoid), lex non cogit ad impossibilia (the law does not compel the impossible), and necessitas non habet legem (necessity knows no law).[135] These deeper principles imply that while the availability of any common law defence in New Zealand will prima facie be determined by whether it conflicts with the express terms of the Crimes Act or with any other legislation, as a general rule no one should ever be compelled by the threat of legal sanctions to do something that he is powerless to do, or be punished when he fails to do the thing he cannot avoid.

The proviso in s 20 has been invoked to prevent the common law defence of duress of circumstances from being available in New Zealand when based on direct or indirect wrongful threats of violence made by persons not present, on the basis that the statutory defence of compulsion in s 24 Crimes Act reflects the extent to which the Legislature was willing to countenance any such common law defence.[136] Similarly, in *Bayer v Police*,[137] the Court of Appeal, without referring to the express terms of s 20, refused to allow a defence of honest belief in the existence of circumstances justifying the need for protection

---

133 [1984] 2 NZLR 396 (CA).

134 Ibid at 397.

135 *Halsbury's Laws of England*, vol 44(1), (4th ed reissue), § 1448. For discussion of general principles regarding involuntariness and impossibility see § 2.3ff.

136 *Kapi v MOT* (1991) 8 CRNZ 49 at 54 (CA). See also *R v Witika* [1993] 2 NZLR 424 at 433ff, (1992) 9 CRNZ 272 at 281ff (CA).

137 [1994] 2 NZLR 48 at 50 (CA).

of another to a charge of trespass on the grounds that the language of s 3(2) Trespass Act 1980 did not make any allowance for the defendant's belief.

By contrast, in *Finau v Dept of Labour*,[138] it was held that allowing the defence of impossibility did not create an inconsistency with the terms of s 14(5) Immigration Act 1964. In the High Court, on an appeal by the Crown, it had been held that to allow an acquittal on the basis of impossibility would have entitled the appellant to a plea of autrefois acquit in the event of a fresh prosecution. It would, in effect, have conferred on her a new immigration status, contrary to the scheme of the Immigration Act under which only the Minister could confer a new status upon an immigrant. However, in allowing the appeal, the Court of Appeal rejected this argument and held that a plea of autrefois acquit would not have been a defence to a subsequent charge of remaining in New Zealand beyond the expiry of the permit, once it became possible for the appellant, after the birth of her child, to leave the country.

It is submitted that, wherever possible, the latter approach to interpretation is to be preferred. While a relevant statutory inconsistency may mandate refusing to allow a common law defence in an appropriate case, this step should not lightly be taken. The importance of preserving the fundamental principles of responsibility and culpability in the law require that a statutory inconsistency should only be found where the interests of the State clearly outweigh the interests of personal liberty, so that it is necessary to deprive a defendant of a defence which would otherwise be available.

---

138 [1984] 2 NZLR 396 (CA).

12

Mistake

The law regarding mistake in the criminal law gives expression to two fundamental principles of criminal responsibility. The first is that moral obligation is determined not merely by the actual facts but also by the actor's perception of them.[1] D should be acquitted of theft if, mistakenly believing an umbrella in a stand to be his own, he walks off with it. He lacks the mens rea, of intent permanently to deprive the owner of possession, because he believes he is the owner. The second is that ignorance of the law (that is, of the content of a penal statute) is no excuse for an offence committed against that express prohibition. The fact that D did not know, for example, that theft was a crime in the jurisdiction in which she is charged is no excuse at law. The doctrine concerning ignorance of law gives support to the principle of legality by declaring, in effect, that no person may substitute her own mistaken view of the penal law for what the law has been declared to be by competent officials:

> To permit an individual to plead successfully that he had a different opinion or interpretation of the law would contradict the Moore postulates of a legal order.[2]

These principles define the parameters of mistake as an exculpatory condition in the criminal law, although it is by no means clear that all mistakes of fact are relevant in assessing criminal liability. Some may be disregarded

---

1   Hall, *General Principles of Criminal Law* (2nd ed), Indianapolis, Bobbs-Merrill, 1960, 363.
2   Ibid at 383.

because even when taken into account, the offender still had the mens rea to commit the crime in question. Suppose, for example, that D, intent on breaking and entering house X in order to steal property, enters house Y by mistake. He is still liable for conviction for burglary because, despite his mistaking the identity of the house, he both intended to commit a crime of burglary and achieved his object. His mistake is, therefore, irrelevant. This type of mistake is sometimes characterised as a mistake as to a *quality* of an element of the actus reus, as opposed to a mistake as to the actus reus *element* itself.[3] The mistake is irrelevant because it does not affect the attribution of mens rea, since A intended to commit the crime regardless of his mistake. Conversely, as we shall see, there may be other situations involving mistake of law where both mens rea and actus reus are present yet for other reasons it is determined that conviction is inappropriate. This applies particularly to situations involving "officially induced" error of law.

In the course of this chapter both of these principles will be examined in greater depth, in order to ascertain the scope of exculpatory mistakes and to locate the concept of mistake within a broader theory of criminal responsibility.

12.1 MISTAKE OF FACT

We have seen in our discussion of mens rea that a necessary element of most offences, other than those of "strict" or "absolute" liability, is a proposition concerning the particular state of mind that must be proved before the offence can be said to have been committed. The principal mens rea "types" are intention, knowledge, and recklessness, although sometimes negligence may be sufficient mens rea for a crime. Where the required state of mind is absent at the time the offence was committed, the offender is entitled to be acquitted, even where the absence of mens rea was the result of a mistake of fact. For this reason it is sometimes said that mistake of fact is a good *defence* to a criminal charge in that it may be effective in negating the mens rea in respect of the offence charged. Imagine, for example, that D, while walking in the park in the early evening sees a stick lying at the base of a tree. Without examining the stick, he breaks it in half intending to take it home for firewood. There is no prohibition against gathering firewood in the park. Unfortunately, it turns out the "stick" which D breaks is a valuable carved walking stick owned by V, who had placed it on the ground while he climbed the tree to retrieve his hat blown off by the wind. D cannot be guilty of the crime of wilful damage[4] because he lacked the necessary knowledge that the "stick" was a valuable artifact and therefore had no intention to damage property. The mistake negated the mens rea for the offence

However, to suggest that mistake is a "defence" to a crime is likely to be misleading, because it may suggest that the accused has an evidentiary burden to discharge in order to raise the defence of "mistake" as a live issue before his

---

3   Allen, *Textbook on Criminal Law* (2nd ed), 1991, 72. See also *R v McCullum* (1973) 57 Cr App R 645 (CA); *R v Ellis* (1986) 84 Cr App R 235, [1987] Crim LR 44 (CA).

4   Section 11 Summary Offences Act 1981.

defence can be considered by the jury. That is not the case. Mistake, being a denial of the accused's belief in the facts which would otherwise make his actions a crime, is a mens rea element which must be disproved by the prosecution beyond a reasonable doubt. Of course, it may be incumbent on the accused to draw the court's attention to the possibility of a mistake, since otherwise the court may never know of it; but once this is done, the onus lies on the prosecution to refute that possibility.

The general rule concerning mistake of fact has long been recognised at common law, where mistake is seen being embodied in the maxim: actus non facit reum nisi mens sit rea. In *R v Tolson*,[5] Cave J said:

> At common law an honest and reasonable belief in the existence of circumstances, which, if true, would make the act for which a prisoner is indicted an innocent act has always been held to be a good defence. This doctrine is embodied in the somewhat uncouth maxim "actus non facit reum, nisi mens sit rea". Honest and reasonable mistake stands in fact on the same footing as absence of the reasoning faculty, as in infancy, or perversion of that faculty, as in lunacy.

Although the Judge uses the language of "defence", it is implicit in this passage that mistake goes to the very heart of mens rea, since an honest belief in the existence of circumstances which, if true, would make an act innocent, represents the very absence of a culpable mental state to which criminal liability may attach. It follows that if D, as a result of a factual error, honestly believes that the act he performs is no crime because he believes it to be a *wholly different kind of act* — for example, shooting at a "stump" in the forest for target practice, the "stump" being a crouching person, or putting "sugar" into another's tea, the "sugar" being caustic soda — he should not be liable for the crime charged where conviction depends on proof of an intention to do the unlawful act. In both of the examples, D's act would have been completely innocent if the facts had been as he believed them to be. He may, conceivably, be guilty of an offence of negligence if his mistake was also related to a failure to perform some legal duty which he had acquired. But that would be an issue quite independent of his liability for the offences requiring proof of intention or recklessness.

In the now celebrated case of *DPP v Morgan*,[6] where the three accused had claimed, implausibly, that they honestly believed the victim was consenting to intercourse with them because her husband, who was present, had said that she "enjoyed a struggle", the House of Lords considered the relevance of mistake in the context of the common law crime of rape. Lord Hailsham said:

> Once one has accepted . . . that the prohibited act in rape is non-consensual sexual intercourse, and that the guilty state of mind is an intention to commit it, it seems to me to follow as a matter of inexorable logic that there is no room either for a "defence" of honest belief or mistake, or of a defence of honest and reasonable belief or mistake. Either the prosecution proves that the accused had the requisite intent, or it does not. In the former case it succeeds, in the latter it fails. Since honest belief clearly negatives intent, the reasonableness or otherwise of that belief can only be

---

5   (1889) 23 QBD 168 at 181, [1886-90] All ER Rep 26 at 34.
6   [1976] AC 182, [1975] 2 All ER 347 (HL).

evidence for or against the view that the belief and therefore the intent was actually held . . .[7]

Morgan continues to be the principal authority on exculpatory mistakes in the English common law jurisdictions, although its authority in the context of rape has, as we shall see, been seriously eroded by statutory developments in New Zealand.

An exculpatory mistake will be relevant in one of two situations:

(i)   Where it relates to a *definitional element* of the offence; or

(ii) Where it relates to an *excusatory claim*.

In New Zealand it is not possible to say with any certainty what the principal difference between these categories is. Typically, a mistake as to a definitional element would need, as in *Morgan*, only to be honestly made to negate the mens rea for the particular offence. For the reasons expressed by Lord Hailsham in the passage cited, the reasonableness of the mistake is irrelevant. Conversely, a mistake as to an excusatory claim, being a mistake as to a *non-definitional element* of the offence involving an admission that the accused had performed the actus reus and mens rea of the offence but was seeking to avoid liability of other grounds (for example duress of circumstances), would normally be required to be reasonable.[8] However, in each case significant exceptions to the general rule have now so undermined the foundation for the distinction that it is no longer possible to articulate a clear principle for distinguishing between mistakes in each class. It is necessary to look at each case in the light of its own facts to determine which category it falls within, then decide whether a subjective or objective approach to the particular mistake is required.

12.1.1 Mistakes negativing mens rea

Where the mistake goes to a definitional element of the offence, *Morgan* is authority for the general principal that if the law requires intention or recklessness with respect to some element in the actus reus, a mistake, whether reasonable or not, which precludes both states of mind will deny criminal liability.[9] In *Morgan* the three accused sought, unsuccessfully, to deny the mens rea of rape by claiming that because of a mistake honestly made by them, they believed the victim was consenting to intercourse when she was not. However, had his claim been believed, his conviction would have been quashed. The mens rea for rape at common law was intention to have sexual intercourse with a woman without consent, or being indifferent whether the woman was consenting, absence of consent being an element in the actus reus of the

---

7   Ibid at 214, at 361.

8   See, for example, *R v Graham* (1982) 74 Cr App R 235, [1982] 1 All ER 801 (CA), where it was held that the accused may only rely on a common law defence of duress where his belief, that he would be killed or seriously injured unless he committed the offence, was reasonable.

9   Smith and Hogan, *Criminal Law* (7th ed), London, Butterworths, 1992, 216.

offence; therefore his mistake, if believed, would have meant that he lacked mens rea.

In New Zealand an honest belief in consent, *simpliciter*, will no longer be a good defence to a charge of rape by sexual violation, because the Legislature has moved to close the perceived gap left by *Morgan* by requiring that the accused have "reasonable grounds" for believing that the woman is consenting to "sexual connection".[10] Effectively, this now makes rape a crime of negligence, rather than of recklessness or intent. As such, apart from manslaughter, it is virtually the only serious crime in New Zealand where a mistake negativing mens rea must be "reasonable" as opposed to being simply "honestly" held.[11] In every other serious crime, where the offence requires proof of recklessness or intent, a mistake, to exonerate, need only be honest (although it has been said that the reasonableness or otherwise of a belief may be an important index whether the belief was genuinely held[12]).

This principle has been firmly established in a line of decisions of the High Court and Court of Appeal, although the line itself is a somewhat circuitous one. In *R v Wood*,[13] the appellant had been charged with cultivating cannabis. Her defence was that she believed that the seeds from which the plants had been grown were "supertom" tomato seeds. The case was decided on an evidentiary point which need not concern us. However, in a postscript to the decision the Court was required to reconsider its earlier decision in *R v Strawbridge*,[14] concerning the nature of the belief required where an exculpatory mistake arises. *Strawbridge* involved similar facts to *Wood*. The accused had been charged with cultivating prohibited plants, namely cannabis. She admitted cultivating a number of plants which it was accepted were cannabis but said that she honestly believed they were not cannabis plants. The Court concluded for various reasons, including the severity of the penalty, that the offence created under the Narcotics Act 1965 was not one of absolute liability and adopted a "half-way house" approach. It said that in order to present a prima facie case it is not necessary for the Crown to establish knowledge on the part of the accused and in the absence of evidence to the contrary knowledge on her part will be presumed, "but if there is some evidence that the accused believed *on reasonable grounds* that her act was innocent, then she is entitled to be acquitted unless the jury is satisfied beyond reasonable doubt that this was not so".[15] In *Strawbridge* the Court adopted the reasoning of Lord Diplock in *Sweet v Parsley*[16] that "it is open to an accused person to point to evidence

---

10 Section 128(2)(b) Crimes Act 1961.

11 For a discussion of the significance of "honest" in this context, see *Adams* § CA20.35. It is doubtful whether "honest" adds anything to the subjective test of belief, but for a contrary opinion see *Millar v MOT* [1986] 1 NZLR 660 at 678, (1986) 2 CRNZ 216 at 236 (CA) (per Casey J).

12 *R v Wood* [1982] 2 NZLR 233 at 237 (CA).

13 Ibid.

14 [1970] NZLR 909 at 916 (CA).

15 Ibid at 916. The present status of this case is discussed at § 4.3.2.3.

16 [1970] AC 132, [1969] 1 All ER 347 (HL).

which tends to show that he or she did not know that the plant which was being cultivated was a prohibited plant".[17]

This reasoning was implicitly adopted in *Wood*. However, on the question of the *nature* of the belief required in such a case (ie whether reasonable or not), the Court of Appeal concluded that in view of the decision in *Morgan* it was clear that there was no obligation on the part of a defendant to prove that she had reasonable grounds for the "honest" belief that the plants were other than cannabis plants. The conviction was quashed and a retrial ordered.

12.1.1.1 *The burden of persuasion*

These cases alert us to an important qualifying principle concerning exculpatory mistakes. Where the mistaken belief attaches to an actus reus element of a crime in which mens rea is an essential ingredient of the offence, the accused's belief in relevant facts need only be subjectively honest, unless the crime is one of negligence (for example, sexual violation). In such cases where intention or its counterpart, knowledge, is an express element in the definition of the offence, the Crown must affirmatively prove the existence of such intention or knowledge, and negate any exculpatory belief held by the accused, beyond a reasonable doubt. Strictly speaking, in a case where the prosecution must prove mens rea, it is unnecessary for the accused to discharge even an evidentiary burden in respect of such knowledge or intention, because it is the obligation of the prosecution to prove all aspects of mens rea, including the negation of any affirmative exculpatory belief.[18]

Nevertheless, it is difficult to see how, in such a case, the Crown could acquire awareness of such an exculpatory belief in order to negate it, unless the accused herself had adduced some evidence of it in the first instance. In practice, it is only when there is some evidence of an exculpatory belief that the Crown will be called on to negate it.[19] In *R v Thomas*,[20] which involved a prosecution for obstruction of a police officer in the execution of duty (a crime requiring proof of mens rea), the Court of Appeal held that where "honest belief" is an available defence, it is for the prosecution to prove that the accused had no such belief *once an evidentiary basis for it has been established*. This is clearly the case where the offence has been characterised as a "true" crime but the mens rea requirement is not stated expressly in the statute. In such a case, in the absence of some evidence to the contrary it may be assumed that mens rea, in the form of intention or guilty knowledge, existed; but if there is any evidence to the contrary (for example, the accused adduces evidence of an

---

17 *R v Strawbridge* [1970] NZLR 909 at 916 (CA).

18 § 4.1.

19 *R v Nazif* [1987] 2 NZLR 122 at 128 (CA).

20 [1991] 3 NZLR 141 at 143, (1991) 7 CRNZ 123 at 126 (CA). See also *Waaka v Police* [1987] 1 NZLR 754 at 759, (1987) 2 CRNZ 370 at 375 (CA). Discussing the mental elements of the offence of assault on a police officer under s 10 Summary Offences Act 1981 the Court of Appeal said: "Knowledge or its equivalent may be assumed . . . unless there is a foundation in the evidence for a contrary view."

honest belief in facts which, if true, would make his act innocent) the onus falls on the prosecution to prove such knowledge affirmatively in the normal way.[21]

This is demonstrated in *R v Metuariki*.[22] There the appellant was appealing against his conviction for supplying a Class A controlled drug to an undercover constable. He had gathered, and sold to the constable, a bag of mushrooms which he knew as "magic mushrooms" and had been told that he could get high on them. However, he denied any knowledge that the mushrooms contained a controlled drug (psilocybine) under the Misuse of Drugs Act 1975. His defence was that he honestly believed on reasonable grounds that he could quite innocently have possession of the mushrooms with their particular properties. Applying *Strawbridge* as modified by *Wood*, the Court of Appeal held that to establish a prima facie case against the accused, the Crown had to prove that the accused supplied the mushrooms and that they were a controlled drug. His knowledge that he was dealing with such a drug would then be presumed unless he could point to some evidence that he *honestly* believed his action to be innocent. The Court accepted that the appellant had made a "good faith" mistake as to an element in the definition of the offence. His mistake was not one of law; rather, he was asserting an honest, but mistaken, belief as to the character of the plant material and it was for that reason a mistake of fact.

In such cases, involving true crimes, although reasonableness is not a required element of the accused's belief, it will be relevant to the credibility of the claim.[23] So if D breaks into the home of V, a complete stranger, in the early hours of the morning while V is still asleep, it would be straining the credulity of the jury for him to assert, on a charge of indecent assault, that he honestly believed that V was consenting to the conduct, despite the fact that honest belief in consent is a defence to such a charge.[24] The patent unreasonableness of the claimed belief will be the strongest evidence that it was not in fact held by the accused at the time of the act of assault.

12.1.1.2 *Mistake and recklessness*

Mistake may also be relevant to whether an accused has acted recklessly, in cases where recklessness is sufficient mens rea for the offence charged. The issue arose in an interesting way in *R v Hay*.[25] In that case the accused, together with some associates, had removed a stolen car to a workshop owned by the employer of one of the associates with a view to stripping the car. While the accused was working with a grinder, sparks from the machine had ignited petrol on the floor of the workshop, which the offenders had spilt while siphoning the car's petrol tank. H was charged with arson in relation to the

---

21 See *Millar v MOT* [1986] 1 NZLR 660 at 665, (1986) 2 CRNZ 216 at 221 (CA). Also §§ 4.1.1.4, 4.3.2.2.

22 [1986] 1 NZLR 488, (1986) 2 CRNZ 116 (CA).

23 *R v Metuariki* [1986] 1 NZLR 488 at 490, (1986) 2 CRNZ 116 at 118 (CA). See also *R v Nazif* [1987] 2 NZLR 122 at 128 (CA): "The reasonableness or otherwise of such belief will be material to the question of whether the accused in fact held it." (per Somers J).

24 *R v Nazif* [1987] 2 NZLR 122 at 128 (CA).

25 (1987) 3 CRNZ 419.

damage to the building, which required proof that he caused the event "by an act which he *knew* would probably cause it, being reckless whether that event happens or not".[26] His defence was that although he turned his mind to the possibility, he did not go ahead with an act which he knew would probably cause damage; rather, he went ahead with an act that he *thought would not* cause damage.[27] Recognising that the sparks might ignite the petrol, he had (he said) turned the machine in a different direction to avoid that possibility. The Court accepted this argument, on the basis that a person who adverts to the question of risk and decides (mistakenly) that there is none should not be held reckless, "the fact that a person is mistaken in that belief does not mean that he is reckless".[28]

This implies that where a person consciously addresses a particular risk but honestly (if wrongly) concludes that it does not exist or will not eventuate, she cannot be guilty of reckless conduct.[29] Recklessness, as we saw in § 3.2, requires that a person foresees a risk (which it is unreasonable to run), and chooses to run it: a definition that is incompatible with a positively held belief that there is no risk. However, in any case where the risk is adverted to but the defendant concludes it is negligible only, as opposed to being non-existent, there is always a danger that she may be wrong in her judgment and the risk, considered objectively, is an unreasonable one to run. So in *Jefferson v Ministry of Agriculture and Fisheries*,[30] where the accused was charged with applying a herbicide in a reckless manner so that damage resulted to vegetation on a neighbouring property, it was held that the accused had been reckless. Upholding the conviction Barker J decided that the District Court Judge had been correct to hold that the risk of damage to other properties was more than negligible and that the appellant had erred in deciding to proceed after considering the risks. The point here is that while a mistake about the *amount* of risk will be taken into account by the court, the court imposes its own judgment about the *reasonableness* of running the risk that the accused perceives. A mistaken *evaluation*, whether the perceived risk is a reasonable one, affords the accused no defence.

12.1.2 Mistake about a claim of justification

It is commonly said that where an accused asserts an honestly held belief as to a matter of justification, the belief need not be reasonable. This is the position in the UK[31] and in New Zealand, at least as regards self-defence.[32] However, this principle does not apply to defence of a dwellinghouse (also a matter of justification), because the statute requires that D's belief that there is no lawful

---

26 Section 293(1) Crimes Act 1961.

27 *R v Hay* (1987) 3 CRNZ 419 at 421.

28 Ibid.

29 See *R v Stephenson* [1979] QB 695 at 703, [1979] 2 All ER 1198 at 1203 (CA).

30 12/8/86, Barker J, HC Rotorua M286/85.

31 See *Albert v Lavin* [1982] AC 546, [1981] 3 All ER 878 (HL).

32 *R v Thomas* [1991] 3 NZLR 141 at 144, (1991) 7 CRNZ 123 at 127 (CA): "Subjective honest belief . . . is sufficient" (per Casey J).

justification for the breaking and entering be based on "reasonable and probable" grounds.[33] On the other hand, where the defence is one of compulsion under s 24 Crimes Act 1961 — a matter of excuse rather than justification — the "belie[f] that the threat will be carried out" need not be reasonable, although its reasonableness or otherwise will be relevant to whether it was honestly held.

The reason why only a subjectively "honest" belief is required in respect of self-defence is because under the statutory framework, the justification of self-defence goes to the definition of the offence charged. A person acting in self-defence does not intend to act unlawfully, whether or not his belief in the circumstances giving rise to the need to use defensive force is reasonable. Indeed, if the facts are as D believes them to be, provided he does not use excessive force, then judged objectively, he is deemed to be upholding a fundamental value of the criminal law by preventing what he believes to be an unlawful assault. That belief negates the intent to act unlawfully and as such need only be honest.[34]

12.1.3 Mistake as to a non-definitional element

Unless a statute commands otherwise, where a defence is characterised as a matter of excuse rather than justification, and the offence is intentionally committed but is sought to be excused because there was no choice (as in cases of "duress of circumstances" or necessity), the issue of mistake or honest belief is treated differently to cases where the justification goes to an element of the mens rea.[35] In *Kapi v MOT* the Court of Appeal held that the common law defence of necessity, to the extent it is available in New Zealand, requires at least a belief formed on reasonable grounds of imminent peril of death or serious injury. The Court was unwilling to contemplate judicially amending the mental element in necessity to bring it into line with the self-defence test, because that would effect a change in the law which the Court considered was the Legislature's responsibility.

This type of defence is sometimes termed "confession and avoidance", because prima facie commission of an offence is conceded but criminal responsibility is avoided because of the exigent circumstances or threats.[36] Where an accused makes a mistake in relation to an element of an *excusatory* defence, it has been held at common law that the mistake must be reasonable.[37] The reasons why the belief must be reasonable in such circumstances are seldom clearly articulated. None the less, the law requires that if a person is to be excused for a crime which, but for the element of overwhelming fear and compulsion, they would otherwise have been judged to be fully responsible

---

33 Section 55 Crimes Act 1961.

34 Cf *Beckford v R* [1988] AC 130, [1987] 3 All ER 425 (PC).

35 *Kapi v MOT* (1991) 8 CRNZ 49 at 56 (CA) (per Gault J).

36 The concept is summed up in the Latin aphorism *coactus volui*. Literally, "at his will but coerced".

37 See *R v Graham* [1982] 1 All ER 801, (1982) 74 Cr App R 235 (CA); *R v Howe* [1987] AC 417, [1987] 1 All ER 771 (HL).

for, the belief which motivated such a clear breach of the law must be objectively reasonable.

One reason why the belief in necessity must be reasonable appears to be that, unlike other cases where an honest mistake defence might excuse by negating the mens rea of the offence in question, the claimed belief in circumstances justifying necessity does not actually negate mens rea for the offence in the sense of creating a belief in a state of affairs which if true would make the act innocent. The effect of the belief is simply to establish the existence of an additional exculpatory condition on account of which the act done with intent may be judged to be non-culpable. It would seem perfectly acceptable to say that the additional exculpatory belief, if it is to have this effect, should be reasonable.

12.1.4 Mistake and regulatory offences

In New Zealand, reasonable mistake of fact is a good defence to a public welfare regulatory offence.[38] The Court of Appeal in *Millar v MOT*[39] has held that a defence of honest and reasonable mistake is available is respect of some modern statutory offences and is incorporated within the general defence of total absence of fault which is available in New Zealand for all public welfare regulatory offences.[40] However, the recognition by the Court of a separate category of absolute liability would seem to imply a narrow band of liability in respect of which even a reasonable mistake of fact will not support a defence. Fortunately, with recognition of the category of strict liability, absolute liability offences are likely to be rare.[41]

12.1.5 Mistake and statutory defences

Occasionally a case may arise where the statute creating an offence provides that specified facts provide a defence, but makes no express provision for mistaken belief in the existence of such facts. This may occur in respect of both statutory offences of strict liability and statutory offences requiring proof of mens rea. An example of the former would be a prosecution under s 15 Resource Management Act 1991 for discharging a contaminant into the environment. A charge under s 15 alleges an offence of "strict" liability, in respect of which it is not necessary for the prosecution to prove that the defendant intended to commit the offence.[42] Section 341 of the Act sets out a number of statutory defences, including necessity, natural disaster, mechanical failure, and the defence that the defendant's "conduct" was reasonable in the circumstances.[43] However, there is no provision that "reasonable belief" or

---

38 *Civil Aviation Dept v MacKenzie* [1983] NZLR 78 at 81, also reported as *MacKenzie v Civil Aviation Dept* (1983) 1 CRNZ 38 at 41 (CA) (per Richardson J).

39 [1986] 1 NZLR 660, (1986) 2 CRNZ 216 (CA).

40 Ibid at 665, at 222.

41 *Civil Aviation Dept v MacKenzie* [1983] NZLR 78 at 85, also reported as *MacKenzie v Civil Aviation Dept* (1983) 1 CRNZ 38 at 45 (CA). See § 4.3.3.2(d).

42 Section 341 Resource Management Act 1991.

43 Section 341(2)(a)(ii).

"reasonable mistake" is a defence to such a charge. It may be argued that in this case a mistake of fact defence is excluded both as a matter of necessary implication from the structure of the statutory defences and as a matter of construction concerning the importance attached to protection of the country's natural and physical resources in the Resource Management Act. Arguably, it would contradict the purposes of the Act if a defendant was able to defend herself on the basis that she honestly and reasonably believed that her actions would not allow contaminants to escape into water, when that Act has expressly provided that a person may discharge a contaminant without intending to do so,[44] and still be guilty of an offence under the Act. Since belief is a cognate of intention it would seem highly likely that the Legislature also intended to exclude any defence based on a mistaken belief.

An example of the second variety, involving an offence of mens rea, is provided by *Bayer v Police*,[45] a case concerning a prosecution for trespass under s 3 Trespass Act 1980. The accused, an opponent of abortion, had entered the premises of an organisation licensed to perform abortions and, with some fellow protesters, had effectively blocked access and refused to move when warned to leave by the occupier. Continuing to remain on any place after having been so warned is an offence under s 3(1) of the Act. However, by subs (2) it is a defence if the accused proves that it was "necessary for him to remain" for the protection of himself or another or for some other emergency. The accused's counsel argued that since the justification to use force in the defence of another (the accused believed that her actions were aimed at the protection of unborn children) provided by s 48 introduced a subjective element of "honest belief", the accused should, under s 3(2) Trespass Act, also be able to rely on an honest if mistaken belief in the existence of circumstances which, if true, would provide a defence to a charge laid under s 3(1). The Court of Appeal rejected this argument and held that the language of the subsection, creating a limited defence in defined circumstances, does not make any allowance for the defendant's belief. The Court has since reiterated this approach in *O'Neill v Police*.[46]

This means that not only will an honest but mistaken belief in the necessity to remain on property be irrelevant on a charge of trespass, but so will a belief formed on reasonable grounds.[47] Although it would seem that the courts have adopted this narrow approach in order to prevent the kind of interference with lawful processes associated with abortions,[48] the approach taken in *Bayer* and *O'Neill* necessarily applies to all cases of trespass under s 3. Consider the following example. D, having trespassed onto V's land in order to bypass a flooded stream, then concludes on reasonable grounds that it is necessary to remain on V's land in order to avoid being trapped by the rising waters of the stream. V warns him to leave but he remains and is eventually arrested and

---

44 See *McKnight v NZ Biogas Industries Ltd* [1994] 2 NZLR 664 (CA).

45 [1994] 2 NZLR 48 (CA).

46 22/11/93, CA392/93 on appeal from *Police v O'Neill* [1993] 3 NZLR 712.

47 See Orchard, "Mistake and Statutory Defences" [1994] NZLJ 92.

48 Ibid at 94.

charged with trespass. According to the authority of *Bayer* and *O'Neill*, D's belief in the necessity to remain is wholly irrelevant. What determines liability is simply the question whether it was "necessary" to remain, seemingly a purely objective test. If, however, D had unlawfully entered V's house in order to seek protection from what he honestly and reasonably believed to be the imminent arrival of an overwhelming flood, his honest belief on reasonable grounds of imminent peril of death or serious injury would have been a good defence to the charge of being found on property without reasonable excuse.[49]

Such a distinction is clearly unsatisfactory. It has been correctly observed that if there is a principle of the common law by which belief in facts which would constitute a defence is itself a defence, this should be available *generally* under s 20 Crimes Act 1961, unless such a principle is inconsistent with the relevant legislation.[50] On the facts given in the example above it is difficult to imagine how allowing a defence of honest and reasonable belief in the necessity to remain on land could possibly create an inconsistency with the Trespass Act 1980.

However, there is a more fundamental objection to the Court of Appeal's approach in these cases. It is arguable that necessity is not a concept that can be completely objective. Whether something is "necessary" is, by its nature, a matter of perception. As a criminal law concept, the doctrine of necessity is a tacit admission of a person's impotence against some great evil, *or what he perceives to be a great evil*, assailing him, and a measure of that person's moral obligation *in extremis*.[51] It is surely unavoidable that, in determining whether something is "necessary", an accused must address his mind to the conditions which dictate that judgment and decide, as a matter of reflection and intuition, that a particular response is called for. The relevant ethical principle is that moral excuse is determined not by the actual facts but *by the actor's reasons for acting*.[52] In turn, the reasons for which the accused acts can only be supplied by his beliefs. Accordingly, to require a person to make a determination that a course of conduct is necessary without the person's subjective belief intruding into that process is both logically unsound and ethically questionable. It effectively imposes absolute liability in respect of a mistake, contrary to general principles of criminal responsibility; since if the actual facts determine our duties, we will be under a moral obligation without knowing it and perhaps even without being able to discover it.[53]

In the case law, the most frequent situation that arises involving the defence of mistake of fact concerns apparently necessary self-defence.[54] In these cases, as has been noted, if D's mistake stimulates his attack, undertaken in apparently necessary self-defence, he may claim a defence. This should alert us to the possibility that in any case where necessity is claimed, there is a similar

---

49 See s 29 Summary Offences Act 1981; *Kapi v MOT* (1991) 8 CRNZ 49 (CA).

50 Orchard, "Mistake and Statutory Defences" [1994] NZLJ 92 at 93.

51 Hall, *General Principles of Criminal Law* (2nd ed), Indianapolis, Bobbs-Merrill, 1960, 416.

52 Ibid at 363.

53 Ibid.

54 Ibid at 364.

danger that the individual's perception of the relevant "necessity" may also be driven by a fundamental mistake of fact. If the courts insist that the determination of necessity under s 3 Trespass Act is to be based on a purely objective standard, the effect will be to deny the "scope for the beneficial operation intended for the subsection"[55] contrary to the apparent intention of the Legislature. It is surprising that even an unreasonable mistake should excuse the serious harms inflicted by self-defensive measures, while the trespasser, who causes a much less serious harm, is put to the strict burden of proving her defence to a rigid objective standard.

It is not clear from the trespass cases whether the limitation on a "subjective mistake" defence, implied where the underlying defence is specified by statute, is created, operates as a general rule. However, for the reasons given here, such a limitation should not be supported on general principles.[56] Consistency with other general statutory defences, in particular self-defence, defence of property,[57] and compulsion would seem to demand that a defence of mistaken belief in facts constituting a defence ought to be a defence, even if it is necessary to incorporate within it an objective requirement of reasonableness.

12.2 IGNORANCE OF LAW

It is a general principle of law that ignorance of the law does not excuse, and that an honest and reasonable, but mistaken, belief that conduct is not criminal is no defence.[58] In New Zealand this principle is reflected in s 25 Crimes Act 1961, which states:

> **Ignorance of law**—The fact that an offender is ignorant of the law is not an excuse for any offence committed by him.

The principle derives from the natural law precept that every person who has attained the age of reason is supposed to know that he should not do to another what he would not have done to himself.[59] In the context of modern criminal law, the principle can be traced back to the Latin maxim ignorantia juris neminem excusat and relies on an obvious fiction, namely, that everyone is presumed to know the law. Despite the fiction, however, the rule reflects a commonsense principle that incorrectly thinking something legal should be no defence to a person who violates a rule of law.[60] One reason for this is the requirement for certainty in adjudication. The requirements of a legal order

---

55 *Bayer v Police* [1994] 2 NZLR 48 at 50 (CA).

56 Orchard, "Mistake and Statutory Defences" [1994] NZLJ 92 at 94. Orchard argues that there is authority from which it is possible to extract support for the existence of a common law principle that an honest but mistaken belief in facts which would constitute a statutory defence may itself be a defence if it is based on reasonable grounds.

57 See *R v Keating* (1992) 76 CCC (3d) 570 and *R v Born with a Tooth* (1992) 76 CCC (3d) 169 (CA), where it was held that necessary defence of property included cases where the accused reasonably believed, or honestly believed, in the existence of the requirements for a defence.

58 See *Johnson v Youden* [1950] 1 KB 544, [1950] 1 All ER 300.

59 Hobbes, *Leviathan* (Oakeshot ed), 1995, 191.

60 *Anon* (1871) 7 Mad 35; cited in 14(1) *English and Empire Digest*, (1977 Reissue) § 123.

necessitate that no one individual should be permitted to substitute his or her view of the criminal law for what the law has been declared to be. To allow such a concession arguably contradicts the principle of legality.[61]

Operation of the principle is confined to ignorance of criminal laws, and may include misapprehensions concerning either the existence of the law, or of its meaning, scope, or application. By contrast, misunderstandings of civil law rights may often lead to acquittal. If D takes V's umbrella, believing that it is rightfully his and not realising that the "contract" under which he bought it was invalid for some reason, his mistake about his rights under property law may be introduced in denial that he had the mens rea for theft.

In practice, situations involving ignorance of law seldom involve clear-cut cases where the accused claims ignorance of a penal provision that is well-known to almost everyone — for example, that taking the property of another without their consent is an offence, or that striking someone with the intention of injuring them is a crime. For the most part, the issues arise in circumstances where the boundaries between mistake of fact and ignorance of law seem to merge, so that it is not clear whether the honest belief arises from a mistake of fact, a mistake of law, or a combination of the two. In *De Malmanche v McKenzie*,[62] the issue was whether the accused's honest belief that games of chance (which he had permitted on premises he occupied) were not illegal was a defence to prosecutions under s 7(1) Gaming and Lotteries Act 1977. The accused believed that because certain modifications had been carried out to gaming machines in his tavern and they were operated in a particular way, the machines complied with the law. However, Judge Kerr held that a mistake in interpreting the law or failing to read and understand the appropriate law was no defence and said:

> [He] is not saying that he did not know there were gaming machines in the tavern. He is saying he did not know the machines in the tavern were machines prohibited by the law ... [A]lthough [he] might be said to have an "honest and reasonable, but mistaken belief" that belief is not in a state of facts, but rather in the application of the law to what he allowed to occur in the tavern.[63]

A mistake of law may be found where an accused either misreads a statute or fails to read it carefully.[64] Additionally, where an accused knowingly handles a substance which she knows to have particular characteristics but which she does not know to be a statutory poison, it will be no defence that she knew it by another name. That is ignorance of the law.[65] However, where an accused attributes her lack of guilty knowledge to something other than mere ignorance that a particular substance is proscribed, her mistake may qualify as a mistake of fact but not ignorance of law. An example of a mistake of fact would occur if the accused were to say, "I did not know that it was the

---

61 Hall, *General Principles of Criminal Law* (2nd ed), Indianapolis, Bobbs-Merrill, 1960, 382, 383.

62 [1989] DCR 567.

63 Ibid at 570.

64 *Johnson v Youden* [1950] 1 All ER 300 at 303, [1950] 1 KB 544 at 547.

65 *Police v Taggart* [1973] 1 NZLR 732.

controlled plant cannabis; I thought it was a tomato plant". It would, however, be a mistake of law if the defendant were to say, "I knew it was cannabis, but did not know that cannabis is a controlled plant".[66]

Similarly, where (for example, on an immigration charge) an accused honestly, but mistakenly, believes in a set of facts which if true would constitute a legal entitlement — eg that he had permission to enter the jurisdiction — it would not be a question of his not knowing that there was a prohibition on entering the jurisdiction without a permit. His belief would simply be mistake of fact, in that the facts that he believed existed were inconsistent with the application of the prohibition.[67]

12.2.1 Mistake of law and mens rea

Generally, a mistake of law cannot excuse a crime. So if D, with mens rea, causes the actus reus of an offence she is, according to normal principles of criminal liability, guilty of an offence. She cannot then claim that she did not know that the actus reus was prohibited by the criminal law. However, it is sometimes contended that in certain circumstances a mistake of law may negative the mens rea of an offence. For example, the actus reus may be defined in such a way that a mistake of law may result in D's act not being intentional with respect to some element of it, so that D lacks mens rea.[68] In these cases the accused's mistake, reasonable or otherwise, may be a defence.[69] However, the principles and constraints under which this concession operates are not always clearly articulated in the case law, and there is potential for confusion. In *Booth v MOT*,[70] the appellant had been charged with driving while disqualified. After the disqualification had been pronounced in open court, no one had taken the appellant's licence from him, and after waiting half an hour he left the Court. Two days later he was stopped by a traffic officer and charged with the offence. His defence was that he believed he was entitled to drive a motor vehicle as he was still in possession of his driver's licence. The trial Judge treated the mistake as one of law and convicted the appellant. On appeal, the issue was whether the appellant's mistake was one of law and whether the prosecution had established mens rea.

It was conceded that the appellant knew that he had been disqualified from driving, but believed that the disqualification did not commence until he had surrendered his licence or had been requested to do so. There was no doubt as

---

66   Ibid.

67   See *Kumar v Immigration Dept* [1978] 2 NZLR 553 at 557 (per Richardson J).

68   Smith and Hogan, *Criminal Law* (7th ed), London, Butterworths, 1992, 83.

69   See *R v Barrett & Barrett* (1980) 72 Cr App Rep 212 at 216, [1980] Crim LR 641 at 642 (CA). In that case, the Court affirmed that an honest but mistaken belief about one's legal rights can afford a defence. However, the Court was clearly of the view that the relevant mistaken belief would be a mistake about civil law rights, rather than about the criminal law. In any event, the defence does not extend to situations where the rights in question have been the subject of litigation and a court of competent jurisdiction has stated what the rights are, but the losing party "out of obstinate blindness" continues to behave as if the court has never declared those rights.

70   [1988] 2 NZLR 217.

a matter of law that the disqualification commenced at the making of the order.[71] In formulating its approach, the Court considered a passage from Smith and Hogan in which the authors suggest that in certain circumstances a mistake of law might negate the mens rea for a particular offence.[72] The view of the Court was that since the offence of driving while disqualified was one requiring proof of mens rea, the issue was whether the Crown had proved as a fact that the appellant was disqualified and that he *knew* he was disqualified. Holland J said:

> Although the time of the commencement of the disqualification was a matter of law which the appellant in some circumstances must be deemed to know, the issue before the Court on a charge of driving while disqualified was what was the actual state of mind of the accused. If there is evidence from which a Court can infer that the accused did not know that the disqualification was in force at the time, and the Crown has failed to prove his state of knowledge to the contrary, then the Crown has failed to prove that element of mens rea which is a necessary ingredient of the crime.[73]

The critical question, it would seem, is whether the appellant's mistake about the time of *commencement* of the disqualification was a relevant mistake of law sufficient to justify an acquittal. Clearly the Court thought it was a relevant mistake about legal rights sufficient to negative mens rea, on the basis that the mens rea for the offence is an intention "to drive [conduct] while disqualified [circumstance]". By implication, the Court rejected the alternative view, that the "mens rea" was in two parts, comprising (i) an intention to drive, and (ii) strict liability as to being disqualified.

However, in so deciding, the Court did not consider whether the mistake about disqualification was one about rights under the civil or criminal law. In our view, this distinction is crucial. It is perhaps unfortunate that, in citing the passage from Smith and Hogan, Holland J failed to include the following section which, with respect, does clarify the distinction being advocated here and which, if applied to the facts of *Booth*, may have produced a different outcome. The authors say:

> The crucial question will be, what is the *mens rea* required by the crime? A mistake negativing *mens rea* as to some element of the *actus reus* is no defence if the law does not require *mens rea* as to that element . . .
>
> This principle will operate only when the definition of the *actus reus* contains some legal concept like "property belonging to another". It has no application where the law fixes a standard which is different from that in which D believes. . . . The principle is probably also confined to the case where the legal concept belongs to the civil law — as the notion of property ownership does — and not to the criminal law. Suppose that X obtains goods from P by deception and gives them to D, who knows all the facts. We have already seen that it will not avail D to say he does not know handling stolen goods is a crime. Equally, it is thought it will not avail him to say that he did not know that it is against the criminal law to obtain goods by deception

---

71   See s 36 Transport Act 1962.

72   *Criminal Law* (7th ed), London, Butterworths, 1992, 83.

73   [1988] 2 NZLR 217 at 220.

and that goods so obtained are "stolen" for this purpose. "Stolen" is a concept of the criminal, not the civil law, and ignorance of it is no defence.[74]

Taking up Smith and Hogan's example, even though the legal status of property as "stolen" has civil law implications, it is a designation that arises primarily from the application of the relevant criminal law rules. Similarly, disqualification is a legal status that arises primarily as a consequence of criminal activities and legal processes. Applying this rationale to the facts in *Booth*, it surely must be said that the appellant's mistake was about a concept of penal law. It was not the same sort of mistake about civil law as that contemplated in the example given. As such, it could even be said that it was a "pure" mistake of law, because there was no factual error,[75] for example, concerning the date when the period of disqualification began, but simply an erroneous opinion about certain legal requirements of the disqualification order itself.

Whatever sympathy the Court may have felt for the appellant, it is doubtful whether his was the sort of legal mistake that justified an acquittal. It is, in any event, a result which is difficult to reconcile with the express terms of s 25 Crimes Act.

However, there is a more fundamental objection to the decision in *Booth*. By allowing the appeal and quashing the conviction, the Court effectively permitted the appellant to substitute his erroneous view of the penal law ("disqualification commences when the licence is physically removed from the defendant") for what the law has been declared to be by competent officials ("the period of disqualification shall commence on the date of the making of the order") thus arguably challenging the Rule of Law itself.[76]

Some support for the approach contended for here may be derived from *MOT v Wilke*,[77] where on a prosecution for driving while disqualified it was held that mens rea related to factual beliefs and not to a belief in, or knowledge of, the law. There the District Court refused to follow *Booth*, preferring the view that the application of ignorance of law as an aspect of mens rea is probably confined to ignorance of civil law.[78] More generally, the courts are unwilling to contemplate defences that may be characterised as "pure" mistakes of law. So it will not be a defence that the defendant, while aware that the person being assaulted was a police constable, entertained an incorrect understanding of the law regarding the extent of a constable's powers.[79] Similarly, where the appellant, on a charge of unlawfully conducting a bingo hall, claimed that

---

74 Smith and Hogan, *Criminal Law* (7th ed), London, Butterworths, 1992, 84, 85.

75 Unlike *Millar v MOT* [1986] 1 NZLR 660, (1986) 2 CRNZ 216 (CA).

76 See Hall, *General Principles of Criminal Law* (2nd ed), Indianapolis, Bobbs-Merrill, 1960, 383: "A legal order implies the rejection of such a contradiction. It opposes objectivity to subjectivity, judicial process to individual opinion, official to lay, and authoritative to non-authoritative declarations of what the law is. This is the rationale of *ignorantia juris neminem excusat.*"

77 [1992] DCR 104.

78 Ibid at 112.

79 *Waaka v Police* [1987] 1 NZLR 754, (1987) 2 CRNZ 370 (CA).

his belief that the Criminal Code was inoperative in certain circumstances was a mistake of fact, it was held that the mistake was one of law and as such no defence.[80]

12.2.2 Exceptions to the "ignorance of law" principle

The case law supports two major exceptions to the principle that ignorance of the law is no excuse. These concern so-called "officially induced" error, and ignorance of laws which have not been published or which are "non-discoverable". We will briefly consider each exception.

12.2.2.1 *"Officially induced" error* [81]

Although ordinarily a mistake of law cannot be successfully raised as a defence to a criminal or *quasi*-criminal charge or regulatory offence, an officially induced error of law may, in some circumstances, constitute a valid defence. The complexity of modern legislation makes it reasonable to assume that a responsible citizen will have a comprehensive knowledge of the law. However, this complexity does not justify rejecting the rule "ignorance of the law is no excuse", which encourages citizens to be responsible, and which is an essential foundation to the rule of law.[82] Rather, the complexity and extensiveness of regulation should be seen as one motive for creating a limited exception to the ignorantia juris rule, in the form of officially induced error. As the State's involvement in the day-to-day lives of people increases, and as the number of officials from whom advice can potentially be sought increases, the likelihood multiplies that an official will be relied on for advice about an enactment which has criminal implications.[83]

The claim that an accused was induced to commit a crime by relying on the erroneous advice of an official responsible for the administration of the law in question has found favour in appellate courts in both the US and Canada, but has not found ready acceptance in the UK and the Australian states. Its status as a defence in New Zealand is currently uncertain. The "defence" raises a number of important questions. First, should an official ever have the power to declare authoritatively what the law is? Secondly, if it is permissible for officials effectively to declare the law in certain defined situations, who qualifies as a relevant official for the purposes of the rule? What obligations lie on a defendant to ascertain whether the interpretation of the law offered by an official is correct? Should the giving of such erroneous advice amount to an excuse or is it best left as a matter going to penalty in an appropriate case?

The principal rationale for the rule is that a person should not be held to be criminally liable where his conduct is in direct consequence of an authoritative

80   *R v Jones* (1991) 8 CR (4th) 137 (SCC). See also *Inspector of Factories v Tarbert St Food Centre (1985) Ltd* [1989] DCR 471, where an error was ruled to be a "pure" mistake of law when the accused took advice from a senior employee of a large wholesale concern as to the legal requirements of the Shop Trading Hours Act 1977.

81   For a more comprehensive treatment of this topic see Brookbanks, "Officially Induced Error as a Defence to Crime" (1993) 17 Crim LJ 381.

82   *R v Jorgensen* (1995) 102 CCC (3d) 97 at 111, [1995] 4 SCR 55 at 77 (SCC) (per Lamer CJ).

83   Ibid.

declaration of what the law is, albeit a declaration that is wrong. It is arguable that the doctrine of ignorantia juris actually upholds the rule of law (the principle of legality) by requiring that only formal or authoritative declarations can give expression to what the law is, and not leaving the determination of law to the discretion of officials. It follows that, to permit an individual to plead successfully that he had a different interpretation of the law, even if officially induced, would contradict the Rule of Law. None the less, in our view the challenge to the principle of legality is insufficient to justify convicting the blameless when a person acts in good faith on the advice of a "law-declaring" official; because the person is not purporting to substitute his view of the law for what the law actually is. Rather, he is acting on an interpretation of the law which has been presented as authoritative.

Moreover, although the basic policy behind the mistake of law doctrine is that all people should know and obey the law at their peril, in certain situations there may be an overriding societal interest in having individuals rely on authoritative pronouncements of officials whose decisions we wish to see respected. Therefore a rule which states, "a person ought not to be punished who reasonably relies on a judicial decision or other official declaration of the law later held to be erroneous", may constitute a valid exception to the general principle. It would, we think, be unjust if a person were to be held criminally responsible who had acted in reasonable reliance on judicial or other official opinion advising that such conduct is legal. A test question is revealing: could the individual reasonably be expected to have been more conscientious or dutiful?[84]

An example illustrating the application of our test question is *R v Laniel Canada Ltd.*[85] In that case, the appellant had been convicted of having kept devices for gambling contrary to the Criminal Code. He argued that he had obtained a licence to conduct and manage a lottery scheme, which included gambling in a public place of amusement, from the Lottery and Races Board. The licence authorised the company to "carry on the business of amusement machines". The Court noted that the regulation concerned *amusement* machines, without mentioning *gambling* machines; which, it held, did not exclude the possibility that an amusement machine within the meaning of the provincial regulation could, for the purposes of the criminal law, be a gambling machine and not only an amusement machine. The Court refused to accept the appellant's argument that he had been "led into error by an official" who only gave him a licence for an amusement machine. The Court said:

> The provincial statute and relevant regulation in the present case cannot be interpreted as permitting the licensee to carry on the business of amusement machines to successfully argue that he was led into error by a civil servant who acted under a statute whose area of concern is clearly distinguishable from that of the criminal law.[86]

---

84 See Briggs, "Mistake of Law", thesis submitted for the degree of Master of Laws, University of Otago, 1994, 67.

85 (1991) 63 CCC (3d) 574.

86 Ibid at 576.

404

Evidently, the appellant had failed to make a reasonable inquiry whether the licence it had obtained included the right to possess machines used specifically for gambling

By contrast is the case of *R v Dubeau*.[87] There the accused had been charged, among other things, with carrying on a business including selling firearms and ammunition without a permit. He pleaded officially induced error, on the basis that before he had commenced the garage sales at which these weapons and ammunition were to be sold, he had made inquiries of the local police firearms officer concerning the legality of selling firearms at a garage sale and, if permissible, how many could be sold without obtaining a "dealer's permit". He was told by the firearms officer that selling guns at a garage sale could be done without a permit and that there was no limit on the number of guns sold. In addition, the appellant had written to the head office of the police department requesting information about a dealer's permit, but because of an oversight, the request had been overlooked.

In the Ontario Court (General Division), Ferguson J held that the appellant's reliance on the advice from the firearms officer was reasonable, taking into account (1) the *complexity* of the relevant law, and (2) the *duty* of the firearms officer to respond to general inquiries from the public. The Court held that the appellant's failure to disclose the fact that he intended to conduct a series of garage sales did not amount to a deliberate withholding of information and that he was not "careless or negligent" in failing to make that disclosure. In finding in the appellant's favour on the issue of officially induced error, the Court acknowledged that the defence had been "clearly recognised" by the Ontario Court of Appeal in *R v Cancoil Thermal Corp*,[88] where the Court of Appeal said:

> The defence of "officially induced error" is available as a defence to an alleged violation of a regulatory statute where an accused has reasonably relied upon the erroneous legal opinion or advice of an official who is responsible for the administration or enforcement of the particular law. In order for the accused to successfully raise this defence, he must show that he relied on the erroneous legal opinion of the official and that his reliance was reasonable. The reasonableness will depend upon several factors including the efforts he made to ascertain the proper law, the complexity or obscurity of the law, the position of the official who gave the advice, and the clarity, definitiveness and reasonableness of the advice given.

The defence of officially induced error has been given further endorsement by the Supreme Court of Canada in *R v Jorgensen*.[89] It would now seem,

---

87   (1993) 80 CCC (3d) 54.

88   (1986) 27 CCC (3d) 295 at 303, 304. For a more detailed analysis of that case see Brookbanks, "Officially Induced Error as a Defence to Crime" (1993) 17 Crim LJ 381 at 388.

89   (1995) 102 CCC (3d) 97, [1995] 4 SCR 55 (SCC). See also *Postermobile plc v Brent London Borough Council* 8/12/97, QBD, where local authority officers represented that planning consent was not required for temporary advertising hordings. It was held that subsequent prosecutions for failing to obtain planning consents were an abuse of process: "It was not as if they had requested planning advice from one of the council's gardeners" (per Lord Justice Schiemann).

contrary to some early opinions about the scope of the defence, that officially induced error is equally applicable to "true crimes" with a full mens rea component"[90] as it is to regulatory offences, although for certain crimes, such as those involving "moral turpitude" the chances of success of such an excuse will be negligible.[91] The Court in *Jorgensen* established a number of criteria which must be satisfied before the defence will be available.[92] They are summarised as follows:

(1) Once the court has determined the error is one of law, the accused must demonstrate that she considered the legal consequences of her actions. Requiring an accused to consider whether her conduct might be illegal and seek advice as a consequence, ensures that the incentive for a responsible and informed citizenry is not undermined.

(2) It must be demonstrated that the advice came from an appropriate official. This avoids the obvious injustice of the State approving conduct on the one hand and seeking to impose a criminal sanction for that conduct with the other. Generally, Government officials who are involved in the administration of the law in question will be considered appropriate officials. The official must be one whom a reasonable individual in the position of the accused would normally consider responsible for advice about the particular law in question (for example a Motor Vehicle Registrar). The advice of officials at any level of government may induce an error of law, provided that a reasonable person would consider that particular Government organ to be responsible for the law in question.

(3) Once an accused has established that he sought advice from an appropriate official, he must demonstrate that the advice was reasonable in the circumstances. Since an individual relying on advice has less knowledge of the law than the official in question, the individual must not be required to assess reasonableness at a high threshold. Thus, if an appropriate official is consulted, the advice obtained will be presumed to be reasonable unless it appears on its face to be utterly unreasonable.

(4) The advice obtained must have been erroneous, a fact which does not have to be demonstrated by the accused. In proving the elements of the offence, the prosecution will have already established what the correct law is, from which the existence of the error can be deduced. Nevertheless, it is important to note that when no erroneous advice has been given, the excuse cannot operate.

(5) To benefit from the excuse, the accused must demonstrate reliance on the official advice. This may be shown by proving that the advice was obtained before the actions in question were commenced and by showing that the questions posed to the official were specifically tailored to the accused's situation.

---

90   Ibid at 111, at 77 (Lamer CJ).

91   Ibid at 112, at 78.

92   Ibid at 112-114, at 78-81.

(6) Officially induced error of law functions as an excuse rather than a full defence. It can only be raised after the Crown has proven all elements of the offence. To rely on the excuse, an accused must show, after establishing that she made an error of law, that she considered her legal position, consulted an appropriate official, obtained reasonable advice, and relied on that advice in her actions. The accused, who is the only one capable of bringing this evidence, is solely responsible for it. Ignorance of the law is not encouraged because informing oneself about the law is a necessary element of the excuse.

(7) As the excuse does not affect the determination of culpability, it is said to be procedurally similar to entrapment. As excuses, both claims concede the wrongfulness of the action but assert that under the circumstances it should not be attributed to the actor. The successful raising of an officially induced error of law argument will lead to a judicial stay of proceedings rather than an acquittal. Because a stay can only be entered in the clearest of cases, an officially induced error of law argument will only be successful in the clearest of cases.

(8) The question whether officially induced error constitutes an excuse in law is a question of law or of mixed law and fact. While a jury may determine whether the accused is culpable, and hence whether the argument is necessary, it is for a judge to determine whether the precise conditions for the excuse are made out. Only the trial judge is in a position to determine if a stay should be entered. The elements of the officially induced error excuse are to be proven on a balance of probabilities by the accused.

This represents the clearest summary to date of the scope and application of the offence of officially induced error in any Commonwealth jurisdiction and, we would submit, provides a valuable model for the development of the doctrine in New Zealand.

12.2.2.1(a) *Officially induced error in New Zealand*

The availability in New Zealand of a common law defence of officially induced error remains unclear. In *Tipple v Police*,[93] involving prosecutions for sales in breach of the Arms Act 1983, which had allegedly been condoned by the police, Holland J suggested, somewhat tentatively, that "such a principle" may need to be applied in an appropriate case if there was no other way of achieving justice. In the event, he preferred to apply s 19 Criminal Justice Act 1985. This hardly represents a strong endorsement of the doctrine. The defence does not appear to have been considered in any other appellate court in New Zealand. However, to the extent that the doctrine has developed as a common law defence in other jurisdictions, it may be argued that the defence is preserved in New Zealand through the operation of s 20 Crimes Act 1961.

A possible obstacle to the development of the defence in New Zealand is the ruling in *Waaka v Police*,[94] to the effect that the defence of total absence of fault cannot extend to pure mistakes of law. Where a court has categorised an

---

93   [1994] 2 NZLR 362, (1993) 11 CRNZ 132.
94   [1987] 1 NZLR 754 at 759, (1987) 2 CRNZ 370 at 375 (CA).

officially induced error as a pure mistake of law, in the context of a public welfare regulatory offence, it may therefore be difficult to contend that the mistake ought to be excused. However, since officially induced error is distinct from a defence of due diligence[95] or absence of fault, its application to situations involving pure mistakes of law may be unobjectionable. Indeed, the essence of the claim, and a principal rationale for the doctrine, is that the offender was misled about the scope or content of a particular law by one who, in the nature of her office, ought to have been better informed — a very different explanation than absence of fault. There would seem to be little justification for limiting the operation of the doctrine to mixed mistakes of law and fact. Doing so would seem to undermine the foundation of the excuse.

It must be doubted, therefore, whether in light of recent Canadian developments the District Court decision in *Inspector of Factories v Tarbert St Food Centre (1985) Ltd*[96] can stand. In that case it was held, applying the dictum of Cooke P in *Waaka v Police*,[97] that since the defence of officially induced error rested on a pure error of law, it was unavailable to the defendant. Two comments should be made.

First, it is clear from recent developments in Canadian criminal law that any attempt to limit the operation of the defence of officially induced error to mixed mistakes of law and fact is misconceived. It is clear that the doctrine, which operates as a carefully carved exception to the ignorantia juris principle, applies to any relevant mistake of law, subject to the limitation mentioned above that its likelihood of success with crimes involving moral turpitude will be nearly nil.

Secondly, the comments of Cooke P in *Waaka* were limited by the context to a consideration of the general principle concerning ignorance of law, and did not address the specific claims of officially induced error. In any event, it is arguable that Cooke P was doing no more than reiterating, in a different form of words, the statutory requirements of s 25 Crimes Act, which prevents mistakes regarding the content or effect of penal law from being a defence to crime. Taken at its face value, the statement "the defence of total absence of fault cannot extend to pure mistakes of law" would seem to eliminate all defence claims involving any error of civil or criminal law, including those which give right to such defences as colour of right. Given the context in which the statement was made, and the lack of a clear signal to this effect, it is unlikely this was the Court's intention.

12.2.2.2 *Non-publication*

There is some authority at common law for the view that inability to know of the existence of a statutory prohibition, either because it has not been published or because the accused was physically absent from the jurisdiction when the law was passed, may be a defence to a criminal charge.[98] However, the better

---

95   *R v Jorgensen* (1995) 102 CCC (3d) 97 at 112, [1995] 4 SCR 55 at 78 (SCC) (Lamer CJC).
96   [1989] DCR 471.
97   [1987] 1 NZLR 754 at 759, (1987) 2 CRNZ 370 at 375 (CA).
98   See *Burns v Nowell* (1880) 5 QBD 444 (CA).

view would seem to be that a criminal intent need not involve knowledge on the part of an accused that his acts were against the law and constituted a crime.[99] In *R v Bailey* D, the captain of a ship at sea, fired on another ship, unaware of a new law which rendered firing on another ship unlawful. He was convicted, even though it was impossible for him to know the law. The Judges recommended a pardon. The principle which justifies conviction in such a case is that the prosecution is only required to prove that the accused brought about the actus reus of the particular offence with the required mens rea. It is not necessary to prove that the accused knew that what he was doing was contrary to law. So, in *Barronet's* case,[100] where the accused, French nationals, were charged with duelling, the fact that they did not know that duelling was an offence in the UK was held to be no defence to the charge. It has also been held that a mistaken belief that a prosecution will not be instituted in respect of the offence is not a defence.[101]

In all these cases, however, the relevant law had at least been published. Moreover, in the modern age of sophisticated access to information, merely being outside the jurisdiction is today no bar to knowing the law. By contrast, when it is *impossible* for the accused to become aware of what the law is because, for example, a particular regulation has not been issued at the time of the alleged offence, it may be a defence that the accused was unaware that the particular prohibition applied to him or her.[102] In Canada, the rigours of the principle concerning ignorance of law have been relaxed where commission of the offence is dependent on a regulation which has not been published in the *Canadian Gazette*. In those circumstances, no person can be convicted of an offence consisting of a contravention of the regulation unless reasonable steps have been taken to bring the purport of the regulation to the notice of the persons likely to be affected by it.[103] There does not appear to be any comparable provision under current New Zealand law, although the current proliferation of regulatory legislation containing penal provisions may indicate a need to consider the creation of a similar rule for New Zealand.

In our view, non-publication of a law should afford a defence. In substance if not in form, it amounts to retrospective criminalisation. Arguably, conviction for contravening an unpublished law may be inconsistent with s 27 New Zealand Bill of Rights Act 1990, which enshrines a right to observance of the principles of natural justice by any tribunal. It would certainly be inconsistent with the Rule of Law, which, as we saw in chapter one, demands that the State give citizens fair warning of offences, so that they may have a proper opportunity to comply with the law.[104]

---

99   *Halsbury's Laws of England*, vol 11(1), (4th ed reissue), § 20.

100   (1852) 22 LJ MC 25

101   *R v Arrowsmith* [1975] QB 678, [1975] 1 All ER 463 (CA). However, a promise to that effect made by a police officer, which is then broken, could conceivably provide a ground to challenge the proceedings on the basis of abuse of process.

102   See *Lim Chin Aik v R* [1963] AC 160, [1963] 1 All ER 223 (PC).

103   *R v Molis* (1980) 55 CCC (2d) 558, [1980] 2 SCR 356.

104   § 1.4.3.

13

Self-defence and Defence of Property

13.1 SELF-DEFENCE

The law of self-defence reflects the commonsense notion that a person who is attacked may defend herself and will be legally justified in repelling force with force. This is regarded as one of the great principles of the common law.[1] However, questions remain about the nature of the justification which self-defence confers and about whether, for example, the actions of a person who falsely believes she is acting in self-defence can ever be justified. While New Zealand law admits a justification for all acts done in legitimate self-defence, there is still an arguable case for saying that a person who mistakenly thinks she is justified should merely be excused — because justification, by its nature, renders an act permissible.[2] By contrast, a person who kills someone whom she

---

1 See Criminal Code Bill Commission, *Report of the Royal Commission Appointed to Consider the Law Relating to Indictable Offences: With an Appendix Containing a Draft Code Embodying the Suggestions of the Commission*, London, Eyre & Spottiswode for HMSO, 1879, 11.

2 Husak, "The Complete Guide to Self-defence" (1996) 15 Law and Phil 399 at 402.

mistakenly believes was threatening her life should hardly be told that her act is permissible; yet at the same time, it may be equally counter-intuitive to suggest that she should be held responsible for a crime.

Despite the fact that these sorts of questions abound in self-defence theory, and that they are an ongoing source of controversy for legal philosophers, the *availability* of self-defence is essentially a very practical matter. According to one writer, it is grounded in the "morally distinctive" feature of the use of defensive force against an unjust immediate threat. That is to say, D's act is one of self-defence when it directly blocks the infliction of unjust harm.[3] It would seem to follow that defensive force may be permissible even when the person posing the threat is not culpable. Even a child, a sleepwalker, or an insane person can compromise his right to life simply by becoming an unjust immediate threat to the life of another person.[4] Self-defence preserves the right, though not the unqualified right, of any person to protect himself against a perceived unjustified threat to life or limb.

Because the employment of *lawful* force is not an offence, it is legitimate to say that D should be acquitted because an element of the actus reus is missing, namely an *unlawful* act.[5] This analysis applies regardless of whether the assailant is killed or merely injured. However, the law has always required that wherever force is used to prevent the infliction of harm, the force used is limited to that which is *necessary* to prevent the mischief threatened. Thus there is a tension between the justified use of force, and its limitation to what is necessary or reasonable.

This tension defines the principal elements of self-defence. Where D uses more force than the law allows in what would otherwise be legitimate self-defence, he is liable for the excess of force used. In such circumstances, the force is deemed to be unlawful, and D's act is deprived of the legal status of having been committed in self-defence. There is no intermediate category of exculpation. His conduct either qualifies as self-defence or he is liable for the full consequences of whatever offence he may have committed.

13.1.1 Legislative history

Prior to 1 January 1981, the New Zealand law on self-defence was characterised by a series of complex statutory provisions originating in the Criminal Code Act of 1893 and re-enacted in the Crimes Act 1908.[6] A Bill introduced into Parliament in 1959 slightly modified the provisions in the 1908 Act relating to self-defence, and the resulting law was duly re-enacted as ss 48-50 by the Crimes Act 1961. In their various re-enactments, these provisions distinguished between provoked and unprovoked assaults, and contained separate provisions for the defence of persons under protection. The laws were difficult

---

3   Uniacke, *Permissible Killing: The Self-defence Justification of Homicide*, Cambridge, Cambridge University Press, 1994.

4   Husak, "The Complete Guide to Self-defence" (1996) 15 Law and Phil 399 at 401.

5   *Beckford v R* [1988] AC 130, [1987] 2 All ER 425 (PC); Allen, *Textbook on Criminal Law* (3rd ed), 1995, 164.

6   Sections 73-76 Crimes Act 1908.

to apply in practice and left defendants who were responsible for minor acts of provocation largely unprotected by the law if they chose to defend against an anticipated retaliation. Furthermore, the old law was unclear regarding by what standard the need for defensive force was to be judged — ie according to the subjective perceptions of the defendant, or by an objective test.

However, the greatest problem in the old law was the inherent difficulty in any fact situation of deciding who started the particular incident,[7] which meant that it was often very difficult for a judge to decide whether to direct a jury to proceed under s 48 (self-defence against unprovoked assault) or s 49 (self-defence against provoked assault). The judges were unusually critical of the provisions. In *R v Kerr*[8] Richmond J, delivering the judgment of the Court of Appeal, spoke of the "quite incomprehensible" tests and distinctions laid down by the former ss 48 and 49, and urged that the sections be replaced by a simpler form of legislation that could be applied in a "commonsense" way. An earlier Memorandum prepared by Richmond J and Speight J at the request of the then Chief Justice, Sir Richard Wild, had also called for a simplification of the law.

Of course, and as the Memorandum acknowledged, the then-existing law had been drafted as it was for a reason: to prevent juries from having too much latitude when determining the availability of the defence, particularly in cases where D's actions caused death or grievous bodily harm. It was recognised that changing the law would require a policy decision whether it was desirable to seek greater simplicity at the price of fewer statutory constraints.[9] After considering various options for reform, the Criminal Law Reform Committee eventually opted for simplification, through the codification of a comprehensive provision to the effect that, *whatever the antecedent circumstances,* the use of force is justified in self-defence or in the defence of another, provided the amount of force used is (objectively) reasonable in light of the defendant's (subjective) perception of the circumstances. This option was favoured because it would "require no abstruse legal thought and no set words or formula to explain it; and only commonsense is needed for its understanding".[10] It was anticipated that the new formulation would simplify the task for both judge and jury. The jury would be required to decide the question of reasonableness in the light of the judge's summing up of the evidence, while the judge would no longer be faced with varying statutory tests and distinctions which were perceived to be extremely difficult to explain to a jury.[11]

---

7   See Criminal Law Reform Committee, *Report on Self-defence*, Wellington, Criminal Law Reform Committee, 1979, 4.

8   [1976] 1 NZLR 335 at 344 (CA).

9   Memorandum of the Judges prepared for the Criminal Law Reform Committee, cited in Criminal Law Reform Committee, *Report on Self-defence*, Wellington, Criminal Law Reform Committee, 1979, 4, 5.

10   Ibid at 8.

11   The Committee rejected the notion of providing, additionally, a list of evidentiary guidelines for the court, on the basis that doing so could introduce into the law complexities of interpretation and a further body of case law when the question in self-defence is one of fact to be decided in the light of an infinite variety of circumstances in different cases.

13.1.2 The statutory test

The present test for self-defence is defined in s 48 Crimes Act 1961, as amended by the Crimes Amendment Act 1980. It provides:

> Everyone is justified in using, in the defence of himself or another, such force as, in the circumstances as he believes them to be, it is reasonable to use.

Essentially, the section comprises two elements, one subjective and the other objective. The first part of the section poses a subjective question: what did the accused *believe* the circumstances to be? If the accused is able to establish a sufficient evidential foundation to the effect that she believed the circumstances were such that she was about to be killed or seriously injured, the trial judge is bound to put the defence to the jury.[12] Once it has been accepted that the jury could at least entertain a reasonable doubt about the accused's state of mind, then that becomes a material issue in relation to the second element of the section, which requires the jury to consider whether the force used was *reasonable* given the circumstances that the accused thought existed.[13]

13.1.2.1 A broad application

Because of the very broad way in which the new statutory test has been formulated, it has given juries significantly more latitude when considering claims of self-defence. This can be illustrated by considering the case of *R v Ranger*.[14] At first instance, the appellant was convicted of the murder of her de facto husband. She had armed herself with a kitchen knife following an argument in the bedroom, during the course of which she was struck by the deceased. Carrying the knife behind her back, the appellant had returned to the bedroom where she used it to stab the deceased in the shoulder. The deceased left the house with the knife still in his body and died a short time later.

At trial, defence counsel did not raise the defence of self-defence, preferring to rely on provocation. However, evidence was given by the accused at the trial that during the struggle the deceased had reached under the bed, where the accused knew firearms were kept, having immediately beforehand threatened to blow both the appellant's and her son's heads off. On appeal, the Court of Appeal held that although this evidence would be far from adequate to discharge a legal burden of proof, because the accused was required to establish only an evidential foundation for the defence, no burden of proof fell on her.[15] Therefore, because there was evidence properly capable of establishing a foundation for the defence, even though it had not been put forward by defence counsel, the trial judge had a responsibility to place it before the jury.

The Court allowed the appeal and ordered a new trial. It accepted that in the circumstances, in which the accused believed that the lives of herself and

---

12   See *R v Tavete* [1988] 1 NZLR 428, (1987) 2 CRNZ 579; also *R v Ranger* (1988) 4 CRNZ 6 (CA).

13   *R v Ranger* (1988) 4 CRNZ 6 at 9 (CA).

14   Ibid.

15   See § 4.1.

her son were in peril because of the deceased's threats to shoot them, it was not impossible that a jury could be left in reasonable doubt whether a pre-emptive strike with a knife would be reasonable force in the circumstances.

The case demonstrates that under the present law, an intention to kill or cause serious bodily injury is consistent with legal self-defence. A person *may* intend to kill her assailant if she believes that killing the assailant is the only means of avoiding the threatened harm; although the use of fatal force will necessarily give rise to careful consideration by the jury of the issue of proportionality. On the basis that an agent intends those aspects of her act which in the circumstances she believes are necessary for the achievement of her aim,[16] many of the deaths caused by self-defence may be described as intentional, since they are necessary to attain the end of self-preservation.[17] Furthermore, *Ranger* demonstrates that far from requiring retreat as a legal element, it is clearly open for those employing self-defence sometimes to use pre-emptive force, and even to benefit from the defence in cases where it has not been expressly pleaded.

13.1.3 Belief in circumstances justifying force

Although self-defence may be characterised as an "actus reus" defence (since it prevents D's conduct from being "unlawful"), the mental element is nonetheless critical. The question which necessarily arises is, *what were the circumstances believed by the accused to exist?* A cardinal principle of criminal responsibility is that moral obligation is dependent not merely upon the actual facts but also upon the actor's perception of them.[18] This principle is of particular importance in the context of self-defence where, typically, the stress of a violent confrontation or emergent threat becomes a fertile environment for mistakes to be made. Often an offender, mistakenly believing he is about to be unjustly attacked, may use or threaten the use of lethal force when, in reality, the victim's conduct is lawful. Self-defence in such circumstances may be characterised as *putative* self-defence, because it is supposed or imagined.

In order to deal with problems that can arise with putative self-defence, the Law Reform Commission of Victoria recommended in a 1991 report that the common law condition that the victim's conduct be unlawful should no longer be a requirement of the plea of self-defence.[19] Fortunately, the same reform is not required in New Zealand. Section 48 contains no requirement that the victim's actions be unlawful; rather, it allows the use of putative self-defence in any circumstances where the accused believes he is about to be unjustly

---

16 Cf Uniacke, *Permissible Killing: The Self-defence Justification of Homicide* Cambridge, Cambridge University Press, 1994, 405.

17 For fuller discussion, see § 3.1.

18 Cf Hall, *General Principles of Criminal Law* (2nd ed), Indianapolis, Bobbs-Merrill, 1960, 363; also §§ 1.2.2.1, 2.

19 Law Reform Commission of Victoria, Report no 40, *Homicide*, Melbourne, Law Reform Commission of Victoria, 1991, 99; cited in Uniacke, *Permissible Killing: The Self-defence Justification of Homicide* Cambridge, Cambridge University Press, 1994, 37.

assaulted. An illustrative case is *R v Terewi*,[20] in which the appellant had threatened to shoot police officers who visited his home, thinking they were people he had earlier met at a hotel and who had caused him trouble. Although the question of mistake was not directly in issue, the Court of Appeal, in allowing the appeal against conviction for threatening to cause grievous bodily harm, held that it was "totally unlikely that the Legislature intended the new section to restrict the former availability of self-defence".[21] The Court may be taken implicitly to have approved the notion that a mistake of fact will not necessarily negate a claim of self-defence. This approach has been confirmed in subsequent case law.[22] Because s 48 is no longer confined to defence against unlawful assault, even in cases where the victims are police officers acting lawfully, the accused may be justified in using reasonable force in self-defence or defence of another, if as a result of a mistake of fact the accused believes the force used by the police is such that it would be unlawful. In *R v Thomas*[23] the accused had intervened to assist the "victim" of what she believed to be an unlawful police "beating". In fact the police were conducting a lawful arrest. However, because the accused had an honest, albeit mistaken, belief that the police were using excessive force, the Court of Appeal held that the defence in s 48 was available.[24]

13.1.3.1 *Unreasonable mistakes*

There is no requirement that D's mistake must be a reasonable one. But it must, of course, be genuine. Although the judge must rule on whether there is evidence of self-defence to go to the jury and is bound to put the defence where there is a sufficient evidential foundation, the jury may still reject the defence if the evidence fails to disclose a reason for the accused to believe that the victim was posing the danger claimed.[25] An unreasonable belief is not *per se* fatal to the defence, although the more unreasonable the accused's belief is that he is under attack, the less likely the jury is to believe it.

In this context, the meaning given to "believe" is critical. That it is a subjective mental state is not in dispute. But what it implies *as* a subjective state of mind does not appear to have been judicially considered in respect of self-defence in New Zealand. To believe is to have faith in, or to put trust in, the existence of something. It is the acceptance of a state of affairs as true or existing.[26] Such a state of mind would seem normally to be inconsistent with a fanciful, unreasonable judgment that a person may be under attack by an

---

20 (1985) 1 CRNZ 623.

21 Ibid at 624.

22 See, for example, *R v Thomas* [1991] 3 NZLR 141; *R v Petel* [1994] 1 SCR 3; *R v Nelson* (1992) 71 CCC (3d) 449, 13 CR (4th) 359.

23 [1991] 3 NZLR 141, (1991) 7 CRNZ 123 (CA).

24 However, compare *Williams v Police* [1981] 1 NZLR 108 at 113-115 where it was held that an accused was not justified in interfering with the arrest of another even if it was unlawful. This authority must be regarded as having been overtaken by *R v Thomas*.

25 *Burns v HM Advocate* (1996) The Juridical Review 416.

26 See § 3.4.

unjust immediate threat. In *Burns v HM Advocate*,[27] the appeal was disallowed because although the trial Judge misdirected himself in requiring that the accused must not have instigated the trouble in order to be able to claim self-defence, there was in fact no miscarriage of justice since there was no evidence to suggest that the accused *had* been acting in self-defence. The case could also have been decided, it is submitted, on the basis that D did not "believe" that the deceased was about to kill or seriously injure him, and therefore D could not be said to have been defending himself against an unjust threat.

13.1.3.2 *Mistakes induced by intoxication*

The rule that a mistake of fact does not necessarily negate the availability of self-defence is now well-established in English common law. In *R v O'Grady*,[28] the English Court of Appeal held that a sober man who mistakenly believes he is in danger of immediate death at the hands of an attacker is entitled to be acquitted of both murder and manslaughter if his reaction in killing his supposed assailant was a reasonable one. However, the same case makes clear that in England a defendant is not entitled to rely on a mistake of fact which has been induced by voluntary intoxication.[29] The reason for this ruling appears to lie in public policy concerns that a person who has voluntarily consumed alcohol should not be able to take advantage of mistakes made by him while in that state — which, by its nature, involves an element of dangerousness.[30] Nevertheless, English authority on this point has never been accepted in New Zealand as determining the relevance of the defendant's intoxication.[31] In any event, it is doubtful whether, in the context of self-defence, there is any room in New Zealand for the approach taken in *O'Grady*, given that s 48 expressly requires the conduct to be assessed according to the circumstances as the accused believed them to be. The question does not appear to have been directly discussed in the Court of Appeal. However, there are cases where self-defence has been held to be available, despite the fact that the accused was intoxicated when using force and was mistaken as to the circumstances.[32]

In principle this seems to be correct. If, as is the case in New Zealand, a defendant may adduce evidence of intoxication to support her claim that the required state of mens rea was absent,[33] it would seem appropriate to allow the same evidence on the question of a mistake about the necessary use of force in self-defence.

---

27 (1996) The Juridical Review 416.

28 [1987] QB 995, [1987] 3 All ER 420 (CA).

29 Ibid.

30 See *DPP v Majewski* [1977] AC 443, [1976] 2 All ER 142 (HL).

31 See also chapter 9.

32 *R v Ranger* (1988) 4 CRNZ 6 (CA); *R v Thomas* [1991] 3 NZLR 141, (1991) 7 CRNZ 123 (CA); *R v Terewi* (1985) 1 CRNZ 623. See also *Tuialli v Police* 19/3/87, Greig J, HC Auckland AP310/86; *Deans v Police* 5/3/87, Holland J, HC Christchurch AP7/87; *King v Police* 5/8/87, Quilliam J, HC Dunedin AP11/87.

33 See *R v Kamipeli* [1975] 2 NZLR 610 (CA).

13.1.4 Reasonable force

As was noted above, the test for self-defence in New Zealand involves both a subjective and an objective element. The subjective element, we have seen, concerns the actual belief of the defendant about the circumstances confronting her. The objective element concerns the requirement that the defensive force must have been "reasonable",[34] albeit reasonable in the circumstances as perceived by the defendant.

Generally, in a jury trial it will be for the jury to determine whether the force used was reasonable (or whether there is at least a reasonable doubt about this). Indeed, the question of the reasonableness of the force used may be regarded as exclusively a jury question and never a point of law for the judge to decide.[35] By the same token, to the extent that the reasonableness of force used is a jury question, it cannot be open to a defendant to claim that she *thought* the force used was reasonable. To allow such a concession would largely defeat the purpose of the objective element. Earlier judicial dicta which suggested that the test is whether the defendant believed the force used was reasonable must now be regarded as wrong.[36] In *R v Murray*,[37] Eichelbaum J stated:

> It would be a startling, not to say dangerous, proposition that the assessment of reasonable force was left subjectively to each individual accused.

Accordingly, the suggestion in *R v Scarlett*,[38] that the accused's belief that the force was reasonable constitutes a defence, does not represent the law in New Zealand. However, an accused's unreasonable belief that the force was *necessary* may still support the defence, provided the belief is honestly held.[39] That is to say, a belief may support the defence where an accused has unreasonably, albeit honestly, thought that the facts of the situation were such that force was his only option.

At the same time, the defence will be negated where the accused acts independently of the claimed belief and in a manner which suggests that it was not the belief, but rather revenge or retaliation, that was the true motivation for an act of aggression. In *R v Savage*,[40] the deceased, a hotel patron, had been violent and abusive toward the accused. Before the fatal incident the accused had asked another patron for a knife. A fight ensued, in which the accused was seen to deliver an upward blow to the chest of the deceased who was not in

---

34 Per s 48.

35 *A-G for Northern Ireland's Reference (No 1 of 1975)* [1977] AC 105 at 137, [1976] 3 WLR 235 at 246 (HL) (Lord Diplock).

36 See *R v Robinson* (1987) 2 CRNZ 632 at 635 (CA). The aberrant dictum in *Robinson* has been explained as being "clearly a slip in quoting s 48". See *R v Wang* [1990] 2 NZLR 529 at 536, (1989) 4 CRNZ 674 at 678 (CA).

37 22/10/87, Eichelbaum J, HC Wellington T26/87.

38 [1993] 4 All ER 629 at 636, (1994) 98 Cr App R 290 at 296 (CA).

39 See *Tuialli v Police* 19/3/87, Greig J, HC Auckland AP 310/86. See also the commentary on *R v Scarlett* in [1994] Crim LR 288; and White, "Going over the Top: Self-defence and Excessive Force" (1994-95) 5 King's College LJ 112.

40 [1991] 3 NZLR 155 (CA).

possession of a weapon at the time of the killing. The accused claimed to have been acting in self-defence when he saw the deceased pull a knife from his back pocket. In rejecting the appeal, the Court of Appeal said:

> when the knife was used, the accused must have seen himself as under a real threat of danger, and not *merely think there may be* some future danger to him. [41]

The dictum implies that "merely thinking that there may be" danger does not satisfy the requirements in s 48 that the accused "believes" danger exists, and that he acts "in the defence" of himself.

Generally, however, New Zealand courts have shown a remarkable degree of liberality in determining the nature and degree of force that is consistent with lawful self-defence, and have readily acknowledged that extreme circumstances may demand extreme measures. [42] In *Dixon v Police*, [43] for example, it was held that striking the victim in the arm with a knife in response to an attack with a heavy electric flex was consistent with a genuine belief that the defendant was in danger. The Court appeared to be uninfluenced by the fact that the defendant had a ready means of escape and could have avoided the confrontation. [44] Similarly, in *King v Police* [45] Quilliam J held the accused was justified when he smashed a beer handle in the face of his assailant, inflicting severe injuries. The assailant had grabbed the accused, who had a broken arm, by the throat while he was seated. In *Deans v Police*, [46] an appeal against conviction on a charge of assault was allowed on the basis that there was a reasonable doubt whether the complainant (a hotel bouncer) may have been pushed through a hotel window justifiably as a result of a "pushing off" by the accused which was no more than a reasonable response to an unlawful assault. The Court held that the District Court Judge had misdirected himself because he had only satisfied himself as to the physical fact that the defendant had pushed the complainant through the window, and had not considered whether the Crown had disproved self-defence.

13.1.4.1 *Proportionality*

The moral right to self-defence is not unlimited. It is confined to the use of reasonably necessary force. [47] This means that the law does not permit the use of *any* means to ward off unjust harm. The qualifying principle is that of proportionality. Suzanne Uniacke illustrates this principle by suggesting that a defender is not entitled to aim at an attacker's heart if she can shoot him in the

---

41 Ibid at 158. (Emphasis added.)

42 *Jenkins v Police* (1986) 2 CRNZ 196.

43 13/2/86, Jeffries J, HC Palmerston North AP5/86, see [1986] NZ Recent Law 233.

44 The Court's approach could not be justified on the ground that a homeowner has no duty to retreat from his own home, since the right of a householder to "stand fast" only applied where it was necessary to use deadly force against an intruder. There was no evidence here that the victim intended to break into the defendant's home.

45 5/8/87, Quilliam J, HC Dunedin AP11/87.

46 5/3/87, Holland J, HC Christchurch AP7/87.

47 Uniacke, *Permissible Killing: The Self-defence Justification of Homicide*, Cambridge, Cambridge University Press, 1994, 31.

leg and doing so is, in the circumstances, sufficient to defend herself.[48] Of course, the example presupposes that the accused is aware that the lesser degree of force will disable the aggressor and terminate the attack, and chooses instead to use a significantly greater measure of (lethal) force. It leaves open the possibility that D may shoot to kill if she (perhaps wrongly) believes that the degree of force used *is* necessary to repel the attack, and that shooting V in the leg will not stop him (eg because she thinks he has a gun).

The need for proportionality dictates that there is no general right to use force in self-defence irrespective of other morally-relevant considerations. For example, D cannot use lethal force against V as a means of preventing V from stepping on D's toe — even if that means is the only one available.[49] In addition, to be reasonable within the scope of s 48, the force used must also be *indispensable* or *unavoidable*; because necessity is, together with proportionality, an essential element in self-defence. This principle is expressed at common law on the basis that the mischief sought to be prevented could not be prevented by less violent means; and that the mischief done by, or which might reasonable anticipated from, the force used is not disproportionate to the injury or mischief which it is inflicted to prevent.[50] In practice, the requirement for necessity operates as an important litmus test for the dictates of proportionality. While it is true to say "if stunning one's assailant will suffice for self-defence, one must not shoot him through the heart" because that offends against the proportionality principle,[51] the action is legally countermanded more specifically because it is unnecessary. In practical terms the more extreme an action taken in self-defence is, relative to the threat offered, the easier it is to conclude that the action was unnecessary. Conversely, it would seem that the more extreme the danger facing the accused (or facing someone under his protection), the less the courts will be inclined to minutely examine issues of proportionality, and the more inclined they will be to accept the necessity of the accused's actions. Thus, in one case where an elderly man attacked, and unintentionally killed, his son-in-law with a wooden baton in order to protect his daughter from physical abuse, the Court, in directing the accused's discharge, stated that "actions are not to be weighed too finely or nicely".[52] Similarly, in *R v Murray*,[53] in an oral ruling on whether the defence of self-defence should be put to the jury, Eichelbaum J stated:

> one is reluctant to give any encouragement to the notion that the production of a dangerous knife or other weapon can be regarded as a reasonable response to an attack by a single person using bare hands. However, here there is available evidence of additional elements, namely a disparity in size and age, that the accused

---

48   Ibid.

49   Ibid at 31, 32.

50   Criminal Code Bill Commission, *Report of the Royal Commission Appointed to Consider the Law Relating to Indictable Offences: With an Appendix Containing a Draft Code Embodying the Suggestions of the Commission*, London, Eyre & Spottiswode for HMSO, 1879.

51   Finnis, *Fundamentals of Ethics*, Oxford, Clarendon Press, 1983, 85.

52   See *R v Brown*, HC Auckland.

53   22/10/87, Eichelbaum J, HC Wellington T26/87.

had rapidly got the worst of the encounter, the other party's known karate skills . . . do not think I can go so far as to say that it is impossible that a jury would entertain a reasonable doubt.

In that case, the accused had fatally stabbed the deceased in the neck with a knife after he had been severely assaulted. He had escaped from the attack and had gone into a bedroom where he obtained a hunting knife with the aim of "scaring off" the deceased. The fatal stabbing occurred when a further fight took place, in which the accused received a number of solid blows. Although the force used was fatal, it could not be said that it was irrefutably disproportionate, given the exigencies of the situation.

The need for a proper synthesis of the elements of necessity and proportionality has been recognised by the Privy Council in R v Palmer, in a well-known passage from the judgment of Lord Morris:

> If there is some relatively minor attack it would not be common sense to permit some action of retaliation which was *wholly out of proportion* to the *necessities* of the situation. If an attack is serious so that it puts someone in immediate peril then immediate defensive action may be necessary. If the moment is one of crisis for someone in imminent danger he may have to avert the danger by some instant reaction. If the attack is all over and no sort of peril remains then the employment of force may be by way of revenge or punishment or by way of paying off an old score or may be pure aggression. There may no longer be any link with a *necessity* of defence. Of all these matters the good sense of a jury will be the arbiter. There are no prescribed words which must be employed in or adopted in a summing-up. All that is needed is a clear exposition, in relation to the particular facts of the case, of the conception of *necessary* self-defence. If there has been no attack then clearly there will have been no need for defence. If there has been attack so that defence is reasonably necessary it will be recognised that a person defending himself *cannot weigh to a nicety the exact measure of his necessary defensive action.* If a jury thought that in a moment of unexpected anguish a person attacked had only done what he honestly and instinctively thought was necessary that would be most potent evidence that only reasonable defensive action had been taken. [54]

The passage affirms the conventional requirements of self-defence, namely, necessity and proportionality; but allows a degree of latitude to the defendant who, faced with a grave threat, must determine for herself the measure of force necessary to repel the threatened attack — without the advantage of on-the-spot guidance from a court. That is not a matter which can be weighed with fine scales.

13.1.4.2 Requirement that the threat be unjust

Although the case law is not clear on this point, it would seem implicit in the notion of necessary self-defence that the accused must have been or have believed herself to be the victim of an *unjust* threat. This appears to be a necessary qualification of the right of self-defence. Uniacke gives the example of a hijacker holding hostages at gunpoint as human shields, who picks off a police sharpshooter about to fire at him.[55] Such a person may act out of fear,

---

54   [1971] AC 814 at 831, 832, [1971] 1 All ER 1077 at 1088 (PC). (Emphasis added.)

55   Uniacke, *Permissible Killing: The Self-defence Justification of Homicide*, Cambridge, Cambridge University Press, 1994, 36.

may have a very strong, even an irresistible, desire to defend his life, but cannot plead self-defence. It is generally accepted that self-defence is not legally permissible against the necessary and proportionate self-defence by the victim of D's culpable attack.[56] To allow an aggressor the *right* to use self-defence against a person defending herself against an unjust attack is inconsistent with a fundamental justification for killing in self-defence, namely that an aggressor killed in self-defence has compromised his right not to be attacked. V, in turn, cannot both be justified in using necessary defensive force and at the same time be said to have forgone his right to be free of attack. Public policy, too, would seem to demand that an unjust aggressor not be entitled to plead self-defence. To not enforce such a limitation on the defence would imply that the State is willing to offer impunity to any unjust aggressor simply because her victim used force to defend himself.

This is not to say, however, that force, or a threat to use it, is necessarily unjust because it arises in the context of a broader enterprise of an unlawful nature. Unjust aggression against D may occur even where D herself is already engaged in criminal activity. Suppose, for example, that in the course of their committing a violent assault on an innocent victim, A, the principal offender, turns and begins to attack B, a co-offender (whom he perhaps perceives to be unwilling to enter fully into the assault in progress). In these circumstances, the fresh assault of A upon B is clearly *unjust* and there would seem no reason in principle why B should be deprived of the right to use necessary and proportionate force to defend against A's attack; regardless of his complicity in the original assault. The determinative questions are likely to be whether D has *foreseeably* and *wrongfully* created the circumstances in which he is endangered by V,[57] and whether the danger is being posed by V's justified response to those wrongfully-created circumstances.

13.1.4.3 *Retreat*

Under New Zealand law there is no absolute rule that a threatened person has a "duty to retreat", although failure to show an unwillingness to fight, or failure to take an opportunity of avoiding the use of force, will be relevant to the question whether the accused acted in reasonable self-defence. According to natural law theorists, such as Samuel von Pufendorf,[58] self-defence should always be tempered by restraint, and should be available as a last resort only when one's safety cannot otherwise be secured. However, even natural lawyers qualify this proposition. Pufendorf stated that a person is not required to flee imminent danger where this would expose the person to attack from behind. Neither, he suggested, is a person always *required* first to retreat rather than

---

56   See, for example, Low, *Criminal Law*, 1990, 166; and LaFave and Scott, *Criminal Law* (2nd ed), St Paul, Minnesota, West Publishing Co, 1986, 455, 459.

57   Uniacke, *Permissible Killing: The Self-defence Justification of Homicide*, Cambridge, Cambridge University Press, 1994, 84.

58   Pufendorf, *De Officio Hominis et Civis Juxta Legem Naturalem Libri Duo*, vol 2, ch V, New York, Oxford University Press, 1927, 3-36; cited in Uniacke, *Permissible Killing: The Self-defence Justification of Homicide*, Cambridge, Cambridge University Press, 1994, 66.

stand and fight, because to do so might weaken the position from which she is able to defend herself.

Pufendorf suggests another useful qualification. While the criterion that defensive force be necessary and proportionate does not mean that D must never expose himself to danger by simply going about his business, it does mean that if a person *impermissibly* courts a risk to his life, he cannot plead self-defence when it then comes to the point that he must kill to save himself. This implication was relevant in *R v Savage*,[59] where the accused, following extreme provocation by the deceased, but before the fatal incident, had asked another hotel patron for a knife. In a subsequent fist fight the deceased was stabbed fatally. In disallowing the appeal against conviction, the Court of Appeal stated:

> the law is that a threat which does not involve a present danger can normally be answered by retreating or adopting some other method of avoiding the present danger.[60]

The Court of Appeal went on to say that:

> whether a person is justified in fighting or should have retreated depends on the jury's view of what was reasonable in the circumstances.[61]

Rather than exercising restraint, D had sought out the very danger that he claimed in justification. His claim must therefore fail: D may not deliberately generate his own defence.[62]

At common law it had been held, in *R v Julien*, that while a person threatened need not "take to his heels and run",[63] it is necessary that he demonstrate that he is prepared to temporise and disengage and perhaps make some physical withdrawal. This approach aims to prevent the application of force wherever possible, and requires retreat, rather than force, as a first resort. However, in *R v McInnes*,[64] the English Court of Appeal qualified its earlier ruling in *Julien*, by holding that a direction on the requirement to retreat should not be in "too inflexible terms". The Court expressed its preference for the view that failure to retreat is only *an element* in the consideration upon which the reasonableness of an accused's conduct is to be judged. While, as noted earlier, there is no statutory duty to retreat in New Zealand, the approach taken in *McInnes* is relevant in this country also, in that failure either to show an unwillingness to fight or to take the opportunity to avoid using force will be relevant to the question whether the defendant acted in reasonable self-defence.[65] In *R v Terewi*,[66] for example, it was held that retreating, or some other

---

59 [1991] 3 NZLR 155 (CA). See § 13.1.4.

60 Ibid at 158.

61 Ibid at 159.

62 Cf Robinson, "Causing the Conditions of One's Own Defense: A Study in the Limits of Theory in Criminal Law Doctrine" (1985) 71 Virginia LR 1.

63 See *R v Julien* [1969] 2 All ER 856 at 858, [1969] 1 WLR 839 at 843 (CA).

64 [1971] 3 All ER 295 at 300, [1971] 1 WLR 1600 at 1607 (CA).

65 See also *R v Bird* [1985] 2 All ER 513, [1985] 1 WLR 816 (CA).

66 (1985) 1 CRNZ 623 at 625.

method of avoiding, a threatened danger will normally be appropriate where the threat does not involve immediately present danger. A proper jury direction would include a statement that ease of escape is one of the factors which the jury should consider when determining whether D's actions were reasonable in the circumstances.[67]

Despite all this, it appears that a person may still be justified in holding her ground, even when an opportunity for escape exists, where the aggressor is actively using a weapon and is in an aggressive and hostile mood. In *Dixon v Police*,[68] the victim had stood in front of the accused, who was standing on his front doorstep, and had swung a heavy electric flex at him. The accused had then struck the victim in the forearm with a knife. In holding that the appellant had acted reasonably in the circumstances as he believed them to be, the Court acknowledged that:

> He was being attacked by a man wielding a heavy electric cord which is not an ineffective weapon. He had a genuine belief he was in danger and I think rightly so.[69]

However, while the Judge was no doubt justified in finding that the appellant genuinely believed himself to be in danger, it is arguable that the Judge may have misdirected himself by failing to give adequate consideration to the issue of necessity. The issue, as was noted above, is not just whether the force used was proportionate (arguably the case here) but also whether it was *necessary* or *unavoidable*. Yet on the facts of the case it apparently *was* avoidable, since the appellant had available the option of walking back into his house and shutting the door, thereby disengaging from the conflict. In these circumstances consideration of the related issue of proportionality becomes unnecessary, since the failure of the appellant to satisfy the requirements of necessity should have meant the defence was unavailable.

The facts of *Dixon* may for illustration be contrasted with those of the Canadian case of *R v Weshaver*,[70] in which failure to retreat was also held not to preclude the accused from relying on statutory self-defence. There the accused, who had been convicted on a charge of assault causing bodily harm, had struck the assailant three times with a heavy wooden doorstop. His appeal against conviction was allowed, on the basis that the accused was being threatened by a powerful and aggressive adversary who had consumed a large quantity of alcohol and was in an uncontrollable rage. The Court held that no properly directed jury could have been satisfied beyond reasonable doubt that the accused had used more force than necessary to defend himself. It appears in that case that the requirement of necessity was satisfied, because there was no clear option available that would have enabled the appellant to disengage from the conflict. The force used was indispensable.

---

67   *R v Whyte* [1987] 3 All ER 416 at 419, (1987) 85 Cr App R 283 at 286 (CA); *R v Savage* [1991] 3 NZLR 155 (CA).

68   13/2/86, Jeffries J, HC Palmerston North AP5/86.

69   *Dixon v Police* [1986] NZ Recent Law 233 at 234. See § 13.1.4.

70   (1993) 17 CR (4th) 401 (SC).

Clearly, failure to show an unwillingness to fight or to take an opportunity of avoiding the use of force may be relevant to the question whether the accused acted in reasonable self-defence. However, it has been acknowledged by the courts that seriousness, in terms of anticipated injury, is often a matter in the eye of the beholder.[71] It may be argued that a person cannot be blamed who, in an intuitive response to threatened violence, uses a degree of force that would have been unacceptable if there had been opportunity for cool reflection and careful deliberation. In a simple case like *Jenkins*,[72] where the Court allowed that throwing a milk bottle at the feet of pursuing assailants was a reasonable response to the fear of further serious assault and a legitimate basis for claiming self-defence on a charge of disorderly behaviour, the principle is capable of a straightforward application. However, it is not an unqualified principle and, arguably, the more violent the response to the perceived aggression, the more carefully a jury will be required to look at whether the accused actually *believed* that the force was necessary against an unjust assault, or whether he *merely thought that there may be* some future danger to him.[73]

13.1.4.4 Pre-emptive strike

The formal requirements for self-defence allow the use of force to resist or repel an unjust immediate threat. This does not necessarily imply, however, that the defender must have begun to experience an actual assault before the use of self-defensive force can be justified. In some circumstances the law allows the use of pre-emptive force to repel or disable the aggressor before he is able to mount an attack. The theoretical basis for allowing a pre-emptive strike is that the person who intends to launch an unjust attack and has armed himself for that purpose, is an aggressor even before having struck a blow.[74] It follows that such a person may also be resisted before the blow is struck. The critical question is, then, at what point may an intended victim use force to prevent an anticipated unlawful attack from occurring? On this point the law in most jurisdictions is unclear, although it now seems to be generally conceded that a pre-emptive strike is sometimes permissible, at least in principle.

Amongst the early natural law accounts of self-defence, Grotius takes the view that while the threatened injury must constitute "a present danger", "imminent in point of time", this condition may be fulfilled where there is a manifest intention to kill on the part of someone who takes up weapons.[75] Uniacke suggests that the condition could also be fulfilled where the victim of an ongoing or intermittent attack uses force against an aggressor who has paused to reload a weapon, or has stumbled, or temporarily lost

---

71 *Jenkins v Police* (1986) 2 CRNZ 196 at 198.

72 Ibid.

73 *R v Savage* [1991] 3 NZLR 155 (CA).

74 Uniacke, *Permissable Killing: The Self-defence Justification of Homicide*, Cambridge, Cambridge University Press, 1994, 70.

75 Grotius, *The Rights of War and Peace*, transl William Whewell, Parker, 1853 at 61-68; cited in Uniacke, *Permissible Killing: The Self-defence Justification of Homicide*, Cambridge, Cambridge University Press, 1994, 70.

consciousness.[76] It is important to note that while Grotius appears to endorse the view that self-defence is sometimes permissible to anticipate an unlawful attack, he warns that in general *mere fear* does not give a right of killing for prevention.[77] The reason for this limitation is that where the danger is uncertain, or can otherwise be averted, recourse should be had to other means of avoidance (such as retreat) or to legal remedies. These limitations suggest that the right of pre-emptive strike is of limited application, and should not be used as a mask for retaliation or as a means of resolving D's misplaced anxiety concerning a future, possible or even imaginary attack. Because it is a representative form of self-defence, it must also be subject to the same essential elements: necessity and proportionality.

The case law on pre-emptive strike in New Zealand, although scanty, has laid down some clear limits to the doctrine. The issue appears first to have been considered by the Court of Appeal in *R v Terewi*.[78] There the Court cited with approval a passage in Glanville Williams' *Textbook on Criminal Law* to the effect that pre-emptive strike is allowable, subject to the qualification that the danger threatened must be or appear imminent.[79] This is consistent with the first of Grotius' suggested limitations. In *Terewi*, the Court emphasised that there was no general right of pre-emptive attack in self-defence; rather, any right of pre-emptive strike must exist only within the wider rule that the force used in self-defence must not exceed what is reasonable in the circumstances. Accordingly, we may state these limitations in terms of two broad conditions. Pre-emptive strike should not be allowed where:

(i)   The danger is not imminent, or

(ii)   Where retreat or disengagement is a reasonable possibility.

The permissibility of pre-emptive strike has already been discussed in relation to *R v Ranger*.[80] There the Court of Appeal stated:

> If this accused did really think that the lives of herself and her son were in peril because the deceased, enraged after the struggle, might attempt to shoot them with a rifle near at hand, then it would be going too far, we think, to say that the jury could not entertain a reasonable doubt as to whether a pre-emptive strike with a knife would be reasonable force in all the circumstances.

In allowing the appeal and ordering a new trial, the Court emphasised that it was *the circumstances as the accused believed them to be* which were determinative whether the force used was reasonable.

The issue of pre-emptive strike also arose in *R v Wang*.[81] In that case, the accused had stabbed her husband to death while he was asleep in a drunken state after he had threatened to kill the accused and her sister and after threatening to blackmail another sister. The question on appeal was whether

---

76   Ibid.

77   Ibid.

78   (1985) 1 CRNZ 623.

79   See Williams, *TBCL*, 503.

80   (1988) 4 CRNZ 6 at 9 (CA). See § 13.1.2.1.

81   [1990] 2 NZLR 529 at 535, (1989) 4 CRNZ 674 at 679 (CA).

the trial Judge was right to refuse to allow self-defence to go to the jury. The trial Judge had found that, having regard to the fact that the accused's husband was asleep and intoxicated, and that she was able to tie him up without waking him, "a reasonable person in her position had a number of alternative courses open to her". By implication, she was in no immediate danger and killing her husband could not be regarded as a reasonable course of action. Significantly, the trial Judge did not rule out the possibility that a pre-emptive strike, even with a knife, could in certain circumstances qualify for consideration as self-defence. Instead, he held that to accede to the accused's suggestion that such an action was justified in the present circumstances would have amounted to "a return to the law of the jungle". Even giving the jury every latitude in taking the most favourable view of the accused's honest, if mistaken, view of the circumstances, no jury could regard the accused's reaction as a reasonable one.

The Court of Appeal agreed, and for the same reasons as the trial Judge found that self-defence was not open to the appellant. Regarding the issue of pre-emptive strike, the Court held that what is reasonable force must depend on the *imminence* and *seriousness* of the threat, and upon the *opportunity to seek protection* without recourse to the use of force. If a person has other alternative courses of action other than the use of force, and the threat by V cannot be carried out immediately, then it would be unacceptable to make a pre-emptive attack.

At the same time, the Court did not seek to generalise its refusal in *Wang*, and indeed approved the dictum of Lord Griffiths in *Beckford v R*, that "a man about to be attacked does not have to wait for his assailant to strike the first blow or fire the first shot; circumstances may justify a pre-emptive strike".[82] However, in order properly to reflect society's concern for the sanctity of human life, the Court concluded that where there has not been an assault, but merely a *threatened* assault, killing in self-defence or in defence of another can only be justified where there is an *immediate* prospect of *life-threatening violence*.

It would seem, therefore, that while pre-emptive strike may be permissible in certain circumstances, it cannot be used as a mask for revenge or retaliation. Neither may it be employed as a means of eliminating a future anticipated lethal attack that is not imminent in point of time and where other means of avoidance are available.

13.1.4.5 *Self-defence and battered women*

One particularly troubling area, in which the issue of pre-emptive strike frequently arises, concerns situations where battered women have killed their sleeping spouses in circumstances where the victim does not pose an objective imminent threat to their life or safety. In some Canadian and US jurisdictions, courts have been willing to extend the self-defence doctrine to cover these situations, on the grounds that a battered woman should not have to wait until a deadly attack occurs before she can act in self-defence.

Suppose the following scenario:

---

82   [1988] AC 130 at 144, [1987] 3 All ER 425 at 431 (PC).

D is a battered woman who has lived in an abusive relationship for a period of years. After a bout of drinking the abusing male partner, P, returns home and commences physically and mentally abusing D. P then announces that he is going to bed, or simply falls asleep in a drunken stupor on the couch, having previously warned D that he intends to "deal" with her in the morning. D, by now emotionally and mentally exhausted, and fearing the prospect of another violent beating the next day, decides that the only way to deal with the problem is to kill P while he is unconscious and not presenting an immediate threat to her. She takes a kitchen knife and stabs P to death while he sleeps.

Is this self-defence? According to conventional self-defence theory the law must say no. The danger to D is not immediate in point of time, and it cannot be said that she is without recourse to other means of avoidance. She could, for example, leave the house, or even seek assistance from the police. Even granted that she is to be judged by the circumstances as she believes them to be, it is impossible to view her response as either *necessary*, in the sense of being unavoidable and indispensable, or *proportionate*, in the sense that a reasonable person in the accused's position would not have considered that the injury inflicted in avoiding the threatened harm was disproportionate.

Despite these implications of the conventional analysis, the approach of the courts to this problem has varied significantly in different jurisdictions. In the now celebrated case of *R v Lavallee*,[83] the Supreme Court of Canada appeared to lend its weight to the notion of "battered woman syndrome", characterised by a condition of "learned helplessness", when allowing the appeal of a woman who had shot her abusive partner in the back of the head as he was leaving a room, after he had issued the challenge "either you kill me or I'll get you". The question on appeal (against the decision of the Manitoba Court of Appeal overturning the accused's acquittal) was whether there was sufficient evidence of self-defence, in the form of expert psychological evidence regarding "battered woman's syndrome" to allow the defence to be put to the jury.

In allowing the appeal and reinstating the acquittal, the Supreme Court held that the definition of what was a reasonable response to the apprehension of death must sometimes be adapted to circumstances which are foreign to the hypothetical reasonable man. The Court held that, in light of the condition of the defendant, it might not be unreasonable to apprehend death or grievous bodily harm before the physical assault is in progress.

However, there are problems with this analysis. In giving more weight to the accused's subjective beliefs and to the somewhat imprecise concept of "learned helplessness", the Court appears to have overlooked, or at least heavily discounted, the formal requirements of necessity, proportionality, and an objectively imminent threat. Arguably, rather than applying existing law, it has tailored a new defence specific to battered women.

New Zealand courts have not been so ready to accommodate the claims of battered women within the rules of self-defence. In *R v Wang*,[84] the Court of Appeal rejected self-defence because the wife was not held hostage and was

---

83   (1990) 76 CR (3d) 329, [1990] 1 SCR 852 (SCC).
84   [1990] 2 NZLR 529, (1989) 4 CRNZ 674 (CA).

free to seek protection in other ways. The Court emphasised the need for "immediacy of life-threatening violence", in any case where an assault is merely threatened, to justify killing in self-defence.[85] Under New Zealand law the courts, when considering the use of pre-emptive force by battered women who kill their abusers, seem to be more inclined to ask whether there was a crystallised, immediate danger that needed to be averted by instant action. If the circumstances are such that no jury could entertain a reasonable doubt on the point, the defence should be withdrawn from the jury.[86]

Of course, the court must still consider the circumstances believed by the accused to exist, when determining the reasonableness of the force used. Thus evidence that the accused suffered from battered woman syndrome may be relevant in determining the imminence and degree of force that the accused might have anticipated, and also as part of a response to any suggestion that the accused should simply have left the victim.[87] However, the question whether her response was reasonable remains ultimately *objective*. By continually relating the issue of the accused's subjective belief back to an objective evaluation of the reasonableness of the force used in light of that belief, New Zealand's judges have sought to give proper weight to the requirements of necessity and proportionality, while not entirely ignoring the special claims presented by these cases.

Nonetheless, the question remains whether the existing self-defence rules are adequate to deal with the unique difficulties presented by cases of battered woman syndrome. Indeed, it is doubtful whether they should be characterised as cases of self-defence at all, since the formal requirements of unjust aggression, imminence of threat, necessity, and proportionality seem to be lacking in each case. Yet this is one area where "conflicting moral and ideological forces [have driven] the law in [a] particular direction".[88] It might be preferable to think of these cases as situations of (say) *self-preservation*, which raise legal considerations different to those typically presented by cases of self-defence against immediate unjust aggression. Given the fact that cases of spousal killings involving battered woman syndrome do not really fit happily within the conventional canons of self-defence, a case might even be made for the return to a form of the old common law plea of *se defendendo*, which provided for the concept of *excusable* homicide, a category of liability occupying a halfway house between total liability and total acquittal.[89] The plea operated by way of confession and avoidance; asserting *se defendendo* conceded the illegality of the killing, but sought to avoid the capital penalty, routine for ordinary cases of murder.[90] Applied in the context of battered woman

---

85 Ibid at 539, at 683.

86 See *R v Ranger* (1988) 4 CRNZ 6 at 9 (CA); *R v Wang* [1990] 2 NZLR 529 at 535, (1989) 4 CRNZ 674 at 679 (CA).

87 See *R v Oakes* [1995] 2 NZLR 673 (CA); also *R v Gordon* (1993) 10 CRNZ 430 (CA).

88 Fletcher, *A Crime of Self-Defense: Bernard Goetz and the Law on Trial*, New York, 1988, 27.

89 Fletcher, "Defensive Force as an Act of Rescue" in Paul, Miller Jr, and Paul (eds), *Crime, Culpability, and Remedy*, Oxford, Basil Blackwell, 1990, 171.

90 Ibid.

syndrome killings, the defence would be required to concede the illegality of the killing, but evidence of battered woman syndrome could be adduced on the question whether the offender was fully culpable for the offence, in much the same way as evidence of "abnormality of mind" is used in the English defence of diminished responsibility to reduce murder to manslaughter.[91] It is interesting to observe that in *R v Gordon*,[92] where the appellant sought to introduce battered woman syndrome as evidence supporting self-defence to a charge that she murdered her husband, the Court of Appeal noted that if New Zealand had had a statutory defence of diminished responsibility, the appellant would have been a candidate for it. Although self-defence failed in that case, and the murder conviction was upheld because of evidence that the appellant intended to kill her husband and had arranged for a "hit man" to do so, the judgment helpfully shows the unsatisfactory state of the law, which currently imposes a mandatory punishment for culpable homicide, even though it is acknowledged that the offender may not have been fully responsible for her crime.

It is submitted that there is room for acceptance of a new palliative defence of *excusable self-protection*, supplementing the existing rules on self-defence, which would allow juries more latitude in dealing with spousal homicides involving battered woman syndrome, and would overcome some of the anomalies created by the present law, without compromising the elements of statutory self-defence.

13.1.5 Excessive force

In a sense, the law gives conflicting signals concerning the degree of force which is permissible in self-defence. On the one hand it states that the defence must fail if the force used by the accused is excessive. On the other hand, the courts will not "weigh to a nicety" what is reasonable defensive force.[93] However, the underlying principle would seem to be that because a person who repels an unjust attack is upholding the law, and as such is justified, where force used in self-defence is disproportionate to the threat offered, the defender himself acts unlawfully and may forfeit the protection that the law otherwise confers. Such a person is then liable for using an excess of force beyond that which the law allows. In New Zealand, authority for punishing excess force is provided by s 62 Crimes Act 1961, which indicates that wherever the law permits someone to use force, she is liable for the consequences of force used beyond that which the law allows. In *R v Godbaz*,[94] the Court of Appeal held that excessive force in repelling an assault was not protected by self-defence and itself constituted an assault. Thus, applying s 62 in a case where excessive force has been used in self-defence resulting in the death of the original aggressor, the offender will be liable for murder (unless she can avail herself of some other defence, such as provocation). For example, this may

---

91 Section 2 Homicide Act 1957 (UK).
92 (1993) 10 CRNZ 430 (CA).
93 See *Palmer v R* [1971] AC 814 at 832, [1971] 1 All ER 1077 at 1088 (PC).
94 (1909) 28 NZLR 577 (CA).

occur where the original aggressor (V) unjustly attacked D with fists, whereupon D responded by shooting V with a pistol.

To say that the force used was excessive is to say that D's response to the unjust attack was disproportionate to the threat it presented. In either case, D has proceeded beyond the status of a victim to become an aggressor, and as such is liable for the consequences of his unlawful acts.[95]

13.2 DEFENCE OF PROPERTY

The traditional response of the common law to the right of an individual to protect his property is reflected in the following statement:

> the house of every one is to him as his castle and fortress, as well for his defence against injury and violence, as for his repose . . .[96]

The maxim, "an Englishman's home is his castle", survives today in common speech and is a principle still recognised by the courts.[97] In *McLorie v Oxford*,[98] Donaldson LJ observed that the rule is subject to exceptions, but that they are few; even in the context of search and seizure, it is for the police to justify a forcible entry. As his Honour said:

> Such is the importance attached by the common law to the relative inviolability of a dwelling house that we cannot believe that there is a common law right without warrant to enter one either in order to search for instruments of crime, even of serious crime, or in order to seize such an instrument which is known to be there. Certainly if there were, we would expect it to be reflected in the books and it is not.[99]

Generally, the right to defend property reflects the commonsense notion that a person who owns or has an interest in land as an occupier should have the right forcibly to remove an intruder, even though the force used may otherwise be an assault. The cases, for the most part, fall into two categories: (a) where an occupier uses force to prevent the entry of an intruder, who may or may not be known to the occupier; and (b) where the occupier seeks to prevent an unlawful intrusion upon his rights by agents of the State (including police, customs, or immigration officers). At the heart of the "right" to defend property is the interest of civilised society in upholding and protecting the legal institution of ownership, which itself implies the right to exclude all others lacking a legal interest from that property, either with the assistance of the State or by resort to self-help. Similarly, the law grants security of possession to

---

95 Uniacke notes that the designation "aggressor" can shift during the course of a conflict from the instigator to the other party, eg when the instigator publicly and sincerely attempts to withdraw, or to introduce peaceful negotiations aimed at settlement, and the victim then unreasonably continues the hostility: Uniacke, *Permissible Killing: The Self-defence Justification of Homicide*, Cambridge, Cambridge University Press, 1994, 71.

96 *Semayne's Case* (1604) 5 Co Rep 91a at 91b, 77 ER 194 at 195.

97 *R v Stanley* (1977) 36 CCC (2d) 216 at 226; *Morris v Beardmore* [1981] AC 446, [1980] 2 All ER 753 (HL).

98 [1982] QB 1290 at 1296, [1982] 3 WLR 423 at 427.

99 Ibid at 429, at 1298.

a possessor, including the right to exclude all others, save perhaps the owner, from entry to the property possessed.

The issue of defence of property brings into focus a difficult question of how to balance the interests of the community in peace and good government, and the interests of a private occupier in protecting his personal space. In general, the balance is found by distinguishing between using force to *claim* property, and using force to *defend* property already in D's possession. Blackstone expressed the basic philosophy of the law in these terms:

> the public peace is a superior consideration to any one man's private property; and as, if individuals were once allowed to use private force as a remedy for private injuries, all social justice must cease, the strong would give law to the weak, and every man would revert to a state of nature: for these reasons it is provided, that this natural right of reception shall never be exerted, where such exertion must occasion strife and bodily contention, or endanger the peace of society.[100]

Normally, in respect of both movable and real property, disputes should be resolved by the courts rather than by resort to self-help. However, where there is an imminent danger of damage to or loss of property or possession at the hands of a wrongdoer, the courts may be unable to provide the relief needed in time, and the occupier/owner of property may find herself so placed that the exigencies of the situation demand immediate action to protect the interests threatened. What should be the response of the law in such circumstances?

The law recognises the paramountcy of human life and safety, even for a wrongdoer, over the security of another's property. For this reason, the provisions in the Crimes Act 1961 governing defence of property, as we shall see, generally limit the use of force in protecting property to that which does not actually cause bodily harm to the trespasser.[101] The only exception to this rule concerns the defence of a dwellinghouse, whereby a person in "peaceable possession of a dwellinghouse" may use "such force as is *necessary*" to prevent the forcible breaking and entering into the house.[102] The reasons for this exception will be discussed below. More generally, the rationale for limiting the permissible use of force to protect property is expressed in the following passage:

> the life of a man is a thing precious and favoured in law; so that although a man kills another in his defence or kills one *per infortun'*, without any intent, yet it is a felony, and in such a case he shall forfeit his goods and chattels for the great regard which the law has to a man's life. [103]

Similarly, while no longer asserting that people have quite so absolute a right to life, when drafting the provisions of the Draft Code of 1879,[104] the

---

100 3 *Blackstone's Commentaries*, 4-5.

101 See, for example, Crimes Act 1961, ss 52 (defence of movable property against trespasser), 53 (defence of movable property with claim of right), 56 (defence of land or building).

102 Section 55 Crimes Act 1961.

103 *Semayne's Case* (1604) 5 Co Rep 91a at 91b, 77 ER 194 at 195.

104 Criminal Code Bill Commission, *Report of the Royal Commission Appointed to Consider The Law Relating to Indictable Offences: With an Appendix Containing a Draft Code Embodying the*

Criminal Code Bill Commissioners were concerned to ensure that the Code reflected the proposition that force used in defence of person, liberty, or property against illegal violence must be proportionate to the injury or mischief which it is intended to prevent.[105] It followed that the use of lawful force was subject to the restriction that the force used was necessary, that is to say that the mischief sought to be prevented could not be prevented by less violent means.[106] This principle still informs the current approach of the law in this area.

13.2.1 Structure of the current New Zealand law

The present New Zealand law concerning defence of property has remained largely unchanged since 1893, when the Criminal Code Act was first enacted. The relevant statutory provisions, now contained in ss 52-56 Crimes Act 1961, have been subject to minimal revision over the last 100 years. It is arguable that the present law is unnecessarily cumbersome and complex, with five sections dealing with defence of property, and three devoted exclusively to defence of movable property. In addition, the legislation makes separate provision for the peaceable entry on any land or buildings and the right to exercise a right of way.[107] The law could surely be rendered in a more compendious and simple form, consistent with the reforms that have significantly simplified the law on self-defence. However, the relative dearth of reported cases where the defence of property has been judicially considered would suggest that this is not a controversial area of law and that, despite their relative complexity, the provisions are readily applied.

13.2.2 Defence of land or building and defence of movable property (ss 52, 53, 56)

Because of the common limitations on the use of force which apply to these sections, it is convenient to deal with them together. The defence provided in ss 52, 53, and 56 allows everyone "in peaceable possession of any movable thing" (ss 52 and 53) or "land or building" (s 56) to use "reasonable force" to defend such property provided the force used does not include striking or doing bodily harm to the trespasser.

Taking as representative of these the defence of movable property, allowed by s 52, the section contains four elements. This means that before an accused can benefit from it, the jury must at least have a doubt about all four. If a jury is convinced beyond any reasonable doubt that any one element is missing the defence must fail.[108] The four elements are:

(i) The accused must be in possession of a movable thing;

Suggestions of the Commission, London, Eyre & Spottiswode for HMSO, 1879, C-2345. The Draft Code was the basis of the Criminal Code Act, 1893 and of subsequent enactments of the Crimes Act.

105 Ibid at 44.

106 Ibid at 11.

107 Sections 57 and 58 Crimes Act 1961.

108 See *R v Born with a Tooth* (1993) 76 CCC (3d) 169 at 177.

(ii)   His possession must be *peaceable;*

(iii) He may use *reasonable force* to resist the taking of the thing by a trespasser;

(iv)   He may not *strike* or *do bodily harm* to the trespasser.

There would appear to be no reported case law in New Zealand on this section. "Movable property" is not defined in the Act but would seem to encompass tangible personal property. Although the section is silent on the point, it is submitted that the standard to be applied in determining whether the nature of situation that is claimed to justify the use of reasonable force is a subjective one; thus if D honestly believes V is a trespasser and meets the other criteria of the subsection, the actions taken by D in defence of property will be justified.

13.2.2.1 *"Reasonable force"*

Assuming the accused honestly believes the circumstances are such that some force is justified, the force used to resist the trespasser must be objectively reasonable. It will not be enough that the accused *herself* thought the force used was reasonable, if an ordinary person in the same circumstances as the accused perceives would not have used that degree of force.[109] As a general rule, in a jury trial it will be for the jury to determine whether the force used was reasonable (or whether there is at least reasonable doubt about this).[110] So if D, resisting what she rightly believes to be an attempt to execute an invalid search warrant, pushes V, a police constable, in the chest, that will not be an unreasonable use of force.[111] Further, some degree of manhandling may well come within the definition of reasonable force if a person has already been requested to leave, provided the trespasser is neither struck nor injured.[112] The force used must be reasonable. There is some authority for the view that the pointing of a gun by a physically weak person may be justifiable to prevent the taking of property,[113] although firing at a person to prevent him from taking the property would probably constitute an unreasonable use of force, whether or not the trespasser is injured.[114]

The Canadian equivalent of s 52 contains a provision that where a person in peaceable possession of personal property lays hands on it, a trespasser who persists in attempting to keep it or take it from him will be deemed to have committed an assault without justification or provocation.[115] Although the New Zealand section does not contain the same provision in express terms, it is arguably an implicit element. Where an issue of defence of property has

---

109   *R v Wang* [1990] 2 NZLR 529 at 534, (1989) 4 CRNZ 674 at 679 (CA).

110   See *R v Ranger* (1988) 4 CRNZ 6 at 9 (CA).

111   *Galvin v Police* 22/4/86, Bisson J, HC Rotorua M44/85.

112   See *Deans v Police* 5/3/87, Holland J, HC Christchurch AP7/87.

113   See *Martin's Annual Criminal Code* 1997, Aurora, Ontario, Canada Law Book Co, 1996, CC/83.

114   See *R v Baxter* (1975) 27 CCC (2d) 96 (Ont CA); also *R v Figueira* (1981) 63 CCC (2d) 409 (Ont CA).

115   Section 38(2) Criminal Code 1954 (Canada).

degenerated into physical conflict between the trespasser and the person in possession, the continued unlawful attempts by the trespasser to gain possession may become a criminal assault against which the possessor may use reasonable force in self-defence.[116] This situation was contemplated by the drafters of the Draft Code, who said:

> If the trespasser resists, and in so doing assaults the party in possession, that party may repel the assault and for that purpose may use any force which he would be justified in using in defence of his person.[117]

It is submitted that this statement reflects the current law.

13.2.2.2 No "bodily harm"

There is no direct authority on the meaning of "strike or do bodily harm" in s 52. However, case law on the meaning of "actual bodily harm" may be relevant. "Actual bodily harm" comprises any type of injury, however minor or temporary, though more than transient or trifling,[118] which is calculated to interfere with the health or comfort of the complainant.[119] In *R v McArthur*,[120] McMahon J held that a victim could not be said to be "injured" when there was no evidence of broken bones, cuts, lacerations, or bruising.

Although the provisions clearly allow the use of *some* physical force, the degree of permissible force used must necessarily be minimal if it excludes such injuries as cuts and (non-trivial) bruising, and if it must also fall short of any "striking". It may be that the only types of force contemplated by the sections are minor technical assaults in the nature of pushing, or the confrontational standing of one's ground to physically prevent the trespasser achieving his object. The Criminal Code Commissioners suggested that the defence of possession of either goods or land against a mere trespass does not, strictly speaking, justify even a breach of the peace: the party in lawful possession "may justify gently laying his hands on the trespasser and requesting him to depart".[121] However, even this attempt partially to stipulate the ambit of the defence in advance may be unhelpful, since the availability of the defence will depend on the facts of each case. It is possible, for example, that even a mild push or the threat to use force could be unreasonable, when a simple request might have persuaded the trespasser to leave the premises or to desist from asserting a claim to property. In the absence of a striking or an

---

116 Section 48.

117 Criminal Code Bill Commission, *Report of the Royal Commission Appointed to Consider the Law Relating to Indictable Offences: With an Appendix Containing a Draft Code Embodying the Suggestions of the Commission*, London, Eyre & Spottiswode for HMSO, 1879, 45.

118 *R v Donovan* [1934] 2 KB 498 at 501 (CCA).

119 *R v Miller* [1954] 2 QB 282 , (1953) 38 Cr App R 1. See also *R v Dawson* (1985) 81 Cr App R 150 (CA) (emotional disturbance not itself actual bodily harm but shock causing physical harm is).

120 [1975] 1 NZLR 486 at 487.

121 Criminal Code Bill Commission, *Report of the Royal Commission Appointed to Consider the Law Relating to Indictable Offences: With an Appendix Containing a Draft Code Embodying the Suggestions of the Commission*, London, Eyre & Spottiswode for HMSO, 1879, 45. See also *De Lambert v Ongley* [1924] NZLR 430.

infliction of bodily harm, whether the force used was permissible will ultimately depend upon what the tribunal of fact considered was reasonable in the circumstances of the case.[122]

13.2.2.3 *"Peaceable possession"*

Another element common to the defences in ss 52-56 is the requirement that the person defending be in "peaceable possession"of the property concerned. The meaning of the phrase does not appear to have been considered directly by a New Zealand court. However, it is thought that "peaceable possession" need not be lawful possession. It suffices that the accused has actual control of the property.[123] In Canada, "peaceable possession" has been held to mean a possession hitherto not seriously challenged by others.[124] In *R v Born with a Tooth*,[125] the appellant together with a group of Peigan Indians had confronted police and environmental officers who had crossed land occupied by the Indians, in order to repair a dyke on land that had been surrendered to the Alberta Government. The appellant's defence to a charge of pointing a rifle at police officers was that he was in peaceable possession of the land and that the officers had not given reasonable notice of their intention to come on the land. He claimed he was entitled to use reasonable force to eject the trespassers. Because a proper explanation of the defence had not been put to the jury, the Court allowed the appeal and ordered a new trial. However, the Court observed that the demand that possession be "peaceable" greatly limits the defence. It is not enough for an accused to show that he kept the peace while on the land. Peaceable possession means that the possession has not provoked a breach of the peace[126] and that it is acquiesced in by all other persons.[127] For the purposes of the Code, it was held to mean a possession not seriously challenged by others before the incident in question. The key to peaceable possession is whether the possession is such, and the challenge to it is such, that the situation is unlikely to lead to violence.[128]

13.2.2.4 *"Claim of right"*

An element common to the defences in ss 53 and 54, and specifically exempted in s 54, is the requirement that there be peaceable possession of a movable

---

122 But see *R v Dupuis* [1974] RL 379 (Que Prov Ct), where a restaurant owner threw an 11 year old boy out of his establishment, the boy having made a nuisance of himself. The boy fell and broke his wrist, yet it was held the force used was reasonable. See also *Marguson v Grant* (1921) 57 DLR 710 (CA): a woman who refused to quit the defendant's premises on request suffered a wrenched arm when turned out by the defendant. Use of force held not unreasonable.

123 *Adams* § CA56.05. See also *Paxhaven Holdings Ltd v A-G* [1974] 2 NZLR 185; *Foster v Warblington Urban Council* [1906] 1 KB 648, [1904-07] All ER Rep 366 (CA).

124 *R v Born with a Tooth* (1992) 76 CCC (3d) 169.

125 Ibid.

126 See Stephen, *A History of the Criminal Law of England* vol III, London, Macmillan, 1883, 13.

127 *Black's Law Dictionary*, (6th ed) St Paul, Minnesota, West Publishing Co, 1990.

128 *R v Born with a Tooth* (1992) 76 CCC (3d) 169 at 178. See also Law Reform Commission of Canada, report No 30, 1987, 38.

thing with "claim of right". Claim of right is not defined in the Crimes Act 1961. However, it is generally thought that the expressions "colour of right" and "claim of right" are synonymous, and that in defining "colour of right" the statute also defines "claim of right".[129] If so, in the context of ss 53 and 54, claim of right requires an honest belief that D's possession is justified and encompasses not only a belief in a state of facts which would at law justify or excuse the possession, but also a belief based on ignorance or mistake of law. The test is a purely subjective test, of honesty of D's claim. In *Murphy v Gregory*,[130] Henry J said:

> Where an accused person really believes he has the right asserted, it is a good defence even if he is mistaken both in fact and in law . . . It is for the prosecution to prove there was no colour of right. If a prisoner puts forward, however wrongheadedly, an honest claim of right, he ought to be acquitted.

As *Murphy v Gregory* indicates, even a "wrongheaded" claim of right will suffice: thus the "claim of right" requires only an honest belief that D has a lawful right to do what she is doing, not a belief in a right that is actually recognised by law.[131] However, an honest belief that the accused had a *moral* right to act as she did, as opposed to an honest belief in a *legal* right, will not suffice.[132] So if D, seeking to prevent police officers from seizing his car as evidence in a hit and run accident in which D was not involved, asserts that such a seizure may occur only "in the hours of daylight", his honest, albeit wrongheaded, belief would constitute a claim of right and may underwrite his defence to a charge of obstruction arising out of his refusal to let an officer enter the car at 9 pm for the purposes of removing it into police custody. If, on the other hand, he asserts that, whatever the powers of the police, they ought not to be allowed to take the car "because he had paid for it", that would constitute a claim of moral right which is no defence.

In the example above, where D has a valid claim of right, D has not simply made a mistake of law, which would be no excuse (as s 25 makes clear).[133] This is because his mistake is not about the specific law of the offence with which he is charged (ie obstruction). Rather, the mistake relates to the general enforcement powers of a constable, which forms the backdrop of his defence, and not to an element of the offence of obstruction. Thus, in our view, the situation in our example is distinguishable from the facts of *Van Gaalen v Police*.[134] In that case, the Court of Appeal held that s 53 could not create a defence to a charge of assaulting a traffic officer under s 63(1) Transport Act 1962. The Court held that to give effect to s 53 in the circumstances in which the appellant had grabbed the traffic officer to prevent him from removing the

---

129 *Adams* (2nd ed) § 48. For discussion of "colour of right", see § 17.3.2.

130 [1959] NZLR 868 at 872. See also *R v Bernhard* [1938] 2 KB 264, [1938] 2 All ER 140 (CCA); *Wicks v Police* (1984) 1 CRNZ 328; *Brown and Edney v Police* (1984) 1 CRNZ 576.

131 *Walden v Hensler* (1987) 163 CLR 561, 75 ALR 173 (HCA).

132 See *R v Hemmerly* (1976) 30 CCC (2d) 141 (Ont CA); *Harris v Harrison* [1963] Crim LR 497 (PC).

133 See further chapter 12 (mistake of law).

134 [1979] 2 NZLR 204 (CA).

rotor arm from his car's engine, would defeat the intention of Parliament to empower officers to take appropriate steps where necessary to immobilise vehicles for reasons of public safety. By contrast, in the example above, it is precisely in such circumstances that s 53 is designed to provide protection to someone seeking to protect his interests in private property. Since the context did not involve any issues of public safety, it could not be claimed that D's assertion of the statutory defence defeated the legislative intention inherent in the offence of obstruction. Indeed, it is arguable that in the circumstances contemplated by our example, the interests of the police in law enforcement and the interests of D in protecting his property are evenly matched. The issue for the Court should then simply be to determine whether it is satisfied beyond reasonable doubt that all the elements of the defence are present. Only if it is convinced beyond reasonable doubt that one or more of the elements are missing should D be convicted.[135]

13.2.3 Defence of dwellinghouse (s 55)

The elements of the defence defined in s 55 are different to those in the other sections. They are as follows:

(i)   The accused must be in possession of a *dwellinghouse*;

(ii) His possession must be peaceable;

(iii) He may use force to prevent forcible breaking and entry of the dwelling;

(iv) The force used must be *necessary* for that purpose;

(v)   He must believe on *reasonable and probable grounds* that there is no lawful justification for the breaking and entry.

Of note under this section is the fact that the peaceful possessor may use *necessary* (not just reasonable) force to prevent forcible entry. The use of "necessary" without any words of qualification implies a subjective standard (ie what the accused considered was necessary). Unlike s 48, there is no statutory requirement that the force used be reasonable. It is implicit, however, that the force must be necessary *for the specified purpose*, ie to prevent the break-in and for no other reason. For example, if D, exercising lawful force to prevent V from breaking into his home, then inflicted a severe beating on V in order to punish him for upsetting the tranquillity of D's otherwise peaceful existence, the beating clearly would be unnecessary and that element of the defence would not be established. D would be liable to prosecution for assault to the extent that the injury inflicted during the beating exceeded what was necessary to prevent the break-in.[136] Indeed, in *R v Frew*[137] Tipping J held that although the expression used in s 55 is not "*reasonably* necessary", that may nonetheless be the effect of the provision. His Honour doubted whether any difference was intended between the "reasonable" force in s 56 and the "necessary" force in s 55. He did not, however, attempt to offer any guidance on the question of what constituted necessary force.

---

135 See *R v Frew* [1993] 2 NZLR 731 at 734, (1992) 9 CRNZ 445 at 448.

136 See s 62.

137 [1993] 2 NZLR 731 at 736, (1992) 9 CRNZ 445 at 451.

In our view, the question of the correct categorisation of the standard to be applied in determining whether force is necessary (ie whether it is objective or subjective) is of some importance. The pattern of s 55 is not similar to that of the amended s 48.[138] There is, we submit, no warrant for importing an objective standard of liability into a penal statute in the absence of a clear justification for doing so. In the absence of qualifying words the Legislature must be presumed to have intended to differentiate between ss 55 and 56 by imposing an objective test of force in one context but not in the other. In the circumstances, given the lack of clarity in the statute, "necessary" should be given its natural meaning of "needful to be done", which is, with respect, an eminently subjective determination. This approach also makes sense in the context of the provision itself. Once the occupier has determined, reasonably, that the breaking and entering is unlawful, she may use whatever force is "needful" to prevent the breaking and entering from occurring or continuing, subject to her considering whether the mischief could be prevented by less violent means. Failure to assess whether a less violent solution was available could be evidence from which the tribunal of fact may infer that the accused did not really believe the force used was necessary at all. But at all points the inquiry should be a subjective one, which does not depend on inquiring whether a reasonable person in the shoes of the accused would have considered the force necessary.

Although the statute does not attempt to define what counts as necessary force, as a matter of general principle the force used in defence of the dwelling must be proportionate to the mischief sought to be prevented, and must be such that the mischief could not be prevented by less violent means.[139] The question of the nature and degree of force permissible in the defence of a dwellinghouse was considered in *R v Frew*.[140] There the accused was charged with wounding with intent to injure. After having been burgled, and anticipating the return of the burglars, he hid in his house with two loaded guns. When the burglars returned, D, without warning, shot one of them in the knee. At a police interview he claimed that he was trying to stop the burglars, retrieve stolen property, and make the house safe for his children. At the trial the Crown sought to have the accused's defence under s 55 withdrawn from the jury on the basis that no jury properly directed could see the accused's actions as being "to prevent" the forcible breaking and entering of the dwellinghouse.

The Court observed that it is only within the time frame between when the forcible breaking and entering begins and ends that the person in peaceable possession can logically take action to prevent such breaking and entering. It held that, whereas in the crime of burglary the entry may be complete upon "penetration" (of the house), the same analysis cannot apply to breaking and entering under s 55: "to hold that the breaking and entering was already

---

138 See *Adams* § CA55.04.

139 Criminal Code Bill Commission, *Report of the Royal Commission Appointed to Consider the Law Relating to Indictable Offences: With an Appendix Containing a Draft Code Embodying the Suggestions of the Commission*, London, Eyre & Spottiswode for HMSO, 1879, 11.

140 [1993] 2 NZLR 731, (1992) 9 CRNZ 445.

complete at [the point of penetration] would be to rob s 55 of most of its intended effect. It would put a quite unreal premium on the precise timing of the force used by the householder."[141] The Judge then directed the jury that at the time the shot was fired, the breaking and entering was still occurring and, subject to the other constraints in the section, the accused was entitled to use force to prevent its continuance. He concluded that the section was not limited to repelling intended burglars from entering, but included the prevention of their continuing with the burglary after having entered.

13.2.4 Reform

In *Frew*, Tipping J observed that the ground covered by s 55 and the adjoining sections of the Act would benefit from legislative clarification and harmonisation at an early date.[142] We agree. There would seem to be little justification for having five separate statutory provisions dealing with defence of property when the subject-matter is substantially the same. What is needed is a simple form of words that is capable of being readily explained to a jury, and which encompasses the essential elements of defence of movable property, land, and buildings. Whether there is a need for a separate generic defence of "defence of dwellinghouse" is debatable, when the modes of modern habitation are so diverse. A defence that seeks to preserve the interests of all citizens to secure *habitation*, as opposed to the protection of only one particular form of residence, would seem to be preferable. A more open-ended defence would also enable well-intentioned third parties, eg neighbours or members of a neighbourhood watch group, to take appropriate action to prevent entry or occupation of a residential home where the owners are absent and known not to have consented to the entry on to their property by named or unnamed persons.

---

141 Ibid at 735, at 450.
142 [1993] 2 NZLR 731 at 736, (1992) 9 CRNZ 445 at 451.

14

Culpable Homicide

Part VIII of the Crimes Act 1961 provides for various crimes against the person. These include three which are described generally as "culpable homicide", and more specifically as murder, manslaughter, and infanticide. Murder is punished by a mandatory sentence of life imprisonment (s 172)[1] whereas

---

1   Normally release on parole will be considered after 10 years, but under s 80 Criminal Justice Act 1985 (as amended in 1993) if the circumstances of the offending were "exceptional" the court may order that D serve a minimum period of more than 10 years: see *R v Parsons* [1996] 3 NZLR 129 (CA); *R v Wilson* [1996] 1 NZLR 147 (CA).

manslaughter carries a maximum of life, the penalty in a particular case being at the discretion of the court (s 177).[2] The maximum penalty for infanticide is 3 years' imprisonment (s 178). When an accused is charged with murder, if the evidence warrants it, she may be acquitted of murder but convicted of manslaughter, or infanticide, but not, on that charge, of any other offence (s 339). Homicide that is not culpable is not an offence (s 160(4)),[3] but homicide is, of course, an essential element of any offence of culpable homicide.

14.1 THE ELEMENTS OF HOMICIDE

Homicide is defined by s 158 as "the killing of a human being by another, directly or indirectly, by any means whatsoever". There are three important elements of this definition: (i) the causing of death (ii) of a person (iii) by another person. We shall consider these elements separately.

14.1.1 The offender

In s 158, "by another" means "by another human being", so that a corporation cannot actually commit homicide.[4] Probably a corporation can be guilty of manslaughter as a secondary party, but possibly not murder, for it cannot be subject to the mandatory penalty,[5] and the general power to impose a fine under s 26(1) Criminal Justice Act 1985 might not apply when imprisonment is mandatory.[6]

14.1.2 The victim

The victim must be a living human being at the time of the killing. The destruction of a child before or in the course of birth, or of a foetus, may be the offence of killing an unborn child (s 182),[7] or procuring abortion (s 183), but it is not homicide. This follows from s 159:

> Killing of a child—(1) A child becomes a human being within the meaning of this Act when it has completely proceeded in a living state from the body of its mother,

---

2   Manslaughter is a crime which varies enormously in gravity, and the judge's discretion as to penalty is correspondingly large; in exceptional cases the maximum of life may be justified: *R v Wickliffe* [1987] 1 NZLR 55 at 62-65, (1986) 2 CRNZ 310 at 316-320 (CA), or, at the other extreme, no penalty: *R v Yogasakaran* [1990] 1 NZLR 399, (1989) 5 CRNZ 69 (CA).

3   But in addition to murder, manslaughter, and infanticide, some unlawful killings may be offences under other legislation: for example, ss 55 and 56 Transport Act 1962; s 53 Arms Act 1983.

4   *R v Murray Wright Ltd* [1970] NZLR 476 (CA); cf *R v P & O European Ferries (Dover) Ltd* (1990) 93 Cr App R 72, [1991] Crim LR 695.

5   Cf *R v Murray Wright Ltd* [1970] NZLR 476 at 480 (North P).

6   Section 44(3) Criminal Justice Act 1954 expressly provided for fining a corporation when imprisonment was the only prescribed penalty. This was overlooked in *Murray Wright Ltd*, ibid, but s 26 of the 1985 Act does not include such a provision, and applies only when imprisonment "may" be imposed.

7   See *R v Henderson* [1990] 3 NZLR 174, (1990) 6 CRNZ 137 (CA) for the uncertain scope of s 182, which depends on when a foetus becomes a "child" within the "ordinary and natural meaning of the word" (26 weeks' gestation was clearly enough).

whether it has breathed or not, whether it has an independent circulation or not, and whether the naval [sic: navel] string is severed or not.

(2) The killing of such child is homicide if it dies in consequence of injuries received before, during, or after birth.

Subsection (1) follows common law authority in requiring that the child be wholly expelled from the mother's body,[8] but need not have breathed,[9] and the umbilical cord need not have been severed.[10] Whether a child is born "in a living state" may depend on whether its heart was functioning,[11] and there is no requirement that it had any hope of survival.[12]

Subsection (2) allows a case to be homicide if a born and living child dies as a result of events before, during, or after birth. This too is consistent with the common law, but it applies only when death results from "injuries". Thus it covers the case where the child was directly injured before birth, or suffered physical injury,[13] including infection,[14] as a result of injury to the mother. However, doubts may arise if D induces premature birth and the child then dies because of inadequate development,[15] including cases where this results from injury to the mother (the most natural interpretation of "injuries" in s 159(2) requiring injuries to the child).[16] But even in these cases the death of the child will be the result of physiological processes, and perhaps these may be sufficient post natal "injury" for s 159(2) to apply. At common law, however, it was not regarded as manslaughter if death resulted from a mother's inadequate preparation before birth,[17] and in such a case there might not be a "killing" under the Act.

If the child suffered a fatal injury as a result of an unlawful and dangerous act aimed at either the mother or the unborn child the killing will be manslaughter, although the House of Lords has held that it cannot be murder at common law unless, perhaps, D intended that the child should die or suffer serious harm after birth.[18] However, the terms of the codification of the doctrine of transferred malice in s 167(c) appear to allow a finding of murder if

---

8   *R v Poulton* (1832) 5 Car & P 329, 172 ER 997.

9   *R v Brain* (1834) 6 Car & P 349, 172 ER 1272; but compare *R v Handley* (1874) 13 Cox CC 79.

10   *R v Trilloe* (1842) 2 Mood 260, 169 ER 103; the provision as to circulation is now seen as based on a misconception as it is established that a living child has an independent circulation before birth: Report of the Royal Commission on Contraception, Sterilisation and Abortion (1977) 279, quoted in *R v Henderson* [1990] 3 NZLR 174 at 181, (1990) 6 CRNZ 137 at 144 (CA).

11   Williams, *TBCL* 290. Difficulties of proof are likely: *Adams* § CA159.07; *R v Castles* [1969] QWN 77.

12   *R v West* (1848) 2 Cox CC 500.

13   For example *R v Martin* (1995) 13 WAR 472.

14   *R v Prince* (1988) 44 CCC (3d) 510 (Man CA).

15   Cf *R v West* (1848) 2 Cox CC 500.

16   Cf *A-G's Reference (No 3 of 1994)* [1997] 3 All ER 936, [1997] 3 WLR 421 (HL).

17   *R v Izod* (1904) 20 Cox CC 690.

18   *A-G's Reference (No 3 of 1994)* [1997] 3 All ER 936, [1997] 3 WLR 421 (HL).

D acts with murderous mens rea towards the mother, but by accident that conduct brings about the death of the child after a live birth.

The question may also arise whether V was no longer alive when D acted. In the past, death was often equated with the cessation of heartbeat and breathing, but these may stop temporarily and developments in medicine and technology enable them to be maintained mechanically. The generally accepted medical opinion now is that death occurs when none of the vital centres in the brain stem is functioning (in which case, in the absence of mechanical intervention, there will be an irreversible loss of heartbeat and breathing).[19] There is no doubt that such "brain death" will mean that in law a person is dead, but it is uncertain whether it is essential for legal death.[20] The Crimes Consultative Committee recommended that the Act provide that a person is dead if there is either irreversible cessation of all brain stem functions or irreversible cessation of all spontaneous circulatory or respiratory functions.[21] However, in the absence of brain death it may be doubted whether a finding of death would ever be possible if circulation and breathing are artificially maintained,[22] although it has been anticipated that there will be increasing pressure to treat as dead those whose brain stem has not been destroyed but whose brain has been so damaged that they are irreversibly unconscious.[23]

14.1.3 Causation

The definition of homicide requires that an offender "kill" another, which means "cause the death" of another,[24] although this may be done "directly or indirectly, by any means whatsoever". In most cases no issue of causation will arise, and it will not be necessary for the judge to give directions on it.[25] Where, however, causation is in issue the judge should explain the applicable principles,[26] it being a question for the jury whether D's conduct was a factual and sufficient cause of death.[27] But if on the evidence or admitted facts the only reasonable view is that D's conduct was a significant cause the judge may so

---

19 For a brief discussion, see Skegg, "The Edges of Life" (1988) 6 Otago LR 517 at 519-522.

20 There are suggestions that it is in *Airedale NHS Trust v Bland* [1993] AC 789 at 856 (Lord Keith) at 863 (Lord Goff), [1993] 1 All ER 821 at 859 (Lord Keith) at 865 (Lord Goff) (HL); but Thomas J regarded it as an open question in *Auckland Area Health Board v A-G* [1993] 1 NZLR 235 at 246, 247, (1992) 8 CRNZ 634 at 645, 646.

21 Crimes Consultative Committee, *Crimes Bill 1989: Report of the Crimes Consultative Committee presented to the Minister of Justice April 1991*, Wellington, Dept of Justice, 1991, 42, 103.

22 Cf the definition of death quoted by Facer, "Do We Need a Legal Definition of Death" [1975] NZLJ 171 at 173.

23 Skegg, "The Edges of Life" (1988) 6 Otago LR 517 at 522.

24 *R v Storey* [1931] NZLR 417 at 465 (Reed J); *R v Grant* [1966] NZLR 968 at 973, 974 (CA).

25 *R v Pagett* (1983) 76 Cr App R 279 at 285.

26 Ibid at 288.

27 *R v Storey* [1931] NZLR 417 (CA); *R v Fleeting (No 1)* [1977] 1 NZLR 343 at 346; *R v Tomars* [1978] 2 NZLR 505 at 511, 512 (CA); *R v Kirikiri* [1982] 2 NZLR 648 at 651.

direct and withdraw the issue from the jury.[28] Conversely, a conviction cannot be sustained if on the evidence a reasonable jury could not have found sufficient cause established.[29]

The general principles of causation apply to homicide, and these have already been examined.[30] In summary, while there may be other causes of death, an offender's act or omission must contribute to it in a significant way. There are also a number of particular statutory provisions, which will now be considered.

14.1.3.1 *Year and day rule*

Section 162 retains the ancient common law rule that there is no criminal responsibility for a killing unless death occurs within a year and a day after the cause of death.[31] This period is reckoned inclusive of the day of the last contributing unlawful act, or on which a relevant omission ceased. Modern developments in medicine make long postponement of death possible, but D will not be freed from responsibility merely because survival beyond the statutory period was precluded by the withdrawal in good faith of life support.[32]

The abolition of this arbitrary rule was proposed in the Crimes Bill 1989, and by the Crimes Consultative Committee,[33] and has been effected in England.[34]

14.1.3.2 *Killing by influence on the mind*

Although psychiatric injury can constitute the "injury" or "actual bodily harm" required for some offences, mere emotions such as fear, distress, or panic will not,[35] and in the context of homicide a special rule is imposed by s 163. It provides that there is no criminal responsibility for killing by "any influence on the mind alone", or by causing some fatal disorder or disease by such influence; unless it is done by wilfully frightening a child under 16[36] or a sick person,[37] in which case the killing is a culpable homicide.[38]

---

28 *R v Blaue* [1975] 3 All ER 446, [1975] 1 WLR 1411 (CA); *R v Malcherek* [1981] 2 All ER 422, [1981] WLR 690 (CA); in such a case absence of causation directions will not involve a miscarriage of justice: *R v McKinnon* [1980] 2 NZLR 31 (CA).

29 *R v Jordan* (1956) 40 Cr App R 152 (CCA).

30 § 2.2.

31 *R v Dyson* [1908] 2 KB 454, [1908-10] All ER Rep 736 (CA); Yale, "A Year and a Day in Homicide" (1989) 48 CLJ 202.

32 *R v Trounson* [1991] 3 NZLR 690 at 696 (CA).

33 Crimes Consultative Committee, *Crimes Bill 1989: Report of the Crimes Consultative Committee presented to the Minister of Justice April 1991*, Wellington, Dept of Justice, 1991, 51, 52.

34 Law Reform (Year and a Day Rule) Act 1996 (UK); see *Smith and Hogan*, 339, 340.

35 *R v Mwai* [1995] 3 NZLR 149 at 153-155, (1995) 13 CRNZ 273 at 278-280 (CA); *R v Ireland*, *R v Burstow* [1997] 3 WLR 534, [1997] 4 All ER 225 (HL).

36 Cf *R v Towers* (1874) 12 Cox CC 530.

37 Cf *R v Hayward* (1908) 21 Cox CC 692.

38 Section 160(2)(e); see § 14.4.2.3.

14.1.3.3 *Acceleration of death*

In so far as everyone dies at some time, every killing is an acceleration of death. This is recognised by s 164, under which D kills V although the effect of the "bodily injury" caused to V "was merely to hasten his death while labouring under some disorder or disease arising from some other cause". The same rule applies at common law. It is a particular application of the principles that independent contributing causes do not excuse, and D must take the victim as he finds him. Causation is not excluded merely because V would not have died but for some disorder,[39] or because a disorder would have soon caused death in any event.[40]

Even so, V's ill-health may be relevant to whether D is criminally responsible. Ignorance of it may result in absence of the fault needed for liability,[41] and in some cases the shortening of life in the course of medical treatment will be lawful. As to this, s 164 expressly applies to causing death by act or omission, but on the issue of lawfulness the law draws a distinction according to whether conduct is classed as an act or omission. Both withholding and withdrawing treatment are classified as omissions, and even though quick death may be inevitable, and intended, a doctor may lawfully withdraw life support if a competent patient consents, or if the patient is unconscious and according to responsible medical opinion its continuation would not benefit the patient.[42] In contrast, even with the consent of the patient it is not lawful for a doctor, or anyone, to do a positive act (such as injecting a drug) in order to bring about death, notwithstanding that the motive is to end suffering.[43] Such an act is, however, lawful if the doctor's purpose is to relieve pain, even though a known incidental effect will be to shorten life, provided the doctor acts in the patient's best interests and in accordance with responsible medical opinion.[44] In directing the jury in *R v Adams*[45] Devlin J appeared to distinguish between a doctor accelerating death permissibly by "minutes or hours" and impermissibly by "weeks or months". In either case there may be a significant acceleration of death and it is doubtful whether principles of

---

39   Cf *R v Renata* [1992] 2 NZLR 346, (1991) 7 CRNZ 616 (CA).

40   For example *R v Dyson* [1908] 2 KB 454, [1908-10] All ER Rep 736 (CA).

41   Cf *R v Dawson* (1985) 81 Cr App R 150, [1985] Crim LR 383 (CA).

42   *Airedale NHS Trust v Bland* [1993] AC 789, [1993] 1 All ER 821 (HL); *Auckland Area Health Board v A-G* [1993] 1 NZLR 235, (1992) 8 CRNZ 634; Skegg, "Omissions to Provide Life — Prolonging Treatment" (1994) 8 Otago LR 205. When a competent patient requests discontinuance there will also be a duty to comply, and, perhaps, when the treatment is of no benefit to the incompetent: *Bland* at 883, at 882 (Lord Browne-Wilkinson).

43   Section 63 Crimes Act 1961; *Airedale NHS Trust v Bland*, ibid at 859, 865, 866, 892, 893, at 867, 890, 891.

44   *Airedale NHS Trust v Bland*, ibid at 867-870 (Lord Goff); in his seminal directions in *R v Adams* [1957] Crim LR 365, 375 Devlin J put it succinctly: "he was entitled to do all that was proper and necessary to relieve pain and suffering even if the measures he took might incidentally shorten life."

45   Ibid at 375.

causation, or mens rea, satisfactorily explain these instructions.[46] But the more quickly death is accelerated the more likely is the inference that the real purpose was to kill, and that makes the act unlawful, even if the motive is to end suffering.

14.1.3.4 Causing preventable death

Section 165 provides that:

> Every one who by any act or omission causes the death of another person kills that person, although death from that cause might have been prevented by resorting to proper means.

For example, an injury which results in death kills V even though death could have been prevented by proper treatment, which is not provided because of a doctor's negligence,[47] or even because V refuses treatment in the knowledge that death might follow.[48] Everyone has the right to refuse medical treatment,[49] and the exercise of it does not relieve another of responsibility for the result. Nor is the chain of causation broken by the lawful withdrawal of life sustaining treatment.[50] This might also be the case when treatment was unlawfully prevented or terminated by another, and injuries caused by D were the physiological cause of death ("that cause" in s 165). Such intervening unlawful conduct would, however, also be a cause of death,[51] and if it was intentional and truly voluntary it might arguably prevent attribution to D.[52]

14.1.3.5 Death resulting from treatment

What is the position if the most immediate cause of death was treatment which was applied in response to injury inflicted by D? The general principles governing intervening causes have been outlined earlier.[53] Nineteenth century case law suggested that medical treatment might never break the chain of causation, but it has since been recognised that there may be exceptional cases where it does. The question is governed by s 166:

> **Causing injury the treatment of which causes death**—Every one who causes to another person any bodily injury, in itself of a dangerous nature, from which death results, kills that person, although the immediate cause of death be treatment, proper or improper, applied in good faith.

---

46   Cf Smith and Hogan, *Criminal Law* (7th ed), London, Butterworths, 1992, 332; Williams, *TBCL*, 385; Beynon, "Doctors as Murderers", [1982] Crim LR 17 at 18; "a few moments" would no doubt be insignificant: see § 2.2.2.1.

47   *R v Evans and Gardiner (No 2)* [1976] VR 523; *R v Bristow* [1960] SASR 210.

48   *R v Blaue* [1975] 1 WLR 1411, [1975] 3 All ER 446 (CA); *R v Holland* (1841) 2 Mood & R 351, 174 ER 313.

49   Section 11 New Zealand Bill of Rights Act 1990.

50   *R v Trounson* [1991] 3 NZLR 690 at 696, (1991) 8 CRNZ 491 at 497 (CA); *R v Malcherek* [1981] 2 All ER 422, [1981] 1 WLR 690 (CA).

51   *Airedale NHS Trust v Bland* [1993] AC 789 at 866 (Lord Goff) [1993] 1 All ER 821 at 868 (Lord Goff) (HL).

52   See § 2.2.3.2(b). But it is doubtful whether a mere omission to perform a legal duty could have this effect: see s 160(2)(c), § 14.4.2.5; also § 2.2.4.2.

53   § 2.2.3.2(a) (*Foreseeable and Innocent Intervention*), § 2.2.3.2(c) (*Foreseeable and Culpable Intervention*).

This has been regarded as declaratory of the common law,[54] but as it applies only if death "results" from injuries caused by D, its only clear effect is that causation is not necessarily excluded when proper or improper treatment is the immediate cause of death. There may, however, be cases where it does have this effect.

Two types of case are to be distinguished. First, the killing is attributable to D's conduct if injury inflicted by D was a significant physiological cause of death, even if its effect was aggravated or accelerated by treatment, and even if that treatment was "thoroughly bad".[55] Such a case is at most one of multiple causes and resort to s 166 is unnecessary. In principle D should be responsible (in terms of causation) even if the original injury was not dangerous, and even if the subsequent "treatment" was not applied in good faith, and may have been intended to kill.[56] Secondly, the harm inflicted by D may not be a physiological cause and may have resulted in death only in the sense that had it not been for that harm V would not have been subjected to the treatment which killed. At common law there is authority that D is responsible in such a case even if the treatment was negligent,[57] but this is qualified by R v Jordan.[58] There the wound inflicted by D was held not have caused death, it having practically healed at the time of death, which resulted from pneumonia caused by "palpably wrong" treatment. This has always been regarded as a very exceptional case,[59] and its effect was further confined in R v Cheshire,[60] where it was said that negligent treatment should not relieve D of responsibility unless it "was so independent of his acts, and itself so potent in causing death, that [the jury] regard the contribution made by his acts as insignificant".

The only reported New Zealand decision on the application of s 166 to this type of case is the pre-trial ruling in R v Kirikiri,[61] where the original injury seems not to have been a physiological cause of death (which resulted from asphyxiation caused by a mishap in the course of treatment). Jeffries J held that it was a question for the jury whether the injury remained "an operating cause of death", rather than merely part of the history. This test is open to the criticism that it allows the jury to find that the chain of causation was broken by treatment directed at the injury notwithstanding that the treatment was not

---

54   R v Kirikiri [1982] 2 NZLR 648 at 651.

55   This was the position in the leading case of R v Smith [1959] 2 QB 35, [1959] 2 All ER 193; § 2.2.3.2(c); the position is the same when V's own imprudent conduct, such as drinking or physical exertion, worsened his condition: R v Wall (1802) 28 St Tr 51; R v Flynn (1867) 16 WR 319.

56   See § 2.2.2.3.

57   R v Cheshire [1991] 1 WLR 844, [1991] 3 All ER 670 (CA); R v Davis and Wagstaffe (1883) 172 ER 1196, 15 Cox CC 174, 6 C & P 177.

58   (1956) 40 Cr App R 152 (CCA); § 2.2.3.2(c).

59   R v Smith [1959] 2 QB 35 at 43, [1959] 2 All ER 193 at 198; R v Evans and Gardiner (No 2) [1976] VR 523 at 531 (where it was unsuccessfully argued that negligent failure to diagnose and treat broke the chain of causation).

60   [1991] 1 WLR 844, [1991] 3 All ER 670 (CA). This judgment provides excessively uncertain guidance: Smith and Hogan, 351, 352.

61   [1982] 2 NZLR 648; § 2.2.3.2(c).

negligent. The issue involves a question of policy as well as fact, and other authority would allow such a result only if the treatment was at least negligent, and probably grossly negligent.[62]

Section 166 applies only if the injury was "in itself of a dangerous nature". In *Kirikiri* this was also treated as a question of fact for the jury, and the meaning of the term was not discussed. It may require an injury which would create a real risk of death if untreated. When the injury was not itself dangerous, and did not actually contribute to death which was caused by treatment, it seems to be implicit from the terms of s 166 that the chain of causation will be broken,[63] although in principle this should not be the case when the treatment was a reasonably foreseeable response to the injury.[64]

14.1.3.6 *Inducing victims to kill themselves*

This kind of case is expressly provided for in the definition of culpable homicide. Under s 160(2)(d), culpable homicide includes the killing of a person "by causing that person by threats or fear of violence, or by deception, to do an act which causes his death". Although this is a rule of causation as well as of culpability, it is convenient to leave examination of it to the discussion of involuntary manslaughter.[65] However, it is necessary at this point to consider the case where D induces V to commit suicide.

At common law suicide by a sane person of responsible age was a felony, being regarded as self-murder. It followed that secondary parties to it were guilty of murder.[66] In New Zealand, suicide has not been a crime since the enactment of the Code of 1893, for the statutory definition of homicide has always been confined to the killing of a human being "by another".[67] If, however, D actually kills V with the latter's consent that will be homicide, and V's consent to death provides no defence to a charge of murder or manslaughter (s 63). It has also been argued that a person who deliberately assists or induces another to commit suicide might still be convicted of murder, on the basis that this can be regarded as a "killing" of another within s 158.[68] However, it is submitted that as a general rule this is wrong. At common law, liability of a party assisting or procuring suicide did not depend on D being held to have "killed", but rather on the theory that D was a secondary party to

---

62 Cameron (1983) 7 Crim LJ 68, where it is also noted that the jury acquitted D of murder and convicted of attempted murder only; as well as its major effect on penalty such a result can allow an offender to benefit under the victim's will, intestacy, or insurance cover.

63 Common law authorities on this are inconsistent: *R v McIntyre* (1847) 2 Cox CC 379; *R v Clark and Bagg* (1842) 6 JP 508; cf *R v Davis and Wagstaffe* (1883) 15 Cox CC 174, 6 C & P 177, 172 ER 1196.

64 §§ 3.2.3.2, 3.2.3.2.3.

65 § 14.4.2.2.

66 *R v Croft* [1944] KB 295, [1944] 2 All ER 483 (CCA).

67 Attempt to commit suicide was an offence under the Acts of 1893 (s 173) and 1908 (s 193), but this is not retained in the 1961 Act.

68 *Adams* (2nd ed) § 1211-1213; in *R v Hinchcliffe* (1906) 8 GLR 652 (SC) Cooper J directed that the Code provisions had not excluded such liability.

the suicide's crime.[69] If a person deliberately kills herself by an act which is "free, deliberate and informed", there is a novus actus interveniens which breaks the chain of causation and prevents a secondary party being held to have "killed".[70] It may, however, be otherwise if V was insane, or below the age of responsibility, and it may be culpable homicide under s 160(2)(d) if D induces suicide by threats or fear of violence, or by deception.

The Act also makes specific provision for parties to suicide, and this reinforces the conclusion that they are not generally guilty of homicide. Under s 179, a secondary party to suicide is guilty of a crime punishable by up to 14 years' imprisonment and, under s 180(2), if someone kills herself pursuant to a suicide pact, a survivor of the pact is punishable by a maximum of 5 years' imprisonment.

14.2 CULPABLE HOMICIDE

For a homicide to be an offence, it must be "culpable homicide" within s 160(2). In most cases this will require that a person is killed by an unlawful act or an omission to comply with a legal duty. Apart from cases of infanticide, any culpable homicide will be the offence of manslaughter or, if it is committed with the appropriate mens rea and not under provocation, it will be murder: s 160(3). Issues as to the scope of culpable homicide under s 160(2) will almost always arise when a killing might not have been murder or manslaughter under provocation, and the question is whether it was at least manslaughter (or "involuntary manslaughter"). Detailed consideration of the scope of s 160(2) will, therefore, be deferred until after discussion of the mens rea of murder, and manslaughter under provocation.

14.3 THE MENS REA OF MURDER

Historically, at common law the mens rea of murder was described as "malice aforethought". This included a number of different states of mind, but in England the effect of s 1 Homicide Act 1957 is that some of these no longer suffice, and there it is settled that it now consists of an intention to kill or cause grievous bodily harm to a person.[71] In New Zealand, however, the relevant states of mind are specified in four paragraphs in s 167, and in a "further definition of murder" contained in s 168. The scope of the crime depends on the interpretation of these provisions.[72] They are alternatives so that, subject to any defences, an unlawful killing is murder if any one of them applies.

---

69 *R v Croft* [1944] KB 295, [1944] 2 All ER 483 (CCA); *R v Dyson* (1823) Russ & Ry 523, 168 ER 930; *R v Russell* (1832) 168 ER 1302, 1 Moo & R 356.

70 § 2.2.3.2. It is this principle which creates the need for rules governing secondary liability.

71 *R v Cunningham* [1982] AC 566, [1981] 2 All ER 863 (HL), applying *R v Hyam* [1975] AC 55, [1974] 2 All ER 41 (HL) and *R v Vickers* [1957] 2 QB 664, [1957] 2 All ER 741 (CCA); see also *A-G's Reference (No 3 of 1994)* [1997] 3 WLR 421 at 427, 430-434, [1997] 3 All ER 936 at 944-948 (HL).

72 Cf *R v Piri* [1987] 1 NZLR 66 at 76-83 (CA).

14.3.1 Intentional killing

Section 167(a) provides that culpable homicide is murder "if the offender means to cause the death of the person killed". This requires "an actual intent to kill".[73] There is an absence of authority, but "means" in its ordinary sense would appear to require that the killing be a purpose and object of the offender, although perhaps it would suffice that he knows it to be an inseparable consequence of his object.[74] However, it will probably be unnecessary to resolve this question because the further paragraphs of s 167 cover cases where killing is not truly intended, but there is a deliberate taking of risk.[75]

14.3.2 Reckless killing

Under s 167(b), culpable homicide is murder "if the offender means to cause to the person killed any bodily injury that is known to the offender to be likely to cause death, and is reckless whether death ensues or not". At common law, it suffices that death was caused by an act done with intent to cause grievous bodily harm (meaning "really serious" bodily harm),[76] and it is not necessary that D intended to endanger life.[77] By contrast s 167(b) expressly requires that the intended injury be "known to the offender to be likely to cause death". This was given a strict interpretation by the Court of Appeal in *R v Dixon*,[78] where V had died as a result of a series of assaults by D, including punching and kicking. It was held that under s 167(b), at the time of conduct contributing to death, D must have "actually appreciated", or had a "conscious appreciation of", the likelihood of causing death; it was not enough that D ought to have been aware of this, or had "the necessary general knowledge to have appreciated the risk if he had paused to think about it". The Court doubted whether the additional requirement that the offender be "reckless whether death ensues or not" really adds anything, although it might emphasise the "conscious appreciation" required.[79]

This interpretation was reaffirmed in *R v Harney*,[80] where D had killed V by stabbing him in a street brawl. It was held that in s 167(b) "reckless" could not refer to a failure to give thought to an obvious risk, but rather "means that there must be a conscious taking of the risk of causing death". The Court added that the inclusion of the term points up the contrast between paras (a) and (b): "The one is aimed at deliberate killing, the other at deliberately taking the risk of killing." On the other hand, "likely" does not mean that D must have thought that a killing was more likely than not, it sufficing that it was

---

73   *R v Aramakutu* [1991] 3 NZLR 429 at 432, (1991) 7 CRNZ 114 at 117 (CA).

74   Cf § 3.1.4.

75   *R v Piri* [1987] 1 NZLR 66 at 82 (CA).

76   *DPP v Smith* [1961] AC 290, [1960] 3 All ER 161 (HL); *R v Cunningham* [1982] AC 566 at 574, [1981] 2 All ER 863 at 865 (HL).

77   *R v Cunningham*, ibid.

78   [1979] 1 NZLR 641 at 647 (CA).

79   Cf *R v Cooper* (1993) 18 CR (4th) 1 at 7 (SCC).

80   [1987] 2 NZLR 576 at 579, 580 (CA).

recognised as a "real or substantial" risk, as "something that might well happen", or as a risk which was more than negligible or remote.[81]

Whether the requisite intent and knowledge is established will often be a matter of inference from what was said and done, and from the circumstances. If D had launched a sustained attack on V, it may be open to the jury to infer that whichever act caused death was accompanied by mens rea, even if the particular act cannot be identified.[82] However, given that s 167(b) needs to be relied on only if D might not have meant to kill, it will often be at least arguable that D lacked the requisite knowledge, even if a weapon was used, especially if the act may have been an instinctive, unthinking reaction in the heat of the moment.[83] If the injury intended was not of a kind which would normally be expected to kill it is likely that the inference of knowledge will not be possible.[84]

14.3.3 Transferred mens rea

Paragraphs (a) and (b) of s 167 are in terms confined to cases where D means to kill or injure the person killed. However, the principle of transferred mens rea (see § 3.7) is applied by s 167(c), under to which it is murder if D acts with one of the states of mind specified in paras (a) and (b) "and by accident or mistake kills another person, though he does not mean to hurt the person killed". A case will be one of mistake when D injures the intended victim, except that he mistook the latter's identity, and it will be a case of accident when D aimed at one person but unintentionally killed another.[85]

Three particular cases require further mention.

First, there may be cases where D has no particular victim in mind and indiscriminately attacks a group (perhaps by shooting or the use of explosives). If someone is killed, it is neither necessary nor appropriate to rely on para (c), for if D meant to kill or injure anyone she will have meant to kill or injure whoever was in fact killed.[86]

Second is the case of bungled suicides. Homicide is confined to the killing of a human being other than the offender (s 158), from which it follows that paras (a) and (b) of s 167 require an intention to kill or injure someone other than D. There is little doubt that this is the state of mind required for (c) to operate, in

---

81   *R v Piri* [1987] 1 NZLR 66 at 78, 79 (CA); *R v Harney* [1987] 2 NZLR 576 at 581 (CA); cf *R v Gush* [1980] 2 NZLR 92 at 96 (CA).

82   *R v Ryder* [1995] 2 NZLR 271, (1995) 13 CRNZ 81 (CA); *Meyers v R* (1997) 71 ALJR 1488; cf *R v McKeown* [1984] 1 NZLR 630 (CA).

83   *R v Harney* [1987] 2 NZLR 576 at 581, 582.

84   Cf *R v Pira* (1991) 7 CRNZ 650; difficulties of proof may also arise from the requirement that the prescribed mens rea must accompany an act which contributes to the death: see § 14.3.6.

85   For example *R v Droste* [1984] 1 SCR 208, (1984) 6 DLR (4th) 607 (SCC); this may include a case where the death results from the intervening act of another which is not such as to break the chain of causation between D's act and the death: *Adams* § CA167.09, citing *R v Pagett* (1983) 76 Cr App R 279, [1983] Crim LR 393 (CA); *R v Mitchell* [1983] QB 741, [1983] 2 All ER 427 (CA).

86   *A-G's Reference (No 3 of 1994)* [1997] 3 WLR 421 at 434, [1997] 3 All ER 936 at 948 (HL).

which case it will not apply if D's object was confined to suicide, or self-injury, and another was accidentally killed.[87]

Thirdly, if an attack on a pregnant woman is followed by the birth of a live child, and the child then dies as a result of injury to it before or after birth, this is homicide of the child.[88] It should be noted, in contrast to the view stated here, that in *A-G's Reference (No 3 of 1994)*[89] the House of Lords held that at common law the fact that D acted with murderous intent directed at the mother would not make such a killing of the child murder, it being thought that the "fiction" or "doctrine" of transferred mens rea should not be taken so far. But such a case would seem to be within the natural and ordinary meaning of the terms of s 167(c), which do not suggest that V must have been a living human being at the time D acts. On the other hand, if the only injury intended by D was to the foetus and not the mother, and the later birth and death of the child was an unintended (though possibly foreseen) result, none of paras (a), (b), and (c) would apply, for D did not mean to kill or injure a "human being".[90] It appears, however, that such a case could be within s 167(d), which is now to be considered.

14.3.4 Killing in furthering an unlawful object

Section 167(d) provides that culpable homicide is also murder:

> If the offender for any unlawful object does an act that he knows to be likely to cause death, and thereby kills any person, though he may have desired that his object should be effected without hurting any one.

Under this provision, D may be guilty of murder even though she did not intend to kill, or even injure, anyone, if she deliberately risked life for an unlawful end. For example, if D sets an explosion in a jail with the object of enabling prisoners to escape and the explosion kills a guard (or a prisoner), D will be guilty of murder if she foresaw a killing as a real risk, although she may have hoped it would not eventuate. Such killings were murder at common law, although in England, legislative and judicial developments have meant that this is no longer the case.[91]

The earlier New Zealand codes included the words "or ought to have known" after "knows", but these words were dropped in 1961, it being evidently decided that objective tests of the kind endorsed in *DPP v Smith*[92] should be eschewed.[93] Now, as under paragraph (b), liability under s 167(d)

---

87   *Adams* § CA167.10; contra *Re Brown and R* (1983) 4 CCC (3d) 571.

88   § 14.1.2.

89   [1997] 3 WLR 421, [1997] 3 All ER 936 (HL); contra *R v Kwok Chak Ming* [1963] HKLR 226 at 349; cf *R v Martin* (1995) 13 WAR 472.

90   The position at common law was left open in *A-G's Reference (No 3 of 1994)*, ibid at 428, 429, at 942, 943; it was said to be murder in *R v West* (1848) 2 Car N 784, but this was an effect of the defunct felony murder rule, which does not apply in New Zealand. As to manslaughter, see § 14.4.2.1.

91   See *R v Piri* [1987] 1 NZLR 66 at 79-82 (CA).

92   [1961] AC 290, [1960] 3 All ER 161 (HL).

93   *Downey v R* [1971] NZLR 97 (CA); *R v Piri* [1987] 1 NZLR 66 at 77.

requires that in doing the act which causes death D consciously appreciates that death might well result, or that death is a real or substantial risk.[94] It suffices, however, that the death of anyone is known to be a real risk, so that there is no need for a separate provision for cases of transferred mens rea.

With the adoption of a subjective test of knowledge, the essential difference between paras (b) and (d) of s 167 is that (b) applies where D means to cause bodily injury to someone, whereas (d) applies although D has some other unlawful object.[95] Paragraph (d) will be most clearly appropriate when D's unlawful object does not include any form of personal injury, but the courts have not confined it to such cases. If the only identified unlawful object is the same personal injury which in fact caused death it would be confusing to attempt to apply (d) as well as (b), and it has been held that as the concluding words of (d) would make no sense in such a case this paragraph cannot be applied to it.[96] However, para (d) will apply if D, with the requisite knowledge, causes death by an assault, and does this act with the unlawful object of effecting some further hurt or injury. In *R v McKeown*,[97] D bound and gagged V with the object of then indecently assaulting her. V subsequently died of asphyxiation as a result of the gag. It was possible that para (b) did not apply, for in binding and gagging the victim D might not have meant bodily injury; but it was held that, if the required knowledge accompanied the conduct, para (d) did apply, notwithstanding that the unlawful object included hurt or injury to V. There was, moreover, no requirement that D foresaw precisely how death would occur (in this case, by asphyxiation).

For para (d) to apply there must have been both a fatal act and an unlawful object, but these need not involve two different offences, or even be "clearly distinct". In *R v Aramakutu*[98] D lit a fire with the unlawful object of damaging a house, and an occupant died as a result. Provided the requisite knowledge was proved, this was murder under s 167(d), even though the act and the object were aspects of the one offence of arson. In Canada it has been suggested that in this context an "unlawful object" must involve "a serious crime, that is an indictable offence requiring mens rea".[99] It is doubtful whether such a precise definition would be regarded as appropriate in New Zealand, but it may be

---

94 *R v Fryer* [1981] 1 NZLR 748 (CA); *R v Piri* [1987] 1 NZLR 66 at 77, 79, 82, 84.

95 *R v Aramakutu* [1991] 3 NZLR 429 at 432, (1991) 7 CRNZ 114 at 117 (CA).

96 *Downey v R* [1971] NZLR 97 (CA), as explained in *R v McKeown* [1984] 1 NZLR 630 at 634, 635 (CA); in *Adams* § CA167.14 it is further suggested that para (d) cannot apply if the fatal injury was one of two or more objects D sought to achieve by the act which caused death.

97 Ibid; cf *R v Hakaraia* [1989] 1 NZLR 745 (CA).

98 [1991] 3 NZLR 429, (1991) 7 CRNZ 114 (CA); see also *Stuart v R* (1974) 134 CLR 426, 4 ALR 545 (HCA); *R v Gould and Barnes* [1960] Qd R 283. The latter decision held that murder could be found under an equivalent provision when an unlawful abortion resulted in the death of the mother; if such an act resulted in the birth of a living child who then died as a result of injuries caused by the abortion, it appears that that could also be murder, provided D had known that the act was likely to cause the death of a human being: cf n 90.

99 *R v Vasil* (1981) 58 CCC (2d) 97, [1981] 1 SCR 469 (SCC).

that it does require some kind of criminal offence.[100] On the other hand, para (d) can apply even though the object was capable of being lawful, but on the facts is unlawful because of the means used to try to achieve it. For example, in *R v Piri*[101] D's object was to obtain information from V, which in itself could have been lawful, but was not because of the means used to achieve it (tying V to a tree, and leaving her exposed to·the elements, which caused death).

14.3.5 The further definition of murder

At common law, under what was known as the felony murder rule, a killing while furthering another offence was murder even though neither death nor personal injury was intended, although ultimately this was restricted to killings in the course of violent felonies.[102] In England this principle was abolished by s 1 Homicide Act 1957, but a much modified version of it survives in New Zealand in s 168 Crimes Act 1961.[103]

Section 168 significantly enlarges the crime of murder by expressly providing that certain unlawful killings are murder whether the offender meant to kill or knew that death was likely to ensue. The effect of the rather precise provisions of s 168(1) is that an unlawful killing is murder if the following conditions are met:

(a) Death resulted from grievous bodily injury which D had meant to cause, or from D's administering any stupefying or overpowering things to, or wilfully stopping the breath of, any person; and

(b) D acted either

(i) for the purpose of resisting lawful apprehension in respect of any offence; or

(ii) for the purpose of facilitating the commission of a listed offence, or for the purpose of facilitating the flight or avoidance of detection of the offender upon the commission or attempted commission of a listed offence.

The listed offences are found in s 168(2), and are treason (s 73), communicating secrets (s 78), sabotage (s 79), piracy (ss 92, 93), escape from prison, lawful custody or detention (ss 119-122), sexual violation (s 128), murder (s 167), abduction and kidnapping (ss 208, 209), robbery (s 234), burglary (s 241), and arson (s 294).

In contrast to the felony murder rule at common law, under s 168 it is not enough that D kills while committing one of the specified offences, or while resisting arrest. It is also essential that D meant to cause grievous bodily injury

---

100 Cf the discussion of "unlawful act" in s 160(2)(a): § 14.4.2.1.

101 [1987] 1 NZLR 66 (CA); see also *R v Hakaraia* [1989] 1 NZLR 745 (CA); conversely the fact that the object involved an offence may show that the fatal act was unlawful: *R v Hamilton* [1985] 2 NZLR 245 (CA), where the act was firing a gun with the object of frightening another.

102 *A-G's Reference (No 3 of 1994)* [1997] 3 WLR 421 at 431, [1997] 3 All ER 936 at 945 (HL).

103 *R v Piri* [1987] 1 NZLR 66 at 79-82 (CA); s 167(d) can also be traced to this rule: *Downey v R* [1971] NZLR 97 at 100 (CA).

(that is, really serious bodily harm),[104] or did one of the other specified acts for a prescribed purpose. So, for example, killing as a result of the accidental discharge of a gun during a robbery is not murder under s 168, although D may be convicted under s 167(d) if, in presenting the gun, he knew that there was a real risk of accidental discharge and consequent death.[105] Although it is not made express, the terms of s 168 appear to extend to a case where D aims at one person but accidentally kills another.[106] Additionally, where the provisions as to flight or avoidance of detection are relied on, it will not be necessary to show that D was in fact being pursued, and the killing need not occur "immediately" after the offence.[107]

Where the actual killer is guilty of murder under s 168, a secondary party may be equally guilty under s 66(1) if he intentionally assisted or encouraged the intentional infliction of grievous bodily injury, or one of the other specified acts, knowing that one of the specified objects was being pursued, even if he may not have foreseen a killing.[108] The Court of Appeal has also held that a killing need not be foreseen when s 66(2) is relied on, but that is controversial.[109]

14.3.6 Concurrence of mens rea and actus reus

The general need for such concurrence has already been considered in § 3.8. In the context of murder, it requires that an offender had one of the required states of mind when she was responsible for an unlawful act or omission which caused or significantly contributed to the death. This can cause difficulty when there were a number of violent acts, for it may be necessary for the jury to identify which act or acts caused death, and to determine D's state of mind at that time, something that may be an impossible task.

There are a number of ways in which this problem may be overcome. It will not be necessary to identify the particular act which caused death if it can be inferred that, whichever act it was, it was accompanied by murderous mens rea.[110] If death resulted from a continuing act (for example, strangulation), it will suffice that the actor had such mens rea at some point during that act,[111] and if there is nothing to suggest that D's state of mind varied during a rapid series of acts, one of which caused death, it will be enough if the jury find that D acted with mens rea during those acts.[112] Moreover, it will be murder if mens

---

104 See *DPP v Smith* [1961] AC 290, [1960] 3 All ER 161 (HL), and the definition of "to injure" in s 2; *R v Mwai* [1995] 3 NZLR 149, (1995) 13 CRNZ 273 (CA).

105 *R v Wickliffe* [1987] 1 NZLR 55, (1986) 2 CRNZ 310 (CA).

106 Cf *R v Rowe* (1951) 4 DLR 238, [1951] SCR 713 (SCC).

107 Ibid.

108 *R v Hardiman* [1995] 2 NZLR 650, (1995) 13 CRNZ 68 (CA).

109 Ibid; *R v October and Kirner* 31/7/96, CA477; 510/95; Orchard, "Strict Liability and Parties to Murder and Manslaughter" [1997] NZLJ 93.

110 *R v Ryder* [1995] 2 NZLR 271, (1995) 13 CRNZ 81 (CA); *Meyers v R* (1997) 71 ALJR 1488.

111 *R v Cooper* (1993) 18 CR (4th) 1, [1993] 1 SCR 146 (SCC); see § 3.8.1.1.

112 *R v McKeown* [1984] 1 NZLR 630 (CA): this applied where D had struck, bound, and gagged V, who died of asphyxiation caused by the gag.

rea accompanied an act of D which was a contributing cause of death, even if it did not exist when D did another (and possibly the last) contributing act;[113] and the earlier act will be a sufficient contributing cause if its effect was to incapacitate, and thus prevent V from escaping the effects of the later conduct.[114]

In addition, strict concurrence might not be required if death followed a series of acts which constituted "one transaction", which included acts which contributed to death as well as acts which did not, if, before the killing, D acted with mens rea during part of the transaction. However, as has been explained, this principle has been allowed only restricted application in New Zealand. In *R v Ramsay*[115] the Court of Appeal thought that it can apply only if one or more offenders carried out the single transaction in furtherance of a "preconceived plan". Moreover, although the Court accepted that the principle might apply if D had meant to kill, so that s 167(a) applied, it held that the principle could not apply when paragraphs (b) or (d) were relied upon; for their terms require knowledge of the risk of killing at the time of the act which caused or contributed to death. The force of both these aspects of *Ramsay* has been doubted,[116] but the judgment appears to remain authoritative.

14.4 MANSLAUGHTER

Apart from the special case of infanticide,[117] any culpable homicide which is not murder is manslaughter. Although it is not terminology used in the Act, an unlawful killing is commonly called "involuntary" manslaughter if it is not murder because of the absence of a required intent, and "voluntary" manslaughter if it is not murder despite the fact that D may have killed with such intent. In many jurisdictions, legislation provides for a verdict of (voluntary) manslaughter in cases of diminished responsibility, where the person who killed was not insane within s 24 but nevertheless suffered such abnormality of mind that his impaired mental responsibility was substantially impaired.[118] This partial defence is not recognised in New Zealand,[119] where there are only two forms of voluntary manslaughter: unlawful killings under provocation (s 169), and killing pursuant to a suicide pact (s 180). Only the first will be examined here.

---

113 *R v Wickliffe* [1981] 1 NZLR 55, (1986) 2 CRNZ 310 (CA): pointing a loaded gun was a contributing cause, although the final cause was an unintended firing of it; cf *R v Cooper* (1993) 18 CR (4th) 1, [1993] 1 SCR 146 (SCC).

114 *R v McKinnon* [1980] 2 NZLR 31 at 36, 37 (CA); see § 3.8.1.3.

115 [1967] NZLR 1005 (CA); see § 3.8.1.3.

116 *Adams* § CA167.17; in *Ramsay* it was also held that whether a series of acts was "indivisible" was for the jury. The *Thabo Meli* approach involves "pitfalls" which a judge may be wise to avoid: *R v Menzies* 16/10/97, CA222/97.

117 See § 14.5.

118 For example, in England, s 2 Homicide Act 1957; *Smith and Hogan*, 216-221; Williams, *TBCL*, chapter 30.

119 For example *R v Burr* [1969] NZLR 736 (CA); diminished responsibility was provided for in the Crimes Bill 1961, but was deleted when Parliament rejected capital punishment: (1961) 328 NZPD 2680 at 2990, 2991.

14.4.1 Provocation

As a general rule, the fact than an accused's conduct was provoked by another is no defence to any crime. Murder is the single exception, in that, although it is not a complete defence, a killing which would otherwise be murder is reduced to manslaughter if it is committed as a result of provocation. This common law rule is codified in s 169.[120]

The partial defence of provocation developed at common law from the late sixteenth century.[121] Initially the judges ruled on a case by case basis whether particular conduct amounted to sufficient provocation, but in the nineteenth century a general rule was articulated: there had to be "a serious provocation ... which might naturally cause an ordinary and reasonable man to lose his self-control and commit such an act".[122] In addition, however, the judges continued to rule that some acts might or might not justify a verdict of manslaughter. In particular, as a general rule some physical violence was required, and words alone could never suffice "save in circumstances of a most extreme and exceptional character".[123] Section 169(2) largely dispenses with particular rules of this kind, and instead provides two general tests which have to be satisfied:

169. Provocation—
(2) Anything done or said may be provocation if—

(a)   In the circumstances of the case it was sufficient to deprive a person having the power of self-control of an ordinary person, but otherwise having the characteristics of the offender, of the power of self-control; and

(b)   It did in fact deprive the offender of the power of self-control and thereby induced him to commit the act of homicide.

Paragraph (a) imposes an objective, or evaluative, condition that requires an estimation of the effect of the provocation on the self-control of a hypothetical "ordinary" person, and para (b) requires that the provocation actually deprived

---

120   Section 169(1) says that this "may" be the effect of provocation, but it is not discretionary: *R v Leblanc* (1985) 22 CCC (3d) 126 (Ont CA). It has been suggested that provocation within s 169 should also reduce attempted murder to attempted manslaughter, for murder is not "the offence intended": cf s 72(1). The weight of authority is against such a possibility: *R v Laga* [1969] NZLR 417; *McGhee v R* (1995) 183 CLR 82, 69 ALJR 650 (HCA); *R v Campbell* (1977) 38 CCC (2d) 6 (Ont CA); *R v Bruzas* [1972] Crim LR 367; but see *R v Smith* [1964] NZLR 834; *R v Duvivier* (1981) 5 A Crim R 89 at 107.

121   Kaye, "The Early History of Murder and Manslaughter" (1967) 83 LQR 365 and 569 at 589.

122   *R v Welsh* (1869) 11 Cox CC 336 at 338 (Keating J).

123   *Holmes v DPP* [1946] AC 588 at 600, [1946] 2 All ER 124 at 128 (HL) where it was held that a spouse's confession of adultery could not be enough, although the finding of a man committing adultery with the accused's wife had long been sufficient, for "there could not be greater provocation than this": *R v Manning* (1672) T Raym 212, 83 ER 112; *sub nom Maddy's Case* 1 Vent 158, 2 Keb 829, 86 ER 524.

the offender of the power of self-control, and by that means led to the killing.[124] Before considering these in more detail, it is convenient to deal with three more particular matters.

14.4.1.1 *Function of judge and jury and burden of proof*

It is expressly provided by s 169(3) that whether there is any evidence of provocation is a question of law, meaning that it is a question for the trial judge, and by s 169(4) that, if there is such evidence, whether the requirements of subs (2) are met is a question of fact, meaning that it is a question for the jury.

The judge should not leave provocation to the jury unless there is sufficient evidence to raise the issue, or evidence supporting "a credible narrative of causative provocation".[125] This will require some evidence of specific acts or words of provocation resulting in a loss of self-control,[126] although in some cases it will suffice that the nature of the conduct or words can be inferred from the evidence.[127] The accused is not, however, required to prove the defence,[128] neither is it essential that D should give evidence of provocation and loss of self-control: in some cases, even if it is inconsistent with evidence from D, there may be sufficient material supporting the defence within the evidence adduced by the prosecution, the defence, or a combination of both.[129] The question for the judge is whether the evidence is reasonably capable of leading a jury to find it reasonably possible that both the tests in s 169(2) are satisfied. If, but only if, this is the case, the jury should be directed on the defence, which succeeds if the jury find that both tests are satisfied, or is of the view that this is a reasonable possibility.[130] If on the evidence the issue is fit to be left to the jury,

---

124 A similar dual test applied under the developed common law: *Holmes v DPP* [1946] AC 588, [1946] 2 All ER 124 (HL); and under the rather differently worded provisions of the earlier Codes: s 165 Criminal Code Act 1893; s 184 Crimes Act 1908.

125 *R v Matoka* [1987] 1 NZLR 340 at 344 (CA); this is a favoured formula in New Zealand, apparently designed to prevent speculation; cf *Lee Chun-Chuen v R* [1963] AC 220 at 229, [1963] 1 All ER 73 at 77 (PC): "All that the defence need do is to point to material which could induce a reasonable doubt."

126 *R v Acott* [1997] 1 WLR 306, [1997] 1 All ER 706 (HL); under NSW legislation it seems that "a specific triggering incident" is not needed if loss of control follows a history of abuse: *R v Muy Ky Chhay* (1994) 72 A Crim R 1 at 13, 14. It is unlikely that this can apply in New Zealand. See § 14.4.1.3.

127 *R v Anderson* [1965] NZLR 29 at 35 (CA).

128 *R v Kahu* [1947] NZLR 368 (CA).

129 *R v Nepia* [1983] NZLR 754 at 756 (CA); *R v Matoka* [1987] 1 NZLR 340 (CA).

130 *R v Nepia* [1983] NZLR 754; in England the effect of s 3 Homicide Act 1957 is that the defence must be left to the jury if on the evidence D may have been provoked actually to lose self-control: *DPP v Camplin* [1978] AC 705 at 716, [1978] 2 All ER 168 at 173 (HL); in New Zealand the defence should be withdrawn either if there is no evidence supporting this (for example *R v Matoka* [1987] 1 NZLR 340 (CA); *R v Mita* [1996] 1 NZLR 95), or if no reasonable jury could find that the objective test may have been satisfied: for example *R v Anderson* [1965] NZLR 29 at 38, 39 (CA); *R v Tai* [1976] 1 NZLR 102 (CA); *R v King* (1987) 7 CRNZ 591 (CA). However, the defence is not lightly to be taken away from the jury: *R v Taaka* [1982] 2 NZLR 198 (CA); *R v Nepia*.

the judge should direct on it even if it was not raised as an issue during the trial.[131]

14.4.1.2 *Anything done or said*

Under s 169(2), "anything done or said" may be provocation, provided only that the two general tests are satisfied. This broadens the defence in a number of ways.

Some formulations of the common law required acts done "to the accused",[132] but this is not required by s 169. So, for example, an assault on another may constitute provocation to D;[133] and it is not necessary that it be intended or foreseen that D might be provoked.[134] An act of provocation need not be violent (for example, it might be a gesture), and a requirement in the earlier Codes that it be "wrongful" has not been retained. This may have merely meant that there had to be an element of "offensiveness",[135] but with its deletion there is no doubt that lawful conduct may be provocation, although s 169(5) expressly provides that the lawful exercise of any "power conferred by law" cannot suffice.[136]

The earlier Codes qualified the common law rule that words alone were not enough, by allowing an "insult" as possible provocation. Now, under s 169, "anything . . . said" may qualify; thus the defence may be based, for example, on verbal taunts, threats of violent or non-violent action,[137] or even on the reporting of a provocative incident.[138]

Of course, the mere fact that the possibility of the defence is not excluded does not mean that it will necessarily be viable when D reacts violently to lawful or verbal conduct. In each case, the two tests in s 169(2) must still be met, and, although the particular circumstances must be considered, it may well be found that the objective test could not be satisfied if, for example, the

---

131 *R v Sarah* (1990) 5 CRNZ 663 (CA); but if counsel consider that there may be such evidence they have a duty to draw this to the judge's attention: *R v Cox* [1995] Crim LR 741, [1995] 2 Cr App R 513 (CA).

132 For example *R v Duffy* [1949] 1 All ER 932 (CCA); but sexual conduct with, or violence against, a spouse, child, or sibling could suffice: *R v Manning* (1672) T Raym 212, 83 ER 112; *R v Fisher* (1837) 8 C & P 182, 173 ER 452; *R v Harrington* (1866) 10 Cox CC 370, 92 ER 349; *R v Terry* [1964] VR 248; or a false imprisonment of a stranger: *R v Tooley* (1709) 2 Ld Raym 1296, 92 ER 349.

133 For example *R v Taaka* [1982] 2 NZLR 198 (CA); cf *R v Pearson* [1992] Crim LR 193 (CA).

134 *R v Campbell* [1997] 1 NZLR 16, (1996) 14 CRNZ 117 (CA); *R v Taaka*, ibid; *R v Twine* [1967] Crim LR 710 (CCA); cf *R v McGregor* [1962] NZLR 1069 at 1073 (CA).

135 *Stingel v R* (1990) 171 CLR 312 at 322, 97 ALR 1 at 7 (HCA).

136 This will include lawful arrest; in the case of illegal arrest, s 170 provides that this does not necessarily suffice, but if the illegality is known to D it may be evidence of provocation; even if D does not know of the illegality no doubt the manner of such arrest might also provide such evidence.

137 For example *R v Nepia* [1983] NZLR 754 (revelation of adulterous relationship plus a threat of loss of access to children).

138 Cf *R v White (Shane)* [1988] 1 NZLR 122 (CA) (a report to D of the rape of his sister, plus an insulting reference to her).

provocation was a mere admission of unfaithfulness,[139] or an intimation of a decision to end a relationship,[140] or took the form of force in self-defence.[141]

14.4.1.3 *Cooling time*

Classic provocation directions require "a sudden and temporary loss of self-control" which may be negated by a lapse of time between the provocation and the killing.[142] A time lapse has dual relevance. Together with the offender's behaviour during the interval, it may indicate that she was not in fact deprived of self-control at the time of the killing.[143] Alternatively, it may be such that an ordinary person would have regained control.[144] This aspect of the law has been criticised for failing to recognise sufficiently that people's reaction times vary. In particular, it has been said that by reason of national or racial temperament some people are "slow burning" and prone to brood for a time before losing control,[145] and that delayed reaction is also typical of battered women.[146]

The previous Codes expressly required that the offender act "in the heat of passion caused by sudden provocation . . . on the sudden and before there has been time for his passion to cool". The 1961 Act contains no reference to suddenness or time lapse, but in *R v McGregor*[147] the Court of Appeal rejected a submission that this had become irrelevant, and upheld directions requiring that the provocation and the killing be "reasonably related in time". But the Court did accept that it is not necessary as a matter of law that the provocation occur "immediately" before the killing, and other cases confirm that "cooling time" is a flexible and uncertain consideration. When there has been more than one provocative incident, it is the period after the last which is important[148] and, although the longer the delay the more likely it is that the defence will fail, there are cases where the defence is for the jury even though a few hours pass before the killing.[149] In cases where time lapse is regarded as significant, the courts also commonly have regard to how the offender acted in that time, even when the objective test is emphasised;[150] although neither the lapse of some

---

139 *R v Anderson* [1965] NZLR 29 (CA).

140 *R v Tai* [1976] 1 NZLR 102 (CA).

141 *R v Fryer* [1981] 1 NZLR 748 (CA).

142 For example *R v Duffy* [1949] 1 All ER 932 (CA).

143 For example *R v Mita* [1996] 1 NZLR 95.

144 For example *R v Erutoe* [1990] 2 NZLR 28 at 35, (1990) 5 CRNZ 538 at 545 (CA).

145 Marsack, "Provocation in Trials for Murder" [1959] Crim LR 697.

146 Nicholson and Sanghvi, "Battered Women and Provocation: The Implications of *R v Ahluwalia*" [1993] Crim LR 728; *R v Muy Ky Chay* (1994) 72 A Crim R 1 at 11.

147 [1962] NZLR 1069 at 1078, 1079 (CA).

148 For example *R v Taaka* [1982] 2 NZLR 198 (CA), where a fight between D and the victim may have "revived" provocation from 13 days before.

149 *R v Mita* [1996] 1 NZLR 95 at 101 (Fisher J), citing *R v Taaka* [1982] 2 NZLR 198 (CA); cf *R v Ahluwalia* [1992] 4 All ER 889, (1993) 96 Cr App R 133 (CA).

150 For example *R v Anderson* [1965] NZLR 29 at 38, 39 (CA); *R v Erutoe* [1990] 2 NZLR 28 at 35, (1990) 5 CRNZ 538 at 544, 545 (CA); *R v King* (1987) 7 CRNZ 591 (CA).

hours nor intervening conduct of some complexity and apparent deliberation are necessarily fatal to the defence.[151]

Notwithstanding this flexibility, the courts continue to hold that "a sudden and temporary loss of self-control" is essential,[152] although with the abandonment of a requirement of immediacy the meaning of this is obscure. In *R v Mita*[153] Fisher J suggests that the defence will be "untenable" unless it was a real possibility that between the provocation and the killing the offender "was in a continuous state of hot blood", or "uncontrolled anger", but this deprives rejection of the need for an immediate response of much of its effect, and seems incompatible with some cases where the defence has been held viable.[154] Alternatively, in *R v McGregor*[155] there is a suggestion that "a sudden transition" to loss of control is necessary, but this would not allow for those whose emotions are "slow burning" and develop gradually before control is eventually lost.[156] The better view seems to be that such directions merely serve to emphasise that it is not enough that the offender was made extremely angry, and that true "loss of self-control" is needed.[157]

14.4.1.4 *Actual loss of self-control*

This is the most fundamental requirement and, notwithstanding the different order in the statute, it is best to deal with it before the objective test, which imposes a limit on the defence.[158]

Under s 169(2)(b), the provocative conduct or words must "in fact deprive the offender of the power of self-control", and in that way bring about the killing. The jury should have regard to any fact, circumstance, or personal attribute of the offender which makes this more likely, whether or not it is relevant to the objective test. This may include, for example, the offender's ill-

---

151 For example *R v Taaka* [1982] 2 NZLR 198; *R v Ahluwalia* (1993) 96 Cr App R 133, [1992] 4 All ER 889 (CA).

152 *R v McGregor* [1962] NZLR 1069 at 1079; *R v Ahluwalia* (1993) 96 Cr App R 133 at 138, [1992] 4 All ER 889 at 895 (CA); *R v Thornton (No 2)* [1996] 2 All ER 1023 at 1030.

153 [1996] 1 NZLR 95 at 99, 100.

154 For example *R v Taaka* [1982] 2 NZLR 198 (CA); *R v Ahluwalia* (1993) 96 Cr App R 133, [1992] 4 All ER 889 (CA).

155 [1962] NZLR 1069 at 1078; cf *R v Thornton (No 2)* [1996] 1 WLR 1174 at 1183, [1996] 2 All ER 1023 at 1031.

156 In *R v Tai* [1976] 1 NZLR 102 at 107 (CA) it was recognised that such an attribute might be relevant to the time factor; and the 1961 Act was intended to allow for "brooding" offenders: (1961) 328 NZPD 2681.

157 Cf *R v McGregor* [1962] NZLR 1069 at 1078; *R v Ahluwalia* (1993) 96 Cr App R 133 at 138, [1992] 4 All ER 889 at 895 (CA).

158 Cf *R v McCarthy* [1992] 2 NZLR 550 at 558, (1992) 8 CRNZ 58 at 67 (CA); *R v Mita* [1996] 1 NZLR 95 at 99.

temper, irascibility, or voluntary intoxication,[159] her history or psychological condition,[160] or mistaken belief regarding the circumstances.[161]

It is not, however, possible to describe precisely what is involved in loss of "the power of self-control". The criterion will be negatived if the killing was "deliberate and premeditated", but positive descriptions of what is required always employ highly metaphorical language: for example, D must act "in hot blood", "in the heat of passion", "while not master of his or her mind".[162] The precipitating emotion will often be anger or resentment, but it may be fear or panic.[163] However, in no case is any such feeling sufficient in itself, it being essential that the result is "an emotional state which the jury are prepared to accept as a loss of self-control".[164]

Moreover, loss of self-control is a question of degree.[165] In particular, although a provoked unlawful killing will merely be manslaughter if D acted without the mens rea required for murder,[166] the defence of provocation is not excluded by the fact that D acted with intent to kill, or with other murderous mens rea.[167] Indeed, the defence only applies to "culpable homicide that would otherwise be murder" (s 169(1)), and strictly it should not be considered before murderous intent is found to be established.[168] Furthermore, as is implicit in the rule that provocation merely reduces the crime to manslaughter, a finding that provocation "did in fact deprive the offender of the power of self-control" does *not* prevent him from being responsible for his conduct, since that conduct was nonetheless deliberate and voluntary. In *R v Campbell*[169] D had killed the victim

---

159 *R v Barton* [1977] 1 NZLR 295 (CA); Orchard, "Provocation — The Subjective Element" [1977] NZLJ 77.

160 *R v Thornton (No 2)* [1996] 1 WLR 1174 at 1182, [1996] 2 All ER 1023 at 1030 (CA) (battered woman's syndrome); cf *R v Taaka* [1982] 2 NZLR 198 (CA) (a "brooding" temperament, which could explain delayed reaction).

161 *R v White (Shane)* [1988] 1 NZLR 122 at 126 (CA).

162 *R v Muy Ky Chhay* (1994) 72 A Crim R 1 at 8, 9 (NSW CCA); cf *R v Mita* [1996] 1 NZLR 95 at 100.

163 *Packett v R* (1937) 58 CLR 190 at 217 (Dixon J); *Van Den Hoek v R* (1986) 161 CLR 158 at 167, 168, (1986) 69 ALR 1 at 8 (HCA) (Mason J); from which it follows that provocation is not inconsistent with self-defence: *R v Pita* (1989) 4 CRNZ 660 (CA); cf *R v Oakes* [1995] 2 NZLR 673 (CA); *R v Thornton (No 2)* [1996] 2 All ER 1023, [1996] 1 WLR 1174 (CA).

164 *R v Muy Ky Chhay* (1994) 72 A Crim R 1 at 14.

165 *Phillips v R* [1969] 2 AC 130 at 137, 138, [1969] 2 WLR 581, 585 (PC).

166 *R v Bruzas* [1972] Crim LR 367.

167 *R v Barton* [1977] 1 NZLR 295 at 299 (CA); see also *A-G of Ceylon v Perera* [1953] AC 200, [1953] 2 WLR 238 (PC); *Lee Chun-Chuen v R* [1963] AC 220, [1962] 3 WLR 1461 (PC); *Parker v R* [1964] AC 1369 at 1391, [1964] 2 All ER 641 at 651 (PC); in *Holmes v DPP* [1946] AC 588 at 598, [1946] 2 All ER 124 at 127 (HL) there was a dictum to the contrary, which perhaps echoed the historical theory that provocation rebutted the "presumption of malice" which the early common law applied to render voluntary killings murder: 1 Hale PC 455.

168 *Johnson v R* (1976) 136 CLR 619 at 633, 643, (1976) 11 ALR 23 at 33, 41 (HCA); *Masciantonio v R* (1995) 183 CLR 58 at 66, (1995) 129 ALR 575 at 580 (HCA).

169 (1997) 15 CRNZ 138 (CA); this was an appeal following a conviction of manslaughter on a retrial ordered in *R v Campbell* [1997] 1 NZLR 16, (1996) 14 CRNZ 117 (CA).

after conduct which D interpreted as a sexual advance. He gave evidence that he was unable to stop what he was doing, and there was medical evidence that it was unlikely that he could control his actions, because of the effects of post traumatic stress disorder from which he suffered after being sexually abused as a child. The Court of Appeal held that the evidence justified a verdict of manslaughter as a result of provocation, but that the accused remained criminally responsible unless he was insane or had acted in a state of automatism, which required conduct that was "not subject to any conscious control". Neither of these defences was available. Despite the medical evidence, the accused had been aware of his acts, which could only be regarded as "deliberate voluntary acts".

14.4.1.5 *The objective test*

What was done or said must also have been, in the circumstances of the case, sufficient to deprive of the power of self-control "a person having the power of self-control of an ordinary person, but otherwise having the characteristics of the offender": s 169(2)(a).

The Act appropriately applies the standard of an "ordinary", not a "reasonable", person. The test is not concerned with reasoning or reasonable conduct (needless killing in the throes of passion is the antithesis of reasonable conduct).[170] The purpose of this additional test is to keep the defence within bounds by ensuring that a killing will not be reduced from murder to manslaughter unless the provocation was "grave and weighty".[171] It does this by imposing a standard which denies the defence "not to all those who react unreasonably to provocation, but only to those whose reactions show a lack of self-control falling outside the ordinary or common range of human temperaments".[172] Application of the test requires the jury to make a decision on a question of opinion.[173] In the following sections, we consider the factors relevant to that decision.

14.4.1.5(a) *Proportionality*

The terms of s 169(2)(a) require only that the hypothetical person might have been deprived of "the power of self-control", but it is well established that the question is a more particular one. The provocative conduct must be compared with the offender's reaction, and the test to be applied is whether a person of ordinary self-control might have so lost control as a result of that provocation as to form a murderous intent, and also to act on it in a way akin to the offender's reaction. For example, in *R v Anderson*[174] the woman with whom the accused lived made a remark which indicated that she had been unfaithful. The accused responded with a brutal and prolonged beating, which continued for

---

170 Cf *R v Morhall* [1996] AC 90 at 97, 98, [1995] 3 All ER 659 at 665, 666 (HL); *Stingel v R* (1990) 171 CLR 312 at 328, 329, (1990) 97 ALR 1 at 11, 12 (HCA).

171 *R v McGregor* [1962] NZLR 1069 at 1075 (CA); *Johnson v R* (1976) 136 CLR 619 at 635, (1976) 11 ALR 23 at 35 (HCA).

172 *R v Enright* [1961] VR 663 at 669; *Stingel v R* (1990) 171 CLR 312, (1990) 97 ALR 1 (HCA).

173 *Phillips v R* [1969] 2 AC 130 at 137, [1969] 2 WLR 581 at 585 (PC).

174 [1965] NZLR 29 at 38 (CA).

up to an hour in more than one location, and which resulted in death. The defence, it was held, was not available because no person of ordinary self-control could have been led by this kind of provocation "to the degree and method and continuance of violence" which had killed the victim.

The High Court of Australia has said that the question whether an ordinary person might have formed a murderous intent is more important than whether such a person might have acted in the way the offender did. Nevertheless, it has retained both requirements, although emphasising that the question is whether an ordinary person could (not would) have so acted, and it is the "kind and degree" of violence which matters, rather than its continuance or precise physical form.[175]

In the past, there have been suggestions that the defence could succeed only if there was some "reasonable relationship" or "proportion" between the provocation and the offender's reaction:[176] "Fists might be answered with fists, but not with a deadly weapon."[177] However, it is now clear that there is no such rule, although such "relationship or disproportion . . . is a factor, and indeed a weighty factor, to be considered by the jury in determining whether there [is] provocation".[178] It is sometimes suggested that it is a factor which might suggest that the offender did not act by reason of the provocation,[179] but the very ferocity and continuance of an attack may also positively support the claim of loss of self-control.[180] It is more likely that proportionality will be relevant to the question whether the offender's reaction exceeded the possible reaction of an ordinary person, the jury being entitled to take the view that people are liable to react with more or less violence according to the gravity of the provocation.[181]

14.4.1.5(b) The circumstances of the case

The objective test requires the jury to consider the provocation in its context and to assess its gravity. Section 169(2)(a) expressly incorporates "the circumstances of the case".[182] This will include information given to the

---

175 *Masciantonio v R* (1995) 183 CLR 58 at 69, 70, (1995) 129 ALR 575 at 582, 583 (HCA).

176 *Mancini v DPP* [1942] AC 1 at 9, [1941] 3 All ER 272 at 277 (HL): "the mode of resentment must bear a reasonable relationship to the provocation . . ."

177 *R v Duffy* [1949] 1 All ER 932 at 933 (CCA).

178 *R v Noel* [1960] NZLR 212 at 219 (CA); *R v Dougherty* [1966] NZLR 890 (CA); in *Phillips v R* [1969] 2 AC 130 at 138, [1969] 2 WLR 581 at 586 (PC) the Privy Council was less emphatic in describing it as "merely a consideration which may or may not commend itself to them". It may not always be an appropriate or useful consideration: *R v Campbell* [1997] 1 NZLR 16 at 26, (1996) 14 CRNZ 117 at 127 (CA).

179 For example *R v Savage* [1991] 3 NZLR 155 at 160 (CA); *R v Campbell* [1997] 1 NZLR 16 at 25, 26, (1996) 14 CRNZ 117 at 127, 128.

180 *Masciantonio v R* (1995) 183 CLR 58 at 68, 69, (1995) 129 ALR 578 at 582 (HCA); *R v R* (1981) 28 SASR 321 at 327, (1981) 4 A Crim R 127 at 132; Orchard, "Provocation — The Subjective Element" [1977] NZLJ 77 at 79, 80.

181 *Phillips v R* [1969] 2 AC 130 at 137, 138, [1969] 2 WLR 581 at 585, 586 (PC); *Masciantonio v R* (1995) 183 CLR 58 at 67, 129 ALR 575 at 581 (HCA).

182 Cf *R v Morhall* [1996] AC 90 at 98, 99, [1995] 3 All ER 659 at 666, 667 (HL) ("the entire factual situation").

accused, by the victim or others, about surrounding circumstances or earlier events,[183] as well as the past and present relationship between the victim and the offender, which may be important. For example, a history of antagonism between them, or abuse by V, may lead to a build up of emotion and so aggravate the effect of an ultimate provocative incident that, even if the incident by itself may appear comparatively trivial, it may in the context be serious, and cause "slumbering fires of passion to burst into flame".[184] Alternatively, D's experience of V's past conduct may lead to anticipation of a particular degree of violence and abuse.[185]

14.4.1.5(c) Characteristics of the offender[186]

After the adoption of the "reasonable man" test, English judges consistently held that the reasonable man was not to be invested with any particular features of the accused's personality. In particular, it was irrelevant to the test that the accused was unusually excitable or pugnacious, or bad-tempered and wanting in "mental balance";[187] and this was so whatever the cause: for example, whether it be mental deficiency,[188] pregnancy,[189] or drunkenness.[190] In *Bedder v DPP*[191] it was confirmed that the same was true of physical disability, it being held that the offender's sexual impotence was to be ignored in assessing a reasonable person's likely response to taunts of impotence. For Lord Simonds LC this followed from the purpose of the reasonable man test:

> Its purpose is to invite the jury to consider the act of the accused by reference to a certain standard or norm of conduct and with this object the "reasonable" or the "average" or the "normal" man is invoked. If the reasonable man is then deprived in whole or in part of his reason, or the normal man endowed with abnormal characteristics, the test ceases to have any value.[192]

There seems to be no doubt that the same principle applied in New Zealand to the unqualified "ordinary person" test in the statutes of 1893 and 1908,[193] but in 1961 Parliament refined the test so that it requires the provocation to be

---

183 *R v White (Shane)* [1988] 1 NZLR 122 at 126, 127 (CA); *R v Matoka* [1987] 1 NZLR 340 at 344 (CA); but see § 14.4.1.6, regarding mistake.

184 *R v McGregor* [1962] NZLR 1069 at 1080 (CA); *R v Pita* (1989) 4 CRNZ 660 at 665, 666 (CA); *R v Tai* [1976] 1 NZLR 102 at 107 (CA); cf *R v Thornton (No 2)* [1996] 2 All ER 1023 at 1030, [1996] 1 WLR 1174 at 1182, 1183 (CA); Wasik, "Cumulative Provocation and Domestic Killing" [1982] Crim LR 29.

185 Briggs, "Provocation Re-assessed" (1996) 112 LQR 403.

186 Orchard, "Provocation — Recharacterisation of 'Characteristics' " (1996) 6 Canterbury LR 202.

187 *Mancini v DPP* [1942] AC 1 at 9, [1941] 3 All ER 272 (HL); *R v Lesbini* [1914] 3 KB 1116 (CCA).

188 *R v Alexander* (1913) 9 Cr App R 139 (CCA).

189 *R v Smith* (1914) 11 Cr App R 36 (CCA).

190 *R v McCarthy* [1954] 2 QB 105, [1954] 2 All ER 262 (CCA).

191 [1954] 2 All ER 801, [1954] 1 WLR 1119 (HL).

192 Ibid at 804, 1123; cf *R v Raney* (1942) 29 Cr App R 14 at 17, where the fact that D was one-legged was regarded as relevant to whether a blow to his crutch might be provocation.

193 As to ill-temper and drunkenness, see *R v Jackson* [1918] NZLR 363.

sufficient to deprive of the power of self-control "a person having the power of self-control of an ordinary person, but otherwise having the characteristics of the offender". The intention was at least to overturn the effect of *Bedder*, and it has been described as an "important clarification".[194] But the courts have experienced some difficulty in interpreting and applying this revised test.

The Court of Appeal first considered the new test in *R v McGregor*,[195] where it described the relevance of an offender's "characteristics" with two different propositions: (i) they might weaken the power of self-control otherwise to be expected of an ordinary person,[196] but (ii) they may be taken into account only insofar as they made the words or conduct more provocative to the offender.[197] The Court also thought it necessary to impose various limitations on the meaning of "characteristics", in order to prevent the unintended obliteration of the ordinary person test.

The dual approach to relevance in *McGregor* was confusing, and the judgment was severely criticised by Sir Francis Adams, who regarded it as having introduced unnecessary complexity, particularly as a result of giving — in proposition (i) — no effect to the words "but otherwise".[198] More recently, in *R v McCarthy*[199] and *R v Campbell*,[200] the Court of Appeal has acted on these criticisms and has held that under s 169(2)(a) the question is "whether a person with the accused's characteristics *other than* any lack of the ordinary power of self-control could have reacted" as the accused did. This interpretation follows the words of the statute, and gives effect to the theory underlying it as explained by Adams:[201]

> A homicide committed under provocation results from a conflict between (a) the offender's sensitivity or susceptibility to the provocation, and (b) his power of self-control.

Under s 169(2)(a) the offender's actual power of self-control, or level of self-restraint (element (b) in Adam's explanation), is irrelevant and the jury is required to imagine a person with the power of self-control of an "ordinary person", or "normal self-control". The offender's personal characteristics are not relevant to this, and characteristics which do no more than negate the possession of such a level of self-control must be ignored: these include, for

---

194 (1961) 328 NZPD 2681.

195 [1962] NZLR 1069 (CA).

196 Ibid at 1081: "The offender must be presumed to possess in general the power of self-control of the ordinary man, save insofar as his power of self-control is weakened because of some particular characteristic possessed by him."

197 Ibid at 1082: "The words or conduct must have been exclusively or particularly provocative to the individual because, and only because, of the characteristic."

198 *Adams* (2nd ed) § 1264-1269.

199 [1992] 2 NZLR 550 at 558, (1992) 8 CRNZ 58 at 67.

200 [1997] 1 NZLR 16 at 25, (1996) 14 CRNZ 117 at 126, 127, where the emphasis in the text is added by the Court.

201 *Adams* (2nd ed) § 1267.

example, a disposition to lose one's temper readily, unusual pugnacity, or excitability.[202]

However, a particular characteristic may be relevant to an assessment of element (a), how sensitive a person might be to the provocation in question, and, therefore to how she might react to it, even if she has an ordinary power of self control. The nature and degree of a person's mental and emotional response to the provocation may be affected by a personal attribute of the offender. It may so aggravate the effect of the provocation that even normal self-control might be overcome, although such control would not be in the absence of such aggravation. For example, a young man who is impotent and sensitive about this may feel taunts about it differently, and perhaps more deeply, than one who was not in fact impotent. Indeed, there may be cases where the very nature of the provocation cannot be properly understood without regard to some personal attributes: for example, the offender's race in the case of a racial slur, the offender's ability to understand the meaning and significance of allegedly provocative words,[203] or the gender of the parties in the case of a sexual assault or advance.[204]

This interpretation of s 169(2)(a) is consistent with the approach to the "ordinary person" test now taken in England and Australia, where the personal characteristics to be taken into account are those which in the view of the jury affect the "gravity", or the "content or gravity", of the provocation.[205]

Where there is evidence of a characteristic which might have such an effect this should be explained to the jury,[206] and if the jury are invited to take into account proportionality of provocation and reaction the judge will need to make it clear that it is the provocation as affected by any relevant characteristics which needs to be considered.[207]

(1) *Normal and abnormal characteristics.* In *R v McGregor*[208] it was recognised that a "characteristic" might be either a physical or a mental quality, or an attribute such as colour, race, or creed. But it was also said that it "must be something

---

202 *R v McGregor* [1969] NZLR 1069 at 1081 (CA); *R v Fryer* [1981] 1 NZLR 748 at 752 (CA); cf *DPP v Camplin* [1978] AC 705 at 716, [1978] 2 All ER 168 at 173 (HL).

203 Cf *R v Lafaele* (1987) 2 CRNZ 677 (CA).

204 *R v Hill* (1986) 25 CCC (3d) 322 (SCC).

205 For example *DPP v Camplin* [1978] AC 705, [1978] 2 All ER 168 (HL); *R v Morhall* [1996] 1 AC 90, [1995] 3 All ER 659 (HL); *Stingel v R* (1990) 171 CLR 312, (1990) 97 ALR 1 (HCA); *Masciantonio v R* (1995) 183 CLR 58, 129 ALR 575 (HCA); see also the majority in *Luc Thiet Thuan v R* [1997] AC 131, [1996] 2 All ER 1033 (PC). That New Zealand law now accords with these authorities was noted in *R v Campbell* [1997] 1 NZLR 16 at 25, (1996) 14 CRNZ 117 at 127 (CA); but there is a doubtful line of cases in the English CA which allow mental abnormality to be considered even if its only effect was to reduce self-control: *R v Parker* [1997] Crim LR 760.

206 *R v Morhall* [1996] AC 90 at 100, [1995] 3 All ER 659 at 668 (HL); *R v Thornton (No 2)* [1996] 2 All ER 1023 at 1031, [1996] 1 WLR 1174 at 1183 (CA).

207 *R v Campbell* [1997] 1 NZLR 16 at 26, 27, (1996) 14 CRNZ 117 at 128, 129 (CA); in *R v Oakes* [1995] 2 NZLR 673 at 681, 682 (CA) a very brief and general explanation was held acceptable, when the point had been at the forefront of the defence.

208 [1962] NZLR 1069 at 1081 (CA).

definite and of sufficient significance to make the offender a different person from the ordinary run of mankind", or different from "the ordinary man of the community".[209] This is misconceived. Although s 169(2)(a) refers to an "ordinary person", what is required is an assessment of the effect of particular provocation on a hypothetical person who has one particular human capacity — an "ordinary" power of self-control.[210] Provided that a personal attribute affects the content or gravity of provocation it may be a relevant "characteristic" even though it is not "peculiar" or other than normal or ordinary.[211] For example, in appropriate cases the offender's race or gender may qualify, as might love for a spouse and children.[212] If fear may have contributed to loss of self-control the comparative size and strength of the parties may be relevant.[213]

(2) *Temporary attributes (including drunkenness)*. It was also said in *McGregor* that a characteristic must have a sufficient degree of permanence to be part of an offender's "character or personality", so that temporary or transitory states of mind (such as a mood of depression, excitability, or irascibility), or conditions (such as drunkenness) were excluded.[214] New Zealand courts have yet to question this,[215] but it raises a difficult question of degree, and reflects a rather narrow interpretation of "characteristics" which ignores the fact that in the assessment of gravity of provocation it is the time of the killing which is important.[216] In *R v Morhall*,[217] Lord Goff considered that some temporary physical conditions may be characteristics (eczema being given as an example), at least if the subject of taunts. He accepted that drunkenness is plainly excluded, but suggested that the basis for this might be the rule of policy that intoxication does not itself excuse offending. The courts have consistently held that drunkenness on the occasion of the killing is irrelevant to the objective

---

209 In *R v Tai* [1976] 1 NZLR 102 at 106 (CA) this was expanded to "an ordinary person in terms of [New Zealand's] mixed society".

210 *R v Morhall* [1996] AC 90 at 97, 98, [1995] 3 All ER 659 at 665, 666 (HL); *Masciantonio v R* (1995) 183 CLR 58 at 66, 67, 129 ALR 575 at 581 (HCA); this standard is sometimes expressed in normative terms: "such powers of self-control as everyone is entitled to expect that his fellow citizens will exercise in society as it is today": *DPP v Camplin* [1978] AC 705 at 716, 717, [1978] 2 All ER 168 at 173, 174 (HL) (Lord Diplock).

211 *R v Hill* (1986) 25 CCC (3d) 322 at 335, 336 (SCC).

212 Cf *R v Nepia* [1983] NZLR 754 at 757 (CA).

213 Cf *R v Oakes* [1995] 2 NZLR 673 at 676 (CA) (in the context of self-defence).

214 [1962] NZLR 1069 at 1081.

215 In *R v McCarthy* [1992] 2 NZLR 550 at 558, (1992) 8 CRNZ 58 at 66, 67 (CA) the Court excluded the effect of alcohol, "being transitory and not a characteristic"; and *Adams* (2nd ed) § 1268 thought it implicit in "characteristics" that "merely temporary or transitory" conditions did not qualify.

216 Orchard, "Provocation — Recharacterisation of 'Characteristics'" (1996) 6 Canterbury LR 202 at 208; Brown, "Killings Non Sedato Animo: A New Test" [1962] NZLJ 489 at 491.

217 [1996] AC 90 at 99, [1995] 3 All ER 659 at 667 (HL); see also *Luc Thiet Thuan v R* [1997] AC 131 at 142, [1996] 2 All ER 1033 at 1042 (PC).

test,[218] although a self-induced addiction or other discreditable attribute, or even intoxication on another occasion, may be a characteristic, if relevant to the gravity of the provocation.[219]

14.4.1.5(d) Relationships between the provocation and a characteristic

In *R v McGregor*, the Court of Appeal stated that there must be some "real" or "direct" connection between the nature of the provocation and the characteristic relied on; the two must be "related", or the provocation must be "directed at" the characteristic.[220] It was apparently thought that a characteristic could not influence the provocative effect of conduct unless such a test was met.

In *R v McCarthy*,[221] however, the Court indicated that the whole of this passage had caused difficulty, and clearly rejected the suggestion that provocation must be "directed at" a characteristic for it to be relevant. In *Luc Thiet Thuan v R*[222] the Privy Council said that such a requirement "may be misleading". It accepted that it would be met "in the great majority" of cases where a characteristic is relevant to the gravity of the provocation to D, but observed that this need not be so, instancing a case where D interprets a remark as referring to a characteristic, when this was not in fact intended. Whether the provocation be by words or conduct, it is clear that it is not essential that the author of the provocation have in mind the characteristic or, indeed, the accused. For example, in *R v Taaka*[223] the primary provocation arose when D discovered V attempting to have intercourse with D's wife, and the characteristic which increased the gravity of the provocation was described by a psychiatrist as "an obsessively compulsive personality . . . directed to his child, his wife [and V]".

In *McGregor*,[224] it was also said that "special difficulties" arise when "purely mental peculiarities" are relied on. This is likely to be so for a number of reasons. How such a condition is likely to affect the gravity of provocation may not be a matter of common sense or ordinary experience, so that expert evidence about this will be needed.[225] Much will depend on the expert's

---

218 This has not been doubted since *R v McCarthy* [1954] 2 QB 105, [1954] 2 All ER 262 (CCA); compare Sir John Smith [1995] Crim LR 891, 892; Orchard, "Provocation — Recharacterisation of 'Characteristics' " (1996) 6 Canterbury LR 202 at 213; intoxication is relevant to the subjective question under s 169(2)(b): *R v Barton* [1977] 1 NZLR 295 (CA).

219 *R v Morhall* [1996] AC 90 at 99, 100, [1995] 3 All ER 659 at 667, 668 (HL) (addiction to glue sniffing, which was the subject of taunts).

220 [1962] NZLR 1069 at 1081, 1082 (CA).

221 [1992] 2 NZLR 550 at 557, 558, (1992) 8 CRNZ 58 at 66, 67; cf *R v Campbell* [1997] 1 NZLR 16 at 25, (1996) 14 CRNZ 117 at 127 (CA).

222 [1997] AC 131 at 148, [1996] 2 All ER 1033 at 1048 (PC).

223 [1982] 2 NZLR 198 (CA).

224 [1962] NZLR 1069 at 1082.

225 At least as a general rule such evidence should not extend to an opinion as to how a person of ordinary self-control might react to the provocation: *R v Turner* [1975] QB 834, [1975] 1 All ER 70 (CA); *DPP v Camplin* [1978] AC 705 at 716, 727, [1978] 2 All ER 168 at 173, 182, 183 (HL).

diagnosis and description of the condition. If this identifies a facet of D's personality or mental make-up which would aggravate his emotional response to the particular provocation, it will be evidence of a relevant "characteristic".[226] But if in substance it is no more than evidence of a short temper or unusual pugnacity, it will not. That was the conclusion in *R v Fryer*,[227] where a psychiatrist had described D as suffering from "a severely disordered personality marked by lack of control when frustrated, violent response to physical threat, and emotional immaturity". Similarly, in *Luc Thiet Thuan*[228] brain damage causing "episodic dyscontrol" did not qualify.

It has been suggested that *Luc Thiet Thuan* holds that mental abnormality is not a relevant characteristic unless the subject of taunts.[229] Certainly, it will be much easier to establish increased provocative effect when a characteristic ("purely mental" or otherwise) is overtly referred to, but such a requirement is not imposed by *Luc Thiet Thuan*, where the evidence did not go beyond identifying a condition which deprived D of a normal power of self-control. We submit that there is no such requirement, although, in the absence of taunts or the like, cases of mental abnormality are liable to present difficulty. If the condition is such that D would feel all or any provocation unusually deeply, it may well be that it should be regarded as in substance no more than evidence of a reduced power of self-control.[230] Even if the abnormality might enhance the provocative effect of only some provocative conduct it might also produce a general reduction in D's power of self-control. Artificial though it might be,[231] the objective test in its present form requires that account be taken only of the enhancement of provocative effect, and not the reduction in the power of self-control.[232]

Section 169(2)(a) does not allow any concession based on reduced self-control even if this arises from brain damage or some other condition which cannot be attributed to any fault of D, and even if it would support a finding of diminished responsibility where that is a defence. In *R v McCarthy*[233] Cooke P remarked that within the limited field of provocation, the unheralded introduction of diminished responsibility may have been the "inevitable and deliberate effect" of allowing for personal characteristics. No doubt this is its effect in those cases where a mental condition increases the gravity of

---

226 Cf the identification of the wife and victim as particular subjects of D's obsession in *R v Taaka* [1982] 2 NZLR 198 (CA); and battered woman's syndrome may qualify on the basis that it heightens awareness of or sensitivity to threatening behaviour: *R v Oakes* [1995] 2 NZLR 673 at 676 (CA).

227 [1981] 1 NZLR 748 at 752 (CA).

228 [1997] AC 131, [1996] 2 All ER 1033 (PC).

229 *Smith and Hogan* 370, 371.

230 Cf *R v Fryer* [1981] 1 NZLR 748 (CA); Orchard, "Provocation — Recharacterisation of 'Characteristics' " (1996) 6 Canterbury LR 202 at 210.

231 Yeo, "Power of Self-Control in Provocation and Automatism" (1992) 14 Syd LR 3.

232 *Stingel v R* (1990) 171 CLR 312 at 332, 97 ALR 1 at 14 (HCA).

233 [1992] 2 NZLR 550 at 558, (1992) 8 CRNZ 58 at 66 (CA).

particular provocation, but it cannot mean that mere diminution of self-control renders such abnormality relevant.[234]

14.4.1.5(e) Age, gender, and race

In England, Canada, and Australia there is one established exception to the insistence of an unvarying standard of an "ordinary" power of self-control: when D is young, the standard is the power of self-control of an ordinary person of D's age.[235] It appears that this will be applied to qualify the "ordinary person" in s 169(2)(a), although age can probably be significant only "at the extremes of senility or obvious youthful immaturity".[236]

There has also been support for including in the description of the applicable standard such other normal attributes as D's gender,[237] and race or "ethnic or cultural background".[238] As to the first of these it would seem neither politic nor justifiable to suppose that the level of normal self-control varies according to sex, although gender may sometimes be relevant to the assessment of the nature and gravity of particular provocation. Regarding the second, in R v McGregor[239] the Court of Appeal had no doubt that it would be irrelevant for D to claim that he belongs to an "excitable race", or a nationality readily accustomed to resort to lethal weapons, and this seems clearly correct unless D's race affects the nature or gravity of the provocation.

However, the position may be different if the issue is whether sufficient time had elapsed for the passion of an ordinary person to cool. If there is evidence that persons of D's gender or race, or with a particular condition (such as battered woman's syndrome), will commonly react to the kind of provocation in question by losing their self-control after a delay, such attributes

---

234 Pace the interpretation of New Zealand law in *Luc Thiet Thuan v R* [1996] 2 All ER 1033 at 1043-1045 (PC); Orchard, "Provocation — Recharacterisation of 'Characteristics' " (1996) 6 Canterbury LR 202 at 206, 207; cf *R v Parker* [1997] Crim LR 760, and commentary. There may be some decisions which are difficult to reconcile with confining the relevance of mental abnormality to an evaluation of the provocative effect of conduct: for example *R v McCarthy* ("excessive emotionalism as a result of brain injury"); *R v Aston* [1989] 2 NZLR 166, (1989) 4 CRNZ 241 (CA) ("paranoid disorder" resulting in distortion of grievances); cf *R v Leilua* 20/9/85, CA19/84, see [1986] New Zealand Recent Law 118 (CA); Stanish, "Whither Provocation" (1993) 7 AULR 381 at 393, 395.

235 *DPP v Camplin* [1978] AC 705, [1978] 2 All ER 168 (HL); *R v Hill* (1986) 25 CCC (3d) 322 (SCC); *Stingel v R* (1990) 171 CLR 312, 97 ALR 1 (HCA).

236 *R v Trounson* [1991] 3 NZLR 690 at 693, (1991) 8 CRNZ 491 at 494 (CA), where the fact that D was 18 was not regarded as significant, although it was otherwise in *DPP v Camplin* [1978] AC 705, [1978] 2 All ER 168 (HL), where D was 16. Abnormal immaturity must probably be treated like any other mental abnormality: *Luc Thiet Thuan v R* [1997] AC 131 at 145, [1996] 2 All ER 1033 at 1045 (PC), doubting *R v Raven* [1982] Crim LR 51.

237 *DPP v Camplin* [1978] AC 705 at 718, [1978] 2 All ER 168 at 175 (HL); *R v Trounson* [1991] 3 NZLR 690 at 693, (1991) 8 CRNZ 491 at 494 (CA); cf Williams, *TBCL* 538, 539.

238 *Masciantonio v R* (1995) 183 CLR 58 at 73, 74, 129 ALR 575 at 586, 587 (CA), per McHugh J dissenting.

239 [1962] NZLR 1069 at 1082 (CA).

should be characteristics relevant to the question of "cooling time".[240] If the issue is whether an ordinary person might have so lost control as to use a weapon, as D did, the comparative stature and strength of the parties might also be relevant.[241]

14.4.1.6 Accident and mistake

Section 169(6) was a new provision introduced in 1961. It provides that:

> This section shall apply in any case where the provocation was given by the person killed, and also in any case where the offender, under provocation given by one person, by accident or mistake killed another person.

This codifies the common law, which allowed the defence in cases of "accident", where D aims retaliation at a person who has provided provocation but unintentionally strikes another,[242] and in cases of "mistake", where D intentionally strikes V in the mistaken belief that V is the person, or one of the persons, who provided the provocation.[243] However, when neither of these possibilities applies the Court in *R v McGregor*[244] thought it inherent in the word "provocation", and the unambiguous effect of subs (6), that the provocation must emanate from the victim. This is consistent with such common law authority as there is,[245] although the restriction is not imposed under modern English legislation.[246] The defence may, however, succeed if V was one of a number who acted provocatively (for example, by attacking D),[247] and it is likely that provocation will be "given by" anyone who is a party to provocative conduct, by acting in concert with, or by aiding, abetting, or inciting, another.[248]

The requirement that provocation be given by the victim perhaps reflects the idea that one justification for the defence is that V was partly to blame, although there is no requirement that V intended to provoke anyone,[249] and at least in England the defence can now be based on conduct which could not be

---

240 This possibility was not excluded in relation to a "brooding personality" associated with race in *R v Tai* [1976] 1 NZLR 102 at 107 (CA); see also Nicholson and Sanghvi, "Battered Women and Provocation: The Implications of *R v Ahluwalia*" [1993] Crim LR 728; Tarrant, "The 'Specific Triggering Incident' in Provocation: Is the Law Gender Biased?" (1996) 26 WAL Rev 190.

241 Cf *R v Oakes* [1995] 2 NZLR 673 at 676 (CA), in relation to self-defence.

242 *R v Gross* (1913) 23 Cox CC 455; *R v Porritt* [1961] 3 All ER 463, [1961] 1 WLR 1372 (CCA).

243 *R v Brown* (1776) 1 Leach 148, 168 ER 177.

244 [1962] NZLR 1069 at 1080 (CA); see also *R v Matoka* [1987] 1 NZLR 340 at 344 (CA).

245 *R v Simpson* (1915) 84 LJKB 189 (CCA); cf *R v Scriva (No 2)* [1951] VLR 298, [1951] ALR 616; see also the terms of the "classic direction" in *R v Duffy* [1949] 1 All ER 932 (CCA).

246 *R v Davies* [1975] QB 691, [1975] 1 All ER 890 (CA); *R v Twine* [1967] Crim LR 710; Smith, "Provocation — The Widened Ambit" [1975] 34 CLJ 188.

247 *R v Brown* (1776) 1 Leach 148, 168 ER 177; *R v Hall* (1928) 21 Cr App R 48 (CCA).

248 *R v Kenney* [1983] 2 VR 470; *R v Tumanako* (1992) 64 A Crim R 149 at 155; *R v Manchuk* [1937] 4 DLR 737, [1938] SCR 18 (SCC).

249 For example *R v Campbell* [1997] 1 NZLR 16, (1996) 14 CRNZ 117 (CA); *R v Taaka* [1982] 2 NZLR 198 (CA); *R v Twine* [1967] Crim LR 710; cf *R v McGregor* [1962] NZLR 1069 at 1073 (CA).

regarded as in any sense culpable.[250] The courts have also accepted that the defence may be available if D lost control because of a mistaken belief about the occurrence, nature, or circumstances of provocative conduct, or in the mistaken belief that the victim was a party to it. But in *R v White (Shane)*[251] a belief as to the circumstances was held not to support the defence unless it was one which an ordinary person might have held. This contrasts with self-defence, which may be based on an unreasonable mistake.[252]

The rule governing abnormal mistakes is qualified if D had a characteristic which may have affected his perception. An extreme example is *R v Campbell*.[253] D had killed the male victim with a number of blows with an axe and there was expert evidence supporting the claim that the lasting effects of childhood abuse may have had the result that when V placed his hand on D's thigh D lost control because he experienced a "flashback" in which he interpreted the act as a homosexual advance by his childhood abuser. This "flashback", or delusion, was to be attributed to the hypothetical person possessed of ordinary self-control. Similarly, in *R v Oakes*[254] it was recognised that, when a woman had killed her partner, the existence of battered woman's syndrome was a relevant characteristic in that it could lead to heightened awareness of or sensitivity to threatening behaviour, including an earlier and greater perception of danger than would be experienced in the absence of the syndrome.

14.4.1.7 Self-induced provocation

In some cases, conduct which leads D to lose self-control may itself be a reaction to D's previous behaviour. In *Edwards v R*[255] D made a blackmail demand of V, but V responded by attacking D with a knife. D wrested the knife from V and stabbed him to death. The Privy Council held that as the attack by V with a knife was an extreme reaction to the blackmail, provocation should have been left to the jury. It was said, however, that "on principle" the defence would not have been available if V's reaction had been no more than a "predictable" response. In *R v Johnson*,[256] on the other hand, the English Court of Appeal appeared to reject this limitation in holding that the defence could not be withdrawn merely because D was led to loss of self-control by V's violent reaction to threatening conduct by D.

---

250 *R v Doughty* (1986) 83 Cr App R 319, [1986] Crim LR 625 (CA) (crying of a baby).

251 [1988] 1 NZLR 122 at 126, 127 (CA); see also *R v Hansford* (1987) 33 CCC (3d) 74, (1987) 55 CR (3d) 347; contrast *R v Kenney* [1983] 2 VR 470.

252 § 13.1.3.1. The difference may cause difficulty if both defences have to be considered: *Adams* § CA169.15; and if there is a mistaken belief that V was a party to provocation which had been offered the case would appear to be within s 169(6), with no requirement of reasonableness.

253 [1997] 1 NZLR 16, (1996) 14 CRNZ 117 (CA).

254 [1995] 2 NZLR 673 at 676 (CA).

255 [1973] AC 648, [1973] 1 All ER 152 (PC); cf *R v Allwood* (1975) 18 A Crim R 120 at 132, 133; *R v Radford* (1985) 20 A Crim R 388 at 401; Ashworth "Self-Induced Provocation and the Homicide Act" [1973] Crim LR 483.

256 [1989] 1 WLR 740, [1989] 2 All ER 839 (CA).

The possible reaction of an ordinary person is a question of opinion for the jury, and in principle the predictability of the provocative conduct should be no more than a factor for the jury to consider.[257] Exceptionally, s 169(5) excludes the defence in the extreme case when the supposed provocation consists of a person "doing anything which the offender incited him to do in order to provide the offender with an excuse for killing or doing bodily harm to any person".

14.4.2 Involuntary manslaughter

"Involuntary manslaughter" describes killings where D is guilty of culpable homicide, but not of murder, manslaughter under provocation, killing or in furtherance of a suicide pact, or of infanticide. Its scope is exceptionally wide and depends on the definition of culpable homicide in s 160(2), which was summarised above in § 14.2. More particularly, s 160(2) provides that:

Homicide is culpable when it consists in the killing of any person —
(a) By an unlawful act; or
(b) By an omission without lawful excuse to perform or observe any legal duty; or
(c) By both combined; or
(d) By causing that person by threats or fear of violence, or by deception, to do an act which causes his death; or
(e) By wilfully frightening a child under the age of 16 years or a sick person.

It is convenient first to consider paragraphs (a), (d), and (e), and then (b) and (c).

14.4.2.1 Killing by an unlawful act: s 160(2)(a)

This is manslaughter at common law and, insofar as it is consistent with the scheme of the Act, it is thought that "unlawful act" is to be given the same meaning as it has at common law.[258]

In the nineteenth century it was at one stage thought that it could be enough that the act was a tort,[259] but in *R v Franklin*[260] Field J ruled that a mere civil wrong was not sufficient. In *R v Lamb*[261] the Court regarded it as settled law that it is irrelevant whether D might be subject to civil liability, and that the act must be "unlawful in the criminal sense of that word". In *Lamb*, D had shot

---

257 Orchard, "Provoked Provocation" (1974) 6 NZULR 63 at 65; cf s 169(4), which seems to make it a jury question, untrammelled by rules as to how an ordinary person might react, as much as s 3 Homicide Act 1957 (UK).

258 Cf *Murray v R* [1962] Tas SR 170 at 173, 192; *R v McCallum* [1969] Tas SR 73 at 84. This might require acceptance that the words are "not otherwise clear in their meaning": *R v Machirus* [1996] 3 NZLR 404 at 410, (1996) 14 CRNZ 172 at 179 (CA). But these provisions were not intended to change the law (Report of the Royal Commission on Indictable Offences, 1879, 23), and this might justify recourse to developing common law interpretation of the same general terms.

259 For example *Fenton's Case* (1830) 1 Lewin 179, 168 ER 1004 (trespass to property by throwing stones down a mine).

260 (1883) 15 Cox CC 163.

261 [1967] 2 QB 981 at 988, [1967] 2 All ER 1282 at 1284 (CA).

and killed a friend when he pointed a revolver at him in jest, and pulled the trigger in the mistaken belief that the gun would not fire. D's conduct did not constitute the offence of assault, for he had not intended V to suffer or anticipate the application of force, and on the basis that his act did not involve any other offence, it was held to follow that the killing was not manslaughter by an unlawful act.[262]

As *Lamb* shows, for an act to be unlawful because it is an offence it will be necessary that D acted with whatever mens rea was required for that act to be an offence,[263] and it must also be done without lawful justification or excuse.[264] It has also been suggested that in principle it must be an offence against the person and not, for example, merely an offence against property.[265] This is not a requirement in New Zealand, where it seems that an act may be "unlawful" if it is an offence of any kind, even if it is an offence of strict or, perhaps, absolute liability. In *R v Myatt*[266] two people had died as a result of a collision between power boats, one of which had been driven by D. One basis on which manslaughter charges were put was that D had committed offences against bylaws and regulations governing power boat use, and the Court of Appeal expressed the view that "unlawful act" included any act in breach of one of the "many provision of Acts, regulations and bylaws which create offences".[267] Moreover, although the unlawful act must be a cause of death there need not be a causal connection between a circumstance that is necessary for the act to be an offence (for example, absence of a licence, or the fact that D acts in a public place), and the death.[268]

The wide interpretation of unlawful act in *Myatt* is, however, qualified by a further requirement: the act must have been dangerous. In Australia the courts have required the act to be "fraught with a risk of serious harm to some person",[269] but in England the test is wider: the act "must be such as all sober and reasonable people would inevitably recognise must subject the other person to, at least, the risk of some harm resulting therefrom, albeit not serious harm".[270]

---

262 D might have been guilty of manslaughter by gross negligence, but there had not been adequate directions on this. In New Zealand, liability on the basis of failure to exercise care could arise under ss 156 and 160(2)(b), although this would now require a high degree of negligence: § 14.4.2.2(c).

263 See also *R v Jennings* [1990] Crim LR 588 (CA).

264 *R v Scarlett* [1993] 4 All ER 629, (1994) 98 Cr App R 290 (CA).

265 *Smith and Hogan* 379.

266 [1991] 1 NZLR 674 at 678-680, (1990) 7 CRNZ 304 at 308-310 (CA).

267 Cf *DPP v Newbury* [1977] AC 500, [1976] 2 All ER 365 (HL); in New Zealand the problematic case of *R v Cato* [1976] 1 All ER 260, [1976] 1 WLR 110 (CA) would involve the offence of administering a controlled drug: s 6(1)(c) Misuse of Drugs Act 1975.

268 *R v Grant* [1966] NZLR 968 (CA).

269 *R v Phillips* (1971) 45 ALJR 467 at 479, [1971] ALR 740 at 758 (HCA); *Wilson v R* (1992) 66 ALJR 517, (1992) 174 CLR 311 (HCA); *R v McCallum* [1969] Tas SR 73 at 88; cf *R v Fleeting (No 1)* [1977] 1 NZLR 343 at 346.

270 *R v Church* [1966] 1 QB 59 at 70, [1965] 2 All ER 72 at 76 (CCA), approved in *DPP v Newbury* [1977] AC 500, [1976] 2 All ER 365 (HL).

In New Zealand, the requirement that the unlawful act be likely to harm another was recognised in *R v Grant*,[271] where it was thought to be the probable explanation of an earlier decision that a particular instance of causing death by driving without a licence was not manslaughter.[272] The principle was confirmed in *R v Myatt*[273] where, however, the Court adopted the English rule that it suffices that there was a risk of some harm, and there need not be a risk of serious harm, although no doubt something more than "trivial or transitory" harm must have been foreseeable.[274] In many cases (including *Myatt*) when an offence has caused death, serious harm will have been foreseeable, but sometimes a conviction will be possible only if a risk of some harm is enough. An example may be *R v Renata*,[275] where D was found guilty of manslaughter when a relatively minor assault resulted in death because V had an unknown abnormal physical condition.

In *Myatt* the Court of Appeal also said that it was not essential that D be in breach of legislation which had public safety as its primary objective: "All that is necessary is that the particular unlawful act is likely to do harm to a particular person or to a class of persons of whom [the victim] is one, which does not mean the public at large in every case."[276] But even this test is too narrow, according to the House of Lords. In *A-G's Reference (No 3 of 1994)*,[277] it was held that a killing will be manslaughter if D intentionally injures a woman who is pregnant, and after birth her child dies as a result of D's assault on the mother. The House confirmed what is implicit in *Myatt*, that D's act need not be directed at the person who dies,[278] and further held that it is enough that the act is likely to harm somebody, even if harm to V, or a class including V, is not reasonably foreseeable. If D's dangerous unlawful act caused the death of the child after it was born, it was no defence that this might not have been reasonably foreseeable.

The act must be accompanied by whatever mens rea is needed to make it an offence, and it is also said that it must be done "intentionally",[279] but on the English authorities the test of dangerousness is objective: it is enough if a reasonable person would have known that the act was likely to harm

271 [1966] NZLR 968 (CA).

272 *R v Faigan*, unreported, 15/7/27 (CA).

273 [1991] 1 NZLR 674 at 679-681, (1990) 7 CRNZ 304 at 309-311 (CA).

274 *R v Creighton* [1993] 3 SCR 3, (1993) 83 CCC (3d) 346 (SCC).

275 [1992] 2 NZLR 346, (1991) 7 CRNZ 616 (CA).

276 [1991] 1 NZLR 674 at 680, (1990) 7 CRNZ 304 at 310.

277 [1997] 3 All ER 936 at 950, 951, 958-960, [1997] 3 WLR 421 at 436, 437, 444-447 (HL).

278 Approving *R v Mitchell* [1983] QB 741, [1983] 2 All ER 427 (CA), where D was guilty of manslaughter when he hit A who fell against V, who died as a result of injuries caused by this; the contrary reasoning in *R v Dalby* [1982] 1 WLR 425, [1982] 1 All ER 916 (CA) is clearly incorrect.

279 *DPP v Newbury* [1977] AC 500 at 506, [1976] 2 All ER 365 at 366 (HL); *A-G's Reference (No 3 of 1994)* [1997] 3 All ER 936 at 960, [1997] 3 WLR 421 at 446 (HL).

somebody.[280] In *Renata*[281] the Court of Appeal did not go further than holding that an assault with intent to cause minor harm was an "unlawful act", but in *Myatt* it had accepted the objective nature of the test of dangerousness.[282] D will be liable if she was aware of the risk of harm to another, or of facts creating the risk, but ignorance will not excuse if a reasonable person (or "reasonable observer") would have recognised the facts or risk.[283] In Canada a narrow exception applies when, without fault, D lacks the capacity to appreciate the risk,[284] and in New Zealand there is a further qualification when harm results from influence on the mind of the victim.[285]

Although since *R v Lamb*,[286] it has been generally assumed that an "unlawful act" must be an offence, some doubt remains whether this is necessarily the case. In particular, it has been suggested that it might be enough if D does something which is in itself not an offence, such as persuading V to undertake severe physical exertion or drink a dangerous quantity of alcohol, with intent to cause death and without justifications or excuse.[287] In *A-G's Reference (No 3 of 1994)*[288] there is also a dictum suggesting that this category of manslaughter comprises killings "where the defendant's act was both unlawful and dangerous because it was likely to cause harm to some person", but it seems that a comma must be inserted after unlawful, for otherwise an offence which is already excessively wide overflows sensible bounds.

Nonetheless, even if an offence is required, if death follows a series of acts by D the immediate cause of death need not necessarily be an offence which is likely to harm another. The killing will be manslaughter if the fatal act was part of the same transaction or series of events as an earlier unlawful and dangerous act committed by D, even if it is disputable whether this was a significant

---

280 *DPP v Newbury* [1977] AC 500, [1976] 2 All ER 365 (HL); *A-G's Reference (No 3 of 1994)* [1997] 3 All ER 936, [1997] 3 WLR 421 (HL); cf *Wilson v R* (1992) 174 CLR 313, 66 ALJR 517 (HCA).

281 [1992] 2 NZLR 346 at 349, (1991) 7 CRNZ 616 at 619 (CA).

282 [1991] 1 NZLR 674 at 678, 679, (1990) 7 CRNZ 304 at 308 (CA).

283 *R v Watson* [1989] 2 All ER 865, [1989] 1 WLR 684 (CA); *R v Dawson* (1985) 81 Cr App R 150, [1985] Crim LR 383 (CA).

284 *R v Creighton* [1993] 3 SCR 3, (1993) 83 CCC (3d) 346 (SCC); it appears that the majority would also ignore D's special knowledge of the activity (eg drug taking) which would increase D's ability to appreciate the risk, but rather discounts the concession by imposing a duty to inform oneself of risks in some cases.

285 See § 14.4.2.3.

286 [1967] 2 QB 981, [1967] 2 All ER 1282.

287 *Adams* § CA160.07, citing *R v Packard* (1841) Car & M 236, 174 ER 487.

288 [1997] 3 WLR 421 at 442, [1997] 3 All ER 936 at 955, 956; cf Stephen, *Digest of Criminal Law*, 1877, 143 where an act "commonly known to be likely to cause harm" is regarded as sufficient, if neither justified nor excused; but by 1883 he had modified this class to acts "commonly known to be dangerous to life": Stephen, *History of the Criminal Laws of England* iii, 16. But he also there included all crimes, torts, acts contrary to public policy or morality, or injurious to the public. There is no modern authority supporting such a sweeping rule.

cause.[289] For example, D might form a mistaken but reasonable belief that his assault has killed V, whom he then kills by disposing of the supposed corpse,[290] or even without such belief he might accidentally cause death in trying to conceal his earlier offence.[291] The killing will not, however, be culpable if the immediate cause was an act by D which was justified or excused, even if this was preceded by unlawful acts by D.[292]

A final doubt concerns omissions. It appears that s 160(2)(a) will apply only when a positive act is a significant cause of death, and a killing by a mere omission will be exclusively within the province of s 160(2)(b).[293] But where there is a positive act, which was unlawful only because of a failure to exercise care, there may now be doubt. At common law even an offence committed by a positive act is not an "unlawful act" in this context if the act would have been lawful but for the fact that it was negligently performed (for example, dangerous driving). In such a case the common law requires gross negligence for manslaughter, and the unlawful act rule does not apply.[294] Where there are applicable code provisions which require gross negligence it would seem that the same rule should apply.[295] However, as will be seen, until recently in New Zealand gross negligence has not been required when there has been a failure to observe a duty of care in relation to dangerous activities, and in Myatt[296] it was assumed that an offence of "positive act" negligence was an "unlawful act" within s 160(2)(a). The law governing such omissions has, however, been changed to require a high degree of negligence,[297] and this question may have to be reconsidered.

14.4.2.2 *Inducing victims to kill themselves:* s 160(2)(d)

It is provided by s 160(2)(d) that culpable homicide includes the killing of a person by "causing that person by threats or fear of violence, or by deception, to do an act which causes his death". This allows for a finding of both causation and culpability in certain cases where the immediate cause of death is an act of the victim in response to conduct of D. For example, V may leap into a river

---

289 Although often it will be a cause: *R v McKinnon* [1980] 2 NZLR 31 (CA); see §§ 3.8, 14.3.6.

290 *R v Church* [1966] 1 QB 59, [1965] 2 All ER 72 (CCA).

291 *R v Le Brun* [1992] QB 61, [1991] 4 All ER 673 (CA); cf *R v Watson* [1989] 1 WLR 684, [1989] 2 All ER 865 (CA); *A-G's Reference (No 3 of 1994)* [1997] 3 WLR 421 at 442, [1997] 3 All ER 936 at 956.

292 *R v Grant* [1966] NZLR 968 (CA); cf *R v Wesley* (1859) 1 F & F 528, 175 ER 838; *R v Setrum* (1976) 32 CCC (2d) 109.

293 *R v Rau* [1972] Tas SR 59 at 62; cf *R v Lowe* [1973] QB 702, [1973] 1 All ER 805 (CA).

294 *Andrews v DPP* [1937] AC 576, [1937] 2 All ER 552 (HL).

295 See *R v Rau* [1972] Tas SR 59; conversely in *R v Phillips* (1971) 45 ALJR 467 at 479, [1971] ALR 740 at 758 (HCA) Windeyer J thought that a grossly negligent tortious act might be an "unlawful act" in such a Code.

296 [1991] 1 NZLR 674, (1990) 7 CRNZ 304 (CA); and in *R v Clarke* [1982] 1 NZLR 654 (CA) the Court of Appeal did not doubt the propriety of charging causing death by reckless driving as manslaughter by an unlawful act.

297 See § 14.4.2.5(c).

and drown,[298] jump from a window and die from the fall,[299] or in attempting to escape might die as a result of an accidental fall downstairs.[300] In most cases V will have sought to escape after threats from D,[301] but the rule could apply if V committed suicide rather than suffer torture, and the extension of it to cases of deception might apply if, for example, V was deceived into consuming poison, or was led to walk into a concealed pit.[302]

Section 160(2)(d) was considered in *R v Tomars*,[303] where after intimidatory driving by D a motorcyclist had swerved in front of another car, and had been killed. It was held that the paragraph would apply if: (a) D had caused V to fear violence; (b) such fear was a "not insignificant" cause of V's driving as he did; (c) such driving by V was the kind of reaction that could reasonably have been foreseen by a reasonable person in D's position, given D's conduct immediately beforehand; and (d) such driving by V contributed in a not insignificant way to his death. Under this test, negligence, or even recklessness, by V or the driver of the other car, would not necessarily exclude such causation.[304]

In some cases where V has acted in fear of D the courts have said that the fear must be "well grounded", and that there must be a "reasonable relationship" between D's conduct and V's reaction, but those requirements are now incorporated in the test of reasonable forseeability.[305] Moreover, although it is sometimes assumed that V must believe that there is "immediate" danger,[306] the essential requirements that V must act as a result of D's conduct and in a reasonably foreseeable way may be satisfied even though V knows D is not able instantly to inflict harm (as when a threat is made through a locked door).[307]

There remains one doubtful question. At common law, a case where V dies as a result of trying to escape from D is treated as being governed by the law relating to manslaughter by an unlawful act, so that for liability D's conduct must be unlawful and such as any reasonable person would realise was likely to create the risk of some harm to a person.[308] In *Tomars* it was recognised that

298 *R v Pitts* (1842) Car & M 284, 174 ER 509.

299 *R v Curley* (1909) 2 Cr App R 109 (CCA).

300 *R v Mackie* (1973) 57 Cr App R 453, [1973] Crim LR 438 (CA).

301 As a matter of construction, it seems that such threats must be of violence, although that need not involve threats of serious injury: cf *R v Mackie* (1973) 57 Cr App R 453 at 461, [1973] Crim LR 438 at 439 (CA).

302 *Adams* § CA160.16.

303 [1978] 2 NZLR 505 (CA); § 2.2.3.2(a).

304 Ibid at 511; cf *R v Storey* [1931] NZLR 417 at 442, 443 (CA).

305 *R v Tomars* [1978] 2 NZLR 505 at 510; the same will be true of requirements that V's response be "proportionate" to the threat, or "within the ambit of reasonableness": *R v Williams* [1992] 1 WLR 380, [1992] 2 All ER 183 (CA).

306 *R v Halliday* (1889) 61 LT 701 at 702.

307 *R v Lewis* [1970] Crim LR 647 (CA); Elliott, "Frightening a Person into Injuring Himself" [1974] Crim LR 15 at 19.

308 For example *R v Mackie* (1973) 57 Cr App R 453, [1973] Crim LR 438 (CA); *DPP v Daley* [1980] AC 237 at 245, 246, [1979] 2 WLR 239 at 245, 246 (PC); *R v Williams* [1992] 1 WLR 380, [1992] 2 All ER 183 (CA).

such cases could be within s 160(2)(a), although in the interests of simplicity it will generally be preferable that the prosecution rely solely on the more explicit s 160(2)(d). This paragraph, it was acknowledged, will not apply if D's conduct was legally justified (eg a threat of reasonable parental discipline), but the Court inclined to the view that apart from that any conduct capable of producing fear of violence could suffice.[309] The requirement that V's conduct be reasonably foreseeable may be justified as an aspect of causation, which para (d) requires, but it may be doubted whether the courts would be warranted in imposing a further gloss requiring D's conduct to be unlawful and likely to cause harm.[310]

14.4.2.3 *Killing by frightening*: s 160(2)(e)

As previously mentioned (§ 14.1.3.2), under s 163 the general rule is that no one is criminally responsible for killing "by any influence on the mind alone", or for killing by any disorder or disease arising from such influence. The abolition of this special rule has been proposed,[311] and in view of modern medical knowledge it appears to be arbitrary. For example, if as a result of D's dangerous unlawful act V indulges in physical exertion which causes death from heart failure there appears to be nothing to preclude liability; but if the same act causes mere fright or emotional stress which produces in V a chemical or physiological process which causes heart failure the rule in s 163 excludes liability.[312] However, ss 160(2)(e) and 163 provide for an exception: it is culpable homicide if D causes death by "wilfully frightening a child under 16 or a sick person", including cases where such conduct produces some fatal disorder or disease.[313] There is an absence of authority on this provision, but it may be that a person will be "sick" if she has a condition making her unusually susceptible to injury or death from fright. "Wilfully" will require that D intend to frighten, or is at least subjectively reckless as to the risk and, although it seems to have been otherwise at common law, the modern approach to mens rea requirements suggests that it should be interpreted as applying to all the elements in s 160(2)(e), so that D must at least be aware of a real risk that V is under 16 or sick.[314] But such "wilfulness" might well take the place of the

---

309 *R v Tomars* [1978] 2 NZLR 505 at 510 (CA).

310 On this view, s 160(2)(d) could well apply if V flees in fear of D, and the physical exertion causes V to die of heart failure: cf *R v Hayward* (1908) 21 Cox CC 692; *Adams* § CA167.16.

311 Crimes Consultative Committee, *Crimes Bill 1989: Report of the Crimes Consultative Committee presented to the Minister of Justice April 1991*, Wellington, Dept of Justice, 1991, 104.

312 This was the conclusion of the Alberta Court of Appeal in *R v Powder* (1981) 29 CR (3d) 183.

313 For cases at common law allowing for a finding of manslaughter where the death of an infant or a person suffering from an abnormal condition had apparently resulted from fright caused by D, see *R v Towers* (1874) 12 Cox CC 530, *R v Hayward* (1908) 21 Cox CC 692.

314 Cf *R v Hayward*, ibid at 693 where Ridley J appears to have directed that even reasonable ignorance of V's illness would not excuse.

elements of unlawfulness and dangerousness required when s 160(2)(a) applies.[315]

14.4.2.4 *Killing by unlawful omission:* s 160(2)(b)

Under s 160(2)(b), it is culpable homicide if D kills by "an omission without lawful excuse to perform or observe any legal duty". The effect of this is that if death results from D's failure to fulfil a legal duty, D may be guilty of manslaughter, and indeed of murder if the requisite mens rea was present.[316] Sections 151-153 and 155-157 Crimes Act 1961 codify certain "Duties Tending to the Preservation of Life" which were recognised at common law, and provide for criminal responsibility where harm may have resulted from a mere omission or, in some instances, from positive conduct which was accompanied by an omission to comply with a legal duty. In practice, most cases of omissions which might involve culpable homicide will be within these statutory provisions. However, s 160(2)(b) refers to "any legal duty" and in *R v Mwai*[317] the Court of Appeal held that the same phrase in s 145 includes duties recognised by the common law as well as by statute, and even, remarkably, the common law version of a codified duty.

It is convenient first to outline the scope of the codified duties, and then to consider the fault required for manslaughter, and the possibility of a defence of lawful excuse. The codified duties fall into two general categories: duties to provide the necessaries of life; and duties of persons who do dangerous acts, who are in charge of dangerous things, or who have undertaken to do things which may prevent danger to life.

14.4.2.4(a) *Duties to provide necessaries*

Under ss 151-153, there may be liability in certain cases where D omits, without lawful excuse, to provide another with the "necessaries of life" (s 151), or "necessaries" (s 152), or "necessary food, clothing or lodging" (s 153). In each case there is criminal responsibility if the result is that V's life is endangered[318] or his health is permanently injured,[319] and it is culpable homicide if death results.

Section 153 imposes the duty and liability on an employer who contracts to provide necessary food, clothing, or lodging for any servant or apprentice under 16. It is of little practical significance today.

---

315 Cf *Adams* § CA160.17; *R v Tomars* [1978] 2 NZLR 505 (CA).

316 For example *R v Gibbons and Proctor* (1918) 13 Cr App R 134 (CCA); *R v MacDonald* [1904] St R Qd 151; such omissions may also support charges of offences of injuring under ss 188, 189 or 190; or, if mere personal endangerment is proved, criminal nuisance (s 145); cf *R v Mwai* [1995] 3 NZLR 149, (1995) 13 CRNZ 273 (CA); *R v Turner* (1995) 13 CRNZ 142 (CA).

317 [1995] 3 NZLR 149 at 156, 157, (1995) 13 CRNZ 273 at 281 (CA).

318 Which occurs when there is a "reasonable possibility" that death will ensue if the duty is not performed: *R v Moore* [1954] NZLR 893 (CA).

319 Under ss 151 and 152 the maximum penalty is 7 years' imprisonment, and 5 years under s 153.

Sections 151 and 152 are more important. These apply to those in charge of helpless people, and to parents and guardians of children. More particularly, D may be criminally responsible if one of the specified results is caused to V by an omission to supply or provide either "the necessaries of life" (s 151) or "necessaries" (s 152), provided that:

(i) D "has charge of" V, who is unable by reason of detention, age, sickness, insanity, or any other cause to withdraw from such charge, and is unable to provide himself with the necessaries of life;[320] or

(ii) D "as a parent or person in place of a parent is under a legal duty to provide necessaries" for V, who is a child under 16 and in D's actual custody, but who need not be helpless.[321]

In this context, "necessaries" in s 152 is synonymous with "necessaries of life" in s 151. These include any thing or service required to sustain life or health, such as medical treatment,[322] food and clothing,[323] lodging or shelter,[324] and, no doubt, heating. The refusal of a parent to consent to surgery on a child may be an omission to "supply" or "provide" a necessary,[325] but it seems that leaving V unconscious where she is asphyxiated by drowning will not.[326]

These sections overlap, in that D may have charge of a helpless person who is also a child covered by s 152; but the parental duty ceases when the child turns 16, whereas the s 151 duty may continue or revive if V is or becomes helpless while in D's charge.[327]

More than one person may owe the duties. In the earlier codes, the parental duty applied only to "the head of the family", but now parents who are living together may both be liable as parents,[328] or one person may have the duty as parent and, if V is helpless, another as a person having charge,[329] or several

---

320 Section 151(1); this "seeks to ensure that those who have the care of one who cannot care for him or herself supply that person with the necessaries of life". *Auckland Area Health Board v A-G* [1993] 1 NZLR 235 at 247, (1992) 8 CRNZ 634 at 647 (Thomas J).

321 Section 152(1); this imposes criminal responsibility but unlike the other provisions it does not create the duty. See also the offences of abandoning a child under 6 (s 154), and cruelty to a child (s 195).

322 For example *R v Moore* [1954] NZLR 893 (CA); *R v Burney* [1958] NZLR 745 (CA); but in *Auckland Area Health Board v A-G* [1993] 1 NZLR 235 at 249, 250, (1992) 8 CRNZ 634 at 649, Thomas J excluded treatment (specifically, ventilation) when the patient was beyond recovery, and it provided no medial or therapeautic benefit, beyond deferring brain death.

323 For example *R v Foster* (1906) 26 NZLR 1254 (CA); *R v Gibbins and Proctor* (1918) 13 Cr App R 134 (CCA).

324 Cf *R v Plummer* (1844) 1 C & K 600, 174 ER 954.

325 Cf *Oakey v Jackson* [1914] 1 KB 216.

326 *R v Phillips* (1971) 45 ALJR 467, [1971] ALR 740 (HCA); and omission to arrange medical attention was not a cause of death.

327 Cf *R v Chattaway* (1925) 17 Cr App R 7.

328 Cf *R v Watson and Watson* (1959) 43 Cr App R 111 (CCA).

329 For example *R v Bubb* (1851) 4 Cox CC 455; *R v Gibbins and Proctor* (1918) 13 Cr App R 134 (CCA).

may jointly have charge.[330] But guilt requires both duty and individual fault, so that even if necessaries are withheld by a number of persons, it may be that only one is guilty.[331]

Section 151 applies when D "has charge of" a helpless person, and it is expressly provided that it applies "whether such charge is undertaken by him under any contract or is imposed upon him by law or by reason of his unlawful act or otherwise howsoever". In some cases "charge" of, and responsibility for, a helpless person may be imposed on D because of their relationship and the circumstances, regardless whether D has *done* anything: for example, when the helpless person is D's spouse or child and is living with D.[332] Alternatively, it may arise from the fact that the helpless person lived with D, who had accepted the responsibility of care,[333] or from the fact that D took control of the helpless person, even temporarily, so that help from others was less likely.[334] The words "or otherwise howsoever" were added in 1961. However, it had already been held that the section applied when D had assumed the responsibility of caring for V voluntarily, and not under contract,[335] and the addition of these words suggests that it may be enough if D in fact has control of a helpless person, even if it is doubtful whether D has accepted responsibility.[336] In *R v Stone*,[337] S had allowed an elderly relative to live in his home, where she became helpless. It was held that a jury could find an assumption of duty by S from the fact that V was a relative occupying a room in his home, and an assumption of duty by S's mistress because she had made some attempt to wash and feed the unco-operative lodger. The case has been criticised,[338] and it is doubtful whether it should have been significant that S was a relative, or that the mistress had done something rather than nothing. Under s 151 S might perhaps be responsible simply because he had control as a result of his occupancy, and others might have "charge" if they share a residence with a helpless person, at least if no one else has assumed full responsibility.

There remain doubtful cases. In particular, it is not clear whether the duty to supply necessaries (which perhaps includes a duty to rescue) might arise simply because D caused V's helplessness (for example, through rendering V

---

330 For example *R v Stone and Dobinson* [1977] QB 354, [1977] 2 All ER 341 (CA).

331 For example *R v Bubb* (1851) 4 Cox CC 455; *R v Conde* (1867) 10 Cox CC 547.

332 For example *R v Smith* [1979] Crim LR 251; *R v Bonnyman* (1942) 28 Cr App R 131 (CCA); *R v Chattaway* (1928) 17 Cr App R 7; *R v Bubb* (1851) 4 Cox CC 455.

333 For example *R v Foster* (1906) 26 NZLR 1254 (CA): grandmother who assumed sole charge of her inadequate daughter's infant; *R v Bubb* (1850) 4 Cox CC 455: cohabitee of an infant's father, who provided means of supporting the child; *R v Instan* [1893] 1 QB 450: niece living with helpless person, who had provided funds for the support of both of them.

334 *R v Taktak* (1988) 14 NSWLR 226, (1988) 34 A Crim R 334; and a kidnapper will clearly have "charge" as a result of unlawful assumption of control.

335 *R v Foster* (1906) 26 NZLR 1254 (CA).

336 Cf *R v Chattaway* (1925) 17 Cr App R 7, where what is required was described as "custody, charge, or care or control".

337 [1977] QB 354, [1977] 2 All ER 354 (CA).

338 Williams, *TBCL*, 262-266.

unconscious by an unlawful act),[339] and perhaps D never has "charge" of a helpless person unless she has a statutory or contractual obligation to provide care, or has assumed responsibility to do so, or at least controls or shares the place where V is.[340] But even if s 151(1) does not apply, there remains the possibility that an equivalent common law duty may be relied upon.[341]

14.4.2.4(b) Duties of those doing dangerous acts and those in charge of dangerous things

These are provided for by ss 155 and 156:

> **155. Duty of persons doing dangerous acts** — Every one who undertakes (except in case of necessity) to administer surgical or medical treatment, or to do any other lawful act the doing of which is or may be dangerous to life, is under a legal duty to have and to use reasonable knowledge, skill, and care in doing any such act, and is criminally responsible for the consequences of omitting without lawful excuse to discharge that duty.

> **156. Duty of persons in charge of dangerous things** — Every one who has in his charge or under his control anything whatever, whether animate or inanimate, or who erects, makes, operates, or maintains anything whatever, which, in the absence of precaution or care, may endanger human life is under a legal duty to take reasonable precautions against and to use reasonable care to avoid such danger, and is criminally responsible for the consequences of omitting without lawful excuse to discharge that duty.

These sections overlap, but neither applies unless there is a reasonable possibility that someone will die if reasonable care is not taken; a risk of injury, even serious injury, is insufficient.[342] In other respects they are of wide application.

Although s 155 specifically applies to the administration of surgical or medical treatment, it also expressly extends to "any other lawful act" which may be dangerous to life; for example, the organisation of a bungy jump.[343] At common law, in *R v Burdee*,[344] an unqualified person was held guilty of manslaughter after the death of an elderly and ill woman was accelerated because she followed D's advice not to eat for 3 days. It may be doubted whether D "administers" medical treatment by merely giving advice, although doing so might perhaps be "any other lawful act" within s 155. It is even possible that liability could still arise on the basis of breach of a duty at

---

339 A duty was recognised in *R v Lanford and Van Den Wiel* (1993) 69 A Crim R 115; there are conflicting dicta in *R v Phillips* (1971) 45 ALJR 467 at 471, 476, 478, [1971] ALR 740 at 745, 753, 756 (HCA).

340 Cf *R v Plummer* (1844) 1 C & K 600, 174 ER 954 (husband refusing shelter to estranged wife).

341 Cf *R v Mwai*, above n 316.

342 *R v Myatt* [1991] 1 NZLR 674 at 681, (1990) 7 CRNZ 304 at 311 (CA).

343 *R v Collett*, unreported T122/90; cited in the Report of Sir Duncan McMullin to the Minister of Justice, on ss 155 and 156 (1995) at 6.

344 (1916) 86 LJKB 871 (CCA).

common law to refrain from incompetent medical advice.[345] Although s 155 applies only if D "undertakes" to do the relevant act, it is probable that this is satisfied if she chooses to do it, even if there was no antecedent promise or agreement to act, and again, any doubts might be resolved by applying the common law.[346]

Regarding s 156, it will be a question of fact whether D has charge or control of the dangerous thing, and there may be more than one person who shares it. Thus, in *R v Turner*,[347] there was sufficient evidence that a factory was under the charge or control of the factory's general manager and also of the managing director of the company which owned it; the latter not having delegated full control to another, and having continued to direct and guide operations.

In *Turner* the Court of Appeal also said that "anything whatever" had been "deliberately chosen as a phrase of wide import", and that it is to be construed, as in the past, as covering things that are dangerous when in operation as well as things which are inherently dangerous in their static condition.[348] The latter could include, for example, explosives, loaded firearms, toxic substances, exposed electric wiring, and things with hidden defects making them dangerous.[349] But many cases will involve things which are dangerous only when in operation, for example, trams,[350] gigs,[351] cars,[352] and speedboats;[353] or things which are dangerous to some because of surrounding circumstances, for example, an unfenced swimming pool in which a child drowns.[354] It was further held in *Turner* that a thing may endanger human life because the thing itself provides the danger (such as a loaded firearm or an explosive), or because it is operated so as to produce something which may do so: for example, a factory producing food for human consumption (as in *Turner*, where contaminated food had been produced), or a factory or quarry producing fumes, smoke, or rocks.

Section s 11 Summary Offences Act 1981 creates an offence of endangering safety, which applies to things which in the absence of care are "likely to cause injury", not just things which may endanger life. There have been decisions

---

345 Cf *R v Mwai* [1995] 3 NZLR 149, (1995) 13 CRNZ 273 (CA); in *Auckland Area Health Board v A-G* [1993] 1 NZLR 235 at 255, (1992) 8 CRNZ 634 at 655 Thomas J did not doubt that the accused in *Burdee* would have accelerated death within s 164, but did not attempt to identify the basis for manslaughter under the Act. In such a case, if V is competent and aware of the risks there may be doubt on the question of causation.

346 Cf *R v Bateman* (1925) 19 Cr App R 8 at 12, 13, [1925] All ER Rep 45 at 48, 49 (CCA).

347 (1995) 13 CRNZ 142 (CA).

348 Ibid at 149.

349 This list is taken from the judgment of Wylie J in *Hilder v Police* (1989) 4 CRNZ 232 at 235; in *Primrose v Police* (1985) 1 CRNZ 621 it was held that a can of petrol was within s 156 when it was thrown on a fire; perhaps it could be dangerous in its "static state".

350 *R v Dawe* (1911) 30 NZLR 673 (CA).

351 *R v Officer* [1922] GLR 175.

352 *R v Storey* [1931] NZLR 417 (CA).

353 *R v Myatt* [1991] 1 NZLR 674, (1990) 7 CRNZ 304 (CA).

354 *R v Turton (No 2)* (1989) 5 CRNZ 274.

that hold s 11 does not apply when danger is created only because of the manner in which the thing is used.[355] These may be doubted, but in any event such a principle has no application to s 156.

However, it remains possible that "anything whatsoever" in s 156 could be confined to things which are "inherently dangerous" in the sense that there is a danger to life if care is not exercised when they are used for the purpose for which they were designed. This would justify the exclusion of things such as candles and pencils which in unusual cases may be used in such a way that death is an unintended consequence.[356] But the judgment in *Turner* does not encourage any gloss on the terms of s 156, and the better view seems to be that it includes absolutely anything provided that in the circumstances of its use there is a real and reasonably foreseeable risk that it will endanger life if it is used carelessly. Moreover, even if for some reason s 156 does not apply, there is a common law duty of the same kind which may. In *R v Mwai*[357] the Court of Appeal thought that bodily fluid containing the HIV virus was a thing within s 156, imposing on D a duty to exercise care to avoid endangering life (at least without the informed consent of an endangered person), by using a condom if engaging in sexual intercourse. But the Court held that in any event a similar common law duty applied, citing, in particular, *R v Burnett*,[358] where D offended by taking a person infected with smallpox into a public place. Such a case is not within s 156, for while bodily fluid may be "anything", a person could not be.

14.4.2.4(c) Duty to avoid dangerous omissions

Section 157 provides that every one who "undertakes" to do any act, the omission of which is or may be dangerous to life, is criminally responsible for the consequence of omitting, without lawful excuse, to do it. No penalty is provided, but it will be culpable homicide if death results, or an offence under s 190 if injury is caused.

An obligation to do particular acts may arise from the undertaking of a general duty of care. For example, in *R v Crump*[359] a number of boys had drowned in an accident which occurred in the course of activities at a bushcraft camp. D, a camp organiser, was charged with manslaughter, it being alleged that in terms of s 157 he had undertaken the duty of ensuring the safety of the boys, and had failed to do so by omitting to repair the handle of the door of the car in which the boys drowned. (The charge failed, however, because it could not be shown that any of the boys would have escaped had the handle been repaired.) No doubt the required undertaking may be express or implied and

---

355 *Hilder v Police* (1989) 4 CRNZ 232 (power boat and para-flying apparatus not included); *Morley v Police* [1996] 1 NZLR 551 (unicycle not included, but ultimately the reason may have been insufficient likelihood of injury).

356 See *R v McCallum* [1969] Tas SR 73; *R v Dabelstein* [1966] Qd R 411 (CCA), where insertion of such objects in a woman's vagina resulted in death; Cf *Timbu Kolian v R* (1968) 119 CLR 47 at 57, [1969] ALR 143 at 150 (HCA).

357 [1995] 3 NZLR 149 at 156, 157, (1995) 13 CRNZ 273 at 281, 282 (CA).

358 (1815) 4 M & S 271, 105 ER 834.

359 [1970] Recent Law 191.

need not be contractual,[360] although s 157 is based on cases at common law where D was held criminally responsible when death was caused by his omitting to perform a contractual duty, as where a mine shaft was left unprotected or unventilated,[361] a railway signal was not turned on,[362] or a level crossing barrier was left up.[363] Some authority suggested that there was no liability if D owed no duty of care to V,[364] but s 157 does not preserve such a distinction. Holding D responsible to the world at large on the basis of a private contract or undertaking may be justified because, but for D's undertaking, the harm would probably have been prevented by someone else's doing the requisite act.

14.4.2.4(d) Other duties

Even if none of these codified duties applies, liability under s 160(2)(b) may arise if death results from a breach of some other statutory duty,[365] or a duty recognised only at common law (§ 14.4.2.4.). For example, although the law recognises no general duty to save life, there will be a duty to try to rescue V from immediate danger if V is a child under D's care, or is a helpless person for whom D has responsibility.[366] The same might be true if V is endangered as a result of D's act, be it lawful or unlawful, as when D accidentally sets fire to a place where V is.[367] Even if none of the code duties apply, such cases might be within s 160(2)(b).

14.4.2.5 Fault required for manslaughter by omission

The mens rea requirement for involuntary manslaughter by omission has been the subject of important statutory modification by the Crimes Amendment Act 1997. For an understanding of this, it is necessary to say something of the history.

14.4.2.5(a) History: liability for mere negligence

In relation to dangerous activities and dangerous things, the terms of ss 155 and 156 (and their predecessors) impose criminal responsibility for failure to have and to use "reasonable" knowledge, skill, care and precautions. This was held to effect a major departure from the common law.

In civil law (subject to the accident compensation legislation), a person is liable to pay compensation for harm caused by her negligence, and for

---

360 *Adams* § CA157.04.

361 *R v Hughes* (1857) 7 Cox CC 301 (CCA); *R v Haines* (1847) 2 C & K 368, 175 ER 152.

362 *R v Pargeter* (1848) 3 Cox CC 191.

363 *R v Pittwood* (1902) 19 TLR 37; cf *R v Pocock* (1851) 5 Cox CC 172 (undertaking to repair a road).

364 *R v Smith* (1869) 11 Cox CC 210.

365 *R v Foster* (1906) 26 NZLR 1254 (CA); cf the differently worded Tasmanian Code, under which only the Code duties apply to culpable homicide: *R v Phillips* (1971) 45 ALJR 467, [1971] ALR 740 (HCA).

366 Cf *R v Middleship* (1850) 5 Cox CC 227 (CA); *R v Russell* [1933] VLR 59 at 75, 81 [1933] ALR 76 at 83, 86.

367 Cf *R v Miller* [1983] 2 AC 161, [1983] 1 All ER 978 (HL); *Green v Cross* (1910) 103 LT 279; § 2.1.1.2(e).

negligence it suffices that she was in breach of a duty of care and failed to exercise "reasonable" care — the degree of care which would be exercised by a reasonable person. At common law, however, if criminal liability for manslaughter by omission is alleged, such "ordinary" or "civil" negligence is not enough. Instead, there must be "a very high degree" of negligence, or "gross negligence". A leading statement of the rule is in *R v Bateman*,[368] where death had resulted from medical treatment:

> In explaining to juries the test which they should apply to determine whether the negligence, in the particular case, amounted or did not amount to a crime, judges have used many epithets, such as "culpable", "criminal, "gross", "wicked", "clear", "complete". But whatever epithet be used, and whether an epithet be used or not, in order to establish criminal liability the facts must be such that, in the opinion of the jury, the negligence of the accused went beyond a mere matter of compensation between subjects and showed such disregard for the life and safety of others as to amount to a crime against the State and conduct deserving punishment.

This test is somewhat circular, and is exceptional in leaving it to the jury to decide what conduct should be criminal, but was reaffirmed by the House of Lords in *R v Adomako*.[369]

In New Zealand this approach did not in the past apply to ss 155 or 156. In *R v Storey*,[370] it was alleged that D was guilty of manslaughter because his negligent driving of a motor car had caused death. The Court of Appeal held that the statutory requirement of "reasonable" care in what are now ss 155 and 156 meant that the same standard applied as governs civil liability, so that "gross" negligence was unnecessary:

> The standard should be neither too high nor too low: it should be a "reasonable" standard, the standard of skill and care which would be observed by a reasonable man.[371]

Of course, for conviction such negligence had to be proved beyond reasonable doubt, whereas proof on the balance of probability suffices to establish civil liability.

The principle in *Storey* imposed liability if D fell in any way below the standard of knowledge, skill, and care which would be exercised by a reasonable person engaging in the activity.[372] When the activity is dangerous to

---

368 (1925) 19 Cr App R 8 at 11, [1925] All ER Rep 45 at 48 (CCA).

369 [1995] 1 AC 171, [1994] 3 All ER 79 (HL); the fault requirement may be described as "recklessness": *Andrews v DPP* [1937] AC 576, [1937] 2 All ER 552 (HL); but conscious awareness of the risk is not needed, and nor need the definition of "reckless" in *R v Lawrence* [1982] AC 510, [1981] 1 All ER 974 (HL) be used: *Adomako*, disapproving *R v Seymour* [1983] 2 AC 493, [1983] 2 All ER 1058 (HL).

370 [1931] NZLR 417 (CA), approving *R v Dawe* (1911) 30 NZLR 673 (CA).

371 [1931] NZLR 417 at 435 (Myers CJ); an anomalous result was that the fault sufficient for manslaughter was identical to that needed for more recently created offences of causing death by dangerous or negligent driving, although they carry must lesser penalties: see now ss 55 and 56 Transport Act 1962. The explanation was that these offences had been created because juries were reluctant to convict for manslaughter in motoring cases.

372 In the case of medical treatment it will normally suffice that D act "in accordance with a practice accepted at the time as proper by a responsible body of medical opinion, even

life, that is likely to be a demanding standard. The mere fact that D makes a mistake or error of judgment does not *necessarily* mean he was negligent[373] — in all the circumstances a reasonable person might have made it — but often it will suffice to show negligence. Expert witnesses on appropriate standards in dangerous activities will be unwilling to acknowledge mistakes and errors as acceptable, and "reasonable" is liable to be seen as much the same as "ideal".

A lower standard does not apply merely because D lacked appropriate qualifications for the activity, and indeed lack of qualifications may show that even embarking on the activity was negligent.[374] On the other hand, a higher standard does not apply merely because D has special skill or qualifications.[375]

What is "reasonable" will, of course, depend on the circumstances. If D has to make an instant decision in an emergency, this will be important on the question whether an appropriate standard was met, although that is its only significance. Section 155 does not apply "in case of necessity", but the exception does not mean that properly qualified people are not required to exercise reasonable skill and care in an emergency; rather, it may exempt from the duty unqualified or insufficiently qualified people who are required to act in emergencies.[376] Liability under these provisions is determined by an objective test, and, as to awareness, it will be enough that a reasonable person would have been aware of the risk in question, whether or not D was aware of it;[377] but if D knew of the risk because of "special knowledge" there might be liability even if a reasonable person might not have been aware of it.[378]

Storey gave effect to the ordinary meaning of the terms of ss 155 and 156, but the result was that a low degree of fault was enough for conviction of a major crime, making New Zealand law markedly more severe than in most similar jurisdictions where the "gross negligence" requirement applies. Similarly-worded statutes in Canada and Australia have been held not to override the common law standard.[379]

---

though other doctors adopt a different practice": *R v Yogasakaran* [1990] 1 NZLR 399 at 404, (1989) 5 CRNZ 69 at 74 (CA).

373   *Long v R* [1995] 2 NZLR 691 at 694, (1995) 13 CRNZ 124 at 127, 128.

374   *R v Bateman* (1925) 19 Cr App R 8 at 13, [1925] All ER Rep 45 at 49 (CCA); *R v Creighton* [1993] 3 SCR 3 at 72, (1993) 83 CCC (3d) 346 at 392 (SCC); cf *R v Webb* (1834) 1 Moo & R 405, 174 ER 140; *R v Burdee* (1916) 86 LJKB 871 (CA); for dangerous acts, the possession of "reasonable" knowledge and skill is expressly required by s 155.

375   *R v Myatt* [1991] 1 NZLR 674 and 682, (1990) 7 CRNZ 304 at 312 (CA).

376   *R v Yogasakaran* [1990] 1 NZLR 399 at 405, (1989) 5 CRNZ 69 at 74 (CA).

377   Cf *R v Burney* [1958] NZLR 745 (CA); it is submitted that a contrary dictum in *R v Edwards* (1991) 7 CRNZ 510 at 513 cannot be right.

378   Cf *R v Dant* (1865) Le & Ca 567, 169 ER 1517; there is a difference of opinion as to the effect of a drug user's acquired knowledge of the effects of drugs in *R v Creighton* [1993] 3 SCR 3, (1993) 83 CCC (3d) 346 (SCC), although the majority emphasise an unvarying standard of care: cf *R v Myatt* [1991] 1 NZLR 674, (1990) 7 CRNZ 304 (CA).

379   *R v Baker* [1929] 1 DLR 785, (1929) 51 CCC 71, affirmed [1929] 2 DLR 282, [1929] SCR 354 (SCC); *Callaghan v R* (1952) 87 CLR 115, [1952] ALR 941, where the High Court of Australia emphasised that the Court was engaged in interpreting "a criminal code dealing with major crimes involving grave moral guilt".

Nevertheless, *Storey* was reaffirmed in *R v Yogasakaran*.[380] In that case, D was an anaesthetist who caused a patient's death when he injected the wrong drug during an emergency in an operating theatre. He had sought the appropriate drug from a drawer in a trolley where it should have been, but the drawer had been improperly stocked by someone who had put the wrong drug there. D was convicted of manslaughter (although no penalty was imposed) and, there being evidence that D had not complied with normal practice when he injected the drug without having checked the label on its container, the conviction was upheld on appeal. The jury had been directed in accordance with *Storey*, which was approved. The Court of Appeal acknowledged that New Zealand law was more severe than elsewhere, but *Storey* accorded with the natural meaning of the statute, which had been drafted at a time when the common law was at best unsettled on the issue. The Court doubted whether the rule produced "unjust results" in practice (and included the present case in this), noting that its severity was "mitigated" by the need to prove causative negligence beyond reasonable doubt,[381] by the caution to be expected of juries, and by the exceptionally wide discretion the judge has in sentencing.

14.4.2.5(b) History: liability for gross negligence

The rule in *Storey* was held to apply where the applicable statutory provision expressly imposes criminal responsibility for a failure to have and to use "reasonable" knowledge, skill, and care. This is done by ss 155 and 156, but not by the other sections which codify duties, and when these were relied upon gross negligence was required.

In *R v Burney*,[382] D's infant had died from malnutrition and infection from a condition which developed a few days before death, and it was alleged that D had offended against s 151 by failing to obtain medical attention early enough. The Court of Appeal rejected an argument that D was guilty only if she knew of V's need. It was held that, whether the charge be manslaughter or endangering life, negligence was sufficient fault, and that ignorance resulting from negligence did not provide a "lawful excuse". The Court added, however, that this was so only if there was negligence "of a high degree"; for *Storey* (above) applied only when the statute defined the applicable standard of care.[383]

---

380 [1990] 1 NZLR 399, (1989) 5 CRNZ 69 (CA); the Privy Council refused special leave to appeal.

381 When V was already gravely ill there may well be doubt whether error in treatment significantly accelerated death: see, for example, *Long v R* [1995] 2 NZLR 691, (1995) 13 CRNZ 124.

382 [1958] NZLR 745 (CA).

383 Ibid at 753, 754; it was held that there had been sufficient evidence of such negligence, and that a direction that D's omission had to be "neglectful and inexcusable" had been adequate. In *R v Witika* [1993] 2 NZLR 424, (1992) 9 CRNZ 272 at 287, 288 (CA) the Court of Appeal rejected a submission that under s 152 it was necessary that D knew V suffered a "life threatening" condition, and approved a direction that what was required was that D "should have known . . . that there was a serious condition requiring treatment". *Burney* was applied to s 157 in *R v Crump, R v Johnston* [1970] Recent Law 191.

In *R v Walker*,[384] what would suffice under *Burney* was described as "negligence of a sufficiently high degree to incur criminal responsibility". There is no doubt that this is the gross negligence required for manslaughter at common law. In essence, this requires the jury to decide whether D's conduct fell below a reasonable standard to such an extent as to be deserving of punishment.[385] While no particular form of words has to be employed in every case when directing the jury, "reckless" has sometimes been thought to be the most appropriate description of the high degree of negligence required.[386]

When responsibility depends on mere negligence, the fact that D suffered from a disability which limited his capacity to meet a reasonable standard of care will be irrelevant to liability, and the public interest may even prevent it from mitigating penalty.[387] When gross negligence is required it is possible, but uncertain, that such a personal characteristic might have to be taken into account.[388]

Adams[389] was sharply critical of the dicta in *Burney* and *Walker*, going so far as to suggest that they were formulated per incuriam. However, his criticisms overlooked the fact that at common law the requirement of gross negligence has been applied to breach of a duty to act, as well as to other forms of manslaughter by negligence,[390] and while it may seem odd to say that negligence by D may provide a "lawful excuse", it makes sense to say that ignorance or incapacity on D's part provides such an excuse, so long as it does not result from gross negligence. The conclusion might also be rationalised on the basis that in this context, when the statute is silent on the issue, absence of gross negligence is an excuse recognised at common law which is not inconsistent with the statute, so that it is preserved by s 20. In any event, the principle supported in *Burney* has now been confirmed by statute.

14.4.2.5(c) A general requirement of gross negligence

In *R v Yogasakaran*,[391] the Court of Appeal doubted whether in practice unjust results followed from the rule that in the context of dangerous activities mere negligence was sufficient fault for criminal liability. Nevertheless, in 1995 the Minister of Justice requested Sir Duncan McMullin, a retired Judge of the Court of Appeal, to consider and report on whether the standard of care applicable under ss 155 and 156 should be changed. Sir Duncan's investigation led him to

---

384 [1958] NZLR 810 at 815, 816 (CA).

385 § 14.4.2.5.

386 *Andrews v DPP* [1937] AC 576, [1937] 2 All ER 552 (HL); *R v Bonnyman* (1942) 28 Cr App R 131 (CCA); the latter case was cited by the Court in *Burney*, above n 381, 754; cf *R v Adomako* [1995] AC 171, [1994] 3 All ER 79 (HL).

387 *R v Abraham* (1993) 10 CRNZ 446 (CA).

388 Orchard, "Culpable Homicide — II" [1977] NZLJ 447 at 450-453; cf the difference of opinion in *R v Creighton* [1993] 3 SCR 3, (1993) 83 CCC (3d) 346 (SCC); in *R v Holness* [1970] Tas SR 74 age was regarded as relevant.

389 *Adams* (2nd ed) § 1107.

390 For example *R v Nicholls* (1874) 13 Cox CC 75; *R v Lowe* [1973] QB 702, [1973] 1 All ER 805 (CA).

391 [1990] 1 NZLR 399, (1989) 5 CRNZ 69 (CA); see § 14.4.2.5(a).

recommend that the law be brought into line with that of the United Kingdom, Australia, and Canada, by making gross negligence essential to criminal liability for breach of any of the duties codified in the Crimes Act. In his view, mere negligence is not a sufficient degree of fault to justify conviction of such a serious crime as manslaughter; and it was anomalous that simple negligence sufficed under ss 155 and 156, but a high degree of negligence was required when ss 151, 152, 153, or 157 were relied upon, especially as there may be cases falling under both groups of sections. Moreover, although the recommended changes would apply to all dangerous activities, there was some evidence that the severe rule in *Yogasakaran* caused particular problems in the medical context: it might lead to the avoidance of justified but risky surgery ("defensive medicine"), the failure to report information and experience from which others could learn, and might even discourage some from practising medicine in New Zealand.

The recommendations in the McMullin Report have been implemented by the Crimes Amendment Act 1997,[392] s 2 of which inserted s 150A into the Crimes Act:

150A. Standard of care required by persons under legal duties—(1) This section applies in respect of the legal duties specified in any of sections 151, 152, 153, 155, 156, and 157.

(2) For the purposes of the Part, a person is criminally responsible for—

(a) Omitting to discharge or perform a legal duty to which this section applies; or

(b) Neglecting a legal duty to which this section applies—

only if, in the circumstances of the particular case, the omission or neglect is a major departure from the standard of care expected of a reasonable person to whom that legal duty applies in those circumstances.

As is clear from the Report and the explanatory note which accompanied the Bill, the purpose of s 150A(2) is to apply to each of the specified sections the requirement that gross negligence is needed for criminal responsibility. This applies for the purposes of Part VIII of the Act, so that gross negligence will be needed if a breach of any of these duties is relied on to support a charge of manslaughter, endangering under ss 151-153, or injuring contrary to s 190. The requirement will not, however, apply if a breach of one of these duties is the basis of some other charge. In particular, it was intended that the ordinary standard of negligence should apply if such a breach is alleged to result in an offence of criminal nuisance, which under s 145 is punishable by a maximum of one year's imprisonment.[393] Section 145 requires that D "knew" that the act or omission in question "would endanger" another's life, safety, or health, but

---

392 For a highly critical, but perhaps jaundiced, appraisal of this reform, see Dawkins, "Medical Manslaughter" [1997] NZLJ 393.

393 Sir Duncan McMullin had recommended that the gross negligence requirement should also apply to s 145, but this was rejected on the basis that ordinary negligence was not an inappropriate fault requirement for this less serious offence.

even if this requires conscious advertence to the risk[394] it will remain the case that when either s 155 or s 156 applies it will suffice that, with such knowledge, D's conduct fell in any way below the standard of care of a reasonable person.

The formula, "major departure" from the standard of care expected of a reasonable person, was recommended by Sir Duncan McMullin, who suggested that while it would bring New Zealand law into line with other jurisdictions it would also "go a considerable way toward removing any circularity of expression or ambiguity arising out of the use of the term 'gross' negligence".[395] This is puzzling. If the law is brought into line with that of other jurisdictions then, whatever the statutory formula, the test of liability is gross negligence. What that involves has been considered in §§ 14.4.2.5(a) and (b), and in *R v Adomako*[396] the House of Lords concluded that whatever descriptive words are employed, it requires the jury to determine whether the breach of a reasonable standard of care was so bad that it should be judged to be criminal and deserving of punishment. This is an inherently uncertain and somewhat circular question but, it was held, it cannot usefully be made more precise. If the requirement is to be expressed in a single word, "reckless" (in its "ordinary sense") is appropriate.[397] It is submitted that directions to this effect will be appropriate when judges come to explain what is involved in "a major departure" from the standard of a reasonable person.

Section 150A applies only to the legal duties "specified" in ss 151-153 and 155-157 of the Act. As has been seen, however, breach of a common law duty

---

394 Although it is doubtful whether this is essential: it may be that it will suffice if D "knew" of the risk in the sense that she knew it would arise *if* an appropriate level of care was not maintained, even if it is not shown that she was aware that this in fact occurred; cf *R v Turner* (1995) 13 CRNZ 142 (CA), where convictions under s 145 were upheld after danger to life had resulted from failure to exercise reasonable care in the operation of a mussel processing factory in breach of s 156. The Court held that it could be inferred that D "must have known" of the risk (ibid at 159) but the basis of this was also described as conduct which D "should have known" (at 153), or "ought to have" realised (at 160) would endanger life.

395 McMullin, *Report of Sir Duncan McMullin To Hon Douglas Graham, Minister of Justice, On Sections 155 and 156 of the Crimes Act 1961*, Wellington, Dept of Justice 1995, 26; the formula had been previously proposed by the Crimes Consultative Committee, in preference to "very serious deviation" which was used in defining criminal negligence in cl 24 of the Crimes Bill 1989, although the Consultative Committee did not recommend applying this to ss 155 and 156. On the other hand, the Criminal Law Reform Committee, in *Report on Culpable Homicide* Wellington, Criminal Law Reform Committee, 1976, 38, recommended that gross negligence should be required in cases within these sections.

396 [1995] 1 AC 171 at 187, [1994] 3 All ER 79 at 89 (HL).

397 Ibid; in this context "reckless" does not require actual awareness of the risk of killing, and in *Adomako* it was held not to be necessary to use the definition in *R v Lawrence* [1982] AC 510, [1981] 1 All ER 974 (HL), rejecting *R v Seymour* [1983] 2 AC 493, [1983] 2 All ER 1058 (HL). *Lawrence* would render D "reckless" if D gave no thought to an obvious and serious risk of injuring another. That would not necessarily involve gross negligence in relation to causing death, and the use of such a definition is likely to be a misdirection, and not merely unnecessary.

may support a charge of culpable homicide.[398] It is implicit in *R v Burney* that in such a case gross negligence has always been required, and this will continue to be the case.

14.4.2.6 *Lawful excuse*

Each of the provisions in Part VIII of the Act which imposes criminal responsibility for omissions requires that D's conduct be "without lawful excuse". The courts have not attempted a comprehensive definition of this phrase,[399] although in *R v Burney*[400] it was said that "it is of the essence of a defence of lawful excuse that the exculpatory reason put forward must be shown to be lawful in its nature, and not to have an unlawful origin." On the other hand, what is required is an "excuse", not a "justification", and this might mean that D may be freed from responsibility even though his conduct was in some sense improper.[401] Indeed, the express terms of ss 155 and 156 allow the possibility of lawful excuse notwithstanding that D has failed to exercise reasonable care, and s 150A(2) (above) imposes a requirement which is additional to those established by the terms of the ensuing sections.

It may be that "lawful excuse" will include any of the general defences (such as impossibility, insanity, automation, self-defence, or defence of property). Their availability, however, is not dependant on such a provision, and the provision is not confined to such cases. It appears to allow a defence in at least two further types of case.

First, D may have been subject to one of the duties and may have failed to perform it in ignorance of the circumstances which required further care or action. When the fault expressly required for any criminal responsibility was an absence of reasonable knowledge and care, such ignorance could excuse if it was reasonable in the circumstances, but in *R v Burney*[402] it was accepted that in other cases it could also excuse provided it did not arise from a high degree of negligence. This result, however, is now achieved more directly by s 150A(2). Moreover, under s 150A(2) the burden of proof will lie on the prosecution, although it may be otherwise when "lawful excuse" is relied upon.[403]

Secondly, D may be aware of the relevant circumstances, and may fail to do what is required by the duty, perhaps deliberately, but there may be circumstances which the court accepts as exculpatory, having regard to the terms and objects of the legislation.

---

398 § 14.4.2.4.

399 *Wong Pooh Yin v Public Prosecutor* [1955] AC 93 at 100, [1954] 3 All ER 31 at 34 (PC).

400 [1958] NZLR 745 at 753, 754 (CA).

401 Cf *R v McFall* (1975) 26 CCC (2d) 181 at 184, 202 (BCCA).

402 [1958] NZLR 745 (CA), § 14.4.2.5(b).

403 *Burney*, ibid at 753. If D does have the burden of proving "lawful excuse", proof on the balance of probabilities will be needed: for example *Sheehan v Police* [1994] 3 NZLR 592, (1994) 12 CRNZ 39. This question also increases the importance of the dubious assumption that general defences are incorporated in the formula: cf *Summary Proceedings*, Wellington, Brooker's, 1994, § SO29.07. For general discussion of the burden of proof in relation to such an "exception" see Orchard, "The Golden Thread — Somewhat Frayed" (1988) 6 Otago LR 615; and see *R v Rangi* [1992] 1 NZLR 385 (CA).

Such circumstances may sometimes rebut an allegation of absence of reasonable care,[404] and at common law they may mean there is no duty to act. They may also be regarded as providing a "lawful excuse". For example, in *R v Mwai*[405] D was held to be in breach of s 156 when, being infected with HIV, he had sexual intercourse without a condom and without revealing his condition. The Court of Appeal said that had he disclosed his condition, so that his partner consented to the risk, it was "certainly arguable" that there would be no further duty to avoid the danger. An alternative view would be that such informed consent would provide a "lawful excuse". That is perhaps a preferable analysis, in that the terms of s 156 do not recognise exceptions to the existence of the duty, and it avoids the need to decide whether "reasonable" precautions or care have been taken, and whether there was a "major departure" from the standard of a reasonable person.[406]

Further examples arise from cases concerning the withdrawal or non-provision of life-prolonging medical treatment. Subject to statutory exceptions, everyone has the right to refuse medical treatment,[407] if she has the mental capacity to make a true choice.[408] Such refusal will undoubtedly provide a "lawful excuse" for not providing treatment which is needed if death is to be avoided. In other cases, modern developments in medicine and technology have led to a recognition that duties to prolong life are not absolute. In some cases a patient may be alive but unable to chose or communicate a choice. Here, although death will quickly follow, it may sometimes be lawful to withdraw life supporting treatment. This will be so if the patient is in a persistent vegetative state and is non-sentient, or is in a closely analogous state, with no hope of recovery, so that there is no medical or therapeutic benefit from maintaining the treatment, and it does not advance the patient's best interests to do so.[409] Even if a fully sentient patient (or those lawfully acting for

---

404 Cf *R v Yogasakaran* [1990] 1 NZLR 399 at 405, (1989) 5 CRNZ 69 at 74 (CA) where the Court held that the exception of cases of "necessity" in s 155 did not free a qualified person from the duty to exercise reasonable care when action in an emergency was required; it is implicit that the mere fact of an emergency would not provide a "lawful excuse" either, although the Court recognised that it would be a "major factor" to be considered in deciding whether the "appropriate professional standard" had been met.

405 [1995] 3 NZLR 149 at 156, (1995) 13 CRNZ 273 at 282 (CA).

406 The consent contemplated in *Mwai* would involve consenting to a risk of an infection which could cause death; it appears to be implicit that this would not be "consent to the infliction of death" within the meaning of s 63.

407 Section 11 New Zealand Bill of Rights Act 1990.

408 Cf *B v Croydon Health Authority* [1995] 1 All ER 683 at 689, [1995] 2 WLR 294 at 299 (CA); parents may also lawfully refuse consent to life prolonging treatment of a child if it is not in the child's "best interests": *Re T (a minor) (wardship: medical treatment)* [1997] 1 All ER 906 (CA).

409 See, for example, *Auckland Area Health Board v A-G* [1993] 1 NZLR 235, (1992) 8 CRNZ 634; *Airedale NHS Trust v Bland* [1993] AC 789, [1993] 1 All ER 821 (HL); the High Court has jurisdiction to declare the withdrawal to be lawful if specified conditions are met (see *Auckland Area Health Board v A-G*); alternatively, in New Zealand it has jurisdiction to confirm the lawfulness of it by consenting on behalf of the patient: *In the Matter of G* 13/12/96, Fraser J, HC Dunedin M126/96.

him) desires treatment, which is necessary if there is to be a chance of survival, it may nevertheless be lawful for health providers to decline to treat, if in conformity with standards and practices commanding general approval within the medical profession a clinical judgment is made in good faith that the treatment is not in the patient's best interests.[410] In assessing the patient's best interests the doctors may take into account pain that the treatment would involve, its prospects of success, and the likely quality of life that would result. Moreover, since resources are finite, it may be that the courts will be unable to avoid the conclusion that even if an individual's "best interests" might favour treatment, its withdrawal may be lawful if a bona fide clinical judgment is made in accordance with generally accepted medical standards and practice that it is not appropriate, having regard to the needs of others who depend on the provider's resources.[411]

14.4.2.7 *Killing by unlawful act and omission*

Section 160(2)(c) expressly provides that homicide is culpable if it consists of killing by a combination of an unlawful act and omission to comply with a legal duty. There is an absence of authority on this paragraph, which may be unnecessarily included, simply owing to an abundance of caution. It perhaps prevents an argument that, if D injures V by an unlawful act, the chain of causation is necessarily broken if V's death might have been avoided had T not failed without lawful excuse to discharge a duty to provide the necessaries of life to V.

14.5 INFANTICIDE

As has been mentioned,[412] in some other jurisdictions there is a partial defence of diminished responsibility, under which murder is reduced to manslaughter if D suffers such abnormality of mind as substantially impaired his mental responsibility. There is no such general defence in New Zealand, but a form of it applies in some cases where a mother who has not fully recovered from the effects of giving birth kills a child. Infanticide is provided for by s 178, and is both a substantive offence and a defence to charges of murder and manslaughter. It is derived from English legislation,[413] and allows for substantial leniency.

---

410 *Shortland v Northland Health Ltd* 10/11/97, CA230/97. The Court said that in these circumstances Northland Health was not "in breach of its duty" under s 151, and that the "extent of the duty" to provide necessaries has to be assessed in the context of a particular case. This perhaps suggests that at least some instances of "lawful excuse" will have the effect that the duty ceases to exist.

411 Cf *R v Cambridge Health Authority, ex p B* [1995] 2 All ER 129, [1995] 1 WLR 898 (CA); in *Shortland v Northland Health Ltd*, ibid, no issue of resource allocation arose, although the Court did comment that the doctors must decide what is best for the patient "in clinical terms and within the resources available".

412 § 14.1.

413 Infanticide Act 1938 (UK), which replaced the Infanticide Act 1922 (UK); for the history, see Seaborne Davies, "Child-Killing in English Law" (1937) 1 MLR 203; O'Donovan, "The Medicalisation of Infanticide" [1984] Crim LR 259.

14.5.1 Scope of infanticide

Section 178(1) provides that:

> Where a woman causes the death of any child of hers under the age of 10 years in a manner that amounts to culpable homicide, and where at the time of the offence the balance of her mind was disturbed, by reason of her not having fully recovered from the effect of giving birth to that or any other child, or by reason of the effect of lactation . . . to such an extent that she should not be held fully responsible, she is guilty of infanticide, and not of murder or manslaughter, and is liable to imprisonment for a term not exceeding 3 years.

The liability of other parties is not affected: s 178(8). The verdict may be returned on a charge of infanticide, or when murder or manslaughter is charged and the evidence supports a finding of infanticide: s 178(2). The dual role of infanticide as an offence and a defence leads to an anomaly in relation to the burden of proof. If D is charged with murder or manslaughter, she will be entitled to a finding of infanticide if there is a sufficient evidential foundation for it, which leaves the jury in reasonable doubt, but if infanticide is charged the prosecution will have the burden of proving all its requirements beyond reasonable doubt.[414] This may be a difficult burden and, if a charge of infanticide is to be defended, consideration may have to be given to charging manslaughter, or even murder, in the alternative.

Infanticide under s 178 is wider than the English equivalent in three significant respects. It extends to the killing of a child under the age of 10 years (rather than under 12 months), the child killed need not be the child whose birth caused mental disturbance, and the child killed need not be a natural child of the mother. Section 178 may apply when D kills "any child of hers", and in *R v P*[415] Heron J interpreted this as including any child "who can, in fact and law and common sense, be said to be hers", not just her natural child. Whether V was such a child will be "largely a question of fact", depending on the particular circumstances "and no doubt the family and social customs of the time". Heron J accepted that it would not suffice that D had temporary care of the child, but *P* was a clear case for the application of s 178: V had been a 5-year-old whom D had cared for as a mother for some 2½ years, and indeed D had been granted custody and appointed guardian of V by the Family Court.

For infanticide to be established, the child must have been alive when D did something which might have caused death.[416] Moreover, a mistaken belief that the child was dead might preclude a finding of infanticide, for it will mean that D did not have the mens rea needed for assault, or, in all probability, culpable homicide (and therefore infanticide) by an unlawful act.[417] In New Zealand, as in England, the legislation is expressed in terms confined to a case where a

---

414 *Adams* § CA178.04.

415 [1991] 2 NZLR 116, (1991) 7 CRNZ 48.

416 Cf s 181, which provides for the offence of concealing the dead body of a child; this requires proof that the child was dead when D acted.

417 *R v G* (1984) 1 CRNZ 275, where such a belief arose from dissociation consequent on child birth; in appropriate cases there might perhaps be culpable homicide on the basis of negligent omission to fulfil a legal duty: *Adams* § CA171.10.

child has been killed. If the child survived, s 178 could have no application to a charge of assault or injury, but in England it has been held that there can be a conviction of attempted infanticide.[418] This would allow appropriate mitigation of what would otherwise be attempted murder, when infanticide was the offence which was in truth intended. However, it contrasts with the prevailing view that provocation is no defence to attempted murder.[419]

14.5.2 Insanity

The fact that the balance of D's mind was disturbed as a result of having given birth will not generally mean that D was insane. However, s 178(3) provides for acquittal "on account of insanity caused by childbirth" if the requirements of s 178(1) are met "to the extent that she was insane". The section goes on to make special provision for the effect of such a verdict, which is similar to the effect of other verdicts of insanity, although s 178(4)(b) requires that D be discharged from custody if two doctors certify that D is no longer insane and has no need for care and treatment in a hospital.

In *R v O'Callaghan*,[420] Quilliam J held that the defence available under s 178(3) is insanity as defined in s 23, although the subsection establishes that the effects of childbirth may be a disease of the mind within s 23. For a finding of insanity, the further requirements of s 23 will have to be satisfied, and D will have the burden of proof. Quilliam J further held that although s 178(3) is expressed to apply "upon the trial" of a woman for infanticide, murder, or manslaughter, it should be read as also applying to a change of attempted murder, although not to alternative charges of assault or injury (to which s 23 alone could apply). This is a complex result, and the interpretation may be doubted.

14.5.3 Conclusion

Depression after childbirth is common, and even psychoses or dissociation may occur,[421] but it is widely thought that the killing of a child is more likely to be the result of social and emotional pressures or personality disorder.[422] In theory, these latter factors will not suffice for s 178 to apply, although sympathy for the mother's plight may mean that the required mental disturbance will readily be found. Retention of the offence/defence (without any special insanity rule) was favoured by the Crimes Consultative Committee, who noted that abolition "would significantly increase the potential penalty for this class of offender, although it is plain enough that a degree of leniency would continue to be extended in practice".[423]

---

418 *R v KA Smith* [1983] Crim LR 739; cf *R v O'Callaghan* (1984) 1 CRNZ 185 at 186.

419 § 14.4.1, n 120.

420 (1984) 1 CRNZ 185.

421 Cf *R v G* (1984) 1 CRNZ 275.

422 Williams, *TBCL*, 694, 695, O'Donovan, "The Medicalisation of Infanticide" [1984] Crim LR 259.

423 Crimes Consultative Committee, *Crimes Bill 1989: Report of the Consultative Committee presented to the Minister of Justice April 1991*, Wellington, Dept of Justice, 1991, 54.

15

Non-fatal Offences of Violence

In this chapter we consider those offences involving the infliction of a physical harm to the person, falling short of murder or manslaughter. Because assault is an included element in many of these offences, we commence our discussion with an analysis of assault, and will consider the other offences in ascending degrees of seriousness. Although "person" by definition includes corporate and unincorporated associations which could conceivably be guilty of committing some of these offences either as principals or parties,[1] in the present context "person" will be limited to human subjects. This limitation excludes unborn children; abortion and related offences will not be considered in the present context.

15.1 ASSAULT

Assault covers a broad range of human conduct. At one end of the scale it may include an unconsented-to kiss on the cheek,[2] while at the other end it may include a grievous physical attack, falling short of murder or manslaughter but nonetheless resulting in severe injury to the victim. However, while such injury is a common feature of many assaults, injury is by no means a *necessary* requirement for an assault at law. This is because under New Zealand law the separate common law concepts of "assault" and "battery" have been incorporated into the unitary concept of "assault". An assault in New Zealand *may* include a battery, which consists of the actual application of unlawful force to another. However, an assault may also consist simply of a *threat* by one person to inflict unlawful force on another, regardless whether the person threatening actually delivers on the threat by physically attacking the victim; provided the assault is accompanied by a relevant "act" or "gesture". In New Zealand, words alone cannot amount to an assault.[3] However, if A, walking down one side of the street, gesticulates in a threatening manner while calling out to B, on the other side of the road, and threatens to "punch your lights out", that will be a relevant assault if A has the ability to deliver on the threat or causes B to believe on reasonable grounds that he has that ability. In *Fogden v Wade*,[4] it was held that walking towards a woman at night and making indecent suggestions to her may constitute an assault. In that case the accused

---

1   Section 2 Crimes Act 1961.

2   *Police v Bannin* [1991] 2 NZLR 237 at 244, (1991) 7 CRNZ 55 at 62; *Hughes v Callaghan* [1933] GLR 330.

3   But compare *R v Wilson* [1955] 1 All ER 744, [1955] 1 WLR 493, 39 Cr App Rep 12 (CCA) ("get out the knives").

4   [1945] NZLR 725.

had not merely spoken to the woman but had moved towards her and she thought that she was about to be molested.

An assault on the basis of threats and gestures alone is possible because of the way in which assault is defined in the Crimes Act 1961. According to s 2:

> Assault means the act of intentionally applying or attempting to apply force to the person of another, directly or indirectly, or threatening by any other act or gesture to apply such force to the person of another, if the person making the threat has, or causes the other to believe on reasonable grounds that he has the present ability to effect his purpose . . .

The definition creates four varieties of assault:

(i)   An application of (direct or indirect) force to another;

(ii) An attempted application of (direct or indirect) force to another;

(iii) A threat (involving an act or gesture) to apply force to another, where D has the present ability to apply such force;

(iv) A threat (involving an act or gesture) to apply force to another, which causes V to believe on reasonable grounds that D has the present ability to apply such force.

The effect of this definition is that, for assault, the threat in case (iii) need not be communicated to the victim. In *R v Kerr*,[5] where the accused was seen by a third person to approach within a few feet of the victim while holding an axe at waist level, it was held that it made no difference that the victim was unaware of the threatening display, because the state of mind of the recipient of the threatening act or gesture need not be a relevant consideration. This is in contrast to the position at common law, where there must be some threatening act sufficient to raise in the mind of the person threatened a fear of immediate violence.[6] However, it would seem that at both common law and in New Zealand there could be no assault if the threat is made, for example, to strike a person with a fist, at such a distance that it was impossible for the blow to strike the victim, or where a firearm is aimed at a range to which the bullet could not possibly carry.[7] In New Zealand, a conviction for assault in such circumstances would be impossible because the accused would lack the "present ability to effect his purpose" and there would be no objective basis for the putative victim to believe that the accused has that ability.

Where there have been threats accompanied by relevant acts or gestures, the threats need only cause the person threatened to believe on reasonable grounds that the threatener has the ability to effect his purpose — even if he does not in fact have that present ability. On this basis, pointing an unloaded gun at another person may constitute an assault if a reasonable person would have believed that it was loaded and the accused had the present capacity to use it to kill or injure.[8] By contrast, where an allegation of assault is based

---

5   [1988] 1 NZLR 270, (1987) 2 CRNZ 407 (CA).

6   *Halsbury's Laws of England*, vol 11(1), (4th ed reissue), § 488.

7   Ibid.

8   See *R v St George* (1840) 9 C & P 483, 173 ER 921.

simply on D's conduct it is D's ability as the threatener to carry out her threats that will be determinative. In *Stephens v Myers*, Tindall CJ said:

> It is not every threat, where there is no actual personal violence, that constitutes an assault, there must, in all cases, be the means of carrying the threat into effect.[9]

15.1.1 Mens rea

At common law, an assault may be committed intentionally or recklessly. In *R v Venna*,[10] it was held that a physical injury inflicted deliberately *or* recklessly on a constable attempting to arrest the accused constituted the offence of assault occasioning actual bodily harm. The accused had lashed out with his legs and injured the hand of a constable who was trying to pick him up after falling or being knocked to the ground. The English Court of Appeal held that there was no reason "in logic or in law" why a person who recklessly applies physical force to the person of another should be outside the criminal law of assault.

However, in New Zealand s 2(1) requires that the act of applying, attempting to apply, or threatening to apply force to the person of another must be done "intentionally". Recklessness will not suffice. This would imply that if, assuming the facts in *Venna*, D had lashed out with his feet, knowing the arresting officer was close to him and knowing that by lashing out he would probably kick the officer, D could not in New Zealand be guilty of any offence requiring proof of an assault. An intentional application of force to the person of another (or an intentional attempt to do so) must be proved before an accused can be guilty of an assault within the definition of s 2(1).[11]

It follows that an accidental or fortuitous application of force will not suffice. Similarly, generalised threats unrelated to a particular victim will not amount to assault simply because they happen to cause alarm. Thus if D, while in a drunken state, begins to shout loudly and issue broad, non-specific threats ("I'm going to shoot you all") while walking down the street unarmed, he cannot be convicted of assaulting V, who is alarmed by the threats, because he lacks both the intention to apply force and the present ability to carry out the threats.

Neither could D be guilty of assault if, seeing V lying in the gutter, he were to kick her inert body while believing that she was dead. Even if V was conscious and affected emotionally by D's acts, there would be no assault because there must be an intention to apply force to, or to threaten, a living person. A belief that the victim is dead will negate the requisite intent.[12]

There is no assault where the threatening gesture is accompanied by words indicating that there is no intention to carry out the threat. In *Tuberville v*

---

9   (1830) 4 C & P 349, 172 ER 735.

10   [1976] QB 421, [1975] 3 All ER 788 (CA).

11   Of course, reckless conduct may be an important evidential factor from which the relevant intention may be inferred: *R v Young* 9/7/92, CA86/92.

12   *R v G* (1984) 1 CRNZ 275 at 280.

Savage[13] a man who had put his hand menacingly on his sword and said, "If it were not assize time, I'd run you through the body", was held not to have committed an assault. His words showed that he did not intend to assault the victim, despite his menacing gesture.

15.1.1.1 *Transferred malice*

Where a person, intending to apply force to one person, unintentionally strikes another, two offences of assault may have been committed. There could be an *attempted* assault on the intended victim and assault by the application of force on the second person, through the doctrine of transferred malice. In *R v Latimer*, Lord Coleridge CJ stated:

> It is common knowledge that a man who has an unlawful and malicious intent against another, and, in attempting to carry it out, injures a third person, is guilty of what the law deems malice against the person injured, because the offender is doing an unlawful act, and has that which judges call general malice.[14]

Where D does an act intending to cause injury to or at least to assault someone, but has no particular victim in mind (for example, if he simply fires a gun into a crowded supermarket), he may be charged with wounding with intent or injuring with intent. If D wounds V mistakenly believing him to be P, he may still be guilty of wounding V with intent.[15] He intended to wound a human being: the mistake is irrelevant.

However, the doctrine of transferred malice does not extend to the situation where D intends to commit one offence but commits a totally different offence; for example, when he throws a stone at a window for the purposes of criminal damage which misses and hits V by mistake.[16] The element of intent to assault or injure a human being, necessary for an assault, would be lacking and recklessness if established would, in any event, be insufficient mens rea for an assault in New Zealand.

15.1.2 Force

The statutory expression "force to the person of another" has been given a wide interpretation both at common law and under the Crimes Act 1961. "Force" does not necessarily imply violence and it is not necessary for violence to be established under an assault charge.[17] Force, like violence, involves a gradation of physical conduct from one end of the spectrum to the other. While the use of force may include the exercise of physical power to inflict physical injury or

---

13 (1669) 1 Mod R 3, 86 ER 684.

14 (1886) 17 QBD 359.

15 *R v Smith* (1855) 1 Dears 559, 169 ER 845; *R v Stopford* (1870) 11 Cox CC 643. See also *R v Mc Masters* [1920] GLR 351; *Chandler v R* 10/2/93, Greig J, HC Napier AP4/93. For further discussion of transferred mens rea, see § 3.7.

16 See *R v Pembliton* (1874) 12 Cox CC 607.

17 *R v Raponi* (1989) 5 CRNZ 291 at 296. See also *R v Terewi* (1985) 1 CRNZ 623, where "force" was held to include a threat to use physical power, so that self-defence is available against threats as well as against actual force.

damage to persons, that degree of force is not *necessary* for an assault. In *Raponi* Wylie J said:

> A mere touching can amount to an assault . . . [A] pat on the bottom or a kiss can be an assault, the mere brushing of some part of a person's body can be an assault . . .[18]

However, the reason why such conduct amounts to an assault is not simply because it involves an element of force, but also because the physical conduct is unlawful. Unlawfulness will turn on whether the physical contact was consented to, and whether the accused intended to act in a manner that is unlawful. Touching someone in order to attract their attention, or as a social greeting, or in the course of conversation, or while standing in a crowded bus or train, are all physical contacts that are normal aspects of daily living. They are not unlawful, either because there is an implied consent to such activity or because there is a general exception embracing all physical contact which is generally acceptable in the ordinary conduct of daily life.[19] So merely tapping a person on the shoulder to get their attention is "a trivial interference with a citizen's liberty" and not an assault.[20] For there to be an assault the prosecution must establish that the defendant's intention in applying force was such that the force was unlawful.[21]

However, where such an intent is present, the least touching of another person, whether or not in anger, will amount to an assault. The amount of force used is immaterial.[22] Thus a tap on the shoulder which is known to be unwanted would be an assault. The breadth of this principle is said to reflect the fundamental nature of the interest so protected.[23]

> [T]he law cannot draw the line between different degrees of violence, and therefore totally prohibits the first and lowest stage of it; every man's person being sacred, and no other having a right to meddle with it, in the slightest manner.[24]

The effect is that everybody is protected not only against physical injury but against any form of physical molestation.

At common law it was sometimes stated that a battery could only be committed where the action was "angry, or vengeful, or rude or insolent",[25] effectively a requirement that the conduct be "hostile". However, this would no longer seem to be a formal requirement, the better view being, as already noted, that the accused's conduct must be intentional and without consent or

---

18   Ibid.

19   *Collins v Wilcock* [1984] 3 All ER 374 at 378, (1984) 79 Cr App R 229 at 234.

20   *Donnelly v Jackman* 1970] 1 All ER 987, [1970] 1 WLR 562.

21   See *R v Kimber* [1983] 3 All ER 316 at 319, (1983) 77 Cr App R 225 at 229 (Lawton LJ).

22   See *Cole v Turner* (1704) Mod 149, 87 ER 907: "The least touching of another in anger is a battery" (Holt CJ). See also *Police v Bannin* [1991] 2 NZLR 237 at 244, (1991) 7 CRNZ 55 at 62.

23   *Collins v Wilcock* (1984) 79 Cr App R 229 at 234, [1984] 3 All ER 374 at 378.

24   *3 Blackstone's Commentaries* 120.

25   See Hawkins 1 PC, chapter 62, s 2.

other justification.[26] At this end of the spectrum the practical distinction between conduct which is lawful and unlawful may be between conduct which is broadly acceptable according to social convention and conduct which is unnecessarily intrusive and may properly be called "rude" or "insulting".[27] However, conduct which might otherwise be regarded as a "meddling" in the autonomy of another person, may still be lawful if it is done bona fide for the purpose of offering consolation or comfort.[28]

15.1.2.1 *"Applying" force*

Because the definition of assault requires an act of intentionally "applying" force to another person, using force to pull away from another person falls outside the concept of applying force, and will not constitute an assault.[29] (However, if D, by pulling himself free from an unlawful arrest by P, causes P's death, his conduct may still constitute manslaughter.[30]) If the alleged assault goes no further than a "bracing and leaning of a body to resist a push" that action may not of itself constitute the direct or indirect application of force necessary for an assault;[31] although if the facts show that the accused physically thrust his body forward, thereby forcing the victim back, that would constitute an assault.[32]

15.1.3 Assault by omission

Because the definition of assault requires an "act" of the accused, the commonly-held view is that an assault cannot be committed by a simple omission.[33] We have already expressed doubt about this interpretation.[34] At common law there is some authority for the view that the word "assault" does not necessarily imply an assault, though it may be narrower than "cause" in requiring the causation of some physical impact upon the body of another. This could occur where, for example, the victim is caused to jump out of a window or run into some protruding object.[35] In *Wilson* the Court of Appeal held that "infliction" of grievous bodily harm may occur without an actual assault, for example, where the accused has done something intentionally which, though not a direct application of force to the body of the victim, does directly result in

---

26 *T v T* [1988] Fam 52 at 64-67; *R v Brown* [1994] 1 AC 212 at 244, [1993] 2 All ER 75, 90 (HL). See also *Hughes v Callaghan* [1933] GLR 330 (kissing a 4-year-old girl on the cheek without her consent held to be an assault even though act was not " indecent, violent or hostile").
27 *Hughes v Callaghan* [1933] GLR 330 at 331.
28 Ibid.
29 *R v Sherriff* [1969] Crim LR 260.
30 See *R v Porter* (1873) 12 Cox CC 444.
31 *Mitchell v Police* (1989) 5 CRNZ 190.
32 Ibid at 191.
33 See, for example, *Adams* § CA196.10.
34 § 2.1.1.3.
35 See *R v Wilson* [1983] 1 All ER 993; *R v Jenkins* [1983] 1 All ER 1000, (1983) 76 Cr App R 313 (CA).

force being applied to the victim's body, so that she suffers harm.[36] There would seem to be no reason in principle why the statutory requirement for an "act" must be construed narrowly to exclude the possibility of assault by omission. Indeed, to insist on this requirement produces anomalies in the law. It has, for example, been held that if D digs a pit with the intention that P should fall into it, and he does, that is an assault.[37] Similarly, if D is sitting in a corridor and anticipating the arrival of P who is running towards him, puts out his leg with the intention that P should trip over it, and he does, that would clearly be an assault.[38] Smith asks:

> Should it not equally be an assault if D, having dug the pit with no criminal intention, decides to leave it uncovered so that P will fall into it, which he does. Or if D's legs are already extended and he decides not to draw them back, so that P will fall over them?[39]

By analogy with the reasoning in cases such as *Wilson* (above), if it were accepted that "act" in s 2 simply means "conduct" and includes both acts ("willed muscular movements") and omissions, the concept of "apply[ing]" force could also be given an extended meaning to include not only the physical application of force but also conduct which results in force being applied to the victim's body. Such an approach would avoid the necessity of adopting the legal fiction of a "continuing act" to transform a simple omission into a relevant "act" for the purposes of establishing liability for an assault.[40] The approach would also, it is submitted, make better sense of the concept of applying force "indirectly", which is particularly apt to describe the results that occur when someone omits to perform a particular duty.

15.1.3.1 *Directly or indirectly*

Many unlawful acts may be committed through the innocent agency of other persons or objects. This is especially true of assault, for which there is no requirement that the accused must actually touch the body of another. Whereas an assault by direct application of force implies that the person who intended the application of that force was the same person who actually applied it by the use of his body, an assault by the indirect application of force implies that the person who intended the application of force gave effect to his intention through some instrumentality *apart* from his person.[41]

The case law is littered with examples of indirectly caused assaults. They include causing a victim to suffer an impact by knocking away another

---

36 See *R v Salisbury* [1976] VR 452, cited with approval in *R v Wilson* [1983] 1 All ER 993 at 998.

37 *R v Clarence* (1888) 22 QBD 23 (Wills J).

38 Smith, *Liability for Omissions in the Criminal Law* (unpublished paper), 16.

39 Ibid. Of course, where the assault is by omission (as in this example), criminal liability would follow only if D is under a legal duty to prevent the assault from occurring (for example, if D is P's parent). For discussion, see § 2.1.1ff.

40 See *Fagan v Metropolitan Police Commr* [1969] 1 QB 439, [1969] 3 All ER 442; § 2.1.1.2(d).

41 *R v S* [1994] DCR 76.

supporting person or object,[42] striking a horse so that its rider is thrown,[43] causing people to be crushed by creating a crowd panic,[44] and pouring acid into a machine which squirts it on to the victim when the victim activates the machine.[45] Similarly, if D, while walking down the street, deliberately "shoulders" P causing her crash into V, who falls and is injured, D would be guilty of two assaults, one by "directly" applying force to P and the other by "indirectly" applying force to V (assuming he intended to apply force unlawfully to both). P would be both the innocent agent through whom the assault on V is committed as well as the object of a direct assault. In *R v S*[46] it was held to be an assault where S caused an 8-year-old boy to jab himself with a pencil. Liability was determined on the basis of an intentional application of force, indirectly via the medium of an innocent agent, against "the person of another" — who happened to be the innocent agent himself.[47]

15.1.4 Consent

At common law, assault and battery are defined so as to require only the threat or application of "unlawful" force. This means that wherever the act charged is in itself unlawful, it is unnecessary to prove absence of consent by the victim in order to convict the offender.[48] However, as we have already seen, there may be many acts which in themselves are harmless and lawful, and which become unlawful only if they are done without the consent of the person affected. An innocent act of familiarity or affection in one case may, in another, be an assault for the simple reason that consent was known to be absent. Where, in such a case, there is a reasonable possibility that V consented, the onus of negativing consent lies on the prosecution. Unless a jury is satisfied beyond reasonable doubt that the victim did not consent, the accused is entitled to an acquittal.[49]

Since the mens rea of assault is intention, the prosecution must also prove that the defendant *intended to apply force to the person of the victim without his consent*. If she did not intend the whole of this italicised phrase — and in particular, if she did not realise he had not consented — she is entitled to an acquittal, and the prosecution will have failed to prove the charge. In respect of ordinary assaults, it is the defendant's subjective belief, not the grounds on which it was based, which goes to negative the intent.[50]

---

42   *R v McMasters* [1920] GLR 351. The accused was charged with assaulting his wife and child after he knocked his wife down with his hand when she was carrying the baby. It was conceded that he had not intended to hit the child and since assault may not be committed recklessly, it is unclear what was the actual basis for liability.

43   *Dodwell v Burford* (1661) 1 Mod 24, 86 ER 703.

44   *R v Martin* (1881) 8 QBD 54.

45   *DPP v K (A minor)* [1990] 1 WLR 1067, (1990) 91 Cr App R 23.

46   [1994] DCR 76.

47   Ibid at 84.

48   *R v Donovan* [1934] 2 KB 498 at 507.

49   Ibid. See also *R v May* [1912] 3 KB 572.

50   See *R v Kimber* [1983] 1 WLR 1118 at 1121, 1122; also the discussion of intention and circumstances at §§ 3.1.5, 3.4.

15.1.4.1 *Withdrawal of the consent defence*

We have noted that the statutory definition of assault in s 2(1) does not make any reference to consent. Nor is consent part of the definition of other assault crimes where consent might, conceivably, be a defence.[51] Rather, because consent is a common law justification, excuse, or defence, it is preserved by s 20 to the extent that it is not inconsistent with the offence charged. Appropriately, such inconsistency with the language of the statutory offence will not be readily found if the particular provision charged is one where consent has traditionally been available as a defence, and where to remove the issue of consent from the jury would be to remove the only real issue and amount to a direction to convict. In *R v B*,[52] the accused faced alternative charges of sexual violation and indecent assault of his 17-year-old intellectually impaired granddaughter. The trial Judge withdrew the defence of belief in consent on the charges of indecent assault, not because the complainant was incapable of consenting, but on the grounds of public policy, maintaining that as one of "the most vulnerable of all members of society", the complainant was entitled to protection from sexual predation. However, the Court of Appeal considered that the trial Judge had gone too far in this ruling and considered that effectively directing a jury to convict was a course that was rarely permissible.

It is arguable that, apart from those cases where the statute expressly excludes the defence of consent, the practical effect of modern case law developments is to maximise the availability of a consent defence rather than to reduce its ambit. In *R v B* the Court was clearly unwilling to extend the public policy rule to cases of diminished capacity, and was cautious in describing the scope of those authorities which do limit the availability of consent as a defence. Traditionally, the common law refused to allow consent to charges like assault and homicide arising from particularly violent encounters, such as duelling or fencing with naked swords.[53] The justification for disallowing consent in such cases, and in other activities like fist fights and prize fights, was the common incidence of terrible injuries being inflicted and the fact that the lives of the participants were endangered or sacrificed.[54] This was said to be contrary to the "public interest". The distinction between a prize fight and blows struck in the course of other legal sports was that in the former, the blow was said to be struck in anger and likely to do "corporal hurt", while in the latter the blow was struck "in sport" and not intended to cause bodily harm.[55] For this reason in *R v Donovan*,[56] where the appellant was charged with caning a 17-year-old girl for the purposes of sexual gratification, it was held that because the blows struck were likely or intended to do bodily harm, the act

---

51 See, for example, s 188 ("Wounding with intent") and s 196 ("Common assault").
52 (1993) 11 CRNZ 64. See also Casenote, "Indecent assault — Withholding consent defence" [1994] NZLJ 317.
53 See *Re Barronet* (1852) 1 E & B 1, 118 ER 337; *R v Orton* (1878) 14 Cox CC 226.
54 *R v Coney* (1882) 8 QBD 534 at 544 (Matthew J).
55 Ibid (Cave J).
56 [1934] 2 KB 498.

was per se unlawful and could not be rendered lawful simply because the person who was the subject of the beating consented to it.

At common law, until recently the general approach of the courts has been that it was not in the public interest that people should try to cause, or should cause, each other actual bodily harm "for no good reason".[57] The courts distinguished "minor struggles" which, by implication, could not be the subject of assault charges where the parties consented, from fights in which actual bodily harm was intended and/or caused, which were unlawful regardless of consent.[58] This limitation on consent did not, however, affect the legality of properly conducted games and sports, lawful discipline, reasonable surgical operations, or dangerous exhibitions.[59] In each such case, the exercise of a legal right, or (as the case may be) necessity in the public interest, was seen to be sufficient justification even where actual bodily harm occurred.

15.1.4.2 Consent to deviant sexual acts

However, in recent years a new testing-ground for the doctrine of consent has emerged in relation to sado-masochistic and other unusual consensual acts of a sexual nature; one which has caused the courts to radically rethink the parameters of proscribed consensual sexual activity. The result of these developments is that the courts appear to be increasingly willing to accommodate a defence of consent even in cases involving actual bodily harm, provided the alleged conduct is consensual, private, and does not involve significant intentional injury.

The challenge first emerged in *R v Brown*,[60] a case involving a group of sado-masochists, in which the House of Lords held that it was contrary to public policy to extend the exemptions concerning consensual violent acts to sado-masochistic conduct, particularly in light of the risk of serious injury and possible corruption of others, notwithstanding that the case involved consensual sexual activity by adults in private.[61] In *Brown* the majority, following the decision in *R v Donovan*,[62] approved the proposition that it was immaterial that the victim had consented to the infliction of bodily harm. The Court's reasoning was that sado-masochistic libido does not provide the requisite "good reason" for allowing consent to excuse or justify the deliberate causing of non-trivial bodily harm.

However, in *R v Wilson*[63] the English Court of Appeal took a much broader approach to the issue of consensual infliction of bodily harm. There the accused, at his wife's instigation, had branded his initials on her buttocks with

---

57   *A-G's Reference (No 6 of 1980)* [1981] 1 QB 715 at 719, [1981] 2 All ER 1057 at 1059.

58   Ibid.

59   Ibid. Other instances where consent may make the infliction of bodily harm lawful include ritual circumcision, tattooing, ear-piercing, and violent sports: *R v Brown* [1994] 1 AC 212 at 231, [1993] 2 All ER 75 at 79 (HL) (Lord Templeman).

60   [1994] 1 AC 212, [1993] 2 All ER 75 (HL).

61   See Dawkins, "Criminal Law" [1997] NZ Law Review 42ff.

62   [1934] KB 498.

63   [1996] 3 WLR 125 (CA).

a hot knife. He was charged with assault occasioning actual bodily harm. The trial Judge ruled that despite the wife's consent he was bound by the majority decision in *R v Brown*, and had no alternative but to convict. In allowing the appeal against conviction, the Court made the following observation:

> We are abundantly satisfied that there is no factual comparison to be made between the instant case and the facts of either *R v Donovan* . . . or *R v Brown* . . . Mrs Wilson not only consented to that which the appellant did, she instigated it. There was no aggressive intent on the part of the appellant. On the contrary, far from wishing to cause injury to his wife, the appellant's desire was to assist her in what she regarded as the acquisition of a desirable piece of adornment, perhaps in this day and age no less understandable than the piercing of nostrils or even tongues for the purpose of inserting decorative jewellery . . . Does public policy or the public interest demand that the appellant's activity should be visited by the sanctions of the criminal law? The majority in *R v Brown* clearly took the view that such considerations were relevant. If that is so, then we are firmly of the opinion that it is not in the public interest that activities such as the appellant's in this appeal should amount to criminal behaviour. Consensual activity between husband and wife in the privacy of the matrimonial home, is not, in our judgment, normally a proper matter for criminal investigation, let alone criminal prosecution.[64]

Although the Court expressed its desire that the law should be allowed to develop on a case-by-case basis rather than upon "general propositions" to which exceptions can arise,[65] it is nevertheless possible to draw from the decision some guidelines regarding the circumstances in which consent may be a defence to the infliction of actual bodily harm. At the least, it appears that an exception will be made:

(i)   Where the "victim" not only consents to but instigates the accused's conduct;

(ii) Where there is no aggressive intent on the accused's part;

(iii) Where the appellant's desire is to assist his partner in acquiring a desirable piece of personal adornment;

(iv) Where the conduct is consensual activity between "husband and wife" in the privacy of their own home.

These concessions seem to create a surprisingly broad exception to the general rule that infliction of injury for no good reason cannot be consented to. For a start there would seem to now be no limitation on the nature of the consensual injury inflicted where the above conditions are met. For example, there appears to be no reason why W should not be permitted to carve his initials on his wife's buttocks or even to burn them on with acid, provided the injury was of a similar degree of severity.

Other questions arise. Would consent have made the conduct lawful if, for example, W's intention was not to assist his wife in acquiring a personal adornment, but rather to make her an object of titillation for friends who were invited to their home for a private "viewing" of her adornment, or for the publication of her personal adornment in a magazine devoted to body

---

64   Ibid at 127, 128.

65   Ibid at 128.

marking? In other words, does the qualification that the act must occur in private limit the exposure of the results of the consensual activity after the event? There is also a troubling question concerning the Court's use of the notions of "intent" and "desire" in the passage quoted. Suppose that W had caused serious injury to his wife when he branded his initials on her buttocks. Would the injury have been any less "intended" because, as he claimed, his "desire" was to assist her to acquire a personal adornment? According to conventional theory, there could be little doubt that W intended to cause his wife actual bodily harm, regardless whether his intent was "aggressive". His claimed "desire", on this view, would have constituted his motive (not intent) for acting as he did; and, as such, was or should have been irrelevant in determining criminal responsibility.

15.1.4.3 *Public policy*
On the issues of public policy and public interest, the Court's arguments do raise a difficulty. Its refusal to visit the accused's actions with the sanctions of the criminal law is advanced on the basis that "consensual activity between husband and wife in the privacy of the matrimonial home" is not the law's business. While admirably libertarian in spirit, this is not to say, however, that *all* activity between spouses in the privacy of the home is permissible, since such a broad extension would have to include conduct in the nature of domestic violence which is now regularly the subject of criminal prosecution. The problem with permitting any kind of bodily harm to be inflicted by one person upon another, within the cloak of "privacy", is the danger that the claimed consent is a mere phantom, the submissive party being either too terrified or so inured to the overbearing demands of his partner that complaint that he was not consenting is not considered to be a realistic option. The difficulty is exacerbated by the fact that the defence applies to "private" conduct — the very location where there is no way of independently testing whether the victim's "consent" was genuine. The rule now established by the Court arguably leaves the victims of such abusive relationships exposed to even greater or more exquisite degrees of physical violence without effective protection from the criminal law.[66]

15.1.4.4 *Consent and sport*
Apart from contexts where consent is no defence, we have seen that an assault will normally only occur where the act done is contrary to the will and without the consent of the victim. However, at common law it has long been recognised that a blow struck in sport and not intended to cause bodily harm does not constitute assault even though not expressly consented to. This exception may be explained either on the basis that some physical conduct is impliedly consented to during sport, or because, subject to the context provided by the agreed rules of a game, such physical contact falls within a general exception

---

66   For an alternative view of the decision, see Dawkins, "Criminal Law" [1997] NZ Law Review 20 at 45, 46.

which embraces physical contact acceptable in the ordinary course of playing the particular sport.[67]

The reality of much modern sport appears to strain the application of these simple precepts. Many sports, including acknowledged contact sports like rugby, rugby league, ice-hockey, boxing, kick-boxing, and other new generation "gladiatorial" sports, may involve extreme violence resulting, not infrequently, in serious disabling injury and even the death of the participants. In such circumstances, where death is the result of an accident the person responsible for the injury would not normally be liable for manslaughter,[68] although it could rarely be said that violence sufficient to cause death was "permissible" within the rules of a particular sport.

A sport or a game will not necessarily be lawful (where consent may be a defence) simply because it is conducted according to the rules. However, it is not clear when such activity becomes unlawful. An earlier suggested limitation was that it may be unlawful if "the risk of death or serious injury" is normally associated with it, or if it is regarded as "essentially dangerous, and ... it is more probable than not that serious injury may result".[69] The relevant association may be provided by the fact that exposure to serious risk is part of the purpose of the activity. In *R v McLeod*[70] M was giving an exhibition of his skills as a marksman at a "Wild West " show. He invited W to take a seat about 21 feet away from him with a view to shooting the ash from the cigarette he was smoking. However, W moved his head and the bullet passed through his cheek causing a serious but not dangerous injury. M was charged with a number of offences including assault, assault causing actual bodily harm, and actual bodily harm under such circumstances that if death had occurred he would have been guilty of manslaughter. Although it was accepted that the accused had fired with the full consent of W, it was held that because a lethal weapon was used in risky circumstances, if death had occurred M would have been guilty of manslaughter and he was duly convicted. The Court appeared to distinguish between death resulting from the "wilful and wanton act[s]" of impermissible "sports" (fighting without gloves, using weapons of an "improper and deadly" nature) and accidental death resulting from permissible sports (football, wrestling, boxing with gloves). The injury to W could hardly be described as an accident, since the very purpose of the exhibition depended upon the fact that W was put in some danger of being injured.

However, such distinctions are increasingly difficult to draw given that dangerous sports and competitive endeavours are now commonplace and generally accepted. The notion of "extreme" sport has redefined the conventional physical limits of many sports, and many new non-contact

---

67 *Collins v Wilcock* [1984] 3 All ER 374 at 378, (1984) 79 Cr App Rep 229 at 234 (Goff LJ).

68 *R v McLeod* (1915) 34 NZLR 430 at 434.

69 *Adams* § CA63.08.

70 (1915) 34 NZLR 430.

competitor sports regularly involve activity which courts a risk of death. In these cases it is very difficult to draw a line between permissible conduct and conduct which may be outlawed for public policy reasons because of its inherent dangerousness. For many such sporting endeavours, it is the possibility of breaking the conventional boundaries of human endeavour to do the very thing that would, for an earlier generation, have been regarded as "impossible" and inherently perilous that provides the very justification for the sport. People, presumably, contract to engage in such activities and consent to the risk of death or serious injury because such risks are part of the attraction of the particular activity.

If society is prepared to lend its tacit, albeit uncomprehending, approval to consensual participation in "extreme" sports where, even without competitive contact, the risk of at least serious bodily injury is high, it seems difficult to deny the right to other sportsmen and women to participate in contact sports where the risk of dangerous and intentional injury is also present. This does not mean that it is impossible to regulate the illicit use of violence in particular sports through the rules of a game, but does suggest that it is becoming increasingly difficult to ban sporting activities simply because they are "essentially dangerous" and likely to cause serious injury. Boxing is the classic case. Boxers intend to injure and impliedly consent to injury, and it can no longer be claimed that the law gives protection in respect of unintended injuries or that no intentional injury is permissible.[71] The suggested prohibition against fighting "in a spirit of anger or in a hostile spirit and with the predominant intention of inflicting substantial bodily harm so as to disable or otherwise physically subdue the opponent"[72] may well suggest the upper limits of permissible physical conduct in a boxing match. But it is an unhelpful limit. Determining when that "spirit of anger or hostile spirit" is present, or the point at which intervention is appropriate to prevent one opponent from "hurting" the other, can only be a fraught exercise when the object of the contest is to batter (therefore hurt) the opponent into submission.

It may be that, apart from the most aggressively violent behaviour (for example biting off part of an opponent's ear, a deliberate head high tackle, deliberately breaking an opponent's limb, etc), the regulation of what is permissible, and therefore may be consented to, is best left to be determined by the application of the rules of a particular sport or code. Because the range of conduct that may be consented to in the name of sport generally is so much broader than could ever have been contemplated at common law, there is a danger that the legal proscription of particular types of conduct will impact much more severely on one type of activity than on another where the relative degree of risk of harm is in each case identical. Arguably, the criminal law should only be involved in the regulation of sporting activity where the intentional activity is so obviously a breach of the rules of the game and contrary to notions of fair play that any reasonable person would recognise it

---

71 See *Adams* § CA63.08.
72 *Pallante v Stadiums Pty Ltd (No 1)* [1976] VR 331.

as unacceptable, particularly where it involves the infliction of grave injury, and/or injury that could result in the death of the victim. Beyond this, the law may be better to defer to those actually involved in the playing of a particular sport to determine what, if any, should be the boundaries of lawful physical contest.[73]

15.2 WOUNDING WITH INTENT

The offence of wounding with intent (s 188 Crimes Act 1961) is the most serious of the various offences of assault and injury to the person with which a person may be charged under the Crimes Act. As we shall see, the offence defined in the section involves a number of discrete mens rea and actus reus elements, including (among the actus reus elements) some concepts which have become legal terms of art. In this discussion, we will examine the separate meanings given to the concepts of "grievous bodily harm", "wounding", "maiming", and "disfiguring", each of which expresses a different way in which the offence may be committed.

The terms of s 188 are as follows:

Wounding with intent—(1) Every one is liable to imprisonment for a term not exceeding 14 years who, with intent to cause grievous bodily harm to anyone, wounds, maims, disfigures, or causes grievous bodily harm to any person.

(2) Every one is liable to imprisonment for a term not exceeding 7 years who, with intent to injure anyone, or with reckless disregard for the safety of others, wounds, maims, disfigures, or causes grievous bodily harm to any person.

In effect, the section defines three separate offences: wounding with intent to cause grievous bodily harm (s 188(1)), wounding with intent to injure (s 188(2)), and wounding with reckless disregard for the safety of others (s 188(2)). One element common to each offence is "causing grievous bodily harm", the meaning of which is now examined.

15.2.1 Grievous bodily harm

Section 188 does not define grievous bodily harm. Neither is the expression defined elsewhere in the Crimes Act 1961. However, the meaning of "grievous bodily harm" has been considered at common law, where it is said that the words are to be given their "ordinary and natural meaning".[74] In *R v Ashman*,[75] it was said of the expression that:

It is not necessary that such harm should . . . be either permanent or dangerous, if it be such as seriously to interfere with comfort or health it is sufficient.

However, it will be a misdirection, when summing up to a jury on a charge of wounding with intent to cause grievous bodily harm, to invite the jury to convict if the only intent established is to interfere seriously with health or

---

73   For a discussion of when unlawful acts may occur within a lawful game, see *Adams* § CA63.09.

74   *DPP v Smith* [1961] AC 290 at 334, [1960] 3 All ER 161 at 171.

75   (1858) 1 F & F 88, 175 ER 638.

comfort.[76] It is now common for juries to be directed that "grievous bodily harm" means really serious bodily injury.[77] On this basis, a broken nose has been held to be grievous bodily harm;[78] although a nose injury causing bleeding need not necessarily result in a fracture for grievous bodily harm to be found, provided the injury could be said to have caused "really serious harm".[79] Injuries such as fractures, injuries to any organ, disfigurement, or physical incapacitation may all be included within the expression.[80] In *Ashman* it was held that a blow to the temple of the victim, caused by powder from a gun discharged by the defendant, which caused a weakness to the victim's eye for some months following the discharge, was sufficient to constitute grievous bodily harm. Grievous bodily harm also accommodates "prospective" harm, in the sense that it need not be limited to the immediate consequences of external assault or injury as might typically result from a blow. Although in the generality of cases the effect is instant (a blow causes a wound), the consequences may be delayed, for example where an offender infects another person with the HIV virus through unprotected sexual intercourse.[81] In such cases the grievous bodily injury is established even before those prospective consequences eventually occur.

Whether an injury amounts to "bodily harm" will depend on the nature of the injury and its consequences whether short- or long-term. At the opposite end of the spectrum from prospective harms, the fact that the victim recovered completely from the injury, or was left with only a cosmetic disability, will be irrelevant if the immediate consequences of the injury interfered temporarily with his health in a relevant way. For example, a compound fracture of an arm or leg would constitute a "really serious bodily harm" even if the fracture healed completely and left no visible scarring or disability. The existence of pain, affecting a person's ability to function fully, will be relevant in determining whether "bodily harm" has occurred.[82]

15.2.1.1 *Psychological and emotional harm*

The expression "bodily harm" is not defined in the Crimes Act 1961. An issue which therefore arises is whether the expression is apt to include psychological harm. In *R v McCraw*,[83] where the accused had written obscene and threatening letters to several women threatening to rape them, the Supreme Court of Canada upheld a conviction for threatening to cause serious bodily harm. It did so on the basis that rape was likely to have serious psychological consequences for the victim, as well as possible serious physical effects. Since "bodily harm" was defined in the Canadian Criminal Code to mean "any hurt or injury", the

---

76   *R v Metharam* [1961] 3 All ER 200.

77   See *DPP v Smith* [1961] AC 290 at 334, [1960] 3 All ER 161 at 171 (Viscount Kilmuir).

78   *R v Saunders* [1985] Crim LR 230.

79   See *R v Waters* [1979] 1 NZLR 375 at 380 (McMullin J).

80   Carter and Harrison, *Offences of Violence*, London, 1991, § 3.29.

81   *R v Mwai* [1995] 3 NZLR 149 at 153, (1995) 13 CRNZ 273 at 278 (CA).

82   *Wayne v Boldiston* (1992) 85 NTY 8 (NT SC).

83   (1991) 7 CR (4th) 314.

Court could see no reason in principle why psychological harm should be excluded. Similarly, in *R v Miller*,[84] evidence that the victim had been in a "hysterical and nervous condition" was held to be sufficient evidence to leave the case to the jury on a charge of assault occasioning actual bodily harm. The Judge ruled that "if a person is caused hurt or injury resulting, not in any physical injury, but in an injury to the state of his mind for the time being, that is within the definition of 'actual bodily harm'". This decision received qualified approval by the English Court of Appeal in *R v Chan-Fook* where, delivering the judgment of the Court, Hobhouse LJ said:

> The body of the victim includes all parts of his body, including his organs, his nervous system and his brain. Bodily injury therefore may include injury to any of those parts of his body responsible for his mental and other faculties . . . Accordingly the phrase "actual bodily harm" is capable of including psychiatric injury. But it does not include mere emotions such as fear or distress or panic nor does it include, as such, states of mind that are not themselves evidence of some identifiable clinical condition . . . [J]uries should not be directed that an assault which causes a hysterical and nervous condition is an assault occasioning actual bodily harm. Where there is evidence that the assault has caused some psychiatric injury, the jury should be directed that the injury is *capable of amounting to actual bodily harm*; otherwise there should be no reference to the mental state of the victim following the assault unless it be relevant to some other aspect of the case . . .[85]

This appears also to be the law in New Zealand. In *R v Mwai*,[86] the Court of Appeal acknowledged the artificiality of separating the mind from the physical body, holding the two to be "inseparable". It approved the approach taken in *Chan-Fook*, and held that in a charge under s 188(2), grievous bodily harm includes really serious psychiatric injury identified as such by appropriate specialist evidence.[87] However, the point did not require final determination in *Mwai*, because the Court found that once the jury were satisfied about causation, the infection of the victim with HIV was so obviously the causing of grievous bodily harm that no mental harm needed to be added to the offence to be established.

Where psychiatric injury is relied upon as a basis for an allegation of bodily harm, but the issue has not been admitted by the defence, expert evidence should be called by the prosecution. The matter should not be left to be inferred by the jury from the general facts of the case, and in the absence of appropriate expert evidence a question whether the assault occasioned psychiatric injury should not be left to the jury.[88]

15.2.1.1(a) The "silent caller"

The harassment of women by repeated silent telephone calls, sometimes accompanied by heavy breathing, has become a significant social problem in

---

84   [1954] 2 QB 282, [1954] 2 All ER 529.
85   [1994] 2 All ER 552 at 558, 559 (emphasis added).
86   [1995] 3 NZLR 149 at 155, (1995) 13 CRNZ 273 at 280 (CA).
87   Ibid.
88   *R v Chan-Fook* at 559.

many countries. One question which arises is whether the making of a series of silent telephone calls can amount to an assault even where no physical violence has been applied directly or indirectly to the person of the victim. This issue has been considered by the House of Lords in *R v Ireland*,[89] in relation to the question whether the causing of psychiatric injury by such conduct could amount to "inflicting" grievous bodily harm. Concluding that it could, Lord Steyn said:

> The answer to [the] question [whether a silent caller may be guilty of an assault] seems to me to be "yes, depending on the facts". It involves questions of fact within the province of the jury. After all, there is no reason why a telephone caller who says to a woman in a menacing way "I will be at your door in a minute or two" may not be guilty of an assault if he causes his victim to apprehend immediate personal violence. Take now the case of the silent caller. He intends by his silence to cause fear and he is so understood. The victim is assailed by uncertainty about his intentions. Fear may dominate her emotions, and it may be the fear that the caller's arrival at her door may be imminent. She may fear the *possibility* of immediate personal violence. As a matter of law the caller may be guilty of an assault.[90]

In New Zealand, although words alone cannot constitute an assault because of the requirement in s 2(1) for threats "by any act or gesture", it does appear from the decision in *R v Mwai* (above) that psychological damage (other than transient fear, distress or panic) caused by the actions of the caller will amount to bodily harm in terms of s 188. The issue for the jury would be whether the accused intended to cause injury in that sense by making the silent call.

15.2.2 "Wounds"

At common law, in order to constitute a wounding there must be an injury to the person by which the skin is broken; the continuity of the whole skin must be severed, not merely that of the cuticle or upper skin.[91] However, the skin severed need not be external, so that striking someone in the face causing the inside of his mouth to bleed will be a relevant wounding.[92] On the other hand, it will not be sufficient to prove that a flow of blood was caused, unless there is some evidence to show where the blood came from.[93] Although it is not necessary that the wounding should have been caused by an instrument (an injury caused by a kick may be a wounding[94]), an injury that merely causes internal bleeding would not constitute a wound because there is no breaking of the skin. Thus, if D throws a blunt object at V which strikes him above the eye, causing a black eye and redness in the eye due to the rupture of an internal

---

89   (1997) NLJ 1273.

90   Ibid at 1273, 1274.

91   *Halsbury's Laws of England*, Criminal Law, Evidence and Procedure, vol 11(1), (4th ed reissue), § 470. See *R v Wood* (1830) 1 Mood CC 278, 168 ER 1271; *Moriarty v Brooks* (1843) 6 C & P 684, 172 ER 1419; *R v Beckett* (1836) 1 Moo & R 526, 174 ER 181.

92   *R v Smith* (1837) 8 C & P 173, 174 ER 448.

93   *R v Waltham* (1849) 3 Cox CC 442.

94   *R v Duffill* (1843) 1 Cox CC 49.

blood vessel, that would not constitute a wounding because there is no severing of the skin.[95] However, provided there is a severing of the skin there will still be a wounding whether or not there is a flow of blood.[96] It is therefore important in a prosecution for wounding with intent to establish the nature of the injury by medical evidence.

The common law meaning attributed to "wound", namely a breaking of the continuity of the skin, has broadly been adopted by New Zealand courts. In *R v Waters*,[97] where the accused had, inter alia, attacked the complainant, banging her face against the floor and causing her nose to bleed heavily, McMullin J was not prepared to rule that internal bleeding which came from the nose could never amount to a wounding, since it was a question of fact for determination in each case. He said:

> A breaking of the skin would be commonly regarded as a characteristic of a wound. The breaking of the skin will be normally evidenced by a flow of blood and, in its occurrence at the site of a blow or impact, the wound will more often than not be external. But there are those cases where the bleeding which evidences the separation of tissues may be internal.[98]

15.2.2.1 *"Indirect" wounding*

Since there is no requirement that a wound must be caused by any particular instrument or object, it would seem to follow that a wound may be caused indirectly. This could occur where, for example, D deliberately pushes V on to a sharp object, like a broken bottle, which causes the wound, or where D throws the same object at V causing injury. There is no legal requirement that the assailant and victim must be in direct contact before there can be a wounding. A wounding could also occur where an object already attached to the person of the victim is used as an instrument to cause injury to the victim. For example, if V is holding a fork and D deliberately knocks her arm so that V is impaled on her own fork, that would be a relevant wounding by D. In *R v Sheard*[99] the victim, who was wearing a hard-rimmed hat, was struck on the head. The resulting injury caused by the effect of the impact of the hard rim was held to be a wounding.

15.2.3 *"Maims"*

At common law, "maim" means "depriving another of the use of such of his members as may render him the less able in fighting, either to defend himself or to annoy his adversary".[100] In New Zealand it has been held to involve the cutting or taking away of some part of a person, and has a connotation of permanence.[101] It would, therefore, presumably make no difference to a charge

---

95 See *C v Eisenhower* [1984] QB 331, [1983] 3 All ER 230.

96 *R v Devine* (1982) 8 A Crim R 45.

97 [1979] 1 NZLR 375 (CA).

98 Ibid at 378.

99 (1837) 2 Mood 13, 169 ER 6.

100 *4 Blackstone's Commentaries* 205.

101 *R v Rapana and Murray* (1988) 3 CRNZ 256 at 257 (Williamson J).

of maiming that the part violently removed was successfully reattached by surgery. The essence of the offence is the non-consensual removal of a body part, regardless of its consequences. Because of its association with combat defence using hand weapons, the concept may have less relevance in present times than once it had.[102]

15.2.4 "Disfigures"

At common law, "disfiguring" consisted of some external injury which may detract from personal appearance.[103] The natural and ordinary meaning of "disfiguring" is "to deform or deface; to mar or alter the figure or appearance of a person".[104] In *R v Rapana and Murray*,[105] the victim alleged he had been disfigured when he was forced to submit to a tattooing down one side of his face using a broken pen and a needle. At the time of trial there were no longer any marks on his face as a result of the incident. The issue for the Court was whether disfiguring necessarily connotes some permanent disfigurement rather than merely temporary change. Noting that the natural meaning of the word "disfigure" does not involve permanent injury or damage, the Court held that the word should be accorded the same meaning in the context of s 188(2).[106] Provided the two essential elements are proved — namely, a disfiguring and an intent to injure — the concept is apt to cover situations like acid throwing and involuntary tattooing where there has been an initial injuring but no permanent damage or marking.[107]

15.2.5 "Injure"

Injury is relevant only to the lesser offence defined in subs (2). The term is defined in s 2(1), and means "to cause actual bodily harm". It appears that the expression does not require proof of physical injury, and may include injury producing an hysterical or nervous condition. Thus, if D physically assaults V in a manner which causes only minor physical injury but in a manner which is highly intimidatory and as a result of which V suffers a psychological injury in the nature of shock or hysteria, the resulting mental injury would amount to "actual bodily harm"[108] provided it could be said to be more than trifling or

102 In ancient times, the punishment for mayhem was the loss of the like part: *4 Blackstone's Commentaries* 205, 206.

103 See Butler and Garsia, *Archbold Criminal Pleading, Evidence and Practice* (36th ed), London, Sweet & Maxwell, 1966, § 2654. This definition no longer appears in the most recent edition of *Archbold* (Richardson (ed), *Archbold Criminal Pleading, Evidence and Practice*, London, Sweet & Maxwell, 1998) because in 1967, s 18 Offences Against the Person Act 1861 (UK) was amended to delete reference to disfiguring. However, the term still appears in a number of English provisions, in particular those relating to explosives or corrosive substances: see ss 28 and 29 Offences Against the Person Act 1861 (UK).

104 *Shorter Oxford Dictionary* (3rd ed), vol 1, 566.

105 (1988) 3 CRNZ 256.

106 Ibid at 257.

107 See *R v James* (1980) 70 Cr App R 215 (CA); *Burrell v Harmer* [1967] Crim LR 169.

108 See *R v Miller* [1954] 2 QB 282 at 292, [1954] 2 All ER 529 at 534.

transitory.[109] However, for the reasons discussed earlier in relation to psychological and emotional harm,[110] although psychiatric injury may suffice, other cognitive or emotional reactions like fear, distress, or panic do not.[111]

15.2.6 Mens rea

The offences defined in s 188 involve two alternative mens rea states. The crime of wounding with intent to cause grievous bodily harm in subs (1) may only be committed intentionally. Recklessness on the part of the accused will not suffice. However, the crime defined in subs (2), of wounding with intent to injure, may be committed either intentionally, or "with reckless disregard for the safety of others".

15.2.6.1 *"With intent"*

The Crown carries the legal burden of proving the specific intent to cause grievous bodily harm, or the intent to injure, as the case may be. It will not often be the case that the defendant makes a statement that she intended to cause really serious harm. Evidence of intent usually rests on circumstantial evidence (the nature of the assault and the physical environment in which it occurs), or is inferred from the acts and statements made by the accused before, at, or after the event. In *R v Taisalika*,[112] where the accused had struck the complainant on the side of the head with a glass causing a serious injury, it was held that the nature of the blow and the gash it produced to the complainant's head were factors which pointed strongly to the necessary intent. However, to establish intent under the section it will not be enough to prove that the accused had foreseen that such harm was likely to result from his acts, or that he had been reckless whether such harm would result.[113] This is because the intent required to be proved for a charge of aggravated wounding has traditionally been regarded as an intent to produce a "particular evil consequence",[114] the equivalent of "malice aforethought".[115] Of course, although the required intent cannot be proved by foresight that serious injury is likely to result from a deliberate act, foresight and recklessness are evidence

---

109 *R v McArthur* [1975] 1 NZLR 486.

110 See § 15.2.1.1.

111 *R v Chan-Fook* [1994] 1 WLR 689, [1994] 2 All ER 552 (CA). See also *R v Burstow* [1996] Crim LR 331.

112 25/6/93, CA94/93.

113 *R v Belfon* [1976] 1 WLR 741, [1976] 3 All ER 46 (CA). See §§ 3.1.3, 3.1.7. On the other hand, the mere fact that the accused does not recall whether he had the necessary intent at the relevant time would be insufficient to establish a lack of intent. Loss of memory of past events is not the same as lack of intent at the time: *R v Taisalika* 25/6/93, CA94/93.

114 *Hyam v DPP* [1975] AC 55 at 86, [1974] 2 All ER 41 at 62, 63 (HL) (Lord Diplock).

115 Ibid.

from which that intent may be inferred. But they cannot be equated, either separately or in conjunction, with intent to do grievous bodily harm.[116]

It is worth noting that where an intention to cause grievous bodily harm is proved, and death results, the accused may be guilty of murder on the basis of the constructive intent provision in s 167(b) ("means to cause to the person killed any bodily injury that is known to the offender to be likely to cause death").[117] However, where death does not result, proof of an intent to cause grievous bodily harm will not be sufficient to support a conviction for attempted murder; to prove an attempted murder nothing less than an intent to kill will do.[118]

What makes the offence in s 188(1) so serious, warranting a maximum sentence of 14 years' imprisonment, is not what D actually does, but rather the intent with which he does it. Consequently, the offence may be committed even though V suffered only minor harm. If D, intending to stab V violently in the abdomen, succeeds only in inflicting a superficial cut to a finger, he may still be guilty of wounding with intent to cause grievous bodily harm.[119]

15.2.6.2 "Reckless disregard"

The alternative offence defined in s 188(2) may be committed where the accused wounds, maims, disfigures, etc "with reckless disregard for the safety of others". Reckless disregard contemplates a wanton indifference to the interests of others, but within the hierarchy of offences created by the section implies a mental state less culpable than intending to cause grievous bodily harm. This is reflected in the penalty prescribed in the section (a term of imprisonment not exceeding 7 years). In New Zealand recklessness invariably requires subjective foresight, unless the statutory context clearly requires that a different meaning be given to the concept.[120] For the purposes of s 188, therefore, recklessness requires foresight of dangerous consequences that could well happen, together with an intention to continue with that course of conduct regardless of the risk.[121]

An intentional or reckless frightening, without more, is insufficient for s 188(2); the person charged must be proved to have been aware that the consequences of her voluntary act might be to cause some injury to the victim, though not necessarily grievous bodily harm.[122] An example of a reckless

---

116 *R v Belfon* [1976] 3 All ER 46 at 53, [1976] 1 WLR 741 at 749 (CA). For a critique of the decision in *R v Belfon*, see Buzzard, "Intent" [1978] Crim LR 5, and Smith "'Intent': A Reply" [1978] Crim LR 14.

117 In such a case, for murder to be proved the prosecution would also need to prove the accused's subjective knowledge that the death of the victim was a real risk: *R v Gush* [1980] 2 NZLR 92 at 96 (CA).

118 *R v Belfon* [1976] 3 All ER 46 at 52, [1976] 1 WLR 741 at 748 (CA).

119 See *R v Hunt* (1825) 1 Mood 93 at 96, 168 ER 1198 at 1200: "if there was an intent to do grievous bodily harm, it was immaterial whether grievous bodily harm was done".

120 *R v Harney* 1987] 2 NZLR 578 at 579 (CA). See § 3.2ff.

121 Ibid.

122 Cf *R v Sullivan* [1981] Crim LR 46 at 47 (CA).

wounding would be where D, standing in the middle of a crowd, begins to swing a heavy chain, with the intention of intimidating those around him. If V, standing in the crowd, is then struck by the chain and injured, D will be guilty of wounding V with reckless disregard if — and only if — D foresaw that someone could well be injured by his actions and continued swinging the chain regardless of the risk. Notice that, as usual under the doctrine of transferred mens rea,[123] it is not necessary that D should have foreseen that V, in particular, might be struck by the chain.

15.3 INJURING WITH INTENT

This crime is defined in s 189 Crimes Act 1961. The offence contains elements which are endemic to the crime of wounding with intent, discussed above, and which will not be separately considered. It is sufficient to note that, as with a prosecution under s 188, proof of an assault is not necessary. Nor is it relevant that the injury actually caused with the requisite intent was not a serious bodily harm.[124]

15.4 INJURING BY UNLAWFUL ACT

This offence is one of the few provisions of the Crimes Act 1961 that allows prosecution for negligent acts alone. Its terms are set out by s 190:

> Injuring by unlawful act — Everyone is liable to imprisonment for a term not exceeding 3 years who injures any other person in such circumstances that if death had been caused he would have been guilty of manslaughter.

The offence has its origins not in English law but in the Draft Code of 1879, where it was entitled "Negligent Acts punishable with two years imprisonment".[125] The section aims to punish negligent conduct that results in injury such that the offender would have been liable for manslaughter if death had been caused. In a sense, the title "injuring by unlawful act" is a misnomer, since an omission without lawful excuse to perform a legal duty would clearly suffice, as would any of the forms of conduct specifically qualifying as culpable homicide by virtue of s 160(2). An unlawful act is a sufficient but not a necessary condition of liability under the section.

The ambit of s 190 is unclear. The section says nothing about the manner in which the injury must be caused. In particular, like s 188, there is no reference to assault or the use of violence. The fact that the offence occurs in a statutory context of serious offences against the person is not conclusive that proof of an assault or something akin to assault is required. Since grievous bodily harm may be caused otherwise than by wounding and may even result from an act which is not an assault (where, for example, someone creates fear in another

---

123 § 3.7.

124 See *R v Hunt* (1825) 1 Mood CC 93 at 96, 168 ER 1198 at 1200: "if there was an intent to do grievous bodily harm, it was immaterial whether grievous bodily harm was done".

125 Section 201 Draft Code. See also s 186 Criminal Code Act 1893.

causing him to attempt to escape, suffering serious injury in the process),[126] the same must also be true of "injuring" under s 190. What is implicit in the section is that the accused caused the injury either by a direct act or by some culpable omission, whether or not the victim suffers permanent damage as a result. Because the present section omits the proviso whereby its predecessor under the Crimes Act 1908 was made inapplicable to the "duty" provisions in ss 151 to 154, it is arguable that an omission to perform a legal duty could now provide the basis of a prosecution under the section. Suppose the following example:

> D is the operator of a "Bungy-jumping" operation which uses a large crane suspended over an enclosed harbour area as a platform from which patrons jump. V, whom D has personally attended in attaching the bungy cord to her ankles, jumps after receiving assurances from D that the jump is "perfectly safe". However, at the end of the jump and after the jump cord has taken up the tension, the bindings around V's ankles slip and she plunges into the sea. V, who cannot swim, is saved from drowning by an assistant of the company who dives into the water and manages to pull V to safety. V suffers from water ingestion and is profoundly distressed by the experience but suffers no lasting consequences from her ordeal.

In such circumstances a prosecution under s 190 would be possible. V has suffered "injury" in that she experienced interference with her health or comfort, albeit not permanently. Furthermore there could be little doubt that had she died D would have been liable for manslaughter as a person in charge of a dangerous thing who failed to take "reasonable precautions against and to use reasonable care to avoid such danger".[127]

The question of liability under s 190 arose in a similar way in *Primrose v Police*.[128] In that case, the appellant encouraged another youth to throw a can of petrol belonging to the appellant into a bonfire, as a result of which the youth suffered serious injury. The Court accepted that the appellant had shouted at the boy to get away, but the warning was not heeded. Hillyer J held that, had death resulted, manslaughter would have been committed. Because there was an omission without lawful excuse to perform or observe a legal duty, as a result of which someone was injured, it was held that the conviction under s 190 was justified.[129]

By its nature, the section is concerned with seriously negligent acts that could have resulted in the victim's death. Where it is not possible to establish

---

126 *R v McCready* [1978] 3 All ER 967 at 970, [1978] 1 WLR 1376 at 1381 (CA).

127 Section 156 Crimes Act 1961.

128 (1985) 1 CRNZ 621.

129 Cf *R v McLeod* (1915) 34 NZLR 430 (CA), in which it was held that shooting the ash off a cigarette held in the mouth of a consenting victim, where the victim was wounded in the cheek, was a "risky" event such that it would have been manslaughter if death had ensued. Bodily injury inflicted in such circumstances would constitute careless use of a firearm under s 53 Arms Act 1983 (hence, an unlawful act) and would be manslaughter under s 53(4) in the event of death ensuing.

such a high degree of negligent risk-taking, it may be appropriate to charge the lesser negligence offence in s 13 Summary Offences Act 1981.[130]

15.5 AGGRAVATED WOUNDING

The crime of aggravated wounding or injury is defined in s 191 Crimes Act 1961:

> **Aggravated wounding or injury**—(1) Every one is liable to imprisonment for a term not exceeding 14 years who with intent—
>
> (a) To commit or facilitate the commission of any crime; or
> (b) To avoid the detection of himself or of any other person in the commission of any crime; or
> (c) To avoid the arrest or facilitate the flight of himself or of any other person upon the commission or attempted commission of any crime—
>
> wounds, maims, disfigures, or causes grievous bodily harm to any person, or stupefies or renders unconscious any person, or by any violent means renders any person incapable of resistance.
>
> (2) Every one is liable to imprisonment for a term not exceeding 7 years who, with any such intent as aforesaid, injures any person.

In essence, an offence is committed when one person harms another with any of the intents set out in s 191(1). The element of aggravation in the title relates not to the nature of the harm inflicted (though this will determine whether the offence is under s 191(1) or s 191(2)), but rather to the reasons for the offending; being to facilitate the commission of a crime, or to avoid detection or arrest. The section bears some parallels to the further definition of murder in s 168, which allows a prosecution for murder where the accused causes the death of the victim for purposes similar to those specified in s 191(a)-(c), although in that context the accused need not mean to cause death or know that it is likely to ensue.

15.5.1 Mens rea

To establish liability under the section, the prosecution must first prove that the accused intended to do one of the things specified in s 191(1)(a)-(c). Because the intent nominated is a further or "ulterior" intent,[131] recklessness will not suffice for this aspect of the mens rea. But once that "preliminary" intent is established, is it necessary for the prosecution to prove in every case that the accused *intended* to inflict the particular type of injury alleged (wounding maiming, stupefying, etc)? The statute is silent on this question, which was considered by the Court of Appeal in *R v Tihi*.[132]

In *Tihi*, the accused and his associates stole a taxi after evicting its driver, with a view to driving to another part of the country. In the course of evicting the driver a co-accused had put his arm around the driver's neck and held a small knife against it. The driver was unaware of the knife but received a small cut near his eye. The co-accused gave evidence that he had no intention of

---

130 As occurred in *Police v Primrose* (1985) 1 CRNZ 621.
131 See § 3.1.7.
132 [1989] 2 NZLR 29, (1989) 4 CRNZ 289 (CA).

cutting the victim and was unaware he had done so until he saw him wiping his cheek with a handkerchief. The issue for the Court was whether, under s 191(2), it was necessary to prove intent or some other form of mens rea in respect of the injury itself, in addition to the intention to commit the crime of unlawful taking. The Court agreed that a purely accidental injury could not attract criminal liability since, if mens rea were irrelevant, the "curious" result would be that purely accidental harm inflicted in the circumstances mentioned in the section would attract a maximum prison term of 14 (or 7) years.[133] The Court was unwilling to find that the offence imposed strict liability in respect of the occurrence of injury, because that would run counter to the well established presumption in favour of mens rea in all criminal offences. In the words of Casey J:

> The introductory phrase "with intent to" in subs (1) establishes a connection between the harm and the conduct described in paras (a), (b) and (c), in that it must have been inflicted as part of the offender's purpose of implementing that conduct, tending to the conclusion that he must at least have turned his mind to the risk of harm . . . Accordingly, before he can be guilty, it must be shown that the accused either meant to cause the specified harm, or foresaw that his actions were likely to expose others to the risk of suffering it.[134]

This means that either intention or recklessness will suffice as the mens rea required for wounding (etc), notwithstanding that recklessness will not suffice for the other mens rea element, required under subs (a)-(c).

15.5.2 "Violent means"

The offence under s 191 may be committed where an accused uses "violent means" to incapacitate another while intending to commit a crime, avoid detection, or escape. In *R v Crossan*[135] it was held that the words "by any violent means whatever" (used in the predecessor to s 191[136]) are unfettered by any context which might throw a gloss upon the words or limit their meaning. In *Crossan*, the accused, intending to have sexual intercourse with the victim against her will, had threatened to shoot her with a loaded revolver unless she submitted to sexual intercourse. The Court held that while a mere threat *simpliciter* would not amount to "violent means", a threat made with a loaded revolver in such a way as to lead the person to believe that it would be used, could have the effect of rendering a person "incapable of resistance" as effectively as if the person were physically incapable, and was properly described as a "violent means". This approach was approved in *R v Claridge*[137] where the accused, while attempting to escape from prison, had struck a prison officer with an iron bar causing him to fall from a prison wall and sustain injuries. It was held that the purpose of the attack was obviously to render the officer incapable of resistance and that to so attack another with an iron bar

---

133 [1989] 2 NZLR 29 at 31, (1989) 4 CRNZ 289 at 291 (CA).
134 Ibid at 31, 32, 291, 292.
135 [1943] NZLR 454.
136 See s 195 Crimes Act 1908.
137 (1987) 3 CRNZ 337 (CA).

was to employ violent means. It is worth noting that the Court in that case did not consider it necessary to decide the question raised above, in § 15.5.1, whether the several acts (wounding, maiming, etc) required any intent; since once the "violent means" was established, and the causal link between such means and incapacity to resist is present, the necessary intent is "self-evident".[138]

15.5.3 Proof of offence

A person may only be found guilty of an offence under s 191(1)(c), or indeed under the corresponding s 192(1)(c) governing aggravated assault (below), if there is proof of the commission or attempted commission of a crime by the person committing the assault or by the person whose arrest or flight he intends to avoid or facilitate.[139] This restriction derives from the original provision in the Draft Code of 1879 from which the present section evolved, which referred to the "flight of the *offender* upon the commission or attempted commission" of a crime.[140] That format required proof that the person whose flight is facilitated actually committed or attempted to commit the crime.[141] Thus if D is acquitted of robbery, he could not then be convicted on a count of wounding with intent to avoid arrest or to facilitate his flight upon the commission or attempted commission of robbery.

15.6 AGGRAVATED ASSAULT

This offence, created by s 192, was substantially redrafted in 1961. It now provides:

> **Aggravated assault**—(1) Every one is liable to imprisonment for a term not exceeding 3 years who assaults any other person with intent—
> (a)   To commit or facilitate the commission of any crime; or
> (b)   To avoid the detection of himself or of any other person in the commission of any crime; or
> (c)   To avoid the arrest or facilitate the flight of himself or of any other person upon the commission or attempted commission of any crime.
> (2) Every one is liable for imprisonment for a term not exceeding 3 years who assaults any constable or any person acting in aid of any constable, or any person in the lawful execution of any process, with intent to obstruct the person so assaulted in the execution of his duty.

The provision defines two quite distinct offences, namely aggravated assault and assault with intent to obstruct a person in the execution of his duty. The offence defined in subs (1) requires that the accused assault some other person, and the aggravating features are identical to those specified in s 191(1)(a)-(c). As with s 191(1)(c), the offence in s 192(1)(c) requires proof of the commission or attempted commission of a crime by the person committing the

---

138 (1987) 3 CRNZ 337 at 340 (CA).

139 *R v Wati* [1985] 1 NZLR 236 at 238, (1984) 1 CRNZ 380 at 382 (CA).

140 See Draft Code of the Royal Commission on the Law Relating to Indictable Offences, 1879 (C 2345) s 188.

141 *R v Wati* [1985] 1 NZLR 236 at 238, (1984) 1 CRNZ 380 at 382 (CA).

assault or by the person whose arrest or flight he intends to avoid or facilitate.[142]

15.6.1 Assault with intent to obstruct

This offence is defined in subs (2). The offence first requires proof of an assault. For an aggravated assault then to be established, the subsection requires proof of two separate intents on the part of the person charged: the ordinary intent involved in the definition of assault in s 2, and the further intent that the assault was with intent to obstruct the person so assaulted in the execution of his duty. The "crucial" words, "with intent to obstruct the person so assaulted in the execution of his duty", must be read as a "composite description" of the further intent required by the subsection.[143] The Crown must prove (i) that the defendant assumed (in the sense of having a positive state of mind in relation to the matters) that the person she assaulted was a constable who was acting in the execution of his duty, and (ii) that she did intend to obstruct him in the performance of his duty.[144] Thus if D's evidence is that she did not give any thought to whether V was a constable in the execution of his duty, and assaulted him because she believed that, whoever he was, he was acting in a highhanded manner, she cannot be guilty of an assault under s 192(2) because knowledge or belief that the victim was a constable in the execution of his duty is the essence of the offence. On the other hand, evidence that the accused wilfully shut his eyes to the likelihood that the person assaulted was a constable, or was indifferent to that fact, may be evidence from which relevant knowledge could be inferred.[145]

The section does not expressly require that the person assaulted must be acting in the execution of his duty. It may be that the offence is committed if the offender believes the person assaulted to be acting in the execution of his duty and intends so to obstruct him, even if it should later transpire that for some technical reason the victim was not in fact acting in the execution of his duty.[146]

15.6.1.1 *Mistake*

Evidence of the state of mind of a defendant, including evidence of any mistaken beliefs on his part, whether of fact or of law, may be relevant to the question of intent. For example, evidence that D was honestly mistaken about the facts and believed the person he struck to be a trespasser would be relevant to the existence of the intent required in the subsection. Faced with such evidence, the Crown may be unable to prove that the defendant had the requisite state of mind for an offence under s 192(2). However, it will be no

---

142 Ibid.

143 *R v Simpson* [1978] 2 NZLR 221 at 223 (CA). See also *R v Reynhoudt* (1962) 107 CLR 381, [1962] ALR 483 (HCA).

144 *R v Simpson* at 225.

145 *Waaka v Police* [1987] 1 NZLR 754 at 759, (1987) 2 CRNZ 370 at 375 (CA). See the discussion of wilful blindness, at § 3.4.1.

146 *R v Simpson* [1978] 2 NZLR 221 at 225.

defence to a prosecution under the section if it is proved that the accused knew that the person being assaulted was a constable who was acting in the execution of his or her duty, but made a mistake about the legal extent of the constable's powers in the circumstances.[147] Such a mistake would be characterised as a "pure" mistake of law, ignorance of which is no excuse (at least, when the ignorance is in respect of the very offence committed by the offender).[148]

15.6.1.2 Honest belief that V is using excessive force

What is the legal position when D sees police officers restraining another person and intervenes because she believes (mistakenly) that the police officers are using excessive force in effecting an arrest? This issue arose in R v Thomas,[149] in which the accused and her friends intervened when they saw police officers restraining another person. At the hearing, the accused said she knew the persons effecting the "arrest" were police officers and as such were entitled to use force in effecting an arrest. However, she intervened because she believed, as a matter of fact, that they were using excessive force and were, therefore, acting in excess of their duty; thus justifying her intervention "in the defence of . . . another".[150] In the Court of Appeal (by way of case stated), it was held that the mens rea requirement that an accused must know the police officer is acting in the execution of his duty is not met by the prosecution's simply proving that the accused knew the police officer was exercising a "prima facie legitimate type of police power such as arrest". The Court held that an honest belief in a state of affairs (such as excessive use of force by the police officer) which, if true, would make the defendant's act innocent or justified, is a good defence to a charge of obstruction.

In that case, both the defences of mistake of fact and self-defence were available and were successfully pleaded. Significantly, the decision in Thomas admits the possibility that there may be some circumstances where a citizen may challenge the manner in which an enforcement officer is exercising a legitimate power without being guilty of obstruction. A person observing a police arrest will not necessarily become an "officious bystander"[151] by virtue

---

147 Waaka v Police [1987] 1 NZLR 754 at 759, (1987) 2 CRNZ 370 at 375 (CA).
148 Ibid. See § 12.2.
149 [1991] 3 NZLR 141, (1991) 7 CRNZ 123 (CA).
150 Section 48 Crimes Act 1961.
151 The High Court Judge, on appeal from the District Court, had implied that the accused in R v Thomas had acted as an "officious bystander" when she sought to challenge the way in which the arrest was being effected, honestly believing that the police were acting in excess of their powers. It may be that the Judge was over-influenced by the fact that the accused and her associates had been drinking to excess prior to the incident, and considered that for this reason they lacked the capacity to make a reasoned judgment in the matter. However, the defence of honest mistake of fact has never been prefaced by a requirement that the person making the mistake must be sober, although evidence of intoxication may be considered together with other matters in determining whether the accused actually held the belief claimed.

simply of acting according to a genuine belief that the police are using excessive force. This makes good sense. Otherwise, if a member of the public were never able to challenge how a police officer exercised an admitted police power, in circumstances where there were indications that the officer was going beyond the legitimate bounds of her authority, it is arguable that the public's ability to protect itself against misuse of police power would be severely compromised.[152] In effect, such a limitation would amount to a substantial fettering of the ability of genuinely concerned citizens to intervene and prevent what they believe to be a real and unjustified risk of serious danger to a victim as a result of excessive police conduct.[153]

However, there are limits to the ability of a citizen to intervene in such a case. If, for example, there was evidence that the intervener wilfully shut her eyes to the question whether the person effecting the arrest was a police officer acting in the execution of her duties or was indifferent to these matters, this is likely to negate her claim of honest belief.[154] Moreover, as was noted above, if D was aware that the victim was a police constable but entertained an incorrect understanding of the law regarding the extent of the constable's powers, that would constitute a mistake of law and would be no defence.[155]

15.6.1.3 *Self-defence*

The above analysis is buttressed by the law regarding self-defence. The "fundamental right" of self-defence cannot be excluded by the general provisions of the Summary Offences Act 1981. In *Thomas*, the accused claimed self-defence under s 48 Crimes Act 1961 on the basis that she was entitled to use reasonable force in the defence of another person whom she believed was the victim of excessive force (being used by the police in making an arrest). It was her belief that the police were acting unlawfully and were not acting in the execution of their duty. In such circumstances, all that is required is a subjective honest belief on D's part. Provided the degree of force used is reasonable in the circumstances *as she perceives them*, there is no reason why self-defence or defence of another should not justify the use of force that would otherwise be an assault, given that the accused did not realise the officer was acting in the execution of his duty.[156]

15.6.1.4 *In the "execution of duty"*

Whether a constable is acting in the "execution of his duty" will depend upon an examination of the facts in each case. Generally, a police officer acts in the execution of her duty from the point at which she commences a lawful task

---

152 Compare *R v Thomas* [1991] 3 NZLR 141 at 143, (1991) 7 CRNZ 123 at 125 (CA) (Casey J): "One has only to ask what would be the position if a bystander saw an outraged constable continuing to beat an unconscious suspect over the head."

153 Ibid at 143, 144, 125, 126.

154 See *Waaka v Police* [1987] 1 NZLR 754 at 759, (1987) 2 CRNZ 370 at 375 (CA); *R v Thomas* [1991] 3 NZLR 141 at 143, (1991) 7 CRNZ 123 at 125, 126 (CA).

155 See s 25 Crimes Act 1961; also *Waaka v Police* [1987] 1 NZLR 754 at 759, (1987) 2 CRNZ 370 at 375 (CA).

156 *R v Thomas* [1991] 3 NZLR 141 at 144, (1991) 7 CRNZ 123 at 125, 126 (CA).

connected with her functions as a police officer. She continues to act in the execution of that duty for as long as she is engaged in pursuing that task and until it is completed.[157] The concept of "execution of duty" is an important constitutional protection against excessive or inappropriate police intervention, and an implicit recognition of the fact that police powers of arrest or search are enormously wide and potentially intrusive into almost every area of human activity.[158] In New Zealand, a prosecution for obstruction or assault of a police officer requires knowledge on the part of the offender that the person assaulted was both a constable and acting in the execution of her duties. Because of the enormously variable circumstances in which a police officer may be required to intervene in the course of her professional occupation, the question whether the officer is actually acting "in the execution of her duty" may often be unclear to an observer. In most cases, the question will be determined by the terms of the enactment under which she purports to act, and by whether her conduct conformed with any statutory duty imposed upon her.[159] In some cases, the "execution" of a duty may involve the right of entry to premises for the purposes of detecting breaches of a particular statute, and may be accompanied by a requirement of "reasonable grounds" for suspecting that a particular activity is taking place.[160] Although a wrongful trespass committed by a constable may take her outside the course of her duty, a trivial trespass, amounting to only a "trivial interference with a citizen's liberty", does not.[161]

The obligations of the police in the execution of their duties under statute are well expressed in the following passage from the judgment of Myers CJ in *Burton v Power*:[162]

> The Police are charged with the preservation of order and peace within the country, and it is their duty to carry out that charge with moderation, fairness, and discretion, and within the law. So long as they do that, they are entitled to and should receive the support of the Courts and of every good citizen. If they carry out their duties unfairly and immoderately, the Court would not hesitate to express its condemnation of their action and would see that no person suffered by reason thereof. But, on the other hand, it is the duty of every citizen, especially in times when susceptibilities and passions are likely to be aroused, with the likelihood of resultant breaches of the peace, to refrain from conduct calculated to produce that kind of disruption within the country.

---

157 *DPP Reference No 1 of 1993; R v K* (1993) 118 ALR 596 at 601 (FCA).

158 Cameron and Young (eds), *Policing at the Crossroads*, Wellington, Allen & Unwin in association with Port Nicholson, 1986, 25.

159 See, for example, *Donaldson v Police* [1968] NZLR 32 (s 3(eee) Police Offences Act 1927 held to imply a duty "to enforce the law" and to prevent the obstruction of the highway).

160 See, for example, *Neiman v Police* [1967] NZLR 304, interpreting ss 208 and 209 Sale of Liquor Act 1962.

161 *Donnelly v Jackman* [1970] 1 All ER 987 at 989, [1970] 1 WLR 562 at 565. See also *Pounder v Police* [1971] NZLR 1080 at 1085.

162 [1940] NZLR 305 at 307, [1940] GLR 192 at 193.

15.7 OFFENCES AGAINST CHILDREN

The Crimes Act 1961 defines a number of offences involving non-fatal assaults that specifically proscribe assaults on and mistreatment of children. Section 194(a), which defines the offence of assaulting a child under the age of 14 years, does not appear to have a common law equivalent and was unknown in earlier enactments of New Zealand's criminal legislation. It was first enacted in Police Offences legislation in 1952.[163] The general law relating to criminal assaults applies to assaults under this section. Prima facie, this would include the possibility of consent as a defence, since the section does not expressly exclude a defence of consent. However, since the offence is designed to protect children below the age of 14 years, it is submitted that the principles governing sexual offences against young persons apply also to s 194,[164] and that, for the purposes of this offence, child victims are legally incapable of consenting to an assault.

Where the evidence of an assault goes no further than an allegation that the accused was "hitting the child when [the child was] going berserk", where the hitting involved two smacks with an open hand on the child's bottom, there may be no justification for treating the incident as anything more than a "pat on the bottom". While evidence of a technical assault, it may not merit the stigma of a conviction and may justify a discharge without conviction.[165] However, the Court in *Hende* noted that unauthorised acts of discipline against children should never be treated lightly, and prosecution in such cases may be justified in the interests of the community.[166]

15.7.1 Discipline of children

The extent to which children may legitimately be disciplined by the use of corporal punishment is governed by s 59 Crimes Act 1961. Essentially, the section permits parents and persons "in the place of the parent" to use force to discipline a child. The expression "in the place of the parent" is exclusive of teachers from whom the right to use corporal punishment has now been removed by legislation.[167] The prohibition against the use of corporal punishment by teachers, private school managers, early childhood centre employees or owners, and others employed as supervisors or controllers of children enrolled in or attending a school, is absolute.[168] Such a person may only use force by way of correction or punishment if that person is also a guardian of the student or child.

The absence in the statute of any reference to "legal" guardian leaves open the question whether a teacher acting as a de facto guardian of a student or child would be authorised by the exception[169] to administer force by way of

---

163 See s 5 Police Offences Amendment Act (No 2) 1952.

164 Cf §§ 16.6-8.

165 *R v Hende* [1996] 1 NZLR 153 at 158 (CA).

166 Ibid.

167 See s 59(3) Crimes Act, as inserted by s 28(3) Education Amendment Act 1990.

168 See s 139A Education Act 1989.

169 Section 139A(1) and (2) Education Act 1989.

correction or punishment in an appropriate case. Since the intent of the section would appear to be to prohibit the use of force by way of discipline outside a domestic setting, it may be that a person who was caring for a student or child, effectively in loco parentis, who was also involved in teaching the child, would be protected provided the force used was reasonable in terms of s 59(1). The possibility awaits consideration by the courts.

15.7.1.1 *Scope of permitted discipline*

Where force by way of discipline is authorised, the force used must be reasonable in the circumstances. In *R v Drake*,[170] a mother administered severe blows to her 8-year-old child, causing the child's death. It was held that the punishment and its result were so "monstrously disproportionate" to any offence committed by the child that it was evident that the punishment was actuated by malice and not by a desire to discipline. The Court held that, in determining whether it was solely correction that was administered, it is necessary to consider both the events at the time and the relationship between the parent and child prior to those events. In addition, factors like the gravity of the child's offence, the character of the child, and the likely effect on the character of the child may be relevant to the question whether force was applied by way of correction.[171] In the absence of any exemption grounded in the purpose of correction, the use of force upon a child becomes a non-consensual criminal assault.

15.7.1.2 *What is "reasonable" force?*

Force used for the purpose of correction must be "reasonable in all the circumstances". Severe beatings will never be reasonable.[172] The word "reasonable" in the Canadian equivalent to s 59 has been held to mean "moderate" or "not excessive", and it has been suggested that whether force is excessive should depend primarily on the age and physical condition of the child.[173] However, it is surely the case that determining whether the force used has exceeded what is reasonable in the circumstances requires the court to consider such matters as the nature of the offence calling for correction, the age and character of the child, the likely effect of the punishment on the particular child, the degree and gravity of the punishment, the circumstances under which it was inflicted, and the injuries (if any) suffered.[174]

15.7.1.2(a) *Cultural characteristics*

It would now appear to be a requirement of New Zealand law that in determining what constitutes reasonable force in s 59 Crimes Act, a court may not exclude from its consideration a defendant's cultural background where relevant. This issue was considered in *Erick v Police*,[175] in which a father had

---

170 (1902) 22 NZLR 478 (CA).

171 *R v Halcrow* [1995] 1 SCR 440 (SCC), affirming (1993) 80 CCC (3d) 320.

172 *Adams* § CA59.04.

173 *R v Halcrow* (1993) 80 CCC (3d) 320 (Southin JA).

174 *R v Dupperon* (1984) 16 CCC (3d) 453, 43 CR (3d) 70.

175 26/2/85, HC Auckland M1734/84, [1985] NZ Recent Law 227.

struck his 6-year-old son numerous times about the back and face with a belt when the child had been persistently disobedient. "Extensive injuries" were inflicted, although there was no permanent damage. On appeal, the High Court upheld the conviction and agreed that the force used by way of correction was unreasonable. It expressed the view that in determining the reasonableness of domestic discipline, a court may consider the "cultural characteristics" of the family or group concerned. It appeared to accept that what might be judged by the broader "New Zealand standard" as excessive force, may well by a more robust Niue yardstick represent correction that was not unreasonable in the particular cultural circumstances, and that such discipline might be administered by a variety of instruments, including sticks, belts, and "anything that is handy".

To fail to consider relevant cultural circumstances may well result in the application of an unduly rigid objectivism when determining the defendant's criminal responsibility.[176] Moreover, "reasonable in *all* the circumstances", if given a broad interpretation, is apt to include characteristics pertaining to defendants' families as well as to defendants themselves. There is merit in the view that since legal provision is made for defendants' ethnic and other characteristics in the context of the provocation defence, it would be appropriate to allow recourse to similar personal characteristics where domestic correction is the issue under s 59.[177] However, by the same token subjective personal characteristics should not be allowed to overwhelm the objective character of the standard. In the final analysis, the criminal law exists to *stipulate* standards of conduct, not to permit citizens to act by their own mores, however ingrained or respectable those personal standards may be. Defendants ought to be held to a general standard that is applicable to all New Zealanders.[178] The "reasonable" New Zealander is a person not of exclusively British blood or background but an ordinary person in terms of a population of markedly mixed racial origins with a substantial Polynesian minority.[179]

15.8 ASSAULT BY A MALE UPON A FEMALE
Section 194(b) defines the separate offence of assault by a male on a female. On such a charge it is necessary for the prosecution to establish both an assault and

---

176 See Comment, *Erick v Police* [1985] NZ Recent Law 227 at 228. It has been suggested that a reference to "reasonable under the circumstances" in s 43 Canadian Criminal Code (the equivalent of s 59), although imposing an objective standard, permits some element of subjectivity to be considered: *Martin's Annual Criminal Code 1997*, CC/88.

177 Ibid.

178 See *R v Baptiste and Baptiste* (1980) 61 CCC (2d) 438, where it was held that in determining whether the force used was reasonable under the circumstances, the court must consider the customs of contemporary Canadian community, not the customs of the accused's former country where corporal punishment may have had greater acceptance.

179 *R v Tai* [1976] 1 NZLR 102 (CA).

the respective sexes of the two persons involved.[180] Absence of consent is not included as an express ingredient of the offence but is implicitly available because of the requirement for proof of an assault.

15.8.1 Mens rea

The mental elements of a charge under s 194(b) require the prosecution to prove that the accused intended to apply force to the complainant (the assault requirement), and that he knew she was a female. Normally, it will be assumed that the accused knew the victim was a female, but if the question is raised the prosecution must prove such knowledge.[181] There is normally no need for the prosecution explicitly to show that there was no consent, or no belief in consent, unless there was something to which the accused could point to raise a reasonable doubt on that issue.[182] The fact that an accused suffers from an impaired mental state will not necessarily exclude the requisite intent in a charge under the section. In *Police v Bannin*, the circumstances, in which the accused held the victim while she struggled to escape, were held to be sufficient to have created within him the realisation that he was holding her against her will, notwithstanding his impaired mental state, and were, impliedly, sufficient evidence of an intention to assault.[183] However, intent is a factual question to be determined in every case where mental state may be in issue, and should not be assumed simply because the offender is capable of apparently purposive actions. In such a case, expert psychiatric testimony will normally be required to assess the offender's state of mind at the time of the offence and to guide the court on the broader issue of the offender's criminal responsibility.

15.9 CRUELTY TO A CHILD

Although the same wrongdoing may fall within a range of other offences, cruelty to a child is also a substantive offence created by s 195 Crimes Act 1961. For a charge of wilfully neglecting a child three elements must be proved:[184]

(i)   That the parents had custody of a child under 16 years;
(ii) That the child of whom they had custody was wilfully ill-treated or neglected;
(iii) That the wilful ill-treatment or neglect is in a manner likely to cause the child unnecessary suffering, actual bodily harm, injury to health, or any mental disorder or disability.

In *Police v L*,[185] there was agreement that wilful neglect is not proved simply by proving negligence on the part of the parents.[186] Indeed, the meaning of

---

180   *Police v Bannin* [1991] 2 NZLR 237 at 244, also reported as *B v Police* (1991) 7 CRNZ 55 at 62.

181   *Chandler v R* 10/2/93, Greig J, HC Napier AP4/93.

182   *Police v Bannin* [1991] 2 NZLR 237 at 245, also reported as *B v Police* (1991) 7 CRNZ 55 at 62, 63.

183   Ibid at 255, 74.

184   See *Police v L* [1993] DCR 617 at 620 (Judge Erber).

"wilfully neglects" has been considered at length by the House of Lords in *R v Sheppard*.[187]

15.9.1 "Wilfully neglects"

In *R v Sheppard*,[188] parents had been charged with wilfully neglecting their infant child. The majority held that the offence of wilful neglect was not one of strict liability to be judged by the objective test of what a reasonable person would have done. Rather, the prosecution is required to prove not only that the child needed adequate medical care, but also that the defendant had deliberately or recklessly failed to provide such care. A genuine lack of appreciation that the child needed medical care, or a failure through stupidity, ignorance, or personal inadequacy to provide that care are good defences. The word "wilful", which describes the state of mind of the actual doer of the act, was held to imply more than merely a "voluntary" act, and extends not only to the doing of the act itself but to the consequences to which the positive acts give rise.[189] In *R v Hende*,[190] the New Zealand Court of Appeal approved Lord Diplock's construction of the meaning of "wilfully". Eichelbaum CJ, delivering the judgment of the Court, said:

> In our view, the appropriate constructional approach is to regard the words "ill-treats . . . the child . . . in manner likely to cause him unnecessary suffering . . ." as a composite expression, which "wilfully" qualifies as a whole.[191]

In *Police v L*,[192] Judge Erber held that wilful neglect is proved if the parents were reckless whether harm was the consequence of their failure to provide care. Such recklessness will be established when it is proved that the parents, *being aware* both that care was required for the child and that a failure to provide or obtain it could well result in harm to the child, refrained from providing or obtaining such care despite that risk of consequential harm.[193] Normally for a prosecution to be brought under the section there would need to be some evidence of gross and habitual abuse or neglect sufficient to justify a claim that the child had been cruelly treated. Mere inadequate parenting should not qualify as wilful neglect where the parent(s) have done their best to make adequate provision for their children but have been prevented from doing so by insufficiency of financial means or lack of domestic support.

---

185 [1993] DCR 617 (Judge Erber).

186 See *MacKenzie v Hawkins* [1975] 1 NZLR 165.

187 [1981] AC 394, [1980] 3 All ER 899 (HL).

188 Ibid.

189 Ibid at 404, 405, 904 (Lord Diplock).

190 [1996] 1 NZLR 153 (CA).

191 Ibid at 156.

192 [1993] DCR 617.

193 Ibid. See also § 3.6.

15.9.2 "Neglects"

In *Sheppard* Lord Diplock held that to "neglect" a child is to omit to act, to fail to provide adequately for her needs; meaning, in the context of the statute, her physical rather than her spiritual, educational, moral, or emotional needs.[194] The actus reus in a case of wilful neglect is simply a failure, for whatever reason, to provide a child, whenever she in fact needs something, with the thing she needs. Because the crime of cruelty to a child is a generic offence, a relevant failure need not be limited to medical aid, and could include a range of necessities including food, clothing, and accommodation. It is arguable that the New Zealand provision also extends to a failure to provide adequate emotional support to a child, if a consequence of such failure has been to cause "any mental disorder or disability". In *Police v L*,[195] a consequence of the alleged neglect was that the three children (ages 5, 3, and 2) were developmentally delayed and severely understimulated, were not toilet-trained, and in the case of one child appeared to be intellectually handicapped and autistic. However, in the absence of cogent evidence in relation to "mental disorder or disability" this question was not pursued at the hearing.

15.9.3 "Custody, control or charge"

A condition precedent to criminal responsibility under the section is that the accused has "custody, control, or charge" of the child.[196] Although the question of whether a person is in "custody, control, or charge" of a child has been held to be one of fact,[197] it is suggested that the legal meaning of the words, in so far as they may be ambiguous, must necessarily be a matter of law.[198] In the comparable Canadian provision, "guardian" is defined to include a person who has *in law or in fact* the "custody or control" of a child.[199] In *Thompson v Grey* the claim that there must be some legal relationship, such as parent and child or guardian and ward, was rejected. The view of the Court was that the word "care" was apt to include those having the temporary care of children and that the words of the statute extended to "persons with whom they (the children) live and who have in fact charge of them and who in fact control them".[200] This interpretive approach, which places the protective responsibility for children with those who have the *actual* custody and care of them, is consistent with modern legislation aimed at the protection of children. It emphasises the practical status of a child as a "member of [a] family" requiring protection, rather than the formal legal status of the carer.[201]

---

194 *R v Sheppard* [1981] AC 394, [1980] 3 All ER 899 (HL).
195 [1993] DCR 617.
196 See also s 10A(b) Summary Offences Act 1981 ("a person to whom the care or custody" of a child has "been lawfully entrusted").
197 See *Thompson v Grey* (1904) 24 NZLR 457.
198 *Adams* § CA195.08.
199 Section 214 Canadian Criminal Code.
200 *Thompson v Grey* (1904) 24 NZLR 457 at 474.
201 See, for example, s 2 Domestic Violence Act 1995, in which "child of the applicant's family" is defined to mean "a child who ordinarily or periodically resides with the

15.9.4 "Ill-treats"

Where a charge alleges the ill-treatment (rather than wilful neglect) of a child, the actus reus is the action of ill-treating (that is, badly treating) the child in a way that is likely, in an objective sense, to cause the child unnecessary suffering.[202] The word "likely" in the section means "such as could well happen", and connotes a real or substantial risk rather than an assessment or balancing of the probabilities.[203] It follows that the *actual* production of "unnecessary suffering", etc is not a necessary consequence of ill-treatment, and does not have to be proved by the prosecution. It is only necessary for the prosecution to prove that there was a *real risk* that those consequences could well result from the conduct alleged. In the majority of cases, of course, it will be the consequential suffering, actual bodily harm, or injury that will have alerted the authorities to the case and provide the impetus for a criminal prosecution.[204]

---

applicant (whether or not the child is a child of the applicant and the respondent or either of them)". Compare also s 178 Crimes Act 1961 ("any child of hers" held to include not only natural children, but also any children who could, in fact, law, and common sense be said to be hers: *R v P* [1991] 2 NZLR 116, (1991) 7 CRNZ 48).

202 *R v Hende* [1996] 1 NZLR 153 at 156 (CA).

203 See *R v Gush* [1980] 2 NZLR 92 at 96 (CA); *R v Fatu* [1989] 3 NZLR 419 at 430, (1989) 4 CRNZ 638 at 648 (CA).

204 Regarding whether "ill-treats" is limited to physical ill-treatment, see the discussion in *Adams* § CA195.10.

16

Sexual Offences

Sexual offences in New Zealand are contained in Part VII of the Crimes Act 1961, which provides the definitions of offences against religion, morality, and public welfare. However, in this chapter we will limit the discussion to crimes of a sexual nature, including sexual violation, sexual intercourse within prohibitions on age and status, and offences of indecency. The chapter will not separately consider offences of bestiality or the "social sanitation" offences associated with prostitution and procuring sexual intercourse. Nor will the innovations in sexual offences committed outside New Zealand be considered here.

It should be observed at the outset of the chapter that over the last 12 years New Zealand law on sexual offences has undergone a radical revision and is still undergoing change at the hands of both the courts and legislators. Some of these changes, which will be considered shortly, have been driven by changing social values, and in particular by changing perceptions of the roles and status of women in society. In addition, with an increasing media profile being given to sexual abuse in all its forms there has come a greater awareness of the needs of the victims of sexual offending, which has led to changes in the way in which criminal litigation, especially that involving women and children as victims, is conducted. Not only have there been major changes to the definitions of substantive sexual crimes, but in addition there have been a number of significant changes in the law of evidence and criminal procedure which are principally geared towards making the trial process less distressing for those who are required to give evidence in such cases.

We commence this discussion by looking first at the most serious of the "new generation" of sexual offences, sexual violation, which now includes the traditional offence of rape.

16.1 SEXUAL VIOLATION

Traditionally, the crime of rape has been regarded as the most serious sexual offence. The punishment of rape has varied at different times, reflecting different attitudes towards its seriousness. Before the Norman Conquest the offence was punishable with death. However, during the reign of William the Conqueror the offence was punished by mutilation involving castration and the loss of the eyes.[1] During the reign of Edward I the offence was reduced to a trespass with a punishment of only 2 years' imprisonment and a fine. However, this remarkable leniency was short-lived, and in 1285 rape became a capital felony, remaining so until the nineteenth century.[2] In England the maximum punishment for rape is life imprisonment, while in New Zealand the offence is now punishable by imprisonment for up to 20 years.[3]

Prior to 1985, when major amendments were made, the Crimes Act 1961 listed sexual crimes under various descriptions contained in ss 128 to 144, commencing with rape and concluding with sodomy and bestiality. As a result of the 1985 amendments a new s 128 was substituted. This replaced the former provisions governing rape and substituted a generic crime of "sexual violation". The amended s 128 does not merely extend an existing concept: it has introduced entirely new concepts of sexual violation and sexual connection, with specific definitions of the latter "for the purposes of this section". The new s 128 reads:

128. **Sexual violation** — (1) Sexual violation is —
(a)   The act of a male who rapes a female; or
(b)   The act of a person having unlawful sexual connection with another person.

(2) A male rapes a female if he has sexual connection with that female occasioned by the penetration of her genitalia by his penis —
(a)   Without her consent; and
(b)   Without believing on reasonable grounds that she consents to that sexual connection.

(3) A person has unlawful sexual connection with another person if that person has sexual connection with the other person —
(a)   Without the consent of the other person; and
(b)   Without believing on reasonable grounds that the other person consents to that sexual connection.

(4) A person may be convicted of sexual violation in respect of sexual connection with another person notwithstanding that those persons were married to each other at the time of that sexual connection

(5) For the purposes of this section, "sexual connection" means —
(a)   Connection occasioned by the penetration of the [genitalia] or anus of any person by —
(i) Any part of the body of any other person; or
(ii) Any object held or manipulated by any other person, —
otherwise than for bona fide medical purposes:

---

1   *Ancient Laws and Institutes of England 1840: The Laws of King William the Conqueror,* London, Great Britain Public Records Office, 1840, XII, XVIII cited in Rook and Ward, *Sexual Offences,* London, 1990, 23.

2   Ibid.

3   Section 128B Crimes Act 1961 as substituted by s 2 Crimes Amendment Act (No 3) 1993.

(b) Connection between the mouth or tongue of any person and any part of the genitalia of any other person:

(c) The continuation of sexual connection as described in either paragraph (a) or (b) of this subsection.

The section is complemented by a definitional section, s 127:

127. Sexual intercourse defined—For the purposes of this Part of this Act, sexual intercourse is complete upon penetration; and there shall be no presumption of law that any person is by reason of his age incapable of such intercourse.

16.1.1 The elements of sexual violation

From this definition a number of specific points in the crime of sexual violation can be identified. It is useful to list them.

First, the section defines a new *generic* offence of sexual violation which is gender non-specific; ie the offence is not limited to unlawful conduct by a male against a female but may embrace any combination of genders on the part both of the assailant and of the victim of a relevant sexual assault. Secondly, the crime of rape, a gender and anatomically specific offence, is included as a particular subspecies within the generic definition of sexual violation. Where rape is alleged, that offence may only be committed by a male against a female, although a female may still be a secondary party to such an offence.[4] Thirdly, the defence of believed consent will only be available where the accused is able to adduce *reasonable grounds* for his or her belief in consent. Fourthly, the offence of sexual violation by unlawful sexual connection is not anatomically specific but may involve any non-consensual "connection" involving penetration of any part of the genitalia or anus, or oral contact with any part of the genitalia of either the offender or the victim, whether male or female.[5] Fifthly, penetration in turn is not anatomically specific, and may be effected by non-human objects. Sixthly, the offence may be committed by a husband against his wife or vice versa while they are married to each other.

16.1.1.1 *Meaning of "genitalia"*

In the legislation which this section replaces, the crime of rape was defined as the act of a male person having sexual intercourse with a female without her consent. Under both old and new law, sexual intercourse is complete upon penetration.[6] However, "penetration" itself is not defined. Accordingly, the common law definition still applies, according to which penetration will be complete if any part of the man's penis is "within the labia or pudendum . . . no matter how little".[7] The replacement in 1994 of "vagina" by "genitalia" in

---

4 See *R v Ram* (1893) 17 Cox CC 609.

5 For an examination of the law of rape from a male perspective see Morgan-Taylor and Rumney, "A male perspective on rape" (1994) NLJ 1490.

6 Section 127 Crimes Act 1961.

7 *R v Lines* (1844) 1 Car & Kir 393, 174 ER 861; approved in *R v Karotu* (1994) 11 CRNZ 691 at 694 (CA) (Casey J). For a further discussion of the meaning of "penetration" in this context see *Adams* § CA127.05.

subss (2) and (5)[8] now means that any penetration of the vulva will suffice for the crimes of rape and sexual violation by unlawful sexual connection.

The consequences of this change in the law may be seen by considering the decision of the Court of Appeal in *R v Karotu*,[9] a case involving an appeal under the earlier law against conviction on counts of sexual violation by unlawful sexual connection. The appellant practised a form of traditional island therapy known as "riring", which involved massage. The conduct alleged included massaging the clitoris of one complainant, and massaging and having oral contact with the genitalia of the other. On appeal to the Court of Appeal on a question of law, the question for the Court was whether sexual connection under s 128(5)(a) could be proved where there had been no penetration of the vagina but only penetration of the vulva. The Court held that the word "vagina" in s 128(5) should be interpreted according to its clearly understood medical meaning — that is, "the membranous canal leading from the vulva to the uterus" — and that the word should not be given a more liberal interpretation so as to embrace the whole of the genital area within the labia.

However, by substituting "genitalia" for "vagina", the effect of the 1994 amendment appears to supersede *Karotu*, such that wherever sexual violation by unlawful sexual connection is now alleged, the merest invasion of the genitalia, whether or not this involves penetration of the vagina, will suffice. As Casey J noted, referring to the law before 1994, rape is dealt with in s 128(1) as a separate kind of sexual violation which, as observed above, required connection occasioned by the penetration of a woman's vagina by a man's penis without her consent.[10] His Honour observed:

> While it may be readily assumed that Parliament did not intend to alter the law about rape, it by no means follows that the intrusion into a woman's genitalia by parts of another body (other than the mouth or tongue) or by objects, was intended to constitute sexual violation rendering the offender liable to imprisonment for 14 (now 20) years, *no matter how slight that penetration might be*. It is not unreasonable to think that Parliament was content to leave non-vaginal penetration in those cases punishable as indecent assaults, as they always have been. [11]

Obviously, the 1994 amendment has therefore changed the law significantly, and future offenders should not suppose that leniency will be extended to them on the basis that the alleged violation involved only "slight", non-vaginal, penetration that might previously have been treated simply as an indecent assault. Whatever may have been the legislative intent regarding non-vaginal penetration prior to 1994, it is now clear that *any* non-consensual invasion of the genitalia, including of the vagina and the vulva, will constitute unlawful sexual connection. Thus the previously vital distinction between vaginal and non-vaginal penetration for the purposes of intrusion by "another

---

8   As amended by s 2 Crimes Amendment Act 1994.

9   (1994) 11 CRNZ 691 at 694 (CA).

10   Ibid at 695.

11   Ibid (emphasis added).

body . . . or by objects" is no longer valid and will not support a defence to a charge of sexual violation.[12]

16.1.1.2 *The "continuation" of sexual connection*

The provision for continuation in s 128(5)(c) requires a brief comment. We know from s 127 that, as a matter of legal definition, sexual intercourse is complete upon penetration. This means that if D decides to have sexual intercourse with P without her consent the act of rape is complete once D has penetrated P. As we have already observed, the slightest degree of penetration will suffice. But what happens if, after D has penetrated P in an act of consensual sexual intercourse, P withdraws her consent? If the act of sexual intercourse is "complete" upon penetration and up to that point P consents to the conduct, can one say that D has raped P because at the point P withdraws her consent but D continues with the act of intercourse? Apparently so, according to their Lordships in the Privy Council decision in *Kaitamaki v R.*[13]

In *Kaitamaki*, D had been charged with one count of rape. He had broken into a house and allegedly twice raped the young woman occupier. There was no dispute that intercourse had taken place twice, but D's defence was that the woman consented or that the appellant honestly believed she was consenting. At the trial D gave evidence that after he had penetrated the woman for the second time he became aware that she was not consenting but that he did not desist from intercourse. The jury was directed that if the appellant continued the act of intercourse having realised that the woman was not consenting, it then became rape. On an appeal against conviction, the appellant argued that for the purposes of the Crimes Act 1961 a man who penetrated a woman with her consent could not become guilty of rape by continuing the intercourse after a time when he realised the woman was no longer consenting. Rape, it was contended, was penetration without consent and once penetration was complete the act of rape was concluded.

The Court of Appeal rejected this argument and dismissed the appeal. On appeal to the Privy Council, the appeal turned on the meaning of "complete" in s 127. Their Lordships, agreeing with the majority decision of the Court of Appeal, held that "complete" is used in the statutory definition in the sense of *having come into existence*, but not in the sense of having come to an end. Sexual intercourse is a continuing act[14] which only ends with withdrawal, because the offence of rape was defined by s 128(1) as "having" intercourse without consent. It followed that the appellant had been rightly convicted and the appeal was dismissed.

The reference in s 128(5)(c) to "continuation of sexual connection" is clearly intended to incorporate the principle laid down in *Kaitamaki*, so that by implication any offence involving "sexual connection" will continue until the accused desists from the activity which constitutes the actus reus of the offence.

---

12 See also *R v Randall* (1991) 55 SASR 447, 534 A Crim R 380; *R v Manuel* 11/3/94, T180/93.

13 [1984] 1 NZLR 385, [1984] 2 All ER 435 (PC).

14 See above, §§ 2.1.1.2.4, 2.1.1.3.

It will not be a defence to say that the victim consented to the initial act of sexual connection if consent is withdrawn while the connection persists.[15] It may be thought that this ruling might create hardship, particularly in situations involving sexually inexperienced persons who, in situations of sexual connection falling short of actual intercourse, do not desist immediately when consent to continuing intimacy is withdrawn. While the courts are mindful of the difficulties created by such cases, they will nonetheless be concerned to uphold the intent of the legislation, which is to protect people from sexual exploitation when they have either not consented to sexual activity or withdrawn consent that earlier was perhaps given. The purpose of the law is to uphold the right to personal autonomy in matters of sexual intimacy, and to punish those who fail to respect that right in others.

16.1.1.3 *Consent*

Before looking at the ways in which the statute deals with the issue of consent, it might be useful to make some general observations about consent. The requirements of consent have been usefully summarised in the following passage:

> Consent must be a free and voluntary consent. It is not necessary for the victim to struggle or scream. Mere submission in consequence of force or threats is not consent. The relevant time for consent is the time when sexual intercourse occurs. Consent, previously given, may be withdrawn, thereby rendering the act non-consensual. A previous refusal may be reversed thereby rendering the act consensual. That may occur as a consequence of persuasion, but, if it does, the consequent consent must, of course, be free and voluntary and not mere submission to improper persuasion by means of force or threats.[16]

The essence of true consent is that it is freely given by a rational and sober person so situated as to be able to form a rational opinion upon the matter to which he consents.[17] However, as with so many other concepts within the criminal law, the existence or non-existence of consent is often a matter of perception and it is never possible to determine in advance whether a particular transaction will be consensual or non-consensual. It has been observed that cases in which there is an apparent consent are always attended by circumstances which will enable a jury to determine whether there was or was not consent. The issue is essentially one of fact for the jury.[18] Each case must be considered in the light of its own facts. The problems associated with the meaning of consent in this context are well illustrated in *R v Brewer*.[19] The complainant attended a job interview, during which the accused asked her what she would do to ensure she got the job over another applicant. After indicating that she was desperate for the job, the accused said "well if you take off your top, I can nearly promise you a job". The complainant said she became

---

15   See also *R v Everson* 9/11/95, CA194/95.

16   *Case Stated by DPP (No 1 of 1993)* (1993) 66 A Crim R 259 at 265 (King CJ).

17   *R v M* [1993] DCR 1144 at 1146 (Judge Inglis QC).

18   *R v Cook* [1986] 2 NZLR 93 at 98 (CA).

19   26/5/94, CA516/93.

frightened that the accused would attack her physically if she did not cooperate, whereupon the accused took off the complainant's shirt and fondled and kissed her breasts. The accused then said she would "definitely get the job" if she performed oral sex upon him. The complainant reluctantly complied and shortly afterwards left the room. The accused was charged under s 129A(1)(c) with inducing sexual connection by coercion.

In the High Court, on a pretrial application, Robertson J approved the view that to consent is "consciously to apply one's mind and agree to what another has proposed or desired" and appeared to agree with the proposition that submission arising from a lack of practical choices open to a victim is not consent: "It is yielding out of an inexorable instinct for human preservation."[20]

On appeal against a conviction for sexual violation by unlawful sexual connection, the Court of Appeal accepted that consent would not be vitiated merely because it was induced by promises. Nor, it held, could "desperation for work" be regarded as inducing and negating consent, since the complainant would still have a choice whether to consent or not. However, it agreed that while one can still consent "with reluctance" even though some degree of coercion is present — so long as the decision to consent is voluntary — a consent would not be genuine if the degree of coercion was so great that the complainant was not in a position to make a decision of her own free will. So if D says to P "have sex with me and I will give you the job", the mere proposition will not of itself amount to coercion sufficient to negate consent. The reason for this is that P's choice is not foreclosed, and she still has the capacity to make an autonomous decision whether to have intercourse with D. If, however, D were to say "You will only get the job if you have sex with me now, before X returns" knowing that X was due back very shortly, it would be arguable that the degree of coercion would be sufficiently great to submerge P's free choice and negate consent.

The present law governing the validity of consent dates from 1985. The various matters which do not constitute consent to "sexual connection" (which must be taken to include rape) are now separately defined in s 128A, which reads:

> **128A. Matters that do not constitute consent to sexual connection**—(1) The fact that a person does not protest or offer physical resistance to sexual connection does not by itself constitute consent to sexual connection for the purposes of section 128 of this Act.
>
> (2) The following matters do not constitute consent to sexual connection for the purposes of section 128 of this Act:
>
> (a) The fact that a person submits to or acquiesces in sexual connection by reason of—
>
>   (i) The actual or threatened application of force to that person or some other person; or
>
>   (ii) The fear of the application of force to that person or some other person:
>
> (b) The fact that a person consents to sexual connection by reason of—
>
>   (i) A mistake as to the identity of the other person; or

---

20 *Brewer v R* [1994] 2 NZLR 229 at 236, also reported as *B v R* (T216/93) (1993) 11 CRNZ 419 at 425; Waye, "Rape and the Unconscionable Bargain" (1992) 16 Crim LJ 94 at 94, 95.

> (ii) A mistake as to the nature and quality of the act.
>
> (3) Nothing in this section shall limit the circumstances in which there is no consent to sexual connection for the purposes of section 128 of this Act.

Subsection (3) may be taken as an indication that all matters bearing on the existence of consent will be relevant, and may include any coercion of the complainant such that she could be said not to be in a position to make a decision of her own free will.[21]

16.1.1.3(a) *Failure to "protest or offer physical resistance": s 128A(1)*

The absence of consent, which is an essential element in the actus reus of sexual violation, is not to be equated simply with the use of force. The issue is: did the complainant consent? There may be an absence of consent even though no force is used at all and even though the complainant offers no protest or resistance. The critical issue is not whether the act was against the victim's will, but whether it was without her consent. It is for this reason that it is wrong to assume that the complainant must show signs of injury or that she must always physically resist before there can be a conviction for sexual violation. In *R v Hallett*,[22] several people were charged with the rape of a prostitute outside a brothel. Coleridge J instructed the jury that if there was no resistance on the complainant's part, but the non-resistance proceeded merely from being overpowered by actual force, or from her not being able because of lack of strength to resist any longer, or because she considered that the number of the assailants meant that resistance was useless, then consent was absent and the actus reus was proved.[23]

The Crown is not required to prove a positive dissent by the complainant. In *R v Murphy*[24] the accused was convicted of rape after he had swapped places with another man he found in his bed and had sex with a woman who had been sleeping there. M had returned to his house to find a couple asleep in his bed. He asked them to leave but only the man did so. He claimed she had rolled over and said she "just wanted to sleep". Soon afterwards, M had sex with the woman from behind. No words were spoken, and she did not look at him. In convicting the accused, the jury evidently disbelieved his claim that the woman made the sexual advances and was a willing participant throughout, and preferred the Crown's view that a reasonable person would not get into bed with a woman he had never met before. If that did happen, a reasonable person would then ensure the woman knew it was not the same man she had been in bed with earlier, before any sexual activity took place.

The case illustrates the principle that the fact that a person does not protest or offer resistance to sexual connection does not by itself constitute consent.[25] There was no suggestion that M had used force. However, the Judge directed that if a person consented to sex by reason of a mistaken identity, it was not a

---

21 *R v Brewer* 26/5/94, CA516/93.
22 (1841) 9 C & P 748, 173 ER 1036.
23 Ibid.
24 DC, Whangarei, reported in *New Zealand Herald*, 9/8/96.
25 Section 128A(1).

valid consent.[26] It has also been held that submission to the inevitable, or out of despair when trapped, is not real consent, even if the submission involves a degree of physical assistance given by the victim to the offender.[27] In *Daniels*, the victim assisted one of the offenders by helping him to place his penis in her vagina, an act which in the circumstances of the case was held to be "not truly voluntary".[28]

But where the appellant's own evidence was throughout consistent with a belief in consent and there is nothing in the complainant's evidence or the surrounding circumstances which objectively indicates that the complainant is not consenting, the evidence may be insufficient to support a charge of sexual violation.[29] In *Tawera* the complainant did not request the appellant to stop during 10 minutes in which he performed oral sex on her and had full sexual intercourse, nor was she threatened in any way. She had not attempted to push his head away during oral sex and made no reply when he requested sexual intercourse. Nor did she make any attempt to get off the appellant before the act was completed, or give any overt indication that the appellant should desist. The Court concluded that there was nothing said, done, or exhibited by the complainant from the time the sexual advances commenced to the conclusion of the incident which would outwardly demonstrate she was not consenting. In these circumstances it was unwilling to allow the convictions for sexual violation by unlawful sexual connection and rape to stand, since the evidence was such that the jury was left in a reasonable doubt on the issue of consent.[30] Normally, it will not be enough for a complainant to say "I was afraid of serious bodily harm and therefore consented". It must normally be proved in evidence that the victim had a genuine reason to be afraid, and (where possible) made some attempt to avoid the outrage.[31]

16.1.1.3(b) *Force and fear: s 128A(2)*

Under s 128A(2), consent may be negatived by fear or mistake even though there is no conduct and no misrepresentation by the offender that is intended to extort consent. The essence of consent, as has already been noted, is that it:

> should be freely given ... Although the victim of duress may intentionally submit to another, this submission arises from the lack of practical choice open to the victim.

26　See s 128A(2)(b)(i).

27　*R v Daniels* [1986] 2 NZLR 106 (CA).

28　Ibid at 110.

29　*R v Tawera* (1996) 14 CRNZ 290 (CA).

30　See also *R v Bursey* (1957) 26 CR 167, 118 CCC 219 (Ont CA). It is curious that the defendant in *Tawera* was not also charged with having sexual intercourse with a girl under care or protection under s 131, since the complainant was only 16 and was, at the time of the offence, as far as can be judged, "living with him as a member of his family" (cf s 131(2)). She evidently regarded him as a guardian. Had he been charged under s 131, the fact that the complainant had consented, or that he believed she had, would be no defence.

31　*R v Jones* [1935] 2 WWR 270, (1934) 63 CCC 341.

Submission is not consent. It is yielding out of an inexorable instinct for human preservation.[32]

So if P submits or acquiesces to sexual connection because of the actual or feared application of "force" to P or to another, consent will be negated. In *R v Olugboja*[33] the 16-year-old complainant, having previously been raped by one defendant, was pushed on to a settee whereupon a second defendant had intercourse with her. She did not struggle or resist, and did not cry out for help. The English Court of Appeal held that the events leading up to the intercourse, together with the complainant's reaction to those events, justified the jury's finding that she did not consent, even though she submitted to intercourse without being subjected to violence or threats of violence.

On the other hand, force certainly includes the use of physical coercion or direct physical violence to bring about submission. One exception was said to arise in *Case Stated by DPP*,[34] where it was held that "rougher than usual handling" in the nature of "boisterous playfulness" as a means of attempting to persuade a wife to consent to sexual intercourse will not of itself negate consent, provided that the conduct is actually acceptable to the wife. However, it is difficult to imagine the concept of "rougher than usual handling" having any wider application than within the context of marriage or of a relationship in the nature of marriage. Indeed, the mere touching of a stranger may negate consent.[35] Because of these possible variations, the parameters of (im)permissible force are not clear. In *Olugboja*, the Court assumed that fear may vitiate consent in rape even though it is not a fear of violence, but did not specify the sort of fear that might have that effect. However, the degree of force, the relative strengths, ages, and sexes of the complainant and of the third party, and the relationship between the complainant and the assaulted third party may all be relevant factors in determining whether an application of force will vitiate consent.[36]

Whether psychological pressure alone will vitiate consent is not yet clear. It is possible to imagine a situation in which a person is told that unless she agrees to sexual activity with the offender, whose mana or charisma she admires, something malevolent of a "spiritual" nature might occur. The implied threat is not of force per se, but to invoke "forces" which the complainant fears because of her belief in their power adversely to affect her life. Such a case may turn on whether the threat involves the "fear of the application *of force* to that person or some other person". Mere fear or apprehension that something untoward might happen to the complainant in the event that consent is not forthcoming would not seem to satisfy the requirement that force be "actual" or "threatened". Nor would it seem to

---

32   Waye, "Rape and the Unconscionable Bargain" (1992) 16 Crim LJ 94 at 95. Cited in *Brewer v R* [1994] 2 NZLR 229 at 235, also reported as *B v R* (1994) 11 CRNZ 419 at 424.

33   [1981] 3 All ER 443 (CA).

34   (1993) 66 A Crim R 259 at 266.

35   Bryant, "The Issue of Consent in the Crime of Sexual Assault" (1989) 68 Can Bar Rev 94 at 112.

36   Ibid at 113.

satisfy the requirement under s 128A(2)(a)(ii) of "fear of the *application* of force". What is required, it appears, is a fear that the complainant will suffer some bodily harm, albeit not grave harm, if she does not consent.

16.1.1.3(c) *Mistake as to identity: s 128A(2)(b)(i)*

Consent may also be negated where the complainant makes a mistake about the identity of the person with whom the sexual connection occurs. The reason for this is that consent is not effective if the complainant has not been given an opportunity to make an informed choice as to who she will share sexual intimacies with. Under previous law, the mistake was limited to a mistaken belief that the offender was the complainant's spouse. This limitation has now been removed. However, s 128A(2)(b)(i) will continue to apply to situations where consent is obtained as a result of a man impersonating a woman's husband. In such cases, for personation to occur there must be an intentional passing off by assuming the character of another person, something that can only be established by considering what was in the mind of the accused person (usually as evidenced by his overt acts).[37] Because the Act now imposes an objective standard for belief in consent, it is arguable that there is now an evidential onus on the "imposter" to show reasonable grounds for believing that the woman was not mistaken as to identity.

16.1.1.3(d) *Other mistakes*

Even if a mistake by the complainant is of a kind not covered by s 128A(2)(b), it is still possible that a conscious and unresisting adult is not to be regarded as "consenting" in law. The existence of the provision does not limit the circumstances in which consent is vitiated,[38] and earlier decisions where consent was found to be either valid or vitiated presumably retain their authority unless inconsistent with the new provision.[39] In *Papadimitropoulos v R*,[40] the complainant was a Greek woman whom the accused had fraudulently induced into believing that she and the accused had gone through a ceremony of marriage. She could not speak English. The marriage "proceeding" was only the lodging of the notice of their intention to marry. Following the false marriage, sexual intercourse took place on a number of occasions, although it was clear that the complainant would not have consented to the acts of intercourse if she had not believed she was married. The High Court of Australia affirmed that mistakes about the identity of the alleged rapist and the character of the physical act done would negate any apparent consent of the victim, but that since, here, the victim was neither mistaken whether she was taking part in an act of sexual intercourse nor mistaken about the identity of the defendant, her mistake did not negate her consent. In *Murphy*,[41] on the

---

37 *R v Kake* [1960] NZLR 595 (CA).
38 See s 128A(3) Crimes Act 1961.
39 Orchard, "Sexual Violation: the Rape Law Reform Legislation" (1986) 12 NZULR 97 at 100.
40 (1958) 98 CLR 249, [1958] ALR 21 (HCA).
41 § 16.1.1.3(a).

other hand, consent was negated because it was unreasonable for the accused to have intercourse with a stranger before ascertaining that she knew his true identity. However, where the mistake is directed to the nature of the relationship with the accused person and not the defendant's identity, it will not negate consent.

Similarly, consent will not necessarily be negated simply because the complainant was mistaken as to the accused's purpose. In *R v Mobilio*,[42] the accused was charged with eight counts of rape relating to his activities when employed as a radiographer. It was alleged that on eight separate occasions he had introduced an ultrasound transducer or probe into the vaginas of a number of young women without their consent. Although this procedure was normally practised by passing the probe over the patient's abdomen, it was sometimes performed as an internal examination. Upon referral by their own doctors to the clinic in which the defendant worked, the victims had each consented to the procedure. The Victorian Supreme Court had to decide whether the consent was negated on the basis that the transducer was not being used for medical diagnostic purposes but rather to satisfy the defendant's prurient sexual needs. The Court held that the consent in each case was not negated by a mistake as to the defendant's purpose, but was real even though given for a purpose with an entirely different moral complexion. The fact that the accused acted in a most improper way does not, of itself, negate consent.[43] It must be proved that the mistake was such as to actually negate consent at the time of the act of unlawful sexual connection. It is likely, therefore, that a mistaken belief that a voyeur present at a medical examination is a doctor present in that capacity,[44] or ignorance that a partner is infected[45] with a disease, will continue to fall within the sorts of mistaken beliefs that do not negate consent to sexual connection.

16.1.1.3(e) *Mistake about the "nature and quality of the act": s 128A(2)(b)(ii)*

In the criminal law there is no general rule that fraud vitiates consent. Under the previous law, s 128 provided expressly for only two forms of fraud — personation of the husband, and fraud in respect of the nature and quality of the act. It was thought that no other form of fraud could negative an actual consent to the act of intercourse.[46] The comparable provisions in the present statute refer only to "mistake" about identity and about the nature and quality of the act, which leaves the question: does "mistake" now include consent

---

42 [1991] 1 VR 339, (1990) 50 A CrimR 170. See discussion of this case in Waye, "Rape and the Unconscionable Bargain" (1992) 16 Crim LJ 94 at 99.

43 See *Brewer v R* [1994] 2 NZLR 229 at 235, also reported as *B v R* (1994) 11 CRNZ 419 at 425.

44 See *Bolduc v R* [1967] SCR 677, (1967) 63 DLR (2d) 82 (SCC); also Roberts, "Dr Bolduc's Speculum and the Victorian Rape Provisions" (1984) 8 Crim LJ 296.

45 *R v Clarence* (1888) 22 QBD 23 at 44, [1886-90] All ER Rep 133 at 145: "The woman's consent here was as full and conscious as consent could be. It was not obtained by any fraud either as to the nature of the act or as to the identity of the agent. The injury was done by a suppression of the truth."

46 *Adams* (2nd ed) § 977.

induced by fraud more generally? The issue does not appear to have arisen directly in the case law, but it seems generally to be assumed that the law on this point is unchanged, and that consent given as a result of fraud is a valid consent, unless the induced mistake is about identity or the nature and quality of the act.

This may sometimes lead to difficulties. The fraud is likely to be a significant factor in inducing a consent, but it is not clear that there will be a consequent "mistake" about identity or the nature and quality of the act. For example, it is arguably inapt to suggest that when the complainant in *Flattery*[47] submitted to intercourse in the belief that the defendant was treating her medically, consent was vitiated because she was "mistaken" as to the nature and quality of the act. Rather, it appears that she was induced to consent by a fraudulent representation about the beneficial consequences of the act. Similarly, in *Williams*,[48] where the appellant, a choirmaster, had intercourse with the 16-year-old complainant under the pretence that her breathing was not quite right, and that he had to perform an "operation" to make an air passage to enable her to produce her voice properly, the language of mistake seems inappropriate to describe an affirmative belief *induced by fraud* that she was being medically and surgically treated. What if, on the same facts, the complainant made no mistake as to the nature of the act of intercourse but accepted the choirmaster's assurances that it would, in any event, improve her breathing, and agreed to intercourse on that basis. Clearly, in those circumstances, the fraudulent representation would be an important factor in the girl's consent but it could hardly be said she was "mistaken" as to the nature of the act itself. Yet we would want to ensure that the deceitful choirmaster was unable to benefit from his outrageous misrepresentation and would regard him as a fit object for punishment.

What seems critical in cases of rape where consent is induced under the pretext of "medical treatment" is the element of *fraudulent persuasion*, often involving complainants who are either young and inexperienced or persons who are sexually naive. If a purpose of rape legislation is to protect the sexual autonomy of women then the law should target that conduct which impugns the ability of a woman to make a free and autonomous decision to have sexual intercourse, even in circumstances where there is some understanding of the nature of the act of sexual connection.[49] In essence, consent may be vitiated by other factors, in addition to a mistake.

---

47   (1877) 2 QBD 410.

48   [1923] 1 KB 340, [1922] All ER Rep 433 (CCA).

49   See *R v Harms* [1944] 2 DLR 61, where the victim consented to an act of sexual intercourse after being fraudulently persuaded that it was a necessary part of her medical treatment. The case was held to be rape. But cf *Boro v Superior Court* 163 Cal App 3d 1224, 210 Cal Rptr 122 (1985), where the Californian Court of Appeal held that it was not rape when a quack doctor persuaded a woman that she had a fatal disease which could be treated by sexual intercourse with a donor injected with a vaccinating serum, and had intercourse under the pretence that he was the anonymous donor. It was held the woman understood the nature and quality of the act.

For these reasons we would suggest that the wording of s 128A(2)(b) should be amended to read:

> (i) A mistake *or a belief induced by fraud* as to the identity of the other person; or
>
> (ii) A mistake *or a belief induced by fraud* as to the nature, quality, *or consequences* of the act.

This wording, we suggest, is better able to reflect the diversity of circumstances where consent may be vitiated by fraud than is possible through the limited concept of mistake.

16.1.1.4 *Marital rape*

At common law the traditional rule, until quite recently, was that a man could not rape his wife, save in certain exceptional cases. The common law position was largely based on the view of Lord Hale, who stated that a husband "cannot be guilty of a rape committed by himself upon his lawful wife, for by their mutual matrimonial consent and contract the wife hath given up herself in this kind unto her husband, which she cannot retract".[50] It is only in recent decades that the basis of this rule has begun to be questioned in the common law.

In New Zealand, the common law in this regard is no longer applicable and the issue of spousal immunity is now covered exclusively by statute. Under the former s 128(3) Crimes Act 1961, as amended in 1980, a man could not be convicted of the rape of his wife unless at the time of the intercourse they were living apart in separate residences.[51] This exception was abolished in 1985 when the present s 128 was enacted. Subsection (4) now provides that a person can be convicted of sexual violation in respect of sexual connection with another person notwithstanding that they were married at the time the sexual connection occurred. As well as being no defence to a charge of sexual violation, the fact that the parties are married or have been in a continuing relationship will not warrant a reduction in sentence. There is now, therefore, no distinction in principle to be drawn between sexual violation in marriage and outside of marriage.[52] Furthermore, as *R v D*[53] makes clear, even if D's alleged act of sexual connection is no more than digital penetration of his wife's vagina, there will be no lessening in the seriousness of the charge where the act is itself one of "forceful aggression" and calculated to belittle the wife and degrade her.[54]

16.1.1.5 *Sentencing*

Once an offence of sexual violation has been proved the court is bound, in sentencing, to consider the terms of s 128B(2),[55] which mandates the imposition of a sentence of imprisonment unless "having regard to the particular

---

50 1 Hale PC 629. See Rook & Ward, *Sexual Offences*, London, 1990, § 2.19.

51 See s 189(1) and First Schedule to the Family Proceedings Act 1980.

52 *R v D* [1987] 2 NZLR 272 (CA). For an analysis of the case and its implications for marital rape see Brookbanks, "Sexual Violation within Marriage" [1989] NZLJ 3.

53 [1987] 2 NZLR 272 (CA).

54 Ibid at 276.

55 Inserted by s 2 Crimes Amendment Act (No 3) 1985.

circumstances of the offence or of the offender, including the nature of the conduct constituting the offence, the Court is of the opinion that the offender should not be so sentenced". This provision applies whether or not the offender is married to the victim.[56] In *R v D* there was held to be no mitigation in viewing the incident as an act of aggression rather than as an expression of sexual interest, but leniency could be extended in fixing the term of imprisonment required by s 128B(2) because of factors peculiar to the particular case. In *R v D* these included the fact that the offender was unlikely to re-offend in this way, that he had no proclivity for perversion or sexual violation of victims, and the good reputation of the offender in his local area.[57]

16.1.2 The mens rea of sexual violation

The statutory definition of sexual violation is silent on the required mental element. Sexual violation requires an "act" (s 128(1)), and it is implicit that this must be conscious and voluntary.[58] Apart from this the only specified fault element is that the offender acted "without believing on reasonable grounds" that the other person consented to the sexual connection in question.[59] However, being a "true" crime, it is clear that the offence requires mens rea as to the remaining ingredients of the actus reus, and so cannot be committed accidentally. In effect, since it is usually meaningless to talk of a person *recklessly* having intercourse, the offence requires that D intend to have intercourse with the victim.

Of course, intercourse or sexual connection per se is not a crime, unless it occurs without the consent of the victim. It follows, therefore, that there are two different mental elements in the crime of sexual violation. The first is the *intention* to have sexual intercourse. The second is the *absence of belief, based on reasonable grounds*, in consent. Accordingly, we may say that the offence of unlawful sexual connection (including rape) will be committed where a sane person:

(i) Intentionally has sexual connection;

(ii) In circumstances where the victim does not consent;

(iii) Either without believing that the victim consents, or without having a reasonable belief that the victim consents.

16.1.2.1 *Without believing that V consents*

It follows from this that there are alternative grounds for establishing mens rea on the part of the defendant. Irrespective of whether there are reasonable

---

56 See *R v N* [1987] 2 NZLR 286, (1987) 2 CRNZ 513 (CA), where a sentence of 3 years' imprisonment imposed on the applicant for the sexual violation of his wife was upheld on appeal: "Parliament has made no distinction in the penalties between spousal and other kinds of rape, and the sense of outrage and violation experienced by a woman in that position can be equally as severe." (Casey J at 270, at 515)

57 [1987] 2 NZLR 272 at 275 (CA).

58 Orchard, "Sexual Violation: The Rape Law Reform Legislation" (1986) 12 NZULR 97 at 102. See generally § 2.3.

59 Section 128(2)(b) and (3)(b).

grounds for believing that V has consented, D will have the mens rea of sexual violation if he in fact does not believe V has consented. But what does "believe" actually mean in this context? As a subjective standard, belief requires an assessment of the actual state of mind of the accused. However, argument may arise as to what states of mind qualify as "believing". Would it suffice, for example, on a charge of rape that the accused assumed the victim was consenting but made no inquiry to that effect. Would indifference to whether or not the victim was consenting negate a belief in consent? It would seem that if a person has thought about the matter and has concluded, without doubt, that the other person is consenting, that will constitute a belief in consent.[60] However, where the accused admits to having doubts about whether the victim was consenting, or asserts that he believed she was *probably* consenting, that would seem to raise a serious question whether the accused possessed the requisite belief in consent. Certainly, it would raise a doubt that he "cared" whether or not she consented.

The indifference criterion appears not to be decisive, since it has been held that in "rare cases" a person may not be guilty of rape if, intending to have intercourse with a woman whether or not she is consenting, he mistakenly believes on reasonable grounds that in fact she is consenting.[61] Rather, the standard of belief appears to be that of subjective recklessness.[62] If D recognises that there is a genuine (and not merely "fantastic" or "remote"[63]) possibility that V is not consenting, then he has the mens rea for sexual violation. This is, in essence, the definition of recklessness approved in *R v Morgan*,[64] namely, an "intention of having intercourse willy-nilly not caring whether the victim consents or no".[65]

16.1.2.2 Without believing "on reasonable grounds" that V consents

The mens rea test discussed above, in § 16.1.2.1, used to be the *only* applicable test. Prior to the 1985 amendment, and as a result of the decision in *Morgan v DPP*,[66] the law was that if, at the time of intercourse, the defendant had a mistaken belief that the woman was consenting, he could not be convicted of

---

60 Orchard, "Sexual Violation: The Rape Law Reform Legislation" (1986) 12 NZULR 97 at 103.

61 *R v Brown* (1975) 10 SASR 139 (Bray CJ). See also the comments in *R v Wozniak* (1977) 16 SASR 67 at 71.

62 For further discussion, see above, §§ 3.2, 3.2.3.

63 *R v Wozniak* [1977] 16 SASR 67 at 74.

64 [1976] AC 182 at 215, [1975] 2 All ER 347 at 362 (HL).

65 See *R v Satnam* (1984) 78 Cr App R 149 at 154, [1985] Crim LR 236 at 237 (CA). The Court approved the expression "couldn't care less" adopted in *R v Kimber* [1983] 3 All ER 316 at 320, [1983] 1 WLR 1118 at 1123 (CA) to describe a reckless state of mind. See also *R v Taylor* (1985) 80 Cr App R 327 at 332 (CA). These decisions represent a retreat by the English Court of Appeal from its earlier view, expressed in *R v Pigg* (1982) 74 Cr App R 352, [1982] 2 All ER 591 (CA), that reckless rape could be committed where the accused "gave no thought to the possibility that the woman might not be consenting" (at 362, at 599).

66 [1976] AC 182, [1975] 2 All ER 347 (HL).

rape, even if he had no reasonable grounds for such a belief.[67] While this approach reflects the standard of recklessness now applied by New Zealand courts in respect of the majority of statutory offences,[68] it is no longer the sole basis of liability for sexual violation.

In *R v Clarke*,[69] the New Zealand Court of Appeal affirmed that the present s 128 Crimes Act was introduced to displace the subjective approach enunciated in *Morgan* — namely that honest belief in consent was sufficient to deny mens rea and exculpate the defendant. The statutory test now effectively gives rise to a mixed subjective and objective standard of mens rea.[70] In *Millar v MOT*,[71] Somers J described s 128 as making rape an offence of negligence. Accordingly, sexual violation is now established *either* when the accused was *aware* of the possibility that the victim might not be consenting but persisted regardless, *or* when he was indifferent and gave no thought to the possibility that the victim might not be consenting in circumstances in which a reasonable person would have thought about that possibility, *or* even when he positively assumed that the victim had consented in circumstances in which a reasonable person would have recognised the truth.

In many respects, the present test resembles a mens rea standard of objective, or *Caldwell* recklessness.[72] In jurisdictions where recklessness remains the mens rea requirement for rape, it has often been argued that recklessness should bear that wider meaning. In *R v Kitchener* Kirby P stated:

> To criminalise conscious advertence to the possibility of non-consent but to excuse the reckless failure of the accused to give a moment's thought to that possibility, is self-evidently unacceptable. In the hierarchy of wrongdoing such total indifference to the consent of a person to have sexual intercourse is plainly reckless, at least in our society today. Every individual has a right to the human dignity of his or her own person. Having sexual intercourse with another, without the consent of that other, amounts to an affront to that other's human dignity and an invasion of the privacy of that person's body and personality. It would be unacceptable to construe a provision . . . so as to put outside the ambit of what is "reckless" a complete failure to advert to whether or not the subject of the proposed sexual intercourse consented to it or declined consent. Such a law would simply reaffirm the view that our criminal law, at crucial moments, fails to provide principled protection to the victims of unwanted sexual intercourse, most of whom are women.[73]

As academics have recognised, the justification for importing an objective standard attaching to the accused's belief, contrary to normal principles of

---

67 See, for example, *R v Kaitamaki* [1980] 1 NZLR 59 at 63, 64 (CA).

68 Cf *Adams* § CA20.29.

69 [1992] 1 NZLR 147 at 149 (CA).

70 Ibid.

71 [1986] 1 NZLR 660 at 677, (1986) 2 CRNZ 216 at 234 (CA).

72 [1982] AC 341, [1981] 1 All ER 961 (HL); above, § 3.2.1.

73 (1993) 29 NSWLR 696 at 697. Approved in *R v Tolmie* (1995) 84 A Crim LR 293 at 303.

criminal liability,[74] in respect of one of the most serious crimes, is based on sexual violation's being a special case:

> In the absence of consent the conduct involved is a very serious intrusion on the person of another, and the crime is unusual in that the attitude and conduct of the complainant is of central importance. Moreover, there will often be a clear risk of absence of consent, and it will usually be easy for the other person to ascertain the true position. In these circumstances a "casual assumption" that a partner is willing, in the absence of struggles and screams, is said to be unacceptable, and there is sufficient culpability if a belief in consent is not supported by reasonable grounds. Full recognition of personal autonomy in sexual relations is widely thought to require this conclusion.[75]

With the 1985 amendment, the New Zealand legislature has given statutory endorsement to these arguments. This means that where an accused has not considered the question of consent, and a risk that the complainant was not consenting to the sexual intercourse would have been obvious to someone with the accused's mental capacity if they had turned their mind to it, the accused is to be taken to have satisfied the requisite mens rea for s 128. The same standard would also apply to situations where consent has been withdrawn during sexual connection, such that the accused was not continuing with the reasonable belief that the victim was in fact consenting.[76]

16.1.2.2(a) "Reasonable grounds"

As we have said, the requirement in s 128(2) and (3) that there be "reasonable grounds" for a belief in consent signals a rejection of the rule in *Morgan* and establishes reasonableness as a substantive requirement of mens rea. However, it is likely that in practice this change will have limited impact on verdicts, because the reasonableness or otherwise of an alleged mistake has always been relevant when assessing an offender's credibility. When actual absence of consent is proved there will seldom be a real possibility of mistake, whether reasonable or unreasonable.[77] In addition, the requirement for a "reasonable" belief in consent implies a "hard" objective standard.[78] There is no warrant for reading it down to "reasonable in the circumstances as he believed them to be" or in some other way bringing in a subjective approach to justify the accused's belief.[79] This means that there is no room for intoxication as a factor in

---

74 Cf Hall, *General Principles of Criminal Law* (2nd ed), Indianapolis, Bobbs-Merrill, 1960, 363: "moral obligation is determined not by the actual facts but by the actor's opinion regarding them."

75 Orchard, "Sexual Violation: The Rape Law Reform Legislation" (1986) 12 NZULR 97 at 103.

76 *R v Tolmie* (1985) 84 A Crim LR 293 at 305.

77 Orchard, "Sexual Violation: The Rape Law Reform Legislation" (1986) 12 NZULR 97 at 105.

78 As opposed to a "soft" objective standard, which would allow the tribunal of fact to consider the issue of reasonableness in the light of the accused's actual beliefs and other external conditions that might modify his beliefs.

79 *R v Clarke* [1992] 1 NZLR 147 at 149. It is, nevertheless, true to say that the test for belief in consent imposes a "mixed subjective and objective mens rea formula" which the

determining whether reasonable grounds existed for the accused's subjective belief that the victim was consenting.[80] So if D, while drunk, has sexual connection with P, and mistakenly interprets her non-resistance as consent, the fact that he was drunk is not an issue that the jury may make allowance for when determining whether his belief that P consented was reasonable. The test is, therefore, whether a reasonable *sober* person would have believed that the victim was consenting — not whether the drunken defendant reasonably believed she was consenting.

Note that, on this question, the prosecution bears the burden of proving that the accused did not believe on reasonable grounds that the complainant consented.

16.1.2.2(b) *Relevance of personal "characteristics"*

The insistence on a strict objective standard in this context does not necessarily mean that subjective characteristics are never relevant in evaluating the accused's belief. However, the extent to which they may be relevant is, at this stage, a matter of some uncertainty. References in present case law to factors that might be considered to be relevant "characteristics" to be taken into account in applying the objective test are oblique at best, and do not provide a conclusive basis in precedent for departing from a purely objective test. It is in any event clear, on the authority of *R v P*,[81] that intellectual impairment and blind lust are, together with intoxication, factors that are irrelevant to the question of reasonable grounds. The defendant in *R v P* was a 30-year-old moderately intellectually disabled man who was convicted of sexual violation by rape of a 30-year-old intellectually disabled woman. He had an IQ in the range of 48-50 points. Although the Court held that the defendant's intellectual disability was irrelevant in determining the objective element within belief in consent, it was a relevant "special circumstance" in determining whether or not he should be sentenced to imprisonment.[82] However, given that objective liability is generally prefaced upon the normative response of a sane, sober *adult* in the situation of the accused, we might expect that some concession could be made to an offender who suffered from a severe intellectual impairment, or to one whose very youth and inexperience in sexual matters and in interpreting such subtle indicia as consent, might mean that he is more likely to make a mistake that would not be made by a mature adult.

In respect of the latter category, there are at least grounds for arguing that in judging belief in consent the question is whether a "mature male" or a "reasonable adult" might have grounds for believing in consent.[83] This might be taken to imply that the *age* of the offender is a relevant characteristic in assessing reasonableness. Clearly sex could not be a relevant characteristic in

---

courts generally avoid when legislation does not expressly provide for it. See *Millar v MOT* [1986] 1 NZLR 660 at 668, (1986) 2 CRNZ 216 at 225 (CA).

80   Ibid.

81   (1993) 10 CRNZ 250 at 253, 1 HRNZ 417 at 420.

82   Ibid. See s 128B(2).

83   See *R v Cox* 7/11/96, CA213/96.

this context, given the now gender-neutral character of the offence of sexual violation. But beyond these two examples little is clear. Some commentators have favoured an "individualised" approach to whether a mistake is reasonable, rather than a purely objective test, which would allow consideration to be given to the "attitudes and capabilities of the defendant which he cannot be expected to control", perhaps even including intoxication.[84] Others would allow consideration of "physical or mental disabilities" of the accused, but exclude intoxication.[85] It would seem that the Minister of Justice at the time anticipated that some personal factors, such as mental deficiency, would be taken into account.[86]

The categories of what might qualify as relevant personal characteristics are not closed. It is open to the courts to determine whether a particular factor is relevant to the assessment of reasonableness. Some assistance in this regard might be gained from the decision of the English Court of Appeal in *R v Bowen*,[87] where, in the context of duress, their Honours ruled on the characteristics that may be relevant in determining whether a person of *reasonable firmness, sharing the characteristics of the accused* would have committed an offence.[88] The Court accepted that mere pliability, vulnerability, and timidity are not relevant characteristics that may be vested in the reasonable person; but listed age, sex, pregnancy, serious physical disability, recognised mental illness or psychiatric condition, and *mental impairment* as factors that might be taken into account as affecting the person's ability to resist pressure.[89] By the same token, characteristics due to self-induced abuse, such as alcohol, drugs, or glue-sniffing were held not to be relevant.

While there are obvious differences in the social policy objectives undergirding the defences of duress and consent, the purpose of the objective standard is the same in each case; namely, to hold people to a standard of conduct that applies universally and generally supports the Rule of Law. This purpose is not compromised where limited exceptions to a general rule of liability are drawn which recognise the special susceptibility to error of particular classes of persons. Apart from the possible exception of sex, for the reason already mentioned, there would seem to be no reason in principle why the other relevant listed characteristics — including age, recognised mental illness or psychiatric condition, and mental impairment — should not be

---

84 See, for example, Pickard, "Culpable Mistakes and Rape: Relating Mens Rea to the Crime" (1980) 30 Univ Tor LJ 75.

85 Temkin, "The Limits of Reckless Rape" [1983] Crim LR 5.

86 (1985) 465 NZPD 6435. For further discussion of the merits of allowing for individual peculiarities within a negligence test, see above, § 3.5.2.

87 [1996] 4 All ER 837, [1996] 2 Cr App R 157 (CA).

88 Under the common law defence of duress a jury is required to consider, amongst other things, whether a sober person of reasonable firmness, sharing the characteristics of the accused, would have responded to the situation of emergency by acting as the accused acted: *R v Graham* [1982] 1 All ER 801 at 806, [1982] 1 WLR 294 at 300 (CA); *R v Martin* [1989] 1 All ER 652, (1989) 88 Cr AppR 343 (CA).

89 *R v Bowen* [1996] 4 All ER 837 at 844, [1996] 2 Cr App R 157 at 166 (CA).

accepted as characteristics modifying the reasonableness test in the context of s 128. Since the Minister has already foreshadowed a political intention that some personal characteristics should be taken into account, the suggested list would properly recognise the special limitations of those classes of people who might be expected to make mistakes in this area, without seriously undermining any value the objective requirement might have.[90]

If this is accepted as a legitimate approach to the issue of belief in consent, some modification to the present law may be necessary. In particular, notwithstanding *R v P* (above), on the basis of the comments in *Bowen*[91] there appears little justification for holding that *intellectual impairment* can never be relevant when determining reasonable grounds. While courts may legitimately exclude merely below-average intelligence *per se* as a relevant factor on the basis that other mental characteristics such as inherent weakness, vulnerability, and susceptibility to threats are inconsistent with the requirements of an objective test,[92] genuine intellectual disability is a substantial disability, and people with mental retardation have a reduced ability to cope with and function in the everyday world;[93] an inability that involves no ascription of fault on their part.

16.2 INDUCING SEXUAL CONNECTION BY COERCION

Supplementing the crime of sexual violation, s 129A defines the separate offence of inducing sexual connection by coercion. This is a new crime and may be committed by any person who has sexual connection with another person (as defined in s 128(3)), knowing that the other has been induced to consent by one of certain specified kinds of express or implied threats. These include threats:

(i)   To commit an imprisonable offence "not involv[ing] the actual or threatened application of force to any person" (subs (a));

(ii)   To make an "accusation or disclosure" about misconduct likely to damage the reputation of another (subs (b));

(iii) To make improper use of any "power or authority" arising out of an occupational or vocational position to the "detriment" of another (subs (c)).

The threat need not have been made by the offender. Neither must the circumstances indicate that the threat was the reason why the complainant consented.[94] This may be a justification for the offence's being one of subjective mens rea, in that the defendant must *know* that the threat induced the complainant's consent. "Knowledge" here carries its usual meaning, requiring

---

90   See Orchard, "Sexual Violation: The Rape Law Reform Legislation" (1986) 12 NZULR 97 at 105.

91   [1996] 4 All ER 837, [1996] 2 Cr App R 157 (CA).

92   Ibid at 843, at 165.

93   *R v P* (1993) 10 CRNZ 250 at 252, 1 HRNZ 417 at 419.

94   Orchard, "Sexual Violation: The Rape Law Reform Legislation" (1986) 12 NZULR 97 at 105.

more than mere recognition of a possibility: the defendant will have the requisite knowledge only if she is sure of the reason for consent, or "knew what the answer was going to be" if inquiry was made.[95]

Section 129A describes an acquiescence to sexual connection induced by a specified relevant threat as "consent". Provided no other factors are present, such as violence, it appears that sexual violation is not committed because that offence can only be committed where consent is absent. It is clear, therefore, that there are important differences between the two offences. Although the offence is purely indictable,[96] it is punishable by a maximum term of imprisonment of 14 years in contrast to the maximum penalty of 20 years for sexual violation.[97] Furthermore, the offence defined in s 129A is not subject to the statutory presumption in favour of imprisonment for sexual violation,[98] and has not been made subject to a separate provision regarding attempts.[99] Its separation from sexual violation suggests that the two crimes are to be regarded as significantly different.[100]

16.2.1 Threats to commit an imprisonable offence: s 129A(1)(a)

One implication to be drawn from s 129A(1)(a) is that, if the specified threats in that section do not vitiate a consent, nor do threats to commit some lesser wrong — which, if successful in inducing consent to sexual connection, would therefore fall outside the scope of either s 128 or s 129A. Suppose, for example, that A threatens B that unless she has intercourse with him he will commit a non-imprisonable summary offence (say, offensive behaviour, or fighting in a public place[101]), knowing that it would cause B great shame or embarrassment.

The offences defined in s 129A give particular expression to the offence of extortion by threats in s 238. In the context of s 129A, as with s 238, to "threaten" carries its ordinary meaning of to "make clear an [unwelcome] intention".[102] The relevant threat may be either express or implied, and it will be a question for the jury whether on the whole of the evidence the conduct of the accused (or another) included a relevant threat.[103] Evidence at the trial that the accused intended no threat may be inadmissible, the question for the jury being whether his conduct, including his language at the time the alleged

---

95   Ibid. See *R v Crooks* [1981] 2 NZLR 53 at 56-59 (CA); § 3.4.

96   See the First Schedule to the Summary Proceedings Act 1957.

97   Section 128B(1).

98   See s 128B(2).

99   Under s 129, the attempt to commit sexual violation is punishable by 10 years' imprisonment. The absence of a similar provision for attempting to induce sexual connection by coercion means that the maximum penalty for an attempt is 7 years (per s 311 (1)).

100 Orchard, "Sexual Violation: The Rape Law Reform Legislation" (1986) 12 NZULR 97 at 101.

101 Sections 4 and 7 Summary Offence Act 1981. Both offences are punishable by a fine not exceeding $500.

102 *R v Wyatt* (1921) 16 Cr App R 57 at 60 (CCA).

103 See *R v Collister* (1955) 39 Cr App R 100 (CCA).

threat was expressed, induced the victim to consent to intercourse taking place.[104] However, because the essence of the offence is "inducing" consent to sexual connection it will be necessary for the prosecution to prove a clear causal nexus between the alleged threat and the consent. A relevant threat in the absence of evidence of induced consent will be insufficient under s 129A to establish liability.

16.2.2 Threats of accusation or disclosure: s 129A(1)(b)

This subsection covers situations where consent is coerced by a threat to report or recount the commission of an offence or sexual misconduct by another. It criminalises, in effect, a species of blackmail where the demand is satisfied by an act of sexual connection. The subsection covers situations where sexual connection occurs as a result of a threat by the offender to make a disclosure that creates a real risk that the victim's reputation will be damaged. It may include a disclosure of criminal offending by the victim, but could also include such mundane matters as a threat to inform the victim's parents of her previous immorality,[105] or to make a false allegation that he is a thief, thereby affecting his future employment prospects. However, moral or economic pressure alone will not be enough in the absence of a threat of disclosure which induces consent to sexual connection.

16.2.3 Threatened actions involving "detriment" to the victim: s 129A(1)(c)

The elements of the offence under this subsection are:

(i)   There has been sexual connection;

(ii)   The alleged offender knew that the victim had been induced to consent by;

(iii) An express or implied threat;

(iv)   To make improper use to the detriment of the other person;

(v)   Of a power or authority, arising either out of an occupational or vocational position held by the alleged offender, or out of a commercial relationship existing between them.

The subsection is aimed at certain cases of sexual harassment, and covers cases where V is induced to consent by threats — for example of dismissal, educational failure, or eviction — which involve a misuse of D's "power or authority".

A critical element in the subsection is that the threatened action must involve "detriment" to the victim. The meaning of "detriment" was considered in *Brewer v R*[106] where a young woman, "desperate" for employment, complained that she had complied with the sexual demands of her prospective employer because he had promised employment upon compliance. In a pre-

---

104   *R v Plaisted* (1909) 22 Cox CC 5.

105   See Smith & Hogan, *Criminal Law* (7th ed), 1992, London, Butterworths, 461.

106   [1994] 2 NZLR 229, also reported as *B v R (T216/93)* (1993) 11 CRNZ 419. See also *R v Brewer* 26/5/94, CA516/93.

trial ruling Robertson J held that the allegations did not constitute an offence against s 129A(1)(c). The requirements of "threat" and "detriment" meant there had to be some "pressing, urging, forcing or inducing action by improper use of the accused's vocational or occupational position to cause loss or damage to the position of the other".[107] Thus "detriment" cannot be interpreted to mean a "failure to grant a right or a hypothetical benefit"; and on the facts in *Brewer* it was held that the mere abuse, for sexual advantage, by the accused of his position as interviewer of a potential employee did not amount to threatening the victim with any immediate loss or damage, and so no detriment could be said to have arisen.

This may be so, but the insistence that "threat" necessarily implies a "pressing, urging or forcing" seems to go somewhat further than "making clear an intention" to do something unwelcome, a test suggested by the earlier authorities.[108] Apparently, however, it reflects the Legislature's intention regarding s 129A.[109]

A question may arise over the meaning of "improper" in this subsection. Does it mean, for example, that liability under s 129A is excluded if the threatened action was not only legitimate but proper, even though the accused intended the threat to induce sexual favours?[110] The best approach, it is submitted, would be to recognise that in such cases the legitimate power or authority may still be used improperly. This could occur where, for example, a lecturer says to a student "I would normally insist that your essay be handed in on the due date (a true statement and legitimate exercise of authority), but I'll make an exception if you will come home with me tonight" (an inducement to consent and an improper use of authority).[111] The focus in such cases should not be upon whether there might be a legitimate basis for the threatened action, but rather whether the accused has used her "authority and control" over the victim to induce consent.[112] In our example, the lecturer's threat is to exercise her authority to further a purpose for which the authority was not intended. Hence the use is improper.

16.3 ATTEMPT TO COMMIT SEXUAL VIOLATION

Attempt to commit sexual violation is defined as a separate offence in s 129 Crimes Act 1961. It specifies a penalty of up to 10 years' imprisonment for anyone who attempts to commit sexual violation or assaults anyone with intent to commit sexual violation. The section defines two separate offences.

---

107 *Brewer v R* [1994] 2 NZLR 229 at 235, also reported as *B v R (T216/93)* (1993) 11 CRNZ 419 at 424, 425.

108 See *R v Wyatt*(1921) 16 Cr App R 57 at 60(CCA).

109 *Brewer v R* [1994] 2 NZLR 229 at 234, also reported as *B v R (T216/93)* (1993) 11 CRNZ 419 at 424 (Robertson J).

110 Orchard, "Sexual Violation: The Rape Law Reform Legislation" (1986) 12 NZULR 97 at 102.

111 See *R v Nichol* (1807) Russ & Ry at 130, 168 ER 720 (CCR).

112 See Bryant, "The Issue of Consent in the Crime of Sexual Assault" (1989) 63 Can Bar Rev 94 at 128, fn 171.

However, there is no special definition of the elements of an attempt under s 129, so that the general definition of an attempt in s 72 applies. Accordingly, for an attempt, the act of the accused must be sufficiently proximate to the offence of sexual violation. Proof of an attempted physical penetration is not required if the actions of the accused can properly be regarded as more than mere preparation and show that the accused has embarked on committing the crime.[113] Thus the act of the accused in "jabbing" his erect penis against the complainant's vaginal area will constitute the actus reus of attempted sexual violation.[114] It is no defence that he was incapable of carrying out the final act of penetration.[115]

16.3.1 Mens rea

The mens rea of attempted rape has been a matter of some controversy, because of the difficulty raised by the more general question whether recklessness is consistent with the concept of attempt.[116] The English Court of Appeal has concluded, at least for the purposes of the crime of rape, that recklessness is sufficient in respect of the "circumstance" that the woman did not consent, but that the "result" − the act of sexual intercourse − must be intended in the full sense.[117] In *Khan*,[118] Russell LJ held that the mens rea for attempted rape is precisely the same as for the substantive offence at common law, namely an intention to have intercourse plus a knowledge of, or recklessness about, the woman's absence of consent. The only difference between the two offences is that, in rape, sexual intercourse takes place while in attempted rape it does not. According to Russell LJ:

> No question of attempting to achieve a reckless state of mind arises: the attempt relates to the physical activity; the mental state of the defendant is the same. A man does not recklessly have sexual intercourse, nor does he recklessly attempt it. Recklessness in rape and attempted rape arises not in relation to the physical act of the accused but only in his state of mind when engaged in the activity of having or attempting to have sexual intercourse.[119]

So an attempt at sexual violation may occur where an accused intends to commit sexual violation and is recklessly indifferent whether there is an absence of consent,[120] provided he goes beyond the stage of preparation. Unlike

---

113 *A-G's Reference (No 1 of 1992)* [1993] 2 All ER 190, [1993] 1 WLR 274 (CA).

114 *R v Khan* [1990] 1 WLR 813 at 816.

115 Ibid.

116 For arguments favouring the inclusion of recklessness in attempts, see Williams, "The Problem of Reckless Attempts" [1983] Crim LR 365. See also Smith and Hogan, *Criminal Law* (7th ed), London, Butterworths, 1992, 306. Contrary views have been expressed by other distinguished commentators, regarding which see *R v Khan* [1990] 2 All ER 783 at 786, [1990] 1 WLR 813 at 817 (CA) (Russell LJ).

117 See *R v Millard and Vernon* [1987] Crim LR 393 (CA) (Mustill LJ); approved in *R v Khan* [1990] 2 All ER 783 at 787, 788, [1990] 1 WLR 813 at 818, 819 (CA).

118 [1990] 2 All ER 783 at 788, [1990] 1 WLR 813 at 819 (CA).

119 Ibid.

120 See *R v Evans* (1987) 30 A Crim R 262. Compare *R v Zorad* [1979] 2 NSWLR 764 at 773; also *A-G's Reference (No 3 of 1992)* [1994] 1 WLR 409, (1994) 98 Cr App R 383 (CA).

the crime of attempted murder, which cannot be committed recklessly[121] and has a *unitary* mens rea element (namely an intention to kill), the crime of attempted rape and, in the New Zealand context, sexual violation, has a *bifurcated* mens rea. Thus an intention to have intercourse without consent, which goes to the actus reus of the offence, is not inconsistent with reckless indifference to the views of the victim. This second element, the absence of consent, may be characterised as an additional circumstance of the offence for which recklessness will suffice:

> If a man sets out to perform an act of intercourse on a woman with reckless indifference to her wishes but fails to achieve penetration his effort to do so has in every sense been an attempt to do something which is prohibited by law. He has attempted rape.[122]

A proper jury direction on a charge of attempted sexual violation should therefore include words to the effect that, when he made the attempt to penetrate the victim or otherwise to have sexual connection with her, the accused was either aware that the victim was not consenting, or realised that she might not be consenting and was determined to have sexual connection whether or not the victim was consenting.[123] It follows that there will be no offence if, at the time of the act of attempted sexual intercourse, the accused honestly believed that the complainant was consenting, or had considered the risk that she may not be consenting but had affirmatively concluded that the risk was negligible — whether or not he had reasonable grounds for so concluding.

16.4 EVIDENTIARY MATTERS

There are four provisions in the Evidence Amendment Act (No 2) 1985, relating to evidential questions in the prosecution of sexual offences, which we will now briefly consider.

16.4.1 Address and occupation of complainant

Section 139 Criminal Justice Act 1985 prohibits the publication of the name of the complainant in the case of certain specified sexual offences, and of any name or particulars likely to lead to the complainant's identification. This provision is itself reinforced by the terms of s 23AA Evidence Act 1908. The effect of the section is that, except with the leave of the judge, the complainant shall not be required to state his address or occupation in court; that no one involved in the proceedings, including lawyers and court staff, is to disclose the information in court; and that no evidence is to be given or sought relating to such matters. The judge is prevented from giving leave unless the information is of "such direct relevance"[124] to facts in issue that to exclude it would be

---

121 See *R v Mohan* [1976] QB 1; [1975] 2 All ER 103 (CA); *R v Whybrow* (1951) 35 Cr App R 141 (CCA).

122 *R v Evans* (1987) 30 A Crim R 262 at 273 (Bollen J).

123 See *R v Zorad* [1979] 2 NSWLR 764.

124 Section 23AA(3) Evidence Act 1908.

contrary to the interests of justice. The purpose of the provisions is to minimise the risk or fear that the complainant might be subject to harassment or attack.[125]

The amendment in 1986 deleted reference to the complainant's name from s 23AA (2)(c). The reference to "name" in the section heading is now redundant. The change reflects the fact that it would not be practicable to give the accused fair notice of the allegations against him if it were not possible to disclose the complainant's identity.

16.4.2 Delay in making complaint

At common law, in cases of rape and other sexual offences against females, the fact that a complaint was made by the victim (to a person to whom the complaint would naturally be made) shortly after the alleged occurrence and the particulars of the complaint, to the extent that they relate to the charge against the accused, could be given in evidence on the part of the prosecution. The purpose of such evidence was to establish the credibility of the complainant's testimony to the facts alleged, in that it showed consistency on her part.[126] It was also considered to be evidence negativing consent, where consent was in issue.[127]

Under the previous law, if there was no complaint at the first reasonable opportunity, it was likely that the defence would suggest that the failure to complain diminished the credibility of the complainant's evidence. However, in practical terms it was often likely that the failure was simply the result of trauma suffered by the victim rather than evidence of consent. The fact that there may be a reason for not complaining in such circumstances is now recognised by legislation. Section 3 Evidence Amendment Act 1985 has enacted s 23AC Evidence Act 1908, which, although it does not alter the existing law on recent complaint, provides that should the issue be raised, the judge is authorised to tell the jury that there may be "good reasons" why the victim of a sexual offence refrained from or delayed in making a complaint. This means that a judge has a discretion to make a comment where appropriate in a particular case, without being required to make a formal direction. An amendment to the section in 1995 extended the protection to complaints alleging an offence under s 114A Crimes Act (sexual conduct with children outside New Zealand); see s 2 Crimes Amendment Act 1995.

16.4.3 Character of the complainant

In the past, where consent was the central defence in a rape trial, it was a common tactic and permissible for defence counsel to endeavour to elicit information regarding the past sexual experience and reputation of the

---

125 Orchard, "Sexual Violation: The Rape Law Reform Legislation" (1986) 12 NZULR 97 at 109.

126 McGechan, *Garrow and McGechan's Principles of the Law of Evidence* (7th ed), Wellington, Butterworths, 1984, 57.

127 See *R v Lillyman* [1896] 2 QB 167, [1895-9] All ER Rep 586; *R v Osborne* [1905] 1 KB 551, [1904-7] All ER Rep 54.

complainant.[128] Obviously, where the defence was able to impugn the character of the complainant by showing her generally to be a person of "loose" morals, it might thereby raise a doubt in the mind of the jury whether her claimed refusal to consent on the present charge was believable.

However, since 1977 the common law right to cross-examine a complainant in a rape trial regarding her sexual experience with anyone other than the accused, or about her sexual reputation, has been severely restricted. These restrictions were first introduced by the Evidence Amendment Act 1977, which created s 23A Evidence Act 1908, applying specifically to the crimes of rape, attempted rape, and assault with intent to commit rape, as well as being a party to and conspiring to commit any such offence. In 1985, a new s 23A was substituted by s 2 Evidence Amendment Act (No 2) 1985, and further amended by s 2 Evidence Amendment Act 1989 and s 2 Crimes Amendment Act 1995. The present s 23A, which now applies to any offence "of a sexual nature", prohibits any question or evidence relating to the complainant's sexual experience or reputation, except by leave of the judge. Leave may be granted only if the information is of such direct relevance to facts in issue that to exclude it would be contrary to the interests of justice.[129] For this purpose, it will be insufficient that the information raises an inference as to the "general disposition or propensity" of the complainant in sexual matters. Leave is not required under the section if the purpose of the evidence is to rebut evidence of the proscribed kind which has been given, or if the accused is alleged to have been a party to another's offence and the evidence concerns the complainant's sexual experience with that other.[130]

Although these provisions would appear to have been effective in excluding evidence of the complainant's sexual experience in the majority of trials,[131] the criteria of "direct relevance" and "the interests of justice" in s 23A(3) may create uncertainty over their application in a particular case. Cross-examination is now permissible only if the judge is satisfied that the conditions referred to in s 23A(3) are met.

These criteria, which are said to constitute a "strong test",[132] were considered in *R v Duncan*.[133] In that case, defence counsel sought to put to the complainant that she had written letters making allegations against a boarder in her home similar to those made against the accused, and further that she had previously told her mother that she had been interfered with when much younger. The Court acknowledged that, given the severe limitations on cross-examination imposed by s 23A, such questioning can be relevant, particularly in child abuse cases, where it may be necessary "to explore the possibility of

---

128 *Garrow & McGechan's Principles of the Law of Evidence* (7th ed), Wellington, Butterworths, 1984, 170. See also *R v Bills* [1981] 1 NZLR 760 (CA).

129 Section 23A(3) Evidence Act 1908.

130 Section 23A(4) Evidence Act 1908.

131 Orchard, "Sexual Violation: The Rape Law Reform Legislation" (1986) 12 NZULR 97 at 110.

132 *R v McClintock* [1986] 2 NZLR 99, (1986) 2 CRNZ 158 (CA).

133 [1992] 1 NZLR 528, also reported as *R v D* (1991) 7 CRNZ 446 (CA).

fabrication to gain attention or through malice, or transferred attribution from actual offender to present accused . . . There can be occasions when questioning along these lines, far from being a character-blackening exercise of little relevance, is well justified in the overall interests of justice".[134] Leave for such examinations may be granted where the examinations are more than "mere fishing expeditions".[135]

In *R v Accused (CA92/92)* [136], the Court of Appeal held that the existence of a second complaint of an indecent assault allegedly made on the complainant by a person other than the accused some months earlier than the offence alleged, and bearing a "remarkable" similarity to the present complaint, prevented the examination sought from amounting solely to a "fishing expedition", and justified the application for leave to cross-examine. The Court observed that while the legislation set out to protect complainants, "it was not intended to avoid exposing the prosecution case to legitimate scrutiny".[137]

16.4.4 Corroboration

At common law, the established practice was that when a sexual offence was charged the judge was required to warn the jury to the effect that it was "unsafe" or "dangerous" to convict on the uncorroborated evidence of the complainant. However, the judge could add that the jury may convict in the absence of corroboration if it were convinced of the essential truth of the complainant's evidence. "Corroboration", in this context, came simply to mean independent testimony which supported or strengthened evidence from which the accused's guilt could be inferred.[138]

Nonetheless, in respect of sexual offending, the rules regarding corroboration have been severely criticised,[139] particularly in so far as they supported a presumption that the evidence given by a complainant was inherently unreliable. Consequently, the requirement for corroboration was eventually abolished by s 3 Evidence Amendment Act 1985, which enacted s 23AB Evidence Act 1908. The section provides that where a person is charged with an offence of a sexual nature, corroboration is unnecessary before that person may be convicted; and the judge is not required to give a warning to the jury relating to the absence of corroboration.

The section reflects Parliament's recognition that there is no special danger in sexual cases calling for special caution before acting on the word of the complainant alone. The judge remains free to comment on the absence of

---

134 Ibid at 535, at 454.

135 Ibid.

136 [1993] 1 NZLR 553 at 557 (CA).

137 Ibid. For a more detailed examination of the relevant case law and principles applicable to this area of the law see *Adams* § CA128.06A.

138 As to the meaning of corroboration, see *DPP v Kilbourne* [1973] AC 729 at 750, 751, [1973] 1 All ER 440 at 456 (CA); also *R v Poa* [1979] 2 NZLR 378 at 383 (CA).

139 Orchard, "Sexual Violation: The Rape Law Reform Legislation" (1986) 12 NZULR 97 at 112.

supporting evidence, if she thinks that the particular case calls for such comment.[140]

It should be noted, however, that s 23AB was largely a superfluous creation. In *Daniels*, the Court of Appeal observed that s 23AB appeared to have been drafted on the mistaken assumption that, prior to the amendment, corroboration of the complainant's evidence was necessary for the accused to be convicted. In rejecting this proposition, the Court noted that what was necessary was merely a warning to the jury of the danger of convicting on uncorroborated evidence. Trial judges were nonetheless free to go on to tell juries that they were fully entitled to convict without corroboration if, having borne the warning in mind, they were convinced of the essential truth of the complainant's account. While no formal warning is now "required", the section clearly preserves a discretion to warn in an appropriate case; although, where the judge does decide to comment on the absence of supporting evidence, no particular form of words is now required. [141]

16.5 INCEST

The crime of incest is defined in s 130 as follows:

(1) Incest is sexual intercourse between —
(a)   Parent and child; or
(b)   Brother and sister, whether of the whole blood or of the half blood; or
(c)   Grandparent and grandchild —
where the person charged knows of the relationship between the parties.

16.5.1 Definition

At one time punishable as a capital offence,[142] the offence of incest it is now punishable by up to 10 years' imprisonment in respect of offenders over the age of 16 years.[143] Unlike the English legislation, which defines separate offences of incest by a man and incest by a woman,[144] and which may only be committed by a member of the opposite sex against a victim within the prohibited degrees of blood relationship, the New Zealand offence is gender non-specific within the degrees prohibited by s 130(1)(a) and (c), and on the face of it would appear to allow for an incestuous relationship between same-sexed partners. Arguably, however, to allow such an interpretation would be to give a wholly different meaning to incest quite unlike that contemplated by the common law, and would be contrary to the presumed intention of Parliament. It is not stated, but in our view should be assumed, that the expression "sexual intercourse" as used in s 130(1) has exclusive reference to sexual connection between a male and a female. This argument is supported by the fact that gender-specific language is used of the brother-sister relationship in s 130(1)(b); and by the fact that the Legislature has used the term "sexual intercourse" rather than the

---

140   *R v Daniels* [1986] 2 NZLR 106 at 111, (1986) 2 CRNZ 164 (CA).
141   Section 23AB(2) amended by s 8(3) and (4) Crimes Amendment Act 1995.
142   See *Adams* § CA130.08.
143   Section 130(2) Crimes Act 1961.
144   See ss 10(1) and 11(1) Sexual Offences Act 1956.

gender neutral concept of sexual connection as defined in s 128(5), implying that the latter concept does not apply to s 130, and that incest can only be committed between a male and a female.[145]

16.5.2 Elements of the offence

For the offence of incest there must be:

(i)   Sexual intercourse;

(ii)   Within a prohibited relationship; and

(iii) Knowledge of the relationship between the parties.

Since incest requires proof of sexual intercourse, it can only be committed by penetrative intercourse. As with other crimes involving sexual intercourse, the offence is complete upon penetration.[146] However, for the purposes of this section sexual intercourse is sufficiently proved by penetration of the vulva by the penis, and penetration of the vagina is not required.[147] The offence may also be prosecuted as an attempt where the prosecution is able to prove conduct going beyond mere preparation (whether or not it is able to prove an attempted physical penetration) which shows that the accused had embarked on committing the crime[148] (for example, where the victim's father had climbed into her bed and had begun to position his body with a view to intercourse taking place).

16.5.2.1 *Knowledge*

The section requires that the accused "knows" of the relationship between the parties. This suggests that the mens rea of the offence involves two elements: the accused must (i) *intend* to have unlawful sexual intercourse (ii) *knowing* that he or she is related to the other. Accordingly, the offence is not one that can be committed while the accused is unconscious or is otherwise unaware of what he is doing. The section does not require that the accused must know that the other party is within a *prohibited* relationship as such, only that they are related in a particular way (parent/child, brother/sister, etc). To require the prosecution to prove as part of its case that the offender knew the relationship was one prohibited by law would contradict s 25 Crimes Act 1961, which specifies that the fact that an offender is ignorant of the law is no excuse. However, lack of knowledge of the *existence* of the relationship would be a good defence, amounting to a lack of mens rea.[149] In *R v Carmichael*,[150] the

---

145 See also *R v N* (1992) 9 CRNZ 471.

146 The expression "sexual intercourse", as used in s 127, remained unchanged by the 1985 amendment, reflecting the common law understanding of sexual intercourse as involving penetration *at least* of a woman's labia by a man with his penis. At common law there was no need to prove penetration of the vagina itself.

147 *R v N* (1992) 9 CRNZ 471 at 473.

148 See *A-G's Reference (No 1 of 1992)* [1993] 2 All ER 190, [1993] 1 WLR 274 (CA).

149 See *R v Baillie-Smith* (1977) 64 Cr App R 76, [1977] Crim LR 676 (CA). There a conviction of incest was quashed because the Judge failed to leave to the jury the critical question, namely whether the defendant at the material time realised it was his daughter and not his wife with whom he was having intercourse.

150 (1940) 27 Cr App R 183 (CA).

English Court of Appeal held that in order to rebut evidence of knowledge that a child born to his wife during wedlock is his daughter, the accused may not only testify denying paternity, but also prove that his wife had told him he was not the father. The Court also allowed that, as evidence of the sincerity of his belief, the accused could testify that he had told his second wife he was not the father, even though this evidence would tend to illegitimise the child, whom he had previously acknowledged as his daughter.

16.5.2.2 *Proving the relationship*

Generally, an admission by the defendant will be sufficient evidence of the relationship.[151] However, an admission may be insufficient in the absence of evidence that the accused had intercourse with the victim's mother at the time of conception. So, in *R v Hemmings*,[152] where the defendant's partner was the daughter of a woman who was married to another man at the time of her conception, it was held that there must be sufficient evidence, regardless of any admission, to rebut the presumption of legitimacy which arises when there is evidence that the child was born or conceived during marriage. The Court held there was not "a particle of evidence" that the mother had committed adultery with the accused.

16.5.2.3 *Mode of proof*

Proof of the relationship and age of the parties is normally achieved by certificates of marriage and birth. The nomination of the age of 16 as the cut-off point of liability for incest is evidently intended to protect both boys and girls under that age, with the result that where a person under the age of 16 permits a man or a woman to have incestuous intercourse she commits no offence. In effect, the nomination of the age of 16 establishes an irrebuttable presumption that a child or young person below that age is incapable of committing incest regardless of how active the child might have been in promoting the activity. Intercourse may be inferred from the circumstances, and proof that the parties were together in bed may be supplemented by evidence of earlier incidents of sexual passion.[153]

There is no separate statutory offence in New Zealand of inciting a person under the age of 16 to have incestuous intercourse. It would, nevertheless, be possible to prosecute such an offence where there was evidence, in terms of s 66(1)(d), that the accused had been a party by inciting, counselling, or procuring the commission of the crime of incest (to be committed by the older party), regardless of whether the full offence is actually committed.

---

151 *R v Jones* (1933) 24 Cr App R 55 (CA); *R v Seaton* [1933] NZLR 548 at 557 (CA) (Myers CJ).
152 [1939] 1 All ER 417 (CA).
153 *R v Ball* [1911] AC 47 at 71 (HL); *R v Bloodworth* (1913) 9 Cr App R 80 (CCA). See also *R v Stone* (1910) 6 Cr App R 89 (CCA).

16.6 SEXUAL INTERCOURSE WITH A GIRL UNDER CARE OR PROTECTION

This offence is defined in s 131 Crimes Act 1961. The gravamen of the offence is that the complainant was living under the same roof as the accused when they had sexual intercourse; thus the offence is intended to protect young persons vulnerable in a family situation,[154] and targets offending that involves "the negation of parental responsibilities".[155] In alleging an offence against s 131, the prosecution is required to prove:

(i)   A man having or attempting to have intercourse with any female under the age of 20 years;

(ii) Such female was not his wife or de facto wife; and

(iii) Either

    (a)   Such female was the step-daughter, foster daughter, or ward of the accused; and

    (b)   At the time of the intercourse or attempted intercourse the male and female were members of the same domestic situation and living in the same domestic situation at the relevant time; or

    (c)   The female was not his step-daughter, etc, and not was living with him as his wife; and

    (d)   The female was, at the time of the intercourse or attempted intercourse a member of the same domestic situation and living in the same domestic situation as the accused; and

    (e)   The female was under the accused's care and protection.

In effect, there are two separate offences defined in the section, which are distinguished by virtue of the nature of the relationship between the offender and the victim. In the first subcategory, the victim must be in a relationship as stepdaughter, fosterdaughter, or ward of the accused, and be living with him as a member of his family. In the second subcategory, the victim has no formal relationship with the accused but is living with him as a member of his family and is under his care and protection. In the first it is the *protected relationship* which constitutes the essence of the offence; in the second, it is the *protected status*, although both subcategories are indicative of a dominating influence and dependence.[156]

The requirement that the victim be living with the offender "as a member of his family" is common to both subcategories, and therefore central to the offence as a whole. This is one aspect of the particular vulnerability recognised by s 131 which arises from the closeness of the living circumstances and the constraints upon complaining and escaping. The phrase "living with him as a member of his family" suggests a reasonable length of time and degree of continuity,[157] and has been held to mean "as if she were a member of the family

---

154 *X v Police* (1993) 10 CRNZ 385 at 388.

155 *S v Police* (1990) 7 CRNZ 173 at 174.

156 *R v H* [1993] 1 NZLR 129 at 131.

157 Ibid at 131.

of which he is a part"[158] or as referring to the relationship in which the persons concerned are living in the same domestic situation. In relation to the accused, a family is "his" if he is a member of the group of people who comprise it.[159] Although short periods of time (for example, periods of one, 2, and 4 days) may not be sufficiently long to constitute "living with" another "as part of his family", periods of 7 weeks, 10 days, and 14 days have been held to qualify, even where the accused came to where the victim was living so that the victim became part of one family.[160]

16.6.1 Party liability

Unlike the offences defined in ss 132 to 134, which specify that the girl shall not be charged as a party to an offence committed upon or with her against the section, such a prosecution is not excluded by s 131, even though she cannot commit the offence as a principal.[161] However, it would presumably be a very rare case where it would be necessary to consider a prosecution, given that the aim of the legislation is to *protect* vulnerable young people in family situations from sexual exploitation, an aim which is hardly consistent with prosecuting them for the offending behaviour.

16.7 SEXUAL INTERCOURSE WITH A GIRL UNDER 12: S 132

One measure of the seriousness with which the above offence is regarded by the Legislature is the fact that it is purely indictable and punishable by up to 14 years' imprisonment. By contrast, the alternative offence of attempting to have sexual intercourse with a girl under 12 in s 132(2) has a right of election and carries a maximum penalty of 10 years.[162] The aim of the section is to protect female complainants who are especially vulnerable to sexual exploitation by reason of their age. Where the girl does not consent, a charge of sexual violation will also lie under s 128. However, under s 128 the offender would be able to defend on the grounds of a reasonable belief in the victim's consent.[163] By contrast, it is no defence under s 132 that the girl consented, or that the accused believed she was over the age of 12 years.[164] Neither can a defendant charged under s 132 escape conviction merely because the evidence at trial shows that a charge of sexual violation would have been justified.[165]

Proof of the age of the victim is, of course, crucial in this offence, since it is the age of the victim that underlies the wrongful nature of the defendant's

158 Ibid (Hardie Boys J).
159 Ibid at 134 (McKay J).
160 Ibid at 131.
161 *R v Tyrrell* [1894] 1 QB 710, [1891-4] All ER Rep 1215.
162 First Schedule to the Summary Proceedings Act 1957.
163 See s 128 (3) Crimes Act 1961.
164 Section 132(3). Note that s 132 is silent on the question of the accused's *belief* in consent. Thus it does not expressly eliminate the possibility of a defence of honest belief in consent. However, such a defence appears to be impliedly excluded by the fact that, if such consent existed *in fact*, it would constitute no defence.
165 Compare *R v Neale* (1844) 1 C & K 591, 174 ER 951.

conduct. It will generally be necessary to adduce some evidence in addition to the girl's verbal statement of her age to prove that she is in fact under 12.[166] Where there is doubt whether the girl was under the age of 12 when intercourse occurred, the difficulty may sometimes best be resolved by charging the lesser offence created by s 134, of having sexual intercourse with a girl between 12 and 16. The latter offence is electable, and is concurrent with the more serious offence in s 132.

16.7.1 Sexual intercourse and attempts

As with other offences under Part VII, where "sexual intercourse" is required, it will be sufficiently proved by penetration of the vulva of the victim. There is no need to prove penetration of the vagina.[167] Nor are rupture of the hymen or ejaculation necessary elements of the offence.[168] This being the case, since the full offence may be committed by any degree of penetration of the victim's genitalia, the offence of attempting to have sexual intercourse with a girl under the age of 12 years under s 132(2) will be complete where there is conduct, being more than mere preparation but falling short of actual penetration of the victim, that shows that the accused had embarked on committing the crime with intent to have unlawful sexual intercourse.[169]

16.8 INDECENCY WITH A GIRL UNDER 12: S 133

This offence is an electable offence with a penalty of up to 10 years' imprisonment. The essence of the offence is indecency,[170] which may occur in the context of an assault or as an ostensibly consensual act. It is the element of indecency which distinguishes the offence from common assault and makes it a rather more serious crime. Section 133 defines three distinct offences; namely, indecent assault of a girl under 12, a male doing an indecent act upon a girl under 12, and a male inducing or permitting a girl under 12 to do an indecent act with or upon him. Force is not required for any of these categories, and it is the absence of force which will generally distinguish an offence under this section from sexual violation. However, a charge of sexual violation will also be available where consent is absent; by contrast, the fact that the girl consented will not be a defence to a charge under s 133.[171]

While the offence principally targets indecency by male offenders, it is clear that the first variety of offence created by s 133 may be committed by a female as a principal offender, since the statute specifically refers to "every one".[172] Any of the three offences nominated may be committed by a female (other than the complainant) as a secondary party, pursuant to s 66(1).

---

166 *Inglis v Police* (1986) 2 CRNZ 463 at 465.

167 *R v N* (1992) 9 CRNZ 471 at 473.

168 See *R v Hughes* (1841) 9 C & P 752, 174 ER 861; *R v Lines* (1844) 1 C & K 393.

169 *A-G's Reference (No 1 of 1992)* [1993] 2 All ER 190, [1993] 1 WLR 274 (CA).

170 *R v Court* [1989] AC 28 at 33, [1988] 2 All ER 221 at 222 (HL) (Lord Griffiths).

171 Section 133(2).

172 In *R v Hare* [1934] 1 KB 354, [1933] All ER Rep 550 (CA), "whosoever" was held to include a woman even though the offence involved was indecent assault on a male.

573

16.8.1 Indecent assault of a girl under 12: s 133(1)(a)

Indecent assault is a species of assault more generally. The essential requirements of an assault are that the accused must have:

(i) Intentionally applied or attempted to apply force to the person of another, directly or indirectly; or

(ii) Threatened by an act or gesture to apply force to the person of another, and

(iii) Has, or causes the person being threatened to believe on reasonable grounds that he has the ability to effect his purpose.[173]

For the purpose of assault, even the slightest touching may constitute force, and at common law the least touching of another in anger was a battery.[174] However, to be an assault the touching must be intentional, and the offence cannot be committed accidentally.[175] It follows that, in the present context, because a typical case of indecency involves some form of physical contact there will usually be force sufficient for an assault. However, even where there is no physical contact between the accused and the victim, the threatened application of force, which causes the victim to believe in the accused's ability to carry out such an assault, may in an appropriate case amount to an indecent assault. This could occur where, for example, a man indecently exposes himself to a young girl while walking towards her and making indecent suggestions.[176]

16.8.1.1 *Mens rea*

The mens rea of an indecent assault by its nature implies some extra mental element beyond what is required for common assault. In *R v Court*,[177] Lord Griffiths held that the "extra" mental element necessary for an indecent assault should be that which constitutes the essence of the offence. In the case of an offence of indecent assault, the mens rea was said to be an intention to do something "indecent" to the woman, in the sense of an affront to her sexual modesty; or an intent to do that which the jury find indecent.[178] In the case of an offence under s 133, the same mens rea would apply, with the rider that the intention to do anything indecent which affronts the girl's sexual integrity should suffice, particularly given that the offence may be committed without the victim's being aware of the indecency having occurred.

An indecent assault may occur under the section in circumstances where, as in *R v Kerr*,[179] the victim was unaware of the threat. In that case the accused

---

173 See s 2 Crimes Act 1961.

174 See 3 *Blackstone's Commentaries* 120; *Cole v Turner* (1705) 6 Mod 147, Holt KB 107, 90 ER 958.

175 *R v Court* [1989] AC 28 at 34, [1988] 2 All ER 221 at 223 (HL) (Lord Griffiths). His Lordship cites the example of accidentally ripping a woman's clothing while attempting to force an exit from a train.

176 See *R v Rolfe* (1952) 36 Cr App R 4 (CCA). See also *DPP v Rogers* [1953] 2 All ER 644, [1953] 1 WLR 1017.

177 [1989] AC 28 at 34, [1988] 2 All ER 221 at 223 (HL).

178 Ibid.

179 [1988] 1 NZLR 270, (1987) 2 CRNZ 407 (CA).

was seen to lower his trousers and approach the sleeping victim with an axe held at waist height. He was held to be guilty of assault with a weapon even though the victim was unaware of his approach and there was no physical contact. All that seems to be required in such cases is that the accused, by a threatening act or gesture, displays hostility towards another.[180] There is no requirement for evidence that the accused's conduct created a fear of violence in the mind of the victim; where the alleged assault is based upon a "threatening by any act or gesture" by the accused to apply force, the state of mind of the recipient of the threatening act or gesture is irrelevant.[181] In the example given above in § 16.8.1, it would equally have been an indecent assault if the victim had had her back to the accused and had been completely unaware of his indecent words and conduct.

16.8.1.2 "Indecently"

It is a question of fact for the jury whether an assault committed by the defendant was indecent. In *R v Dunn*, the Court of Appeal approved a jury direction on the meaning of "indecent" in the following terms:

> It is the modern and popular use and acceptance of that term today. We are talking in this case of "now", the present day application of that word. It is used in a criminal statute so it must be something which will warrant the sanction of the law, not some trifling or unimportant episode, something sufficient to invoke the law that must appeal to you as a matter of common sense . . . The criminal law deals with matters of substance and that is what you have to deal with here. Now "indecent" is a word which very largely speaks for itself. It is a word . . . which the statute uses and it is not qualified in the statute in any way at all.[182]

Whether ordinary people would consider an act indecent will sometimes depend on the purpose with which the action is carried out. In *R v Court*,[183] the House of Lords held that smacking a girl a number of times outside her shorts on her buttocks for no apparent reason is an equivocal action. However, because there was evidence that the accused's purpose was to satisfy a "buttock fetish", it was held to be an indecent assault. The Court held that on a charge of indecent assault it was necessary for the prosecution to prove not only that the accused intentionally assaulted the victim but that in doing so he intended to commit an assault which right-minded persons would think was indecent. Note, however, if the outward nature of the assault is *incapable* of being regarded as indecent, the undisclosed intention of the accused cannot make the assault an indecent one.[184]

An assault that is not inherently indecent may be rendered indecent by its surrounding circumstances. In *Inglis v Police* it was held that a kiss on the lips of a 7-year-old girl alone in a bedroom with a 20-year-old youth, was indecent. Hillyer J said:

---

180 Ibid.

181 Ibid at 274, at 411.

182 [1973] 2 NZLR 481 at 482, 483.

183 [1989] AC 28, [1988] 2 All ER 221 (HL). See also above, § 3.3.

184 Ibid at 33, at 222 (Lord Keith).

This was not the sort of innocent peck on the cheek frequently given to children, nor does it appear that the appellant was in the position of an aged uncle or aunt who commonly demonstrate affection in that way.[185]

Similarly, in *Police v B*,[186] a 22-year-old man who kissed a 14-year-old girl on the stomach, thigh, and knee while she lay on his bed under a duvet, was held to have committed an indecent assault having regard to the "time and place and circumstances".

In *Beal v Kelley*,[187] an indecent assault was held to have occurred where the appellant pulled a boy towards himself, having just asked the boy to handle his exposed penis. The assault itself was not indecent, but the element of indecency was sufficiently established by proof of the circumstances surrounding the assault. Touching naked young boys on the hands, arms, and torso,[188] and a grown woman's embracing and cuddling a young girl,[189] are both situations where the courts have determined that the accompanying circumstances may render the conduct indecent.[190]

In the UK, the courts have recognised the existence of a category of indecent assault where, rather than being inherently indecent or rendered indecent by its accompanying circumstances, the assault is, at most, *capable* of being considered indecent.[191] Where, as in *R v Court*, an equivocal act could have either an innocent explanation — for example horseplay or physical discipline — or an indecent one, the spanking administered by the accused was said to be *capable* of being considered indecent. Whether it would be considered indecent by right-minded persons would depend on a variety of factors, including the relationship between the parties, and importantly, the reason why the appellant acted as he did.[192]

The effect of the decision in *Court* is that evidence of motive may be admissible on the issue of indecency only if right-minded persons *may* consider the assault indecent, and would want to know why the defendant acted as he did before reaching a conclusion.[193] However, such evidence would be irrelevant and inadmissible if right-minded persons would not consider the assault indecent.

It needs to be remembered, however, that consideration of motive is only relevant in circumstances where the act on the face of it does not clearly manifest an intention to, in some way, affront the sexual modesty or integrity

---

185 (1986) 2 CRNZ 463 at 466 (HL). Compare *R v Leeson* (1968) 52 Cr App R 185, [1986] Crim LR 283 (CA) where it was held that an assault by kissing a girl against her will was rendered indecent by accompanying suggestions that she should submit to sexual intercourse.

186 [1994] DCR 581.

187 [1951] 2 All ER 763, (1951) 35 Cr App R 128.

188 *R v Sutton* [1977] 3 All ER 476, [1977] 1 WLR 1086.

189 *R v Goss and Goss* (1990) 90 Cr App R 400 (CA).

190 See *Rook & Ward on Sexual Offences*, London, 1990, 4ff, and cases discussed there.

191 *R v Court* [1989] AC 28 at 35, [1988] 2 All ER 221 at 224 (HL) (Lord Griffiths).

192 *Rook & Ward on Sexual Offences*, London, 1990, 6.

193 Ibid.

of the victim. It will not apply where the act of the accused unequivocally shows such an intention, as where there is a deliberate indecent touching or where the circumstances surrounding the act manifest such an intent. In such cases the indecency of the assault may be inferred from the nature of the act itself; as when a woman induces an underage boy to have intercourse with her,[194] or where a man inserts his finger into the vagina of a 15-year-old girl.[195]

16.9 SEXUAL INTERCOURSE OR INDECENCY WITH GIRL BETWEEN 12 AND 16: s 134

As with the offence defined in s 133, this provision contains a number of distinct offences. They include:

(i)   Having sexual intercourse with a girl over the age of 12 but under the age of 16 (s 134(1));

(ii) Attempting to have sexual intercourse with any such girl (s 134(1));

(iii) Indecently assaulting any such girl (s 134(2)(a));

(iv) Being male, doing an indecent act on any such girl (s 134(2)(b);

(v)   Being a male, inducing or permitting any such girl to do an indecent act upon him (s 134(2)(c)).

However, unlike s 133, in respect of which the defences of consent and belief in the age of the girl are expressly excluded, s 134 contains elaborate provisions governing both consent and belief in the girl's age. We may surmise that, since the offence carries a right of election, is punishable by a maximum of 7 years' imprisonment, and provides for a defence of consent (albeit in limited circumstances), it is regarded by the Legislature as a less serious offence than the other offences we have considered involving juvenile female victims. Nevertheless, the purpose of the provision is to protect young girls from the type of misbehaviour and control defined in the statute. The courts take the view that illicit (even though consensual) sexual conduct with girls under 16 is a serious matter, and that the sexual exploitation of such persons while deliberately running the risk that they may be under 16 is likely to lead to a "substantial" prison sentence.[196]

The essential elements of the offences defined in s 134, including sexual intercourse, attempt, and indecency have already been considered above, in discussing the offences in ss 128 to 133, and will not be considered further in this context.

16.9.1 Consent

Unlike the other offences regarding juvenile female complainants, however, consent is relevant to s 134. The issue of consent arises in two distinct ways. Subsection (3) provides that it will be a defence to a charge under the section if *the person charged* proves that the girl consented and that he is younger than the

194 *R v Hare* [1934]1 KB 354, [1933] All ER Rep 550 (CA).

195 *R v McCormack* [1969] 2 QB 442 at 445, [1969] 3 All ER 371 at 373 (CA) (Fenton Atkinson LJ).

196 *R v Calder* (1989) 5 CRNZ 159 at 161 (CA).

girl. Under subs (4), a more rigorous consent is provided for where the person charged proves that the girl consented, that he was under 21 at the time of the offence, and that he had "reasonable cause" to believe, and did believe, that the girl was of or over 16 years of age.

In both s 134(3) and (4), it is expressly provided that, notwithstanding proof by D of the complainant's consent, the defence will be negated if the prosecution in turn proves that the consent was obtained by a false and fraudulent representation as to the nature and quality of the act.

16.9.2 Proof of age

In any prosecution under the section, proof of age is an important element. It is now an essential element in each of ss 133(1)(a), 134(2)(a) and 135. The fact of a child's age may be proved by any lawful evidence.[197] The question of how age should be proved in such cases was considered in *R v Forrest & Forrest*,[198] where the appellants had been charged under s 134 with having sexual intercourse with a girl under 16. There was no dispute that intercourse had taken place. The principle issue for the court was whether the Crown had established that the girl was under 16. The only evidence led by the Crown regarding the girl's age came from the girl herself, who produced what she claimed to be her own birth certificate. The Court held that in such a case the issue of proof of age is a matter to which the prosecution "should seriously address itself", adducing the best evidence possible. Since this was not done the appeal was allowed and the convictions quashed. North P said:

> In a case where exactitude is important, in which it is sought to prove a person's age by his own production of his own birth certificate, it should surely be possible for the deponent to testify. . . as to the day on which he has habitually celebrated his birthday, to the age at which he first went to school, and in what year, and similar details as to leaving school, or other matters supporting, though from the mouth of the deponent himself, his identification of himself with the person named in the certificate. [199]

At common law, evidence must be given identifying the person concerned with the person to whom the certified copy of a birth certificate relates.[200] Age may also be proved by direct evidence from someone who was present at the birth[201] or from witnesses who had seen the child and were able to testify to what they believed was his or her age.[202] Since the Crimes Act does not specify how the age of the complainant must be proved, we would suggest that all of these methods may be a legitimate means of proving age in a particular case.

---

197 *R v Cox* [1898] 1 QB 179 at 180, [1895-99] All ER Rep 1285 at 1287.
198 [1970] NZLR 545 (CA) (North P).
199 Ibid at 547.
200 *R v Bellis* (1911) 6 Cr App R 283 (CCA).
201 See, for example *R v Nicholls* (1867) 10 Cox CC 476 (CCA).
202 *R v Cox* [1898] 1 QB 179, [1895-99] All ER Rep 1285.

16.9.3 Proving the consent-based defence

The defence provided in subs (3) requires that the person charged must "prove" that the girl consented and that the accused was younger than the girl. This suggests that the onus on the accused in this regard is a legal (persuasive) onus and not merely an evidentiary onus, requiring the accused to establish these facts on the balance of probabilities. Parliament has made the conduct a crime and expects citizens engaging in sexual activity with young persons to make a reasonable effort to ascertain the age of prospective partners. It is rather more than a casual requirement.[203] However, in order to establish the defence of consent the accused is bound to address the issue of the girl's age, since proof of his younger age is a co-requisite of proof that she consented. He cannot prove he is younger unless he has first established her age.

Whether an accused did take reasonable steps to ascertain the complainant's age will depend on the circumstances. In *R v Osborne*[204] it was held that there must be an "earnest " inquiry or some other compelling factor that obviates the need for an inquiry. An accused may only discharge that requirement by showing what steps he took and that these steps were all that could reasonably be required of him in the circumstances. It will not be sufficient to state that further inquiries were not made because they would open the accused to ridicule, embarrassment, or rejection.[205] On the other hand, in order to rely on the defence, the accused need not necessarily directly ask the victim her age or ask collateral questions that would disclose her age. The age differential between the accused and the victim may be considered in determining whether the steps taken were reasonable; the greater the disparity in ages, the more inquiry will be required.[206]

In proving the defence under subs (4) the accused must, in addition to proving that the girl consented, prove that he had "reasonable cause" to believe, and did believe, that the girl was 16 or over. Belief may be inferred from the circumstances, including the conduct of the accused and the girl, and need not be sworn to by the accused. Both the belief of the accused and reasonable cause for the belief must be established by some evidence, so that the accused makes it appear to the jury that he did believe on reasonable cause that the girl was of or over the age mentioned.[207] In such a case, the personal appearance of the girl will be a material piece of evidence, though not necessarily proof, to establish the cause and belief. The jury must be satisfied on the balance of probabilities that the girl's appearance, taken together with any other available evidence including the accused's testimony (whether sworn or unsworn), establishes both the accused's belief and reasonable cause for that

---

203 *R v Osborne* (1992) 17 CR (4th) 35. See also the discussion in *Adams* § CA134.19.

204 (1992) 17 CR (4th) 350 at 363 (Goodridge CJN).

205 Ibid.

206 *R v K (RA)* Unrep, 22/2/96, NBCA; cited in *Martin's Criminal Code 1997*, Toronto, 1996, cc/247.

207 *R v Perry and Pledger* [1920] NZLR 21 at 23 (CA).

belief. However, belief may be negatived where there is evidence that the accused never directed his mind to the question of age.[208]

Even though, as we have said, the burden of proving the consent-based defences provided in s 134(3) and (4) falls upon the accused, it appears that the negating proviso (that the defence is excluded if it is proved that consent was obtained by a false representation, etc[209]) must be proved, where relevant, by the prosecution beyond reasonable doubt. It would be inconsistent to require the accused to prove that the consent was not obtained by a false and fraudulent representation as to the nature and quality of the act when the Act specifically requires the *positive proof* of that element. Requiring the accused to so prove would also be hard to reconcile with s 141 (indecent assault on man or boy), where the negation of consent obtained by false and fraudulent representation (etc) is clearly part of the actus reus to be proved by the prosecution in the normal way.

16.9.4 Time limit

Section 134(7) specifies that no one shall be prosecuted for an offence against the section unless the prosecution is commenced within 12 months of the time when the offence was committed. The indecent assault offence under subs (2)(a) is expressly excluded from this limitation. Both at common law and by statute in New Zealand, the day on which the offence was committed is excluded; thus, if the offence were committed on 10 September in one year, prosecution may be commenced on or before 10 September the following year.[210]

While this formula would appear to be simple to apply where there is a single charge and proceedings are commenced promptly, the situation may be more complex where there are multiple charges arising out of the same transaction, and informations are laid at different times. In *R v G*[211] the accused faced several sexual offending charges. Counsel applied for a discharge in respect of two charges made under s 134(1) on the basis that they were barred by lapse of time in virtue of s 134(7). Informations charging sexual violation by rape had been laid within a month of the alleged offences, but the accused did not face a charge under s 134(1) until some 13 months after the events, when the Crown solicitor presented an indictment charging an offence disclosed in the depositions for the sexual violation charges. In granting the application, Neazor J held that since the elements of sexual violation by rape were different from those of the offence defined in s 134, the prosecution could not be saved by s 339(1), which allows the accused to be convicted of any crime included in the commission of another crime. His Honour also rejected the proposition that a committal on depositions, the evidence of which would support a charge

---

208 *DPP v Cole* (1994) 100 NTR 1.

209 § 16.9.1.

210 *Radcliffe v Bartholomew* [1892] 1 QB 161, [1891-4] All ER Rep 829; Section 25(b) Acts Interpretation Act 1924.

211 (1992) 8 CRNZ 577.

under s 134, should be regarded as the commencement of a prosecution under s 134. His Honour said:

> The committal is specifically related to the charges set out in the informations and it is on those charges that the accused was committed to the High Court for trial ... It is a strange use of language ... to suggest that a prosecution has been commenced against the accused by virtue of the committal and the effect of s 345(1) in any case where the new charge is not an included offence within the terms of s 339. If it is not such an offence, unless an indictment is presented containing a specific charge and the accused is arraigned on it he will never in any sense have been charged with such an offence or even have been in danger of being convicted of such an offence.[212]

16.10 INDECENT ASSAULT ON WOMAN OR GIRL: S 135

An assault is essential to a prosecution under this section, there being no proscription of consensual indecent conduct (unlike the offences in s 133 (1)(b) and (c) and s 134(2)(b) and (c)). The elements of the offence that must be proved by the prosecution are:

(i) That the accused assaulted a female of or over the age of 16.[213]

(ii) That the assault, or the assault and the circumstances accompanying it were indecent.

(iii) That the accused intended to commit an assault which in its nature or because of the circumstances was indecent.[214]

Indecent assaults are considered in detail above, in § 16.8.1. In *Milne v Police*,[215] where the appellant had kissed the complainant on the lips after he had asked whether he could do so and she had said "no", it was held that the word "indecent" is to be given the meaning accorded to it in general use. What is indecent is to be judged in light of time, place, and circumstances.[216] Gault J held that a kiss, even unwelcome, upon an adult in many circumstances, although objectionable, will not be indecent. However, in the circumstances of the case he was unwilling to depart from the trial Judge's finding, and in reliance on *Inglis v Police* agreed that a kiss was an indecent act.[217]

16.10.1 Consent

Consent is a defence to a charge under s 135. However, unlike sexual violation, which requires proof of a "belief on reasonable grounds" (s 128(2)(b) and (3)(b)) before the defence will be available, for indecent assault an "honest" belief as to consent is sufficient. The essence of a charge of indecent assault is that the prosecution must prove that the defendant intended to touch the victim without her consent. If he did not intend to do this, or if he did not so intend

212 Ibid at 579, 580.
213 On the meaning of assault, see *R v Kerr* [1988] 1 NZLR 270 at 274, (1987) 2 CRNZ 407 at 411 (CA); also the discussion above, § 16.8.1.
214 *R v Court* [1989] AC 28 at 34, [1988] 2 All ER 221 at 223.
215 (1990) 6 CRNZ 636.
216 Ibid. See also *R v Dunn* [1973] 2 NZLR 481 at 483 (CA).
217 (1986) 2 CRNZ 463.

because he believed (albeit wrongly) that she was consenting, the prosecution will have failed to prove the charge. It is the defendant's belief, not the grounds on which it was based, which goes to negative the intent.[218]

This principle was applied in *R v Nazif*,[219] where the 61-year-old offender had allegedly indecently assaulted a 16-year-old girl, with whom he was acquainted. As she left his shop the accused grabbed her hand and holding her with one hand, started kissing her neck while putting his other hand first on her breast then on her genitals. On appeal against his conviction, the appellant argued that the trial Judge had misdirected the jury when he said that "If you believe a person is consenting to an assault that consent must be based on reasonable grounds". The Court of Appeal disagreed and held that, except in cases where it is otherwise provided by statute or where there are "other more dominant public interest features", it would be contrary to principle that a person who believes the victim of an assault consented to it should be found guilty of an assault. As Somers J said:

> Where there is evidence of such belief it will be for the Crown to negative it. The reasonableness or otherwise of the grounds of such belief will be material to the question of whether the accused in fact held it.[220]

The fact that indecent assault offences do not involve a "dominant public interest feature" would seem to be the principal reason why the Legislature has chosen not to redefine them as offences that may be committed negligently, by requiring proof of a belief based on objectively reasonable grounds. At present, an honest belief in consent will be a good defence to any sexual assault charge other than sexual violation, unless the defence of consent has itself been excluded expressly by statute.

Recklessness whether the victim consented will also be sufficient mens rea for indecent assault.[221] Although the issue has not been definitively settled, it is probable that only subjective, or *Cunningham*[222] recklessness will suffice. In *R v Kimber*, the English Court of Appeal indicated that a defendant is reckless about consent if he "couldn't care less whether or not the victim is consenting."[223] The implication of this is that *Caldwell* recklessness[224] is not enough: the defendant *must have realised* that the victim might not be consenting but decided to go ahead anyway.[225]

---

218 *R v Kimber* [1983] 3 All ER 316 at 319, [1983] 1 WLR 1118 at 1121, 1122 (CA).

219 [1987] 2 NZLR 122 (CA).

220 Ibid at 128.

221 *R v Kimber* [1983] 3 All ER 316 at 320, [1983] 1 WLR 1118 at 1123 (CA).

222 See § 3.2.1.

223 *R v Kimber* [1983] 3 All ER 316 at 320, [1983] 1 WLR 1118 at 1123 (CA).

224 See § 3.2.1.

225 *Rook & Ward on Sexual Offences*, London, 1990, 19; *R v Bonora* (1994) 35 NSWLR 74. However, for a contrary approach see *DPP v K* [1990] 1 All ER 331, (1990) 91 Cr App R 23; also *Fitzgerald v Kennard* (1995) 38 NSWLR 84, (1995) 84 A Crim R 333.

16.10.2 A lesser included offence?

One issue which the courts have had to consider is whether indecent assault is a lesser included offence within the definition of sexual violation. Important consequences turn on this where, for example, on a charge of sexual violation there is doubt whether penetration has occurred. Can the court substitute a charge of indecent assault on the grounds that the physical elements of indecent assault are necessarily included in the offence of sexual violation?

It would seem not. The issue arose in *R v Norris*.[226] At the close of the prosecution case on a charge of sexual violation, there was doubt whether penetration had been established. Section 339 Crimes Act 1961 permits a conviction of any crime "included" in the crime charged, where the evidence does not prove the crime actually charged but does prove the included, lesser, offence. Tipping J held that while at first glance it would seem that indecent assault must necessarily be included within a charge of sexual violation, on analysis it is clear that the mental element of sexual violation is different from that of indecent assault. For the former, the Crown must show that the complainant did not consent and that the accused did not believe on reasonable grounds that the complainant was consenting. However, in the case of an indecent assault, while lack of consent must also be proved, an honest belief in consent alone is sufficient to exculpate. Accordingly, it could not be said that the commission of sexual violation necessarily includes the commission of indecent assault. A person may be convicted of sexual violation but on the same facts be acquitted of indecent assault.

The decision in *Norris* may be compared to *R v Leonard*.[227] In that case, the accused, having pleaded guilty to one charge of sexual violation and five charges of indecent assault, applied for leave to appeal out of time against the conviction for sexual violation, on the ground that he should not have pleaded guilty to that charge because the victim had clearly consented. The accused, a 63-year-old man, had kissed the 11-year-old complainant on the vagina but over her underpants in circumstances where there could not have been sexual connection. The Court accepted that since consent had been freely given, and in the absence of any other evidence to support the charge of sexual violation, this was an exceptional case in which the accused upon the admitted facts could not in law have been convicted of sexual violation. But Sir Gordon Bisson, delivering the judgment of the Court, then ruled:

> However, there is no doubt that the particular conduct the basis of the charge of sexual violation on the admitted fact amounted to an indecent assault. We substitute a conviction of indecent assault for that of sexual violation.[228]

The Court cited no authority for this ruling. In light of the ruling in *Norris*, it is arguable that the Court misled itself in assuming that the fact that the "particular conduct" founding the sexual violation charge "included", or in the Court's words "amounted to", an indecent assault; and that the Court failed to

---

226 (1988) 3 CRNZ 527.
227 6/6/91, CA179/90.
228 Ibid at 3, 4.

distinguish between the common physical elements of both crimes and the differing mental elements. On the authority of *Norris*, it cannot be said that indecent assault is a lesser included offence within the crime of sexual violation. Although the outcome would seem to be correct, it is arguable that the proper procedure would have been for the Court to amend the count of sexual violation to one of indecent assault, per s 335(1), "so as to make it conformable with the proof".

16.11 SEXUAL OFFENCES AGAINST THOSE WITH MENTAL DISABILITY

Section 138 Crimes Act 1961 makes it an offence to have sexual intercourse with a severely subnormal woman or girl. Section 142 also makes it an offence to have anal intercourse with a severely subnormal "person", where the offender knows or has good reason to believe that the person upon whom the act is committed is severely subnormal. These are the only offence provisions which specifically proscribe sexual conduct with intellectually disabled persons.[229] The Mental Health (Compulsory Assessment & Treatment) Act 1992 has not carried over the offence of having sexual intercourse with a mentally disordered female, formerly provided for by s 113 Mental Health Act 1969, which targeted the sexual abuse of patients by hospital employees. The current legislation does not proscribe any form of sexual contact with patients.

The rationale for s 138 is, first, to protect vulnerable people from exploitation and, secondly, to guard against all the problems that can arise when a severely subnormal woman becomes pregnant.[230] While the social purpose of the provision seems clear enough, difficulties in interpretation have arisen because the section uses language and concepts that have no parallel in modern mental health legislation. For example, whereas in the 1969 Mental Health Act the definition of "mentally disordered" included the "mentally subnormal", defined as those suffering from subnormality of intelligence as a result of arrested or incomplete development of mind, the new Mental Health (Compulsory Assessment and Treatment) Act 1992, which repeals the 1969 Act, contains no definition of "mentally subnormal". In *R v Bowman*,[231] Judge Morris dealt with these interpretative difficulties by finding that the present section, together with s 20(b) Acts Interpretation Act 1924 enabled the prosecution to proceed on the basis that the repeal of the 1969 Mental Health Act does not affect the Crimes Act provision in so far as the 1969 Act has been "applied, incorporated or referred to".[232] This does indeed appear to be the best approach to the problem.

The phrase "severely subnormal" has no interpretative history in New Zealand. However, in England, where "severe mental impairment" is defined to mean "a state of arrested or incomplete development of mind which

---

229 Contrast the position in English law, where both the Mental Health Act 1959 and the Sexual Offences Acts of 1956 and 1967 define a range of offences that may be committed against those who are mentally handicapped or psychiatrically unwell.

230 *R v Whittaker* 27/8/97, CA23/97.

231 15/5/96, DC Auckland T404/95. See also *R v Whittaker* (1996) 14 CRNZ 64 (Doogue J).

232 Section 20 (b) Acts Interpretation Act 1924

includes severe impairment of *intelligence* and *social functioning*",[233] it has been held that severe impairment is to be measured against the standard of normal people.[234] This means that a person whose incomplete development produces severe impairment of intelligence and social functioning compared to normally developed members of the public, but only moderate impairment when compared with other mental defectives, is still to be regarded as suffering from severe impairment.[235]

16.11.1 Mens rea

In New Zealand, severe subnormality is defined in the statute as meaning "incapable of living an independent life or of guarding herself against serious exploitation or common physical dangers". To be guilty of an offence under the section, the accused must "know" or "have good reason to believe" that the woman is severely subnormal.[236] "Know" and "believe" imply subjective mens rea. The language of the corresponding English statute, "if he does not know and has no reason to suspect her to be a defective",[237] has been held to imply a subjective test as to what the accused knew or had reason to suspect, and not an objective inquiry regarding what an ordinary reasonable person ought to have known or believed.[238] Such knowledge may be inferred from surrounding facts, eg the accused's acknowledgement in a diary that the complainant was simple-minded and intellectually disabled, and his knowledge of her circumstances through close contact with her family.[239] The mere fact that the accused had no hostility towards the complainant, or his contention that he did not appreciate that the complainant was severely subnormal, will not necessarily negate mens rea, provided there is evidence that he realised she was suffering from a major degree of mental handicap.[240]

It would seem that the requirements for knowledge and belief in s 138(1) are to be read disjunctively, so that an accused may be guilty if he lacked the relevant knowledge but clearly had good reason to believe that the complainant was severely subnormal.[241] In *R v McNally*,[242] the accused sought to defend a charge under the section involving an 18-year-old complainant with a mental age of 12 years, on the basis that he regarded his involvement with her an extramarital affair with a young woman whom he thought was an ordinary person, possibly slow, but definitely not subnormal. The explanation was clearly rejected by the jury. On appeal, McKay J said:

---

233 Section 1 (2) Mental Health Act 1983 (emphasis added).
234 *R v Hall* (1988) 86 Cr App R 159 (CA).
235 *Rook & Ward on Sexual Offences*, London, 1990, 210.
236 *R v Whittaker* 27/8/97, CA23/97.
237 Section 7 (2) Sexual Offences Act 1956.
238 *R v Hudson* [1996] 1 QB 448 (CA).
239 *R v Whittaker* 27/8/97, CA 23/97.
240 Ibid.
241 Ibid.
242 6/4/93, CA 441/92.

It is quite unreal to describe these offences as if they were instances of extra marital consensual sex. This was not a single isolated offence, but one which was repeated. It is difficult to see how McNally could have been other than well aware of her subnormality, and the issue of his knowledge has been settled by the jury's verdict. He took advantage of her in circumstances involving a gross breach of trust.[243]

16.11.2 Consent

Section 138 is silent on the question of consent. However, the protective nature of the offence would seem to imply that consent is no defence. The essence of the offence is knowingly having intercourse with a severely subnormal woman: the notion of a reasonable belief in consent would seem to be incompatible with that analysis. If the accused possesses the relevant knowledge or belief in the woman's mental subnormality, it should make no difference to liability that he believed, reasonably or otherwise, that the complainant was consenting. Neither would it be a defence for the accused to prove that he did not know the victim was a girl, but thought that she was a woman. The mistake would be deemed to be irrelevant because of his knowledge of the relevant subnormality.

16.12 ANAL INTERCOURSE

This is a new offence, enacted by s 5 Homosexual Law Reform Act 1986. The section repeals and substitutes the provisions relating to sodomy, which under the old law was a crime regardless of the consent of the other person. Consensual anal intercourse is now criminal only if the person upon whom the act is committed is either under the age of 16 or severely subnormal. Like the crime of sexual violation, the offence defined in s 142 is gender neutral. It is, however, expressly limited to acts of anal intercourse, and therefore cannot be committed where both parties are female. A woman might, nevertheless, be charged as a party under s 66(1) where the victim is either under the age of 16 or severely subnormal.

16.12.1 Mens rea

The offence of anal intercourse is structured similarly to the offence created by s 138 (sexual intercourse with a severely subnormal woman or girl). Accordingly, the mens rea of the offence is committing an act of anal intercourse *knowingly* upon a person under the age of 16 years, or upon a severely subnormal person. For the reasons discussed in relation to s 138, consent should be no defence where the victim is severely subnormal. In our submission, knowledge of the disability is incompatible with consent and would necessarily negate any consent defence which would otherwise have been available to the accused. Similarly, consent will be no defence in the case of a victim under 16 years of age — since in the absence of consent, the offence would be one of sexual violation against s 128.

---

243 Ibid at 5.

16.12.2 Actus reus

Because the offence is defined in terms of an act of anal "intercourse", the actus reus will not be satisfied by an act of sexual connection falling short of actual intercourse, notwithstanding that such conduct may be punishable as an attempt. Although "intercourse" is not defined in the section, what is implied is penile penetration, any degree of which will be sufficient for liability.[244]

16.13 OTHER SEXUAL OFFENCES

For reasons of space, it is not proposed to deal separately with the remaining sexual offences in Part VII. In some, like the relatively uncommon offences of conspiracy to induce sexual intercourse (s 136), and inducing sexual intercourse under pretence of marriage (s 137), once sexual intercourse is proved liability will be determined on the application of general principles concerning conspiracy and the making of false representations. Others, including the offences of indecent act between woman and girl (s 139), indecency with boy under 12 (s 140), indecency with boy between 12 and 16 (s 140A), and indecent assault on man or boy (s 141), contain elements which are common to a number of offences already discussed at length in this chapter, and need not be further considered here.

---

244 See *R v Kaitamaki* [1984] 1 NZLR 385, (1984) 1 CRNZ 211 (PC).

17

Theft and Receiving

17.1 THE CORE OFFENCE OF THEFT

Theft is at the heart of property offences. Indeed, while stealing is criminalised in various specialist forms, including "theft by failing to account" and "theft as a servant", and in aggravated forms such as robbery, many of these variants can only be established if it is first proved that the defendant has also committed a simple theft. The definition of theft itself is set out in s 220(1) Crimes Act 1961:

> Theft or stealing is the act of fraudulently and without colour of right taking, or fraudulently and without colour of right converting to the use of any person, anything capable of being stolen, with intent—
>   (a) To deprive the owner, or any person having any special property or interest therein, permanently of such thing or of such property or interest; or
>   (b) To pledge the same or deposit it as security; or
>   (c) To part with it under a condition as to its return which the person parting with it may be unable to perform; or

(d)   To deal with it in such a manner that it cannot be restored in the condition in which it was at the time of such taking or conversion.

17.2 THE ACTUS REUS

It follows from the definition above that the actus reus of theft is the "taking or converting of anything capable of being stolen". It may be divided broadly into two elements: (a) taking or converting of a thing, (b) which is capable at law of being stolen. We begin with the second of these.

17.2.1 What is capable of being stolen?

The core definition of what things are capable of being stolen is stated in s 217, with some additional items specified in ss 218 and 219. Section 217 reads:

> Every inanimate thing whatsoever, and every thing growing out of the earth, which is the property of any person, and either is or may be made movable, is capable of being stolen as soon as it becomes movable . . .

Whether something is capable in law of being stolen depends, firstly, upon the *physical* nature of the thing, ie its corporeal characteristics, and secondly, upon the *legal* nature of the thing, ie whether it is capable of being owned and is in fact owned by ("is the property of") someone. Unlike the old common law rule, there is no further requirement that the thing stolen have any economic value, although value will often be relevant to sentencing decisions.[1]

17.2.1.1 *Physical characteristics*

According to s 217, "every inanimate thing whatsoever, and every thing growing out of the earth, which . . . either is or may be made movable" is capable of being stolen. This includes pieces of paper such as a cheque,[2] documents of title to land,[3] gas,[4] and water in pipes.[5] However, an "inanimate" or "growing" *thing* must have a physical existence: thus it is impossible to steal a chose in action (including a debt),[6] an idea, or information per se.[7] But there may be theft of the paper which represents the chose in action, information, etc so theft of a cheque is theft of the piece of paper, and not theft of its proceeds.[8]

---

1   See s 227.

2   *R v Bennitt* [1961] NZLR 452.

3   *Bishop v NZ Law Soc* [1932] NZLR 1516.

4   *Oliver v Taylor* (1896) 15 NZLR 449.

5   *Ferens v O'Brien* (1883) 11 QBD 21.

6   Cf *R v Bennitt* [1961] NZLR 452; *Mead v R* [1972] NZLR 255 (CA). The origin of this rule is attributed to Coke CJ in *Cayle's Case* (1584) 8 Co Rep 32a, 77 ER 520.

7   Cf *Oxford v Moss* (1978) 68 Cr App R 183, [1979] Crim LR 119. Confidential information in the form of proofs of a university examination paper, which the student subsequently returned, did not amount to property for the purposes of s 4(1) Theft Act 1968 (UK), notwithstanding that it included choses in action and *in*tangible property.

8   *R v Bennitt* [1961] NZLR 452. Note, however, that the value of a stolen cheque is the value attaching to the rights which it confers, which may therefore be more than the value of the paper itself.

Exceptions to this rule are electricity, which is deemed by s 218 "to be a thing capable of being stolen",[9] and equitable interests falling under ss 222-224.

The criterion that the item stolen must have a physical existence means that the protection afforded by s 217 does not extend to a number of things regarded as "property" in civil law. This is something of a curiosity, since the purpose of theft is to regulate interferences with property rights. The restriction seems rather anachronistic, the by-product of an age when value resided primarily in tangible property. In the modern world, the increasingly cybernetic nature of our wealth suggests that reform of the definition is warranted.

At common law, land and anything affixed to land cannot be stolen.[10] Under the Crimes Act, land itself remains incapable of being stolen (except under the separate s 223) but under s 217 any *part* of land (including soil) or anything attached to or growing out of land can now be stolen as soon as it is made movable.[11]

17.2.1.2 Capable of legal ownership

Section 217 requires not only that the thing by its physical nature must be capable of being stolen, but also that it must be the property of some person. This means that it must be prima facie capable of being owned. Some things, though corporeal, cannot be owned at all. At common law this included wild animals (ferae naturae) when at large,[12] and the human body, even when deceased;[13] so a human corpse cannot be stolen, although the corpse of a farm animal can.[14] The position with regard to animals is now covered by s 219 (see § 17.2.1.3). However, the question of the human body or body parts is not covered in the Crimes Act, and remains uncertain. There is an interim right to possession (not ownership) of a corpse which vests in those charged with its burial.[15] Apart from this, the courts have sometimes recognised a limited possessory right in a corpse or body part if being used as a medical specimen or exhibit as in a museum, at least where the item has undergone a lawful

9   Cf *R v Koura* [1996] 2 NZLR 9, (1996) 13 CRNZ 463 (CA).

10 In this sense, real property resembles a chose in action — compare Gray, "Property in Thin Air" (1991) 50 CLJ 252, who points out that the notion of property in a resource is not absolute, but relative; and therefore questions the rigid dichotomy between contract and property.

11 In *R v Tainui* [1967] NZLR 364, mineral ore was held as capable of being stolen as soon as it became movable, even though the ore was only made movable in order to steal it. (Cf the remainder of s 217, omitted in the text above.)

12 Even a landowner does not own or possess the wild animals on his land. Cf *R v Howlett and Howlett* [1968] Crim LR 222.

13 *Williams v Williams* (1882) 20 Ch D 659 at 662f, [1881-1885] All ER Rep 840 at 843f. (Extending to a corpse the logic of the proposition that a live human body cannot be subject to ownership.)

14 *R v Edwards* (1877) 13 Cox CC 384.

15 *Calma v Sesar* (1992) 106 FLR 446; *Dobson v North Tyneside HA* [1996] 4 All ER 474, 478.

application of skill (eg embalming);[16] and the Human Tissues Act 1964 allows certain persons a right of possession to a body in particular circumstances.

But the fact that there may be certain limited rights to a corpse or parts thereof does not resolve the question of ownership. The problem can be summarised as follows. First, although there may be possessory rights in some circumstances, it appears those rights do not amount to full ownership.[17] And if body parts are incapable of being owned, then it would seem that, like the corpse itself, they cannot be stolen.

On the other hand, such limited rights as may be had in body parts might nonetheless amount to a "special property or interest therein" within the meaning of s 220(1)(a). We consider the significance of this possibility below, in § 17.2.1.3(b), but arguably, a taking in contravention of such rights may be sufficient for theft.[18] If so, a second problem for the law is to identify *when* such possessory rights can arise. For example, it remains unclear under present law whether anyone has a property right to a body part designated for transplant surgery; and thus whether such items can be stolen. It is certainly arguable that such body parts deserve the protection of the criminal law.[19]

17.2.1.3 *Actually owned by someone*

In addition to being *capable* of being owned, the thing stolen must also in fact *be* owned. Thus wild animals cannot be stolen unless they have been held in a state of confinement, so that rights of ownership have arisen.[20] Intentionally abandoned goods are res nullius and cannot be stolen.[21] However, courts are reluctant to find that goods have been "abandoned" rather than merely lost: abandonment is a technical status, and it will not suffice, for example, merely

---

16 *Doodeward v Spence* (1908) 6 CLR 406, [1909] ALR 105. In that case, Griffith CJ was careful not to say that a corpse could be owned, but rather that it could be in the lawful possession of someone, and that the law would protect that lawful possession. Note that preserving a brain in paraffin before a post-mortem examination does not turn it into an item in which others could have a right of possession or property: *Dobson v North Tyneside HA* [1996] 4 All ER 474.

17 Quaere human hair manufactured into wigs, or sperm in a sperm bank. It appears that there may be property rights in the by-products of the living body: in *R v Welsh* [1974] RTR 478, a man was convicted of theft of a urine sample. Cf *R v Rothery* [1976] RTR 550, [1976] Crim LR 691; also *Herbert* (1960) The Times, 22 December, (1960) 25 J Cr L 163 (cutting off hair — though surely an offence against the person rather than property?). Smith opines that body parts even if originally res nullius should, as in the case of wild animals, be able to become property by *occupatio*: Smith, "Stealing the Body and its Parts" [1976] Crim LR 622. This seems to be consistent with the reasoning of Griffith CJ in *Doodeward v Spence* (1908) 6 CLR 406, [1909] ALR 105. See also Matthews, "Whose Body? People as Property" (1983) 36 CLP 193.

18 Cf the reasoning in *R v Ellerm* [1997] 1 NZLR 200 (CA), criticised at § 17.2.1.3(b).

19 See Lavoie, "Ownership of Human Tissue: Life after *Moore v Regents of the University of California* [1989] 75 Va LR 1363; *Adams* § CA217.08.

20 Section 219.

21 Also a common law rule: *Ellerman's Wilson Line Ltd v Webster* [1952] 1 Lloyd's Rep 179, 180.

to put rubbish out for collection,[22] or to bury a dead animal.[23] Normally, as in these examples, some right in the subject-matter will be preserved. Abandonment of ownership requires a giving up of the owner's physical control of an item, accompanied by the cessation of any intention to possess that item — ie a relinquishing of all rights over it.[24]

Of course, an honest belief that the goods have been abandoned (rather than lost) *is* a defence to a charge of theft.[25] However, this is because of the lack of mens rea, rather than the absence of an actus reus.

17.2.1.3(a) *Ownership distinguished from special property rights and interests*
It is important to note the difference in wording between ss 217 and 220. Section 217 provides that the thing stolen must be "the property of any person". It is unnecessary to be able to identify the owner: it suffices to prove that the thing is owned by *some person*. Nevertheless, it seems clear from this wording that for the thing to be capable of being stolen there must in fact exist an owner, even if the owner is unascertainable.

The mens rea provisions in s 220, however, introduce a different property concept. Section 220(1)(a) requires an intent to deprive, not necessarily the owner, but merely "any person having any special property or interest" in the thing. P has a special property or interest in something whenever P has a proprietary right of possession (a special property) or an equitable proprietary interest in that thing.[26] One common example is a lien, which is a right to possession enforceable against anyone, including the owner, until a condition is satisfied. A repairer of goods, for example, has a lien over the improved goods until the repair is paid for.[27] A bailee of goods also has a special property therein.[28]

As with liens and bailments, most forms of special property involve a right to possession enforceable against the whole world, including the owner. However, this is not a necessary feature. The preferable view would seem to be that a thief in possession of stolen goods has a better possessory right to the goods than a stranger, even though she may not be able to maintain that right

---

22 *Williams v Phillips* (1957) 41 Cr App R 5. As long as the rubbish remained on the owner's premises it was not abandoned; property in it passed when collected by the local authority.

23 *R v Edwards* (1877) 13 Cox CC 384.

24 Cf Hudson, "Abandonment" in Palmer and McKendrick (eds), *Interests in Goods*, London, Lloyd's of London Press, 1993; *The Crystal* [1894] AC 508; *Keene v Carter* (1994) 12 WAR 20.

25 *R v White* (1912) 7 Cr App R 266.

26 See § 17.2.2.2(b).

27 *R v Cox* [1923] NZLR 596 (CA).

28 As was held in *R v Brown* [1948] NZLR 928 (CA), where D, a search officer employed by the New Zealand Railways Board, was convicted of theft of a quantity of cutlery consigned to the railway for transportation. See also *R v Ellerm* [1997] 1 NZLR 200 at 208 (CA).

against the true owner.[29] Thus the stranger who takes those goods from the thief can himself be guilty of a theft.[30]

17.2.1.3(b) When there is no owner, but special property rights exist

The interrelationship between ss 217 and 220 poses difficult problems in cases where there is no owner, but someone has a lesser property right in the thing taken. A good example is the right to possession of a corpse for the purposes of burial.[31] Since possession is one of the rights of ownership, this would amount to a "special" property right, enforceable by proprietary remedies, which falls short of ownership.[32] A second example of this sort may be abandoned goods in which another person has acquired some limited rights. This was said to have occurred in *R v Ellerm*,[33] a decision considered later in this section.

Prima facie, such things cannot be stolen since they are not "*the* property of any person", as required by s 217. One way around this problem might be to disregard ownership, and consider the fact of possession or other interest, which creates a "special property" in the thing, to be sufficient for theft.[34] However, this appears to be contrary to a strict construction of s 217. Moreover, it is inconsistent with the clear distinction drawn in ss 220(1)(a) and 225 between ownership and lesser interests in property. Perhaps most importantly of all, the function of s 220(1)(a) is merely to specify one of the mens rea conditions for theft. (The three alternative forms of mens rea, stipulated in s 220(1)(b)–(c), make no mention of special property.) The subsection is therefore irrelevant to proof of the actus reus. We submit that the better analysis of the Act is that the thing stolen *must* be *owned by* someone (s 217) although the theft may be from someone with a lesser property interest (s 220).

In the context of the human body, the consequence of this interpretation would be that to find theft the courts would have to become more willing to recognise ownership of body parts, especially where legitimate work has been done on the item (eg by preparation of a kidney for transplantation); although property in such things might vest only in certain eligible persons and be accompanied by stringent duties.[35] Indeed, perhaps it is time that the old rule

---

29 This view was preferred by Donaldson LJ in *Parker v British Airways Board* [1982] QB 1004 at 1009, [1982] 1 All ER 834 at 837; cf *Bird v Fort Frances* [1949] 2 DLR 791; *Buckley v Gross* (1863) 3 B & S 566, 122 ER 213. Contra *Garrow and Turkington*, § 220.7.

30 This is so whether or not the stranger thereby commits theft also against the owner.

31 See § 17.2.1.2.

32 Compare de Stoop, "The Law in Australia Relating to the Transplantation of Organs from Cadavers" (1974) 48 ALJ 21 at 22.

33 [1997] 1 NZLR 200 (CA).

34 Cf *Adams* §§ CA217.08, 217.08A, 217.11.

35 Arguably, if ownership is regarded as having the largest bundle of rights available in respect of something, the extent of those available rights will naturally vary for different items — thus the fact that the bundle will be a small one in the case of body parts may still be consistent with the ascription of ownership. Contra, however, if the maximum bundle available lacks rights which are fundamental to any concept of ownership: cf Honoré, "Ownership" in Guest (ed), *Oxford Essays in Jurisprudence: first series*, London, Oxford University Press, 1961, 107 at 108-110.

that there can be no property in a body or its parts — a rule of dubious ancestry[36] — was itself abandoned.

More straightforwardly (and more generally), there is a case for statutory reform. Section 217 could be amended to require only that the thing stolen be something in which someone has *a* property right, whether possession or control, or a proprietary right or interest.[37] However, there is also something to be said for the view that interference of such things as body parts, in which there are — quite properly — no ordinary rights of ownership, is not really the sort of wrongdoing for which property offences are the suitable means of control, and that offences of this type warrant separate criminalisation.[38]

Unfortunately, despite the supposed lack of an owner, the Court of Appeal found that a theft had been committed in *Ellerm*.[39] In that case, D had dishonestly recovered rimu logs from the bed of a lake. The logs had apparently been abandoned by their original owner some decades ago, after sinking during storms that arose while the logs were being towed across the lake. The lake itself was the property of the Crown, which exercised an active management of the lake and lakebed.

On these facts, the Court of Appeal upheld D's conviction. However, although the decision seems to be correct, its reasoning may be doubted. On the footing that the original owner's interest in the logs had been abandoned in law,[40] the Court held that the Crown's role as owner and manager of the land upon which the logs lay "falls short of any ownership in the logs in the lake, but arguably gives a right to their possession".[41] After reviewing the authorities, their Honours concluded that:

> it is clear that the owner or occupier of land who has manifested a sufficient intention to exercise control over the land and the things which might be on the land has rights over chattels on that land (even if they are not attached to or imbedded in the land). Those rights may be categorised as a "special property" in the chattels . . . or as possession . . . In s 220 the words "the owner, or any person having any special property or interest" encompass persons having a wide range of proprietary and other interests in things capable of being stolen. They are not confined just to owners having general property . . . The words must be taken to extend to lawful possession as, for example, in a bailee. They must also extend to the interest of an owner or occupier of land exercising actual control over what is on it as in the cases referred to. Even if that interest is something less than legal ownership no miscarriage of justice can flow from that in this case.[42]

---

36 Compare Smith, "Stealing the Body and its Parts" [1976] Crim LR 622 at 623-624.

37 Cf s 5(1) Theft Act 1968 (UK).

38 To be found in s 150.

39 [1997] 1 NZLR 200 (CA).

40 [1997] 1 NZLR 200 at 204 (CA).

41 Ibid at 205.

42 Ibid at 208.

It is submitted that this reasoning is flawed. Certainly, if the interest that the Crown acquired in the logs was less than legal ownership, then it would amount to a special property sufficient for s 220(1)(a). But proof of s 220(1) merely establishes mens rea. The prosecution must also prove the actus reus requirements of theft, including those of s 217 — that is, that the logs were capable of being stolen, and therefore that they were *the property of someone*, and not merely things in which someone else had a special property interest. One wonders how the Court's reasoning would have provided any basis for deciding the case if D's intent had not been to deprive permanently (s 220(1)(a)), but merely to pledge the logs temporarily and then return them to the lake (s 220(1)(b), in which special properties are irrelevant)? The Court appears to have substituted analysis of mens rea for that of actus reus.

The better analysis is that if there was no legal owner then the logs could not be stolen,[43] but D was properly convicted because the Crown owned the logs. Ownership of items which are abandoned or otherwise res nullius vests in the first person to take possession of them.[44] Possession itself is taken by intentionally exercising control over the items. The occupier of land may do this either by (a) restricting public access to the land upon which the items lie,[45] or (where the land is open to public access) by (b) manifesting an intention to exercise control over the land and the things thereon.[46] Certainly the Crown had done sufficient to satisfy (b).[47] It was therefore in possession of the rimu logs, and thus their owner.

17.2.2 Taking or conversion

Apart from being capable of being stolen, the goods must also be taken or converted by D. This requirement substantially restricts the scope of theft and the range of property interests that it protects. Those interests not covered by s 220 are protected (if at all) by other sections in the Crimes Act. For convenience, we present here a brief summary of the wrongs addressed in this and the next chapter, grouped loosely according to the property interest that the wrongdoing violates:

---

43 Contra *Adams*, § CA217.11. Reliance upon English cases such as *R v Woodman* [1974] QB 754, [1974] 2 All ER 955 is misplaced in this respect; the Theft Act 1968 (UK) requires only that the property "belong to another", and s 5(1) provides that for the purposes of theft, "property shall be regarded as belonging to any person having possession or control of it, or having in it any proprietary right or interest".

44 Unless the items are attached to or buried in land, in which case they automatically become the property of the occupier of the land: *South Staffordshire Water Co v Sharman* [1896] 2 QB 44, [1895-1899] All ER Rep 259; *Waverly Borough Council v Fletcher* [1996] QB 334, [1995] 4 All ER 756.

45 *Parker v British Airways Board* [1982] QB 1004 at 1013, 1019 (Donaldson LJ), 1020 (Eveleigh LJ), 1021 (Sir David Cairns), [1982] 1 All ER 834 at 840, 844 (Donaldson LJ), 845 (Eveleigh LJ), 846 (Sir David Cairns).

46 Cf *Parker v British Airways Board* [1982] QB 1002 at 1018, [1982] 1 All ER 834 at 844b; *Tamworth Industries v A-G* [1991] 3 NZLR 616 at 620.

47 [1997] 1 NZLR 200 at 204, 205 (CA).

(i) *Unlawful interference with possession*: a "taking" under s 220. Answer: D's taking of possession was consensual.

(ii) *Possession lawfully obtained but the goods subsequently misappropriated in contravention of V's legal rights of ownership or possession*: a "conversion" under s 220. Answer: D acquired ownership as well as possession.

(iii) *Possession lawfully obtained but the goods subsequently misappropriated in contravention of V's equitable rights of ownership*: a theft by person required to account (chapter 18).

(iv) *Possession obtained with consent, where the consent was induced by a fraud*: an obtaining by false pretences (chapter 19).

(v) *Possession and ownership obtained by fraud*: an obtaining by false pretences (chapter 19).

17.2.2.1 *Taking and the protection of possession*

The first element of a theft by taking is that there should be a physical "taking". Section 220(5) requires that, to be taken, the item must be moved, so a failure to return goods acquired in circumstances not amounting to theft does not constitute a taking, although it may amount to conversion.[48] Unlike the common law, which required a "taking and carrying away", it is enough for theft under s 220 if the thing is moved only slightly — it does not have to be carried away. In *R v Coslet*, for example, it was held sufficient that D moved a parcel from one end of a wagon to the other;[49] the same conclusion was reached in *R v Taylor* when D pulled a pocket-book partly out of another person's pocket.[50]

Since theft by taking is an interference with *possession*, it follows that it may be committed not only against an owner, but also against any other person in possession of the thing. In particular, D can be guilty of theft if he takes something with intent to deprive someone who has a "special property or interest" in the thing for the purposes of s 220(1)(a). We have seen[51] that such an interest may exist, for example, where a person is a bailee of the goods. An important consequence of this is that theft from the possessor may even be committed by the owner.[52] This would typically occur in a case where someone has a lien over goods. In *R v Cox*,[53] a garage repairing a car had a lien over the car, which D dishonestly retrieved. D was convicted of theft, as the lien had

---

48 Cf *Police v Subritzky* [1990] 2 NZLR 717. D allowed her 4-year-old daughter to keep a toy which the child had (without D's knowledge) taken from a shop.

49 (1782) 1 Leach 236, 168 ER 220.

50 [1911] 1 KB 674. See also *R v Amier* (1834) 6 C & P 344, 172 ER 1269, in which D broke into a house and proceeded to take money from a room, but when detected threw the money under the grate in the same room. This was held sufficient to constitute stealing, if the money was taken with dishonest intent.

51 *R v Brown* [1948] NZLR 928 (CA); see § 17.2.1.3(a).

52 Something confirmed by s 225(a).

53 [1923] NZLR 596 (CA).

conferred a possessory interest amounting to a "special property or interest" in the car. Similarly, in *Larkin v Brown* P retook a horse which was arguably subject to an auctioneer's lien. D arrested him for theft of the horse, whereupon P sued D alleging false imprisonment and assault. The Court held that the lien, if established, would give the auctioneers a special interest in the horse, and thus that D would be justified in arresting P.[54]

17.2.2.1(a) *Answer: D's possession was by consent*

Theft by taking under the Crimes Act effectively replaces the common law offence of larceny, which required a taking without the consent of the owner; in other words, a *trespassory* taking. Correspondingly, the second element of a theft by taking is that the taking should be unauthorised.[55] This reflects the property law rule that rights of possession give title only against a *wrongdoer*.[56] If D acquires possession of goods with the consent of the person from whom they are obtained then there is no taking, even if the consent is obtained by false pretences.[57] (Although there may be a subsequent theft by conversion,[58] and the charge of obtaining by false pretences may also lie.[59]) However, consent must be distinguished from submission: a "consent" obtained by threats is not, in law, an effective consent; and things obtained by such means can be stolen by a taking.[60]

One interesting case is that of a supermarket. The House of Lords has held in *Morris*[61] that a shopper acts with the implied authority of the supermarket owner when he takes goods from the shelf, puts them on his trolley, and takes them to the checkout counter to pay the correct price. The shopper obtains an authorised possession, although property does not pass until the price is paid

---

54 (1906) 8 GLR 654.

55 Obviously, this exempts from liability a person authorised to take something from someone in possession who does not consent, eg an owner who recovers goods from a bailee at will or a thief. In such cases D merely exercises her property rights. Contra *R v Turner (No 2)* (1971) 55 Cr App R 336, an unsatisfactory decision rightly criticised by, among others, Smith, *The Law of Theft* (7th ed), 1993, § 2-54, and Smith, *Property Offences: the protection of property through the criminal law*, London, Sweet & Maxwell, 1994, at 4-43; the decision can be distinguished if necessary on the basis of the language of the Theft Act 1968 (UK). For the proposition that theft presupposes an infringement of civil law rights, see further § 17.2.2.2(d).

56 Cf *Jeffries v Great Western Ry Co* (1856) 5 El & Bl 802 at 805, 119 ER 680 at 681.

57 Section 220(2).

58 Thus a receiver, who does not commit theft by taking, may convert the goods. See § 17.4.

59 Section 246. See chapter 19.

60 *R v Parker* [1919] NZLR 365 (CA). This is implicit in offences such as robbery (s 234), which presuppose that D commits a theft. Cf *R v Mitchell* [1988] 2 NZLR 208, (1988) 3 CRNZ 515 (CA); Lanham, "Duress and Void Contracts" (1966) 29 MLR 615.

61 [1984] AC 320, [1983] 3 All ER 288. Cf *Dronjak v Police* [1990] NZLR 75 at 77, (1988) 3 CRNZ 141 at 143.

and a contract is concluded between the customer and cashier.[62] It follows from this that, in effect, the prospective shoplifter has a period of grace while still in the supermarket. Since her possession is authorised,[63] she can only be convicted of theft when she later *converts* the goods by smuggling them beyond the point of sale without permission.

17.2.2.2 *Conversion and the protection of property rights*

Under the common law, where a person legitimately in possession of goods later decided to appropriate them to his own use there could be no larceny, since there was no taking and carrying away contrary to the will of the owner. This problem was resolved in the New Zealand Criminal Code of 1893, and its modern successor the Crimes Act 1961, by extending the basic offence of theft to include *conversion* of property — a fundamental change in the law of theft. It is usually said that there is a conversion whenever a person (however innocently she obtained possession) acts inconsistently with the rights of the owner[64] and without authorisation to do so.[65] Examples include deliberate destruction of or damage to something, the sale or attempted sale of it,[66] granting a chattel security over something that was not yours,[67] and obliterating the identifying marks on something.[68] If D has possession of a thing for particular, limited purposes, then using it for other purposes will amount to conversion.[69]

---

62 Cf *Davies v Leighton* (1978) 68 Cr App R 4, [1978] Crim LR 575. The decision in *Morris* has since been overruled by the House of Lords in *DPP v Gomez* [1993] AC 442, [1993] 1 All ER 1, which decided that a person who takes possession, even with consent, commits theft if he does so with the intent permanently to deprive. However, these decisions turn on the meaning of "appropriation" in s 1 Theft Act 1968 (UK). The NZ statute distinguishes between taking and conversion, both of which connote acts *unauthorised* by the owner; thus the decision in *Gomez* would appear to be irrelevant in this context.

63 In *Dobson v General Accident Fire and Life Assurance Corp plc* [1990] 1 QB 274 at 289, [1989] 3 All ER 927 at 937, Bingham LJ suggests that "it might be said that a supermarket consents to customers taking goods from its shelves only when they honestly intend to pay and not otherwise". That view, however, should be doubted, for two reasons. First, it would largely obliterate the distinction between theft and obtaining by deception. Ex hypothesi, V would never authorise dishonest conduct or consent to a dishonest transaction if she knew the full facts. Secondly, the analysis would extend the scope of theft too far into the realm of preparatory activity, rendering theft primarily a "mind" crime. (These very criticisms may be levelled at English law following *Gomez* [1993] AC 442, [1993] 1 All ER 1.)

64 *R v Maihi* [1993] 2 NZLR 139 at 141, (1992) 9 CRNZ 304 at 306 (CA); *R v Ilich* (1987) 162 CLR 110 at 115-117, 124, (1987) 69 ALR 231 at 235, 236; *Adams* § CA220.05; Turner, *Kenny's Outlines of Criminal Law*, Cambridge, Cambridge University Press, (17th ed), 1958, § 245.

65 *McNicholl v Police* (1990) 6 CRNZ 603 at 605.

66 *Clouston v Bragg* [1949] NZLR 1073.

67 *R v Dunbar* [1963] NZLR 253 (CA). (D had the loan of a boat, which he pledged as security for a financial transaction.)

68 *R v Russell* [1977] 2 NZLR 20 (CA).

69 Cf *Clouston v Bragg* [1949] NZLR 1073, where a car dealer sold a car having been given possession only by the owner.

In order to be a conversion, D's act must amount to a *usurpation* or denial of O's rights, eg by the assertion of an inconsistent right. Sometimes this may depend upon the intention with which D's act is done: thus merely putting the item in a drawer for safekeeping, as opposed to keeping the thing for oneself, is not a conversion.[70]

The mere decision to convert is not sufficient for theft. There must be conduct as well.[71] However, the conduct may be a continuing act or omission, as distinct from a fresh positive act,[72] and need not involve moving the goods. For these purposes, keeping property lawfully obtained is sufficient. In *R v Oram*,[73] a finder of lost goods who decided to keep them, when it was reasonably easy to trace the owner, was therefore held guilty of conversion. And in *Police v Subritzky*,[74] failing to return an item taken innocently by D's child was held to be theft. Likewise, borrowing a thing and then keeping it having decided not to return it may amount to conversion — on the basis of the keeping rather than the borrowing.

17.2.2.2(a) *Criminal conversion versus tortious conversion?*

No definition of conversion is given in the Act, but it should not be assumed that the requirements of criminal conversion are the same as for the tort of conversion.[75] In particular, the tortious action lies only if the plaintiff has actual possession or an immediate proprietary right to possession.[76] Thus even the owner, if she is not in possession and has no immediate right to possession, cannot sue in conversion.[77] Moreover, an owner is capable of converting her own goods, if someone else has an indefeasible possessory right.[78]

---

70 *Police v Moodley* [1974] 1 NZLR 644.

71 *R v Maihi* [1993] 2 NZLR 139, (1992) 9 CRNZ 304 (CA). Compare *Broom v Police* [1994] 1 NZLR 680, (1993) 11 CRNZ 20.

72 See § 2.1.1.2(d), and more generally, § 2.1.1ff.

73 (1908) 27 NZLR 955.

74 [1990] 2 NZLR 717.

75 *Rogers v Arnott* [1960] 2 QB 244 at 249, [1960] 2 All ER 417 at 418, 419.

76 Even a contractual right to delivery is insufficient to give a proprietary right in the goods, and thus will not support an action in conversion: *Jarvis v Williams* [1955] 1 All ER 108, [1955] 1 WLR 71; Watts, "The Tort of Conversion and Equity's Rules against Merger" [1994] NZ Recent LR 336 at 337, 338, criticising *Campbell v Dominion Breweries Ltd* [1994] 3 NZLR 559 (CA).

77 *Gordon v Harper* (1796) 7 TR 9, 101 ER 828; *Wertheim v Cheel* (1885) 11 VLR 107; *Nyberg v Handelaar* [1892] 2 QB 202, [1891-1894] All ER Rep 1109; Warren, "Qualifying as Plaintiff in an Action for a Conversion" (1936) 49 Harv LR 1084. An example would be during a fixed term bailment, where the proper remedy at common law would be an action on the case. Note, however, that the bailor will characteristically have a reversionary right to possession. Where the bailee (as opposed to a stranger) deals with the goods in a manner inconsistent with the terms of his possessory right, the right to possession revests in the owner forthwith and conversion lies: *Penfold's Wines Ltd v Elliott* (1946) 74 CLR 204 at 217, 218, 241, 242, [1946] ALR 517 at 522, 533, 534; *Citicorp Australia Ltd v BS Stillwell Ford Pty Ltd* (1979) 21 SASR 142 at 144; *North General Wagon and Finance Co v Graham* [1950] 2 KB 7; *Milk Bottles Recovery Ltd v Camillo* [1948] VLR 344, [1948] ALR 418.

78 See § 17.2.2.2(c).

At civil law, therefore, conversion presupposes that P has possessory title to goods, but not necessarily ownership. This should be contrasted with the conventional view that criminal conversion requires an act inconsistent with the *owner's* rights to the goods.[79]

The civil law's emphasis on possession rather than ownership parallels that found in the crime of larceny. It is the product of the priorities of very early common law, and to some extent of the constraints imposed by old forms of action. Indeed, originally, the law had little cognisance of a concept of ownership apart from possession or the right to possession.[80] By the nineteenth century, however, it was recognised that both ownership and possession should be protected by property offences. Theft by bailees was first criminalised specifically in 1867,[81] and it is clear that the criminalisation of "conversion" in the Criminal Code Act 1893 was an innovation designed to cover theft by bailees along with other misappropriations by possessors.[82]

For all this, however, given that the Code and its successors provided no definition of conversion, reference to its civil law meaning may sometimes be appropriate. Two main questions arise regarding the scope of criminal conversion:

(i) What sorts of acts by D will count as potential conversions; and

(ii) What sorts of rights are protected by conversion? (ie for what range of rights would their infringement count as a conversion?)

The first question was discussed above, in § 17.2.2.2. The civil law is particularly relevant on this issue, since both varieties of conversion presuppose an action which usurps or denies another's rights. Indeed, all the accepted examples of conduct amounting to a criminal conversion would also constitute a tortious conversion.[83]

It is on the second question — infringement of *whose* rights — that criminal and civil law diverge. Nonetheless, even here we think that where the civil action would not lie, the extended definition of criminal conversion should be treated with caution. Suppose, for example, that D sells goods to P. Before they are collected and paid for, however, D resells them to T. In this case, P is the owner of the goods, but has no immediate right to possession, since the seller has a lien for the unpaid purchase price. Neither D nor T converts the goods;[84] and, it is submitted, neither commits the actus reus of theft.

That is a case where the owner has as yet no possessory rights. Conversely, can there be a criminal conversion against someone with an indefeasible

---

79 See § 17.2.2.2.

80 Pollock and Maitland, *The History of English Law* (2nd ed), 1911, vol I, 57, vol II, 153ff.

81 Larceny Act 1867, s 3; cf 20 & 21 Vic c 54, s 4 (1857). See the discussion in Stephen, *History of the Criminal Law of England* vol III, London, Macmillan, 1883, chapter 28.

82 Cf *Adams* (2nd ed) §§ 1679, 1727.

83 For example, wrongfully keeping the goods (detinue); disposing, or dealing with goods so that P's title to them is lost; altering a chattel so as to change its identity, or unauthorised use it in defiance of the owner's rights.

84 *Lord v Price* (1874) LR 9 Ex 54; *Short v City Bank of Sydney* (1912) 15 CLR 148, [1912] ALR 408; *Kahler v Midland Bank* [1950] AC 24, [1949] 2 All ER 621.

possessory title but not ownership? The answer in the civil law is clearly yes, and it is submitted that in principle the response of the criminal law should also be yes. Normally, this question will be irrelevant since a conversion against the possessor will also usurp the rights of the owner. The exception is if the conversion is committed by the owner herself. We consider this possibility below, in § 17.2.2.2(c).

17.2.2.2(b) *Protecting other property rights?*
Conversion may therefore be regarded primarily as an offence against *title* in something, complementing theft by taking, which is an offence against *actual possession*. This leaves the more general question: in what way are other property rights protected by the law of theft?

In fact, only three types of property right exist in personal property: (i) ownership, (ii) possession, and (iii) equitable charge. As we have seen, ownership and possession are ably protected by s 220.

Equitable proprietary rights present more difficulty. An equitable owner in actual possession of the goods may be stolen from, by either taking or conversion.[85] But there is no such thing as equitable possession, and it seems clear that s 220 does not protect equitable interest-holders in property who do not have possession or an immediate right to possession. Neither was it intended to. The section was not designed to prohibit all infringements of property rights, merely to protect legal ownership as well as possession.[86] Thus if D is the legal owner of property subject to a trust, dishonest dealing with it to the prejudice of the beneficial owner is normally not theft under s 220, and falls to be considered under other sections of the Act.[87] (Indeed, some of these other offences would be otiose if equitable property rights were protected by s 220.)

It appears that an equitable interest, like a possessory right, may be a "special property or interest" falling within the definition of s 220(1)(a). But once again, it must be emphasised that s 220(1)(a) is concerned only with D's *mens rea*. Infringement of a special property does not constitute the actus reus of theft unless it also amounts to a taking or conversion. This requirement, misunderstood in *Ellerm*,[88] was also neglected in *Police v Hawthorn*.[89] In that case, D was the managing director of a company which owned four cars, over which P, a bank, had a debenture. D purported to sell the cars. He was held liable to be convicted of theft, on the footing that the debenture was capable of

---

85 Cf *Healey v Healey* [1915] 1 KB 938.

86 Apart from adding conversion to the basic offence, s 220 thus corresponds substantially to the common law offence of larceny, which, we have noted, did not protect equitable property rights. Why did the common law not protect against breach of trust? The rationale was apparently that people "could protect themselves against breaches of trust by not trusting people — a much easier matter in simple times, when commerce was in its infancy, than in the present day". Stephen, *History of the Criminal Law of England*, vol III, London, Macmillan, 1883, 151.

87 For example, the related offence of theft by a person required to account under s 222 (see § 18.1); or other offences involving fraudulent conduct (chapter 19).

88 See § 17.2.1.3(b).

89 [1981] 2 NZLR 764.

giving a right to possession (ie created a conditional right to possession) in the cars.

The soundness of the decision must be doubted. Even conceding that the debenture conferred an equitable interest in the cars, two further things had to be established. First, such an interest must be a "special property or interest" if D is to be convicted on the basis of his intention to deprive the bank of that interest. Quilliam J explicitly held that this was so, and that a contingent rather than immediate proprietary right to possession was sufficient to create a special property or interest in the cars.[90]

Secondly, D must have converted or taken the cars. Unfortunately, his Honour did not even advert to this requirement. On the assumption that D acted with the authority of his company, there was neither a taking nor a conversion against the owner.[91] Yet it seems clear that there was no conversion against the bank, since the nature of the bank's interest in the cars was insufficient to support such a claim. Criminal conversion lies only for the usurpation of ownership or possessory title. Thus the basis of D's conviction (at least, for theft) is obscure.

17.2.2.2(c) Conversion by an owner?

We saw earlier[92] that an owner can commit theft by taking from someone in possession. Can the owner commit a theft by conversion? Prima facie, O cannot not infringe the rights of the owner since she *is* the owner. However, s 225(a), which states that theft may be committed by the owner against someone with a special property or interest, suggests conversion by the owner should be possible, since the section does not differentiate between theft by conversion and theft by taking. Moreover, s 220(4) explicitly states that the thing converted need not be in D's possession.

In practice, conversion by an owner is normally impossible. The owner generally has a right to possession, and we have seen that mere infringement of a lesser property interest is not conversion. Thus the fact that D has title to the goods will generally be a full answer to the claim that he has converted them.

There are two exceptions. First, it is submitted that an owner is capable of converting his own goods, if someone else has an indefeasible possessory right to them.[93] Suppose, for example, that the owner recovers goods from a bailee during a continuing bailment.[94] He converts the goods if he then retains or deals with them in such a way as to deny the bailee's possessory title.

---

90   More precisely an "interest", since "special property" is an old term applying to possession — as opposed to "general property", ie ownership. See *Clerk and Lindsell on Torts* (17th ed), London, Sweet & Maxwell, 1995, § 13-61.

91   [1981] 2 NZLR 764 at 766: the District Court Judge determined, and it was accepted before the High Court, that D had not stolen from the company.

92   See § 17.2.2.1.

93   Cf, in tort, *City Motors (1993) Pty Ltd v Southern Aerial Super Service Pty Ltd* (1961) 106 CLR 477, [1962] ALR 184; *Roberts v Wyatt* (1810) 2 Taunt 268, 127 ER 1080; *Howe v Teefy* (1927) 27 SR (NSW) 301.

94   For example, the owner may legitimately recover goods from a thief who stole them from the bailee.

More importantly, an owner may convert goods where she is *an* owner but not the only one.[95] In particular, s 225(d) provides that, where property is co-owned, theft may be committed by one of the co-owners against the others. This will often be the case with partnership property and property belonging to members of a club. It is also likely to occur with respect to family property. Until recently, s 226 provided that one spouse could not commit theft of the property of the other, where they were living together. This exemption was, however, abolished as from 1 September 1995.[96]

17.2.2.2(d) *Answer: no conversion if D becomes the owner as well as possessor*

Leaving those exceptions aside, a parallel can be seen between taking and conversion. A taking requires a wrongful interference with possession, so cannot be committed where D is authorised to acquire possession. Alternatively, where possession is authorised,[97] D may still commit theft by conversion. *But if D also acquires ownership in the goods there can be no conversion.*[98] Thus there can generally be no theft at all where D obtains both possession and property. For example, suppose that P sells goods on credit to D. P delivers the goods and transfers property in them to D, who subsequently forms the intent not to pay for them. D does not commit theft. (Although, if she has obtained the property by fraudulent misrepresentations, she may be guilty of obtaining by false pretences under s 246.)

In order to determine whether conversion has occurred in a given case, it is therefore essential to determine whether title has passed to D. The criminal law provides no answer to this question, which must be decided by reference to civil law rules. We consider these rules in more detail below.

The importance of this point cannot be overstated. Consistency of criminal law and civil law concepts is essential in theft, which after all is concerned with the protection of property rights.[99] It would be more than odd if D could be convicted of theft when she had not in fact interfered with V's property rights. As Williams writes, "the object of the law of theft is to attach a penal sanction to certain violations of property rights; so (it may be urged) if there is no violation of property rights under the general (civil) law, there should be no

---

95 Compare *Coleman v Harvey* [1989] 1 NZLR 723 (CA).

96 By s 4(1) Crimes Amendment Act 1995.

97 Or obtained innocently, such that the taking is not a theft — including an unauthorised taking (the actus reus) where D at that time lacked mens rea.

98 *McDuff v Hammond* (1911) 30 NZLR 444; *R v Muir* (1910) 29 NZLR 1049 (CA) .

99 Cf Smith, "Civil Law Concepts in the Criminal Law" (1972B) 31 CLJ 197. Though see *Rao v Police* (1988) 3 CRNZ 697 at 699, 700; also *R v Morris* [1984] AC 320 at 334, for the dubious (and unnecessary) claim that the criminal law should not be concerned with the niceties of the civil law. The approach taken in *R v Walker* [1984] Crim LR 112 and in *R v Tillings & Tillings plc* [1985] Crim LR 393 is to be preferred. Compare too *Dobson v General Accident Fire and Life Assurance Corp* [1990] 1 QB 274 at 289, [1989] 3 All ER 927 at 937: whether property belongs to another "is a question to which the criminal law offers no answer and which can only be answered by reference to civil law principles".

theft".[100] It was said in this text, as far back as chapter one, that there ought to be no criminalisation without harm.[101] In theft, the relevant harm is infringement of another's property rights. Protection against that harm *is the very purpose* of criminalising theft. The rights (specifically, ownership and possession) which are protected are creatures of civil law. Therefore, unless those civil law rights are in fact infringed, the harm does not occur and theft should not lie.

17.2.3 Has ownership passed?

In determining ownership of property for the purposes of conversion, there are two principal problems. The first is to ascertain whether title has prima facie passed, or whether D merely has possession. Here one needs to look at the terms of the agreement between P and D, in particular whether P has reserved property rights in the goods. Secondly, even where a prima facie transfer of title has been identified, the transferor's intention may be vitiated, eg by duress or a mistake. Obtaining by duress will normally be a theft by taking, since P's consent will be negated for *both* ownership and possession. Obtaining pursuant to a mistake, on the other hand, does not constitute theft by taking. Where the mistake is induced by D's fraud or false pretences, the offence is the separate crime of obtaining by false pretences.[102] But, whether or not the mistake was induced by D, where the mistake is regarded as "fundamental" this may negate the transferor's consent to the transfer — and therefore the passing of title — altogether.

17.2.3.1 *Has ownership passed, prima facie?*

The general rule is that title passes if and when the transferor so intends it to pass.[103] This general rule is subject to a number of provisos. The first is that the transferor, if she is not herself the owner of the goods, must have authority to pass title on behalf of the owner.[104] Secondly, as we have mentioned, the intention to pass title may be negated by a mistake[105] or by duress.[106] Finally, in many standard situations the transfer of property is affected by statutory and common law rules.

It is not possible here to give a comprehensive account of the civil law regarding transfer of property. Rather, we propose to discuss some of the more common types of case, and to illustrate the relationship between the relevant civil law rules and the criminal law of theft.

---

100 Williams, "Theft, Consent and Illegality" [1977] Crim LR 127, 138. Per Smith, *Property Offences: the protection of property through the criminal law*, London, Sweet & Maxwell, 1994, at 5-49, "if the civil law sees no reason to permit the owner to complain of an interference with his property why should the criminal law do so?"

101 See § 1.2.1.

102 See chapter 19.

103 Cf *Fawcett v Star Car Sales Ltd* [1960] NZLR 406 (CA).

104 See § 17.2.3.3.

105 See § 17.2.3.2.

106 See § 17.2.2.1(a).

17.2.3.1(a) *Contracts for sale and the reservation of title*

Where ascertained goods are sold, the rules on passing of title are to be found in the Sale of Goods Act 1908. The basic rule, stated in s 19, is that where there is a contract for the sale of specific or ascertained goods, property in them passes when the buyer and seller so intend. In the case of sale of unascertained goods, s 18 provides that no property in them is to be transferred to the buyer unless and until the goods are ascertained.[107] Section 20 provides that if there is no agreement then property passes at the time the contract is made.[108]

One consequence of s 19 is that a seller may insert a reservation of title clause into a contract of sale. Indeed, s 21(1) provides explicitly that the seller may reserve the right of disposal of the goods until certain conditions are fulfilled. Where goods are sold subject to a reservation of title clause, commonly known as a Romalpa clause,[109] property ostensibly remains in the seller until the buyer has paid for the goods, so that although the buyer has possession, unauthorised dealing with the property could amount to theft by conversion. The English courts have traditionally been reluctant to recognise a reserved property right in the seller. But New Zealand courts have been more willing to adhere to the spirit of s 19 and allow the seller to retain property rights in the goods. In *Pongakawa Sawmill Ltd v NZFP Ltd*,[110] for example, the Court of Appeal held that property in goods supplied under a contract of sale passed when the parties intended, and the seller could impose a condition that it should not pass before payment. The effect of this is that, at least in the straightforward case of unmixed goods, a charge of theft by conversion may lie where D, having taken possession of goods subject to a Romalpa clause, then usurps P's rights of ownership over those goods, eg by granting a security over them before they have been paid for,[111] or by selling them without authority.[112]

The position is less clear with respect to an authorised commingling of P's goods with D's, or their consumption during the production of new goods. It is possible for the Romalpa clause to vest an absolute legal interest in the resulting goods in P, according to the proportion of the product that P's goods have contributed.[113] But successful instances of this being done are rare, and

---

107 The provision was held in *Jansz v GMB Imports Pty Ltd* [1979] VR 581 to be absolute, and so to prevail over any contrary expressed intentions of the parties. For a modern case see *Re Goldcorp Exchange (In Receivership)* [1994] 3 NZLR 385, [1995] 1 AC 74 (PC): buyers had no legal or equitable interest in an undifferentiated bulk of gold bullion.

108 Provided the goods are specific and deliverable, and the contract is unconditional. Other rules in s 20 apply where these criteria are not met.

109 *Aluminium Industrie Vaassen BV v Romalpa Aluminium Ltd* [1976] 2 All ER 552, [1976] 1 WLR 676. See generally McCormack, "Reservation of Title in England and New Zealand" (1992) 12 LS 195; Watts, "Reservation of Title Clauses in England and New Zealand" (1986) 6 OJLS 456; Ong, "Romalpa Clauses" (1992) 4 Bond LR 186.

110 [1992] 3 NZLR 304 (CA).

111 *R v Nottingham* [1992] 1 NZLR 395 (CA).

112 Cf *Hendy Lennox (Industrial Engines) Ltd v Grahame Puttick Ltd* [1984] 2 All ER 152, [1984] 1 WLR 485 (D's credit period had expired and S had demanded delivery up).

113 *Coleman v Harvey* [1989] 1 NZLR 723 (CA); *Ahead Group Ltd (in rec) v Downer Mining Ltd* 26/8/91, Wylie J, HC Auckland CP1304/91. In England, if the goods are consumed

clauses which attempt similar feats (but, for example, limit the interest according to D's indebtedness) are likely to be held to create a disguised charge over the new goods.[114] In that case the clause is void for non-registration,[115] and D may deal with the goods as his own without fear of conversion.

P cannot claim a legal title in the proceeds of sale,[116] although she may sometimes be vested with an equitable interest,[117] interference with which would potentially amount to an offence under s 222 rather than s 220.

17.2.3.1(b) *Receptacles and containers*

The owner of a vending or similar machine, such as a coin-operated telephone, becomes the owner of any money as soon as it is inserted.[118] This is explicable on the general rule: the depositor intends to pass ownership when he inserts a coin in prepayment. Even if the machine malfunctions and he does not get what he pays for, his remedy is a refund, not a retrieval of the particular coin inserted. It is thus the actus reus of theft to retake money from such a machine, except by authorised means (eg pressing the refund button).

Similarly, when petrol is sold at a service station, ownership passes when the petrol is pumped into the tank of the vehicle. Thus a motorist who fills his tank intending to pay for the petrol, but then decides not to pay for it and drives off, commits no theft.[119] He already owns (and has possession of) the petrol before he forms the mens rea of theft, and is simply a dishonest debtor.

However, if a person puts a valuable ring in a desk drawer, and after death her executor sells the desk, the buyer may not keep the ring on finding it since it was not included in the sale,[120] and a dishonest failure to do so would constitute theft by conversion. Ownership of the ring remains in the executor since he does not intend to pass title thereto when he sells the desk.

---

rather than merely commingled, it has been held that P's asset is not susceptible of continuing ownership, and that any title to the new product may vest in P only by virtue of its being granted by D: *Clough Mill Ltd v Martin* [1984] 3 All ER 982, [1985] 1 WLR 111 (where the clause was found on the facts to create a charge rather than to transfer outright ownership to P). The position would be the same if title to mixed products vested entirely in P.

114 Cf *Kruppstahl AG v Quitmann Holdings Ltd* [1982] ILRM 551; *Re Peachdart Ltd* [1984] Ch 131.

115 Per s 103 Companies Act 1955; Companies (Registration of Charges) Act 1993.

116 Goode, "The Right to Trace and its Impact in Commercial Transactions" (1976) 92 LQR 360 at 367ff. Quaere, however, *Trustee of the property of FC Jones and Sons (a firm) v Jones* [1996] 4 All ER 721, [1996] 3 WLR 703.

117 *Len Vidgen Ski & Leisure Ltd v Timaru Marine Supplies (1982) Ltd* [1986] 1 NZLR 349. Such instances will be rare — cf *Re Andrabell Ltd* [1984] 3 All ER 407 — and are more likely to involve a charge which is void for non-registration: *E Pfeiffer Weinkellerei-Weineinkauf GmbH & Co v Arbuthnot Factors Ltd* [1988] 1 WLR 150.

118 *Martin v Marsh* [1955] Crim LR 781; *Hollings* (1940) 4 J Cr L 370; cf *R v Jean* [1968] 2 CCC 204.

119 *R v Greenberg* [1972] Crim LR 331; *Edwards v Ddin* [1976] 3 All ER 705, [1976] 1 WLR 942.

120 *Thomas v Greenslade* [1954] CLY 3421; *Moffatt v Kazana* [1969] 2 QB 152, [1968] 3 All ER 271.

17.2.3.1(c) *Sale or return contracts*

Section 20, Rule 4 Sale of Goods Act 1908 provides that where goods are delivered to the buyer on "sale or return" or similar terms, the property passes to the buyer either:

(i)   When the buyer signifies approval or acceptance to the seller or does any other act adopting the transaction; or

(ii) If the buyer does not signify approval or acceptance to the seller, but retains the goods without giving notice of rejection then, if a time has been fixed for the return of the goods, on the expiration of that time, and if no time has been fixed, on the expiration of a reasonable time.

The relationship between the parties is that of bailee and bailor, but an act indicating election on the part of the bailee to buy the goods, or an act inconsistent with the lack of title in the bailee will have the effect of adopting the transaction and property in the goods will pass. This may happen, for example, where the bailee pledges the goods with a third party, or grants a bill of sale over them.[121] Under an ordinary bailment such conduct would constitute a conversion,[122] but in this case it operates to effect a transfer of property and so cannot be theft by the bailee-purchaser.

17.2.3.1(d) *Hire purchase*

In a hire purchase agreement, possession passes but the property in the goods remains with the seller until all instalments have been paid. Thus an on-sale by the possessor will be theft by conversion.

17.2.3.2 *Is the passing of title negated by mistake?*

O's consent to the transfer of title may be negated by a "fundamental" mistake, whether or not induced by fraud or misrepresentation. A mistake is fundamental if and only if its existence makes it reasonable to say that there is no intention on O's part to transfer *this* property to *this* person.[123] According to the High Court of Australia, what this means is that a mistake is sufficiently fundamental if it is "as to the identity of the transferee or as to the identity of the thing delivered, or as to the quantity of the thing delivered".[124] However, applying this test is not always clear-cut.

17.2.3.2(a) *Property*

Mistake as to the identity of the property will always defeat consent. In *R v Davies*[125] the proprietor of a nursing home induced two old ladies to endorse

---

121   *Australasian Finance Co Ltd v Tunley* (1935) 30 MCR 29.

122   *R v Dunbar* [1963] NZLR 253 (CA).

123   Williams, "Mistake in the Law of Theft" (1977) 36 CLJ 62 at 64.

124   *Ilich v R* (1987) 162 CLR 110 at 126. In other cases, a person who knows his receipt is pursuant to another's mistake may have an affected conscience, such that the receipt is held on trust for the mistaken transferor: eg *Chase Manhattan Bank NA v Israel-British Bank (London) Ltd* [1981] Ch 105, [1979] 3 All ER 1025. Misappropriation of the receipt would not be theft, since s 220 does not protect equitable interests (see § 17.2.2.2(b)). However, it may be an offence against s 222 (theft by person required to account). See §§ 18.1.2.5, 6.

125   [1982] 1 All ER 513, [1982] 74 Cr App R (S) 302.

cheques made out to them by signing on the back, and then paid the cheques into his own account. The victims had not known that they were endorsing cheques, but merely thought that they were signing pieces of paper. For this reason property in the cheques never passed to D, who was thus rightly convicted of theft. Here the mistake was obviously fundamental: in each case V believed the property to be a valueless piece of paper, whereas in reality it was a bill of exchange — a different type of thing altogether.

Other cases of mistaken identity may not be so clear-cut. In *R v Ashwell*[126] D asked K for the loan of a shilling. K mistakenly handed over a sovereign. D discovered this some time later, at which time he decided to retain the coin for himself. The Court was unable to agree whether title in the coin had passed, the difficulty being whether the relevant consent by K at the time of the transaction related to the coin *qua* coin, or the coin *qua* sovereign. Clearly K intended to hand over "the coin he was holding", but he did not mean to transfer "a sovereign". The decision is complicated by the fact that, at common law, larceny did not lie if D had already received possession of the goods, which he subsequently converted. Thus in such a case it was necessary to prove that even *possession* did not pass, at least until D discovered what he had actually received. Such distortion is not necessary under s 220, which requires only that D did not receive ownership. It is submitted that the better view is that K transferred mere possession and not ownership of the sovereign to D, and that under modern law D may be convicted of theft by conversion.

17.2.3.2(b) *Quantity*

If the owner intends to deal only with a specific number of goods handed over, then there is no consent as to the excess. But if O's intention is to hand over a group of things, mistake as to the number of items in the group does *not* negative the intention to hand them all over.

An example of the former variety is *Russell v Smith*:[127]

> D was a driver for a haulage company. He was instructed to collect a one-ton load of pig meal from P. P, when loading the meal, inadvertently loaded an additional eight sacks. When D discovered the error, he appropriated the eight sacks and sold them.

P intended to give D the number of sacks corresponding to one ton of meal; there was no intention to put the additional sacks on the lorry. Thus P remained owner of the eight sacks, which D converted when he sold them. Contrast this decision with an example where P offers to sell D all the pig meal then stored at his warehouse; which P mistakenly thinks amounts to one ton's worth, when in fact it is eight sacks more than that weight. In the latter case, D acquires ownership of the entirety. The excess is his to keep.

The distinction at work here is between a mistake which simply motivates or underlies P's intention to pass title to certain goods, and one which negates P's very intention to pass title in those goods which were in fact delivered. It is,

---

126 (1885) 16 QBD 190. Cf *R v Hehir* (1895) 18 Cox CC 267.
127 [1958] 1 QB 27, [1957] 2 All ER 796.

in short, the difference between a mistake as to *what* P is passing to D, and a mistake as to *why* he is doing so.[128]

Suppose that C is a wages clerk. When making up the pay packets one week, he accidentally puts a $100 note, which has stuck to another note, into D's packet, which now contains $250 instead of $150. Upon discovering the error, D resolves to say nothing and spends the money. He is guilty of converting the $100 note. Compare, on the other hand, *Moynes v Coopper*,[129] where a wages clerk miscalculated the amount due to D. Although the employee was thus overpaid, the clerk intended to pay the amount of money actually paid. Hence title in the whole amount paid passed to D, and D could not be convicted of theft.

17.2.3.2(c) *Transferee*

Mistake as to the identity of the other party may vitiate consent, but only if the identity was crucial to O's decision to give consent.[130] In *R v Hudson*, D received and paid into his bank account a cheque which was inadvertently made out to him, but obviously intended for someone else with the same surname. He was convicted of stealing the cheque.[131]

It seems that a mistake about the transferee's identity supplies the best explanation of another well-known case, *R v Middleton*.[132] In that case, D went to withdraw 10 shillings from his Post Office savings account, which had at that time a balance of 11s. The Post Office practice was to pay out withdrawals pursuant to a warrant obtained by D and a letter of advice from the Postmaster General sent direct to the relevant branch. Unfortunately the clerk consulted the wrong letter of advice, which related to a different account-holder, and paid out £8 16s 10d. The Court of Criminal Appeal held that D was properly convicted of larceny, as the clerk's intention to pass title to the money was vitiated by his mistake. Since the clerk clearly did intend to give D £8 16s 10d, and not 10s, he made no mistake about the nature or quantity of the property

---

128 Analogous to the distinction in contract law between a mistake "in the motive or reason for making an offer", and a mistake in the terms of the offer itself: *Imperial Glass Ltd v Consolidated Supplies Ltd* (1960) 22 DLR (2d) 759.

129 [1956] 1 QB 439, [1956] 1 All ER 450. See also *Ilich v R* (1986) 162 CLR 110.

130 Thus *Cundy v Lindsay* (1878) 3 App Cas 459, [1874-1880] All ER Rep 1149 may be distinguished from *King's Norton Metal Co Ltd v Edridge Merrett & Co Ltd* (1897) 14 TLR 98, where the rogue's assumed name was of no particular significance.

131 [1943] KB 458, [1943] 1 All ER 642. But this is not an absolute rule, at least where the parties deal face to face. In *Ingram v Little* [1961] 1 QB 31, [1960] 3 All ER 332 a contract for sale of a car to a rogue under a false name (whose cheque bounced) was held void, but in *Lewis v Averay* [1972] 1 QB 198, [1971] 3 All ER 907 a similar sale to a rogue believing him to be a certain TV actor was held valid. Possibly the only explanation for this anomaly is that in the latter case there was no actual misrepresentation by the buyer. Even before these cases, the considerable difficulties in this area of law had been pointed out by Williams, "Mistake as to Party in the Law of Contract" (1945) 23 Can Bar Rev 271; cf Sutton, "Reform of the Law of Mistake in Contract" (1976) 7 NZULR 40.

132 (1873) 12 Cox CC 417.

transferred.[133] Rather, his mistake is best seen as being about D's identity, which he had mistaken for that of the person named in the letter of advice.[134]

In 1972, the English Court of Appeal purported to follow *Middleton* in *R v Gilks*.[135] G placed various bets at a betting shop, including one on "Fighting Taffy", which was unplaced in a race won by "Fighting Scot". When he went to collect his winnings on the various bets he had placed, the bookmaker mistakenly thought G had backed the winner, and calculated and paid out an amount well in excess of G's true winnings. G, realising the mistake, decided to pocket the entirety. He was convicted of theft, on the footing that *Middleton* had established that in such cases property in money paid by mistake does not pass. It is submitted, however, that this reasoning is flawed. The bookmaker's error was an antecedent one of calculation, of the type that occurred in *Moynes v Coopper*, and not of the sort found in *Middleton*. He paid G exactly the amount he intended to.

17.2.3.2(d) *Other mistakes*

Other mistakes, which simply affect the reasons why the original owner consented, do not negative passing of possession or title. An example would be the mistake made by a supermarket cashier as to the price of goods. In *Dronjak v Police*[136] D bought a stereo which had two price tags on it. In showing the cashier the lower of the two tags (which was in fact incorrect), thus buying at a gross undervalue, he was found guilty of obtaining by false pretences[137] but not of theft. Similarly, in *Dip Kaur v Chief Constable for Hampshire*[138] D was in a shop

---

133 Per Bramwell B (dissenting): "No doubt the clerk did not intend to do an act of the sort described, and give to Middleton what did not belong to him. Yet he intended to do the act he did. What he did he did not do involuntarily, nor accidentally, but on purpose." (1873) 12 Cox CC 417 at 428.

134 (1873) 12 Cox CC 417 at 419: the clerk "certainly meant that the prisoner should take up that money, though he only meant this because of a mistake he made as to the identity of the prisoner with the person really entitled to that money". Cf Orchard, "The Borderland of Theft Revisited" [1973] NZLJ 110 at 112; Smith and Hogan, *Criminal Law* (1st ed), 1965, 354. On whether the facts really support such a finding, contra the dissent by Cleasby B (1873) 12 Cox CC 417 at 441, 442: "The conclusion of law [that there was a taking *invito domino*] would be quite correct if it could be correctly said that the amount was intended for another. The clerk ought to have intended that amount for another, and would have done so if he had properly informed himself of the facts, but unfortunately for the prisoner the clerk did not properly inform himself of the facts, and therefore he intended the prisoner to receive the larger amount. The clerk intended A to receive what he ought to have intended B to receive, but it was not the less his intention that A should receive what he handed over to him." See Turner, "Two Cases of Larceny" in Turner and Radzinowicz (eds), *The Modern Approach to Criminal Law* (1948) 356 at 359.

135 [1972] 3 All ER 280, [1972] 1 WLR 1341. See the criticism by Smith in [1972] Crim LR 586; Orchard, "The Borderland of Theft Revisited" [1972] NZLJ 110 at 111ff. Compare *R v Prince* (1868) LR 1 CCR 150.

136 [1990] 3 NZLR 75, (1988) 3 CRNZ 141.

137 But see discussion of the case on this point at § 19.1.1.1(b).

138 [1981] 2 All ER 430, [1981] 1 WLR 578. The decision appears now to be inconsistent with English law in the wake of *DPP v Gomez* [1993] AC 442, [1993] 1 All ER 1, but remains relevant in New Zealand.

where she found a pair of shoes, one of which was marked for sale at £6.99, the other at £4.99. She took the shoes to the cashier, hoping that the cashier would see the lower (incorrect) price. She was charged £4.99. Her conviction for theft was quashed, for the reason that the cashier's mistake (in thinking £4.99 was the correct price) did not negate her intention to sell the goods to D for £4.99; thus, when D left the shop, she owned the shoes and could not steal them.

17.2.3.3 *Was the transferor authorised to pass title?*
Property will not pass if the transferor does not have the owner's authority to pass title. In *R v Bhachu*, a dishonest cashier acted in collusion with D by "selling" the goods to her at a price below the authorised price.[139] In such a case, the cashier does not have the authority to pass title on O's behalf, and the goods are converted by D when she takes them out of the shop.[140] However, a mere error on the part of an agent does not mean that the agent's conduct is unauthorised, even if the recipient is dishonest.[141]

17.3 MENS REA
There are three elements to the mens rea of theft.[142] The defendant's actions (i) must be fraudulent; (ii) must be without colour of right; and (iii) must be either with intent permanently to deprive (s 220(1)(a)) or with one of the criminal intentions defined in the subsequent subsections. We consider these elements in turn.

17.3.1 Fraudulently
"Fraudulently" in this context means dishonestly. The leading authority is *R v Coombridge*, where the Court of Appeal stated:

> We think that in order to act fraudulently an accused person must certainly, as the judge pointed out in the present case, act deliberately and with knowledge that he is acting in breach of his legal obligation. But we are of opinion that if an accused person sets up a claim that in all the circumstances he honestly believed that he was justified in departing from his strict obligation, albeit for some purpose of his own, then his defence should be left to the jury for consideration provided at least that there is evidence on which it would be open to a jury to conclude that in all the circumstances his conduct, although legally wrong, might nevertheless be regarded as honest. In other words the jury should be told that the accused cannot be convicted unless he has been shown to have acted dishonestly.[143]

In *R v Williams*, the Court of Appeal declared the above to be "how the test has been applied in this country for many years".[144] The test is subjective. It is a

---

139 (1976) 65 Cr App R 261. Cf *R v Tideswell* [1905] 2 KB 273.

140 In such circumstances, the cashier herself converts the goods when she offers to sell them at an undervalue.

141 *R v Jackson* (1826) 1 Mod 119, 168 ER 1208; *R v Prince* (1868) LR 1 CCR 150.

142 For discussion of the doctrine of recent possession and its evidential role in the proof of mens rea, see § 17.4.3.

143 [1976] 2 NZLR 381 at 387 (CA).

144 [1985] 1 NZLR 294 at 308 (CA). In particular, the Court of Appeal in *Williams* declined to adopt the mixed objective-subjective test of dishonesty established by the English Court

defence that D had an *honest belief* that she was entitled so to act. Therefore, the necessary fraudulence is negatived if D believes, even mistakenly, that her actions were *morally* justified.[145] D's belief does not have to be reasonable. A jury may be less likely to credit her with honesty if the facts did not warrant her belief,[146] but if there is a reasonable possibility that D did so believe then she must be acquitted.

17.3.2 Without colour of right

"Colour of right" is defined in s 2, and means an honest belief that the taking or conversion of the thing is *legally* justified,[147] even where the belief is based on ignorance, mistake of fact, or even mistake of law. "The essence of the defence of colour of right is honesty of purpose" and it is for the prosecution to prove the absence thereof.[148] Examples of colour of right defences are found in *R v Bernhard*,[149] where a woman who blackmailed her former lover thought she had a right to the money claimed; and in *R v Skivington*,[150] where D held up a wages clerk and demanded his wife's wages. Though this was an assault, it was held that there was no theft and therefore no robbery, since he believed he had a lawful claim.

Skivington demonstrates that since colour of right is a defence to theft, it is also a defence to any other crime in which the intent to steal is a necessary element, eg robbery, burglary, and demanding money with menaces. In these cases, since D believed he was entitled to the money, the charge fails for lack of intent to steal; it is irrelevant whether D believed he had a right to use force.

Although D's belief need not extend to justification of the action taken to obtain the thing, the "colour of right" must relate to the thing stolen. If D believes that she has a right to X, this is a defence to any charge alleging intent to *steal* X, as the requisite intent is simply not there. But that belief does not

---

of Appeal in *R v Ghosh* [1982] QB 1053, [1982] 2 All ER 689, according to which dishonesty is determined according to the ordinary standards of reasonable people, qualified by the proviso that the defendant must have been aware that his behaviour would be regarded as dishonest according to those standards. But is there any such thing as a common standard of (dis)honesty shared by all? In a multicultural society with wide internal socio-economic variation, that is surely unlikely. For discussion, see Halpin, "The Test for Dishonesty" [1996] Crim LR 283, and references there cited; also Smith, *Property Offences: the protection of property through the criminal law*, London, Sweet & Maxwell, 1994, at 7-47ff.

145 Cf, in Canada, *R v Hemmerly* (1976) 30 CCC (2d) 141 at 145.

146 Cf *Cheape v NZ Law Soc* [1955] NZLR 63 at 68, where the conduct was said of itself to be "altogether inconsistent with honesty and fair dealing", and therefore fraudulent.

147 Cf the definition of "justified", also in s 2: "not guilty of an offence and not liable to any civil proceeding".

148 *Murphy v Gregory* [1959] NZLR 868 at 872: "Where an accused person really believes he has the right asserted, it is a good defence even if he is mistaken in both fact and in law."

149 [1938] 2 KB 264, [1938] 2 All ER 140. V agreed to pay his mistress (D) a sum of money, which he did not; she then threatened to expose him to his wife and the public unless he paid up. D was acquitted of demanding money with menaces with intent to steal, as she — mistakenly — thought she had a valid claim to the money.

150 [1968] 1 QB 166, [1967] 1 All ER 483.

entitle her to steal Y in order to obtain X; and a belief of right to take X does not per se prove or imply an additional belief of right to take Y. In *Wicks v Police*,[151] D received by mistake and kept a barrister's file, and attempted to use it to force the barrister to settle a tort claim. He was convicted of theft: although he believed that his tort claim was justified, he admitted that he had no right to the file.

The distinction, however, is a narrow one. In *Wicks*, D was guilty of theft, whereas the defendant in *Bernhard* was not. Yet both are essentially cases of blackmail, the legal difference being that D's conduct in *Bernhard* did not constitute any crime apart from blackmail.[152] But where (unlike *Skivington*) D's independent crime is merely another theft — and that by way of set-off, as it were — it is more difficult to see a substantial moral difference between the two.

17.3.2.1 *Distinguishing colour of right from fraudulence*
We may therefore distinguish between the defences of a belief in a *legal* right to the thing allegedly stolen, which operates through the "colour of right" defence, and a belief in a *moral* justification for the act. Belief in moral justification may, but will not necessarily, include a belief that D is legally entitled to the thing taken. Where D knows that he has no legal right to the thing, his belief in a moral right alone is not sufficient for the colour of right defence,[153] although it would usually mean that D was not fraudulent. The decision in *R v Minhinnick* was therefore probably correct in the result it reached, but doubtful in the reasoning:

> D, a Maori, covertly removed a New Zealand Cross, then worth $10,000, from the Rotorua Museum. He was aware when he did so that his actions were contrary to law, but was inspired by cultural and spiritual beliefs that, he felt, obliged him to take the medal and return it to his ancestral burial ground.[154]

The Court held that D had a colour of right defence. However, he did not claim to be *legally* right. Thus the true defence was that he did not act fraudulently.

17.3.3 Intent to deprive permanently
The standard intent required for theft is the intent *permanently to deprive* the owner, or other person with an interest or property in the goods, within the meaning of s 220(1)(a). The intention need not be for D to keep the thing for himself: it is sufficient that D intends the victim to be (or is morally certain the

---

151 (1984) 1 CRNZ 328. By way of comparison, had D been charged with demanding with intent to steal (s 239), he would have had a colour of right defence.

152 On the particular facts of the case, in New Zealand D would have committed an offence under s 238(1)(a), for which colour of right is not a defence: *R v Cargill* [1995] 3 NZLR 263, (1995) 13 CRNZ 291 (CA).

153 *R v Hemmerly* (1976) 30 CCC (2d) 141. D, a drug dealer, was convicted of robbery; in his defence he argued that he was entitled to the money taken, as the victim owed it to him. However, it was clear that D did not believe he had a legal claim to the money; and although belief in a moral right might negative a fraudulent intent, it was held not to do so in this case.

154 [1978] NZLJ 199.

victim will be[155]) permanently deprived of the thing. Therefore D is guilty of theft where he steals to give to another, he himself receiving no benefit.[156] But even if fraud and absence of colour of right are proven, there is no theft where D intends to deprive only temporarily. Where a joyrider intends to take only temporarily, even for a period of several days, he is not guilty of theft of the car although there may be theft of the petrol consumed during the joyride.[157] Regarding the car itself, there is a separate offence of car conversion under s 228.[158]

In other cases, where s 228 does not apply, this can lead to quite a fine distinction between the intent to deprive only temporarily and the conditional intent to deprive permanently. As we saw in §3.1.8, a conditional intent is treated in law as sufficient for intention. To illustrate the implications of this, consider the facts of two cases. In *R v Hare*,[159] D found a letter containing important business information. He wrote to the sender demanding money for its return, and threatening to send copies to interested persons if money was not paid. D was convicted of theft. By contrast, in *Broom v Police*,[160] D recovered a stolen bicycle, and negotiated its return in response to an advertisement by the owner, in which a reward was offered. D's conviction for theft was set aside on appeal, on the footing (inter alia) that he had no intent to deprive the owner permanently.

The difference between these cases is that in *R v Hare* the defendant meant not to return the letter unless a ransom was paid. By contrast, Broom apparently had no thought of not returning the bicycle — he was merely temporarily withholding it in the hope of negotiating a reward. More generally, if the possessor attempts to extract a reward but means to return the thing even if uncompensated, the proper charge would lie under s 262.[161]

17.3.4 Alternative theftous intents

As an alternative to s 220(1)(a), D may be guilty of theft where she intends to pledge the thing or deposit it as security (s 220(1)(b)); or to part with it under a condition as to its return which she may not be able to fulfil (s 220(1)(c)), for example by pawning it knowing she may not be able to redeem it;[162] or to deal

---

155 See § 3.1.4,7.

156 *Leakey v Quirke* [1918] NZLR 550.

157 *R v Bailey* [1924] QWN 35; cf *Neal v Gribble* [1978] RTR 409, (1978) 68 Cr App R 9.

158 Cf *Murphy v Gregory* [1959] NZLR 868.

159 (1910) 29 NZLR 641 (CA). Cf *Wicks v Police* (1984) 1 CRNZ 328.

160 [1994] 1 NZLR 680, (1993) 11 CRNZ 20. Cf *R v Gardner* (1862) 9 Cox CC 253.

161 Cf *Broom v Police* [1994] 1 NZLR 680, (1993) 11 CRNZ 20, where it was regarded as crucial that the owner had already offered the reward that D sought to collect.

162 Cf *R v Medland* (1851) 5 Cox CC 292, where D pawned property belonging to her landlord. The actual indictment was for larceny, which required an intent permanently to deprive. Counsel for D submitted that this intent did not exist because she did intend to redeem the property. However, it was held that there could be no intention to redeem under circumstances that render it very improbable, or at least uncertain, that such ability would ever exist. This reasoning should be doubted, since it is clearly possible to intend to do something even if success is unlikely. (If an unskilled player lands a treble-

with it in such a manner that it cannot be restored in substantially the original condition (s 220(1)(d)), for example where D wrongfully feeds V's oats to V's horses.[163] For these variants there is no need to prove an intention by D permanently to deprive.[164]

17.4 RECEIVING PROPERTY DISHONESTLY OBTAINED

"There would not be so many thieves if there were no receivers."[165] The crime of receiving is in many ways a special case of being an accessory to theft,[166] one which deserves independent criminalisation because of the important role that fences — and indeed end-purchasers — of stolen goods play in the economics of the offence. It should be noted, however, that although receiving is normally (and historically) associated with theft, the modern offence can be committed in respect of *anything* obtained by crime. Thus one who launders the proceeds of an illegal drug deal may be guilty of receiving under s 258.[167] The section, which is drafted in remarkably wide terms, provides that it is an offence whenever someone:

> receives anything stolen or obtained by any other crime, or by any act wherever committed which, if committed in New Zealand, would constitute a crime, knowing that thing to have been stolen or dishonestly obtained . . .

The penalties are the same as for theft of something of equivalent value,[168] reflecting the perception that receiving is a form of participation in theft. In this respect the statute has obvious limitations: its association with theft makes it a somewhat inflexible tool for prosecuting those who deal in the proceeds of crime more generally. Neither does the Act draw any distinction between the lay receiver who might once in her lifetime buy stolen goods for her own

---

twenty at darts, her feat may still be intended.) Section 220(1)(a) would now be appropriate only if it was "morally certain" that she would not be able to redeem it — as to which the discussion at § 3.1.4,7 — or if she actually meant the landlord never to have the property back.

163 *R v Morfit* (1816) Russ & Ry 307, 168 ER 817. For other examples, see *R v Richards* (1844) 1 Car & Kir 532, 174 ER 925; *R v Cabbage* (1815) Russ & Ry 292, 168 ER 809; *R v Duru* [1973] 3 All ER 715, (1973) 58 Cr App R 151; *R v Smails* (1957) 74 WN (NSW) 150.

164 *R v Tennent* [1962] NZLR 428 at 431 (CA).

165 *R v Battams* (1979) 1 Cr App R (S) 15 at 16. See generally Smith, *Property Offences: the protection of property through the criminal law*, London, Sweet & Maxwell, 1994, chapter 30.

166 Indeed, this was how it was first criminalised, in 1692, 3 & 4 W & M c13 (receivers deemed to be accessories). Earlier law disclosed an offence only if D actually received or abetted the thief himself: *Dawson's Case* (1602) 2 Bracton 337 at 339, 80 ER 4. The old position is now reversed, and receiving the thief does not constitute receiving the goods stolen: *R v Wiley* (1850) 4 Cox CC 412, 169 ER 408.

167 *Stevens v Police* (1988) 4 CRNZ 69. Section 258 thus supplements s 257A (money laundering) as well as s 11 Misuse of Drugs Act 1975. Enactment of the offence considered in Howarth, "Handling Stolen Goods and Handling Salmon" [1987] Crim LR 460 would be unnecessary in New Zealand.

168 Cf ss 258(1)(a), (b), and (c) with ss 227(ba), (c), and (d).

consumption, and the professional criminal receiver who maintains an organisation and thus supports the theft industry.[169]

Section 258 stipulates three key elements of receiving. The actus reus elements are: (a) that D receives something, and (b) the thing received was stolen or obtained by crime. The third component relates to mens rea: (c) when he receives it, D *knows* the thing was stolen or dishonestly obtained.

17.4.1 The actus reus

17.4.1.1 *Receiving something*

The property must be received from another person.[170] However, D need not take personal physical custody of the goods. The requirement of "receiving" is satisfied whenever D has (joint or sole) possession *or* control over the stolen property, *or* aids in concealing or disposing of it.[171]

Regarding the first of these alternatives, "possession" is established by showing (i) that the goods are either in D's immediate physical custody, or located at a place over which D has control (eg in D's house).[172] In either case, proof of possession also requires that the prosecution show a mental element, (ii) an intent by D to possess the goods.[173] Thus D cannot be in possession of property that he does not know exists. Suppose, for instance, that T, having stolen a wallet, disposes of it by slipping the wallet into D's bag without D's knowledge. In such a case, for the purposes of receiving D does not take possession of the wallet, at least until she knows she has it. Similarly, if goods stolen by another are found in D's house, it must be shown either that D had arranged for them to be delivered there[174] or, alternatively, that D had realised the goods were present and intentionally exercised control over them.[175]

If D lacks actual custody of the stolen goods, he may nonetheless be found to have "control" over them. This occurs when custody is in the hands of an

---

169 Cf Hall, *Theft, Law and Society* (2nd ed), 1952, chapter 5; Klockars, *The Professional Fence*, New York, Free Press, 1974; Chappell and Walsh, "Receiving Stolen Property: The Need for a Systematic Inquiry into the Fencing Process" (1974) 11 Criminology 484; Blakey and Goldsmith, "Criminal Redistribution of Stolen Property: The Need for Reform" (1976) 74 Mich LR 1512. The difference would, however, normally be reflected in sentencing.

170 *R v Seymour* [1954] 1 All ER 1006, [1954] 1 WLR 678 at 679. This decision represented an attempt by the Court of Criminal Appeal to correct the tendency to find someone guilty of receiving, rather than theft, whenever they were found in "recent possession" of stolen goods. (See § 17.4.3.) Lord Goddard CJ emphasised that to find someone guilty of receiving, the jury must be satisfied that D received from *someone else*: "If he is the thief, he cannot be guilty of receiving because a man cannot receive from himself, but must receive the property from somebody else." Thus where the evidence is as consistent with theft as it is with receiving, the indictment ought to contain a count for theft and a count for receiving.

171 Section 260.

172 *Police v Emirali* [1976] 2 NZLR 476 (CA); *Rose v Loo Kee* [1927] GLR 403 (drugs).

173 *Dong Wai v Audley* [1937] NZLR 290.

174 *R v Lloyd* [1992] Crim LR 361.

175 Cf *R v Cavendish* [1961] 2 All ER 856, [1961] 1 WLR 1083.

agent or servant acting under D's direction; through whom D exercises control over the goods.[176]

It is not necessary for a finding of possession that D should know the thing was stolen — such knowledge goes rather to the mens rea of receiving.

17.4.1.2 *Stolen or obtained by any crime*

The thing received must be the actual thing that was first unlawfully obtained, not its proceeds or a substitute.[177] Arguably, there is a case here for statutory reform; the present law may be too generous to those involved in laundering the proceeds of theft, since it confers an immunity from prosecution upon subsequent participants in the laundering "chain", once the original item is exchanged.[178] However, D need not receive the whole of the thing stolen. It is sufficient, for example, that D receives parts of a car which has been stolen (eg the wheels or radio), or parts of a stolen stereo system, such as the tape deck or amplifier. Furthermore, the property need not be in the same state or condition as it was when stolen. A stolen car can be received even though substantially damaged in an accident before it arrives in D's hands. Similarly, s 258 would apply to the receipt of mutton from a sheep which was alive when stolen.[179]

It is not necessary to prove the identity of either the person who actually committed the crime, or the owner of the property.[180] Provided the evidence discloses that the property was obtained by theft or another crime, even the acquittal of the particular person charged with committing that theft is

---

176 Cf *R v Smith* (1855) Dears 494, 169 ER 818; *R v Miller* (1854) 6 Cox 353; also, in the context of the Misuse of Drugs Act 1975, *R v Cox* [1990] 2 NZLR 275, (1990) 5 CRNZ 653 (CA); *R v Cossey* (1990) 6 CRNZ 185 (CA); *R v McRae* (1993) 10 CRNZ 61 at 66, 67.

177 *R v Lucinsky* [1935] NZLR 575, [1935] GLR 515 (CA). (D received banknotes of different denominations from those actually stolen. The Court of Appeal ruled that he was not guilty of receiving within the terms of s 258.) Cf *R v Walkley* (1829) 4 C & P 132, 172 ER 640.

178 Contrast s 24(2) Theft Act 1968 (UK). It is possible that the civil law may be in the process of filling this lacuna. Common law tracing now allows P to claim the proceeds of an unauthorised exchange-transaction: see *Trustee of the Property of FC Jones and Sons (a firm) v Jones* [1996] 4 All ER 721, [1996] 3 WLR 703. On this analysis, the victim of a theft acquires title in the exchange proceeds, and subsequent handlers may be guilty of theft. It is not yet clear, however, whether the common law claim crystallises immediately, or only after demand for the proceeds is made, or alternatively whether it is merely a form of transferred money had and received (ie non-proprietary).

179 *Cowell and Green* (1796) 2 East PC 617.

180 *R v Carr & Wilson* (1882) 10 QBD 76. (Bonds stolen from an English ship moored in Holland, thief and circumstances of the theft unknown.) In *R v Fuschillo* [1940] 2 All ER 489, 27 Cr App R 193, D was charged with receiving a large quantity of sugar, although it was not proven who had stolen them or from whom they were stolen. The Court of Criminal Appeal applied dicta in *R v Sbarra* [1918-19] 2 All ER Rep Ext 1453, (1918) 13 Cr App R 118, to the effect that "the circumstances in which a defendant receives goods may of themselves prove that the goods were stolen, and, further, may prove that he knew it at the time when he received them. It is not a rule of law that there must be other evidence of the theft".

irrelevant to the charge of receiving.[181] However, it *is* essential to prove that the property was stolen,[182] or obtained by some other *crime*. So, for example, where the person charged with originally stealing a thing is acquitted (or cannot be charged at all) on the ground of legal incapacity such as minority or insanity, the receivers cannot be convicted in the absence of other evidence showing the property to have been obtained by a crime.[183] An illustration of this is the case of *R v Farrell*,[184] in which the person from whom D received a stolen cheque was acquitted of theft on the ground of insanity. Consequently, the Court held that the evidence against D lacked an essential ingredient of the receiving charge, namely that the cheque was "obtained by any crime". In such a case D's subsequent dealing with the cheque might, of course, be a conversion sufficient for D himself to be charged with theft under s 220.

17.4.1.2(a) *Goods which are no longer stolen*

Goods are no longer stolen, and cannot be received, once they re-enter into the possession of the legal owner or a person authorised by the owner to possess the goods.[185] This may occur in two ways. First, the goods may be restored to the original owner or to an authorised possessor. Suppose, for example, that the police recover stolen goods but then, with the consent of the owner, return them to the location where they were discovered in order to trap a would-be receiver. In that case, the subsequent purchaser cannot be convicted of receiving.[186] However, if the owner does not know of the recovery and no agency exists between the owner and the police, the goods remain stolen as they have not in those circumstances been restored to the owner.[187]

Alternatively, someone else may acquire legal ownership of the goods, usually by purchasing them in good faith. Normally in such cases the rule nemo dat quod non habet will prevent third parties from acquiring ownership, since at law a person cannot transfer to another any better title to goods than

---

181 *R v Dee & Hennessy* (1875) 3 NZCA 58. Neither is a conviction admissible against the receiver. See *Adams*, § CA258.10.

182 "Stolen or" is an insertion. The original wording of s 258(1) provided only that the offence was committed by receiving anything obtained by any crime. This was amended in 1985, in response to the decision in *Anderson v Police* [1983] NZLR 509 (CA). The charge in that case failed, as the prosecution had not proven beyond reasonable doubt that the thing received had been theftously *taken* (such that it could be said to have been "obtained" by a crime), rather than legitimately obtained and then *converted* by a dishonest employee or hirer.

183 *Walters v Lunt* [1951] 2 All ER 645, (1951) 35 Cr App R 94. (Property received from a child aged 7: no conviction for receiving since the child, being under 8 years old, could not be guilty of larceny.) See Brown, "Receiving Goods Stolen by Children or the Insane" [1979] NZLJ 506.

184 [1975] 2 NZLR 753; following the rule in *Walters v Lunt* (op cit fn 183).

185 Section 261.

186 *R v Dolan* (1855) Dears 436, 169 ER 794; *R v Schmidt* (1866) LR 1 CCR 15; *R v Hancock* (1878) 14 Cox CC 119.

187 *Fry v Police* [1975] Recent Law 295.

she has herself.[188] However, there are some exceptions to this, most of which are contained in the Sale of Goods Act 1908.[189]

17.4.2 Mens rea

D must know that the thing was stolen or dishonestly obtained. It is not necessary that D should know the particular way in which the thing was obtained,[190] but he must know it was obtained by a crime. "Dishonestly" here means *criminal* dishonesty: "in an Act dealing entirely with crimes, 'dishonestly obtained' must refer to criminal and not merely immorally dishonest acts".[191] In particular, "dishonestly obtained" adds no colour of its own, and does not mean that the crime must have involved dishonesty as defined in s 2 of the Act.

D must have the requisite knowledge at the time the thing was received.[192] If D receives property innocently, he is not guilty of an offence under this section. However, retaining property after discovering that it was obtained by crime may amount to theft by conversion.[193]

17.4.2.1 *Knowing that thing to have been stolen or dishonestly obtained*

The meaning of "knowledge" was considered in §3.4, where it was said that knowing means "knowing, or correctly believing". In essence, this requires that D must accept, or assume, or have no serious doubt, that the goods he receives were obtained by crime. We have nothing to add to the principles stated there. It may, however, be helpful to reproduce here statements from the leading authorities under s 258. The central case is *R v Crooks*. According to Mahon J:

> The gist of the crime of receiving is the receipt of stolen goods then "knowing" that they have been dishonestly obtained. A person is said to "know" something when he has ascertained, by physical or mental perception, a state of facts or circumstances which creates in his mind a certainty that the point of his inquiry is free from doubt. If this were the test of criminal liability for the crime of receiving, then the only sure method of proof would be to establish that the suspected receiver actually saw the goods being stolen. It was for this reason that the word 'knowing' came to be treated in the common law concept of receiving as "believing".[194]

For an early example of this approach, one may look to the 1859 case of *R v White*:

---

188 Sections 23 and 26(1) Sale of Goods Act 1908.

189 For example, if the rogue has obtained a voidable title to the goods that has not been avoided at time of on-sale (ss 25 and 26(2) Sale of Goods Act 1908), or is fraudulent buyer in possession (ss 26(2), 27(2)), or is a mercantile agent with authorised possession (s 3 Mercantile Law Act 1908).

190 *Stevens v Police* (1988) 4 CRNZ 69; compare *DPP v Nieser* [1959] 1 QB 254, [1958] 3 All ER 662.

191 *R v Creamer* (1912) 32 NZLR 449 at 454, 15 GLR 246 at 249 (CA).

192 *R v Johnson* (1911) 6 Cr App R 218; *R v Smith* (1935) 25 Cr App R 119; *R v Tennet* [1939] 1 All ER 86.

193 *R v Stone* [1920] NZLR 462, [1920] GLR 357 (CA).

194 [1981] 2 NZLR 53 at 56 (CA). See also *R v Simpson* [1978] 2 NZLR 221 at 225 (s 192(2)).

The knowledge charged in this indictment need not be such knowledge as would be acquired if the prisoner had actually seen the lead stolen; it is sufficient if you think the circumstances were such, accompanying the transaction, as to make the prisoner *believe* that it had been stolen.[195]

17.4.2.1(a) *Belief and wilful blindness*

The meaning of "belief", too, is considered in *R v Crooks*:

Belief is the result of a subjective evaluation of evidence or information which has produced acceptance of a proposition, or of the existence of a set of facts. Where a belief is founded not upon evidence or information from other persons but is derived from intuitive assessment of a set of circumstances, then it is not in the true sense a belief at all. It is only an opinion or, in the present context, a suspicion, and the fact that a receiver merely suspects goods to be stolen cannot make him liable.[196]

However, what, if D suspects the goods are stolen and deliberately refrains from inquiring any further into the question? In this situation D's mental state may be described as one of *wilful blindness*. Does D's failure to make that further inquiry itself establish the requisite knowledge or belief? As we stated in §3.4.1, generally the answer is no. That wilful blindness is not an alternative form of knowledge[197] was made clear by the English Court of Appeal in *R v Griffiths*:

To direct the jury that the offence is committed if the defendant, suspecting that the goods were stolen, deliberately shut his eyes to the circumstances as an alternative to knowing or believing the goods were stolen is a misdirection. To direct the jury that, in common sense and in law, they may find that the defendant knew or believed the goods to be stolen because he deliberately closed his eyes to the circumstances is a perfectly proper direction.[198]

The New Zealand Court of Appeal in *R v Crooks* came to a parallel conclusion, with the similar qualification that a failure by D to make some inquiry may, in certain circumstances, be taken into account in considering whether the prosecution has proved beyond reasonable doubt the existence of knowledge or belief. The jury should be directed on the following lines:

If the jury are satisfied that the defendant, whilst lacking direct knowledge on the point, nevertheless formed the view when receiving it that the property had been dishonestly obtained, then they are entitled to consider the question why he made no inquiry. If they come to the conclusion that the defendant deliberately abstained from inquiry because he knew what the answer was going to be, then they will be entitled to infer that his omission to inquire stemmed not from mere suspicion, but

---

195 (1859) 1 F&F 665, 175 ER 898 (Bramwell B; emphasis added). See also *R v Nosworthy* (1907) 26 NZLR 536, 9 GLR 434 (CA).

196 [1981] 2 NZLR 53 at 57 (CA).

197 As might be suggested by somewhat ambiguous dicta in *Atwal v Massey* [1971] 3 All ER 881, (1971) 56 Cr App R 6 (DC).

198 (1974) 60 Cr App R 14 at 18. Similarly, in *R v Smith* (1976) 64 Cr App R 217 at 220, Lawton LJ stated: "We are satisfied that except in most unusual cases juries are capable of understanding what is meant by the word 'believing' . . . Phrases such as 'suspecting that the goods were stolen and then wilfully shutting one's eyes to the obvious' should not be used as a definition of 'believing'."

from an actual belief on his part that the goods had been dishonestly obtained. But if the jury should decide that the state of mind of the defendant was such that he merely entertained a doubt as to whether or not the property had been honestly obtained, then they must not use against him, as evidence of guilt, the fact that he failed to inquire. This is because he may have abstained from inquiry because he was gullible, or careless, or believed that his suspicion about the transaction might in fact be unjustified. Having put aside the failure to make inquiry, the jury must then come to a decision, on all the other relevant circumstances, as to whether guilty knowledge on the part of the defendant has been proved beyond reasonable doubt by the Crown.[199]

In this context, it is important to remember that the test for guilty knowledge is *subjective*. In *Atwal v Massey*,[200] it was held to be a misdirection for the jury to be told that the circumstances were such that they could hold that D *ought* to have realised the dishonest origin of the property. This could easily have been misunderstood as meaning that D would be liable if a reasonable person in his situation would have made an inquiry.

Nonetheless, it seems that there is still limited room for the wilful blindness doctrine, as the basis for inferring a belief that goods were stolen. It operates where D believes the goods are almost certainly stolen, and where any slight doubt on the matter could easily be resolved by his further inquiry. If D deliberately refrains from making that inquiry, he is to be attributed with knowledge. For a modern statement of the doctrine, one may look to *Severinsen v Dept of Social Welfare*, where the Court observed:[201]

(i) That the doctrine of wilful blindness concerns deemed knowledge and it is of very limited scope.

(ii) That it only applies to a situation where it can almost be said that the defendant actually knew the particular fact which is in issue.

(iii) That the gist of the doctrine is:

(a) That the defendant suspected the fact in issue; and

(b) That he realised the probability of the fact in issue or realised the need for an enquiry on his part; and

(c) That he deliberately refrained from making enquiries for fear that he may learn the truth or because he wanted to be able to deny knowledge.

(iv) That the following are not sufficient for a finding of wilful blindness:

(a) Ignorance of the facts

(b) Mere suspicion

(c) Reasonable grounds for suspicion

(d) That a reasonable person would have enquired

---

199 [1981] 2 NZLR 53 at 59 (CA).

200 [1971] 3 All ER 881, (1971) 56 Cr App R 6 (DC).

201 31/5/94, Penlington J, HC Hamilton AP1/94, at 19.

(e) There has been an honest mistake, however that mistake has been made.

We endorse propositions (i), (ii), and (iv) of this analysis unreservedly. The one qualification we would express is over the requirement "that he realised the probability of the fact in issue or realised the need for an enquiry on his part". It is submitted that — as we argued in § 3.4.1, and as the quotation above from *R v Crooks* suggests — the degree of D's certainty must be greater than this to count as knowledge.

17.4.2.2 *Dishonesty on the part of the receiver?*

Dishonesty is not required explicitly by s 258, but it appears to be an established element of the crime that the goods should have been dishonestly received. It is submitted that this is the best interpretation of a statement by the Court of Appeal in *R v Crooks*,[202] that the receiver must have had the intention of appropriating such goods for the benefit of himself or of some other person. The problem with the Court's phrasing is that someone (even a police officer!) who chases a thief and recovers property for the owner receives that property for the benefit of another. Such persons should not, of course, be guilty of an offence — because their actions are not dishonest.

The view taken here is consistent with the case law. In *R v Matthews*[203] the English Court of Criminal Appeal held that a person who has received stolen property intending to hand it over at once to the police or the true owner could not be guilty of receiving stolen property. In *R v Monson*,[204] D was charged with receiving stolen goods. His defence was that he was so drunk that he could not form any intent at all. The jury delivered a verdict of "Guilty, but without criminal intent"; apparently they believed that D had been drunk, and that he might have intended to return the property. The Court of Appeal held that the jury's words amounted to a verdict of not guilty, since criminal intent at the time of receiving the goods was an essential ingredient of the crime of receiving stolen property.

17.4.3 Evidence of criminality: the doctrine of recent possession

The "doctrine" of recent possession is a common sense rule that the proof of possession by D of property recently stolen is sufficient evidence to justify a finding that D is either the thief or a dishonest receiver.[205] It has been described as:

a convenient way of referring compendiously to the inferences of fact which, in the absence of any satisfactory explanation by the accused, may be drawn as a matter of common sense from other facts, including, in particular, the fact that the accused has

---

202 [1981] 2 NZLR 53 at 62 (CA).

203 [1950] 1 All ER 137, (1949) 34 Cr App R 55 at 58.

204 [1939] GLR 253.

205 For more detailed discussion, see Adams, "Recent Possession" [1967] NZLJ 399 at 495, 511; *Adams* § CA220.19; *Garrow and Turkington* § 220.15.

in his possession property which it is proved had been unlawfully obtained shortly before he was found to be in possession of it.[206]

Although in some jurisdictions it has been held that the rule is limited to theft, its application to receiving may be justified on the pragmatic ground that criminal receivers can rarely be detected in the act of receiving, so that direct evidence is rarely available.[207]

The classic direction is found in *R v Aves*:

Where the only evidence is that an accused person is in possession of property recently stolen, a jury may infer guilty knowledge (a) if he offers no explanation to account for his possession, or (b) if the jury are satisfied that the explanation he does offer is untrue. If, however, the explanation offered is one which leaves the jury in doubt as to whether he knew the property was stolen, they should be told that the case has not been proved, and therefore the verdict should be Not Guilty.[208]

The doctrine of recent possession has been held compatible with s 23(4)(b) New Zealand Bill of Rights Act 1990, which gives persons arrested or detained the right to refrain from making any statement, and with s 25(c) and (d), which refers to the right to be presumed innocent until proven guilty according to law, and the right not to be compelled to be a witness or to confess guilt.[209]

17.4.3.1 *Proof of guilty knowledge under s 258(2)*

It is also worth mentioning the provision in s 258(2) that, in proving guilty knowledge, the prosecution may give as evidence (a) the fact that other property obtained by crime was in D's possession within the period of 12 months before D was charged with the current offence,[210] or (b) the fact that D was convicted of the crime of receiving within the period of 5 years before

---

206 *DPP v Nieser* [1959] 1 QB 254 at 266; [1958] 3 All ER 662 at 668, 669. See also *R v Raviraj* (1986) 85 Cr App R 93 (CA): the doctrine is only an extension of a general proposition that guilt may inferred from unreasonable behaviour by the accused in response to his being confronted with facts which prima facie suggest his guilt.

207 Hall, *Theft, Law and Society* (2nd ed), 1952, 175. However, where the actus reus of receiving is constituted only by concealment or disposal (see § 17.4.1.1), actual knowledge must be proved and the doctrine of recent possession does not apply: *R v Hyde-Harris* [1968] NZLR 315.

208 [1950] 2 All ER 330, 34 Cr App R 159 at 160. See also *R v Ketteringham* (1926) 19 Cr App R 159; *R v Hepworth* [1955] 2 QB 600, [1955] 2 All ER 918; *R v Cash* [1985] QB 801, [1985] 2 All ER 128 (CA).

209 *R v Clarke* 16/12/93, CA417/93.

210 The wording is very similar to that of s 19 Prevention of Crimes Act 1871 (UK) on which the Court in *R v Ballard* (1916) 12 Cr App R 1 at 4 commented that the reason for the provision was probably that in many cases there was not sufficient evidence of guilty knowledge, especially as at the time a prisoner could not give evidence: "Parliament said, 'Where you find a man in possession of stolen property he may be unfortunate, and not guilty, but if you find other stolen property in his possession it may not be easy to believe that it is merely a coincidence.' "

being charged with the current offence. Note that paragraph (a) does not involve proof of a previous crime but only proof of two of its elements: possession, and the fact that the car was stolen.[211]

---

211 *R v Cooke* [1990] 2 NZLR 257 (CA). For a detailed treatement of this section, see *Adams* § CA258.19ff; *Garrow* § 258.12ff.

18

Other Forms of Stealing

18.1 THEFT BY PERSONS REQUIRED TO ACCOUNT

In the previous chapter, we saw that theft under s 220 Crimes Act 1961 requires a taking or converting, and therefore protects only persons in possession, or with legal rather than equitable ownership, of the property stolen. What, then, if a person such as stockbroker, solicitor, or estate agent, having received property in a fiduciary capacity, fraudulently misuses it for his own benefit? Since the fraudsters in such cases have legal ownership of the property entrusted to them, dishonest dealings with this property fall outside the scope of ordinary theft.

Interference with equitable ownership is addressed with supplementary offences, which are enacted by ss 222, 223, 224, and 230. Of these, ss 223, 224, and 230 create very specific property crimes, and are considered together in § 18.2. The main offence is theft by a person required to account (s 222).[1] The section provides in part that:

> Every one commits theft who, having received any money or valuable security or other thing whatsoever on terms requiring him to account for or pay it, or the

---

1   Indeed, fraudulent activities of trustees and other fiduciaries which might fall under ss 223, 224, and 230 are likely also to be offences under s 222. However, s 222 potentially applies in a much wider range of situations. See generally Smith, "Theft by Persons Required to Account" [1980] 1 Canterbury LR 15. For illustrative cases see *Adams* (2nd ed) § 1820.

proceeds of it, or any part of such proceeds, to any other person, though not requiring him to deliver over in specie the identical money, valuable security, or other thing "received, fraudulently converts to his own use or fraudulently omits to account for or pay the same or any part thereof, or to account for or pay such proceeds or any part thereof . . .

Two different offences are created here: fraudulent conversion and fraudulent failure to pay.[2] The essential elements are (i) receipt by D of some form of property; (ii) on terms requiring the recipient to account; (iii) conversion to D's own use, or failure to account for the property; and (iv) fraudulence. The first three elements are actus reus requirements, among which the principal difficulty here lies in determining when D has a duty to account, such that (ii) is satisfied.

As will be observed below, the question when a duty to account exists is an extremely technical one, which has been complicated by recent moves in the civil law, especially in the area of constructive trusts. Unfortunately, the civil law developments have generally been motivated by concerns to protect the rights of creditors, a concern that should not necessarily dominate the criminal law. In light of these trends, it is arguable that s 246 should be revised by stating more clearly the situations where a duty to account arises, in order to avoid its becoming a creditors' device.

18.1.1 The duty to account distinguished from mere personal liability

Where T gives D property intending that D should at some stage pass that identical thing either back to T or on to another person, D may be a bailee or trustee of that property. In that case D lacks legal or equitable ownership of it. If she is not the legal owner, then conversion of the property will be an offence under s 220 Crimes Act 1961.[3] If she is not the equitable owner, she will owe a duty to account under s 222.[4]

However, where T gives D money for a specific purpose it is often assumed that D will not pass on the exact banknotes, cheque, etc that T gives her. T intends rather that D should pay out an equivalent sum. In this situation D is the outright owner, but may still have a duty to account within the terms of s 222.

A duty to account does *not* exist where the relationship between D and the transferor of the property is that of debtor and creditor, such that the transferor's remedy against D is merely in personam.[5] The duty to account

---

2   *R v Walker* [1946] NZLR 512, [1946] GLR 214 (CA); *R v Irvine* [1976] 1 NZLR 96 (CA).

3   Not under s 222: *Adams* (2nd ed), § 1807; *Adams* § CA222.16; contra Smith, "Theft by Persons Required to Account" [1980] 1 Canterbury LR 15 at 27.

4   Unless the terms of her trusteeship require her to "deliver over in specie the identical money, valuable security or other thing received", in which case s 222 is precluded and the proper charge is under s 224 (if money) or s 230. See the references in the preceding footnote.

5   *Mead v R* [1972] NZLR 255 at 261 (CA). Compare the proviso contained in the second paragraph of s 222, which governs the explicit case where there is a proper entry of the amount of money or proceeds in a debtor-creditor account. However, the duty to

must also be distinguished from a *liability to account* where someone has a cause of action in a civil claim against D for money had and received.[6] In this case the action is also in personam, and until the claim is made the money remains the untrammelled property of D.[7] In fact, a claim in personam may arise on the same facts as the claim in rem based on a duty to account. This appears to have occurred in *Reading v A-G*,[8] where an army sergeant received thousands of pounds in commissions for his complicity in enabling illicit substances to be smuggled through Cairo. The Crown confiscated the money, and the House of Lords held that it was entitled to keep it. The principal ground for the decision seems to be that the Crown would have had a good claim against D for an account of the money received; however certain of their Lordships envisaged a proprietary claim as an alternative, since D was in a fiduciary position with respect to his employer. More recently, Lord Templeman in *A-G for Hong Kong v Reid* explicitly acknowledged the possibility of the remedies existing as alternatives, as long as they did not result in double recovery.[9]

In theory, the difference between a duty to account and a liability in personam is clear enough:

> The distinction is between property to which the recipient is both legally and beneficially entitled, and which he may therefore dispose of as his own, subject only to such contractual or other liabilities as this may involve, and, on the other hand, property of which he may be the legal but is not the full beneficial owner, and is not entitled to dispose except in accordance with the terms.[10]

However, it is not always a simple matter to distinguish them in practice. Professor J C Smith, discussing the corresponding (former) English offence of fraudulent conversion, suggests the following test where money is transferred:

> Was the transferee permitted, under the terms of the contract, to use the money as he thought fit; or was he obliged to apply it in a particular way or to retain an

---

account still applies where there is no "proper entry", as where D supplies false accounts to her creditor: *R v Kirk* (1901) 20 NZLR 463 (CA).

6 On the claim for money had and received, see Scott, "The Recovery of Money: Recognising the Potential of the Claim for Money Had and Received" (1994) 8 Otago LR 239.

7 Cf *Police v Leaming* [1975] 1 NZLR 471 at 473.

8 [1951] AC 507, [1951] 1 All ER 617.

9 [1994] 1 NZLR 1 at 4, [1994] 1 AC 324.

10 *Adams* (2nd ed) § 1803. Garrow has suggested the following elaboration, which was approved by the Court of Appeal in *Mead v R* [1972] NZLR 255 at 261 (CA): "The money or property must have been received upon terms which require the receiver to pay the money over or to hand over the property or its proceeds to any other person. The section expressly states that the obligation need not require the handing over of the identical money or property in specie. Accordingly a case would come within the section even if the accounting party was entitled to mix the moneys received with his own. The arrangement must, however, create a duty to account as distinct from a mere debt." It is not obvious how far this definition advances our understanding of the concept.

equivalent sum, either in his possession or in a bank? Only in the latter event can the transferee commit fraudulent conversion.[11]

The distinction is often relevant in a civil law context, especially in an insolvency, where it may be important to decide whether the money forms part of a debtor's general assets to be distributed among creditors, or whether it may be recovered intact by the transferor.[12] In the criminal context, a simple example may be found in the travel agency business. A travel agent generally receives money from customers in return for a collateral obligation to provide the ticket, and may use the money received from customers as he chooses. It was held in *R v Hall*[13] that this creates a debtor-creditor relationship. In that case, D had received deposits for air tickets and paid the money into a general trading account; he then failed to supply tickets to the clients. Although his conduct was "condemned as scandalous", in the absence of special arrangements imposing on him an obligation to deal with clients' money in a particular way, he had no duty to account and therefore did not commit theft. By contrast, in *R v Brownrigg*[14] D, a rogue posing as a travel agent, stated that the money would be kept in a trust account and repaid if a booking could not be obtained. In these circumstances D had a duty to account and was convicted of theft.

18.1.2 Practical applications of the distinction

Section 222 Crimes Act 1961 requires the property to be transferred "on terms" requiring D to account. Obviously this condition is satisfied where the terms are expressly agreed. But is a formal agreement necessary? The court in *R v Scale* thought the application of s 222 "debatable" where the duty did not arise from "a term, whether express or implied, or some express agreement between the recipient of the money and some other person", but left the issue open.[15] It is submitted that the better view is that no express agreement is required. This seems to be at least implied in *Police v Leaming*, where Speight J appears to accept that even in the absence of a particular term, the law might in an appropriate case find an obligation to account.[16]

---

11 Smith, "The Scope of Fraudulent Conversion" [1961] Crim LR 741 at 797, 800. This test was adopted in *Stephens v R* (1978) 139 CLR 315 at 334, (1978) 52 ALJR 662 at 669. For a useful illustration, compare *R v Hotine* (1904) 68 JP 143 with *R v Donald Smith* [1924] 2 KB 194.

12 For example in the *Quistclose* line of cases: *Quistclose Investments Ltd v Rolls Razor Ltd* [1968] 1 All ER 613, [1968] 2 WLR 478.

13 [1973] QB 126, [1972] 2 All ER 1009.

14 [1933] NZLR 1248 (CA).

15 [1977] 1 NZLR 178 (See § 18.1.2.5).

16 [1975] 1 NZLR 471 at 473 (See § 18.1.2.4). Compare the civil case *Westpac Banking Corp v Savin* [1985] 2 NZLR 41 (CA), which concerned litigation following the financial collapse of A Ltd. A had acted as an agent selling boats belonging to S and B. One of the issues was whether A was under a duty to keep the proceeds of these sales separate from its own funds. In the absence of express agreement on this question, the Court of Appeal held that it was entitled to look to the surrounding circumstances to ascertain the parties'

Assuming the view taken here is correct, in what circumstances will a duty to account be imposed? This question is particularly difficult because of the lack of relevant case law. In fact, *Leaming* and *Scale* appear to be the only decisions in which this aspect of s 222 has been considered. In much of the discussion that follows, therefore, we must rely on decisions from other jurisdictions, and on civil law cases.

In both *R v Scale* and *Police v Leaming*, one crucial factor is identified as being a *fiduciary element*. However, a precise definition of this concept is as elusive as the distinction it purports to elucidate. Indeed, it may be that "fiduciary" should be defined differently for different purposes. In the context of s 222, where misuse of the property amounts to theft, the "fiduciary element" refers to a particular obligation that D has *with respect to the property*; such that D does not hold the property absolutely and unencumbered. In this situation, there is a three-way relationship between D, the property, and the person to whom he owes the duty to account.

The fiduciary element or obligation under s 222 should be distinguished from what the civil law knows as a fiduciary *relationship*. As it happens, one way of establishing the fiduciary element for s 222 might be through finding a constructive trust, for which a fiduciary relationship between T and D is normally required. But finding this more general fiduciary relationship is not *necessary* under s 222.

That said, what are the characteristics of the fiduciary obligation in the context of s 220? Smith and Hogan have emphasised that the obligation must be "a *legal* obligation, a moral or social obligation will not do".[17] While an important admonition, as a definition this would be somewhat circular, since the very finding that D owes a duty to account means that the obligation is regarded as a legal one, and not merely moral. Something more is obviously required. We need to know *when* there will be a legal obligation.

18.1.2.1 *Is a trust required?*

Some authorities have suggested that a fiduciary obligation under s 222 exists only where equity would find an express or constructive trust.[18] The force of this suggestion stems from the view that the law of theft exists to protect property interests, rather than to prevent fraudulent dealings generally. A trust beneficiary is regarded in equity as being the owner of the property. In equity therefore the trustee has no property in the goods; and so it makes sense to suggest that he could be guilty of theft, where, as Speight J pointed out in *Police v Leaming*, "the underlying concept is that the property in the hands of the

---

intentions, and concluded that A was not entitled to pay the sale proceeds into its general trading account.

17   *Criminal Law* (7th ed), 1992, 523, commenting on s 5(3) Theft Act 1968 (UK). Cf *DPP v Huskinson* [1988] Crim LR 620. See also Smith, "The Scope of Fraudulent Conversion" [1961] Crim LR 741 and 797, 799ff.

18   For example *Adams* (2nd ed) § 1802. Cf *Police v Leaming* [1975] 1 NZLR 471 at 473; also Smith, "Theft by Persons Required to Account" (1980) 1 Canterbury LR 15 at 23-25.

alleged thief is not his money but his principal's money which he has misapplied".[19]

However, there are several problems with the analysis that s 222 exists solely to protect equitable owners.

First, it implies that for a fiduciary obligation to exist there must be a corresponding beneficial interest held by some other person. Even ignoring for a moment the complex area of constructive trusts, there are situations in which we would hold D to be under a fiduciary obligation even where she had legal *and equitable* ownership of a thing. There is authority for the proposition that the residuary legatees of an estate have no proprietary interest before the estate is administered,[20] but we would think the executor guilty of theft were he dishonestly to appropriate the estate property to his own use. Another example is provided by the *Quistclose*[21] line of cases, where the transferees of money were obliged to keep it separate and to use it for specific purposes, even though there was no beneficial interest vesting in the intended recipients, nor, initially, in the transferors.[22]

Turning from arguments of principle to the structure of the statute, it is clear that legal rights of property and possession are protected by s 220. That ss 222-224 exist as separate theft offences at all suggests a deliberate extension of the offence of theft to protect more amorphous rights in certain defined situations. This does not preclude s 222 from being the equitable-ownership counterpart of theft, but may mean that we should be slow to regard s 222 as simply the progeny of s 220, and therefore subject to the same type of approach. This proposition is supported by *R v Tennet*,[23] in which the Court of Appeal considered the interrelationship between ss 220 and 222. In that case, a solicitor had misapplied money and shares given to him by clients. However, it was doubtful whether he had formed an intent permanently to deprive. He

---

19   [1975] 1 NZLR 471 at 473.

20   *Commr of Stamp Duties (Queensland) v Livingstone* [1965] AC 694, [1964] 3 All ER 692.

21   *Quistclose Investments Ltd v Rolls Razor Ltd* [1968] 1 All ER 613, [1968] 2 WLR 478.

22   Additionally, the proposition that s 222 protects only a defined property interest becomes a doubtful one when one considers that, even where D expressly holds on trust and thus has only legal ownership of the property, it may be difficult to locate precisely the beneficial ownership of the property. One example is a discretionary trust for a very large class (*Vestey v IRC (Nos 1 and 2)* [1980] AC 1148, [1979] 3 All ER 976); another is a charitable or private "purpose" trust where the object of the trust is to carry out a purpose, rather than benefit ascertainable individuals; another is a solicitor-client relationship which (see § 18.1.2.2) probably falls within s 222 even though it may not be possible to identify the beneficial ownership of the fund. If one cannot identify a specific person or persons who are the beneficiaries under the trust, whose property interest is being protected by s 222? Even the question whether a trust creates a right in rem at all is a complex one, and the dividing line between property and contract can be extremely fine. It may therefore be problematic to define s 222 by reference to equitable property rights which are of notoriously uncertain scope. Indeed, the trust requirement has been criticised as importing an unnecessary complexity into the administration of the criminal law: per Gibbs J in *Stephens v R* (1978) 52 ALJR 662 at 668, 669, (1978) 139 CLR 315 at 333, 334.

23   [1962] NZLR 428 (CA). See also *Mead v R* [1972] NZLR 255 (CA).

was convicted of an offence under s 222, the trial Judge taking the view that intent permanently to deprive was not an element of the offence. On appeal, it was argued that s 222 was simply a variety of theft and accordingly the mens rea requirement of s 220 should apply. The court rejected this argument, deciding that the offences were separate and independent, so that no intent permanently to deprive was required. Although the two offences may overlap, their constituent elements are not, and should not be regarded as, identical.

It is submitted that the better interpretation of the scope of s 222 is therefore to be found in *R v Scale*, where the Court of Appeal declined to require a trust, holding that a duty to account exists whenever there is "a 'fiduciary element' or the 'earmarking' of the property in the hands of the accused".[24] In our view, an "earmarking" of property by the transferor may give rise to a duty to account without the need to establish a trust or a more general fiduciary relationship between D and another. The existence of a trust is thus *sufficient but not necessary* to establish the fiduciary element, and consequently a duty to account, under s 222.

Beyond this proposition, however, it is difficult to state any general principle. Indeed, the best way of approaching the section is to look at the specific situations in which it is applied. These may broadly be grouped into two categories. The first is where V deposits property with D on the understanding that D is to transfer an equivalent sum representing the property or the proceeds thereof either back to V or to a third party. This situation, where the property is clearly earmarked, typically includes cases of agency. The second category is where T transfers property to D intending that D should take absolutely, but where the fiduciary nature of D's relationship with V is such that D may be required to hold on trust for V.

18.1.2.2 *Property deposited with an agent*

This is a paradigm case for the application of s 222. Where money or other property is received by an agent such as a stockbroker or solicitor, s 222 will apply if the agent has a fiduciary obligation with respect to that property. Obviously, such an obligation may arise by express agreement between the parties. Where there is no express agreement, the court will have to look at all the circumstances of the case to identify the parties' intentions.[25] However, some generalisations may be made in particular situations.

As we have seen, money paid to a travel agent is generally not received in a fiduciary capacity. By contrast, certain businesses are legally required to pay clients' money into a separate account. Section 56 Real Estate Agents Act 1976 requires an estate agent to pay any money received in his capacity as such either to "the person lawfully entitled thereto or in accordance with his written direction or, where he is in doubt about the question of entitlement, into his

---

24 [1977] 1 NZLR 178 at 181, 182. The test stated in *R v Scale* was applied without discussion by the Court of Appeal in *R v Cameron* [1981] 1 NZLR 515 (CA). (Dealer who sold a van on commission received proceeds "earmarked" for his principal, and so was held properly convicted of theft under s 222.)

25 Cf *R v Kirk* (1901) 20 NZLR 463 at 473.

trust account". Section 55(2) requires money to be kept in a trust account pending payment. Failure to comply with these requirements constitutes an offence under the Act, and may also constitute theft under s 222. Another example is a solicitor-client relationship. Under s 71 Law Practitioners Act 1955, a solicitor is obliged to pay all money received for or on behalf of a client into a separate general or trust account.

Where a person has entrusted property to an agent or factor to be sold, the general rule is that the ownership of the goods remains in the principal until the sale takes place. Upon sale, the principal then has an equitable proprietary interest in the proceeds.[26] This rule applies not only to agents who receive proceeds on behalf of a principal,[27] but also to trustees, and anyone else in a fiduciary position, whether or not the transaction is authorised by the principal. In *Re Hallett's Estate* D, a solicitor, had been given bonds by T to hold as bailee, and later sold the bonds without T's authorisation. It was held that T was beneficially entitled to the proceeds if they were identifiable, Jessel MR observing that "there is no distinction, therefore, between a rightful and a wrongful disposition of the property, so far as regards the right of the beneficial owner to follow the proceeds"; and, later, "has it ever been suggested, until very recently, that there is any distinction between an express trustee, or an agent, or a bailee, or a collector of rents, or anybody else in a fiduciary position?"[28]

Where, on the above basis, T as principal is the equitable owner of proceeds of sale, D as fiduciary necessarily has a duty to account to T. If D at that point misappropriates the proceeds, he will be liable to conviction under s 222.

18.1.2.3 *Making a profit from abuse of fiduciary position*

If an employee has authority to deal with her employer's chattel for a profit, eg where she is a shop assistant, property in the payment passes directly to her principal.[29] However, the position may be different where the employee deals with her employer's goods outside the scope of her authority. In the nineteenth-century case of *R v Cullum*,[30] the captain of a barge carried cargo contrary to his instructions, and appropriated the resulting profits. It was held that he did not receive the profits "on account of" his employer, but on his own behalf, although he was no doubt obliged in quasi-contract to account to his employer for the money received.[31] The employer therefore had a claim in

---

26   Cf *Foley v Hill* (1848) 2 HL Cas 28, 9 ER 1002; *Palette Shoes Pty Ltd (In liquidation) v Krohn* (1937) 58 CLR 1, [1937] ALR 432; *King v Hutton* [1900] 2 QB 504 at 507, (1900) 83 LT 68 at 70; *Westpac Banking Corp v Savin* [1985] 2 NZLR 41 at 49 (CA).

27   See also *R v Martini* [1941] NZLR 361, [1941] GLR 145 (CA) (premiums given to a life insurance agent), and *R v Chard* 12/4/95, CA454; 527/94 (insurance broker).

28   (1879) 13 ChD 696 at 709, [1874-80] All ER Rep 793 at 796.

29   *R v De Banks* (1884) 13 QBD 29. (D was requested to sell V's horse; he then misappropriated the proceeds. The Court held that D was a bailee of the proceeds and so guilty of larceny.)

30   (1873) LR 2 CCR 28. Cf *A-G's Reference (No 1 of 1985)* [1986] QB 491, [1986] 2 All ER 219.

31   Note that "account" here is used in a different sense to that in s 222 — cf Speight J in *Police v Leaming* [1975] 1 NZLR 471 at 473.

personam for an amount equivalent to the employee's profits, but no claim to the proceeds themselves, which were received as the property of the employee.

On this analysis, Cullum would not be guilty of theft of the proceeds of his misconduct, under either s 220 or s 222.

But such a fact situation may now give rise to a constructive trust.[32] Goff and Jones write that "a fiduciary who uses his position of trust to acquire a benefit for himself holds that benefit on constructive trust for his beneficiary".[33] This rule applies, for example, where a person in a fiduciary position derives a profit from the unauthorised use of another's property;[34] or acquires confidential information which he exploits for his own profit;[35] and it has recently been held that a constructive trust will also arise where a fiduciary receives a secret bribe or commission.[36] A constructive trust would give the beneficiary an equitable proprietary right in the benefit acquired, thus bringing s 222 within range. The question becomes, therefore, whether D is a fiduciary. In this context, a fiduciary has been described as:

> simply, someone who undertakes to act for or on behalf of another in some particular matter or matters. That undertaking may be of a general character. It may be specified and limited. It is immaterial whether the undertaking is or is not in the form of a contract. It is immaterial that the undertaking is gratuitous. And the undertaking may be officiously assumed without request.[37]

However, as we have remarked already, the concept of a fiduciary relationship is notoriously amorphous, and it is difficult to avoid the

---

32   Smith, "Constructive Trusts in the Law of Theft" [1977] Crim LR 395 at 398.

33   Goff and Jones, "The Law of Restitution" (4th ed), London, Sweet & Maxwell, 1993, 647.

34   Ibid at 661. See also Goode, "The Right to Trace and its Impact in Commercial Transactions" (1976) 92 LQR 360 at 528, 534, 535; Youdan (ed), *Equity, Fiduciaries and Trusts*, Toronto, Carswell, 1989, 97, 223; Birks, *An Introduction to the Law of Restitution*, Oxford, Clarendon Press, 1989, 388; Goode, "Ownership and Obligation in Commercial Transactions" (1987) 103 LQR 433 at 442-445.

35   Cf *A-G v Guardian Newspapers (No 2)* [1990] 1 AC 109 concerning use of confidential information in the book *Spycatcher*; *Diamond v Oreamuno* 301 NYS 2D 78 (1969): D, a director, speculated in the company's shares, using unpublished information about a potential take-over bid. See also generally Jones, "Unjust Enrichment and the Fiduciary's Duty of Loyalty" (1968) 84 LQR 472.

36   *A-G for Hong Kong v Reid* [1994] 1 NZLR 1, [1994] 1 AC 324; see § 18.1.2.4.

37   Finn, *Fiduciary Obligations*, Sydney, Law Book Co, 1977, 201. See also Shepherd, "Towards a Unified Concept of Fiduciary Relationships" (1981) 97 LQR 51 at 75, who proposes the following definition:

"A fiduciary relationship exists whenever any person receives a power of any type on condition that he also receive with it a duty to utilise that power in the best interests of another, and the recipient of the power uses that power."

Underlying this, however, is a concept of property, and the recovery is restitutionary, not compensatory (ibid at 78):

"The basic idea is that, where A transfers an encumbered power to B, B in no sense receives anything of his own. It is A's power, and he has only really lent it to B, such that, at least in equity, the use of this power by B is really the use by A. If A used the power, he would receive all of the profits, and so should receive all of the profits when B uses it as well."

conclusion reached by Goff and Jones that "a fiduciary relationship is a condition which is easily satisfied and which conceals the conclusion that the particular plaintiff should be granted an equitable proprietary remedy".[38]

As a general rule, an agent[39] or a company director[40] holds a fiduciary position. It appears that the same is not true for a mere employee. In the context of bribes, discussed below, a number of cases suggest that a fiduciary relationship does not ordinarily exist between employer and employee. However, it is arguable that there should be a fiduciary relationship.[41] A fiduciary relationship has been held to arise "whenever the plaintiff entrusts to the defendant a job to be performed",[42] and in *Liggett v Kensington* Gault J remarked that "generally it is appropriate to look for circumstances in which one person has undertaken to act in the interests of another or conversely one has communicated an expectation that another will act to protect or promote his or her interests".[43] Nonetheless, we incline to the view that since employees act under specific instructions they should not normally be regarded as fiduciaries.[44]

18.1.2.4 *Employees who take bribes*

In *Police v Leaming*,[45] it was held that an employee who accepted a secret commission was not in a fiduciary relationship with his employer, and that his retention of the money was therefore not a failure to account within the meaning of s 222, and his conviction for theft under that section was accordingly quashed. Speight J relied on the authority of *Lister and Co v Stubbs*,[46] in which a foreman in a textiles firm received substantial secret

---

38   *The Law of Restitution* (4th ed), 1993, 93f.

39   *Boston Deep Sea Fishing and Ice Co v Ansell* (1888) 39 Ch D 339 at 354ff, [1886-90] All ER Rep 65 at 68ff.

40   *Regal (Hastings) v Gulliver* [1942] 1 All ER 378. Shares intended to be acquired by directors at par to avoid them giving a guarantee of the obligations under a lease were sold at a profit, and the directors were held to be liable to the company for the proceeds of the sale. See also *Phipps v Boardman* [1967] 2 AC 46, [1966] 3 All ER 721.

41   Smith, "Constructive Trusts in the Law of Theft" [1977] Crim LR 395 at 398; "Theft by Persons Required to Account" [1980] 1 Canterbury LR 15 at 21.

42   *Reading v R* [1949] 2 KB 232 at 236 (per Asquith LJ). Decision affirmed sub nom *Reading v A-G* [1951] AC 507, [1951] 1 All ER 617.

43   [1993] 1 NZLR 257 at 281 (CA).

44   Cf Waters, "Banks, Fiduciary Obligations and Unconscionable Transactions" (1986) 65 Can Bar Rev 37 at 53, 54; it may be otherwise in the case of senior officers of a company who are charged by their employer "with initiatives and responsibilities far removed from the obedient role of servants." *Canadian Aero Service Ltd v O'Malley* (1974) 40 DLR (3d) 371, [1974] SCR 592.

45   [1975] 1 NZLR 471. *Lister v Stubbs* was also followed in *Mayall v Weal* [1982] 2 NZLR 385.

46   (1890) 45 ChD 1. In Australia the decision has been described as anomalous and confined to its own facts: *DPC Estates Pty Ltd v Gray and Consul Development Pty Ltd* [1974] 1 NSWLR 443 (NSW Court of Appeal). For criticism of *Lister v Stubbs*, see Goff and Jones, *The Law of Restitution* (4th ed), London, Sweet & Maxwell, 1993, 669; Oakley, *Constructive Trusts* (3rd ed), 1997, 135. But Birks, *An Introduction to the Law of Restitution* (1989), argues at 378ff that a constructive trust must be founded on a proprietary base, and there is

commissions under an arrangement with one of the suppliers. The English Court of Appeal held that D did not hold the receipts in the capacity of trustee. The relationship between D and his employer was that of debtor and creditor; it was not that of trustee and cestui que trust. As Cotton LJ said:

> the moneys which under this corrupt bargain were paid by [the suppliers] to the Defendant cannot be said to be the money of the Plaintiffs before any judgment or decree in some action has been made.[47]

In *Police v Leaming*, Speight J concluded:

> The illicit commissions cases related to money which is paid to the agent by a third person, to persuade him to act contrary to his duty. It was never intended by the third person to be paid for the benefit of the principal nor was it ever known by the principal to be in existence or likely to be in existence. The reason that the principal can claim it is that it is a form of unjustifiable enrichment received by the agent but it is a claim made by the principal for money which a Court of Equity would hold he was entitled to — it is not an action to "recover" something which is properly his.[48]

His Honour distinguished the case at hand from that of *Reading v A-G*,[49] where the employee was "not merely a servant but an officer of the Crown and for this reason held by many of their Lordships to be in a special fiduciary relationship to the Crown".[50]

Originally, there were two possible explanations for the decisions in *Lister* and *Leaming*: (i) that no fiduciary relationship in general existed between P and D; or (ii) that receipt of a bribe should not in principle give rise to a constructive trust. The latter proposition now seems unsustainable following the decision of the Privy Council in *A-G for Hong Kong v Reid*.[51] In that case, the main question for the Court of Appeal had been whether the Hong Kong Government held a proprietary interest in bribes received by D while a Crown servant of the Colony of Hong Kong. It was common ground before the Court that D was a fiduciary; the issue was whether he was also a constructive trustee of the money received. The Court of Appeal considered themselves bound by the authority of *Lister v Stubbs*, and concluded that, in light of the precedent:

> it would be contrary to principle to hold that a principal acquires a proprietary interest in property never previously belonging to the principal at the moment when the registered proprietor learns that the moneys used to purchase the property come from a corrupt bargain made by the principal's fiduciary.[52]

---

therefore an essential distinction between an enrichment received by D directly from the briber and an enrichment resulting from D's misuse of trust property.

47 (1890) 45 ChD 1 at 12, 13.

48 [1975] 1 NZLR 471 at 473, 474. Cf *Powell v MacRae* [1977] Crim LR 571: "by no stretch of language could it be said that the money 'belonged to' the employers."

49 [1951] AC 507, [1951] 1 All ER 617.

50 [1975] 1 NZLR 471 at 474. The position of the employee in *A-G for Hong Kong v Reid* (below in this section) may be similarly distinguished.

51 [1994] 1 NZLR 1, [1994] 1 AC 324 (PC); [1992] 2 NZLR 385 (CA). Noted by Smith, "*Lister v Stubbs* and the Criminal Law" [1994] 110 LQR 180; Devonshire, "Last Rites for *Lister v Stubbs*?" [1994] 5 Canterbury LR 374.

52 [1992] 2 NZLR 385 at 393.

The Privy Council disagreed, overruling *Lister v Stubbs* and holding that:

As soon as the bribe was received it should have been paid or transferred instanter to the person who suffered from the breach of duty. Equity considers as done that which ought to have been done. As soon as the bribe was received, whether in cash or in kind, the false fiduciary held the bribe on a constructive trust for the person injured.[53]

What emerges from the case is that a fiduciary who receives, for himself, a bribe or commission paid for the misuse of his position will hold the money on constructive trust for his principal. However, since it was conceded that Reid was a fiduciary, the question whether an employment situation will necessarily give rise to a fiduciary relationship was not considered.

18.1.2.5 *Property obtained by mistake*

In all the situations discussed so far, it appears that the duty to account is based on either an express earmarking of the property by the transferor, or the existence of a more general fiduciary relationship between D and another person. *R v Scale*[54] presents a rather different type of case: where D obtains property without either of these features, but simply pursuant to V's mistake.

Where D has induced the mistake, there may be an offence of obtaining by false pretences under s 246. Alternatively, the character of the mistake may be such that ownership of the item does not pass,[55] in which case D may be guilty of theft by conversion under s 220. However, as we saw earlier, if property does pass D cannot subsequently commit theft under s 220. In *R v Scale*, the trial Judge attempted to circumvent this outcome by using s 222.[56] D had received a cheque mistakenly made out to his company, and, aware of the mistake, paid it into the company account. At first instance, he was convicted of converting the money to his own use under s 222. However, on appeal the conviction was quashed: the common law obligation to repay money received by mistake did not impress the property with a constructive trust, but merely created a debtor-creditor relationship.

This decision must now be reconsidered in the light of *Chase Manhattan Bank NA v Israel-British Bank (London) Ltd*,[57] where Goulding J held that the person who pays money to another under a mistake of fact retains an equitable proprietary right or interest in the money, as opposed to a purely personal right. This principle was accepted by the Court of Appeal in *Liggett v Kensington*.[58] If such an analysis is valid, s 222 would appear to be applicable, just as it is for constructive trusts founded on a fiduciary relationship.[59]

---

53 [1994] 1 NZLR 1 at 4, [1994] 1 AC 324 at 331.

54 [1977] 1 NZLR 178 (CA).

55 § 17.2.3.2.

56 [1977] 1 NZLR 178 (CA). This possibility is canvassed by Orchard, "The Borderland of Theft Revisited" [1973] NZLJ 110 at 115, 116.

57 [1981] Ch 105 at 119, [1979] 3 All ER 1025 at 1032. (Plaintiff bank paid $2 million by mistake to another bank for the account of D bank, which then went bankrupt. P sought to recover the overpayment.)

58 [1993] 1 NZLR 257 at 268ff (CA). The decision in that case was overturned by the Privy Council in *Re Goldcorp Exchange Ltd (In Receivership)* [1994] 3 NZLR 385, [1995] 1 AC 74

The essential difficulty here — and also with the bribery cases earlier — is that a fiduciary relationship has traditionally been a prerequisite to the availability of equitable "proprietary" remedies. The authority commonly cited as establishing this rule is *Re Diplock*,[60] in which the English Court of Appeal interpreted an earlier decision by the House of Lords[61] as stating that an initial fiduciary relationship was necessary for equitable tracing. The heresy of Goulding J in *Chase Manhattan* was to depart from the orthodox interpretation of these two cases, preferring the view that "the fund to be traced need not . . . have been the subject of fiduciary obligations before it got into wrong hands. It is enough that . . . the payment into wrong hands itself gave rise to a fiduciary relationship."[62]

18.1.2.6 Constructive trusts without fiduciary relationships: when D's conscience is tainted

More recently, doubt has been cast on the reasoning in *Chase Manhattan* by the House of Lords in *Westdeutsche Bank v Islington LBC*. According to Lord Browne-Wilkinson, Goulding J's decision was "based on a concept of retaining an equitable property in money where, prior to the payment to the recipient bank, there was no existing equitable interest".[63] None the less, it was said, the case may have been correctly decided: retention of the money once the recipient became aware of the mistake may provide the foundation for a constructive trust.

On this approach, it is not the mistake *by itself* that gives rise to a constructive trust, but also the fact that the recipient knows about it; thus he cannot, in conscience, keep the money. Viewed this way, Goulding J's judgment is not an isolated one. In a similar vein, Bingham J in *Neste Oy v Lloyds Bank plc* remarked that "the receiving of money which consistently with conscience cannot be retained is, in Equity, sufficient to raise a trust in favour

---

(PC), but their Lordships did not express an opinion as to the correctness of the decision in *Chase Manhattan* (see [1995] 1 AC 74 at 103).

59   *Smith and Hogan* come to a similar conclusion (see at 542, 543). The decision in *Chase Manhattan* is criticised in Goff and Jones, *The Law of Restitution* (4th ed), 1993, 131, but defended by Birks, *An Introduction to the Law of Restitution*, 1989, 377. See also Birks, "Misdirected Funds: Restitution from the Recipient" (1980) LMCLQ 296, and *Agip (Africa) v Jackson* [1990] Ch 265.

60   [1948] Ch 465, [1948] 2 All ER 318 (CA); sub nom *Ministry of Health v Simpson* [1951] AC 251, [1950] 2 All ER 1137 (HL).

61   *Sinclair v Brougham* [1914] AC 398, [1914-15] All ER Rep 622. The reasoning in that case was said no longer to be sound by the House of Lords in *Westdeutsche Bank v Islington LBC* [1996] AC 669 at 709-714, [1996] 2 All ER 961 at 992-996 (HL). At the same time, however, "Your Lordships should not be taken to be casting any doubt on the principles of tracing as established in *In re Diplock*". (at 714, per Lord Browne-Wilkinson).

62   [1981] Ch 105 at 119, [1979] 3 All ER 1025 at 1032.

63   [1996] AC 669 at 714, [1996] 2 All ER 961 at 997. If this criticism is correct, the owner of an undivided interest cannot transfer legal title and retain the previously non-existent equitable interest. See, however, *Abbey National Bldg Soc v Cann* [1991] 1 AC 56, [1990] 1 All ER 1085, which does allow charge by reservation; followed in *Australian Guarantee Corp (NZ) Ltd v Nicholson* [1996] 1 NZLR 167.

of the party for whom or on whose account it was received".[64] Whatever its status in England,[65] this principle appears to have been adopted by the Court of Appeal in New Zealand. In *Elders Pastoral Ltd v BNZ*,[66] it was held that "the constructive trust . . . has come to be used as a device for imposing a liability to account on persons who cannot in good conscience retain a benefit in breach of their legal or equitable obligations".

We conclude that while a *substantive* constructive trust is founded upon an existing fiduciary relationship, the constructive trust is now, alternatively, available as an equitable *remedy* to effect the demands of conscience even in the absence of a fiduciary duty. The civil law has therefore changed. Since offences of theft are designed to protect proprietary interests, it necessarily follows that this change, which alters the scope of proprietary interests, in turn affects the reach of the criminal law.

However, in the context of s 222, departure from the strict requirement of a pre-existing fiduciary relationship is dangerous, because it muddies the waters between the institutional or substantive constructive trust, whereby the court purports to recognise an existing property right, and the remedial constructive trust, which is a redistributive device to reverse unjust enrichment.[67] The divide between these two types is in our view crucial to the application of s 222.

We submit that property impressed merely with a remedial constructive trust should *not* be the subject of a duty to account under s 222. The purposes for which the civil law imposes a remedial constructive trust are characteristically irrelevant to the criminal law.[68] Very often, the leading consideration is whether V should have a prior claim in insolvency over a third party, T. It is not obvious that the question whether D steals from V should be determined by the unrelated issue of priority between V and T. One may go

---

64 [1983] 2 Lloyds Rep 658 at 666. Cf also Millet J in *Agip (Africa) v Jackson* [1990] Ch 265 at 290, [1992] 4 All ER 385 at 402.

65 Compare *Halifax Building Soc v Thomas* [1996] Ch 217 at 229, [1996] 2 WLR 63 at 72, where the Court of Appeal declined to apply *A-G for Hong Kong v Reid* in a situation where there was no fiduciary relationship.

66 [1989] 2 NZLR 180 at 193 (per Somers J).

67 Cf Gault J in *Liggett v Kensington* [1993] 1 NZLR 257 at 281 (CA): "Finding of a fiduciary duty simply as an expedient to justify a constructive trust no longer is necessary. A remedial constructive trust may be imposed in the absence of a fiduciary duty. The cases to date have held that course justified in certain circumstances when it would be unconscionable for the party into whose hands the property came to retain it against the claimant, for example where the money has been appropriated for the use and benefit of the payee in breach of trust; where a payment was made by mistake; where moneys were deposited pursuant to void contracts; where moneys were paid in circumstances in which it was inevitable that there would be a total failure of consideration." See also the discussion by Rotherham, which predates this case and the decision by the Privy Council in *A-G for Hong Kong v Reid*: Rotherham, "The Redistributive Constructive Trust: 'Confounding Ownership with Obligation'?" [1992] 5 Canterbury LR 84.

68 Per Smith, "Constructive Trusts in the Law of Theft" [1977] Crim LR 395 at 400: "the civil law imposes constructive trusts in situations, and for multifarious reasons, which may have nothing to do with the purposes of the criminal law." See also his *Property Offences*, 1994, § 4-90.

further — it would be *bizarre* were the criminal character of D's behaviour to depend on that concern.

In any event, it is unclear that D's behaviour in *Scale* should be criminalised at all. As Holt CJ once remarked, "shall we indict one man for making a fool of another?"[69] If V foolishly and mistakenly gives D an unjustified windfall, her proper remedy is in money had and received. The criminal law should not wade to her rescue. That, of course, is a case where D did nothing wrong in gaining his windfall. But even if D acquires his enrichment by means of wrongdoing — eg by accepting a bribe — the proper approach is to look at that initial wrongdoing. Thus, in *Police v Leaming*,[70] Leaming should have been prosecuted under the Secret Commissions Act 1910 for taking a bribe, and not for subsequent theft of the proceeds.[71]

The better approach to s 222 is to insist on a pre-existing fiduciary obligation — which would include a substantive constructive trust — or some other earmarking of the property. This would certainly be more faithful to the intentions of those who originally drafted the offence. Moreover, it has the advantage of giving greater certainty to the law, and increasing the level of fair warning available to prospective thieves.[72] If even Lord Wilberforce might say that the making of a secret profit "is no criminal offence whatever other epithet may be appropriate",[73] one can hardly expect the man in the tavern to foresee the possibility and criminal implications of a remedial constructive trust.[74] Taking studious advantage of another's mistake is hardly admirable; but the criminal law is not the place to resolve the issues it raises.

The distinction we have argued for can be reconciled with the language of the Crimes Act 1961. Section 222 requires that the property be *received on terms* requiring D to account. This wording suggests that the duty to account must attach, as a term, at the time of receipt. As we saw earlier, the requirement is satisfied where there is a pre-existing fiduciary relationship or a clear earmarking of the property when D acquires it. But there are two reasons why a remedial constructive trust does not satisfy that same requirement. First, it is

---

69 *R v Jones* (1703) 2 Ld Raymond 1013, 92 ER 174.

70 See § 18.1.2.4.

71 Another example might be knowing receipt in cases of commercial fraud, which may lead to a constructive trust. On this analysis, the receivers would also become guilty of theft.

72 See § 1.4.3.

73 *Tarling (No 1) v Government of the Republic of Singapore* (1979) 70 Cr App R 77 at 111, [1978] Crim LR 490. Despite this statement, making secret profits has been held indictable as conspiracy to defraud: *R v Button* (1848) 3 Cox CC 229; *R v Rashid* [1977] 2 All ER 237, [1977] 1 WLR 298; *R v Doukas* [1978] 1 All ER 1061, [1978] 1 WLR 372; cf also *Adams v R* (1994) 12 CRNZ 379 (PC) (conspiracy to defraud where there was concealment of information regarding secret profits — see § 19.3). Even so, it is submitted that such conduct, if criminal in nature, should be regarded as a variety of fraud, rather than subsequent theft of the proceeds thereof.

74 "There are topics of conversation more popular in public houses than the finer points of the equitable doctrine of the constructive trust." *A-G's Reference (No 1 of 1985)* [1986] QB 491 at 506, [1986] 2 All ER 219 at 225.

not founded upon a *term* governing the receipt by D, but arises simply because it is unconscionable for D to retain the property against the claimant. Secondly, the timing is arguably wrong. Unlike an institutional constructive trust, it appears that the subsequent imposition of a redistributive constructive trust might not prevent D from *acquiring* beneficial ownership of property, such that he could be convicted under s 222; since such a trust, being a discretionary remedy, may operate prospectively rather than ab initio.[75]

18.1.3 Mens rea

In *R v Tennent*,[76] the Court of Appeal made it clear that s 222 Crimes Act 1961 is not subject to the same mens rea requirements as simple theft under s 220. For this offence, all that is required by way of mens rea is a fraudulent intent.[77] The definition of "fraudulent", which was laid down by the Court of Appeal in *R v Coombridge*[78] is discussed earlier in § 17.3.1.

Perhaps the most important implication of this analysis is that there is no requirement that D must intend permanently to deprive.[79] However, an intention to repay or replace the property taken may often negative the dishonesty implicit in a fraudulent intent.[80] It should also be emphasised that the mens rea requirement is a fraudulent *intent*. Mere carelessness or forgetfulness is insufficient. In *R v Reisterer*, for instance, the Court of Appeal pointed out that the conduct of the appellant may have been "reckless and censurable from a business point of view, but whether it was criminal is another matter".[81]

The second difference from s 220 is that no express mention is made of colour of right.[82] However, it is not clear that this omission will have much practical effect, since a belief that D has a legal right to the thing taken[83] would tend also to negative dishonesty, thus providing evidence that D did not act fraudulently.

---

75 Palmer, *The Law of Restitution* vol I, Boston, Little Brown, 1978, 171, Supplement (1990) 10; Waters, "The Constructive Trust in Evolution: Substantive and Remedial" (1991) 10 Estates and Trusts Journal 334; contra Cope, *Constructive Trusts* Sydney, Law Book Co, 1992, 17, 33.

76 [1962] NZLR 428 (CA).

77 See also *R v Williams* [1985] 1 NZLR 294 (CA) (s 224); *R v Martini* [1941] NZLR 361 (CA) (s 222); and *R v Coombridge* [1976] 2 NZLR 381 at 387 (CA) (s 222).

78 [1976] 2 NZLR 381.

79 Cf *R v Martini* [1941] NZLR 361 (CA).

80 Cf *Nelson v R* [1902] AC 250.

81 [1962] NZLR 1040 (CA). This passage was omitted from the official report, but is recorded in *Adams* § CA222.18.

82 This point was made by Richmond P in *R v Coombridge* [1976] 2 NZLR 381 at 387.

83 On the meaning of "colour of right" see § 17.3.2.

18.2 RELATED OFFENCES

Besides s 222, the Crimes Act 1961 contains three other offences involving the fraudulent misappropriation of property that D has received legitimately. These are briefly described below.

18.2.1 Theft by person holding power of attorney

Section 223 creates a theft offence where someone entrusted with the power of attorney for the disposition of any property (whether real or personal, and whether or not capable of being stolen within s 217) fraudulently disposes of the property or fraudulently converts the proceeds of the property to purposes other than those for which he was given the power of attorney. The expression "power of attorney" is not defined by the section, but refers to a formal written appointment of an agent, and is generally in the form of a deed, although no particular form is required by s 223. It is not sufficient to show that D had a power of attorney with respect to T, and that D dealt fraudulently with T's property: it must be shown that D dealt with the property concerned *by virtue of* being T's attorney,[84] ie there must be a causal connection between the power and the transfer of the property to D.

18.2.2 Theft by misappropriating proceeds held under direction

Section 224 applies where D receives money or a valuable security, or holds a power of attorney for the sale of property, with a direction that the proceeds or part thereof should be applied to a specific purpose or paid to a specific person. D commits theft when he fraudulently[85] deals with the money or proceeds outside the scope of the direction.[86]

18.2.3 Criminal breach of trust

Section 230 creates the offence of criminal breach of trust (not theft) where a trustee with intent to defraud[87] and in breach of trust converts trust property to purposes not authorised by the trust. This might seem to provide a more straightforward answer than does s 222 to the problem posed by dealings with

---

84 *Police v Borick* [1990] 2 NZLR 431, (1989) 5 CRNZ 620. (D had a power of attorney from an elderly woman, and purchased a painting from her at a gross undervalue. He was convicted of fraudulently disposing of the property under s 223.)

85 The section adds "in violation of good faith and contrary to the direction". However, as *Adams* comments (§ CA224.07), "Given the definition of 'fraudulently' adopted in *R v Coombridge* [1976] 2 NZLR 381, it is debatable whether these words now add anything to the required mental element." See § 17.3.1.

86 Eg *R v Tennent* [1962] NZLR 428 (CA). (D, a solicitor, received money from clients to be applied for particular purposes. In violation of his instructions, D appropriated the money to other purposes.) See also *R v Prast* [1975] 2 NZLR 248 (CA); *Cheape v NZ Law Soc* [1955] NZLR 63.

87 Regarding which see the discussion of mens rea in s 246 (obtaining by false pretences): see § 19.1.2. Cf *R v Smillie* [1956] NZLR 269.

equitable interests, which are not captured by s 220. However, the section is limited to certain specified categories of trustees, such as trustees upon express trusts, executors, administrators, and official liquidators. Like ss 223 and 224, it is therefore of rather narrow scope.

19

Deception and Fraud

Stealing is not the only way of usurping another's property rights. Sometimes, V might have cause to complain even though D has neither taken nor converted V's goods. Instead, the wrongfulness of the acquisition may be more subtle. It may, for example, lie in the fact that D duped V into parting with his property consensually, or in the fact that she fraudulently gained from the use of V's assets even though V suffered no loss. In common with theftous offences, wrongdoing of this sort involves dishonest behaviour by D regarding the property of another. However, its prevention requires the enactment of offences which differ substantially from traditional forms of theft.

The extent to which such offences are necessary has sometimes been questioned.[1] For example, although acquisition by deception may not give rise

---

1   See, for example, *R v Jones* (1703) 2 Ld Raymond 1013, 92 ER 174; *R v Goodhall* (1821) Russ & Ry 461, 168 ER 898.

to tortious claims in trespass or conversion,[2] other civil law remedies, such as deceit, are usually available to the aggrieved party. In addition, much commercial wrongdoing is controlled by administrative regulation of the marketplace, buttressed by the civil sanctions available to professional bodies. Given such existing sanctions, and the commitment in New Zealand to a broadly liberal economic philosophy, is it really essential to fence in the marketplace with criminal law?

The answer is yes. Our rights to private property are part of the very fabric of modern New Zealand.[3] Property relations are shared elements which help to structure our interpersonal relations within the community. As such, they are integral to our membership of society, and to the understanding we have of our own lives. In particular, one feature of our participation in a broadly liberal society is the autonomy we have in respect of our property — the freedom to use, control, and dispose of that property as we wish.

Of course, there are limitations to our autonomy as proprietors. Even the freedoms of contract and testament are substantially constrained by law. Neither may we use our assets to fund criminal activities, and we are compelled by the State to contribute through taxation to certain communal goals which may not be of direct personal benefit to us. Nonetheless, the importance of individualism to the New Zealand polity means that personal property rights have attracted better protection from the criminal law than many more abstract social or community values, such as an unpolluted environment or a well educated populace. By contrast with these examples, the occurrence of harms is more readily criminalised and prosecuted when there is an identifiable victim whose concrete individual rights have been transgressed.[4]

This imbalance may be reason for complaint, but not on the basis that property rights deserve reduced protection. Indeed, the harms involved in property offences shade into those addressed by offences against the person, and any suggestion that offences against property are concerned solely with material loss would be misleading. The violation of our homes by a burglary, for example, may cause psychological injury and distress quite independent of the quantum of loss. Offences such as theft, deception, and blackmail are generally categorised as property offences, and understandably so, for they involve wrongful acquisition of property. But they are also, in a very real sense, offences against the person. In each case, the conduct prohibited can be seen as an attack upon the victim's entitlement to dispose of his property by his own full and informed choice. Thus, the conduct represents an attack upon the victim's rights of free will and autonomy, and upon his freedom to exercise

---

2   Since possession and/or title will normally have passed, at least prima facie. See §§ 17.2.2.1(a),(d), 17.2.3.

3   Cf Waldron, *The Right to Private Property*, Oxford, Clarendon Press, 1988; Ryan, *Property and Political Theory*, Oxford, Blackwell, 1986; Nozick, *Anarchy, State and Utopia*, Oxford, Blackwell, 1974; Epstein, "Property as a Fundamental Civil Right" (1992) 29 Cal West LR 187.

4   A similar problem arises for fraud: see § 19.3.

control over his own situation. Blackmail, for instance, involves D infringing V's legitimate control over his own affairs by imposing her free will in place of his. This subjugation of V resembles an assault as much as it does a "property" wrong. Deception, understood in this sense, is a crime partly because it entails the manipulation or exploitation of another. Unlike the corresponding civil law remedies, property offences, in differing ways, protect the individual's entitlement to respect as an autonomous member of our society.

19.1 OBTAINING BY FALSE PRETENCES

The operative provision creating the offence of obtaining by false pretences is s 246 Crimes Act 1961, read in conjunction with s 245. An offence under s 246 is committed if D, with intent to defraud by a false pretence, either obtains title or possession to anything capable of being stolen or procures the delivery of anything capable of being stolen to anyone other than himself (s 246(2)), or induces another person to deal in some way with a valuable security (s 246(1)). There are four core elements of the offence:

(i)   A false pretence;

(ii)   Intent to defraud;

(iii) An obtaining of title or possession, or a procurement of delivery, of something capable of being stolen (s 246(2)); or an inducement of another to deal with a valuable security (s 246(1));

(iv)   Causation or reliance.

19.1.1 False pretence

A false pretence is defined in s 245. It consists of (i) a representation which is known by the representor to be false, or (ii) a promise which the promisor intends not to perform; which in either case is (iii) made with fraudulent intent to induce reliance. The last requirement overlaps with s 246, which expressly requires an intent to defraud as well as a false pretence. It appears that the effect of this repetition by s 246 is to add a causal requirement: that D must intend to defraud *through the false pretence*.[5] For convenience, we will defer for separate consideration the subjective element of fraudulent intent, and omit it from the present discussion of "false pretence" simpliciter.

19.1.1.1 A representation

In accordance with s 245(1), the representation must be either of a past or present fact, or about a future event, or about an existing intention, opinion, belief, knowledge, or other state or mind. The broad definition helps to simplify some of the complexities found in contract law, according to which a statement of opinion or a statement about future events would not normally amount to misrepresentation. However, the definition does not entirely dispose of those difficulties, and guidance in this area may still be obtained from the civil law. In particular, in order to qualify under s 245, the representation must be capable of being false. This means that it must contain, expressly or

---

5   See § 19.1.4.

impliedly, a proposition of fact. For example, if D states to V, "the owner has authorised me to sell this car", he asserts a fact which may be true or false. That is a plain case of a representation. But other statements are less clear-cut. Suppose that D says to V, "it is a good car for its age". This seems to express an opinion, rather than state a fact.[6] Even though s 245(1) deems statements about opinions to be representations, the opinion itself is not capable of being false. It is similar if D's statement is about a future event: the assurance that "New Zealand will win the next America's Cup competition" is prima facie no more than a prediction. Such a proposition may *become* false, but is usually not false when made.[7]

In cases such as these, it will be necessary for the prosecution to establish a further, *implied* representation by D in order to satisfy the actus reus. There are two standard implied representations in this situation. The first is *that D herself genuinely holds that opinion or believes that prediction*. This is a representation about D's existing mental state, and as such is capable of being false:

> it is very difficult to prove what the state of a man's mind at a particular time is, but if it can be ascertained it is as much a fact as anything else. A misrepresentation as to the state of a man's mind is therefore, a misstatement of fact . . .[8]

The second representation is normally inferred only if D is in a better position to express the opinion or prediction than V. In such cases, there is usually an implicit representation that D's view is a reasonable one given the information available to him. A useful statement of this rule may be found in the words of Bowen LJ in *Smith v Land and House Property Corp*:

> if the facts are not equally known to both sides, then a statement of opinion by the one who knows the facts best involves very often a statement of a material fact, for he impliedly states that he knows facts which justify his opinion.[9]

Assistance may also be gleaned from *NZ Motor Bodies Ltd v Emslie*.[10] In that case, D prepared (for the purpose of a takeover by P) a budget forecasting turnover and profit. The budget contained gross inaccuracies. Although the prediction may have been believed by D,[11] the Court held that it involved a false representation, since the making of the forecast implied that present facts existed which justified its conclusions.

As in the civil law, an exaggeration of quality is not a false pretence unless carried to such an extent as to amount to a fraudulent misrepresentation of

---

6   An analysis that is reinforced by s 245(4): "Exaggerated commendation or depreciation of the quality of anything is not a false pretence unless it is carried to such an extent as to amount to a fraudulent misrepresentation of fact."

7   See the note by White, "Trade Descriptions About the Future" (1974) 90 LQR 15.

8   *Edgington v Fitzmaurice* (1885) 29 Ch D 459 at 483.

9   (1884) 28 Ch D 7 at 15. Cf *Brown v Raphael* [1958] Ch 636, [1958] 2 All ER 79.

10   [1985] 2 NZLR 569.

11   And therefore was probably not a false pretence for the purposes of s 245. The case involved a claim for damages for negligent misrepresentation; on these facts, it would appear not to disclose a criminal offence, since D (who did not prepare the forecast personally) did not realise the forecast was ungrounded.

fact.[12] The question here is whether the statement goes beyond praise which does not appear to be serious or more than a mere opinion. A description of land as "fertile and improveable" has been held to be mere sales talk.[13] However, a statement that use of a carbolic smoke ball will prevent influenza is a more specific claim and may amount to a representation.[14]

19.1.1.1(a) *Implications from conduct*

Implicit in the foregoing section is that the law does not restrict its analysis of representations merely to the literal meaning of express words used by D. Rather, the test is "what meaning was actually conveyed to the party complaining".[15] This rule is buttressed by s 245(2), which states that the representation may be "by words or otherwise"[16] and thus need not be express.

The representation may, for instance, be constituted by conduct. In *R v Barnard*,[17] D, by wearing a university cap and gown, was held to have falsely represented that he was a member of Oxford University, in order to obtain credit from a tradesman; whether or not he had made such a claim by words, his conduct alone constituted a false pretence.[18]

According to Lord Reid, writing a cheque implies a representation that it will be honoured when presented for payment.[19] Since this is a prediction of future events, a further representation must be implied from it that the drawer of the cheque presently intends and expects that it will be honoured when presented.

---

12   This rule is stated in s 245(4), but appears simply to express the common law rule in contract, rather than to override or extend it.

13   *Dimmock v Hallett* (1866) LR 2 Ch App 21. See also *R v Bryan* (1857) Dears & B 265, 169 ER 1002.

14   *Carlill v Carbolic Smoke Ball Co* [1893] 1 QB 256, [1891-94] All ER Rep 127.

15   *Bisset v Wilkinson* [1927] AC 177 at 183. See *R v Taylor* [1991] 1 NZLR 413 at 417 (CA); *R v Cooper* (1877) 2 QBD 510 at 513.

16   Cf *R v Giles* (1865) Le & Ca 502 at 508, 169 ER 1490 at 1493. For comprehensive discussion of representations implied from conduct, see Smith, *Property Offences: The Protection of Property Through the Criminal Law*, London, Sweet & Maxwell, 1994, § 17.5.

17   (1837) 7 C & P 784, 173 ER 342.

18   See *R v Parker and Bulteel* (1916) 25 Cox CC 145: a banker who keeps his doors open and continues to trade may thereby represent that he is solvent.

19   *DPP v Turner* [1974] AC 357 at 367, [1973] 3 All ER 124 at 128. (Note that this representation encompasses the implied representations stated in the old case of *R v Hazelton* (1874) LR 2 CCR 134. It is submitted that the earlier case may now be disregarded.) Cf *R v Gilmartin* [1983] QB 953 at 962, [1983] 1 All ER 829 at 835, per Goff LJ (in the context of ss 15 and 16 Theft Act 1968 (UK)): "by the simple giving of a cheque, whether postdated or not, the drawer impliedly represents that the state of facts existing at the date of delivery of the cheque is such that in the ordinary course the cheque will on presentation for payment on or after the date specified in the cheque, be met." Thus the test is "not the known state of the appellant's account at the moment the cheque was issued, but whether it had been proved that he did not honestly believe that the cheque would in the ordinary course be met." *R v Miller* [1955] NZLR 1038 at 1049 (CA). See also the discussion in Smith, *Property Offences: The Protection of Property Through the Criminal Law*, London, Sweet & Maxwell, 1994, § 17.52.

Another common situation is the use of a credit card or bank card, which involves a representation that the person using it has authority to do so.[20] Similarly, countersigning a traveller's cheque amounts to a representation that D is the person authorised to sign and use it.[21]

Where D purports to sell goods to V, there is usually an implied representation that D has the capacity to pass ownership of the goods,[22] and that the goods are genuine.[23] Conversely, where D buys or orders goods, she impliedly promises (and represents her intention) to pay for them; and where payment on the spot is expected (eg at a restaurant or service station), she impliedly represents also that she has the ability to pay. Therefore, where D takes a taxi, she implies by her conduct that she has money for the fare.[24]

19.1.1.1(b) *Implications from silence*

As in contract law, silence or non-disclosure will generally not be regarded as representation.[25] However, the general rule is qualified in some circumstances. One exception occurs where D's conduct gives rise to an implied representation that is false, and which D silently fails to refute.[26] A controversial example of this is the case of *Police v Dronjak*,[27] in which D allowed a supermarket cashier to charge an incorrect price, by not pointing out the presence of another, higher price tag on the goods. This decision is questionable, as it effectively creates a higher duty of disclosure in the criminal law context than is imposed in the context of civil obligations.[28] Consistency with the civil law is essential in s 245, since it would be wrong to find D guilty of obtaining by deception something for which he is entitled to sue under a valid contract. Nonetheless, the controversy over *Dronjak* is restricted to whether D's presentation of the goods

---

20 *MPC v Charles* [1977] AC 177, [1976] 3 All ER 112; *R v Lambie* [1982] AC 499, [1981] 2 All ER 776. These decisions, however, fail to address the causation point (§ 19.1.4), that the vendor accepting the card may rely only upon the minimum representation required to validate the charge transaction — ie that the customer is the person named on the face of the card (itself an implied representation: *R v Abdullah* [1982] Crim LR 122). See Smith, "The Idea of Criminal Deception" [1982] Crim LR 721.

21 *R v Griffiths* [1960] NZLR 850 (CA).

22 *R v Sampson* (1885) 52 LT (NS) 772. Cf *Eichholz v Bannister* (1864) 17 CB (NS) 708 at 723, 144 ER 284 at 290, "in almost all the transactions of sale in common life the seller by the very act of selling holds out to the buyer that he is the owner of the article he offers for sale".

23 *R v Jean Jacques Williams* [1980] Crim LR 589.

24 *R v Waterfall* [1970] 1 QB 148 at 150, [1969] 3 All ER 1048 at 1049 (Lord Parker).

25 Cf *Smith v Hughes* (1871) LR 6 QB 597, [1861-73] All ER Rep 632. Unless D is under a duty of disclosure, for example arising from a contract to which he is party: *R v Firth* (1990) 91 Cr App R 217. The relevant principles here are those governing liability for omissions: considered at § 2.1.1.2.

26 It is clear that D can expressly negative the usual implications of his conduct: cf *R v Douglas* (1972) 8 CCC (2d) 275.

27 [1990] 3 NZLR 75, (1988) 3 CRNZ 141. See § 17.2.3.2(d).

28 Cf *Adams* § CA245.11. Of course, it would be otherwise if D had himself actively interfered with the price labelling, as occurred in *Rao v Police* (1988) 3 CRNZ 697. See also the discussion at § 19.2.3.

to the cashier amounts to a representation that the price tag showing is the only or correct tag. Once this proposition is conceded (as, with respect, it should not be), the second principle — that D may be convicted for deliberately failing to correct a misapprehension he creates — would appear unobjectionable.

A second exception to the general rule is the case of half-truths, where D's silence has the effect of distorting the meaning of some positive representation that she makes. It seems clear that an incomplete representation accompanied by silence as to material facts can be a false representation, if there is an implication from the circumstances that all material information has been disclosed. Thus it is a misrepresentation for a vendor to state that the properties are let, and omit the further truth that the tenants have been given notice to quit.[29]

Thirdly, the failure to negate an understanding that is implied from a course of dealing may also result in a false representation. In *R v Silverman*,[30] D had been convicted of obtaining property by deception under s 15 Theft Act 1968 (UK) by grossly overcharging for rewiring and redecoration of a house. Although the conviction was quashed on other grounds, the English Court of Appeal held that in the situation of mutual trust, which had built up over a number of years, D had impliedly represented that his firm was going to get no more than a modest profit from the work. Watkins LJ referred to dicta of Lord Reid in *DPP v Ray* that "a man intending to deceive can build up a situation in which his silence is as eloquent as an express statement".[31] In practice, this sets a standard which very much resembles the test applying in civil law; something that might otherwise be inappropriate except for the buttressing of a fraudulent intent requirement, without which there can be no offence.

In contract law, a misrepresentation may be inferred from a failure to disclose a change in circumstances which makes false a representation that originally was true.[32] It appears that this rule does not apply in the criminal law. In *Nelson v R*,[33] D made an insurance claim for theft of her car, truthfully stating that she did not know who had taken it. Before the claim was settled, she discovered that a friend had arranged for the removal and burning of the car; but she did not tell the insurer this. The Court of Criminal Appeal held that her conduct did not amount to a false pretence. The rule of equity, that a person has a duty to disclose in a pre-contractual situation where a statement inducing a contract becomes false prior to conclusion of the contract, "is not a

---

29 *Dimmock v Hallett* (1866) LR 2 Ch App 21. Compare *R v Kylsant* [1932] 1 KB 442, [1931] All ER Rep 179; *R v Bishirgian* [1936] 1 All ER 586; also *The Siboen & the Sibotre* [1976] 1 Lloyds Rep 293.

30 (1988) 86 Cr App R 213, [1987] Crim LR 574; also *R v Stevens* (1844) 1 Cox CC 83.

31 [1974] AC 370 at 380, [1973] 3 All ER 131 at 133.

32 *With v O'Flanagan* [1936] Ch 575, [1936] 1 All ER 727.

33 [1987] WAR 57. The original conviction was under s 409(1) Criminal Code (WA), which is essentially the same as s 246.

rule which has anything to do with the criminal offence of obtaining something by a false pretence".[34]

However, the failure to disclose a change of circumstances or of intention may amount to a distinct misrepresentation where the original representation is repeated, or may be regarded as continuing. An example of the latter is *DPP v Ray*,[35] where D ordered food in a restaurant, ate the meal, then decided to leave without paying. The majority of the House of Lords held that by entering and ordering the meal D had represented that he intended to pay for it. (Under s 245, an alternative analysis is that D *promised* he would pay for it.) This representation was analysed as an ongoing one, sustained by D's subsequent behaviour: "by continuing in the same role and behaving just as before he was representing that his previous intention continued".[36] The representation became false at the moment that D decided not to pay; thereafter, D may rightly be convicted of obtaining anything that he subsequently ordered by deception.

19.1.1.2 *Known to be false*

The representation must in fact be false.[37] There can be no false pretence where the representor makes a statement believing it to be false, when it is in fact true.[38] Apart from this requirement, the prosecution must also establish that the D *knows or believes* his representation is false. As was stated earlier, in § 3.4, absolute certainty is not required.[39] Wilful blindness regarding the falsity of the statement will also be enough.[40] However the test of D's knowledge or belief is purely subjective. A belief, however unreasonable, that the representation is true will prevent the defendant's conduct from amounting to a false pretence.[41]

---

34   [1987] WAR 57 at 60 (Burt CJ). The application of the equitable law rule was also rejected by Lord Hodson in *DPP v Ray* [1974] AC 370 at 389, [1973] 3 All ER 131 at 142; although his Lordship was in the minority, this specific point does not seem to have been disputed by the majority.

35   [1974] AC 370, [1973] 3 All ER 131; for criticism see [1974] Crim LR 181-183 (in fact, D ordered nothing subsequent to his deciding not to pay). Compare *Fagan v Metro Police Commr* [1969] 1 QB 439, [1968] 3 All ER 442; see § 2.1.1.2.(d); White, "Continuing Representations in Criminal Law" (1986) 37 NILQ 255.

36   [1974] AC 370 at 386, [1973] 3 All ER 131 at 139 (Lord Morris).

37   *R v Spencer* (1828) 3 C & P 420, 172 ER 483. Since this is an element of the actus reus, the onus lies on the prosecution to prove the falsity of the representation. However, proof may be either by direct evidence or by inference from the circumstances: cf *R v Mandry and Wooster* [1973] 3 All ER 996, [1973] 1 WLR 1232; *R v Kingston* (1905) 24 NZLR 431.

38   *R v Deller* (1952) 36 Cr App R 184. D sold a car purportedly free of encumbrances, believing that in fact he had only the use and possession of the car under a hire purchase agreement. Though made dishonestly, D's representation might indeed have been true; the purported sale and hiring back to D was arguably a sham concealing the true transaction of a loan on the security of the car, which would have been void for non-registration.

39   See also § 17.4.2.1; *R v Crooks* [1981] 2 NZLR 53 (CA).

40   § 3.4.1.

41   *R v Conrad* [1974] 2 NZLR 626 (CA). Of course, whether there were reasonable grounds for D's belief may be considered by the jury when deciding whether D in fact had that belief.

On the other hand, where D subsequently realises that her original representation was false, the doctrine in *R v Miller* may well place her under a duty to counteract the effects of that initial, innocent deception.[42] At present, this possibility remains moot: there is no case in which it has been held that the rule in *Miller* carries over into deception.

19.1.1.3 *Or a promise which the promisor intends not to perform*

The inclusion by s 245(1) of promises within the range of false pretences reverses the common law rule that it is no crime to obtain something by means of a promise that D does not intend to perform.[43] The mere fact that a promise is not performed does not prove that D *intended* to break it.[44] On the other hand, it is no defence that the performance of D's promise would have been impossible[45] or illegal.[46]

19.1.2 Intent to defraud

The principal mental element for an offence under s 246 is an "intent to defraud by any false pretence". The requisite criminal intent therefore consists of (i) an intent to defraud the victim, and (ii) an intent that the fraud should be by means of a false pretence.[47] In addition, it has been held implicit in an intent to defraud that there must be (iii) an element of dishonesty.[48] Thus the authorities relevant to the interpretation of "fraudulently" in the context of theft are salient also to s 246.[49]

Regarding (i) an "intent to defraud", the meaning of this phrase will also be discussed in § 19.3.4 (conspiracy to defraud). The term "defraud" suggests harm to the victim, and raises the question whether D must intend that V be "deprived" of anything. It appears that the answer is no: it is sufficient that V's interests or rights are (deliberately and dishonestly) risked, whether or not they are, in fact, eventually compromised.[50] Indeed, the gist of the deception offence in s 246 is the obtaining of an advantage for D, rather than the deprivation of a victim per se; thus there seems no reason why actual deprivation should be required. Conversely, where a dishonest deprivation of V is intended without any benefit to D or another, it would usually be more appropriate to charge under one of the fraud offences, such as conspiracy to defraud.

---

42 [1983] 2 AC 161, [1983] 1 All ER 978 (HL); discussed at § 2.1.1.2.(e).

43 *R v Goodhall* (1821) Russ & Ry 463, 168 ER 899.

44 Section 245(3).

45 *R v Giles* (1865) L & C 502, 169 ER 1490.

46 *R v Binley and Walsh* (1912) 32 NZLR 159; *R v B* (1953) SR (NSW) 497.

47 Cf *R v Wakeling* (1823) Russ & Ry 504, 168 ER 920, in which D was not guilty of obtaining by false pretences a benefit conferred as a result of a pretence made for other reasons.

48 *R v Speakman* (1989) 5 CRNZ 250 (CA).

49 § 17.3.1.

50 Cf s 246(1), which adds the words "or cause loss to any person", suggesting that not all defraudings cause loss — otherwise it is difficult to see how this adds anything to the mens rea requirement, since a dishonest causing of loss will necessarily amount to a defrauding. Perhaps the emphasis here is that *any person* may be defrauded or suffer loss, and not merely the victim of the deceit. See also § 19.3.3.1.

Nonetheless, in the context of s 246, this difficulty will not generally arise, since someone will, consequent upon the actus reus of the section, normally have parted with a property interest in something capable of being stolen, or will have become liable under a valuable security, thus prejudicing her rights and interests therein, and so in any case would fall within any definition of fraud requiring a person to be deprived "of something which is his or of something to which he is or would or might but for the perpetration of the fraud be entitled".[51]

Apart from the foregoing question, some further points may be made of the intention to defraud under s 246. First, the section expressly recognises that the effect of the fraud may be that the victim is induced to deliver something to another person. It is not necessary, therefore, that a defendant should intend to benefit personally from the fraud. In *R v Potter*,[52] D's brother obtained a driving licence when D impersonated him at the driving test. Both were convicted of procuring a driving licence by false pretences. D's intent to defraud was established by his intent to induce, by deception, the county council to give his brother a driving licence.

The case of *Potter* illustrates that D may be convicted of obtaining even where the thing obtained has little or no economic value to the victim, provided it is capable of being stolen.[53] Nor must D intend anyone to suffer a net economic loss. There may be an intent to defraud even though the victim in fact obtained real consideration for the thing given to D, provided the transaction was induced by D's false pretence. In *Welham v DPP*, D had witnessed forged hire purchase agreements, on the basis of which finance companies advanced large sums of money. In his defence he asserted that he did not intend to deprive the finance companies of any economic advantage, but merely to enable the borrowers to circumvent credit restrictions. Lord Denning, rejecting the argument that an intention to defraud involves an intention to cause economic loss, remarked that "if a drug addict forges a doctor's prescription so as to enable him to get drugs from a chemist, he has, I should have thought, an intent to defraud, even though he intends to pay the chemist the full price and no one is a penny the worse off".[54]

Implicit in this passage is that, where D borrows money by false pretences, an intention to repay does not negative the intent to defraud. The locus

---

51   *Scott v Metropolitan Police Commr* [1975] AC 819 at 839, [1974] 3 All ER 1032 at 1038 (Viscount Dilhorne).

52   [1958] 2 All ER 51, [1958] 1 WLR 638; see also *Alexander v Police* 27/4/94, McGechan J, HC Wellington AP8/94.

53   See also commentary to *R v Moses and Ansbro* [1991] Crim LR 617: defendants who had fraudulently obtained National Insurance numbers could in principle have been charged with obtaining property by deception, since they had obtained plastic number cards bearing their National Insurance numbers.

54   [1961] AC 103 at 131, [1960] 1 All ER 805 at 814. See also *R v Hammerson* (1914) 10 Cr App R 121; *R v Naylor* (1865) LR 1 CCR 4. In *R v Potger* (1970) 55 Cr App R 42, D falsely represented that he was a student taking part in a competition to sell magazines. The fact that the magazines would have been delivered and would have been worth the purchase price did not prevent his conduct from being dishonest.

classicus of the common law on this point is to be found in the direction to the jury given by Channell J in *R v Carpenter*:

> If the defendant made statements of fact which he knew to be untrue, and made them for the purpose of inducing persons to deposit with him money which he knew they would not deposit but for their belief in the truth of his statements, and if he was intending to use the money so obtained for purposes different from those for which he knew the depositors understood from his statements that he intended to use it, then . . . we have the intent to defraud, although he may have intended to repay the money if he could, and although he may have honestly believed, and may even have had good reason to believe, that he would be able to repay it.[55]

19.1.3 The subject-matter of the deception

The offence under s 246 may be committed in two ways. The first, an obtaining of title or possession or a procurement of delivery under s 246(2), is relatively straightforward.[56] However, it should be noted that s 246(2) only covers things "capable of being stolen" within the meaning of s 217.[57] There can, for example, be no obtaining of an equitable interest or a spes successionis under a will – as where D induces T to make his will in favour of D instead of C (the classic example here being of Jacob and Esau). In such a case there might be a conspiracy to defraud,[58] although the scope of that offence is limited to acts committed by two or more people in concert. Where D acts alone and obtains a chose in action, it may be necessary to charge an offence under s 246(1).

19.1.3.1 *Dealing with a valuable security*

Section 246(1) makes it an offence to induce by deception the treatment (execution, endorsement etc) of a valuable security. The purpose of this section is to deal with the following type of problem. Where D by a false pretence induces V to make a cheque in his favour, the obtaining of the cheque qua chose in action will not be an offence under s 246(2), since for an obtaining under this subsection the thing must be capable of being stolen, which means that it must belong to another. However, the chose in action represented by the cheque has never belonged to anyone but D.[59] Of course, D may be charged with obtaining the cheque qua piece of paper,[60] or with obtaining the money if and when the cheque is cashed. But the former may be seen as rather artificial, and the latter would not work where, for example, the chose in action could

---

55 (1911) 76 JP 158 at 160, 22 Cox CC 618 at 624. Approved in *R v Kritz* [1950] 1 KB 82, [1949] 2 All ER 406. Cf *R v Greenstein* [1976] 1 All ER 1, [1975] 1 WLR 1353.

56 Note, in the case of procurement of delivery, that the recipient may be an innocent party: *R v Duru* [1974] 1 WLR 2. There is no requirement in s 246 that the person from whom the goods are obtained should have had title or a particular interest therein.

57 Discussed at § 17.2.1.

58 Cf *R v Tillings* [1985] Crim LR 393.

59 This lacuna is illustrated in *R v Danger* (1857) 7 Cox CC 303. *Danger* was subsequently confirmed in *R v Preddy* [1996] AC 815, [1996] 3 All ER 481.

60 Cf *R v Bennitt* [1961] NZLR 452; *R v Duru* [1973] 3 All ER 715, [1974] 1 WLR 2; *R v O'Connell* (1992) 94 Cr App R 39, [1991] Crim LR 771; *R v Caresana* [1996] Crim LR 667.

not be "transformed" into something capable of being stolen (eg documents of title to land). Section 246(1) is therefore a more satisfactory solution.

"Valuable security" is defined in s 2 as including "every document forming the title or evidence of the title to any property of any kind whatever; and also includes any negotiable instrument, bill of exchange, cheque, or promissory note". An offence under s 246(1) is committed not only where the victim of the false pretence becomes liable under the valuable security, but also where a third party incurs liability thereunder, for example where V possesses a cheque made out to him by C, and D by false pretences induces V to endorse that cheque and give it to D (or E).[61]

19.1.4 Causation

Section 246(2) provides that the thing must be obtained "either directly or through the medium of any contract obtained by the false pretence". Although the language does not explicitly state that where the thing is obtained "directly" it must be by means of the false pretence, the causal requirement is to be implied. In order for the false pretence to cause the obtaining, it must *both* deceive the representee, *and* be an operative cause of the obtaining of the thing (or of the procurement of its delivery to another person).[62] In other words, there must be *inducement* of or *reliance* by the representee. There is therefore no offence under s 246 where the representee is aware of the falsity of the representation, but hands over the property anyway, although in this situation there may be an attempt to obtain.[63] The condition of reliance is satisfied where the deceptive representation was *one* of the reasons for which the representee acted as she did, even if not the *only* reason.[64] However there is no reliance where she is indifferent to[65] or unaffected by[66] the representation, even if she believes it.

---

61 Compare the facts of *R v Davies* [1982] 1 All ER 513, [1982] 74 Cr App R 94.

62 Cf *R v King* [1987] QB 547, [1987] 1 All ER 547. Thus the deception must not be subsequent to the obtaining: *R v Brooks* (1859) 1 F & F 502, 175 ER 827; *R v Collis-Smith* [1971] Crim LR 716.

63 *R v Hensler* (1870) 11 Cox CC 570. D wrote a begging letter claiming (falsely) to be a shipwrecked and destitute widow. The recipient of the letter sent 5 shillings despite knowing the falsehood of D's claims. D could not be guilty of obtaining by false pretences but was convicted of attempting to obtain.

64 Compare *R v Hamilton* (1991) 92 Cr App R 54, [1990] Crim LR 806; *R v Gauci* (1995) 79 A Crim R 506 at 509; *R v English* (1872) 12 Cox CC 171; also the discussion of multiple causes at § 2.2.2.3.

65 *R v Laverty* [1970] 3 All ER 432, (1970) 54 Cr App R 495; *R v Dale* (1836) 7 C & P 352, 173 ER 157; *R v Strickland* (1850) 14 JP 784. This traditional view of the causation requirement no longer represents the law in England, following the decisions in *MPC v Charles* [1977] AC 177, [1976] 3 All ER 112 and *R v Lambie* [1982] AC 449, [1981] 2 All ER 776 (noted at § 19.1.1.1). These more recent cases effectively dilute the requirement to find a false representation by D which is an operative cause of the obtaining. As such, it is submitted that they are mistaken, and that the traditional approach is to be preferred in New Zealand.

Note that the requirement of inducement does not mean that the false pretence must be a credible one. If V did in fact believe the representation, it does not matter that a reasonable person would not have believed it.[67]

Although the false pretence must cause the delivery or obtaining of the thing, it need not do so directly. For example, the offence can be committed where the false pretence causes the representee to initiate a process whereby the thing is delivered, even where the thing is actually obtained from someone other than the representee.[68] In *R v Bennitt*,[69] D falsified timesheets, thus obtaining an overpayment of wages. The Supreme Court held that the original false representation operated through each stage of the transaction; there was a nexus in the chain of events from D's representation to the eventual receipt of the cheque.

Sometimes, however, the final transaction by which something is obtained may be too remote from the original representation for causation to be established. This was said to be the case in *R v Clucas*, where D through a false pretence induced V, a bookmaker, to accept a bet on credit. The horse he backed won, but the money he received was held not to be obtained by a false pretence — the effective cause of the obtaining was not D's representation but the fact that the horse won.[70] Most situations of this type arise when the immediate cause of the obtaining is some event contemplated in a contract.[71] Where that contract is itself induced by a false pretence, the difficulty about causation is now expressly resolved by the language of s 246(2).

The need for deception and reliance excludes from s 246 the unauthorised obtaining of money from an automatic teller machine, since it has been held

---

66 For example if she "confirms" the truth of the representation by her own enquiries, without relying on the fact that D has made it: *R v Roebuck* (1856) D & B 24, 169 ER 900; *R v Winning* (1973) 12 CCC (2d) 449.

67 *R v Piri Hira Hoani* (1915) 34 NZLR 902; *R v Giles* (1865) Le & Ca 502, 169 ER 1490; *R v Jessop* (1858) D & B 442, 169 ER 1074.

68 Cf *R v Kovacs* [1974] 1 All ER 1236, [1974] 1 WLR 370; *R v Charles* [1977] AC 177, (1976) 68 Cr App R 334; *R v Clarkson* [1987] VR 962 at 980, (1987) 25 A Crim R 277 at 296.

69 [1961] NZLR 452.

70 [1949] 2 KB 226, [1949] 2 All ER 40. With respect, it is doubtful whether the horse's victory was a *novus actus interveniens*, since that was precisely the subject-matter of the wager. (Contrast *R v Lambassi* [1927] VLR 349, [1927] ALR 295.) The case may be distinguished if necessary from *R v Button* [1900] 2 QB 597, where D's representation that he had never won a race before enabled him to gain a long start and thereby win two races. Here the causal connection was more straightforward, since the representation made it more likely that D would win the race itself.

71 Compare the unreported UK case of *R v Lewis* (1922) Russell (12th ed) vol 2, 1186 n 66, discussed in *R v King* [1987] QB 547, [1987] 1 All ER 547. D obtained a teaching post through a forged teacher's certificate: the view was taken that her salary was obtained as a result of performing the obligations of her post, and not of the false pretence. See too the criticism of *R v Miller* (1992) 95 CR App R 421, [1992] Crim LR 744 by Smith, *Property Offences: The Protection of Property Through the Criminal Law*, London, Sweet & Maxwell, 1994, § 17.125.

that a machine cannot be deceived,[72] and does not "rely" on representations, but simply delivers money in response to a certain input. The offence in this case would fall within s 229A (taking or dealing with documents with intent to defraud, the document in question being the bank card).

19.2 OBTAINING CREDIT FRAUDULENTLY

A related offence is created by s 247, which provides that it is an offence to obtain credit by means of any false pretence or any other fraud. Although restricted to obtainings of credit the section, in some respects, has a wider scope than s 246: it applies to an intangible thing (s 246 covers only "things capable of being stolen", which as we have seen does not include a chose in action), and it uses the term "fraud" rather than the narrower "false pretence"[73]. The elements of this offence have been summarised by Mahon J in *Police v Griffiths*:

> there are four ingredients of liability under s 247 of the Crimes Act. The offender must incur a debt or liability, he must obtain credit in respect of that debt or liability, he must obtain that credit by false pretences or other fraud, and he must at the time when he obtains the credit have intended not to pay the debt or otherwise to defraud the creditor.[74]

19.2.1 Debt or liability

The debt or liability must be legally enforceable against D; there is therefore no offence where the credit is obtained under a contract which is void[75] or illegal.[76]

19.2.2 Obtaining credit

The credit obtained must be in respect of a monetary obligation.[77] Thus if D receives a benefit in return for an obligation to perform services or deliver goods in the future, he does not obtain credit within the terms of s 247 − the proper charge would be under s 246(2), in respect of the initial benefit obtained. The credit obtained need not be pursuant to a specific contract,[78] or for any minimum length of time. Thus filling one's tank at a self-service petrol station

---

72 *Kennison v Daire* (1985) 38 SASR 404 at 406. After D's bank account had been closed, D withdrew money from an ATM with his cashcard. Per King CJ: "The crime of obtaining money by false pretences requires, in my opinion, the intervention of a human being who is induced by the false pretence to part with money. A machine cannot be deceived by a false pretence or other fraud." D could not therefore be convicted of obtaining by false pretences, but was instead convicted of larceny. Cf dicta in *Davies v Flackett* [1973] RTR 8, [1972] Crim LR 708.

73 See § 19.2.3.

74 [1976] 1 NZLR 498 at 499.

75 *R v Leon* [1945] KB 136, [1945] 1 All ER 14.

76 *R v Garlick* (1958) 42 Cr App R 141.

77 Per Lord Dilhorne LC in *Fisher v Raven* [1964] AC 210 at 231, [1963] 2 All ER 389 at 394; followed in *R v Kinsman* [1969] NZLR 678 (CA). In England the decision in *Fisher v Raven* has been overturned by s 360(2)(b) Insolvency Act 1986 (UK).

78 *R v Kinsman* [1969] NZLR 678 (CA); *R v Peters* (1886) 16 QBD 636.

constitutes an obtaining of credit at least until the filling is completed and one is due to pay.[79]

There is no "obtaining" where D merely gets an extension of time to pay an existing debt. However there is a sufficient "obtaining" where D incurs a fresh liability even where this is simply a substitute for an old debt, for example executing a bill of sale to pay off an overdraft,[80] or making use of a bank overdraft facility to draw a cheque paying a credit card bill. On the other hand, where D pays for goods by drawing a cheque which he knows will bounce, the offence is obtaining goods, rather than credit, by false pretences.[81]

It appears that the credit must be extended to D personally, and not obtained for another.[82] However, in situations where D incurs joint or derivative personal liability (eg by obtaining credit on behalf of a partnership of which he is a member), the relevant authorities are open to reconsideration,[83] and it may be that D's misconduct will be held to fall within the section.

19.2.3 By false pretences or other fraud

The elements of false pretence and causation in s 247 are identical with those in s 246, and are discussed earlier.[84] Fraud may occur without any representation,[85] and has been interpreted in Canada as including any dishonest conduct or scheme.[86] *Garrow and Turkington* concludes that the following example would therefore fall within the scope of s 247:

> Thus if a shopkeeper, without any misrepresentation by words or conduct on the part of the customer, mistakes him for someone else and therefore gives him credit the customer, if he is aware of the mistake and accepts credit intending not to pay, is guilty of [obtaining credit by] fraud, although there is no false pretence on his part.[87]

With respect, we doubt that the extension of s 247 goes quite so far as *Garrow and Turkington* suggests. That would be to impose criminal liability without any positive action whatsoever by D; and indeed to create an inconsistency with the civil law. We cannot improve on the statement of this point by Smith:

> Whether such "passive acquiescence in the self-deception" of another could be held to amount to deception by conduct is doubtful but certainly arguable; but a holding that it constituted an offence would be incongruous in the extreme when viewed in the light of the civil law. The civil court, in allowing D to [enforce the contract] would be assisting him to obtain what, according to the criminal court, would be the proceeds of his crime. This would be an absurdity which the courts could scarcely

---

79   Cf *R v Jones* [1898] 1 QB 119.

80   *R v Thornton* [1964] 2 QB 176, [1963] 1 All ER 170.

81   *R v Cosnett* (1901) 20 Cox CC 6, 65 JP 472.

82   *R v Bryant* (1899) 63 JP 376; *R v Steel* (1910) 5 Cr App R 289.

83   *R v McLean* [1928] NZLR 454, [1928] GLR 311; *R v Hamer* [1954] Crim LR 209.

84   §§ 19.1.1 and 19.1.4, respectively.

85   And, therefore, without any deception. A similar rule applies in conspiracy to defraud; see § 19.3.2.

86   *R v Olan, Hudson & Harnett* (1978) 41 CCC (2d) 145, 86 DLR (3d) 212; *R v Sebe* (1987) 35 CCC (3d) 97.

87   § 5247.2(3).

allow . . . It is true, of course, that statutes creating criminal offences affect the civil law. A statute prohibiting a particular result invalidates any contract to bring about that result. But the law of theft and associated offences assumes the existence of a body of civil rights and duties; it exists to protect those rights and it is the business of the criminal courts to protect them, not to change them.[88]

Fraud, while not depending on a representation, at least requires some conduct or scheme going beyond merely taking advantage, sub silentio, of another's spontaneous mistake.

19.2.4 Mens rea

The requirement of an intent to defraud is an implicit element of s 247.[89] It is not sufficient that D obtains credit merely by a deception or other dishonest conduct.[90] Suppose, for example, that D uses a ruse to borrow a sum of money from V to which he believes he is otherwise entitled (perhaps as a result of a disputed earlier debt). Although he commits the actus reus of an offence against s 247, he lacks the mens rea.

Note that the fraudulent intention must exist at the time when the credit is obtained: a later decision not to repay is insufficient.[91]

19.3 CONSPIRACY TO DEFRAUD

New Zealand lacks a general criminal offence of fraud. So too does the common law, according to which the defrauding of one individual by another does not *per se* constitute a crime.[92] For the most part, fraud is criminalised through more specific offences, which address particular forms of economic activity when done with a fraudulent intent.[93]

However, the common law does recognise an offence of *conspiracy* to defraud, operative where the fraud involves two or more persons acting together.[94] The same crime has remained unchanged since codification in New Zealand, when (as s 284 of the Draft Code) it was regarded by the Criminal

---

88 "Civil Law Concepts in the Criminal Law" [1972] 31 CLJ 197 at 219.

89 *Police v Griffiths* [1976] 1 NZLR 498.

90 *R v Muirhead* (1908) 73 JP 31, 1 Cr App R 189; *R v Brownlow* (1910) 4 Cr App R 131, 26 TLR 345.

91 *R v McKay* [1961] NZLR 256 (CA).

92 *R v Wheatly* (1761) 2 Burr 1125, 97 ER 746. An exception was the old offence of Cheat, which was confined to fraud "in a subject concerning the public, which, as between subject and subject, would only be actionable by a civil action . . ." *R v Bembridge* (1783) 22 St Tr 1, 99 ER 679 (Lord Mansfield).

93 Notably, in the Crimes Act 1961, ss 250-256 specify particular fraud offences: false statement by promoter (s 250); falsifying accounts relating to public funds (s 251); false accounting by officer or member of body corporate (s 252); false accounting by employee (s 253); false statement by public officer (s 254); issuing false dividend warrants (s 255); concealing deeds and encumbrances (s 256). Other relevant statues include the Companies Acts 1955 and 1993, and the Securities Act 1978.

94 *R v Hevey* (1782) 1 Leach 232, 168 ER 218. See Hadden, "Conspiracy to Defraud" [1966] 24 CLJ 248; Gillies, "The Offence of Conspiracy to Defraud" (1977) 51 ALJ 247.

Code Commissioners as declaratory of the common-law offence. Section 257 provides that anyone commits an offence:

> who conspires with any other person by deceit or falsehood or other fraudulent means to defraud the public, or any person ascertained or unascertained, or to affect the public market price of stocks, funds, shares, merchandise, or any thing else publicly sold, whether the deceit or falsehood or other fraudulent means would or would not amount to a false pretence as hereinbefore defined.

Although its importance has diminished with the enactment of separate statutory offences, conspiracy to defraud remains a catch-all offence covering conduct that does not fall under other substantive fraud offences. The scope of the crime is extremely wide, because of the broad definition of fraud, and the fact that the conspiracy need not be to commit an offence, but may also be to commit a civil wrong[95] or perhaps certain kinds of moral wrongs.[96] For these reasons, the offence might be thought prima facie objectionable and one to be used sparingly. Its broad drafting offers little guidance to prospective offenders — by contrast, a series of offences each of which specifies an actus reus more narrowly offers better guidance to citizens, by warning clearly that proposed conduct falls within the reach of the criminal law.[97]

Even more importantly, the offence makes illegal conduct by two defendants that may not be criminal when done by only one. It is hard to see how that distinction between individual and group, and its very serious consequences, are justified. Why does the moral character of (say) a lawful deceit change, *so much so that it becomes a crime*, simply because it is perpetrated by two rather than one?[98] The distinction created by s 257 is, moreover, difficult to reconcile with the crime of conspiracy under s 310, which requires that the conduct conspired at should itself be an offence.

Aggravating these problems is the difficulty of drawing a boundary between mere sharp practice in the commercial sphere, and criminal dishonesty. The two shade into each other, and in practice it may be the element of conspiracy that redesignates a transaction from unscrupulous to

---

95 *R v Warburton* (1870) LR 1 CCR 274; *R v Weaver* (1931) 45 CLR 321 at 334, [1931] ALR 249 at 251. In *R v Potter* [1953] 1 All ER 296, a recalcitrant debenture-holder entered into an agreement whereby he was guaranteed an additional 7s in the £ on his debentures from an outside source, in return for his agreement to a scheme whereby all debenture holders were to agree to a composition of 8s in the £. D's counsel argued that the private agreement was merely unenforceable or void as a fraudulent preference, and did not constitute an indictable offence. Cassells J disagreed, holding that there was an indictable offence of conspiracy; although at trial both defendants were acquitted.

96 *R v Timothy* (1858) 1 F & F 39, 175 ER 616; *Heymann v R* (1873) LR 8 QB 102 at 105; cf *R v Weaver* (1931) 45 CLR 321 at 346, 347, [1931] ALR 249 at 256, 257 (but see at 349, at 259). See § 19.3.3.3.

97 See the discussion of fair warning at § 1.4.3.

98 For an argument that the moral character of the wrong changes when there is conspiracy, see Dennis, "The Rationale of Criminal Conspiracy" (1977) 93 LQR 39. But Dennis does not suggest that the moral character of the defendants' activities changes so drastically that a conspiracy to do a mere civil wrong (let alone lawful acts) should be criminalised.

illegal. Perhaps as a consequence of this, in the public mind fraud has tended to lack the graphic moral character of theft or receiving, and there is a continuing debate whether commercial malpractice is a proper subject for "public law", or whether it should primarily be dealt with by civil law mechanisms; particularly since such wrongdoing is often perceived to be victimless, in that there may be no identifiable individual who is directly and immediately out-of-pocket as a result of the defendant's activities.[99] Even where the activities are regulated by criminal law, the law's control mechanisms are different to those for street crime, in terms of the social standing of the suspects, and in terms of the comparative immunity of "white-collar crimes" from police surveillance or normal crime prosecution.[100] Nonetheless, serious commercial fraud has increased considerably, and is extremely costly to society in economic terms. No doubt this is attributable to the evolution of commercial practices.[101] Modern credit economies enable fraudsters to manipulate wealth in large denominations, without being constrained by having to deal with its physical manifestation. The techniques of wrongdoing multiply as the variety and complexity of financial transactions increases, requiring specialist knowledge to initiate, process, and above all, monitor. This changing nature of commercial and financial life presents at least one reason for retention of a fall-back crime such as conspiracy to defraud, since it may be impossible for specific legislation constantly to keep up with the mutating ways in which fraud may be committed, especially given modern communications and computing innovations, and the globalisation of securities and other markets.[102]

The elements of conspiracy to defraud under s 257 are:

(i)   An agreement or conspiracy between 2 or more persons;

(ii)   That contemplates using deceit, falsehood, or fraudulent means;

(iii) To defraud the public or a person, or to affect the price of anything sold publicly; and

(iv)   Mens rea.

We consider these elements in turn.

19.3.1 Conspiracy with another person

The law on this point is the same as for ordinary conspiracy under s 310.[103] There must be an act of agreement, constituting a *joint decision* to commit the fraud. Preliminary negotiations or discussions regarding the possibility of

99   See § 19.3.3.1.

100 Levi, *Regulating Fraud: White-collar Crime and the Criminal Process*, London, Tavistock, 1987, 15.

101 Cf Lanfrentz, "Defalcations" 24 Journal of Accountancy 254.

102 See Sullivan, "Fraud and the Efficacy of the Criminal Law: a Proposal for a Wide Residual Offence" [1985] Crim LR 616; McBarnet and Whelan, "The Elusive Spirit of the Law: Formalism and the Struggle for Legal Control" (1991) 54 MLR 848; Smith, "Conspiracy to Defraud: Some Comments on the Law Commission's Report" [1995] Crim LR 209.

103 See the more detailed discussion in § 6.2.4; also Orchard, "'Agreement' in Criminal Conspiracy" [1974] Crim LR 297 and 335.

doing something fraudulent, which do not crystallise into any firm decision, are insufficient.[104] Neither is there a conspiracy where the parties each have the same thought or intention, but have not communicated this to each other: a concurrence between two people of "mere wicked thoughts not intended to be acted upon"[105] will not do. The joint "decision" required for conspiracy only exists if there is both agreement to defraud between the parties and a common intention to carry out that agreement.[106]

In general, there are three kinds of conspiratorial agreement. The simplest variety is where each conspirator is aware of the existence of all the others and knows that they are parties to the agreement. The second, more complex, case is the "wheel" (or "cartwheel") conspiracy, where A, B, and C (the spokes) are all individually in contact with D (the hub), but have never met each other.[107] The third variant is the "chain" conspiracy, where A contacts B, who contacts C, who contacts D, and so on.[108] However, it is important not to roll up a number of separate transactions in one conspiracy charge. This point is made in *R v Griffiths*,[109] where a lime supplier (Griffiths), his accountant, and seven farmers whom Griffiths supplied, were charged with conspiracy to defraud the government of subsidies. Their convictions were quashed on appeal, as there was no evidence of any collusion between the farmers, either directly or through the intermediation of Griffiths, but only of separate conspiracies between the supplier and individual farmers.[110]

Like conspiracy per se, a conspiracy to defraud, once formed, does not admit of withdrawal. After an agreement is reached, and the other elements are established, the crime of conspiracy to defraud is complete and it is irrelevant that subsequently one or all of the parties decide to abandon the agreement.[111]

---

104 This is the explanation of *R v Walker* [1962] Crim LR 458. D had participated in discussions about a planned payroll robbery, but later withdrew. His conviction was quashed as it was not proven that the discussions had progressed beyond the stage of negotiation before his withdrawal. See § 6.2.4; also *R v Barnard* (1979) 70 Cr App R 28.

105 *R v Banks* (1873) 12 Cox CC 393 at 399.

106 *R v Sew Hoy* [1994] 1 NZLR 257, (1993) 10 CRNZ 581 (CA).

107 Cf *Ex p Coffey, Re Evans* [1971] NSWLR 434.

108 *R v Ardalan* [1072] 2 All ER 257, [1972] 1 WLR 463. Note, however, the cautionary words of Roskill LJ (at 262, at 470) that "words or phrases such as 'wheels', 'cartwheels', 'chain', 'sub-conspiracies' and so on are used only to illustrate and clarify the principle and for no other purpose".

109 [1966] 1 QB 589, [1965] 2 All ER 448.

110 Ibid at 599, at 455: "It is right and proper to say that the judge correctly pointed out the principle, saying that the Crown had to prove that the conspirators put their heads together to defraud the Ministry. The trouble is that it never seems to have been considered ... whether or not in this case each farmer put his head together with Griffiths' head without any thought of a general conspiracy." Hence, although each defendant may have conspired separately with Griffiths, the convictions were unsafe since the defendants should not have been joined in a conglomerate charge.

111 Cf *R v O'Brien* (1954) 110 CCC 1 at 3, 4, [1954] SCR 666 at 669 (Taschereau J): "If a person, with one or several others, agrees to commit an unlawful act, and later, after having had the intention to carry it through, refuses to put the plan into effect, that person is nevertheless guilty."

19.3.2 By deceit, falsehood, or other fraudulent means

The modus operandi of a conspiracy to defraud is specified by s 257 in very broad terms. In essence, the conspiracy must involve the use of "fraudulent means"; which is not defined at all, but which expressly (and obviously) includes the use of deceit or falsehood. A "fraudulent means", however, does not *require* that there be a falsehood, or that anyone must be deceived.[112] In *Scott v Metropolitan Police Commr*,[113] for example, the defendants bribed cinema employees to let them borrow films, which were then copied in breach of copyright. Their behaviour was certainly fraudulent, even though it involved neither falsehood nor deceit.

19.3.3 The object of the conspiracy

An offence under s 257 may be committed in either of two forms: by conspiring to defraud some person or persons, or by conspiring to affect the price of anything publicly sold. Of these alternative objects, in practice the first is much the more significant.

19.3.3.1 To defraud the public, or any person

The paradigm case will be where D conspires to obtain a benefit at the expense of another's assets. In many cases this can, and should, be charged under s 310; as either conspiracy to steal, or conspiracy to obtain property by deception. However, the offences of theft under s 220 and obtaining under s 246 both require that the subject matter be something capable of being stolen. Conspiracy to defraud is not limited in this way: thus it encompasses depriving someone of land, or an equitable interest, or even persuading a testatrix to change her will in favour of the defendants.[114] The latter example would not be theft even of an equitable interest under s 222,[115] since the (erstwhile) potential beneficiaries under a will have merely a spes successionis, and are not deprived of any proprietary right.

The range of s 257 is therefore very wide. Moreover, as the wording of the offence makes clear, the essence of defrauding is deprivation of or prejudice to the victim's interests. So it is not necessary that the purpose of the conspiracy

---

112 Cf § 19.2.3; also s 257 itself, which states that an offence subsists "whether the deceit or falsehood or other fraudulent means would or would not amount to a false pretence" (defined in s 245; at § 19.1.1). Contrast the definition by Buckley J in *Re London & Globe Finance Corp Ltd* [1903] 1 Ch 728 at 732, which (wrongly) suggests that deceit is *necessary* for fraud: "To deceive is, I apprehend, to induce a man to believe that a thing is true which is false, and which the person practising the deceit knows or believes to be false. To defraud is to deprive by deceit: it is by deceit to induce a man to act to his injury. More tersely it may be put, that to deceive is by falsehood to induce a state of mind; to defraud is by deceit to induce a course of action."

113 [1975] AC 819, [1974] 3 All ER 1032. See also *R v Walsh and Harney* [1984] VR 474, (1983) 9 A Crim R 307; *R v Horsington and Bortolus* [1983] 2 NSWLR 72; *R v Weaver* (1931) 45 CLR 321 at 334, [1931] 37 ALR 249 at 251; *R v Sinclair* [1968] 1 WLR 1246; *R v Hollinshead* [1985] AC 975, [1985] 2 All ER 769.

114 *R v Tillings* [1985] Crim LR 393.

115 Chapter 18.

should be to benefit anyone.[116] In *Welham v DPP*, Lord Radcliffe pointed out that:

> Although in the nature of things [defrauding] is almost invariably associated with the obtaining of an advantage for the person who commits the fraud, it is the effect upon the person who is the object of the fraud that ultimately determines its meaning.[117]

The law thus looks at the intended effect of the fraud on the victim, irrespective of whether the defendants sought thereby to make a gain.

Further, if we concentrate upon the victim, we find that she may be defrauded even if she suffers no loss. It is sufficient that the conspiracy *puts at risk* the economic, or property, interests or rights of the victim.[118] In *Scott* (§ 19.3.2), a conspiracy to defraud was established notwithstanding that the breach of copyright caused no direct pecuniary loss to the cinema owners, and merely had the potential to deprive them of profits. Similarly, in *Adams v R* it was said that there may be a conspiracy to defraud based upon an agreement dishonestly to conceal information where the conspirator is under a duty to disclose it, or upon an agreement dishonestly to withhold information from persons entitled to require its disclosure;[119] whether or not those persons suffer financial harm as a result.

These examples involve conspiracies to defraud "persons ascertained or unascertained". Alternatively, the fraud may be on the "public" at large, where no individual's particular interests (actual or potential) are jeopardised. "Where the intended victim of a 'conspiracy to defraud' is a person performing public duties as distinct from a private individual it is sufficient if the purpose is to cause him to act contrary to his public duty."[120] Consequently, there may be a

---

116 Cf *R v Cope* (1719) 1 Str 144, 93 ER 438.

117 [1961] AC 103 at 123, [1960] 1 All ER 805 at 808. (D was charged with uttering forged documents with intent to defraud, contrary to s 6 Forgery Act 1912 (UK).) Cf Viscount Dilhorne in *Scott v Metropolitan Police Commr* [1975] AC 819 at 839, [1974] 3 All ER 1032 at 1038: "'to defraud' ordinarily means, in my opinion, to deprive a person dishonestly of something which is his or of something to which he is or would or might but for the perpetration of the fraud be entitled."

118 *R v Allsop* (1976) 64 Cr App R 29. The victim may, of course, be the public at large, and the interest threatened may not be actionable by any private individual; thus, in *R v Walters* [1993] 1 NZLR 533 (CA), a conspiracy to breach provisions of the Fisheries Act 1983 which protected a valuable natural public resource was held to fall within s 257.

119 (1994) 12 CRNZ 379 at 390, [1995] 1 WLR 52 at 65 (PC). The Privy Council held that a conspiracy to defraud existed where company directors dishonestly agreed to conceal information relating to secret profits, so as to impede action by the company to recover those profits. However, there must still be an intention to act to the prejudice of some extant right: "A person is not prejudiced if he is hindered in inquiring into the source of moneys in which he has no interest. He can only suffer prejudice in relation to some right or interest which he possesses."

120 *Scott v Metropolitan Police Commr* [1975] AC 819 at 841, [1974] 3 All ER 1032 at 1040 (Lord Diplock).

conspiracy fraudulently to obtain a driving licence,[121] an IRD number,[122] confidential information,[123] or membership of a society.[124]

19.3.3.2 To affect the market price of any thing publicly sold

According to *Adams*, there are no modern examples of prosecutions under this arm of s 257.[125] In general, dishonest manipulation of a market price will now fall within insider trading regulations, and is better dealt with under that head by specialist legislation. Given its potential effect on otherwise justifiable business transactions and upon the free operation of the market, it may be questionable whether criminal law is an appropriate tool at all for market regulation of this sort;[126] and it is certainly desirable to control wrongdoing with more sensitive legislation, which admits of appropriate exceptions for legitimate transactions, than with a blunt and overbroad mechanism such as s 257 provides.

19.3.3.3 Illegality of object?

As was pointed out earlier (§ 19.3), and unlike conspiracy under s 310,[127] the object of a conspiracy to defraud need not itself constitute an offence when done. This, perhaps, is an inevitable consequence of finding a conspiracy to defraud where V's interests are merely put at risk — in the absence of a crystallised loss or gain, the contemplated activities may well be insufficiently harmful to attract the wrath of criminalisation. Nonetheless, it is submitted that the scope of s 257 should be confined to conspiracies at least to commit a legal wrong, and that conspiracy to commit a moral wrong, simpliciter, should not fall within the section.[128]

19.3.3.4 Impossibility

What happens where the means chosen by the conspirators fail to work, as when the conspiracy is to defraud by deceit but the intended victim is ultimately not deceived, or because of some fact or circumstance unknown to the conspirators could not be deceived in the way they intended? The question

---

121 *R v Potter* [1958] 2 All ER 51, [1958] 1 WLR 638. And see *Alexander v Police* 27/4/94, McGechan J, HC Wellington AP8/94.

122 *R v Moses & Ansbro* [1991] Crim LR 617 (National Insurance number).

123 *DPP v Withers* [1975] AC 842, [1974] 3 All ER 984.

124 Cf *R v Bassey* (1931) 22 Cr App R 160, where an unqualified student acting alone, who attempted to gain admission to the Inner Temple by the use of forged references and degree certificates, was held to have defrauded the Benchers of that Inn.

125 § CA257.06. Earlier authorities on conspiracies to rig markets include *R v De Berenger* (1814) 3 M & S 67, 105 ER 536; *R v Esdaile* (1858) 1 F & F 213, 175 ER 696; *R v Burch* (1865) 4 F & F 407, 176 ER 622; *R v Gurney* (1869) 11 Cox CC 414; *R v Aspinall* (1876) 1 QBD 730; *Scott v Brown, Doering, McNab & Co* (1892) 2 QB 724, [1891-94] All ER Rep 654. For an account of a case that in New Zealand might have fallen within s 257, see Pugh, *Is Guinness Good for You? The Bid for Distillers*, 1987.

126 For discussion, see Gillen, "Sanctions Against Insider Trading: A Proposal for Reform" (1991) 70 Can Bar Rev 215; Carlton and Fischel, "The Regulation of Insider Trading" (1983) 35 Stanford LR 857.

127 See § 6.2.1.

128 Cf Williams, *CLGP*, §§ 222, 226.

of impossibility arose in *Sew Hoy*.[129] The defendants' company had imported clothing described as women's clothing. Customs officials inspected the shipment, discovered it to be men's clothing (on which the duty payable was higher than for women's clothing), and classified it as such. When asked to produce further documentation, the defendants again produced documents alleging the clothing to be women's, thereby intending to deceive the customs officials. However, their plan did not, and could not, succeed, since the officials already knew what the shipment contained. Although the method employed to deceive the officials failed, the defendants were found guilty of conspiracy, a distinction being drawn between an agreement which if carried out *necessarily* could not achieve its objective because of legal or physical impossibility, and an agreement which might have worked, but which failed because of the behaviour of some person external to the agreement.[130]

19.3.4 Mens rea

The mens rea of s 257 is sometimes described as an "intent to defraud". In fact, the mens rea components of a conspiracy to defraud are rather more specific than this:

(i)   Fraudulence, and

(ii) Intention to carry out the agreement.

The first element, fraudulence, is essentially a question of dishonesty.[131] There seems to be no reason why this element should be interpreted any differently within s 257 than it is for theft under s 220. As such, the crucial factor in determining dishonesty will be D's subjective intentions.[132] It is no defence that D does not know the contemplated actions are unlawful, or even

---

129 [1994] 1 NZLR 257, (1993) 10 CRNZ 581 (CA).

130 Cf *R v Bennett* (1979) 68 Cr App R 168; thus the Court of Appeal distinguished *DPP v Nock* [1978] AC 979, [1978] 2 All ER 654, in which the means employed were physically incapable of achieving the purpose intended. For further discussion of impossibility in conspiracies, see § 6.2.10.

131 *R v Sinclair* [1968] 1 WLR 1246; *R v Allsop* (1976) 64 Cr App R 29 (CA); *R v Landy* [1981] 1 All ER 1172 at 1181, [1981] 1 WLR 355 at 365.

132 See § 17.3.1. Cf *R v Landy* [1981] 1 All ER 1172 at 1181, [1981] 1 WLR 355 at 365: "The dishonesty to be proved must be in the minds and intentions of the defendants. It is to their states of mind that the jury must direct their attention. What the reasonable man or the jurors themselves would have believed or intended in the circumstances in which the defendants found themselves is not what the jury have to decide; but what a reasonable man or they themselves would have believed or intended in similar circumstances may help them to decide what in fact the individual defendants believed or intended." In the UK this analysis has since been rejected and replaced with a partly objective test: *R v Ghosh* [1982] QB 1053, [1982] 2 All ER 689. Although the *Ghosh* approach has been rejected in both New Zealand and Australia in relation to theft, it seems that Australia has accepted it in the context of conspiracy to defraud: *R v Walsh* [1984] VR 474; *R v Eade* (1984) 14 A Crim R 186; noted (1985) 9 Crim LJ 177.

that he positively believes they are lawful.[133] However, this would tend to show that his intent was not dishonest.[134]

Secondly, there must be an intention on the part of the alleged conspirator to carry out her part of the agreement.[135] Thus there is no conspiracy by D if he appears to agree, but secretly intends to frustrate the execution of the plan;[136] nor if D is indifferent to the success or failure of the conspiracy, and simply does not intend to participate in carrying it out.[137] Furthermore, it is apparently insufficient that D acquiesces passively in an agreement, in relation to which he has no influence or input: D's agreement must be of real consequence to the conspiracy.[138]

As with all crimes where motive is not part of the mens rea, a benign motive or purpose will not of itself foreclose an agreement to defraud from constituting a conspiracy. It is sufficient that the agreement exists and that D intends to carry it out, for whatever reason.[139]

It might be thought that conspiracy to defraud requires, perhaps in addition to the above two elements, a separate intent to defraud. Not so. Proof of an intention to carry out the agreement to defraud is, of itself, sufficient to establish an intent to defraud; thus, in the context of conspiracy, the requirement of an intent to defraud adds nothing to the two elements identified here. In particular, since fraud may be committed simply by placing another's rights or interests in jeopardy, an "intent to defraud" means simply a (dishonest) intention to act to the potential prejudice of another person's rights[140] — ie to carry out the agreement. This includes deliberately putting V's rights at risk, whether or not actual loss is intended. As the English Court of Appeal stated in *R v Sinclair*:

> To cheat and defraud is to act with deliberate dishonesty to the prejudice of another person's proprietary right. In the context of this case the alleged conspiracy to cheat and defraud is an agreement by a director of a company and others dishonestly to take a risk with the assets of the company by using them in a manner which was

---

133 *Churchill v Walton* [1967] 2 AC 224, [1967] 1 All ER 497.

134 But not in every case: for example, certain forms of insider dealing or market manipulation (see § 19.3.3.2) have sometimes been found not to be unlawful (a finding that often leads to law reform). Yet they may be dishonest.

135 *R v Gemmell* [1985] 2 NZLR 740, (1985) 1 CRNZ 496 (CA); approving *R v O'Brien* [1955] 2 DLR 311, [1954] SCR 666.

136 *R v Anderson* [1986] AC 27 at 38ff, [1985] 2 All ER 961 at 965ff.

137 *R v Thomson* (1965) 50 Cr App R 1.

138 Per Fisher J in *R v Richards [Conspiracy]* (1992) 9 CRNZ 403; § 6.2.5.1. See generally Orchard, "The Mental Element of Conspiracy" (1985) 2 Canterbury LR 353.

139 *Wai Yu-tsang v R* [1992] 1 AC 269, [1991] 4 All ER 664; considered in *R v Gunthorp* 9/6/93, CA46/93. See also the discussion of *R v Smith* [1960] 2 QB 423, [1960] 1 All ER 256; chapter 3.

140 *Wai Yu-tsang v R* [1992] 1 AC 269 at 276, [1991] 4 All ER 664 at 668 (Lord Goff). Cf the reasoning in *R v Walters* [1993] 1 NZLR 533 (CA).

known to be not in the best interests of the company and to be prejudicial to the minority shareholders.[141]

---

141 [1968] 1 WLR 1246 at 1250. See also *R v Olan, Hudsson & Hartnett* (1978) 41 CCC (2d) 145, [1978] 2 SCR 1175. Per *R v Allsop* (1976) 64 Cr App R 29 at 31, 32 (CA): "If the deceit which is employed imperils the economic interest of the person deceived, this is sufficient to constitute fraud even though in the event no actual loss is suffered and notwithstanding that the deceiver did not desire to bring about an actual loss... Interests which are imperilled are less valuable in terms of money than those same interests when they are secure and protected. Where a person intends by deceit to induce a course of conduct in another which puts that other's economic interests in jeopardy he is guilty of fraud even though he does not intend or desire that actual loss should ultimately be suffered by that other in this context."

INDEX

vicarious liability – *continued*
corporations *see* **corporations**
delegation principle, 5.2.1
due diligence defence, 5.2.2.1
master-and-servant, 5.2
principal-and-agent, 5.2
regulatory offences, 5.2
"scope of employment" rule, 5.2.2
victim
actus reus, contribution to, 2.2.3.3
secondary liability of, 5.1.4.2
victimless crime
conspiracy to defraud, 19.3
voluntariness, 2.3
disinhibition, 2.3.1.2
impulsive action, 2.3.1.2
voluntary acts
behavioural element in actus reus, 2.1.2
possession, 2.1.2.2
states of affairs, 2.1.2.1

"wheel" conspiracy, 19.3.1 *see also*
conspiracy to defraud
wilful blindness
false pretence, 19.1.1.2
receiving, 17.4.2.1(a)
recklessness, 3.2.3, 3.4.1
wilful damage
mens rea, 3
wilfulness
mens rea, 3.6
"with intent", 3.1.7
wounding with intent
defined, 15.2
disfiguring, meaning of, 15.2.4
grievous bodily harm, 15.2.1
silent telephone calls, 15.2.1.1(a)
indirect, 15.2.2.1
injure, meaning of, 15.2.5
maim, meaning of, 15.2.3
mens rea, 15.2.6
"with intent", 15.2.6.1
wound, meaning of, 15.2.2